THE BLACK WATCH

Victoria Schofield is a historian and commentator on international affairs, with specialist knowledge of South Asia. In addition to *The Highland Furies: The Black Watch 1739–1899*, she is the author of *Kashmir in Conflict, Afghan Frontier, Wavell: Soldier and Statesman* and *The Fragrance of Tears: My Friendship with Benazir Bhutto*. She read Modern History at the University of Oxford and was President of the Oxford Union. In 2004–05 she was the Visiting Alistair Horne Fellow at St Antony's College, Oxford. She has contributed to *The Sunday Telegraph*, *The Times* and *The Independent* as well as BBC World TV, BBC World Service and other news outlets.

By the same author

The United Nations

Bhutto, Trial and Execution

Every Rock, Every Hill: The Plain Tale of the North-West Frontier & Afghanistan

Kashmir in the Crossfire

Kashmir in Conflict: India, Pakistan and the Unending War

Old Roads, New Highways, Fifty Years of Pakistan (Ed.)

The House That Fell Down

Wavell: Soldier and Statesman

Afghan Frontier: At the Crossroads of Conflict

Witness to History, The Life of Sir John Wheeler-Bennett

The Highland Furies: The Black Watch 1725–1899

The Royal Navy in War and Peace: O'er the Deep Blue Sea by Vice Admiral B.B. Schofield (Ed.)

The Fragrance of Tears: My Friendship with Benazir Bhutto

THE BLACK WATCH

FIGHTING IN THE FRONT LINE 1899–2006

VICTORIA SCHOFIELD

FOREWORD BY HRH THE PRINCE OF WALES

An Apollo Book

First published in 2017 by Head of Zeus Ltd
This paperback edition first published in 2022 by Head of Zeus Ltd,
part of Bloomsbury Publishing Plc

1 3 5 7 9 10 8 6 4 2

A catalogue record for this book is available
from the British Library.

Typeset by Broadbase
Maps by Jamie Whyte

ISBN (PB) 9781784979980
(E) 9781784979966

Printed and bound by CPI Group (UK) Ltd,
Croydon, CR0 4YY

Head of Zeus Ltd
5–8 Hardwick Street
London EC1R 4RG

WWW.HEADOFZEUS.COM

To the fallen of The Black Watch

Without courage there cannot be truth;
and without truth there can be no other virtue.
Sir Walter Scott

Contents

Foreword

by HRH Prince Charles, Prince of Wales & Duke of Rothesay

All those with an interest in the military history of the United Kingdom of Great Britain and Northern Ireland and in the story of The Black Watch will have been eagerly awaiting, as have I, the appearance of the second volume of the official history of The Black Watch (Royal Highland Regiment), of which my great grandfather, King George V, my grandmother, Queen Elizabeth The Queen Mother and I, myself, have had the privilege of being Colonel in Chief. The first volume covered the period from the formation of the Regiment in 1739 until 1899, just before the beginning of the Second South African War. The remarkable and exciting story of the Regiment's first 160 years was expertly brought to life through the words of numerous Black Watch officers and men as they soldiered across the globe. Expectations for this second volume were high, not least because very many of those who helped create the Regiment's history in the 20th and 21st century are alive and able to recall events at first hand.

I am delighted that the expectations have been more than matched by this concluding volume. It appears in the midst of our commemorations of the First World War. Not surprisingly that terrible conflict occupies a significant part of the book, as too does the Second World War. Never before, and we must hope never again, have such very large numbers been required to wage war with the Nation's enemies. Never before, and we must hope never again, did so many Black

Watch men make the ultimate sacrifice on our behalf. Quite rightly, their extraordinary deeds are given much prominence in a story that is as humbling as it is inspirational. We read, too, of the more recent exploits of the Regiment whether in Korea, Northern Ireland, Iraq or Afghanistan. We do so with pride and admiration.

As the last Colonel in Chief of The Black Watch (Royal Highland Regiment), and now as the Royal Colonel of The Black Watch 3rd Battalion Royal Regiment of Scotland, I could not be more pleased that all those who have worn the Red Hackle over the years now have an authoritative Regimental history that is told in their honour; an honour which they richly deserve.

Charles

Preface

by Lieutenant General Sir Alistair Irwin, KCB, CBE

On 28 March 2006 The Black Watch (Royal Highland Regiment) joined the other remaining Scottish infantry regiments to form the Royal Regiment of Scotland. As the last Colonel of the Regiment I had the unhappy duty of attending a parade in Palace Barracks in Belfast to mark the moment at which the old became the new. For those who were serving it was a time to mourn the passing of the Regiment that they had specifically chosen to join but it was also a time to set the eye firmly on the future. For those no longer serving the day was one of infinite sadness and regret but also one of immense pride in having been part of a legend, part of a Regiment that had made its name famous around the world. In the 267 years since its formation in 1739 The Black Watch played a prominent and gallant part in the unfolding history of the United Kingdom of Great Britain and Northern Ireland, forging a record of service and a reputation of which no one could fail to be proud.

Quite rightly the Regimental Trustees of The Black Watch were determined to do all that they could to ensure that their Regiment's history and legacy should be preserved and honoured. Among the measures they took was to launch a project to expand the Regimental Museum in Perth and to use this as the basis for an educational outreach programme that would serve to inspire future generations of young Scots to live their lives in the spirit of selfless service and ambition to excel that had so characterised the life of the Regiment over the years.

As I have stated in the Preface to the first Volume, the Trustees also decided to commission a new history of the Regiment, of which this is the second and final volume. There have of course been many previous histories, each of them with their admirers but most now out of print. The author, Victoria Schofield, had already produced a fine biography of the most famous of the sons of The Black Watch, Field Marshal Earl Wavell. The Trustees were delighted when she agreed to turn her attention to the Regiment to which that great soldier had belonged. She was invited to produce a work that was at once readable and scholarly. The history of the Regiment was to be set in the context of events beyond the Regiment and the emphasis was to be on the experiences of the officers and men who had served, for it was they who had created the history; the Regiment of itself had no meaning without the men who lived and breathed it. Above all the author was required to ensure that as much as possible of the material she used was from contemporary primary sources including diaries and letters and that these and other sources should be properly noted in the book, something that no previous history of The Black Watch has done.

As a result of these stipulations we have already seen in the first volume, published in 2012, a story that is full of human interest as it traces the progress of the Regiment from its earliest days until the end of the 19th century. We now have the conclusion of the story, starting with the Second South African War and taking us up to the merger into the Royal Regiment of Scotland and the first six years of the Black Watch battalion of the new Regiment. The narrative does not pretend to follow every operation and encounter, but rather to tell the story of how the Regiment did its duty. Like the first volume, this book is about the officers and men, what they thought, and how they lived and fought. Similarly, periods of peace on garrison duties are as much part of this story as the conflicts; in the process absorbing new light has been cast on the life and times of The Black Watch.

The Regimental Trustees dedicate this history to all the officers and men who have served in The Black Watch since 1739 and especially to those many thousands who laid down their lives in the service of the Crown. They hope that members of the regimental family will take pleasure in this record of their beloved Regiment. And they hope that the wider readership will understand why those of us who have served in The Black Watch are so closely at one with Sir George Murray, a former Colonel, who said in 1844: 'How high an honour I shall always esteem it to have been for upwards of twenty years the colonel of a regiment, which, by its exemplary conduct in every situation, and by its distinguished valour in many a well-fought field has earned for itself so large a share of esteem and renown.'

Acknowledgements

In writing The Black Watch's official history, I should like to thank the Trustees of The Black Watch Regimental Trust (absorbed into The Black Watch Regimental Association in 2016), for the confidence they placed in me to commit to paper the story of their famous and much-loved regiment. The challenge of recreating the lives of numerous officers, non-commissioned officers and private soldiers against the backdrop of the momentous events of the twentieth century, including two World Wars, has been both daunting and a privilege.

To the modern-day reader, the casualties during the First World War, in particular, are unimaginable. What dominates the history, however, is the sense of duty, loyalty and friendship felt by officer and soldier alike. Whether in the mud of Flanders or the heat of Mesopotamia in the First World War, the desert of North Africa, the torrential rain of the jungles in Burma, the freezing cold of the mountains in Italy, or on the beaches of Normandy in the Second World War, or in Korea, Kenya, Northern Ireland, Iraq, the courage and bravery of the thousands of men who served in The Black Watch is absolute. The narrative is drawn from their words, describing their hopes, fears and hardships, as related in their diaries, letters and memoirs. The story is further embellished with the memories of those alive today, including veterans of Dunkirk in 1940, Alamein in 1942, Monte Cassino and D-Day in 1944. As the reader will notice, many of those who feature rise to seniority, as they progress in time through the narrative. The stories of others are cut short, their lives ending sometimes within hours or days of reaching the front line, sickness, accidents and friendly fire all taking their toll in addition to those killed on the field of battle.

During my several years of research, I am especially grateful to Lieutenant General Sir Alistair Irwin, KCB, CBE, who not only requested me to write the Regiment's history, but who has been unfailingly supportive, both reading the manuscript and making many helpful comments. I am also indebted to Lieutenant Colonel Roddy Riddell, Vice-Chairman of The Black Watch Association, and his wife Jenny, for their generous hospitality during my countless visits to Perth to research in the archives at The Black Watch Museum, Balhousie Castle and for their constant support and encouragement. The limitless assistance of Thomas B. Smyth, both as the Archivist at The Black Watch Museum and after his retirement, has been invaluable. My thanks also to Major General Andrew Watson, CB, Brigadier Garry Barnett, OBE, Brigadier Duncan Cameron, OBE, Brigadier Edward de Broë-Ferguson, MBE, Major General Mike Riddell-Webster, CBE, DSO, Major General James Cowan, CBE, DSO, and Major Hugh Rose, all of whom contributed to my knowledge and understanding as well as offering me hospitality. I am grateful to Colonel Alex Murdoch, Chairman of The Black Watch Association, and Major Ronnie Proctor, MBE, Secretary of The Black Watch Association for their advice.

My access to The Black Watch Museum at Balhousie Castle, Perth, has been infinite and I am grateful for permission to quote from numerous primary sources in the archives, as well as being able to use a number of illustrations from the photographic archive. The staff at Balhousie Castle has been consistently helpful in facilitating my research. In particular I should like to thank the former Museum Manager, Emma Halford-Forbes and the Archivist, Richard Mackenzie, as well as Maureen Brace, Linda Campbell and Lorna Tunstall. In addition I should like to thank all those Black Watch serving and retired officers and men who have shared their recollections with me, as listed in the bibliography, as well as the descendants of others, who opened their homes to me, often producing yet more invaluable source material. My thanks to them for permission to cite from their private collections. I am also grateful for permission to quote from archives in other libraries as listed in the bibliography and I am ever thankful to the London Library for its liberal lending policy and for being granted Thomas Carlyle membership for the duration of writing this history.

Lastly I should like to thank my agent, Sara Menguc, for her steadfast support, both practical and emotional; Anthony Cheetham and Richard Milbank, at Head of Zeus, for retaining their longstanding enthusiasm for publishing the history of The Black Watch, Clemence Jacquinet for overseeing production, and Avril Broadley for typesetting the text; my copyeditor, Janey Fisher, for conscientiously bringing the manuscript and notes into a consistent whole as well as providing an excellent index, and Jamie Whyte, whose beautifully drawn maps complement the narrative perfectly. I should also like to thank my wide circle of friends who have retained their interest in my subject matter for a number of years, many of them suggesting additional avenues of research and providing introductions. My final thanks are to my extended family, my husband, Stephen Willis, my adult children, Alexandra, Anthony and Olivia, all of whom have helped me to ensure that this tremendous undertaking came to fruition.

Regimental Title Changes

Since the six Independent Companies were raised from Highland clans in 1725 and formed into a regiment in 1739, there have been several changes of title:

1725 The Independent Companies or The Black Watch

1739 The Earl of Crawford's Highlanders, or The Highland Regiment, listed as the 43rd Regiment of Foot

1741 Lord Sempill's Highlanders, or The Highland Regiment, listed as the 43rd Regiment of Foot

1745 Lord John Murray's Highlanders or The Highland Regiment, listed as the 43rd Regiment of Foot

1749 Lord John Murray's Highlanders or The Highland Regiment, listed as the 42nd Regiment of Foot

1751 The 42nd Regiment of Foot, The Highland Regiment

1758 The 42nd or Royal Highland Regiment of Foot, also known as Royal Highlanders following the grant of the title 'Royal'

1861 42nd Royal Highland Regiment of Foot, The Black Watch

1881 The Black Watch (Royal Highlanders)

1935 The Black Watch (Royal Highland Regiment)

2006 The Black Watch, 3rd Battalion The Royal Regiment of Scotland (3 Scots)

1786 The 2nd Battalion (raised in 1779) became the 73rd (Highland) Regiment of Foot

1816 The 73rd Regiment of Foot

1862 The 73rd (Perthshire) Regiment of Foot

1881 The 2nd Battalion The Black Watch (Royal Highlanders)

Battle Honours

In The Black Watch Museum at Balhousie Castle, Perth, there are several stands of the Regimental and Sovereign's Colours which have been laid up as tradition dictates after another stand has been presented. The oldest surviving are the tattered Colours carried throughout the Peninsular Wars and at Waterloo in 1815. Traditionally emblazoned on the Colours are the Battle Honours awarded during specific operations, campaigns and wars. In addition to the Sphinx superscribed 'Egypt', granted after the Battle of Alexandria in 1801, the Regiment gained the following Battle Honours during its 267-year history; ten from the First World War and ten from the Second World War (indicated in bold) were inscribed on the Sovereign's Colour.

Guadeloupe 1759, Martinique 1762, Havannah, North America 1763–64, Mangalore, Mysore, Seringapatam, Corunna, Busaco, Fuentes d'Onor, Salamanca, Pyrenees, Nivelle, Nive, Orthès, Toulouse, Peninsula, Waterloo, South Africa 1846–7, 1851-2-3, Alma, Sevastopol, Lucknow, Ashantee 1873–4, Tel-el-Kebir, Egypt 1882-1884, Kirbekan, Nile 1884–85, Paardeberg, South Africa 1899–1902.

The Great War: Retreat from Mons, **Marne 1914, 18,** Aisne 1914, La Bassée 1914, **Ypres 1914, 17, 18,** Langemarck 1914, Gheluvelt, Nonne Bosschen, Givenchy 1914, Neuve Chapelle, Aubers, Festubert 1915, **Loos, Somme 1916, 18,** Albert 1916, Bazentin, Delville Wood, Pozières, Flers-Courcelette, Morval, Thiepval, Le Transloy, Ancre Heights, Ancre 1916, **Arras 1917, 18,** Vimy 1917, Scarpe 1917, 18, Arleux, Pilckem, Menin Road, Polygon Wood, Poelcapelle, Passchendaele, Cambrai 1917, 18, St Quentin, Bapaume 1918, Rosières, **Lys,** Estaires, Messines 1918, Hazebrouck, Kemmel, Béthune, Scherpenberg, Soissonnais-Ourcq, Tardenois, Drocourt-Quéant, **Hindenburg Line,** Épehy, St Quentin Canal, Beaurevoir, Courtrai, Selle, Sambre, France and Flanders 1914–18, **Doiran**

1917, Macedonia 1915–18, Egypt 1916, Gaza, Jerusalem, Tell'Asur, **Megiddo,** Sharon, Damascus, Palestine 1917–18, Tigris 1916, **Kut al-Amara 1917,** Baghdad, Mesopotamia 1915–17.

The Second World War: Defence of Arras, Ypres-Comines Canal, Dunkirk 1940, Somme 1940, St Valéry-en-Caux, Saar, Bréville, Odon, Fontenoy le Pesnil, Defence of Rauray, Caen, Falaise, **Falaise Road,** La Vie Crossing, Le Havre, Lower Maas, Venlo Pocket, Ourthe, Rhineland, Reichswald, Goch, **Rhine,** North-West Europe 1940, 44–45, Barkasan, British Somaliland 1940, **Tobruk 1941,** Tobruk Sortie, **El Alamein,** Advance on Tripoli, Medenine, Zemlet el Lebene, Mareth, **Akarit,** Wadi Akarit East, Djebel Roumana, Medjez Plain, Si Medienne, **Tunis**, North Africa 1941–4, Landing in Sicily, Vizzini, Sferro, Gerbini, Adrano, Sferro Hills, **Sicily 1943, Cassino II,** Liri Valley, Advance to Florence, Monte Scalari, Casa Fortis, Rimini Line, Casa Fabbri Ridge, Savio Bridgehead, Italy 1944–45, Athens, Greece 1944–45, **Crete,** Heraklion, Middle East 1941, Chindits 1944, **Burma 1944.**

The Hook 1952, Korea 1952–53.

Al Basrah, Iraq 2003.

Maps

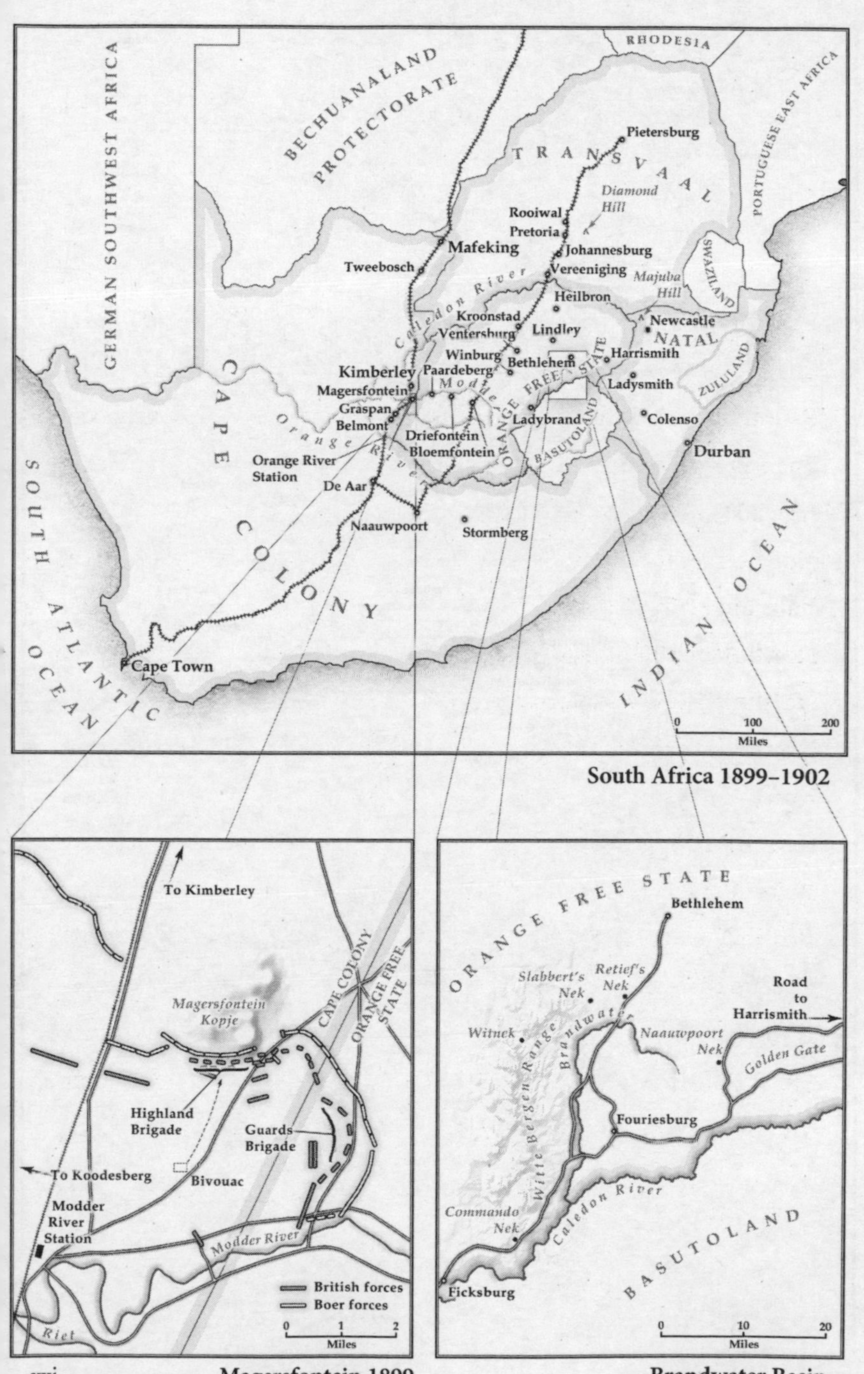

South Africa 1899–1902

Magersfontein 1899

Brandwater Basin

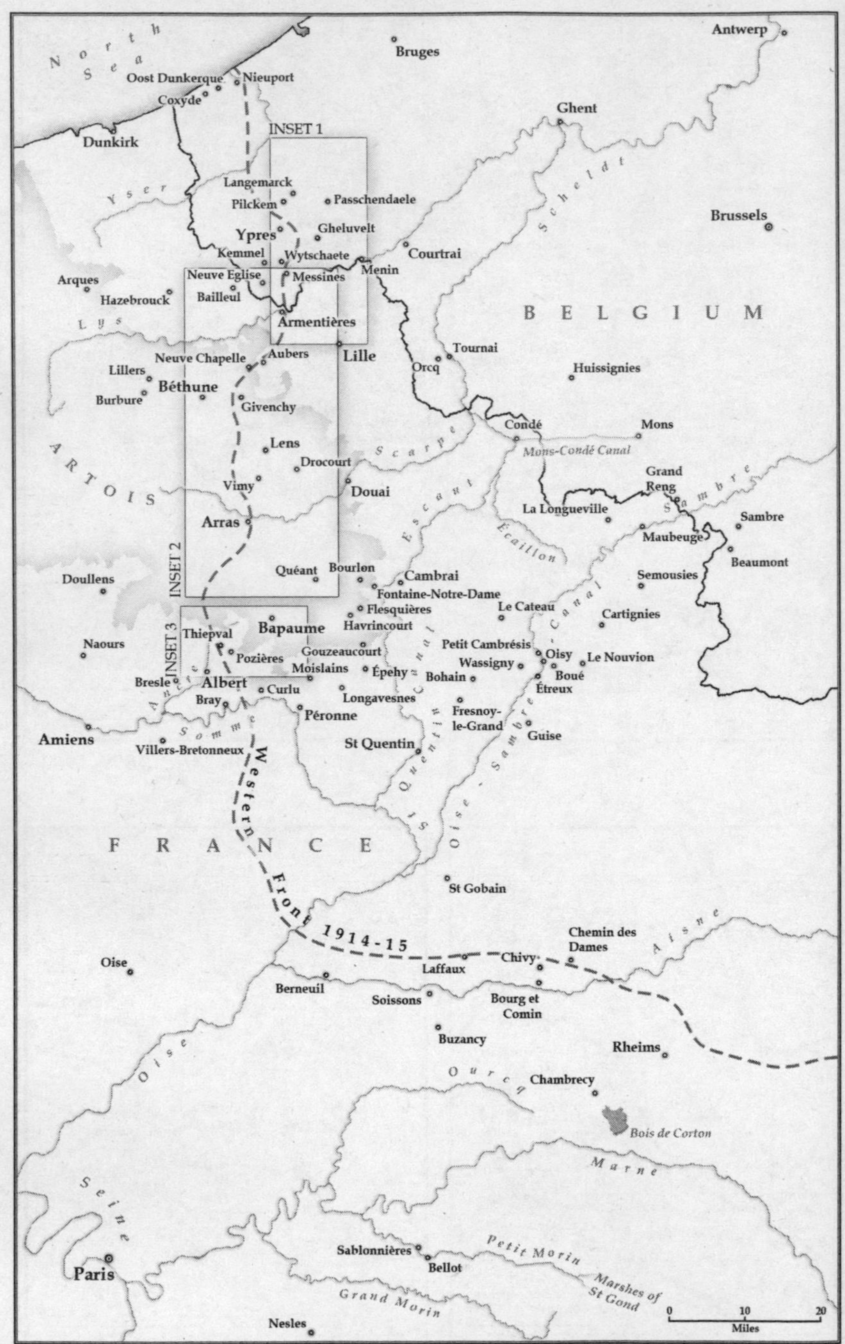
North Sea
Oost Dunkerque
Nieuport
Coxyde
Dunkirk
Bruges
Antwerp
Ghent
INSET 1
Yser
Langemarck
Pilckem
Passchendaele
Ypres
Gheluvelt
Kemmel
Wytschaete
Courtrai
Menin
Brussels
Scheldt
Arques
Hazebrouck
Neuve Eglise
Bailleul
Messines
Armentières
BELGIUM
Lys
Neuve Chapelle
Aubers
Lille
Tournai
Orcq
Lillers
Béthune
Burbure
Givenchy
Huissignies
Lens
Drocourt
Condé
Mons
Mons-Condé Canal
Scarpe
ARTOIS
Vimy
Douai
Arras
Escaut
Ecaillon
Grand Reng
La Longueville
Sambre
Maubeuge
Beaumont
INSET 2
Doullens
Quéant
Bourlon
Cambrai
Fontaine-Notre-Dame
Flesquières
Havrincourt
Le Cateau
Semousies
Cartignies
INSET 3
Thiepval
Bapaume
Naours
Pozières
Gouzeaucourt
Petit Cambrésis
Oisy
Wassigny
Le Nouvion
Bresle
Albert
Moislains
Épehy
Bohain
Boué
Étreux
Ancre
Bray
Curlu
Longavesnes
Péronne
Fresnoy-le-Grand
Guise
Amiens
Somme
Villers-Bretonneux
St Quentin
St Quentin Canal
Oise-Sambre Canal
Western Front 1914-15
FRANCE
St Gobain
Chemin des Dames
Aisne
Oise
Chivy
Laffaux
Berneuil
Soissons
Bourg et Comin
Buzancy
Rheims
Ourcq
Chambrecy
Bois de Corton
Marne
Seine
Sablonnières
Bellot
Petit Morin
Marshes of St Gond
Paris
Grand Morin
Nesles
0
10
20
Miles

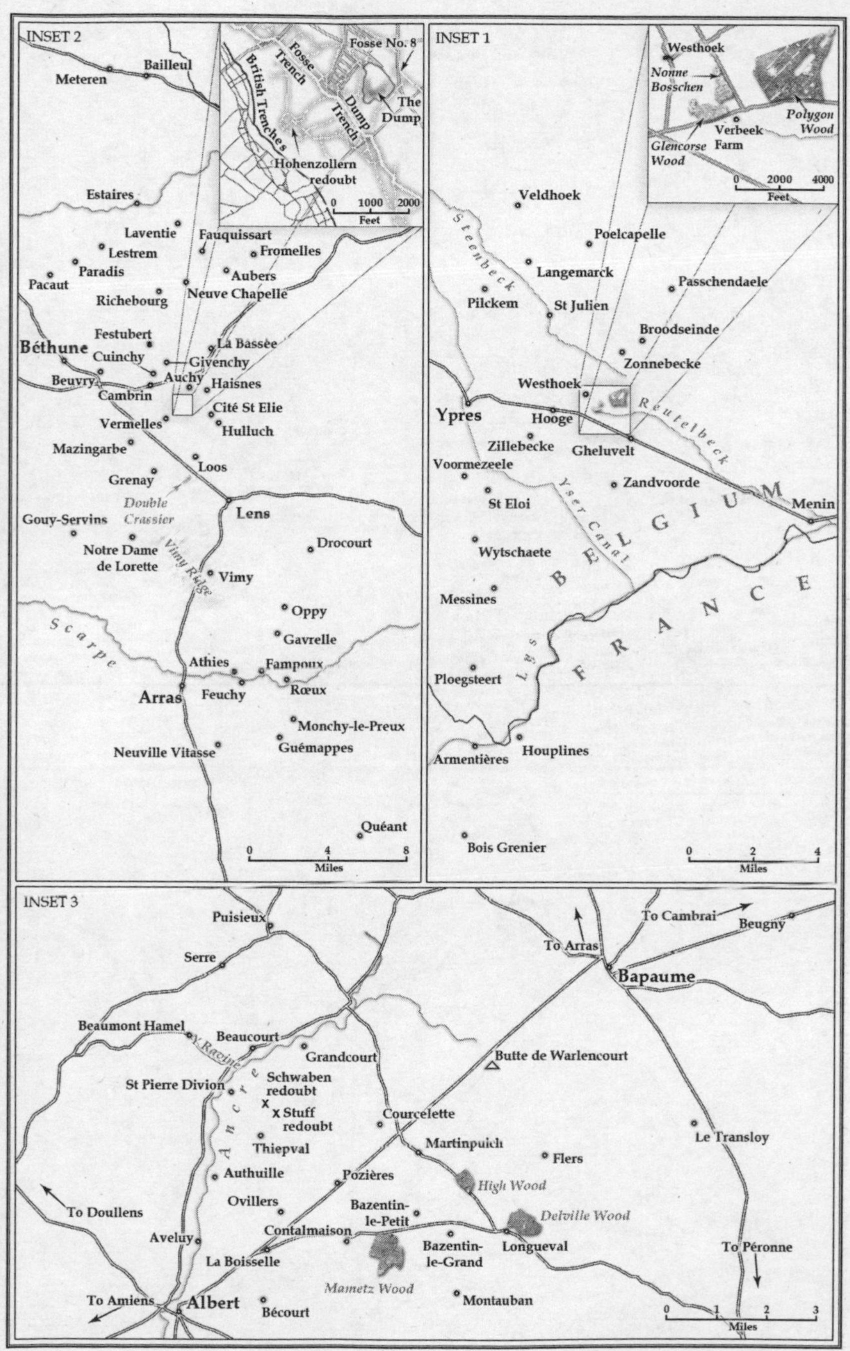

The Western Front 1914–18

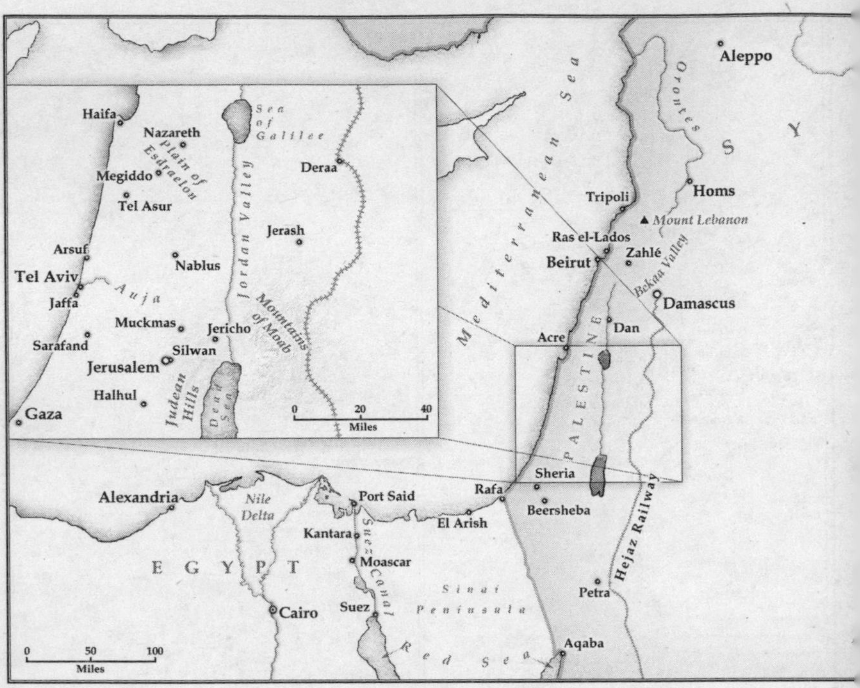
Aleppo
Orontes
S Y
Homs
Mediterranean Sea
Tripoli
Mount Lebanon
Ras el-Lados
Zahlé
Beirut
Bekaa Valley
Damascus
Dan
Acre
PALESTINE
Sheria
Rafa
Beersheba
Hejaz Railway
Alexandria
Nile Delta
Port Said
El Arish
Kantara
Suez Canal
Moascar
EGYPT
Sinai Peninsula
Petra
Cairo
Suez
Aqaba
Red Sea
0 50 100
Miles
Haifa
Nazareth
Plain of Esdraelon
Megiddo
Tel Asur
Sea of Galilee
Deraa
Jordan Valley
Jerash
Arsuf
Nablus
Tel Aviv
Jaffa
Auja
Mountains of Moab
Muckmas
Jericho
Sarafand
Silwan
Jerusalem
Judean Hills
Dead Sea
Halhul
Gaza
0 20 40
Miles

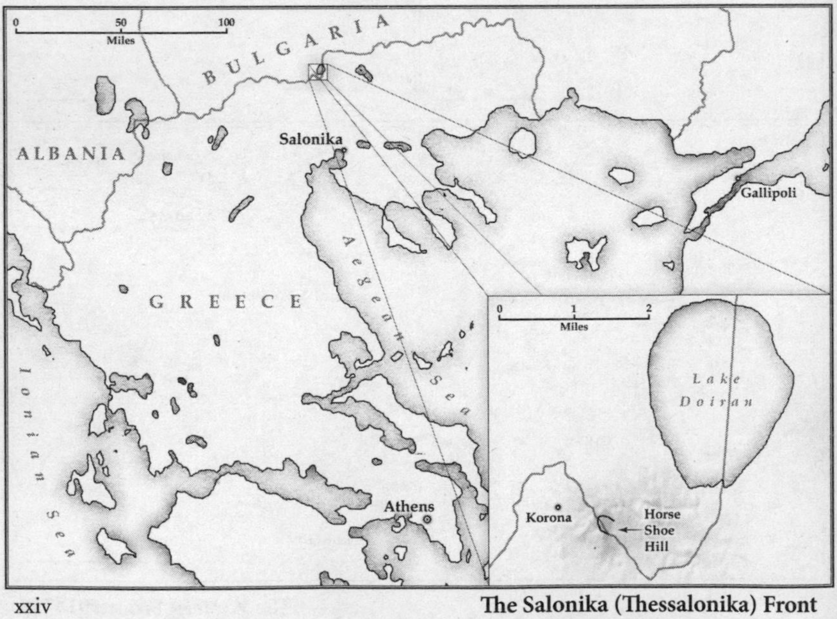
0 50 100
Miles
BULGARIA
ALBANIA
Salonika
Gallipoli
GREECE
Aegean Sea
Ionian Sea
Athens
0 1 2
Miles
Lake Doiran
Korona
Horse Shoe Hill

The Salonika (Thessalonika) Front

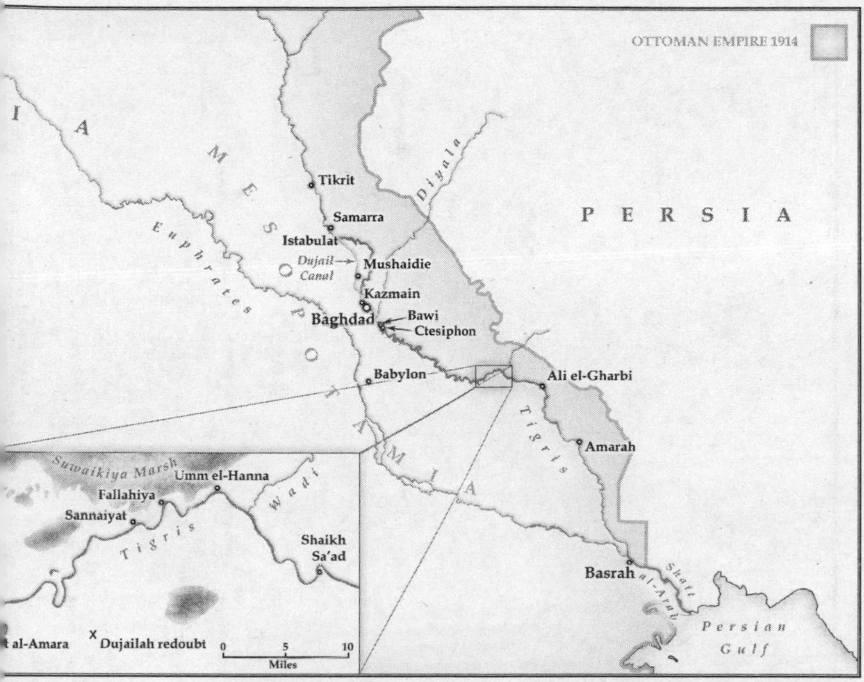

Ottoman Empire: Palestine, Syria and Mesopotamia 1916–18

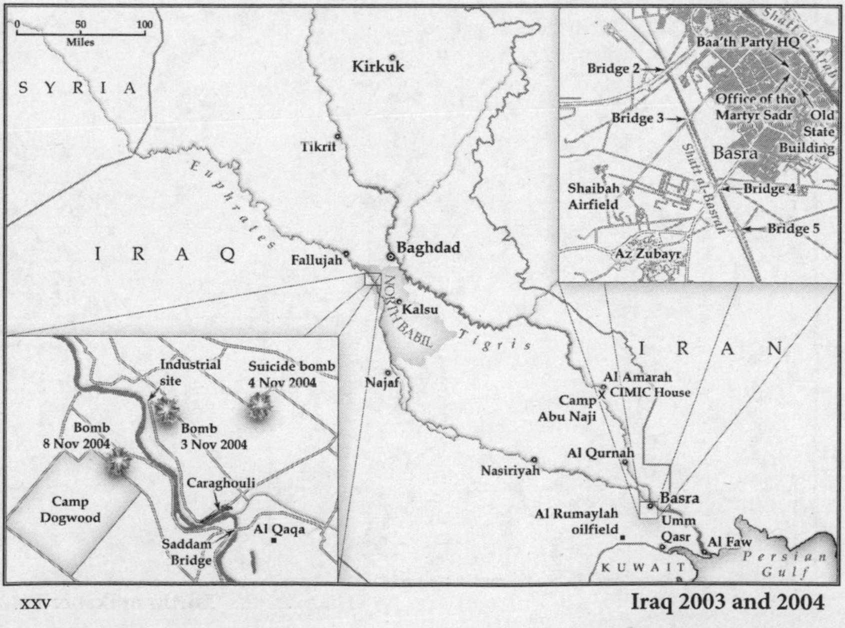

Iraq 2003 and 2004

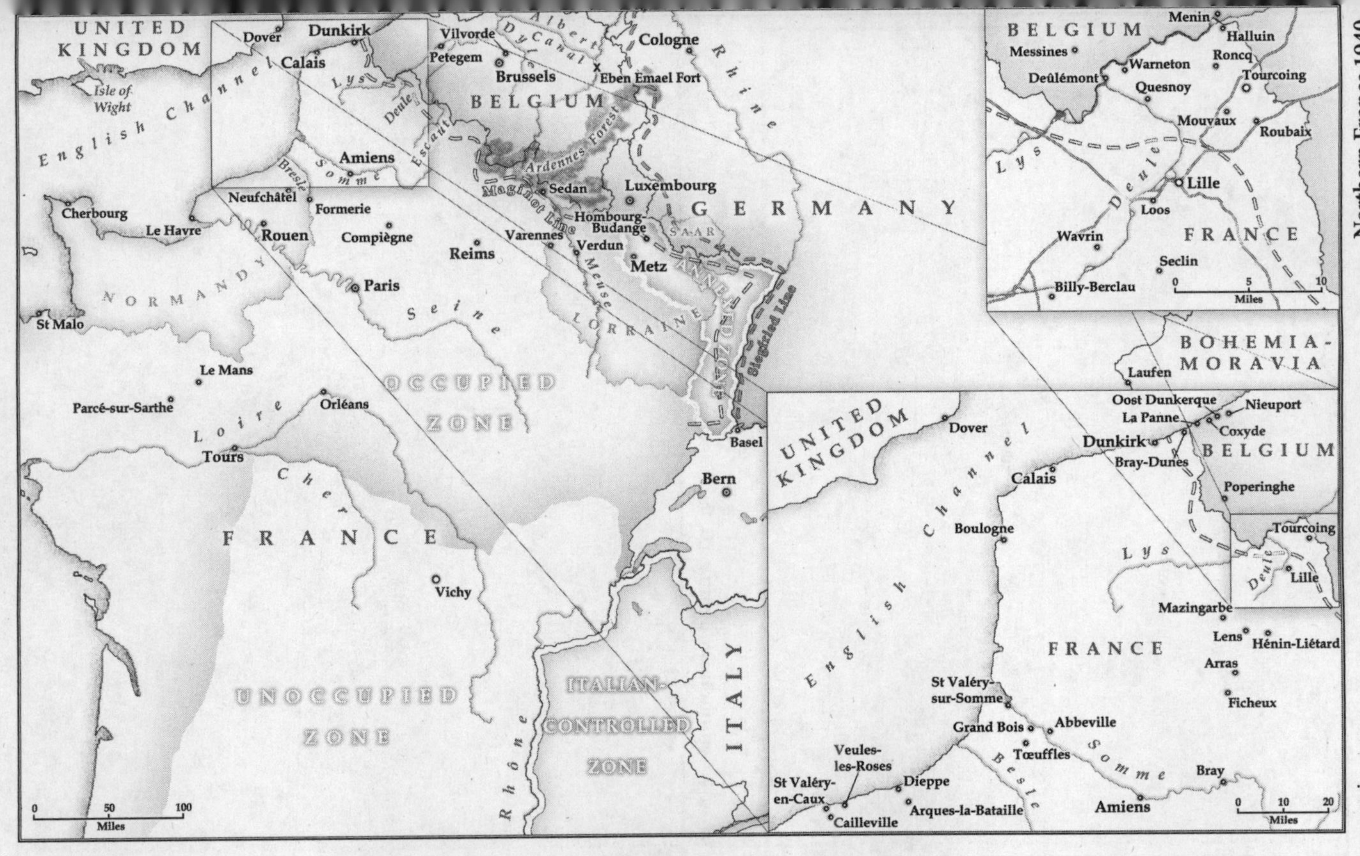

Northern France 1940

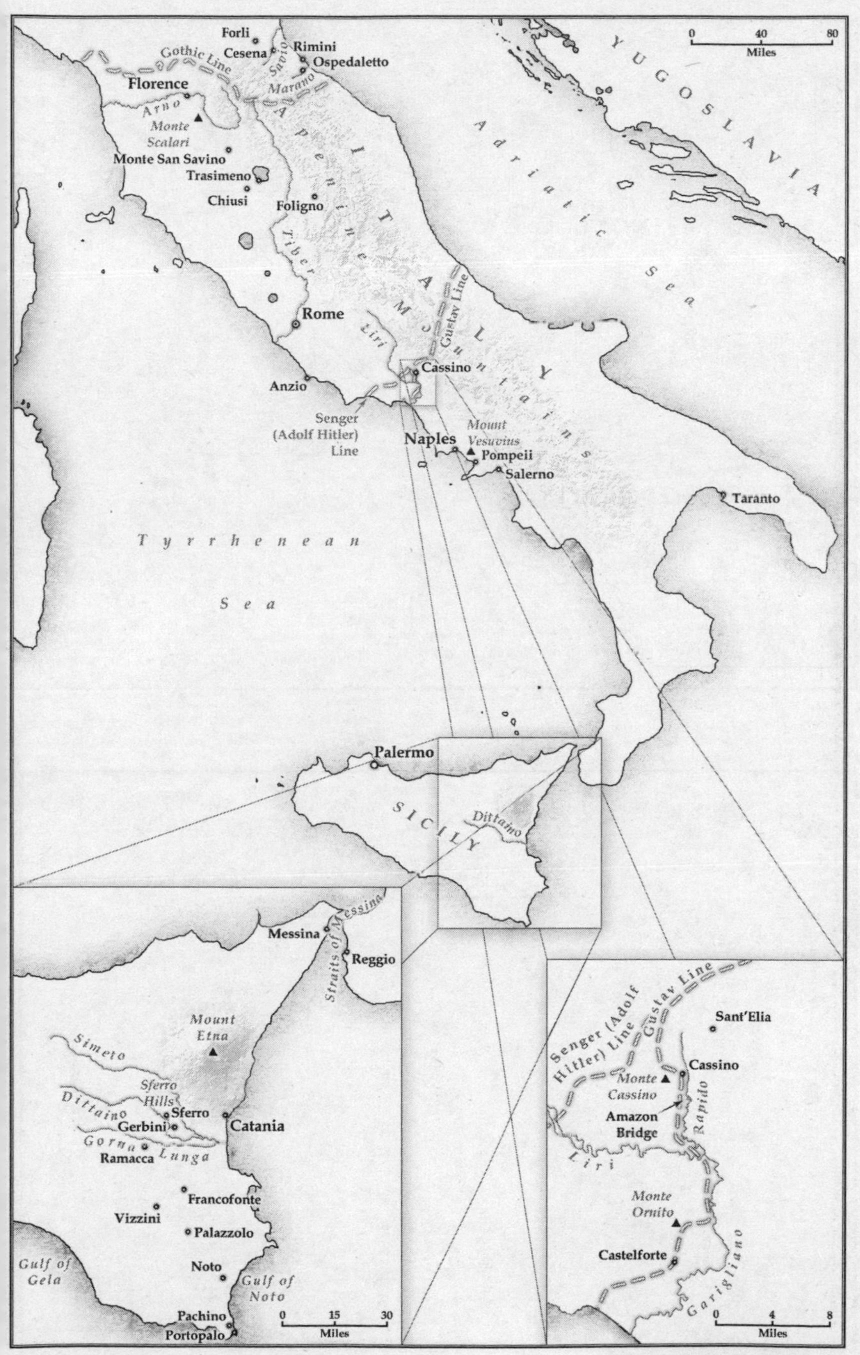

Italy and Sicily 1943–44

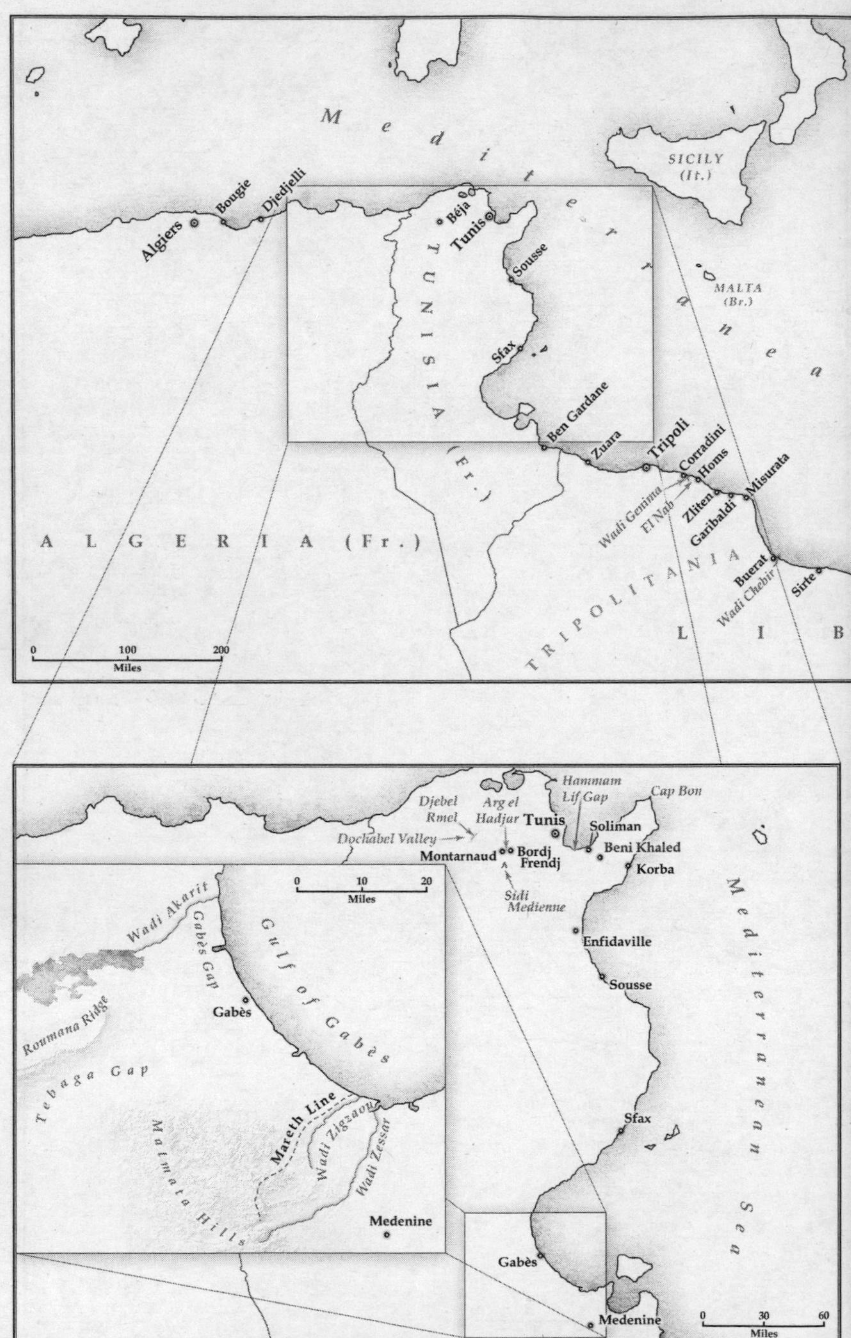

Mediterranean
SICILY (It.)
MALTA (Br.)
Algiers
Bougie
Djedjelli
Béja
Tunis
Sousse
Sfax
TUNISIA (Fr.)
Ben Gardane
Zuara
Tripoli
Corradini
Homs
Wadi Genima
El Nab
Zliten
Garibaldi
Misurata
ALGERIA (Fr.)
TRIPOLITANIA
Buerat
Wadi Chebir
Sirte
LIB
0
100
200
Miles
Djebel Rmel
Arg el Hadjar
Hammam Lif Gap
Cap Bon
Tunis
Soliman
Dochabel Valley
Montarnaud
Bordj Frendj
Beni Khaled
Korba
Sidi Medienne
Enfidaville
Sousse
Sfax
Mediterranean Sea
Gabès
Medenine
0
30
60
Miles
0
10
20
Miles
Wadi Akarit
Gabès Gap
Gulf of Gabès
Gabès
Roumana Ridge
Tebaga Gap
Mareth Line
Wadi Zigzaou
Wadi Zessar
Malmata Hills
Medenine

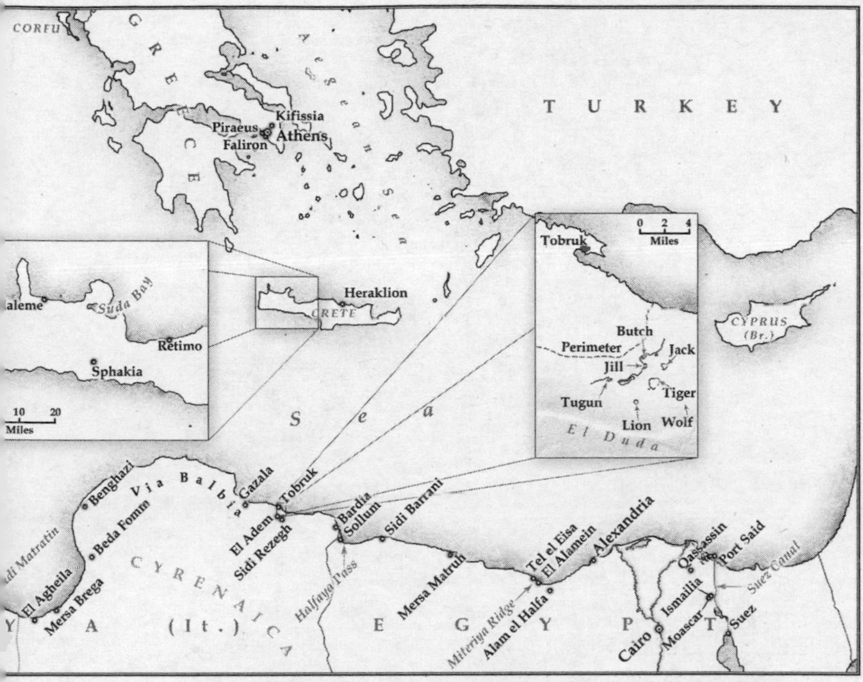

North Africa and the Mediterranean

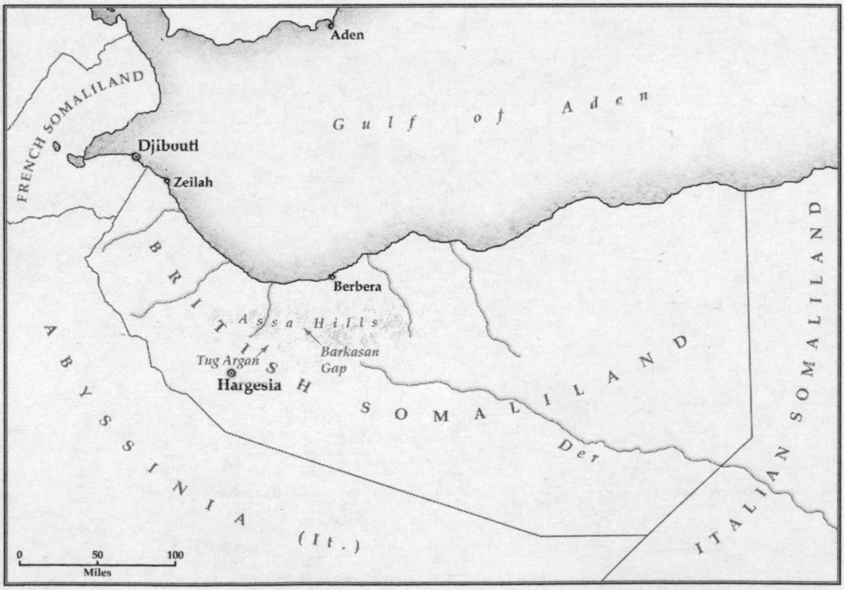

British Somaliland 1940

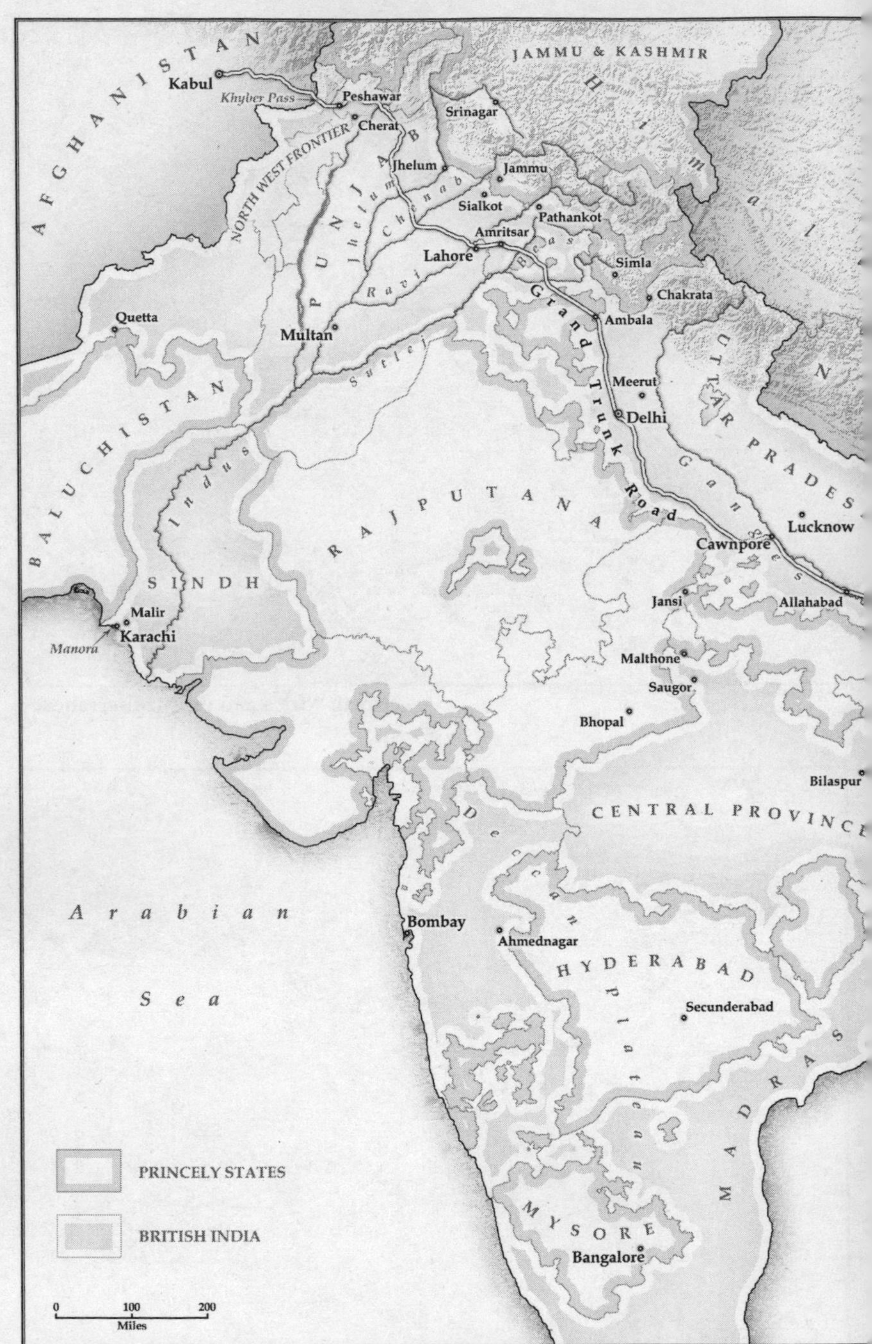

AFGHANISTAN
Kabul
Khyber Pass
Peshawar
Cherat
NORTH WEST FRONTIER
JAMMU & KASHMIR
Srinagar
Himalaya
PUNJAB
Jhelum
Jammu
Sialkot
Pathankot
Jhelum
Chenab
Amritsar
Beas
Lahore
Simla
Ravi
Chakrata
Grand Trunk Road
Ambala
Quetta
Multan
Sutlej
UTTAR PRADESH
Meerut
Delhi
BALUCHISTAN
Indus
RAJPUTANA
Ganges
Lucknow
Cawnpore
SINDH
Jansi
Allahabad
Malir
Karachi
Manora
Malthone
Saugor
Bhopal
Bilaspur
CENTRAL PROVINCE
Deccan plateau
Arabian Sea
Bombay
Ahmednagar
HYDERABAD
Secunderabad
MADRAS
PRINCELY STATES
BRITISH INDIA
MYSORE
Bangalore
0
100
200
Miles

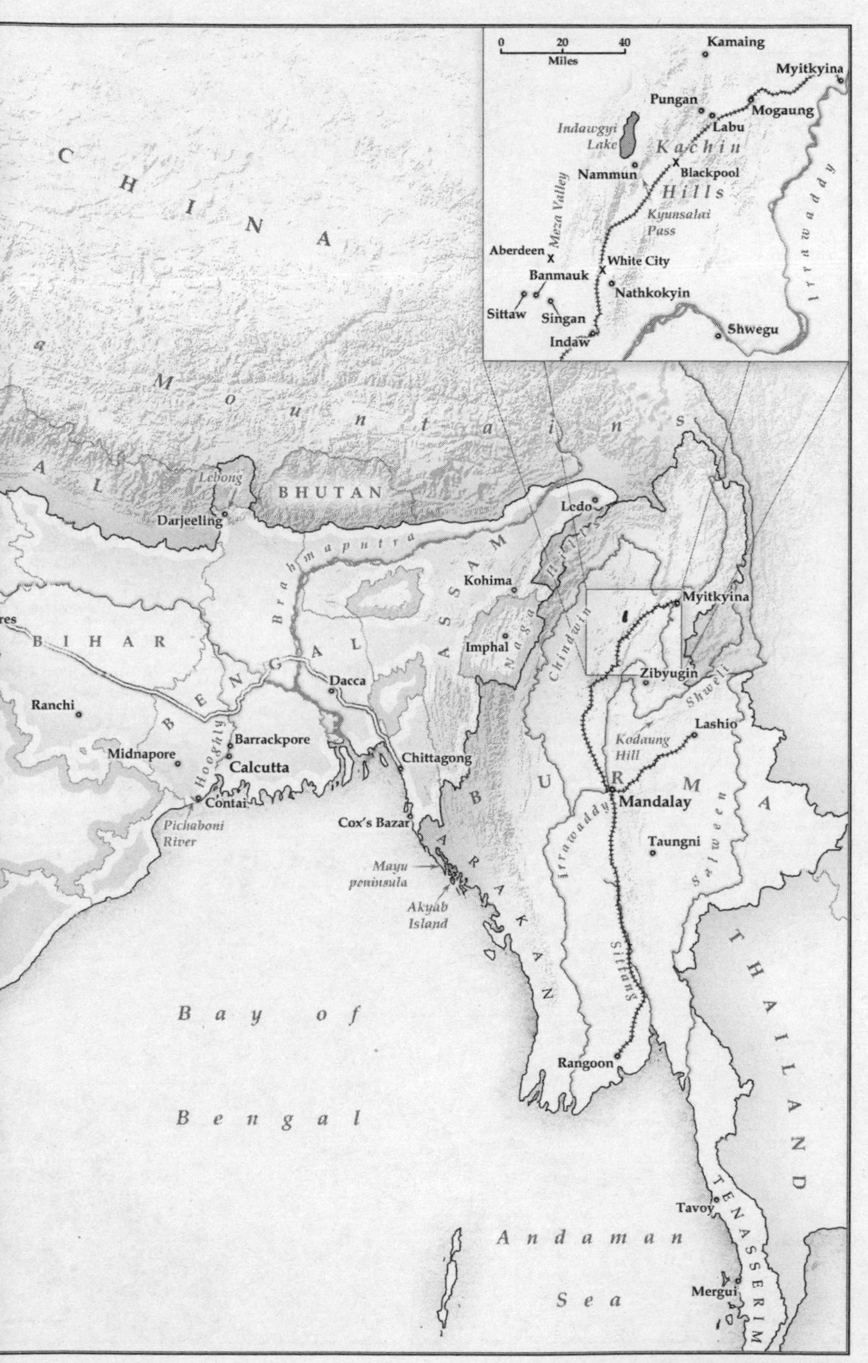

Northern India and Burma pre-1947

0
50
100
Miles
North
Sea
ENGLAND
Colchester
London
Tilbury
Thames
Dover
Southampton
Newhaven
Portsmouth
Isle of
Wight
English Channel
Amsterdam
NETHERLAN
Arnhem
Waal
's-Hertogenbosch
Kle
Maas
Geertruidenberg
Afwaterings
Canal
Vught
Schijnde
Haaren
Eindhove
Antwerp
Weert
BELGIUM
Dunkirk
Calais
Brussels
Louvain
Liège
Namur
Meuse
PAS DE CALAIS
Somme
Ardennes
Forest
Luxembo
St Valéry-en-Caux
Dieppe
Cailleville
Pierre-le-Viger
Cherbourg
Utah
Beach
Omaha
Beach
Le Havre
FRANCE
Mauny
Seine
Bayeux
Verrières Ridge
Falaise
Orne
Paris
Juno
Beach
Gold
Beach
Sword
Beach
Bény-sur-Mer
Douvres
Bayeux
Amfreville
Chateâu
Saint-
Côme
Pegasus
bridge
Bréville
Caen Canal
Caen
Colombelles
Fontenay-le-Pesnel
Bois
de
Bavent
Odon Valley
Orne
Rauray
0
3
6
Miles
Marche
Ourthe
La Roche-en-Ardenne
Hives
Huberr
Lavaux
Nisran
St Hubert
0
4
Miles

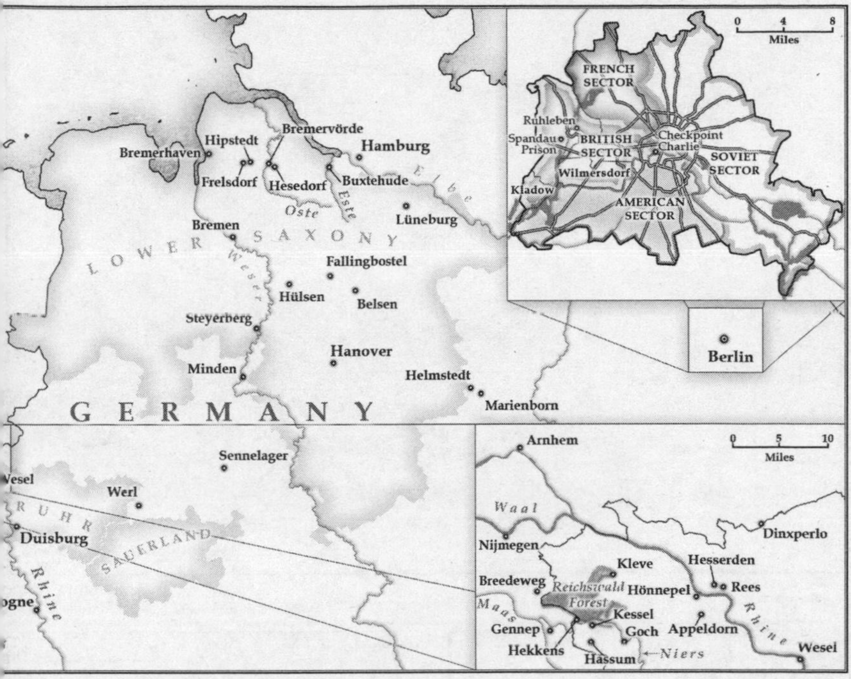

Bremerhaven
Hipstedt
Frelsdorf
Bremervörde
Hesedorf
Hamburg
Buxtehude
Elbe
Este
Oste
Lüneburg
Bremen
LOWER SAXONY
Weser
Fallingbostel
Hülsen
Belsen
Steyerberg
Hanover
Minden
Helmstedt
Marienborn
GERMANY

0 4 8
Miles
FRENCH SECTOR
Ruhleben
Spandau Prison
BRITISH SECTOR
Checkpoint Charlie
SOVIET SECTOR
Wilmersdorf
Kladow
AMERICAN SECTOR
Berlin

Sennelager
Wesel
Werl
RUHR
Duisburg
SAUERLAND
Rhine
ogne

Arnhem
0 5 10
Miles
Waal
Dinxperlo
Nijmegen
Kleve
Hesserden
Rees
Breedeweg
Reichswald Forest
Hönnepel
Maas
Kessel
Appeldorn
Rhine
Gennep
Goch
Hekkens
Hassum
Niers
Wesel

Northern Europe

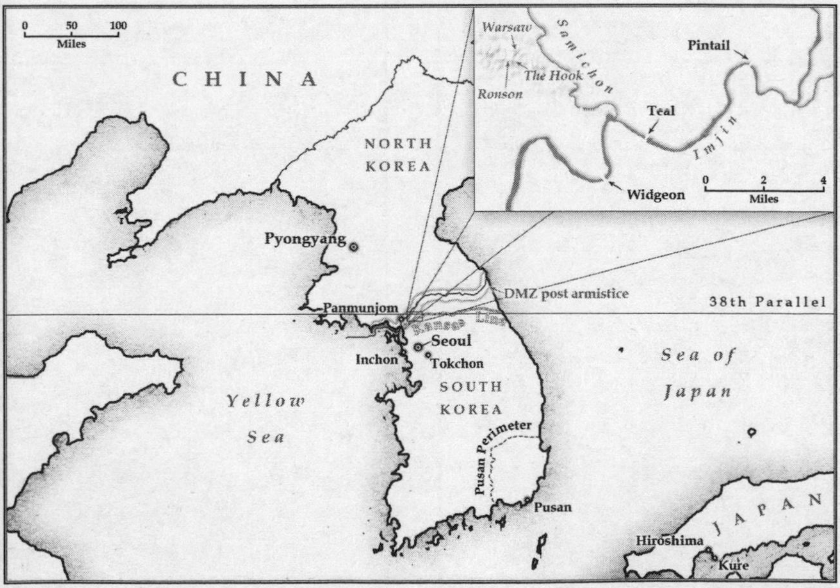

0 50 100
Miles
CHINA
Warsaw
Samichon
The Hook
Ronson
Pintail
Teal
Imjin
Widgeon
0 2 4
Miles
NORTH KOREA
Pyongyang
DMZ post armistice
38th Parallel
Panmunjom
Kansas Line
Seoul
Inchon
Tokchon
Sea of Japan
Yellow Sea
SOUTH KOREA
Pusan Perimeter
Pusan
JAPAN
Hiroshima
Kure

Korea

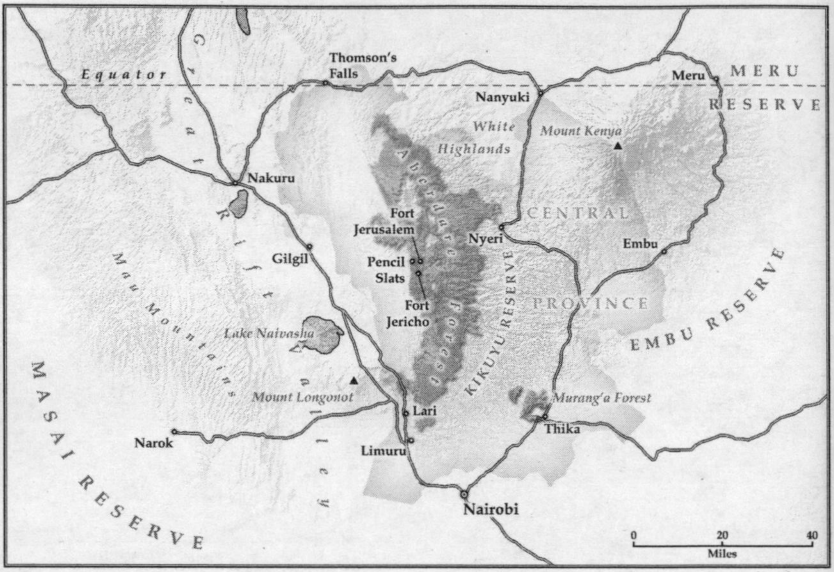

Kenya 1953–55

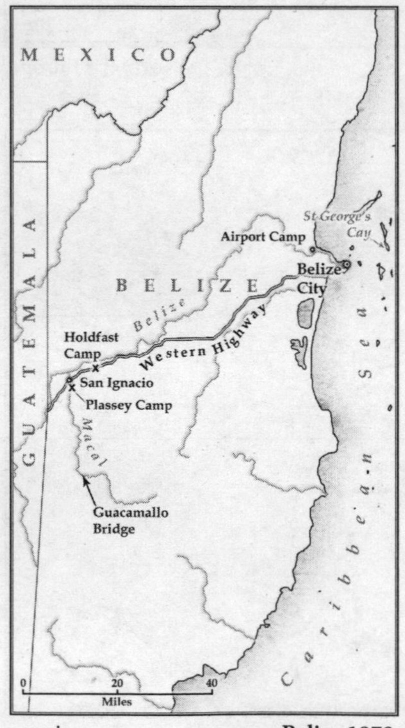

Belize 1979

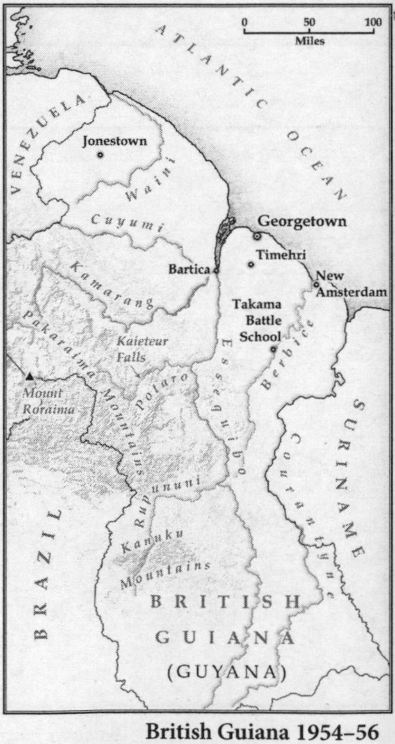

British Guiana 1954–56

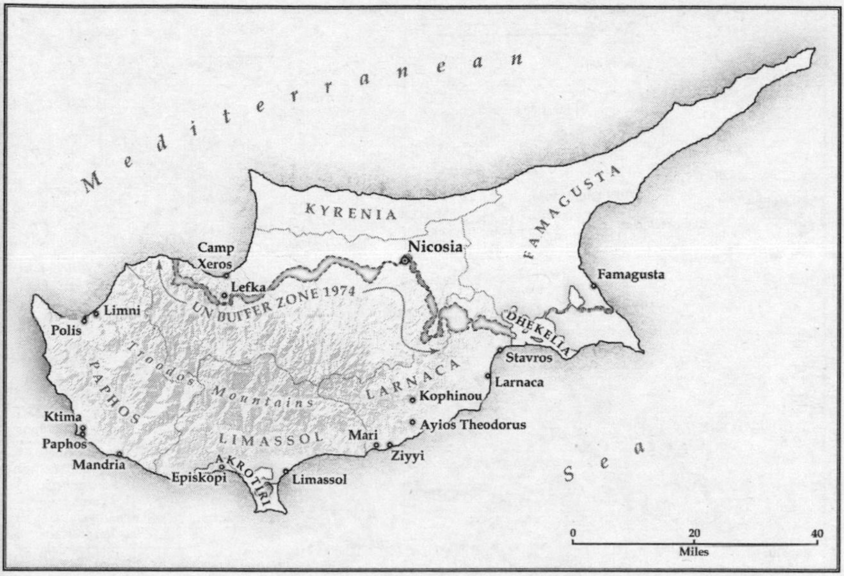
Mediterranean
Sea
KYRENIA
FAMAGUSTA
Camp Xeros
Nicosia
Lefka
UN BUFFER ZONE 1974
Famagusta
Limni
Polis
DHEKELIA
Troodos Mountains
PAPHOS
Stavros
Larnaca
LARNACA
Kophinou
Ktima
Paphos
Ayios Theodorus
LIMASSOL
Mari
Ziyyi
Mandria
AKROTIRI
Episkopi
Limassol
0
20
40
Miles

Cyprus 1958–61, 1967–68

0
50
100
Miles
SERBIA
MONTENEGRO
Pristina
KOSOVO
Podgorica
Stmlje
Skopje
ALBANIA
MACEDONIA
Vardar
Adriatic Sea
Tirana
GREECE

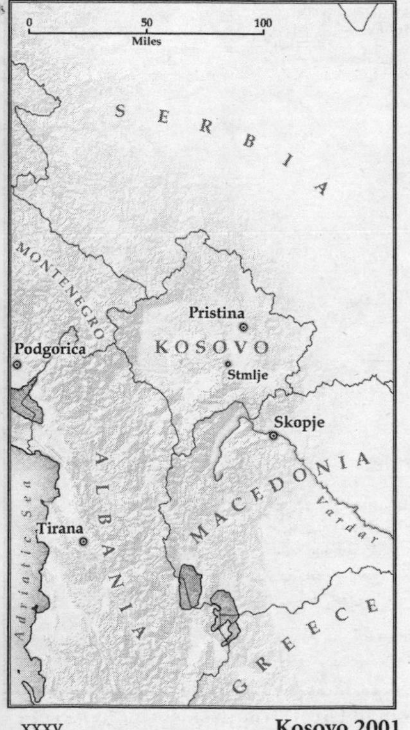

Kosovo 2001

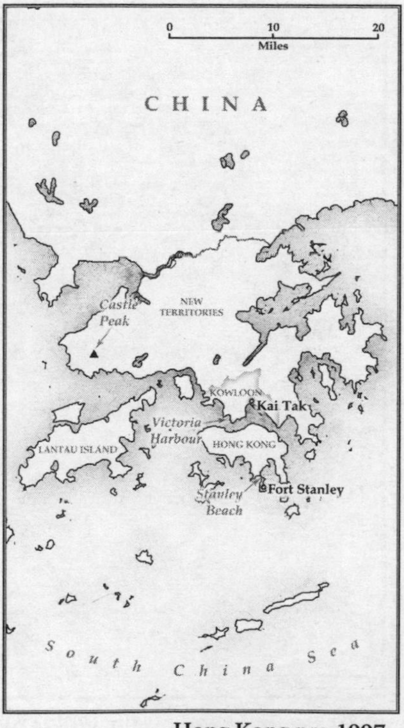
0
10
20
Miles
CHINA
Castle Peak
NEW TERRITORIES
KOWLOON
Kai Tak
Victoria Harbour
LANTAU ISLAND
HONG KONG
Fort Stanley
Stanley Beach
South China Sea

Hong Kong pre-1997

The United Kingdom of Great Britain & Northern Ireland & the Republic of Ireland

1

Chasing Back the Boers

Tell you the tale of the battle,
Well there ain't so much to tell;
Nine hundred went to the slaughter
And nigh four hundred fell;[1]

Soldiers of the Empire

'It was something wonderful the way the railway lines were laid,' marvelled twenty-two-year-old Lance Corporal James Williams, describing the unfamiliar landscape of southern Africa. 'In some places the railway was cut through the mountains, then again it would be on the mountainside, then away down in the valley, with the mountains towering aloft.'[2] Having come by sea from Britain, over a thousand officers and men serving with the renowned Scottish regiment, The Black Watch (Royal Highlanders), had arrived in Capetown in mid-November 1899. Their destination was several hundred miles to the north where they would join the Highland Brigade, positioned south of Kimberley in Cape Colony. The fighting in which The Black Watch's 2nd Battalion was soon to take part would result in an exceptional number of casualties, such as rarely experienced during the 160 years since the Regiment was raised in 1739. Even so, as those in the British Army understood, regardless of the cost, duty to Sovereign and Regiment was paramount; as in the previous century, their actions were in the service of the British Empire, whose colonies, scattered across the globe, rendered approximately one-quarter of the world map pink.[3]

In the late nineteenth century a new set of strategic relationships was emerging which had the potential to undermine Britain's imperial ascendancy. The Triple Alliance, formed in 1882, bound together the recently federated German Empire, the 'dual' monarchy of the Austro-Hungarian Empire and the newly established Kingdom of Italy in a defensive relationship. Meanwhile Tsarist Russia, under the Romanovs, was shifting allegiances. Having accepted a bilateral defensive alliance with Germany in 1887, the relationship had soured. In January 1894 Russia entered into a joint military convention with France. Paramount among the provisions of the 'Dual' or Franco-Russian Alliance was agreement that if a member of the Triple Alliance attacked either country, a joint counter-attack would be made. In addition, despite a tradition of friendship pre-dating the Napoleonic Wars and the links between their respective royal families, the German and British Empires were becoming maritime rivals.[4]

As Queen Victoria entered the twilight of her long reign, and before European relations reached breaking point, important among Britain's colonial concerns was retaining authority in South Africa where tensions had developed between the Boers, the Afrikaans-speaking population of Dutch origin, and the British settlers. After fighting began in 1880, culminating in a Boer victory at Majuba Hill in 1881 (known as the First South African War), the Boers had secured the independence of the Orange Free State and the Transvaal (together also called the South African Republic) while Cape Colony and Natal remained under British administration. But the discovery of gold in the Transvaal in 1886 led to an influx of non-Boer *uitlander* migrant workers, whose lack of full voting rights was seen by the British government as an opportunity to regain political control of the Transvaal. On 29 December 1895 the Cape Colony's Prime Minister, Cecil Rhodes, sent a force led by Dr Leander Starr Jameson to foment unrest as part of a plan to seize Johannesburg and the goldfields. Failing in his objective, Jameson was forced to surrender, the ill-fated sequence of events a disaster for Anglo-Boer relations which led to Rhodes' resignation.[5]

Relations further deteriorated in June 1899 with the collapse of the Bloemfontein conference, instigated by the President of the Orange Free State, Martinus Steyn, in an attempt to resolve the *uitlander* issue, and attended by Sir Alfred Milner, High Commissioner for Southern Africa and Governor of Cape Colony, and the President of the Transvaal, Paul Kruger. On 9 October the Boer leaders gave a forty-eight-hour deadline for the withdrawal of British troops stationed on the borders of the Transvaal and the Orange Free State. When the ultimatum expired at 5 p.m. on 11 October they declared war.[6]

By the time the 2nd Black Watch arrived in South Africa, the Boers had invaded Natal and Cape Colony and were attacking British garrisons at Kimberley, Mafeking (Mahikeng) and Ladysmith.[7] An immediate priority was to relieve Kimberley, to which end Lieutenant General Sir Redvers Buller, commanding British forces in South Africa, sent the 1st Infantry Division. Included in the Division was the Highland Brigade, commanded by former Black Watch officer, Major General Andrew (Andy) Wauchope, and the Guards Brigade.[8]

On reaching De Aar, the officers and men of the 2nd Black Watch were given special 'mobilisation' clothing suited to the approaching summer. Instead of their customary doublets and bonnets, the soldiers were issued with 'Indian khaki drill jackets and Indian white helmets with khaki covers and pugris and small red hackles'; their haversacks and spats were dyed in coffee in the cookhouse. Sharpened broadswords were left behind. Instead the officers were given standard-issue rifles.[9] Moving briefly to Naauwpoort the soldiers were taken onto the veldt 'and exercised in skirmishing'.[10]

As they journeyed onward to the Orange River Station to join the Highland Brigade, 'our eyes met an awful scene,' recorded Lance Corporal Ernest Brown. Piled high were the clothes of dead officers and men, who had fought in the recent battles at Belmont and Graspan, 'covered with blood and bullet marks. It was then we realised our reasons for being in such a country. Our thoughts and all turned at once to our loved ones at home and wondered if we would ever return again.' Their objective was to reach the Modder River Station, south of Kimberley, where Lieutenant General Lord

Methuen, commanding the 1st Infantry Division, had taken up position. 'It was from there our hardships came,' continued Brown. 'The smell of the place was awful on account of the shallowness of the graves round about in every direction.'[11] Arriving at the camp on 6 December, the soldiers found morale was low. Although their Boer adversary, General Piet Cronjé, had been forced to withdraw during recent fighting, British losses had been considerable and the Boers had now taken up a position on a range of hills (*kopjes*) at Magersfontein 6 miles away, blocking the way to Kimberley.[12]

Magersfontein: 'Not The Black Watch, we don't retire!'

'On Sunday the 10th of December 1899 we, "The Highland Brigade" formed up to attack,' continued Williams.[13] The Guards Brigade was in reserve. First, however, twenty-four field guns bombarded the Boer positions. 'Having thus given the Boers due warning that we were likely to make an attack first thing in the morning,' observed Captain Charles Stewart, 'we retired a short way and bivouacked all packed together one regiment behind another.'[14] Wearing khaki aprons to hide the front of their kilts, viewed from behind 'they were still unmistakably Scottish.'[15] 'Heavy rain thunder & lightning,' noted Private Finch. 'One blanket between two men. About midnight we were roused & orders quietly whispered.' 'Monday 11th, still raining and pretty well soaked,' Stewart continued.[16]

The Brigade's objective was the east point of the main ridge. The Black Watch was on the right, with the 2nd Seaforth Highlanders in the centre, the 1st Argyll and Sutherland Highlanders on the left and the 1st Highland Light Infantry in reserve; they were later joined by the Gordon Highlanders who had only just arrived.[17] 'We kept our places by the guide of each company holding a bit of string with knots every 10 yds. No light or noise of any kind,' related Stewart. 'We scrambled over rocks and dykes, and I fancy the regiments behind were in a most fearful muddle as some of the Seaforths suddenly got mixed in my company.'[18] Having decided not to advance in open order, permitting space between the ranks, for fear of losing direction,

General Wauchope marched at the head of the compact column.[19] 'Not one of us knew what we were going to do,' Stewart continued. 'Lord Methuen, I hear, altered his plans twice but as always decided on a direct frontal attack without previously reconnoitring the ground thoroughly and without any preparatory artillery fire, as the fire on Sunday only warned them to clear out while it was going on.'[20]

By daybreak 'the column had only reached a belt of scrub some 600 yards from the foot of the kopje,' recorded Lieutenant Arthur Wauchope, the General's cousin, attributing their slow progress to the fact that 'the magnetic compasses were deranged, either by the thunderstorm or by the ironstone in the rock.'[21] Unknown to the assailants, instead of adopting the normal tactic of positioning his force on the summit of the hills, Cronjé, advised by his field general Koos de la Rey, had ordered his soldiers to take up position at the base where they had dug 'the most elaborate entrenchment and so wired them that you couldn't rush them.'[22] 'As soon as they thought we had come near enough they opened on us a most murderous rifle fire for which of course through somebody's neglect we were quite unprepared. We at once got the order to lie down, it being the only thing we could do at the time, to see if the fire would slacken a little.'[23] 'The Boers opened fire right into the midst of us knocking us over like rabbits before we could fire a shot. Even if we had fired, we would have shot our own men,' Private James McFarlane wrote in a letter to his sister. 'We were so close together, it is a terrible sight, men falling all around & the groans were terrible.'[24]

Both General Wauchope and the 2nd Black Watch's Commanding Officer, Lieutenant Colonel John Coode, were killed in the initial advance and so 'no coherent action took place.'[25] '[We] got no command off any one, only had to charge in our own tinpot way,' recorded Private James Williamson. 'We pulled up the barb[ed] wire and rushed on the Boers.'[26] 'Then the confusion started,' noted Brown. 'One regiment got mixed up with another, and some made an attempt to retire, some extended to the right, and left, many charged the trenches again and again only to a murderous death.'[27] Having realised that the forward troops were pinned down, Methuen ordered the Gordon Highlanders to advance. They too were cut down. 'A poor thin line of Gordons came up and went on a little way but they were of no use,' commented Captain Archibald Rice Cameron, whose company was in the rear, the fighting he experienced 'mild and unexciting.'[28]

Despite the order to retire, three companies of The Black Watch remained until the evening 'as no order of any sort ever reached them.' 'Hardly a man who had been standing upright but what was shot down,' related Private James McFarlane. 'The bullets were falling in hundreds around me, and poor men falling at every step… To tell the truth, I did not care much whether I was shot or not, I was so far through. I don't know how I escaped, it was just luck.' Having received a few bullet holes through his belt, he was fearful of not being so lucky again and asked his sister to ensure that his daughter, 'little Annie', was brought up 'in a proper manner' and sent to a school for soldiers' children.[29]

Unable to advance forward or move backwards, Captain Charles Stewart was 'so sleepy, I went to sleep about 3 in the afternoon.' He awoke to find that the Boers had emerged from their trenches. Seeing their opponents were now 'comparatively harmless', 'two of them came down with water-bottles. I yelled at them to go away, but couldn't stop them so they just gave the wounded water and took stock of us. They then got an interpreter who said they wouldn't fire on the wounded if they lay still.' Later Stewart went to parley with the Boers to obtain help for the wounded. 'They seemed quite a decent lot that I saw though I hear some pretty low things done by them.'[30]

Many of the wounded had multiple injuries. 'I got hit with a Mauser bullet in the left thigh while carrying a wounded comrade,' related Lance Corporal Brown. 'My second in the back and travelled out from the lower part of my stomach which was very painful. My third was in the thigh and my fourth in the elbow. I was in a very great pain all day – lay in the field for 29 hours.' Piper David Welch was hit 'first in the groin by a piece of shell, and, after lying for about twenty minutes, I received another piece of shell in my back… I lay all that day and night, and part of the next day without water, except what the Boers brought out to me.' Hit by a bullet at the top of his left thigh, Lance Corporal Williams thought he had been kicked by a mule. 'We received orders not to use our water bottles, as we would not get any more 'till we reached Kimberley, which was 22 miles away. Jings, we never saw Kimberley 'till 3 months later.'[31]

Among the severely wounded officers was Lieutenant Arthur Wauchope, whose leg was fractured. He had also received 'two other hits in the same leg.' 'I am afraid I shall be laid up for some time as the bone of my upper arm is broken,' Captain Archibald Cameron informed his father from hospital. Lieutenant Archibald Bulloch behaved 'like a hero,' recorded Stewart. 'He was hit in 3 places, head arm and ankle, and kept talking quite coolly to the men near him, telling them what to do.' Lieutenant Sydney Innes was so seriously injured that he was invalided home.[32] Having been wounded early on in the battle, the Adjutant, Captain William 'Anak' Macfarlan continued to fight on until the end. 'Old Anak bagged four Boers before they got him,' recorded his 'best friend', Lieutenant Freddie Tait, Macfarlan's actions later described 'by a Perthite who was there':

'Form a line here, men, we'll hold them,'
Macfarlan's tall form stood erect,
Volley on volley we gave them
Until their fierce fire we checked.[33]

The reality had been somewhat different. From a force of over 14,000, there were nearly 1,000 casualties, mostly from the Highland Brigade, compared with less than a hundred fatalities in the 8,000-strong Boer force. 'We have not realized yet all the gaps in the poor Regiment. It is dreadful to think of their being cut to pieces for no purpose,' Captain Cameron wrote to his father.[34] 'Our Brigade was simply thrown away,' commented Lieutenant Tait, well-known as an amateur golf champion, who had himself been wounded in the thigh. 'Hundreds of splendid fellows were killed and wounded, and nothing gained in the end.'[35] Recorded as missing was the Royal Ancient Golf Club's caddie master, Private John McGregor. Together with other fallen officers and men Major General Wauchope was buried at sunset 'in a blaze of African splendour' on 13 December, his body having been retrieved under a flag of truce. 'How grim and stern these dead men looked as they lay face upward to the sky,' noted the correspondent for the *Daily News*.[36]

In the aftermath of defeat, reprimands followed. 'The Black Watch behaved as they should I think,' Captain Stewart recorded, 'but I heard some queer stories of other regiments. The way we were supported in one place was being fired at in the back by some other corps. Then I suppose our own guns in the afternoon didn't know we were as close up as they burst some shells bang over us killing some of my men.' 'The real truth is that the 3rd Regiment, the Argyll & Sutherland, bolted at the commencement and I fancy carried the Highland Light Infantry with them – the latter Regiment subsequently reformed,' Cameron informed his sister. 'Had the Argyll and Sutherland been fresh I have no doubt they would have been as good as anybody, but like all the troops who had been engaged in Methuen's previous reverse at Modder River they were in a somewhat demoralised condition.'[37]

Wauchope was also criticised for being slow to deploy. 'It was a great mistake on the General's part to march us up in a compact body. We should have been extended long before we came up,' observed Private James McFarlane. 'It was only precious lives and noble heroes just running simple and plain into the jaws of death,' recorded Lance Corporal Brown. 'As regards myself, I shall never, never, forget the disaster of my noble Regiment and the remainder of the Highland Brigade.'[38]

Hearing of the disaster Queen Victoria was: 'very anxious to know how wounded are going on.'[39] When news of the 2nd Black Watch's losses reached India, the men were 'wild and want to do various impossible things,' Captain Adrian Grant Duff wrote in his diary; 'they have requested that the whole of the grant for the New Years dinners may be devoted to the fund for the widows and children also a day's pay.'[40] A British defeat at Stormberg in Cape Colony the day before Magersfontein and at Colenso in Natal on 15 December meant that the second week of December was solemnly called 'Black Week'. Nearly half a century later, Archibald Wavell, still a schoolboy at Winchester College in 1899 but soon to be commissioned into the Regiment, visited the Magersfontein battlefield. 'There was 'no good reason,' he observed 'why the *kopje* should have been attacked directly for the relief of besieged Kimberley, which was the objective of Methuen's force. It would have been easy enough to make a turning movement round it. But turning movements were not in the fashion of some British Generals at that time. They seem to have been regarded rather in the same light as diverging from the straight line out hunting to go through a gate instead of jumping the fence immediately in front, however stiff it might be.'[41]

By Modder's stream we laid the Hieland bold Brigade,
At head we laid him who shall guide thro' Death to Victory;
An' the War-pipe's wild Lament told the Sacrifice was made.[42]

1900: Koodesberg and Paardeberg, the Horse Mountain

In the New Year, the Prime Minister, Lord Salisbury, proposed to revitalise the South African campaign. While General Buller retained command in Natal, the new Commander-in-Chief was Field Marshal Lord Roberts, known as Bobs Kandahar for his affability with private soldiers and his success against the Afghans in the 1878–79 Afghan War.[43] Travelling with Roberts was his Chief of Staff, Major General Horatio Herbert Kitchener, honoured as Baron Kitchener of Khartoum for his victory at Omdurman in 1898.[44] Roberts' strategy to relieve Kimberley was to bypass Magersfontein. In order to draw the Boers away from Natal and Cape Colony, the British force would then strike eastwards to capture Bloemfontein, capital of the Orange Free State.

Wauchope's successor in command of the Highland Brigade was Major General Hector MacDonald, Gordon Highlanders, while Lieutenant Colonel Archibald Carthew-Yorstoun took command of the 2nd Black Watch.[45] To bring the Battalion up to strength the 3rd

(Militia) Battalion sent drafts of reservists. Each of the six Volunteer Battalions, raised and affiliated to The Black Watch in the previous century, sent volunteers to three service companies which served with the 2nd Black Watch throughout the war. Only those who were marksmen or first-class shots, aged between twenty and thirty-five, were accepted.[46] A volunteer cavalry regiment, the Imperial Yeomanry, was also raised.

The Highland Brigade's next action was in early February at Koodesberg Drift, west of Magersfontein on the Riet river. The march was exhausting. 'If you could see the dust. Hundreds fell out,' Private McFarlane wrote home. 'The Boers kept sniping at us, and we at them, all day.' One of the two officers killed in the 2nd Black Watch was the amateur golf champion, Lieutenant Tait. After three days' skirmishing, on 7 February the Boers withdrew, the Highland Brigade returning to the Modder River Camp.[47] Meanwhile, the Cavalry Division, under the command of Major General Sir John French, was moving to outflank the Boer forces and capture Kimberley.[48] Realising that he was in danger of becoming caught in a trap, Cronjé's only escape was to withdraw east to Bloemfontein, taking up position at Paardeberg, where he had assembled some 5,000 men, 400 wagons, women, children and cattle, in anticipation of reinforcements arriving from Bloemfontein.

Cronjé's options narrowed when all available British forces converged on Paardeberg.[49] At 6 a.m. on 18 February the Highland Brigade advanced, encountering heavy fire from the Boers who held both sides of the Modder River. In an attempt to gain the advantage a detachment, commanded by Captain Stewart, crossed the river by linking arms in the water and 'hanging their ammunition pouches round their necks'. But yet again they encountered heavy Boer fire.[50] At dusk a general retirement was ordered. As a result of casualties sustained, which included the 2nd Black Watch's Commanding Officer, Lieutenant Colonel Carthew-Yorstoun, instead of attacking again Roberts ordered continual bombardment until Cronjé and his burghers could withstand no more.[51] On 27 February, the ninth anniversary of the British defeat at Majuba Hill, the Boers surrendered.

'Such an anniversary for Amajuba,' recorded Stewart, 'Cronjé and 3,700 Boers prisoner.' 'Tons' of ammunition and large quantities of stores were taken.[52]

Observing events from India, Grant Duff, 1st Black Watch, enthused: '*Tout vient à qui sait attendre.*' By comparison, his 'trivial existence' consisted 'of Parade before often after breakfast, Polo on Monday Wednesday & Friday and occasional games of hockey'.[53]

On 7 March, British forces again forced another withdrawal at Poplar Grove, opening the way to Bloemfontein, the Boers retreating 'in such haste as to leave their dinners cooking in the deserted camp'. As they departed, the British force shadowed them, clashing at Driefontein, the last line of defence before Bloemfontein. When night came, with their line broken to the north, the Boers again withdrew, the British soldiers arriving in Driefontein 'very hungry as nothing except biscuit since very scanty breakfast'.[54]

At Paardeberg, like eagles in the sun
With bloody plumes the Black Watch stand
The field is fought and won.[55]

Bloemfontein: 'Flags flying and bands playing'

Five months after the declaration of war, Roberts marched into Bloemfontein, followed by the Highland Brigade. 'The shops were all besieged,' Stewart observed. 'Prices are high – we bought tea cakes for 1/- and the Plums are 6d. Whiskey 9/- a bottle is sold out… Peace and quiet have been the order of the last few days and very welcome they are. On Friday the pipers played in the market square and I noticed several civilians looking on rather dejectedly, though the vast majority wore miniature Union Jacks.'[56]

Meanwhile, a draft of over 400 men had arrived at Capetown to reinforce the 2nd Black Watch. 'As we came off the ship we got grapes handed to us from ladies,' recorded Private Francis O'Brien.[57] 'What struck me as very interesting & peculiar at first was seeing so many different nationalities represented,' remarked Private John

McEuan Crearar, 1st Volunteer Company. 'Dutchmen, Englishmen, Germans, Italians, Malays, Chinese, Indians, Kaffirs & many others too numerous to mention, all jabbering in their various respective languages.' 'It seems like fairyland to me with all the queer characters going about,' noted another volunteer from Dundee.[58] Moving onwards to Naauwpoort, their appearance was in stark contrast to the veteran soldiers who had 'nothing but the clothes they stand up in, and these are all in rags'. On 12 April, the new arrivals entered Bloemfontein with 'flags flying and bands playing'.[59]

For the next six months the Highland Brigade had 'continual hard marching and occasional fighting' throughout the Orange Free State.[60] The weather had turned cold. 'Our blankets were stiff with the frost,' recorded Corporal Duff '& the cold was so intense that we had to run about before we could get our legs thawed.'[61] 'Reveille at 4.30 a.m. Shortly after we marched off and after a twelve mile march we heard guns firing to our front,' recorded Private Charles Rufus Critcher, describing an encounter with the Boers. 'The Black Watch were leading and presently we crossed the open Veldt and could see a large kopje in front of us. The artillery was searching the hill with their shrapnel and the cavalry went galloping round the kopje to flank them. We formed up for attack… our skirmishers advanced and the Boer commenced to fire on them… presently we advanced to the support of the firing line and the bullets began to sing around us.'[62]

Having driven the Boers off the hill, known as Bavian's Berg, their actions earned a commendation from Roberts: 'Black Watch distinguished themselves and were very well led.' 'We have had a very exciting time of it chasing back the Boers from hill to hill,' the Dundee volunteer informed his family from Winburg.[63] To counter the heat, 'colonial felt slouch hats were now taken into wear, and generally approved of, though hardly sufficiently thick to keep off the heat of the sun in hot weather.'[64] Queen Victoria's birthday was celebrated on 24 May with 'an issue of rum to drink her health in.'[65]

Trekking across the South African veldt had its hazards. Setting out from Winburg at the end of May, 'we were settled down for the night, we thought at a grand place for camping with plenty of water,' recorded Private O'Brien. While the soldiers were enjoying a swim and a wash, they received word that the advance guard of Seaforth Highlanders had been attacked. 'Everything was packed up in a hurry and we got some bullie beef which we ate on our way out of camp.' By the time they reached the Seaforths, 'everything was quiet,' but the presence of the Boers meant further attacks were likely. Continuing on to Lindley the following day, they had not gone 'more than a mile and a half when we found as we expected that the enemy had taken up a position in the ridge which we had to pass... We had to retire very quickly for our own good.' 'The bullets flew around us like hail. I dropped behind an ant hill,' recorded Private Critcher. 'It was very trying to the nerves lying without being able to fire, hearing the bullets whistle round you and having the wounded fellows groaning with pain.' By the time they reached the ridge where the Boers had taken up position, they had gone. Moving onwards, they reached Lindley before nightfall. 'I fell asleep thinking of wife and children and home and did not forget to offer a short prayer to my maker for being spared while others fell.'[66]

The following day, the 2nd Black Watch was ordered to remain as the rearguard: 'As The Black Watch were coming along a very heavy fire was being set into them.' Having been ordered to begin firing, 'our rifle fire seemed to have great effect because the Dutchmen cleared off at the double... This was my first shot I had got at the Boers,' continued O'Brien. As they marched onwards, the Boers continued to shell the advancing troops. 'When we were about six miles from Heilbron the Boers had taken up a position on our right commanding the road. Our guns put in a lot of good work while we got along the road right until dark when we were troubled no more by the Dutchmen who like ourselves would be glad of a rest.'[67]

On arrival at Heilbron the Highland Brigade was badly short of food and the men were put on half-rations, the ability to forage denied to them by the presence of the Boers on the surrounding hills who 'fired at you if you went outside the outpost line & would of course just disappear if you sent a force against them,' and who, as

Captain Stewart recorded, were still talking of 'sweeping us into the sea.' By 6 June Cameron was recording 'butter and sugar end.'[68] Two days later, Methuen arrived with a convoy 'composed of about 120 wagons with 10 days rations for our brigade'. But the Boers had captured a smaller convoy of supplies which included a delivery of mail. 'I felt bitterly disappointed for I have been looking forward to letters from home, being anxious to know that all the dear ones are well,' Private Critcher confided to his diary. Later, all registered letters and telegrams 'from various captured people' were returned.[69]

Meanwhile, on 5 June Roberts marched triumphantly into Pretoria, capital of the Transvaal, the Boers having proposed peace talks following an armistice agreed on 30 May. Johannesburg had also been captured and, to the west, after 217 days, the siege of Mafeking had been lifted, with the soldiers 'delighted at the good news'.[70] But the Transvaal Boers, now led by thirty-seven-year-old General Louis Botha, were not vanquished; nor were those in the Orange Free State, which, in late May, the British had named the Orange River Colony, causing further disaffection.[71] Without an agreed peace, the Highland Brigade was operating in circular movements, sometimes engaging the Boers, at others finding they had slipped away. 'Well of all unexciting cold blooded things recommend me to a modern battle – why you get more excited riding to a meet and I haven't found a man who thought otherwise,' Captain Stewart was writing from Heilbron in late June. 'No doubt in the old days when you got to close quarters and could hit somebody it was exciting, but I'm blowed if this game is.'[72]

Brandwater Basin: 'Three loud cheers'

After the capture of Bloemfontein, President Steyn, his senior burghers and their families, together with Christian de Wet and several thousand 'Free State' fighters had taken refuge in the Brandwater Basin, south of Bethlehem. Contoured like a huge horse-shoe formed by the Witte Bergen range, it extended from Commando Nek opposite Ficksburg in the west, to Slabbert's Nek and Retief's Nek, a narrow passage between the cliffs in the north. From there the outline of the horse-shoe continued south-east through Naauwpoort Nek and Golden Gate in the west. Through the centre ran the Brandwater river, a tributary of the Caledon river forming the boundary with the British protectorate of Basutoland, which bordered Natal and Cape Colony. In the heart of the basin was the village of Fouriesburg, where Steyn had established a provisional government. Although well-protected, four main points of entry provided access with two additional wagon routes in the east.

Roberts' strategy was to assemble sufficient troops to encircle the basin and force the Boers' surrender. 'Our convoy is the longest I have seen yet, being 7 miles in length. We have Black Watch, Seaforths, H.L.I. [Highland Light Infantry], 1 Battery of R.H.A [Royal Horse Artillery]. Details of Lancers 18th Hussars, Household Cavalry and mounted Infantry all for General French['s] Cavalry Brigade,' recorded Critcher on 1 July. 'We are now a large & motley crew collected here,' observed Cameron. 'The nights have been cold & frosty but the days warm & sunny.'[73] 'A very wearisome march and the cavalry burning every patch of the veldt which is like tinder,' related Stewart, referring to the scorched earth policy adopted by Roberts as collective punishment to the Boer farmers for aiding Britain's adversaries and in an attempt to deny them food.[74] The burning of farms, meant that thousands of women and children were forced to live in refugee or 'concentration' camps.

On 22 July 1900, Roberts' field commander, Lieutenant General Archibald Hunter, set out for the Brandwater Basin. Although Steyn, accompanied by Christian de Wet and nearly two thousand men, had escaped a week previously, there still remained over four thousand Free State Army fighters, commanded by de Wet's successor, General Martinus Prinsloo.[75] Of the various passes, Hunter ordered Commando Nek and Witnek in the west to be blocked, while two brigades of infantry would mount an attack on Slabbert's Nek in the centre. Hunter's own force, including the Highland Brigade, would attack Retief's Nek, while additional forces would move towards Naauwpoort. Although this left Golden Gate in the east unguarded until reinforcements arrived, Hunter guessed, correctly, that the

Boers would be unlikely to exit from the east. 'Marched off at 11.15 a.m. towards Retief's Nek,' Captain Cameron noted in his diary. 'Battn with two guns and cavalry was on left flank – little sniping – ground difficult for guns… took over an hour to get down bluff in single file. Poured with rain and was bitterly cold – did not reach camp till 9.30 p.m. and then it snowed.' After dawn on Monday 23 July the attack began with a heavy bombardment. 'Battn detailed to take kopje on left of [Retief's] nek.' But their advance was delayed 'as had no artillery to help us'. Eventually in the late afternoon, half of the Battalion advanced, supported by volleys from the other half. 'Carried kopje in 20 minutes and opened heavy fire on Boers as they rode away.'[76]

By mid-afternoon the following day, both Retief's Nek and Slabbert's Nek had been captured, the two forces meeting up inside the basin. 'We saw plenty of signs of the Boers' hasty flight and I also saw a string of our poor fellows buried under a tree. Lonely and silent are their graves,' observed Private Critcher.[77] With all possible exits now blocked, Prinsloo and what remained of the Free State Army was trapped. On 29 July he sent a message under a white flag offering to surrender, the process lasting a number of days on what became known as Surrender Hill east of Fouriesburg, where he had taken refuge. Over four thousand Boers surrendered their weapons, although Hunter allowed the burghers to keep their carts and covered wagons. On hearing of the surrender, the soldiers gave 'three loud cheers'. Served with rum, Private Skidmore noted in his diary, they 'lay down for the night, next morn[ing] we indulged in washing as we had not washed for a week'. The 2nd Black Watch had lost two officers and seventeen men.[78]

On 4 August Hunter's force reached Harrismith. 'The population consisted chiefly of English & Scotch subjects', related Private Crearar, 'who were almost mad with enthusiasm when they heard the Bagpipes skirling in the distance… we were greatly amused at the ceremony of raising the British Standard by an old Scotch Doctor over 70 years of age who pitched into a young influential-looking Boer for refusing to take his hat off while the anthem was being sung.'

'During the afternoon a good crowd of Boers came and gave up their arms & ponies,' related Private Critcher. 'I had a long conversation with several of them and found them very intelligent and thoroughly sick of the war and glad to see us there for they have had it rough just the same as we have.'[79]

With Steyn and de Wet still at large, fighting continued. For the next two months, the Highland Brigade was in the Kroonstad and Winburg districts 'encountering the Boers and capturing some wagons.'[80] On 14 August, Critcher was recording how, while escorting a convoy and passing to the left of Spitz Kop 'without the slightest warning and when in an exposed position, the Boers commenced shelling the convoy with 4 guns from the distant kopjes. There was nothing to be done but gallop out of range with the wagons as we were helpless for the time.' By sunset, once the artillery was brought forward, the Boers 'as usual had flitted.' Another action on 13 September resulted in the capture of thirty-three Boer wagons 'loaded with clothes and comforts. I got a fair share of loot and marched into camp with one of the captured wagons.'[81]

Meanwhile, Roberts had been pursuing the Transvaal Boers. His victory at Diamond Hill in June, ensuring that the Boers could not recapture Pretoria, marked a turning point. In August his army linked up with Buller's forces in Natal and on 1 September 1900 the Transvaal was annexed to the British Crown. Since the Boer leaders refused to surrender, guerrilla warfare continued.

The Highland Brigade was still operating in and around Kroonstad. 'The great pleasure of this place', Cameron informed his mother, 'is the Scottish Hospital. It looks so comfortable that one longs to be ill when one sees it. On Friday we played the members of it at cricket. On Saturday they gave some Highland games for the Brigade & stood us tea & the Militia Band played & everything was peaceful; one wished one could have asked de Wet to come & perhaps he might have seen how much more pleasant peace is than War.'[82] But, as the soldiers realised, the difficulty of ending the war arose from their inability to defeat the Boers decisively. 'As the Boers won't fight (not that I want them to do anything desperate) and we can't catch them,

I don't see how we are going to end this show,' Cameron wrote home. 'We picture ourselves for years trekking round the Free state, till we become a phantom brigade like the Flying Dutchman; nothing to be seen, but at night the wailing of pipes and loud curses will be heard at night… to the terror of the inhabitants.'[83]

Returning to Bloemfontein, 'the Brigade was broken up & its various Regiments sent to garrison towns in the Cape and Orange River Colonies,' recorded Private Crearar.[84] Since it had become too hot for felt hats, helmets 'were now taken into wear.' In early October the 2nd Black Watch went to garrison Ladybrand, east of Bloemfontein, 'as the Boers in that district who had surrendered had risen again.' 'On arrival at Ladybrand', continued Crearar, 'every available man was sent to build walls across the streets, dig trenches, & put up barb wire Entanglements. When these fortifications were completed the town had the appearance of a Chinese puzzle.'[85]

With both the Orange River Colony and the Transvaal nominally under British authority, at the beginning of November Roberts handed over as commander-in-chief to Kitchener. Before leaving he acknowledged the difficulties of the campaign:

> There has been no rest, no days off to recruit, no going into winter quarters as in other Campaigns which have extended over a long period. For months together in fierce heat, in biting cold & in pouring rain you, my comrades, have marched & fought without a halt & Bivouacked without shelter from the elements & you frequently have had to continue marching with your clothes in rags & your boots without soles, time being of such great consequence that it was impossible for you to remain long enough in any one place to refit. When not engaged in actual Battle you have been continually shot at from behind kopjes by an invisible enemy to whom every inch of the ground was familiar & who from the peculiar nature of the Country were able to inflict severe punishment while perfectly safe themselves.[86]

Since November, for the first time in The Black Watch's history, a Regimental Mounted Infantry detachment had been raised, and which had 'several brushes with the enemy.'[87] Leisure activities included 'fishing, swimming, visiting farms,' related Private O'Brien. 'We caught eighty-nine fish one day.' He was also pleased to record receiving turkey and plum pudding from the Captain 'for our Christmas Dinner. We got presents from different farms in the shape of cakes and fancy bread.'[88]

1901–02: 'Seasons may roll'

The new year was shaped by the news of Queen Victoria's death on 22 January. From their postings in South Africa and in India, The Black Watch marked her passing by attending church ceremonies. 'She came to the throne amid profound indifference. She leaves a world in tears,' observed Grant Duff in India. Officers would now have their commissions signed by the new King, fifty-nine-year-old Edward VII.[89]

Throughout 1901 Kitchener's strategy was one of containment, overseeing the building of protective circular blockhouses in locations under frequent Boer attack, such as railways. He also expanded Roberts' scorched earth policy. But, as the number of dispossessed families increased, the camps became overcrowded and conditions deteriorated. With insufficient food, medicine and doctors, and poor hygiene, disease spread.[90] The 2nd Black Watch remained at Ladybrand, its duty, as before, to prevent the Boers from seizing supplies and destroying communications. The British proclamation on 7 August 1901 'threatening severe penalties on all who failed to surrender by the 15th of September' proved 'a complete failure.'[91]

In September the Battalion went to northern Natal. 'Arrived at New castle & had breakfast,' recorded Corporal Duff. 'Glad to get out of the train after our 50 hours ride & almost 600 miles from Ladybrand.' But, as Captain Stewart had observed, travelling by train was far preferable to marching. 'A train seemed a terribly quick method of locomotion after so long a time, 14 miles an hour, about a day's march.'[92] Divided into detachments, they operated on the Natal and Zululand borders, where Botha had gathered a force of nearly two thousand men 'with the evident intention of making a second invasion.'[93] While some soldiers were engaged in building blockhouses, others joined a corps of irregular mounted scouts commanded by Lieutenant Colonel Michael (Mike) Rimington. Popularly known as Rimington's Tigers from their custom of wearing wild-cat skins around their hats, their official name was Rimington's Guides.[94] The cavalry, observed newly commissioned Second Lieutenant Archibald Wavell, had plenty of action, but the infantry – the 'foot sloggers' – had to do a lot of 'trekking' and little fighting and so it was 'not very exciting work.'[95]

On 13 November 1901, having offered itself for active service in South Africa, the 1st Black Watch received orders to leave India. Embarking on board the S.S. *Armenian* on 6 December, 'after a calm though very hot voyage of 17 days,' they reached Durban, proceeding up country by train. Stationed at Harrismith, their duties included constructing blockhouses and guarding the railway line, while individual companies were sent to join various companies on operations. Soon after the Battalion's arrival a detachment was sent to Elands River Bridge, 'a march of about 18 miles which the men covered well taking into consideration that it was the hot season of the year and that the men had been three days in the train.'[96]

Both the 1st and 2nd Black Watch spent Christmas 1901 in South Africa. There was 'very little difference', recorded Second Lieutenant James Blair, who had joined the 2nd Black Watch at Ladybrand in July, between Christmas Day and any other day.[97]

Throughout early 1902, while the 1st Black Watch remained in Harrismith, the 2nd Black Watch was still working in detachments on the Natal border. Soldiering, remarked Second Lieutenant Wavell, was unpredictable and tiring. 'Last night, I thought I was going to get some sleep at last as no orders to move had come. But at 3.15 a.m. this morning a sergeant put his head into my bivouac and told me reveille was at 3.45 and parade at 4.50 a.m. We started about 5.a.m.

and got here at 12 noon about. It is very nearly 20 miles so it was pretty good marching.'[98] Successes were notable. 'Today has been a great day as we have at least come in contact with the Boers and we bagged 3 with 6 or 7 rifles, 30 or 40 saddles and a few horses,' noted Blair. A month later he was recording that 'it simply poured all last night, & I found a nice little puddle under my valise this morning when I woke up. I felt very sorry for the men as they had no tents.'[99]

Fatalities, although not frequent, still occurred. 'Some Boers tried to break through our line on high ground between Elands River & Bethlehem,' recorded Major Hugh Rose, describing an encounter in late March while in command of a group of the Battalion's Military Band, manning a blockhouse. 'Being foiled, they fired at the shining roof of this blockhouse from some 1500 yards away. A chance bullet entered the collarbone of Lance Corporal Walter Scott of the Band, & came out at the base of his spine. He fell dead in the arms of "Punch" Wilson.'[100]

At the beginning of March the Boers had achieved an unexpected success when, during an attack on a convoy at Tweebosch, Methuen was captured. But his injuries, which included a broken leg, were so severe that de la Rey released him so he could be treated in hospital. A month later Boer forces were beaten at Rooiwal, signifying the last major battle of the war, after which talks for 'a perpetual treaty of friendship and peace' began in earnest. On 31 May, the second anniversary of Roberts' entrance into Johannesburg, Milner and Kitchener, on behalf of Great Britain, signed the Peace of Vereeniging; Steyn was unwell and so de Wet signed on behalf of the Orange Free State. Schalk Burger, Acting President, signed for the Transvaal. All Boer fighters had to surrender themselves and their weapons. Everyone had to swear allegiance to the Crown; no one would receive the death penalty and a general amnesty would apply. After three years' fighting the British government had achieved its objective: both Boer republics reverted to British imperial authority.[101]

'Heard peace was declared,' Wavell recorded in his diary on Sunday 1 June. 'Whether the war is over or not is a different matter,' observed Blair. 'It was very curious that, when the news was given out, there was not a sound of rejoicing.'[102] 'We spend an idle life,' Captain Grant Duff was writing on 10 June. 'I read & do German. A tooth has been bothering… the nights are bitterly cold & I should be glad to get the men back to tents & extra blankets.'[103] On 27 June, while, unusually, the two battalions were stationed together at Harrismith athletic sports were held 'at which our men & those of the 73rd [2nd Battalion] won nearly everything.' A football match between officers and sergeants led to Wavell injuring his shoulder and collar bone, resulting in his return home to convalesce.[104]

In September 1902 orders were received to transfer as many men as possible from the 1st to the 2nd Black Watch for service in India. 'I think they might have let our men go home for a month or so first, some of them have been abroad a long time,' noted Grant Duff. 'And,' he continued, emphasising the different sense of belonging which existed between the two battalions, 'they resent being sent to the 73rd [the 2nd Battalion] as they say that they only extended to serve with their own regiment. It is a rotten system.'[105] 'Late in the day we came to this country,' Lieutenant Colonel Edward Grogan observed in his Farewell Order, relinquishing command of the 1st Black Watch to Lieutenant Colonel Alexander Gordon Duff, 'and consequently our opportunities have been few, but the most has been made of them.'[106] Leaving Harrismith in late September, the 1st Black Watch returned to Britain. Of those who had left Scotland to serve in Egypt and the Sudan in August 1882, only Lieutenant Colonel Duff, Quartermaster William Bruce Ferguson Davidson and Drummer William (Barney) Reilly were still in the Regiment.[107]

'Poorer in men, richer in heroes'

The Black Watch's losses during the South African War numbered fourteen officers and 198 men killed, seventeen officers and 370 men wounded, the majority at Magersfontein.[108] Nearly 8,000 British and Dominion lives were lost in action, while almost twice as many died of disease, total casualties recorded as 52,156.[109] From a smaller fighting force, Boer losses were over 9,000, over half of whom died in action. An estimated 24,000 had been transported abroad and nearly 30,000 had died in the concentration camps, used to detain not only white Boers and their families but thousands of Black Africans, an unknown number of whom died.[110] Numerous memorials were raised throughout the British Empire, the first being the granite memorial cross in South Africa, unveiled by Lord Milner in 1902, its inscription reading: 'Scotland is poorer in men, but richer in heroes.'[111]

On 5 May 1903 a memorial window and plaque with the names of the fallen was unveiled at St Ninian's Cathedral, Perth. 'Greater love hath no man than this, that a man lay down his life for his friends,' declared the Very Reverend V. L. Rorison, Dean of St Andrews, citing the words of St John's Gospel.[112] A week later, the 2nd Black Watch travelled by special train to Dalkeith Palace for the presentation of South African War Medals, Edward VII praising The Black Watch for having shown its 'old spirit'.[113] In August Earl Roberts opened the Wauchope and Black Watch Memorial Home in Perth.[114] In February 1905 another memorial was unveiled by the Duke of Atholl, Lord Lieutenant of the County, in St John's East Parish Church, Perth, the benediction given by the former chaplain of the Highland Brigade, the Reverend James Robertson.[115] In 1908 Edward VII opened the Queen Victoria School in Dunblane as a memorial to those killed. Two years later a memorial 'to the memory of Officers, Non-Commissioned Officers & Men of The Black Watch who fell in the South African War' was unveiled on the Mound in Edinburgh.[116]

For as long as life lasts must be warfare.
Till th' strivings of nations shall cease,
Till th' sword be beat into a ploughshare,
And thro' the wide world shall be peace.
Then forward! March forward! Men of Motherland,
Th' Union Jack of Freedom to float o'er the Rand.[117]

2

Balancing Power

You can speak about your First Royals or your Irish Fusiliers
The Aberdeen Militia or the Queen's Own Volunteers
Or any other Regiment that's lying far awa'
Come gie to me the tartan o' the Gallant Forty Twa![1]

The genesis of world war

While Mary, the wife of the former caddie master, John McGregor, 'missing, presumed killed' at Magersfontein, was struggling to get a war widow's pension, the European balance of power had again begun to shift. In 1904 French and British representatives signed a series of documents, embodied in the Entente Cordiale, recognising each other's respective spheres of influence in their colonial empires. Pre-dating this new relationship, the Triple Alliance between Germany, Austria-Hungary and Italy had been renewed in 1902. When, in July 1905, the Tsar attempted to revitalise Russia's relationship with Germany by signing the Treaty of Björkö which was to be a mutual defence accord with his cousin, Kaiser Wilhelm – both grandsons of Queen Victoria – his ministers rejected it on the grounds that Russia could not give the same assurances to both France and Germany 'whose interests were mutually antagonistic'.[2] Two years later, with the signature of the Anglo-Russian Convention in August 1907, a halt was called to Russia's rivalry with Great Britain in the 'Great Game' enacted in Central Asia. Given Russia's prior convention with France, this Triple Entente created a formidable counter-weight to the Triple Alliance. Throughout this period, Great Britain's own competitive relationship with Germany was accelerating. As early as 1904 'it was borne in upon me that we would most certainly be at war with Germany within ten years,' commented Major Hugh Rose, recalling his service as private secretary to the Governor who was also Admiral of the Indian Ocean in Mauritius. 'What made me so sure of the ten years was a "graph" of our respective fleets.'[3]

In view of Britain's experiences in South Africa, which had demonstrated that a prolonged offensive required reinforcements beyond the capacity of the regular reserve, Britain's military establishment was being overhauled. An important component of the reforms, put forward by the newly appointed Liberal Secretary of State for War, Richard Haldane, was the creation of an Expeditionary Force composed of six (later reduced to four) infantry divisions and one cavalry division, which could fight overseas, theoretically anywhere, but optimised for war on the continent.

With the passage of the Territorial and Reserve Forces Act in 1907, transferring the rifle volunteer and yeomanry forces into a new Territorial Force for home defence, The Black Watch gained four more battalions from the Volunteer battalions: the 4th (City of Dundee), 5th (Angus & Dundee), 6th (Perthshire) and 7th (Fifeshire) Battalions, forming The Black Watch Brigade.[4] Included in the 6th Black Watch was a 'self-contained' Irish company, raised and based in Ireland, originating from the early 1900s when 'a number of men from Dublin – civil servants, bank and insurance men – were on a cycling tour in Scotland.' Having met some members of a volunteer battalion attending their annual camp, Private George Farrar, who joined the Dublin section of the Irish company in 1909, noted that the convivial evening the men spent together had persuaded them to join the Perthshire Territorials.[5] Eighteen-year-old Alfred Anderson enlisted in the 5th Black Watch in 1912 'chiefly to attend the annual camp – as a holiday'.[6] 'Each of these battalions was to carve out of history an individual page of its own', wrote a future Colonel of the Regiment, Bernard Fergusson, later Lord Ballantrae, 'to be bound into the book of the History of The Black Watch as a whole.'[7]

In terms of weaponry, fighting the Boers had revealed the need for accurate marksmanship, which contributed to the remodelling of the Lee Enfield rifle in use by the British Army since the 1880s. In 1904 a new, lighter 'short rifle' model was introduced known as the Short Magazine Lee Enfield (SMLE) Mark I. Its system of charger loading increased the rapidity and accuracy of sustained fire, enabling a well-trained soldier to fire twenty to thirty rounds at a target within a minute.[8] The training of Black Watch officers at the School of Musketry at Hythe in Kent had a 'cascade' effect throughout the Battalion.[9]

Scotland and Ireland: Routine and ceremony

During the first decade of the twentieth century the soldiers of The Black Watch were barely aware of the shifting European relationships which would affect their lives so dramatically. For those not on active service, life was one of routine and ceremony. A highlight for twenty-five non-commissioned officers (NCOs) at the end of 1900 had been travelling to Sydney, Australia, as part of an Imperial Corps representing the British Army at the country's federation into the Commonwealth of Australia on 1 January 1901. During their three-month stay – the Regiment's first visit since the 73rd's posting in 1810 – 'the men of The Black Watch detachment distinguished themselves in many of the sports held in honour of the Imperial Corps, W. Ross, formerly pipe-major of the 2nd Battalion, winning every open piping competition.'[10]

'There are some curious new orders,' Captain Adrian Grant Duff was noting of the 1st Black Watch's existence in Scotland in November 1902. 'Men are allowed to stay out till reveille without a pass which does not seem to me desirable… Young boys are better under a certain amount of restraint especially in the surroundings of a garrison town.'[11] In 1903 one company, under the command of Major Hugh Rose, provided the Royal Guard at Ballater during the Royal Family's summer holidays at Balmoral. The first time the Regiment had done so was in 1900 when a company was despatched from the 3rd (Militia) Battalion. In the years to come, providing the Royal Guard at Ballater was to become a regular occurrence, engendering special memories for those selected.[12]

Another memorable occasion was the visit in August 1904 of the military band and seven pipers, under Major Rose's command, to Toronto, where they had been invited to play at the Canadian National Exhibition before touring the country, the party 'most enthusiastically received and feted in the Cities of Montreal Toronto Winnipeg and Ottawa'. Included in the delegation greeting them were several veterans who had served in the Regiment in the late 1870s and settled in Canada.[13] As a memento, the Exhibition directors presented Rose with a 'fine silver' Canadian punch bowl, inscribed with the words: 'Presented to the Officers' Mess, 42nd Royal Highlanders, The Black Watch.'[14] After the tour Rose recorded how while 'prowling round the Toronto Fair', he was 'much impressed by an invention called the "Sub-Target" [gun machine] for training recruits to fire accurately'. Back home he bought one 'and never was money better spent'.[15] The link with Canada was enduring: in 1905 the oldest Highland Regiment in Canada (known since 1904 as the 5th Regiment Royal Scots of Canada, Highlanders), became affiliated to the Regiment, assuming the name 5th Regiment Royal Highlanders of Canada in 1906. The following year The Black Watch's name was included, the Regiment becoming the 5th Regiment Royal Highlanders of Canada (Black Watch).[16]

In September 1904 the 1st Black Watch moved to Fort George. Its last posting there was during the Napoleonic Wars in 1791–93. Two years later, the Battalion moved to Ireland, the soldiers stationed in barracks on the open plains of the Curragh, County Kildare. 'At that time gambling was frequent among the men,' recorded Private William Buchanan (Tug) Wilson, who had enlisted in The Black Watch in 1908. 'At nights after lights out, a blanket would be put round the barrack room table and a candle lit, then the gamblers would commence… they would have a man watching for the approach of the Provost Sergeant or any of his Regimental police.'[17] While in Ireland, having observed how sailors trained 'at the double',

Major Rose determined to improve the soldiers' fitness. 'Our scheme was not popular at first, as you may imagine; men with adipose tissue, and beer drinkers, etc. found the doubling about a great trial, so we introduced weekly runs of 6 to 7 miles, in which everyone had to take part... The boozers found that good health was a better egg than a "head" in the morning, and the Battalion became very much more sober.'[18]

In September 1909 the 1st Black Watch moved to the 'wild district' of Limerick where the 2nd Black Watch had served in the 1890s, Rose taking command of the Battalion in May 1910.[19] The soldiers had initially felt unwelcome because, according to Private Wilson, 'a Scots Cavalry Regt' had painted yellow the monument of the nationalist leader and campaigner for Catholic emancipation, Daniel O'Connell. 'The Celts of Ireland were about as unforgiving as we Celts of Scotland.' The Regiment's reputation improved when the soldiers helped in 'battling the flames' of a serious fire in Limerick in June 1911. 'The people of Limerick took the Battalion to its heart and I'm sure as Scots, we were not associated with our countrymen who had painted the Dan O'Connell monument yellow any more.'[20]

India: 'A grand lot of chaps'

Until the 1907 military convention with Russia, defence of India against a presumed Russian threat was Britain's main military concern. Of secondary importance, nearly fifty years after the Indian Mutiny, was internal security. To supplement the Indian Army, British regiments were required, rotating between locations, which provided greater variety and experience.[21] By the time the 2nd Black Watch began its service in India in October 1902, General Kitchener had been appointed Commander-in-Chief, under the Viceroy, George Nathaniel Curzon: both were anxious for reform.

The Battalion's first ceremonial duty was taking part in the magnificent Delhi Durbar to celebrate the coronation of King Edward VII and Queen Alexandra as Emperor and Empress of India. The festivities, lasting two weeks, included sports, military bands and exhibitions, and culminated in a coronation ball on New Year's Day 1903. Representing the King and Queen were the Duke and Duchess of Connaught, and the events were attended by most of the rulers of the Indian Princely states riding on elephants. To young soldiers sighting India for the first time the spectacle must have been dazzling.

After two years in Ambala (Umbala) on the Grand Trunk Road, in 1904 the Battalion moved to Peshawar, following in the footsteps of the 1st Black Watch in 1865.

To determine the level of efficiency, during the winter of 1904/5 each battalion was required to undertake the Kitchener or Commander-in-Chief's Test, which included transport duties, loading animals with kit, tools, ammunition rations and tents, and 'miscellaneous duties' such as 'knotting' and 'bayonet fighting'. One test required the soldiers to march for 15 miles with 100 rounds of ammunition in order to defend a position at the top of a steep hill and 'retirements covered by rear guards'.[22] Whereas the Gordon Highlanders, also posted to Peshawar, took the test seriously, The Black Watch did not, finding itself ambushed by the Gordons![23] According to Lieutenant the Hon. Malise Hore-Ruthven, when the results were published, the 2nd Black Watch came bottom. 'It was not so much that we were badly trained, as not trained at all. A grand lot of chaps, scrambling along mostly in blissful ignorance of how ignorant we were.'[24]

The men could, however, be proud of their sporting successes. In March 1905 the Battalion football team won the Murray Cup at Lucknow, beating the Royal Irish Rifles; it also won the open shooting competition for the Division. Sport for the officers ranged from the Peshawar Vale Hunt to golf, polo, cricket and hockey. 'Deeply regretted by all who knew him' was the death in March 1905 of Lieutenant Robert Macpherson Robertson 'from the result of a Polo accident'.[25] As always, illness reduced their ranks, the number of those falling ill with fever in the winter of 1906 meaning that the Battalion only mustered 450 men out of a total strength of nearly 1,100.

Moving to the hill station of Cherat for the summers 'the cemetery of the sixteen men of the 42nd who died there in 1867 was put in order and permanently preserved.'[26] To amuse their fellow officers, Lieutenants Archibald Wavell and Charles Henderson, (known as 'Long Man' to distinguish him from the shorter Lieutenant Neville Henderson), together with Lance Corporal McDonald, edited a newspaper, the *Cherat Times and Jalozai Chronicle, A family journal for the million*, with 'notes and news', whose 'crude' humour appealed to the men, and in which Wavell could indulge his fondness for writing doggerel:

Tin huts do not a station make,
Nor wooden sheds a Club;
I'd all the "social joys" forsake,
Could I but find a pub! [27]

On 18 November 1907 the 2nd Black Watch moved from Peshawar to Sialkot in the Punjab, taking part in the Jhelum–Sialkot manoeuvres the following year. All ranks were commended for 'keenness, good work and discipline'.[28]

The first Colonel-in-Chief

On 6 May 1910, after just over nine years on the throne, Edward VII died. No sooner had George V's coronation ceremony taken place at Westminster Abbey on 22 June 1911 than the King and Queen left for India. Their presence at the Delhi Durbar was the only time in Britain's imperial history that a reigning monarch visited India. Among those present was the 2nd Black Watch, whose ranks had recently been filled with a draft of 112 NCOs and men from the 1st Black Watch, one of whom was Private Tug Wilson, who had joined the pipe band. 'I was not so enthusiastic about drafts. However an old soldier of the pipe band said foreign service should be the lot of every man who wanted to see something, so on foreign service I did go'.[29]

During the celebrations the King presented new Colours to the Battalion, the first since Belfast in May 1889 when his late brother Albert, then Prince of Wales, had presided.[30] Having been present at the 1889 ceremony, George V began: 'Remember that this is no common flag which I am committing to your keeping. A Colour is a sacred Ensign; ever, by its inspiration, though no longer by its presence, a rallying-point in battle. It is the emblem of duty: the outward sign of your allegiance to God, your Sovereign, and Country: to be looked up to, to be venerated, and to be passed down untarnished by succeeding generations.' Reminding young soldiers of the Battalion's past exploits, he continued: 'As the 73rd you made your name first in India, so it is fitting that you should receive your new Colours in this place.'[31] Among his listeners was twenty-two-year-old the Hon. Fergus Bowes-Lyon, commissioned into the Regiment in 1910.

The Black Watch was also granted the privilege of providing a Guard of Honour on the steps where the King and Queen were crowned. 'The smartest and tallest men of the battalion were chosen… and it was a splendid sight seeing them fully dressed on practice parade,' observed Wilson.[32] Subsequently, on the King's orders, 108 'Coronation' medals were issued to those who had taken part.[33]

By the time the King returned to Britain, the 1st Black Watch was in Edinburgh. 'We did Guard duties at the entrance to the Castle, in Crown Square and at Holyrood,' related Private Frank MacFarlane. 'There were shooting ranges at Arthur's Seat and we would march there through the town with a Piper.' In July and August they went to Stobbs Camp near Hawick. 'It was lovely weather… we did field manoeuvres and a lot of rifle practice and route marches. Ten miles the first day, 15 miles the next and 20 by the end of the week all in full kit with a rest for 10 minutes every hour. Along with the cross country running it got you into full fitness.'[34] They also enjoyed highland games, including 'tossing the caber' and 'throwing the hammer', five-a-side football and five-a-side hockey as well as boxing.[35]

On 3 September 1912 an enduring link between the Royal Family and the Regiment was established when George V assumed the honorary role of Colonel-in-Chief of The Black Watch (Royal Highlanders); soon afterwards, for the first time in nine years, a company provided the Royal Guard at Ballater. The following year the Battalion journeyed south. 'There were great crowds to see us off and the whole of Edinburgh knew we were leaving,' continued MacFarlane. 'We travelled overnight, arrived at Aldershot and marched to Oudenarde Barracks.'[36] One of the Battalion's first duties was sending a contingent to take part in the funeral at St Paul's Cathedral of Field Marshal Viscount Wolseley: 'easily our best soldier since Wellington,' remarked Major Adrian Grant Duff.[37] 'London was covered in dense fog that day,' related MacFarlane. 'Some of the streets were paved with wooden blocks to keep down the noise of horses and carriages.' At Aldershot 'a big change' was initiated when the eight companies in the Battalion were 'doubled up' to form four. 'And to give the officers experience in handling a much larger body of men they developed a scheme whereby one Regiment would amalgamate with another. The HLI [Highland Light Infantry] was the one we were amalgamated with… the HLI were quite a good Regiment, but there was the usual banter between the Regiments of course: "… the HLI the dirty crew, they lost their kilts at Waterloo."'[38]

George V's inspection of the 1st Black Watch in May 1913 provided the opportunity for him to be presented with certain 'regimental ornaments', paid for by officers, past and present, in recognition of his position as Colonel-in-Chief. One of them was a dirk, copied from an 18th century model.[39] Subsequently the King approved the addition of *North America 1763–64* to the Regiment's Battle Honours 'in recognition of services rendered during the war against the Red Indians' 150 years previously.[40] A highlight of 1913 was taking part in the Grand Manoeuvres in September 'before all the crowned heads of Europe. We went from Aldershot all the way up to Banbury Cross – every road was blocked with troops and transport,' observed MacFarlane. 'We used no mechanised transport on these exercises, it was all horse-drawn.'[41]

The European Crisis

In Europe tensions between the Triple Alliance and the Triple Entente were increasing. In the corridors of Whitehall and at numerous meetings of the Committee of Imperial Defence, discussions focused not on whether but how a European war would be conducted. Illustrative of their deliberations was a three-page 'secret' memorandum, 'Military Aspects of the Continental Problem', written in 1911 by Home Secretary Winston Churchill, in which he suggested that the decisive theatre would be along the borders between France, Belgium and Germany. Given Germany's ability to mobilise superior numbers of troops, he thought that France's only option would be to fight a defensive war. Instead of 'being frittered into action piecemeal', his suggestion was for a British Expeditionary Force (BEF) to be 'assembled around (say Tours) by the fortieth day, in rear of the French left' by which time, assailed by both France and Russia, Germany's forces would be 'extended at full strain', providing the opportunity for a 'decisive trial of strength.'[42] Major General Henry Wilson, Director of Military Operations, disagreed, suggesting that if the BEF took up a position alongside the French immediately war was declared 'the chances of repulsing the Germans in the first shock of battle were favourable. Every French soldier would fight with double confidence if he knew he were not fighting alone.'[43]

A ringside observer to events at the War Office was Major Grant Duff, who, as military assistant secretary to the Committee of Imperial Defence, had been given responsibility for designing and editing 'The War Book'. This was a manual which outlined the procedures to be followed by government departments, including the War Office, the Admiralty, Colonial and Indian Offices and the Treasury, on the outbreak of war. 'I have been delving mainly into Co-ordination,' he observed on 11 March 1912, shortly before the first edition of the War Book was completed in May. 'The Admiralty, who sit up and purr on the slightest provocation, have now come to see the usefulness of my proceedings.'[44] In the months to come, further revisions to the War Book were made. 'One excellent result of the co-ordination committee is that most if not all the departments have also drawn up War Books for internal office use setting out the precise action to be taken and assigning the responsibility & indicating where everything & everybody is to be found etc.' Of importance was 'trying to crystallize some ideas as to what the effect of a big European war is likely to be on our industry & trade & on the internal situation generally.' But, he remarked, 'it is not easy to get any very convincing results with so many speculative factors.'[45]

Wavell, promoted captain in March 1913, was also at the War Office. Having left the 2nd Black Watch in India to attend Staff College, he had spent a year in Moscow learning Russian. He was then assigned to the Russian section, attending manoeuvres in the Caucasus mountains in 1912 and in Kiev in 1913. Assessing Russia's military potential, he noted that the Russian soldier was 'a first class' fighter, but higher command was weak and the army was short of equipment. He was also following events in Ireland where, throughout the summer of 1914, Home Rule was being hotly debated.[46]

Meanwhile, the 'European Crisis' was evolving. Those who had been thinking war was inevitable did not predict that the catalyst would originate in the Balkans. On Sunday 28 June 1914 the Archduke Franz Ferdinand of Austria, and his wife Sophie, Duchess of Hohenberg, were assassinated while visiting Sarajevo, capital of Bosnia-Herzegovina. That the assassin, Gavrilo Princip, was a member of the Young Bosnia Revolutionary Movement, which had links to neighbouring Serbia's Black Hand nationalist organisation, triggered a series of diplomatic exchanges between the European foreign ministries, their respective accords increasing the potential to widen the conflict. On 23 July (as British officials were engaged in an abortive conference at Buckingham Palace on Ireland) the Emperor of Austria-Hungary, Franz Joseph I, sent Serbia a harsh ultimatum, supported by Germany. Three days later, Austria-Hungary ordered partial mobilisation, declaring war on Serbia on 28 July. The following day Tsar Nicholas partially mobilised the Russian Army in support of Serbia. On the same day Britain's War Office issued a Precautionary Order to all Army units. All leave was cancelled and officers and men were ordered to return to their barracks. 'All glittering articles of your uniform had to be dulled and then "all bayonets to be collected and sharpened",' commented Private MacFarlane.[47]

On 30 July the British Government rejected Germany's proposal for Britain's neutrality. The following day Russia ordered general mobilisation and Germany proclaimed a state of *Kriegsgefahr* ('danger of war'). On 1 August Germany declared war on Russia and full German mobilisation was ordered. On the same day the British government ordered naval mobilisation. 'We shall face the situation with much greater calm when we know that our land forces are all mobilized and at their war stations,' proffered the Military Correspondent of *The Times*. With Britain's involvement still unclear, he continued: 'Even if the need for these services does not arise – and it will be the less likely to arise if we are known to be prepared.'[48] To avoid fighting a war on two fronts and adhering to suggestions made by the former Chief of the Imperial German general staff, Field Marshal Alfred von Schlieffen, German strategy required a rapid strike against Russia's ally, France, before turning east.[49] Circumventing France's fortified frontier, the main thrust of Germany's attack would be through Belgium, with or without its permission. On 3 August Germany declared war on France; on the same day the British Government ordered general mobilisation, *The Times* now proclaiming that 'the great catastrophe has come upon Europe'.[50]

In Britain, opinion remained divided. 'We are going to suffer, I am afraid, terribly in this war, whether we are in it or whether we stand aside,' Foreign Secretary Sir Edward Grey stated in the House of Commons. Mindful of the 1839 treaty guaranteeing Belgium's neutrality (supported by Britain, France, Italy, Austria and Prussia), the position of Belgium precluded Britain's 'unconditional neutrality'. Failure to act, Grey concluded, would mean sacrificing 'our respect and good name and reputation before the world, and [we] should not escape the most serious and grave economic consequences.'[51]

On 4 August the Prime Minister, H. H. Asquith, addressed the House of Commons, explaining how the King of the Belgians had appealed to Great Britain for diplomatic intervention on behalf of his country following Germany's demand (and Belgium's refusal) for free passage. Simultaneously, continued Asquith, the Belgian Legation had sent a telegram informing him that Belgian territory had been violated. Britain's ultimatum to Germany stipulated that German troops should be withdrawn from Belgium by midnight Central

European time (11 p.m. GMT).[52] Once the ultimatum expired, 'a sheaf of cipher telegrams' was despatched to Britain's colonies and embassies around the world, informing their officials that a state of war now existed between them and the German Empire.[53]

As the crowds cheered in excitement outside Buckingham Palace, few shared the foreboding of the King who warned of a 'terrible catastrophe but it is not our fault'.[54] 'We had the greatest confidence in ourselves as a Battalion,' commented Private MacFarlane. 'We believed that a British soldier was worth three Germans – it didn't turn out that way, but the morale in the Battalion was very, very high.'[55]

Marching, marching,
On the old-time track;
Soldier's song upon my lip,
Haversack upon my hip,
Pack upon my back;
Linton on my left hand,
On my right side Jack –
Marching, marching,
Steel swung at my thigh,
Marching, marching,
Who so gay as I?
(Left, left!) [56]

3

1914: The Great War

Twas in August 1914 (the Black Watch lay encamped),
When we loosed the British Bulldog, and off to war he tramped.[1]

Halt the Greys, Steady the Bays, and let the Black Watch through.[2]

August 1914: Setting Europe on fire

'With the utmost reluctance and with infinite regret,' Prime Minister Asquith announced, 'His Majesty's Government have been compelled to put this country in a state of war with what for many years and indeed generations past has been a friendly Power.'[3] The order to mobilise, received on 4 August by the 1st Black Watch at Oudenarde Barracks, Aldershot, signalled a period of frenzied activity. According to Army Regulations, those under nineteen were debarred from service abroad and so 200 reservists and an additional 300 men were needed to bring the Battalion up to a wartime strength.[4]

'The spirit of the regiment was up to fever heat,' recorded Private Tug Wilson, serving with the 2nd Black Watch in Bareilly, India. 'What a change was noticeable on the regiment during those waiting days which seemed to take weeks in passing... all were now anxious to get across to Europe in time to take part in the fight and we did not want the war to be over before we got there.'[5] Balaclava helmets for warmth and pay books and identification discs were issued. Those away from the Regiment were disappointed. Among them was Captain Wavell at the War Office, informing his sister that he was 'too utterly depressed, for it seemed to him that it would never be possible to make up for missing the beginning.'[6]

Divided into I and II Corps, the British Expeditionary Force totalled approximately eighty thousand men, the respective commanders being Lieutenant Generals Sir Douglas Haig and Sir James Grierson (replaced by Lieutenant General Sir Horace Smith-Dorrien after Grierson died unexpectedly on 17 August).[7] The 1st Black Watch, formed into four companies, A, B, C and D, was in 1 Guards Brigade, 1st Division, I Corps, the Brigade including the 1st Coldstream Guards, the 1st Scots Guards and the 2nd Royal Munster Fusiliers. The BEF's commander-in-chief was Field Marshal Sir John French, veteran of the Second South African War.[8] French's counterpart in command of the French Army, consisting of approximately 1 million men, was General Joseph Joffre who had fought in the 1870–71 Franco-Prussian War.[9] As the BEF was preparing to leave Britain, Joffre was already concentrating his forces close to the Franco-German and Franco-Belgian borders.

On 8 August the 3rd (Special Reserve) Battalion (formerly the 3rd (Militia) Battalion), under the command of Lieutenant Colonel R. C. Campbell-Preston, mobilised at The Black Watch regimental depot, Perth, entraining that evening for its 'war-station', Nigg, Ross-shire.[10] In addition to coastal defence to guard against a German invasion, the 3rd Black Watch trained soldiers for drafting overseas as reinforcements. Private Jim Braid, who had run away from home in Fife to join the Army, described their days 'trench digging and route marching: they don't march up here, they gallop, nearly everybody was dropping out.' The food was 'very poor… nearly all tinned meat and stinking. We have sometimes an apology for ham. What a disgrace. It is enough to sicken a dead dog.'[11]

The four Territorial Battalions, the 4th (City of Dundee), the 5th (Angus & Dundee), the 6th (Perthshire) and the 7th (Fife) were immediately mobilised for home defence. Within weeks each was recruiting a second battalion.[12] Among those joining the 4th Black Watch was a group of journalists who called themselves 'from some headline, "Writers and Fighters Too"', recorded Linton Andrews, news editor of the *Dundee Advertiser* and so one of the 'Fighter Writers'.[13] The soldiers, who, in all Scottish regiments acquired the name 'Jocks', were 'all sorts and conditions… drawn from all classes – professional men, mill-hands, clerks, labourers,' noted Joseph Gray, a writer and illustrator for the *Dundee Courier,* who also joined the 4th Black Watch.[14]

To provide the numbers that Kitchener, the new Secretary of State for War, believed would be necessary, a 'New Army' of volunteers was raised. This included the 8th, 9th and 10th (Service) Battalions The Black Watch, with an 11th (Service) Battalion later formed at Nigg. To clothe and arm the New Army, quantities of equipment were procured. As the demand for manpower increased, new recruits learnt only the basics of marching and drilling. Since numbers often exceeded supplies, the men were invariably wearing civilian clothes and drilling with broom handles.[15] Many third-generation Scots living in Canada and South America volunteered to fight in Scottish units, including more than fifty joining The Black Watch from Argentina.[16] A shortage of officers and NCOs meant that retired regular soldiers returned to active service. Eighty-year-old Mark Axe, a veteran of the Crimea and India, was even accepted as a recruiting sergeant in Montecute, Somerset.[17]

On 11 August, the 1st Black Watch was inspected by the King. Two days later the Battalion left Aldershot. 'The pipes and drums were playing, but there was no brass band because their instruments were left in store and the men were now stretcher bearers,' commented Private MacFarlane.[18] Embarking at Southampton, 'after a night's sail' they reached Le Havre.[19] 'The unloading of all the transport and horses took about five hours and it was very nearly six before we marched off,' related Lieutenant Lloyd Rennie. 'I've never seen such enthusiasm as the inhabitants displayed, one could not hear the pipes for cheering, "Heep Heep-ing", "Vive l'Angleterre", the Marseillaise, etc.'[20]

Before leaving the rest camp at Harfleur the men wrote 'farewells' home. 'Here we are all the married and engaged men writing to their wives and fiancées & not knowing what to say because all letters are censored,' Lieutenant Victor Fortune wrote on a postcard to his wife,

Eleanor.[21] 'I don't think I have any more news to give you', wrote Lieutenant Lewis Cumming, 'but I hope that when we finish this show to march down the Unter den Linden to the tune of "Highland Laddie" with the old Forty Twa… ever your loving Lewis.' His postscript was less cheerful: 'Or if I do get "killed" I think it rather a good thing to remember the couplet: "For how can man die better/Than facing fearful odds,/For the ashes of his fathers,/And the temples of his Gods?"'[22]

On 16 August the Battalion moved off by rail for Le Nouvion 'with 50 men in every horsebox,' recorded Private John Laing.[23] Although the officers were 'fairly comfortable', Rennie conceded that the men 'were very crowded', but they 'soon cheered up when we began to pass stations crowded with excited people, with fruit, cigarettes and tobacco for the men, and the train began very soon to look more like a Carnival car at Nice so covered was it with flowers and tri-colour flags.' Marching on to Boué, through 'pretty wooded country, mostly pasture and orchards', the Battalion had purchased a white horse, called 'Allez-vous en', to pull their mess cart.[24]

On 21 August, as the BEF began to move forward on the left of the French Fifth Army, the Battalion reached Cartignies, where it remained overnight. Continuing onwards, '[we] caught our first glimpse of the enemy in a Taube Monoplane which passed over us,' commented Captain A. D. C. Krook.[25] 'We heard guns firing that day evidently from NW of Maubeuge which caused great excitement,' recorded Rennie. By the early hours of the following day [23rd] they had reached Grand Reng in Belgium.[26] 'Footsore and weary; people very glad to see us; opened their licensed houses and gave us refreshments,' observed Laing. 'We spent the day cleaning up, dressing feet, sleeping and feeding,' recorded Krook.[27]

The Retreat from Mons

The Allied objective was to check the German advance through Belgium, while Joffre's French armies carried out the main offensive to the south. By the third week of August British troops were holding a line from the Belgian city of Mons, 30 miles south-west of Brussels, along the Mons–Condé Canal. While II Corps had taken up position curving westwards along the canal and encircling the city, the line of I Corps followed the Mons–Beaumont road north-east of Maubeuge. To the BEF's right was General Charles Lanzerac's Fifth Army while on the left was the French Cavalry Division, commanded by General André Sordet, with the Belgians between them and the coast. 'But no possible disposition of the two corps could have availed against the six or more German corps', recorded the 1st Black Watch War History, 'who unknown to our forces, were streaming south-westwards from Brussels.'[28]

On 23 August in the first major action of the war, Britain's first military engagement in northern Europe since Waterloo ninety-nine years ago, British and German forces clashed at Mons. The battle, which had begun with a German artillery bombardment at dawn, was followed by an assault from troops storming the canal. Initially, the Germans' tightly packed ranks presented relatively easy targets for the British riflemen and the first assault was repulsed with heavy German losses. But, as the attacks continued throughout the day, the British position became untenable. Although the 1st Black Watch was not engaged, it 'fully expected to be attacked during the night of the 23rd or at dawn on the 24th.'[29] 'We were ordered out, and took up an entrenched position, digging ourselves in all night,' continued Captain Krook. 'Just had about 2 hours sleep when we are ordered to stand to arms but found it a false alarm,' continued Laing.[30]

Late on the same evening Sir John French received news that the French Fifth Army was going to begin a general withdrawal. Realising that the British right flank would be exposed, he had no option but to conform. 'Started to retire back into France but only to act as bait and draw enemy away from road to Paris,' recorded Private Mitchell.[31] Rennie continued: 'We had to hold a main road and had it very nicely held with barbed wire and two machine guns, but the only people we had to deal with were refugees, a most pathetic sight, carrying their children, some in farm carts but most of them on foot and all absolutely terrified.' The following day they watched an artillery duel between the French and Germans on their right front, 'which was very interesting as it was the first time we had seen anything of the kind. We withdrew about ten that morning... That was our first taste of 'the retreat'.[32] 'We marched on about another ten miles to La Longueville where we again billeted, and were once again on French soil,' observed Krook. The French civilians, not yet understanding the reason for the retreat, greeted them 'with the cry of "Perfides".'[33]

By the night of 26 August the Battalion was in billets in Petit Cambresis. 'There were few of us who did not suffer hallucinations, imagining that troops of Cavalry were going past. We had some cases of dysentery, due to eating fruit out of the orchards as we marched by,' recorded Jack Campbell, Royal Army Medical Corps attached to the 1st Black Watch.[34] The following day 1 Brigade was ordered to hold a rearguard position, with the aim of keeping the Germans north of Etreux until the 1st and 2nd Divisions had passed through. 'We dug ourselves in and waited till everyone was through, and got absolutely drenched to the skin by a thunderstorm,' continued Rennie.[35]

Once orders were received for the rearguard to withdraw, the 1st Black Watch moved off. Reaching 'the exposed portion of the road to Guise', the Battalion came under 'sharp Artillery and rifle fire' with seven men 'slightly' wounded and three missing, one presumed dead, the Regiment's first casualties of the war. 'It was rather a poor show from our point of view as we had to keep on retiring and could not go for them as it was a retirement. Our gunners were simply splendid, they came galloping back and opened fire.' Marching onwards through Guise, and still unaware that the 2nd Royal Munster Fusiliers, which had also formed part of the rearguard, had been virtually wiped out near Oisy, Rennie described the day's events as 'distinctly rattling. We fell in our bivouac about eleven o'clock – everyone dead beat and were rejoiced to find that the cookers and mess cart had been there some time and that there was a hot meal for us. We got hold of some straw and slept like logs until three a.m. when we got up and marched off again.' The following day Rennie was recording the 'good work' of the 2nd Dragoons (Royal Scots Greys) and the 12th (Prince of Wales's Royal) Lancers against a German cavalry brigade:

'The Greys did dismounted work and stampeded the German-led horses, and then the 12th [Lancers] got in amongst them with the lance, and the Greys remounting finished the good work with the sword.' But, he emphasised, the 'pretty story about The Black Watch charging, holding on to the Grey's horses' was 'a complete fabrication from start to finish.'[36]

Reaching St Gobain the men were given a day's rest. 'Made some "kail" and "spuds" with a chicken we were lucky to get,' related Laing. 'Turned out at 4 p.m. to hear the King's, Kitchener's and Government's thanks for our splendid work and marching. We had done 135 miles in eight days under a broiling sun.'[37] At St Gobain, Grant Duff had permitted their heavy greatcoats to be handed in: 'but the coats could not be transported and had to be burnt. Their want was soon badly felt.' Soon afterwards extra wagons were provided enabling their packs to be carried which made 'a great difference to the marching and fighting power of the men.'[38] Their onward progress 'was slow, through heavy forest. Firing heard not far off. In contact with enemy in the afternoon,' recorded Private Mitchell on 1 September.[39] 'We have only been under fire once for about half an hour,' Lieutenant Lewis Cumming wrote home, informing his parents that the 'most welcome' item they had sent were some socks 'as marching is very hard on them.' His next request was for 'mixed chocolate or chocolate peppermints'.[40]

On 3 September the BEF, now increased with the addition of III Corps, crossed the Marne. Two days later the soldiers halted at Nesles, south-east of Paris. Overall losses during the 'retreat from Mons' had been considerable. II Corps's defensive stand at Le Cateau on 26 August – which had prevented the retreat from becoming a rout – had resulted in over seven thousand casualties. Although the Germans had been prevented from outflanking the French Fifth Army, the threat remained: 'It is the thirty-fifth day', Kaiser Wilhelm II was recording on 4 September, 'we are thirty miles from Paris.'[41]

The Miracle of the Marne

As the Germans pushed forward to Paris, they changed direction to the south-east, hoping to cut off the retreating French. This movement, however, exposed the German right flank. On the same day as the Kaiser was noting their successes, Joffre ordered the French armies and the BEF to counter-attack. 'Retirement ends and offensive assumed,' noted the 1st Black Watch's War Diary.[42] On 5 September, a day earlier than Joffre intended, following a precipitate withdrawal of the German First Army, the combined French and British forces attacked the Germans along the River Marne: their actions were defined by the Marne's tributaries, the Ourcq, the Grand and Petit Morins and the marshes of St Gond. 'This is the first day of our advance after a retiring action that created a World's Record for marching,' commented Private Mitchell on 6 September. 'This was the turning point as the enemy thought they had nothing else to do but march to Paris but,' observed Private Laing, 'instead of them chasing us we are after them now.'[43] The 1st Black Watch's part in the offensive action took place on 8 September against German troops east of Sablonnières on the road to Bellot. 'My company was advance guard and a platoon vanguard when we ran into some of the Pomeranian German Guard Jägers who were entrenched in an orchard at the entrance of the village,' related Lieutenant Rennie. 'My platoon was in front and we started the fun. However [they] did not wait for the bayonet and either gave themselves up or shammed dead.' While two companies engaged the Germans in the trees, a third successfully outflanked them on the road.[44] 'Village cleared and 40 Germans captured – M.G. doing good execution,' noted the War Diary, as well as recording the death of two Black Watch officers and ten other ranks, with eighteen wounded. 'After a desperate fight,' continued Laing, '[we] gained considerable ground.'[45]

The following day the Battalion re-crossed the River Marne. 'This is great partridge country rather like Norfolk I fancy,' Lieutenant Cumming was writing home. 'So far as I can see this show may go on indefinitely, although we know probably less than you.'[46] Despite a spirited resistance from the Germans, the First Battle of the Marne, known as the 'miracle of the Marne', prevented the Germans reaching Paris. To the south the Allies' position was assured by Joffre's counter-attack with six French Field Armies which left nearly 20,000 dead (compared with less than 2,000 from the BEF). After visiting the front in person on 11 September, General von Moltke, Chief of the German General Staff, ordered a general withdrawal along a front of nearly 250 miles north-east to the River Aisne, 'the lines so reached' to be 'fortified and defended'.[47]

The Aisne: 'Full of the scream of shrapnel'

Having withdrawn across the Aisne, the Germans had taken up position on high ground along an old Roman road, known (in honour of Louis XV's daughters) as *Chemin des Dames*. 'We crossed the Aisne on Sunday, 13th', explained Rennie, 'and came in for the usual "Angelus" of shell fire at 6 o'clock, which, however, did not touch us. I was on outpost that night for the 2nd night running and it rained hard and we all got soaked to the skin. Next morning it was still raining and then began the Battle of the Aisne.'[48]

'Reveille at 3.30, breakfasted & marched off, did not go far when we had a very severe shelling,' recorded Private Ogilvie. 'By 7.30 a.m. [I] was in the very thick of it and our company was very nearly wiped out,' continued Laing.[49] To confuse the situation, a thick mist covered the battlefield. 'The Guards went up first and then the Camerons, both having to retire,' related Private Fairweather. 'Although we had watched the awful slaughter in these regiments, when it was our turn we went off with a cheer across 1,500 yards of open country. The shelling was terrifying and the air was full of the scream of shrapnel.'[50] 'Had cover behind houses & high wall & stayed there for [a] bit', Ogilvie continued, 'until Col Grant Duff came back & formed us up; after that we were extended in skirmishing order.' They then found themselves moving forward with the Cameron Highlanders, who were 'a little in advance of us when the Col[onel] called out "to never mind the Camerons go right through them". After that he gave us the order "forward the 42nd" & off we went, it was awful going, our feet sticking deep in the mud & could hardly get them out again, however we got over the field onto the road covered with mud from head to foot & when we got to the road we found the Scots & Coldstream Guards & some other Regiments all lying there & very little room for us when we got there.'[51] Fairweather was one of the many wounded:

> Only a few of us got up to 200 yards of the Germans. Then with a yell we went at them… and it was then my shout of '42nd for ever' finished with a different kind of yell. Crack; I had been presented with a souvenir in my knee. I lay helpless, and our fellows retired over me. Shrapnel screamed all around, and melinite shells made the earth shake. I bore a charmed life. A bullet went through the elbow of my jacket, another through my equipment and a piece of shrapnel found a resting place in a tin of bully beef which was on my back. I was picked up eventually during the night, nearly dead from loss of blood.[52]

At 3 p.m. Laing was 'still in the thick of it, cut off from the battalion don't know where and how they are getting on.' Private Small was advancing 'across very open country – we had not gone far when shot & shell were falling amongst us like hail, men were falling like ninepins.' Seeing his 'master (P.K.)' – Second Lieutenant Patrick Kinloch Campbell – fall, he went to help him. 'He told me to leave him as the firing was dreadful – of course I would not do so – I could not leave him wounded & bleeding – he was very angry at first – but I was angry too – & I would not leave him until I had a field dressing on his knee. We then bade each other goodbye & good luck – he was very grateful to me.' To Small's surprise, later in the day, he saw 'the bold P. K. coming up into the firing line again – & there he remained all that day fighting with only one good leg under him.'[53]

Others were less fortunate. 'Sir, your son was killed in my presence on the afternoon of the 14th Sept while both of us were scouting across the Chivy Valley,' Corporal Petrie informed Lieutenant Cumming's father. 'His death sir was instantaneous and he had no pain for he was hit in a most vital part.' 'He died magnificently', his younger brother, Kynoch, 1st Cameron Highlanders, told their step-mother, quoting the same verses from Macaulay's 'Horatio', 'and if you realise how many others are killed fighting for their country it is not so bad as it might be.'[54]

The Battalion's Commanding Officer, Lieutenant Colonel Adrian Grant Duff, had also been killed. The adjutant, Lieutenant Guy Rowan-Hamilton, was near by:

> We had been having rather a bad time. The whole brigade was scattered about and we had no reserve to meet an impending German attack – The General ordered my C.O. to collect all the men he could officers, servants, regimental scouts, some stragglers, signallers, etc [we] went up on the ridge, & we opened fire. Very shortly we came under very heavy shell-fire and [one] man shouted to me that the Colonel was hit. I went over to him, & he told me that he was hit in the stomach. As we were under very heavy fire, I thought it best to get him out at once so with the assistance of another man, we helped him out of the firing line. There was a very steep bit of hill to get him down but eventually we got him down into the cave where brigade headquarters had been & there we put him down upon the straw & someone fetched the doctor. He told me then that I must go back again to the party I had left on the hill.[55]

By the time Rowan-Hamilton returned, Grant Duff had died.

Another fatality was Major Lord George Stewart-Murray. Initial reports were that he was only wounded: 'so he must have been picked up by the stretcher bearers of some other brigade,' his younger brother, James, 1st Cameron Highlanders, wrote to their father, the 7th Duke of Atholl. But 'it was with the deepest sorrow that the Regiment was eventually forced to realise that there was no hope of his return.'[56] 'Only 51 of our company answered the roll call out of 250 men,' observed Private Small. 'We spent the night of the 14th digging and collecting dead and wounded – the collecting had to be abandoned owing to the fire kept up on the stretcher parties,' related

Captain Krook.[57] '10 p.m. got a drop of tea not very warm but very thankful of it all the same,' recorded Private Laing, 'still raining very hard, got warned that the enemy were going to attack our position and that we were not to retire at any cost, every man to die at his post as we were holding the main position.'[58]

After a 'wet and beastly night' patrols were sent out in the early morning. '5 a.m. just like hell can't get a move at all, shelling us continually,' continued Laing.[59] Once again they were subjected to German artillery fire. 'We went over the ridge to meet the enemy advancing & we were doing grand work – firing as hard as we possibly could at their infantry & we were winning quite easily when all at once a perfect fusillade of shells dropped right amongst us,' recorded Private Small. 'Almost at once I was blown in the air by the explosion of a shell – my nose, ears & mouth were bleeding but otherwise unhurt.' Lieutenant P. K. Campbell was again wounded, this time in the leg and shoulder. As an aside, Small wished to record how Campbell suffered throughout the campaign from 'bad feet caused by wearing civilian shoes. I asked him to discard them altogether & wear a pair of ordinary Private's shoes – he did so & now wears nothing else – Privates socks as well.'[60]

The fighting on 14 and 15 September had resulted in nearly 600 casualties in the 1st Black Watch. Lieutenant Lloyd Rennie had been 'hit through the arm about 12 and got into the dressing station about four that afternoon.' Corporal George Snelling had both hands blown off and died later.[61] Major James Murray, who had assumed command of the Battalion after Grant Duff's death, had tears in his eyes 'as he stood looking at what was left of us, & some of the boys wept openly & unashamed when they discovered that their pals were numbered amongst the dead.'[62] By 16 September it was 'still raining hard, battle still proceeding, enemy still trying to shell us out,' Private Laing recorded. '7.am. got a tot of rum I can tell you we were sore in need of it.'[63]

The 1st Black Watch spent the next four days 'digging in'. Three days later the Battalion was relieved. 'We were very glad at the prospect of getting a rest & a good wash & clean up for none of us had had a wash since 10th of the month,' recorded Private Ogilvie.[64] Marching to Berneuil, the Battalion then took over the line on the heights on both sides of the Chivy Valley. 'The next day we heard that the Camerons who had taken over our cave [near Bourg et Comin] were buried by two direct hits,' wrote Captain Krook.[65] Among the twenty-nine officers and men killed was the 1st Cameron Highlanders' acting Commanding Officer, Captain Douglas Miers.[66]

Since the Battle of the Aisne, the opposing Allied and German armies had become engaged in a race to outflank each other in the gap between the Aisne and the sea to the north. As agreed between General Ferdinand Foch, formerly commanding the French Ninth Army, now Commander of Army Group North, and Field Marshal Sir John French, the British Army's focus of attention would be a bleak part of Flanders. By suggesting that the British move to this sector, French anticipated not only shortening the BEF's lines of communication but also being better able to defend the Channel ports in northern Belgium. At its maximum in 1914, the British line extended for 25 miles.[67]

'Sardines, Potted meat, Osborne Biscuits, Strawberry Jam, Marmalade, In tins for preference, Cocoa - would be very nice,' Fortune (promoted captain after the Aisne) was requesting his family on 30 September. 'Also pair of jaeger drawers for wear with kilt.'[68] 'Sunday 4th [October],' recorded Private Laing. '5.30 a.m. bombarding us, as thick as they can throw them over, managed to get breakfast but just in time for shells were coming rather near.' On 16 October the Battalion was relieved, having spent '18 days and nights in trenches "a record I suppose for British troops"... havn't had a night's sleep since I went to trenches.'[69]

Meanwhile, with Antwerp under siege since August, Belgian resistance was weakening. On 9 October the independent force which had been operating in Belgium under Lieutenant General Sir Henry Rawlinson's command was transferred to the BEF, constituting IV Corps. Its presence in Belgium was too late to save Antwerp, which fell the following day. To make up for continuing losses in the BEF, fresh drafts continued to arrive, the demand for junior officers being especially high. By mid-October almost all trained officers below the rank of major and all trained soldiers remaining in Britain had left for France.[70]

The 2nd Black Watch had also been ordered to France from India as part of the Indian Corps. 'We marched to the station at night, with the pipes playing, through throngs of natives lining the road with torches to give us a parting farewell,' recorded Private Wilson. 'We of the 2nd Black Watch were part of the Bareilly Brigade, 7th Meerut Division.' Leaving Karachi on board the S.S. *Elephanta*, their progress was slowed by the presence of German light cruisers operating in the Indian Ocean. On arrival in Marseilles on 12 October, the men were issued with a 'broderick' (field service) cap, 'as worn by the English Regiments,' with the Glengarry being discontinued in order to avoid their identification as Scottish regiments. 'Indignation ran high that such an insult should be offered to The Black Watch and Scotland, but this had to be swallowed.'[71] They also received new rifles since those brought from India 'did not take the latest mark of ammunition.'[72] Travelling up to the front, the soldiers were 'absolutely stormed by spectators all offering fruit or wine or whatever they fancied we might need – eggs were frequently displayed,' Wilson observed, although as 'disciplined veterans' they could not be tempted 'not on parade anyway'. 'The discipline was very severe,' recalled Private James McGregor Marshall. 'But it learned [us] something we knew nothing of in civil life – clean living – religious prestige – for all were Presbyterians – duty – & loyalty to Scotland – to be spick & span on parade.'[73]

Battle of Ypres: Langemarck and Gheluvelt

In order to form a defensive line in front of the Channel ports, the BEF's II and III Corps had taken up a position, extending for about 20 miles from La Bassée canal to Neuve Eglise. I Corps was at Hazebrouck, while IV Corps was positioned to guard the roads leading to the ancient town of Ypres. 'We marched through Ypres at about 8 o'clock on a dry morning in mid October, 1914,' related

Private MacFarlane. 'The town was practically intact; the famous Cloth Hall had only a few bullet holes in it and the place was full of people… we did not stop but marched through and on to the big white chateau at Hooge by nightfall. From there we branched to the left, through Pilckem and on to Passchendaele… in 1914, it was all green crops in the fields with cattle, horses, pigs and sheep, although a lot of them were lying killed certainly.'[74] Supported by French and Belgian cavalry and other units, both Foch and French favoured an attack into Belgium to capture Bruges. But instead of the weak opposition they expected, Moltke's successor, General Erich von Falkenhayn, had assembled a formidable force which included the German Sixth Army under the command of Rupprecht, Crown Prince of Bavaria, as well as several reserve corps of volunteers.

On 20 October, before Allied forces could move off, the Germans attacked on a wide front from Gheluvelt to the mouth of the Yser. While the 2nd Division moved steadily forward to meet the advancing Germans, the 1st Division's movement was constrained by German attacks against the French 'which modified the advance so as to create, on this day, the curious line afterwards called "the Ypres Salient"'.[75] The 1st Black Watch was in brigade reserve at Pilckem. When, two days later, the Cameron Highlanders and the Coldstream Guards came under heavy attack, the Battalion was sent forward. Reaching the Steenbeck river 'the enemy continually attacked during the night and all next day.'[76] Among those killed was Lieutenant C. L. C. Bowes-Lyon, who had only arrived in France in mid-September.[77] Although the German advance had been halted, the respite was brief.

The Battalion was then ordered to take up position in another threatened area along the road between Zandvoorde and Gheluvelt, sustaining severe casualties during a German bombardment of its entrenched position. Having failed to penetrate the British line on a wide front, Falkenhayn ordered a more localised attack at Gheluvelt, where the German Group Fabeck, commanded by General Max von Fabeck, broke through. Fighting alongside the Coldstream Guards, the 1st Black Watch's B and C Companies were overrun, while A and D Companies drove off a frontal attack.[78] Having come 'face to face' with some Germans, Captain Krook was taken prisoner: 'I had my notebook and pencil in my hands and I must admit that I was taken by surprise – they fired at me and one downed me with the butt end of his rifle – and that was the end of the fight for me.'[79]

During the night of 30/31 October, the British line was withdrawn to the small hamlet of Veldhoek, between Gheluvelt and Hooge.[80] Under frequent German shellfire, on 1 November Major Murray was wounded, whereupon command passed to Lieutenant Colonel Charles Edward Stewart, 2nd Black Watch, recently arrived from India. On 2 November, the Germans again broke through British lines along the Menin Road, the 1st Black Watch helping to restore the line 'by a brilliant counter-attack', as the three Company commanders, Captains Victor Fortune, Lloyd Rennie and Harold Amery, led their respective companies forward. Both Rennie and Amery, who had just rejoined the Battalion after recovering from wounds received on the Aisne, were again wounded, on this occasion, in Amery's case, fatally.[81]

Among the new units arriving in France was the 5th Black Watch which embarked on Sunday 1 November. In contrast to the popular image of streets lined with weeping mothers and sweethearts as they departed, Private Alfred Anderson remembered being driven through deserted streets before dawn in trucks to a station closed to the public. 'Our pride, was however, overshadowed by the realisation of our unpreparedness,' recalled Second Lieutenant Hugh Quekett, a former clerk in the London Stock Exchange. 'Even steadiness on the parade ground could not compensate for the fact that none of our new recruits had ever handled a rifle let alone fired one, as was the case with most of the others already in the regiment.' Two days later they were enduring bitterly cold nights in a tented camp at Le Havre, before moving into the line opposite Neuve Chapelle as part of the 8th Scottish Division. The soldiers' main activity was turning the roadside ditches into more effective defences.[82]

Nonne Bosschen: Black Watch Corner

The 1st Black Watch had remained in the line at Ypres, 1 Brigade being now under the command of Brigadier General Charles FitzClarence, who had been awarded the VC during the Second South African War. On 8 November German forces attacked north of the Menin Road, occupying the trenches held by the 1st Loyal North Lancashire Regiment, 2 Brigade, 1st Division. Two companies of the 1st Black Watch counter-attacked and re-occupied part of the Lancashires' trenches. 'Stiff battle [in the] afternoon', noted Private Mitchell, 'piles of German dead'.[83] Day after day there was 'heavy shelling'. 'Then came the fatal 11th, the enemy opened fire on us even after daylight, using every kind of shell possible for them to use; there was no doubt the enemy had the range of every trench,' related Private Andrew Mackie, describing the bombardment as the 'heaviest shell fire possible to be under.'[84]

To supplement their forces the Germans had brought up two fresh divisions including the Prussian Guards. Advancing through the early morning mist, they moved into No Man's Land between the Menin Road and Polygon Wood. Near by were the smaller woods of Nonne Bosschen (Nun's Wood) and Glencorse Wood, in front of which ran a small stream, the Reutelbeck. Facing the Germans were the depleted forces of the BEF. 'In front of us was the Prussian Guards and with their big tall helmets they all appeared to be seven feet tall. They came on, not in extended order, but they were marching practically shoulder to shoulder shouting, "Hoch!" and they were singing "*Die Wacht am Rhine*",' recalled Private MacFarlane. 'There were some huge specimens of men amongst them, but a bullet stopped them however big they were… the first wave was practically decimated altogether. However they did get into the trenches.'[85]

The positions held by the 1st Black Watch, between the 1st Camerons and the King's Regiment (Liverpool), 2nd Division, were all overrun. 'When I looked out to my dismay, I saw that the Germans were in our trenches not only in the front trenches but they also occupied the rear ones… I don't know how I looked but

I felt that my heart had dropped to the soles of my feet,' recorded Private Mackie, who spent the rest of the war as a prisoner. 'Owing to the heavy shelling a great amount of trench in B Company's line was destroyed,' related Lieutenant Colonel Stewart.[86] The Germans' onward sweep was immediately challenged by a strongpoint (*point d'appui*) held by Lieutenant Francis Anderson and forty members of C Company. Situated near the south-west corner of Polygon Wood, lying hidden in a hollow and protected by barbed wire, the men's presence surprised the approaching Germans. Forced to split up into small groups in order to pass either side, they suffered a number of casualties before escaping into the woods.[87]

Another party of Germans had advanced towards the 1st Black Watch's Battalion Headquarters, shared with the 1st Camerons, near Verbeek Farm. Although the Germans temporarily occupied the farm, they failed to take the Battalion Headquarters, their advance halted by Corporal Robert Redpath. With twenty men, he took cover behind some farm buildings, ordered rapid fire and killed two Germans, those following on making 'no attempt to follow their comrades', according to Stewart, who had received a slight wound in the head.[88]

In the early afternoon, a mixed force, including members of The Black Watch, advanced into the wood, clearing the ground from Verbeek Farm to the position held 'with the greatest gallantry' by Anderson and C Company: 'this little corner being known on all later maps as "Black Watch Corner"'. Anderson's strongpoint later became 'a salient feature of defensive warfare'.[89] By the end of the day Captain Fortune was the only uninjured officer. '[He] managed to get us all gathered together again… there was probably about 150 of us,' related Private MacFarlane, who believed that 11 November 1914 was 'the day the war should have finished… it was one of the most horrible days of my life... all the men you knew and had known for several years they were lying dead around about you.'[90] Other fatalities included Lieutenant Alexander (Allie) Lawson who, after more than nineteen years' service, had recently been granted a commission: struck by a shell, 'he was killed instantaneously, and suffered no pain,' Fortune informed Lawson's wife.[91]

The following day, 12 November, was a 'quiet day – practically no shelling.'[92] Having attempted to organise a counter-attack at 2 a.m. to win back the lost front trenches, Brigadier General FitzClarence was shot by a German sniper. The next day the 1st Black Watch was withdrawn. 'I met the Battalion, quite by chance, a few days ago,' former Commanding Officer Lieutenant Colonel Hugh Rose, now serving at HQ III Corps, wrote on 20 November. 'Marvellous lads to have gone through all they have and look so fit on it.'[93]

The Battle of Nonne Bosschen, as it was known, constituted the last major German offensive of the First Battle of Ypres, Moltke lamenting to the Kaiser about 'the utter failure to be successful'.[94] 'It was here that the battle was won. It was here that the battle and war itself was very nearly lost,' commented historian Lyn MacDonald. 'The salient held. The line stood.'[95] Losses on both sides were unprecedented. The Germans' superiority in numbers was not matched by their experience, and British machine-gun fire and the use of barbed wire proved strong impediments. Among the German dead were twenty-five thousand student soldiers, known as the 'innocent of Ypres', who were buried in mass graves at Langemarck.[96] The effect on the BEF had been devastating; henceforward the war would be fought not by the Regular Army, which had all but ceased to exist, but by hastily trained recruits joining regular battalions, together with territorials and Kitchener's New Armies.

In late November Field Marshal Sir John French thanked the 1st Black Watch for its 'splendid work', reminding his listeners that 'The Black Watch – a name we know so well – have always played a distinguished part in the battles of our country.'[97] On 3 December the King inspected the Battalion. Nearly a century later, on 4 May 2014, a memorial, representing a sergeant of The Black Watch standing poised for battle, was unveiled on the south-west corner of Polygon Wood to commemorate the Regiment's stand at Black Watch Corner.[98]

Givenchy: 'Bullets whizzing over our heads'

By the time the 2nd Black Watch was brought forward, the struggle to prevent a German breakthrough at Ypres was at its height. The 7th Meerut Division had therefore 'to be employed to meet an emergency,' commented Major Arthur Wauchope. The Division took over the extreme right of the British line north of Givenchy 'within shouting distance' of the French. 'Expectation ran high among us as we could hear the rifle bullets whizzing over our heads or the distant noise of a German big gun,' related Private Wilson. The weather had already become cold and wet, the construction of trenches in terrain below sea level now 'a matter of unending struggle against water and mud,' continued Wauchope.[99]

On 23 November, a German attack along 'almost the whole front of the Indian Corps' resulted in units of 58th (Vaughan's) Rifles, also in Bareilly Brigade, being forced from their trenches. The 2nd Black Watch was immediately engaged in the counter-attack, successfully re-occupying the trenches. Wauchope described carrying 'the war into the enemy's line' when, accompanied by Second Lieutenant Neil McMicking and ten men, he attacked a German trench, 'the Germans in it bolting.'[100] After a brief respite in reserve, the Battalion then reinforced a section of the line at Festubert, which included the infamous 'Hell Corner'. Running close to a German trench, its perilous location was demonstrated when, on 27 November, the Battalion lost its first officer, Captain Charles Eric Strachan, killed while attempting to silence a German machine gun near his trench. 'Most hated' were the grenades hurled into the trenches, 'bomb right' or 'bomb left' being 'a constant cry by day and night, and woe to him who was slow to pay heed to that warning.'[101]

As the Germans continued to target the front held by the Indian Corps, including the use of mines, so the various battalions tried to resist them. Among the fatalities was Lieutenant William Maitland who had just joined the Battalion on attachment from the Seaforth Highlanders. A surgeon in civilian life, 'one of his party (since dead) had been hit and Maitland finding himself unable to tie him up in the narrow trench had lifted him onto the ground behind, when he was himself hit.'[102]

To support the Indian Corps, units of the 1st Division had been ordered into the line at Givenchy. The 1st Black Watch arrived at Béthune in the early hours of 21 December, having endured a 'very trying' march for over 20 miles in 'much-needed' but uncomfortable new boots; the weather was 'wet and stormy.'[103] The following day an attack was ordered at Givenchy and Festubert where the Germans had broken through. Although 1 Guards Brigade, supported by the French Territorials, re-took Givenchy, some ground near Festubert was left under German control. 'Snipers were active on both sides, and the Battalion trenches were frequently shelled with sudden and heavy bursts of fire.'[104] 'It's very cold here now and rather rough luck, we spent the 3 preceding days & Christmas Day in the Trenches,' Sergeant John Wallace informed Evie Marindin, Major Arthur Marindin's wife, who was running a Comforts Fund for the soldiers. Describing their Christmas dinner, he continued: 'It consisted of 3 soups, that is to say, 3 different sorts of soup tablets put into one pot, a real good mixture, tomato, pea soup & oxtail… That was followed by a good greasy mutton stew.'[105] 'All the ranks did get a brass presentation box from Princess Mary containing chocolate, cigarettes and a Christmas card,' recorded Private MacFarlane.[106]

The 2nd Black Watch spent Christmas in reserve. 'What new fields to conquer awaited us afterwards was in the hands of the Gods,' recorded Private Wilson. 'We wore our Balmoral bonnets with a khaki cover recently issued and in them was the old red hackle – we were restored into our pride as Scots once more.' Billeted in empty sheds and hay lofts, 'or whatever suitable quarters could be found,' the men enjoyed 'a happy rest there, away from the turmoil we had recently been through – and we had good training ground.' There was also some illicit activity. 'All soldiers are not Angels and in the Black Watch they were no exception to the general rule,' continued Wilson, describing how men confined to the guard room for 'field punishment' invariably managed to absent themselves in the evening to the local *estaminet* by putting straw against the back mud wall, boring themselves out and then returning before being missed. 'The sentry was on the front entrance never suspecting what the prisoners were up to – I wonder!'[107]

Although each winter of the Great War had its hardships, the first was characterised by insufficient equipment and munitions; the men even lacked enough spades to build dugouts. 'I think everybody's at heart, very fed up,' continued Wallace. 'It's not as though one can get at them at all, there are certainly bayonet charges, but so few & far between, & the big guns & machine guns play such havoc, that the pleasure of fighting is reduced to nil.'[108] 'The bitterly cold, damp Christmas day was spent in the trenches,' wrote Second Lieutenant Quekett, 5th Black Watch, still in the sector opposite Neuve Chapelle. 'This was the time when we were accused of "fraternising" with the Germans, when in fact our particular part of the front was only 100 yards from them and they maintained almost complete silence. No rifle fire, no shell fire, an uncanny feeling until the Germans started singing Christmas carols followed by bursts of laughter in which we decided to join in with our own carols.'[109]

A period of truce permitted the burial of the dead. After four months in France, out of one thousand casualties in The Black Watch over one-third were fatal, including Private George Reid, 1st Black Watch, one of eight brothers serving in different regiments, who died of his wounds on New Year's Eve.[110] At midnight Lance Corporal Dugald McLeod, 1st Black Watch, stood in the trenches, playing the familiar pipe tune, *In the Garb of Old Gaul.*[111]

There were some who ne'er came back again;
there are some without a scratch;
But all of them have gained great fame –
the gallant, brave Black Watch.[112]

4

1915: Trench Warfare – Hell on Earth

We were excited and eager to do that for which we had joined the Army. Moreover, there was the thrilling anticipation of being in at the great final victory of the War. Vain Hope![1]

Another funeral passes. Each is a son – God pity the poor mothers.[2]

'Mud, shell fire, hell let loose'

Early 1915 was cold and wet. 'Got up at 7 a.m. had a glass of cognac, got breakfast, gave the place a clean up,' Private John Laing, 1st Black Watch, wrote in his diary on New Year's Day. 'Rifle fire not quite so heavy but artillery going for all they are worth.' 'Mud. Shell fire. Hell let loose, Singing, women, drinking – when you got the chance – not too often – anything to forget where you were and so the weeks go on,' recorded Private James Marshall, 2nd Black Watch. 'The war will be over in twelve months so they tell us – but we know better.'[3]

After five months both the Allied and German armies remained entrenched in two opposing lines, protected by barbed wire. In between lay No Man's Land. While the German trenches constituted a defensive position designed to maintain and consolidate their territorial gains in Belgium and France, initially the Allied trenches were built as temporary structures to protect the troops until the next offensive. As the war became more static, the simple trenches became more complex, deeper and with a growing number of communicating passages. Place names, reminding the soldiers of home, were allocated to the various routes.

Without duckboards or proper drainage, during winter the trenches became rivers of mud. 'We, as Highlanders, were particularly affected,' related Second Lieutenant Hugh Quekett. 'The straps of the spats, attached between sole and heel of the shoe, would not stand up to its constant immersion in the mud and water with the result that many of our shoes were sucked off without any hope of recovery... We still had the Lee Enfield long rifle left over from the Boer War, which used to get clogged with mud, making it totally unusable.'[4] Sanitary conditions remained poor, the latrines frequently flooded and treatment of 'trench' foot was rudimentary. Any minor infection could lead to gangrene requiring amputation. 'In France the lice were the bugbear,' recorded Private Jock Dawkins. 'Before one could sleep one had to go all over your shirt and burn the bounders with a lighted candle.'[5]

Stretching under No Man's Land, an extensive network of tunnels was being created in order to place mines under the trenches of their adversaries. The work was carried out by tunnelling companies, formed as specialist units of the Corps of Royal Engineers. 'We had mines running from our trenches right under the German trench ready to blow up at any time,' related Private Jim Braid, 1st Black Watch. 'They are very eerie,' recalled Second Lieutenant Lionel Sotheby. 'The air is very foul and the sides of the tunnel drip with moisture. At each end there is a little recess made, and a hole about 6 inches in diameter is bored 12 feet into solid earth. Here we have to place men to listen for the enemy mining or counter-mining.'[6]

Throughout January 1915 the 1st Black Watch was in and out of the line in the Givenchy sector. Having failed to break through at Ypres, it was not long before the Germans tried again. 'Yesterday at about 8 a.m. when we were peacefully in billets sleeping', recorded one platoon commander, 'a terrible cannonade started. I got up and dressed immediately and found that the Germans had attacked and that we were to move at once.' The destination was Cuinchy, south of Givenchy. 'The Germans had rushed the Coldstream and Scots Guards trenches and had captured them, at all costs we had to retake them.' A combined force moved forward to re-establish the original line. 'I with two platoons – 100 men – was to start the attack, so off I went, I'll never forget it as long as I live. We started running by "dashes", 50 men at a time, the usual way.' But the Germans were in too strong a position. 'We had not got 100 yards when every man in my half company was either killed or wounded. God knows how I escaped, I got up and advanced after the fourth dash and found myself advancing by myself in a withering fire of rifles, machine guns and shell and I never got a scratch. I looked round, saw I was by myself and dropped flat in the mud.' Realising further advance was futile the young Black Watch officer 'gradually crawled' on his stomach back to the British line. 'I am not nearly clever enough with my pencil to describe to you the modern battle in the field,' he continued. 'It is hell on earth, no other thing is suitable to call it. Shrieks - cursing - with such a terrific noise of those wicked shells whistling, machine guns cracking and the noise of rifle fire.'[7]

After another attempt in the afternoon, the 1st Black Watch was withdrawn. 'I wish never to hear a shell again', wrote the platoon commander. 'Of course for my first day in action it was a bit thick because it was supposed to be worse even than Ypres, in other words one of the fiercest attacks in the war.' Six officers and 205 other ranks in the Battalion were killed or wounded. 'That's enough isn't it? To see one's men and brother officers knocked down like that makes one sick.'[8] Among the dead was Lance Corporal John Morrison, a former gamekeeper, who 'got a bullet in the leg. Nevertheless, he crawled to the assistance of his officer, also wounded, and was in the act of helping him to remove his pack when he was fatally shot.'[9]

Withdrawn from the line for training, fatalities could be accidental. On 16 February Major James Murray, who had commanded the Battalion after Grant Duff's death in September before Lieutenant Colonel Stewart arrived, and Sergeant Hart were both killed 'by the premature explosion of fuse when at experimental bomb throwing.'[10]

In late February the 4th Black Watch left Scotland. Arriving at a rest camp near Boulogne, the men were glad of warm sheepskin coats: 'it was very funny to see us running about in the dark with the white jackets on, everyone shouting "Baa Baa"', related Lance

Corporal Alex Thomson. 'Shouts of laughter broke out as we looked at our comrades,' commented Private Joseph Gray, describing a mixed consignment of coats. 'One man's coat was black and white, another's entirely white, another sported about like some primeval animal in a great black shaggy coat two or three sizes too big for him. Arctic explorers – Eskimos – trappers from the Far West – we looked anything but soldiers.'[11]

Neuve Chapelle: 'A roar that shook the earth'

In early March the 2nd Black Watch moved into the line at Rue du Bois, running in a north-easterly direction from Béthune to the front line; the men were kept busy digging trenches and reconnoitring in preparation for a planned attack on the village of Neuve Chapelle. If successful, British forces could move on to take Aubers Ridge, enabling them to obstruct German lines of communication between La Bassée and Lille. Also taking part in the attack was the 4th Black Watch, which had joined the 2nd Black Watch in the 7th Meerut Division, and the 5th Black Watch, which was already in the line near Neuve Chapelle in the 8th Division. 'We were excited and eager to do that for which we had joined the Army,' recalled Lance Corporal Andrews, 4th Black Watch. 'Moreover, there was the thrilling anticipation of being in at the great final victory of the War. Vain Hope!'[12]

On 10 March 'there was a silence – a few guns fired – then – with a roar that shook the earth, every gun in the district opened fire,' related Thomson. 'The crash of that awful salvo must have struck terror into the hearts of the enemy even more than to us who were more or less prepared for it. Daylight was beginning to strengthen and we could see the fresh troops that had been brought up, making ready to go forward to the attack.' We lay appalled while the terrible bombardment thundered on – unceasing, one diabolical volume of ear-splitting sound,' recorded Private Gray. 'German dead were flung into the nearer points of our trenches by the terrible explosions.'[13]

In the late morning units of the 7th Meerut Division moved forward to consolidate the positions gained by other divisions in the initial assault while the 2nd Black Watch was fighting to hold its position along the Rue du Bois. In the 4th Black Watch's first action, the Commanding Officer, Lieutenant Colonel Harry Walker, led the soldiers forward to occupy the captured trenches. 'There was no battle joy in our hearts, but we would not fail our comrades of the 2nd Black Watch, or those poor Indians who were so baffled under bombardments,' observed Andrews. 'The German trenches entered by the men of the 4th… were in a terrible condition, so great was the havoc wrought by the bombardment. Barbed wire entanglements, thought by the Huns to be impregnable, had been blown to pieces, so that not even the supports were left standing… Terribly mutilated dead lay all around,' continued Gray. Among 'many gallant deeds' was that of Private Dolan, who, seeing 'a comrade, Private Rafferty, badly wounded in both legs,' had gone to help him until the stretcher bearers arrived.[14] Two days later in thick fog a German counter-attack against the 2nd Black Watch's positions was repulsed. The Battalion suffered over 160 casualties, including at least one fatality while bringing in prisoners.[15]

Duties for the 5th Black Watch included bringing up supplies, helping with salvage work and guarding prisoners, whom Second Lieutenant Quekett described as 'a motley lot. Most bare-headed but a few still wearing the spiked helmets so prized as souvenirs by the British Army. When we reached the rendezvous all were without headgear and certain haversacks showed a distinct bulge!'[16] The soldiers also had to bury their dead, including one of the Battalion's 'most popular characters': stretcher bearer Piper Arthur Howie 'shot through the heart, in the act of bearing a badly wounded man to the rear.'[17]

'The battle of Neuve Chapelle had ended with a British gain of 1200 yards on a front of 4000 yards,' Gray reported. 'One of the most strongly defended positions on the Western front had fallen into our hands, and it had been proved that the German line could be broken at any time if only our infantry were supported by adequate artillery fire.'[18] But the cost was severe, with more than ten thousand casualties, British and Indian, with a comparable number of Germans. The fighting at Neuve Chapelle was one to which Gray returned, recreating the scenes of devastation on canvas.

For the rest of March the 'usual routine' continued, with brief periods of rest.[19] 'It was little wonder that our marching lacked dash and spring,' continued Gray. 'A number of the men dropped out, and rejoined the battalion later. Others suffered such agony owing to their feet being swollen through standing for days on end in freezing water, that they had to slit up their boots. Others again could not wear their boots even when cut up, and they bound up their feet in odd stockings, mufflers, or body belts, and limped along in the rear. The Fourth looked like a regiment of tramps – weary, battered tramps at that.'[20] Briefly, two companies of the 2nd Black Watch were attached to the 58th Vaughan's Rifles, Bareilly Brigade, composed mainly of Indian soldiers. While the Pathans (Pashtuns) 'were unequalled in "stalking"', noted Major Wauchope in command of the detachment, 'the Highlanders gave the necessary steadiness and feeling of security to the whole patrol.'[21]

Mindful that those fighting were now mostly territorial forces, in early April Sir John French, accompanied by Haig, inspected the troops, expressing his admiration for the soldiers' 'courage,… self-denial and… splendid fighting spirit.' But, as the horrors of the protracted fighting became apparent, Private William Cuthill, 4th Black Watch, wrote home advising his parents not to let his brother enlist. 'It is not war here, it is pure murder. You don't get a fighting chance, you have simply got to wait and chance your luck.'[22]

Meanwhile 'nothing of importance' had happened to the 1st Black Watch, positioned north of Festubert. The weather remained cold, with the occasional snowfall 'but it improved as time passed.' A new weapon was being brought into service: the trench mortar. Called the 'stove-pipe', it was designed to be more effective in destroying strong-points. The 1st Black Watch's first 'bombing officer' was Lieutenant Jock Haldane who 'with his detachment moved about the line, firing his stove-pipes from different positions.'[23] 'Very quiet in the morning,' Private Laing recorded in his diary on 11 April. 'Having grand weather – 11 am our artillery sent over a good many shells. Enemy's artillery kept very quiet, too much aeroplanes going over their lines they don't want to give their gun positions away that is how they are so quiet for it is not often the case on a Sunday.'[24] This was his last entry; later that day he was killed.

On 22 April the Germans launched a second offensive against Ypres in an attempt to reduce the 'bulge' of the salient. Although none of The Black Watch battalions was engaged, news spread of the Germans' use of gas for the first time. 'What do you think of the Hun's latest frightfulness, asphyxiating gases,' Lieutenant Colonel Hugh Rose was asking. 'War is surely bad enough as it is but if it is going to be a question of gases and poisons – all Nations should chip in to suppress this diabolical innovation on the part of the Hun.'[25] The gas attack had created a 4-mile gap in the sector held mainly by French Algerian and Moroccan troops, but the Germans had insufficient forces to break through. In late April and May gas was again released. Although Allied troops were better prepared, their attempts at counter-attacking failed with the result that by the end of the Second Battle of Ypres, the German front line had crept closer to Ypres, leaving Langemarck, St Julien and Zonnebecke behind German lines.

In early May the 6th and 7th Black Watch left for France to join the 1st (later numbered the 51st) Highland Division.[26] As they boarded the train, Private George Farrar observed their Commanding Officer 'Auld Robbie' – Lieutenant Colonel Sir Robert Moncrieffe – standing alone with his wife. 'As he said his final goodbye he stood back, gave her a smart salute and, with a loud voice which many of us heard [said] "Goodbye, my dear, my place is with my men in the battle-field."' Disembarking at Boulogne the Division moved to the 'battle zone'. If only, continued Farrar, just the 6th Black Watch had been on the march 'it might not have been so bad. But as the whole division was on the move in a confined space the result was chaos. Every time we got to a cross roads we had to halt to let transport go through, after each halt we had to hurry to catch up with the unit in front.'[27] 'My dear Crissie,' Colour Sergeant Alick Guthrie was writing to his wife. 'Here we are "somewhere in France"... There are very few men to be seen about the countryside, and the women who turn out to see us march thro' the villages are very quiet and sedate looking, many of them dressed in mourning.'[28]

Aubers Ridge: The push in the spring

While fighting was going on at Ypres, British forces were brought into action to support the French to the south at Vimy Ridge and Notre Dame de Lorette. The objective was the capture of Aubers Ridge guarding La Bassée to the south-west and Lille to the north-east. The importance of the region lay in its proximity to the coalfields of the Lens area. Operations again took place along the Rue du Bois, and at a road junction known as Chocolate Menier Corner. Included in the action in their respective divisions were four Black Watch Battalions, Second Lieutenant Quekett describing how, after Neuve Chapelle, the 5th Black Watch had moved to a part of the line near Fleurbaix 'to be fattened up for the next attack.'[29]

'Naturally there was great excitement as it was now evident that the much talked of "push in the Spring" was about to commence and that we were to take part in it,' recorded Lance Corporal Thomson, 4th Black Watch. 'Throughout the day we were issued with all the odds and ends necessary to keep our equipment and rifles in order for some time – oil, rifle rag and the like.' In case of a gas attack, they were given respirators. '[They] were of such an elementary character that I fear they would have been of little service. They consisted of a small piece of cloth stretched over a wire frame which fitted across the nose and mouth and was tied in position by means of two tapes passing behind the head. The cloth had to be dipped in a specially prepared solution and was supposed to be kept damp.'[30]

'The night of the 8th of May came dark and forbidding,' reported Private Gray. 'An eerie wind moaned fretfully through the trees as we lined up quietly in the road. Conversation was short.' Thomson spent the night with others lying in the open 'packed like sardines and all feeling the cold bitterly. The dawn lightened in the eastern sky and the whole world seemed at peace; but me, lying there, waiting, knew too well that before long the awful hand of war would swoop down upon us, claiming its victims amid the uproar and the shrieks and agony of battle.'[31]

'Dawn of great day,' Piper Dan McLeod, also in the 4th Black Watch, was noting in his diary on 9 May. 'Bombardment started 7 minutes to 5 o'clock. Germans retaliated very heavily. It was awful. We lay in reserve trench.' Lance Corporal Andrews brought out his notebook 'and scribbled a few words… "Under bombardment. Nerve-racking medley of roar and clatter. We are lying as low as possible"'.[32] The heavy bombardment was intended to destroy the Germans' wire and front-line trenches but 'the barbed wire was of an entirely new kind, which was constructed by thick barbed cables' and less easily destroyed. The German front-line trench was a 'blind' one, full of more barbed wire, while the German soldiers had remained 'comparatively safe in deep dug-outs constructed of concrete.'[33] 'When the barrage ceased we jumped out of our trenches and proceeded in short rushes over no man's land where we were met with outbursts of machine gun fire,' Quekett recalled. 'It was on our third rush forward that I was hit in the right hip and knocked over by the impact.'[34] The 2nd Black Watch had also been ordered forward 'but the enemy fire was so heavy that it collapsed before 30 yds had been covered. A wide and deep ditch, filled with water and mud, running parallel to the front, further impeded the advance.'[35]

In the heat of battle, those in the rear were unsure what was happening. 'A wounded Seaforth passed by and told us that the first three lines had been captured and in our relief we cheered loudly,' Thomson wrote in his diary.

> Alas our happiness was short lived. More wounded passed us and from them we learned the awful state of affairs in the firing line. Our attack had been a failure… The Germans had opened artillery fire and were battering our front line and supports to pieces. Everything was in confusion. The day was lost!!!… There were wounded men everywhere. Gurkhas and British, English and

> Scotch all lay together. Equipment, rifles, trench stores and ammunition was lying scattered all over the trench… no one seemed to know where we were to go and we seemed to be more in the way than of any use. We were told to go down to the front line – then to stay where we were – then again to go somewhere else.[36]

Not surprisingly he described the situation as 'topsy turvy'. Even those in the reserve trenches were 'under terrible fire', recorded McLeod. 'Five Stretcher Bearers wounded. Nearly 200 casualties.'[37] After the initial advance failed, the 5th Black Watch remained in the assembly trenches, suffering both from heavy German shell fire and 'through [British] shells dropping short.'[38]

Despite rising casualties, Haig ordered another assault in the afternoon, bringing forward, among others, the 1st Black Watch, their pipers playing 'to within 100 yds of enemy lines.'[39] 'Suddenly at 3.59 p.m., there was a flash of bayonets all along the line,' observed a brigade staff officer, describing the 1st Black Watch's advance 'with their officers five paces in front of their platoons, and their pipers playing in front.' Amid the noise, there was a sound like the clapping of hands but which they soon realised was machine gun fire: 'The bit of line that I could see through my glasses suddenly began to fall, the falling moving along from right to left. At first I believed they were lying down by order. I did not realise how quickly people could be killed.' Although some members of the Battalion reached the German lines, they were 'unsupported, and our guns had to bombard for an extra half-hour to let them out again. Two companies disappeared and the remainder were sorely shattered. The whole affair was absolute carnage', related an officer in the 1st Scots Guards, 'sending brave men to certain death, and, my God, they met it like men, too.' 'You talk about murder, you ought to have been there,' commented Private Braid. 'They were throwing bombs at us. There were some of our chaps blown to atoms at this juncture, that made the rest of us retire.'[40]

Even the Germans conceded the bravery of their enemies, describing how the British had sent 'one of their best Highland regiments to the front, the best they have anywhere. The Black Watch advanced. The gallant Scots came on, but even their really heroic bravery was in vain, for they were not able to turn the fate of the day.'[41]

Haig had no alternative but to order a withdrawal. 'To have pressed the attack would have meant the annihilation of all,' observed Gray. Survivors were ordered to lie down in No Man's Land until they could crawl back to the British line under cover of darkness. 'The scenes in the trenches as night fell were very painful. The stretcher-bearers had great difficulty in moving the wounded owing to the narrowness of the trenches… We were not allowed to remove our boots and equipment, and lay down as we were. Rain had fallen again during the evening. It was very cold. We were physically very tired, but the events of the day had made such a deep impression that few of us found it possible to sleep.'[42]

The action at Aubers Ridge achieved no strategic success. 'The old fault, wire not cut,' observed Sotheby. 'Next time the Germans will get it. Given a chance with wire down and at close quarters, they will be slaughtered, and I feel quite mad at it, and long for a decent smash at them.'[43]

Two VCs were awarded to Black Watch soldiers, one to forty-seven-year-old Corporal John Ripley, 1st Black Watch, 'the first man of his battalion to ascend the enemy's parapet, & from there he directed those following him to the gaps in the German wire entanglements. He then led his section through a breach in the parapet to a second line of trench.' Having established himself 'with seven or eight men' he held the position 'until all his men had fallen and he himself was badly wounded in the head.'[44] The second VC was won by Lance Corporal David Finlay, 2nd Black Watch, who had been in command of a bombing party, ten of whom were killed or wounded. Having ordered the two survivors to crawl back, he helped two wounded men, carrying first one, then the other to safety while under fire.[45]

In the 4th Black Watch there were two instances of fathers and sons serving together, in both cases losing a family member. 'There was a sergeant-major who put a white cross on the grave of his son, and a private who put a cross on the grave of his father,' observed Lance Corporal Andrews.[46]

The recent fighting had revealed a shortage of heavy weapons, shells and trench weaponry. *The Times'* military correspondent highlighted the lack of an unlimited supply of high explosives as 'a fatal bar to our success'. His comments were picked up in a leader article: 'This is a war of artillery, and more and more it is coming to depend upon the supplies of ammunition... British soldiers died in vain on the Aubers Ridge on Sunday because more shells were needed.'[47] What became known as the 'shell crisis of 1915' caused such outrage that Asquith agreed to re-form the Cabinet as the first Coalition ministry, which included one Labour and nine Conservative Members of Parliament. The Liberal politician David Lloyd George was appointed minister-in-charge of a new munitions department. Having already endured the losses at Neuve Chapelle, the news of Aubers Ridge created strong anti-German feeling in Scotland, where riots took place in Perth on the same day as the *Perthshire Advertiser* bemoaned 'the sacrifice of hundreds of grand young lives'.[48]

Festubert: 'Ground all trembling with bursting shells'

After the failure at Aubers Ridge another offensive was planned. The objective was again to divert attention from the French at Vimy Ridge by a renewed attack in the area around Festubert. In I Corps, the 2nd and 7th Divisions would carry out the attack, with the 47th and 1st Canadian Divisions, supported by the newly arrived 51st Highland Division, in reserve. To the north was the Indian Corps with the 2nd and 4th Black Watch in the 7th Meerut Division.[49] But, despite an exceptionally heavy bombardment, which began on 13 May, insufficient high-explosive shells meant that, as previously, it failed to make serious inroads into German defences.

The ground attack began on the evening of 15 May. Although suffering heavy casualties from Germany artillery fire while crossing No Man's Land, the 2nd Division managed to occupy German front and support-line trenches. The following day, the 7th Division was brought to the front, I Corps bearing the full weight of the advance. 'Enemy still shelling heavily, ground all trembling with bursting shells & splinters flying all over,' observed Lance Corporal David Simpson, 2nd Black Watch, in line again at the Rue du Bois.[50] Despite German resistance, a gap had been created forcing them to withdraw to a new line over a thousand yards to the rear, which, with the arrival of reinforcements, they managed to hold. On 19 May, the 1st Canadian and 51st Highland Divisions were ordered to move forward to relieve the 2nd Division, the soldiers passing through an 'extremely shallow' communication trench, 'only a few feet deep', according to Private George Farrar, 6th Black Watch. 'We were ordered to keep well down so that we more or less proceeded on hands and knees.'[51]

Instead of taking part in the next attack, ordered for 23 May, the 51st Highland Division was moved from I Corps to the Indian Corps, which had been spared the heavy fighting. Having taken up position in an area of uncleared battlefield, Farrar volunteered to be part of a burying party to get his first experience 'over with'. 'About six of us were sent out in front with instructions to bury on the spot.' They were ordered to 'keep well down when a flare went up,' which happened soon after they had set off.

> By its light I saw that I had dropped beside a decapitated head. When the flare died down I dug a hole, pushed the head into it and covered it over. I then ran a few yards & dropped into a trench where I saw a German officer – or what was left of him. He wore riding boots, white breeches & had a belt round his waist, but above there was nothing. His body had gone & maybe the head belonged to him. We soon covered him and gradually worked our way along the trench covering everything we saw. I don't know how long we were out there or how many we buried but when we got back to our trench I felt that I had had my share of grave digging for a very long time.[52]

After two days, the 6th Black Watch was relieved by the 7th, which also had the sorrowful task of burying the dead. Heavy rain added to the 'general discomfort'. Colour Sergeant Guthrie wrote home: 'We are resting for two days and then back again to the trenches... The Germans gave us a hot time with shell fire and their famous "black Marias" these are the high explosive shell guns, fortunately their aim is not as good as our gunners, otherwise they should have wiped us out.'[53]

By 25 May the line had advanced less than 2 miles, with over 16,000 casualties (the French sustaining over 100,000 in their larger offensives in what was known as the Second Battle of Artois) compared with a total of 50,000 German casualties at Vimy Ridge and Festubert. For once, casualties in The Black Watch were minimal.[54] 'During the day it was usually very hot, but intensely cold at night,' commented Private Gray, 4th Black Watch. 'The guns thundered on unceasingly, and each morning the aeroplanes flew overhead.'[55]

All named heroes

Among reinforcements arriving in France were members of Kitchener's New Armies. In the 9th Division was the 8th Black Watch. 'Just off, don't worry I shall pull through, please God,' Lieutenant Jack Mackintosh was writing to his 'Mother Darling' in April.[56] 'The sea voyage caused more uneasiness than 10,000 Germans would,' remarked Orderly Room Sergeant Adam Macgregor Wilson. 'All lights out and everybody wondering when *that* torpedo would strike.' Reaching Boulogne they travelled onwards in crowded trucks: 'what sardine would envy us?' Wilson observed how the people seemed 'quiet & depressed. Not at all like the gay debonair French I have read so much of – But, my own countrymen would be depressed & have a grim determination if they were within 18 miles of – some call it hell – others say it more forcibly – names a pencil would fain write.'[57]

Moving to billets near Arques and then Bailleul, training began at once. 'Oh – Yawn – another day again and pouring rain,' recorded Wilson. 'Well, it might be worse. Much better that it rains water than shells... and if it were not for the strange tongue I could almost believe that I am still at home.' But, he acknowledged, there was a marked difference. 'Still the ambulances pass with their freight of sadness. The eternal stream. But how much more sad is the thought of those who have been left. Finding their last resting place in foreign soil. The luxury of a coffin is denied.' In a later entry he continued: 'A sad thing in connection with the graves is shown on three crosses "Grave of a Soldier" – that's all – all named heroes. Somebody will mourn for them in their unknown graves.'[58] 'One does not seem to think a great war is being waged all round, except for the troops,' Lieutenant Mackintosh informed his sister. 'It is only the roar of the guns incessantly day and night and the strings of Red Cross vans bringing in wounded that brings it home to one.'[59]

After spending early May 're-organising and re-fitting', the 8th Black Watch moved to Armentières. 'I have just returned from the trenches. We went in for a night (24 hrs) for instructional purposes and to get blooded as they call it,' wrote Mackintosh. 'It was a time of regular spells in the trenches interspersed with brief periods, in reserve or at rest,' recalled seventeen-year-old Second Lieutenant Neil Ritchie who, although under age, had joined the 1st Black Watch. 'It did, however, give one the opportunity of getting used to a life of discomfort, exposure to almost constant danger and made a young officer realise his responsibilities towards his men, their well-being, their comfort and their safety.'[60]

'They are very much alive these Germans', observed Wilson, 'and to show your head above the sandbags for more than a few seconds is courting death in the truest sense.' On 16 June Captain Robert Forrester, 1st Black Watch, did just that when the Battalion was in the line at Cuinchy. Looking over the parapet 'for barely 5 seconds', he suddenly fell 'like a log' into the trench below. 'I had heard a great crack which the German bullet makes at close range, and so knew what had happened,' recorded Second Lieutenant Sotheby standing near by. 'There he lay at my feet, a great hole behind the left eye, his eye shot out and most of his brains hanging out, a great stream of blood rushing out. The bullet had come out of the other side of the head and must narrowly have missed me too.'[61]

After Festubert, the 6th and 7th Black Watch's activities were limited to small operations. 'We are in the same position as last, only our Company is more advanced in the firing line,' Guthrie was writing in mid-June. 'The big Guns have been pounding away at the enemy's lines all day and they in return have been hammering us.'[62]

At the end of June the 51st Highland Division moved north to Laventie, taking over the line at Fauquissart. 'The front line here was much better than at Festubert,' observed Farrar. 'Instead of a narrow trench which had been dug down into the wet clay we were behind breastworks which had been raised above the ground level – well built and properly traversed. They were very dry and what was more important well-sheltered from the Germans. There was a good deal of patrol work in the area – otherwise it was quiet.'[63] 'The big Guns are "lying low" on both sides, possibly it is the calm before the storm bursts,' wrote Guthrie in another letter home, describing how 'after a night of work & silence at daybreak the men began shouting all sorts of things to the enemy over the way, inviting them to come out for a mornings shooting, whilst they on their part sent replies back in pure English one being distinctly heard to say "it's all right Scottie take off your boots & go to bed".' Later in the day they requested 'Piper Ferguson to tune his pipes & give us a number of selections, so you can see,' he assured his wife, 'while we are engaged in serious work, the men are in good spirits... we have practically not had our boots off for the last eleven days & feet are not in consequence in the best of order.'[64]

In the hope of avoiding 'unpleasant' battalion duties, Private Farrar had decided to join the battalion 'bombers'. In contrast to the early primitive bombs, consisting of little more than an empty jam jar filled with rusty nails and an explosive with a fuse lit by a match, 'the Batty time-fuse bomb had just arrived – this was a cast-iron canister about the size of a 1lb jam pot – the outside was cut with squares of about 1 inch so that the bomb would burst into suitable fragments.' The explosive was already in the canister but 'the rest of the bomb was in the form of spare parts'.

We had to cut our own fuses, put them into detonators and after

> attaching a patent lighter to the fuse, wire the whole lot together – … the tricky part was fixing the detonator to the time fuse… [In the absence of tools] the detonator was put in the mouth & we bit on the part where it overlapped the time fuse until we were sure that we could not pull it out. Our instructor (an NCO who had been to the Bombing School at Béthune) told us to bite firmly but gently. 'Don't bite too hard or you'll blow your bloody head off!'[65]

Transporting these amateur bombs was 'a nightmare. They were carried in long narrow boxes… the way they rattled about was enough to terrify anybody.' Predictably there were accidents: the 1st Black Watch's bombing officer, Lieutenant George Mitchell, was killed by an explosion. A keen boxer from Yorkshire, he had gained an enthusiastic following before the war by travelling to Paris to fight (and lose) against the French champion boxer, Georges Carpentier.[66]

Throughout the summer the 1st Black Watch continued to rotate in and out of the line in the sector south of Givenchy. The formation of the Guards Division in August meant that the Battalion was no longer brigaded with the 1st Coldstream and 1st Scots Guards; instead they were joined in 1 Brigade by the 8th Royal Berkshire and the 10th Gloucestershire Regiments. Throughout June, July and August the 2nd Black Watch spent sixty days in the trenches compared with thirty-two out of the line, but no events 'of any particular importance' altered the routine.[67] The 4th Black Watch was likewise spared any 'severe actions', Gray noted. 'By this time we were beginning to feel like old soldiers & began to live a little more luxuriously,' related Lance Corporal Thomson. 'A double page of *The Times* began to appear as a tablecloth & the bread was placed on the "table" cut & buttered. The cake too, was neatly sliced & the cheese had the skin off it.' Although morale remained remarkably high, Captain Patrick Duncan could not help questioning how men 'professing the same Christianity should, after 1900 years of teaching, bring such desolation… It is far worse than the middle ages, when those fighting were ignorant religious fanatics but at this time of day both sides have been educated and know better.'[68]

The 8th Black Watch had remained near Festubert. 'Nearly a year has passed since the first shot was fired,' Adam Macgregor Wilson was writing on 1 July. 'About this time last year I was engaged in the very peaceable pursuits of making hay and now I am listening to the roar of the cannon belching forth destruction. What a contrast.' On 6 July he was noting: 'They are still blowing Festubert to pieces or rather they are blowing the small pieces of Festubert to smaller pieces.' 'The whole of this place is one huge cemetery', he continued: 'the legs of dead soldiers stick out in places – a man's head & shoulders – a pair of boots with feet in them – a man's hand grimly bent to shape pointing the way… – a grim jest, truly.' Describing some of his dead comrades, he said they were 'butchered' not killed: 'one had only two legs – no body or head – another only a few mangled remains which we put and tied in a waterproof sheet. The other was without head or shoulders… Hell couldn't be worse.'[69]

Meanwhile, on 8 July 1915 the 9th Black Watch left Scotland, joining the 15th Scottish Division. 'If the worst comes to the worst you can secure my gold watch & chain,' Sergeant Joe Barber told his brother. 'You might ask Father at a suitable time if my money in the savings bank could be got by him without any statement by me.' 'We had rather a bad crossing, nearly all the men were ill,' Major Jack Stewart, the Battalion's second-in-command, informed his wife. 'We had no adventures of any kind, except that I woke up in the middle of the night and mistook the kicking of the mules on the horse-deck for guns going off and wondered how the dickens we could have got to the battle line without my knowing it.'[70]

Following agreement between General Foch and Field Marshal Sir John French that the British line would again be extended, at the end of July the 51st Highland Division was ordered south, for the first time taking over the Méricourt–Ribermont region of the Somme. 'After the flat and marshy plains of Flanders, the well wooded slopes of the Somme area were a pleasing change & we felt cheered up at the prospect of staying some time in the neighbourhood,' related Farrar, who was amused to record the departing French General's reaction to their kilts: '*C'est bon pour l'amour, mais ce n'est pas bon pour la guerre*!'[71] In the absence of an offensive, the soldiers followed a routine of ten days in the line, ten days out. 'The getting to the Fire Trenches was pretty stiff and was done at the double,' observed Colour Sergeant Guthrie. 'The Trenches have all been renamed such as Fair Maid Str. Dundee Avenue, Arbroath Road, Scouringburn, Kirriemuir Road, etc etc. there are so many it is quite a maze & one could quite easily lose himself until he gets to know his way about.' 'We were constantly under fire from whizz bangs, aerial torpedoes which made a terrific noise,' recorded Farrar, 'and huge trench mortars which we called flying dustbins – as soon as one of these was fired we could watch its progress through the air – turning over and over – and coming so slowly that we could guess where it would fall and take shelter accordingly'.[72]

All along the Western Front, the placing of mines continued. The 6th Black Watch had its first experience on 8 August when, before midnight, the Germans exploded two mines underground at L'îlot, a small salient near the village of La Boisselle. Known by the British as the Glory Hole, its furthest point was only a few yards from the German front line. One of the casualties was Private W. Nicholson; blown out of the front trench, he was taken prisoner but died four days later.[73] Since many in the 7th Black Watch came from the coal-mining region of Fife, they proved ideal recruits for the tunnelling companies. Among them was Second Lieutenant Herbert Humphrys, a former mining engineer. On 26 August he went down a mine at La Boisselle 'without any safety apparatus' to rescue a soldier overcome by gas. Three days later he attempted a similar rescue but was himself overcome. 'If he hadn't roped himself, he would have been done for,' his Company commander, Captain Peter Alabaster, Royal Engineers, wrote home, describing Humphrys as 'an A1 chap'.[74]

Loos: 'Dead Highlanders in Black Watch tartan'

In September, the relative calm along the Western Front was shattered. With French, British and Empire forces still engaged at

Gallipoli, Kitchener had promised to maintain pressure on Germany by ordering another offensive. While French forces would launch an attack in Champagne, a combined British-French assault would be made in Artois: the British First Army were to attack the town of Loos, north of Lens, while the French Tenth Army launched an offensive to the south. Opposing them was the German Sixth Army, commanded by Crown Prince Rupprecht and IV Corps, German First Army, under General Friedrich Sixt von Armin.

The British attack was to be made between Givenchy and Grenay with Loos in front, overlooked by a redoubt on 'Hill 70'. Two corps of the British First Army were positioned side by side with the village of Vermelles in between. Six Black Watch battalions were to be engaged. Facing the German trenches on the left, in I Corps, the 2nd and 9th Scottish Divisions were opposite the towns of Auchy and Haisnes; jutting into No Man's Land opposite the 9th Division's position was the Hohenzollern redoubt, bordered by the 'Little Willie' and 'Big Willie' trenches. Behind lay Fosse Trench and Dump Trench in front of a large slag heap, Fosse No. 8. Next to the 9th Scottish Division was the 7th Meerut Division, facing Cité St Elie and the northern half of Hulluch village. 'Photography of the enemy's trenches from the air had only just been introduced,' related Major Wauchope, who had taken command of the 2nd Black Watch in early September. To prepare for the attack he had ordered a plan of the German trenches to be reconstructed behind British lines. 'Over this the Battalion practised.'[75]

In IV Corps, the 1st Division was facing Hulluch, while the 15th Scottish Division was opposite Loos village and Hill 70 behind which was Cité St Auguste. On the extreme right was the 47th Division, whose objective was two mining spoilheaps known as Double Crassier. The 5th Black Watch was still under strength after Aubers Ridge and so the only platoon taking part was the Grenadier platoon of bombers, which carried out a diversionary attack at Bois Grenier in the Neuve Chapelle sector.[76]

'Everything is now arranged for the big attack,' Captain J. S. S. Mowbray was informing Captain Edward Murray, whom he had replaced in command of D Company, 8th Black Watch, in July after Murray was wounded. 'We are here in trenches handed over by the French.' 'At this particular part of the line the trenches are dug 6' [ft] deep from the surface and with the parapet are easily 9' [ft]', observed Private Ireland. 'They are splendid trenches; the only fault that they are too narrow and great difficulty will be found carrying wounded down them. This is the greatest place yet we have been for communications and lines of trenches. It is a fair mangle. Without a doubt the shortest way out would be 3½ miles.'[77]

'There is a move coming off soon but I must not write anything about it in case this book were to fall into other hands,' Adam Macgregor Wilson confided to his diary on 15 September. 'I won't say too much but many of the battalion will make this last journey… What a funny world – yet most of us know that it may be our turn & think absolutely nothing of it. It's fine to live, and live on, then go home to the loved ones & be happy; but if instead of that – death – well if it is to be it will & what's the use of grousing.' 'Not long now. We are all very cheerful. It is funny how we all chaff one another about our chances,' Lieutenant Sidney Steven, 4th Black Watch, wrote home a week later. 'Friday, 24th September, dawned a bleak day – rain poured steadily down,' recorded Private Gray. 'The men know that on the morrow their battalion was to take a leading part in a great battle.' 'Just a few lines to report good health as usual,' Sergeant Barber, 9th Black Watch, wrote to his parents, warning them that 'if the letters are few & far between don't become alarmed. We are expecting great things & everyone is in great spirits.'[78]

On 25 September 1915 Sir John French launched the largest offensive on the Western Front since the outbreak of war, the number of guns used during the bombardment against the German trenches exceeding that at Neuve Chapelle. 'Our artillery these past few days have made the earth fly over their way and for one to look across it seemed as if life could not live under such conditions,' continued Private Ireland. Low-bursting shrapnel fire was used to cut the German wire. 'On the 15th Division front this had been fairly well done, but further north, on the 1st Division front, it was not successful, which fact had a great bearing on the whole operation,' commented Wauchope.[79]

Emulating the Germans at Ypres in April, about 140 tons of chlorine gas was released, the men having spent the preceding days 'digging places for the cylinders all along the front': 'great secrecy', related Lance Corporal Forman, 8th Black Watch, 'this being the first time the British had used gas. But it never surprised the Germans; they had better gas-masks than we had. In fact we suffered more than they did.'[80] Lieutenant Colonel Walker, 4th Black Watch, had instructed all the men in the front trenches to have 'their smoke helmets on 10 minutes before the gas cylinders are opened. Men must not go into dug outs, shell holes, ditches or sally ports for 20 minutes after the gas has been cut off, as the gas being heavy fills up all such places.' 'Hardly slept all night,' recorded Piper McLeod. 'Cannot give much idea of times. Bombardment for about 10 minutes. Smoke and gas.'[81]

'Then: Over the Top with the best of luck!' continued Lance Corporal Forman. 'Our headgear was a glengarry – we didn't have tin hats in those early days – we had 120 rounds of ammunition, entrenching tools, iron rations and other odds and ends. Our training for moving forward in those [days] was by short rushes of about 30 yds and then drop down. The Germans soon got the hang of that. He would wait till we got up again then sweep us with machine guns. Each time some would fall, never to get up again.'[82]

By 7 a.m. the German stronghold of the Hohenzollern redoubt and the 'Little Willie' trench had been taken. A combined force of the 8th Black Watch and 5th Camerons then moved on to take Dump Trench. But casualties were severe, with officers and men 'mown down'. Lieutenant Jack Mackintosh was 'killed at the first German trench… He was in great spirits and he died nobly at the head of his platoon,' Lance Corporal McGee informed Mackintosh's sister. Company Sergeant Major Ernest Hamilton was fatally wounded in the stomach: 'he was rather a stout man and, as I opened his kilt to use his Field Dressing, he was burst right open. Bullets were hitting all around and I had to carry on,' related Forman, noting the irony of having been told before the battle that there would be no resistance for 5 miles 'as the Germans would all be gassed. What a hope!'[83]

Temporarily the Germans fell back to their support trenches, the 8th Black Watch occupying the German front line having advanced beyond Dump Trench. 'The trenches we had left had no proper shelter or cover but here [were] well made dug outs about a dozen steps down, with wire beds to sleep on.' As darkness approached, 'things were quieter.' It had also begun to rain, the discomfort compounded by the Germans' decision to open a sluice, which flooded a communication trench. At midnight the Battalion was relieved. There were 'no officers in my company left to give us orders,' commented Forman. '1 Sgt and myself L Cpl and about 30 men.' They decided 'to send a man back to Headquarters for instructions' and about 2 a.m. we had orders to fall back to our original front line trench. What an awful sight for dead and dying every few yards we took – wounded shouting "Stretcher Bearer!" "Stretcher Bearer"!' Among the severely wounded was the 8th Black Watch's Commanding Officer, Lieutenant Colonel Lord Sempill, who was replaced by Major J. G. Collins. Captain Mowbray was killed when an 'unlucky shell' pitched into D Company when in the front line.[84]

The 2nd Black Watch had also moved forward. '[Piper] Simpson and I struck up "Happy we've been a'thegither" just to show them we were not downhearted and then the order to advance came,' recorded Piper Alexander MacDonald. 'At last we charged out at the head of our Company playing "Heilan Laddie". The Germans were assailing us with machine guns, rifle fire, and goodness knows all what, but we stuck to it.'[85] They too experienced the gas. 'The Black Watch, being on the leeward flank, suffered more severely from it than the remainder of the Brigade,' noted Wauchope. 'No gas seems to have reached the enemy trenches.' 'Owing to the wind being unfavourable, many casualties were caused amongst the attackers. In fact, half the Officers and many men were out of action before the enemy front line was reached. Direction was only maintained with difficulty on account of the smoke, which, however, gave a certain measure of protection from the heavy rifle and M.G. fire.' But despite 'the distress caused by the gas', the Battalion advanced to the German trenches, driving them back 'with bayonet and bomb'.[86]

'Just as we gained the 2nd line poor Simpson was shot down but I kept playing as we dashed forward and attacked the 3rd line,' Piper MacDonald's account continued. 'We took this also and the next, but at both we were hotly assailed with bombs.'[87] To the right, the Garhwal Brigade had been less successful, leaving Bareilly Brigade exposed. At 1300 'an orderly withdrawal was carried out with great steadiness and the original British line was reached and held.' 'You cannot imagine such a sight as the return from the trenches when relieved!' commented Second Lieutenant Malcolm Thorburn, 2nd Black Watch. 'Clogged with mud, some with no hats, some with German helmets, some with their smoke helmets – cheery, but dead-beat. What trophies they got – Iron Crosses, helmets, coats, books – you have no idea what.'[88]

Having captured the German front line, the 4th Black Watch had moved forward to occupy the support trenches.'The enemy were evidently taken by surprise… The Germans surrendered in Batches and small parties of them with hands up and pale faces were quickly sent back to our lines… for the most part the prisoners were young men, well-built, but very anxious for mercy.' But the area had not been sufficiently 'mopped up and many casualties were inflicted by snipers who had been overlooked.' When the Germans brought up their heavy artillery, the position could not be held. 'The Fourth hung on doggedly in an inferno of bursting lyddite and poisonous fumes,' related Private Gray.[89]

At 'about 11 o'clock the Germans counterattacked in very strong force,' wrote Piper McLeod in his diary. '*No reinforcements for us.* 8th Gurkhas retired on our right flank. Germans bombing round. Just in time a few of us nipped over the parapet and made a run. Most of them knocked out by rifle and machine gun fire… Managed to crawl into small shell hole.' 'Suddenly the Germany artillery fire ceased,' reported Private Gray, 'and masses of grey-clad forms loomed ahead out of the smoke as the enemy advanced, outnumber[ing] our men 20 to 1… the thin line of the Fourth was now divided into isolated groups of the survivors, who, disdaining surrender, continued the battle against hopeless odds.'[90] Crawling back to the British line, Piper McLeod 'came upon Colonel Walker. Very seriously wounded and impossible to bandage him up.' At dusk he returned with stretcher bearers who brought Walker in 'and as many men as I knew where they were.' Walker's wounds proved fatal. 'The saddest task any regiment can have is to bury its colonel,' observed Thomson who had just returned from leave and missed the battle. 'And when the First and Second in command Colonel Walker and Major Tosh were laid together in a neat little graveyard at Pont du Hem everyone present (all that remained of the Battalion) was deeply moved.'[91]

Among the many private soldiers killed in the 4th Black Watch was nineteen-year-old William Cuthill. Lieutenant Harvey Steven was greeted with the news of the death of his older brother, Lieutenant Sidney Steven, when he joined the Battalion a few days later. 'Sid, with his company following him, was attacking the second line of trenches when he came upon seven Germans,' Harvey informed their mother. 'The report I have is that he shot six of them with the six rounds of his revolver but the seventh shot him through the thigh. It was a ghastly wound.' Barely two weeks later Harvey Steven himself was killed. 'It had been a grand advance but at great cost,' noted the 4th Black Watch's War Diary, the objective being to draw German troops from 'more vital parts of the battlefield' and give assistance to the British divisions fighting near Loos.[92]

To the right the 1st Black Watch, 1st Division, had advanced towards Hulluch north of Loos. As Second Lieutenant George Young described,

> I was soon moving once the attack began. We had to pass some horrible sights. Men with their faces smashed in or legs torn off or their bodies so mutilated as to be unrecognisable… we found the gas was still about and had to use our helmets… [I] had to keep going the whole night encouraging and directing the men with bullets flying all over the place. Rain began as the darkness came down, and the wet appeared to bring the gas out of the ground, adding much to the discomfort of the troops.[93]

Held up by the uncut wire, although reinforcements were sent up, the Division made limited gains. Among the wounded was Second Lieutenant Neil Ritchie who was sent home to convalesce.[94]

On the 1st Division's right was the 15th Scottish Division, with the 9th Black Watch, which was spared the same ill-effects from the release of gas. The Division's first objective was the heavily fortified redoubt known as the Jew's Nose, on the Lens Road. Within five minutes the German front and support lines were taken but casualties were heavy with three Company commanders killed, four other officers, all four Company Sergeant Majors and over 200 men. Major Henderson's last words were recorded as 'Keep going'.[95] 'No one present will ever forget that attack,' recorded the War History. 'It seemed impossible that these lines of disciplined soldiers had been, twelve short months before, almost all civilians. Perfect steadiness prevailed, regardless of the heavy fire which, coming more especially from the "Lens Road Redoubt", swept the ground over which they had to cross… not a line wavered or stopped.' 'The dead Highlanders, in Black Watch tartan, lay very thick. In one place, about 40 yards square, on the very crest of the ridge, and just in front of the enemy's wire,' recorded Brigadier General Henry Thuillier, later to command the 15th Scottish Division. 'They were so close that it was difficult to step between them. Nevertheless the survivors had swept on and through the German lines.'[96]

'We did our job,' affirmed Major Jack Stewart. 'Of course the rest of the Brigade were with us but we, the 9BW, almost unaided rushed the HUN trenches (three lines of them) fought our way through the town [Loos] & up to a certain hill [Hill 70]… The Regiment was absolutely magnificent and they've written a page of BW history that will rank with Ticonderoga.' The arrival of reinforcements, including more ammunition and machine guns, which the soldiers carried up to the front line 'in the face of heavy and continuous fire', rendered 'magnificent service to the hard-pressed Highlanders'.[97]

So great were the 9th Black Watch's casualties that when the Battalion was withdrawn to its former billet in Mazingarbe, a farmhouse known as Black Watch Farm, there was room for the Battalion in a place 'which prior to the battle had been scarcely large enough to take in A Company alone.'[98] Among those killed was Sergeant Joseph Barber, who had promised his gold watch and chain to his brother 'if the worst comes to the worst.'[99] 'They will be remembered as long as the BW is a Regiment. Ah 42nd, you have reason to be proud of your 9th Bn,' Stewart wrote home. 'The Hun fought splendidly, but gave in in vast numbers when he was actually collared… I took one prisoner myself poor devil, he was trembling with fright.' 'Poor' Lieutenant Sharpe was shot 'after he had lowered his revolver when a Hun officer held up his hands.'[100]

Having become isolated from his platoon, Private Jock Young, 9th Black Watch, and another soldier 'held on grimly till the end came.' Seeing a German bomb at their feet, Young picked it up intending to throw it 'back at the Hun from whom it came'. Before he could do so, it exploded in his hand. Taken prisoner, he was escorted to a dressing station behind German lines and questioned about the initials 'RH' on his shoulder straps. 'Royal Horse' was his response. 'The examiner seemed doubtful & said he had never heard of such a regiment.' In reply, Young explained that it was originally a cavalry regiment 'but as there was little use of cavalry' it had been re-formed into infantry 'putting them into kilts as they were all Scotch'. When asked if the Scottish were tired of the war, he replied: 'Yes, but they believed the only thing to do was to fight hard to get it over.' Having been well-treated by the German doctors, Young was thinking 'what a strange world' it was. 'Only yesterday they had schemed & fought to kill each other, today, they had on more than one occasion been kind.'[101]

One action which captured the imagination was that of a young French girl, Emilienne Moreau, who, with her mother, 'even under the awful shellfire that was going on, kept bringing coffee to the wounded.' While the 9th Black Watch's medical officer, Captain Frederick Bearn, was tending the wounded, shots were being fired from a nearby house by two snipers. 'This little girl then calmly took Bearn's revolver and walked into the house where the Germans were by the back door.' Having fired two shots she returned. Handing back the revolver, she remarked: '*[ils] son[t] fini* (they are finished)… I think she was pretty plucky, don't you?' Stewart asked his young son in a letter home. When the story of Mademoiselle Moreau's action spread, she became known as the 'Lady of Loos'.[102]

By the following day, the most advanced positions were held by the 9th Scottish Division, elements of which had reached the outskirts of Haisnes beyond the Hohenzollern redoubt. 'A Brigade relief came and led us back to the British old fire trench,' recorded Wilson, 8th Black Watch. 'I see the new Brigade fighting in front bombing the enemy from the Hohenzollern redoubt – a shell bursts & a man vanishes in parts – shells burst perilously near.'[103]

Early on the morning of 27 September, as the Germans fought to regain the Hohenzollern redoubt, a mixed force of 8th Black Watch and 5th Cameron Highlanders was sent forward under the command of Captain Fergus Bowes-Lyon. 'The enemy had a heavy gun hitting the communication trench and it was a proper death-trap,' recalled Lance Corporal Forman. 'You had to wait till [the] shell had burst and then make a dash for it, quite a few got caught and pieces of men were lying around, heads, arms, legs and torsos.' Among them was Bowes-Lyon. '[He] must have died instantaneously from concussion when his leg was blown off,' Lieutenant Gilroy assured his mother, Lady Strathmore, '& can never have known anything about his leg at all. It was terribly hard luck on him as he had come all through the attack on the 25th without a scratch, and had, I hear, done excellent work.'[104] Also killed in the late afternoon was Major Collins, upon whose death command fell to the adjutant, Captain J. L. S. Ewing. The fatal wounding of the bombing officer, Lieutenant P. H. Forrester, and others meant the 8th Black Watch had no trained bombers and so men in the rear trenches had to be shown 'how to light and throw grenades' before moving forward 'to keep up the fight'.[105]

The next day the 8th Black Watch was withdrawn; as the soldiers marched out of range of fire, Forman recalled that 'one Jock had some bagpipes he had picked up… He struck up the tune: "Eh! Jock are yer glad yer listed! How do you like the soldiers noo!"'[106]

An estimated 20,000 officers and men were casualties at Loos. The Germans called the battle *Der Leichenfeld von Loos* (the Field of Corpses of Loos). 'We went into action about 170 strong and I brought about 80 out,' commented Second Lieutenant George Young, 1st Black Watch, describing his company's strength.[107] Both the 2nd and 4th Black Watch were so badly depleted that the two battalions were amalgamated under Wauchope's command. Realising that there had been many 'whose gallant acts' at Loos might go unrewarded, he ordered medallions to be 'specially struck', forty-four of which were later presented to NCOs and private soldiers for 'valuable services' and 'gallantry'.[108] Reflecting on the battle, Major Stewart, 9th Black Watch, was thinking that he would never be the same again. 'One has heard the saying "who dies if England lives" but I confess I never actually KNEW what it meant till last Saturday. The heroism of our people was nothing but marvellous.'[109] 'From what I can ascertain, some of the divisions did actually reach the enemy's trenches,' Rawlinson informed Lord Stamfordham, George V's Private Secretary. 'For their bodies can now be seen on the barbed wire.'[110]

After the battle

During 1915 the Regiment had suffered its severest losses to date with over five thousand officers and men wounded, missing or killed. On 21 September the 10th Black Watch arrived in France and was billeted in Villers-Bretonneux, 'destined to become famous as the turning-point of the enemy's final advance in March 1918'. So great was the demand for reinforcements that the 11th Black Watch could not be brought up to strength, acting instead as a training battalion.[111]

In early October the Germans retook part of the Hohenzollern redoubt. While the 46th Midland Division attempted to regain the lost ground, the 1st Division attacked the German line south-west of Hulluch. 'Casualties had gradually diminished my two platoons to 37 strong all told,' related Second Lieutenant Young, 1st Black Watch.

> At two o'clock I gave the order to advance and got over the parapet. It was a wonderful sight. As far as the eye could see was one long line of men dashing into the cloud of smoke caused by our gas

> and by smoke bombs. On the right my fellows went splendidly but near me somehow they became very thin… then a whack on the ribs as if someone had hit me with a flat board. I collapsed into a shell hole and made myself as scarce as possible dimly realizing that I was wounded. There was no pain at first and I felt a strange elation at having experienced a new sensation.[112]

As the pain increased Young took a morphia pellet and waited for an opportunity to crawl to safety and a dressing station. 'I watched [the] sun, thinking what a glorious sunset it was and yet deploring the length of time it took for darkness to fall.' By evening every officer who had gone 'over the top' was a casualty, and the battalion eventually re-organised in the former British front line. Although the 46th Division was partially successful, casualties were heavy. The 1st Division hardly made 'any headway' against the German barbed wire.[113]

The sector to which the 2nd and 4th Black Watch had been assigned opposite Givenchy was 'a red inferno'.[114] Not only was the area heavily mined, but German snipers dominated the British line. 'Their look-out men were so well posted and so efficient that when a Highlander fired a single shot a dozen bullets immediately struck the loophole he had fired from,' observed Wauchope, still in command of both battalions.[115] On 8 October the Germans blew up two mines, breaching the line. 'Terrific explosions. Heavy shelling,' recorded Piper McLeod, who had just been promoted lance corporal. But against 'steady fire' the Germans were unable to capitalise on the breach and were driven back.[116] In early November twenty-year-old Lieutenant Charles Somers Cocks, 2nd Black Watch, was describing 'mud and bitter cold. Waders issued but little use.' 'We are holding a bit of line which varies from 150 to 250 yards from the Allemands,' remarked a new arrival, Lieutenant Archibald Bryant (Brykie) Cumming. 'There is a stream in front about 5yds wide and 9ft deep unfortunately containing many of our regiment and also Seaforth, which have been there since the beginning of the summer. Poor devils.'[117]

With the arrival of reinforcements, the 4th Black Watch was re-formed again as a separate unit, commanded by Major G. A.

McL. Sceales, 1st Argyll & Sutherland Highlanders. As Private Miller recalled, '480 men were needed to make up the tremendous losses the 4th had sustained. As I was now 18, I was allowed to go with these reinforcements.'[118] Assigned to 44 Brigade, 15th Scottish Division, the soldiers were in the same division as the 9th Black Watch. Their time was 'devoted to cleaning uniform, etc.'[119] The 8th Black Watch had taken up a position between the railway and road running between Ypres and Courtrai. 'Heavy gunfire tearing great gaps in the front line, exposing us to German snipers, most of our losses here were caused by snipers,' related Lance Corporal Forman. With the approach of winter came the rain, 'the trenches filling 1 to 2 feet with muddy water and we had no proper winter clothing.' During November the Battalion 'kept popping in and out of the line.'[120]

The 10th Black Watch's stay on the Western Front was brief. On 10 October Great Britain had declared war on Bulgaria, whose forces, alongside German and Austrian troops, had entered Serbia. To forestall any further advance by the Bulgarians, the Salonika Expeditionary Force, augmented to four divisions, was established. Travelling via Alexandria to join the force, the Battalion, as part of 26th Division, disembarked at Salonika on 24 November, before moving inland. 'The only form of training was route marches across the hills, as any instruction which involved standing was out of the question owing to the weather.'[121]

The 51st Highland Division, meanwhile, had remained in the Somme sector. 'We, that is 30 of our Co[mpan]y, were at the "Baths" today,' Colour Sergeant Guthrie was recording in early October. 'The water was drawn in barrels from some old cesspool, emptied into boilers to be heated, then into tubs. We were each allowed one and a half inches of water, did not cover the feet, but it was enough as the smell was strong enough to kill anything… The rest of our men are stoutly refusing to go near them.' Their routine consisted of ten days in the trenches and ten days out, being called out 'at any hour, *at short notice.* In fact we are at times called out – the men think without reason – but it is really for a test and to train the men for any eventuality.'[122]

On 25 October the 6th Black Watch was chosen to represent 153 Brigade during another visit by the King to the Western Front at Méricourt.[123] The Battalion's last spell in the trenches was at Authuille, north of Albert. 'The weather was bad and to make matters worse the enemy celebrated St Andrew's night by a four hours' bombardment of the front line'. The 7th Black Watch had been undertaking a similar routine, before beginning a period of retraining, which signified the 51st's Division's 'first long rest' since arriving in France in early May. On 25 December Lieutenant Colonel Moncrieffe relinquished command of the 6th Black Watch 'for which he had done so much'.[124]

Having lost Prime Minister Asquith's confidence, on 10 December Field Marshal Sir John French handed over command. His successor was General Douglas Haig.[125] For all battalions on the Western Front, trench warfare had become routine. Some aspects had improved: not only were the trenches deeper and better drained, but the parapets were theoretically 'bullet proof'. 'Brodie' steel helmets had been issued and dugouts gave better protection from the elements and against grenades and shrapnel; reliefs took place more frequently.[126] Training was carried out in a vast 'Bullring' at Étaples, near Boulogne. 'The bayonet fighting is the most energetic,' related Corporal Ian Maclaren, 'charging of dummies in most realistic fashion.'[127] An unusual volunteer was Private Hamilton (Hammie) Donald, the son of a Dundee seaman shipwrecked off the Japanese coast and married to a Japanese fisherman's daughter, whose family 'longed to help in some way'. Travelling from Japan at his own expense, he reached Scotland in late 1915, receiving a commission on 6 July 1916 as a second lieutenant in the 4th Black Watch.[128]

Reinforcements wanted

In November the 2nd Black Watch left France. 'Word has come through things are not too bright in the east – reinforcements wanted,' noted Private James Marshall. 'We entrain for a warm climate and so have done with wet trenches, thank Heaven,' Lieutenant Cumming wrote home. Passing through Lillers, where the 1st Black Watch was stationed, the two battalions met for the first time since South Africa in 1902.[129] After embarking at Marseilles in early December, Cumming was having second thoughts about their destination: 'France has such heaps of advantages. Whiskies and sodas any time you wished, mail every day, leave every three months. After all what is an occasional heavy shelling with those advantages compared to a de'il o' a thirst, mosquitoes and heat.'[130]

Entering the Persian Gulf on Christmas Day, Second Lieutenant Robert Morrison noted the irony of celebrating Christmas during wartime: 'Instead of having "Peace and Goodwill towards Men," there we were, "strafing" each other.' Arriving at Basrah (Basra) on 31 December, the Battalion transferred to river steamers and barges for the 50-mile journey up the Shatt al-Arab. 'With memories of the winter mud of Flanders many welcomed the change to an eastern theatre,' observed Major Wauchope, 'where there would always be sun and warmth, no mud, and an adversary who could be driven into the open and fought and beaten in the old style. Such optimists soon had a bitter disillusionment.'[131]

Marching, marching,
On the same old track;
Sorrow gnawing at my heart,
Mem'ry piercing like a dart;
Care perched on my back;
Linton on my left hand –
But, alas! Poor Jack!
Marching, marching,
Quietly does he lie,
Marching, marching,
Who so sad as I? [132]

5

1916: Attrition

From six a.m. till afternoon,
We marched till we were out hose and shoon,
We climbed a mountain, descended a glen,
We tramped, we walked, we crawled, and then,
With a mighty effort of body and will,
We arrived at the village of Blanqueville.[1]

Mesopotamia: The relief of Kut

While stalemate continued along the Western Front, British and Empire forces were fighting Ottoman Turkey, which had declared war against the Allied powers in November 1914. Although their joint naval campaign to seize the Dardanelles and the land invasion of the Gallipoli peninsula had failed, other offensives were being undertaken. In October 1914 the Indian Expeditionary Force D (known as the Mesopotamian Expeditionary Force) arrived from India to protect Britain's interests in the Persian Gulf. After Turkey's declaration of war, the force was increased and the port city of Basrah was occupied, and the Turks withdrew into Mesopotamia, the area of land between the Tigris and the Euphrates rivers. In September 1915 Lieutenant General Sir John Nixon, who had taken command of the Mesopotamian Force in April, ordered an attack on Baghdad. Despite initial successes, fierce fighting forced Major General Charles Townshend, in command of the 6th Poona Division, to withdraw downriver from Ctesiphon to Kut al-Amara. The Turks, commanded by the German Baron von der Goltz, went in pursuit and took up a position at Shaikh Sa'ad, 25 miles south-east of Kut, cutting off the 6th Division.[2]

Townshend's assessment was that a relief force would have to reach him by 10 January before his supplies ran out. Nixon immediately began assembling the Tigris Force, commanded by Lieutenant General Sir Fenton Aymler. 'In view of the apparently immediate need,' observed Major Wauchope, in command of the 2nd Black Watch, instead of organising the force in Egypt 'the transports had been passed straight through the canal independently, and the troops in a similar fashion up the Tigris from Basrah.' This meant large numbers of troops were without their artillery, hospital facilities or transport.[3] Included in Tigris Force was the 7th Meerut Division, commanded by Major General Sir George Younghusband, which was making its way up the Tigris from Basrah.[4]

'Hogmanay – New Year's Day – which is always a Scotch festival, we kept up in fine style,' recalled Private John Haig, 'singing all the songs we could think of as we plugged along the Tigris in flat-bottomed barges.' Those like Private James Marshall who had never travelled east were assailed by 'strange sounds – strange languages – strange people – the old world or where civilization started.'[5] On 3 January they halted at Amarah, where the men did field work on the sand, 'just to show that we hadn't forgotten the way to attack. And didn't it rain! Drops as big as shrapnel bullets fell all around us, and soaked us through and through in less than ten minutes… I couldn't help thinking about Neuve Chapelle, where the lead was coming over us every bit as thick as the rain, and the Black Watch advanced through it all as steady as on parade. They didn't mind lead and bullets a bit, but they cursed that rain something shocking!'[6]

Travelling onwards, their destination was Ali el-Gharbi, about 50 miles from Kut. '6th Jan. started marching at 8.30 a.m. 20 miles, awful dust,' recorded Lieutenant Somers Cocks. 'Many men fell out.' 'I've done some marching in my time – out in India, and France, and at home – but never anything like that. It was hot – seemed as if the sun had made a bet to scorch us up,' Haig continued. 'We were fully loaded – packs, rifles, pouches and bandoliers full of ammunition, water bottles and haversacks full, and our blankets on our shoulders. The very rifle barrels got hot, and if you touched them with your bare hands they raised a blister, while the water in our bottles was luke-warm.'[7] Aymler's first attack, which included 'all of the 7th Division available', on 4 January had failed. On 7 January another attack was ordered, the force now including the 2nd Black Watch. 'It seemed really funny to hear the guns in this strange land… Everything seemed at least a thousand years old, and if the enemy had been armed with bows and arrows we shouldn't have been a bit surprised.'[8]

Shaikh Sa'ad: 'The ground was dyed crimson'

When the 2nd Black Watch was ordered forward, the soldiers were in the middle of a late breakfast. 'The fires had scarcely been lit and the bully beef tins were not yet opened,' commented Wauchope. 'The Battalion advanced at great speed in four lines of platoons in fours, at forty paces interval.' 'It was a terrific affair,' related Lieutenant R. H. Dundas. 'The Turks in a trench, ground dead flat with no cover at all… their rifle fire was like hail. I can't conceive how I escaped and the hard ground made the bullets ricochet. We went at a fearful pace: and I was so parched and exhausted that death would have been welcome!'[9] The Battalion's hurried entry into the battle meant that 'no information with regard to the enemy was available, nor was any preliminary reconnaissance possible… magazines were only charged whilst advancing to the attack. The only order given as to the objective was to attack where the fire was thickest! After 200 yds advance, Battalion came under long range rifle fire, and 400 yds further on the attack had to be carried on by short rushes. The sun was in the attackers' faces, and this fact, and the mirage, made observation of fire and location of the Turkish trenches impossible.' By the time they reached to 'within 400 yards of the enemy lines,' all Company commanders 'save one' were wounded, including Wauchope, Captain D. C. Hamilton-Johnston taking command of the Battalion.[10]

'Men were dropping like flies,' recorded Lieutenant Brykie

Cumming, who had been wounded in the groin by a shrapnel pellet. 'Not because the shooting was good – but the volume of it... Saw Lt Hutchison badly wounded head & stomach – awful sight all blood. He died later, having never regained consciousness.' Second Lieutenant Robert Morrison was 'badly shot in stomach, died later.' 'A high explosive burst amongst the section in front of me laying out the lot,' recorded Second Lieutenant Bowie. 'At the same time I was spun right about & dropped. I rose up and saw that a great deal of my left arm had been blown off just below the elbow. The blood was spurting in different jets & I stuck the finger of my right hand in the hole... holding the blood back in this fashion for nearly an hour.'[11]

'I'm only telling the cold truth when I say that the ground was dyed crimson. Shrapnel shells and bullets were making the air black,' related Private Haig, wounded in the thigh. 'Got bullet through left arm, broken and knocked down,' recorded Lieutenant Somers Cocks. 'Remained on flat ground under heavy fire till 4 pm, then doubled back to ditch 300 yds. 4.30 went back to 1st aid post. Walked back across desert, arrived at river 8.30.' When Haig reached the dressing station, he found 'over half the battalion there as well. There was nobody to attend to us, and we had to do what we could for each other. It was pitiful and we cried like school kids who've lost their mothers.'[12] Although the men were tired, those fit enough had to work through the night. 'First I patrolled our right flank to find who was there,' recorded Dundas. 'Then sent to find our transport. I didn't [find it] but walked many miles by compass (invaluable) and stars... masses of wretched wounded everywhere, groaning and crying for help: I bandaged one or two, and carried some in. But they mostly lay out with no coats in great cold till 4 a.m. or so. Then at last we got up water, food (one sandwich since 8 a.m. but I was saved by a box of Bovril tablets) a coat and priceless rum all round.' 'End of 1st day of battle of Shaikh Sa'ad... spent rotten night, no sleep, morphia,' continued Somers Cocks, noting the following day 'no dressing, no food, no doctor, men dying', while Second Lieutenant Bowie recalled that 'they made arrangements for 250 casualties, they have got nearly 4500 instead.'[13]

As Tigris Force was badly reduced, it took up a defensive position. 'We got our line fairly well dug; and have held it all this baking day,' Dundas recorded on 8 January, 'lying flat in our scrape with bullets skimming a foot over. If we attack tomorrow the battalion will pretty well cease to exist at present.'[14] But although the attacking force had again failed to dislodge the Turks' left flank, it achieved some success on the right and on 9 January the Turks retired. In the aftermath, both officers and men criticised their ordeal as well as the 'confused haste' with which Tigris Force had been assembled.[15] '(1) A damn bad show,' noted Lieutenant Cumming in a series of numbered 'Remarks' in his diary. 'No one knew anything; (2) A disgrace to British Generalship (3) someone needs to show up the awful organisation (4) Turks burst their shrapnel too low otherwise there would have been more killed & more severe wounds (5) went into action 700 appx probably under (6) 47 killed appx. (7) wounded 422. (8) 18 out of 24 Officer casualties & 3 killed (9) hosp staff hopelessly few. Appx 1 Doctor for 600 wounded.'[16] 'The home people would be quite shocked,' Bowie recorded in his diary. 'What food it would be for The Daily Mail & such like papers. But everything here is kept remarkably quiet. The [Censor] at Basra evidently knows his job.'[17]

On 13 January the 7th Meerut Division was again ordered to attack the Turks, now entrenched upstream on the banks of the Wadi river, a tributary of the Tigris. While one brigade made a direct assault, the remainder attempted to outflank the Turks further upstream. Yet again they stood firm. Since the 2nd Black Watch was not part of the assaulting force, which was heavily defeated, its casualties were minimal. The continuing reverses caused Nixon to be replaced by Lieutenant General Sir Percy Lake, formerly Chief of the General Staff in India.[18]

Umm el-Hanna: 'Sheer suicide'

After resisting Tigris Force at the Wadi, the Turks again withdrew to a stronger position on the left bank of the Tigris at Umm el-Hanna. 'Though the frontage of the position was less than a mile, it was impossible to turn either flank, for the right rested on the Tigris and the left stretched to the edge of the Suwaikiya marsh.'[19] On 20 January the 2nd Black Watch moved forward to the advanced trenches. Short of bayonets and grenades, success depended on the supporting units moving up quickly from behind.

'So far rather exciting,' Dundas was writing on 21 January. 'Bombardment all day, every 2 hours and at 10 p.m. and 1 a.m… now we are dug in. But it's brilliant moonlight and we'll be seen. They are keeping up a furious rifle and machine gun fire (the idea was that the guns would silence both. They haven't): and I think the attack four hours hence will be sheer suicide… it'll be just like the 7th, but worse.' The ensuing battle fulfilled his fears: 'The Turks far from being cowed were giving us a tremendous rifle and MG fire: and getting over our little parapet into it was disagreeable (this was my first experience of going over: there was no top on the 7th!) It was too far for one rush: and the men lay twice in shallow ditches… all this time the air was thick with bullets and we lost a lot.' When the Turks began bombing the trenches, it was hard to retaliate. 'Only bombers can stop bombers: we had very few bombs (15 in all I believe) and very bad ones,' continued Dundas, who had been wounded in the arm. 'It appeared that our splendid CO H.J. [Hamilton-Johnston] had been hit and died of wounds.'[20] Among other fatalities was twenty-three-year-old Sergeant David Finlay who 'died fighting with the same cool courage' that had won him his VC at Aubers Ridge on 9 May 1915.[21]

Conditions for the survivors were miserable: 'at 12 cold rain began, and went on all day. We sat in pools absolutely numbed till about 6, (and many wounded must have died). At dusk we went back to our line… That walk was a nightmare. The earth was flooded all over, and every 100 yds [on the bank] was a ditch or nullah with water up to the knees and steep banks of pure slime: all this the wounded had to traverse, for 2 or 3 appalling miles.' Staggering onwards, they found there was no transport 'only pools of mud.' Eventually Dundas got on a boat. With nothing to eat but a dry biscuit and 'a tiny tin of potted meat' all day, when he reached the field hospital and was put into bed with 'hot brandy and a hot meal and clothes' it was like 'falling suddenly into Heaven'. Reviewing the day's events, he concluded: 'Artillery poor, attack in daylight hopeless with weak battalion, no bombs, no supports, men too far from objective to rush (in one swoop)... What happens now I don't know – there was a 6 hour armistice yesterday to get in our wounded.' He couldn't see 'the least prospect of our getting to Kut in time to relieve it.' On 25 January he spent the day 'writing letters for men... It's pathetic how they all say it's nothing serious or worth worrying about.'[22]

The 2nd Black Watch lost 60 per cent of its fighting strength. Briefly the Battalion came under the command of the only unwounded officer, Second Lieutenant Thomas Henderson, who brought the Battalion out of the line, until the transport officer, Second Lieutenant Stewart-Smith, could take command the following day. 'Exclusive of the transport, 29 officers and nearly 900 ORs had landed at Basra three weeks earlier. There now remained... two combatant officers and 130 men, and of these not all were unwounded.'[23]

On 4 February, the remnants of the 2nd Black Watch and 1st Seaforth Highlanders were formed into a Highland Battalion, commanded by Lieutenant Colonel W. M. Thomson, Seaforth. 'We were fortunate in being extremely friendly with the Seaforth Highlanders so the Highland Battalion worked quite well,' commented Second Lieutenant Neil Ritchie, who, after being wounded at Loos, had been with the 3rd (Special Reserve) Battalion in Nigg, until, 'out of the blue', he was sent to the 2nd Black Watch. He too sensed 'the general opinion' that they were going 'to a nice easy front' about which no one knew much 'except what they had read in *The Arabian Nights*'.[24] For the rest of the month the Highland Battalion remained entrenched opposite Umm el-Hanna, the strain 'exceptional, the labour continuous and the hours of rest few'.[25] Another attempt to rout the Turks on 8 March, known as the Battle of the Dujailah Redoubt, failed; the Highland Battalion was still in line opposite el-Hanna and did not take part. Despite his earlier pessimism, Townshend was still holding out in Kut, having estimated that by slaughtering all remaining animals he had sufficient supplies until mid-April.

Sannaiyat: 'Do or die'

At the beginning of April, a strengthened relief force attacked Fallahiya and Sannaiyat where the Turks had taken up position, having again withdrawn along the banks of the Tigris from Umm el-Hanna. 'This is apparently to be a do or die show so we'll show 'em how we do both or either,' Lieutenant Cumming informed his family on 6 April, having spent three months in India recuperating after his January wound.[26] But, although the Fallahiya position was taken relatively easily, ignorance of the terrain and the strength of the Sannaiyat position again meant heavy losses. A second attempt was made on the morning of 9 April. So great were the losses of the assaulting division, that the 7th Meerut Division was ordered forward. 'This was a difficult task, as it had to be carried out at short notice, in the dark, amid the confusion consequent on the failure of the attack, and in face of an exultant enemy.'[27]

During the night of 10/11 April working parties dug a new line. 'Here I am at it again and last night we had to go out and dig in 150 yards nearer Johnny Turk. We were under fire the whole time and it was not very nice,' Cumming informed his parents. Parties of stretcher bearers and volunteers also had to recover the dead. 'One night I went collecting dead and clearing up the battlefield. It's a rotten job especially as some of the bodies were out for some time… well cheerio, awfu' fit, heaps of love from Brykie. Heaps of biscuits and chutney are always acceptable.' He wrote home again on 21 April: 'The heat here is pretty annoying and the dust appalling. Beyond a certain liveliness there is nothing doing. We occasionally give the Turk a hot time with shells etc, and yesterday had a fine bombardment. The fireworks are all on our side as he has next to no artillery… please send some writing paper and also envelopes which won't stick owing to heat. Not foreign thin ones.' He ended this letter with a less cheerful PS: 'I am just trusting that God will be as good to us all as He always has been and that I may be returned to you safe and sound by His Own Goodness and Mercy.'[28]

Townshend's position was now critical, as 24 April had been

assessed as the day his supplies would definitely run out. Having almost broken through Turkish lines on 17 April, a final assault was ordered for the 22nd. With one section of the terrain waterlogged, the assault could only be delivered on a single brigade front, the Highland Battalion in the lead. Despite taking the front-line trenches, they could not be held. 'The supply of grenades, always meagre during these operations, had run out', explained Wauchope, 'and the majority of the rifles had become so clogged while the men were wading through the deep mud that the bolts jammed and the rifles could not be fired.'[29]

By the end of the day the Highland Battalion was reduced to a 'mere skeleton'. Among those killed were twins, Second Lieutenants David Horace and George John Anderson, who had joined the 2nd Black Watch from Corsica. Lieutenant Brykie Cumming was 'leading his men very gallantly when he received a wound which proved mortal,' the Commanding Officer, Thomson, informed his mother.[30] 'I may say that just before your son went out of the trench to the attack he gave his letter case and diary to his soldier-servant with instructions to give them to me if he did not come back – so that is how I got them,' explained the Chaplain, Andrew Macfarlane. 'Somehow he seems to have anticipated that he was not coming through this battle.' 'The casualties were such that by the end of April I found myself, then a junior 2nd Lieutenant,' related Ritchie, 'as the senior officer of The Black Watch left in that theatre of war.'[31]

No further action to relieve Kut was possible, although there was an unsuccessful attempt to send supplies by river. On 26 April Townshend began negotiations for a surrender, the British Government offering £2 million for the release of the officers and men. But the Turks refused and so, on 29 April, Townshend had to surrender unconditionally. He remained in captivity in Istanbul (later taking part in the negotiations for an armistice in October 1918). His surviving troops were sent to Anatolia, where over half died in prison.[32] Of the relieving force of 19,000 men, bolstered to 30,000, approximately 23,000 had been killed or wounded. It was no consolation that their adversary, Baron von der Goltz, had died of typhus in Baghdad on 16 April. In the aftermath of the worst capitulation in British history, Lieutenant General Sir Frederick Stanley Maude was put in command of the Tigris Force, assuming command of all Allied Forces in Mesopotamia in late July.[33] 'We spent the summer of 1916 in the Sannaiyat position in a sedentary role,' related Ritchie, 'gradually building our strength so that we could attack and drive the enemy northwards.'[34]

The Western Front: 'Long spells in the trenches'

By 1916 military manpower shortages caused by the high casualty rate and reduced numbers of volunteers led to the Military Service Act being passed on 2 March. All men aged between eighteen and forty-one were liable to be called up unless married, widowed with children, serving in the Royal Navy, a minister of religion or working in a specific exempted occupation.[35]

With the 2nd Black Watch in Mesopotamia and the 10th in Salonika, seven Black Watch battalions were active on the Western Front. At the beginning of the year the 1st Black Watch moved twenty-nine times in and around Loos where the trenches 'were good, and the line usually quiet'.[36] The 4th and 5th Black Watch were still understrength and, in preference to being drafted into other Black Watch battalions, on 15 March they were amalgamated into the 4/5th, joining the 39th Division.[37] Among those in the 4th Black Watch invalided home was Joseph Gray; having sent back reports to the *Dundee Courier*, he became the official war artist for the *Graphic,* basing his drawings on his original sketches.[38] Operating in the Neuve Chapelle sector 'we now commenced the long spells in the trenches again,' commented Miller. 'Although I was a trained machine gunner I had avoided the gun section as I did not like to carry the heavy gun the long distances entering and leaving the trenches, but now a new unit, the Machine Gun Corps, was started and the infantry were issued with the new Lewis Gun which was much lighter, and I joined the Lewis Gun section… During the spring and summer we worked every section from Festubert, Richebourg to Givenchy.' One episode when he was off-duty caused 'a bit of trouble':

> We only had a dugout for four and during the day when fifth was off duty, the fifth one had nowhere to go. It had been raining hard all day and I was fifth man, so to get shelter I went along the trench to the bomb store which was very dry and I slept on top of the bombs, but it had been decided that we would be relieved without giving us notice and I was missing. All the trench was searched and the team had to leave without me, and when I woke and returned to the post, I thought I had had it as the men in the trench wore trousers. I felt sure they were Germans. 'Are you Miller?' I was asked and told 'to get down to Givenchy village quick before you are reported missing.'[39]

On rejoining the Battalion he was again reprimanded 'for sleeping in a place which might go up and leave no trace of me at all'!

In early March the 51st Highland Division, with the 6th and 7th Black Watch, relieved the French in the sector where a 'labyrinth' of trenches criss-crossed the scarred terrain, wrested from the Germans the previous year. Included in the sector lay Vimy Ridge, the Battalion going into line at Neuville St Vaast. 'We have now taken over the new part of the line and at present our men are in reserve position and it is a pretty safe spot,' Colour Sergeant Alick Guthrie wrote home. 'There are still a few people hanging on to their homes I suppose because they have no place else to go. But the houses are practically all empty and broken down.' As elsewhere the proliferation of mines posed a continuous threat, an explosion causing a fight 'as to which side should occupy the lip of the crater, and thus gain a good observation post of the trenches opposite.'[40]

Having spent January in billets near Bailleul, the 8th Black Watch, 9th Scottish Division, went into the line in the Ypres sector at Ploegsteert or 'Plugstreet' as the men called it, while Ypres was known as 'Wipers'. 'Everyone in trenches stands to twice a day,' related Second Lieutenant Hubert Clement,

> just before dawn & dusk, the idea is to be prepared in case the enemy should attack & it is a convenient opportunity for seeing

> that the men have their rifles & bayonets in good order & for getting the trench 'house-maided' in the morning. Cleanliness in trenches comes even before Godliness & one cannot be too particular especially in hot weather. After the trench has been tidied up the men go back to their dug-outs to sleep till breakfast arrives, except of course the sentries. No cooking is allowed in the front line trenches but there is usually a place in the support line or the reserve where a cookhouse can be built & the men in the front line send down there for their meals.[41]

The 9th Black Watch, 15th Scottish Division, had spent early 1916 in the Mazingarbe and Hulluch sector. With 'shell-shock' a little understood condition, on 15 February Private John Docherty became the first Kitchener volunteer upon whom Haig upheld the death sentence for desertion.[42] After a period in reserve, by April the Division was back at Loos, a gas attack causing several casualties and some fatalities. 'The war on our front is getting so that we can send out little parties into the Hun trenches, chuck bombs into their duck boards, kill or capture anyone who interferes and nip back to our own line before the old thing has time to do anything!' Major Stewart, who had taken command of the Battalion in January, informed his wife. 'All this is exceedingly annoying to the ponderous, slow thinking Teuton mind and he is rapidly losing his "morale" and we on the other hand, just like a naughty boy who goes on doing what he oughtn't to do without reproof are getting more and more impish and mischievous.'[43] Stewart's self-confidence was soon shattered by General Haig's next offensive, to be carried out under General Sir Henry Rawlinson's command on the Somme.

The Somme: 'An absolute inferno'

The objective of 'The Big Push' in the summer of 1916 was to break through the line in the triangle of land bordered by the Somme and Ancre rivers. While British troops attacked across the Albert–Bapaume road north to Serre, French divisions would assault

German lines along a front stretching from Curlu to Péronne. Haig then envisaged a rapid advance beyond the German trenches into open country. 'Unless I am much mistaken, we shall see some real active service before the summer is out,' Second Lieutenant Clement was writing home on 7 June. 'Personally the sooner we get into a "strafe" the better pleased I shall be as I want to have a go at the Boche.'[44]

Originally planned to begin on 1 August, the date for the new offensive was brought forward to 1 July to reduce pressure on French troops fighting to hold Verdun. The opening attack, focusing around strategic locations beyond Albert, started after the largest bombardment ever recorded, over 1.5 million shells being fired at the German lines during the preceding week. 'It seemed as though nothing could live, not an ant, under that stupendous artillery storm,' commented journalist Philip Gibbs.[45] In reserve 'at instant call', the 8th Black Watch was back from the firing line 'but [we] can hear the big guns when there is anything of a bombardment,' Clement informed his sister on 30 June. 'At night the whole sky is sometimes lighted up by gun flashes – it's like exaggerated summer lightning.'[46]

The bombardment was far less successful than anticipated. Along most of the front, the wire remained uncut and the creeping barrage intended to protect the advancing troops invariably failed. As they crossed No Man's Land, British forces presented an easy target for the German machine-gunners, who had sheltered underground in dugouts 30 feet deep. On the first day alone approximately 58,000 British and Empire casualties were recorded, one-third of whom were killed including 60 per cent of all officers involved.[47]

Spared the heavy fighting of the first day, on 4 July the 8th Black Watch moved forward, going into the line at Montauban on the 8th: 'guns on every side of us, French & English. The noise is deafening,' remarked Commanding Officer Lieutenant Colonel Charles Gordon, who had ear protectors 'on most of the day & jolly good things they are.'[48] The 1st Black Watch had also reached the Somme, marching to Naours on 6 July. 'The route from Doullens passed through scenes of great activity; motor convoys, in an endless file, were taking fresh formations to the battlefield, and on the return journey, bringing out all that was left of the division which had been in the line since the first attack a week before.' On 10 July the Battalion moved to Bécourt, beyond which the Allied front line had now advanced. Within hours of taking up position in front of Contalmaison Wood, the soldiers were engaged in resisting a German counter-attack, successfully taking the wood and nearby villa as well as capturing four German guns.[49]

On 14 July Haig ordered an assault on the villages of Bazentin-le-Petit, Bazentin-le-Grand and Longueval adjacent to Delville Wood with High Wood beyond. Among the forces attacking Delville Wood and Longueval, initiating the battle's second phase, was the 8th Black Watch. Second Lieutenant Hubert Clement described the day's events:

> The attack was launched at 3.25 a.m. There was no proper bayonet charge as our artillery had been bombarding the barbed wire & the front of the village with terrific intensity for the previous 14 hours. We just walked forward through the little that was left of the wire and into the ruins of the village. Our job was to clear a sector of the village of what Huns remained, by bombing them out. The place was an absolute inferno – you could [not] hear yourself shout for the noise of the shells bursting on all sides. I staggered forward as best I could & put a bomb into one likely looking cellar. Then on turning a corner I came upon a group of men who seemed to be Boches & they seemed to recognise me as an enemy; so I took the pin out of one of my bombs as quickly as I could & threw the bomb into the middle of them. Whether it was a bit of my own bomb which hit me or whether one of them fired at me at the same moment or whether I was hit by a bit of an exploding shell, I don't know, but the next instant I felt a sudden jab & felt myself going round & round.[50]

'The Battle swayed backwards & forwards,' explained Gordon, praising the South African Brigade which had attacked through Delville Wood for 'fighting perfectly grandly.'[51] By 18 July the

Germans had regained Delville Wood, and most of Longueval, leaving the assaulting forces, including those of the 8th Black Watch, 'woefully reduced'. 'For 5 days they had fought incessantly with no sleep & little food & no hot meal, the men were dead beat,' Gordon's letter continued.[52] The following day the 9th Scottish Division was relieved. Moving north to take up a position at Gouy-Servins, the 8th Black Watch passed through billets occupied by the 9th Black Watch; now under the command of Lieutenant Colonel Syd Innes, the 9th was travelling to the Somme from the Hohenzollern sector. A welcome halt enabled the two battalions to meet.[53]

By now Haig's general offensive to break through the line had become fragmented into a series of separate actions in the attempt to capture strategic locations from which a further advance could be made. A two-day subsidiary attack at Fromelles north of the Somme on 19 and 20 July, involving the Australian Imperial Force in its first military action on the Western Front, was designed to support the Fourth Army on the Somme but had little effect in drawing away German troops. A greater success was the capture of Pozières by units of the Australian 1st Division on 23 July. Operations, however, were hampered by poor communications, bad weather and lack of supplies.

The 51st Highland Division reached the Somme sector in late July. 'I felt like a deserter going home for a commission when they went to the Somme,' recalled George Farrar, promoted lance corporal 'to keep us off any unpleasant fatigues on the way home'.[54] On 22 July an attack on High Wood was launched as part of a continuing attempt to secure the high ground around Delville Wood. The 6th and 7th Black Watch were mainly occupied providing working and carrying parties before moving into line four days later. On the evening of 30 July another assault was ordered and both the 6th and 7th Black Watch were engaged. Advancing under the protection of a creeping barrage, as so often happened, the soldiers were met by heavy German rifle and machine-gun fire. Having advanced further than the other battalions, the 6th became isolated. Exposed to continuous fire, the two leading companies were 'almost annihilated', the survivors digging themselves in until they could return to the original front line under cover of darkness. 'So hot' was the German fire against the 7th Black Watch that its two advancing companies suffered heavy casualties; the 7th's Commanding Officer, Lieutenant Colonel Allen, was wounded the day before.[55]

At the beginning of August the 51st Highland Division was relieved. The results of the fighting were 'disappointing and dispiriting to all,' commented the Division's 1921 historian, Major Bewsher. The Division had sustained over 3,500 casualties including 150 officers. Although more than half of High Wood had been occupied, the Germans still held a 'formidable' redoubt in the eastern corner.[56] After this relatively brief action, the Division was sent north. 'Feeling fit as a ferret Mother and no need to worry,' Corporal Ian Maclaren, 6th Black Watch, wrote to his mother in Aberfeldy on 11 August 1916, as the 51st Highland Division was moving in stages to Armentières. 'The worst things out here are lack of sleep and feeling very drowsy, but after one night's good sleep and a wash feel just as well again.'[57] Having gone into the line at Houplines, an unsuccessful raid into No Man's Land at the end of August resulted in twenty-three casualties. The Division remained in the Ypres sector throughout September, both battalions going in and out of the line around Houplines.[58]

On 14 August the 9th Black Watch went into the line north of Contalmaison, where the men were heartened to see two of the guns recently captured by the 1st Black Watch. During another attempt to breach the line initial success was followed by the inability to consolidate. Captain Bearn, the medical officer, who had been famously assisted by the 'Lady of Loos' in 1915, was so severely wounded that he never returned to the front.[59] Severe fighting, meanwhile, was continuing around High Wood, as the Germans fought to hold the areas to the north and west. After fighting at Contalmaison in July, the 1st Black Watch had moved up to the former German line south of Bazentin-le-Petit. On 19 August the Battalion, which had suffered heavy losses during an attack the previous day, moved into brigade reserve at Mametz Wood before returning to fight again at High Wood.

In Britain, recruits were kept informed of the battle's progress. 'We are marched to the Palladium Cinema Theatre in forenoon to witness the film "The Battle of the Somme",' Private H. L. Junks, 4th Reserve Battalion The Black Watch, recorded in his diary on 11 September.

> It makes us realise more than anything else has what a terrible war it is. One almost shudders as he looks on the pictures of the shells and other instruments, the invention of which is solely for the purpose of killing. Amongst the many scenes we see the troops climbing out of their trenches to the attack. They don't all get over the parapet for several of the men are seen falling back and rolling down into the trench as soon as their heads appear above the parapet. They lay motionless! In another picture we see a number of them being knocked out as they thread their way thro' barbed wire entanglements.[60]

The strain for some proved too great. On 18 September while the 7th Black Watch was still in the Ypres sector, Private Peter Black was shot for desertion. Second Lieutenant Robert Badenoch, who had recently joined the Battalion, was thankful to have escaped the 'very unpleasant experience' of witnessing the execution since he was out on a working party.

> The whole Company were turned out at dawn to watch. He had been a 4th Black Watch man at present serving with the 7th. The procedure was that the whole Coy [Company] was paraded at dawn, a firing party was chosen consisting of men who had originally been in the 4th Battn. There were so many live rounds and so many blanks, the idea being that no one knew who had shot the man. That may be alright in theory but not in practice because as soon as the rifle is fired the soldier knows by the kick of the rifle whether it was 'live' or blank. The Officer-in-Charge was the man's platoon officer, in this case a farmer near Windygates in civilian life, and if the job is muffed, it is his responsibility to go forward and finish the job with his revolver.[61]

During the Somme offensive, the 4/5th Black Watch had been kept in the Neuve Chapelle sector. To coincide with the opening battle, on 1 July the 39th Division had made a feint attack on the Festubert–Givenchy front, 116 Brigade advancing over two lines of German trenches. 'During the night we took over from them,' recalled Miller. 'And in the morning a number of bodies were seen lying in No Man's Land. As the day went on, it was found that a number were still alive. An officer of C Company went out and brought the first one in and, as no firing started, it was not long before men were going out to bring as many as possible while the good mood lasted.' It was only a matter of time before the Division was ordered south. 'Early in August we were moved to the Somme area and we had to walk making nearly 20 miles a day. This was a test of endurance.'[62]

In late August orders were given to prepare for an attack north of the Ancre river, the previous fighting having taken place to the south. The objective was the strongly held German position opposite Beaumont Hamel in the Ancre valley. Included in the attacking force was the 4/5th Black Watch. Lieutenant Colonel Sceales issued a special order 'in which he expressed the certainty, on the eve of going into action, that Scotland would once more have reason to be proud of the 4th and 5th Black Watch.'[63] On 3 September the attack began. 'Heard terrific bombardment at 5 a.m.,' Pipe Major McLeod noted in his diary. 'No definite news. We all went about the camp very much down in the mouth. The news did not seem very bright. Our bombardment ceased about 1 p.m. which I thought was a bad sign. Spoke to some of the wounded. Heard pipers had done grand. News came that the Black Watch had got over to third line. They held on until ordered to "Retire". Some held on until night.'[64] The fighting was described as being 'of a particularly grim and determined nature. Men on both sides firing point-blank at each other from twenty yards range.'[65] Casualties were severe. When one of the dugouts was blown in and the men buried, Miller described how, after the alarm was raised, 'the expert diggers set to [to] save them.' Since there was only space for four men to work at one time 'they went all out. As soon as they were exhausted they fell back and the next four moved in… My share was to bring up supplies of water and have it there for the men who were working, and to clean the faces and throats of the rescued. The first four were not badly hurt but, as we got deeper, the injuries became worse and the last four were dead.'[66]

On the same day as the 4/5th attacked Beaumont Hamel – 2 September – the 1st Black Watch was ordered to attack High Wood. Supported by the 1st Camerons, the advance was again halted, trench mortar shells falling short, which left the flank positions exposed. Suffering heavy casualties, the depleted battalions had to withdraw.[67] The 1st Division was then sent to army reserve at Bresle, before returning to the line opposite Flers. The death of Black Watch officer Brigadier Charles Stewart, 154 Brigade, 51st Highland Division, hit by 'a chance shell burst' in Houplines on 14 September, had resulted in an immediate change of command in the 1st Black Watch. Hamilton, who had succeeded Stewart in command of the Battalion in January 1916, again succeeded him in command of 154 Brigade. This left thirty-three-year-old Victor Fortune in command of the 1st Black Watch, having risen from the rank of captain to temporary lieutenant colonel in two years.[68]

Meanwhile, on 8 September the 9th Black Watch had been part of another attack on High Wood, but was prevented from consolidating by 'enemy pressure'. The Battalion then moved back to the Martinpuich sector before being relieved, having spent forty-four days in the line. Its casualties during the recent fighting were recorded as twenty-three officers and 456 men.[69]

'Just one mass of shell holes'

Haig's third offensive on the Somme began on 15 September. For the first time thirty-six armoured vehicles, known as 'tanks', were used, initiating a new age of mobile warfare.[70] An early success was the capture of High Wood. During this last phase the 1st Black Watch fought only one engagement while in the line at Flers on 25 September when the Germans made a 'strong bombing attack, entering our lines'. The attack was 'driven off' and a counter-attack made. Ten prisoners were taken and '40 enemy killed'. Black Watch fatalities included the 'popular' Captain William Debenham MacLaren Stewart; having recovered from wounds received in May 1915 while serving with the 2nd Black Watch, 'Deb' had returned to the front with the 1st Black Watch. 'He was throwing a bomb when a bullet hit his arm and the bomb dropped + killed him,' recorded Second Lieutenant Leonard Sarjeant, who had just joined the 1st Black Watch after spending the early part of the war in the London Scottish Regiment and been wounded at Loos.[71] Having served with Stewart, Sergeant Wilson wrote a poem 'to the Loving and Glorious Memory of our Comrade':

We'll meet the Celtic Warrior
Up in the mystic blue!
For life is no long barrier
Till death's call comes to you! [72]

In late September the 1st Black Watch moved out of the line. 'Nothing much doing,' commented Second Lieutenant Keith Arbuthnott, who had recently joined the Battalion. 'Went to the Follies in the evening. V. good show.' Although the 1st Black Watch returned to the Somme at the end of October, the winter of 1916 was judged 'uneventful'. 'Raining + dull,' Sarjeant wrote on 24 October. 'Lecture by C.O. on Discipline, Cheerfulness + decentralisation of command.'[73]

The 4/5th Black Watch had continued to rotate in and out of the line. On 10 October, the Battalion was ordered to Thiepval to hold the recently captured south face of the Schwaben redoubt, one of two strong points on the ridge overlooking the Ancre valley, the other being the Stuff redoubt. Four days later an assault was made on the redoubt's north face. 'As two Lewis Gunners were left out of every attack so that there were always some gunners left, it was my turn to be left out of this one,' recalled Miller, 'and this was certainly one to be out of as it was defended with all the skill and courage the Germans had, and our boys had a tough time taking it and we had 240 casualties.' Described as a 'soldier's battle', nearly all the officers of the attacking companies were either killed or wounded. Among the nine wounded officers was Major Geoffrey Bowes-Lyon, a cousin of Fergus, who had been killed at Loos in 1915.[74] Miller's account continued:

> Our strength was made up in two days and we returned to hold the position we had taken, and when you were on top of the hill you saw why it was so important, as we could now see for nearly 10 miles over the German lines to Grandcourt and looking back we could look out over our lines to Albert. We were only 48 hours in this position and it was about the worst time we ever had, as the Germans were shelling us the whole time and tried on the second day to take it back, but we were able to hold on and keep them down the hill.[75]

At the end of September the 8th Black Watch had been ordered back to the Somme, going into the line at Flers. The 9th Scottish Division's role, in conjunction with others on the right and left, was to attack the Butte de Warlencourt, an old burial mound off the Albert–Bapaume road which, since the recent fighting, had given the Germans a dominating position over the new British line. On 12 October the main attack began but, as with previous attempts on the Butte, the attacking troops failed to make any significant gains. The next few days were spent in clearing the ground 'during which operation many bodies of men belonging to The Black Watch Territorials were found and buried.' A follow-up attack was again met by a fierce German counter-attack, as a result of which the Germans successfully occupied part of the British line until they were driven out. Much of the battle was fought in pouring rain.[76] Although attempts to take the Butte continued, the 9th Division played no further part, and on 20 October it moved to High Wood. The 8th Black Watch had lost over 200 men killed, wounded or missing between 10 and 20 October (from a total casualty list of over three thousand in the Division between 12 and 24 October). After recuperating in Albert, the Battalion went into billets near Arras: 'unusually quiet and peaceful. Scarcely a shell was heard all day.'[77]

The 9th Black Watch spent most of October in and out of the line in the Somme sector as well as a period of rest at Bresle and in divisional reserve. 'The bosches [sic] often come over and surrender because they are fed up with the war,' Lieutenant Ernest Reid informed his younger brother, Ronald, on 28 October.[78]

The 51st Highland Division had returned to the Somme in early October as part of the Reserve Army, sent to make up for the losses in Rawlinson's Fourth Army. Returning to the line, the soldiers experienced the 'vilest of weather' against which they had the 'poorest kind of protection.' 'In this sector the trenches had been named after characters in French history, the pronunciation of whose names tried the Jocks very high,' commented Bewsher.[79] Haig's orders were for the Reserve Army (designated the Fifth Army on 30 October) to attack again in the Ancre valley. In preparation for an attack on Puisieux, the 7th Black Watch practised assaulting an area marked out with tapes, 'the artillery barrage being represented by men carrying flags.' Although the attack was abandoned the method later became part 'of the recognised preparation in the Division for all attacks'.[80] 'A good deal of our time is spent tramping about the roads,' Private William Couston told his mother in mid-October. 'We have shifted again yesterday afternoon & are now in bivouacs again in an open field. While I am writing an artillery duel is going on overhead. Am afraid Fritz must be having rather an unpleasant time. Most of his shells – almost all fall far short. So much the better you will say… Our bivvies consist of a tarpaulin stretched over a piece of wood as a ridge pole. We lie on the ground on our waterproof sheets… we have no time to wash our socks let alone darning them.'[81]

The Division's role was to take part in a last attempt to gain ground before the winter. With German forces occupying the high ground above the Ancre river, Beaumont Hamel, a name which was to become a byword for the Highland Division's fortitude, had been repeatedly attacked since the beginning of July but the Germans had stood firm. A particular feature of the village's defence was a 'troublesome' obstacle to the south, known as the Y Ravine, whose steep sides ran towards the British line and which was strongly fortified.

Although 'urged to attack with three infantry brigades,' the Divisional commander, Major General G. M. Harper, chose to attack with only two brigades, keeping one in reserve.[82] 'The attack on Beaumont Hamel was on 13th November and it was a very foggy morning,' continued Second Lieutenant Badenoch, who recalled a runner arriving in the middle of the night 'with a message from Brigade to Coy Commander,' marked 'Urgent Secret and Confidential'. When the envelope was opened 'the message read "there will be an issue of chewing gum on 'Y' day." Please note a ration of chewing gum is one half stick per man!!!' The 6th Black Watch was part of the assaulting force, while the 7th Black Watch was mainly acting 'as carrying parties taking supplies to the forward areas. I remember my platoon's job was to carry sacks of Mills bombs up to the front and I am glad my imagination did not work overtime, because if the pin had come out of one bomb, there is no saying what havoc would result.'[83] Sergeant Mitchell, 6th Black Watch recalled that:

> None of us slept much that night. But everybody was in wonderfully bright spirits… about 5 a.m. we had a hot drink served out to us… everything was timed to the second. On our left a large mine was touched off, and the artillery began to play on the Hun front line, together with the trench mortars and Stokes guns which did magnificent work… as for weather, it was so misty we could hardly see ten yards in front of us. This made it very difficult to keep our direction, but we knew which way to go, and so we started creeping forward.'[84]

Although the Germans were taken by surprise, stiff resistance meant that Y Ravine was not forced until the afternoon, the attack costing the 6th Black Watch 'dearly'. One fatality was Corporal Maclaren, who had told his mother he was feeling 'fit as a ferret' in August. 'Our Battalion was the first to advance in the thick mist and half light of the early morning,' Lieutenant Colonel John Wylie informed Mrs Maclaren. 'And when all the officers of the company except one had been killed or wounded, Ian was leading the men of his platoon with the utmost gallantry… I could scarcely tell you how vexed I am that he has made the supreme sacrifice in doing his duty so nobly.'[85]

Among the dead in the 7th Black Watch was Private Baron Hubert de Reuter, whose grandfather, a German entrepreneur, had founded the Reuters News Agency in London in 1851. 'He would have gained a very high decoration had he lived,' commented his Commanding Officer, Lieutenant Colonel G. R. H. Cheape.

> He was with his platoon in the attack and through his courage and resource they captured 97 Germans. The whole of the platoon went over the first line of German trenches into the second. De Reuter went down a 20-foot dug-out and shouted out in German asking if any men were there. No answer, so he threw two bombs round the corner and then again shouted – 'Anybody there?' The answer came – 'One officer and thirty-five men.' Then he made [them] file out past him. He then found that some Germans had been passed over in the first line, and were shooting from behind and from the right rear, so he put the German officer on the parapet, threatening him with his bayonet and made him order the men to surrender. Sixty-two men came over.[86]

This action meant that one sergeant and twenty men had captured one German officer and ninety-seven German soldiers. But, having carried three badly wounded men to relative safety while under heavy machine-gun fire, de Reuter was fatally wounded.[87]

After the action at Beaumont Hamel the 51st Highland Division was relieved, the soldiers passing through Ovillers, Pozières and Courcelette, 'all villages which had been literally raised to the ground by shelling,' related Badenoch. 'The countryside was devoid of landmarks and was just one mass of shell holes.'[88] Known as the Battle of the Ancre (but by the 51st Highland Division as the Battle of Beaumont Hamel), the taking of Beaumont Hamel and Beaucourt on the Ancre signified the last major action on the Somme. As Major Bewsher commented:

> The battle of Beaumont Hamel was the foundation stone on which the reputation of the Highland Division was built. General Harper's leap-frog system of attack had been proved; his attack with two Brigades instead of three had been fully justified, and an experience had been gained from which the future training of the Division was evolved... the results of the capture of Beaumont Hamel were far reaching. It was undoubtedly the loss of this stronghold and its immediate effects which largely determined the German High Command to evacuate in the following spring the salient formed in their lines during the battle of the Somme.'[89]

After over four months' fighting, however, the Allied front had barely advanced 7 miles at its furthest point and there had been no breakthrough. The cost for gaining this devastated piece of land was high: total Allied casualties were estimated to be over 600,000, the Germans at least 400,000. 'The Somme marked the end of an age of vital optimism in British life that has never been recovered,' observed historian John Keegan in 1998.[90]

Mesopotamia: 'Burning sun'

During the summer of 1916 the Highland Battalion had remained entrenched in front of Sannaiyat. 'Even in France the heat, the lack of air, and all the smells inseparable from trench warfare were disagreeable enough on a hot summer's day. In Mesopotamia the sick returns show how severely these conditions re-acted on the health of men with no means of escape from the burning sun,' commented Wauchope, who had recovered from his Shaikh Sa'ad wound and returned to Mesopotamia in late May, resuming command of the Highland Battalion. In early July, with the arrival of reinforcements, the 2nd Black Watch and 1st Seaforth Highlanders were re-formed, a proposal for one battalion to rest and reorganise in India being rejected on the grounds that their close ties meant they would prefer to reorganise together. As the weather became cooler, Lieutenant General Maude had begun re-establishing lines of communication and administrative services as well as training troops for a 'vigorous' offensive. 'His labours were ceaseless,' continued Wauchope, 'but he found time to visit many battalions. Maude never left the lines of The Black Watch without making every man feel that no event could shake his faith in the resolution and leadership of the General.'[91]

Before leaving to join the 2nd Black Watch at its depot in Poona, India, Lieutenant Alexander Blair wrote the customary farewell letters only to be opened in the event of his death. 'When you get this letter,' he told his six-year-old son, Neville, 'God will have considered it best for me to come up and see him, and as you know, once one does that one never comes back.' Reminding him that, if this happened, he would be the only man left to protect his mother, he encouraged his young son not to forget

> the fine Scotch Regiment to which I belong and of which I am so proud: Remember that 'The Black Watch' is the Head of all the Highland Regiments; that is why we are called the Royal Highlanders. I don't know whether you will ever be a soldier: it is too early to decide such matters yet: I don't necessarily want you to be one, although it would be nice if you, when you grow older, decided to be one. But remember this, that whatever work you decide to do, when you grow up, you must also give up some of your time to learn *How to Defend your Country* and *Mummy* should any naughty person or persons come along and want to hurt them. *That is Your Duty* and a *Charge I Lay* upon you to do.[92]

The charge laid upon Neville Blair, a future Commanding Officer in The Black Watch, was immediate. Blair set sail on 5 January 1917 and died of meningitis in Bombay (Mumbai) on 13 March.

'Now I know otherwise'

In Britain the reaction to the Somme had an unforeseen outcome. Although the front line had moved forward a few miles, the rolls of honour appearing daily in the newspapers could not conceal the tremendous losses and a group in parliament had begun questioning Asquith's seeming complacency with the direction of the war (despite losing his own son Raymond at the Somme in September). On 7 December Lloyd George took over from him as Prime Minister, relinquishing the position of Secretary of State for War which he had assumed on Kitchener's death in June 1916. Not wishing to comply with the suggestion that Britain should sue for peace, he proposed taking a more active role in decision-making regarding the conduct of the war. Rather than insisting, however, as the Generals believed, that the war could only be won on the Western Front, he proposed making the Ottoman Empire's defeat a British war aim, a requirement which would necessitate retaining enough troops in the region to make this possible.[93]

After the Somme, the 1st, 6th and 7th, and 9th Black Watch had remained in the sector in their respective divisions. 'It is next to impossible to keep clean here,' Private Couston was informing his mother in mid-December. 'We have to wash our faces in the water from a shell hole.' 'The trenches were in a shocking condition with water and mud and I remember before going into the line we were issued with thigh gum boots,' related Badenoch.[94] Having taken part in an attack on St Pierre Divion on the Ancre river, south-east of Beaumont Hamel, the 4/5th Black Watch was sent to Ypres: the 'Sinister Salient'. The 8th Black Watch's deployment in Arras had been relatively peaceful but, as the fighting at the Somme lessened, the sector became more active.[95]

The 10th Black Watch was still operating on the Salonika Front, engaged in intermittent fighting around Lake Doiran and at Horse Shoe Hill. As they dug for protection the soldiers found statuettes, copper ornaments and a ten-foot long mammoth tusk. 'Mind you label it as having been dug up by the 10th Battalion the Black Watch,' requested Lieutenant Archibald Don, who had an interest in geology and arranged for several items, including sections of the tusk, to be sent to the Sedgwick Museum in Cambridge. He did not live to see the artefacts in place, dying of malaria on 11 September.[96]

By the end of the year two more battalions had joined The Black

Watch. Already in May the 12th (Labour) Battalion had been established and was operating in France. In October, in common with other yeomanry regiments, the Scottish Horse Yeomanry was converted into an infantry battalion, becoming the 13th (Scottish Horse) Black Watch and ordered to Egypt for the defence of the Suez Canal before joining the 27th Division in Salonika. 'The weather here is a bit different from Egypt,' commented Private Sandy Stratton. 'It's pretty warm during the day but dashed cold at night which is nothing if it remains dry.'[97] The Fife & Forfar Yeomanry, which, like the Scottish Horse, had fought as dismounted infantry at Gallipoli, became the 14th (Fife & Forfar Yeomanry) Black Watch. 'We were proud to link our record to the long and glorious record of the Black Watch,' commented Major Douglas Ogilvie.[98]

During 1916 5,498 officers and men in the Black Watch battalions serving abroad were recorded as killed, died of wounds, were missing or wounded.[99] 'From time to time one hears of people who have been invalided home suffering from nervous breakdown – I do not mean shell-shock,' observed Second Lieutenant Hubert Clement. 'In many cases they have not been through any particularly trying experiences such as an attack or even a raid but usually they are people who have been at the front for some time.' Explaining how before coming to France he thought they were either highly strung or had suffered a breakdown from drinking too much, he continued: 'Now I know otherwise. The chief factor of such a nervous breakdown is what I would call "Front line tension". It is the feeling that everyone with any sense of responsibility has when holding part of the front line – a feeling that can be compared to no other experience that I know of.' Emphasising the burden on junior officers, Clement continued: 'One has to be prepared for any emergency at all times by day & more especially by night, and the average subaltern cannot help feeling rather weighted down by the thought that the lives of his platoon may be entirely dependent on his presence of mind.' When the weather was fine, 'and with plenty of food & a certain amount of sleep you can fairly easily overcome any depression of spirits due to this nervous tension more especially when you know that you will be relieved within at most six days. But what must it feel like to have not a platoon but a company under your control and instead of summer weather, weeks of cold & wet?'[100]

Are you not weary in your distant places,
Far, far from Scotland of the mist and storm,
In drowsy airs, the sun-smite on your faces,
The days so long and warm?
When all around you lie the strange fields sleeping,
The dreary woods where no fond memories roam,
Do not your sad hearts over seas come leaping
To the highlands and the lowlands of your Home?[101]

6

1917: Blown to Pieces

There runs a road in Flanders
A broken thing of mud,
Where holes yawn wide and cannot hide,
The dull red slime of blood.[1]

'Brutal and mechanical warfare'

Conditions on the Western Front remained bleak. 'The 1916–17 winter was the worst experienced in France,' commented Private William Cameron, Scottish Horse, who had joined the 7th Black Watch. 'This is the 11th day of frost,' Lieutenant Arbuthnott, 1st Black Watch, was recording on 28 January. 'Getting a bit fed up with it.' 'In daylight one is always under German observation,' remarked Reverend Coll Macdonald, Chaplain to the 8th Black Watch, describing how one night a machine-gun swept a part of the road he was on 'and made me run as I didn't run since I was a boy.'[2]

In Salonika, the 10th and the 13th Black Watch remained in defensive positions. 'Each week I start to write I wonder what on earth I can say to fill up a page or two,' Private Stratton wrote home.[3] While the 11th Black Watch had been sending drafts of soldiers overseas, the 12th was undertaking general labouring work in France, including building a light railway on the outskirts of Arras. When the Labour Corps was formed in January 1917, the Battalion became its 5th and 6th Companies.[4]

Meanwhile, the German Chief of the General Staff, Paul von

Hindenburg, had instituted 'unrestricted submarine warfare', aimed at starving Britain into defeat. Although this prompted the United States' entry into the war on 6 April, the Germans hoped to secure a decisive victory before American troops reached Europe. From the Allied perspective, the prospect of American assistance was heartening, provided they could hold out until the Americans arrived.[5]

Sapping Turkish strength

Entrenched at Sannaiyat, the 2nd Black Watch celebrated New Year's Day 1917 with Regimental sports and a concert, the sergeants receiving a pint of champagne, the soldiers a bottle of beer. After the humiliation of Kut in 1916, Lieutenant General Sir Stanley Maude proposed to invigorate the campaign in order to march on Baghdad, sapping 'the enemy's strength by constant attacks'.[6] Once again the 7th Meerut Division, reorganised as the 7th Indian Division, I Indian Army Corps, was in the forefront of operations. The 2nd Black Watch, 21 Brigade, was fighting alongside the 9th Bhopal Infantry, the 20th Punjabis and the 1/8th Gurkha Rifles, with whom 'a great friendship' was established.[7]

Plans were also being made to attack Turkish positions in Palestine. Lieutenant General Sir Archibald Murray, in command of the Egyptian Expeditionary Force (EEF), had already captured most of the Sinai peninsula thereby safeguarding the Suez Canal. Although divergent viewpoints existed both among members of the War Cabinet and between the Allies about the merits of focusing attention on the Western Front in preference to the Near East, in early 1917 agreement was reached for Murray to continue operations.[8] In addition, sanction was given to foment a revolt among the Arabs, led by twenty-eight-year-old T. E. Lawrence, on secondment from his position as intelligence officer in Cairo. His first objective was to disrupt Turkish supply lines by attacking the Hejaz railway which ran from Damascus to Medina.[9]

On 17 February Maude ordered an attack on Sannaiyat. Although the two assaulting battalions in 21 Brigade reached the first two lines of Turkish trenches, when the Turks counter-attacked they could not be held. The 2nd Black Watch was then ordered to move forward, but 'the confusion was so great that a well-organised attack was impossible,' observed Wauchope, the Battalion's Commanding Officer. Five days later another attack was made, but the Turks again counter-attacked. 'It was not till the 23rd that the enemy's third and fourth lines were secured. None of our men will ever forget the scene on that clear morning, nor the feeling of freedom and elation as the companies gained trench after trench. The Sannaiyat position, which had held us back for ten long months, which had lost us Kut and before which so many lives had been given in vain, was now in our hands. The enemy had escaped with his guns, but 'many trenches were found to be filled with Turkish dead, rifles, boxes of ammunition and a few heavy trench mortars whose shells had caused so much trouble and loss during the past six months.'[10]

The Turks were now 'in full retreat', with the way open to Baghdad. Continuing onwards past Ctesiphon, by 7 March Maude's forward troops were at the Diala river where a Turkish rearguard was blocking their way. 'General Maude determined to turn the line of this obstacle by crossing to the right bank of the Tigris, and ordered a bridge to be thrown at Bawi.'[11] 'On the evening of March 10, 1917 we crossed the Tigris from the left to the right banks and did a longish march of about 15 miles to a position within a few miles of Baghdad on the right bank of the river Tigris,' recalled Lieutenant Ritchie, now the Battalion's adjutant. 'We bivouacked there for the night in an absolutely dreadful sand storm in extreme discomfort and very short of rations and water.' At daybreak, as the dust storm lifted, they saw 'the most wonderful sight of the sunrise striking on the golden domes of the mosques at Kasiemain [Kazmain]. A great sight and we felt we were getting back to some sort of civilisation again.'[12]

The next day the 2nd Black Watch led the advance on Baghdad. While one patrol captured the bridge over the Maudiya canal, another, commanded by Second Lieutenant Benjamin Houston, reached the city's outskirts. 'We reported having captured Baghdad railway station early in the morning and subsequently found that it was the wrong station and not the main one so we had to send in a further fighting patrol under Lt Houston to occupy the station itself,' continued Ritchie. 'This was done without any opposition from the enemy. Other regiments have claimed to have been first into Baghdad, but there is no doubt that we were the first as this signal was quoted, I recollect, in General Sir Stanley Maude's despatch reporting the capture of the city.'[13]

'The battle beyond'

Having withdrawn from Baghdad, the Turks had taken up position 20 miles to the north at Mushaidie on the right bank of the Tigris, near the railway station. On the night of 13 March the 7th Indian Division was ordered to move forward for an attack the following day. 'Water bottles were filled, and enough water was carried on mules to refill them once on the next day.'[14]

Instead of attacking close to the river, where an assault might be expected, Maude ordered the main attack in the desert region astride the Baghdad railway; when 28 Brigade's advance was slowed by Turkish rifle fire, 21 Brigade, with the 2nd Black Watch, was ordered into action. Despite the lack of artillery support and rising casualties, 'all along the front of the Battalion small sections still continued to rise up, make a rush forward and fling themselves down, weaker perhaps by two or three of their number, but another thirty yards nearer the enemy,' related Wauchope, describing how one platoon changed commanders 'six times in as many minutes'. By early evening Turkish resistance was weakening. A final bombardment of Turkish lines was the prelude to another advance: 'the Battalion rose as one man, and, their bayonets gleaming in the setting sun, rushed across the open, with the Gurkhas on their left.' But, he continued, 'there was little work for the bayonet. The Turk fled as our men closed.' Praised by the Corps Commander for 'a fine determined attack', the 2nd Black Watch's casualties constituted over one-third of those who took part. As after Loos in 1915, Wauchope awarded medallions in recognition of 'the battle beyond Baghdad'.[15]

In early April operations were resumed, the Turks having fortified themselves across the Dujail canal behind the ancient fortifications of the Median Wall at Istabulat; beyond lay the railhead at Samarrah (Samarra). 'A very well-selected position it proved, and a very difficult one to attack.' Before the assault Wauchope suggested constructing a line of 'strong points… about a mile ahead of our line, and that when these had been made good, a second line 800 yards in advance of the first should be constructed, so that by this means the final assault might be made from a comparatively short distance to the enemy's main position; also artillery officers would be able to locate definitely the enemy's main trenches, and guns could be brought up within 2000 yards before the infantry assault.'[16] Wauchope was no longer commanding the Battalion. Promoted temporary brigadier general, on 20 April he took command of 8 Brigade, 3rd Lahore Division, also in I Indian Army Corps; his successor as Battalion commander was Jack Stewart who had commanded the 9th Black Watch on the Western Front before being evacuated home due to illness in June 1916.

Within hours of assuming command Stewart received orders that the assault was to take place at dawn on 21 April, 21 Brigade being ordered to lead the attack east of the Dujail. Advancing rapidly, with the Gurkhas on the right, the Battalion's first objective, a strong redoubt on the east of the canal, was taken just over an hour after the first opening salvos were fired but the advance had been so rapid that it outpaced the artillery's ability to provide support. Having counter-attacked, the Turks reoccupied the redoubt. Almost at once, a renewed assault was made and the redoubt regained: 'that day the Highlanders without help won a victory that only those who saw it can realize was among the most gallant gained in this war,' commented an artillery officer who witnessed the assault. 'The redoubt we had to take was the KEY to the whole Turkish position,' related Stewart, 'and had the enemy had even half an hour in which to reinforce the work… things might have gone very differently.'[17]

'Conspicuous bravery, coolness and resource in action,' earned Private Charles Melvin one of the four VCs awarded to members of The Black Watch during the war.

> On reaching the enemy trench, he halted and fired two or three shots into it, killing one or two enemy, but as the others in the trench continued to fire at him, he jumped into it, and attacked them with his bayonet in his hand, as, owing to his rifle being damaged, it was not 'fixed'. On being attacked in this resolute manner most of the enemy fled to their second line, but not before Pte, Melvin had killed two more and succeeded in disarming eight unwounded and one wounded. Pte Melvin bound up the wounds of the wounded man, and then driving his eight unwounded prisoners before him, and supporting the wounded one, he hustled them out of the trench, marched them in and delivered them over to an officer.[18]

Casualties again amounted to over a third of the Battalion's strength. Among those who fell was Company Sergeant Major Duncan Palmer, 'an old soldier' who had retired from the Army in 1912. At the outbreak of war he was working as a storekeeper on a cattle ranch in Patagonia, being one of the more than fifty men who travelled from Argentina to serve in The Black Watch.[19]

An assault on the Turks at Istabulat the following day enabled the 2nd Black Watch to pass through to attack Samarrah, only to find that the Turks had left. While in Samarrah Lieutenant Ritchie, together with pioneer Sergeant Milligan, acquired a large bell. 'This is not the Baghdad bell itself but it comes from Samarra railway station,' explained Ritchie. 'Bells were placed in all the railway stations and were all of a similar type and all had "Baghdad" on them as far as I know.' The capture of Samarrah marked the end of a campaign which had begun at Sannaiyat.[20] 'I really marvel now how I managed to command the 9th Bn; this is absolute child's play to it,' Stewart informed his wife in early May, requesting her to send him 'occasionally a steak & kidney pudding (tinned). Crosse & Blackwell make them I think: we live on bully beef and biscuits and whatever we can get locally.'[21] On 25 July Private George Cutmore was shot for desertion by firing squad. 'He was caught a long way down the line and brought back here with the usual result,' commented Stewart.[22]

While Maude had been successful in Mesopotamia, Lieutenant General Murray was moving into Palestine, starting with an assault on the ancient city of Gaza. In early March the 14th Black Watch moved to Kantara and then El Arish on the border at Rafa, playing a subsidiary role. Two attacks, on 26 March and 17–19 April, failed, as the Turks were too strongly entrenched. The next three months were spent digging trenches. 'Our camp was pleasantly situated on a sandy plain, within half a mile of the sea, and dotted with scattered fig-trees just beginning to show a few leaves. The climate was perfect, but the water arrangements were most difficult,' commented Ogilvie.[23]

During April and May in Salonika, the 10th and 13th Black Watch in their respective divisions had been trying to break through the Bulgarians' defensive line. Among those honoured with the Military Medal (MM) for 'conspicuous coolness and gallantry' during frequent skirmishes in No Man's Land was Private John Campbell, 13th Black Watch, who organised the rescue of a wounded scout 'in spite of there being about 25 Bulgars in the vicinity.'[24] On 8 and 9 May the 10th Black Watch took part in assaults on the Lake Doiran line but 'the enemy artillery, both in calibre and volume of fire, had been much underestimated'. The Battalion lost half its strength with 300 casualties.[25] The day before the attack Private Archibald Brown had deserted. Once captured, he was shot 'at 04.30' on 1 June.[26]

'The weather is still as warm as ever & as usual the mosquitoes come along with it. They're nothing like so thick as they were in Egypt however,' Private Stratton, 13th Black Watch, was writing home. 'At night when not inside a bivouac, mosquito net, hut or dugout, every man must wear his veil down, gloves on, and arms covered up,' stipulated the 13th Black Watch's Commanding Officer, Lieutenant Colonel Railston. 'Sentries and patrols will have the front part of their veil lifted up to enable them to see and will put the grease provided on their faces.'[27]

Arras: 'Much to be feared'

On the Western Front, a German withdrawal had begun behind the recently constructed and fortified Hindenburg Line (*Siegfriedstellung*). Stretching from Arras to Laffaux, near Soissons on the Aisne, the objective was to shorten German lines of communication and alleviate an increasing shortage of manpower. No Man's Land now constituted an extended wasteland of destroyed bridges, roads and railways. 'The Bosche has left very little for us except booby traps. It is an extraordinary feeling walking about the ground so lately held by the enemy,' Lieutenant Arbuthnott noted on 18 March.[28]

Instead of continuing operations in the shattered region beyond the Somme, France's new Commander-in-Chief, General Robert Nivelle, proposed a major Allied offensive, in which British and Empire forces, supported by the French, would attack Vimy Ridge and Arras in the north. Meanwhile the main French effort would be along the *Chemin des Dames* on the Aisne, where Nivelle promised a breakthrough or *rupture*. Lieutenant General Sir Edmund Allenby, commanding the Third Army, was to command the attack in the north.[29]

Four battalions of The Black Watch were to be engaged, including the 6th and 7th brought up from the Somme. According to Second Lieutenant Douglas Wimberley, Queen's Own Cameron Highlanders, also in the 51st Highland Division, they were being assigned some of the hardest campaigns, the Germans putting the Scottish soldiers first in their order of *Furchtbarkeit* 'much to be feared' (lit. 'frightfulness').[30] Also involved in the offensive was the 8th Black Watch, already at Arras, and the 9th Black Watch, which had moved there in early March. Opposing them were the German Sixth and Second Armies, General Alexander von Falkenhausen reporting directly to General Erich Ludendorff, Hindenburg's deputy.[31] Instead of assaulting an extended front, as at the Somme, Allenby planned to attack a relatively narrow stretch from Vimy Ridge to Neuville Vitasse, south of the Scarpe river. As usual the offensive would begin with a heavy bombardment and mine explosions. Gas was also used.

'It was known that an attack was coming off in the Arras sector and I remember taking out a working party to dig an enormous grave in preparation for the killed,' related Second Lieutenant Badenoch, 7th Black Watch. 'It was not exactly a very cheerful thought.'[32]

Zero hour was 5.30 a.m. on Easter Monday, 9 April. While the 7th Black Watch was among those moving forward to attack pre-assigned objectives on Vimy Ridge, the 6th Black Watch was in reserve. 'It was a most thrilling experience & I am glad to say I had no fear,' recorded Private Cameron, describing his first experience going 'over the top'. Predictably, machine-gun and sniper fire as well as uncut wire proved serious obstacles. A sudden snowfall altered the contours of the landscape, not only revealing the soldiers' movements but also obscuring identifiable landmarks.[33]

A key objective for the 8th Black Watch was the capture of the Arras–Douai railway. Moving forward against heavy machine-gun fire, the soldiers reached the railway, while other battalions passed through to take the towns of Athies and Fampoux. The 9th Black Watch, meanwhile, was attacking east of Feuchy village, leading to Monchy-le-Preux, the town's elevated position making it an important objective. 'Over we go at 5.30 a.m., Captain Reid in advance,' related Private Alexander Black, Captain Ernest Reid's soldier-servant. 'The noise was indescribable, the barrage fairly going; hell let loose, men falling over barbed wire in shell holes, wounded and killed. What an awful sight! Still on we go. Fifteen yards to our right Lieutenant Cuthbert is down wounded and dies from the effects within 25 yards of our own trench. Mr Reid still leads the way, encouraging the boys to advance and holding in check rash members of our company from going too far as they were in danger of our own barrage.'[34] Casualties in the 8th and 9th Black Watch were heavy, with half the 8th Black Watch's complement killed or wounded within 15 minutes on the first day.[35] During the advance, Reid was wounded. Although rescued from the field of battle by Private Black, as so often happened in the grime of war Reid, aged twenty, died nine days later from septicaemia. Among those killed in the 9th Black Watch was the Roman Catholic Chaplain, Captain Herbert Collins, who 'was ever to be found in the front line with a haversack full of cigarettes, his own gift to the men'. Although losses in the 6th and 7th Black Watch were relatively light, the 'devoted' medical officer Captain Edward Blair was killed while attending a wounded man during a heavy bombardment.[36]

The next two weeks were spent alternating in and out of the line in a continual attempt to improve their positions. A key feature was Greenland Hill, which gave the Germans a visual advantage over the surrounding terrain. Zero hour for another assault was in the early hours of 23 April during which the 6th Black Watch managed to establish itself on Greenland Hill's lower slopes. Subjected to 'murderous' machine-gun fire, the 7th Black Watch was unable to move forward until, after several hours, a tank made its way across No Man's Land. 'As soon as the tank crossed the German wire and trench, the enemy in the front line put up their hands.'[37] 'I may tell you, without giving away any secret, that the Battn has been in action twice within the last fortnight,' Private William Couston, 7th Black Watch, was writing home, noting that his letters were not being censored because all the officers were at the front. 'I have not been with them on either occasion as I have been left behind in charge of the Brigade stores, etc. I consider myself very fortunate indeed; tho I had rather been with the boys in the "push" I shall get back to the Battn when they come "down the line" for a breathing space before the next "racket"… It is pleasant in the sunshine and the guns are a mere rumble in the distance.' When his mother wrote 'with a list of killed & wounded' Couston was 'indeed sorry… especially fellows whom I know.'[38]

The 9th Black Watch was also back in the line, Sergeant Gibb distinguishing himself by working his way around the end of a trench and destroying 'an enemy machine gun and its crew who were holding up the advance.'[39] At the end of April, the 8th Black Watch was brought forward for another assault on Greenland Hill. 'Dear G, just a scrawl to let you know we're going up the line first thing in the morning,' Lieutenant Clement was informing his sister on 28 April. 'Have had a very slack time here… jolly glad to be going. Much love Hubert.' 'The moon went down about 3.00 a.m. and the attack started at 3.45 a.m.

in pitch darkness,' recorded the War Diary. 'Further troubles were created by all troops losing direction as they were absolutely unable to see where they were going… owing to heavy casualties both in Officers and men, it is impossible to collect anything like a correct story, but it appears likely that only a few scattered parties of men reached the German line and these were captured or killed.'[40]

'Things were pretty well mixed up,' the 8th's Commanding Officer, Lieutenant Colonel Abercromby, informed Hubert Clement's sister, Gertrude. 'A few hours after the attack your brother, who was with me at Battalion's HQ, went forward to our front line to find out exactly what had happened. This was about 7 a.m. We heard nothing of him, and others went forward to try to find him. They could not do so, and it was not till after dark that we did find him. He had been shot in the head and death must have come at once… Clement was one of the best men I have seen out here, and seemed to have no fear whatever.'[41] 'If war were as in the old days the Scottish Regiments would face and beat twice their number of Huns. But alas! war is brutal and mechanical and the only romance is in eloquent perorations at home and in comfortable newspaper offices,' Reverend Macdonald told his son, Angus, emphasising in another letter to his wife that religion was 'very real here – not many miles from the front and with the prospect of a very near acquaintance soon.'[42]

Fought between 9 April and 16 May, the Battle of Arras ended in stalemate, resulting in an estimated 158,000 Allied casualties as against 130,000 German. Nivelle's operation on the Aisne had resulted in 200,000 French casualties (with 29,000 killed). Although not as ruinous as Verdun, his failure to deliver the promised *rupture* resulted in a dramatic loss of morale. Relieved of his command on 29 April, Nivelle was replaced as Commander-in-Chief by the Chief of General Staff, sixty-one-year-old General Philippe Pétain. The change of command did not instantly remedy the breakdown of French fighting spirit: approximately 30,000 French troops left the front line in what became known as the 'mutinies of 1917'. Discipline was only restored in August after over three thousand men were court-martialled and forty-nine executed.[43]

'I soon got used to the monotonous routine and began to distinguish between the various shells. I also learnt the different noises made by our own and the Bosche machine guns, grenades, sling bombs etc.,' commented Lieutenant José Penney who joined the 7th Black Watch after Arras. 'There were any amount of bodies built into the trench and trampled into the mud, particularly under the duckboards at Roeux... and soon one got familiar, but never reconciled to that unforgettable smell – which haunted one for days.'[44] The strain was constant. In June Second Lieutenant James Bell Salmond, 7th Black Watch, suffering from neurasthenia, was sent to the Craiglockhart War Hospital, the military psychiatric hospital near Edinburgh for those with shell-shock. He was joined by Lieutenant Wilfred Owen, attached to the 2nd Manchester Regiment. Together they produced a magazine, *The Hydra*, until both returned to their units.[45]

The 1st Black Watch, which had been in the Somme sector, had moved north to Ypres. 'Nothing unusual. – Terrific heat of past fortnight continued,' Second Lieutenant George Young recorded in early June. On the 7th the British Second Army captured the Messines-Wytschaete Ridge, denying the Germans the high ground south of Ypres and forcing them to move troops north from Arras and the Aisne. 'Brigade manoeuvres with "tanks" and aeroplanes,' commented Young, while the 1st Black Watch were mainly engaged in reconnaissance. The Battalion then moved to the Nieuport, Oost Dunkerque and Coxyde sectors where the country was 'flat with a fringe of sand dunes running along the coast... The Bosche use Minenwerfer, Sausages [mortar bombs] & Pineapples [grenades] here and do a fair amount of shelling,' commented Lieutenant Arbuthnott.[46]

Ypres: The road to Passchendaele

In the aftermath of Arras, Haig's plan was to break through to the Belgian coast and destroy Germany's submarine shelters, from where attacks on British shipping had reached an alarming rate. Anticipating that morale would be low after German reverses at Messines, his objective was to take the Passchendaele Ridge which gave the Germans a strategic observation point. Simultaneously Pétain would undertake another offensive at Verdun. Neither Lloyd George nor General Foch (appointed Chief of General Staff when Pétain replaced Nivelle as Commander-in-Chief), favoured the offensive, preferring instead to wait until an all-out attack could be made the following year with the Americans. By the time the British War Cabinet gave its approval on 25 July, the heavy artillery bombardment had already begun.

The battle was fought in three phases with several subsidiary operations, the first phase lasting throughout July and August with fighting at Pilckem Ridge, Westhoek and Langemarck. Of the five Black Watch battalions involved, the 4/5th Black Watch had already spent early 1917 at Ypres in positions formerly occupied by the French. 'When we sat at night round a small fire the rats came out and joined us and we concluded that the French must have made pets of them,' commented Miller, 'but that did not last with us and the rats soon kept away when they had been chased with bayonets a few times.'[47]

The 1st Black Watch had a different assignment as part of an amphibious force which would land on the Belgian coast. Operating in great secrecy as part of Operation Hush (first considered in early 1915), training took place in Clipon Camp, west of Dunkirk. By the end of July the force was ready but British forces had first to advance on land.

The section of the line allotted to the 6th and 7th Black Watch was north of Ypres. 'Last preparations,' Lieutenant Penney was writing on Tuesday 24 July. 'Everybody is now covered with gaudy coloured distinguishing marks. I have 2 blue stripes on my arm for the battalion; a green strip on my shoulder for the company and a red one on the back of my collar for the second wave of the attack. You see talking is apt to be fragmentary during a barrage.' To compound the difficulties of the assault, the weather was appalling. 'Still raining anything,' Penney recorded on 30 July. 'Water and mud everywhere.' Yet despite the conditions 'everyone is pleased to get at the job after all these weeks of waiting... I spent a long night laying out tapes to direct the advance – a ten yard tape had to be laid out from each gap in the wire and laid on the correct bearing and checked by compass, to guide the men and make sure they started off straight… Anyone who is late may lose the barrage which is timed to fall on certain areas at certain times.'[48]

After a ten-day bombardment, during which an estimated three thousand guns fired over four million shells, on 31 July the infantry assault began under the cover of a heavy barrage.

> At about 3.49 everything became deathly still – not a shot or a gun anywhere and just on time the barrage came down… it was of course still dark and the shell bursts seemed to make it still darker. I never heard a noise like it in my life – couldn't have believed it possible. The air was just singing and humming and crackling with shells. Speaking or even shouting was simply a waste of time. Behind us and for miles to the north and to the south every gun in the place was going like the hammers of hell – simply ripping. I felt as if I had just drunk four bottles of fizz![49]

'Zero hour, the Battalion crossed No Man's Land,' recorded the 9th Black Watch's War Diary. 'From there on the fighting till the objectives were reached was continuous. The opposition was due chiefly to snipers & M[achine] Guns in shell holes.' 'Great battle started,' recorded Pipe Major McLeod, 4/5th Black Watch. 'The 39th Division was going over in three waves and the 118 Brigade was the third,' related Miller. 'This meant that we started last and had to go over all the ground already covered and to start our fighting after passing through all the shell fire on the others.' During the advance Miller was hit by a piece of shrapnel and evacuated to a casualty clearing station. 'I used to wonder what all the padres did when the fighting was on but I found them here helping the wounded in every way they could by serving food, supplying Field cards to write home and writing them if that was necessary. They were doing a very good job which was a great help to the lads.' 'Band take up rations to front line. Myself in charge. Hot time,' continued McLeod.'[50]

On the 51st Highland Division's front, the 7th Black Watch was one of the leading battalions, the 6th Black Watch assigned to pass through. 'This was the best engagement I ever was in, our artillery was using all kinds of shells including liquid fire etc. There were also mines put up on the enemy & really it was just like a firework display,' recorded Private Cameron, who had returned to the front after a month in hospital with swollen feet. 'No Man's Land was an awful mess of mud and water. There was wire everywhere – all broken and torn… it was quite dark until we got to the German support line,' recorded Penney. 'Everything was battered to pieces and nothing was recognisable – even whole farms had disappeared… I never saw such a wreck of countryside. Shell holes literally were so close that they cut into each other. There were a few roots of trees and hedges but all roads had disappeared.'[51]

'Towards three o'clock in the afternoon the enemy was observed massing near Langemarck village,' recorded a member of the 6th Black Watch. 'Counter-attack after counter-attack was delivered and repulsed. The enemy waited for further reinforcements which could be clearly seen coming up, again attacked and was again repulsed. But the plight of the mere handful of the 6th whose lot it had been to push forward into that advanced position was momentarily becoming more desperate. Ammunition was running short.' With both flanks exposed, the Battalion's only option was to withdraw to an abandoned German 'pill box' with a commanding position over the Steenbeck river. 'Those who came through bear witness that it was one of the most terribly exciting moments of their lives. Stumbling through the mud, falling, rising, pressing on, while the enemy, barely 100 yards away, stood up and took deliberate aim at them – one of the memories of the Great War which no length of time will ever blot out.'[52]

'We had nothing much to do in the afternoon, except clearing up and salvaging – still pouring,' continued Penney who had been wounded in the leg and felt 'done to the world'. The following day 'it was still pouring. Our shelter had now two feet of water in it… we made stepping stones out of empty rum jars – pretty wobbly ones, if you didn't get straight on to them.'[53] In early August the 51st Highland

Division was withdrawn, returning to the line at Poelcapelle in September.

As at the Somme, the swift breakthrough the Generals had hoped for evolved into a series of battles fought in the towns and villages beyond Ypres. Describing operations, Lieutenant Colonel Sceales, 4/5th Black Watch, was scathing in his criticism of going into battle with understrength battalions: 'The obvious ridiculous situation of a battalion 961 strong on paper having so many men extra-regimentally employed in or out of the battle, that the platoon strength in these operations averaged 20 and 21, thus reducing the new fighting organisation to almost a farce… had tanks been able to come forward they would have inflicted enormous casualties on the assembling Bosches.' 'Usual. German Gotha-type aeroplanes over dropping bombs,' Pipe Major McLeod was recording on 31 August. 'Saw them bursting about a kilo away.'[54]

Among 1st Black Watch fatalities was Captain Duncan Murray-Menzies, serving as a reconnaissance officer with the recently formed Tank Corps. 'We spoke to him but he did not answer or move,' Lieutenant Edward Wolf informed Murray-Menzies' mother. 'He was always a daring lad and had a heart like a lion and no fear,' his soldier-servant, Private James Wallace, related, describing how Murray-Menzies was repairing one of the tanks in No Man's Land when 'he was seen to fall shot through the forehead, he was killed instantly.' 'He frequently put me to shame with his absolute disregard of danger,' observed the Commanding Officer, Victor Fortune. 'In fact I always used to rag him about it and how he frightened me and he was always so particular that anybody with him did not expose himself to unnecessary danger.' As so often happened, the Murray-Menzies family, who had already lost a son at Givenchy in January 1915, had the harrowing news that Duncan's body could not be buried. 'It is lying beside his derelict tank close to a ruined farm house which is still in the hands of the enemy.'[55]

Before the fighting in the Ypres salient reached its dismal conclusion, the 51st Highland Division was moved to the Somme, having taken part in a last action in late September 'on a Sector of the

Langemarck-Gheluvelt line which had resisted capture for more than a month, an incursion into hostile territory and the consolidation of important hills south west of Poelcapelle and Bacaroise House.'[56] The 15th Scottish Division had been moved to the Arras sector, the 9th Black Watch engaged mainly in 'raiding the enemy lines and keeping up that aggressive spirit for which it was famed.' On 16 October the last Black Watch deserter during the war, Private Norman Taysum, was shot at Arras; ninety-one years later posthumous pardons were granted to 306 men executed for cowardice, among them the five soldiers of The Black Watch.[57]

The 8th Black Watch, meanwhile, had moved from Arras to the Somme sector in late July, going into the line at Havrincourt village, where the soldiers spent time 'deepening & improving outpost to front lines'. In late September the Battalion moved north to take part in the fighting at Ypres, where the 4/5th Black Watch were still engaged. Operations now aimed at pushing through to Passchendaele with battles fought at Broodseinde and Poelcapelle. 'Big attack,' Pipe Major MacLeod was recording on 9 October. 'Heavy bombardment started 5.10 a.m. Parties from Battalion working on railways. Aeroplane bombs dropping very near through the night.'[58] Two days later around midnight and 'under torrents of rain along the slippery duckboards' the soldiers moved towards their assembly positions. 'The forming-up positions were heavily barraged with gas and H.E. by the enemy's guns; many of the taping parties were killed or wounded, and all had to wear their respirators for several hours,' recorded the 9th Scottish Division's historian, Major Ewing.[59] Although some progress was made, German resistance was sufficient to prevent consolidation. Among the 'outstanding features of the attack,' the 8th Black Watch's War Diary recorded 'the difficulty, almost the impossibility, to recognise objectives; almost all landmarks being obliterated by shell fire... the enemy shelling was continuous, heavy and well placed... the weather conditions and the necessary exposure entailed thereby were of the worst kind.' 'No man could progress at more than a snail's pace, and sheer exhaustion was a factor more potent than the enemy in bringing the advance to a standstill,' continued Ewing.

Communications had also broken down 'since the pigeons were unable to fly against the strong wind that prevailed, and the men who had charge of the messenger dogs all became casualties.' Guns had also got stuck in the mud and 'leadership, marked more by valour than by discretion, caused an unnecessary number of battalions to be involved in wasteful and confused fighting.'[60]

'In perusing' the list of dead, Reverend Macdonald found that:

> almost all the Gaelic men were killed or wounded. Ossian's lines remain true – they also went forth to the war and seldom returned. It was the same at Loos. The poor Highland lads gave themselves generously, and only a small remnant remains in regiments which were genuinely Highland in 1914 and early 1915. They have a greater pride of race than the Germans themselves and once engaged they never falter till they fall or reach their objective. If only we had an army of them, all would be well. Much of the élan of the Canadians is due to their strong mixture of Highland blood, and the dash of the French is probably traceable in their Celtic ancestry.'[61]

Having spent part of October on 'road repair' the 4/5th Black Watch returned to the line on 1 November. 'Believe me the Salient at Ypres was the abomination of desolation,' remarked Lieutenant Badenoch, now with the 4/5th Black Watch. 'The countryside had no landmarks, it was just a mass of shell holes and some stunted trees. The front line could not be reached except in the dark and then over duck boards walking in single file and woe betide anyone who got off the duck board track, as the shell holes were a mass of mud and water and deep. There was no system of trenches', he noted, and 'the front was held by isolated posts. Conditions had to be seen to be believed. Virtually the only shelter we had was a sheet of corrugated iron over the front of the trench. A kilt was certainly not the most suitable dress for these conditions!!'[62]

A 'terrible job' remained burying the dead. 'We were each told to take a section of men and one NCO, draw rubber gloves, sandbags, and an extra rum ration for the men, and take our sections out to the battlefield area,' recalled Lieutenant P. King, 2/5th East Lancashire Regiment. 'They were mostly Scottish soldiers – Argyll and Sutherland Highlanders, and Black Watch… Some had been lying there for months and their bodies were in an advanced state of decomposition; and some were so shattered that there was not much left… where the bodies were so broken up or decomposed that we couldn't find an identity we just buried the man and put "Unknown British Soldier" on the list… The smell was appalling and it was deeply depressing for the men.'[63]

After taking part in the attack on the Passchendaele Ridge, the depleted 8th Black Watch moved to the Coast Defence sector near Oost Dunkerque. 'Last night we were ferociously bombed, the windows rattling and the house quaking. One poor fellow of my B.W. boys was killed just as he reached the camp after a week in the trenches,' continued Macdonald. 'I believe this was a quiet sector till we arrived, but no one can complain of inactivity now. One can't have everything and though shell and bomb keep us lively here, we have on the other hand healthy sea breezes and excellent billets.' The War Diary merely recorded: 'Weather for month very mild, and fairly dry.'[64]

Since no breakthrough at Ypres had been achieved, on 14 October Operation Hush was cancelled, the 1st Division moving to Ypres to take part in the last stages of the fighting. This included another attempt on Passchendaele carried out in early November by units of the Canadian Expeditionary Force, who finally took the ridge on the 10th. A week later the 1st Black Watch moved up to the front line to relieve the 1st Cameron Highlanders. On their right, the 2nd Rifle Brigade was relieving the 42nd Royal Highlanders of Canada. Realising that they had just missed fighting 'side by side', Fortune wrote to the 42nd's Commanding Officer saying that they were looking forward 'to meeting you all again in the near future either in the mud or in billets.'[65]

In the aftermath, Haig's decision to attack in Flanders, rather than further south where the weather might have been better, became a matter of public debate, as did undertaking an offensive so soon after Nivelle's failed operations instead of waiting for

American reinforcements. Known also as the Third Battle of Ypres, Passchendaele was described by the soldiers as 'the battle of mud'. As at the Somme in 1916, the cost was disproportionately high: an estimated 310,000 casualties on the Allied side (perhaps half of whom were killed); 90,000 were reported missing and although some of these were buried in unknown graves, 42,000 bodies were never recovered. 'Many were simply blown to pieces.'[66]

Cambrai: 'Dead country'

After being withdrawn from Ypres at the end of September, the 51st Highland Division had moved south near the newly fortified German position along the Hindenburg Line. For the first time the soldiers witnessed the impact of what the Germans called 'a dead country' after their withdrawal earlier in the year. 'No village or farm was left standing, no road was left passable, no railway track or embankment was left in being. Where once were woods, there are gaunt rows of stumps; the wells have been blown up. In front of our new positions runs like a gigantic ribbon our Empire of Death.'[67]

On 13 November, the anniversary of the capture of Beaumont Hamel, there was 'a general holiday… a special dinner was given to the men at mid-day.'[68] A week later the Division was engaged in a surprise attack against the Hindenburg Line, involving tanks. As Haig outlined in his despatch, the purpose was 'to gain a local success at a point where the enemy did not expect it. Our repeated attacks in Flanders, and of our Allies elsewhere, had brought about large concentrations of the enemy's forces on the threatened points, with a consequent reduction in the garrisons of certain other sectors of the line.' Of these, the front opposite Cambrai had been selected 'as the most suitable for the surprise operations in contemplation.'[69]

The 6th Black Watch was part of the first wave, while the 7th would follow on. Over seventy 'rover' tanks to crush the wire and 'fighting' tanks to attack the trenches were detailed to each brigade. 'For two or three nights prior to the battle we couldn't get sleeping for the terrible noise of heavy transport,' recorded Private Cameron, 'and on going outside one night the roads were thick with hundreds of "Tanks" and Heavy Guns etc. etc. going up to take their various positions for the Day of Battle.' On 19 November the infantry moved up 'in Fighting Order & lay all night in a large field until our artillery "kicked off at 6-30 am" next morning,' continued Cameron. 'It was a fine sight to see the tanks oblivious to danger, ambling along in front of us & attacking anything from a pillbox to a heavy howitzer gun pit.'[70]

'All Infantry got away at their correct distances as tanks moved off without any trouble,' recorded the War Diary. 'It was a well carried out attack & it was about noon when we (A Company) got to our objective the famous "impregnable" Hindenburg Line,' related Cameron.[71] The 7th Black Watch moved off in the second wave but its progress was less straightforward. 'Infantry following the tanks captured Hindenburg support at about 10.35 a.m. All the tanks that reached this position were knocked out by an anti-tank battery… the wire between Hindenburg support and Flesquières trench was uncut, there were no tanks on our front, the village of Flesquières was still in the hands of the enemy; there was no artillery barrage. Consequently further advance at this time was impossible.'[72]

'Shortly after 1 p.m. [on the 20th] the weather changed, and rain began to fall,' continued the 6th Black Watch's War Diary. 'The afternoon was spent re-organising, cleaning arms etc.' preparatory to further operations the following day. 'Zero hour' was fixed for 6.45 a.m. Finding that the Germans had withdrawn from Flesquières, the 51st Highland and 62nd Divisions moved forward to Fontaine-Notre-Dame, creating a breach in the German line. 'We lay in dug-out in the Hind-Line for a day & next night we were marched from the village of Flesquières (which our Division captured) right into the shell hole front line between Bourlon Wood & the village of Notre Dame Fontaine [sic],' continued Private Cameron. 'Our boys were dead beat from exhaustion & want of food etc.'[73] On the evening of 21 November, the 6th Black Watch went into divisional reserve 'in readiness to move forward for action at ½ hours notice… companies partially equipped with the enemy tools.' The 7th had remained in the line 'to deal with the enemy's counterattack which, however, did not develop. Weather dull. Several showers of rain.'[74]

At night on 23 November the 51st Highland Division was relieved by the Guards Division. Private Cameron described the new arrivals as 'dead beat' after a three-day 'forced' march, the offensive's gains being swiftly lost when the Germans counter-attacked. 'This I believe had a lot to do with the big failure on this front (when Gerry broke through) no sufficient fresh reserves.'[75] Having already recaptured Fontaine-Notre-Dame, by early December, the Germans had forced the evacuation of the positions gained: 'a sombre sunset after a brilliant sunrise,' noted military historian Captain Basil Liddell-Hart in 1930, citing Major General Harper's decision to place too great a distance between tanks and infantry as the reason for the high fatalities caused by German machine gun fire.[76]

Despite some Allied successes on the Western Front, Russia's struggle against the Central Powers in the east was collapsing. Rioting in Petrograd had led to armed clashes, the unrest culminating in Tsar Nicholas' abdication and the end of the Romanov dynasty, known as the February Revolution. Although the new government, led first by Prince Georgy Lvov and then by the Menshevik leader, Alexander Kerensky, had pledged to continue the fight, the Petrograd Soviet of Workers and Soldiers' Deputies proposed a ceasefire. In April, facilitated by Germany, the Bolshevik leader, Vladimir Lenin, returned from exile in Switzerland, calling immediately for an end to Russia's participation in the war.

The failure of Kerensky's July Offensive, an attack by General Brusilov on Galicia, a region straddling the border of modern Poland and the Ukraine, weakened Kerensky's government, revealing the loss of morale and discipline in the Russian Army. Compounded by economic hardship, further rioting in Petrograd paved the way for a Bolshevik takeover in October. In December 1917 Lenin agreed an armistice with Germany and peace negotiations began at Brest-Litovsk. Russia's withdrawal from the war and Italy's crushing defeat at Caporetto in November gave Hindenburg the opportunity to focus attention on the Western Front before the Americans arrived.[77]

Jerusalem by Christmas

The Egyptian Expeditionary Force, meanwhile, had been continuing operations in Palestine. In late June Murray was replaced by General Allenby, former commander of the Third Army on the Western Front. Having been encouraged by Prime Minister Lloyd George that Jerusalem would be a 'fine' Christmas present for the British nation, Allenby had been organising a new offensive designed to drive the Turks from their defences on the southern frontiers of Palestine and open the way to the Holy City. 'The plan itself was simple, as are almost all good plans in war,' observed Wavell, who had been promoted brevet lieutenant colonel while serving as liaison officer between Allenby and the CIGS, General Sir William Robertson. 'To concentrate a superior force against the enemy's left flank, while inducing him to believe that his right would again be attacked.'[78]

Together with other units, the 14th Black Watch had spent most of September and October training before moving to Abu Sitta, where the attacking force was assembling. 'Dawn brought in a new vision,' recalled Corporal David Livingstone, who had recently arrived from Britain. 'Rock, sand, but no water in sight… Away to the N. West the flash and thunder of the guns at Gaza could be seen and heard, but this was nothing to the flash and thunder of heaven's artillery – a tropical thunderstorm which broke at 2 a.m. and continued for over 2 hours … one good result of the storm, plenty of water, and we just swallowed pints of it, sand and all.' Moving up to 'Dundee Wadi', the Battalion was busy road making: 'a couple of good hours hard graft saw a fairly good road fashioned and before we had finished, the artillery and transport were coming along.'[79]

The operation began with an attack on Beersheba on the night of 30/31 October 'so timed that the light of the full moon favoured this night approach. The weather, however, was sultry and airless, and a dense pall of dust lay heavy on the marching columns,' Wavell noted. 'Wednesday 31st. broke on us with striking suddenness, the crashing report of a naval gun bringing every man to his feet,' continued Livingstone. 'The reason – the great movement and attack on Bir-Shaba (Beersheba)… had begun, and I was witness of a sight that few men have seen… a battle in which everything is visible to the observer.' The capture of Beersheba was 'the first stroke in the great business. Many Turks passed through the lines that day, and a more nondescript crowd I have seldom seen.' Once the cavalry had passed through, the 74th Division moved up, taking over an outpost position on 2 November. 'Not a tree or shrub could be seen… [the] most trying experience, however, was the terrible scarcity of water,… the water came all the way from Egypt, across the Sinai desert in a pipe laid by the EEF and that along with the railway was one of the great achievements in this theatre of war… the Battalion engaged mopping up Turkish lines for a couple of days.' To the soldiers' surprise, 'Johnny Turk' as they called their opponents 'had been quite comfortable here, even to the extent of a Singer Sewing Machine, and a dozen or so of hens.'[80]

Following the success at Beersheba, the main assault on Gaza was launched on 6 November. At the same time the 14th Black Watch took part in an attack on a Turkish defensive position at Sheria, between Gaza and Beersheba. '[The] action began about 5.30 a.m. and proved a decided hot business for the men… Many officers and men were lost that morning.' Among them was Corporal Livingstone's 'esteemed' Company commander, Major Osborne 'and my platoon commander, Lieutenant Kinniburgh.'[81] At the end of the day the Commanding Officer, Lieutenant Colonel John Gilmour, was wounded 'to whom was due no small part of the credit for the victory. His brilliant leadership and dash' earning him a bar to his Distinguished Service Order (DSO).[82] Ten days later Jaffa fell, the 14th Black Watch again making roads so that the guns and transport could pass through. 'Road making was made fairly easy owing to the large amount of stones available, the valleys and hills being literally covered with a stone, cream in colour and fairly hard. The legend was told out there that this was the Manna of Moses' time turned to stone, and the quantity certainly gave credence to the tale. From here we set out on our final journey in the Holy Land and incidentally our last brush with the Turk.'[83]

By dawn on 9 December the Turks had left Jerusalem. Two days later General Allenby entered the Holy City on foot through the Jaffa Gate, which was the main entry to the old walled city and traditionally only opened to a conqueror. To the 14th Black Watch 'fell the honour of supplying the first Christian guards over the holy places in Jerusalem after a Moslem occupation of seven centuries.'[84]

The 14th Black Watch's last action in 1917 was capturing the hill of Shafa. 'We started the advance just after dark, and all went well until we had almost reached the objective... when we suddenly bumped right into the Turk. Both sides were rather taken by surprise, and our men at all events were thoroughly excited and firing wildly in the dark without much chance of hitting anything... shortly before midnight, the excitement calmed down a bit... scouts, sent out to the front, reported that the Turk had cleared right off the whole hill.' The last two days of 1917 were spent clearing the battlefield and reorganising.[85]

In Mesopotamia, at the beginning of November, in response to a 'hostile attack' from Turkish forces entrenched at Tekrit (Tikrit), Maude ordered a counter-attack, resulting in Tekrit's capture. The 2nd Black Watch was not 'closely engaged' and on 12 November the attacking force returned to Samarrah. Shortly afterwards Maude died of cholera, his death 'keenly felt'.[86] In early December, the 2nd Black Watch received '*very* sudden' orders to move 'that very afternoon, and it [was] during the following three days we marched 67 miles on our flat feet,' Stewart told his wife. The weather was bitterly cold. 'Twice have I had about quarter of an inch of ice on my bucket in the morning and on one of these occasions we had 15 degrees of frost, this is hardly imaginable after the heat of August.' Proceeding by train and river they halted at Basrah to await further instructions on their next posting. 'Where that spot is I cannot tell you firstly because, though I have a good idea I am forbidden by the censor and secondly because no names can be mentioned until 10 days after one has arrived at the place. This actual letter will not be posted until we arrive at our new destination.'[87]

On the Western Front, recovery from the losses at Ypres was gradual, with all battalions needing reinforcements. 'It was not without forgery and finesse that I got to France,' related Private Eric Linklater, who had falsified his age (indicating that he had been born in March 1898 instead of 1899) and amended the records of his poor eyesight. 'And twenty-four hours after landing I was heartily sorry for my cleverness. It was December, and the camp on the hill above Boulogne was cold and crowded.' He was posted to the 4/5th Black Watch, where 'for a few weeks we occupied the lonely and abominable mudpits that made a front-line at Passchendaele or laid duck-boards at night and saw them shot to pieces in the morning.'[88]

'It has been a raw December day – frost gone and mud, thick, greasy, glutinous holds us in its foul grip,' commented Reverend Macdonald, describing the 8th Black Watch's location at Gouzeaucourt near Cambrai, where the 9th Scottish Division had moved in early December. 'The war is raging fiercely in this region and there is little time or opportunity of writing letters and you must not be surprised or jump to any miserable inferences if you don't hear frequently from me.'[89]

During 1917 the eleven Black Watch battalions overseas recorded 5,728 officers and men killed, wounded or missing.[90] 'Once more Christmas has come round,' Private Stratton was writing from 'an old Greek village' where the 13th Black Watch was in billets. 'Another Christmas spent abroad.'[91]

A skull rose out of the mud one day;
(Passchendaele was the name of the place):
And the winter waters were oozing down,
When a skull appeared – with part of a face.
… So many had died who had passed that way;
Blown to pieces in dead of night:
Killed by a bullet at dawn of day:
Or stumbled to death 'neath a Very light.[92]

7

1918: Weary of War

Weary of War, I stand – a watcher – in a shell-torn land,
The Earth is scarred; all holes, no road, a path of chalk;-
Cobwebs of barbed-wire where'er I walk;
The daylight dies and dusk begins to fall,
And all is silent as the grave. 'Tis War.[1]

War is a fool's game and despite all poets, historians and journalists have written there is neither sense nor glory in it.[2]

A shell-torn land

By the beginning of 1918, unknown as yet to the combatants, the war was entering its final year. As American soldiers prepared to cross the Atlantic, on 8 January President Woodrow Wilson proclaimed his 'Fourteen Points', pledging the right of 'self-determination' to those fighting against their oppressors. Meanwhile, on 3 March the new Bolshevik government signed a peace treaty with the Central Powers at Brest-Litovsk, concluding Russia's participation in the war and providing Germany with the opportunity for a final push on the Western Front before United States troops arrived. Compared with the 20 to 25 miles originally assigned to the BEF in 1914, British divisions were now defending up to 123 miles from the Ypres salient as far south as Péronne and St Quentin, six (rising to nine) Black Watch battalions in their midst.

'We spent the winter until some time in January 1918 going out and in at various parts,' related Lieutenant Badenoch, 4/5th Black Watch in the Ypres sector, 'and I think I was one of the few junior Officers who survived each tour.'[3] The 1st Black Watch, now under the command of Lieutenant Colonel Lewis Pugh Evans, VC, was also still in the Ypres salient.[4] 'Heavy snow today so the parades were mostly off. Everyone seems very fed up with life just now,' Lieutenant Arbuthnott was writing on 8 January. 'In the morning we broke the ice on shell holes to get water for washing and shaving,' recorded a new arrival, eighteen-year-old Private Albert Hay. Although living conditions had improved, repeated shelling had destroyed the drainage system and the countryside remained waterlogged, working parties constantly having to repair 'the ravages of weather'. Lice were a persistent menace. 'Old soldiers, tough as saddlery, rose cursing and afraid, and we youngsters were ravished more deeply, and far more often, than Lucanian girls by Spartacus's insurgent gladiators,' remarked Private Linklater.[5] In late January the 4/5th Black Watch moved from Ypres, joining the Fifth Army in the Somme sector. On the day of departure, it poured with rain. 'A highly intelligent company commander had told us to take off our kilts, and wear them as capes about our shoulders. So we said good-bye to Passchendaele with a flutter of grey shirt-tails dancing behind our bums,' related Linklater, noting that the mud of the Somme was 'a paler, more sympathetic mud than the dark and evil mud of the Salient.' 'Here I had one of the worst nights I ever had as, out of 16 NCOs, I was chosen to go to the trenches on 31st January to take over and guide the Battalion in when they came next day,' recalled Miller, back with the 4/5th after being wounded at Ypres. 'This was the fateful day and every machine gun that rattled and every shell that whistled over, I thought was meant for me. This was the nearest I got to understanding the poor fellows who were shell-shocked. On this new front, both sides were making regular bombing raids to find out what units were holding the line and where the attacks were to be made.'[6]

Both the 51st Highland and the 9th Scottish Divisions had remained in their advanced positions in the Somme sector. 'Well mum I am back to the old daily routine again – back to the line,' Private William Couston, 7th Black Watch, was writing home on 8 March. 'Such a glorious morning it was, [with] a light touch of frost in the air – just fine for marching.' 'One day is so like another just now that I have no news worth writing,' the Reverend Macdonald was telling his wife. 'One gets tired of the useless weather topic and impressions of present and prospective war activities are forbidden.'[7] To the north, the 15th Scottish Division, with the 9th Black Watch, was holding the line near Arras.[8]

The Kaiserschlacht (the Kaiser's Battle)

On 21 March General Ludendorff launched what proved to be the last major German assault on the Western Front, 'on the issue of which depended the fate of Germany and the world,' in the opinion of the 9th Scottish Division's historian, Major Ewing. 'At first the omens seemed favourable to the enemy for a thick mist, hovering over ridges and valleys, allowed his grey-clad men to leave their trenches without detection.'[9] Attacking along a 20-mile front, the German objective was to break through at the junction of the French and British armies near St Quentin and capture Amiens. Codenamed Operation Michael and later known as the Third Battle of the Somme (also the Kaiser's Battle), supplementary offensives were intended to divert forces from the main attack. Black Watch battalions were among the thousands of soldiers resisting the onslaught, once more fighting to defend strategic locations by which the different parts of the battle became known: Bapaume, Pozières, Lys, Estaires, Messines and Kemmel Ridge.

Positioned in support at Longavesnes, north-east of Péronne, when the barrage began the 4/5th Black Watch immediately stood to arms, the sound of firing making it appear 'as if every second German had a machine gun.'[10] The following day the line broke 'and the Germans came through,' related Miller.

> Now started the most fantastic ten days of the war as we tried to stop the German advance. When the Germans came forward they stopped and sent a party to cut us off and we had to run again. This went on – run two miles, come back a half mile, take up another position, wait again and repeat same three times a day. On the third day everybody was on edge and when the 4/5th held

> a position before Bray, two Germans on a motor cycle made us all run by getting along the end of our trench and firing wildly along and shouting at the same time.[11]

The destruction of the bridges over the Somme temporarily halted the Germans but on the night of 25 March a crossing was made, forcing the 39th Division to withdraw. 'Day after day we dodged and came back until 31st March, when we passed through a line of Australians… We had retired 120 miles, but must have covered twice that distance… [with] all retreats and the returns we made. As all the units were hopelessly mixed, each one was given a gathering point and the 4/5th gathered together at their point 120 men out of the 750 who took up position on 21st March.'[12]

The Commanding Officer of the 4/5th Black Watch, Lieutenant Colonel T. D. Murray, had been evacuated, suffering from exhaustion and gas poisoning. 'I don't imagine for one moment that I should have survived had I been with the Battn,' commented Badenoch, who was on leave. 'For it took an awful mauling.'[13] Although involved 'in some disagreeable episodes' Private Linklater's main recollection was 'of consuming, with great relish, a bottle of looted champagne and a jar of the best plum jam I have ever tasted; of sleeping very comfortably between two convenient graves in a shattered churchyard; and of listening, during a whole day of battle, to an Irish man discussing his next war.'[14]

In its advanced position near Cambrai the 51st Highland Division was also struggling against the German advance. 'Precisely at 5 a.m. our Artillery opened heavy fire, and almost immediately the enemy put down an intense barrage… the morning was dull and a thick ground haze with the smoke and dust from bombardment made visibility very bad… gas was mixed with H.E.,' recorded Major Campbell who had temporarily taken command of the 6th Black Watch. Although the Division maintained its position, when others in the line fell back, the danger of being outflanked by the advancing Germans meant the front line battalions had to withdraw. 'Parties of the enemy were also pushing up the valley towards Bapaume and we were almost surrounded,' continued Campbell. By 27 March he was reporting that 'the men had little food and everyone was done up, but we pegged away, hoping for rest soon.'[15]

The 7th Black Watch had been similarly exposed. 'Dawn broke [on the 24th] and we were still holding the line – but Jerry's artillery had arrived and began now, and continued the whole time, to liven things up,' related Private Josiah Ashworth, who was wounded and taken prisoner. Since the German barrage had destroyed the front line trenches, leaving C and D Companies isolated, a 'last stand' was made at Louverval. Second Lieutenant Gilmour Cumming, aged twenty, was 'last seen with a handful of men entirely surrounded fighting gamely. All this garrison perished.' Over two-thirds of the 7th Black Watch's officers and men were killed, wounded or were missing. So great were the losses that the Battalion ceased to exist as a unit, becoming part of '51st Division Force'.[16] Among the wounded officers was the Commanding Officer, Lieutenant Colonel McClintock, command passing to Major Keir, who had been with the Battalion since 1914.[17]

Private Couston was writing to his mother from hospital:

> I hope you have not been worrying about my not writing sooner; but to tell the truth I have little energy… you need not be alarmed about me. I am getting along first rate & am in good hands. You will have got my p.c. by this time with the news. Am wounded in the head & in rather a nasty place – behind the left ear. Fortunately the wound is slight. The machine gun bullet went thro' the top of my left ear – glanced along the bone down towards the neck. Had it gone the least fraction of an inch deeper I would not be writing this letter. The doctor said I had a marvellous escape & you may be sure I am very thankful. I was wounded at close range too – less than 200 yards – when the Germans were almost on the top of us… it seems like Paradise here – in bed between the sheets.[18]

The 8th Black Watch had just gone into the line near Gouzeaucourt when the attack began. 'A desperate resistance was offered by the posts, and great rents were ruthlessly torn in the ranks of the invaders, but yard by yard the Germans tightened their hold,' recorded Ewing, the 8th's losses recorded as exceeding '50 per cent of the infantry, but the rest were in good heart.' After a week's intensive fighting, on 1 April, the 9th Scottish Division entrained for Flanders, the Battalion brought up to strength by young boys who, although 'splendid examples of the beneficial effect of good feeding, regular exercise, and military discipline on young Scotsmen', had no experience of active service.[19]

The 9th Black Watch in the Arras sector had not been in the immediate firing line. But, by the end of the day on 22 March, to conform with the movement further south, the 15th Scottish Division had withdrawn to a new defensive position, the Germans moving forward to occupy the now vacant front line trenches. The relative quiet was soon broken when, on 28 March, having failed to capture Amiens, the Germans attacked Arras. Although repulsed, Allied casualties were heavy, the 9th Black Watch included. Lieutenant Colonel Innes had already been evacuated due to ill health, but his successor, Major William Binnie, was wounded as was his successor, Captain Story-Wilson, who remained in command until relieved by Lieutenant Colonel Dudgeon, Cameron Highlanders. Despite needing rest, 'owing to the gravity of the situation and to the lack of the reserves', the 15th Scottish Division remained in the line, its endurance praised by the Corps Commander, Lieutenant General Sir Charles Fergusson, whose son, Bernard, was later to receive a commission in the Black Watch: 'I knew you could be relied upon to stick it out to the end… I want the honour of holding Arras to be yours alone.'[20]

At the end of March the severely depleted 39th Division was moved to Flanders. Encountering the remnants of a Guards battalion, a piper began to play 'Highland Laddie'. 'We were a tatterdemalion crew from the coal-mines of Fife and the back-streets of Dundee,' related Private Linklater, 'but we trod quick-stepping to the brawling tune, kilts swinging to answer the swagger of the Guards, and the Red Hackle in our bonnets like the monstrance of a bruised but resilient faith.'[21] On arrival at Arques in early April, a composite brigade was formed, its strength amounting to 'barely' 700 men, the 4/5th having only one officer and 30 other ranks. 'There was only a skeleton left,' recorded Badenoch 'My platoon was now a mixed lot consisting of some Black Watch, some Sussex and some Warwicks.'[22]

'For the next two or three weeks the war was in a state of singular confusion,' Linklater continued. 'We were in the neighbourhood of Ypres again – at Zillibeke and Voormezeele – and wherever we went we were digging trenches and fighting off an enemy who generally appeared from some entirely unexpected quarter. It was the season for low-lying fog, and on one occasion we refrained, in the nick of time, from opening fire on a battalion of Cameron Highlanders who, in the most mysterious fashion, came charging towards us out of what we thought was the German line.' General Haig's 'celebrated' order 'in which he said we were fighting with our backs to the wall' was met with 'laughter from one end of the country to the other. For we had no such illusion of support, and were more likely to be fighting with our backs to the enemy, since the Germans often appeared on both sides of us.'[23]

The 1st Black Watch, still holding the northern area of the Ypres salient, was subjected only to artillery fire, and its casualties had been light, the soldiers' activity confined mainly to conducting raids or countering those from the Germans. But as the Germans began to focus attention on Flanders in order to reduce pressure on the now exhausted German troops on the Somme, the Battalion was ordered to move south. 'Here we are for the show,' Lieutenant Arbuthnott was noting on 3 April. 'On this march it was very evident that the Germans were making progress because the roads were almost blocked with civilians making their way rearward with all they could take of their possessions,' recorded Private Hay, who had just finished Siege Camp 'for special training in bomb throwing and musketry' as well as attending 'gun class' for training in the use of a Lewis machine-gun. 'Some were driving cows while they were laden with huge packs containing clothes and valuables, while others pushed small wheeled carts piled high with all manner of goods, and the scene was extraordinary with Béthune on fire away on our left and shells bursting in the village of Beuvry on our front.'[24] The 51st Highland Division was near by, having arrived in Burbure in late March before moving to Pacaut and going into line at the River Lawe, a tributary of the River Lys. Although 'some three thousand men' had joined as reinforcements, there were few new officers; moreover, the authorities had confused the situation 'by posting Gordons to Black Watch battalions, and Seaforth to Argylls'.[25]

On 9 April the Germans began their second offensive, Operation Georgette, attacking Allied forces between Ypres and Béthune. Having crossed the River Lawe, they broke through to Estaires, causing high casualties among the divisions of the *Corpo Expedicionário* Português (CEP, the Portuguese Expeditionary Force), between La Bassée Canal and Armentières. Flanked by the 50th and 55th Divisions, the 51st Highland Division was moved up in support.[26] For the next two days, severe fighting continued at Lestrem and Paradis. 'All available men of 6th and 7th Black Watch were collected and formed up; ammunition was issued and a stand made. Machine guns were of great assistance here,' noted Major Campbell on 11 April. But the Germans 'pressed their advantage on each flank', the terrain hindering resistance since it was intersected 'by a river, marshes and small canals'.[27] The following day Campbell was reporting: 'enemy on our left in large numbers shelled our line and rear very heavily, and seemed to have guns well forward. Machine guns were enfilading us, and we were forced to withdraw.'[28]

Both the 6th and 7th Black Watch again endured severe losses; the 'Battle of the Lys' was considered to have been 'the most trying ordeal' the 51st Highland Division had so far experienced.[29] Twenty-six-year-old Lieutenant Colonel Neil Campbell, who had been temporarily absent due to injury, was among the fatalities. So weakened were the 6th's ranks that a mixed force of Black Watch and Gordon Highlanders, known as 'Fleming's Force', was briefly formed under Lieutenant Colonel Fleming's command. On 23 April the 6th Black Watch was reorganised, Lieutenant Colonel Francis Rowland Tarleton assuming command. After a brief spell in the Labyrinth (for the third time) at Vimy Ridge, the Division 'side-stepped' south to

Oppy and Gavrelle, before being withdrawn for training.[30]

The 8th Black Watch had also been under fire when the 9th Scottish Division was called in to support the 19th Division at Messines, which together with Wytschaete had briefly fallen into German hands. 'This is a bitterly cold day,' Reverend Coll Macdonald was writing on 14 April, 'and one can only pity the poor fellows who are lying out in shell holes.'[31] Soon afterwards the Battalion was involved in renewed fighting as the Germans fought for the high ground around Kemmel Ridge, but they failed to capture the strategically important rail centre of Hazebrouck. By early May the 8th Black Watch had been withdrawn, moving to the sector around Meteren.

The 1st Black Watch had gone into the line at Givenchy. 'At 5 o'clock in the afternoon of the 16th of April the Colonel visited our Platoon and said we would shortly be in the front line and he expected us to uphold the great traditions of our Regiment,' recorded Private Hay. 'Then we were each given a hundred extra cartridges to bring our supply up to two hundred and twenty per man and in addition I carried six Lewis Gun Magazines each containing forty-seven rounds.' Although the first few miles in daylight were 'fairly easy… when it became dark and we had to dodge shell-holes, barbed-wire, and other obstacles we soon became tired out with our burdens of ammunition, etc.' Occupying the same positions as in 1915, the defences had been strengthened. 'The little hill, which since 1914 had given such high tactical value to Givenchy, had been tunnelled from an entrance in the slope facing Moat Farm to an exit in the front line,' continued Hay. Even so, the width of the front to be held meant that there was no battalion reserve and parts of the line had not been sufficiently wired. 'Our trench was in fairly good condition but it was so shallow that we could see over the parados without standing up on the firestep.'[32]

Almost at once the soldiers were informed that an attack was imminent. 'When it became dark in the evening of the 17th we could see lights moving behind the German lines and we could quite distinctly hear the sound of iron-shod wheels on the roads,' noted Hay. 'Our artillery opened fire and we saw the flash of shell bursts in the distance… The German artillery soon replied… then our artillery stopped firing and the enemy fire became more intense until by 1 a.m. the bombardment was terrific.' 'By this time the forward defences no longer existed,' recorded the Battalion's report.[33]

'Shells of every size were dropping all round us and the noise was deafening, while we were compelled to wear our Gas respirators to enable us to breathe in the gas and smoke, although there did not appear to be many gas shells,' Hay related.

> One can tell a gas shell burst by the dull, liquid sound it makes; the gas being in liquid form until it is free and makes contact with air… We knew the Germans were 'over the top' when we saw the SOS signals of the men on our right. These SOS signals were a call to our artillery to open fire, and they responded at once, and the first that we saw of the enemy when they appeared in the distance, was just a grey wave with gashes being smashed in it by our shells. The SOS signals at that time were lights fired from a rifle and suspended in the air by a parachute, they were coloured red over green over red and they floated for a short time before dying out.[34]

In the midst of the fighting Hay recollected hearing the remark: 'Latest Bulletin, All quiet on the Western Front, and the spirit of the troops is excellent.'[35]

In the late afternoon news was received that 'nearly every member' of the 1st Black Watch's A and C Companies had been killed, wounded or taken prisoner. 'Their front line posts were so close to the German line that the attacking troops were amongst our men before they had time to realize that the barrage had lifted… The Germans had to use flame throwers before the men in the tunnel surrendered, but these men had no chance whatever as all the tunnel entrances were in German hands very soon after the beginning of the attack.' A counter-attack by the 1st Loyal North Lancashire Regiment was 'too late to save any of our men, and it was next day before they were able to recover any of our dead,' observed Hay, recording more casualties than the number lost in the South African War. 'In the evening we could plainly see small parties of the enemy carrying their wounded from No Man's Land into their front line and we allowed them to carry on this work in peace, but many were left lying out as we heard them calling "Kamerad, mercy Kamerad" all through the night while we worked at building up the broken down parapet of our trench which had been blown in… Not since the 9th of May 1915 had the Battalion endured such a day… but the enemy had been held.' Although there appeared to be little chance of another attack, the soldiers had to keep their boots on and equipment ready. 'The enemy left us in peace until the morning of the 20th, when we were again heavily shelled but fortunately none of the shells dropped in the trench we occupied,' Hay observed. 'The weather at this time was dry but very cold at night, and we found it difficult to keep warm even during the day time because enemy aeroplanes were about frequently, trying to discover the disposition of our troops in the line taken up on our right since the last attack… The ground was so much cut up by shell holes and large craters that it must have been very difficult for the stretcher bearers to find and also to carry in the wounded men as they could only work during darkness.'[36]

On 21 April the 1st Black Watch was relieved; 15 officers and 366 men had been killed wounded or were missing. One of the wounded was Lieutenant Arbuthnott who was taken prisoner. The Battle of the Lys (Béthune) was a sequel to Kemmel Ridge and Lys (Lestrem). 'Thursday April 25th was a cleaning and inspection day, and we had a hot bath while our kilts and tunics were fumigated,' Hay continued.

> The fumigation process took place in a large tank-like contraption on a steam lorry when steam was admitted to the tank after the door had been tightly closed on our clothing. This treatment made our things feel dry and brittle, and it probably affected the length of life of garments so treated, but it certainly killed all vermin and that was a good thing, although it was impossible to keep clean for more than a few days. The bath was only an all-over wash while we stood in iron tubs of cold water, and when everyone was ready the man in charge opened a tap, and water from a large boiler ran

> along pipes and descended on us from sprays. Then, when we had dried ourselves we filed past a window and each received a clean towel, shirt, and a pair of socks, and by this time our other things were ready so we dressed and then marched back to camp.[37]

By late April, the German advance had been stemmed. 'So ended the most fierce and intense grapple of the British and Germans,' reflected Winston Churchill, emphasising that 120 German Divisions 'had repeatedly assaulted 58 British.' Over 300,000 British officers and men had been killed, wounded or were missing or taken prisoner, constituting over one-quarter of the force under Haig's command on 21 March.[38]

Numbers in both the 4/5th and the 9th Black Watch had been so reduced that on 16 May the 9th was absorbed by the 4/5th, which was transferred to the 15th Scottish Division, while the 39th Division was reduced to cadre.[39] 'Our [Lieutenant] Colonel [Archie Bulloch] and Adjutant were both from the 9th and I was given B Coy but don't ask me why I think I must have been the senior Lieutenant in the Coy because it could not have been for my warlike abilities,' related Badenoch. Moving south, the Battalion went into the trenches near Fampoux, east of Arras.[40]

Meanwhile, the 9th Black Watch's training staff, composed of ten officers and fifty-one other ranks, became a training cadre for American troops arriving in France. 'We had first the 77th Division,' related Miller, 'which was recruited from New York and were very difficult, as many could not speak English and after 4 weeks we had the 30th Division, which was a territorial [National Guard] division from Carolina and Tennessee. These were great men and afterwards played a good part when the war entered its final stages.'[41] In late May the training cadre moved to Aldershot and was formed into the 2/9th Black Watch, absorbing the recently formed 15th Black Watch.[42]

Palestine: The fortress of Arsuf

The 2nd Black Watch's third theatre of operations was Palestine. Having left Mesopotamia at the end of 1917, the 7th Indian Division had gone to re-train in Egypt. 'We are having perfectly glorious weather, cloudless skies and just hot enough in the middle of the day to make a helmet necessary,' observed Lieutenant Colonel Stewart. In March the Division set out from Moascar camp across the Sinai. 'The only thing of moment that happened during our rail trip across the desert was that the Colonel lost his boots.' According to Captain Ritchie, Stewart objected to the sound of snoring and grabbed a pair of boots to throw at the perpetrator of the offending noise. Missing his target, the boots (his own) were propelled out of the truck![43]

By the time the Division reached Palestine, the Egyptian Expeditionary Force's defensive line encompassed the Jordan Valley including Jericho, Jerusalem and Jaffa. 'We are bumping Abdul back at quite a good rate,' observed Stewart. 'The only thing that makes it appear slow is that we can only advance just as quickly as we can make the roads through the Judaen hills to get our guns along.' Among the road makers was the 14th Black Watch. 'Saw "Johnny" get a terrific hammering,' Corporal David Livingstone was recording in early March. 'Another 4 days on road-making, and then on the line of march, and finally into the line on 19th March below Tel Asur, 4,000 ft up, and as cold as blazes at night. Here I got a glimpse of the Dead Sea, and away to the East the mountains of Moab. Down in the valley one could glimpse in the distance the city of Nablus, the ancient Seschem of the Bible.' 'Here we are firmly fixed on historic soil!' Stewart enthused in another letter home. 'By Jove, WHAT oranges we get, I eat eight or 20 of them a day.'[44] Although he could not reveal their location, they were close to the front line at Sarafand.

On 31 March steel helmets with a khaki covering were issued as protection from the heat.[45] With malaria prevalent, to reduce the number of mosquito bites, kilts were replaced by long trousers. Since the Auja river was liable to cause the parasitic infection, bilharziasis, the soldiers were forbidden to swim or wash in it. But, recalled

Ritchie, the morning dew was so heavy that 'you could roll about in the long grass, get yourself completely wet and then having soaped yourself all over, remove the soap by rolling in the wet grass again.'[46] At the beginning of April the Division went into the front line. 'Abdul sometimes "gets the wind up",' Stewart was informing his wife, 'and sends over hundreds of shells, but so far they have done no harm, the noise however is a nuisance and disturbs one's slumbers somewhat.' When the Battalion went into brigade reserve, although 'things are not quite so strenuous,' they still had to keep on the '*qui vive*'.[47]

So great, however, was the demand for reinforcements on the Western Front that Allenby's planned offensive in the spring had to be postponed. Among the forces sent to Europe was the 14th Black Watch. Reaching Alexandria on 1 May 'we discarded our Eastern Kit and were provided with kit for France which now proved to be our destination,' recorded Corporal Livingstone, confessing that his greatest fear while in the 'land of the Pharoahs' had been 'sand snakes and scorpions, of which there were plenty'.[48] Allenby and the remaining troops had now to wait, digging in for the summer in southern Jordan in an area where, according to the official military handbook, 'nothing is known of the climate in summer-time, since no civilised human being has yet been found to spend summer there.'[49]

By early June the 2nd Black Watch was at Arsuf on the coast, a position which was, according to Wauchope, 'thoroughly unsatisfactory' since it was 'overlooked by the enemy'. On 8 June the Battalion was involved in a minor offensive, known as the Action of Arsuf, to improve their line. While the Guides Cavalry attacked two elevated features, dubbed 'the 'North and South Sisters', the 2nd Black Watch captured a line of high ground (Point 170), west of the North Sister. Despite a heavy bombardment and an attempted counter-attack, the Turks failed to dislodge the Guides, who had taken the Sisters, their resistance bolstered by the 2nd Black Watch's reserve company. 'The Turks are very chastened out here, they are always taking the knock, and don't like it one little bit,' Lieutenant Colonel Stewart was recording on 23 July. 'Throughout the period, of course,' related

Ritchie, 'we were building up for a major offensive which was to take place later at the beginning of the autumn.'[50]

March to victory: 'Many dead lying about'

Having contained the German attack on the Western Front, the Allied forces were still fighting subsidiary offensives, their numbers at last strengthened by 318,000 American troops, who reached Europe in March, the vanguard of 1.3 million landing in August.[51] Four more Black Watch battalions had also arrived: the 14th, which was engaged 'in intensive training', giving the men 'the first taste of work with the Tanks,' recorded Corporal Livingstone, who 'had a turn round in one of those monsters, and it was an experience. The Battalion also gave a Demonstration for the edification of Canadian and Australian troops of operating in the open to which we had been accustomed out East.'[52]

After nearly three years in Salonika, on 7 June the 10th Black Watch moved to Sergueux, 50 miles south-west of Amiens. Its responsibilities included securing supply lines, camps and stores in the rear, as the British Army had grown from a force of 120,000 men and 53,000 horses in 1914 to 3 million men and half-a-million horses by 1918.[53] Following in the 10th's footsteps was the 13th Black Watch. 'At present we are laying well out of the way, really resting, & I don't think we'll be doing much else for some time yet,' commented Private Sandy Stratton.[54] In late July the 2/9th Black Watch came from Britain, returning to the front around Loos and the Hohenzollern sector in mid-August.[55]

After the heavy fighting at Givenchy, the 1st Black Watch had moved to Cambrin in early May, moving in and out of the line in the Hohenzollern sector with 'intervals of rest'. 'Each day I took a turn of one hour on sentry duty along with a man of the other gun team, and each night half of the available number of men was on duty in the trench while the others slept near at hand on the tunnel staircase,' related Private Hay. 'We changed over at one o'clock and my turn of duty was from one a.m. until five.'[56] Since June the Battalion had been under the command of Lieutenant Colonel Francis Anderson, one of the original members of the BEF whose *point d'appui* had proved so effective at Nonne Bosschen in November 1914. A welcome distraction for a composite company was representing The Black Watch at France's Bastille Day celebrations in Paris on 14 July.[57]

In response to a request for reinforcements from Foch, created Marshal of France on 6 August, Field Marshal Haig had agreed to send four divisions to Rheims: the 51st Highland and the 15th Scottish Divisions and the 34th and 62nd Divisions. Before they arrived, German forces attacked Rheims, resulting in a change of plan whereby the 15th Scottish Division joined the French Tenth Army near Soissons. 'I don't know what the reason was,' related Badenoch, in command of B Company, 4/5th Black Watch and promoted a temporary captain in June, 'unless it was to boost the morale of the French, which had shown signs of cracking.' Encountering some newly arrived Americans 'one Yankee shouted as he was passing "Give them hell Jock" and a very weary and disgusted voice behind me replied: "Aye – efter fower years" which I thought a very apt reply.'[58]

On 28 July the 4/5th Black Watch took part in an attack on the village of Buzancy. 'The countryside was completely new to me and had never been fought over,' continued Badenoch. 'The attack was timed for 12.30 p.m. and we were guided to the jumping-off place. It was not a case of climbing over the parapet and advancing in extended order. There were no trenches so it was a matter of going forward at first in single file. We had to go along a narrow road bordered on one side by a cornfield and on the other side by the ground dropping away very steeply.' B Company's job was to pass through 'the gates of an old Chateau and mop up the Village of Buzancy or part of the village then take up a position on the open ground beyond.' Having captured a number of prisoners, they reached their objective 'with a greatly reduced number of men. My Coy [Company] was on the extreme right of the British Divisions and we were supposed to join up with the French, but no French were to be seen. They were certainly conspicuous by their absence. After we got to our objective I spotted a group of soldiers dressed as far as I could see in Grey-Blue.

They were on the high ground to our right and about 4-500 yds ahead. They waved to us and beckoned us to come on.' As the senior of the only remaining two officers, Badenoch ordered the other, Lieutenant McGregor, 'to take a few men and go forward and reconnoitre to see if they were the missing French. He moved forward and got quite close when a machine gun fired on us and we had to lie flat on our faces. McGregor and his men were taken prisoner so that answered the question as to who they were.'[59]

Realising their right flank was unprotected, 'we decided in the absence of [the] French we should have to retire. When we got back to the gates of the Chateau the Bosches had already got a machine gun trained on the gates and I'm afraid there may have been a few casualties there… we had commenced the operation with 4 officers and 128 other ranks, and when I got back I was the only Officer and I had 8 men. During the night we collected in all about 30 men.' The following day 'what was left' of the Company was relieved.[60] On 1 August another assault was made, the Battalion getting 'smashed up again,' recorded Pipe Major Dan McLeod.[61] The next day the Germans withdrew. 'About a week after we attacked I was over the ground again,' continued Badenoch, concluding his account of what became known as the Battle of Soissonnais (Buzancy) 'and it was a ghastly sight. It was the height of summer and the killed had lain out for a week. Faces, legs and hands were as black as coal and unrecognisable.' The action at Buzancy marked the beginning of Germany's withdrawal from the area. A month later, General Gassouin, commanding the 17th French Division, headquartered at Buzancy, ordered the construction of a monument commemorating the place where 'the traces [were] still fresh of the exploits of your Scottish soldiers'. Noting that the monument was supposed to be on the furthest point of the advance, Badenoch observed: 'That was not the case… but the monument was certainly on the ground B Company attacked over.' In recognition of the 4/5th Black Watch's role in holding the front line when the retirement began, Lieutenant Colonel Bulloch was awarded the Chevalier of the Legion of Honour, France's highest decoration.[62]

The 51st Highland Division, meanwhile, was near Rheims, its destination the dense woodland of the Bois de Corton. With heavy congestion on the roads, the Division had arrived within hours of a planned attack on 20 July, in which both the 51st and the 62nd Divisions would be engaged. Leading the attack in 153 Brigade was the 6th Black Watch, which advanced against heavy machine-gun fire. Despite reaching its objective, '[the] situation on the right was still obscure,' noted Lieutenant Colonel Tarleton, 'and 7th Black Watch and 7th Gordon Highlanders should have passed through us but did not do so. Enemy appeared to be bringing forward Machine Guns and subjecting us to heavy fire. Some 7th Black Watch and 7th Gordon Highlanders appeared to have joined our front line. Many German aeroplanes kept flying round the woods at a very low altitude and were firing at whatever targets they saw.' After retaining its position 'without food or water for one day and one night' the 6th Black Watch was relieved. There was, however, little respite. On 22 July, the French moved up to attack the German line, while the 6th Black Watch was ordered to push through to occupy its previous position. Yet again, the Germans resisted and so 'no appreciable progress' was made. Five days later another attempt was made to clear the Germans from the wood, the 6th Black Watch again leading the attack. On this occasion there was 'very little opposition or perhaps nil' since the Germans had withdrawn 'though unfortunately we had about 40 casualties from guns of our own barrage firing short.' On 28 July, as the 4/5th Black Watch was attacking Buzancy, a further advance was made to the village of Chambrecy, the 6th Black Watch again bearing the brunt of the fighting. 'A German barrage came down on them, though up to then things had been absolutely quiet, and Machine Gun fire opened on them from both sides of the Valley. I saw we were in a trap,' continued Tarleton, 'but to come back would have been fatal, and to push on seemed to be the only possibility; this, the Battalion did, in most gallant style.' Although there were 'many' casualties from German artillery and machine-gun fire, the Germans did not counter-attack, the 6th Black Watch withdrawing in the early hours of 29 July. With the Germans 'in full retreat' and the French no longer needing British support, the 51st Highland Division was withdrawn.[63]

Having moved to the Meteren sector, south of Ypres, the 8th Black Watch spent the summer in and out of the line. 'We met another B.W. Battalion on their way up and I rather think they will have our old trenches to defend,' Reverend Coll Macdonald informed his wife. 'They were asking very eagerly about the sector of the line we left. I always think it unfair to say anything to dishearten in-going troops, and I painted life… as rosily as I could, only warning them to take no liberties or linger on their way in or out.'[64] On 19 July the Battalion took part in an attack on Meteren. 'Enemy plane over our Lines evidently did not spot anything unusual, the camouflage on the Outposts proving effective,' observed the War Diary.[65] But German machine gun and sniper fire together with uncut wire meant that their advance was held up until the Germans withdrew in response to pressure 'on the neighbouring sectors'. The Battalion's losses were recorded as 'heavy'.[66]

Palestine: Megiddo, 'the death-blow'

After spending the summer in the Jordan valley, Allenby was preparing to complete his planned offensive against the Turks in Palestine and then move into Syria. 'Strictly Secret' instructions were issued, which included the order that 'special precautions' should be taken 'to prevent any chance of prisoners falling into the hands of the enemy'. Throughout the operation the 'strictest water discipline [was] to be enforced.' 'If shells fall short men will light flares and try to indicate their positions to any Aeroplane. This only to be done by order of an OC Coy.'[67]

Allenby's *coup de grâce* against the Turks, involving cavalry and infantry, included a march of more than 50 miles to enter the plain of Esdraelon, north of the ancient fortress of Megiddo, cutting off Turkish lines of retreat. 'There is no parallel in military history to so deep an adventure by such a mass of cavalry against a yet unbroken enemy,' commented Wavell, still serving as Allenby's liaison officer.

'The long Turkish domination of Syria and Palestine, and the military power on which it was founded were to be given the death-blow in the grand manner.' Allenby again adopted various ruses to mislead the Turks, creating the illusion that the attack would be inland rather than along the coast. 'The greatest precautions were taken to prevent the enemy from gaining the slightest inkling of our concentration both of guns, men and horses on the last two days,' related Stewart. 'For weeks beforehand, Battalions and other units had been occupying twice their usual camping grounds, battalions were camped in half-battalion camps, each occupying the space necessary for a complete battalion, thus deceiving any Turkish airmen who might have wandered over our lines with a view to spying out the land. As a matter of fact, our Air Service was so good that no enemy plane showed its nose anywhere near us during the week previous to the attack.'[68] Before the main offensive on 19 September there were two preliminary operations: the first was carried out by T. E. Lawrence, leading the Arabs, who cut communications at the Deraa junction on the Hejaz railway; the second was an attack on Nablus.

The 2nd Black Watch was ordered to take the Turkish front line system 'on a frontage of some 500 yards, with its left on the point where the enemy trenches formed a right angle,' observed Stewart. So that 'nothing should be left to chance, several rehearsals of the attack were carried [out] both by day and night on ground well behind our own position, where the lines of enemy trenches were marked out with flags… At Zero hour, 04.30 on the 19th, the artillery bombardment commenced. To us who had been waiting anxiously for some minutes, it seemed as if some button had been pressed which discharged every gun on the 15-mile front… The change from silence to pandemonium was startling to say the least.' Since it was still dark, all they could see were 'the vague figures of men in the immediate vicinity moving in their lines on a compass bearing almost due North. The noise made by our guns precluded all ordinary conversation and it was only by shouting that one could be heard at all. Very little retaliatory fire came from the enemy. They seemed dazed with the volume of our fire and too much alarmed by the width of the attack to know exactly what to do.' Stewart was relieved, once the bombardment started, that 'at last' he could smoke![69]

'It was one of the most remarkable sights of my life to see two whole divisions of cavalry… going through us in line of squadrons and disappearing into the distance to complete the victory which we had started by breaking through the enemy's position. We then swung round towards the east and went in to the Jordan hills where we had one or two fairly stiff minor engagements,' related Ritchie, who was awarded an immediate MC. Traversing the hills, they reached the road to Nablus 'proceeding along it through the most amazing sight of devastation resulting from air bombing of the enemy's mostly horse-drawn transport which was trying to escape northwards.' As part of the leading infantry, they followed as fast as they could behind the cavalry 'which entailed hard marching day after day without any rest… but it was wonderful to be chasing a defeated enemy'. Short of water, the men were on strict rations. The speed with which they advanced also meant 'it was next to impossible to keep ourselves supplied… we wore out our boots and shirts and as a result found marching extremely arduous and indeed painful. However, the Navy were able to put ashore dumps of material for us which we gladly picked up and used as we went on.' At the end of September the Battalion reached Haifa 'just in front of Lawrence's Arabs from the desert. We were fortunate in this for otherwise the whole place would have been utterly looted.'[70]

At Haifa the men could rest, bivouacking near the sea before continuing northwards to Acre. By 10 October they were in Beirut where 'signs were first noticed of a serious type of malaria which accounted for much sickness in the Battalion. At the same time of course other troops of ours further inland were closing on Damascus.' After halting east of Tripoli, the 2nd Black Watch moved to Ras el-Lados on the road to Homs, having advanced 297 miles in twenty-six marching days in pouring rain or 'unbearable heat'.[71] By the end of October Allenby's forces were in Aleppo. They had moved the front forward 350 miles, captured 75,000 prisoners and 360 guns, suffering a 'little over 5,000' casualties.[72] On 30 October an armistice was signed with

Turkey, hostilities ending at noon the following day. Bulgaria had sued for peace a month earlier.

Hundred Days offensive: 'Dash and fury'

After Ludendorff's failure to consolidate, the Allied forces in Europe had lost no time in fighting back. On 8 August a surprise attack on the Somme, using 500 tanks, and advancing more than 7 miles on the first day, succeeded in breaking through the German line. The Battle of Amiens, as it became known, caused upwards of 30,000 German casualties (compared with less than 10,000 Allied), and was described by Ludendorff as 'The Black Day of the German Army'. As a result, morale plummeted and a steady German withdrawal began. Although not engaged in the initial advance, over the next three months nine Black Watch battalions fought in several actions, many of which again became Battle Honours, among them Épehy, St Quentin Canal, Selle and Sambre.[73]

At the beginning of September the 1st Black Watch left the Hohenzollern sector and entrained for Arras. 'Orders and counter orders followed each other in rapid succession,' related Private Hay.

> It was not until daylight was fading that we finally marched off by companies with the knowledge that the village of Guémappe was our immediate destination, and that our first job was to support the Canadians in their attack on the Drocourt–Quéant Switch Line. The roads were choked with traffic, but for a few miles the traffic was all going in one direction and the road was wide enough to allow motors and horses to proceed past us without our having to take to the fields until the returning transport began coming and the road became a succession of shell holes. Then to add to our discomfort German aeroplanes bombed the road, and they did it very accurately considering the darkness.[74]

The attack by the Canadian 4th Division and British 4th Division on the line between Drocourt and Quéant was so successful that the

1st Division was not required to advance until the afternoon. 'We watched a steady stream of prisoners, wounded and unwounded, passing rearward. A good many Canadians had been killed or wounded, and those of the wounded who were unable to walk were carried by Germans.'[75]

After fighting at Buzancy in late July the 4/5th Black Watch had moved to the Loos and Hulluch sectors, where September passed 'quietly'. By early October, as the Germans continued to withdraw along the front, the 15th Scottish Division moved forward conforming with the advances to the north and south. Having crossed the Haute Deule Canal on 12 October, it reached the western bank of the River Scheldt ten days later. 'Here the advance was held up for about a fortnight. The enemy had destroyed all the bridges across the canal and river, and it was evident that they intended to make a stand on the eastern bank of the Scheldt and Escaut rivers,' commented the War History.[76] The 6th and 7th Black Watch, meanwhile, were undertaking operations in the Fampoux sector at Arras, their actions forming part of the second Battle of Arras and of the Scarpe.

'Sat Sept 1st. Great news from Somme, also good advance on our front,' Private James Jack was writing from behind Ypres, where he was serving as a stretcher bearer at the casualty clearing station. Among those going in pursuit from Moislains was the 14th Black Watch. 'All were startled just at daybreak [2 September] by the breaking of a terrible barrage from our guns,' related Corporal Livingstone. 'My first impression on waking was the shrill whistles of the gun leaders, and then a minute later the whole of hell seemed let loose for with a terrific roar and a myriad flashes battery after battery let loose on the enemy entrenchments. This continued for over an hour and only eased off with the coming of daylight. This was my first experience of what was known as a barrage.' Despite heavy casualties from German machine-gun and artillery fire, the attacking troops advanced some 6 miles. 'Had the pleasure at this stage of inspecting a Bosche dugout. The place was a veritable fortress at least 30 feet down, and was fitted in the most approved fashion,' continued Livingstone. 'Electric light was installed throughout and even was laid on to the trenches above.

Really the Bosche did things in style.'[77]

Having moved into the line at Ypres, in the early hours of 28 September the 8th Black Watch took part in an attack on the Passchendaele Ridge in conjunction with the Belgian Army. Despite fierce German resistance, for the next two weeks the advance continued, numerous Belgian villages falling to the Allied forces, while the Battalion alternately moved forward, passed through or acted in support. On 14 October St Eloi was captured, followed by an attack across the River Lys. A month later, the 8th Black Watch was withdrawn from the line and saw no more action.[78]

'For nearly a whole day we marched to catch up with the scene of hostilities, and for the first hour or two we passed over the ground which had been taken by the 46th Division,' Private Hay, 1st Black Watch, was writing on 16 October describing the Battalion's movement forward to the St Quentin Canal.

> I counted ten disabled tanks and saw many groups of new crosses alongside the road. We marched through Fresnoy-le-Grand to Bohain, a town which had been in German hands from the beginning of the war; here the repatriated country people could be seen coming back to their homes, trundling their few remaining goods in wheelbarrows or on carts; the old "lines" and "areas" which the Battalion knew so well had now been left behind and the feeling that the last days of the war were in sight grew steadily in everyone's mind. The houses and streets were little damaged, and the Battalion found billets in various buildings.[79]

The 6th and 7th Black Watch spent the last months of the war fighting beyond Arras on the Scarpe river at Monchy-le-Preux. On 16 October, in recognition of the 6th Black Watch's actions in late July in the Bois de Corton, known as the Battle of Tardenois, the French Government conferred on it the Croix de Guerre. The General Officer Commanding the French Fifth Army, General Adolphe Guillaumat, described how 'this battalion *d'elite* under the brilliant command of Lieutenant Colonel Francis Rowland Tarleton, has given splendid proof of its dash and fury [*d'un entrain et d'un mordant admirables*] in the course of several hard fought battles between 20th and 30th July 1918. After seven days of furious fighting in spite of exhaustion and heavy losses caused by most intense enemy machine gun fire, it successfully stormed a wood splendidly fortified and stubbornly defended by the enemy.' 'Illumined copies of the French Order of the Day,' were given to all those 'who have served with the Battalion from Mobilisation till the date of the Armistice.'[80]

'It has been a case of here to-day & away to-morrow sort of game & I honestly think that [they] should have supplied us with bikes & motor ones at that in order to allow us to keep in touch with "Jerry"', Private Stratton, 13th Black Watch, was telling his father in early October. Having reached Selle, the Battalion crossed the river on 17 October 'in thick mist and smoke barrage', its objective being Le Cateau. 'Considerable resistance was experienced at railway line and advance was held up for some hours by M.G. fire from station buildings.'[81] Meanwhile, the 1st Black Watch remained engaged in its advanced position beyond the St Quentin Canal. 'At a late hour on the 18th [October] orders came through for an attack on Wassigny, the town where Sir Douglas Haig first established his Headquarters in 1914,' related Private Hay. 'The time of the attack was postponed until several hours after daylight, so that the ground might be examined.' Describing it as 'completely successful', he observed that the French had carried out a 'parallel operation, but did not join hands… till a late hour that night and we did not see them until next forenoon.'[82]

'Great advances along the whole front,' Private Jack was again enthusing on 22 October. 'Can scarcely hear the guns here at Ypres.' Among those killed the following day while attacking 'an enemy position' at Orcq in Belgium was eighteen-year-old Second Lieutenant F. K. Cumming, 14th Black Watch, whose brother 'Brykie' had been killed in Mesopotamia in April 1916; their mother once more received a condolence letter informing her how 'very gallantly' her son had died 'leading his men forward to the attack… he was smiling in death, so it seems reasonable to hope that he died happy in the knowledge of duty well done.' On 1 November 'the enemy put over a few shells,' resulting in the death of the 14th Black Watch's adjutant, Captain R. H. Colthart: 'a great loss' to the Battalion.[83]

The 1st Black Watch's last assault in the 'advance to victory', later known as the Hundred Days Offensive, was crossing the Oise-Sambre Canal on 4 November. 'All night long we heard loud explosions and saw buildings on fire out in front, and it was evident that the enemy was withdrawing to the east of the Oise-Sambre Canal,' noted Hay. 'The whole line of battle kept decreasing in length as the Belgian frontier was approached.' The Battalion returned to rest at Wassigny but barely had the soldiers settled into a barn when a shell came through emitting mustard gas. 'We did not feel any ill effects until a few hours later when our eyes were affected. Only two of us, myself and one other, were so bad that we required attention.'[84]

On 9 November the 13th Black Watch reached Semousies, close to Maubeuge and the Belgian frontier. After meeting initial resistance from German machine-gun fire, the Germans 'suddenly abandoned their position and withdrew'. 'The first day they had pretty stiff opposition but after that it was almost plain sailing,' wrote Private Stratton, who was 'battle surplus' and 'left behind'.[85] 'It was obvious that the Germans were on the way out,' related Captain Badenoch, 'and during the latter days of October and early November they were moving out of a place in the morning which by night we had occupied.'[86] To compound Ludendorff's problems on the ground, severe food shortages had finally taken their toll on morale, leading to strikes and protests throughout Germany. On 3 November German sailors had mutinied at Kiel. Rumours during the preceding days had left the war-weary soldiers on both sides hardly daring to believe the fighting could end. 'On the evening of Thursday, November 7th, I was at a concert in the camp when the Camp Commandant announced that an Armistice with Germany had taken place,' related Private Hay, recuperating from the effects of mustard gas at a convalescent camp in Le Havre. 'But this was contradicted next morning.[87]

Armistice: 'War napoo!'

'Events have marched on the wings of a hurricane growing in force and momentum month by month, week by week, day by day,' Prime Minister Lloyd George at last proclaimed in London on 9 November. 'Dirty day, but severe fighting still going on. More about peace. Fritz applies for armistice,' recorded Private Jack. 'I for one shall never forget the reception we Scots received from the inhabitants,' recalled Corporal Livingstone, describing the 14th Black Watch's entry into Tournai on 10 November. 'It is said that we were the first Scottish Troops to pass through the town during war-time since the time of Wellington and Waterloo, but for the statement I cannot vouch, nevertheless it looked like it. Flags and bunting everywhere, and God only knows where the Belgians had managed to conceal all the stuff during the four years of German occupation. There it was, however. We reached the town just as the Churches were coming out and the sight of the kilts completely captivated the onlookers, especially the ladies, and many a Tommy that morning felt embarrassed at the attentions, osculatory and otherwise, of mademoiselle.'[88]

'Mon Nov. 11th Germans sign armistice. Hooray, War napoo [finished],' Private Jack was at last able to record.[89] Livingstone continued his account:

> A curious stillness crept over the land. No one could fitly describe that eerie sensation, distant guns became silent and all was peace, and passing as we were over the original battle front where the first clash of the war took place between the enemy and the BEF and where now the shell holes were rapidly filling up and become overgrown with weeds and herbage of various kinds, it was ironical that this was the end. A halt was called, and everyone was curiously still, the strangeness of the atmosphere affecting man and beast alike. Just at 11.10 the Brig Major rode down the columns and imparted the glad tidings that hostilities had ceased as from 11 a.m. and an Armistice had been signed. Minutes passed before we realised what the news meant, but the feelings of the men burst

forth in wild cheering which might have been heard in Cupar.[90]

'On the day that actually saw the cessation of hostilities I was on special police duty at the camp entrance,' continued Private Hay. 'In the evening I was allowed out on pass and went down to the town where there was general rejoicing but in a subdued sort of way, and it seemed that the situation had not been quite realised but rather that fighting might commence again in a few days.' 'That it is all finished is more than I can really imagine & yet it is scarcely possible that the Germans would get an armistice unless peace was a certainty,' observed Private Stratton.[91]

'I remember the announcement was received very quietly. I don't even remember a cheer given. We marched into a place called Huissignies and the Belgians were very enthusiastic that night, but it did not last long,' recalled Badenoch, noting that two officers were sent to Perth to bring back the Regimental Colours, B Company being made Colour escort. 'It was quite a ceremony for my Company to march the Colours on to the parade ground and then escort them back later while the remainder of the Battalion stood at "Present Arms".' 'It was a lovely autumn day and it seemed that the sun shone brighter with the glad report,' recalled Sergeant Miller. 'After dinner Jim Phillip, who was now Major second-in-command of the battalion, told me to get the lads out to make a bonfire and we would have a show with all the flares and Very lights we had.'[92]

The 2nd Black Watch was still at Ras el-Lados. Its main preoccupation was now the Spanish 'flu 'raging all over the world', observed Captain Ritchie, who was in hospital when the Armistice was signed. 'These are days of excitement,' POW Private Josiah Ashworth was writing on 12 November. 'Yesterday the paper was eagerly bought and read, for it contained the conditions of the Armistice. They are certainly very stiff and will not allow of Germany taking up hostilities after the termination of the Armistice… but of course the point which affects us "Gefangeners" [prisoners] is our return – to our great joy – to our dear old "Blighty". It seems almost too good to be true.' Remembering those killed at Meteren in July, on 13 November

Second Lieutenant Garnet Alexander Farmer, 8th Black Watch, accompanied the chaplain to place crosses on their graves.[93] 'After more than four years of war,' declared Field Marshal Haig in a Special Order of the Day, 'the enemy has been forced to ask for an armistice and has accepted the terms dictated by the Allies. Hostilities have been suspended and we may look forward to the early conclusion of a just and honourable peace.'[94] Ludendorff, who had been dismissed by Kaiser Wilhelm, fled to Sweden in disguise. Days later the Kaiser left Germany for exile in Holland, never to return. In 1918 a total of 6,607 Black Watch officers and men were recorded as killed, wounded, died of their wounds or were missing. 'War is essentially a sad thing,' concluded Albert Hay, 'and more so than ever before, was war a sad thing in the years 1914 to 1918 because of the terribly inhumane methods adopted by the combatants to maim and kill each other… [and] because of the impression, still remaining, that so many brave men laid down their lives for nothing.'[95]

The battle's won – though won in seas of blood.
The object's gained – a thousand yards of mud.
Yet more than mud; the stage of noble drama,
Where gallant men have proved this awful day
That Britain's glory shall not fade away.
'Retire to rest, lads, weary and worn; you're Scotch,
However thinned, you're still the Old Black Watch.'
'Tis War.[96]

8

Their Name Liveth For Evermore

There is no returning on the road of life;
The frail bridge of Time, on which we tread,
Sinks back into eternity at every step we take.[1]

No wonder we lacked leadership in those post-war years.[2]

Thankful villages

There were no 'thankful villages' in Scotland after the Great War. Every town, village and settlement had lost someone from their midst; the same was true for Northern Ireland. Only a handful of villages in England and Wales could be thankful that their inhabitants had escaped bereavement.[3] Over one million soldiers in the United Kingdom and the British Empire had been killed, were missing or had been taken prisoner during four years of what became known as the Great War. Over two million had been wounded. 50,000 had been commissioned or enlisted in The Black Watch, two-thirds of whom had been wounded; 8,960 were recorded as killed in action or died of their wounds.[4] Only one officer and twenty-nine other ranks served continuously in the 1st Black Watch. Among them was Lance Corporal Frank MacFarlane, who recorded that *Allez-vous en*, the white horse which had pulled the Battalion's mess cart since 1914, came 'through the entire war'. In the 2nd Black Watch six officers and forty-six other ranks served continuously.[5]

'Things were very quiet as the war was over and we were waiting to return to the UK,' observed Captain Ritchie, who, after recovering from Spanish 'flu and enjoying some leave, had returned to the 2nd Black Watch in early 1919. Reflecting on his service, he noted that out of the five new subalterns at Nigg in 1914, three had been killed and one had lost a leg, leaving him as 'the only one surviving relatively unscathed.[6] The death of the Earl and Countess of Strathmore & Kinghorne's fourth son, the Hon. Fergus Bowes-Lyon, meant that Countess Strathmore did not reappear in public until 1923 when her daughter, Lady Elizabeth, married Prince Albert, Duke of York.[7]

Demobilisation took place on a large scale: the 1st Black Watch returned to Britain in April, the 2nd in June, having been absent from Britain since leaving for South Africa in 1899. 'We got a great civic welcome. A very touching finish to the First World War,' continued Ritchie.[8] The 3rd (Special Reserve) Battalion, which had moved to Ireland in November 1917, returned to Scotland in March 1919. The New Armies were disbanded and the Territorial Battalions reduced to cadre. 'I joined up two months after the war started,' commented Miller, 4/5th Black Watch, 'and was home two months after it finished, to get back to the old life again.'[9] Briefly re-established as part of the newly named 'Territorial Army' in 1921, the territorials were again merged as the 4/5th and 6/7th. 'As always, the Territorials withered first in the frost of military penury,' commented Eric Linklater, author of The Black Watch's history published in 1977.[10]

In addition to the four recipients of the Victoria Cross, numerous officers and men were awarded the DSO, Military Cross (MC), Distinguished Conduct Medal (DCM), or Military Medal (MM), as well as being Mentioned in Despatches. Brevet Lieutenant Colonel Victor Fortune, the only officer of the 1st Black Watch who left Britain in 1914 and had survived the war unharmed, was awarded the DSO for 'highly successful command and leadership during active operations' in 1916 and was Mentioned in Despatches four times. Major Sydney Innes was awarded the DSO and bar while commanding the 9th Black Watch. Having lost ten of his 'true' friends in South Africa, he lost another ten 'really good regimental friends' during the Great War.[11]

'For some years after the War, like many, many others who had been there a long time, I woke almost every night in terror from a nightmare of suffocation by gas, or of being trapped by a bombardment from which I ran this way and that, or of fighting a bayonet duel with a gigantic Prussian Guardsman,' related Linton Andrews who resumed his career in journalism. Having been advised by the 'specialists' to forget the war, he burnt nearly all the hundreds of letters he had sent home. 'There were my War diaries. There were souvenirs, maps, battalion orders, German badges, the usual trophies and mementoes. I put them away in a worn-out trunk.' A decade later he retrieved them, compiling a history of his three years with the 4th Black Watch: *Haunting Years*. Of the other 'Fighter Writers' in the 4th Black Watch, Joseph Lee was already well-known for his illustrations and poems, published in *Ballads of Battle* (1916) and *Workaday Warriors* (1917). In addition to publishing the history of the 4th Black Watch in the *Dundee Advertiser*, artist Joseph Gray portrayed the realities of war in his paintings of the Battle of Neuve Chapelle.[12]

On 27 September 1919 at the annual general meeting of The Black Watch Association, Sir John Maxwell, Colonel of the Regiment, suggested reorganising the Association's duties, 'in this its 46th year of its existence', to acknowledge the wartime contribution of the affiliated territorial and volunteer regiments.[13] At another meeting in December it was agreed to observe 5 January as 'Red Hackle Day'. The choice of date arose from the prevailing belief that the Regiment had been granted the right to wear the Red Hackle after the action at Geldermalsen on 5 January 1795. Although the belief was subsequently challenged, the tradition of observing a day of entertainment endured.[14] Following publication of two editions of *The Black Watch Chronicle* in 1913 and 1914, it was proposed to have a quarterly regimental magazine, known as *The Red Hackle*, recording past and present-day activities, the first edition issued in April 1921. For twenty-five years Captain Sammy Watson, formerly with the 7th Black Watch, was the Association's Secretary, retiring in 1946.[15]

Finally the Association suggested instituting 'a Black Watch War Memorial… a building of practical utility rather than a statue or monument' which was to be a 'Holiday Home' primarily for the widows and children of those who had fallen in the war as well as for veterans. 'Fortune favoured them in their quest,' when a large mansion, Dunalistair House, at Broughty Ferry, Dundee was offered 'at a very reasonable price'. Mrs Ethel Shepherd, 'an able administrator, possessed of great charm, tactful and with a grand sense of humour,' served as matron until 1946. In 1923 Lady Strathmore presented a memorial crest to Dunalistair.[16] A year later as part of a tradition to preserve the Regiment's heritage, a collection of Regimental artefacts was 'modestly assembled' in a small ration store at the Queen's Barracks depot in Perth under the auspices of Major Jock Fowler, the only officer who had served in the 1st Black Watch throughout the war.[17]

1919: India, Allahabad

After six months in Aldershot, the 1st Black Watch sailed for India on board the S.S. *Kashmir*. 'When we turned in many of us found a hammock a very uncomfortable thing to sleep in,' related Albert Hay, promoted corporal. 'I finished a restless night by getting some sleep on a table and I continued to make my bed on the table each night throughout the voyage, or on deck on fine nights.' Arriving at Bombay in late September, the soldiers went by train to Allahabad, a staging post on the Grand Trunk Road linking Peshawar to Lahore, Delhi and Dacca [Dhaka]. Remote from the more volatile North-West Frontier and Afghanistan, which, briefly in 1919, engaged Britain in a Third Afghan War, life in India was largely ceremonial. 'The rainy season had just ended when we reached India,' continued Hay, 'and it was still very hot during the day so we had not much work to do, while our parade dress consisted only of a thin khaki shirt with short sleeves, cotton drill shorts, hose-tops, puttees, and boots, or stockings and shoes. We slept for an hour or two in the afternoons and played football and hockey in the evenings.' An hour's 'educational training' formed part of 'the daily programme for NCOs and men in the British Army.'[18] From Allahabad, one company went to Benares (Varanasi), another to Cawnpore (Kanpur), where a memorial church had been built to commemorate the dead of 1857.

On 12 December 1921 the Prince of Wales visited Allahabad during his Royal Tour of India. Although a boycott, inspired by Mohandas K. Gandhi and his movement of non-cooperation to achieve *swaraj* (self-government), caused some embarrassment, *The Red Hackle* down-played the opposition. 'The Indian population of the city, coerced into a *hartal* [strike], abstained from greeting the Prince, but their absence served to emphasise the loyalty of the European residents and the Indians of the Civil Lines and Cantonments.' The Prince gained 'universal applause for his excellent play' during a polo match between his staff and the Allahabad Gymkhana Club. In the cooler weather a Rifle Club was formed but lack of funds prevented them from enjoying 'any shoots until next cold season'. On New Year's Eve 1921 a 'very successful smoker' was held in the Corporals' Mess leaving visitors 'secure in the knowledge of what Hogmanay means to the Scotsman'.[19]

1920: New Frontiers, Germany and Upper Silesia

After leaving Palestine in 1919, the 2nd Black Watch was re-formed, incorporating the 3rd (Special Reserve) Battalion. While it was stationed in Maryhill Barracks, Glasgow, in March 1920, orders were received to proceed to Germany to form part of the Army of Occupation of the Rhineland. There was no repetition of 'The Black Watch Revolt' the previous year, when a draft of about 200 men 'Scottish and for the most part' belonging to The Black Watch had resisted returning to Europe in June 1919 so soon after the end of the war.[20] Billeted in former German army barracks in the Marienburg quarter of Cologne, Lieutenant Colonel Arthur Wauchope again took command. The arrival of wives and families made the provision of billets and the appointment of a Billeting Officer 'a necessity'.[21] After an absence of over ten years Archibald Wavell had rejoined the Battalion. Despite having lost his left eye in the trenches in 1915, he retained a love of football. Captain Ritchie, who had served as adjutant since 1917, witnessed an occasion when, in the absence of sufficient men, Wavell offered to stand in. 'He took off his puttees, put his glass eye in a drawer and went out on to the square.' Having played 'a very fine game', he returned to his desk, put back his glass eye and continued with his work. 'That is the sort of thing that endeared him to the men.'[22]

Under the terms of the Treaty of Versailles, a plebiscite was to be held to determine whether Upper Silesia, which Germany considered an essential part of its territory to meet its obligations regarding reparations, should become part of the newly established Republic of Poland. As a key industrial area, 'Silesia resembled a child whose parents – Poland and Germany – were not overflowing with affection for one another,' remarked Sergeant Erskine. 'Nevertheless, both countries wanted the child for the wealth it could give them.' In early March 1921 the 2nd Black Watch moved to Lublintz (Lubliniec) in Upper Silesia, where it was to form part of the British Silesian Plebiscite Force under Wauchope's command, Archie Bulloch taking command of the Battalion. Although Lublintz afforded 'few, if any, of the necessaries for a gay life,' they soon made it 'lively and habitable with football matches and impromptu concerts.'[23]

The Battalion remained for only a week; severe industrial unrest in Britain had caused 'a depletion in the Army of the Rhine, and our return [to Cologne] was desirable,' continued Erskine.[24] When the plebiscite was held on 20 March over 700,000 votes were cast in favour of Silesia being part of Germany compared with nearly 500,000 in favour of Poland. The result, however, was contested and in late April fighting broke out, which developed into the Third Silesian Uprising. To restore order, the British Upper Silesia Force (UpSi), was dispatched; composed of troops from the Army of the Rhine and reinforcements from Britain, it included the 1st and 2nd Silesian Brigades, the 2nd Black Watch being part of the 1st Silesian Brigade. Billeted on the outskirts of Oppeln and moving to Vossowska, detachments operated throughout Upper Silesia. During protracted negotiations, the soldiers had to keep the peace between opposing factions, their duties combined with sporting events and entertainment. 'A Concert Party (The Red Hackles) has been started in the Battalion and gives a weekly performance. It has brought to light any amount of talent and is rapidly developing into a first-rate company.' Dances were less successful 'owing to the absence of the ladies at Cologne'. In winter the soldiers enjoyed ice-skating, ice-hockey and some cross-country running. At New Year, they 'fed and sang and danced to good purpose.'[25]

Although a general amnesty was proclaimed, no agreement on Upper Silesia's future could be reached, and so the issue was handed to the League of Nations, which decided to award nearly a third of the territory to Poland together with half of its nearly 2 million inhabitants. In April 1922 the 2nd Black Watch moved to Tarnowitz (Tarnowskie Gory), which had been allocated to Poland, the hand-over ceremony taking place on 25 June.[26] As the soldiers realised, not everyone rejoiced at becoming Polish. While in Tarnowitz Sergeant Tom Kempshall had befriended a young girl who wanted to go to Germany. Together with some fellow soldiers, they bought her a train ticket to Breslau. Subsequent events made Kempshall wonder whether they had done the right thing:

I wonder what happened to Anna;
An orphan of Tarnowitz town:
Who got away safely to Breslau
Before the new frontier clamped down…
We have oft wondered since if our actions
(And our motives could not have been higher)
Had helped in a way to take Anna
From the frying-pan into the fire.[27]

1922: India, Quetta, Multan, Chakrata

After three years in Allahabad, in November 1922 the 1st Black Watch moved to Quetta, Baluchistan (Balochistan), where a Staff College had been established in 1907. Travelling by troop train, it took three to four days to cover a distance of over a thousand miles. Quartered first in Kitchener Barracks before moving to Roberts Barracks 'all are pleased to be here, for though it is mighty cold, especially at night, yet it is more or less a home climate, and it may be said that of all stations in India, Quetta most nearly resembles Scotland. This was well brought home to us all last week by a free issue of four inches of snow!' When the weather improved, the soldiers were reminded of 'Spring in the Highlands of God's Own Country.' But, as they soon realised, their posting was in 'a harsh, dusty, stony place – a fit cradle for the people reared in that region.'[28] Sergeant Tom Kempshall, who had transferred from the 2nd to the 1st Black Watch, again expressed his thoughts in verse:

Bitterly cold are the nights there
After the heat of the day;
A land with bare rock as a background;
A land that is dusty and grey…
Baluchistan – vicious and spiteful
And seemingly hostile to life:
The Afridi's the man with the rifle:
The Baluchi's the man with the knife.[29]

In December 1925 the 1st Black Watch moved to Multan in the Punjab, the Battalion's arrival coinciding with the installation of electric lights and fans. As usual, their activities revolved around sport and training. One member of The Black Watch remembered the customary move to the hills for what it revealed about their Commanding Officer, Archie Bulloch who, having briefly commanded the 2nd Black Watch in Upper Silesia, took command in June 1926. 'We had detrained at Pathankote early in the morning and were getting ready for the four days' march ahead of us. Chaos appeared to reign supreme – the regimental cooks were preparing breakfast over open wood fires on the platform; the bullock-carts which were our transport, locked wheels, and the drivers screamed at each other; at least three dogfights were in progress; cocks crowed, chickens squawked, Sergeants swore and my platoon (detailed as baggage-guard) looked fed up. Amidst all of this confusion,' the writer continued, 'I saw the tall, still figure of my new Commanding Officer propping up a pillar on the Station Rest House verandah and reading an Edgar Wallace novel – completely unperturbed but not aloof.'[30]

The 1st Black Watch's next posting in March 1928 was to Chakrata in northern India 'having covered a distance of 420 miles by road since leaving Multan.' During the two-year posting, the warrant officer in charge of education, Frederick George Woolnough, contributed articles on historical and military matters to the English language newspapers as well as stories featuring the fictitious Saman Khan, an egg and poultry merchant in Quetta, published in the *Chronicle* (Delhi).[31]

1922: Britain, peacetime soldiering

In July 1922 the 2nd Black Watch had returned to Britain. Posted to Bordon in east Hampshire, 'one would imagine that barracks, bearing so high sounding a name as "Guadaloupe", would be modern and luxurious. Alas! Such is not the case: the only modern thing is the freedom with which fresh air is admitted to all buildings,' commented *The Red Hackle*.[32] The Battalion's presence coincided with a series of reforms affecting the British Army. In August 1921 Prime Minister Lloyd George had appointed Sir Eric Geddes chairman of a committee on National Expenditure. Among his recommendations was the reduction of defence expenditure. Known as the 'Geddes Axe', numerous officers and men were discharged, the loss of 'many good sportsmen' in The Black Watch 'keenly felt'. Others transferred to the 1st Black Watch in India, the departure of 220 other ranks in September 1922, leaving 'a big hole in our establishment.'[33]

In keeping with the newly fashionable activity of flying, several members of the Battalion 'have lately forsaken Mother Earth for the skies round Farnborough, and all profess to be happier among the clouds than down below. This may be so, but their pea-green faces on return to Barracks rather belies the tale.' Training exercises for the territorial battalions were regularly held, the summer of 1922 favouring the 4/5th with 'excellent weather.' When the 6/7th Battalion's turn came, the summer had become 'the coldest and wettest within the memory of all serving Ranks.' An important calendar event was the King's Review on 19 May 1923 at Aldershot, The Black Watch, 'like most of the regiments', having its two 'strongest' companies on parade.[34]

Soldiering in Britain in the mid-1920s, however, had none of the urgency of the Great War. 'Now that the Army has settled down into the narrow channel of peace-time soldiering, it becomes increasingly difficult to find matter of sufficient interest to put into print. At the moment, the writer would like a war, an earthquake, or a rebellion to help to loosen his pen,' commented the author of the 2nd Black Watch's notes in *The Red Hackle,* irreverently describing a 'typical' roster of duties during brigade training on the Sussex downs: '00.30 hours, Lie down, wrap single blanket round body; 00.31 hours, Wind blows blanket over head; 00.32 hours, Tuck blanket under feet; 00.33 hours, Wind blows blanket off face; 00.34 hours, Rain soaks blanket and face; 00.35 hours, Wind blows blanket clean away; 00.36 hours, Swear, give up trying to sleep and go in search of a hot drink.'[35]

On 21 October 1925 the 2nd Black Watch left Bordon for Fort George, which gave the soldiers their first glimpse 'of real hills and sea'. But, despite its remote location, the Battalion enjoyed 'every modern convenience. Few barracks can speak of cooking done by electricity or have hot water night or day.'[36] In September 1926 the 2nd Black Watch was invited to participate in a combined operation at sea with the Royal Navy, involving the battle cruisers, HMS *Hood* and HMS *Repulse*. The objective was to practise landing in the ship's boats on an open beach, and then advance across about 6 miles of countryside to destroy an 'enemy' wireless station. Although delayed by a heavy sea, the training exercise – the forerunner of what was to become an essential feature of combined naval and military warfare – was judged successful, the experience providing 'a change in our somewhat placid existence.'[37] In the autumn the Battalion provided a company for the Royal Guard at Ballater, thirteen years after the Regiment had last had the honour. After over four years in Fort George, in February 1930 the Battalion moved to Meanee Barracks, Colchester.

Despite a drop in recruitment during the 1920s and a feeling that 'young men of to-day are all out for a change' those with family links still chose commissions in The Black Watch, including, in time, both sons of the 1st Black Watch's current Commanding Officer, Lieutenant Colonel Guy Rowan-Hamilton. Among those commissioned in the early 1930s were four Second Lieutenants (all of whom were later to command a battalion): Neville Blair, who had followed his father's advice and joined the 'Head of all the Regiments'; Bernard Fergusson, whose father, General Sir Charles Fergusson, had commanded the 5th Division, II Corps in 1914; Patrick Campbell-Preston, whose father, Colonel R. C. Campbell-Preston, had commanded the 3rd (Special Reserve) Battalion for thirty-four years; and David Rose. Although Rose's family regiment was The Highland Light Infantry, his father, 'a Brigadier of the old school', had insisted that each of his four sons, known as the 'Wild Roses', join a different regiment 'to avoid any conflict between the call of duty and filial loyalty in time of war.'[38] Second Lieutenant David Walker had wanted to join the Royal Navy: 'the thought of the Navy was heaven. The thought of the Army was hell'. Having failed to gain entry, he went to Sandhurst, obtaining a commission in January 1931 in his 'home' Regiment, The Black Watch: 'If one must be a soldier, that was the kind of soldier for me.' Another 'son' of the Regiment was Second Lieutenant Neill Grant Duff, whose father, Lieutenant Colonel Adrian Grant Duff, was killed at the Battle of the Aisne in September 1914. 'I am having great fun riding everyday,' he informed his sister in October 1931. 'Tomorrow I have got a day's shooting which will be fun.' Although he believed the Army was 'probably better prepared for what it is likely to have to do than it has ever been before,' Grant Duff recognised the challenges of peacetime soldiering. 'The idea of war conditions is entirely foreign to the average man. It is almost impossible to take precautions against imaginary bullets, air-craft, shellfire, gas, etc. But this is what one must endeavour to do, otherwise men will only learn by bitter experience.'[39]

Invariably young officers lived above their means. 'My pay was £12 per month,' related Rose, 'my Mess bill was always a pound or two more. We had to pay "extra messing" which was about eight shillings a day.' To keep him in credit his mother provided an allowance of £250 a year. 'This kept us solvent, with sometimes recourse to a small overdraft.' Looking back, Rose was amused to note that Fergusson and Campbell-Preston had jointly purchased a car for £23 but 'it stood outside the Mess for several weeks, polished but unused, for they hadn't the cash to fill it with petrol. Petrol was one shilling and sixpence a gallon.' As Fergusson explained: 'A Second Lieutenant drew 9s. 10d. a day. Even if you neither smoked nor drank, your mess bill, including your share of entertainment and your subscriptions, gobbled it all up.' Life for other ranks was tougher, the commitment being to enlist for '7 and 5': seven years with an option to serve for five more.[40]

In October 1933 the 2nd Black Watch returned to the familiar quarters of Maryhill Barracks, Glasgow. 'It looked like Barlinnie Prison,' noted Rose. 'There was no central heating, but each Barrack Room had a small fire at each end. Officers had fireplaces in their bedrooms, but we seldom bought a bag of coal, unless we were reading for the Staff College. We just kept our greatcoats on if we were writing a few letters. There were no plugs for electric fires.' One activity in Glasgow was the construction of tennis courts and football pitches as well as the usual route marches, recalled Private Dave Hutton, who had enlisted in 1934, having first wanted to join the Scots Greys because of their scarlet uniforms and grey horses. 'I had to wait six months to get a kilt because I was so thin.'[41] In May the Battalion travelled to London to participate in the Royal Tournament, first held in 1880 as the Grand Military Tournament, when the soldiers gave a 'historical display' of famous incidents in the Regiment's history. The Battalion was back in Scotland in June giving a similar display at the Scottish Military Pageant in Edinburgh, winning 'high praise from the Press and public.' All was not pomp and circumstance. The 2nd Black Watch's presence in Glasgow coincided with the Great Depression. 'Quite apart from the gloom of rain and fog, the people were in despair,' described Rose, '[they] were thin and pale and sour.'[42]

1930: India, Meerut and Barrackpore

By October 1930 the 1st Black Watch had moved to Meerut in Uttar Pradesh. Although conditions were 'far from comfortable,' recalled Captain Ritchie, who had been at the Staff College and rejoined the Battalion in March 1930 as second-in-command to Lieutenant Colonel Alwyn Vesey Holt, 'on the whole the men behaved very well' especially if kept busy during the hot summer months. Throughout the Battalion's time in India, the soldiers found themselves having to act as 'a potential riot squad against internal trouble and external threat. I say *potential* because in my five years there before the war we were never called out to aid the civil power,' observed Lieutenant David Walker, who emphasised that whereas Indians 'worked for us in numerous ways. We did not work for them at all.' In the absence of military operations, they had 'polo to learn, golf of a sort to play, squash, occasional tennis, soccer with the Jocks. It was almost totally a physical life.' Ritchie claimed responsibility for introducing pig-sticking: 'a magnificent sport, and of course, a rather risky one as one had to ride over wild country following the pig with a spear. You just had to put your reins down on the horse's neck and let the horse choose the route and everything else. The country over which one galloped was really very dangerous indeed and one often turned upside down!'[43]

There was also music. Under the guidance of its President, Captain Alan Duncan, a former chorister at St Paul's Cathedral, the Band 'became very good,' related Second Lieutenant Alec Brodie, describing how Duncan ran the Battalion Concerts, 'taking a leading and very comical part himself.' One production was Gilbert and Sullivan's *The Gondoliers*.[44] At Meerut the Battalion was 'fortunate' to have 'as successive companions two British cavalry regiments, the 10th Hussars and the Royal Dragoons, both allies of the foot-slogging Black Watch,' recalled Walker. 'We dined together, drank together at the club, and generally had a good time together. I cannot remember that we had anything to teach them, but they had much to teach an aspiring horseman.'[45]

After four years in Meerut, in October 1934 the 1st Black Watch moved to Barrackpore, near Calcutta (Kolkata), site of the East Indi Company's first military cantonment and 'the only place (excep jungles) of some charm that I knew in the plains of India,' continue Walker. 'The golf course, dotted with big trees, ran along the banks the Hooghly river.' Despite varied activities 'the humdrum routine' their existence remained. While the 'thankless brunt of maintaini discipline' was born by the warrant officers and NCOs, 'the offic were protected, somewhat apart. We could be easy and friendly w everyone. It was a society of trust and some affection, but a tr egalitarian society it was not.' The hill station to which the Batta travelled in summer was Lebong, 1,000 feet below Darjeeling. Lei activities included roller-skating at the Darjeeling Club or vis 'new acquaintances at their tea gardens,' which was like 'living saturated cloud cocoon.'[46] New Year's Day 1935 was spent taking in the traditional Proclamation Parade on the Maidan in Cal Another celebration was George V's Silver Jubilee in May. Re from their horizons was the 'very serious affair' that occurred afterwards when the town of Quetta was destroyed in a devastating earthquake causing an estimated 30–60,000 casualties.[47]

The Royal Highland Regiment

On 11 December 1934 General Sir Archibald Rice Cameron, Colonel of the Regiment, was informed by the War Office that the King 'has been graciously pleased to approve that in future "The Black Watch (Royal Highlanders)" should be designated "The Black Watch (Royal Highland Regiment)".' Recording the news in *The Red Hackle*, the editor emphasised that this was not 'an innovation' but a reversion to the name given by George II when the title 'Royal' was granted in 1758.[48]

The following year a company of the 2nd Black Watch again provided the Royal Guard at Ballater. 'I dined one night with the King,' recorded Lieutenant Rose, describing how the ageing monarch told him to 'tuck into the grouse'. 'He spoke to me just like a father. I was entirely at ease with him. Only a year later I was to slow march behind his coffin with a fine body of NCOs and men at my back.' George V, the Regiment's first Colonel-in-Chief, died on 20 January 1936: 'We slow marched all the way to Paddington Station. His Majesty was on his way to Frogmore… We were in the place of honour, our arms reversed, immediately behind the coffin.' 'What a blow to Empire, one feels it terribly inside one's tummy,' recorded Lieutenant Neville Blair, '30-minute guns from castle, one for each year of reign.' Edward VIII's abdication so that he could marry Wallis Simpson meant that his brother Prince Albert (Bertie) ascended the throne as George VI in December. On 11 May 1937, Queen Elizabeth became the second Colonel-in-Chief of The Black Watch.[49]

The 1st Black Watch left India in December 1936, 'thus completing 17 years service'. Sailing from Bombay, its destination was Khartoum, individual companies posted to Gebeit, 'a small world in itself' near the Red Sea, and Atbara in north-eastern Sudan, 'an asshole of a place, a railway junction with nothing much more than a No.1 and No.2 Club,' according to Second Lieutenant Richard Fleming, one of four subalterns posted from the 2nd Black Watch to the 1st.[50] As it was now an administered colony, following the turbulence in the 19th century, duties were mainly ceremonial. 'We have taken quite kindly to Badminton, but the Golf Course is seldom visited. It is situated on an uninspiring stretch of desert, where a driver and putter are the only effective weapons… Our connection with the great outside world is slight, and news filters through but slowly.'[51]

1937: Palestine, milk and honey

After the collapse of the Ottoman Empire, in 1922 Britain had obtained a 'mandate' from the League of Nations legitimising its administration in Palestine. In accordance with the provisions, and in the spirit of Balfour's 1917 declaration indicating Britain's support for the creation of a Jewish homeland 'it being clearly understood that nothing shall be done which may prejudice the civil and religious rights of existing non-Jewish communities in Palestine', Jews from Europe had begun arriving in Palestine.[52] Their influx led to increasing violence. In 1936 hostilities erupted into a nationwide rebellion and the call for a general strike by the Arab Higher Committee, the main political organisation representing the Arabs, led by the Grand Mufti of Jerusalem, Hajj Amin al-Husayni. To restore order, Prime Minister Stanley Baldwin sent two divisions of the British Army to Palestine. By October a ceasefire had been arranged, assisted by the rulers of Iraq, Saudi Arabia, Transjordan and Yemen. In November, Lord Peel, Chairman of a Royal Commission of Inquiry, visited Palestine. After listening to the testimony of the protagonists, the Peel Commission recommended partitioning Palestine, giving the Jews land in the north, leaving a corridor of access to the Holy City of Jerusalem, and granting the Palestinians land in the south. No workable agreement, however, could be reached.

In September 1937 the 2nd Black Watch was deployed to Palestine, the officers and men 'inoculated and vaccinated and medically examined, and fitted out with strange and exotic clothing.' 'Embarkation leave' meant that some missed the King and Queen's visit to the Battalion. Those present remembered 'bad luck' in the weather 'but Her Majesty braved it'. Since it seemed unlikely that the Colours presented by George V in 1911 at the Delhi Durbar would survive another foreign posting, in September new Colours were presented to a detachment of the Regiment at Balmoral. 'For many of you Foreign Service will be a new experience,' said the Colonel-in-Chief, Queen Elizabeth, mindful that the Battalion's last foreign posting was over 15 years ago. 'These Colours... will be treasured for the fact that they have been received at your Majesty's own hands,' Lieutenant Colonel Alexander McLeod responded.[53]

Two former Black Watch officers were already in the Middle East: General Sir Arthur Wauchope, British High Commissioner in Palestine and Transjordan since 1931, and Major General Sir Archibald Wavell, appointed General Officer Commanding (GOC) British Forces in the Middle East in August.[54] Having advertised their telegraphic address as 'Milk and Honey, Palestine', the officers and men were soon aware of the dissensions in their new environment.

On 26 September the Assistant British District Commissioner of Galilee, Lewis Andrews, accused of supporting Zionism, was murdered in Nazareth. The following day, the Arab Higher Committee was banned and several members arrested, the Mufti escaping to Europe.[55] As a result of the disturbances, the Battalion went first to the military camp in Sarafand. 'The Arabs had captured the old city of Jerusalem and there was a real rumpus going on with about five British battalions fighting to take it back,' explained Sergeant Harold (Nobby) Clark. 'We had to wait until that was over.' On 14 October the Battalion moved to Talavera Barracks in Jerusalem. 'We were exceedingly busy owing to the disturbances which are much in vogue. A little sightseeing has been done and much photography.'[56]

The prevailing discontent made an even greater impression when, on 5 November 1937, two Black Watch privates, Thomas Hutchison and Albert Milton, were shot below the West Wall of the Old City. 'So there was hell,' commented Sergeant Clark. 'Everyone was recalled to barracks, the Black Watch Jocks were screaming "let's get at these people" but we were kept locked up in barracks.' Once the police had located the suspected culprits in Silwan, a cordon was placed around the village. The only available battalion to conduct the search was the 2nd Black Watch. Understanding the mood of the soldiers both Wavell and Lieutenant Colonel McLeod were concerned they might run amok, the firm presence of the Regimental Sergeant Major, Jimmy Findlay, keeping them in check. 'We were all steaming,' Private Dave Hutton recalled, 'but the CO came out and gave us a lecture – to keep calm.'[57]

'I must admit I spent an unhappy night, as I knew I had taken a certain risk,' Wavell later wrote. 'There were a great number of people, both in Palestine and at home, who were only too ready to accuse British troops of atrocities, and I did not want my old regiment involved in what might well be a serious incident.' Lieutenant Bernard Fergusson, the Brigade Intelligence Officer, recorded that of all the major crises which faced Wavell, he never saw him show greater anxiety. 'Very stupidly they fired on us,' commented Sergeant Clark, describing the Battalion's presence in the village. But 'with impeccable discipline' the troops did not respond, an eyewitness remarking: the 'Jocks are good forgivers.'[58] The Palestinian version of events went unrecorded. Strict British censorship ensured that Palestinian (Arabic-language) papers were closed for long periods of time and 'the Palestinian Arabic Press was unable to make critical comment on British military activities in the country after 1936.'[59]

In early 1938 a draft of 200 men including five officers from the 1st Black Watch, which was on its way home after its brief posting in the Sudan, arrived in Jerusalem. Lieutenant Fleming, a former 2nd Black Watch officer, was 'literally welcomed back into the arms of the 73rd. There was a very hidebound atmosphere pertaining to the 42nd... we [in the 73rd] were all young, somewhat wild and certainly carefree. It seemed that every officer was a character in his own right, and that few, if any, could be classified as the typical somewhat dull Wellington/Sandhurst stereotyped infantry officer.' Also in the draft was Wavell's son, twenty-one-year-old Second Lieutenant Archie John Wavell, commissioned into The Black Watch in 1936. 'He was loved by his platoon and got them all doing Shakespearean plays, which in those days was thought to be most peculiar.'[60] Back in Britain, the 1st Black Watch was quartered in Dover Castle, last garrisoned by the Regiment in 1856. '"Dug in" is quite a suitable description, as the whole place is honeycombed with tunnels in which it is possible to wander for hours and eventually get lost.'[61]

With tensions continuing between the Palestinian Arabs and the Jews, the 2nd Black Watch took part in numerous operations 'surrounding villages while the police searched the houses for arms, ammunition and undesirable characters.' They also escorted convoys and participated in 'organised drives over large areas of mountainous country with the aid of donkeys.'[62] 'Signalling in those days was very much a case of the morse code, heliographs and flags,' recalled Fleming. 'There were indeed field telephones with their yards of telephone wire, which had to be laid out from one station to another, so [they were] easy to get entangled and or broken. Although there were wireless sets, they had not yet got down to the level in infantry battalions.'[63]

'It was not a question of being stationed in Jerusalem,' recalled Clark, now sergeant major. 'You were always in a constant state of alert, you would have a company on stand-by, ready to move in 20 minutes, fully equipped which could stay wherever it went for two or three days before needing to be resupplied. We travelled Palestine from Dan to Beersheba from Jaffa to Jerusalem to Jericho.' 'You knew before you went out on patrol there were rules of engagement,' recorded Hutton, 'unless you came under fire but if you saw someone with a weapon you could challenge him.' Throughout the tour Jewish settlers continued to arrive 'in small boats and sometimes larger ships, which they would run aground on the shore, and then leave. The Black Watch would be called down to Haifa or Tel Aviv when this happened but the immigrants had always disappeared,' continued Hutton, wondering if, in sympathy, the soldiers intentionally arrived late.[64] When not on patrol, officers enjoyed 'bathing at Jaffa or playing polo at Sarafand,' with expeditions to the Roman town of Jerash in Transjordan and 'one of the wonders of the world': Petra.[65]

On 1 March 1938 Wauchope retired as High Commissioner for Palestine and Transjordan, the 2nd Black Watch providing a Guard of Honour. Wavell, promoted lieutenant general, returned to England taking up the position of General Officer Commanding-in-Chief, Southern Command. Before leaving he gave 'three most interesting discussions' on the 1917 Palestine campaigns, drawing on his own observations as liaison officer.[66] Soon afterwards, his son, Second Lieutenant Wavell returned home, having been injured when the Battalion's armoured car hit a land mine.[67] In October 'a very lovable human character', Lieutenant Colonel Neil McMicking, took command of the Battalion. An incident, among many, endeared him to the Battalion: one night he was waiting in his car outside the King David Hotel when 'some of his very inebriated young officers stormed out,' related Fleming. 'Seeing what they thought was a taxi [they] piled in, tapping the driver on the head and shouting "Barracks umshi, ya wallah"! Without a word Neil drove them home.'[68]

'Living or dead we are comrades all'

In the aftermath of the Great War, the first task of the Imperial War Graves Commission was to oversee the burial of the millions of dead whose resting place was in 150 cemeteries along the Western Front. Over 300,000 names of those with 'no known grave' were also inscribed on 'Memorials to the Missing' in the French and Belgian countryside. Thousands more were buried with the dedication 'known only to God' inscribed on the headstones. Having seen one such grave in a garden near Armentières in 1916, at whose head was 'a rough cross' inscribed with the words 'An Unknown British Soldier' and in brackets beneath 'of the Black Watch', a former army chaplain, the Reverend David Railton, wrote to the Dean of Westminster in London, suggesting a symbolic grave might be established within the Abbey's precincts. The outcome was the dedication of the 'Tomb of the Unknown Warrior' in Westminster Abbey on 11 November 1920. The Black Watch was represented by an officer and two other ranks.[69] In May 1922 George V made a 'solemn pilgrimage' to Belgium and France. 'A generation of our manhood offered itself without question, and almost without the need of a summons,' he proclaimed at Terlinchtun Cemetery, Boulogne. 'We can truly say that the whole circuit of the earth is girdled with the graves of our dead… in the course of my pilgrimage, I have many times asked myself whether there can be more potent advocates of peace upon Earth than this massed multitude of silent witnesses to the desolation of war.'[70] The King also visited the Tyne Cot Cemetery and Memorial to the Missing on the outskirts of Ypres, where the names of nearly 300 officers and men of The Black Watch are among the 34,000 names inscribed on the walls. A further 200 names are commemorated on the Menin Gate, constructed at the entrance to Ypres and listing 50,000 officers and men who died before 15 August 1917. So too on the Loos Memorial, commemorating over 20,000 officers and men.[71]

Of the 4,000 names on the Memorial to the Missing of the Marne at La Ferté-sous-Jouarre, east of Paris, commemorating those of the British Expeditionary Force killed in the first three months of war, sixty-nine belong to The Black Watch. To commemorate the shared actions of the 1st Black Watch and the 1st Cameron Highlanders at High Wood 'a flat square slab of dark grey granite, with a St Andrew's Cross engraved on either face and the Regimental Crests and appropriate mottoes of the Black Watch and Cameron Highlanders' was erected on the east side of High Wood. Unveiled on 13 July 1924, 'the changes effected by Nature's healing hand, the voluptuous vegetation of France, and the industry of the French peasants and builders rendered the country[side] hardly recognisable.'[72] Further afield, in northern Greece, a red sandstone memorial was unveiled in 1926 at Doiran to those of the British Salonika Force who died in Macedonia and Serbia. The Scottish War Memorial in the grounds of St Andrews Scots School in Olivos, Buenos Aires, lists 522 names, including 10 from The Black Watch.[73]

Of the memorials in Britain one was dedicated at Dundee in May 1925 to the 53 officers and 863 NCOs and men of the 4th Black Watch with the inscription, 'Living or dead we are comrades all'. There is also a memorial tablet at the Royal Military College, Sandhurst.[74] On 14 July 1927 the Prince of Wales opened the Scottish National War Memorial at Edinburgh Castle, where an alcove, known as Black Watch Bay, displays a tablet 'to the memory of the 566 officers and 9459 other ranks who gave their lives for King and country in the Great War.'[75]

The largest memorial, to the 'Missing of the Somme', was the immense triple arch, designed by Sir Edwin Lutyens, near Thiepval, on whose columns several hundred more names of The Black Watch were inscribed with over 70,000 others. Inaugurated by the Prince of Wales on 1 August 1932, a decade after his father had made his solemn pilgrimage, he again emphasised that 'these myriads of names carved in stone… must form no mere Book of the Dead if, in the words which in honest faith we have cut deep and clear, they are to "live for evermore". They must be, and I believe they are, the opening chapter in a new Book of Life – the foundation and guide to a better civilization, from which war, with all the horror which our generation has added to it, shall be banished.'[76]

Seven years later the world was again at war.

All that they had they gave – they gave; and they shall not return.
For these are those that have no grave where any heart may mourn.
…
All that they had they gave – they gave
In sure and single faith.
There can no knowledge reach the grave
To make them grudge their death
Save only if they understood
That, after all was done,
We they redeemed denied their blood
[A]nd mocked the gains it won.[77]

9

1939: Marching Off to War

This country is at war with Germany. You can imagine what a bitter blow it is to me that all my long struggle to win peace has failed.[1]

The Black Watch were marching off to war! We were cheered all the way and there were tears from the womenfolk.[2]

The King's enemies

Britain's declaration of war on 3 September 1939 was the culmination of months of avoidance. It 'all but coincided,' wrote Bernard Fergusson in his history, *The Black Watch and the King's Enemies*, with the 200th anniversary of the signature of 'Letters of Service' to the Regiment's first Colonel, John Lindsay, the Earl of Crawford.[3] As in 1914, Britain's adversary was Germany, now under the dictatorship of Adolf Hitler and the National Socialist (Nazi) Party. In October 1933 Germany had withdrawn from the League of Nations; in 1935 German forces moved into the Ruhr, occupied by French and Belgian troops since 1923 to enforce German payment of reparations. Italy's fascist dictator, Benito Mussolini, had likewise become belligerent, sanctioning the invasion of Ethiopia (Abyssinia) in 1935. The following year the two leaders endorsed a treaty, establishing a Rome–Berlin Axis, which was converted, on 22 May 1939, into a political-military alliance, called the Pact of Friendship and Alliance between Germany and Italy (better known as the Pact of Steel).

Since returning to Britain, the 1st Black Watch had been in Dover Castle 'endeavouring to master the technicalities of modern formations, new weapons and learning to drive the large number of trucks and motor cycles which have been thrust at us. We are finding the change from the spear and the camel to the bren and the truck takes up all our time.'[4] European relationships, however, were continuing to unravel as Hitler's ambition to establish a Third Reich brought him into conflict with his neighbours. In March 1938 the *Anschluss* with Austria was announced. Hitler then turned his attention towards Czechoslovakia. On 15 September a state of national emergency was declared in Britain. 'All ranks were recalled from leave till further notice.' Despite an attempt at appeasement, it soon became evident that the 'peace in our time' secured by Prime Minister Chamberlain by signing the Munich agreement with Hitler, French President Edouard Daladier and Mussolini at the end of September, was temporary. By early October, although the state of emergency 'ceased to exist', the need to prepare for war remained, and 'the pleasant routine of peace-time soldiering' became 'a thing of the past'.[5]

'The equipment was quite pathetic,' commented Lieutenant Colonel C. G. (Steve) Stephen, formerly Royal Fusiliers, who had taken command of the 1st Black Watch in June 1938. 'There were 22 bren guns in the unit, no mortars, no anti-tank guns; anti-tank rifles were represented by gas piping stuck into a piece of wood and carriers by 15-hundredweight trucks carrying blue flags. Despite it all a considerable amount of training took place, to the amusement of the German, Italian, Turkish and Egyptian Military Attachés who could not make out whether we were bluffing or in quite such a parlous condition as was apparent.'[6] In spite of the uncertainty, a planned Black Watch pilgrimage to France and Flanders took place in late August 1939, the 'highlight' being 'an international reunion of old soldiers, Allies and ex-enemies, on the field of Waterloo.' Returning to Brussels, veterans placed wreaths at the foot of the Unknown Soldier's Grave and the British monument, still perhaps hoping another war would be averted. Yet, even as the veterans were visiting the battlefields, on 22 August the code word again placing the British Army in a state of emergency had been received, initiating 'a period of 5 or 6 days of restless waiting', while the Battalion proceeded with 'its mobilisation arrangements.'[7]

When German tanks rolled into Poland on 1 September the British and French governments, as guarantors of Poland's integrity, had no option but to declare war. 'We have a clear conscience, we have done all that any country could do to establish peace,' Chamberlain said on 3 September, addressing the British public on the radio. 'The situation in which no word given by Germany's ruler could be trusted, and no people or country could feel itself safe had become intolerable.' 'The expected news was received that Great Britain was declared to be in a state of war with Germany and 15 minutes later the first air raid warnings gave forth their dismal wail,' recorded Stephen. 'The drill for taking cover was carried out quickly and the All Clear followed shortly after.'[8] On the same day, the National Service (Armed Forces) Act was passed enforcing conscription on all men aged between eighteen and forty-one.

Inevitably there was a sense of *déjà vu*. 'My darling Neill,' Adrian Grant Duff's widow Ursula wrote to their son on 5 September, 'I promise you that as long as I live, I won't forget what we are fighting for & will do my utmost now, & all the time, to keep that steadily in mind & to allow no bitterness towards the innocent in Germany – darling I am very proud of you – I don't mean because you have gone – but chiefly because you take the trouble to see clearly – as far as in you lies – & that is a great deal further than most people will ever get – but I also hope that you will help many others to see as you do – your very loving Mummy.'[9] Also in the 1st Black Watch was Second Lieutenant Angus Rowan-Hamilton, soon to be joined by his brother Second Lieutenant Denys Rowan-Hamilton, whose father had been with Grant Duff when he was killed in 1914.

The Phoney War

As in 1914, the British Expeditionary Force would take up a defensive position alongside the French. Composed of General Headquarters, I, II and III Corps, the BEF was commanded by the former Chief of the Imperial General Staff, General Viscount Gort. The Commander-in-Chief of Allied Forces was the French General, Maurice Gamelin. A veteran of the First World War and credited with modernising the French Army in the 1930s, Gamelin had overseen the completion of the Maginot Line, named after France's former Minister of War, André Maginot, and consisting of a series of bunkers and large forts, known as *ouvrages*. Together with the region's natural defences, including the Ardennes forest, the line was considered impregnable. Once hostilities began, several lines were instituted. The front line, or *Ligne de contact*, was signified by a series of outposts with two main objectives: 'first to prevent the enemy getting information about the Maginot forts and secondly to get early information of any attack in strength.' Behind the *Ligne de contact* was the *Ligne de recueil* (Retreat), 'usually about halfway between the outposts and the Maginot'. Behind the fortress line lay the *Ligne d'arrêt*.[10]

Corresponding with the Maginot Line was the German Siegfried Line. Known in Germany as the *Westwall*, it was originally part of the First World War Hindenburg Line, but had been reconstituted by Hitler in the late 1930s. Composed of thousands of bunkers, tunnels and tank traps, it stretched for over 390 miles from the Netherlands to Switzerland. No fortifications existed between Germany and Belgium, the Belgians being reluctant to identify themselves too closely with the French lest this made them vulnerable to a German attack through the Netherlands. Germany's re-militarisation in 1936 of the Rhineland, occupied by the Allies since 1918, had prompted King Leopold II to proclaim Belgium's neutrality.

On 8 September, as divisions of the French Army were beginning to occupy their defensive positions, the 1st Black Watch marched out of Dover Castle. 'And so its last march out of Dover Castle took place by the same gate and same road as depicted in the famous print of the 42nd carrying out their last route march before embarking for the Crimean war,' commented Stephen. 'The pipes and drums were represented in fact at the head of the unit but the restless farm horses were only represented by a rather dilapidated 15-hundred weight truck, which had some mechanical trouble on the hill outside the Castle.'[11]

After being under canvas a few miles from Dover, on 25 September the soldiers entrained for Aldershot. Following an inspection by Lieutenant General Alan Brooke, II Corps Commander, Stephen was informed that the Battalion in full drill order, with the pipes, drums and military band, would be visited by the King and Queen during which the Regiment's Colonel-in-Chief, Queen Elizabeth, would inspect the Battalion. (As Stephen related, she was told by the King 'this is your regiment, you inspect it'!) The order, however, caused some concern because the spare instruments had already been packed up to be sent to the depot in Scotland and had to be retrieved. The parade, noted Lieutenant Noel Jardine Paterson, 'went off all right except for a slight muddle at the end, when instead of the expected "Order Arms" we got "Left Turn" a command which only the front two companies managed to hear and execute, the remainder doing a somewhat complicated "order arms, turn left, slope arms: all in one"!'[12]

To prevent the soldiers from being identified as Scottish – which might give information to German intelligence regarding British deployments, and consequently fighting qualities – prior to departure they were ordered to wear 'battledress' trousers instead of their kilts. Not everyone was happy. 'But damn it, we *want* to be identified,' Company Sergeant Major 'Big Mac' MacGregor was recorded as saying. As recompense, the King directed 'that a tartan patch of the Black Watch tartan should be worn on the left arm of the battle dress, so, as he said, "to retain a piece of the regimental tartan". He also said that officers would wear metal badges of rank on their battle dress as a privilege.' As a result, 3,000 tartan patches were made and sewn on the left arms one inch below the shoulder strap, the convention later adopted by all Black Watch units.[13]

From mid-September onwards, contingents of the BEF had been arriving in France. 'One special correspondent of a Paris newspaper writes that he met a British officer, a veteran of the last war, who apologised for his rusty French, but added: "All the same, I can still remember one phrase, *On les aura* [We will get them]".'[14] The 1st Black Watch's turn to embark came on 5 October. With nearly two thousand men crammed into the RMS *Mona's Queen*, many had to stand all night, with numerous cases of seasickness. On arrival 'arrangements for the reception of units arriving in Cherbourg appeared to have broken down,' observed Stephen. 'Practically no food could be obtained and our cookers which had been brought to France in an unauthorised manner, came in very handy.'[15]

Travelling overnight by train to Le Mans, a 10-mile march took them to billets at Parcé-sur-Sarthe, from where the adjutant, Lieutenant Berenger Colborne Bradford, known as Ben by his family, Bill by everyone else and never by his given name, wrote home. Adopting a pre-arranged method of communication, he began: 'I am not allowed to say where I am which is a pity.' The inclusion of this sentence was an indication for his parents to search for his location in the sentences which followed, distinguishing marks over certain letters spelling it out. As the war progressed, Bradford continued the practice, which proved 'rather more useful' as his fortunes varied. 'The people in Parcé were extremely pleased to see British troops and did all they could to make the unit comfortable,' recorded Stephen. 'One of the officers went so far as to sing the *Marseillaise* at a small dinner party. This did not go quite with the bang intended, as the inhabitants of Parcé were Royalists.'[16]

Posted to fill the gap in the French line of defence at Lens opposite the Belgian frontier, the BEF spent its first two months in France building defences on the otherwise unfortified frontier. Billeted in the mining town of Hénin Liétard 'apart from a certain amount of excitement among the civilian population at the arrival of British troops, with the obvious hope of making a bit of money, all was peace and quiet,' continued Stephen. 'My French is improving slightly,' Bradford was informing his parents on 16 October. 'Can you send me "Brush up your French"?' Censorship of letters remained a necessary obligation, Jardine Paterson commenting on the quantity of letters written by the soldiers which took up to two hours a day to censor. 'It was not a nice job having to read the letters through and sign them at the bottom and on the envelope but we got used to it in time.'[17]

On 1 November the men practised firing with two-inch mortars 'but only smoke ammunition could be used because there was no H[igh].E[xplosive],… [a] 'state of affairs' which existed throughout the BEF until its withdrawal from France in 1940,' commented Stephen.[18] 'We are at present in comfortable billets,' Lieutenant Grant Duff was writing on 3 November. 'We are in good spirits. We have enough work & recreation to keep us happy. It must be a new experience for nearly all of us, & so far we have had an easy time.' 'During the day we used to wear battledress but in the evening we changed into jacket and trews which was a good thing and much more comfortable,' related Jardine Paterson.[19]

Champagne, Bradford told his family, only cost about 4s 6d a bottle: 'it doesn't cost you much to be out for the evening. In between we get filthy digging trenches in water-logged ground.' News that an assassination attempt on Hitler on 8 November had failed was disappointing. 'I wish that bomb had got Hitler the other day,' Bradford confided in another letter to his parents, referring to the attempt made by the thirty-six-year-old carpenter-cabinet maker Georg Elser, who had placed a time-bomb inside a wooden pillar near where Hitler was to make a speech in Munich.[20]

In preparation for moving across the Belgian frontier 'should the enemy invade Belgium' the soldiers had to practise 'embussing' as well as general training, 'such as digging and wiring by night, and occupying trenches for 24 hours, and then being relieved by other units. I suppose it is a good thing,' Bradford was writing at the end of November, 'though it has been so wet and the ground is so sodden, that I sometimes have me doots. It is very difficult for the men to get clean again with only one pair of boots and one suit [of battle dress].' The soldiers did not do 'anything special' for St Andrews's Day, although the men were let off 'night-digging, and we are going to have a piper in our Mess, and a haggis I believe'.[21]

Living near by in Lens was the 'Lady of Loos', Emilienne Moreau, who had shot two German soldiers while helping the 9th Black Watch's medical officer, Captain Bearn, in 1915. 'Owing to her association' Bradford, accompanied by Captain Campbell-Preston and Lieutenant Jardine Paterson, went to meet her: now in her late thirties and married, she produced the medals she had received 'which she kept hidden in her house'. They also visited Mademoiselle Henriette Hennequet at 'The Black Watch Farm' in Mazingarbe, where the 9th Black Watch had been billeted. 'Mlle Hennequet had a Black Watch Regimental history on her bookshelf,' recorded Stephen, 'and was extremely pleased to see the officers. She was actually able to pick out several 9th Bn officers from a photograph which was shown her.' Groups of men also visited Loos 'and although the battlefield had practically returned to its normal appearance, the various positions were pointed out and a description of the fighting given.'[22]

On 6 December, during a visit by the King, a parade was held at Seclin, near Lille. 'The Brigade detachments were drawn up on either side of the road and H.M. walked slowly along talking to officers as he passed. His inspection produced tremendous enthusiasm, in fact you could hear the cheering from the Bdes he passed some half mile away.' Rumours were already 'afoot' that a move was to be made to the Saar area in Lorraine, bordering German Saarland and scene of a failed French attack against the Siegfried Line in September, the objective being to give the soldiers some 'combat experience'.[23] On 10 December the 1st Black Watch entrained for Metz. Attached to the French 12 Brigade, they were billeted in a French cavalry barracks north of the town and in a nearby hospital.

'The terrain at the Saar front was attractive,' related Campbell-Preston, 'undulating grass country with large woods and small villages, which were evacuated at four hours' notice on the outbreak of war. There was therefore a number of domestic comforts to be found in these villages but they were often spoilt by the squalor and dirt left there by the original French troops and some British units as well.' In mid-December the Battalion moved up to the Maginot Line. 'We have been having bitter weather during our march up and snow and frost,' Bradford wrote soon after their arrival, requesting his parents to send a bottle of *Regesan* Chilblain Liniment. 'The forts themselves were extremely interesting,' observed Stephen, 'having been dug into the features chosen for that purpose, and they were classified from their size and the number of men that occupied them as one, two, three or four class of fort. The large fortresses gave one the impression of being in a London tube station. They were completely underground and no man ever showed his head above ground. All observation and firing was carried out with the aid of periscopes.'[24]

The 1st Black Watch's presence on the Maginot Line coincided with a visit by the Prime Minister, Chamberlain, accompanied by Gamelin on 18 December during which he inspected a French battalion. Stephen, who was present, noted that the soldiers were a 'sorry sight but had been issued with new great coats and steel helmets for the great occasion'. Seeing the defences of the Maginot Line, Chamberlain was encouraged to think that 'neither side could or should attempt to break through the fortified lines'.[25]

'We were up in front of the Maginot Line for over 2 weeks,' Bradford informed his family; '10 days in second line and five in the front line, where we were about 1,000 yards from the Germans. They patrol right through to the second line, and we patrol a bit too. You could see them wandering about, or digging, and also their O.Ps [Observation Posts] but no one seemed to do much about it. Occasionally we shelled each other, but no shells must land near villages by mutual agreement.' The weather remained bitterly cold. Since there was insufficient anti-freeze for the motor transport, they had 'to keep fires going under vehicles which were required to be in instant readiness'.[26]

Christmas Day was 'held very quietly' because of the Battalion's impending move into the *Ligne de Contact* between 26 and 31 December, the occupation of which gave 'the unit a good deal of valuable experience. The majority had been shot over for the first time but they came out of it in good heart, though somewhat thinner than they went in, owing to the great difficulty of getting rations up over the snow bound roads and large distances.' Bradford was anticipating 'a somewhat belated New Year's Day in due course... I hope we shall soon settle down "into winter quarters" like Hannibal as I'm sure it would be better than fighting in this weather.'[27]

By the end of 1939 Hitler had not moved against the Maginot Line and British soldiers found themselves in a period of 'phoney war', or, as described by the First Lord of the Admiralty, Winston Churchill, the 'twilight war.'[28]

Palestine: The Arab rebellion

The 2nd Black Watch heard the news of the declaration of war from a distance, Germany presenting no immediate threat. 'I was on detachment at Allenby Bridge on the Jordan [river] when Britain declared war on Germany and the Second World War began,' recollected Captain David Rose. 'We had been the only battalion in Palestine at the start of the Arab rebellion, with platoons and companies scattered literally from Dan to Beersheba. Now there was a steady build up of Yeomanry and several other regiments.' Before war was declared, the Battalion had been preoccupied keeping the peace between the Arab and Jewish communities. In late July 1939, in a continuing attempt to reduce the flow of weapons among the Arab population, two companies of The Black Watch had been ordered to surround the villages of Halhul and Muckmas near Jerusalem. While A Company went to Muckmas, B Company went to Halhul. The strategy adopted was to enforce 'a strict regime and work the able-bodied men very hard, with restricted rations of food and water,' related Rose, second-in-command, A Company. 'When they became cooperative and started handing in their weapons, the restrictions would be modified.' While the men were interned in a wire compound, old men, women and children were kept separately in a school.[29]

Having established the procedure, A Company's Officer Commanding (OC), Major Lindsay-Orrock-Graham-Scott, returned to Jerusalem leaving Rose in charge. 'At about midnight I was aroused by the Guard Commander. "Mr Rose, there is a terrible carry-on down at the cage, I think you had better come."' On arrival, Rose found the men groaning, shouting and 'convulsed with malarial rigor'. Having ordered water to be distributed, each man was given a blanket. When Rose made his report, Lindsay-Orrock-Graham-Scott was 'furious and red in [the] face. In future I was to obey orders to the letter.' The following day 'in the appalling heat and dust' the search for rifles continued but none was produced. 'The night which followed was a repeat performance, but worse. I again rescinded the orders.' Once more Lindsay-Orrock-Graham-Scott 'blew up, turning bright purple but this time I stood up to him. "When you are not here, I consider that I am in command. Please take me to see the Colonel."' Having seen Lieutenant Colonel Neil McMicking, he was assured that his complaint about the restrictive conditions of the Arab villagers would be reviewed by the Brigade Commander, Brigadier Tidbury. To Rose's dismay, the following day McMicking handed him the same orders, signed by the Brigadier. 'I was horrified – they were entirely unchanged. I folded up the letter and put it in my pocket.'[30]

B Company was undertaking a similar operation at Halhul. 'We surrounded the village, cleared it of inhabitants and searched each house in the normal way. A few decrepit weapons were found,' related Captain Neville Blair. When a member of the brigade staff visited Halhul in the evening, Blair reported that 'the whole op in all its details had gone very successfully. Arrangements to feed the men and women were in hand and working.' One platoon, commanded by Lieutenant Lord Douglas Gordon, 'bivouacked in an empty house on the edge of the village near the school and the wired pen, and the rest of B Coy returned to barracks.' But, realising that the conditions under which the Arabs were held were extremely severe, Blair told McMicking how he 'disliked the op,' suggesting that either he or the second-in-command, Major Adrian (Hammy) Hamilton, should come to Halhul 'to see for themselves. Hammy came and did not like what he saw, but still the op went on.'[31]

The operation, however, was immediately suspended when five Arabs were reported to have drowned after jumping down a well at Halhul. At the subsequent court of enquiry, Blair exonerated Gordon, as commander of the platoon stationed near by, and McMicking cleared Blair. Recalling the event in later life, Blair continued: 'The Brigadier's evidence was horribly twisted and he made no bones about it that five Arabs' deaths required more than a subaltern's [Gordon's] bowler hat. The captain [i.e. Blair] must surrender his.' While the court of enquiry was taking place, the Divisional Commander and Military Governor of Jerusalem, General Sir Richard O'Connor, arrived. 'He was cross that he had not been informed of the Court or of the operation. He failed to understand why the Brig had not told him.' When O'Connor insisted on accepting full responsibility for what had occurred in his area of divisional command, according to Blair, Tidbury said 'that he had misjudged the consequences of his orders'.[32]

The operation in Muckmas was also cancelled. Before leaving Rose assembled the villagers 'and with my Arab and Jewish interpreters beside me, gave them a short talk on the need for cooperation. Then I gave the women the unexpended portion of the day's ration of bread, margarine and potatoes.'[33] But the harsh methods had repercussions. In addition to those who drowned in the well, fifteen Arabs were recorded as having died due to being left out in the sun with insufficient water. There were also claims from the villagers that one of those who drowned at Halhul had been beaten by the soldiers, the events subsequently classified as one of two incidents which 'arguably meet the definition of an atrocity'. Although no civil inquest was held, the High Commissioner for Palestine and Transjordan, Sir Harold MacMichael, agreed that compensation of over £3,000 should be paid to the families in Halhul. Reflecting on the incident in later life, Neville Blair's daughter, Juliet, recalled how her parents used 'this episode in discussions about the occurrence of and responsibility in war for atrocities. They were, quite admirably, trying to show me how complex decisions and responsibility can be. When is an order totally unacceptable and what do you do about it? This is of course an enduring issue.'[34]

Despite the distance of the European war from Palestine, and Mussolini's reluctance to enter the war on the side of his Axis ally, the proximity of Italy's colonial possessions with those of Britain was menacing. Italy controlled the three provinces of Libya (Cyrenaica, Tripolitania and Fezzan) bordering Egypt, while its annexation of Ethiopia threatened British-held Sudan, and, indirectly the Suez

Canal. Somalia, on the Indian Ocean up the coast from Kenya, was an Italian Trust Territory bordering the British Somaliland Protectorate and French Somaliland.

On 25 September the 2nd Black Watch was relieved from its 'anti-rebel operations' and sent from Jerusalem to Beersheba to begin training for 'European warfare.' By mid-October, the Battalion was back in Jerusalem. 'During the phoney war,' commented Lieutenant Richard Fleming, 'nothing very much happened and both the two contestants, Arab and Jew, sought to gain favour with us, the British.'[35]

The depot, territorial battalions and home defence

As in 1914 a tremendous influx of manpower was required to bring the territorial battalions up to strength. The Black Watch depot was immediately expanded under the command of Lieutenant Colonel Alwyn Vesey Holt, who had preceded Stephen in command of the 1st Black Watch. 'Living conditions for the troops were appalling,' observed Lieutenant David Walker who had returned from Canada after serving as ADC to the Governor-General, Lord Tweedsmuir (the well-known author, John Buchan). 'But [they] gradually improved in that long cold winter under Colonel Vesey.'[36] As in Europe, the freezing winter in Britain combined with a serious 'flu epidemic made it difficult to maintain sufficient men on duty.

Both the 4/5th and 6/7th Territorial Battalions were re-formed as separate battalions, the 4th again recruiting in its traditional area of Dundee. The 5th Black Watch had neither regular officers nor NCOs, except the Regimental Sergeant Major.[37] The Battalion's first week of the war was spent in Arbroath 'where we reported to the Drill Hall every morning and went home at night,' recalled Private Edward Meekison, who had joined up in May, believing 'that war with Germany was a distinct possibility.' When they left Arbroath 'the whole town turned out to see us go – it was Saturday and the Black Watch were marching off to war! We were cheered all the way and there were tears from the womenfolk.'[38] The Battalion then spent six months at Alloa on the north bank of the Firth of Forth. Posted to the 9th Highland Division as a training battalion, the 'two greatest enemies were boredom and a sense of frustration'. Those whose families came from industrial towns and ports 'had also to endure the anxiety caused by frequent reports of air raids' upon places where their families lived. There was 'a shortage of instructors and equipment necessary for training.'[39]

On 2 September the 6th Black Watch assembled at Perth. 'Each Company as they arrived were turned out on to the Show Ground, East of the South Inch, to dig slit trenches for occupation in the event of air raids,' observed Captain Brian Madden, who had retired from the Army in 1938 on medical grounds but rejoined the following year, being appointed the Battalion's adjutant.[40] The rest of September was spent equipping and taking part in training exercises, carried out on the South Inch, before moving to Aldershot. 'Having been awarded the Croix de Guerre during the First World War the officers and men wore the flashes on their shoulders with great pride,' related Second Lieutenant Henry McKenzie Johnston, who described the relationship between all ranks 'like a Highland family business. A man's a man for all that. There was very good discipline but the feeling between officers and men was as between friends.'[41]

'Monday was a busy day; all the Drill Halls were collecting men and issuing them with kits,' noted Second Lieutenant David Russell, describing the 7th Black Watch's early days in Kirkcaldy following orders for mobilisation. The Battalion's duties involved detachments on Guard Duty at various places designated as Vulnerable Points (VPs) throughout Fife and Perthshire, including the north and south approaches to the Forth Bridge, which experienced its first air raid on 16 October. By mid-October the detachments at the VPs had been replaced by members of the Local Defence Volunteers, forerunners of the Home Guard, leaving the 7th Black Watch free to train at Kirkcaldy, which mainly entailed 'marching, arms drill, and gas drill'. The greatest endurance test was the cold. 'Coal was not issued in sufficient quantities to keep a place like the Palace Hotel warm, and parades in Service Dress, as was then still worn by officers, with eight or ten inches of snow on the ground were chilly.' On 23 October, the

7th Black Watch moved to Callander in Perthshire. Its operational role was as a Mobile Striking Force, 28 Brigade, which included the 10th and 11th Argyll & Sutherland Highlanders, 9th Highland Division.[42]

Both the 4th and 6th Black Watch were assigned to the 51st Highland Division which, since 1937, was commanded by former Black Watch officer, Major General Victor Fortune. Emulating its First World War composition, the 51st's three brigades were numbered 152, 153 and 154. One aspect of the soldiers' behaviour which Fortune wanted to correct was 'the present custom of the 1939 soldier of whistling at women wherever they see them… it is one of the characteristics of the (present day) soldier as opposed to the 1914 one who was not so well looked after but had better manners.' On 15 September he thanked 'all ranks of the old 51st Highland Division, Territorial Army, for their loyal and devoted service up to the present day' while emphasising that they still had much to learn 'before we take the field – and this must be fully realised by all – but the Highland Division has inherited a tradition from 1918 which is second to none. This will inspire us all both during the coming days of training and finally when we are called upon to prove ourselves on the Field of Battle.'[43]

To meet the growing demand for manpower for home defence, the territorial associations had already asked the local area councils of the Royal British Legion Scotland to send branch delegates to a conference to discuss the best way to raise national defence companies, where all men were 'given to understand that they joined up as privates irrespective of any previous rank.'[44] On 2 November, having been mobilised as the 62nd Group of National Defence Companies of the Territorial Army, the 8th Battalion The Black Watch was formed, headquartered at Kirkcaldy. Since a condition of joining up was to have served in the First World War, the Battalion's members were 'no longer in the first flush of youth,' observed Lieutenant Colonel Baxter, Honorary President of Fife and Kinross Area Council, who took command of the Battalion. The Battalion also included men who were deemed unfit for overseas service and had transferred from other territorial battalions. Medical standards were initially 'a bit too lenient, it being laid down that the loss of any eye, arm or leg did not disqualify men from service.' Equipment was often improvised and 'supplies appeared to be non existent.' It was not until November that the War Office considered it necessary to provide a Quartermaster, the hour bringing 'forth the man and CQMS Mustard was found.'[45]

Similarly, on 11 November 1939 the 61st Group of National Defence Companies, headquartered in Dundee, became the 9th Battalion The Black Watch, commanded by Lieutenant Colonel G. F. Underwood.[46] Following a request from the 12th Battalion (Tyneside Scottish) Durham Light Infantry to be affiliated with a Highland Regiment, on 20 December it became the 1st Battalion The Tyneside Scottish, The Black Watch (RHR) 'thus adopting the Black Watch Tartan and Red Hackle.'[47]

Lean, wind, lean,
For summer has been.
Cry, plover, fly,
For the year must die.[48]

10

1940: A Colossal Military Disaster

When we had a ten-minute halt during these night-marching withdrawals, one had to keep awake oneself in order to be sufficiently alert to wake one's soldiers at the end of the break. It was agony.[1]

The fog of war

After nearly three weeks on the Saar front during one of the coldest winters on record, in early January the 1st Black Watch began the move to Tourcoing, close to the Belgian frontier. Arriving late in the evening of 3 January, they were housed in 'most excellent and centrally placed billets'. When the weather improved the soldiers resumed wiring and digging defensive positions. 'This was undoubtedly the most pleasant time we spent in France although by no stretch of imagination could it be said to have been good training for the fighting which we all supposed would happen in the not far distant future,' related Lieutenant Jardine Paterson.[2] While out on patrol in early February, 'a brush' with some smugglers netted a sack containing 'four bottles of Benedictine, two of rum, two of Pernod and one of brandy.' After this 'valuable haul', commented Lieutenant Colonel Stephen, 'there was a long list of volunteers to carry out these frontier patrols.'[3]

In early March the 1st Black Watch was ordered to exchange places with the 6th Black Watch, 51st Highland Division, which had landed at Le Havre in mid-January, the purpose being to strengthen a purely territorial division with regular troops.[4] The changeover was accomplished on the roadside at Wavrin, south of Lille, the 6th Black Watch, now in the 4th Division, proceeding to Tourcoing to take over the 1st's former billets. 'There were few dry eyes and quite a few tears shed as the sound of bagpipes faded into the distance,' recalled Private George Morrison Daily, 6th Black Watch, a former apprentice ships' joiner. 'We are now in Victor's Division,' commented Bradford. 'It is great fun having all our own kith and kin round us. If only we were all in the kilt, what a fine show we would make.'[5]

Hitler, meanwhile, was maintaining a defensive position in Europe, turning his attention instead to Scandinavia. On 9 April German forces invaded Denmark and Norway, where their mission was swiftly accomplished. In the interim, General Gort had prevailed upon the French High Command to increase the force sent to the Saar from a brigade to a division. Initially, the 5th Division was selected but it was diverted for action in Norway and so the 51st Highland Division was chosen instead. In mid-April the '51st Divisional Group', renamed the Saar Force on 1 May, travelled by train to the Saar, taking over a sector north-east of Metz at Hombourg-Budange. Due to ill-health Stephen had to return home, and on 29 April the Battalion came under the command of Major George (Honey) Honeyman. 'There are rumours about Italy entering the war against us,' Grant Duff was informing his sister on 3 May. 'I don't much like the Italians what ever they do.'[6]

Having already served in the Saar, the 1st Black Watch considered themselves 'old hands'. Campbell-Preston noticed certain changes: 'the outposts had been altered and strengthened and there was a much more active policy of patrolling. Each battalion had a special fighting patrol of about 16 men commanded by a subaltern. They were armed with Tommy guns and grenades and were specially selected and trained for night work.' He also noted that 'about 20 different battalions had been in the line, so many new and redundant signal lines had been laid.' When an inspector from the War Office checked them, 'he told us that the Germans had been tapping our lines and getting information. We used a rough code for all spoken messages but usually in the heat of the moment we forgot it.' Little was known about German positions. 'Their main outpost line was considered to be 3–5 miles to the north. There was therefore a large No Man's Land which the Germans patrolled, their units including local men who knew the countryside, while a story circulated 'that their best patrol commander was the station master from Grindorf station.'[7]

'The first night we were in the trenches I was on barbed-wire patrol,' related Private Alan Brierley, 'which meant checking the wire around the perimeter for breaks.' Having just returned from a morning patrol, the patrol was attacked by German mortars, and several men, including Brierley, received shrapnel wounds. 'Eventually, one of our patrols cleared out the wood they were firing from.' While one of the wounded was being evacuated, the Germans started mortaring again. Observing the stretcher bearers drop their charge and run, Brierley went to help. 'But there was a big lump of shrapnel sticking out of his side and I knew he was a "goner".'[8]

The 6th Black Watch, 4th Division, had moved south of Tourcoing to Mouvaux. 'Rows of pill boxes and barbed wire, not much protection from the Panzers of the Wehrmacht,' commented Private Daily. 'Just drilling, throwing hand grenades about, not loaded of course,' observed Private Jamie Garvie who had succeeded in coming overseas with a glass eye; on falling sick, he went to the medical officer. 'I told him about me having a glass eye. He wouldn't believe me till he asked me to take it out and when I did so he told me off about being in France.'[9]

The battle for France: 'Blood, toil, tears and sweat'

After eight months of 'phoney war', or as the French called it, *drôle de guerre*, Hitler instigated Operation *Fall Gelb* (Case Yellow). Although initially Germany's invasion plan, formulated in 1939 by General Franz Halder, envisaged a straightforward movement through Belgium, pushing Allied forces back to the Somme, it was now proposed to make a two-pronged armoured assault.[10] While Army Group

A would attack through the Ardennes forest, Army Group B would make a diversionary attack through Belgium, luring Allied forces north. Supported by General Heinz Guderian's panzer divisions, already used so effectively in Poland, the reality of the German 'blitzkrieg', as it became known, proved more successful than the original plan. Having occupied Luxembourg on the evening of 9 May, in the early hours of the next day German paratroopers captured the strategically located Eben Emael fort on the Belgian–Dutch border near the Albert Canal. They also landed at The Hague in the Netherlands.

General Gamelin responded by initiating the 'Dyle plan' (Plan D): the advance of the bulk of the French Army to the River Dyle to strengthen Belgian resistance and prevent the Germans from making a 'sickle sweep' into France. 'A struggle to the death has begun between ourselves and Germany,' he announced. 'For all the Allies the watchword must be: Coolness, Vigour and Faith.'[11] 'No one could have been expecting the attack judging from the fact that only the previous afternoon our Divisional Commander had come to say goodbye to us before going home to another appointment and that we had also that afternoon held a conference to decide who was next on the roster for UK leave,' remarked Captain Madden. 'But several times that night, some of us had been woken up by quite unusual air activity overhead and had wondered what was going on. Then we listened in to the early morning news from the BBC on the 10th and heard that the Germans had struck.'[12]

Faced with the disastrous situation in Norway and unable to gain the Labour Party's support if he continued as Prime Minister, Neville Chamberlain resigned. His successor was Winston Churchill who set up a National Coalition government, selecting Clement Attlee, leader of the Labour Party, as Lord Privy Seal. When, on 13 May, the House of Commons was summoned to give the new government a vote of confidence, the audience thrilled to Churchill's rhetoric. 'I have nothing to offer but blood, toil, tears and sweat… You ask, What is our policy? I will say: It is to wage war, by sea, land and air, with all our might and with all the strength that God can give us… You ask,

What is our aim? I can answer in one word: Victory.'[13]

On the continent, the BEF had begun to leave its fortified positions and move north. The 4th Division was in reserve and so the 6th Black Watch's role was, Madden related, 'not very exciting. There was a good deal of map reading and telephone calls but night found us still at Mouvaux with no definite time of moving.' 'Quiet but cold, one or two air raids, ordered to "stand to" at 08.40. Lay all night with equipment on with 4 hand grenades and amm[unition],' noted Private Garvie. On 12 May the 4th Division moved forward. 'Left France at 8.30 in troop carriers, travelled nearly all night, crossed frontier at 10 o'clock.' The local people showered us with flowers and kisses and cheered us on our way. We got as far as the outskirts of Brussels and formed a thin line of resistance,' recorded Private Daily.[14] Two days later, Captain Ian Macrae recorded making their first contact with the Germans 'when five Messerschmitt 110s passed low enough to fire on the second-in-command and the Sergeant Major. Fire was returned by all Anti-Aircraft Bren posts within sight without, however, any visible results.' Already thousands of Belgians were fleeing; Garvie described the 'pitiful sight' of 'children in arms of mothers, old men and women… motor cars full with mattresses on top,' and 'streams' of Belgian soldiers retreating 'with white flags on rifles'.[15]

No sooner had the Allied movement of troops begun, than the next stage of Hitler's *Fall Gelb* began: the surprise advance of German Army Group A, commanded by General Gerd von Rundstedt, through the Ardennes forest. Having crossed the River Meuse at Sedan, wreaking havoc in the French Second and Ninth Armies, Rundstedt benefited from his sudden success by turning northwards to the French coast and putting his forces in position to encircle the Allied armies.

Ordered to hold a bridgehead south of Vilvorde, Madden was struck by the sight of Germans shelling a road in the distance: 'hopelessly unreal in that lovely countryside… There appeared to be complete silence except for the explosion of each shell – the guns were too far away to be heard, and nobody could be seen.' Unable to retrace their steps, the 4th Division's route took them in a more northerly direction to Petegem, which they found had been evacuated 'very hurriedly, cigarette ends had burned themselves out on tables, half empty glasses had been left and even half-finished games of draughts. Some of us went round releasing tame rabbits and canaries and picking up what stores we could carry. It was our first sight of an utterly deserted town,' recorded Madden. They moved on 'over a horribly difficult route,' where the congested roads slowed their progress.[16]

As the Allied troops continued to withdraw, on 17 May the 1st Battalion The Tyneside Scottish, The Black Watch, which had only arrived in France in late April, was ordered forward to protect the BEF's lines of communication. Still only partially trained, it had been intended to assist with airfield construction while undertaking further training. Instead the soldiers found themselves engaged in heavy fighting south of Arras at Ficheux, where ninety-three men were killed on 20 May, others dying later, with hundreds wounded or taken prisoner.[17]

Still hoping to stem the tide of the German advance, on 21 May Gort ordered a series of counter-attacks, including one at Arras, which were to be coordinated with the French First Army. If successful they could join up with the remainder of the French forces, now under the command of seventy-three-year-old General Maxime Weygand who had replaced Gamelin on 18 May. The 6th Black Watch was ordered to meet the threat of German forces on the 4th Division's left. 'Movement began just before dark along a road which was being very heavily shelled and to most of the Battalion this was their first real taste of battle,' recorded Madden. 'Was shelled terribly while in trenches,' noted Private Garvie. 'We were seated in an open truck, when a shell exploded behind us and poor Pat Murphy, a nice lad from Ireland was hit,' recorded Private Daily. 'He was killed instantly, right in front of our eyes. We buried him by the road side, with a marker to identify him.'[18]

Having been ordered 'to press forward to conform with troops on our right', the 6th Black Watch was again subjected to shelling 'as heavy as anything that occurred in after years,' continued Madden, describing events on 23 May. 'Altogether it was a most unpleasant day with a good deal of confusion largely due to the complete lack of communications.' That night the Battalion was again on the move. 'By now we were getting very tired indeed having had practically no sleep for over a week and some men went to sleep while actually marching. It is a horrible feeling and the only remedy is to be dragged along by your fellows.'[19]

In Britain the relative complacency of those on home defence was shattered. 'We were immediately put on the alert and speedily moved under canvas to the Crook of Devon, Perthshire, in ideal summery weather. There we were reinforced by drafts from other Regiments,' recalled Company Quartermaster Sergeant Meekison, 5th Black Watch. 'From May to October sporadic night air raids took place, the enemy's bombing being incredibly bad and no damage done to any of the battalion's posts and happily very little to civilian life or property,' recorded Lieutenant Colonel Baxter, 8th Black Watch.[20] Among new arrivals in France was Private Andrew Meldrum, a former bricklayer at Rosyth Naval base, who was 'aghast' at seeing urinals in the open road near the base camp in Rouen. He was ordered to join the 51st Highland Division, but 'Gerrie's attack by the stukas' prevented contact with either the 1st or 4th Black Watch, so 'the officer in command decided that the best thing to do was to make for the coast.' From St Malo they returned home. 'So much for my first taste of war.'[21]

The road to Dunkirk

As the German Army Groups A and B converged, the Allied forces were being surrounded on three sides, their supply lines severed. Once Boulogne and Calais fell, Gort's only option was to order a withdrawal to the port of Dunkirk. On the morning of 24 May, the 6th Black Watch struggled across the Belgian–French border into Halluin taking up quarters in a carpet factory. 'As soon as we got there the electric current was cut off but not before we had heard on the BBC that the Boche was in Boulogne, or in other words, right round behind us,' commented Madden. 'This was our first news of how badly things were going, as up to that point we had been told that we were only moving back to conform with the Division on our right.' 'Billeted in a sort of rug factory,' Garvie wrote in his diary, later informing his family that this is where he had broken his glass eye.[22] While at Halluin the senior officers heard that their destination was Dunkirk 'but this information was not to be divulged any lower.' After a brief rest, on 26 May, the 6th Black Watch moved into brigade reserve at Roncq.[23] No sooner had they begun to dig in than they were ordered to move north-west to counter the Germans who were moving towards Messines.

The action on 27 May proved to be 'the one really interesting battle of the 3 weeks retreat,' continued Madden. 'We were practically on an island bounded on the north by the Menin–Warneton canal, on the west by the River Deule and on the south by another canalised river. All bridges to the north had been blown, but those at Warneton, Deûlèmont and Quesnoy were open, the latter two being used by the 3rd Division who were moving across our rear… the thing therefore became a race. As the Germans moved westward so we leap-frogged our troops to the left, always hoping to get into position before the Boche made an attempt to cross.' But instead of attempting to cross the canal where the 6th Black Watch was in position, the Germans 'drove straight for the 5th Division' holding the line of the Canal de Ypres, crossing the almost dry canal, close to Warneton. An 'excellent' counter-attack by the 6th Black Watch restored the position.[24] The respite was brief and when the Germans again attacked 'things did not look very happy as there was a good deal of disorganisation.' 'It was a 'terrible ordeal,' noted Private Garvie. 'All regiments mixed through one another.'[25]

In the early hours of 28 May Belgium surrendered. Meanwhile British and French troops continued to withdraw. 'The main body of the Battalion moved off on horribly overloaded trucks, even lying on the roofs and sitting on the wings but soon we came across some spare ones and the run from there to Poperinghe went smoothly,' recorded Madden, confessing that as the adjutant 'leading the column,' he was 'in perpetual fear of taking a wrong turn… asking strange civilians for guidance was a dangerous move.' After Poperinghe 'there was a hold up for hours as another Division (believed to be the 3rd) was also passing through it. If the Boche had known there would have been grave trouble, but he only put in an odd round over Poperinghe that night. Morning of the 29th found us very little further on and still moving two or three abreast in very short bursts. Yet again, no bombing took place on a truly wonderful target.' Reaching the Dunkirk perimeter, the Battalion concentrated at Oost Dunkerque, before moving on to Coxyde.[26]

'At this stage we began to see the abandoned lorries of the BEF,' recalled Captain Macrae. The next rendezvous point was along the Nieuport road. Almost at once the 6th Black Watch was involved in preventing the Germans crossing a bridge in 'almost exactly the area' where the 6th's Commanding Officer, Lieutenant Colonel Archibald Carthew, had served as a subaltern during the First World War.[27] Having 'pushed Gerrie back,' Private Garvie encountered a dead German: 'quite young, no more than 17 or 18. Searched him for souvenir (nothing), got his helmet only to lose it again, made our way back, lost road.' In an unusual encounter Garvie then described being helped by two Germans. 'Digger Dickson got his arm torn on barb[ed] wire; meet two German sentrys; Digger spoke to them in German and they directed us to where we wanted to go.'[28]

'Details of what we were to do on the beaches seemed to show that everything was well organised and we were quietly confident,' continued Madden. 'Alas, for the bitter revelation!' 'Got on beach sometime in the early morning,' continued Garvie. '[We] could see nothing but soldiers by the thousands – [being bombed] and machine gunned… we clustered together and fired up at them and they soon stopped machine gunning us; [instead] they went for the ships and men that were in small boats. Our officer ordered us to form in tens then started to walk from Nieuport a distance of 8 or 9 miles along the sands.' Having reached La Panne along the coast from

Nieuport Bains 'we found very heavy shelling of the town in progress and a complete blockage to all traffic,' recorded Madden. 'We were told to debus, smash up our vehicles as far as possible and get on to the beaches.' On arrival they found that all 'beach organisation' had broken down. 'The Navy were a mile offshore but there appeared to be no way of reaching them. An odd boat or two were found and a few people got off that way but most of us walked some miles along the beach to Bray-Dunes where we sat down for an hour or more in roughly dug trenches. Two horses were found and an endeavour was made by their optimistic riders to swim them out but they didn't see eye to eye with this idea and it had to be abandoned.'[29]

At Bray Dunes the men found that a pier had been constructed on the tops of lorries but the tide was too far out for embarkation. They were then ordered to split up into parties of 40 men and head for Dunkirk. 'Enemy aircraft were overhead all the time with very few of our own fighters about, though those that were put up a very gallant show,' recorded Madden. As they marched, the soldiers sang the traditional regimental song: 'the Gallant Forty-Twa'. 'On the way we passed a number of French troops busily engaged in skinning dead mules presumably for their midday meal and as we got close to Dunkirk the desolation and destruction grew more and more pronounced. Out at sea were several wrecked destroyers, while Dunkirk itself was a grim if fine sight with clouds of black smoke going up from bombed oil tanks.'[30]

'We made our way to the beach where thousands of men from all regiments waited in hope to get away across the Channel,' recorded Private Daily. 'The German planes kept swooping down, strafing us as we dived into the sand dunes to hide from the hail of bullets. It would have been pandemonium in our sector, if it had not been for the efforts of a young British officer who was riding up and down the beach on a large white horse, trying to organise things. I don't know who he was but he should have been awarded a VC. I will never forget seeing this horse and young rider amidst all the chaos.' 'Troops were all over the beaches,' recorded twenty-year-old Private George Grant. 'It was every man for himself to get to the boats.'[31]

'We had been waiting a long, long time, when I happened to look over the side of the pier and spotted a wee fishing vessel at the foot of a metal ladder,' continued Private Daily, who had been queuing for a place on one of the ships. 'I walked back to where my mate was waiting and quietly fetched him back to the metal ladder. I asked the skipper of the boat if he would take us. He would take men but not equipment, so we had to dump all our gear and surplus equipment over the side into the sea. Imagine my heartache as this included my mouth organ, which I used to play, whenever possible to my mates in the platoon. Still, we shimmied down the ladder to the fishing boat which was ready to cast off... As we came on board he gave a blanket each and said "come on boys you will be all right now".'[32]

Less fortunate were those in the ship that Daily and his companion had been waiting to board. When it was hit by dive bombers 'all the men on board were thrown into the water.' Although Daily recalled that their fishing vessel was buzzed by a German plane, it seemed 'that he did not want to waste his ammo on such a small target, not when there were greater ones to be had.' Having fallen asleep during the journey, he awoke in Dover harbour. 'Can anyone imagine the relief, the wonderful feeling that we were safe and sound in our ain country. On the way over we had acquired a French soldier, he was swimming the Channel to safety and the fisherman obliged by bringing him on board.' On landing, ladies from the Women's Volunteer Service (WVS) provided cups of tea and postcards to send home. 'They couldn't do enough for us,' recalled Private Grant. 'At every stop we were fed and feted,' recorded Madden, 'and it really seemed as if we were a victorious Army coming home.' In the confused fighting around Dunkirk, two platoons of C Company had become separated. Reported as missing, their loss elicited a number of condolence letters until it was discovered that they had reached England two days before the main Battalion.[33] After twenty-four hours' leave, the Battalion went to Ryde on the Isle of Wight. 'It was amazing to all meet up again after all that we had been through.'[34]

During the nine-day evacuation, approximately 200,000 British soldiers and nearly 140,000 French had been rescued. All heavy equipment and vehicles had been abandoned, leaving the British Army effectively 'disarmed.' On 4 June, Churchill addressed the House of Commons. Describing events in France and Belgium as 'a colossal military disaster,' he again exhorted Britons to continue the fight. 'We shall fight on the beaches, we shall fight on the landing grounds, we shall fight in the fields and in the streets, we shall fight in the hills; we shall never surrender.'[35]

Surrender at Saint Valéry-en-Caux

Despite Churchill's defiant words, the 51st Highland Division's position was precarious. 'The nightingale has been singing within a few yards of where I have been for the past two days,' Captain Grant Duff had written optimistically to his mother on 23 May. With talk 'of the war being over this year… [in] the belief that the Germans cannot take a knock,' he wondered whether, if the war did end with the collapse of Germany 'what other collapses will that bring in its wake? And what part is Russia going to play in the next 25 years?'[36] Little did they realise that it was they, not the Germans, who would take a 'knock'. Having remained in the Saar, General Fortune had to conform with French movements and withdraw. The Division was then ordered to move to Normandy to assist in pushing back the Germans, who had established bridgeheads at St Valéry-sur-Somme and Abbeville.

Leaving the Verdun area on 26 May, 'after a long march to the station' some units of the 51st Highland Division, including the 1st Black Watch, boarded the train at Varennes, which took a circuitous route via Orleans and Tours to Neufchâtel. 'Two blissful uneventful days in train, moving well south of Paris,' observed Honeyman.[37] Other units had gone in motor transport by road, circumventing Paris to the north, the Division re-united in woods overlooking the River Bresle. 'By then it was raining fairly hard,' recalled Captain Bradford, observing that the 'entire Battalion was working from only five Michelin maps'. Placed under French command, on the night of 29 May the 1st Black Watch was ordered to relieve a French unit near Toeuffles south of Abbeville. 'French troops were huddled about everywhere and very jittery,' continued Honeyman. 'We were lucky not to have been shot at. Found eventually that they had vacated their positions on the high ground overlooking the plain of Abbeville long before the Battalion could possibly arrive, and, at one period, we had no protection in front of us at all. These French troops, in fairness, had had a bad hammering all the way from Belgium… By this time the inhabitants had all fled. Horses, Pigs, Cows etc, were plentiful and cellars were well-stocked. All orchards in blossom and countryside beautiful.'[38]

The following day a company of the 1st Black Watch was ordered to support 'a French attack in a forlorn attempt to push the Germans back across the Somme,' recorded Second Lieutenant Freddy Burnaby-Atkins. 'We got to the forward edge of the copse in sight of the Grand Bois from where we came under heavy fire and were pinned down, unable to cross the open ground between the copse and the big wood. (There was no artillery or friendly aircraft). We remained prone, in that position for at least an hour.' Eventually, Burnaby-Atkins received a message saying that 'the French attack had failed and that my platoon was to withdraw'.[39] By 1 June, the 51st Highland Division was in the front line taking over positions formerly held by the recently formed 4e Division Cuirassée commanded by Brigadier General Charles de Gaulle. Having already made two attacks in an attempt to dislodge the Germans, de Gaulle shared his experiences. 'He told us exactly where the difficulties were and suggested how we should do it,' related Lieutenant Colonel Swinburn, Fortune's Chief of Staff. Although de Gaulle left the front to become Under Secretary of State for National Defence soon afterwards, the future President of France later praised their 'comradeship in arms on the battlefield'.[40]

On 4 June, as Churchill was describing the 'colossal military disaster' which had befallen British and Allied troops at Dunkirk, a renewed attempt was being made to dislodge the Germans from the bridgehead at Abbeville. Bradford and Campbell-Preston, who were both Etonians, joked beforehand that it was doomed to failure since it was taking place on the Fourth of June, traditionally an Eton holiday.[41] Unfortunately the attack did fail, resulting in a heavy defeat for the 4th Seaforth and 5th Gordons in the 51st Highland Division.

When, the following day, the Germans counterattacked, the 7th Argyll & Sutherland Highlanders bore the brunt, leaving Fortune frustrated at the pressure being placed on the Division: 'I have been holding a ridiculous front since 31 May in addition to having a troublesome battlefront in the middle of it,' he informed Lieutenant General James Marshall-Cornwall, the British representative on the Staff of the French Tenth Army, in a letter written at midnight on 5 June. Explaining the 'trying & tiring' time they had experienced on the Saar, he said the men 'are now quite dead beat. I am only too ready to keep a sense of proportion but I owe my soldiers some loyalty, and I quite candidly state it is sheer murder to keep us on a 19 mile front 24 hours longer.' His request was for half of the front they were holding to be taken over by another unit, and for some 'air! in our favour'. While being sympathetic, all Marshall-Cornwall could do was to ask Fortune 'to hang on to the Bresle line at all costs,' which he believed would not be attacked 'for a day or two, anyway.'[42]

The Germans, however, were in full pursuit. With the disintegration of Allied forces at Dunkirk, *Fall Rot* (Case Red), a rapid advance across the Somme, was instigated. 'From then on till 12th June was one series of withdrawals by night over unknown ground or across country roads to positions often with inadequate time for reconnaissance, and an endeavour to stem the tide and get some rest by day,' recorded Honeyman. 'There was a pattern to those nights and days,' observed Captain David Walker, who, after briefly being at the depot at Rouen, had volunteered to join the 1st Black Watch. 'At Dusk, or soon after, the German attack would peter out and our orders to move back would come. After the Somme, the rivers which made our defensive lines were all small and all flowed across our front from right to left towards the sea. So we would march ten miles or so, reaching the inconsiderable stream that was to be our next defence line as dawn was breaking. The Jocks could rest a little, waiting for breakfast.' Having sited their platoon positions and dug slit trenches, they slept 'until the enemy began arriving.' According to Walker, the

Germans facing his part of the line were not 'particularly aggressive. They advanced by day and stopped for a good night's sleep while we withdrew in another bad night's march.'[43]

'The weather was very hot with short nights, usually leaving us very little time in which to do the distance in darkness,' recorded Honeyman. 'Never was there time for any written orders, and it was a case usually for hurried verbal orders at dusk for the move back as soon as it got dark (about 2200).' 'It was our backs that were to the wall,' related Private James Clarke. 'The marching by night was terrible as most of us were walking as if in a trance for lack of sleep.' 'When we had a ten-minute halt during these night-marching withdrawals, one had to keep awake oneself in order to be sufficiently alert to wake one's soldiers at the end of the break. It was agony,' recalled Burnaby-Atkins.[44]

On the evening of 9 June Fortune addressed his brigade commanders at 154 Brigade's headquarters, Arques-la-Bataille, south of Dieppe. With rumours already circulating that their line of retreat had been cut by the advancing Germans, he explained that their only escape was towards Le Havre.[45] Since time was critical, he planned to send an advance force to hold a line of defence around Le Havre through which the remainder of the Division would pass. Named Ark Force and commanded by 154 Brigade's Commander, Brigadier Arthur Stanley-Clarke, it included nearly half the Division; mindful of fighting still to come, all regular battalions, the armoured regiment and most of the anti-tank guns were retained, so while the 4th Black Watch escaped with Ark Force the 1st Black Watch remained.[46]

The following day Fortune gave orders for the evacuation: 'The Navy will probably make an effort to take us off by boat, perhaps tonight, perhaps in two nights. I wish all ranks to realise that this can only be achieved by the full co-operation of everyone. Men may have to walk five or six miles. The utmost discipline must prevail.'[47] But, among their German pursuers, Erwin Rommel's 7th Panzer Division had advanced so rapidly that even Le Havre was no longer an option.[48] By the evening of 10 June, Fortune's last hope was to make for the coastal town of St Valéry-en-Caux, 30 miles east.

With the remnants of the 51st and the dispirited French troops from IX Corps, commanded by General Marcel Ihler, all converging on St Valéry, the scene was chaotic. 'There were hundreds and hundreds of dumped trucks, cars, guns and equipment for some miles,' commented Bradford. 'All the main roads were simply choked with French troops on foot, and refugees, occasionally we passed piles of them dead at the roadside, having been machine-gunned from the air or just rolled aside by tanks,' recorded Private McCready.[49] Fortune's attempts to regulate the influx by ordering the 51st along the coastal road so that the French could approach St Valéry from the south and south-east were ignored.

On 11 June, having established his headquarters in the village of Cailleville, 3 miles from St Valéry-en-Caux, Fortune moved closer to oversee the evacuation. Hemmed in by the approaching Germans, a combination of German aerial attacks and poor visibility sealed the Division's fate. 'St Valéry-en-Caux... was the end for us as word came that the Navy could not get us away,' continued Private Clarke. Only where the Royal Navy could land beach parties was escape now possible. 'Seven of us eventually reached the coast [at Veules-les-Roses],' recalled Lieutenant Sandford. 'We must have climbed over 30 barbed-wire fences and we wriggled over about 4 roads flat on our stomachs... How we were not seen or heard is a miracle.'[50] Private McCready was among those descending the cliffs. 'Someone started making a rope of rifle slings and I joined in. By the time we had it made, it was daylight and the enemy were shelling from both sides. I was fourth man on the rope and it was two-and-a half hours before I got down. The first man to go met his death as the slings snapped, but it was either chance it or get caught so over I went, what a drop; and bullets spattering all over.' Having made it to the bottom 'without mishap', he struggled along the beach, littered with dead, and got onto a boat. 'The ships put up a terrific barrage and brought down two planes. How I got on the ship is still a bit of a dream to me, but get on I did, and soaked to the skin and simply covered with mud.'[51]

Most were not so lucky. 'On the night of June the 11th my company and a strong German force blundered into each other in the darkness, on a road near Veules-Les-Roses,' related Private Robert Mitchelson.

> At a range of 10 yards approx., we fought it out. Tho' for myself, I could not do much, as I was rendered hors-de-combat very early. I was on the flank nearest the Germans & was unlucky to have a hand-grenade explode practically at my feet. The blast completely bowled me over & on getting to my feet, I was shot at close range by a German soldier. Luckily for me, he was a bad shot & secondly, it was a revolver instead of the usual Tommy gun. He got me in the right arm. I considered I had better call it a day, being as I had lost a finger, broken another, badly torn another, had nearly all my teeth blown [out], plus a bullet in the arm & a few shrapnel wounds. So when I went down for the second time, I stayed there for the full count.

When Mitchelson recovered consciousness he found the fighting was over and he was standing 'in a road of dead.'[52]

On the morning of 12 June, 'after a night of rain', the Germans again shelled and mortared British and French positions. 'Gradually tanks encircled the locality and infantry infiltration progressed,' related Honeyman. Eventually their ammunition ran out. Second Lieutenant Alastair Telfer-Smollett was killed 'in a gallant effort' to bring up the guns of the anti-tank platoon. At 'about 09.30' Honeyman recorded receiving orders to capitulate. 'As the final attack was coming in, Colonel Honeyman was standing near me,' related Second Lieutenant Angus Irwin, later awarded the MC for leading 'the Bren gun carriers under his command into the line of fire to rescue their wounded companions.' [He] 'said, I never thought this would happen, certainly not that I would ever have to chuck the can in but I'm afraid we're going to have to give up to save lives because we're completely surrounded. He then sent some runners to give the order to cease fire.'[53] Bradford heard news of the surrender from Major Tom Rennie 'at about 10.00 hrs... Various men were absolutely in tears on getting this order.' Destroying what equipment they could, the British troops were assembled on a hill.[54]

From his Divisional Headquarters, Major General Fortune had been summoned to the town square, where he was met by Rommel and Marshal Ihler, whose capitulation and surrender of the French forces had forestalled any attempt to continue fighting. Having formally accepted Fortune's surrender, Rommel invited him to share a meal but Fortune declined.[55] 'Our arms and equipment were taken off us and most of the men lost their haversacks and everything else, as the Germans ordered them to throw them down as well,' continued Bradford. 'We had no option but to do as ordered,' related Private Clarke. 'We were lined up on the road where we were searched by the Germans. I don't know about the rest of the lads but I felt about 2 feet tall as they helped themselves to anything they fancied.'[56]

One of the twenty fatalities in the 1st Black Watch on 12 June was Captain Neill Grant Duff who had not received the order to cease fighting and 'was leading his Company to a new position to engage the enemy who were threatening to outflank the rest of the Battalion. He was shot from a Tank & killed instantaneously,' Fortune later informed his mother, Ursula. 'The Regiment will always remember with pride that his Father died leading the 42nd in 1914 & that he 26 years later was killed at the head of his Company of the 42nd.'[57] 'We had been through so much together that it doesn't seem right that I am left,' Second Lieutenant David Campbell, who was near by when Grant Duff was hit, told his widow, Barbara.[58]

In the aftermath of the surrender at St Valéry, Churchill described being 'vexed that the French had not allowed our division to retire on Rouen in good time, but had kept it waiting till it could neither reach Havre nor retreat southward.' That the 51st Highland Division remained under French command hindered any possibility of its speedy evacuation. Its presence also signalled to the French that they still had British support, which was undoubtedly Churchill's intention. In hindsight, the 51st Highland Division's loss gave rise to speculation that it had been 'sacrificed' for the greater good of the Allied war effort.[59]

France's defeat was now inevitable. On 14 June German troops reached

Paris, marching triumphantly up the Champs Elysées. On 22 June, in the same railway carriage in the forest of Compiègne where Germany's representatives had agreed to the 1918 armistice, Hitler, accompanied by his senior generals, obtained France's surrender. The country was to be divided into an occupied zone in the north and west and an unoccupied zone (*zone libre*) in the south with its capital at Vichy, administered by eighty-four-year-old Marshal Pétain. Italy, which had entered the war on 10/11 June, had control of a zone in the south-east. Hitler's victory in France and Belgium had cost both sides heavily in lives and equipment. Included in the many ships sunk was the RMS *Mona's Queen*, which had transported the 1st Black Watch to France in October 1939.

The march into captivity

The German conquest of France and Belgium had resulted in the capture of over a million prisoners-of-war, of whom approximately 11,000 belonged to the 51st, mostly taken at Saint Valéry-en-Caux. In addition to Victor Fortune and his GSO2, Major Tom Rennie, captured Black Watch officers included the 1st Black Watch's Commanding Officer, Honeyman, the second-in-command, Major Dundas, the adjutant, Bill Bradford, and all the surviving Company commanders, including Captain Campbell-Preston who had been wounded in the head on 10 June.[60] 'It was all over and the column straggled, passing death in the covered huddle of two Frenchmen behind their anti-tank gun, passing a German tank on the top of which a black-uniformed officer pointed here and there issuing orders with those barking screams so peculiar to Germans,' related Walker. 'I broke my automatic, compass and binoculars so that the Boche shouldn't use them,' commented Bradford.[61]

'Next it was the march to captivity and it was a hard slog especially as you tried to help lads who were wounded,' related Private Clarke. 'Many fell by the wayside and never rose again.' Having passed north of Rouen, they spent the night of 13 June at Formerie. 'The guards at this camp were particularly brutal and unpleasant. When I took some drinking water over to some of our men, who had been marched in about 1400 hrs, and were tired and hot, one of the guards knocked me over with his rifle, and poured away the water in front of the men,' recorded Bradford. 'Naturally,' he continued, 'escape was always in our thoughts, but we had been so tired that we couldn't do anything.' Having agreed a plan with Second Lieutenant Campbell, on 19 June he saw a chance during a halt near the village of Billy-Berclau. At the last minute Campbell changed his mind and Jardine Paterson refused a spur-of-the-moment invitation. 'So I went off alone… I got off the road without being noticed, and into the wood, which was very swampy. I lay down with my mackintosh over my head to keep off the clouds of mosquitoes… I didn't hear the column go off, but after about one and a half hours, I crept back onto the road, and found it clear.'[62]

Bradford was not the only one to escape at that time. Majors Rennie and Mackintosh-Walker (who had been commanding the 4th Camerons) also escaped, twenty-seven-year-old Bradford later confessing that he had refused to go with them because he thought they were too old (at thirty-nine and forty respectively) to get anywhere![63] Taking four weeks to bicycle to Marseilles, under Italian administration, Rennie and Mackintosh-Walker went to the US and British Consuls, who loaned them some money. Having acquired visas for Spain and Portugal, they made it to Lisbon, flying back to Britain on 4 August. Bradford's progress, mostly on foot, was slower. Having reached Marseilles and hearing that Rennie and Mackintosh-Walker had already passed through, he crossed to North Africa. After first attempting to get onto a boat from Morocco, he eventually escaped from Algiers in a fishing boat, reaching Gibraltar in June 1941 and Britain in early July.[64]

Sergeant David Philp and Privates James Clarke and Davie Wilson fell out from the line of march, hiding in a church until the column of prisoners had moved off. Having reached Marseilles, they went their separate ways, Clarke to the Seaman's Mission, where he encountered Reverend Donald Caskie, who became known as the 'Tartan Pimpernel' for helping servicemen of all nationalities escape to Britain, making his way home via Gibraltar.[65] Philp spent most of the war on the run in France, eventually joining the French resistance and hiding out in the hills until meeting up with British forces in 1944. Wilson was recaptured and shot.[66]

Thousands continued to be force-marched through France and Belgium: 'swaying and jostling in endless queues under pouring rain,' recalled Second Lieutenant John Moon. 'A queue for a square inch of mouldy bread, some lukewarm smelly water, another for a little dirty coloured liquid with dabs of yellow grease floating on its surface.'[67] Reaching the Rhine 'we were crammed on to boats to go up river, and to move by cattle truck to a final first stop at Laufen on the left bank of the Salzach, which had been the frontier with Austria,' noted Walker. 'Journey's end for the present' was Oflag VIIC in Bavaria, one of a growing number of *Offizier Lager* in Germany and Poland. Even more numerous Stalags (*Stammlager*) housed NCOs and enlisted men.[68] 'The German Commandant spoke to us on one of our muster parades,' commented Colour Sergeant McKenzie, sent to Stalag XXA at Thorn in Poland 'and informed us that we were not to worry as we would be well looked after and would be home again by Christmas when the war would be over. This was taken as a standing joke by the troops although the Germans actually believed this would come to pass.'[69]

Given the option to work on the land, in factories or down the coal mines, Lance Corporal John Grieve from Fife chose to work in the mine where it was 'warm when it was cold above ground and dry when it was wet above ground.' He kept informed of world news by an illegal radio, which picked up *London Calling* at midnight. Their meagre supplies were supplemented by Red Cross parcels and mail from home every three weeks. 'Washing facilities were very primitive and we were only allowed a very small issue of water which was run into a long wooden trough and here men were expected to wash themselves and keep clean,' related Colour Sergeant McKenzie.[70]

While imprisoned in Oflag VB at Biberach in September 1941 twenty-six men escaped by tunnelling out of the camp including Lieutenants Freddy Burnaby-Atkins and Angus Rowan-Hamilton.

But although Rowan-Hamilton made good his escape, Burnaby-Atkins and another officer were apprehended on the Swiss border. 'You can imagine the terrible anti-climax of being caught so near "home" after we'd lasted out 10 nights,' Burnaby-Atkins informed his mother. 'I'd hoped I might get back to join you in the north for my 21st birthday – but not this time, I'm afraid.'[71] A 'serial escaper' who kept being recaptured was Captain Nigel Thornycroft, Pioneer Battalion, attached to the 51st Highland Division. 'To take his mind off his troubles, he wrote a book on toilet paper with the stub of an illegal pencil, describing… the Norfolk coastline, where he used to shoot geese before the war.'[72] Second Lieutenant John Moon escaped with two other officers but, after six weeks, was recaptured. Another escaper, Private Cameron Walker, was taken in by the Hubert family in Normandy, staying with them throughout the war.[73]

Lieutenant Kenneth Henry Sutherland, whose father had commanded the 2nd Black Watch in 1919, escaped from the 'subterranean' camp of Stalag XXI at Posen in Poland. 'Ken and three companions, with the knowledge of the Polish underground, had themselves bricked-up by their friends into the walls of the fort. The Germans failed to find them and when the coast was clear they emerged to undertake the journey of escape to Sweden.' Having lived off the land for over a year, on 24 September 1942 Sutherland was recaptured. Interrogated by the Gestapo, he was forced to watch the 'unspeakable treatment' of other political prisoners. In 1943 he was sent to Oflag IVC, Colditz Castle, near Freiburg. 'He arrived in a state of shock and malnutrition,' related Burnaby-Atkins, also now in Colditz as were Pat Campbell-Preston and David Walker. Himmler's warning in 1943 that 'under certain circumstances' escaped prisoners would be shot 'put a stop to escaping for almost all of us… So, perhaps ignobly, we stopped trying.'[74]

Wounded prisoners had different opportunities. In April 1941 while in hospital in Paris, Sergeants Frederick Henry Gare and David Adamson Reid used their bedsheets to escape from an upstairs window. Making their way to Tours, their journey on foot took them across the Cher river into Vichy France. Although they had to separate, both eventually made it back to Britain, via Spain and Gibraltar.[75]

Despite the temptation to escape, Major General Fortune spent the rest of the war as a prisoner of war, working to ensure better conditions for the officers and men, one initiative being the 'complete transformation' of the surrounding moat at Oflag IX A/H in Spangenberg near Kassel, to make a rudimentary cricket pitch. Born out of captivity was the 'Reel of the 51st Highland Division', which remains one of the most popular Scottish dances, the idea of having the St Andrew's Cross as part of the formation symbolising the 51st Highland Division and Scotland in adversity.[76]

Somaliland: 'No big butcher's bill'

In April 1940 'owing to the war scare with Italy' the 2nd Black Watch was ordered to move from Palestine to Egypt. 'This was very bad news for us,' related Captain Gerald Barry, one of a draft of Rhodesians who had only just arrived, 'since not only were we tired after our long journey, and had no clean clothing to speak of, to change into, but we particularly wanted to see something of Palestine and Jerusalem.'[77] Stationed at Moascar on the Suez Canal, since Britain was not yet at war with Italy the soldiers were under orders 'not to provoke hostility and I expect they were too,' related Captain David Rose. 'We had to follow all the ships that came through the canal,' recalled Corporal Dave Hutton, 'especially the Italian ones coming from Somalia, with Italian soldiers, in case anyone went over the side and swam ashore.' On one occasion Rose recalled seeing 'a gathering of Jocks on the bank apparently in deep discussion. A big Italian troop ship was approaching. The Jocks all "fell in" in a single rank. The Sergeant or Corporal in charge gave the order. "About Turn – Bum-bags down – Touch your toes – Bum Bags up – About Turn – Fascist Salute – Fall Out." They were obviously delighted with their well thought-out insult and jumped into the water. There was no response from the ship.'[78]

Italy's entry into the war on 10/11 June changed Britain's priorities throughout North Africa and the Middle East. 'There was a scare that a bombing attack by Italy was going to take place,' noted Barry. 'Everyone went rushing to their posts until it was proved to have been a bogus one.'[79] France's capitulation also had an impact on her colonial possessions. At the beginning of July the Battalion was suddenly ordered to embark at Port Suez 'for an unknown destination,' recalled Lieutenant Richard Fleming.[80] Bound for Djibouti, their objective was an abortive attempt to prevent the new Vichy government surrendering French Somaliland to the Italians. Once the Franco-Italian armistice was signed on 25 June, the Battalion was diverted to the British Protectorate of Aden 'to await developments'. Stationed at Crater, in an ancient volcano, 'everyone was ankle deep in lava.'[81]

On 3 August Italian troops, commanded by General Gugliemo Nasi, crossed into the British Somaliland Protectorate defended by a 4,000-strong Somaliforce, under the command of Brigadier A. R. Chater. They were 'a very mixed bag of troops indeed', commented Fleming. 'There were Indians, East Africans, Northern Rhodesians and of course the Somaliland Camel Corps.' By 5 August the Italians had taken the port of Zeilah on the coast and the town of Hargeisa, forcing the defending troops to fall back on Tug Argan in the Assa hills overlooking the main road to Berbera. To bolster the defence the 2nd Black Watch was sent from Aden as Force Reserve. 'The Italians are known to have strong forces, several white Battns, of Blackshirts, also some native Irregulars, some tanks and artillery,' commented Captain Barry. 'They also have complete air superiority and send over bombers and fighters as they please.' As the British position deteriorated, General Wavell, C-in-C Middle East, dispatched Major General Reade Godwin-Austen to Berbera to take over command from Chater.[82] Unable to resist the superior Italian force, on 15 August he was ordered to evacuate the territory, with the 2nd Black Watch fighting a rearguard action.[83]

'The next job for the battalion was to hold the Barkasan Gap, so as to give time for the withdrawal of the troops in front of us,' related

Captain Rose. 'It was a poor prospect. For the next two days we were very busy digging our fighting trenches and cutting thorn bushes to camouflage them. We had no air support, no tanks and only one Bofors gun with a dozen shells… we had no machine guns.'[84] What assistance they did have came from the Royal Navy whose ships in the Gulf of Aden gave supporting fire from the sea.[85] 'We eventually found ourselves holding a 'thin red line of defence in a two mile wide defile with a road running up the centre,' related Fleming. On 17 August they were attacked 'by hoards of Italian troops, many of them black and being driven forward by shambok wielding white officers. How lucky we were that we were able to hold our position.'[86]

'We opened fire and they all ran into each other and the troops scattered for cover and more trucks came up behind. Now everyone was firing,' related Rose. To his horror, some members of the Battalion started withdrawing. 'This was absolutely not allowed without express orders. I got very angry and jumped out of my trench, waving my pistol I shouted to them to turn around and get back into their trenches, fix their bayonets and then come with me.' During the action, Rose was 'bowled over with a shot through my shoulder and went arse-over-tip like a shot rabbit… someone helped me to my feet and we returned to our slit trenches in good order and took a breather, waiting for the next attack.' 'We survived God knows how, but we did,' continued Fleming, commending Rose's 'last recorded bayonet charge' in history, which scattered the opposition although he had virtually run out of ammunition. 'The Fog of War is a well known expression, but how easy it should have been for them to have annihilated us.'[87] 'The Italians seemed to be on the point of breaking through', recorded Sergeant Kavanagh, Somaliland Camel Corps, 'and had they done so it would have been disastrous – when the Black Watch fixed bayonets and went for them.'[88]

While The Black Watch engaged the Italians, under the supervision of Commander Maurice Vernon, RN, the evacuation took place, the difficulties increased by the seasonal Kharif wind which made navigation dangerous. Anticipating that the Italians would send out a recce plane to observe their movements, the coxswains of the various boats had been ordered 'to turn around and head for the shore, so the Italian plane would think we were landing troops and not taking them off,' related Vernon. The order turned out 'to be a good one', the appearance of landing reinforcements enabling the evacuation to continue 'for two nights and two days'.[89]

Having evacuated about 2,500 Eritreans who feared being slaughtered by the Italians, Vernon began evacuating the troops. 'As they came down I put them in the boats and sent them off. The army apparently kept no record whatever', but Vernon noticed that with the exception of three or four wounded, 'there hadn't been any Black Watch'. Having informed Godwin-Austen that The Black Watch had not been evacuated, Vernon was unhappy with Godwin-Austen's description of them as a 'write-off' since the bridge by which they might have escaped had been blown. Commandeering two trucks, and, accompanied by Sub-Lieutenant David Mountbatten, Marquis of Milford Haven, he set out to locate them. 'We followed along the road with no headlamps on because I didn't know where the Itis were or whether they'd overrun The Black Watch and I had no idea of the position.' Having reached the blown bridge which meant the Battalion's transport was stranded on the other side, he loaded up the two trucks, calling for additional lorries for the remainder of the men. Two latecomers, who missed getting on a boat, were later found on board, having swum naked to the ship. 'If you let us have a boat, Sir,' they told Vernon, 'we'll go back and get our clothes and so on – we brought our rifles with us.'[90]

Total casualties amounted to thirty-eight dead, including eight from The Black Watch, among them the 'Chieftain', Piper Henry MacDonald, who had just struck up his pipes during the bayonet charge when he was hit. This compared with nearly 500 dead Italians and about two thousand local tribesmen.[91] The loss of British Somaliland without higher casualties, however, angered Churchill, not so much because of any strategic loss but because of the damage to Britain's prestige. Defending the decision to withdraw for which, as Commander-in-Chief Middle East, he was responsible, Wavell reportedly informed the Prime Minister that 'a big butcher's bill was not necessarily evidence of good tactics'. According to General Sir

John Dill, Chief of the Imperial General Staff, this remark 'roused Churchill to greater anger' than he had ever seen before, straining relations between him and Wavell at a critical time in the war.[92] Unaware of his superiors' altercations, Captain Barry believed that more might have been achieved if the Battalion had not 'sat at Aden for a whole month when it could have been digging trenches and putting up wire in Somaliland.' Yet, 'if nothing else', recollected Fleming, 'that first real action of war brought out for me the value of tradition, *esprit de corps*, or however else one likes to describe one's pride in one's unit. There was no thought of fear or cowardice. One was far more fearful of letting down the tradition of one's regiment.'[93]

The 2nd Black Watch then returned 'to the fleshpots of Cairo… Guard duties for our Jocks but fun for us officers,' remarked Fleming. Taking up quarters in the Citadel, 'there is a good NAAFI, a swimming bath, a cinema and other conveniences for the men,' recorded Barry. Like their predecessors, the soldiers enjoyed visiting the pyramids.[94] Training included instructions 'on swimming in full gear,' recalled Private Meldrum, who, having failed to reach the 51st Highland Division in France, had joined the 2nd Black Watch.[95] Before long the soldiers were on the move again, their destination Crete. 'Out onto the blue Med, one would have thought this was a lovely cruise, just lying around on the Deck getting a little Sun-Tan!! It was only a dream,' related John McVay. 'Two planes welcomed our presence with two *torpedoes*, on we sailed, and arrived safely at Suda Bay.'[96] 'Nothing much to be done at that stage,' related Lieutenant Fleming, 'but we did do quite a lot of digging defensive positions against a possible attack from the sea. The Cretans were so pleased to have us among them and were hospitable almost to a fault.' Having sampled the local wine, known as 'krassi', Second Lieutenant Hamish Stewart-Peter recorded how if a soldier had drunk too much, he would be described as being 'krassied up.'[97] 'Air raids were part of the daily routine but the caves, which were numerous, proved to be good protection,' related Private Meldrum, who found that apart from 'the many vineyards on this lovely island', the scenery reminded him of Scotland.[98]

'Though much is taken, much abides'

After the evacuation of Dunkirk the 1st Black Watch began to re-form: 'It was a privilege and an honour to be one of the officers chosen to form the nucleus of the new "Forty Twa"', remarked Second Lieutenant Douglas Tobler. 'For a week or more there was only the Commanding Officer, the Adjutant, one senior Company Sergeant Major and myself to take care of the drafts arriving daily by rail from all over the country.' Briefly under the command of Lieutenant Colonel Edward Gurdon, on 14 August Lieutenant Colonel Stephen resumed command, having been spared capture due to his earlier evacuation. His son, Lieutenant Michael Stephen, became his adjutant. 'Those gloriously sunny months in Callander were busy ones. Excitement was in the air, a freshness and dedication on the part of all ranks to the countless tasks required of them.'[99]

With the Battle of Britain raging over Britain's skies, the requirements of home defence had changed from guarding against sabotage to defending important locations from aerial attack. Pill boxes and trenches were built along the coastline. From the Crook of Devon, the 5th Black Watch went first to Ladybank in Fife, then Tayport and finally Aberdeen, becoming part of the Aberdeen Mobile Column. The Battalion's first taste of aerial bombardment came on 27 August, when bombs were dropped near the camp but no damage was done. A move to Banchory in October 1940 led to the Battalion's 'longest stay in one location'.[100]

The 6th Black Watch remained in the Isle of Wight, where the soldiers made a 'lasting impression': 'we had an infestation of lice; we all had to be disinfected, and they took everything from us. We were left standing there, alongside the road at Havenstreet Station, without any of our clothes, but with just our rifles and 50 rounds of ammunition! Of course, we were in full view of all the passing traffic, including the buses. There we were, 900 stark naked "Scottish" soldiers defending the Isle of Wight!'[101]

From the end of May, the 7th Black Watch was in the Shetlands while the 8th was in Fife. 'The condition of hostilities in European theatres of war necessitated a continual state of preparedness at all posts,' commented Lieutenant Colonel Baxter. 'From May to October sporadic night air raids took place, the enemy's bombing being incredibly bad and no damage done to any of the battalions posts and happily very little to civilian life or property.' Since various posts, including guard duties, were being taken over by the civil military police, the soldiers had more time to train.[102] During the Battle of Britain the 9th Black Watch had become responsible for the defence of five aerodromes in Scotland in addition to other locations including the Tay Bridge.[103] The 10th Black Watch, formed in June from the 50th Holding Battalion at Broughty Ferry, Dundee, was occupying defensive positions in the north of Scotland.[104]

In August 1940 the 9th Highland Division was renamed the 51st Highland Division, 26 and 27 Brigades becoming 152 and 153 Brigades. The 5th Black Watch was assigned to 153 Brigade, with the 1st and 5/7th Gordon Highlanders, while 152 Brigade was composed of the 2nd and 5th Seaforth Highlanders and the 5th Queen's Own Cameron Highlanders. 28 Brigade was merged with what remained of 154 Brigade which had escaped from France, and included the re-formed 1st Black Watch, the 7th Black Watch and the 7th Argyll & Sutherland Highlanders.[105]

For the next two years, the 51st Highland Division, first under the command of Major General Neil Ritchie and then Major General Douglas Wimberley, remained in Britain on home defence, undertaking monotonous guard duties. 'Every man knew that he would have many arduous campaigns to fight, and was eager to undergo the vigorous, exhausting training that he knew he needed. Yet he did not seem to be getting it as he faced a gale on the Tay Bridge, watched the rain pouring off the Pylons at Douglas Wood, or read a Western romance in the Guard Room at the Montrose Airfield.' But, commented John McGregor, who joined the 5th Black Watch as a second lieutenant in August 1941 and was later to write the Battalion's War History, there were advantages: 'young officers and NCOs learned the first elementary lessons of command, its loneliness and the weight of its responsibilities.'[106]

Despite the disasters of 1940, one military success raised Britain's spirits making Churchill purr 'like six cats'. In early December Wavell had launched Operation Compass, an advance into Italian-held Libya. The outcome was better than Wavell's expectations: the planned raid across the desert turned into a major campaign, the first phase of which had gone like 'clockwork'.[107]

Though much is taken, much abides; and tho'
We are not now that strength which in old days
Moved earth and heaven, that which we are, we are;
One equal temper of heroic hearts
Made weak by time and fate, but strong in will
To strive, to seek, to find and not to yield.[108]

11

1941: All Hell Broke Loose

Junkers planes o'er-shade the azure sky,
Out men come like falling rain,
Some to land in quiet olive groves,
Some to hide in golden grain.[1]

Britain stands alone

General Wavell's campaign in the Western Desert may have signified Britain's first victory in an otherwise disastrous confrontation against the Axis powers, but, with Germany dominating Europe, prospects for Britain appeared bleak. Of the Black Watch battalions, only the 2nd was to see almost continuous action in 1941. Weather permitting, the re-formed 51st Highland Division was undergoing rigorous training in Scotland: 'Snow continued to fall on and off till the 7th February when a thaw set in and training again started, to be stopped again by a heavy snow fall on the night of the 20th February,' related Lieutenant Colonel Stephen, 1st Black Watch.[2] Under Lieutenant Colonel Keir Wedderburn's command, the officers of the 5th Black Watch at Banchory were obliged to rise early; their first task of the day after Reveille was Scottish dancing. 'It may not have produced many graceful dancers but it ensured that every Officer was wide awake early,' observed McGregor.[3] In early January the 7th Black Watch moved to Sumburgh, a small village with an aerodrome on the southern point of the Shetlands. 'There were a tremendous number of invasion scares which required Stand-to at all sorts of times, and patrolling of the beaches and beach defences.'[4]

In March 1941 the 4th Black Watch was sent to join the garrison at Gibraltar, where a state of readiness needed to be maintained in case Hitler pressurised Spain's fascist dictator, General Francisco Franco, to join the Axis. The 6th Black Watch moved from the Isle of Wight to be deployed around Newbury, Stockbridge and Camberley.[5] In August 1941 the 8th and 9th Black Watch were amalgamated as the 8/9th commanded by Lieutenant Colonel Underwood, Lieutenant Colonel Baxter retiring 'on account of age'.[6]

In North Africa, Wavell's offensive against the Italians was progressing along the coastline. After the Italians had been overwhelmed at Sidi Barrani on 10 December 1940, in early January 1941 the fortress of Bardia fell. Then came the surrender of Tobruk on 22 January. Early February saw the fall of Beda Fomm and the surrender of the Italian Tenth Army. In Europe, however, there were pressing concerns, especially in the Balkans. In the event German troops entered Bulgaria, Prime Minister Koryzis of Greece had requested Britain's help. Backed by the Foreign Secretary, Anthony Eden, and the CIGS, Sir John Dill, Churchill decided to send a force from North Africa to provide 'succour to Greece'. This would mean halting any further advance across the Western Desert to Tripoli. After a series of consultations, Wavell agreed to the movement of troops. The decision became controversial when Churchill's enthusiasm cooled.[7] On 7 March Operation Lustre began with the departure from Alexandria of Major General Bernard Freyberg, VC, in command of a force of approximately 58,000 men, composed of British, Australian and New Zealand troops. After less than two months, against superior German forces, the Allies had to withdraw from the Greek mainland. Although the Royal Navy succeeded in evacuating most of the men, the loss of heavy equipment, including tanks, was considerable. Having overrun the Balkans, Hitler turned his attention to Crete while continuing to conduct a bombing campaign against the strategically located British crown colony of Malta. To compound Britain's discomfort, a German force had landed in North Africa.

Crete: Blossoming parachutes

Stationed on Crete since November 1940, as the Allied position was worsening in Greece, the 2nd Black Watch moved first to Maleme and then to the airfield at Heraklion. 'I was detailed to go and make a sketch map of Maleme airstrip,' recalled Captain the Hon. Hew Dalrymple, who had joined the 2nd Black Watch after its return from Somaliland. 'I produced nothing intelligible. A camera would have been more useful.'[8] 'Quite an anxious time, as Greece was starting to topple, thus troops and VIPs were arriving mainly by caiques from the mainland,' related Lieutenant Richard Fleming. 'I had to lend my Ford car in order that the King of Greece could be driven west to Suda Bay.' 'We dug deeper and more blasphemously into the hard chalk, more wire miraculously arrived, and the vineyards were wired,' related Second Lieutenant Hamish Stewart-Peter. 'We prepared our defences which were mainly slit trenches,' recollected Private Andrew Meldrum. 'Further forward we strung out a line of tin cans and trip wire and were now ready and waiting for the action to begin.'[9] On 26 March '*Boom* the "Ities" jumped the Naval (Defence) with high speed boats and torpedoed HMS *York*!' recalled John McVay. 'Her sailing days were over!! Our sunbathing days and "Fools Paradise" had ended!!'[10]

At the end of April Freyberg arrived in Crete to take command of all Allied land forces, known as Creforce. Attempts to reinforce the island included re-forming 14 British Infantry Brigade, commanded by Brigadier B. H. Chappel. 'When I tell you that his staff was inadequate to a degree, you will understand why, since I was made the Brigade Major, i.e. the senior staff officer,' continued Fleming. 'Me, who was only 26, never been to Sandhurst, the staff college, and thus had the minimum of training. Only, as I used to claim, quite a good polo player and perhaps one for the girls.' His assessment of his two brigade intelligence officers illustrated his belief that they were 'a bunch of amateurs': Gordon Hope-Morley was 'charming but not trained' and Paddy Leigh Fermor, 'a mad Irishman, very erudite maybe, but quite wild and, at that stage, quite useless!'[11]

Included in the Brigade was the 2nd Black Watch, commanded by Major Andrew Pitcairn, the 2nd Yorks & Lancs, under the command of another Black Watch officer, Major Alistair (Gilly) Gilroy, and the 1st Welch Regiment. Additional battalions were later assigned including the 2nd/4th Australian Infantry Battalion which had escaped from Greece 'but with virtually no equipment. In order to make them effective', Fleming recalled, 'we had to beg, borrow or steal arms and ammunition from the regular battalions, by no means a popular order.' There were also two Greek Battalions, the 3rd and 7th. 'Brave, wonderful fighters but, like the Aussies, very short of equipment.' The atmosphere was tense: 'The "Blitz" is now supposed to be coming in five days' time, both by air and sea,' observed Captain Gerald Barry.[12]

To assess the situation, on 11 May Wavell sent his acting Director of Operations, Brigadier Eric Dorman-Smith, to Crete. While earlier signals received from Ultra decrypts had reported that the Germans were preparing a combined air and sea attack on Crete, the latest intelligence indicated that countering the sea attack would be of secondary importance. 'The entire plan is based on the capture of the aerodromes,' observed Freyberg's Brigadier General Staff, Keith Stewart. 'If the aerodromes hold out, as they will, the whole plan will fail.' This meant that it was necessary to redeploy, especially around Maleme on the west of the island. But no redeployment took place, because, without an alternative source, Ultra intelligence could not be exploited.[13]

On 20 May the Germans attacked. Fifty-one-year-old General Kurt Student, commander of *XI Fliegerkorps*, led the operation, codenamed Operation Mercury. 'The blossoming of the parachutes in the sky was the most beautiful sight,' recalled Lieutenant James Donaldson. 'There was a momentary hush and then I felt a tremendous exhilaration as the whole aerodrome opened up on the descending Germans.' 'We were surprised when we saw what we had been waiting for,' related Private Meldrum. 'Down came the German paratroopers. The air was thick with them and like sitting ducks, they were slaughtered.' 'They came in screaming', recalled Corporal

Dave Hutton describing the arrival of German Stuka bombers. 'Dive bombing all over the place.' Then came the large Junker troop carriers. 'They came in singles and doubles which provided a good target for us and we let them have it.' '"All hell broke loose" from our trenches and holes, everything was spitting death!!' related McVay. 'It was slaughter, they didn't have a chance in hell.'[14]

'On the afternoon of the 20th, I received a warning at 2 p.m. to stand to in battle positions,' related Barry. 'Shortly afterwards, hordes of bombers and Messerschmitts arrived, and proceeded to bomb and machine-gun the aerodrome and all round very heavily for the next two hours… At about 5 p.m. a lot of German troop carriers arrived and proceeded to empty parachutists all round, among us, behind us, and in the valley below us. It was an extraordinary scene. All of a sudden there were about two hundred men dangling on their ropes, descending from a height of about 300 feet all round us, and masses more up the valley.'[15]

'Our troops had a field day and the German losses were terrific,' observed Fleming. 'However, many parachutists were dropped outside our perimeter and were thus able to reform into fighting units.' 'The paras landed everywhere – in the sea, where they drowned; on the beach; in front of them, behind them,' continued Hutton. 'That first day was a massacre for the Germans. The Black Watch buried 1,300 men during the night.' 'The Germans were very brave in the way they tried to collect their gear and shoot back at us,' continued Barry.[16]

'I was in a large cave helping the Company cook make the evening meal,' recalled Piper George Ogilvie. 'It was put into containers and put on our backs & I headed the cooks etc. playing "Brose & Butter" to a meeting place so the troops could get their meal. At the same time I got a good telling off by the CSM for letting the Germans [know] where we was. The pipes stayed silent until I played "Lochaber No More" to bury six of the company that had been killed.'[17]

'Today has been a hard one.' Freyberg cabled Wavell. 'We have been hard-pressed. So far, I believe, we hold aerodromes at Retimo, Heraklion, and Maleme, and the two harbours.' But, he continued, it would be wrong 'to paint optimistic picture… Scale of air attacks upon troops has been severe.'[18] And as events later revealed, Freyberg's inability to mount an effective counter-attack enabled the Germans to retain their foothold at Maleme airport. 'After dark, we could hear all the Germans who had escaped calling to each other all round us in the darkness, just like a dispersed covey of partridges after a day's shoot!' recorded Barry. 'We had to be very careful, not knowing how many there were, or exactly where they were.'[19]

During the night the 2nd Black Watch moved its position inland to the foot of two hills behind the airstrip at Heraklion, known as the Charlies. The ground was too hard to make trenches, but Hutton succeeded in cutting down some olive trees to make a parapet for protection. The following day more paratroopers arrived. '[They] were landing everywhere all round us even in the sea. The sand was covered with dead bodies.' Unable to communicate with Company headquarters, Hutton realised it was 'every man for himself'. Around midday he was wounded in the arm and knee with shrapnel penetrating the side of his body. Loaded onto an ambulance, he thought he would 'live another day'. Lieutenant Donaldson had a near miss. 'Seven bombers came over in close formation and simultaneously each dropped 10 bombs. I saw that the line being taken by the planes was going to pass immediately overhead and it was a most unpleasant few minutes while the bombs came down. I felt that with 70 bombs altogether one was sure to hit but they all missed.'[20]

'These two days were frightfully tiring, and I imagine the Germans must have been very tired too,' commented Barry. 'During the day the valley would ring to the volleys of rifle and machine-gun fire sent hurtling across it by both sides.' After dark the firing ceased. 'It would have inconvenienced both sides equally. For this was the time when whatever had to be done was done, when the casualties were evacuated, the dead were buried, the rations and ammunition distributed.' Barry also heard the 'cries of the defeated' which sounded 'weird and unearthly in the stillness of the night; many of them remained unanswered. Eventually they ceased altogether and silence reigned.'[21] Among the Germans killed were three brothers: descendants of the renowned General Gebhard Leberecht von Blücher whose forces had bolstered those of Wellington at Waterloo in 1815.[22] Dalrymple got his wish for a camera when a captured German handed him a Zeiss Contacts Mark 2 'which at the time was an extremely expensive, complicated focusing mechanism… I carried it through the rest of the war.'[23]

The next few days were 'comparatively' calm, but the Germans were continuing to land troops and equipment. 'So the battle hangs in the balance at the moment, but I do hope they will send us reinforcements from Egypt, for we cannot go on indefinitely without being relieved,' Barry confided to his diary. 'There is no air support here now, and after five days of this, we are indescribably dirty, bearded and very tired.' By 27 May, he was 'still in the same slit trench, after seven days of invasion. The life we lead is terribly tiring. We are compelled to sit in this narrow, cooped up place for sixteen hours a day… I have not averaged three hours sleep for the last week.' The following day was: 'a horrid day! During the morning we watched seventy troop carriers arrive and deposit at least two Battalions over what we call Table Mountain, the flat topped hill east of us. It was an extraordinary sight – plane after plane came in, and dropped their loads in succession, and I suppose there were as many as a hundred men dangling in the air at the same time as each lot arrived.' Still the Germans continued their onslaught. 'After lunch, a real "blitz" started—bombers came over and dropped bombs chiefly round the aerodrome, and finally a fleet of Messerschmitts came round screaming just over our heads, and machine gunned our own positions, as well as dropping bombs. It was, quite frankly nerve-wracking!'[24]

Twice, the Battalion intercepted German supplies. Major Dick-Cunyngham, whose uncle had been in command of the 10th Black Watch in the First World War, took possession of a motor cycle and side-car, while the medical officer, Captain 'Hoot' Gibson, received medical supplies and surgical instruments 'the like of which, he declared, he had never seen since joining the Army.' There were also acts of bravery, such as Lieutenant Stewart-Peter picking up an unexploded bomb on the airfield at Heraklion 'and carrying it to the cliff where he dropped it into the sea.'[25]

Lieutenant Fleming had been sent to the south of the island to meet up with the 2nd Argyll & Sutherland Highlanders, who were arriving to reinforce 14 Brigade. 'We set off in the dark in a southern-westerly direction.' The 'we' consisted of his batman, Eddie Welsh, and a corporal from the Rhodesian platoon, Spiro Divaris, who, being of Greek extraction, was to act as interpreter. Having found their way there, assisted by three Cretan shepherds as guides, the return journey without the Cretans was 'a nightmare… messages kept coming up to us to go slower. The darkness was soon upon us and we had no knowledge of the very rough terrain.' The only 'saving grace' was that Heraklion had been bombed 'unmercifully and so was a heaven-sent landmark to give us somewhere to aim, being a blaze of light.'[26]

After only a week, as the British public rejoiced at the sinking of the German battleship, *Bismarck*, on 27 May, following the loss of HMS *Hood*, General Wavell was reporting to Churchill that Crete was no longer 'tenable' and that their only option was evacuation. 'Alerting the various units was not an easy task,' recalled Fleming, 'but I did manage to contact by telephone all the many units except my own battalion, The Black Watch who were positioned on the extreme eastern perimeter [and] for some reason were out of contact. We had by then started packing up the Brigade HQ, burning all [the documents] so that nothing was left, and sending personnel down to the docks.'[27]

'The decision to leave Crete is a very distressing one,' observed Barry, 'but apparently things have gone very badly at Suda and Maleme which are now untenable… in my haste I forgot to pack my camera, which is very annoying. But I took in my haversack some of my family photographs, and my tartan trews and glengarry, which the Bosche shall not get, my War diary (this book) and small sketches I managed to save.' One act of sabotage before leaving was to pour petrol into jars of rum. 'After dark all my extra ammunition – pinched and collected from here and there, was dumped in the sea,' related Stewart-Peter.[28] 'We have had a pretty tough time,' Freyberg informed Wavell. 'The troops were not beaten by ordinary conditions, but the great aerial concentration against us. The bombing is what has beaten us, the strafing having turned us out of position after position… We were handicapped by lack of transport, communications and lack of staff… I am sorry Crete could not be held. It was certainly not the fault of the troops.'[29]

Two cruisers, HMS *Dido* and *Orion*, accompanied by several destroyers, had been taking the men on board. 'Down at the docks there was a long mole out into the harbour, with the destroyer [HMS *Imperial*] alongside,' continued Fleming. 'Trust me, but I managed to trip on a hawser or something and spread eagled myself, everything I was carrying going to the four winds.' Once on board, Fleming was shown to a wardroom, 'where I literally passed out.' But not for long: his next recollection was being woken by an apologetic naval officer, informing him that *Imperial* had been hit and they would have to abandon ship. 'Up we went to find another destroyer alongside us. We scrambled across to her. This was HMS *Hotspur* who had been ordered to wait and collect all aboard the *Imperial*. How lucky we were.'[30] When the Royal Navy could no longer operate north of the island, the troops had to be evacuated from the south, the soldiers having to cross the mountains to Sphakia. 'It was during the cover of darkness that we crept through the vineyard in single file,' recalled Meldrum. 'We had a few near misses on the road to safety.'[31]

As the convoy of ships made for Egypt, it was subjected to heavy aerial attack. 'They were determined to get us,' recorded Stewart-Peter on board HMS *Orion*. 'Every available Bren went on deck, but in spite of all our armaments, three direct hits were scored. One hit the sick bay, just as it was full of casualties from the first hit.' At this point 'the wardroom then began to fill with bandaged figures, like tottering Klu Klux clansmen… Sometimes only eyes and swollen mouths were showing, the effects of burn and bomb-blast; many were temporarily paralysed in one or more limbs. Part of the ship was flooded and all men possible were moved over to the port side, which trimmed her sufficiently to get to port… It was only when we got about 80 miles from Alex[andria] that we were left in peace, and by then our supply of ammunition was, I believe, very short.'[32] 'I was lucky on board the *Orion*', recalled Donaldson, 'being in a part of the ship that was not directly affected by the bombing, although well-aware that it was going on… The vibration during each raid was such that I wondered how the ship held together and did not open up.'[33] The ship was so badly damaged that she had to be towed into harbour. HMS *Dido* had been similarly attacked, with a direct hit on the gun turret and a second bomb that went through the hole and exploded in the canteen, causing numerous casualties, many badly burnt.

On arrival, Piper George Ogilvie stood on the gun turret of the destroyer, HMS *Jackal*, piping the ship into harbour. In 1954, artist Noel Syers depicted the scene, inspired by Ogilvie's descriptions, but instead of placing the Piper on board the *Jackal* he depicted him on board the *Dido*. 'The artist thought a better painting would result from the Piper playing from a battered man o'war than one that wasn't hit at all,' explained Ogilvie.[34]

Mindful of their losses on Crete, Wavell thanked the soldiers, including those of his own Regiment, the 2nd Black Watch, for their 'great courage and endurance… it must have appeared to many of you that you had been asked to do the impossible and that you were insufficiently equipped and supported. As Commander-in-Chief I accept the responsibility for what was done. It was for strategical reasons necessary to hold the island of Crete if this could reasonably be done.'[35] A severe toll had been taken not only on Allied forces but also on the Germans: Churchill later described how 'German losses of their highest class [of] fighting men removed a formidable air and parachute weapon from all further part in immediate events in the Middle East.' 'When we came back to Egypt,' recalled John McVay, 'we didn't seem to be the same battalion, not much was said.'[36]

While Crete was being evacuated, Corporal Hutton was lying wounded in a field hospital on the island. 'The next thing the Germans came in and said you are now prisoners of war. We felt down in the mouth. It was terrible. That was my life wasted.' Flown to Greece, the wounded prisoners were temporarily housed in an old barracks in Piraeus, the port of Athens. 'I found myself settled in the prison convalescent camp and I feel sure that you know me sufficiently well,' wrote Pipe Major Robert (Rab) Roy, who had been wounded in the chest, 'to understand that I resolved as soon as I was reasonably better I would make an attempt to escape.' Meantime, having brought his bagpipes with him, he started to play them. 'The Germans, except for a little show of interest did not bother.' Roy's chance came in July 'when a storm was blowing and the moon did not rise till 12 Midnight.' Having escaped with four others, they took refuge with some local villagers 'to await an opportunity of getting a boat… at the time of writing I am in Turkey and move tomorrow, 20th September for Egypt… I might mention I escaped with my silver mounted bagpipes!'[37] Those who remained in captivity were moved to Salonika, where Hutton recollected having insufficient food, left-over fruit and vegetables from the market, making tea from lime leaves, and 'green and mouldy' bread made for the defence of Greece 'months before'. Later they were sent to Germany, to the prison camp at Lamsdorf, where Hutton worked in a sugar factory. Although an Escape Committee was formed, when some of those who escaped returned with their heads 'all battered, there was no chance after that'.[38]

Syria: Operation Exporter

France's capitulation had opened its colonies to Axis occupation: in May 1941 German troops used Syrian airfields to support a pro-German Iraqi rebellion, prompting Wavell to order an attack on Vichy-controlled Syria. On 8 June a mixed force of Free French troops, Australians and an Indian Brigade under the command of General Henry Maitland (Jumbo) Wilson advanced into Syria. Although Vichy forces evacuated Damascus, a stalemate ensued, the Vichy remaining entrenched in the Lebanon. Unable to dislodge them, the only troops available to augment the Allied forces were the survivors of Crete. In early July the 2nd Black Watch was ordered to move from Cairo. 'The heat was terrific, reaching 95 degrees, and we came across the black widow spider and the scorpion,' recalled Private Meldrum. 'They fought each other whenever they met and it was a fight to the death. The scorpion won.'[39]

Passing through Damascus, now controlled by the Free French, the 2nd Black Watch was ordered to storm a position leading to the strategically located city of Zahlé between Beirut and Damascus in the eastern foothills of Mount Lebanon in the Bekaa Valley. 'Orders were given to us Company Commanders and we were all set to attack the following day,' recorded Fleming. Lacking reinforcements to maintain their position, however, the Vichy Commander, General Henri Dentz, agreed to an armistice, signed on 12 July, and the attack was called off. 'Thank heavens,' continued Fleming, who realised that they would not have 'stood an earthly chance' of success since they were 'very thin on the ground with little or no artillery support'. 'Apart from a pillbox which we captured there was no action,' recalled Meldrum.[40]

An uneasy interlude followed. 'The Vichy French had not caught on to the fact that they had capitulated; the Free French knew that they had ousted their kinfolk; and the British forces also enjoyed issuing orders. We were *not* to fraternize, we *were* to fraternize. In fact, Order, Counter-order, Disorder, again,' related Fleming, who was among those who volunteered to remain in Syria supervising the return of the Vichy French to France, as agreed under the terms of the armistice.[41]

One of the 'amenities' of Beirut and Damascus was trout-fishing in the Orontes river. 'My new trout rod promises awfully well,' Captain Barry was recording on 15 August. 'Yesterday I made rings out of paper clips and one for the top of the rod and fastened them on and a home made reel out of split pins fastened to the bottom of the rod, around which one can wind the line by hand. The grip was the masterpiece – made out of lavatory paper wound round the rod and adhesive tape covering it over! It works beautifully!' Barry had also been called as the principal witness at a court of inquiry to determine 'how the balance of our Crete Coy [Company] money fell into the sea at Heraklion during evacuation. Old George Rutherford (at that time

CQMS) was carrying it, and it caught on the side of the gangway and fell down the side – in the darkness and general scrimmage it was impossible to recover it.'[42]

While the Battalion, now under the command of Lieutenant Colonel George (Rusky) Rusk, was in Syria, Pipe Major Roy reappeared 'unannounced, and attired in a blue coat and grey flannel trousers, into the lines'. Arriving just as the officers were finishing their dinner, 'the Colonel insisted in opening a bottle of whisky to celebrate the occasion.'[43] In late September the 2nd Black Watch was under orders for a 'secret' destination: the port of Tobruk. Captured by the Allies during Wavell's Western Desert campaign in January 1941, it had been under siege since early April.[44]

Tobruk 'break out'

During the spring and summer of 1941, the Allied position in North Africa had steadily deteriorated. Having diverted troops to Greece in April, Wavell was left with inadequate forces to defend the Western Desert against the German Afrika Korps (later known as the Panzer Group Afrika), commanded by General Rommel. His advance from Tripoli resulted in the Allies being pushed back towards Egypt, leaving Tobruk isolated.[45] Defended by the 9th Australian Division along a perimeter approximately 25 miles from sea to sea, its retention was considered vital; not only was it the only port in North Africa between Alexandria and Tripoli, but it was an impediment to Rommel's further progress towards the Suez Canal. Furthermore, its capture would greatly shorten Axis supply lines. With the port bombed and strafed by the Luftwaffe during the day, supplies and reinforcements could only be brought in at night by the 'Tobruk ferry service', composed of Royal Navy and Royal Australian Navy ships, which also evacuated the wounded.

Coincident with the Syrian operation in mid-June, Wavell had launched Operation Battleaxe: an attack on Axis positions on the Egypt–Libya border at the Halfaya Pass, which Rommel had fortified after an earlier attack in May. Although initially successful,

Allied troops had had to withdraw.[46] A week later Churchill ordered Wavell to exchange commands with General Sir Claude Auchinleck, who had been serving as Commander-in-Chief India, the handover effected in the first week of July. Less than a fortnight previously Germany had invaded the Soviet Union, resulting in Stalin's entry into the war on the Allied side.

Despite the failure of Battleaxe, Tobruk had held out. In October orders were issued to replace the 9th Australian Division with the newly formed 70th British Infantry Division, commanded by Major General Ronald Scobie, which included the 2nd Black Watch in 14 Brigade.[47] Leaving Alexandria on the morning of 22 October, the Battalion reached Tobruk harbour at nightfall. 'The scene that met the eye was not exactly beautiful,' recorded Captain Barry the following morning. 'The wrecks of hundreds of cars and lorries are strewn all over the place, junk of all description as far as the eye can see in every direction.' Their biggest fear, recorded Private Andrew Meldrum 'was not so much the enemy as the booby traps and mines that the Aussies had left behind.[48]

On 29 October the 2nd Black Watch moved up to the perimeter. 'Life was Spartan,' commented Lieutenant John Benson. There was 'practically no drink and one gallon of water per day per man which had to suffice for drinking, cooking, washing including clothes, and for a period I believe we only had three quarters of a gallon.' 'Really this is a filthy place!' Barry was noting on 2 November. 'It is quite impossible to keep clean, and one's hair becomes a clogged mass of dirt. Washing one's head in sea-water with soap is fatal, the whole thing congeals into a mass of semi-glue, through which the comb will not penetrate... how the Australians lived here for seven months under these conditions, I cannot imagine!'[49] Contact with the outside world was spasmodic, only improved when Barry, in command of HQ Company, acquired a radio and compiled its news into a daily newssheet, *Tobruk Truth*.[50]

'Rations in Tobruk consist mainly of bully beef, biscuits, or canned meat and vegetables,' recorded the War Diary on 11 November. 'NAAFI supplies confined to strictly limited rations of cigarettes and matches with very occasional packet of biscuits, tins of fruit or tube of sugar gums. Only communication is by sea and the extremely hazardous voyage is only made when absence of moon will allow ships into harbour unobserved by enemy bombers and "Bardia Bill" a long range gun which consistently shells the harbour.' This gun, comparable to the huge 'Big Bertha' in the First World War, had acquired 'an animate personality in the minds of the troops… He used to join in whenever a ship arrived. If the evening air-raid aroused more attention than usual, Bill would barge in again.'[51]

The Black Watch did not have to wait long for action. Pressed by Churchill to mount a new offensive into Libya, Auchinleck planned Operation Crusader, to be carried out by the Eighth Army, formed from the Western Desert Force. Like Battleaxe its aim was to dislodge the Germans from the Halfaya Pass. In support, the garrison at Tobruk would 'break out'. On 18 November the Eighth Army, under Lieutenant General Sir Alan Cunningham's command, advanced across the desert. Addressing the 70th Division, Scobie assured the men that the 'break out' would only take place once 'the German Armoured Divisions and the other formations on the front had already been thoroughly pounded and smashed.'[52]

'Things were hotting up and there was a terrific tank battle going on on our left flank,' related Meldrum. 'This was at Sidi Rezegh. A push was on. The Tide was turning for us. We were going to break out and meet up with the advance.'[53] Two days after the main offensive had begun, Rusk received the code word 'Pop' indicating that the 'operation will take place tomorrow… At 1700 Bn. commences to move to assembly areas. Very quiet night, no arty [artillery] activity but numerous flares sent up by enemy in all sectors. Tanks move up to assembly area.' 'We took up our position at midnight waiting for the dawn and every man was given a tot of rum' continued Meldrum. 'Everything we had was going over our heads.'[54] The 2nd Black Watch's objective, with the support of the 4th Royal Tank Regiment and the Royal Horse Artillery, was to capture a strongpoint code-named 'Tiger' leading to the ridge of El Duda. First, several Forward Defended Localities had to be taken, of which 'Jill', a 'stout stone sangar about 8 feet in diameter', was in the Battalion's line of advance. To the left the 2nd King's Own Royal Lancaster Regiment would assault 'Butch', while the 2nd Queen's Own Cameron Highlanders would advance on the right.[55]

At zero hour, 6.30 a.m. on 21 November, the 2nd Black Watch, with twenty officers and 580 men, was ready to cross the start line. 'The white tapes had been well laid, & we had no difficulty in finding our proper position. The Battn was lined up in four waves of attack, 75 yards apart between each,' recorded Barry. But 'through absolutely no fault of our own, the attack got off to a bad start,' commented Lieutenant Benson, commanding D Company. 'First the tanks supporting us never appeared... and secondly, because the tanks did not appear we waited for them... darkness or first light plus the tanks were to be our help and shield. We lost both.' Having started late, 'everything went quite well for the first 200 yards.' 'Then the whole world seemed to wake up,' continued Barry. 'Machine guns opened up from the front, as well as all the hostile guns in our area of attack.' Having advanced no more than 400 yards, Benson was hit in the thigh, finding himself 'immobilised'.[56]

'All hell broke loose,' recorded Rusk, who was travelling in a mobile HQ consisting of four vehicles. 'In the succeeding din, smoke, dust and flying ironmongery, I was suddenly diverted from our regular progress by hearing Roy, our Pipe Major's chanter penetrating the blast.' Since he was playing 'Lawson's Men', 'that "puts the leap upon the lame"', Rusk realised that he was 'in the forward C Company area, whose Company March it was.' The sound of the pipes, recorded one soldier 'was instrumental in kindling the spirit with which the whole attack was carried out'.[57]

'Butch on our left had evidently fallen to the King's Own', continued Barry, 'but Jill put up a stiff resistance, and as we approached its wire, it was plain that we had lost a good many tanks on the minefield which had not been thought to exist. Casualties now began to occur, and I saw rifles and bayonets stuck upside down in the ground to denote their positions to the stretcher bearers coming on behind.' This was 'possibly a mistake in the open desert,' commented Benson, 'as I well remember those of us wounded being machine-gunned for a time after everyone had gone through.'[58] For some, the battle went better than expected: 'There was I with my Bangalore torpedo at the ready but my job was a suicidal one,' recollected Private Meldrum. 'I'd to get that torpedo over the wire. God must have been on my side because, that day when we reached the enemy defences, there was no trip wire or mines. The enemy had been prepared to attack but we had beaten them to it. We arrived at their dugouts, firing at anything that moved. All I could see were Italian soldiers surrendering all over the place.'[59]

During the advance Rusk's artillery carrier had blown up. What he described as his second 'horse', in which the adjutant, Captain Mungo Stirling, was travelling, 'came up and was blown to bits by some larger projectile. The Tank liaison light tank went up also.' This meant that of the four vehicles comprising his mobile HQ, Major Birkin's artillery carrier was the 'sole remaining unit… The only course left to me was to jump pillion on top of Birkin and [his driver] Worley. This took up some five valuable minutes, dropping, as we did, behind the main attack, which by then had captured Jill.' Proceeding through the semi-dark, the carrier arrived unexpectedly on their next objective, Tiger. Having reconnoitred the position and found it to be less strongly defended than they expected, Rusk realised 'that something had gone wrong on the left – [there were] no Tanks of C Squadron 4 RTR at Tiger and no Black Watch.'[60] Having gone in search of the supporting tanks, his absence 'for some time' fuelled the rumour that he had been killed, subsequently dispelled when he reappeared, having located the missing squadron of tanks. Once these were redirected on Tiger, the Battalion was able to consolidate its position, which included taking 'about 1,000 prisoners, 12 Field Guns, a Flame Thrower and upwards of 30 Spandau Machine Guns, which we found extremely useful.' By midday 'a square defensive position' had been established around the edge of Tiger, enabling Rusk to release the two artillerymen, Birkin and Worley, 'with all my grateful thanks… from having to cart me around.' On patrolling forward, 'we found the enemy had vanished'.

The advance 3 miles from their start line had cost the Battalion dearly, the effect of the German machine guns devastating. 'Of the 600 men of my battalion who crossed the start-line,' Rusk noted that only '160 survived to consolidate Tiger.'[61] 'What a day we had yesterday!' Barry was writing on 22 November 'from a small shallow dug out' on Tiger. 'I am so weary, I hardly know what to do. My feet are sore and swollen, and I am aching in every limb, as if someone had beaten me with a heavy stick all over the body.'[62]

One of the several hundred casualties was Captain Mungo Stirling, who had been fatally wounded in the stomach.[63] Captain Neville Blair, commanding B Company, had been hit in the shoulder and arm. Taken to the Regimental Aid Post (RAP), he praised the medical officer, Captain Gibson and the Padre, Bill Cochrane, for doing 'excellent work,' observing that the Italian prisoners helped to carry the wounded, although 'the Germans wouldn't.' One German medical officer, however, was also doing 'excellent work,' caring for both British and German casualties. Also wounded was Pipe Major Roy. 'One of the first hail of bullets must have hit him,' recorded Lance Corporal James McGraw. 'He dropped and got up. Then he was hit again and again – he got up the pipes still under his arm. When he was hit a third time he could not get up but he still played lying on the ground.' After being taken to the RAP, Roy continued to play for both friend and foe, acquiring the name 'The Piper of Tobruk.'[64]

Although the 70th Division's attack had taken Rommel by surprise, the 7th Armoured Division's defeat at Sidi Rezegh had jeopardised the operation's gains. While the 2nd Black Watch remained in possession of Tiger, fierce shelling continued. 'We are still on Tiger, and there is no change in the situation,' Barry was commenting on 24 November. 'The 8th Army is still unable to get through to us, in spite of the fact that the BBC announced that the relief of Tobruk was imminent!'[65]

At the Eighth Army's headquarters, Lieutenant General Cunningham was suggesting operations be curtailed. His advice, however, was not acceptable to his superiors and Auchinleck relieved him of his command, calling upon Black Watch officer Major General

Neil Ritchie to take his place. Writing in later life, Ritchie, who had come to the Middle East as Deputy Chief of Staff, General Staff, in June 1941 shortly before Wavell's departure and been retained by Auchinleck, considered the decision was unwise. 'In the light of after-events, my own view is that Auchinleck should have accepted the fact that he must himself take over the command temporarily of the [Eighth] Army whilst asking for a senior general to be sent from home to assume command… this would have been a far more reasonable proposition than putting in a very junior individual to carry out nominal command under his control.'[66]

Briefly, the tide of operations turned. 'A terrific tank battle is raging at this very moment in front of us,' observed Barry on 26 November, describing how at 6.15 that morning the tanks of the Royal Tank Regiment had left Tiger for the capture of El Duda. 'Their silhouettes, with pennants flying, as they moved up to the attack against the dawn sky, made a wonderful spectacle. As they went down into the shallow valley in front, enemy artillery opened up, and soon all hell was raging.' The 70th Division's attack on the El Duda ridge had at last enabled the Tobruk garrison to link up with a small force of New Zealanders from the Eighth Army in the early morning of 27 November. 'This more or less completes the cordon, starting from Tobruk and going south to the escarpment, bottling up the eastern sector,' noted Barry.[67] On 9 December the 2nd Black Watch moved from Tiger back to Tobruk. For the rest of the month sporadic fighting and mopping-up operations continued. Unable to capitalise on his position, in late December Rommel withdrew his forces to Gazala.

After its losses during the break out, the 2nd Black Watch again suffered at sea. Having brought in reinforcements to Tobruk, on 5 December HMS *Chakdina* was hit by an aerial torpedo as it was returning to Alexandria with nearly 400 Allied and Axis wounded. Reflecting on the attack, Benson, one of the 'walking wounded', confessed that the ship was 'a perfectly fair target'. Hastily converted into a hospital ship to accommodate the excessive casualties from Tobruk, 'we were not marked as a hospital ship, and in any case we were carrying several hundred P.O.Ws.'[68] Blair, another 'walking wounded', was in the wardroom, an old first-class saloon on the top deck. Realising the ship had been hit, he went out on deck and found it listing badly. 'I somehow didn't believe it possible the ship was sinking,' he continued. Together with Benson and another 'walking wounded', Gibson, the medical officer, 'we saw two boats being lowered, one for'end the other aft'. When a sailor ran past, they asked what they should do. 'Follow me, if you are wise,' was his response whereupon the sailor climbed over the deck rails.

> We noticed other people then jumping. Hoot [Gibson] climbed over and disappeared into the sea. John [Benson] was on crutches, a leg wound, and I helped him over the rails. Then I followed. I had the impression of running down the ship's side rather than jumping. I remember being impressed with the buoyancy of the life jackets. Then I was suddenly aware of the need of getting as far away from the ship as possible. I was conscious of the bows of the ship coming up until it stuck straight into the air. I thought it was coming over on top of me… When the ship appeared to be perpendicular she just slipped straight down into the water. I think I was drawn under, but then I was conscious of an explosion and I was on the surface again.[69]

Seeing a nearby spar, Blair swam over to it, helping two soldiers to reach it as well. 'One of them pointed out a small raft close to us. We splashed over to it. The two soldiers had drawn themselves up on to it and I was holding on, when up came a head next to me from the sea. A voice called "Neville", the head belonged to John Benson.' Eventually, as the men in the water were singing 'There'll always be an England' and 'Roll out the barrel', the destroyer, HMS *Farndale*, picked them up. 'A rope was flung to our raft. We were hauled up one by one,' continued Blair. 'Neville and I and those of us who were picked up – 30 or 40 perhaps – were lucky indeed,' recorded Benson. 'We were wrapped up in blankets, and lay with our backs to the wall our feet converging into the centre of a tiny room feet touching the middle rather like the face of a clock.'[70] Gibson had also survived as had another wounded officer, Lieutenant Ronnie Macdonald. 'I think he was the only stretcher case who was a survivor,' observed Blair. 'He was able to walk and got up and went on deck when the explosion occurred.' Those who were more severely wounded all perished, including one officer and thirteen men from the 2nd Black Watch. Sailing through the night, they reached Alexandria the following morning. 'We had had a heavy attack at dusk but we had driven them off.'[71]

On 11 December Rusk addressed the depleted Battalion, still in Tobruk: 'I have never felt more proud of anything in my life than of being privileged to command you all on the most severe test of the 21st November. I have never seen the Regiment advance more steadily under fire, even at Loos in the last war, when we lost over 700 casualties. Indeed the fire was enough to stop all but the most determined troops. You were all magnificent and true to the breed. After all, why should it change?' Mindful of those lost, he continued: 'The only pity of it all is the price that had to be paid and it is always the best that pay.'[72]

The 2nd Black Watch returned to Egypt in late December. 'The journey back to the Delta was too miserable to dwell on,' related Captain Bernard Fergusson who had rejoined the Battalion ten days after the battle. Together with Captain David Rose, appointed adjutant on 3 December (in place of the fatally wounded Stirling), he had contacted 'all the base units and headquarters collecting all Black Watch officers and soldiers who had been employed on base jobs' to bring the Battalion back to strength. 'At every stage one looked for some comrade or confidant with whom to exchange grumbles and grouses - only to remember that he was either fighting for his life in hospital or buried in Tobruk.' From Egypt, Blair wrote to the relatives of those in B Company who had been killed. Private John Nisbet's mother responded that his letter 'has comforted me more than words can tell.'[73]

Elsewhere the horizons of the war were expanding. Following Japan's attack on the American naval base at Pearl Harbor in early

December 1941 the United States declared war on the Axis powers. Britain's imperial possessions in the Far East were also under threat: coincident with the bombing of Pearl Harbor, Japanese troops had invaded Hong Kong. On 10 December HMS *Prince of Wales* and HMS *Repulse*, dispatched by Churchill to demonstrate Britain's naval presence in the Far East, were sunk. Having sent General Wavell to India as Commander-in-Chief in June 1941, Churchill agreed to his appointment as Supreme Allied Commander of a new multinational force of Australian, British, Dutch and American troops, ABDACOM, which would oversee operations against the Japanese in Malaya, Singapore and the Dutch East Indies (Indonesia).

'So ends 1941. Looking back on the early days of the war, and all that has happened, I think we are now well on the way to victory,' Captain Barry was writing on 31 December. 'It is hard to see how we can lose. Hitler cannot have much up his sleeve to play now, and American production is well under way.'[74]

Remote from pilgrimage, a dusty hollow
Lies in the Libyan plain:
And there my comrades sleep, who will not follow
The pipes and drums again.[75]

12

1942: The Desert Was Their Battlefield

The Desert was their Battlefield
On the night of the 23rd
As the Regiment went in to fight
The roar of our guns were heard.[1]

The Desert – I had read the book and seen the film
Beau Geste… all fine adventure reading for a young boy
but now – unknown to my friends and I – there was coming
up the biggest test of courage we had ever known.[2]

'The end of the beginning'

The entry of the United States into the war meant that Britain no longer 'stood alone' but the theatre of operations was greater. In late 1941 Japanese troops had moved from French Indo-China (Vietnam) through Thailand and into northern Malaya. Travelling swiftly down the Malayan peninsula, less than a week after crossing the Singapore Straits they forced Singapore's surrender on 15 February 1942. This was followed by the capitulation of the Dutch East Indies and the surrender of United States' forces in the Philippines. With no further role to play as Supreme Commander of ABDACOM, General Wavell returned to India as Commander-in-Chief, shortly before Burma (Myanmar) fell.

As in 1941, the 51st Highland Division, with the 1st, 5th and 7th Black Watch, had been enduring 'months of hard training, summer and winter, and exercises involving moves in lorried transport on a divisional scale over the length and breadth of the northern half of Scotland,' observed Captain Tobler, serving as 154 Brigade's intelligence officer.[3] The 2nd Black Watch was recuperating at Qassassin camp in Egypt after Tobruk. The 4th Black Watch was still in Gibraltar, the soldiers digging trenches and running to keep fit.[4]

In April 1942, the 6th Black Watch moved to Scotland 'and our CO, now Pat Barclay, another regular, decided to test our physical fitness by entraining us to Catterick and then making us march the rest of the way to Stobbs Camp, near Hawick, which I think we did in four days, simply bedding down at night in barns,' related Second Lieutenant Henry McKenzie Johnston. 'Fortunately the weather was good.'[5] In May, the 8/9th Black Watch Headquarters moved to Montrose.[6] In the same month the 1st Battalion The Tyneside Scottish, which had returned from spending over a year in Iceland, was assigned to the 49th West Riding Division; since two of its brigades had also been deployed there, the Division acquired the name: Polar Bears.[7]

With the Eighth Army

Since June 1941 the 51st Highland Division had been under the command of Major General Wimberley. Known as 'Tartan Tam', his tall figure, 'topped with his Jock's Tam o' Shanter' strode 'wherever things had to be done', recorded Lieutenant Peter Watson, 7th Black Watch.[8] In April 1942 the Division received orders to mobilise. Strict secrecy was observed regarding their destination. 'The rumours started when we were issued with pith helmets and K[haki] D[rill] uniforms,' related Private Davy Chalmers, batman to Lieutenant Colonel Tom Rennie, who, after escaping from St Valéry, had been given command of the 5th Black Watch, 153 Brigade. 'We entrained one evening and arrived the next day at the quay side [at] Liverpool, [and were] confronted with the bulk of the *Empress of Australia*. It was a scramble in the evening for a hammock or one slept on the table or on the floor.'[9] Taking the safe but circuitous route around the Cape of Good Hope, they were at sea for nearly two months. 'Drill competitions were held and all men were trained in first aid,' observed Major John Hopwood, 7th Black Watch.[10]

Their destination was North Africa, where Allied forces were under pressure from Rommel's Panzer Army Afrika. The recent fighting at Gazala, resulting in the fall of Tobruk on 21 June, had brought Axis forces within striking distance of Alexandria. Halted by Auchinleck in what was known as the First Battle of El Alamein in July, Rommel dug in, successfully withstanding Allied counter-attacks. In early August Churchill arrived in Cairo to review the Middle East Command, his intention being to separate the Near East from the Middle East. While Auchinleck would retain responsibility for the Near East (Persia and Iraq), General Sir Harold Alexander, who had arrived from India, after overseeing Britain's withdrawal from Burma, would become C-in-C Middle East. When Auchinleck refused, General Jumbo Wilson took over the Near East. Command of the Eighth Army was given to Lieutenant General William (Strafer) Gott but no sooner had he been appointed than he was killed when his transport plane was shot down. Churchill then chose Lieutenant General Bernard Montgomery, who had spent the last two years overseeing defensive preparations in the south of England. Montgomery's assumption of command on 13 August coincided with the 51st Highland Division's arrival in Egypt.[11]

The Prime Minister and his entourage, which included his senior generals, among them Alan Brooke, Chief of the Imperial General Staff, and Wavell, C-in-C India, had then travelled to the Soviet Union to inform Stalin that the Allies were not in a position to open a 'Second Front' in Europe in 1942.[12] On their return, to the 'delight' of his former Regiment, as Tobler observed, Wavell visited the soldiers at Qassassin camp before returning to India: 'Wearing a bush shirt, the erect, stocky figure with its stiff arm and glass eye seemed to be in excellent form, if tired looking, as he stood chatting with our small group.' A priority for the new arrivals was acclimatisation: 'None of us had experience of desert conditions and the kind of warfare we were to meet. We were anxious to learn from others, an attitude which helped later to establish good relations with the veteran Australian and New Zealand Divisions.' 'We were initiated into the tactics and drills of desert warfare,' recounted Major Hopwood. 'In the main these concerned movement by M[otor] T[ransport], desert formations and the general routine of position warfare in the desert.

Essential features were to acquire the proper drills for dispersal and how to live and move… under conditions of heat and lack of water. Proper methods of digging in and the necessity for digging in to avoid air attack and shelling at almost every halt became second nature.'[13] The men also had to become accustomed to the sand and grit which penetrated their clothing, causing skin irritations. 'Sand storms wreaked havoc; the only protection was to wrap yourself in a ground sheet and go to ground.'[14]

'The desert is like the sea and needs deadly accurate navigations, as there is not a single landmark to help you at all, it's as flat and desolate as the moon must be. It's a big responsibility,' wrote twenty-one-year-old Lieutenant George Morrison, describing his duties as a navigating officer in the 7th Black Watch. 'But I'm pretty good at the sun compass now; I've been studying it since we landed. It's an eerie job going out into the unknown and very often the unmapped as well. It means that every man of these hundred men depends on me, the navigator, to guide them perhaps a hundred miles over the desert, and it's my job to keep watching and checking all the way.'[15]

As part of the 60,000-strong Delta Force, the 51st Highland Division was responsible for holding the Delta if the Germans broke through the lines of the Eighth Army. 'Here the Battalion spent a thoroughly unpleasant period bivouacked in orange groves belonging to the King of Egypt,' recorded Hopwood. 'Flies, dirt and Egyptians all vied with each other to take their place as major annoyances in a difficult and unpleasant stay.' 'Our enforced though brief stay there was marked by appalling humidity, day and night,' remarked Tobler. 'It was also about this time many of us had our first experience of that horrible complaint known as "gyppy tummy" which comes on without warning and can leave the victim weakened and depressed for days.' 'It is not so bad out here as it could be and we are always kept busy and the time goes in one way or another,' Private William Fisher informed his wife. 'But we are all waiting for the day when we can get back home again to start our lives over again when we get out of the Army… I am getting quite brown now with the sun and you will not know me when you see me again. forever your Will.'[16]

'The vast canvas of Alamein'

On 30 August Rommel launched Operation Brandung, attacking south of El Alamein at Alam el-Halfa in an attempt to encircle Montgomery's forces before they were reinforced. Having received advance warning through Ultra intercepts, the Eighth Army resisted the attack, which proved to be the last Axis offensive operation in North Africa. Delta Force was then brought forward to take part in Operation Lightfoot, an attack at El Alamein.

First, Montgomery initiated a period of training. 'Each rehearsal of a night-attack was made as near to the real thing as possible,' observed Tobler. 'The area chosen was, in fact, more or less similar to the ground over which the brigade would be attacking. Live ammunition fired over our heads by field artillery and machine gunners simulated the greatest possible realism, as did the firing of bursts of coloured tracer along the brigade and divisional boundaries by Bofors guns of the 40th Light Anti-Aircraft Regiment.' 'Deep dummy minefield belts were positioned in chessboard formation in considerable depth, infantry positions covering anti-tank posts were laid out behind these,' related Hopwood. 'In practice, over and again, deep advances up to 8,000 yards and the subsequent rapid reorganisation of the position once captured were made. This included not only digging ourselves in but laying minefields against counter-attack by the defences and the bringing up of the supporting Arms and digging in anti-tank guns.' Detachments also went to the front line to train with the 9th Australian Division 'who were the most seasoned and experienced fighters and knew the routine of desert existence most thoroughly.' Having encountered the 2nd Black Watch in Tobruk, the Australians made the Black Watch feel 'very welcome'.[17]

At the end of September Montgomery revealed his battle plans, 'opening a new and even more intensive pre-Alamein phase. Forward assembly areas had to be reconnoitred, sites chosen for battle headquarters and elaborate precautions taken to conceal these preparations from the enemy. No movement was allowed by day and all parties at work on slit trenches had to be dug-in and camouflaged by first light, as were stocks of rations, ammunition and stores that formed part of the formidable build-up in the rear areas. Nothing was left to chance,' continued Tobler. An essential 'aid' was the Bagnold Compass, devised by Brigadier Ralph Bagnold, who had explored and mapped most of the desert during the 1930s, later organising the Long Range Desert Group, experts in reconnaissance and intelligence gathering.[18]

Montgomery's preparations included practising a number of deceptions, known as Operation Bertram. Dummy tanks and lorries were used, the lorries made of wood and canvas concealing the field guns. Real tanks were hidden by 'sunshades' made of canvas, giving them 'the innocent look of soft-skinned vehicles,' explained Eric Linklater, visiting the battlefield 17 years later.[19] 'We trained hard on desert formation & in rehearsing our part in the big battle which it soon became apparent was near at hand,' Lieutenant Colonel W. N. Roper-Caldbeck informed General Sir Arthur Wauchope, who had become Colonel of the Regiment in August 1940. 'The Battalion kept very cheerful though the incidence of sick was high – we lost over 70 men to hospital with sandfly fever & Dysentery.' Sadly while practising a night attack through a minefield in early October, Roper-Caldbeck's second-in-command, Major Arthur Wilmot, was killed. 'An error on the part of the gunners caused us to be caught in a concentration and Arthur & 4 men were killed, & 2 more wounded. It was a very grievous blow.'[20]

'Just before the battle sand models were made,' continued Hopwood, 'and all men were thoroughly informed of the plan and how it was hoped the battle would work.'[21] Separating the two armies was the heavily mined No Man's Land, 3–5 miles deep, protected by wire and through which a frontal attack would be launched. With an army of nearly 200,000 men, Montgomery's forces greatly exceeded the Panzer Army Afrika. Bolstered by 500 American Sherman tanks, there was no shortage of equipment and supplies. Absent from the impending battle was Rommel, who had returned to Germany on sick leave on 23 September, his place being taken by Lieutenant General Georg Stumme.

'On the vast canvas of Alamein, the task of the Division, as of every other formation engaged, is a minute part of the whole,' related Bernard Fergusson in his history.[22] After a heavy bombardment, XXX Corps (which included the 51st Highland Division) would advance across the minefields. Flanked by the 9th Australian Division and the 2nd New Zealand Division, the 51st Highland Division's start line was marked out with white tape leading towards imaginary lines, Green, Red, Black and Blue, along which lay strategic locations named after places in Scotland. Only when 'Oban', 'Mull' and 'Findhorn' had been reached would they have crossed the Blue or *Oxalic* Line, where the Germans had established their defensive position on the Miteriya Ridge. 'No details were left to chance and every item of equipment and weapons was carefully thought out by Company Commanders,' recorded Captain David Russell who was later to write the 7th Black Watch's war history. Positioned next to the New Zealanders, the soldiers had agreed that if, 'in the fog of battle', there were any confusion, they would shout 'Jock!' or 'Kiwi!' Once two corridors had been cleared, the tanks of X Corps would follow.[23]

'I feel excessively cheery and optimistic right now,' Lieutenant Morrison was writing in a 'wee' letter to his mother on 16 October, 'and this death business doesn't bother me in the least. So if I do get one – don't be too sad – it's too late to be sad and I wouldn't like it.' Requesting Handel's *Largo* to be played in the Kirk if the worst happened, he reminded her that 'this war is being fought to protect people like you from horrible things, and it's only right that some should have the privilege – yes, the privilege, to give themselves for the cause of the good and the right.' On the eve of battle, Padre Tom Nicol held a communion service 'for anyone wishing to take part', recalled Private Chalmers. 'It was well attended.'[24]

Montgomery's message to the Allied troops was resolute: 'Let no man surrender so long as he is unwounded and can fight.'[25] 'There had been some ribaldry among the Jocks about Montgomery's message, his talk of our place in history, but as the time approached everyone was absorbed in his private thoughts. I have never known such intensity of purpose,' recalled Lieutenant Watson whose role as intelligence officer in the 7th Black Watch was 'to advise the CO on the axis of the battalion's advance. It had to be precise – by compass bearing across the featureless desert, paced out against the clock to keep us behind the "friendly fire" but not so far behind that Jerry had time to get himself organised.' There was to be strict radio silence only broken 'in case of operational urgency,' observed Captain Tobler. 'A tremendous feeling of exhilaration attended this business of navigation. The sun and wind and the great space all played their part.'[26]

On 23 October, in the light of a full moon, the men emerged from their 'burrows, [like] nocturnal creatures'. Moving silently through the gun lines, 'the gunners paused in their preparations to whisper "good luck",' recalled Private Henry Scivity Barker. 'In the Highland Division we wore white St Andrew's Crosses tied to the backs of our packs and, in addition, every man carried a pick or shovel as well as an entrenching tool,' noted Hopwood. 'Extra sandbags were carried below the small pack and steel helmets were covered with a sandbag covering to prevent any shine.'[27] The first stage of the battle was heralded by a tremendous bombardment against the entire 40-mile front, before an even heavier bombardment targeted specific areas. 'Memory becomes a kaleidoscope... suddenly all the guns in the world opening up almost under one's feet in a multitude of flashes so vividly unexpected against the blackness with which one had been struggling.' 'The din of the artillery barrage began at 2140 hours snapping an uneasy hush,' continued Watson, who described his tin helmet metaphorically flying 'six feet in the air as the world erupted in sound and light... the moon – Monty's Moon, we called it – made the desert shine.'[28]

In the Highland Division's sector, a searchlight had been switched on, followed by another. As the beams were lowered, they formed a St Andrew's Cross. 'Scotland for ever and second to none', Wimberley signalled to the troops under his command, after which XXX Corps moved off. 'The infantry went forward into a roaring hail of shell-fire, and as they drew nearer to their objectives the storm was thickened by the bursting of mortar bombs.'[29] 'In this, our first battle, pipers were to play forward and this they did right well,' noted Hopwood, commenting that they suffered such casualties 'that thereafter they could not be spared.' 'It really got us going,' recalled Private Sid Lunn, 5th Black Watch. Their orders not to stop to help the wounded, 'seems barbaric', observed Barker, 'but you soon got used to it and realised that ignorant hands could do a lot of harm.'[30]

'A Company were on the right, B Coy on the left with the [5th Black Watch's] Adjutant, Augur East, as navigating officer in the centre with his compass,' related Private Chalmers. 'Some accompanying him were counting paces (approx 3 paces were 2 yds) as we were to advance fifty yards to the minute to keep up with the creeping barrage. I was with the CO [Rennie] in the centre party and he told me to count the paces as well. This was all very well but suddenly we would head off over to the right to see how A Company were faring, then we would return to the centre, next over to B Company or even make our way back a bit. It certainly kept the brain working', he added, 'though the calculations might not have been correct.'[31] As they advanced, some members of the 5th Black Watch ran into the wire. 'Get a bloody move on, Jock! You're no' cutting hair now!' cried a voice from the dark, addressing the soldier with the wire-cutters, who was the Company's barber![32]

As the attacking forces moved on, 'the air was filled with dust and smoke, the acrid smell of cordite drifted over and the increasing shrill screams of flying shrapnel and ricochets made a cacophony of deadly sound,' recorded Lieutenant McGregor.[33] After capturing Montrose, Arbroath and Forfar, the 5th Black Watch's next objective was Red, the furthest point of its advance, while the 1st Gordon Highlanders passed through to Black and Blue. As Private Chalmers was digging in, making a slit trench for himself and Rennie, 'an 88mm Airburst cracked near by and I dropped to the bottom of the trench'. Noting that the sandbag he had just placed on the edge of the trench 'had a nice hot piece of shrapnel sticking in it' he recognised that 'attending Padre Nicol's service must have paid off'.[34]

Meanwhile, the 1st Black Watch had moved forward, directed through the minefields by the navigators. 'The desert, as you will know', Roper-Caldbeck informed Wauchope, 'gives you no finding marks and even the objective[s] were only slit trenches which were invisible.' Despite the difficulties the Battalion reached its destination on Black so quickly that they 'almost ran into their own artillery'.[35] 'The whistle blew and off we went led by a Piper (what a brave lonely man that Piper was),' recalled Sergeant Robert Penman in the 7th Black Watch, which passed through the positions already reached by other battalions. Although the Red line was reached without incident, securing Black became more perilous because of heavy shelling. 'On and on we went through a night that seemed endless. We finally got the order to dig in.'[36] During the advance, six of the 7th Black Watch's navigating party were wounded, one fatally – Lieutenant George Morrison who had extolled the 'privilege' of giving his life 'for the cause of the good and the right'. 'The worst moment was lying in a dug-out beside my friend, George,' recalled Lieutenant Watson, who had been injured. 'One minute we were chatting, the next I heard a grunt and he was a goner, just like that.'[37]

After reaching Black, the 7th Black Watch's next objective was 'Kirkcaldy' on Blue, at the end of the Miteriya Ridge, a particular objective being a hillock, known as 'The Ben', at the ridge's north-west end. With numbers severely depleted, a composite company was formed, commanded by Captain Charles Cathcart. Encountering fierce opposition, one officer was killed and the remaining four, including Cathcart, wounded, but they had driven the Germans from the ridge, the only part of *Oxalic* captured by the Division that night. 'When morning came he [Cathcart] had 30 men to hold the open, western slope of the ridge throughout the hot day that followed.'[38] After the action Brigadier Howard Kippenberger, 5 New Zealand Brigade, described seeing 'a whole section' of The Black Watch, 'a corporal and seven men, all on their faces.' 'Over the whole battlefield lay the most profound confusion,' commented Hopwood. 'Everywhere shelling had raised a complete fog of war and it was not till after dusk on the evening of the 23rd that the forward companies could be properly located.'[39]

Despite the Eighth Army's apparent success in moving forward, the advance had not been as effective as Montgomery had hoped.

Only the New Zealanders had reached the forward slopes of the Miteriya Ridge, while sustaining heavy losses. X Corps's advance had been even less successful. Montgomery's determination to push the tanks through XXX Corps not only led to serious congestion but resulted in heavy tank losses in areas where they had to fight their way forward.[40] 'Tanks milled backwards and forwards in the attempt to break out and each movement caused further spasmodic shelling,' commented Hopwood.[41] Among those attempting to clear the northern corridor so the tanks could pass through was the 2nd Seaforth, 152 Brigade, held in reserve while the other brigades of the 51st Highland Division had been advancing. As they passed through the lines of the 1st Black Watch 'somebody asked one of their company commanders if the Battalion could do anything to help, but he just laughed and said "No." They went forward steadily into the attack, their Jocks joking with ours as they passed; but fortune was not with them; they melted away under the enemy's fire, and few survived.'[42] Wimberley himself had a 'providential' escape when on the 24th, as he had gone forward to visit his brigade commanders, his jeep was blown up by a mine, which killed his driver and a soldier and seriously wounded another officer. Despite being carried 'quite a long way from the remnants of the jeep' and being knocked unconscious, by the afternoon Wimberley had recovered sufficiently to resume command of the Division.[43]

The Germans had not been without their losses. To assess the situation at the front, also on the morning of 24 October, Lieutenant General Stumme had left his headquarters when his vehicle had been fired upon by British anti-tank and machine-guns. The officer accompanying him had been fatally wounded. Not realising that Stumme had been attempting to jump out of the car and then fallen, the driver returned at speed to base. At first reported missing, Stumme was later found to have died of a heart attack. Rommel was immediately recalled. Flying via Rome, where he requested Italian naval assistance in transporting petrol and ammunition, he resumed command of the newly named German–Italian Panzer Army on 25 October.[44]

By the evening of 26 October the 51st Highland Division had

advanced 6 miles, suffering over two thousand casualties. Although it had achieved its objectives, X Corps's difficulties meant that there was a danger of the advance losing momentum. 'Throughout the course of each day and night we were at Alamein we were shelled in very heavy bouts, the idea being to frighten us and keep us awake both day and night,' recorded Sergeant Robert Penman, 7th Black Watch. 'We had 100% "stand to", that is everyone standing up in their slit trench ready to repel attack from dusk to one hour after dusk and in the morning 60 minutes before dawn, to dawn as this had been the hours the powers that be had decided were the most likely hours for a German counter attack. At night we had 50% "stand to" all night.'[45] To inject renewed impetus, Montgomery decided on a change of plan. Instead of continuing the frontal attack, he conceived Operation Supercharge which would assault Axis forces along the coast. When reviewing his options, however, Rommel had predicted this change in tactics and had already strengthened his position in the north. On the morning of 29 October, Montgomery, advised by his field commanders, again changed direction, ordering the Australian and New Zealand Divisions to attack the boundary between the German and the Italian defensive line. Since these divisions had already lost heavily and needed reinforcing, Montgomery conceded a 24-hour delay, and Supercharge was rescheduled to take place on the night of 1/2 November.[46]

While some units of the Highland Division were included in the advance, the Black Watch battalions remained in line, the number of fatalities in each battalion rising due to shelling and sniper fire. On 28 October Rennie's command post had been hit by a mortar bomb, wounding him in the neck. After receiving medical attention he resumed his duties 'as if nothing had happened'. A day later, the 5th Black Watch had an unexpected windfall when a German jeep, with three Germans, drove into the Battalion's lines. While the soldiers were taken prisoner, their jeep was added 'to the Battalion's growing transport fleet', which, recorded Lieutenant John McGregor, came to include 'one German three-tonner, one armoured car and one gun-towing vehicle'.[47]

On the night of 1 November Operation Supercharge began. More than a week after the opening shots of what became known as the Second Battle of El Alamein had been fired, Allied troops finally broke through the Axis line 'only to be frustrated by the heavy and incessant rain which reduced the tracks to mud wallows', recorded Hopwood.[48] To guard against a counter-attack the 1st Black Watch had been ordered to Tel el Eisa, north of the coastal road. 'So there was no rest!' related Roper-Caldbeck. 'The Bn came in just at dusk, being shelled & stuka-ed on the way but getting off very lightly. We dug in during the night. 2nd Nov. was fairly peaceful & the counter attack did not materialise.'[49] With their defences broken, Axis forces began to withdraw.

'In the last 14 days', observed Major General Wimberley, 'we of the 1942 Edition, have I am sure, reminded Scotland that we too were chipped off just the same block of Northern Granite that provided the best British fighting Division of the last great War.' Reflecting on the battle, Sergeant Penman praised the pipers. 'Back in Blighty I loathed them, they did nothing but practise on their chanters and did no fatigue duties or guard duties. But in battle there was usually a piper with each Forward Company who must have been the bravest man in the Company [with] nothing to defend himself with but his pipes. Then during the fighting they were out looking for the dead and wounded, they went out where our tanks had turned back… [with only] a steel helmet, a stretcher and a red cross on a white arm band to protect them.'[50]

Casualties in all Black Watch battalions had been high. One of the fatalities was twenty-year-old Second Lieutenant Rose, 'little Hughie Rose' of Kilravock, 'just as he was being congratulated by his commanding officer for capturing his objective with his platoon'. The youngest officer in the 1st Black Watch, he was the only son of former Commanding Officer, Lieutenant Colonel Hugh Rose. The 5th Black Watch's B Company lost so many men that it had to be disbanded.[51] Between 24 and 31 October while the 7th Black Watch was in line, its casualties were recorded as seventy-eight killed including six officers, with 183 wounded including thirteen officers.

On 3 November an 'unlucky shell' hit the headquarters of the 1st Black Watch's D Company, setting off the reserve ammunition which 'blew Company Sergeant Major Moyes in half and killed the rest of Company HQ'. The only survivor of this incident was Captain Gerald Osborne, who received 'no more than a scratch on his arm,' recorded Roper-Caldbeck.[52]

Among those honoured, Privates James Joseph Cosgrove and Charles Reid received the MM, their actions recorded as saving the lives of three men who would have bled to death, as well as having brought in many other casualties.[53] During the initial advance Piper Duncan McIntyre, 5th Black Watch, had been hit three times but had continued to play the Company onto its objective, dying where he lay. The following morning when his body was retrieved, his fingers were still on the chanter. His actions were commemorated in a Regimental song, 'El Alamein':

Now I'm going to tell you a story,
Of a boy who was called from his home,
To fight for his King and his country,
And also the Old Folks at home.[54]

'A show of this description brings home to me like nothing else has so far what an appalling waste of life and money and raw materials it all is,' Major Hew Blair-Imrie, 5th Black Watch, was writing from hospital in early November. 'The only redeeming thing about this particular [battle] is that we all know it is the last one in North Africa. We know that Monty has the men materials and ability to drive the enemy right out of North Africa.'[55]

Montgomery, however, had decided against going in hot pursuit and Roper-Caldbeck described the succeeding days as 'very strange... There was no shelling & no gunfire... The desert all round, which for 14 days had been a milling mass of tanks, trucks & lorries was empty, save for the blackened skeletons of burned out vehicles. We suddenly realised that the whole battle had swept forward and we were completely out of it. From being in it, we were as far divorced from it as if we had been back in the Delta.'[56]

'Now this is not the end,' Prime Minister Winston Churchill said, addressing the Lord Mayor's luncheon at the Mansion House in London on 10 November. 'It is not even the beginning of the end. But it is, perhaps, the end of the beginning. Henceforth Hitler's Nazis will meet equally well armed, and perhaps better armed troops… We mean to hold our own. I have not become the King's First Minister in order to preside over the liquidation of the British Empire… Here we are, and here we stand, a veritable rock of salvation in this drifting world.'[57]

The chase across Libya

On 11 November, Armistice Day, Lieutenant General Sir Oliver Leese, commanding XXX Corps, inspected the 1st Black Watch. Roper-Caldbeck found the praise the Battalion received rather 'fulsome. Admittedly, water is hard to come by, & the men had a fortnight's blood & dirt on them, but they should have been a little smarter. No one, however, could cavil at their drill.' When introduced to a soldier who gave his name as Montgomery 'the Corps Commander took a little persuading that no impertinence had been intended, but all came straight in the end.'[58]

During the lull, the soldiers spent time clearing the battlefield, which involved salvaging thousands of jerricans and other equipment which was 'to prove of enormous use in the subsequent advances.'[59] 'Our big guns are keeping Gerry busy,' Private William Fisher, 7th Black Watch, informed his 'darling' wife. 'We are up all night and sleep all day. But it is getting very cold out here.' He also wanted her to let their young son, Billy, know that he had got him a German helmet which he would bring home.[60] 'We have started training again as we learnt a good deal from the fighting,' Roper-Caldbeck informed Wauchope. The battalions also took on reinforcements to make up for those who had been killed. 'I do hope I get some pipers out from home as the 42nd [i.e. the 1st Black Watch] is the worst off Bn in the Div. in this respect, having now only three left.'[61]

On 19 November the 51st Highland Division moved off, 153 Brigade leading. 'None who took part in it will ever forget the exhilaration of that chase across Libya,' commented Bernard Fergusson. The Highlanders, recorded Wimberley, had already become known as the 'Highway Decorators' for their habit of painting 'HD' 'on almost any available surface in the Division's area.' Crossing through the Halfaya Pass which the men called the 'Hellfire', they entered Libya, reaching Tobruk on the afternoon of 21 November, just five months after it had been forced to surrender. Montgomery's objective was the fortified position of El Agheila, where the Via Balbia linked Benghazi and Tripoli along the coast road and which was the furthest point reached by Allied forces in 1941. Cutting across the bulge of Cyrenaica 'reveille would be at 5.30 a.m.; at six would come the order "prepare to move"; five minutes later, "move." A dim red light glowed on the Navigator's vehicle, and the rest would follow it. Soon there would be a little light; at 7.15 a.m. the chilly sun would pop into the sky; then there would be a halt, and the order "brew up!" A hundred little petrol fires would spring into being, and there would be a delicious breakfast of sausages, bacon, biscuits, marmalade and tea.'[62]

Protecting the approach to El Agheila was the village and bay of Mersa Brega, bounded by sand-dunes and a salt marsh. At night, Allied forces occupied the forward slopes of the line of dunes overlooking the village. At daylight they withdrew to the reverse slopes, leaving some observations posts to take note of German movements.[63] To counter the Allied pursuit, the Germans had laid hundreds of deadly 'S' mines, which, when triggered, launched into the air, projecting shrapnel in all directions and causing severe casualties at a distance. 'There were more mines per acre than one would expect to find potatoes in a respectable potato field,' related Private Barker, 'or so it seemed.'[64] Having made contact with the Germans on 8 December 'the process of shrinking No Man's Land' began. 'The enemy were extremely active, and any movement at all in the open attracted heavy and accurate shelling,' related Lieutenant Colonel James Oliver, in command of 7th Black Watch. 'The Germans were on one side of the bay whilst we occupied the other,' continued

Private Barker. 'Strangely enough on occasions sea bathing took place, not at the same time but a form of truce pervaded, neither side fired on the other whilst swimming.'[65]

On 13 December an assault was launched. While the 1st Black Watch approached between the village and the sea, the 7th was ordered to move along the edge of the salt marsh. 'The first two thousand yards advance was uneventful and no enemy interference was encountered,' continued Oliver. Subsequently one of the leading vehicles blew up on a mine, but the remainder got through safely 'although the following day, when other units' transport was moving up and using the same route, quite a number of vehicles were blown up in this area.' Reaching the main road, they found that it had been heavily mined with plate-shaped 'Teller' mines capable of destroying a lightly-armoured vehicle or blowing the tracks off a tank. As soon became evident, the Germans were no longer at Mersa Brega. 'The enemy had slipped away under cover of darkness', Hopwood explained, 'and, in spite of shelling, had been so protected by his minefields that he had managed to pull out unscathed and get clean away before the encircling armour to the south had cut him off.'[66]

The 51st Highland Division then went into reserve, the respite providing the opportunity for some recreation and training, including night exercises to gain greater proficiency in advancing through minefields. Rennie, who took command of 154 Brigade in early December, also evolved drills for '"giant-stepping" across the emptiness of the "no-man's land" of desert to make quicker and more effective contact with the enemy… screens of snipers were to go out to establish contact and, behind this protective screen, we practised moving up and digging in,' related Hopwood, who briefly took command of the 5th Black Watch after Rennie's departure. The Battalion's new Commanding Officer was Lieutenant Colonel Charles (Chick) Thomson, temporarily absent with a throat infection. His second-in-command was Major Hew Blair-Imrie who had recovered from his El Alamein wound.[67]

Meanwhile, the recently formed First Army, commanded by

Lieutenant General Kenneth Anderson, had been preparing for Operation Torch. Planned in Gibraltar, the operation involved a series of landings on the coast of Africa in French-held Morocco and Algeria. Fifty-two-year-old US General Dwight Eisenhower was appointed Supreme Commander Allied Expeditionary Force of the North African Theatre of Operations. During the preparations a sentry of the 4th Black Watch took his duties on garrison duty in Gibraltar so seriously that upon seeing a man in civilian clothes 'looking too closely at military installations', he arrested him without recognising Eisenhower. Fortunately for the soldier, when the error was realised 'Ike treated his arrest as a joke'.[68] Taking part in Operation Torch was the 78th Division, formed in May 1942, with former Black Watch officer Brigadier Keith Arbuthnott in command of 11 Brigade.[69]

In anticipation of an Allied victory in North Africa, on 8 November pro-Allied French forces mounted a coup against the Vichy government in French North Africa. Among the Vichy leaders detained was Prime Minister Admiral François Darlan, who had just arrived in Algiers to visit his son, in hospital with a severe attack of polio. Having chosen to switch his allegiance, Darlan negotiated an armistice with the Allies, who permitted him to become High Commissioner for France in North and West Africa in return for ordering all French forces in Africa to join the Allies. Angered by Darlan's changed loyalties, Hitler ordered the invasion of Vichy France, bringing the whole country under German occupation. When on 24 December Darlan was assassinated, he was succeeded by General Henri Giraud who had recently escaped after two years in captivity in Germany, arriving in Algeria to take command of French units joining the First Army.[70]

With the 51st Highland Division spending its first Christmas in North Africa a variety 'of barely-hoped-for things' turned up, including 'berried holly (camel-thorn and Italian cotton wool dyed with red paint), tables with white-cloths, flowers cut from paper, and real desert flowers.'[71] Church services were held and inter-battalion football matches played. A highpoint was the 5th Black Watch's first performance of *The Agheila Angels* 'to a packed house, who roared their approval, especially at the "Angels" chorus of "volunteer" Officers in make-shift bras and frilly knickers', recalled Lieutenant McGregor. 'The orchestra included an accordion, trumpet, violin, drums and bugle.' 'By what seemed almost a miracle, an excellent Christmas dinner was produced for all, consisting of turkey, plum pudding, and Christmas cake, together with pork and tomato soup,' complemented by 'a large consignment of whisky' which had been ordered for the 7th Black Watch's Officers' Mess and which 'suddenly arrived', according to Russell. Private William Fisher's description was less enthusiastic. 'We had our Xmas, one bottle of beer and piece of Turkey, some plum duff. But it was not much of Christmas as if I was at home. But we are far from civilians and we were lucky to get anything.' While the 5th Black Watch remained at Mersa Brega, the 1st and 7th moved west to Wadi Matratin. 'So 1942 came to an end,' continued McGregor, observing that their Christmas celebrations a year ago in Scotland 'were in another age'.[72]

India: Keeping public order

Before the 51st Highland Division left for North Africa, in February 1942 the 2nd Black Watch was given orders to move from Qassassin to Syria to prepare defensive positions against a presumed German attack through Anatolia. Orders then came to return to Qassassin 'en route for somewhere else. Speculation is of course rife as to where this is to be, but to my mind it's a tenner to an orange that we go to the W.D.,' Barry wrote in his diary. 'I was quite wrong', he commented two days later. 'We are not going to the Western Desert at all, but somewhere East. This is most exciting as it might be India, Ceylon, Burma, or even Madagascar! We are to be issued with drill and topees this afternoon.' Their actual destination was Burma. But once Rangoon had fallen, their ship was diverted to Bombay. From there the various units were sent to camps in the Deccan 'and bidden to study jungle warfare'.[73]

At the beginning of April, after a month in Ahmednagar, the

Battalion moved to Ranchi in eastern India where it was reunited with the Divisional Headquarters, forming part of a mobile reserve for the defence of India; also in the 70th Division was 23 Brigade, while 16 Brigade went to Ceylon. At Ranchi the soldiers witnessed the remnants of the Burma Corps, 'gaunt and ragged as scarecrows', returning home after the 'longest' geographical retreat in history, extending for nearly 1,000 miles through the Arakan jungle.[74]

By May the heat was 'getting unbearable. In this oven in which we live, one longs for the night, and the comparative coolness it brings.' As always, news of the war in Europe and North Africa was eagerly absorbed. The fall of Tobruk to Axis forces in June was 'heart-breaking', Barry recorded. 'I mind this more than the loss of Crete. After all the dead we left there, and other people left there, it is tragic beyond words. It is no use trying to pretend that to us it is merely a horrible place full of dust and sand – it is much more than that.' News from Soviet Russia was getting 'steadily worse… if the Bosche gets Stalingrad then it will be very serious, as the railway which takes the oil from Caspian to Moscow will be cut.'[75]

Events in India were complicated by the growing demand from Indian nationalists for independence. In August an outbreak of 'civil disobedience', designed to force Britain to undertake 'an orderly withdrawal', was launched. Known as the Quit India Movement, it involved attacks on installations and communications, the trouble being more serious 'than has ever been allowed to appear in the paper'. Although there was no widespread rebellion, the movement's partial success meant that instead of military duties, the soldiers had 'the distasteful duty' of keeping public order.[76]

In mid-October the 2nd Black Watch was sent to Contai in West Bengal, where protesters proposed to establish a 'National Government' in parallel to the local district administration.[77] No sooner had the Battalion arrived than it began to rain. 'By 1100 hrs today, a gale of cyclonic proportions was blowing from the N.E. It raged until sunset and not one building in the area for a hundred miles around escaped damage,' recorded the War Diary on 16 October. 'A tidal inundation accompanied the cyclone, breaking the sea wall and sweeping all before it except the strongest buildings on the highest ground.' 'No houses standing, tents covered by a foot of mud and silt, trucks emptied of their loads,' reported C Company's diary, describing 'ships swept a quarter of a mile inland, dead bodies and carcasses of cattle, frogs, fish, snakes and pi-dogs wherever the eye can reach.' 'It was a sad sight to see cattle drowned and people hanging from tree tops,' recorded Private Meldrum, 'some of them already dead. One woman I saw, whom I helped to take down had her inners hanging out.'[78]

With the countryside 'one vast sheet of water with people marooned all over it,' Lieutenant James Donaldson made a valiant attempt to extricate a ration party in two lorries stranded near his platoon post on the banks of the Pichaboni river. 'By means of lashing one lorry to a clump of palm trees and ordering his party to strip and remain concentrated and calm in this vehicle,' the men were saved. The other lorry was already under water, the men submerged up to their necks. When the flood subsided several hours later, Donaldson led them forward. Despite his own exhaustion he and another man 'waded and swam for twelve hours to Bn HQ at Contai to report and obtain rations and equipment,' his actions resulting in the award of an MBE.[79] In another incident Lieutenant Duncan Menzies, an Australian Rhodes Scholar, who had joined The Black Watch in April 1941, rescued his platoon, which had become almost submerged, by directing the men towards higher ground, successfully maintaining 'the morale and safety of his men'. For his actions Menzies was Mentioned in Despatches.[80]

In addition to the heavy death toll among the villagers, 14 soldiers of the 2nd Black Watch had drowned during the floods. To decontaminate the area, large scale burials were necessary, with 152 corpses and 421 cattle buried by the Battalion HQ alone, while the death rate during the cyclone was estimated at 80 per cent. 'Pits were dug for the cattle and the humans were burnt on pyres, as was the custom,' recorded Meldrum. 'It was a shattering experience for us. We had to get used to anything happening in this war.'[81] 'For the next weeks the Battalion was busied in succouring the people whose sedition it had come to suppress,' observed Bernard Fergusson. An appeal to give blood met with an estimated 95 per cent response from The Black Watch.[82] After two weeks, the Battalion returned to internal security duties before resuming jungle training.

Having heard 'great news' of the Eighth Army's attack at El Alamein, the officers and men in India awaited fresh bulletins, Barry describing as 'really wonderful' the news that 'the Axis has been broken and the Bosche and Itis are fleeing in disorder. It looks like a complete rout!'[83] As the war progressed and the history books were written, El Alamein acquired legendary status, Churchill remarking in his official history that 'it marked in fact the turning of "the Hinge of Fate". It may almost be said, "Before Alamein we never had a victory. After Alamein we never had a defeat."'[84]

We are the Black Watch,
Sons of the Red, White and Blue,
We are the Black Watch,
We'll show you what we can do,
Up boys and at 'em,
We'll make that housepainter yell,
Now's the time to join the Black Watch
We are the Ladies From Hell.[85]

13

1943: Fighting in the Front Line

Fighting in the front line of a battlefield is a very frightening and very, very dangerous place to be and when you are wounded the flesh heals up but the mind is scarred forever.[1]

Life is such a very small thing compared to the task in hand.[2]

Casablanca

In January 1943 the Allied leaders assembled in Casablanca, 'a pleasant spot', as Prime Minister Winston Churchill remarked, the warm North African air making a welcome change from the gloom of wartime London in winter.[3] Also present to discuss the future conduct of the war was US President Franklin Roosevelt, together with Generals Henri Giraud and Charles de Gaulle, representing the Free French, accompanied by their respective senior naval and military commanders. Stalin was absent, preferring not to leave the Soviet Union as the battle for Stalingrad reached its climax with the surrender of German forces on 2 February. Codenamed Symbol, the Allied leaders' deliberations produced the Casablanca Declaration, proposing a policy of 'unconditional surrender'.[4]

Operations had first to continue in North Africa. Once Tripoli was taken, the Eighth Army would advance into the French protectorate of Tunisia, joining forces with the First Army, battling for Tunis.[5] Over the next four months, the soldiers would pass through towns they had as yet not heard of but, once captured, the names would be etched for ever in their memories: among them were the 'wadis' or valleys in the North African coastal regions where rivers had run dry. Of these Wadi Akarit beyond Tripoli became notorious for the fierce fighting and the lives lost.

On to Tripoli!

'We had a rotten new year out here. We are still following Gerry all the time,' Private William Fisher was writing home in early January, describing to his wife how he had recently lost some of his 'pals… but it is just your luck out here'.[6] On 5 January the Division began to move towards the salt marsh of Wadi Chebir in the footsteps of advanced elements of the Eighth Army. 'By now the nights were becoming extremely cold,' recorded Major Hopwood. 'The men shivered without their greatcoats and blankets, as only the minimum equipment could be carried forward in the transport.' Progress slowed when they reached 'a mined bottleneck where the desert route debouched onto the main road,' resulting in a number of casualties, including Rennie who was badly injured when his jeep was blown up and his driver killed. 'Enemy air attacks during this period were frequent, especially against recce parties operating in No Man's Land,' recorded Roper-Caldbeck, who temporarily took command of 154 Brigade in place of Rennie.[7]

On 12 January Montgomery issued one of his 'Personal Messages' reminding the soldiers that they were going 'On To Tripoli!'[8] While the 2nd New Zealand and 7th Armoured Divisions proceeded inland, the 51st Highland Division, strengthened by the 9th Londonderry Heavy Anti-Aircraft Regiment, took the coastal road. The operation was to be conducted in four phases: 'Silk', making contact with German and Italian forces at Buerat, and 'Satin' which involved consolidating their position; these two phases would be followed by 'Cotton' and 'Rags', advancing on Tripoli and clearing the coastal road of mines. 154 Brigade moved forward on 14 January, setting in motion 'Silk'. The next phase, 'Satin', 'the capture and exploitation of the enemy's position in Buerat', would be carried out the following night by 153 Brigade.[9] 'At this time, information from Higher

Authority implied that the enemy was going to stand and fight,' continued Roper-Caldbeck. But, as at Mersa Brega, the Germans had withdrawn.[10]

'Cotton', the advance on Tripoli, began on 16 January, with a sense of urgency created by the need to gain control of the harbour before the Germans destroyed it, rendering it unusable for shipping. 'As much as 12 miles were covered in two consecutive hours,' continued Hopwood. Having passed Misurata (Misrata), the Division moved on to Zliten. At Garibaldi 'the country took on a different nature, consisting of an escarpment of small hills… while between it and the sea lay a fertile cultivated plain closely covered with vines and olive groves, dotted with little Italian settlements and pleasant little farmhouses set amongst the groves.'[11] Their progress was slowed by the terrain, which included 'sunken lanes, deep irrigation channels, wadis, and thick palm groves', as well as obstacles left by the retreating Germans.[12]

Having spent the night of 18 January at Garibaldi, the Division reached Homs (Khoms). A rocky feature to the south-west, where German troops were visible 'moving about on the skyline,' blocked their way. 'This was an old Italian barracks sited on an isolated hill beyond Homs and effectively dominating any further advance down the road, which now deviated from the coast and took to the hills in a more direct line for Tripoli,' explained Hopwood.[13] Known as Homs Castle, the soldiers renamed it Edinburgh Castle. During the night of 19/20 January Roper-Caldbeck sent out several patrols to probe its defences but German shelling and sniping was 'very active and accurate', and Lieutenant Bruce Fortune was lucky to survive when a bullet penetrated his liver.[14]

Instead of ordering a frontal attack to dislodge the Germans, Wimberley decided to outflank them. Leaving the 1st Black Watch in front of 'Edinburgh' Castle, the remainder of the brigade would march about 15 miles towards the coast before coming inland to cut the main road at Wadi Genima, a deep gully running from the coast to the hills. Local guides were 'requisitioned' without whom it would have been 'quite impossible' to advance 'as there was no road or track of any kind shown on the map,' recorded Lieutenant Colonel Oliver, 7th Black Watch. On reaching Hamadan, intelligence was received that the Germans had taken up position 'just east of the point at which the outflanking force had been ordered to cut the main road.'[15] Although, before the 7th Black Watch appeared, the Germans had been about to withdraw, they re-occupied their former positions with the result that the Battalion became 'heavily engaged'. Only when Allied reinforcements arrived with heavy machine-guns did the Germans pull back, shelling the positions they had evacuated. Fortunately the number of Allied casualties was reduced because many of the German shells were dud. Although the operation, known as the Battle of the Hills or Corradini, had contributed to the German withdrawal from the *jebel* or mountainous area between Homs and Corradini, the soldiers were disappointed at 'so little tactical success'. Meanwhile the 1st Black Watch had been, in Hopwood's words, 'flogging forward down the coast road' filling up 'innumerable craters and demolitions to make further advance possible'. The 5th Black Watch had also been moving forward, the road from Homs now 'one long traffic jam', observed McGregor.[16]

On 23 January the Eighth Army entered Tripoli. Montgomery's 'Personal Message' to 'all Troops' was laudatory, emphasising that it was only three months since the 'Battle of Egypt' had begun at Alamein. 'This achievement is probably without parallel in history.'[17] Privately, however, he had been critical of the 51st Highland Division, which he believed was 'getting weary, and generally displayed a lack of initiative and ginger' for which he had given Wimberley 'an imperial "rocket"'. Wimberley's response was to swear to himself that 'come what may, I would show the little man what we Highlanders could do.'[18] The 51st Highland Division's entry into Tripoli was delayed for three days because of a shortage of petrol. In a 'triumph of innovation', each section commander was told 'to hitch-hike on any transport that he could… every driver was to "borrow" enough spare petrol to get him forward.'[19]

While the 1st Black Watch was quartered in the town, the 5th found 'residence with becoming dignity in and around General Balbo's former palace,' and the 7th was encamped on the Homs road 'amid the olive groves, vineyards and orchards.' Here the men settled down for 'a period of rest and training which was almost at once rudely interrupted by dock work in Tripoli, for which daily and nightly, large work parties had to be supplied,' recorded Captain David Russell. Those looking forward 'to the flesh-pots' of the captured town were disappointed to find that life was 'pre-eminently military… a certain amount of local red wine was obtainable in varying degrees of purity, but beyond this there were very few attractions, although NAAFI had organised canteens and a cinema', dependent 'on the vagaries of the electric lighting system'.[20]

On 4 February Churchill, who had remained in North Africa after Casablanca, making brief visits to Cyprus and Turkey, witnessed the 'magnificent entry' of the Eighth Army through Tripoli's 'stately streets'. 'The men looked extremely well and had taken infinite trouble over their turnout, and the Quartermaster did wonders in producing clean suits of battledress and new bonnets, while the 1st Battalion kindly lent us new hackles since ours had not yet arrived,' related Russell. 'The parade itself consisted of an inspection and a march past across the Piazza Italia under the ramparts of the old Moorish Citadel, and must have been one of the smartest parades ever held in the middle of a military campaign.'[21]

'I have never felt prouder in all my life,' wrote Wimberley, who led the Division in a bren-gun carrier called 'Beaumont Hamel', in recognition of the Division's action in 1916. 'As the Pipes and Drums played our famous Highland Regiments past in turn to the strains of "Highland Laddie", "Pibroch O'Dhomnuill Dubh", the "Cock of the North" and "The Campbells are Coming", my heart was very full and there were tears in my eyes. However, I was certainly in good company that day. I noticed the same in Alan Brooke's and as for Winston, the tears were running down his cheeks.'[22] 'I addressed about two thousand officers and men,' recorded Churchill. 'I spoke to them about "*Yet nightly pitch our moving tent/ A day's march nearer home*". But they were still a long way from home; nor was the route to be direct.'[23]

On 20 February the British Eighth and First Armies were placed under a new headquarters, 18th Army Group, commanded by General Sir Harold Alexander, Eisenhower remaining in supreme command.[24]

The Mareth Line

While the 51st Highland Division remained on the outskirts of Tripoli, the 7th Armoured Division and other elements of the Eighth Army had been pursuing Axis forces, now operating under the name Army Group Afrika, towards Tunisia. In February, the towns of Zuara, Ben Gardane and Medenine had fallen, all of which were significant outposts of the Mareth Line – a line of fortifications constructed by the French before the outbreak of war to guard against an attack by the Italians in Libya, but held by the Axis since the fall of France. It stretched from the Mediterranean coast to the Matmata Hills, while beyond lay a vast expanse of sand, making any left-flanking movement impossible. 'The role of the Division was now to make its way forward,' explained Hopwood, 'gaining ground each night, until a firm base was established opposite the Mareth Line from which the assault could be delivered.'[25]

By the end of February, 154 Brigade had reached Wadi Moussa parallel to the Mareth fortifications. For the 7th Black Watch this began 'a period of contact with the enemy which remained more or less unbroken, except for a day or two, until the battle of the Wadi Akarit, nearly six weeks later,' remarked Russell.[26] The 5th Black Watch had already begun to send out patrols reporting on Axis defensive positions, their reconnaissance revealing that the Germans were laying new minefields and digging in guns.[27]

On 6 March Rommel's forces made a pre-emptive attack at Medenine. 'At first light heavy enemy artillery and mortar fire. I stood up and watched,' related Private Henry Scivity Barker. 'The shells were falling about two hundred yards in front of us. In anticipation of the attack, the 7th Black Watch had been moved to a stronger defensive position across the Wadi Zessar. 'From a position on the high ground where we had our junction with the right-hand Company of the Queen's [Royal Regiment, 131 Brigade], the Germans and Italians had infiltrated and were able to bring fire to bear across the Battalion area,' related Hopwood, describing the 1st Black Watch's position in what became known as the Battle of Medenine. 'As dusk came the Queen's had all their Companies committed, including their reserve. It was now that Roper-Caldbeck was able to launch his counter-attack… it went forward splendidly into the sunset and the ridge was soon clear and the position restored.'[28] 'We could scarcely believe that this ill-planned and badly supported affair was to be the last word of the famous Afrika Corps,' commented Russell, pointing out that Rommel had lost 'no less than 50 tanks which he could ill afford'. Later in the day, Oliver went forward, seeing 'all the evidence of a very hurried withdrawal by the enemy, both German and Italian, shown by abandoned equipment and infantry guns.'[29]

Disappointed with the failure to forestall the inevitable Allied attack on the Mareth Line, on 9 March Rommel travelled to Europe to persuade Hitler that his position in North Africa would be improved by shorter lines of communication. Hitler, who was still 'very upset and depressed' at Germany's failure at Stalingrad, was 'unreceptive' to his proposal, implying that Rommel had become 'a pessimist'. Ordered to take sick-leave, his place in command of the Army Group Afrika was taken by General Hans-Jürgen von Arnim, commander of the 5th Panzer Army. Rommel never returned to North Africa.[30]

The Allied assault on the Mareth Line was Montgomery's first big operation since El Alamein. Codenamed Operation Pugilist, his 'Personal Message' was insistent: 'the Eighth Army:- (a) Will destroy the enemy now facing us in the Mareth position; (b) Will burst through the Gabès Gap; (c) Will then drive northwards on Sfax, Sousse, and finally Tunis.'[31] As part of the operation, the 2nd New Zealand Division (reinforced as the New Zealand Corps), would make a flanking movement, circumventing the Matmata Hills, to break through the Tebaga gap facing Gabès.

On the night of 20 March the 50th Northumbrian Division began the frontal attack. Heavy rain slowed their advance and the obstacles included deadly quicksands and a deep anti-tank ditch. The 51st Highland Division was among units detailed for a 'pursuit role'. '[We] are still following Gerry and I wish to hell it was finish[ed]', Private Fisher was writing to his 'dear wife' on 22 March, having repeatedly told her how much he wanted to get home 'for I miss you more than the world'.[32] But, owing both to the conditions and the opposition, the 50th Northumbrians failed to establish a firm bridgehead. 'The whole situation appeared chaotic,' noted Russell, 'especially as the infantry in front were being thinned out… had the enemy attacked at this time, there is no doubt that he could have scored a considerable local success.'[33]

In a subsidiary attack on 25 March the 5th Black Watch was ordered to secure 'a dominating feature' called Carrier Hill.[34] With the 50th Northumbrians still unable to break through, Montgomery had withdrawn a number of units to reinforce the more successful New Zealand flanking attack, obliging a German withdrawal from the Mareth Line. Although, briefly it appeared that the Germans might attempt to reoccupy their positions, Allied mortar and artillery fire 'severely punished' them. By 26 March patrols had established that Axis forces had withdrawn to Wadi Zigzaou. The following day Oliver and Hopwood crossed through the Mareth Line, finding 'a tremendous amount of abandoned equipment, both British, German, and Italian… the whole area was strewn with British dead… mines and wire.'[35]

Wadi Akarit: 'Second to none!'

North of Gabès were Wadi Akarit and the Roumana Ridge, where the Army Group Afrika now lay entrenched 'in a final effort to prevent the junction of the First and Eighth Armies'. 'Well let me tell you', Private Fisher was writing on 31 March, 'we never had a break since we landed hear [sic] but we think it [is] about over hear so it might not be long till I [am] home beside you and my wee son.'[36] On 2 April the 7th Black Watch moved forward taking over an area which encompassed 'an Arab tented settlement of considerable size which had large flocks of sheep, goats and camels attached to it,' recorded Oliver, noting that, fearful of being caught in the midst of a warzone, the Arabs made a 'strategic withdrawal… complete with all their animals and belongings… leaving a scrupulously clean area behind them.'[37]

Codenamed Operation Scipio, the next stage would feature an attack by the 50th Northumbrians to the west of the Roumana Ridge, while the 51st Highland Division would assault the ridge and the Wadi. The 4th Indian Division would then move forward. 153 Brigade, less the 5th Black Watch kept as divisional reserve, was to consolidate a line a mile in front of Wadi Akarit. Once the 7th Argyll & Sutherland Highlanders had broken through the Wadi's defences and created a bridgehead, the 7th Black Watch would pass through, joining up with 152 Brigade on the Roumana Ridge.

'We reached the anti-tank ditch to see Oliver standing on the other side of the ditch,' recalled Sergeant Robert Penman. 'I will never forget his words "Come on the 7th, the Argylls have taken 700 prisoners and we will have to do better than that!"' The German artillery was 'tremendous. This was their last ditch stand and they were going to make a fight for it… We (7th Bn) had four miles to walk and every step taking us down the throat of the guns.' Despite securing the bridgehead 'extremely accurate and constant shelling' meant that very little further progress could be made 'and it was not possible to get any anti-tank guns or vehicles forward.'[38]

In the late afternoon reinforcements from the 1st Black Watch had been sent forward. 'Up they got and off they went hundreds of boys like myself embroiled in a conflict that was nothing to do with them in the beginning. I was proud of these youngsters who had nothing to lose but their lives, limbs and their future,' commented Penman. 'Meantime, also, the enemy had infiltrated well past the flank of the 7th Black Watch and got down the anti-tank ditch almost into the Battalion's area', related Hopwood, 'and it was here that some of our stretcher parties were ambushed and shot up by the Germans.' During the battle, Hopwood was seen 'trying to persuade some reluctant tanks to move forward. He eventually climbed on to one of the leading tanks and told the tank commander in pretty typical Hopwood fashion what he thought about him and what he had to do.' During the altercation he was shot through the lung by a German machine-gunner; luckily his wound was not fatal.[39]

On the Roumana Ridge 152 Brigade had encountered severe opposition, the 5th Black Watch being put under its command in order to reinforce the 5th Seaforths which had 'run into trouble'. By the following day the Germans were found to have withdrawn. Casualties were high, the 7th Black Watch having eleven officers and 180 other ranks dead or wounded; one of the fatalities was Private William Fisher who had so longed to go home.[40]

'I doubt if our Empire has ever possessed such a magnificent fighting machine as the Eighth Army,' proclaimed Montgomery. 'You have made its name a household word all over the world.' When Lieutenant General Sir Oliver Leese commended the 51st Highland Division, Wimberley again added his praise. 'We can indeed proudly say that Scotland's troops have once again shown the British Army that they are still second to none.'[41] The Division then moved on to Sfax where 'bathing parties went down to the beach' and life was 'pleasant'. When Montgomery was granted the freedom of the city, the 7th Black Watch provided a Guard of Honour, borrowing kilts from the 1st Black Watch. 'The ceremony was quite impressive, though it seemed somewhat incongruous, coming as it did towards the end of a military campaign,' observed Oliver, who received a bar to his DSO after Wadi Akarit.[42]

Among others in The Black Watch who were honoured, Lieutenant Peter Watson received the MC for guiding the battalion through a minefield gap. Stretcher bearer Private George Clark received the MM, his conduct in 'moving across an exposed slope under mortar fire to give assistance, during which he himself was wounded' upholding 'the high standards which the Stretcher bearers have set.'[43] Wounded in his right hand while out on patrol on 6 April, Captain Ian Reid, 7th Black Watch, was among the prisoners, but not for long. Having managed to escape, he remained 'at large' in Italy for two years.[44] Another POW was Private Bill Johns. A keen musician, he played the accordion throughout his captivity, even entertaining Pope Pius XII on a visit to Campo 66 in Capua where Johns was a prisoner. Observing that the accordion was 'a bit worse for wear' the Pope arranged for him to be sent a new one.[45]

After two years on garrison duty in Gibraltar, the 4th Black Watch returned to Britain in April. Before leaving Lieutenant Colonel B. A. Innes arranged for plaques to be cut into the pillboxes and tunnels telling future generations that they had been constructed by The Black Watch.[46] The 1st Tyneside Scottish, The Black Watch was in Thetford, Norfolk: 'So little time for training by the time the Jocks have attended RSM's parades, Padre's lectures and carried out maintenance etc.,' nineteen-year-old Brian Stewart informed his brother, George, 5th Black Watch, who was describing fighting 'Jerry and Eyties'.[47]

Advancing on Tunis

While the Eighth Army had been moving along the coast to Tunis, passing through Sousse and Enfidaville, the First Army was advancing from the west. Included in its ranks was the 6th Black Watch which had arrived in Algiers in late March to join the 4th Division. The journey by sea took 'nine days after a huge sweep out into the Atlantic, presumably to avoid U-boats which was not entirely successful as one of the ships in the convoy, carrying many nurses, was sunk,' recalled Lieutenant Henry McKenzie Johnston. 'We disembarked wearing greatcoats and full marching order,' related Private Charlie Framp, who had joined The Black Watch from the young soldier's battalion, the 70th Leicestershire Regiment. 'We were thankful for the greatcoats – despite the fact that we'd arrived on the southern shores of the Med it was as cold as the Scotland we'd left behind.'[48] Among those who had 'contrived' to come to Italy with the 6th Black Watch 'at the age of 50' was Sergeant W. B. (Tug) Wilson, a veteran of the First World War.[49]

Having left Algiers on 1 April, the 6th Black Watch moved to the Béja area. 'There was no natural cover here,' observed McKenzie

Johnston, 'which made us very nervous, but fortunately by then, as we discovered, we had obtained virtual air superiority and the Germans had given up mounting air attacks on troop concentrations such as ours, preferring to save their limited resources for occasional hit-and-run raids nearer their own front line.'[50] Ten days later the Battalion was ordered forward through the Dochabel Valley to a line of hills, the Djebel Rmel, on the road to Tunis.

'In single file, platoon by platoon, company by company, the Battalion moved out of the valley and headed for the front line, a piper leading each company,' recorded Framp. 'The hills about us were, appropriately enough I remember thinking, red with poppies.' Spending his first night in the front line he was 'both excited and frightened.' At first light 'the guns of both sides suddenly and savagely opened fire upon each other. It was my first experience of the "morning hate."' During the day they improved on their slit trenches. 'We had dug in on the forward slope – the slope, that is, in full view of the enemy, in our case the Germans on the other side of our valley and also, unbeknown to us, on the two hills either side of us. Completely ignorant of this fact and being the greenhorn troops we were, men were wandering about the hillside as if we were still playing at war back in Scotland.'[51]

The following morning the Germans again started heavy shelling. 'I hardly had time to feel fear,' recalled McKenzie Johnston. As signals officer, he was kept busy maintaining the communication cables which had been laid between Battalion HQ and the various companies. 'At one stage I myself raced over a couple of hundred yards to the forward company, an unpleasant run with shells falling around me, to take an urgent message because both the telephone and the wireless links had ceased to work.' Private Framp's recollection was of trying to get some sleep in the intervals in between shelling 'so to await the next "stonk", call to duty or whatever!'[52] Lance Corporal Charlie Hankins was lucky to survive:

> I heard a mortar bomb screaming down and thought "Hell, that's close." As I dived into the few inches of dugout it hit me in a flash.

> My left leg was completely blown off just a few inches from the groin. My other leg was just hanging on bits of flesh. The side of my left hand was torn off. For a few seconds my eyes dimmed. I turned on my back to try and make my way down the hill. My other leg fell off as I moved down. Then I was hit in the side of the chest with a gunshot and my lung collapsed. I could hardly breathe. There was no pain at that time, it was a lot just to take it all in.'[53]

Casualties at Djebel Rmel were heavy, the Commanding Officer, Lieutenant Colonel Barclay, being among those fatally wounded; since his second-in-command, Major Neil Blair, had been knocked unconscious, command temporarily passed to the adjutant, Captain Brian Madden. Although 'no further incidents of note' occurred, there was at least one 'remarkable demonstration' of toughness when a soldier who had been hit in the leg remained out in the open for two days until he could crawl back to their lines, his water bottle still half full and his emergency ration untouched. When asked the reason for this self-denial, he replied that his orders were that he could only open his rations with an officer's permission and never to do more 'than wet his mouth from his water bottle.'[54] On 19 April the 6th Black Watch was relieved, with American forces later securing Djebel Rmel after a fierce fight.

By late April the focus of the Battalion's operations was a junction known as 'Peter's Corner', where the road to Tunis turned north-east, parallel to which ran a narrow ridge, the Argoub el Hamma, held by the Germans. After a failed attack on 24 April by a company of the 6th Black Watch on the hill of Sidi Medienne, held in greater strength by the Germans than intelligence reports indicated, a full-scale attack was ordered the following day. 'The plan was for the artillery to put a barrage down upon the German wire during the daylight hours when the wire could be seen, so as to blast gaps in it through which we could pass early that same night before the Germans had time to repair the damage,' related Framp, 'The battalion attack was to be a silent affair with no artillery support *immediately* preceding it to warn the enemy of our approach.' Just before dark, the men

ABOVE *On the March, Boer War* by W. Skeoch Cumming. Wearing khaki aprons to hide the front of their kilts, viewed from behind 'they were still unmistakably Scottish'.

RIGHT A blockhouse in South Africa, 1902, by Lt Colonel Hugh Rose of Kilravock, 1929. 'A chance bullet entered the collarbone of Lance Corporal Walter Scott of the Band, & came out at the base of his spine. He fell dead in the arms of Punch Wilson.'

TOP Sounding the Gong, Fort George, Inverness, 1904. Found in 1858 during the Indian Mutiny, the 'Cawnpore' gong remains a prized regimental trophy.

ABOVE India Coronation Durbar 1911. The 2nd Black Watch formed the Guard of Honour for the King-Emperor George V.

TOP Postcard from the Trenches. 'We did our job,' Jack Stewart wrote home. 'Of course the rest of the Brigade were with us but we, the 9BW, almost unaided rushed the HUN trenches.'

ABOVE *4th Black Watch in the Attack, Neuve Chapelle*, 1915, by Joseph Gray. 'There was the thrilling anticipation of being in at the great final victory of the War. Vain Hope!' commented Lance Corporal Linton Andrews.

LEFT Lieutenant N. F. Dixon, 6th Black Watch, in the trenches, wearing sheepskin jerkin and trousers. He was killed in October 1917. 'Arctic explorers – Eskimos – trappers from the Far West – we looked anything but soldiers,' said Private Joseph Gray, 1915.

BELOW 'Soldiering' memoir of Albert H. Hay. 'Shells of every size were dropping all round us and the noise was deafening', he wrote, describing fighting at Givenchy in April 1918.

OPPOSITE, TOP 2nd Black Watch, Colours Party, Palestine 1937. 'We travelled Palestine from Dan to Beersheba from Jaffa to Jersualem to Jericho', said Sergeant Major Nobby Clark.

OPPOSITE, BELOW Pipe Major 'Rab' Roy. Wounded at Tobruk in 1941, after being taken to the Regimental Aid Post, he continued to play for both friend and foe, acquiring the name 'The Piper of Tobruk'.

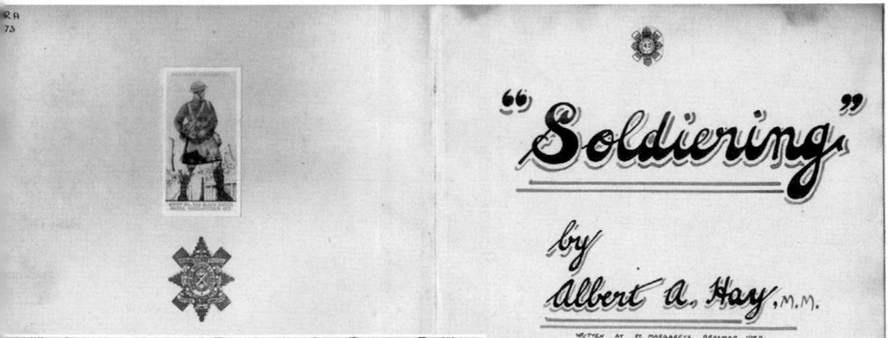

"Soldiering"

by

Albert A. Hay, M.M.

WRITTEN AT ST. MARGARETS, BRAEMAR. 1939.

15th February, 1917 — 31st March, 1921.

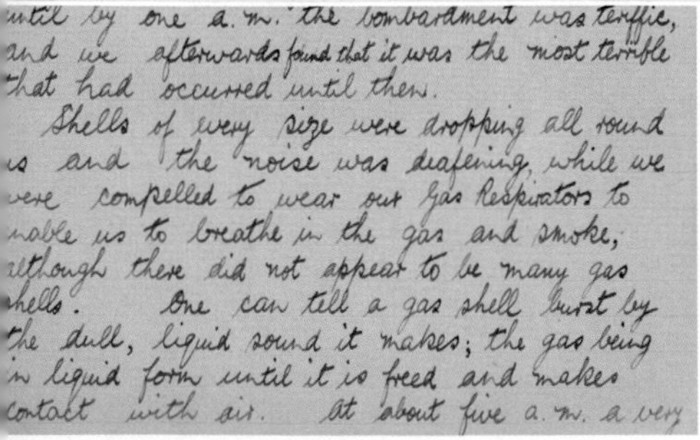

until by one a. m. the bombardment was terrific, and we afterwards found that it was the most terrible that had occurred until then.

Shells of every size were dropping all round us and the noise was deafening, while we were compelled to wear our Gas Respirators to enable us to breathe in the gas and smoke, although there did not appear to be many gas shells. One can tell a gas shell burst by the dull, liquid sound it makes; the gas being in liquid form until it is freed and makes contact with air. At about five a. m. a very

START
LINE
ELGIN
LEVEN
VICTORIA
MONTROSE
COMRIE
DOLLAR
9th AUS.DIV.
FORFAR
TURRIFF
INSCH
KILLIN
CRIEFF
KINTORE

OPPOSITE, TOP *HMS* Dido *arriving in Alexandria*, May 1941 by Noel Syers. 'The artist thought a better painting would result from the Piper playing from a battered man o'war than one that wasn't hit at all,' explained Piper George Ogilvie who piped in HMS *Jackal*, his descriptions of the scene inspiring the artist's imagination.

OPPOSITE, BELOW *The 51st Highland Division plans El Alamein*, by Ian G. M. Eadie. At the end of September 1942, General Montgomery revealed his battle plans, 'opening a new and even more intensive pre-Alamein phase. Forward assembly areas had to be reconnoitred, sites chosen for battle headquarters and elaborate precautions taken to conceal these preparations from the enemy'.

TOP 7th Black Watch preparing for El Alamein, 1942. 'I'm pretty good at the sun compass now; I've been studying it since we landed. It's an eerie job going out into the unknown and very often the unmapped as well,' Lieutenant George Morrison, 7th Black Watch, wrote home. He was killed on 23 October 1942.

ABOVE Privates Bruce and McMichael painting the 'HD' sign. 'The Highlanders', recorded Major General Wimberley, 'had already become known as the "Highway Decorators" for their habit of painting HD on almost any available surface in the Division's area'.

TOP Chindits in Burma, crossing the river, 1944. 'Mules are hard working and hardy but they're not pets,' observed Bill Lark. 'You have to build a relationship and some of them can be stroppy. Very stroppy.'

ABOVE, LEFT *Cassino Town, 1944*, by Geordie Cox. 'I will never forget my first sight of Cassino, as we rounded a corner and saw below us in the moonlight the remains of the town.'

ABOVE, RIGHT Padre Tom Nicol, The United Nations Memorial Cemetery at Pusan, South Korea, July 1953. 'Quartermaster Nobby Clark had arranged that all the Black Watch graves had a red hackle put on top, so we could all see which were Black Watch people,' recorded Lieutenant David Arbuthnott.

'tightened rifle slings, fixed bayonets, climbed from our trenches and moved silently forward to the attack. We, who had only heard about but had not seen the strength of the German barbed wire defences, hoped the artillery lads had made a good job of flattening them. The almost total loss of B Company the previous day was very much to the fore of all our minds.'[55]

'The forward troops crept right up to the wire as the barrage stopped and found several gaps through which they charged with fixed bayonets and a piper playing,' related McKenzie Johnston. 'It gave us great confidence to go forward,' recalled Private George Daily, 'it also must have frightened the hell out of the enemy, as they thought that they were being attacked by the whole of the 51st Highland Division. They beat a hasty retreat, much to our surprise and relief. The power of the pipes!'[56] But, although the front-line German troops had been taken by surprise, they immediately 'opened up a devastating fire upon us,' continued Framp. The artillery barrage against the German wire had not been as successful as they had hoped. 'Loose strands caught up first one leg, then the other. As quick as I freed one the other caught. Lines of tracer bullets from the German trenches shot by me. My brain was numbed with terror as if in a nightmare… grenades were bursting everywhere, whether thrown by Germans or by our own men still behind us, I was unable to distinguish.' Having got through the wire, finding himself further forward than the rest of his platoon he ran back to rejoin them. 'Maybe if I'd stayed where I was I'd have been alright.' A 'stream of bullets' followed his progress, one hitting his left arm, the sensation like being 'savagely struck by a cricket bat'. While making for the Regimental Aid Post, he realised that the Battalion's efforts were not in vain and 'the hill was ours, all firing upon it ceased.'[57]

'The day after the battle, my friend Andy and me were doing a bit of mopping up and found two dead German soldiers in a slit trench, sitting propped up at either end,' recalled Private Daily. 'They both had binoculars round their necks, but such is the callousness of war, and as they had no further use for them, Andy and I purloined them as spoils of war!'[58] The 6th Black Watch remained in the sector until it was relieved at the end of April, German prisoners later observing that the fighting 'was more severe than anything they had experienced in Russia.'[59]

'Driving the enemy into the sea'

For the final breakthrough to Tunis two divisions of the Eighth Army, the 4th Indian and the 7th Armoured, were to assist the First Army in creating a gap in the German defensive positions south of Tunis. 'By this time, however,' remarked McKenzie Johnston, 'German resistance was collapsing and the campaign became fairly fast moving as we occupied position after position with virtually no fighting.'[60] The 6th Black Watch's last action was capturing a feature known as Point 161, at Arg el Hadjar, north-east of the village of Montarnaud; the attack was launched on 6 May. By 7 a.m. the gap was breached, the Germans having already withdrawn. After remaining 'under slight mortar fire' the Battalion moved forward to Bordj Frendj. As the full weight of the First Army was pitched against Tunis, on 10 May the 6th Black Watch's role was 'to cut off the enemy's force by passing through the Hammam Lif gap and then by way of Soliman and Beni Khaled reach the sea at Korba, on the coast of Cap Bon.' Passing through the 'new-won' gap, there was little sign of any Germans 'except for a lot of abandoned vehicles and a few prisoners'. With German resistance broken, on the night of 13 May the 6th Black Watch was informed that it 'might stand down'.[61]

In retrospect Henry McKenzie Johnston remembered more 'scenes and incidents, rather than of war: the wide open, treeless countryside and rather hostile scattered Arab communities; the occasional appearance of a small bird or two to which the warfare surrounding them was evidently unimportant; the chilly nights lying in the open watching the stars – and the often astonishing silence, apart from an occasional distant "crump" of some artillery activity elsewhere.' A more trivial recollection was getting badly sunburnt; since this constituted a 'crime' he had to be treated secretly by the medical officer, suffering 'in silence for a few days as I went about my military duties in agony without showing it. I peeled in strips.'[62]

Meanwhile, the remainder of the Eighth Army had advanced through Sousse and Enfidaville. After its severe losses at Wadi Akarit, the 51st Highland Division was not part of the final movement forward. Instead it took over the positions of the 4th Indian Division and 2nd New Zealand Division in the Enfidaville area before moving to Djedjelli (Jijel) on the Algerian coast to engage in 'mountaineering to keep fit, and combined operations training with the Navy'. 'We did beach landings, wet and dry,' recorded Barker. 'The training had one positive advantage, swimming.' 'It is a mighty country this. You drive for miles and still the hills roll up before you, whereas you could have been twice around Scotland,' observed Private Marchant.[63]

The North African campaign ended with the surrender of nearly a quarter of a million men of the Army Group Afrika including the senior generals. 'Your contribution to the complete and final removal of the enemy from Africa has been beyond all praise,' extolled Montgomery. 'As our Prime Minster said at Tripoli, in February last, it will be a great honour to be able to say in years to come: "I marched and fought with the Eighth Army."'[64]

The First Army was then disbanded. The 6th Black Watch moved to Sousse on guard duty: 'a trying time, which the Jocks hated,' recalled McKenzie Johnston. 'The Italians were very undisciplined and simply would not queue properly for food and water, or keep their areas and latrines clean.' 'The Germans had great contempt for the Italians,' recorded Madden, 'the Italians considerable fear of the Germans' and so they had to be kept separate. 'We gave the Germans wire and told them to erect a barricade between themselves and the Italians. It was up in no time – they weren't going to mix with Mussolini's warriors. We gave the Italians wire and a similar order. Up went the barricade again – anything to make themselves safe from their allies.' The Battalion then moved to Bougie, quartered 'amongst lime and lemon trees,' recalled McKenzie Johnston who accompanied the Padre in his quest to identify and photograph many of the temporary graves. After Bougie, the Battalion was quartered in Djedjelli, in the footsteps of the 51st Highland Division. 'The move was delayed a couple of days', continued Madden, 'as we had a hen hatching and represented to Brigade that she must be allowed to finish the job. Our plea was acceded to at once and three lusty chickens were soon taken on our strength in Battalion orders.'[65]

The invasion of Europe: Sicily

After knocking 'Rommel and his Army "for six" right out of North Africa,' the Eighth Army's next objective was Sicily, where General Valentine von Hube was in command of the island's defence. Included in 'Gruppe Hube' were two German divisions and about 200,000 Italians. Although initially outnumbering Allied forces in men, the Axis forces had fewer tanks, less field artillery and ammunition.[66]

The 51st Highland Division's destination remained secret until the convoys were at sea. 'You will by now have realized,' Wimberley's message said, 'if you had not sensed it before, that we of the Highland Division were chosen, before even the fighting in North Africa ended, to form part of the Empire's spearhead.' 'En route we were issued with a copy of "A Soldiers Guide to Sicily". Quite an impressive booklet giving do's and don'ts when in enemy territory,' noted CQMS Meekison. After a brief stop at Malta, the onward voyage was rough. 'Most of the rest of the lads were seasick, and spent the whole time in their bunks. I suffered dizzy spells but managed to keep going and to hold my food.'[67]

On 'the eve of the Invasion of Europe', Major Bobby Hutchison wrote another letter home, informing his parents that the Division was going to play a leading part, that his Brigade was the assault Brigade and that the 7th Black Watch 'with its fine record' would have 'a most responsible task'. 'There will be sacrifice – I may be one – if this reaches you, you will know that I have finished my work on this earth.' Pointing out that he felt he had received more than he had given, he continued: 'after all life is such a very small thing compared to the task in hand. Just think of this and then pray that my life has gone with the many others before as bricks in the building of a better world.'[68]

On the night of 9/10 July, the immense amphibious and airborne operation was launched. Codenamed Operation Husky, it involved two Task Forces. While the Western Task Force, commanded by General George Patton and consisting of the United States' Seventh Army, landed in the Gulf of Gela, the Eastern Task Force, consisting of the Eighth Army under Montgomery, disembarked in the south-east off the Gulf of Noto, the 51st Highland Division landing near Portopalo. Supported by naval forces transporting the invading armies, simultaneous airborne attacks had begun just after midnight. 'It was good to see the Spitfires and Hurricanes passing overhead to hit enemy targets,' observed Meekison, who helped himself to 'quantities of ripe tomatoes' on arrival. 'This proved to be the first practical use for the steel helmet,' recalled Barker. 'We used them as trugs, i.e. filled them with tomatoes.' To their surprise, their landing was not contested. 'The Italians evidently thought no one would be mad enough to be in the seas on such a night… They evidently underestimated the Scots.'[69] 'The whole of the first day was spent in attempting to find any enemy,' commented Russell. Advancing inland, the weather was 'extremely hot and the roads were dusty'. Each man carried a heavy load, consisting of two days landing rations, respirators, picks and shovels. Passing through Pachino and Noto, they reached Palazzolo where Allied bombing had destroyed much of the town and corpses were still lying on the streets.[70] Their presence was soon challenged when, on 13 July, a German unit ambushed the 5th Seaforth near Francofonte, leading to fierce fighting against the Germans defending the town.

The following day, one of the hottest so far experienced, Wimberley ordered an attack on Vizzini, strategically located on a hilltop dominating the roads below. An earlier attempt by the Malta Brigade had failed. While 153 Brigade was part of the attacking force, battalions from 154 Brigade later moved up. Unfortunately, as Russell explained, either the orders had been misunderstood 'or watches had not been properly synchronized', but, as the 1st Black Watch reached its objective, another heavy barrage 'from somewhere to our left came down slap on top of the 1st Battalion,' resulting in numerous casualties.[71] Having resisted the Allied assault throughout the day, the Germans withdrew under the cover of darkness. 'Vizzini had proved quite a hard nut to crack,' commented Lieutenant McGregor, 5th Black Watch, 'and it was the first taste of street fighting which was to become a Battalion skill in later conflicts.'[72]

During the battle, Meekison was 'safely ensconced behind a hill feature'. Just as they were settling down, 'word came down that there had been a number of casualties requiring evacuation.' When a request came for assistance, he and another soldier volunteered. Unable to proceed until dark 'it was an eerie journey as we had to crawl [in our vehicles] up a difficult winding road lit only by sporadic tracer fire and the occasional starshell, and we were quite sure that we could be heard for miles around.' On arrival Meekison was told that their journey was unnecessary. The stretchers laid out in the church hall had been occupied by 'some tired Jocks, who had fought all day and had taken the opportunity to have a comfortable if brief rest!'[73]

Gerbini and Sferro: 'There will be sacrifice'

'The next week [to] ten days consisted of night attack after night attack; [it] got a bit tiresome,' observed Private Barker. Moving northwards towards the Catanian plain as part of the leading brigade, the 7th Black Watch line of advance was towards the Sferro Hills 'which lay in a commanding position to the west of the Gerbini area, where there was a known German aerodrome being held at the time as part of the German main line of defence.' Unable to cross the plain in daylight, a 'wheel' round towards Ramacca was ordered. 'The plan was for a series of leapfrogs, the [1st] Battalion passing through the other two Battalions to attack its final objective,' explained Hopwood, who had recovered from his Wadi Akarit injury and was now second-in-command, 1st Black Watch.[74]

Their first objective was the village of Gerbini, whose capture would give 'greater depth to the Brigade position'. If they could hold it, Rennie, who had resumed command of 154 Brigade after his January injury, believed they might 'possibly force the enemy to withdraw from his defences to the north which were preventing them from crossing the Dittaino [river].'[75] The operation began on the night of 18/19 July. 'With the coming of dawn, the Battalion's troubles started,' recorded Russell. Hemmed in by German troops, the 7th Black Watch could do little more than send out patrols 'attempting to mop up Spandau posts or other pockets of German resistance.' The 1st Black Watch's attack on the village was strongly resisted. 'The battle for Gerbini airfield was fierce and fluid. We crossed the river, pushed on the cross roads near the airfield perimeter,' recalled Barker, describing their opponents in the 1st Hermann Goering Division as 'fanatical fighters, so much so that we were convinced that they were doped to the eyeballs… The airfield was won and lost five times.'[76] 'More ill luck was to follow,' Hopwood related, when the 1st Black Watch's Commanding Officer, Neil Blair, who had transferred from the 6th to take command of the 1st Black Watch in May, was severely wounded in the leg while 'standing on top of a bank to see what he could of the battle'. When the Germans counter-attacked, the Battalion had to withdraw. The fighting at Gerbini, recorded Rennie, was 'the first occasion during the campaign in Sicily in which the Division encountered really serious opposition.'[77]

The 5th Black Watch had been part of the force advancing towards Sferro, a few miles north-west, having first secured the Sferro bridge and established a bridgehead over the Dittaino. 'The 19th July was to be remembered by the Battalion as one of the blacker days with 14 killed and many more wounded, but all the objectives had been securely held,' recorded McGregor. One of Meekison's lasting memories 'was the sight of Mt Etna's red crater glowing in the dawn as we made our way back from the front, glad to be alive. That was my real baptism of fire, and it gave me a little more confidence in myself in future. I had not been so terribly afraid, and perhaps more so, hadn't showed it.'[78]

The Allied invasion of Sicily had further undermined Mussolini's authority. On 25 July King Victor Emanuel III had him arrested and began secret discussions with the Allies with a view to signing an armistice. After the severe fighting at Gerbini, Montgomery had decided to shift the focus of attack, which meant withdrawing the Dittaino bridgehead held by the 7th Black Watch. 'The Divisional thrust line was altered to an axis further North across the river,' and closer to where 153 Brigade had obtained its 'lodgement' in the Sferro area, explained Hopwood, who had taken command of the 1st Black Watch after Blair was injured. While other divisions would deliver the main assault, the 51st Highland Division was ordered 'to protect the right flank of this advance from the Sferro bridgehead'. First a 'set-piece' attack had to be made on the Sferro Hills. 'Mount Etna is straight in front of us and we only hope we don't have to assault the top of it!' commented Major Archie Murray. Despite putting up stiff resistance, with several attempts at counter-attacking, by the end of the day on 1 August the Germans had withdrawn, the number of weapons and ammunition left behind indicating a hurried departure.[79]

The capture of Sferro Hills signified the final stages of the Sicilian campaign. The ebb and flow of battle had its emotional cost, as Captain Stewart McLaren recorded, including the traumatic experience of withdrawing over ground where they had already fought. Since the ground had been too hard to dig graves to bury their dead comrades, they had built stone cairns around their bodies. Passing again over the same terrain a few weeks later, they saw the cairns had been disassembled and the corpses were lying in the open, stripped of their clothes and shoes by the destitute Sicilians.[80]

The Western Task Force, under Patton's command, had faced far less opposition in its advance across central and western Sicily to Messina and on 10 August General Hube began evacuating German forces to mainland Italy. 'I don't think the end of this phase is far off now,' Lieutenant James Murray, 1st Black Watch was commenting on 15 August. Two days later the German withdrawal was complete, Montgomery announcing: 'the campaign in Sicily is over… we have captured our first slice of the Italian home country.'[81] Later described as 'a strategic and tactical failure', only Eisenhower conceded that the campaign would have achieved speedier success if landings had been made on both sides of the straits of Messina, preventing access to the mainland.[82] Yet the Sicilian campaign prompted Italy's surrender: on 3 September General Guiseppe Castellano signed an armistice on behalf of Mussolini's successor, Marshal Pietro Badoglio, which was made public five days later.[83]

During the thirty-nine-day offensive, the 51st Highland Division recorded 1,436 casualties out of nearly 12,000 men in the Eighth Army killed in action, wounded or missing, of which 402 were from Black Watch battalions.[84] Stories of gallantry were many: stretcher bearer, 'Smokey Joe' Masterton, and Corporal 'Smudger' Smith 'performed heroics,' commented Barker, describing how Masterton 'treated friend and foe equally'. Lance Corporal Francis Barrett, 5th Black Watch, received the MM for demonstrating 'leadership at its best' during the capture of the Sferro bridge. Lieutenant Mike Wingate-Gray, 1st Black Watch, was awarded the MC for knocking out a German machine-gun post at Gerbini.[85] One of those who died in the final stages was Major Bobby Hutchison, who had earlier warned his parents 'there will be sacrifice'.

Once the campaign was concluded Major General Wimberley was ordered to take up the position of Commandant of the Staff College, Camberley. Having commanded the 51st Highland Division for over two years, his Farewell Message reminded his listeners that 'no individual, no Regiment, no Division can afford to rest on its laurels.' He concluded by expressing thanks 'in the farewell words of my great predecessor, Sir Colin Campbell, who led our same famous Highland Regiments to such glory nearly one hundred years ago – "From the bottom of my heart".'[86]

Despite the unanimity of the Allied war effort, in late September an unprecedented incident took place when about 500 newly arrived men refused to follow orders since, instead of being sent to join their own units, the 51st Highland and the 50th Northumbrian Divisions, they had been reassigned to the 46th and 56th Divisions in US General Mark Clark's Fifth Army fighting at Salerno, south of Naples. Promised that once Salerno had been taken, they would rejoin their regular units, the majority acquiesced, leaving 192 men who were charged with mutiny under the Army Act. Among the original mutineers who subsequently agreed to follow orders were 'about 100 Black Watch'. As one of them, Private Alec McMichael, explained, their minds were changed by Lieutenant J. A. Coulter, who was returning to the 7th Black Watch after being wounded in Sicily. '[He] told us that there were men at the front line who need our help… if we did not go to their aid they would be pushed back to the beach and the boats waiting offshore would be used for their escape. We, therefore, would be left on the beach.'[87]

Meanwhile, having briefly crossed over the straits in early September to cover the landing at Reggio on the mainland, the 1st and 7th Black Watch returned to Sicily. The autumn was spent resting and retraining with the opportunity for the men to visit the battlefields of Gerbini and Sferro. One 'interesting occurrence' recorded in the War Diary was the arrest of a deserter, Private Kidd, who, when captured, kept escaping until he was 'securely shackled & placed in his cell, clothed only in his shirt to ensure that no further escape could take place.'[88]

Before leaving Sicily a stone monument in the shape of a Celtic Cross was dedicated at Sferro Hill. 'It poured rain all day & the mud on the hill was terrific,' recorded Lieutenant Murray.[89] The 51st Highland Division, now under the command of Major General Charles Bullen-Smith, King's Own Scottish Borderers, then returned to Britain. Travelling on board 'dry' American troopships, most of the officers made sure to come on board 'well stocked with local Sicilian brandy and wines and nearly everyone had brought home crates of oranges and silk as presents for those at home.'[90] Arriving at Liverpool docks, their destination was the English countryside. 'Pipers Wood Camp [in Buckinghamshire] was not, at first glance on a rainy November day, a very encouraging place in which to house heroes returning to their homeland,' recorded Russell. 'However it was home at last and spirits were high.'[91]

Only the 6th Black Watch remained in North Africa, moving in December to Egypt for training 'in opposed landings on enemy coasts.' Christmas Day, McKenzie Johnston recalled, was spent 'struggling to erect tents in a sandstorm, our only food being cold bully beef in tins which kept getting covered in gritty sand. The Jocks were not pleased.'[92]

Fighting fit in India: Beating the Japanese at their own game

Throughout early 1943 the 2nd Black Watch had been training in jungle warfare. 'And by God did we sweat! It was march, march, march until you were almost dropping,' related Private Meldrum. 'I had become a real fighting Black Watch man by now.' Stationed near Ranchi, they lived in bamboo huts known as 'bashas'; the soldiers ensured that all their 'gear' was inside 'because, if anything was left outside, the ants were quick in demolishing it. One lad left his boots out, only to discover in the morning that the soles had gone.' Another skill was making boats from bamboo canes and groundsheets. After practising crossings in daylight, they did so at night, a 'great tragedy' occurring when two boats collapsed. While those in the leading boat survived, the other boat sank in deeper water and two men were drowned.[93]

In addition to overseeing operations safeguarding the borders of India, the Commander-in-Chief India, General Wavell, had been focusing on a new strategy to retake Burma which included sending a force of irregular troops behind Japanese lines to sabotage communications. Simultaneously the Chinese Fifth and Sixth Armies would advance into Burma from the north. 'The room where we worked in Delhi was covered in maps of Burma,' related Captain Bernard Fergusson, seconded to the Joint Planning Staff. 'The recapture of Burma was the subject which filled our days.' The man called upon by Wavell to lead the expedition was Brigadier Orde Wingate, who had undertaken similar operations during the 1941 Ethiopian campaign to reinstate Emperor Haile Selassie. Codenamed Operation Longcloth, 77 Indian Infantry Brigade's 3,000 members were divided into two groups of seven columns. Their later name, 'Chindits', was a mispronunciation of the Burmese word 'Chinthe', the mythical beast, half-lion, half-griffin, guarding Burmese pagodas. Two Black Watch officers joined the expedition: Fergusson, who wished 'to exorcise the thought that I had spent almost all the war in safe places', and who took command of No. 5 Column; and Lieutenant Duncan Menzies, who had distinguished himself during the floods at Contai, served as Fergusson's adjutant.[94]

On 8 February the expedition set out. Their departure coincided with offensive operations into the Arakan peninsula, the objective of which was to capture the island of Akyab with its port and all-weather airfield on the Mayu peninsula.[95] No military support, however, came from China. Before permitting his armies to advance, Chiang Kai-Shek had wanted assurance that the Allies had air superiority over Burma and the Bay of Bengal; but the withdrawal of the British fleet to the Mediterranean to assist the landings in North Africa meant air superiority could not be guaranteed.[96]

Having crossed the Chindwin river, two columns marched south while five went east, including No.5 Column. The scenery was reminiscent 'of the West Highlands, set up on thrice the scale'.[97] Their objective was to undertake sabotage operations on the main north–south Mandalay–Myitkyina railway. That task accomplished, albeit temporarily because the Japanese quickly made reparations, Wingate's next instructions were to cross the Irrawaddy to cut the Mandalay–Lashio line. This took the isolated columns of Chindits into more inhospitable terrain where they became easy targets for Japanese patrols. Water was scarce and their only recourse was to return to India, splitting up into small groups.

After a difficult crossing of the Shweli river, Fergusson and his group reached the Kodaung Hill Tracts inhabited by the traditionally more friendly Kachins. 'Once there I hoped our troubles would be over.' Sadly, while reconnoitring the village of Zibyugin, Menzies and the other members of his patrol were captured. Later he and another soldier were found tied to a tree, having been used for bayonet practice by the Japanese. Although his companion was dead, Menzies was just alive. His rescuer acceded to his wishes to be given a lethal dose of morphia, before himself being shot by a sniper. Fergusson felt the responsibility of Menzies' death 'acutely... he had a brilliant future before him… he combined in his character all that was best in his Australian upbringing and his pure Highland descent'. By the end of April Fergusson and his remaining men had reached Imphal, others arriving days and weeks later. After over three months in Burma, nearly one-third of the force was killed, taken prisoner or was missing. 'We [5 Column] went into Burma in January 318 strong, and came out at the end of April 95 strong,' recorded Fergusson, who was awarded the DSO.[98] Menzies received the MC posthumously.

'What did we accomplish? Not much that was tangible,' he later wrote. 'What there was became distorted in the glare of publicity soon after our return.'[99] The expedition, however, had taken place at the same time as Operation Chastise, an attack on German dams (publicised as the Dam Busters), and in contrast to the failed campaign to capture Akyab in the Arakan, the stories of the 'wrecking expedition' boosted morale. *The Times* reported that it had proved 'unsupported columns can operate in the jungle with the aid of nothing but wireless and air.' 'Skilfully handled,' observed Lieutenant General Bill Slim, in command of XV Corps which had taken part in the Arakan campaign, 'the press of the Allied world took up the tale, and everywhere the story ran that we had beaten the Japanese at their own game.'[100]

On 1 May 1943 the 2nd Black Watch, now under the command of Lieutenant Colonel George Green, moved from Ranchi to Deula, 40 miles south of Calcutta. 'We had to get back to Calcutta and the business of fighting the enemy,' recalled Meldrum. Briefly the Battalion was sent to Cox's Bazaar in the southernmost tip of Bengal close to the Burmese border, where the soldiers patrolled into Japanese-occupied territory. 'If we were attacked and encircled, we were to stay put and fight it out.' Their task was 'minimal… the Royal Scots whom we were supporting had done a good job.' Travelling back to Deula in late June, the Battalion's next posting was Bangalore.[101]

To meet the growing demands of the South East Asia theatre, in August 1943, a new South East Asia Command (SEAC) was created. Under the command of the Supreme Allied Commander, Lord Mountbatten (promoted acting Admiral), came the newly established Fourteenth Army, commanded by Slim. In early September Green received orders that the 70th Division was being converted into Chindits to take part in a second expedition under Wingate's command. Sanctioned by Roosevelt and Churchill during their August conference in Quebec, Special Force was officially called the 3rd Indian Division, Long Penetration Group, although more familiarly 'Wingate's Chindits'.[102] Disappointed that the 70th Division was to lose its identity as a formation, the men did not 'at first take kindly to the idea' of emulating the 'ragamuffins' of the first operation, recorded Fergusson who visited the various battalions 'to give a clearer impression of what the new form of warfare would entail than the picture built up from the newspaper accounts of the first adventure.' Unlike the first expedition, the Chindits would act under the Fourteenth Army's command structure; at the same time as they set out the deputy commander of SEAC, General Joseph Stilwell, would lead a force of Chinese and American troops (X Force) from India into Burma.[103]

On 2 October 1943 the 2nd Black Watch moved to Jhansi to start 'jungle' training. Unfortunately their anti-malarial pills ran out 'and within a few days we had every hospital for miles full of malarial patients,' recorded Private Fred Patterson.[104] 'Being in the jungle you have no eyes,' recalled Corporal Jim McNeilly, one of fourteen Black Watch soldiers sent on a four-month exercise with a group of Gurkhas.

> You can't see beyond a few feet, so you have to rely on your other senses. If there's a Jap patrol following you, you need to be able to hear it, to hear them talking. Jungle training teaches you to use every possibility, and how to live with rations strictly curtailed. It's a state of mind you have to get into, with your mind being questioned all the time by the jungle's own special noises that you have to learn to recognise, or you'd be a nervous wreck. The other stuff is more straightforward, jungle craft, crossing rivers with livestock, all that.[105]

As 1943 drew to a close, Roosevelt, Churchill and Chiang-Kai Shek met in Cairo to discuss the future conduct of the Pacific war, once again endorsing a second Chindit expedition as one of seven operations to retake Burma. In late November Roosevelt and Churchill travelled to Teheran to meet Stalin. Key among their decisions was to open a Second Front by launching a cross-Channel invasion in 1944.[106] All planning for Operation Overlord came under the Supreme Headquarters Allied Expeditionary Force (SHAEF) based in Middlesex under General Dwight Eisenhower. The newly formed 21st Army Group, consisting of the United States First Army and the British Second Army, was placed under the command of General Montgomery, Leese taking command of the Eighth Army. For the next nine months intensive planning was undertaken in order to enable Allied forces to land in northern Europe.

Fair stood the wind for France
When we our sails advance,
Nor now to prove our chance
Longer will tarry.[107]

14

1944: Only Numbers Can Annihilate

Our war wasn't like the war in Europe; every section, platoon and column had its own war.[1]

I saw the platoon men scramble, 1916 fashion, from the ditches and move forward.[2]

It was difficult to accustom yourself to this type of warfare. Every house and hedgerow had to be fought for.[3]

'The beginning of the end'

By 1944 the outcome of the war looked brighter, even though challenges remained. Although representatives of the Italian government had signed an armistice with the Allies, in retaliation German forces had occupied most of Italy, defeating Italian forces in southern France and the Balkans. Despite the Soviet Union's success in withstanding the siege of Stalingrad, the country was still hard-pressed. In South Asia, Japanese forces were occupying Burma and threatening India. After operations in North Africa and Sicily, the fortunes of 1st, 5th and 7th Black Watch, 51st Highland Division, were now linked to the 21st Army Group. So too would be those of the 1st Battalion The Tyneside Scottish, The Black Watch. Since returning from Gibraltar, the 4th Black Watch had remained in Britain, while the 6th Black Watch was still training in Egypt. The 2nd Black Watch was waiting to move into Burma.

Chindits: Inside hostile territory

With resources diverted to Europe for Operation Overlord, objectives for the Second Chindit Expedition, Operation Thursday, were less ambitious than Major General Wingate hoped. Compared to the first expedition, the scale was much larger, Special Force consisting of 18,000 men, composed of six British and Indian brigades and supporting units.[4] President Roosevelt had sanctioned a task force, including United States Army Air Force (USAAF) bombers, fighters, gliders and transport planes, to reduce the ground forces' dependence on mules and enable evacuation of the sick and wounded by air. Wingate 'had a plan to form us into Angels by making us take wings,' recalled Private Meldrum. 'Our wings were provided for us in the form of American Gliders, WACOS. We had to learn what it felt like to be lifted and dropped by the WACOS.'[5] Important for reconnaissance were the Burma Rifles, the 'Burrifs', a name eventually signifying any friendly Burmese.

The 2nd Black Watch was assigned to 14 Brigade under Brigadier Thomas Brodie, divided into a headquarters and two columns: 73, under Lieutenant Colonel Green, and 42, commanded by Major David Rose. Bernard Fergusson, promoted temporary brigadier, was given command of 16 Brigade. Each column, numbering approximately 400 men with sixty mules, a few horses and some bullocks, was trained to operate separately.[6] 'Our war wasn't like the war in Europe,' observed Frederick Patterson, one of a draft of Black Watch soldiers who had been transferred to the 1st Cameronians and whose brother, Jim, 1st Black Watch, had been killed at Wadi Akarit in April 1943. 'Every section, platoon and column had its own war.' Having been warned that in jungle warfare there was no front line, 'every tree was a potential enemy,' recorded Meldrum.[7]

Before their departure Wingate assembled the officers. 'You could have heard a pin drop throughout his masterly discourse,' observed Rose. 'He described how we would construct a chain of fortresses [blocks] astride the enemy's L[ines] of C[ommunication].' Once established, landing strips would be made for re-supply and the evacuation of casualties. 'To invest and attack these forts would require far more [Japanese] men than their defence and as each attack was mounted, the Japanese would be ambushed and harried by mobile columns of Chindits.' Wingate even described 'how we would eventually plant vegetables to supplement our rations!' But while Rose applauded the plan, he believed those entrusted with carrying it out were not 'supermen, inured to a hard life and frugal living.'[8]

'I had never seen, let alone been into a jungle,' recalled Private William (Cocky) Cochrane. 'I didn't have a clue what was waiting for us when we got there. I knew what a forest was like, but the jungle?'[9] 'We were the ordinary product of urban life,' continued Rose. 'We were not used to killing the food we ate, nor even digging up the vegetables.' In fact, as they discovered, they were to live on American K-rations: 'three neat waxed packets a day. The waxed wrapping was good for starting a fire to heat the water in each man's mug!' 'Those Americans were bloody clever, the whole of the pack was useable,' observed Cochrane.[10]

Departing from northern India in late January, 16 Brigade undertook the arduous journey (400–500 miles) to Burma on foot, its first task being to establish a stronghold in the Meza valley with a landing strip, called 'Aberdeen'. They could then begin sabotage operations. In early March, 77 and 111 Brigades arrived by air. 'We awakened', remarked Patterson, 'with the sudden realisation that we were now approximately 200 miles inside hostile territory.' 77 Brigade immediately began establishing a block on the railway line north of Indaw. Known as White City from the parachutes hanging on the trees, it was the first of Wingate's planned fortresses which would entice Japanese troops into the open so they could be ambushed.[11]

14 Brigade was next to depart. 'The airfield [at Lala ghat] was a hive of activity,' recalled Private Cochrane. 'The muleteers were having a grand old time trying to control their charges, animals were kicking and biting as they were led up the straw covered ramps into the aircraft's interior.' Not only was it 'chaos' loading the animals but the airfield 'looked and smelt like a farmyard'.[12] 'Mules are hard working

and hardy but they're not pets,' observed Piper Bill Lark, who, having put his bagpipes in storage, had become a muleteer. 'You have to build a relationship and some of them can be stroppy. Very stroppy.'[13]

On 23 March the first contingent of 73 Column flew out, the remainder leaving the following day. 'Our plane steadily rose to its ceiling height to fly over the mountains and I earnestly hoped and prayed that the Imperial Japanese airforce was concerning itself with other matters and not the undefended airborne force that was slowly, but surely, flying into its domain,' related Cochrane. 'My first view of Burma was just a mass of trees,' recorded Private Meldrum. 'One had the sensation of running along a green carpet, so close were we to the tree-tops.'[14] Landing at Aberdeen, Wingate greeted the new arrivals, telling Green to congratulate the men 'on being the first Scottish troops to land at a Scottish airport in Burma'. Hours later, on returning to India, his plane crashed near Imphal, leaving the expedition temporarily leaderless, the news of his death kept secret for a week. In Wingate's place, Slim appointed 111 Brigade's Commanding Officer, Brigadier Joe Lentaigne, 'the most balanced and experienced of Wingate's commanders'. As a more conventional soldier he lacked Wingate's flair, Fergusson commenting that Wingate's untimely death 'was also the death of the campaign as he had conceived it'. The Burma theatre was 'in a bad way', as the Chindits' arrival coincided with a concerted Japanese movement across the Chindwin to attack Imphal.[15]

On 26 March 73 Column left Aberdeen, followed by 42 Column, which had had its first experience of Japanese firepower when 'varied calibre bombs' were dropped on Aberdeen.[16] Ordered to cut the Banmauk–Indaw road (in support of an unsuccessful attack by 16 Brigade on the two airfields there), 73 Column had its first encounter with the Japanese near the village of Sittaw when a few shots were exchanged, after which Captain Chesney, the Column's medical officer, performed an emergency operation on a wounded soldier in a nearby copse. Medical conditions were rudimentary: a case of acute appendicitis in 42 Column had to be operated on in the dark during a heavy downpour. 'Such torches as still had batteries were pressed into service, life-jackets were inflated to make a bed for the man…

The Animal Transport Officer was anaesthetist.' Captain the Hon. Hew Dalrymple's contribution was 'a bit of sponge – used as a swab, and the handles of my mess tin bent, so as to hold the wound apart.' The columns' dependence on aerial supply drops 'meant laying out a marker,' continued Dalrymple, consisting of 'an area of 8 fires in an L shape, with 2 at the short end.'[17] 'The long line of the 'L' always would be facing towards India, north from Burma. The short leg was to be the dropping zone,' related Meldrum. One hazard was the 'friendly bomb' when a parachute failed to open, its load falling to the ground at such a speed that it killed a man.[18]

In early April 73 Column had 'a tip-off that a small convoy was coming our way', recalled Corporal Jim McNeilly. Green therefore gave orders to set up an ambush. 'We waited, and three trucks came along, all full of Japs. We blew the first one up with grenades. The second one couldn't move so we took out as many Japs as we could but they fought before they disappeared… the third one reversed right out of it, high speed backwards in the dark round quite a sharp bend.'[19] The Battalion's next operation was destroying an ammunition dump in Singan using combined ground and air attacks for the first time. Once American planes, directed by wireless sets operated by RAF signallers on the ground, had bombed and strafed their targets, the soldiers moved in.[20] During the operation 42 Column came under fire from Japanese concealed in the trees. Although Rose was among the wounded, he refused evacuation until late May when, suffering from severe blood-poisoning, his return home became necessary.[21]

Marching and counter-marching, as the days passed, their activities lacked direction. 'We didn't know where we were going. Nobody told us. We broke camp every morning, marched all day, and camped again. When we were told to stop, we stopped. When we were told to move on, we moved on. All I knew was that we were passing trees. Miles and miles and miles of trees,' observed Lark. Having crossed the same junction for the third time, Green reportedly announced: 'this ought to confuse the Jap: we don't even know where we're going ourselves.'[22] 'We usually marched for fifty minutes, then had a ten-minute breather. The Section would rotate during the march, so that nobody was at the front all the time,' related Cochrane. 'The Bren gun was carried for the fifty minutes, then it was passed to the next man and so on during the day. If there was any action, then whoever was carrying the Bren gun had to fire it. Sometimes, blokes would say that it was alright for them to carry it for longer, I don't know whether it was because they felt sorry for the next man, or if they wanted to fire the Bren in action.'[23]

One piece of equipment the men carried reluctantly was the 'flamethrower'. Known as the lifebuoy 'because that was the shape of the fuel tank, it was deeply mistrusted,' recalled Corporal McNeilly. 'For one thing, it made you a target. If the Japs saw you with it, they'd go for you right away.' It was also unreliable. Having used it once McNeilly's section dumped it 'and used the fuel for cooking.'[24] 'We each had a waterproof oilskin pouch that could be stashed away into one of the oversized pack pouches,' continued Cochrane. 'I had the photos of my wife and daughter, my watch, a local area map, small copies of the gospels of St Matthew and St John and a thin book of Common Prayer.' The rest of the pack was taken up with ammunition and rations, 'but it still weighed more than 70 lbs; we were just human donkeys.'[25]

'Every man had ten rupee coins,' related Lark, 'which were like half-crowns, and when a man was hurt he could use these to buy some safety and care. In such a case we generally all gave the man an extra rupee of our own. And then we sent the Burrifs into the village. They would take their army gear off and sling a dhoti round their middles and go into the villages to get information for us. And they would say, there's a man up the track, look after him, hide him from the Japs.' As the weather became hotter, longer rest periods were essential. Living off their K-rations, if not supplemented by ordinary food, the men suffered from diarrhoea, 'calls of nature' needing to be hidden in the ground. Cigarette ends also had to be hidden, matches 'pressed vertically into the ground so they didn't show.'[26]

During halts 'the drill was automatic,' recorded Private Meldrum. 'Off with your gear then give a hand with the mules.' 'All the mules had their vocal chords cut,' recorded Cochrane, 'so that they couldn't make any noise, it was a terrible thing to do to the animals, but what was the alternative? A mule's braying could put everyone in danger.' Taking mules to water 'was a decidedly dangerous adventure,' related Lark. 'The mule didn't know about snipers and just wanted to get to the water. The muleteer couldn't abandon his beast and couldn't really stop it either, so the Jap had two targets, one very nervous with two legs and one oblivious with four.'[27]

In just over a month 14 Brigade had destroyed nearly two dozen dumps of Japanese supplies, ammunition and fuel as well as cutting the railway line in several places south of Indaw. Under challenging conditions, 73 Column had covered 150 miles since leaving Aberdeen, 42 Column 'slightly less'. A 'great novelty' during a supply drop was 'a certain number of jungle hammocks... of American type, with mosquito netting and waterproof roof,' initially available only for the officers and the wounded or sick.[28]

'Up the Watch!'

Early May saw a change of strategy. Exhausted by its long march in, 16 Brigade had already returned to India to train other units and Aberdeen was closed. Instead of operating as a long range penetration group, Special Force would act as regular infantry attacking fixed targets in support of Stilwell's X Force in the north, where his objective was to open lines of communication to China via Ledo. This meant securing the area between Mogaung and Myitkyina. The first task for 14 Brigade was to assist 111 Brigade, commanded by Lentaigne's successor, Brigadier Jack Masters, to evacuate White City.

On 5 May 'a strong ambush party' from 73 Column was ordered to create a diversion by ambushing the Japanese along one of their transit routes.[29] 'We waited for what seemed like hours and I thought that the Japs must surely know that we were there,' related Cochrane. 'There was no talking and you wouldn't have known that you were part of a force of 200 men.' First to arrive were some bullocks, followed by Japanese soldiers. 'And, would you believe it, an officer on a great white horse, and all these men behind, slugging along with their heads down,' recalled McNeilly. 'We had to wait for the entire Jap column to pass us,' continued Cochrane, 'wait for the signal to fire, then block the road and stop them from escaping. The stopping force at the head of the ambush would do the same, then the idea was to do murder with them trapped in withering crossfire. The Japs were still passing us where we were lying in wait. They were only about 8 ft away from me, I could hear the shuffling of feet, coughing, equipment squeaking and the general noise that can't be stopped when a large group of men are moving!'[30]

Once the first shot was fired at the rider of the white horse, 'it went mad, just mad,' related McNeilly. 'The Japs were screaming, their mules were screaming – theirs had voices, ours didn't – they were braying and kicking.' 'The whole Jap force was in a straightforward panic and just trying to get as far away from the fighting as fast as they could run. They just dumped their packs and in most cases, their rifles, then legged it back down the road and up and over the bank where we were positioned,' continued Cochrane, observing that the Japanese 'weren't the "Supermen" that we had been told we would be up against. They were just scruffy bustards, miles from home, the same as we were, but I've got to admit that I was glad that it was me going through their kit and not the other way around.' Although at least 100 Japanese had been attacked, only fourteen bodies were counted including the officer on the white horse. They then had to move away, carrying their own wounded on hastily made stretchers, lest the Japanese counter-attacked. 'I can only remember being tired all of the time. Mind you, at least we were alive to complain about it all.'[31]

Another ambush north of Nathkokyin had a different outcome, when, having waited for a Japanese column to pass by, the ambush party was itself ambushed. 'It was a right shambles, we were in the same state that the Japs had been in only a couple of days previously,' continued Cochrane. Ordered to storm the positions from where the Japanese were firing, 'we crawled towards the slope and got into position... the signal to attack was going to be a single shot and we were all to lob a grenade up the slope as far as we could... The shot was fired, the grenades were lobbed towards the bunkers and we ducked down. The grenades exploded with red and orange flashes and we got up shouting and roaring.' 'It was every platoon and every section to fight for itself and to find a way back to the rendezvous,' recalled McNeilly. 'There were three rendezvous points at different times, but if you didn't get there you were on your own. They wouldn't wait for you.' One wounded man with a 'smashed' femur was left near a village, the inhabitants promised a reward if they looked after him but he was never heard of again.[32] Despite the losses sustained, White City had been evacuated and a signal came from Special Force HQ: 'the familiar cry with many an old association: "Up the Watch!"'.[33]

A dripping world

As 14 Brigade continued north, the monsoon was at its height. 'You just couldn't ever get dry,' recalled McNeilly. 'A ten mile march to a rendezvous point which would have only taken us a day in April took four days to cover,' remarked Cochrane, observing that although they carried a ground sheet to sleep on 'everything was so wet that half the time it just stopped you from lying directly in the mud.' 'They lived in a dripping world, where every fire successfully lit represented a heavy outlay of patience and ingenuity,' recorded Fergusson, now back in India. Rain and thunderstorms presented 'the threat of starvation… either might prevent the supply planes from flying, and thunder prevented the use of wireless to summon and direct them.'[34] With the rain came leeches. 'How they got through your clothes and in between your toes, I don't know,' remarked Lark. 'But they did. And everywhere else. The boys used to touch them with their cigarette ends and they curled up and dropped off.' Under such conditions, supplies of cigarettes lifted morale. 'When we were in training, in India, the lads used to chuck their cigarette ration because they were so awful.' Realising they would 'come in handy one day', Lark had collected the discarded cigarettes which he later distributed. 'When you've got nothing, anything will do.'[35]

In mid-May, Stilwell's forces took the airfield at Myitkyina, forcing a Japanese withdrawal into the town. To prevent reinforcements reaching them, Special Force was ordered to attack Mogaung and the area south-west of Myitkyina. Establishing 14 Brigade HQ at Nammun south of the Indawgyi Lake, the columns conducted limited operations to gain intelligence. The Brigade's next mission was 'to float in the hills around Blackpool', another block which 111 Brigade had established across the railway line south of Mogaung. The monsoon soon curtailed the use of Blackpool's airstrip and in late May it too was evacuated, the soldiers making their exit across the Kyunsunlai pass to the south-east, which 14 Brigade was holding against the Japanese 'at all costs'.[36] Lacking sufficient stretchers to carry all the wounded, Brigadier Masters considered it more humane to have the dying shot rather than leave them to the mercy of the Japanese. 'One by one carbine shots exploded curtly behind me. I put my hands to my ears but nothing could shut out the sound.'[37]

After over two months in Burma, spirits were low. 'When you rested in a safe area, you were getting respite from the Japs but not from the disease, and not from the general depression,' recalled McNeilly. 'Sometimes we would have a Kirk parade, which was good for morale. Everybody went, whatever their religion, because the singing cheered you up. There we were, singing hymns in the jungle, while the typhus crept up on us.'[38] The presence of two Sunderland flying boats, known as Gert and Daisy, provided 'a new method of evacuating sick and wounded'.[39]

Although Lentaigne was arguing in favour of Special Force's withdrawal because of its weakened condition, Stilwell considered its presence might still be useful. 77 Brigade had already begun attacking Mogaung, where Captain Archie John Wavell, attached to the 1st South Staffordshire Regiment, was among those wounded. 'News this morning that A.J. has lost a hand, but is not considered to be in danger,' noted his father, now Viceroy of India.[40] After being relieved from guarding the Kyunsunlai pass, 14 Brigade had moved closer to Stillwell's forces and 77 Brigade at Mogaung, which was captured on 26 June. The rains made progress 'terrible': '80% of us had raw feet, it was the sand and the mud,' related Captain Graham Bishop. 'The guts shown by all the men was something terrific.[41] On the evening of 12 July Lieutenant William Bowie, who was 'very ill with malaria, dysentery and was also extremely dehydrated' died from a single gunshot, the men believing that he had taken his own life. 'I was very disturbed by the thought that [he] would take his own life,' related Cochrane. 'He was always encouraging us when we thought that we couldn't go on and even though he was suffering from illness himself, he helped to carry sick men's kit.' 'Tragically killed', as recorded in the Battalion's War Diary, a brief burial service was held the next day.[42]

Having been informed of the poor medical condition of the remaining Special Force brigades, the Supreme Allied Commander, Admiral Louis Mountbatten, had prevailed upon Stilwell to send in medical inspectors. 'General health is undoubtedly deteriorating at a rapidly increasing rate due to (1) the frequent occurrence of short rations and (2) the continued wet weather,' noted one of 14 Brigade's medical officers. The condition of 77 and 111 Brigades was even worse and, after arguing with Stilwell, Lentaigne was permitted to evacuate all 'ineffectives' which meant both 77 and 111 Brigades.[43] 14 Brigade (and 3 West African Brigade) would remain until Myitkyina fell and the British 36th Division arrived. 'Sickness has been on the increase and typhus has been taking toll of our already depleted numbers. The weather has been alternately very wet and very hot and we've had some little luxuries to augment our usual "K" rations. On the whole things aren't too bad and we're good for a few miles yet,' the War Diary was confidently noting on 31 July.[44]

Back home glowing reports of the Chindits' activities appeared in the press. 'Lively Offensive Kept Up,' the Scottish *Sunday Mail* was reporting in late July. 'Special Force troops (are) patrolling north of Taung[gy]ni... adding to their recent outstanding work in wiping out strong pockets of resistance in the hills... operating in the most difficult jungle country and in incessant monsoon downpour, they have been driving the enemy relentlessly south.'[45]

After a ten-week siege Myitkyina fell to Stilwell's forces on 3 August. Two days later 73 and 42 Columns united near the railway for a last battle at the village of Labu: 'the most spectacular of all,' related Private Anderson. 'The pipes played during the assault and we had the pleasure of seeing 20 Japs running for their lives,' related Bishop, describing how Green had ordered Piper Bill Lark's bagpipes to be dropped at their base at Pungan the previous week. 'I strongly suspect it was the pipes that frightened them, not the bayonets,' recorded a member of the Yorks and Lancs. 'That piper, unarmed except for his pipes, was as near a hero as anyone I ever knew.' Inevitably there were casualties. 'A machine gun opened up and I was hit in the leg which smashed the bone,' recorded McNeilly. 'One man lost both his legs, and we had to be taken back to the hut where the medics were. They rearranged my leg how it should be and tied my two legs together with string.' As Private Cochrane was helping to wrap Private James Doyle's dead body in some blankets, he couldn't stop 'from shaking like a leaf… I glanced at the other lads and could see that they were taking it the same as I was, all the talk before was just bravado.'[46]

By mid-August 14 Brigade had begun the journey back to India, Lark continuing to play the bagpipes. Two soldiers from Kirriemuir composed a song, parodying the well-known First World War Dundee song, the 'Bombin Raid… Standin in the b-loomin trench wi' the mud right up to here,/All soaking through, aye through and through.' Their words were as follows:

You may have heard of the Naga Hills, Three thousand feet or more,
We climb them step by step till our feet were bloody sore
And soaking through, Aye, soaking through.[47]

On their way out, they passed the 36th Division entering Burma. To the weary Chindits, the men looked like 'toy soldiers, changing the guard at the palace', although Cochrane acknowledged that these men 'were eventually to chase the Japanese out of Burma completely'. Having gone from Mogaung to Myitkyina in jeeps converted to travel along the railway, they completed the journey to Assam by air. The first stage of recuperation was 'blanket' treatment 'to acclimatize us back to eating usual rations, so we were given loads of chicken soup to eat,' related Cochrane. 'I suppose it was all our shrunken stomachs would have been able to have put up with.'[48]

At the rest camp a medical inspection of 14 Brigade, which included 126 men from The Black Watch, was carried out. Although no case of psychiatric illness was recorded, various factors were noted as having affected morale, one of which was the promise of leaving Burma before the monsoon. 'Every job after May was their last job and morale dropped considerably with each promise.' Another factor was that the sections were never up to full strength. Fresh drafts were often untrained in jungle warfare. Had the campaign ended before the monsoon many deaths from illness would have been avoided. K-rations were 'almost unbearable after three months.' Referring to the 'inadequate' medical treatment, the report suggested that there were occasions when it was 'ridiculous to call it treatment at all'. Sick men often had to be turned away by the medical officer 'with the apology that he had nothing to give them. On occasion it was impossible to get even a bandage, parachute cloth having ultimately to be torn up to serve the purpose.' Scrub typhus affected morale considerably combined with the fear of not being evacuated and having to continue in the Column unwell. Those who needed to wear glasses 'went in constant fear of either losing or breaking their glasses, and even with them on the glasses were little better than useless owing to rain and perspiration dimming the lenses.' Despite everything, the men's 'unanimous opinion' was that they would be able to have another 'go' in six months time.[49]

In mid-September the 2nd Black Watch reached Bangalore, where members of the Battalion attended a party at Viceregal Lodge, Simla. Lark was ordered to play the bagpipes 'and say the health in Gaelic, thereupon downing a glass of whisky. I didn't drink, I'd never had whisky. I had no idea what would happen to me if I did have it, so I asked the butler. He fixed me up with a glass of cold tea and I quaffed that.'[50] On 1 October the Battalion assembled for a memorial service for their fallen comrades.[51]

In addition to those who received decorations, all members of Special Force were issued with a Chindit insignia and a letter from Lentaigne: 'You have hit the Jap where it hurts him most – in the guts.' He concluded with a warning:

> You must remember that the fine work you have done is not the end of the war. We have won this round on points – in the next round we will go in for a knock out. You are now fully trained and know your stuff. Your job is to train the new fellows and lead them next time. Teach them to kill with every round. Teach them that the jungle is nothing like as bad as it is cracked up to be. Teach them that though it's a tough job, it's a man's job, a job worth doing and a job that's got to be done if we want to get back to Civvy Street quickly.[52]

Monte Cassino: 'Whoever had that mountain was the master!'

In early March 1944, as the 2nd Black Watch was preparing to enter Burma, the 6th Black Watch arrived in Naples from Egypt. 'I never did get to see the Pyramids, nor a camel for that matter,' commented Private George Daily. 'The harbour was a mess from earlier bombing and the destruction by the retreating Germans,' commented Lieutenant McKenzie Johnston, who remembered enjoying the first bananas 'any of us had seen for a very long time.' On arrival the soldiers were issued with long johns 'which made us wonder where we were going, as we thought of Italy as a warm country. We soon changed our minds when we ended up in the snow-bound mountains,' remarked Private Daily.[53]

Forty miles beyond Naples lay the front line, where a combined Allied force under General Harold Alexander had been battling against the German Tenth Army. While the British Eighth Army, under Leese's command, was concentrated along the Adriatic front, the United States' Fifth Army was in the west.[54] After the failure to capitalise on the Allied landing at Anzio in January and advance directly to Rome, the plan was to break through the heavily fortified German Gustav Line at a narrow gap in the Apennine mountains below Monte Cassino.[55] Two previous assaults in January and February had failed, the second involving the controversial decision to bomb the monastery, mother-house of the Benedictine order, which the Allied leaders mistakenly believed the Germans were using as an observation point.[56]

In the 4th Division, the 6th Black Watch was ordered up to a position in the foothills of Monte Ornito, south of Cassino. Getting to their destination was an ordeal. 'The only paths were goat tracks which twisted and writhed agonizingly up and across the mountain slopes,' recalled Private Charlie Framp. 'It seemed as if we marched miles just to make a few hundred yards upward progress.' Given their proximity to the Germans, 2 miles away at Castelforte, there were several casualties when 'for luck' German shelling of these hidden pathways hit a target, but 'the greatest enemy was fatigue and cold.' 'The ground was so hard it was hopeless trying to dig slit trenches, so we had to construct what was called a sangar for protection from shell fire,' continued Daily. 'This consisted of a layer of large rocks, about two feet high, to form a circular shelter.'[57]

'Blizzards were frequent and icy winds blew the snow through the unprotected openings into the sangars. No hot meals could be brought to us so our diet consisted of frozen bully and rock-hard biscuits,' continued Framp. 'Tea was our life saver and, with all the snow about, water was no problem.' 'As we were at an altitude designated by officialdom as justifying very welcome extra rations,' recorded McKenzie Johnston, 'we had a daily rum ration and masses of chocolate and tins of butter.' Life in the front line was 'usually not too unpleasant,' recorded Commanding Officer Brian Madden, 'except for the night sentries who froze.' 'I would say to myself "if ever I get out of here I will be a different man," every day was a bonus,' recalled Corporal George Grant.[58]

In mid-March a third assault on Cassino was launched. 'We could hear the noise as waves of bombers destroyed the town of Cassino,' McKenzie Johnston recorded. But after a week's intensive fighting, despite obtaining a foothold in the town, a German counter-attack prevented further progress by the Allied troops. While the offensive was taking place, the 6th Black Watch was relieved, the soldiers having a 'magnificent view of an eruption of Vesuvius' as they came down the mountainside.[59] The Battalion's next position was a bridgehead 4 miles north-east of Cassino, near the village of Sant' Elia. Although the sector was relatively quiet, signals officer McKenzie Johnston noted that by midnight on 3 April he had only slept for 15 hours during a 112-hour period. 'The telephone lines between battalion headquarters and the forward companies were constantly being broken by shelling which involved all-night work repairing them… there was a certain beauty in the stillness punctuated at almost metronomic intervals by the eerie calls of scops owls. We even heard a nightingale one night.'[60]

On 7 April the 6th Black Watch was again relieved. Two weeks later, with their boots muffled by sandbags, the soldiers entered 'what was left of Cassino town' to relieve the Coldstream Guards positioned in the cathedral. Since the river had overflowed its banks, much of the town was under water. 'I will never forget my first sight of Cassino, as we rounded a corner and saw below us in the moonlight the remains of the town,' recalled Lieutenant Geordie Cox, who later painted what he saw. 'There was not a single building with a roof and in between the piles of rubble and stark walls with holes where windows had been, there were huge bomb craters mostly half filled with water and the noise of the frogs which had taken up residence there was almost deafening.' 'During the hours of daylight we looked out upon a dead world,' recorded Private Framp. 'Nothing stirred in the ruins. Even so, hidden eyes watched everything.'[61] The only casualty on arrival was Sergeant Tug Wilson who was hit in the groin by a 'friendly fire' smoke canister. 'To be knocked out killing Germans was alright, but to be knocked out in this way was, to his way of thinking, all wrong!' recorded Major Jock MacLaren Stewart.[62]

'Routine (at any rate in the Crypt) was as follows,' related Madden. 'We slept until 1200 hrs; (the Boche evidently did the same, as his harassing fire did not start until about 1400 hrs as a rule), and had breakfast at midday, tea at 1530 hrs, dinner between 1800 and 1900 hrs.' An hour later what they called 'Exercise Flurry' would begin ('a Coldstream name which the Battalion found it could not improve on'). While a smokescreen was laid, porters would arrive and rations would be issued 'until the place was a milling mass of sweating humanity, all very hot from scrambling over the rubble. Then suddenly towards midnight, on a normal night, all would quieten down, and there would be very little for the next twelve hours except the routine of the departure of the stretcher bearers at 0300 hrs.' Outside the cathedral, those positioned in the town lived in sangars made from ruined houses, their vision limited to a few yards. Subjected to shelling from guns and mortars, 'probably the nearest parallel' to their existence was Stalingrad.[63] 'I found life in the crypt unexpectedly comfortable', recalled McKenzie Johnston, 'although depressing being in the dark all the time except for the dim light of candles and hurricane lamps. Ventilation was entirely natural and the air remained surprisingly fresh. I had a stretcher to sleep on with a somehow comforting skull of some long dead monk in a little niche at my head.' On 4 May, the Battalion handed back its position to the Coldstream Guards.[64]

For a fourth attack on Cassino, Operation Diadem, the US Fifth and British Eighth Armies would attack across a 20-mile front from Cassino to the sea, with the Liri river the dividing line between the two armies. Simultaneously, Allied troops would break out from Anzio and cut the road to Rome. 'Only numbers can annihilate,' Alexander reportedly stated, quoting Nelson before the Battle of Trafalgar.[65] The 4th Division's role was to make a bridgehead across the Rapido river, a mile from Cassino. To prevent the deployment of German reserves from the north, Alexander planned various diversions; these included reconnaissance flights creating the illusion of a planned amphibious landing north of Rome.

Late in the evening of 11 May, the German Tenth Army's commander, General Heinrich von Vietinghoff, having informed Field Marshal Albert Kesselring, Commander-in-Chief South, that 'nothing special' was going on, Alexander's offensive began with a massive artillery attack.[66] 'All in the same second every gun on the entire front opened fire. It was as if the very world itself had suddenly ripped apart. As far to the east and west as we could see ran an unbroken line of flashing white fire,' related Private Framp. 'The crashes of hundreds upon hundreds of guns combined to produce a thunder of stupendous dimensions, it was scarcely possible to believe it was the work of men, it seemed it must shake the very stars out of the heavens.'[67]

Attempts to cross the Rapido were hindered by both German batteries behind Cassino and thick fog. While the 4th Division's 10 Brigade achieved 'a rather insecure bridgehead', only a few men from 28 Brigade got across. Fortunately, the Germans did not counter-attack, having been hard hit by the barrage and prevented by the fog and a smokescreen from seeing exactly where to attack. During the lull 'Amazon', the first of several 'Bailey' bridges, was constructed, enabling reinforcements to cross the river, and 12 Brigade, with the 6th Black Watch, which had been in reserve, was then brought forward. Hearing bagpipes, 'our faces brightened,' recorded Lieutenant Frank Sutton, 2nd Bedfordshire & Hertfordshire Regiment, 10 Brigade. 'We had only one Scotch battalion in Fourth Division, the 6th Black Watch.'[68] Once across the river, the Battalion, supported by tanks, prepared to attack German positions. 'I saw the bright gleam of polished steel, describing the movement from scabbards to rifle muzzles, all along the ditch, as the platoons on either side of us fixed bayonets,' related Framp. 'I saw the platoon men scramble, 1916 fashion, from the ditches and move forward, in an extended line with rifles held at high point… all looked equally magnificent as they walked steadily forward into the German fire.'[69]

'Unfortunately shells from at least one of our guns were falling short and causing casualties to our own troops,' related Lieutenant McKenzie Johnston. 'I was standing up beside the bren gun carrier containing the wireless link back to Brigade, frantically trying to get someone to identify the guilty guns, when I was myself hit by one of these shells.' 'Someone shouted across to me from the west bank that they had some wounded to be evacuated,' related Sergeant Bonella. With only one boat left and the current too fast for the men to paddle, 'the only thing I could think of was to tie a length of telephone cable to a hand grenade – I removed the primer, of course – and throw it across the river. We were then able to haul the boat over by cable.'[70] Having gained a strong foothold across the river, the advance up the Liri valley continued. After six days the Germans withdrew, the strength of the Allied attack at last prevailing.

On 18 May a tattered white flag was hoisted over the ruined monastery of Monte Cassino, which had been occupied by the Germans after its destruction. Having at last taken possession of the town, Private Daily observed that 'on the gable end of what is now the "Hotel Continental" some wag had stuck a board with the message: Under New Management.'[71] 'By this time the Battalion was getting very tired,' commented Madden. Included in the reinforcements were members of the Transvaal Scottish, their presence converting the 'paper' alliance between the two regiments into 'one of flesh and blood'.[72] On 23 May Allied troops broke out of Anzio pushing through the German defences north of the Adolf Hitler Line. 'It seemed a long 4 months,' commented Private John Lewis, 8th Black Watch, who had arrived from Algiers in January with a 'platoon size' draft attached to the 2nd Sherwood Foresters, 1st Division.[73]

In hindsight, Monte Cassino was considered a 'hollow victory'. 'Years later I read in a newspaper, that the most sensible thing to have done, was to go round the damned mountain in the first place. Just think how many lives would have been saved, but the powers that make the important decisions wanted to go through, not round Cassino,' observed Daily. The capture of Cassino had come through the quantity of men and equipment rather than tactical brilliance, with Allied tanks greatly outnumbering the Germans. Advocates of the offensive argued that the Italian campaign, of which Monte Cassino was an important objective, kept German divisions out of Northern Europe.[74]

'Chasing Huns all over Italy'

'The way to Rome was now open,' continued Daily, who was surprised, when passing through an Italian village, to hear a voice calling out in a broad Glaswegian accent: 'Ye want yer socks washed?' 'These were Italian women who had spent most of their lives in Scotland but, through no fault of their own, had been repatriated to Italy at the start of hostilities. They had recognised the Black Watch, probably the Red Hackle. They were more used to the Black Watch than they were the Black Shirts of Mussolini.'[75] Although Alexander had wanted to close the gap on the retreating German Tenth Army, which had already withdrawn from Rome, the US Fifth Army's commander, Lieutenant General Mark Clark, preferred to enter Rome, his triumphal arrival taking place on 5 June. Soon afterwards members of The Black Watch passed through; Madden described their visit as 'a little disappointing as the route avoided St Peter's, the Coliseum and other famous places.' 'Population-wise,' commented Private Framp on a later visit, 'it resembled New York more than an Italian city. There were Yanks everywhere, millions of 'em.'[76]

Clark's decision, however, had let the Germans escape. By early June it was evident that the Italian campaign had become secondary to the war in northern Europe, where the Allied invasion of Normandy had just begun. The withdrawal of several divisions to take part in Operation Anvil (later known as Dragoon), the Allied invasion of southern France planned for August, also reduced their fighting strength. So critical were operations in Europe, and so comparatively neglected became the Italian front, that a 'ballad' was popularised:

We're the D-Day Dodgers, out in Italy –
Always on the vino, always on the spree…
Naples and Cassino, taken in our stride
We didn't go to fight, we just went for the ride.[77]

The reality was evidently different. 'Chasing Huns all over Italy' was an exhausting business, related Madden. As the Battalion moved north, Framp remembered 'little files of our lads, widely spaced on either side of the road, helmets angled, rifles slung, tin mugs swinging from packs, plodding patiently on, mile after dusty mile along the alternatively sunlit and then starlit roads of Tuscany.'[78] Once Allied forces had breached the German's next line of defence at Trasimeno/Chuisi, they fell back on Florence and the River Arno. 'Movement across country was difficult also and very hot going, and ambushes had always to be taken into account,' continued Madden, who was wounded on 2 July during a mortar attack. Two days later his successor, Major Jock Stewart, was wounded and command passed to Major Pat Lindsay, but he too was wounded during prolonged skirmishing. Major Ian MacRae then assumed command, followed by Major Robert Pollok-McCall. A new arrival in the Battalion was the Italian liaison officer, Gian Caspare Napolitano, who later fictionalised his experiences in *To War With The Black Watch*.[79]

By the end of July the Allied advance had slowed to a halt south-east of Florence. The 6th Black Watch was involved in attacking several features around Monte Scalari in operations codenamed Corbett. During a 'recce' on 27 July, a 'stonk' came over and Madden, once more in command, was again wounded. Major Graham Macpherson-Smith's succession signified the seventh change of command in less than a month. After three days' heavy fighting, Monte Scalari was taken. During the battle, Private Twells, a stretcher bearer, made nine journeys 'each time carrying a stretcher a distance of one and a half miles, often under heavy fire and involving a total of 5,000 ft of climbing.'[80] With southern Italy under Allied control, it was deemed safe enough for the King to visit, for which the 6th Black Watch provided a Royal Guard at Monte San Savino.[81]

On 4 August Allied troops entered the outskirts of Florence, bringing the Eighth Army close to the Gothic Line, Germany's last major line of defence. The 4th Division had already been withdrawn. Billeted in Foligno, the 6th Black Watch had quarters in a former lunatic asylum: 'the biggest bug home in all Italy', remarked Framp. 'We looked as if we'd all contracted galloping scarlet fever.' The building was speedily evacuated, the 'Corps of De-buggers' remedying the situation.[82]

Instead of attacking the Gothic Line in the centre, General Alexander decided on an assault at the 'Rimini gap' where the mountains fell short of the sea. On 25 August Operation Olive began, and the Germans were taken by surprise while senior commanders were on leave. The failure to make an immediate breakthrough meant bringing the 4th Division into action sooner than expected. 'Bloody morning, had to walk miles because couldn't get even [a] jeep through traffic jams,' Private Wombwell noted in his diary on 1 September. 'Don't like the sight of corpses early in the morning with no breakfast inside me. First area we looked at was full of mines. German warning signs everywhere... even the chickens had only one leg.'[83]

Attempts to force a bridgehead over the Marano river at Ospedaletto were delayed by heavy rain. While they waited, the men played cards. 'At times like these nobody greatly valued the money they carried in their pockets and consequently the gambling was reckless and the stakes, by our usual standards, high,' recalled Private Framp.[84] On 14 September the 6th Black Watch moved off. 'V. bitter fighting,' recorded Wombwell. Framp was among the wounded: 'caught out in the open, on the receiving end of concentrated artillery fire, a man's world becomes reduced to that little patch of it actually occupied by his own body. If the "stonk" or barrage be prolonged more than a few minutes – and under such circumstances minutes become hours – it shrinks still further. Limbs become expendable if they can be utilized, in even the smallest way, to protect the vital parts.' Hit several times, his worst injury was to his leg. 'I thought it had been torn off. I'm sure I must have screamed out with the pain and shock but if I did I don't remember it. I do remember the dreadful piercing screams of the others, one of which was abruptly cut off in mid-scream as more shells fell amongst us.'[85]

Fighting had now moved to the River Savio near Cesena, Rimini being captured by a Greek brigade. While the 2nd Royal Fusiliers established a bridgehead across the river, what remained of the 6th Black Watch moved forward in support. Despite 'an unpleasant amount of shelling and mortaring', the position was held. By 24 October the Germans had been pushed back, the shelling recorded as 'perhaps the severest the Battalion had ever undergone'.[86] On 8 November the 6th Black Watch fought its last battle in Italy at Forli. 'I remember a war correspondent taking a film of me standing up in my bren carrier receiving the cheers of the populace,' recalled McKenzie Johnston, who had recovered from his Monte Cassino wound and was now the Battalion's adjutant. Although they encountered no resistance going through the town, there was 'fierce opposition on the other side involving a good deal of close combat.' After four days the town was secured.[87] The 4th Division was then ordered south before what was expected to be a rest in Palestine.

Reflecting back, McKenzie Johnston's memories were of 'sheltering in a slit trench in a vineyard in glorious autumn weather where I could pluck ripe grapes, spending most of a night in a ruined farm house before a dawn attack, playing poker and drinking rum (when I lost heavily to Archie Callander)', who was killed soon afterwards; 'the chaos when trucks got stuck in mud and all my carefully planned movement orders were thrown into confusion and had to be sorted out by me; trying with little success to sleep in the rain curled up in the cramped space of the bren gun carrier in which was the wireless set communicating with brigade while occasional shells fell around us.'[88] The Italian campaign continued until April 1945. Between 11 May and 5 June Allied casualties were recorded as 44,933 of which 8,645 were killed.[89]

D-Day: 'A solid bridge of ships'

During the fight for Italy, and while operations were continuing in Burma, northern Europe had again become a battlefield. Operation Overlord's objective was to land troops along the Normandy coast, while making the German High Command think that the invasion would be at the Pas de Calais. The US First Army would disembark on beaches codenamed Utah and Omaha, west of Caen, while the Second Army, composed of British and Canadian troops in I and XXX Corps, would land between Bayeux and the Orne river at beaches Gold, Juno and Sword. Planned for 5 June, bad weather postponed D-Day for 24 hours. So unsuspecting were the Germans that Rommel, sent to Normandy at the end of 1943 to oversee the strengthening of Germany's 'Atlantic Wall', was on leave in Germany. Other senior commanders were at a conference in Rennes. It was not until the early hours of 6 June that Field Marshal Gerd von Rundstedt, in command of the German Army in the West, heard reports of a massive airborne assault, the beginning of the Allied invasion.

'Channel looks like a solid bridge of ships,' noted Private Graham Shand, 5th Black Watch, which, under Lieutenant Colonel Thomson's command, was among the first units of the 51st Highland Division to depart.[90] During their passage church services were held. 'Those of us who had been in action realised in some measure what was before us but none had any real idea of how devastating the next six weeks or so would turn out to be,' recollected Company Quartermaster Sergeant Meekison. 'Perhaps it was just as well.'[91] 'Somewhere off the Isle of Wight, the convoy swung to port and the speed increased as it joined the vast armada heading hell-bent for the Normandy beaches,' recorded Captain John McGregor. By dawn on 6 June, they had reached the Normandy coast. But strong on-shore winds 'kept the high tide on full flood... which restricted the clear space for manoeuvring vehicles, especially tanks... The bottleneck on shore created the "traffic jam" in the sea approaches.'[92]

'We anchored quite near to the beaches and for several hours had a grandstand view of the action taking place,' continued Meekison. 'There was also a steady volume of fire from the big Naval vessels, *Warspite* and friends, pounding targets some distance inland, and vehicles were moving steadily off the beaches and out of sight. At long last, our patience which by this time was wearing a bit thin, was rewarded and we saw our 3-tonner heaved over the side along with two others, and scrambled down the side of the ship to join it.' Once on board the landing craft, as they were approaching the beaches 'out of nowhere, swooped a number of German Aircraft, strafing the landing area and dropping bombs.' Forced to heave-to and wait, by the time they landed, darkness had fallen, although the area was brightly lit with anti-aircraft fire. 'Off we dropped down the ramp and into quite deep water which swirled around our legs.' Directed up the causeway, the beach was strewn with the debris of the first arrivals. 'It was a moment of history, the first time the 5th Black Watch had been on French soil since the Great War.'[93]

The next day the 5th Black Watch was ordered to attack the radar station at Douvres. As the soldiers advanced along the road east of

Bény-sur-Mer, contact was made in the nearby woods. 'Suddenly the Company Commanders were yelling "Stop firing!"', related McGregor. It soon became apparent that the 'enemy' was the North Shore Regiment of Canada. Having encountered strong German resistance when they attacked the radar station, the Canadians had withdrawn into the woods where they met the 5th Black Watch. 'It certainly was not the best way for the Battalion to start its European campaign,' continued McGregor, the 'needless action' causing casualties on both sides. The radar station was not captured until reduced by a naval and artillery bombardment nearly two weeks later.[94]

By the time 154 Brigade with the 1st and 7th Black Watch arrived in Normandy in the early hours of D+4 (10 June) a bridgehead had been established 'to include Bayeux and an early attempt to seize Caen had just failed', related Hopwood, the 1st Black Watch's Commanding Officer.[95] Leaving the landing craft, Private Henry Barker recorded 'the wettest of wet landings… The army issue of pocket watches were safely waterproofed in French Letters (condoms) especially used for that purpose – Top Brass think of everything.' 'The sky was filled with protecting balloons and fighter aircraft scoured the skies and swooped in to land at a strip visible not far inland,' continued Hopwood. 'Roads were already being made through the dunes and the whole area filled with directional signs and notices. The first signs of the famous Mulberry [harbour] were in progress and already artificial breakwaters of sunken ships had been constructed; it was from this hive of activity that the men marched into the seemingly peaceful hinterland.'[96]

Also in the 'second wave' was the 1st Battalion The Tyneside Scottish. 'The sea was crammed full of boats and ships of all descriptions as far as the eye could see,' recalled Private Tom Renouf, who had found a piano on board which he played. 'It put everyone at ease, and certainly helped my seasickness'. 'Our Captain, anxious no doubt to ensure that he was able to depart as soon as possible, had erred seriously on the side of caution,' related Lieutenant Brian Stewart. 'We were anchored so far out that each carrier disappeared under water; only the drivers' heads and the exhaust pipes were to be seen above the water line... happily, each emerged and ground its way onto dry land.' 'The local inhabitants seem neither glad nor sorry to see us. I don't think the war has affected them very much here,' Captain Donald Mirrielees wrote home.[97] Initially, the 49th West Riding Division was in reserve, Stewart describing the first few days as 'something of a picnic... with visits to Norman farms, now liberated from "*les sales Boches*".'[98]

The 5th Black Watch had already moved east of the River Orne, where the 6th Airborne Division had established a bridgehead across the Caen Canal at the bridge named 'Pegasus' (after the Division's sign, the mythical flying horse). Placed under the 6th Airborne's command, 153 Brigade was ordered to fill the gap in the line between Château St Côme, Bréville and Amfreville. Having received information from a patrol sent by the 9th Parachute Battalion that, despite the presence of snipers 'they did not think Bréville was strongly held', in the early hours of Sunday 11 June, the 5th Black Watch approached the town from the south-east. Almost at once, A Company came under German machine-gun fire and mortar attack. 'Within seconds most of them were hit and many were killed outright,' with fatalities totalling forty-nine by the end of the day. Among the wounded was McGregor in command of A Company, which had sustained the worst casualties. 'It was a complete disaster which depressed me badly for a long time,' observed Meekison.[99]

Lacking support from artillery or tanks, and on the orders of Brigadier James Hill, commanding 3 Para Brigade, Thomson withdrew to a defensive position at Château St Côme. The following day, intermittent shelling and mortaring continued until mid-afternoon when the Germans launched a heavy barrage, knocking out the remaining anti-tank gun and several bren gun carriers, leaving the Battalion with only small arms and mortars to defend themselves. During fighting that lasted 'some three hours', losses were again heavy. The establishment of a radio link with HMS *Arethusa* offshore and two well-placed salvos on the Germans' position brought some respite. That night the 6th Airborne Division took Bréville.[100]

To the veterans of North Africa, Normandy presented a different battleground. 'With close-wooded country, small fields, thick hedgerows and narrow twisting lanes, there was limited field of observation and little space for flanking movements. The enemy were all around but only seldom seen,' commented McGregor, evacuated to Britain after his injuries. After one week the Battalion's casualties numbered over 300, including 100 dead. These included a number of captured men shot by the Germans in Château St Côme.[101] One had survived, having feigned death. '[He got a] Bullet through [his] helmet and lay 12 hrs. till dark then [came] back to his lines and reported,' noted Private Shand. According to Meekison, the survivor 'was shaking with nerves' and, to avoid panic among the other soldiers, he was sent for psychiatric treatment. When the Battalion's padre, Tom Nicol, visited the graves of the recent fatalities, Meekison accompanied him: 'It was very quiet as we fixed the crosses one by one over the temporary resting places… there were far too many for my peace of mind.'[102]

154 Brigade had also come under the command of the 6th Airborne Division. 'East of the Orne was a very active sector,' related Barker, 1st Black Watch. 'For weeks, six I think, we were under strict instructions not to remove any clothing, especially our boots.' 'The ghastliest hole of all' was an exposed area known as the Triangle bounded by the Bois de Bavent and exposed to the Germans on two sides. 'We came under shellfire fairly frequently but we were well dug in,' related Lance Corporal Andrew Dow who had been transferred from the 7th to the 5th Black Watch after its losses. 'I can remember being impressed with the dugouts as whoever had improved the original slit trench had added a roof of corrugated iron and sandbags.'[103] Among those wounded in the 7th Black Watch was Captain Stewart McLaren, whose knee and leg was penetrated by shrapnel. Evacuated to Scotland, he was advised that amputation of his leg was necessary, but the doctor treating him recognised him as a well-known Perthshire cricketer and contrived to administer the relatively new medication, penicillin, thereby saving his leg.[104]

In the weeks following the invasion, German resistance had been fiercer than expected. 'Gerries over dropping leaflets,' observed

Shand, their contents warning that London and other cities were going to be destroyed by V-rockets and calling on the British soldiers to surrender. A severe storm between 19 and 21 June had delayed the landing of supplies, damaged landing craft, and grounded aircraft. 'Our push into Normandy was slowing to a crawl,' observed Renouf.[105]

Defence of Rauray – fall of Caen – Colombelles

Having failed to take Caen, Montgomery decided on a pincer movement which involved bringing forward the 49th West Riding Division. 'Most of us were 18 or 20 year olds with no combat experience, just our military training to fall back on,' recalled Private Lawton. The 1st Tyneside Scottish was among those carrying out a preliminary action, Operation Martlet. Its object was to secure the high ground on the right flank in preparation for Operation Epsom, the movement of troops into the Odon valley, south-west of Caen, which would outflank the Germans and seize the city. 'As we moved round the end of a row of terraced cottages, I was struck by a feeling of apprehension which was not helped by the smell of burning cordite combined with that of putrefying flesh,' continued Lawton. 'This early in our front line experience, we were not to know that this was far more likely to emanate from dead cattle rather than human remains.'[106]

By nightfall on 25 June the 49th Division had established a line south of Fontenay-le-Pesnel, in front of Rauray. The 1st Tyneside Scottish were under orders to attack the village at dawn, but, lacking sufficient supporting artillery and with the Germans firmly entrenched, they encountered fierce resistance, their visibility impaired by mist and gunfire.[107] Included in the German arsenal was the *Nebelwerfer*, a rocket-propelled mortar nicknamed 'moaning minnie', which 'would become the bane of our lives,' recalled Renouf. 'Being caught in the middle of a stonk was enough to break some men... another unwelcome echo of the Great War came in the form of shell-shock, which could reduce a man to a shambling wreck, no matter who was doing the firing.'[108]

'Our moment came on the morning of the 1st of July,' related Lieutenant Stewart, the anti-tank platoon's second-in-command. 'We had been ordered to take over and defend a position against an expected dawn attack… We hurried back to choose gun positions as best we could from the map since there was no time for personal reconnaissance. Nor was there time to dig effective gun pits by hand, so contrary to the rule-book, I told the gun commanders that they could use their Anti-Tank mines to blow gun pits so that the guns would be "hull down" when the attack came.' At dawn 'Jerry brought a heavy barrage crashing down on our battalion positions... We could hear the rumblings of the approaching Panzers,' Stewart informed his mother. 'The guns were deployed in the classic pattern: each gun facing obliquely across the front, so that it could aim at the side not the massive frontal armour of the enemy tanks and give mutual support to its neighbouring 6pdrs.' By the end of the day, he recorded '32 "dead" German tanks on our battalion front.' Stewart's part in the battle was brought to 'an abrupt end' mid-morning when he was wounded by 'an unfriendly Panzer.'[109]

Casualties in the 1st Tyneside Scottish were so high that a number of reinforcements were needed to bring the Battalion back to strength; by August the requirements of other battalions meant that the Tyneside Scottish was disbanded, its officers and men sent mainly to the 5th and 7th Black Watch and the 7th Argylls.[110] 'I was overjoyed,' related Renouf, who joined the 5th Black Watch. 'At last I had achieved my ambition to join the Highland Division – the "Fighting 51st". Little did I realise that the division had built its legendary reputation on a high level of activity and risk.' Lance Corporal John Samson transferred to the 7th Black Watch, where his service inspired a lifelong interest in the Regiment's history.[111] Despite the heavy losses, Operation Martlet had served its purpose in distracting the Germans from the British main effort, Operation Epsom. By mid-July, after further Allied pressure, the Germans had withdrawn from Caen.[112] Cherbourg had already surrendered to the US First Army on 27 June, although some outlying harbour forts held out for two more days.

On 10 July 153 Brigade, supported by the 7th Black Watch, with tanks and artillery, was ordered to attack the village of Colombelles, east of Caen. 'The Germans were thought to have occupied the tall brick chimneys of the metallurgic factory', explained Captain Brodie, who had replaced the wounded McGregor in command of A Company, observing that his subalterns consisted of a textiles clerk, a chartered accountant and a former detective. How the Germans had climbed the chimneys, he continued 'was never discussed, but the factory stood on high ground and no doubt did provide good observation.'[113] While the 1st Gordons were to advance on the right and attack the village, the 5th Black Watch would move to the north-west corner; the 7th Black Watch would then pass through and occupy the factory, leaving the 5th Seaforth in reserve. 'I can't say I am looking forward to this "do". I've a feeling there may be slaughter,' Shand confided to his diary.[114]

That night the attack began. 'I was lying in a ditch,' related Private Roland Dane. 'We all went very quiet until they started heavy shelling; somebody's arm came into the ditch with me. I don't know whose it was.' As was soon evident, several other observation points were enabling the Germans to dominate the location, and, as the Battalion advanced, they came under heavy artillery and mortar fire, leading to numerous casualties and the loss of all but one of their supporting tanks. 'Never, in all my days will I ever forget this, 11th day of July, 1944,' continued Shand, describing one place as 'a real Hell-hole and dawn being well on its way to daylight we were easy targets for snipers. Their bullets were coming as often as the shells and they were coming like rain the whole time.' The death of Colour Sergeant Andrew Hodge 'really hit me,' related Private Douglas Roger. 'Somebody else is just a name, but we had been through the war since July 1939.'[115] Among the wounded was Brodie, hit in the hand and thigh following a 'salvo' from the moaning minnies, which caused several fatalities. Although the 7th Black Watch was not sent forward, it suffered casualties from shellfire while forming up.[116] Their mission incomplete, 153 Brigade was ordered to withdraw.

Later criticism of the 5th Black Watch's 'fighting qualities' elicited a strong rebuttal from Lieutenant Colonel Thomson who maintained that the plan was 'unsound'. The Brigade's commander, Brigadier 'Nap' Murray, assumed responsibility for agreeing to the operation, the observations of both men at the divisional meeting prior to the attack having been 'overruled'. 'It took the Canadian Army two divisions to take that factory and we went in with one brigade,' commented Dane.[117] In late July Thomson, who had commanded the Battalion since December 1942, returned to Britain to take command of the 10th Black Watch. His successor was Lieutenant Colonel Bill Bradford, who had escaped from St Valéry.[118]

The Falaise push

By late July the Allies were finally breaking into France's heartland. 'Heavy fighting,' Private Shand was noting in his diary. 'Enemy planes drop flares and A.P. [anti-personnel] bombs. The sight is really beautiful if it wasn't so dangerous.[119] News was leaking out of a failed attempt on 20 July to assassinate Hitler, a last-ditch effort by members of the German High Command to disassociate themselves from the Führer and perhaps negotiate a more favourable peace. Among those caught in Hitler's pursuit of alleged conspirators was Rommel, recently hospitalised with head injuries following an attack on his staff car by the RAF.[120]

Having secured a bridgehead south of the Orne, on 6 August Montgomery ordered a drive towards the Seine. The 51st Highland Division, under the command of Major General Thomas Rennie, one of The Black Watch's 'own', now moved from I Corps to the Canadian II Corps, under Lieutenant General Guy Simonds.[121] While British troops directed their attention towards Argentan, the Canadians were ordered to make for Falaise. Simonds' first objective was Verrières Ridge, the Germans' main defensive position after the fall of Caen. His previous attempt in late July had failed with severe casualties, decimating The Black Watch (Royal Highland Regiment) of Canada.[122] Simonds now adopted the innovative strategy of a fully mechanised infantry attack. Travelling in stripped-down tanks converted into armoured personnel carriers called Kangaroos, and following closely behind the tanks, the infantry would gain the advantage of speed and surprise. By directing the beams of searchlights onto low-lying clouds to create 'artificial moonlight' (known as Monty's Moonlight) Simonds had the advantage of being able to advance at night.

In a Special Order of the Day, Rennie made his first address as Divisional Commander. 'In Africa we fought side by side with Australians and New Zealanders. Now we are with Canadians and it is a coincidence that during the closing stages of the Great War we were also fighting beside a Canadian Corps.'[123] In the early hours of 7 August, Operation Totalise began with RAF bombers targeting points ahead of the ground forces.[124] The columns then moved forward, four vehicles abreast. By midday the Germans had been dislodged. 'The front had now broken and the race was on to cut as much enemy off as possible,' recorded Lance Corporal Dow. 'We had our casualties but not as great as the set pieces we had in the desert. It was a different type of war and it was difficult to accustom yourself to this type of warfare. Every house and hedgerow had to be fought for.'[125] One lucky survivor was Sergeant Robert Penman who had been left for dead until another soldier 'noticed a slight movement, found I was still breathing, picked me up like a baby and carried me to the First Aid Station.'[126] After the heat and dust of battle, Captain Donald Mirrielees was longing 'for a good day of mist and rain'. But, he wrote to his sister, 'it is no good thinking of these things until we have got this job finished.' On 29 August he, and five others, were killed during a skirmish at Mauny. Private Renouf was among the wounded.[127]

'What a change has come about in the last few weeks,' announced Montgomery. 'Our Armies are moving relentlessly Eastwards into France. Many hundreds of towns and villages have been liberated.' 'Piobaireachd', the 51st Highland Division's newsletter, echoed his sentiments, describing how British and Canadian forces 'have drawn the ring tighter North-West of Falaise.'[128] A follow-up offensive, Operation Tractable, ended with the Canadians reaching Falaise.

The 'gap' was closed on 21 August when Canadian and Polish troops met up with United States forces advancing from the south. Four days later Allied troops entered Paris. 'The Division has played a major part in the Battle of France,' Rennie announced. 'For fifteen days [it] fought continuously in its most intensive period of fighting in this war. We sustained some 1,761 casualties but took over 1,600 prisoners, in addition to killing and wounding a very large number of Germans and to overrunning great quantities of German equipment… the German is no good when his tail is down.' Mindful that their next objective was St Valéry-en-Caux, he recalled the events of 12 June 1940 when members of the 51st Highland Division were 'sacrificed in a last effort to keep the French in the war… the discipline of that Division remained up to Highland Division standard to the last. I was there, so I know.'[129]

From St Valéry-en-Caux to Le Havre

Although the Germans were withdrawing from France and Belgium to a defensive position along the Siegfried Line, garrisons had been left in the ports eastwards from Le Havre to deny the Allies access to the European mainland by sea. Travelling onwards over congested roads 'the sights were horrific,' recalled Barker, 'dead bodies of men and horses lying on the road side. We couldn't do anything about it, too busy pushing on… The biggest surprise was the amount of horse drawn transport and guns abandoned in fields at the roadside, the smell was everywhere. The sight of dead horses strangely enough had more effect on me than did the soldiers.' Despite the 'utter devastation,' the streets were crowded 'with cheering men, women and children, who showered us with apples and flowers, and during halts pressed bottles of rather bitter cider into the hands of the Jocks seated in their vehicles.' In return the soldiers gave away 'cigarettes, chocolates and sweets.'[130]

As the 51st Division was reaching the outskirts of St Valéry, on 1 September Canadian forces entered Dieppe, where, in August 1942 a disastrous raid had resulted in over half of the 6,000 men who landed becoming casualties. 'So they, like the Highland Division, would be recalling the past.'[131] As they neared the coastline, those present in 1940 pointed out familiar landmarks, Private Shand visiting a graveyard 'of B.W. killed'. At Saint-Pierre-le-Viger the schoolmaster gave Bradford some personal effects, kept safely since 1940.[132] On 2 September the 51st Highland Division re-entered St Valéry-en-Caux, where Rennie established his headquarters in the chateau at Cailleville. 'Our Brigade took up the same position as our predecessors had held in 1940 and in fact our Company Commander made his headquarters in the same farmhouse as he had been in in 1940,' observed Dow.[133]

'This is a very great occasion in the history of our famous Division,' said Rennie on Sunday 3 September, the fifth anniversary of the outbreak of the war, repeating his earlier comments and describing how he had disposed the Division 'as far as is possible in the areas where it fought at St Valéry'. Mindful of the surrender, he continued: 'It had been our task to avenge the fate of our less fortunate comrades and that we have nearly accomplished.'[134] A church parade was held 'in a Catholic Church which had been bombed and had lost its roof,' recollected Dow. 'When collection time came round we all emptied our pockets and enough money was collected to complete all repairs to the church. Money was no good to us anyway, as there was nothing you could spend it on. We never thought of saving it for a rainy day as we were not even sure that we would survive to see that.'[135]

After St Valéry, the Division turned back. 'Our next job was to be the capture of the Port of Le Havre which had been bypassed on the advance and was held by a very determined German general, who had sworn to resist us to the last,' continued Dow, who had temporarily been reduced in rank and was now 'back up to corporal again'. 'It was reckoned to be a very hard nut to crack but our orders were to crack it... Our morale at this time was very high. Just like in the desert we considered ourselves the crack troops... we were the Highland Division and that to us meant something.'[136] Codenamed Operation Astonia, the offensive was to be a combined assault by the 51st Highland and the 49th West Riding Divisions, with supporting units. 'Air photos were available and plans were made in some detail,' Bradford wrote in his diary. 'It rained daily and ground and tracks became increasingly boggy.' By 10 September the weather had turned fine.[137]

The attack that evening, Dow noted was 'to be a set piece effort with an artillery back up (Shades of El Alamein). The first preparation would be a 1,000 plane raid and if that did not make them surrender there would be another 1,000 plane raid before we actually attacked.' The Germans did not surrender and so the ground troops went in. The 49th Division was the first to breach the north-eastern perimeter, followed by the 51st, their advance helped by local intelligence. 'One Frenchman had actually stolen the German fire-plan and presented it to our Intelligence Staff.' On the third day, the German commander, Colonel Eberhard Wildermuth, surrendered; 12,000 Germans were taken prisoner. Among Allied casualties was the 7th Black Watch's second-in-command, Major David Russell, who lost a foot.[138]

'We moved into Le Havre occupying the barracks,' related Barker, now a lance corporal. 'We fell heir to a German officer's Alsatian, he was a bit hostile at first, but food conquers all. We also had a cow and believe it or not we actually managed to milk it. Luxury fresh milk daily.' 'There were signs of devastation everywhere,' observed Dow. 'Buildings were ruined, even graveyards had suffered in the bombing. White flags were everywhere as were cheering civilians. Some sniping was going on in various places but our supporting tanks dealt with them. They didn't stand on any ceremony when they found a building with a sniper. They simply blew the building up.'[139]

Briefly the soldiers enjoyed a rest 'bathing in the sea, and fraternising with the "much-relieved" French people'. 'It was in this area that we saw how the French dealt with females who had been too friendly with the Germans. They used to shave the woman's head and parade her up the street where she was spat on by all and sundry,' continued Dow. Rennie again praised the Division, maintaining that Le Havre's capture would 'speed up the final destruction of the German army.'[140] By mid-September the Allied forces which had landed in Normandy had established contact in the vicinity of the Vosges mountains with those who had been fighting in southern France. The intention was now for both forces to sweep north to the Siegfried Line and enter Germany.

Post-haste to Belgium and Holland

'What a change has come over the scene,' stated Montgomery, who had recently been promoted Field Marshal, on 17 September. 'Today the Seine is far behind us; the Allies have removed the enemy from practically the whole of France and Belgium, except in a few places, and we stand at the door of Germany.' On the same day, he launched the largest airborne operation to date, Operation Market Garden, 'Market' involving two US and one British Airborne Division, and 'Garden', the British XXX Corps, now under the command of Lieutenant General Brian Horrocks. The objective was to capture the bridges across the Waal, Maas (Meuse) and Lower Rhine rivers, including at Arnhem, so that the Ruhr could be encircled from the north. Despite some initial Allied success in taking the bridges between Eindhoven and Nijmegen, the attack was met by determined German resistance. Although a unit of the British 1st Airborne Division reached the northern end of the bridge at Arnhem, delays in the infantry's arrival meant no further advance could be made. On 25 September the airborne units were evacuated. During the week-long offensive, nearly 2,000 British paratroopers and airmen were killed, while 6,000 men were taken prisoner. The US Airborne Divisions suffered over 3,500 casualties and the Germans had an estimated 1,300 dead.[141]

The 51st Highland Division had been retraining. Orders then came for 154 Brigade to undertake a separate assignment. Over 170 miles away a 15,000-strong German garrison was in Dunkirk 'where things were reversed with the Germans inside and us outside,' commented Private Dane. For nearly two weeks the Brigade held the 56-mile perimeter, during which time a 24-hour truce was arranged for the evacuation of nearly 20,000 civilians and seriously wounded German soldiers. A key negotiator, fluent in French and German, was Captain Wingate-Gray, the intelligence officer. Four days later, on 8 October, the Brigade was relieved, Dunkirk remaining under siege until May 1945. 154 Brigade then had a 'top secret' assignation: guarding the Eindhoven airfield, where the King was going to land 'very near the German front line in the Arnhem corridor'.[142]

The rest of the Division had moved 'post haste' to Belgium, passing 'all the well-kept graveyards of the First World War,' as Dow recorded.[143] By mid-October the 51st Highland Division was in Holland, preparing for the next offensive and supported by 33 Armoured Brigade. Montgomery's renewed objective was to gain control of the Maas river and reopen Antwerp to Allied shipping. The operation, codenamed Colin, was under the direction of XII Corps, commanded by former Black Watch officer Lieutenant General Neil Ritchie.[144] The Battle of the Maas, as the offensive became known, coincided with the second anniversary of Alamein on 23 October.

'Into attack at dawn. Just as we start off with tanks across the moors a terrific barrage opens up. We advance over the sandy moors under a smoke screen. Our own barrage is far too close to us – just on us,' related Private Shand.[145] Over the next few days, the Division moved forward in stages. '[It was] a difficult operation as the Boche were dug in on the opposite bank,' related Bradford, describing their progress crossing the Aftwaterings Canal, which ran in an east–west direction through 's-Hertogenbosch. 'Both banks were about 30 ft high. We had some opposition to begin with and lost some men when crossing the Canal but once our men were amongst them, the Boche surrendered easily and we got about 100 prisoners.' During their advance they came upon the concentration camp at Vught, bearing 'mute witness to the horrible things that had happened there,' recorded the 51st Highland Division's 'officer-observer', Captain James Borthwick.[146] Used as a transit camp for Jews, it had also housed Belgian and Dutch political prisoners, most of whom had already been moved to Germany.

Summing up the operation, Rennie described how, between 23 October and 7 November, 'the Division, by its thrust from Schijndel to Geertruidenberg and its activities later east and north of 's-Hertogenbosch, cleared an area of some 300 square miles of

Holland, denied the Germans their bridge escape route at Geertruidenberg, and captured or annihilated most of the German rearguards south of the river Maas.' 'We were sitting in the station at 's-Hertogenbosch discussing what we were going to do in the future,' related Private Dane. 'I wanted to be an electrician, but my parents wanted me to go into market gardening. Soon afterwards our Sergeant got up; advancing about 300 yards, he was shot dead. We never again discussed again what we were going to do in the future.'[147]

By 30 November, St Andrew's Day, after taking part in Operation Ascot to dislodge the Germans from their bridgehead across the Maas to the south, the 51st Highland Division was in the Island: an area of Holland between Nijmegen and Arnhem where the river divides into two channels. On 3 December the Germans opened the sluices. Operation Noah – the Island's evacuation – came into immediate effect. 'The only things above water now are the various farms which are our positions and a village which we hold,' related Bradford. 'The road between is anything up to fifteen inches deep in water, which is rising steadily.' Unable to use their vehicles, they were reliant on 'horses and carts to maintain ourselves with. Luckily, jeeps can still get to Bn HQ.' Having rescued 'dozens' of livestock, there was insufficient feed and so 'they in turn became feed for Jocks,' the surplus slaughtered.[148]

Counterattack in the Ardennes

The German reaction to Allied successes came unexpectedly. On 16 December a major offensive was launched through the forest of the Ardennes, its objective to split the Allied armies before they could close in on Germany. In response, on 19 December the United States Ninth Army, isolated from its 12th Army Group Headquarters, and elements of the US First Army, were placed under Montgomery's command. XXX Corps (once more including the 51st Highland Division) was ordered west of the Maas as a 'Long Stop' to counter-attack German forces crossing the river. 'In the midst of our Christmas preparations,' recalled Meekison, 'we were rudely interrupted by no less than General von Rundstedt who had decided in his wisdom to knock [the] blazes out of the Yanks in the Ardennes areas which he did very successfully, catching them completely by surprise, and making big advances into their territory. Monty had reacted at once and we were ordered to proceed immediately into Belgium and take up defensive positions forward of Louvain.' Lieutenant Colonel Oliver was recalled from leave 'when he was practically stepping onto the plane.' Approaching the Ardennes area, Lance Corporal Dow could sense the civilians' panic. 'The welcome signs, which they had some weeks ago painted up on walls, etc., welcoming the allies were all being carefully eroded in case the Germans broke through.'[149]

'The whole situation was somewhat reminiscent of 1940,' commented Hopwood 'as no one knew where the German columns had reached.' When the threat to Louvain subsided, they moved to Weert on the Dutch–Belgian–Luxembourg border. 'Christmas was within the next day or two, and plans were immediately put into effect to give the lads a bumper Xmas dinner,' recorded Meekison. Church services were 'of course conducted in Flemish, but the hymn tunes were much the same as those Christmas ones we sang at home and we joined in heartily as and when we could. I think it did us all a lot of good to be there along with these very sincere people.' Returning from Church it was 'obvious a flap was on'. The Division was again under orders to move, its destination Liège. 'Our belated Christmas meal was served up in darkness, but was none the less appreciated as most of us were starving.'[150]

The year ended with both the 4th and 10th Black Watch 'draft finding' in Britain to reinforce the depleted battalions overseas.[151] Having reached Taranto in Italy in early December, it appeared that the 6th Black Watch's war was over. 'We handed in our weapons and were billeted near the harbour waiting to be shipped to Palestine,' recalled Captain Mike Honey, Transvaal Scottish, serving with the 6th Black Watch. The Battalion then embarked on board the *Bergensfiord*. Their destination was in fact Greece. 'The Germans had been driven out of the country by then and a small British military presence had been established in Athens which had become surrounded by hostile irregular communist forces,' explained McKenzie Johnston. This was ELAS, the Greek People's Liberation Army, the military wing of the left-wing National Liberation Front (EAM) who were 'intent on taking control'. 'Having done most of the fighting the partisans now wanted a say in how Greece was governed,' recorded Private Daily.[152]

To support the government led by Georgios Papandreou, Prime Minister of the Greek government-in-exile, Churchill had agreed to provide what became known as 'Churchill's Army'. Landing near Faliron (Phaleron), the 6th Black Watch had to secure the main road to Athens so that supplies could be transported from the coast. 'Each house was searched for arms,' recalled Honey. 'It was a laborious business but after a shot or two the "enemy" melted away.'[153] Christmas was quiet with one battalion fatality on 26 December, and another accidental one later that week. 'It was New Year's Eve,' related Daily, 'when Willie McCartney, of our platoon, reported for guard duty.' In the excitement of wishing him 'all the best for the New Year', the soldier McCartney was relieving accidentally pressed the trigger of his gun 'and hit Willy, killing him instantly... we had come through so much together, so many terrible sights, and on the very last day of the year, to lose Willy in such a stupid fashion was too much to bear.'[154]

In northern Europe, on New Year's Eve the 51st Highland Division was manning defences on the Maas river between Liège and Namur. 'Fourteen days after the start of the German offensive, we have regained one-fifth of the ground lost,' enthused 'Piobaireachd'. 'Quite an eventful year,' noted Private Shand. '[General Sir Harold] Alexander has driven right up thro' Italy and thro' the Hitler and Gothic lines. In Burma, the Fourteenth Army holds the upper hand. In China more aid is flowing in with new airfields being made available against Japan. In the Pacific the Yanks are in the Philippines. In W. Europe the German is almost entirely back in his own country.'[155]

Now is the winter of our discontent
Made glorious summer...[156]

15

1945: Unconditional Surrender

We just swept across Germany and whole towns were surrendering.[1]

After months of constant gunfire and all the harsh noises of modern warfare – there was silence.[2]

A structure of peace

By the beginning of 1945 Prime Minister Winston Churchill was confident of victory, boldly encouraging the Germans to submit to unconditional surrender rather than endure the suffering of another year of war. 'We, the Allies, are no monsters,' he stated in the House of Commons on 18 January, 'but faithful men trying to carry forward the light of the world, trying to raise, from the bloody welter and confusion in which mankind is now plunged, a structure of peace, of freedom, of justice and of law, which system shall be an abiding and lasting shelter for all.'[3]

Of the five Black Watch battalions serving abroad, the 2nd was still in India and the 6th in Greece. With Athens once more under Royalist control, the men had been patrolling the mountains where communist partisans had taken refuge. 'We would approach a mountain village, and, as we drew near, the church bells would start to ring,' recalled Private George Daily. 'This was a warning to the partisans to melt away before us.' On 15 January a truce became effective under which ELAS, the Greek People's Liberation Army, would withdraw behind an agreed line while a settlement was agreed. 'This was now the end of active military action,' commented Major McKenzie Johnston. 'Our next job was much more pleasant! Garrison duty on the island of Corfu,' continued Daily. 'It was like landing in Heaven after all the months of Hell.'[4]

Winter warfare

In northern Europe, the 1st, 5th and 7th Black Watch began the New Year on the Maas river. Conditions remained gruelling. 'It was a battle not only against a desperately resisting enemy, but against the elements – the biting wind, the frozen ice-covered roads, the hidden mines,' observed Captain James Borthwick. Having gained experience of 'winter warfare' in Iceland in 1941, Major Aldo Campbell, 5th Black Watch, gave some lectures 'which included tips about coping with the cold.' An unexpected bonus was their proximity to the Americans. 'When the temperatures dropped below a certain point,' recalled Private John Mitchell, 'British servicemen were issued a once per day rum ration... Most of us in the ranks were between 18 & 21 years old and did not drink alcohol.' When the rum ration was handed out, a sergeant would stand at the end of the mess table with a keg of rum and a pail. 'Every soldier was asked if he wanted his rum ration and if he refused it was put in the pail. Around midnight every night an American "patrol" came in, and a British "patrol" went out – the Yanks brought us boxes of fruit cocktail which was a delicacy to us in the British Army during the war.' In return the Americans took 'the rum our men had refused.'[5]

On 7 January the 51st Highland Division left its positions on the Maas as the Allied counter-offensive against the German attack into the Ardennes continued. 'We moved down to the Brigade area of Marche, which was the limit of the German advance,' related Private Barr, 7th Black Watch, describing how, to combat the cold, 'the well-dressed soldier was wearing two pairs of woollen socks, heavy wool underwear; flannelette shirt; wool gloves; boots, and equipment and steel helmet, plus any items available such as scarves and Balaclava helmets.' The weather remained atrocious. 'Carriers just slid backwards and sideways into the ditches,' related Lieutenant Colonel Bradford, 5th Black Watch. 'My feet were like blocks of ice,' recalled Private Roland Dane, a bren gun carrier driver. 'So I put the carrier in first gear, and, with my hand on the steering wheel, I ran alongside; once I got my feet warm I would jump back in.' Showing 'art and ingenuity', related Captain Borthwick, the soldiers created 'a species of "nicky-tams"' consisting of layers of straw and sacking, making them look like they were suffering from elephantiasis.[6]

'We kept the Bren magazines under our greatcoats to prevent them from freezing and had to constantly work the Bren mechanism by hand to keep it moveable in case of need,' recorded Private Stanley Whitehouse, 1st Black Watch. 'Nevertheless the gun still froze up. We were given graphite grease to smear on our sten-gun bolts and rifle bolts… and the grease froze.' 'If anybody sat down you were told that you were to get them up and walk them up and down, not to let anybody sit still,' recalled Private Percy Lawton. 'A hot meal was brought up to us… I ate the stew as quickly as I could, because I was cold and hungry. But when I came to the rice pudding, which was in my other mess tin I found that there was already a thin coating of ice on the top of it. It was still quite warm underneath.'[7]

While 154 Brigade advanced up the main road beside the River Ourthe towards La Roche-en-Ardenne, Rennie had ordered 153 Brigade to take a parallel route across country. 'We walked single file through knee deep snow at night,' remembered Lieutenant William Chisholm, 5th Black Watch. 'I told my platoon to keep walking in the steps of the one in front to save energy in the bitter cold. But always there is one who doesn't listen. He moved out of line to talk to his friend up ahead and fell into a deep ditch full of snow. Unfortunately he carried two lots of PIAT bombs – as we fished him out he lost one lot of three and since we were holding up the whole Company we did not have time to recover them.'[8]

'The plan was for 152 Brigade to continue to advance southwards, covering the right flank,' explained Private Renouf, 5th Black Watch. '154 Brigade would capture La Roche and push forward; and 153 Brigade would advance on the left flank, east of the Ourthe valley.

All three brigades would attack simultaneously, as time was of the essence. The aim was to cut the enemy's main escape route and then link up with American troops driving north, thus preventing the retreat of the front-line German forces.'[9] While the 1st Black Watch attacked La Roche, the 7th would wait until the town had fallen in order to pass through and attack the village of Hives 'and exploit as far as Lavaux'.[10]

On entering the northern part of the town, a platoon of the 1st Black Watch came under German artillery fire. 'Several lads were hit', related Lance Sergeant Rowe, 'among them our 2nd Lieutenant, who was killed. He had just arrived from Scotland and it was his first and last bit of action.'[11] Bringing up the rear was the 1st Black Watch's mortar platoon. 'How naked and vulnerable we seemed to be,' recalled Sergeant Jim Burrow. 'We stood out like a sore finger. I think it must have been in everyone's mind, as it was in mine: Which hill had the "Jerry" artillery observation post? … When would we get the hell off this road?' Seeing an abandoned German tank, Major Ambrose Walton climbed into it. 'The German Officer had left his Binoculars, which I used in future operations.'[12] Only when the 1st Black Watch had 'dealt with the Germans still holding out', could the 7th Black Watch proceed, its progress hindered by numerous road blocks, mines and booby traps. As the battalion neared Hives, a German tank positioned across the only track leading to the village barred their way: 'after confused fighting [they] took some forty prisoners'.[13] It was dark when the supporting vehicles started their journey up the mountain road, Private Charles Gate marvelling at the effect of 'Monty's Moonlight' 'on the huge icicles which hung from a rock face'.[14]

On 12 January 'Piobaireachd' was recording that 'the whole bulge, bounded by La Roche, Marche and St Hubert is being squeezed in.' 'Coldest night I've ever spent. Advance up slope towards Hubermont – pretty anxious time,' Private Shand was writing on 13 January. The 5th Black Watch had temporarily been put under the command of 154 Brigade as it moved forward to consolidate the villages beyond La Roche. 'There were many stops and starts', observed Renouf, 'and there were a few shells coming in our direction… The Company was deployed in defensive positions and told to "dig in". Since the ground was too hard to dig slit trenches, the men lay in the snow 'seeking what cover we could find'.[15] Once Hubermont had been taken, the Brigade advanced to Nisramont, finding that the Germans had vacated it under cover of darkness.

Although fierce fighting between the Germans and Americans continued until the end of the month, the 51st Highland Division, with its three Black Watch battalions, was no longer involved in the Ardennes battle. After reassembling in La Roche, whose destruction Renouf described as 'worse than most of the towns in Normandy – rather of the devastation like Caen', the Division moved northwards to recuperate 'in good warm billets in the local schools and halls'. On entering Haaren on 23 January, the 5th Black Watch received 'a great welcome back,' having liberated the town in October. Bradford was granted the honour of unveiling a memorial plaque to those of the 51st Highland Division who had died capturing the town.[16]

The Ardennes offensive, which became known as the Battle of the Bulge, had resulted in approximately 120,000 German casualties. American casualties were recorded at nearly 8,500 killed, over 46,000 wounded and nearly 21,000 missing. During the month-long offensive, Black Watch fatalities in the 1st, 5th and 7th Battalions numbered less than fifteen. Although the German counter-attack had surprised the Allies 'when the fog, which blanketed the German initial infiltration lifted, and the Allied Air Force got going, the situation was hopeless as far as the enemy were concerned. His lines of communication were battered to pieces.'[17]

The Reichswald: 'Onto German soil for the first time'

On 4 February the 'Big Three' – Churchill, Roosevelt and Stalin – met in the Livadia Palace near Yalta in the Crimea. Yet again they affirmed their commitment to forcing Germany's unconditional surrender. Once achieved, the country would be split into four zones occupied by the Allied forces. Germany would be demilitarised and 'denazified'. Those accused of war crimes were to be brought to justice. Stalin also agreed to enter the war against Japan within three months after Germany's defeat. Roosevelt, however, was a sick man. His death on 12 April meant that his successor, Vice-President, sixty-year-old Harry S. Truman from Missouri, would preside over the conclusion of hostilities.[18]

Having withstood the German counter-attack, Allied forces resumed their advance towards the Reichswald, the 'Imperial Forest', between the Maas and Rhine rivers on the German frontier. 'We returned from Brussels to find the next phase of the war being marked out for us,' commented Andrew Dow, 5th Black Watch. 'This was to be a big one. Onto German soil for the first time.'[19] To the north, Operation Veritable was assigned to the Canadian First Army and part of the United States Second Army, while the southern pincer manoeuvre, Operation Grenade, was to be carried out by the United States Ninth Army, with the objective of dislodging German troops on a broad front on the west bank of the Rhine before attempting a crossing.

Under the command of the Canadian First Army, XXX Corps was to lead the attack, the infantry divisions supported by two armoured divisions as well as specialised units including flame-throwing tanks. Given the narrow 'jumping off' position of each division, Rennie chose 154 Brigade, strengthened by the 5/7th Gordons, for the 51st Highland Division's initial advance. 'The whole thing was gone into in detail with the help of a sand model and large-scale maps,' recorded Russell, in his history of the 7th Black Watch, noting that during the 'intense' preparations, the officers had time for a cocktail party![20] But their German adversaries were not giving in without a fight. Almost at once Operation Grenade had to be postponed when the release of water from the Roer river dams upstream flooded the area and enabled German troops to focus attention to the north, reinforcing the Siegfried Line.

'Huge concentration of warfare. We are in a Nissan hut for the night all teed up for tomorrow's show,' Private Shand recorded on 7 February the night before Operation Veritable was launched.

'Morale not too low.' At 5 a.m. on 8 February, the artillery, supported by the Allied air forces, began its bombardment 'the like of which the Division had not experienced since Alamein.' 'A most hellish racket starts,' continued Shand. 'All the 5.5s in the world appear to be in action.'[21] After over three hours, the 7th Black Watch, positioned on the right, moved forward, A Company taking the village of Breedeweg 'without much difficulty'. 'There was hardly anybody about, which was not surprising after the bombardment,' recorded Private Dane. 'Shell and bomb holes all over. Tricky driving.' 'At first sight [Reichswald Forest] seemed a difficult long stretch of flat open fields, crossing of which appeared to invite disaster,' recalled Lance Corporal Barker, 1st Black Watch. 'However, somehow we made it and dug in at the edge of the forest.' During the advance, the section took seven prisoners, 'one was no more than a schoolboy. The first of the Hitler youth.'[22] In response to a signal from the 1st Black Watch's temporary Commanding Officer, Major Peter Taylor, saying 'positions taken' came Lieutenant General Horrocks' congratulations for being 'first on German soil'.[23]

'About 4 o'clock in the afternoon we got the order to move,' continued Dow, describing how the 5th Black Watch in 153 Brigade could not advance until 154 Brigade had captured its objectives.

> We moved forward under heavy shellfire and between us and the edge of the forest there was a large expanse of open ground. Through the centre of this piece of ground there was strung a barbed wire fence about 4 and a half to 5ft high. Along this fence a German machine gun was firing on a fixed line in spasmodic bursts. The problem was to get across this open ground without being seen and over this fence as soon as possible. We set off in sections, my section leading. We each had a smoke grenade which we threw in front of us as we moved forward. As normal in circumstances like this, we went hell for leather and crossed this open ground and threw ourselves over this fence somehow.[24]

Pushing on towards the edge of the woods, Dow was expecting

'bursts of fire from the enemy'. But none came. Realising they were finally in Germany 'we all felt elated. It had been a long trail from El Alamein.'[25]

To create a secure position from which to advance, Hekkens had to be taken. Situated on the southern edge of the Reichswald at the crossroads of the Gennep–Kleve and Kessel–Goch highways, through which the Siegfried Line ran, the village was heavily defended. By the early evening of 11 February both the 1st and 7th Black Watch 'were firmly established in the village and had taken a couple of hundred prisoners'. Having taken Kessel, 154 Brigade moved on to Hassum to capture the railway station. Although successful, fatalities included Major Ian Molteno, who, despite losing an eye in North Africa, had managed 'by gallant importunism to force his way back to the side of his comrades'.[26]

Meanwhile, the 5th Black Watch was attacking Gennep, west of Hekkens. The challenge now was no longer the cold but a thaw, creating streams of water and mud two feet deep, as the River Niers doubled in width. 'It is about 200 yds wide,' recorded Private Shand, 'and we do it just before daylight. Small paddle boats are used.'[27] Among the fatalities was Major Donald Beales killed by shell fire. The next objective was Goch, 'bastion town of the Siegfried Line', the attack on which began in the early hours of 19 February. 'We had to capture some houses on the outskirts, then, Company by Company,' related Captain Alec Brodie, who had succeeded Beales in command of D Company, 'the whole Battalion passed by, each capturing a bit of the town and letting the next one come through it and capture a bit further on. We took our first bit without firing a shot, and even got a bridge on our left, which everybody thought would have been strongly guarded, and some Boche in a pill box. It was a very dark misty night, and there was a terrific bombardment before we started, so the Boche were rather dazed.'[28]

Finding the houses 'quite unoccupied and unlooted', Brodie even had time to enjoy 'some very nice bottled fruits, including gooseberries', while other troops passed through. Soon afterwards, during residual sniping, he was wounded. After ensuring that his second-in-command, Captain Ken Buchanan, 'was well able to take over', he started 'to limp back across the ploughed fields to Battalion Headquarters.' On the way another 'stonk' came down and he was hit on the sole of his right foot, remarking that the hob nails and thick sole of his boot prevented him receiving 'more than a bad bruise'. The shell was, however, 'red hot' and he was badly burned. 'I tottered on to Battalion HQ, saw the CO Bill Bradford and told him all I could of the state of my Company. He then put me in a jeep to go to the Regimental Aid Post. Believe it or not the wretched thing slithered into the anti tank ditch beside the road, and I had to wade out ankle deep in icy water. This did seem to do my foot good and I managed the walk back to the RA Post.'[29]

On 22 February, having cleared the Reichswald, General Crerar, in command of the Canadian First Army, initiated a new phase, code-named Blockbuster, which involved attacking German positions in the north, with the objective of joining up with the US Ninth Army.[30] Although the Germans had fought to retain a bridgehead at Wesel on the west bank of the Rhine, on 10 March they withdrew.

Crossing the Rhine became the Allies' next objective. First a period of amphibious training began. 'After a short spell in the village near Goch,' continued Dow, 'we were drawn back to an area near the Dutch–Belgian border', where the soldiers were made 'very welcome by the local population… They could not do enough for us and wanted to share what little they had with us.' Training in 'Buffaloes', armoured amphibious vehicles already used during operations in Holland in October 1944, the River Maas was used to simulate the Rhine. 'The river Maas in this particular area was fairly wide but not as wide as what we expected the Rhine to be. We practised this exercise by day and by night frequently. During this period fresh reinforcements had arrived and we had a performance from our own Balmoral Concert Party. Wine and cognac flowed freely. Too freely in some cases.'[31] Among new arrivals in the 7th Black Watch was Second Lieutenant Ian Critchley who wondered if the thirty Jocks in his platoon would think that he, aged just nineteen, would be 'up to' leading them and so, to demonstrate leadership during the amphibious rehearsals, he made sure to disembark first. To help with visualisation, the 7th Black Watch's intelligence officer, Lieutenant Karl Leyser, visited the various companies 'with air photos of each location where we were expected to attack.'[32]

'Over the Rhine'

'In the *west*, the enemy has lost the Rhineland, and with it the flower of at least four armies,' proclaimed Montgomery in a message to the 21st Army Group at the beginning of March. 'In the *east*, the enemy has lost all *Pomerania* east of the *Oder*, an area as large as the Rhineland; and three more German armies have been routed. The Russian armies are within 35 miles of Berlin. Overhead, the Allied Air Forces are pounding Germany day and night... The complete and decisive defeat of the Germans is certain; there is no possibility of doubt on this matter. *21st Army Group will now cross the Rhine...* Over the *Rhine* then let us go.'[33] The code name Operation Plunder covered several operations, including parachute landings on the east bank. XXX Corps, with the 51st Highland Division, was among the assault forces. While 154 Brigade, with the 7th Black Watch in the lead, would cross the Rhine near Honnepel, 153 Brigade would cross on either side of Rees. Once the Division had secured a bridgehead, others, including the armoured divisions, would follow while the Canadians would exploit the terrain northwards. Operating over an area of open fields, interspersed by dykes and farmhouses, an artificial smokescreen would be laid down to inhibit German visibility.[34]

'We knew that crossing the Rhine was going to be a big push. This is what Churchill had said,' continued Critchley, describing the Prime Minister's visit on 4 March, accompanied by Montgomery and Alan Brooke. 'To everyone's amazement, he looked as if he was on holiday. But to see Winston and Brooke certainly had a most heartening effect on everyone.' Lance Corporal Barker had a different opinion of Churchill's appearance: 'Right under the guns of the Siegfried line... Not the most diplomatic of moves, or situation choice, in fact downright crazy. If the Germans had got an inclination, the casualties would have been high.' Two days before the crossing there were 'more visitors (some said invaders), the British Broadcasting Corporation,' continued Barker. 'The propaganda machine had arrived complete with microphones, aerials, tape recorders and a large caravan, similar to a present day mobile home.'[35]

On 23 March, 4,000 guns opened fire in a deafening cacophony of sound lasting four hours. 'The air was filled with the shriek of shells so low in trajectory that you felt you could raise your hand and have it shot off,' related Private Dennis Hall. 'The actual attack happened at last light,' recalled Critchley. 'As we embarked we were given life jackets and when we reached the other side we had to throw them back onto the vehicle... all of us were slightly nervous at jumping off – we were scared of the anti-personnel "schu" mines, but there weren't any. Other platoons were not so lucky.' In the mist and smoke, Critchley's forward section encountered Major Landale Rollo, the 7th Black Watch's second-in-command, who, as the unit landing officer, had been monitoring progress. Critchley's recollection of Rollo's comments gave the 7th Black Watch its place in history: 'You must be the first of the Battalion over [the Rhine]. I must get onto the radio and say you, 7 BW, were the first over.'[36]

'H hour arrived and we moved up to our start line ready to get on our Buffaloes,' recalled Dow. 'Our shells were winging over our heads but there did not seem to be much coming back. We were worried that we might be sunk somewhere in the middle and kept telling the driver to get a bloody move on! Eventually we arrived on the other side and got out of that Buffalo like lightning.'[37] As they moved inland Lieutenant Colonel Bradford was reporting 'considerable trouble' with mines in Esserden which the detector parties had missed, 'or were deeply buried, and two Carriers were lost.' 'The weapons we are finding are not the type expected to defend the Rhine,' observed Private Shand. 'All the rifles are prehistoric – 1891 – and great long things.'[38]

By the morning of 24 March the 1st, 5th and 7th Black Watch had all crossed the Rhine, their fortunes now dependent on the opposition they would encounter on the other side. A 'terrible shock,' related Critchley, was the death of the Divisional Commander, Major General

Tom Rennie, when his jeep received a direct hit from a cluster of mortar bombs. Also killed on 24 March was 'yet another seasoned Company Commander', Richard Boyle, 1st Black Watch, who had served with the 2nd Black Watch in Crete. Having hid in the hills to avoid capture, he had later escaped from Crete by submarine, and then fought at Tobruk in 1941.[39] With the 51st Highland Division now under the command of Major General Gordon MacMillan, the individual brigades moved off to separate objectives, their actions becoming a series of advances, each brigade taking turns to move forward.[40]

One of the 7th Black Watch's objectives was the small Dutch town of Dinxperlo on the German border. 'Fortunately at the time,' related Private Hall, 'this was only lightly defended. However chaos reigned, as there was only one small bridge on the outskirts of the town, and with several battalions and all the supporting vehicles attempting to cross, many of us lost touch with our units.' Sometimes following the railway, at others crossing open country, the men struck a course north-eastwards. Compared with the fighting in previous weeks there was relatively little opposition and, as spring approached, conditions on the roads improved. 'We just swept across Germany and whole towns were surrendering,' recorded Private Derek Howard-Smith, 7th Black Watch. 'Sometimes a group of people came forward bearing a white bed sheet on a pole and walking behind it.'[41]

The Allied presence in Germany presented a new challenge. While the officers were 'comfortable' in their billets, Bradford admitted the difficulty of keeping the soldiers occupied. 'In Holland and France they could always talk to civilians and sit round a fire, but now that we must avoid fraternizing with civilians there really isn't a lot to do in the evenings; the provision of amusement and occupation will be one of our major tasks whenever we settle down for a period.'[42]

Victory in Europe

For all prisoners-of-war the prospect of the Allied advance was heartening. 'About the end of March, it was evident that the Germans were cracking,' recorded Private Robert Mitchelson. 'We have been listening to a constant barrage of artillery and bombing by our own planes and troops… outside the Stalag, everything is in chaos. The Germans seem to have got out and left everything, including their own civilians who are wandering about dazed and hungry.'[43] According to Lance Corporal Grieve, when they realised that Soviet soldiers were approaching the camp, the German guards vanished and so the surviving prisoners liberated themselves, deciding to march west. Corporal Dave Hutton, captured in Crete, and a few others had escaped from their camp in Poland, but were apprehended by Russians who refused to believe they were British. Following the intervention of some Czech partisans and the Czech Red Cross, Hutton got through Soviet lines to the Americans. From Rheims he was flown to Britain.[44] 'At last the boys have reached us,' Mitchelson was writing on 16 April. 'At the time of writing two armoured cars have driven into the camp and everything is pandemonium. It is exactly 9.28 a.m. & after nearly 5 years I find I am a free man again, tho' strangely enough I don't feel any different now than I did days ago. I must be too excited to notice it.'[45]

Not all prisoners got home safely. Private James Clarkin, 1st Black Watch, was one of four who had made 'the long march' from East Prussia but who were summarily shot on 24 April by a German officer at Putlitz. 'The German officer was shouting, *Swinehund Englander* [English pig],' related another prisoner, Bombardier E. E. Rafferty. 'We appealed to him that these men were Scotch and had nothing to do with the war having been prisoners for 5 years.' But their entreaties had failed and the four men were buried with full military honours, the villagers providing materials to make Union Jacks for the four coffins.[46]

By 22 April 1945, ensconced in his *Führerbunker* beneath the Reich Chancellery in Berlin, Hitler was conceding that the war was lost and indicating his intention to commit suicide. Infighting between his potential successors resulted in his rejection of both Hermann Göring and Heinrich Himmler, his choice falling instead on Grand Admiral Karl Dönitz. During the night of 29/30 April, Hitler and his mistress, Eva Braun, were married. She then committed suicide by taking cyanide; Hitler shot himself and their bodies were burnt in the Reich Chancellery garden.

'By now it was obvious that we were nearing the end of the War,' observed Meekison, promoted Regimental Quartermaster Sergeant, 'although there were numerous small actions with resultant casualties. After one of these brushes with the enemy I remember Jock Geddes passing through with an arm wound, quite happily. He made no bones about the fact that although he was temporarily incapacitated he would at least live to see the end of hostilities.'[47] 'Your Fight is Won!' announced 'Piobaireachd' on 5 May. 'All German land, sea and air forces in north-West Germany, in Holland, in Denmark, in Heligoland and in the Frisian Islands have surrendered to Field Marshal Montgomery. The surrender, signed at 1820 hrs last night, will take effect from 0800 hrs this morning, Saturday.' 'The end came quite suddenly,' continued Meekison. 'We were billeted in a nondescript village of a somewhat depressing nature, and watched the Argylls going through it to make further contact with the enemy.' Once official confirmation of the surrender was received 'a rum ration was immediately authorised. By this time all Companies had a good reserve as it was not always possible to make issues when the troops were in action, and as result the distribution on this occasion was a generous one... I think we all got rather tiddly.' 'Men hugged each other and clinked bottles in the air in sheer jubilation,' recalled Renouf. 'It felt like a death sentence had been lifted from our heads.'[48]

On 7 May representatives of the *Oberkommando der Wehrmacht* and the Allied Expeditionary Force together with the Soviet High Command signed the Instrument of Surrender at Rheims, a French representative signing as a witness. The following day, known as VE (Victory in Europe) Day, representatives of the Allied Expeditionary Force and Germany's three armed services signed a second act of military surrender in Berlin, with Soviet, French and American representatives signing as witnesses.

'After months of constant gunfire and all the harsh noises of modern warfare – there was silence,' observed Meekison. 'A somewhat uneasy silence, as we had to occupy our final objective and that meant passing through the enemy lines. Our destination was the Port of Bremerhaven.' 'This journey was a journey which I shall never forget. We started off and our Company was in the leading trucks,' recalled Corporal Dow. 'Each farmhouse we passed was crowded with German soldiers lined up and with their small arms piled in a heap in the middle of the yard. As we drove past the soldiers they all turned their backs on us. Some no doubt with tears in their eyes. They were a defeated army.'[49]

The 1st Black Watch 'came to rest at Hulsen in the Hamburg area,' recalled Barker. 'It was here that what I had avoided for six and a half years came to pass:… a spit and polish parade par excellence. It was the one and only time I wore the kilt. Proudly because I knew it fitted properly.' The 1st Black Watch then moved to Buxtehude, each company taking turns as guards at a German naval shore barracks, now occupied by the Royal Navy and rechristened *Royal Catherine*.[50] The 7th Black Watch had been ordered to Frelsdorf to take over the dump where quantities of German arms, ammunition and motor transport had been collected. 'It was an amazing sight. There were vehicles and guns and weapons and kit of all sorts all over the place,' commented Second Lieutenant Critchley.[51]

On 12 May a Victory Parade was held in Bremerhaven, at which XXX Corps' Commander, Lieutenant General Horrocks, took the Salute. Together with the US Naval and Military Forces, The Black Watch provided a Guard of Honour. On parade were the Massed Pipes and Drums of the 51st Highland Division. 'This was something the Highland Division always took very seriously, so we immediately set about cleaning our uniforms, which were caked with four or five weeks of mud and grime… We even polished our rifles, something we very rarely did, and tried to remember our ceremonial parade training from the distant past,' recalled Renouf. 'The Highland tunes that had haunted the Germans in the First World War and had signalled our own advances in North Africa, Sicily, Italy, Normandy, Holland and Germany now echoed off the ruined walls of Bremerhaven.'[52]

Many members of the German High Command, including Grand Admiral Dönitz had by now been arrested, but Himmler was still at large. From Bremerhaven, men of the 5th Black Watch were posted to Bremervörde, where a checkpoint was established on the bridge over the River Oste. 'We had to keep an eye on the endless flow of refugees, check identity papers and detain anyone who looked suspicious,' continued Renouf. 'But it was an almost impossible task. The crowds flocked over that bridge as if emerging from a football stadium where they had witnessed a heavy defeat… they were a sorry lot, and obviously desperate to escape from the advancing Russians… most of the time we just watched the mob roll past, acting more like spectators than soldiers.'[53] On 22 May it was 'business as usual' when Renouf and his section arrived for their shift. One of those detained in the guard room was a German soldier whose papers identified him as ex-Sergeant Heinrich Hitzinger. Upon further interrogation, he revealed his identity as Himmler. Removed by British Intelligence to a camp in Lüneburg, during a medical examination he bit (accidentally or intentionally) on a phial of cyanide, killing himself instantly. 'At the time we were not particularly interested when we learned the identity of our famous prisoner,' observed Renouf. 'We were much more concerned about the pals we had lost since D-Day. With the benefit of hindsight, though, I can see that capturing him was one of the 5th Black Watch's more significant wartime achievements. After all, Heinrich Himmler was one of the worst mass murderers in human history – and he had almost escaped.'[54]

Soon afterwards the 5th Black Watch moved to a village near Hanover. 'Life at Steyerberg was quite peaceful,' related Meekison. 'There was a wee bit of trouble with the lads when the rather stupid order of no fraternisation was largely ignored, as there were quite a few bonny lassies in the village, who were quite obliging. However, it was recognised that this order could not be enforced, as it was against human nature, and although we never got very friendly with the people, we lived peaceably alongside them.' 'The village was so beautiful that sometimes I wondered if the war had just been a bad nightmare,' related Renouf. 'It was all in such contrast to the horrors we had experienced a few months earlier.'[55] Among them were the concentration camps; Belsen, liberated on 15 April, was a two-hour drive from Steyerberg. 'The cremation furnaces were still there standing stark and menacing,' observed Meekison who, after visiting the camp, was left with the impression of 'absolute disgust at the Nation which had countenanced such bestiality'.[56]

Airborne in India

On 1 February the Chindits were officially disbanded. 'It was the most distasteful job of my career,' Mountbatten, Supreme Allied Commander, later said. 'I only agreed because by that time the whole Army was Chindit-minded.'[57] The 2nd Black Watch's next role was as an airborne unit, becoming part of 14 British Airlanding Brigade, 44th Airborne Division (India), on 1 May. Of those who had served as Chindits, Brigadier Bernard Fergusson had become deputy director of Combined Operations in London in January 1945, taking over as director in July, while Captain Archie John Wavell went to work at the Army Education Centre in Simla.[58] After returning from leave in March 1945, during a medical examination, Private Cochrane was told 'that I wasn't fit for parachute training… so I was drafted away out of the Black Watch for good.'[59]

The Battalion was now based at Secunderabad. The new Commanding Officer, Lieutenant Colonel John Benson (who had survived the ordeal of the *Chakdina*'s sinking after Tobruk in 1941), 'wanted as many as possible to volunteer for parachutists', related a new arrival, Private Edward Graves. 'Those who never cared for this would be glider troops. I decided from the start if I was to go into action it would be by gliders!' Assigned to different companies depending on their qualifications, Graves and several others joined the assault pioneer platoon 'as we knew a little about building work… Sometimes we did route marches that made what was called route marches in Blighty seem like a Sunday morning stroll compared with these… marching night and day over mountains made of solid rock and across bush country where you nearly choked with the dust.' A 'chief worry' was water. 'Our water bottle never held much and what it did was nearly boiling when you got to drink it,' though a 'canvas bag arrangement' helped to keep it cool.[60] In recognition of 'Victory in Europe', two days' holiday were observed on 9 and 10 May, but the soldiers were reminded of 'the hard task still necessary for the defeat of Japan'.[61]

In early June the Battalion moved to Kota Camp, near Bilaspur in the Central Provinces, for jungle training. 'The camp area was in a deplorable state', Private Graves continued, 'and we had to start work straight away pitching and carting our tents in the sweltering heat of the day. It was one of the hardest working days I have experienced and it turned out to be that the next two months were to be the same.' Conditions gradually became more 'bearable': a canteen was opened, some football pitches were made 'and the film shows turned up more often. By now our training had started and this meant being out in the jungle and paddy fields for sometimes three or four days. At the start it wasn't too bad, but soon the monsoons broke and turned what were passible tracks and roads into lanes of thick mud.' On occasion they 'were lucky' to be issued with a tot of rum 'but this was not often.' The monsoon did have the advantage of helping against prickly heat from which many men suffered. 'We used to strip and let rain wash our skins.' Once the monsoon was over, their airborne training began.[62]

As the war in the Pacific reached its climax, on 6 and 9 August two atomic bombs were dropped on Hiroshima and Nagasaki. Japan's surrender was fêted as VJ (Victory over Japan) Day on 15 August, when the soldiers again enjoyed another two-day holiday, this time 'by having a fun fair with elephant rides & pony racing and all sorts of side shows.'[63] 'There was free beer and great bonfires were lighted.' Once the excitement subsided, their duties resumed 'and in the afternoons education classes were started.' Those who had completed their terms of service went home. 'Many good mates were lost but new friendships were being made with chaps of the new drafts that were joining us,' commented Graves, describing their peacetime routine as 'plenty of spit and polish, drill parades and ceremonial guards.' Instead of fighting the Japanese, their aircraft were now used to repatriate Allied POWs and then to train Indians as parachutists.[64]

A minor success while the Battalion remained 'airborne' was refusing to wear a maroon beret, as suggested by Field Marshal Montgomery, now Chief of the Imperial General Staff, in preference to the Tam o'Shanter and the Red Hackle. The prevailing belief among the Black Watch was that the Viceroy, Lord Wavell, had intervened to ensure that his former Regiment did not have to wear 'cherry berets'.[65]

Rolls of honour

Nearly six years of world war left between 60 and 80 million dead, constituting 3–4 per cent of the world's population in 1939. Between September 1939 and August 1945 an average of 27,000 people died daily.[66] Thousands more had been wounded and/or endured captivity. The map of Europe had been redrawn and redrawn again. Despite his pivotal wartime role, in July 1945 Churchill lost the General Election to the Labour party, Clement Attlee, becoming Britain's new Prime Minister.

Compared with the 8,960 recorded fatalities in The Black Watch during the First World War, there were 1,379 during the Second World War. Out of a total of 9,051 casualties in the 51st Highland Division, those of The Black Watch constituted nearly one-third.[67] During and after the war, numerous officers and men in the Regiment were honoured for their gallantry by receiving the DSO (many with an additional bar), the MC and the DCM. The MM was given to over 140 NCOs and men. Many were Mentioned in Despatches.[68] Among those honoured was Major Peter Taylor who had begun the war as a private in the 6th Black Watch and had taken command of the 1st Black Watch as it entered Germany.[69]

Of those who remained as prisoners-of-war, Major General Victor Fortune had repeatedly refused repatriation, even when, in October 1943 over a thousand seriously wounded were released. 'Victor was told to come home with them but only said "I brought out the 51st Div. I intend to take them back". So I need not expect to see him till the end of the war,' his wife Eleanor wrote in January 1944. On 19 April 1945 he was created a Knight Commander of the Order of the

British Empire 'in recognition of valuable services in the interests of British Prisoners of War in Germany' and, for the sixth time in his military career, he was Mentioned in Despatches in October.[70] An outward sign of Lance Corporal John Grieve's liberation was being reunited with his bagpipes. While working in the mines, he had practised the fingering of various tunes on the handle of his pick and so it took just 'ten minutes' to be able to play again.[71]

For service in every major theatre except Norway and Malaya, The Black Watch was awarded 64 Battle Honours. 'As we fought our way across the deserts of North Africa,' recorded Major David Russell, 'the hills and valleys of Sicily, the fields of France and the plains and floods of Belgium and Holland, where our fathers and comrades had fought and died before us in the last world conflict, and over the soil of Germany, the bastion of the "*Herrenvolk*", we fought and died for King and country, and each of us, in our fashion, endeavoured to maintain the great reputation and traditions of our Regiment – "*Nemo me Impune Lacessit*" [No one provokes me with impunity].'[72]

As agreed at Yalta, Germany was divided into four zones of occupation. On 21 August the 21st Army Group was converted into the Headquarters of Britain's zone and renamed the British Army of the Rhine (BAOR), requiring the continued presence of the 51st Highland Division. On 6 December the 4th Black Watch was sent to Palestine. The 6th Black Watch's presence in Greece had become 'very relaxed as the first troops began to be sent home on leave'. Visits to Athens were organised, although, as McKenzie Johnston observed, it was difficult to keep the soldiers occupied and 'we had quite a lot of disciplinary troubles'.[73] In India on New Year's Eve 'the camp was ablaze with bonfires and everyone was full of fun but strange to say after they had brought the New Year in, in the good old style, everyone seemed to wander off to their beds, with the result that about 00.30 hrs the camp was almost deserted.' The next day '90%' of the 2nd Black Watch began 1946 'with a great hangover'.[74]

Since The Black Watch first were formed,
How far afield they've roved.
Yet soon or late they've aye returned,
To the Scotland that they loved.

The pipes would raise a rousing strain,
The Scottish hills to greet,
And Scottish earth resound beneath,
Those homeward marching feet.

And now once more the hackle red,
Lights up our far flung line,
While Libya, Crete and Italy,
Salute the warrior sign.

Still further east where cyclones whirl,
And jungle paths are green,
Unyielding yet to flood or foe.
Is that bright emblem seen.
Though years may pass and wars must end,
And peace be brought to birth,
And home returning wanderers,
Tread firm on Scottish earth.

Then like these men of yesterday,
Set free from War's sad toil,
Men of to-day, as fervently,
Will greet old Scotland's soil.[75]

16
The Illusion of Peace

And the land rested from war.[1]

I look back on my army days with mixed feelings. Terrible, terrible times, and also many good times, when we seemed to spend much of the time laughing and fooling around. I'm glad that I was able to come through when so many young men of my generation died.[2]

The truth is that the human race seems incapable of learning to live in peace with itself.[3]

Returning to Civvy Street

In the aftermath of war thousands of men and women had to pick up the pieces of their civilian lives in a changed world. 'You could not just return to Civvy Street and resume your education. There was a waiting list to get into university so I worked as a labourer on building sites in Musselburgh and then with the electricity board,' recalled Tom Renouf, who celebrated his 20th birthday in July 1945. 'I frequently woke up in a cold sweat as horrific episodes from the war flooded into my mind. But slowly the night terrors began to diminish and I learned how to cope with them.'[4]

Regular soldiers had once more to adjust to peacetime soldiering. The 1st Black Watch was in Germany as part of the British Army of the Rhine (BAOR), where reconstruction had begun with the European Recovery Plan, formulated by US Secretary of State, George Marshall. The Battalion was first stationed at Buxtehude on the Este river in northern Germany, near Hamburg, before moving briefly to Hesedorf in Lower Saxony and then, in June 1946, to

Glamorgan Barracks, Duisburg, in the western Ruhr. The 2nd Black Watch remained in India.

The territorial battalions were again merged or disbanded. Having been posted to Palestine in late 1945, on 11 May 1946 the 4th Black Watch was disbanded two months before the bombing of the King David Hotel in Jerusalem, headquarters of the British Mandatory Authorities, by the militant Zionist organisation, Irgun. The 6th Black Watch was disbanded in Greece, where a 'Service of Thanksgiving and Remembrance' was held in Kifissia on 26 May. 'Madden who had been absent from the Battalion in Northern Europe returned as our CO to wind us up,' commented McKenzie Johnston. 'He was sorry that the Battalion had to go but was delighted that he was the one doing it. The 6th Battalion had been his life.'[5] When, a year later, the Territorial Army was re-formed, the 4th and 5th were combined into the 4/5th Battalion, with Colonel 'Chick' Thomson in command. The 6th and 7th Black Watch became the 6/7th Battalion. Briefly, until 1948, the 51st Highland Division was amalgamated with the 52nd Lowland Division.[6]

Having been Colonel of the Regiment since 1940, General Wauchope handed over to Field Marshal Lord Wavell on 1 March 1946, his 72nd birthday. Wauchope died the following year, Wavell observing that he had lost his 'best friend'.[7]

Divided India: Last days

No sooner was the war over than the demand for India's independence had to be addressed. Still serving as Viceroy of India, Wavell assumed the challenge of overseeing discussions between the two major Indian political parties, the All India Congress Party and the Muslim League, while trying to satisfy the Sikhs in the Punjab. In January 1946 Prime Minister Attlee dispatched the Cabinet Mission to India, or, as Wavell called them, the 'three Magi': Frederick Pethick-Lawrence, Secretary of State for India, A.V. Alexander, First Lord of the Admiralty, and Sir Stafford Cripps. Having failed to achieve consensus between the Indian political leaders, the delegation proposed a settlement, known as the Cabinet Mission Plan. Although accepted in principle, relations between the opposing factions again soured when the Congress leader, Jawarharlal Nehru, disavowed adherence to any agreement once independence had been granted. Declining further attempts at power-sharing, Mohammed Ali Jinnah, leader of the Muslim League, reverted to an earlier demand, endorsed in Lahore in March 1940, for the Muslims of the subcontinent to be allocated independent 'sovereign states' in the north-west and north-east where they predominated, called West and East 'Pakistan'. His call, however, for a 'Direct Action Day' to achieve this resulted in widespread rioting and slaughter in Calcutta, creating even greater communal strife.[8]

In early 1946 the 2nd Black Watch had left Kota Camp in the Central Provinces in India, travelling by train across the 'very desolate countryside' of the Sindh desert. Their destination was Malir Camp, about 17 miles from Karachi where, during the tortuous discussions to transfer power, the Battalion remained occupied with parades and 'normal training'. More exciting was being called to take action when, on 21 February 1946, some mutinous sailors from shore establishments on the Manora peninsula, south of Karachi, took control of the Royal Indian Navy Sloop HMIS *Hindustan* and began firing on anyone attempting to board the ship. 'However mortar and 75 mm gunfire from point-blank range proved too much for them, and the white flag was hoisted.' By the evening 'all was quiet on the "Manora Front"'.[9]

After six months in the 'sand storms of Malir', the Battalion moved to Napier Barracks, Karachi, in July. 'I recall early morning muster parades in which each man was issued with a large tin mug of salted water to be drunk there and then under the watchful eyes of officers and the CSM,' related Second Lieutenant Ian Critchley, now in the 2nd Black Watch after his service in the 7th, and briefly the 4th Black Watch in Palestine. 'Physical fitness was also important and highland dancing.' As always, 'Hogmanay spirit' was 'quite apparent' at the end of the year.[10]

With continuing deadlock over India's future, in March 1947

Wavell was replaced by Admiral Lord Mountbatten, the 2nd Black Watch forming the Guard of Honour for both incoming and outgoing Viceroys. 'At the Guard of Honour for Mountbatten the new Viceroy, the Jocks who were more used to the soldier's soldier Wavell, were astounded by the smell of Old Spice aftershave emanating from the rather sophisticated playboy figure, as he passed down the ranks during his inspection,' commented Critchley.[11] Returning to Britain, Wavell was raised to the peerage with the additional title of Viscount Keren of Eritrea and Winchester. On 19 July, in the presence of the Regiment's Colonel-in-Chief, Queen Elizabeth, and on behalf of The Black Watch, he received 'the Freedom of Entry into the City and Royal Burgh of Perth on ceremonial occasions with bayonets fixed, drums beating and Colours flying', the parade taking place on the North Inch overlooking the River Tay.[12]

Throughout this period, the systematic reduction of the British Army was creating 'great turbulence' among the ranks, observed Critchley. Those who had completed their service returned to Britain. 'The tailor's shop of Ghulam Nabi was kept busy, particularly in the tailoring of cold weather battle dress for those going home. The fashion then was for the Jocks to ask for inserts to be put into the battle dress trouser legs to be up to date for the new look "flares".' Rumours were rife regarding the Battalion's future 'and included postings to Basra, South and East Africa and Bermuda.' There was also talk of disbandment: 'the dread was that we would be posted to a Lowland Regiment'.[13]

In April 1947, amid continuing tensions over India's future, the 2nd Black Watch was deployed to the North-West Frontier Province (NWFP) on a routine relief of the 2nd King's Own Scottish Borderers who, because of the reductions, were being put into 'suspended animation'. 'This journey was 711 miles as the crow flies from Karachi and took 3 days by train. The trains were unspeakably hot but our lives were saved by tin baths filled with ice put in each carriage and refilled at every stop,' continued Critchley.[14] 'A strange tension seemed to hang over the North-West Frontier,' related Lieutenant Colonel Neville Blair, who replaced Benson as Commanding Officer in May.

'By then partition was being mooted as a possible option but no date had been fixed.' 'A lot of the Indians couldn't believe that we were leaving,' commented Lieutenant Geoffrey Cowper-Coles, posted to the 2nd Black Watch, after serving briefly in the 4th in Palestine.[15]

On 3 June Mountbatten announced the plan for creating two new Dominions, the date set for the transfer of power being 14/15 August 1947. Included in the provisions of the 'partition plan' was a referendum to be held in the NWFP, whose inhabitants remained divided on their future allegiance. Despite the state's majority Muslim population, the dominant political figures, the Chief Minister, Dr Khan Sahib and his brother, Abdul Ghaffar Khan, who had opposed British authority since the 1930s in the 'Red Shirt' (*khudai kidmatgar*) movement, favoured remaining with India. 'As a further choice to partition, Ghaffar Khan adopted another cause,' explained Blair. 'He and his "Red Shirts" vehemently sponsored the formation of "Pakhtunistan", an independent state of Pushtu-speaking people.'[16]

In mid-June the Battalion, minus two companies which remained in Peshawar for internal security duties, moved to Cherat, 'a pleasant change' where the soldiers undertook 'mountain warfare' training, and visited the historic Khyber Pass. Another task was researching the names of the 'thirty-odd graves' belonging to the victims of the 1867 cholera epidemic in the Black Watch Cemetery.[17] Before the referendum on partition was held in early July, the Battalion returned to Peshawar to supervise the polling stations. Each company 'mounted in 15 cwt trucks, with a troop of the 19th Lancers in their tanks under command, was given daily a whole series of different polling stations to visit,' continued Blair. 'It was an exhausting and wholly unpleasant operation, in the heat of the day and the awful dust that smothered the Jocks as they drove in their open trucks for miles and miles across the country.' Since no option for Pakhtunistan was given, Ghaffar Khan ordered a boycott, his Red Shirts 'much in evidence,' at the polling stations, matched by the Green Shirts supporting Pakistan. 'Feelings were running very high, and everyone was carrying a rifle. The slightest spark would have set off a conflagration which would readily have passed from polling station to polling station.

Companies had to be very circumspect; their presence and bearing soon produced results.'[18] The boycott meant, however, that the result was recorded as 'unanimously' in support of Pakistan.

Before leaving Peshawar on 10 August, the 2nd Black Watch took part in an 'emotional' parade. 'A fine be-turbaned figure near me, obviously much affected by the spectacle, called out poignantly in a loud voice: "Look, look; never will we see the like again,"' related Blair.[19] Having left a rear party under Major Angus Irwin to conclude the move, again travelling by train, the Battalion reached Karachi in time to participate in the independence celebrations on 14 August.

> That last party under the British Raj at Government House, Karachi, defies description. It was a beautiful night; the floodlighting enhanced the elegance of the surroundings, the large concourse of people – the majority of whom were, perhaps Pakistanis, many in turbans and all, men and women alike, clad in picturesque garments enriched with jewels. Mingled amongst them was a sprinkling of princes and rajahs in even finer garb… Scattered throughout the throng at strategic points, adding a touch of grandeur and ceremonial to the occasion, were those of the Viceroy's Bodyguard resplendent in their magnificent uniform, who had followed the dictates of the Muslim faith and forsaken Delhi.[20]

Among those present was the new Governor-General, Mohammed Ali Jinnah, and Lord Mountbatten, 'still Viceroy for another few hours'. As the hour of Pakistan's creation approached, 'in brilliant floodlighting, the Union flag was lowered and the Pakistan Ensign hoisted in its place.' Mountbatten then travelled back to Delhi for India's independence celebrations the following day.[21]

The Battalion's return to Malir spared the soldiers from witnessing the severity of the communal violence which erupted after partition, unlike the rear party in Peshawar which saw the horrors first hand. 'On 7 September bazaar gossip had caused 2,000 tribesmen to collect in the cantonment area and burn the Sikh quarter and indulge in killings,' related Critchley. 'Thank heaven I never knew what had been going on in Peshawar,' Elizabeth, Major Irwin's wife, wrote to her parents. 'The papers always said it was quiet. They've been having the most terrible time. The Afridis came down into the cantonment and for three days the whole thing was quite out of control Sikhs being murdered right and left, even my poor old Munshi [secretary] was shot by mistake. The entire Hindu canteen staff were murdered except the owner who hid in a tea chest, the manager was chopped up in front of the mess – and the wretched Jocks could only look on.' Among the objects looted was Elizabeth Irwin's 21st birthday present from her husband, stolen from the jewellers. 'Luckily A[ngus] hadn't paid for it!'[22]

Appointed Refugee Officer, Major Angus Irwin was assigned a truck 'with NWFP government written all over it and had a terrific time organizing Hindus and Sikhs in the Fort… Eventually the Afridis went back into the trucks in which they'd arrived and things calmed down a bit as the normal inhabitants without the leadership of the Afridis were not too bad although they have sworn to murder every Sikh in the place.'[23]

Temporarily 'bottled up' in Peshawar, since the railways were not running, in early September the rear party returned to Karachi, witnessing en route the consequences of a recent attack on a refugee train full of Hindus and Sikhs. 'The sight was unbelievable – arms, limbs scattered all over and some of the bodies still twitching and some of them not even properly dead, and strewn all over were their pathetic little bundles and tin boxes… for the first time the Jocks didn't laugh at any rioting they had witnessed… they really sat silently and thought about the tragedy of it all.'[24]

For the remainder of 1947, the Battalion remained in Malir. 'It is believed that we were held there to add an element of stability to the newly-formed State of Pakistan,' observed Blair, noting that they were forbidden to take part in moderating disputes between Muslims and Hindus 'unless a request was especially made seeking the Battalion's help to quell some exceptional violence.' 'We were told you are a foreign army now,' recalled Second Lieutenant Louis Manson, 'there is nothing you can do, nothing you *must* do.'[25]

'The Battalion's particular role,' continued Blair, 'was to provide a protective and stable base to cover the departure of all those Europeans who wished to leave the country.' With a ship leaving Karachi every two weeks, he made it his duty 'to try to see each ship sail, and at each sailing the Pipes and Drums played on the quay-side, to add, I hope, a little gaiety and spectacle to the departure. The majority of the passengers were of course British families leaving for home after a life-time of service in the Sub-Continent... it was a truly dismal sight to see the expressions of awe and sadness on their faces, yet with a hint of wonder of what the future held in store.' Among those leaving by air was Field Marshal Sir Claude Auchinleck, former Commander-in-Chief, India. 'The Field Marshal was undoubtedly very touched by the farewell that the Battalion gave him, and the Pipes and Drums played him away as the aircraft flew aloft.'[26]

With their numbers dwindling Blair found it difficult to keep the soldiers 'employed and contented. By and large, competitions superseded training, to encourage morale and *esprit de corps*.' One of their activities was competing for the new Rhodesian Platoon Drill Competition Shield, presented to the Battalion by the 'magnificent body of Rhodesians' who had joined the 2nd Black Watch in Jerusalem in May 1940. Another diversion, organised by Major Jack Monteith, was going on safari along the Indus river valley to shoot duck and other game birds, which 'gave the Officers and Jocks a change of scene and experience of life in the open beyond the formal confines of the cantonment lines.'[27]

In January 1948 the assassination of Mahatma Gandhi presaged an outbreak of violence. As recollected by Lieutenant Colonel Blair's daughter, Juliet, when her mother heard the news on the radio she feared an outbreak of violence and 'tried frantically to get through to the mess on the phone to let Dad know the news which she thought would not yet have reached him.' Lieutenants Ian Critchley and Rowland Tarleton were in Bhopal, as the guests of Major The Prince Zoda Fakhr-ul-Mulk, Nawab of Bhopal. Having graduated from Sandhurst, the Nawab had spent six months with the 1st Black Watch in Dover before the war, and had 'hoped to return the friendship and hospitality he had received by inviting two officers to Bhopal to shoot tiger.' News of Gandhi's assassination cut their visit short 'as all Bhopal shut down in mourning'.[28]

By the middle of February 1948 preparations were made for the 2nd Black Watch to return home, while a 'large draft' was to join the 1st Battalion The Highland Light Infantry in Jerusalem. Among them was Major Alec Brodie. As tensions between the Arab and Jewish population increased, the British Army's job was to prevent 'one side sniping the other… both sides are too well supplied with automatic weapons, grenades, and small mortars. Battles flare up very suddenly,' related Brodie who received a bullet wound in the shoulder during one such skirmish.[29]

On 26 February the remaining families embarked at Karachi on board the *Empire Halladale*; the following day the Battalion left. Driven 'all spick and span' from Malir to the outskirts of Karachi, the soldiers marched through the city 'with Colours flying and bayonets fixed and led by the Pipes and Drums in full dress,' related Blair.

> Great crowds blocked the streets and the police had difficulty in clearing a passage for us. Very noticeable amongst the throng were many be-turbaned, upstanding men, obviously old soldiers, standing stiffly to attention, who saluted the Colours and myself, as Commanding Officer, as we passed. Somehow the whole scene brought tears to one's eyes, for it became very apparent how much the British Raj was still respected by the general population and was going to be missed.
>
> We marched into the grounds of Government House and the Battalion formed into line in front of a dais. On the arrival of Mr Mohammed Ali Jinnah, the Quaid-e-Azam, to give him his full title, we gave him a Royal Salute. He was very noticeably affected by the tribute, tears coming into his eyes, and in an emotional and broken voice he said that he never conceived that he would be entitled to such an honour. After inspecting the Battalion, Mr Jinnah returned to the dais to address us.[30]

Although Jinnah's prepared speech emphasised that the time had come for the country to stand on its own feet, Blair felt that his ex tempore remarks 'had a slightly different tone' revealing that 'without the devoted help and guidance of the British over the centuries never would Pakistan have now been able to become an independent country. And he continued for quite a while in this vein, there being appreciation, combined with sadness, in his voice that the period of tutorship was now over.'[31]

From Government House the Battalion proceeded to the docks, where the massed pipes and drums of The Baluch Regiment, 'dwarfing those of the Battalion, led us to the quayside. There the Battalion formed a hollow square in front of a dais, behind which was assembled a large crowd.' After a General Salute, taken by Major General Akbar Khan who inspected the Battalion and a message from the Pakistani Prime Minister, Liaquat Ali Khan, as well as a speech by General Khan, the men of the 2nd Black Watch ascended the gangplank. 'As the Colour party entered the *Empire Halladale*, the Battalion flag broke at the yard-arm signifying that the Battalion had embarked.' The 2nd Battalion The Black Watch was the last unit of the British Army to leave Pakistan, sailing on 28 February, the same day as the last British battalion in India sailed from Bombay. Already hostilities between the two new Dominions had broken out over the disputed princely state of Jammu and Kashmir.[32]

Divided Germany: The Cold War

As the Soviet Union, in the firm grip of Joseph Stalin, tightened its control on the countries of Eastern Europe, a stand-off was taking place in Germany. The break came in 1948 when Britain, France and the United States introduced a new currency, the deutschmark. The Soviet authorities responded with the introduction of their own reformed currency which they intended to introduce throughout Berlin, also divided into four zones. On 24 June 1948 all land and water traffic was halted, amounting to a Soviet 'blockade' of West Berlin. To counter this, an airlift was begun.

While the crisis in Berlin was in its early stages, The Black Watch was having to conform to the British government's decision that all British infantry regiments should have only one battalion. On 13 July 1948, at Duisburg, the 1st and 2nd Black Watch were amalgamated. 'On that parade the Regimental Colour of each Battalion was borne down the ranks in the presence of Field Marshal Wavell, who, like his father and his son, was a man of the 2nd Battalion,' recorded Lieutenant Colonel Fergusson, who had taken command of the 1st Black Watch in March. Henceforward the two special trophies of the two Battalions, the gong of the 1st Black Watch captured during the Indian Mutiny, and the Baghdad Bell taken by the 2nd Black Watch in 1917, 'were to hang side by side, as they do to-day, to sound our daily routine.'[33] Despite the solemnity of the occasion, the combined wit of Wavell, Fergusson and Eric Linklater, also present, enabled them to produce a 'Ballade of Bereavement' for Wavell's shaving brush which he had left behind, while fulfilling his obligations as Chancellor of Aberdeen University:

My chin, once glossy as a nectarine,
Now looks like holly on a Christmas card,
Or straggly hawthorns in a woodland scene
Such as is deftly drawn by Fragonard...
I left my shaving brush in Aberdeen.[34]

During his visit, Wavell asked Fergusson to arrange for him to see where the members of the 1st, 5th and 7th Black Watch had fought at Goch, Rees and Appeldorn in 1945. To accompany them, Fergusson selected Lieutenant Critchley, now the 1st Black Watch's intelligence officer, and who had been one of the first across the Rhine with the 7th Black Watch. As they drove through the countryside, Critchley saw what appeared to be the same horse trough in which he recollected 'the Jocks used to wash their mess tins. So we stopped there and had our picnic.'[35] Also while in Germany, as Colonel of the Regiment, Wavell permitted the Battalion's medical officer, Major Kathleen 'Mick' Prendergast, to wear the Red Hackle and a Black Watch tartan skirt: born in Western Australia, she was thought at the time to have been the only woman to be appointed regimental medical officer to a regiment of the British infantry. 'Passionately pro-Black Watch', she remained with the Battalion for five years.[36]

When Wavell visited the Battalion the following year, with the airlift still underway, he and Fergusson flew from Duisburg to Berlin on one of the supply planes. 'I was sitting in the back where there were sacks of flour,' recollected the signals officer, Lieutenant Andrew (Andy) Watson, commissioned into the Regiment in 1946. 'So when I exited from the plane I looked like a snowman!'[37] On 12 May 1949 the Soviets finally lifted the blockade, the 323-day airlift having enabled Britain, France and the United States to maintain control of West Berlin. The confrontation between the Allied 'Western' powers and the Soviet Union marked the beginning of the Cold War. For the next four decades, Europe was divided into opposing blocs, characterised by the division of West and East Germany and frequent references to the 'the iron curtain', a term first used in relation to the division by Churchill at Fulton, Missouri in 1946. Young officers, like Second Lieutenant Bob Tweedy, who had joined The Black Watch for 'family reasons – my elder brother in the 2nd Black Watch had been killed in Crete in 1941 and my uncle Bobbie had died of typhoid in India in 1911', found service in Germany 'grey and bleak', the damage to cities like Duisburg and Dusseldorf 'almost unbelievable'.[38]

In April 1950 the Battalion moved to the newly named Montgomery Barracks in Berlin. As requested by Wavell, who was busy writing his own 'recollections', Bernard Fergusson had been compiling the Second World War history of The Black Watch, entitled *The Black Watch and the King's Enemies.* Having asked surviving senior officers to provide a draft account of their respective battalion's activities, he had also spent time 'scrabbling through dusty files and maps and war diaries', which, he said, 'have brought before me again many fine men of all ages with whom I spent my youth, and of whom it is so hard to be worthy.' Some of the stories he confessed, 'almost make me weep to write of them.'[39] Wavell wrote the Foreword, describing the 'Jock' of today as having inherited 'the spirit and traditions of his Highland forbears - the clan feeling, the toughness, the fierceness in assault, the independence of character, the boundless self-confidence in his own powers in all circumstances and conditions.'[40]

Wavell's health, however, was failing. After an emergency operation, he had a severe haemorrhage, dying in the early hours of 24 May 1950. His funeral on 6 June was the first time that a state river cortège had progressed up the Thames since Nelson's in 1805. Fergusson and a contingent from The Black Watch came from Germany to participate in the service. Of the many distinguished officers who served in The Black Watch, Wavell achieved greatest seniority. Although he never commanded a battalion, his heart, he said, had remained with the Regiment: incorporated in his coat of arms was a private soldier of The Black Watch and a scholar of his school, Winchester College, where he was buried.[41]

Soon after Wavell's funeral, Fergusson handed over command of the Battalion to Major Pat Campbell-Preston.[42] In the constrained environment in Berlin, the Battalion's activities were confined to training in the Grunewald forest, and guard and ceremonial duties. The Black Watch was especially popular because of its 'kilts, pipes and drums,' recorded Private Joe Hubble who recollected performing 'every Guard of Honour.'[43] A visit in October 1950 from The Black Watch (Royal Highland Regiment) of Canada gave the Regiment a lasting trophy: 'a spacious silver cup' which was filled with whisky 'and circulated round the table many times… the formal part of the evening finished with some country dancing, and the remainder of the evening was spent in places informal and abnormal.'[44]

One 'contretemps' with a contingent of Soviet soldiers caused an amusing distraction. 'A whole lot of Russian tanks returning from manoeuvres had accidentally come into the British Sector at some cross-roads on the way back into Berlin,' related Lieutenant Adam Gurdon, whose father, also in The Black Watch, had briefly commanded the 1st Battalion after its return from France in 1940. 'D Company was ordered to man those cross-roads to make sure it didn't happen again… In those days an incident of this sort caused the most terrific kerfuffle and notes of protest flashed from General to

General and from Government to Government; the might of Russian divisions surrounding Berlin were mobilised and everyone managed to get very alarmed.' Having put up a 'formidable' barrier, they continued to man the road. 'Very soon the whole affair became a rather boring chore and the force level was reduced to a reinforced platoon.' To prevent another incursion, it was decided that a white line should be painted on the road to show the border. 'It was whilst the white line was being painted by Private Plotniky, D Company's sanitary man, that one of the Russian sentries refused to move,' continued Gurdon. With a firm resolve to carry out his assignment, the soldier continued painting across the Russian's boot. 'Luckily the Russians thought it was as funny as we did and for some time the gap in the white line remained as a memorial to Plotniky's determination.'[45]

While the countries of Western Europe were adjusting to the new world order, having first established the Western European Defence Organisation in September 1948 and then, with the inclusion of the United States, the North Atlantic Treaty Organisation (NATO) on 4 April 1949, a third world power was rising. On 1 October 1949, after ousting the Kuomintang government of Chiang Kai-Shek, the Communist revolutionary leader, Mao Tse-Tung (Zedong), established the People's Republic of China, triggering fears in western corridors of power that all regions of South East Asia would fall like dominoes to communism. Of immediate concern was the Korean Peninsula.[46]

I watched last night the rising moon,
Upon a foreign strand,
The memories came back like flowers in June
Of home and fatherland.
I dream't I was a child once more
Beside the rolling mill,
When first I saw, in days of yore
The moon behind the hill.[47]

17

Korea: The Forgotten War

There's blood on the hills of Korea
Tis the blood of the brave and true
Of the nations that battle together
Neath the banner of red, white and blue.[1]

It was not going to be a walk in the park, that was for sure.[2]

'The Land of the Morning Calm'

Following the Japanese surrender in 1945, the Korean Peninsula, ruled as a Japanese colony since 1910, became divided into two spheres of influence along the 38th Parallel. While the Soviets supported thirty-six-year-old Kim Il-sung as the premier of the Democratic People's Republic of Korea in the north, United States' troops moved into the south in support of seventy-three-year-old Dr Syngman Rhee, who had served as President of the Provisional Government of the Republic of Korea in Exile during the Japanese occupation, and who again became President in 1948.[3] Both leaders considered themselves the rightful leader of a unified Korea. On 12 December 1948 the General Assembly of the United Nations recognised Rhee's Republic of Korea as the legitimate government. A United Nations Temporary Commission on Korea (UNTCOK) was set up to oversee free and fair elections but the Soviet Union refused to recognise its legality.

On 25 June 1950, alleging that the South Koreans had violated the border, North Korean troops crossed the 38th Parallel, reaching Seoul four days later.[4] In response, the UN Security Council passed

Resolution 84, recommending military intervention. Unusually in its history, the resolution was passed because the Soviet Union had boycotted proceedings in protest at Chiang Kai-Shek's exiled government representing China in the Security Council rather than that of Mao Tse-Tung.[5] In support of the Republic of Korea, by 1 September 1950 the United Nations Command, under US operational command, had deployed 180,000 men, British troops initially forming part of 27 British Commonwealth Brigade.[6]

With the South Koreans pushed back to an enclave 40 miles from the port city of Pusan (Busan), known as the Pusan perimeter, in September a UN counter-offensive, under the command of US General Douglas MacArthur, established a bridgehead on the west coast of Korea, recapturing Seoul and taking the North Korean capital of Pyongyang.[7] But this success had unintended consequences. In late October 1950 Mao Tse-Tung committed over 200,000 'volunteers' of the Chinese People's Liberation Army to support the North Koreans, aided militarily by the Soviet Union, enabling another advance beyond Seoul.[8] By the spring of 1951 the city had again changed hands, with UN forces now holding a line close to the 38th Parallel. On 5 July peace talks began at Panmunjom in a 'peace train' on the railway north of Seoul, its location marked at night by a searchlight shining into the sky.When the talks stalled over the terms for repatriating North Korean prisoners-of-war held by UN forces, fighting resumed along the entrenched line.[9]

1952: The Black Watch deployed

During the war's early stages, the 1st Black Watch had remained in Germany, returning to Buxtehude in October 1951, where they occupied Spey Barracks. Some men, however, had volunteered for service in Korea as reinforcements. Among them was Private Bill Speakman, attached to the King's Own Scottish Borderers. In early November he performed an act of bravery 'in complete disregard for his personal safety' for which he was awarded one of only four VCs given during the Korean War.[10]

With National Service still compulsory, there was a regular influx of 'Nashies' undertaking training in Scotland before joining the Battalion in Germany. 'Some hated it [National Service], others enjoyed it and most tolerated it, but for the majority it was something you just did,' observed Second Lieutenant Peter Stormonth Darling. 'We were at Fort George to be put through our paces, and it was not an enjoyable experience. To make it worse, the winter of 1950/1951 was one of the coldest on record, and those in authority there were not at all of a mind to consider that recruits should be comfortable or warm.' 'There was no doubting that we were well disciplined,' recalled Lance Corporal Jim Laird. 'From Day One at Fort George we had been pressured and efficiently processed to run, stand still, jump, salute, obey without question – or take the consequences. We were brimming with an elite Scottish brand of *esprit de corps*.' Harold Davis looked forward to the adventure and accepted the tough discipline. 'Having played football at a decent level with East Fife, I was used to taking orders as a sportsman, and that side of things came easily for me.'[11]

In Germany, it was 'snowing like mad' when the soldiers were informed they would be deployed to Korea by mid-summer. 'I was excited,' related Private Hubble, 'though I didn't have a clue where Korea was.' 'I would say that we were totally ignorant of anything that was relevant to the war,' continued Laird. 'I think possibly that at the time we were still thinking of it as a follow-on from the war and that in a sense we were fighting for world peace. We felt there was a sort of togetherness against the communist threat, although even from that point of view we were still very mystified about why someone we were fighting on the same side with during the war, an ally, was now an enemy. We were certainly very naïve.'[12] Stormonth Darling was one of several officers whom Lieutenant Colonel Campbell-Preston asked to extend their National Service to serve in Korea. 'I did not want to be killed, and I dreaded the thought of being seriously wounded. But I knew subconsciously and instantly that if I said no, I would regret it for my entire life and should chastise myself for being a coward.'[13]

'It was not Britain at war with our enemy at the gates, but America at war, with a token force from the Commonwealth; a gesture of goodwill,' observed Lieutenant Colonel David Rose, who on 6 April 1952 succeeded Campbell-Preston in command of the Battalion, which had returned to Scotland after over six years' post-war service in Germany.[14] 'The Ministry of Defence sent us a staff officer to lecture us on what to do if captured,' related Lieutenant Critchley, '"the number, rank and name" mantra. Talk of being made a POW was NOT popular with David Rose and he suggested the lecturer leave us alone!'[15] Another visitor was Eric Linklater who had travelled to Korea in 1951 to obtain material for a booklet prepared for the Central Information Office, *Our Men in Korea*. His report 'was not promising', recorded Stormonth Darling. 'He told us of its fearsome climate veering from arctic temperatures in winter to tropical heat and monsoon rains in summer, and of its rugged, largely mountainous terrain.'[16]

Meanwhile, four years after being amalgamated, the 2nd Black Watch was re-formed at Roman Way Camp, Colchester, under the command first of Lieutenant Colonel Neville Blair and then of Lieutenant Colonel Bill Bradford. 'We had quite a job getting ourselves operational because inevitably all the best recruits went to the 1st Battalion going to Korea,' related Lieutenant Andy Watson, who joined the 2nd Battalion from the 1st. 'At one stage I found myself being paymaster, signals officer, messing officer and President of the Regimental Institute all at one time.'[17] One gratification was regaining possession of the regimental silver, including the Baghdad Bell, 'in the safe keeping' of the 1st Battalion since 1948. 'The years of amalgamation have not destroyed the very strong Second Battalion sentiment. A symptom of this is to be seen in the revival of the use of the old number 73. I expect we shall be calling ourselves "the old Mangalores" next.'[18] Having, for the first time since 1935, sent a company to undertake the Royal Guard at Ballater, in October 1952 the 2nd Black Watch was posted to Gort Barracks, Hubbelrath, as part of the BAOR. In July 1953, the Battalion moved to Dortmund.[19]

Before the 1st Black Watch departed to Korea, on 13 May the

Battalion was addressed by the Regiment's Colonel-in-Chief, Her Majesty Queen Elizabeth the Queen Mother, as she had become on the accession of Princess Elizabeth. It was her first public appearance since George VI's death in February, the Pipes and Drums representing the Regiment at his funeral on 15 February. With the country in mourning, the officers and men were still wearing black armbands.[20]

On 25 May an advance party left Britain by air. The rest of the Battalion travelled by sea on board the *Empire Orwell*. For many, active service in Korea would be their first time under fire. 'The ship's doctor had been in the Second World War,' recorded Lieutenant Adam Gurdon. 'There would be no trouble, he said, from "combat stress" if it was nipped in the bud as early as possible. It was therefore the battalion, company or platoon commander's job to spot it before it spread. You identify all the different characters of men in your platoon, the jokers, skivers, liars. As soon as a soldier starts acting out of his particular character, you decide that he needs three days off.'[21] After five weeks at sea, on 20 June the Battalion arrived in Pusan harbour. 'We were greeted on the quayside by an American Negro Band!', Major Angus Irwin informed his wife – an event which revealed not for the last time that the Americans were expecting to see black soldiers in a regiment called The Black Watch. 'It went down very well with the Jocks.'[22]

'The climate in June is tolerable,' observed Stormonth Darling, 'but the stench in Pusan, of which we had had warnings we had never fully believed, was all pervasive and almost unbearable.' The seventeen-hour journey by train to Tokchon 'was the most uncomfortable, as well as the most depressing journey I can remember. We passed through dismal, largely destroyed villages with just a scattering of ramshackle single-storey houses built of earth and straw thatch where we saw mournful-looking old people.'[23] From Tokchon they transferred to Britannia Camp, headquarters of the Commonwealth Division. Those who believed they had assimilated considerable knowledge in the 'I' or Intelligence Section during their outward journey were disappointed to find that 'map reading in Korea was entirely different to anything we had previously learned.'[24]

Already present in Korea was the advance party, whose journey had taken twenty days, 'a fairly lengthy journey for air travel,' as Lieutenant David Arbuthnott noted. On arrival the Battalion was reinforced by 'a splendid bunch' of drafts from the home-going regiments, among whom was Captain Malcolm Wallace, Argyll & Sutherland Highlanders, whose father, Colonel R. F. H. Wallace, 1st Black Watch, was an expert on Regimental dress.[25] The Battalion was supported by a squadron of Royal Engineers and the 'Skins' – the 5th Royal Inniskilling Dragoon Guards. Surplus to requirements was an anti-tank platoon 'since the Chinese were not using tanks', explained Gurdon.[26] For the first time in the Regiment's history, as part of a United Nations' force, in addition to a tartan patch in the shape of The Black Watch badge, they wore a pale blue patch with 'Commonwealth' in gold letters beneath a crown on the shoulders of their battledress blouses.[27]

The overall strategy of the UN force was to maintain a defensive position along the Main Line of Resistance (MLR) stretching for 120 miles from the Yellow Sea in the west, north of Seoul, eastwards to the Sea of Japan. The Commonwealth Division was positioned north of the Imjin river, 'a favourite bathing place', as Arbuthnott noted, behind the front line. The river could be treacherous and on 6 July the Battalion had its first fatality when Private William Kirk drowned.[28] On the south side was the Quartermaster with the Battalion's supplies: 'Three bridges which we named Pintail, Teal and Mallard were our lifeline,' continued Gurdon. 'But since the river also ran through Chinese lines, during the rainy season, when the Imjin rose 20 to 25 feet, the Chinese used to pack rafts with explosives in the hope of destroying the bridges. So we would deploy the Skins to shoot up the rafts before they hit the bridges.'[29]

On 8 July 1952 the 1st Black Watch relieved the 1st Royal Australian Regiment in the front line. 'It was raining,' recalled Sergeant Brian Gait. 'There are only three kinds of weather in Korea, too hot, too cold, or too wet.'[30] 'During this first period of a month,' related Lieutenant Arbuthnott, 'lessons were learnt in the most effective of training areas. The time it took a DF [Defensive Fire] SOS to arrive, the fact that a little red triangle on a fence indicated a minefield… Communication and cooperation between all arms was very good and stemmed from a deep mutual respect.'[31] A routine was soon adopted of 'digging in – strengthening bunkers – improving fighting pits and communication trenches – sentry duties – listening posts at night – patrols and sleep when convenient,' remarked Corporal George Jackson, who had completed his National Service with the Regiment, but the 'trials and tribulations of Civvy Street', had caused him to enlist as a regular soldier.[32] 'Stand to was at 0400, stand down 0500, reveille 1000, breakfast 1030, weapon cleaning and work till lunch at 1400 hrs', related Second Lieutenant Brian Mann, 'improving our positions 1500–1800, a meal at 1900, stand to 2000, with a rigid distribution of paludrine [an anti-malarial drug] – stand down 2100.'[33]

A severe hazard were the minefields 'all around us, and everyone had to learn the way out and – more difficult – the way back again', the perils evident when, on 14 July, Private Martin Hogan was killed when his patrol ran into an uncharted minefield. 'The Chinese were adept at moving the skull and crossbone signs marking the perimeter of the minefields, and patrols would stumble into them,' explained Gait.[34] 'A greater hazard was the barbed wire surrounding our positions,' related Lieutenant Ian Critchley. 'This was a belt of some 50 to 100 yards in depth (not the one-yard Dannert wire coil we were used to in training). The wire dominated our lives in the line (forward positions) for each night parties were sent out to cover the wire especially the routes through such a massive maze but also to repair holes caused by shell fire. The carrying of the replacement wire, angle-iron pickets, wire cutters, and sledge hammers was difficult in the dark, exhausting, the whole operation a terrifying stay in No Man's Land.'[35]

On 25 July Lieutenant Alec Renny-Tailyour was killed. 'I wrote to his mother this evening,' Rose recorded. 'Oh, what a difficult and unpleasant task… It was all so sad because he was killed by a piece of one of our own shells. He called for the fire himself and was not where he should have been. I told him on no account to call down fire unless he was 500 yards back from the target and he really had no need of it at all. I didn't of course put this in my letter.'[36] In early August Second Lieutenant David Nicoll was killed in a minefield while mending the perimeter fence broken by shell fire. 'David was in many ways a gilded youth,' recollected Stormonth Darling, who wrote his obituary for *The Red Hackle*. 'He would have succeeded in whatever path he chose in life.'[37]

While in the front line, the officers and men lived in what they called 'hoochies', their bed frames made from requisitioned metal pickets normally used to stake up the barbed wire. 'I live in a big hole in the ground all roofed in just like a cave,' Major Irwin wrote to his son for his fourth birthday. 'Also living in my hole are the Sergeant Major – and lots of mice!… There are also lots of Jeremy Fishers which come in when it rains and are really rather a nuisance as they hop into the box where my clean clothes are kept! I have to be very careful when I put on my clothes that there aren't any frogs inside them – it would be horrid to have a cold clammy frog in your shirt wouldn't it?'[38]

On 8 August the Battalion moved into reserve, its position taken over by the 'Van Doos', the Canadian Royal 22ème Regiment. 'This pattern of alternate spells in the line and in reserve continued and, in fact, more time was spent out of the line than in it,' observed Arbuthnott. '[There were] no villages or houses but dusty roads leading across the Imjin river to ridges increasing in height to the North.'[39] Although training continued, there was some relaxation. 'Long nights in bed (when not on patrol exercises), an open-air cinema, and leave at Inchon Camp for the lucky ones.' A group from the assault pioneer platoon ran a 'confidence course' in mines and booby traps, an idea developed by the US Marines. 'The enemy on the Marines' front have been in the habit of stealing mines from our own minefields and using them against us, so we thought we had better prepare ourselves in case the same should happen in our new sector.'[40]

Having identified 'a very real need for sing-songs etc,' and in the absence of the military band, Rose purchased instruments from Japan for a 'mountain band' consisting of an accordion, organ, violin and drums.[41] 'Everywhere there was talent at hand. Our Welshmen sang as a team as only Welshmen can. Korean porters were not going to be outdone and also produced a part-song. This started with a very smart salute and had a good swinging rhythm which led one to think that it might well be their National Anthem, but on enquiring it turned out to be – a Love Song!'[42] To buy essentials for the men, two officers' wives, Elizabeth Irwin and Jean Rowan-Hamilton, set up a 'Comforts Fund'. One initiative was a raffle, which resulted in nearly 300 donated prizes.[43]

By the end of August the monsoon had begun, leaving the men 'frightfully busy repairing rain and flood damage and trying to keep the water out of our tents, etc.' Then came the Korean autumn, described by Second Lieutenant Mann: 'with lovely clear days, still warm enough to swim in the Imjin, but very cold at night and the first of our cold weather clothing was issued – thick sweaters that were very welcome.'[44] 'Scrounging' for supplies became an instinct. One of the 'great exponents' was Lieutenant Ian Critchley, the motor transport officer, frequently seen 'driving off with a bottle of gin and returning some time later with valuable loads of wood and spare parts.' Their vehicles, he explained, were in 'a parlous state' and so he had no qualms about 'buzzing around the American area to beg, borrow or steal… once we got a whole engine.'[45] 'Every CO was issued with a heater for his jeep,' recollected Private Hubble, working as the Signals Dispatch Service (SDS) driver. 'Lieutenant Colonel Rose told me that I should have the heater because he knew I was out all night. That was the kind of man he was.'[46]

In early October the Battalion returned to the line. 'Shelling has been heavy lately,' Stormonth Darling informed his father. 'And for the first time in the war British troops have been given steel helmets – an awful nuisance they are, and we are bad at wearing them.'[47] At the end of the month the 1st Black Watch relieved the 1st Battalion 7th Marines, 1st US Marine Division, on a ridge of land known as the Hook, because 'some perceptive, poetic soul had decided it was shaped like a fish-hook.' Protruding into Chinese lines, it was regarded by Stormonth Darling as having 'a provocative sort of "in your face" feel about it.'[48]

The Hook: 'A living hell'

The strategic importance of the Hook lay in preventing the Chinese from advancing to the south and driving a wedge between the Commonwealth Division and the US 1st Marine Division. Protected by two standing patrols, Warsaw, to the north-east, and Ronson to the west, it marked the northern-most part of the Main Line of Resistance.[49] 'We are now in our new place,' Rose was writing to his wife on 4 November, 'the positions were pounded to bits when the Marines had their battle here.' His immediate concern was overseeing repair work on the shattered defences. 'Both sides [had] poured in shells and mortar bombs and pounded it with air strikes as well, so the trenches are all filled in and the barbed wire is all blown to bits.' 'The trenches were full of a cat's cradle of telephone wires; it seemed that Marines did not repair a break in a cable, they just rolled out another drum of cable,' observed Lieutenant Critchley.[50] Working by night to avoid shelling from the Chinese, barely a hundred yards away, and assisted by the Royal Engineers and a Korean workforce, the plan was to create tunnels into which they could withdraw 'so that if they attack again in force, we can fire the artillery on our own position to kill the majority before we have to mop up,' Rose informed the Colonel of the Regiment, Major General Neil McMicking. 'Each tunnel entrance was to be provided with a grenade trap and dog-legs and would be four-foot high and three-foot wide, close-timbered and driven back into the hillside until the overhead cover was a minimum ten feet,' explained George Cooper, troop commander, Royal Engineers.[51]

From 10 November the Chinese artillery bombardment intensified, those on patrol vulnerable to having their positions overrun. 'It was not the best of times to go forward on a walk-about,' commented Lance Corporal Stan Wood, 're-badged' into the 1st Black Watch from the Royal Leicesters and part of a six-man patrol occupying Ronson on the night of 18/19 November. 'The shelling was extremely heavy, and there was no effective shelter.'[52] 'Suddenly a heavy barrage came down all around us,' related Second Lieutenant Sandy Younger in charge of the patrol. Unable to get in touch by wireless with his Company HQ, he decided 'we could *not* be of any real assistance in holding back an attack out here and that we would be of much more use in the Coy position.' As they were withdrawing, Younger was wounded in the leg. 'At this point I found that I had *no* grenades as they had slipped off my belt when we were backing down the trench.' Before he could decide on his next move, two Chinese approached. 'I was defenceless so I shammed dead. The Chinamen came and poked around in my trouser pockets where they found two Sten magazines and my handkerchief which they took. They did not search the top pockets of my jacket. They took off my watch.' Saved from further scrutiny, Younger renewed his attempt to withdraw. 'I met another two Chinamen who saw that I was alive, and I think defenceless.' Fortunately Younger again escaped, making his way back to the Regimental Aid Post.[53] Two members of the patrol had been killed and Lance Corporal Wood wounded.

At the same time, a standing patrol led by Corporal William Kerry had come under attack on Warsaw and was joined by a reconnaissance patrol led by Second Lieutenant John Roger Doig, Seaforth Highlanders. Instead of withdrawing, Doig ordered them 'to fix bayonets and charge the enemy'. 'Kerry rushed forward beside his officer firing his Sten Gun to good effect, but both of them were blown off their feet by a grenade.' Doig's wounds were fatal. After reorganising the men, Kerry obliged the Chinese to withdraw but within no time they returned. Seeing 'swarms of the enemy sweeping up the hill towards him in close formation,' Kerry ordered the soldiers to open fire, bringing 'the enemy to a standstill. A fierce grenade battle ensued.' While the Chinese were attempting to outflank him, Kerry successfully withdrew the patrol, including the wounded. 'It was the most amazing performance,' observed Lieutenant Gurdon, Kerry's platoon commander, and his action was later recognised with the award of a Military Medal.[54]

The attacks on Ronson and Warsaw were the prelude to another Chinese attack on the Hook. 'A tremendous barrage suddenly descended upon us. This lasted half-an-hour and we estimated that some 4,000 assorted shells and mortar bombs arrived during that period.' The artillery barrage was deafening 'and so heavy it literally changed the contour of the hillside,' recalled Second Lieutenant Donald Black. 'I thought the whole hill had blown up,' recorded Sergeant Jackson. 'So many shells landed simultaneously that the ground itself was shaking.'[55] Lieutenant Arbuthnott, the signals officer, remembered the inconvenience caused by the Chinese success in cutting the telephone lines, which meant they could only communicate by wireless. 'All those carefully laid telephone lines were obliterated.'[56] Simultaneously the Chinese began to advance.

Major Irwin, Officer Commanding A Company, was controlling the battle from his command bunker; since he was suffering from a bad cough, he had to relay whispered orders through his second-in-command, Second Lieutenant Geordie Chalmer. As the Chinese moved forward, he ordered the men into the recently-fortified tunnels, before calling for the artillery to fire above the position. 'This stopped the Chinese for a time but more and more poured over no-man's land on to us,' related Rose, who was encouraging Irwin to 'stick it out' while promising reinforcements.[57] 'All the enemy effort was directed at A Company although the other 3 companies were heavily shelled,' Arbuthnott continued. 'In order to clear the enemy from A Company's position the CO ordered the Pipes and Drums and the 3 platoons from B Company to assist.' Two platoons of D Company were engaged.[58]

'We were suddenly told – well, we knew because we heard the shells coming down and so on – that there was quite a big battle going on at the Hook. And we were told: B Company will go back on to the Hook to help reinforce A Company,' related Critchley. Mindful of having spent part of the Second World War as a prisoner-of-war after his capture at St Valéry, Major Rowan-Hamilton, Officer Commanding B Company, promised to 'sell his life dearly'. Unfortunately, while advancing up the hill, a grenade 'practically took off his leg', his batman's swift action in making a tourniquet with his scarf saving it.[59] 'As the night progressed we had some very anxious moments. My reserves were now all used up, so now it was a question of slogging it out,' related Rose.[60]

'The Chinks had been told to take the position regardless of losses, and they were fighting like tigers,' related Private Bob Clark. 'I fired my Bren continuously for what seemed hours, although it could not have been for more than 20 minutes. Cold as the weather was I was sweating like a horse.' Having killed a number of Chinese, his bren gun was blown out of his hands by a shell and his only weapon was a broken spade. 'I turned at a corner in the trench and there was a Chinese armed with a sub-machine gun. Before he could fire I hit him on the face with the spade and killed him.'[61] By dawn the following day, The Black Watch, assisted by the Skins, had succeeded in repulsing the Chinese. In the action The Black Watch lost twenty men out of 800; among them was Private William Robert Shaw 'well known in Perth amateur boxing circles.' Private G. Coley, who had been operating in front of A Company's position in a gun bay, later died of his wounds. 'He was surrounded by empty ammunition belts and Chinese corpses. During the night he had fired thirteen belts of ammunition on free traverse, before the Chinese had finally managed to swamp his position,' recorded Sergeant Gait.[62] When compiling his report Lieutenant John Moncrieff, the intelligence officer, recorded that the Chinese soldiers appeared to have been 'doped' as they fought 'madly in all directions and seemed quite oblivious of all the shells landing around,' opium seeds later being found in a Chinese cigarette packet.[63]

'Perhaps you will have heard before you get this, that my battle came off and we gave them a good trouncing,' Rose informed his brother Rhoddy on 23 November. 'The men are very proud of themselves and rightly so.'[64] Less welcome was the information that Brigade HQ had been warned of the attack two hours in advance, but had failed to pass on the information. Hearing that Brigadier Abdy Ricketts 'didn't see what difference it would have made', Rose responded that 'he did not think seventy-five wounded Jocks not to mention the missing sappers, would agree with him.' Relations with the Brigade HQ remained cool until Ricketts' replacement, Brigadier Joe Kendrew, arrived in late November.[65]

Private Stanley, who had been taken prisoner, managed to escape while being marched back to the Chinese positions. 'On crossing a wire obstacle I got caught up in it and they were all waiting for me to untangle myself… When I got myself free I made a bolt for it. A big shout went up. They threw grenades at me and fired with their burp guns but I got away unscathed.' Less fortunate was Derek Hall who remained a prisoner, collating a book of poems during his captivity:

It's here upon one November night
That first platoon fought its epic fight.
For ten long days the mortars fell
Making this place a living hell.[66]

Meanwhile, more men had been ordered up from the divisional reinforcement company in Kure, Japan. Private Jack Erskine, a former apprentice blacksmith and farrier, was at the cinema when Private Derek Halley, a former shepherd, 'tapped me on the shoulder and said "Come on; we're off." And he dragged me out of the cinema with my friends and we boarded a train for Hiroshima.'[67] The next day they flew to Seoul in Korea.

When news of the battle reached home, numerous donations were sent which 'has done more for the spirit of this Battalion than any of you can comprehend,' Rose wrote in thanks to readers of *The Red Hackle*.[68] Major General McMicking received 'a personal note' from the Queen Mother, informing them how proud she was that the Regiment had 'not only maintained but enhanced' its reputation 'for courage and prowess in battle.'[69] In recognition of his 'great calmness and efficiency under fire', Irwin was awarded an immediate DSO, Rose later receiving a bar to his DSO awarded for his actions in Somaliland in 1940. 'The action seems to have created quite a stir out here and I have been besieged by reporters ever since,' Irwin wrote home.[70] Among others who were given awards was Lieutenant Haw, who received the MC: he walked 'boldly out under fire with a small patrol and brought in three of our wounded who had been lying there throughout the night.' Second Lieutenant Donald Black, whose soldiers in the foremost platoon had been reduced to hurling rocks and fighting the Chinese off with their fists, received the MC, as did Lieutenant Michael Anstice, 5th Royal Inniskilling Dragoon Guards: the guns from his tank, supporting The Black Watch's advance, were 'a deciding factor in the success of the mission.'[71] Sergeant Brian Gait was awarded the DCM: not only had he distinguished himself in command of a platoon on Ronson two days before the battle, but when Ronson was overrun on 18 November, in a decisive counter-attack, he had 'swept forward with his men through heavy enemy shell and mortar fire, killing and chasing the enemy.' Later, he and his remaining men prevented a third attack from penetrating their entrenched line 'and single-handed he beat off one enemy probe which came in around the flank.'[72]

Both sides used propaganda, disseminated in leaflets dropped across their respective lines. While the UN leaflets showed dead Chinese soldiers with their grieving mothers and offered passes for 'safe conduct', the Chinese responded with leaflets carrying stories 'from home', including letters from mothers and sweethearts. 'The Koreans and Chinese don't want to be your enemies,' affirmed one Chinese letter. 'Our enemies and yours are those who sent you here and destroyed your happiness.' Having learnt to distinguish the different Regiments, whenever The Black Watch arrived in the front line, the Chinese played Scottish music. Recalling the propaganda broadcast by Japanese women during the Second World War, the soldiers called the Chinese equivalent 'Tokyo Rose'. 'There was one thing she did say: "If you want us to carry on [don't] fire your rifles",' related Private Halley, '"and if you want us to stop, fire them longer." And of course we were firing like hell, determined [for them] to stop. They were not that daft, because we were merely using up ammunition.' On another occasion, Stormonth Darling remembered hearing the question: '"Black Watch, when are you going to give up?" Needless to say, no one was taken in by any of this. We treated it as a big joke. All the tea in China would not have moved us.'[73]

A dire aspect of their lives was sanitation, which Private Halley described as 'non-existent – anyone asking for the urinals was introduced to The Desert Rose by a soldier who was holding his nose with one hand and pointing to a scruffy arrow signpost with the other… The toilets were just thunder boxes with a canvas covering which sat over holes 8–10 feet deep and the stench was so evil the bile bubbled in your throat until you learned how to endure it.'[74] Rats 'as big as cats… were enough to make your stomach turn,' observed Corporal Harold Davis, who had arrived in Korea with a draft of new recruits in late 1952, 'especially when it was dark and you didn't know whether they were crawling around you or not.' As a result Manchurian fever was 'a massive worry… If you were bitten by one of those blighters, you had a first-class ticket home, no questions asked.'[75]

By the beginning of December, the Battalion was in reserve. 'I must say it is very pleasant to be able to get a good night's sleep with one's boots off,' observed Irwin, who described the floor of his tent being excavated 'about 4 feet deep so as to get the floor below frost level'. Snow had already fallen and on 12 December the Imjin river froze.[76] While officers enjoyed the 'Bath Unit' consisting of three baths, run by the 'popular' Korean, Bertram, 'which go with us wherever we go', soldiers could expect a shower once a month 'if the bath unit came, which was a big marquee with piping from a boiler to about thirty shower roses at a time.'[77]

A big hut, built out of wattle and daub, with ten heaters and seating for one hundred, constituted a cinema, with films such as *The African Queen* and *Ivanhoe* shown two or three times daily. Bridge and canasta competed 'for popular favour.'[78] 'Christmas and Hogmanay were celebrated by the Black Watch in a magnificent fashion that astonished the rest of the Division', recorded Sergeant Gait. Although there was plenty of beer and rum, whisky was in short supply with only two bottles available. 'David Rose pondered the problem and came up with a Solomon-like judgment – he would keep both bottles. During the celebrations the rumble of artillery fire could be heard in the distance but we were in reserve and so all was well.'[79]

On 3 January 1953, the Black Watch returned to the front line. 'Our days were often made more interesting by heavy air strikes on the Chinese positions in good weather, made by carrier based planes of the Fleet Air Arm – they dominated the skies as there was no Chinese air presence,' recalled Second Lieutenant Mann.[80] When in the front line, those in Lieutenant Gurdon's platoon supplemented their meals with plentiful pheasant. 'My platoon radio operator was an underkeeper on a large estate... he used to empty half a can of baked beans on the ground, with a drop of whisky. By the time stand to was over, the pheasant was so inebriated, it didn't know if it was in Korea or Scotland, enabling us to have a jolly good dinner!' Generally provisions were scarce. Tea was served cold, 'only heating it when the need gave us the nerve,' recalled Halley. 'The tell tale smoke generally attracted unwanted attention.'[81]

The weather was bitterly cold. 'For a shave you got a mug full of snow and put it on your stove and melted it,' recollected Lance Corporal Derek Hurst. 'The wind from the north seemed to cut into your face like cuts from a razor,' related Lance Corporal Wood, 'and after several hours on a standing patrol, your legs just did not want to move.' With nights spent 'peering through slits' in order to observe any movement from the Chinese in caves and trenches in the opposite hills, 'by morning our eyes were red raw. Simply standing could be agony.' Flouting the regulations, Private Halley confessed often to 'sitting on empty ammo boxes.' 'You could only leave a sentry on duty for 20 minutes because he had to have his trigger finger uncovered so that he could fire and his ears uncovered so that he could hear,' observed Gurdon.[82] Among many poems written in Korea, Private Ian (Danny) Kaye recorded the sentry's solitude:

Have you known the lonely silence
... at the witching-hour of midnight?
You've patted each grenade ten times,
And even whispered to your Sten
Dozed off – then woke in panic
With fear of death upon you,
And every shape and shadow seems
Chock-full of 'little men'!... I have![83]

At the beginning of February, the Commonwealth Division went into reserve. Positioned much further behind the line '[we] hardly even heard the guns, and could lead a more relaxed life,' related Second Lieutenant Mann. 'A lot of the time was spent in preparing positions on a reserve line', noted Arbuthnott, 'called the Kansas Line.'[84] 'The other night', Irwin was writing in mid-February, 'I woke up in the middle of the night and discovered a Korean thief in my tent – he had just found my wallet when I discovered him & fortunately he dropped it as he made his escape. When I first heard him I reached for my pistol which I have by my bed and fortunately for him I grabbed my torch by mistake.'[85] At the end of the month Brian Mann returned home, having completed his National Service. Like Peter Stormonth Darling, who had left at the end of 1952, he had 'very mixed feelings, of joy but also of sadness, at leaving my Jocks who had been so loyal, courageous and unresentful about the position they found themselves in. It had been a most extraordinary experience for a 19/20 year old straight out of school, and it stretched to the limit whatever qualities of leadership I may have possessed.'[86] Among new arrivals was Second Lieutenant Hugh Blakeney, 1st Argyll & Sutherland Highlanders, attached to The Black Watch. 'Apart from my sword-stick, my only armament was a .38 revolver and about twenty rounds of ammunition.' Having been advised to look to 'the Americans for something with more fire power', in exchange for two bottles of gin, he acquired a semi automatic .300 carbine along with about 300 rounds of ammunition.[87]

1953: The Hook again

In early April the Battalion returned to the Hook. Since Major Irwin had left to take part in the Queen's coronation ceremony in June, Captain Tony Lithgow took command of A Company.[88] With the assistance of the sappers, the network of trenches was rebuilt and strengthened. As usual the Chinese were broadcasting propaganda threatening an attack. 'We were so fed up with it we didn't think anything really would happen,' recalled Private Halley. On 8 May, the eighth anniversary of VE Day, 'we were all standing in the trenches when all the trip flares started going off.' 'The whole place was lit up,' recalled Anthony Laycock in D Company which was defending the flank of the Hook known as the Sausage. Realising that the Chinese were dropping phosphorous shells, he described the scene as 'rather pretty if it wasn't so deadly.' Lonely and frightened, he prayed. 'It had come home to me that I was only 19 and wasn't ready for dying just yet.' 'There were masses and masses and masses of Chinese. They were like ants coming up a hill,' related Private Halley.[89]

When communication was lost with a forward platoon command post, manned by Second Lieutenant Alec Rattray, Corporal Colin Harrison went with a line party to repair the break in the telephone line. To his surprise, having repaired it, there was still no response from the platoon command post. Returning to check what had happened, he saw 'a huge amount of smoke. The command post had been blown up.'[90] Since contact had been lost with the other forward platoon command post, the Royal Engineer troop commander, George Cooper, volunteered to go forward from Lithgow's HQ, 'being blown over on the way by a 20mm mortar bomb exploding at my feet!' On reaching the first command post, he found that the occupants were sitting as he had seen them before the battle 'but all stone dead, killed by [the] blast.' In addition to Rattray, the dead included Private James Irvine, the radio operator and Sergeant Albert (Tug) Wilson, Seaforth Highlanders. Only the runner, Private Lockhart survived, although badly shell-shocked. Proceeding to the next platoon command post Cooper found two soldiers carrying Lieutenant David Haugh. 'He too had had a mortar bomb exploding at his feet but had taken the full blast and died in my arms, with the two Jocks in tears.'[91] When Private Halley saw Sergeant Wilson's body, the 'cruellest irony' flashed through his mind: 'Tug Wilson had once tugged me back to earth for posing as an old soldier when I was nothing more than a nyaff [worthless] person… he had marched me up and down the platform at Inverness Station and hauled me off to Fort George to give me the benefit of his boot, and there he lay lifeless at mine, his unseeing eyes staring at a real old soldier at last.'[92]

Once reinforcements arrived, despite the hazards of near-daylight, Rose ordered 'two strong fighting patrols forward to sweep the battlefield', having promised to put down a smokescreen to protect them.[93] During the battle Corporal Davis went forward into No Man's Land to check the wire and he was wounded in the foot; as he was making for the safety of a trench, a hail of bullets hit him. 'I knew I was in big trouble. I could feel where I had been hit in the stomach and right across my torso. This wasn't the pain of one bullet, like I'd felt before; this was like I'd been ripped open.' Davis was lucky to survive; his recovery took two years. Corporal Jim Laird, who was hit in the spine while 'keeping low' in a trench, was paralysed from the chest downwards.[94]

At dawn the Chinese withdrew, setting off smoke bombs to protect their departure and enabling them to clear away the dead and wounded. 'If they found a wounded Jock', observed Lieutenant Gurdon, 'they did not take them prisoner because they had no medical facilities to look after them, but would most likely put them into a shell hole with a cigarette and some marijuana for us to take away.'[95]

'We've had another battle,' Rose was writing on 8 May, 'not such a heavy one as last time – thank God! This time the enemy tried to come in without a preliminary bombardment. He got to within 20 yards of our trenches and there was some hand-to-hand fighting. We put down everything we have got and it all went splendidly from that point of view,' despite the death of two 'very fine' officers: Rattray and Haugh.[96] Other fatalities on 8 May included Privates James Irvine and Robert McKee.[97]

On the night of 12/13 May, in 'teeming rain', the 1st Black Watch was ordered to withdraw, its place on the Hook taken by the Duke of Wellington's Regiment, 'the Dukes'.[98] Among the 'lessons we learnt', observed Rose, was the 'value of guaranteed wireless communications.' Debriefing showed that many men did not fix their bayonets. 'Had every man done this there were several occasions when a bayonet would have been the best weapon to use.' Rose also considered that after the November battle, they were 'all very tired and considerably disorganized' and had not made proper use of 'a well known tactical principle, the importance of the counter attack,' successfully implemented in May.[99] Among the honours awarded, Rose's second-in-command Major R. A. A. S. (Raas) Macrae, Seaforth Highlanders, received the MBE for having gone forward 'three times during the night into heavy shell and mortar fire to organise reinforcements, the evacuation of wounded and the resupply of ammunition.' Padre Tom Nicol received the MBE for his 'exacting work as a Chaplain on Active Service'. Captain Tony Lithgow received the MC.[100]

Although now in the 'quiet' Yong Dong sector 'nightly there was a great increase in enemy activity and movement forward of our positions,' recalled Lance Corporal Hurst.[101] Anticipating that the renewed shelling presaged another attack, Rose was recalled from leave in Japan. '[Brigadier] Kendrew was worried that the Dukes might not be able to withstand the Chinese and wanted us behind them in order to counterattack.'[102] But the Dukes stood firm, and the Fourth Battle for the Hook took place on 28 May without 'any serious commitment' of The Black Watch; the Chinese were again forced to withdraw.[103]

In celebration of Queen Elizabeth II's coronation on 2 June 1953, a 'display of red, white and blue coloured smoke [was] fired onto successive enemy-held hills by the divisional gunners,' related Arbuthnott. 'It was a fine sight to see the tracer bullets streaming up into the night sky as each platoon passed the signal to the next hill top.'[104] To their surprise, the Chinese observed a truce along the Commonwealth Division's line. 'The Australians in particular had great fun planting Union Jacks all over the Chinese lines. In return the Chinese crept up to our lines and put presents on our wire like lots of pairs of nylons,' recorded Lieutenant Gurdon.[105]

In early July The Black Watch was relieved. 'I am sorry to see you go, because a battle-experienced unit is leaving the Division,' stated Brigadier Kendrew, 'a thing we cannot afford to lose – and also because I will lose a lot of good friends among all ranks.'[106] Travelling south by train to Pusan, the soldiers visited the United Nations Memorial Cemetery. 'Quartermaster Nobby Clark had arranged that all the Black Watch graves had a red hackle put on top, so we could all see which were Black Watch people,' related Lieutenant Arbuthnott who, during Padre Tom Nicol's address, confessed to 'thinking more of the people who had been killed, the friends we'd lost' than 'of God's purpose and religion.'[107] 'The firing party of the Guard of Honour was formed by men from all Regiments who had been put into The Black Watch,' explained Private Hubble, emphasising Rose's decision 'to recognise all detached regiments with us.'[108]

The following day the Battalion left Korea. 'I like to remember the good times, the beautiful sunrises in the "Land of the Morning Calm"', wrote Stan Wood. 'The wonderful starlight in a dark velvet sky, and the moonlight nights… the good comradeship, the willingness to share.' Adam Gurdon remembered the contrasts: 'the Americans who differed from the British, the tremendous heat and the piercing cold, the beauty of the landscape and the ugliness of war.'[109]

The peace train at Panmunjom

Truce negotiations, deadlocked over the issue of 'voluntary' repatriation of POWs, had resumed in April. On 27 July 1953 the Panmunjom Truce was signed. By its terms a 2½-mile Demilitarised Zone (DMZ) was created as a buffer at the 38th Parallel. Since the document was an armistice rather than a peace treaty, the Democratic People's Republic of Korea and the Republic of Korea remained in a state of contained belligerence.

In hindsight, Lieutenant Colonel Rose believed that the UN force never dominated the battlefield. 'With our great superiority of weapons we should have been able to make "no man's land" quite intolerable for the enemy… the fortitude of the Chinese, in the face of our complete domination of weapons, was truly staggering.' That the Korean War was mainly fought at night with semi-trained troops was a disadvantage. 'I think we should have made more use of Artificial Moonlight (searchlights reflected off the clouds). We had the generating capacity and the communications to switch on and off at will. If you can see the battlefield, you need not use thousands of shells and mortar bombs on Defensive Fire, when you are attacked.' 'The Battalion fought an entirely defensive war, holding the hilltop positions that had been captured in 1951,' observed Lieutenant Arbuthnott, who praised the Katcoms, the Koreans Attached to the Commonwealth, who 'quickly became an integral part of whichever platoon they joined.'[110]

An estimated 178,698 South Korean and Allied soldiers died in Korea with an unconfirmed number of between 300,000 and 750,000 North Korean and Chinese. The Black Watch had 66 fatalities, with 200 men wounded and thirteen taken prisoner.[111] Of the 87,000 British servicemen who fought in Korea between 1950 and 1953, over half were National Servicemen like Peter Stormonth Darling and Privates Derek Halley and Richard 'Rocky' Dewar, who died in a 'battle' accident on 2 July. 'The Sergeant asked Rocky to clean the grenades. When he pulled one out of the carrier, the pin came out. He died instantly, holding the grenade near to him to protect the others,' related Halley, who later recorded his experiences as a 'conscript… stolen away and forced to see things, that I would choose not to dwell on for forty years.'[112]

All those who served in the Korean War were awarded a United Nations Medal with a blue and white ribbon, the clasp stating 'Korea' and a Queen's Korean Medal with blue-and-yellow ribbon. The flags of all the countries which supported the United Nations' action still fly at the United Nations Memorial Cemetery, where an inscription in English and Korean has the words 'The Forgotten War' – although those who fought have not forgotten, and anniversary celebrations regularly take place. 'The ideal of democracy, for which you were willing to sacrifice your all 50 years ago, have become universal values in this new century and millennium,' President Kim Dae-Jung said on 25 June 2000, commemorating the 50th anniversary of the outbreak of hostilities.[113] The Scottish Korean War Memorial, a small wooden pagoda surrounded by trees, is situated in Witch Craig Wood, West Lothian.[114] On 3 December 2014 a memorial to 'The Korean War 1950–1953' was unveiled in Whitehall, London.[115] Whereas North Korea, under Kim Il-sung's grandson Kim Jong-Un, remains the world's most closed dictatorship, South Korea has become one of the G-20 major economies in the world, its inhabitants still enjoying the freedom for which soldiers of The Black Watch and others fought and died.

So the Jocks retired to count the cost
And mourn for those that they had lost
But then again another story
They had made their mark on the path to glory.[116]

18

Small Wars: Kenya and British Guiana

It is night in the African jungle
And the sentries pace their beat;
The ambushes strain for the faintest sound
Of advancing Mau Mau feet.[1]

The Mau Mau

The 1st Black Watch's next posting was to have been the 'Canal Zone' in Egypt, but instead the Battalion was diverted to Kenya, a British protectorate since 1895 and a Crown Colony since 1920. In the early 1950s rising discontent among the majority tribal grouping, the Kikuyu, had led to acts of violence by rebel groups. Known as the Mau Mau, the movement was a reaction to colonial rule which had permitted white settlers to occupy large swathes of fertile land in the Central and Rift Valley provinces while the economically deprived Africans were confined to 'Native Reserves'.[2] On 21 October 1952 the Governor, Sir Evelyn Baring, declared a state of emergency but the unrest continued. In March 1953, a group of Mau Mau attacked members of the Kikuyu Home Guard and their families in Lari in the largest 'massacre' to date. As law and order deteriorated, Britain's military presence was increased to approximately 10,000 men.[3]

Leaving Korea in mid-July 1953, the 1st Black Watch's voyage down the coast of China had progressed 'meal by meal rather than mile by mile'. On reaching Mombasa, the Battalion went by train to Nairobi. 'The General [Sir George Erskine] told me that our first task was to re-establish the Police and the Civil Authority in the Kikuyu Reserve,' recorded Lieutenant Colonel Rose, who gave Erskine a 'run-down' of their concerns, including the absence of their wives after over a year on active service. 'Many of our Officers, Warrant Officers and NCOs were entitled to claim home posting', without whom the Battalion would be 'in a sorry plight, but all were very willing to stay if they could be joined by their families.'[4] After some resistance, Erskine agreed, cautioning that the Battalion would still be deployed where necessary.[5]

The Black Watch's immediate area of activity was the Great Rift Valley, north-west of Nairobi, where the individual companies were dispersed in different locations. In addition to their musical responsibilities, the Pipes and Drums undertook guard duties and patrols, moving from company to company. 'You were soldiering first and piping second,' related Piper Harry Ellis.[6] 'I am afraid we are in for a very hard time once we are acclimatised,' Rose informed his wife, Jean, in anticipation of her arrival. 'We work in the mountains in very thick bamboo forests – spells of a week or two, then a few days rest.'[7] So that the men could understand their adversaries, he organised briefings by local civilians. The Mau Mau, they discovered, only attacked isolated farmhouses and local Kikuyu who had joined the Home Guard. For protection 'remote farms were issued with a Verey Pistol', explained Private Alexander Farmer. 'Each had a colour code pattern to set off in the event of trouble. Mobile units stood at readiness and would rush off when the sky lit up. Other times, when Intelligence suspected something might happen, small groups of 3–4 men were sent to spend the night at that particular farm.'[8]

In late August the Battalion moved closer to the Mau Mau stronghold in the Aberdare mountains, west of the Kikuyu Reserve. 'It is hard going, over bad country – mostly jungle, often wet, and always hilly,' commented Rose.[9] A favoured Mau Mau tactic, related Private Bob Mitchell, was to light a fire and then move out. Believing the area to be a Mau Mau 'hide', the RAF would bomb the area, resulting in the death of game and providing the rebels with a supply of food. On one occasion, Major Claud Moir led an attack against a stockade in which a gang of Mau Mau sympathisers was hiding, resulting in 'bows and arrows, spears, knobkerries [and] a shot gun' being thrown out of the stockade before 'about 60 men shambled out with hands above their heads,' recorded Corporal Hubble. 'That is how I became the owner of [a] spear and knobkerrie.'[10]

Operating in companies and platoons, the Battalion's challenge was 'to inflict maximum casualties on first contact, before the gang has dissolved into the thick jungle'. To maintain control of wooded areas, all Kikuyu were forbidden to enter Prohibited Areas. 'Here we can shoot on sight,' continued Rose. 'Where the forest ends we have formed a one-mile belt round the Native Reserve. In this belt no cattle are permitted to graze even by day and no crops may be planted. Here we ambush the gangs when they come out to forage, or to intimidate peaceful members of their tribe into joining their movement.'[11]

On 14 October 'an unfortunate incident' happened following a request for a party of civilian Kikuyu 'to enter the prohibited area to harvest food under the protective supervision of a Police escort. This procedure was practised in order to deny food to terrorist gangs which have sought refuge in the Forest.' Permission was given by Captain Peter Lindsay, D Company's second-in-command 'in operational command of that particular area'. In the early afternoon the 'food harvesting party' of Kikuyu women, escorted by police officers, entered the prohibited area. Soon afterwards a reconnaissance party, led by Sergeant Howie, encountered them 'and, not having been advised of the legitimacy of their presence in the prohibited area, opened fire killing Constable Ngare Wandeto and food harvester Nyambura w/o Mutuhithiri'. At the court of inquiry, the Magistrate established that 'manslaughter' had been committed but since Lindsay was unavailable to testify 'and is reported to be out of the Colony' he could not finalise proceedings.[12] While the general opinion was that Howie's action was 'quite legal' ('instructions having been issued to both Military and Police that fire could be opened upon any unauthorized person found within the limits of the prohibited area'), the Commissioner of Police highlighted the fact that

Emergency Regulation 22A(2) – making it 'mandatory for necessary steps to be taken to ensure the safety of persons authorized to be in the prohibited area' – had been 'disregarded by either Captain Lindsay or a person or person to whom he delegated this responsibility'.[13] Lindsay never appeared before the Magistrate, having been transferred out of Kenya at the end of November 1953, later joining the 2nd Black Watch. Upon a subsequent request for information, the colonial government was informed that 'suitable disciplinary action' by the Brigade Commander had been taken.[14]

On 24 December news was received that a Mau Mau gang had beheaded an African loyalist in Thika, 30 miles from Nairobi, near Battalion HQ and Officers' Mess. While the local police were apprehending the gang, four of them escaped. To assist in their capture, a patrol was deployed under the command of Major the Earl Wavell, who had rejoined the Battalion in November. 'I now heard the African Sgt Major yell to the enemy that they had better give up as white troops had arrived', related Colin MacDonald, a reserve officer in the Kenyan Police. 'One of the enemy replied that they would, but nothing came of it… a few shots were being fired at us at this time… Operations then proceeded until I suddenly heard a shot and saw Major Wavell collapse. When I got to him I found that he had been killed instantaneously… Grenades were now being thrown by the troops and we had to constantly duck to avoid being hit by the fragments, but we managed to drag the body to a hollow to which a stretcher had been brought.' Wavell had been shot through the head. 'He did not have a steel helmet, only his Tam o'Shanter,' observed Piper Ellis, who later wrote a pipe tune, 'Skirmish at Thika', in memory of 'a very brave and efficient soldier'.[15]

'Archie John's death was a sad blow,' Rose wrote to the Regiment's Colonel, Major General McMicking. 'We all feel very deeply for poor Lady Wavell.' 'His death and funeral on Boxing Day hung as a heavy cloud over any Christmas festivities we had hoped to have.'

He found the poetry of Man's endeavor.[16]

1954: 'An unpleasant job'

Hogmanay and New Year's Day 1954 were celebrated 'in the traditional fashion'.[17] The arrival of the Battalion's families towards the end of 1953 had been 'quite wonderful, and of course, made our contacts with the Settlers much easier and more friendly,' related Rose. 'In fact, in retrospect, it is hard to see how we could have done without them.' Security concerns, however, meant that sightseeing was 'severely limited'.[18] On 17 January 1954 'the foundations of congregational life' were laid with the formation of the Kirk Session, the 'first properly constituted Church of Scotland Kirk Session in H.M. Forces', which attested the link between The Black Watch and the Kirk ever since the raising of the Regiment in 1739. Officially placed on the Roll of the Presbytery of Perth, 'the author and motivator' was Bernard Fergusson, who had commanded the Battalion between 1948 and 1951. Regardless of denomination, it was decided that the Battalion's Commanding Officer would always be an ex-officio member of the Kirk Session, even if he had not been ordained an Elder or belonged to a different denomination.[19]

In Britain, operations against the Mau Mau had come under public scrutiny following allegations of police brutality and 'competition between battalions of British security forces serving in Kenya as to the number of Mau Mau shot by soldiers', including the offer of monetary prizes.[20] At the beginning of January 1954 an inter-parliamentary delegation visited Nairobi and the surrounding 'troubled areas'. The delegation concluded that they had not come across any example of brutality either by the Army or the police. 'This is a rough world. In an emergency like this there is a great deal of roughness used at times, but there is a sharp distinction between roughness and brutality.' Shortly afterwards, however, *The Times*'s special correspondent was again reporting that police brutality and malpractices were considered to have occurred on a scale constituting 'a threat to public confidence in the forces of law and order'.[21] Correspondingly, the Mau Mau's tactics were viewed by the soldiers as 'murder of maximum brutality, often preceded by and followed by mutilation of the body – of anyone seen to be standing in its way'. Noting that the Kikuyu 'are amongst the most advanced and intelligent tribes in Africa', Second Lieutenant John Rankin observed that 'the murders and mutilation committed by some of their number defied belief. Individuals took oaths of allegiance to Mau-Mau more often than not under compulsion of varying degrees, the final oath being that of murder accompanied by rituals of unbelievable beastliness. Those individuals who had taken the final oath had rendered themselves unclean so far as their tribe was concerned – the Mau-Mau became their fatherland, so to speak, and in a tribally-based society, their allegiance to it was complete.' 'We have an unpleasant job to do and we are doing it in accordance with the accepted rules of war,' commented the author of the Battalion's notes in *The Red Hackle*.[22]

After patrolling the Kikuyu Reserve, the Battalion moved to the European-settled area at the north-eastern end of the Aberdare Mountains bounded by Nyeri, Nanyuki and Thomson's Falls. 'Everybody was pleased to leave the Native Reserve,' observed Rose. Although they had failed to capture their main opponent in the area, General Kago wa Mboto, who operated from the Murang'a forest, they had achieved some success. 'The Home Guard posts were well established and aggressive and we had formed a close liaison with the Administrative Officers and the Police. The situation was said to be "numb".' The area over which the soldiers were now operating was even greater. 'There are many small Police Posts scattered over the area and a number of Special Mobile Police Squads, as well as the odd Mounted Section, manned by farmers and the Kenya Police Reserve. Our main tasks are to co-ordinate the actions of all these people with our own: to pool and pass on all available intelligence; to concentrate forces of all types when a contact is made or when cattle are stolen. Communications are as usual our main difficulty.'[23] 'From day one we were never allowed anywhere without our rifle and 50 rounds of ammunition held in a canvas bandolier around our waist. This was not because we were in any imminent danger of ambush but to stop any pilfering or stealing of ammunition or rifles left in a tent or elsewhere,' recorded Private Peter Grant.[24]

An added challenge was the military's relationship with the settlers of the 'White Highlands' who were not 'the type (like ourselves)', observed Rose, 'to be pushed around by anyone, so we had to devise a method of approach which would win their co-operation. Each Company Commander was to invite the Settlers and their wives in their area to a social gathering. No one was to be left out. I would of course, attend the party to get to know them and hear their views.'[25] Although most were 'on the whole kind and hospitable', Rankin found that some farmers were annoyed at the security forces' limited success in preventing the theft of stock which the rebels then slaughtered for food. 'In fact, the task was an extraordinarily difficult one in view of the huge areas involved, combined with the fact that the gangs received considerable help from Kikuyu farm labourers who would often turn animals loose and warn the gangs of military or police presence.' In addition, 'natural predation by wild animals was often wrongly attributed to Mau-Mau activity'. Although assisted by local trackers, 'few of them were of much use', since it had been assumed that anyone who was black would be a good tracker even though they had grown up in the backstreets of Nairobi. When a school for trackers was established in Nanyuki the situation improved.[26]

On one occasion Private Alexander Farmer took part in an ambush which involved waiting all night. 'We settled down as best we could... I was lying very close (almost under) the Bren.' In the event Farmer fell asleep, the gunner was supposed to wake him when the Mau Mau appeared. But he failed to do so, and Farmer woke 'to the chatter of the Bren and a handful of hot empty cases' down his neck. 'Everything was just a blur... everyone on their knees blazing away at the group of screaming, shooting, terrified Mau Mau who were approximately 40–50 yards away. There may have been some return fire but I doubt it. Like many incidents of its kind this was over very quickly and I doubt if it lasted a full minute.'[27]

As in Korea, a 'major headache' was 'the never ending cycle of de-mob and new drafts – with at some stages a 60% make up of National Service personnel on a maximum term of 24 months which came down to 21 months or less with the battalion after deducting basic training,' observed Private Peter Grant who arrived in Kenya on National Service in March 1954. 'This meant in real terms every month a percentage of troops was due to return to civilian life to be hopefully replaced by new National Service men with a sprinkling of longer term regulars. It was not that in itself that was the problem but the continual loss of fully trained men, junior NCOs in particular.' There was, however, a useful side-effect to their presence: many were tradesmen – joiners, plumbers, electricians and painters – all of whose skills could be utilised whether it was 'fine tuning' the erection of a hut or making up a shower unit from a pile of pipes.[28]

By the spring most of the large rebel gangs had been broken up. Monitoring his platoon's activities, Second Lieutenant Rankin realised the importance of being sufficiently fit 'to meet the demands of covering long distances, in warm weather at high altitude, often with some days' rations on one's back, in addition to the inevitable military equipment.'[29] An enduring challenge was confronting the wild animals, as Private Grant recalled:

> We had problems with rhinos whilst on patrol to the point where instructions were issued on Part One Orders on what action to take when confronted by a charging rhino. Whoever wrote that order had never met one face to face… The orders were to the effect that we were not to climb the nearest tree or run off in all directions but to let the animal charge and then stand aside at the last minute – the rhino was considered to be very short sighted and its reactions would be too slow to see you jump aside; well that was the theory but few were prepared to put it to the test. On one memorable patrol the call went out, 'Rhino' – chaos and everyone climbed up a tree, unfortunately the same one. Left at ground level was one Captain [David] Severn quite put out but he stood his ground and achieved instant fame for kicking the beast as it went past at 25–30 mph. The theory was proved and patrols tended to stay intact until faced by buffalo which was a much more serious problem and not quite so slow as the rhino.[30]

April 1954 brought the 'unwelcome' news of Operation Overdraft, 'a concentrated patrolling effort in the forest by all available battalions for a week', following the poor response the authorities had received from an earlier Operation, Wedgwood, which invited the rebels to surrender, the idea being that they would emerge with their weapons above their heads, carrying a bunch of green twigs or a branch. 'Our platoon task was to set up a camp at a position called Wuthering Heights,' continued Rankin. An exhausting aspect was having to climb to an altitude of 10,000 feet. 'Carrying compo rations for seven days and our weapons and ammunition, blankets, bivouacs, etc, was a severe test, and during the final two hours we had to rest for five minutes after every five minutes climb.' Having reached the summit, to their surprise and mild annoyance, a light aircraft flew overhead, radioing to ask if they would like their rations dropped 'which would have reduced our loads and general grief considerably'.[31]

In addition to dropping rations and mail, and what Peter Grant called the 'appalling waste of financial resources' of bombing the forest, light aircraft provided an effective way of radio communication, since reception on the ground was frequently impeded by trees and hills. 'On one occasion, [Captain] David Arbuthnott was hovering above my patrol and was able to pass the interesting information to me that we were within fifty yards of a pride of lions and heading straight for it', commented Rankin, 'but of course this may have been David's little joke!'[32] After what turned out to be an 'abortive' climb of Wuthering Heights, they were informed of a Battalion move, some 'clown' floating a rumour the move was to Hollywood 'to make a film of the "battle of the Hook" acting as extras! This rumour died a hard death!'[33]

Operation Anvil: Sweeping the city

The Battalion's destination was Nairobi to take part in a massive 'sweep' of the city, where the rebels 'could move about more or less unmolested.'[34] Taking up quarters in a local school, the officers and stores were 'squeezed' into the school buildings, while the soldiers slept in tents in the playing fields and on the nearby race course. 'By this time the rains had begun and the tents were soon awash. Drainage ditches were dug but these were inadequate and the whole area quickly became a quagmire,' which the soldiers felt must resemble a First World War battlefield. When Private Ellis had to play the pipes at Torr's Hotel in Nairobi he had to be carried in because 'everything was a sea of mud'.[35]

Codenamed Operation Anvil, and beginning on 24 April, the exercise involved the police and several battalions of the British Army. The objective was to cordon off Nairobi 'area by area, whilst the police screened all members of the Kikuyu, Embu and Meru tribes, dividing them into two groups: those suspected of involvement with the Mau-Mau; and non-suspects'.[36] As outlined in a communiqué issued to the press, the aim was 'to re-establish the rule of law in the city and its environs and to restore confidence in those who look to us for protection'. 'You must expect some slight disruption of the many public services in the City,' General Erskine informed the local inhabitants. 'Bus drivers may not be able to report for duty, and you may get your milk rather later than you normally do. We are doing our best to see that this disruption is reduced to the minimum.' 'Operation Anvil was the first time that we were to see our "enemy" up close and personal and probably the first time I gave much thought to what was going on,' related Private Grant who confessed to a general ignorance about the local African population as well as admitting being influenced by the views of the white settlers: 'after all with a few exceptions we were the same nationality, we spoke the same language and they could just as easily have been our family or friends from home'.[37]

'The Jocks did their cordoning job well, and treated the locals with their usual courtesy,' related Rankin, who remembered seeing a Kikuyu woman, who had walked through the cordon 'being gently if uncomprehendingly led back by a Jock who saluted her and said "I'm afraid you can't cross this road at the moment, ma'am."' Having cordoned off their assigned area and rounded up the male inhabitants, the soldiers moved to where screening was done 'at great speed and was apparently pretty arbitrary.' Those the colonial authorities wished to detain were mainly part of the support group or Passive Wing in the Mau Mau structure, responsible for collecting arms and ammunition, oathing supporters and those using 'the usual protection rackets to raise funds' for the Active Wing which went under the name Land Freedom Army who were the forest fighters,' explained Grant.[38]

Those identified as suspected Mau Mau supporters were taken to detention camps, known as 'reception areas', outside Nairobi, while the women and children were either 'repatriated' to the Reserves or, if found to be Mau Mau, sent to prison. 'We left after lunch with a full load of detainees for Mackinnon Road, an old army base north of Mombasa and now turned into a POW camp for want of a better name,' Private Grant informed his father on 6 May, describing the first of several train journeys to the camps. 'We were told we were to transport about 800 but it was well over the 1,000.' On arrival at Mackinnon Road 'the train would stop in a siding adjacent to the camp gates, the detainees were detrained and made to squat on the road outside the camp six abreast, at which point a count was taken and we handed them over to the camp authorities.'[39] With the city emptied of all but loyalist Kikuyu, the operation was deemed a 'success'. Its scale, however, meant that thousands of Africans were detained. Several thousand more were taken to the Reserves, many of whom had never lived there previously, resulting in overcrowding and personal dislocation. Furthermore, allegations of 'inhumanity' in the reception centres provided a damaging legacy.[40]

By late May 1954 the 1st Black Watch was back in the Rift Valley, where patrolling continued.[41] 'It was extremely hard work,' according to Private Grant. 'You would go through a combination of walking through dense trees, which thinned out to an equally dense bamboo belt and then you came to moorland, like the bogs in Scotland. As the altitude increased, so the vegetation changed. There were also deep ravines at the bottom of which were big boulders which had been undercut by the water, creating caves; so you had to go down to check no one was hiding out there.' One assignment was 're-activating' a run-down lookout called Fort Jericho. 'The area of the fort is about 150 ft square, constructed of a bamboo wall all around with a rather rickety watchtower on one corner,' Grant informed his father. 'The inside of the walls are a series of bamboo lean-tos which comprise our living quarters, the roof is made from fronds, grass and anything which could do as thatch and as a result leaks like the devil. The whole fort is surrounded by a ditch that is lined several rows deep with thin split bamboo stakes which are very lethal should you attempt to cross the ditch and are called *panjis*.'[42]

In early June C Company was posted to Narok, both to discourage infiltration into the Masai Reserve by Mau Mau gangs from the Aberdares and Kikuyu Reserve and to deal with those who had already found a safe haven. As recorded by Rankin, the presence of the Pipes and Drums played 'a very considerable part in winning the hearts and minds of the Masai and I am afraid that it was voiced abroad by us that the big drummer had slain in personal combat the leopard with whose skin he was adorned!' Their relationship was also helped by the District Commissioner who had already explained to the Masai that the Scots were not Europeans 'but a fierce warrior tribe who lived in the North of Britain!'[43]

While at Narok their main opponent was Kerito Ole Kesio, who enjoyed a 'Robin Hood' reputation among his followers and became known as General Sungura ('Rabbit') because of his cunning, one of the rabbit's characteristics in African folklore. After his discharge from the King's African Rifles in 1946 for allegedly orchestrating a 'miniature mutiny', his disaffection against colonial authority had intensified when he was asked to pay royalties on trees he was felling for his sawmill business east of Lake Naivasha. After several weeks' patrolling and tracking, and assisted by informants, in early September 1954 'a picked patrol' ambushed Kesio. 'They hid in the back of a lorry which, driven by Kesio's area manager, was to take Kesio supplies at a rendezvous on the Narok-Nairobi road. There they waited for hours until alerted by a whispered "Sasa" (now). In a second the patrol were on their feet shouting "Simama" (stand). But the crawling figure of Kesio was not waiting to "Simama". In a flash he was on his feet, breaking for the bush… only to be shot down by a hail of fire.'[44] 'The manner of his dispatch – betrayal and being shot at point blank range – was somewhat squalid,' observed Rankin. 'Apart from being a ruthless killer, he was admittedly a fine leader who inspired, albeit with fear, the terrorists he led.' A month later Kesio's second-in-command (and former partner in the sawmill business), Mundet Ole Ngapian, was captured by the Masai and handed over to the colonial authorities 'and the number of surrenders increased.'[45]

In mid-November, with the individual companies reunited, 'a rather amusing if exhausting battalion operation' was undertaken which involved bombing an extinct volcano, Mount Longonot, where it was believed that Mau Mau leaders were assembling. 'The plan was that the volcano was to be well and truly bombed after which a Battalion of the KAR were to mop up survivors whilst we (1BW) and the rest of the Brigade cordoned the mountain and cut off any escapers,' explained Rankin. As often happened, the results were negligible, with three rebels killed while others escaped 'in spite of our efforts.'[46]

1955: Operation Hammer: The 'grouse drive'

The Battalion's New Year celebrations were 'somewhat marred' by the death on 1 January 1955 of Private Jimmy Graham and the wounding of another soldier 'as the result of an accidental encounter with a [Kikuyu] Home Guard unit.'[47] Soon after the customary observance of Red Hackle Day, another operation known as Operation Hammer began 'as a follow up to a surrender offer to the gangs.' Describing the operation as 'a huge grouse drive' through the Aberdares involving 'several battalions,' Rankin could not help thinking that it had been 'dreamed up at some office desk', given the logistical problems which 'militated' against its success. As he explained: the plan was 'simply to put every available unit into the Aberdare Forest and sweep it from end to end in an operation lasting two or three weeks.'[48] 'We set out early in the morning with a sharp hoar frost on the ground. After an hour and a half the sun was gaining heat and this, coupled with a steep climb and the altitude, overcame our medical orderly who had to return to base.' 'It was particularly hard going due firstly to our general lack of condition after the Christmas shenanigans,' recalled Private Grant, 'and secondly the altitude around 11,000 feet above sea level.'[49] To add to their labours, the difficult terrain meant there were places where animals could not be used for transportation and 'so we had to carry all our kit plus four days rations. The average load was somewhere in the region of 60lbs, a considerable load at that altitude.'[50]

Despite their best efforts 'across the moorlands, tramping down deep forest clad gorges, crossing rivers innumerable times and sweating and cursing', they failed to encounter any Mau Mau. 'We had three or four days wandering around,' related Lieutenant Adam Gurdon, their efforts rewarded by fishing in streams full of 'the most wonderful trout.' 'Hammer was a hard slog for minimal returns;' observed Private Grant. 'It was never going to be a game changer as Anvil had been and was effectively the last of the big sweeps.' Overall, as Rankin recorded, the operation went 'better than most expected – our Brigade inflicted 40 casualties in one day – but inevitably terrorist activity increased in the Rift Valley'.[51] During the operation members of C Company had been undertaking a 'denying' role from Fort Jerusalem at the top of the Aberdares, and nearby Pencil Slats 'with a discouraging lack of success… As far as we can see the Mau Mau are simply not there, but the animals undoubtedly are!'[52]

D Company then took part in Operation First Flute on Mount Kenya. Operating under the command of the 1st Royal Northumberland Fusiliers, like Hammer the objective was to cordon off part of the forest to prevent the rebels breaking into the settled area. 'If the dearth of Mau Mau was any measure of success, then we were eminently successful: we saw no one.' By early March the Battalion was in Gilgil, where the men could enjoy showers. 'We never had these in our company locations and cleanliness was dependent on a wash in an aluminium basin or an occasional bath begged from a neighbouring farmer!' recorded Rankin.[53]

On Sunday 13 March, shortly before the Battalion's return home, the 'biggest' event recorded in the Church diary was the Service of Dedication of a stained-glass window presented by the Battalion to St Andrew's Church, Nairobi. Unveiled by Lieutenant Colonel Rose, it depicted a Black Watch soldier, flanked by an African with a book in his hand and a white farmer carrying a sheep. On behalf of the congregation 'and indeed of Kenyans of all races', Reverend Calderwood thanked the members of The Black Watch 'for what you have done to help us all during your service here. You have maintained your high traditions as men and as soldiers.'[54] Six days later, a farewell ball took place in Nairobi's City Hall, where the goodbyes including 'a C.O.s parade, a parade for the Brigadier and finally a farewell parade for the C in C followed by a drinks party'. Reflecting on their service in Kenya, Rose described it as 'a wonderful experience for all of us. We had occupied and restored order in the Kikuyu Reserve, we had given assistance and security to the Settlers in the White Highlands and we had started a strategic road over the Aberdares.'[55]

The Mau Mau uprising officially lasted until October 1956, when the capture of the movement's 'titular' head, Dedan Kimathi, signified the conclusion of the military campaign.[56] As was increasingly evident, however, Britain's colonial empire was coming to an end. In December 1963 Kenya achieved its independence, becoming the 19th member of the Commonwealth and the 112th member of the United Nations. Jomo Kenyatta, imprisoned between 1952 and 1959 for alleged links with the Mau Mau, became Prime Minister and then President.

As time passed, the methods used to suppress the Mau Mau, involving alleged mistreatment and severe beatings, led to the military operation in Kenya being known as the 'Dirty War'.[57] On reflection, Peter Grant admitted that the colonial authorities had probably 'over-reacted' by sanctioning the detention of so many men in camps. 'The idea was that they were rounded up and then hooded informers would identify who was Mau Mau, but invariably the informers were settling personal scores and so the system broke down.' He also emphasised the difference between the actions of the military and the police. 'I think people now see the whole as one whereas the army and police were quite different.' Looking back Grant recollected witnessing only one instance of 'near' brutality. 'We had unloaded about 1,000 suspects on a train line when soldiers from another regiment started laying into some African detainees 'with rifle butts, but were quickly halted by the NCOs.' Compared with an estimated 200 killed and nearly 600 wounded British military, police and Kikuyu Home Guard, Mau Mau fatalities exceeded 12,000. Over 100,000 Kenyans were subjected to 'screening' and detained in appalling conditions.[58]

In June 2009, a compensation claim was lodged against the British Government in the High Court in London, demanding a full enquiry into allegations of castration, beatings and rape. The case led to the declassification of several thousand documents held by the Foreign and Commonwealth Office containing information which could embarrass the British Government, other governments, the military and security forces.[59] In October 2012 the High Court gave the claimants permission to claim damages. The ruling, described as 'historic' by the complainants' lawyer, paved the way for further claims against the British Government.[60]

On 2 April 1955 the 1st Black Watch left Kenya. The journey by train from Gilgil was unexpectedly disrupted when, as a prank, an officer of the King's Royal Rifle Corps threw what he thought was a smoke grenade into the compartment of the departing officers. It was in fact 'a mob dispersal grenade' seriously injuring Major Scott Macdonald and Lieutenant Brian Harries and wounding others. Second Lieutenant Rankin had a lucky escape. 'When I took off my kilt I found a very clean hole had been punched through two pleats. The cleanness of the hole indicated that a piece of shrapnel had been travelling very fast at the time and had missed my leg by the proverbial fraction of an inch!' The next few hours of the 16-hour train journey were 'pretty chaotic,' tablecloths from the dining car being used to bandage the wounded. With the smell of smoke filling the air, the officers took off their kilts, which had absorbed the smoke 'very efficiently', and hung out of the train's windows to air them.[61]

At Mombasa the Battalion boarded the troopship, *Empire Halladale*. As Rankin admitted, conditions were more comfortable for the officers and sergeants than for the soldiers 'whose sleeping accommodation lay below decks and was oppressively hot at nights. Tempers became frayed and fights broke out over nothing.' 'It's too damned hot to write,' Private Grant noted in his diary. 'I am soaked through but we are at least out in the briny.'[62] As usual, there was a variety of entertainments: 'almost nightly cinemas, tombola, talent competitions, a tug o' war, a county fair, a ship's concert and daily recitals from the Band and the Pipes and Drums.'[63]

After three weeks at sea the Battalion reached Glasgow. 'The Pipe band was on the main deck, playing "Sailing up the Clyde. Sailing up the Clyde, to your ain fireside,"' related Private Mitchell. 'It was sad too. Nearly seventy Black Watch soldiers had died in Korea; three in Kenya. So it was sad for their families seeing the Battalion coming home. Their loved ones were not coming with them.'[64] The Colonel of the Regiment, General McMicking, immediately came on board and read a message from the Queen Mother congratulating the Battalion 'on the fine way you have carried out your duties overseas.' Lieutenant Colonel Rose – in Rankin's opinion regarded by his junior officers as 'a first cousin (if not closer!) to God' – was shortly to relinquish command to Lieutenant Colonel Henry Conyers (Mick) Baker Baker, so the soldiers lined the ship's rails and gave him 'a great send off'.[65]

Travelling by train to Crail in Fifeshire the 1st Black Watch occupied the barracks briefly used by the 2nd Black Watch before being posted to British Guiana. 'It was back to a very new and different battalion', commented Private Grant, 'many new faces from the Jocks to the CO with very little to do.'[66] For the first time since 1912, the Battalion provided a company, commanded by Major Tony Lithgow, for the Royal Guard at Ballater. 'Fitting them out in No.1 Dress proved to be a complicated business as it consists of a pool of items issued to regiments in turn for such ceremonial occasions, and being in such short supply the jackets are not allowed to be altered. We were therefore faced with the problem of finding men to fit the jackets rather than vice versa, which is a sad state of affairs in these modern times.'[67] As previously, their duties ranged from meeting the Royal Family on arrival, to leading them to Church at Crathie where Queen Victoria had asserted her right to worship as Queen of Scotland every Sunday. A major commitment remained providing beaters for the grouse shooting and attending the Ghillies Ball. 'You were right close to the Royals, they knew you by name,' observed Sergeant Colin Harrison, who danced the 'Dashing White Sergeant' with the Queen Mother. Although no alcohol was permitted during the Royal Family's presence 'as soon as they left at 10 p.m. the bar opened,' observed Lieutenant Gurdon who took over as adjutant in August 1956, 'and the party began.'[68]

1954–56: 'No one quite knew what or where British Guiana was'

After two years in Germany and a brief stay in Britain, in September 1954 the 2nd Black Watch arrived in British Guiana, ceded to Britain by the Dutch in 1814. In the twentieth century rising nationalism had created tensions among the multi-racial population. The general election of April 1953 was won by the left-wing People's Progressive Party (PPP), co-founded by Cheddi Jagan, of Indo-Guyanese origin, and his American wife.[69] Alarmed at the PPP's manifesto, which opposed British colonial rule, in October the British Government suspended the constitution and imposed a state of emergency, which included establishing a military presence. 'No one quite knew what or where British Guiana was, but that did not really matter. Our ignorance instead gave rise to rapturous speculations: galloping pampas with miles of horses, crocodile-fishing and barracuda-hunting; soft-skinned, grass-skirted hybrids; swigs of rum at 1/4d per gallon.' However, 'titbits' of information dulled expectations: 'rainy seasons; no roads to speak of; a muddy beach of some length; and one lonely bath for the whole colony.' As the soldiers soon realised: 'it was not for nothing that the French had Devil's Island just next door.'[70]

With Battalion Headquarters and a contingent stationed in

Balaclava Barracks in the capital Georgetown, the remainder was based upriver at Atkinson Field Air Base Timehri. Communications were virtually non-existent, consisting of one metalled road running from Georgetown east to the border with Dutch Guiana and a semi-metalled road to the airport. With hardly any telephones, radio communication 'was particularly demanding'. 'In case of any trouble,' related Second Lieutenant David Steavenson, 'control of the airport to plan a speedy exit or get reinforcements was considered essential.' Second Lieutenant David Wilson believed, however, that instead of 'the normal procedure of rolling out barbed wire', law and order could more effectively be restored by 'parading the Pipes and Drums so everybody would stop and listen!'[71]

Conditions for the officers and men were basic. 'The house I had to occupy was on stilts at the edge of the jungle, sparsely furnished with little more than table, chairs and a bed,' related Captain Andy Watson, the Battalion's adjutant. Reveille was at 6 a.m. and the soldiers generally worked until midday. 'There seemed to be a lot of drill parades,' observed Private Bob Ritchie, who had joined the 2nd Black Watch in 1953, 'then swimming in the afternoon. The soldiers would get into Georgetown for weekend leaves.' 'One thing which struck me as strange,' recalled Steavenson, 'was that although we were in the middle of the jungle, the officers would always dress for dinner, not just ordinary mess kit, but white tie. It was of course always for "good form".'[72] Until they acclimatised, the men suffered 'all sorts of queer ailments.' One member of the Pipes and Drums developed jaundice, while another's face 'swelled alarmingly but he only had a gum boil'. Fortunately, unlike the country inland, there was little risk of malaria.[73]

'This is a very interesting country and the contrasts are very marked,' Second Lieutenant Malcolm Davidson informed his grandmother. 'Georgetown is a ghastly town. There are many good well-built houses but they lie side by side and intermingled with Indian shacks of horrible filth.' Assuring her that there was 'absolutely no trouble here whatsoever', he confidently claimed that 'so long as there are troops here there will not be the slightest chance of it. The local population are enormously kind to us all'.[74] Despite the heat and the difficult terrain, patrols were sent 'to every part of the country from the Pakaraimas to the Kanukus, from the Waini to the Courentyne'. Assisted by the British Guiana Volunteer Force, the soldiers also undertook expeditions into the Rupununi river region and to New Amsterdam, south of Georgetown. 'I have had a very interesting week,' Davidson was telling his parents in late December. 'We set off on Tuesday last at 4.30 in the morning arrived at a town called Bartica.' Having located some gold mines, abandoned in 1920, they spent two days training 'and being taught how to make everything for ourselves out of wood by a guide we got called Milton… We learned to hunt and trap make beds from bamboo and all about anna[conda]s and snakes.' In contrast, Christmas 1954 'in BG' consisted of 'innumerable processions with Steel bands (made of oil drums) and rather drunk native population.'[75]

The world's widest single drop waterfall, the Kaieteur Falls, was a popular attraction. Having heard that a party of Argyll & Sutherland Highlanders had climbed the trail up the side of the Falls in a record forty-five minutes, Private Robert Howat determined to set a different record by swimming across the Potaro river above the Falls. Although he went into the river well above the 'lip', by the time he had reached the opposite side, the current had taken him to within five yards of the edge of the Falls. Unable to get out of the water because of the jungle growth on the bank, he worked his way further upstream before attempting to return to the opposite bank. Caught again in the current, he was swept even closer to the edge. 'Miraculously he was able to grab hold of some thick weed', at which point some schoolgirls saw him. Together with a local Amerindian, who found some rope, they pulled the exhausted Howat from the water.[76]

Another feat was climbing Mount Roraima, the highest peak of the Pakaraima Mountains, in the south-west bordering Venezuela and Brazil, believed to be the inspiration for Sir Arthur Conan Doyle's *Lost World*. In April 1955, Second Lieutenants David Wilson, Hugh Hunter and Colin Campbell undertook a month-long expedition. Nearing the summit 'the first thing we realized was that we could never say that we were at the top. This was no ordinary mountain with a well defined peak. The plateau itself stretches for sixteen miles… it was like walking on another planet.'[77]

By the end of the posting, as Davidson had predicted there had been 'absolutely no trouble' with the local population. News, however, of impending disbandment 'overcast' their departure 'with the sort of dismay that would be caused by a diagnosis of an incurable and fatal disease in an apparently healthy man', observed *The Red Hackle*. In April 1956 the Battalion returned to Edinburgh. Having organised a '73rd Reunion' in June for members 'past and present', on 1 October the 2nd Battalion was disbanded.[78] For the next fifty years, The Black Watch had only one battalion.

A signaller comes running
To the tented officers' mess;
An urgent call? – a cry for aid?
It's difficult to guess.

The message is handed over
From G.H.Q., it hails:
'Officers attending the Limuru Ball
Must definitely wear tails!'[79]

19

What The Black Watch Does is News

What The Black Watch does is news any day of the week.[1]

Have they told ye, Hielan' laddie,
Since you hae been away',
They've demolished a' the barracks
O' the gallant Forty-Twa?[2]

1956: The four-power city, Berlin

In January 1956 the 1st Black Watch joined the British garrison in Berlin, where Britain, the United States, France and the Soviet Union retained an occupying presence. Stationed at Wavell Barracks, a regular duty continued to be guarding Spandau prison where those condemned of war crimes at Nuremberg were serving out their sentences. Each occupying country guarded the prison for a month. Interaction between soldiers and prisoners was forbidden, but on one occasion Rudolph Hess handed Private Jim Anderson a stray feather from a Red Hackle.[3] On 30 September 1956 Grand Admiral Karl Dönitz completed his ten-year sentence. 'Nobody telephoned the press for a picture scoop of Doenitz walking out,' wrote journalist Philip Howard, undertaking his National Service with The Black Watch. 'For one thing it would not have occurred to us. For another thing it would have seemed unregimental. And the Spandau telephones would not have worked anyway.' In May 1957 Walther Funk, serving a life sentence, was released early due to ill health, leaving Albert Speer and Baldur von Schirach serving twenty-year sentences, and Hess imprisoned for life. While Schirach and Speer 'cultivated their gardens in the exercise yard with a good show of flowers and vegetables... Hess would not garden, but sat slumped on a three-legged stool in the sun.'[4]

A decade since the end of the Second World War, Berlin was considered a 'good posting', observed Second Lieutenant Duncan Cameron, who had chosen a commission in The Black Watch because his namesake and great-great-great uncle had commanded the Battalion during the Crimean War. 'It was long enough after the war for people no longer to be prejudiced against Germany. Although almost nothing had been done to clear the World War 2 damage in East Berlin, it included the old cultural part of the city and we could cross freely to attend concerts, ballet and opera.'[5] The soldiers also enjoyed the sporting facilities built for the 1936 Olympic Games. Since space for manoeuvres was limited, training took place at Sennelager in northern West Germany.

In the autumn of 1957 the Pipes and Drums and Regimental Band toured the United States. 'With the aplomb of seasoned world travellers, the pipers and drummers handled their TV appearances and news interviews with matchless tact and diplomacy.'[6] Having weathered rising East–West tensions following the Soviet Union's invasion of Hungary the previous year, in November the 1st Black Watch returned to Edinburgh, its first posting to 'Auld Reekie' since 1911. A highpoint in the Battalion's sporting achievements was the athletic team winning the Army Inter-Unit Athletics Championship at Aldershot in July 1958; it was 'the first time that the name of a Scottish regiment appeared on the championship shield since the competition started in 1920,' recorded Cameron, a distance runner and one of the team's forty athletes.[7] After a year in Edinburgh, in November 1958 the Battalion sailed for Cyprus. The journey on board the *Empire Fowey* was 'strangely flavoured with visions of Dunkirk and of transport in the First World War.'[8]

1958: Cyprus and EOKA

Under British administration since 1878 – when Sergeant Samuel McGaw, VC, 'the stoutest man in the Forty Twa', had died of 'heat apoplexy' – Cyprus had been declared a Crown Colony in 1925.[9] Thirty years later British authority was being challenged by the Enosis (Union) movement, whose goal was unification with Greece. Britain's refusal to consider any alteration to Cyprus's political status had resulted in the formation of a nationalist organisation, the EOKA, led by Colonel Georgios Grivas, a former Greek army officer of Cypriot birth.[10] Although the Greek Government had remained aloof from the growing conflict, in August 1954 Field Marshal Alexander Papagos, under pressure from the leader of the Greek-Cypriot community, Archbishop Makarios III, brought the issue before the UN General Assembly. In the ensuing debate, Turkey, a member of NATO since 1952, opposed any proposal for Cyprus which would result in a union with Greece, declaring that if Britain withdrew from Cyprus political control should revert to Turkey as previously under the Ottoman Empire.[11] In an attempt to reduce support for the Union movement, Makarios was exiled to the Seychelles in March 1956, whereupon Grivas took control of both military and political campaigns, while the demand for Enosis was replaced by calls for independence.

By the time The Black Watch reached Cyprus, EOKA activity had been contained, but a state of emergency still existed, with demonstrable hostility between the Greek and Turkish communities. 'You knew exactly which house was pro-Greek or Turk because it flew either the Greek or Turkish flag,' related Lieutenant Cameron. 'The doors were either red to indicate allegiance to the Turkish flag or light blue to show loyalty to Greece,' observed Captain Watson, who had returned to the 1st Battalion after the 2nd's disbandment.[12]

Garrisoned at Limni, near the copper mines and the north-western town of Polis, 'the camp was thick with mud and we lived in eight-man tents,' recorded Private Christopher Rose who had joined up as a volunteer in 1957: 'Winter dress was very relaxed and there was virtually no "bull". No parades either. No parade ground… The field latrines took some getting used to.' A bonus to their existence was the Indian catering staff. 'Because the regiment had a long association with India, we showed no surprise, when our caterers from the Empire joined us.' Ghulam Nabi immediately 'set up shop': 'At reveille, his employees did the rounds of our tents, serving buns and tea, for a small price. This meant we didn't have to go off to breakfast. On patrol the soldiers were even more grateful when, 'dying of thirst... suddenly, out of nowhere would appear one of Mr Nabi's *chai wallahs*, with a tea urn on his back. Gunga Din be praised!'[13] 'Superb' weather on 25 December made it hard to realise that it was Christmas 'but the goat-herds with their flutes and the ancient wooden ox-drawn ploughs were a biblical reminder.'[14]

In the New Year the Battalion took part in Operation Mare's Nest in the Troodos mountains in western Cyprus, 'to carry death and destruction to the mountain stronghold of the terrorist organisation.'[15] Involving three other battalions, reaching their destination seemed more perilous than the operation. 'We set off in a large number of vehicles to our first staging post, the Rest House at Stavros. The journey to this charming place was terrifying. Most of the way was over roads only just wide enough to take a 3-ton truck and never were we without a big drop to one side or the other. To those who had nerves of steel it must have been most enjoyable as the scenery was exceptional.' Predictably some vehicles fell 'victim to the atrocious conditions,' leaving the men temporarily stranded.[16] The attempt to land troops by helicopter – 'a new experience for us' – had to be abandoned because of high winds 'except for one luckless fellow', described by Rose, 'who had been the first to descend, without his rifle. He spent the night alone on the targeted mountain before being relieved the next morning.' The 'luckless fellow' was Lance Corporal Bruton, who had 'nothing but the clothes he stood up in and a bar of chocolate.'[17]

Setting up camp was also a challenge. 'The only possible site was a knife-edged ridge overlooking one of the villages we were to watch. We overcame the lack of flat ground by following the local example of digging terraces into the side of the hill.' Having established themselves, the soldiers began sweeping their operational area. 'This consisted of a large hill spur towering above us. We soon found a large number of unoccupied caves and two old hides which contained various odds and ends of clothing and cooking equipment. Although instinctively suspicious of our area we did not find any terrorists.'[18] After two weeks the Battalion returned to Limni.

Meanwhile, peace talks were taking place. On 11 February 1959 a settlement was reached in Zurich between representatives of the Greek and Turkish governments regarding their respective Cypriot communities. A week later an agreement was made between Britain, Turkey, Greece and the two Cypriot groups. Grivas went into voluntary exile in Greece. With the official ending of the Emergency, Makarios was released, returning to Cyprus to a rapturous welcome in Nicosia on 1 March 1959, at which The Black Watch provided a Guard of Honour. The agreements paved the way for the drafting of a constitution which would culminate in Cyprus's independence.

In hindsight, Private Rose admitted having had no sympathy for the EOKA. 'Our army had suffered a lot at the hands of the terrorists and our job was to put an end to that.' He considered, however, that their own behaviour was perhaps 'a bit over the top, sometimes. Even aggressive. Whenever we searched a church (a favourite EOKA hiding place for weapons), for example, our Bren gunner placed his weapon on the pulpit to cover the worshippers. And when we were on patrol, we never thought twice about helping ourselves to whatever fruit we found in a farmer's field. One night we found ourselves stranded in a field and slept there. In the morning we discovered we were in the middle of a watermelon field, so that took care of breakfast. I also remember taking my rifle and going through orange groves, plucking fruit as the mood took me.' Since they were 'not much kinder' to the animals, they were ordered 'to try to stop driving over so many animals. I think there was a competition amongst the drivers to see who had the highest kill rate in a month.'[19]

In the spring of 1959 the Battalion moved to Camp Xeros, near Lefka

(Lefke). 'We were still living in tents,' continued Rose, 'but now we had a parade ground and donned khaki drill to look smart again.' Occasionally, provided they wore 'trews and blue bonnets', they were allowed into the town. 'We sampled the local beer (quite awful) and local wine (even worse), but both were very cheap and affordable to the ill-paid National Service soldiers.' A nearby mobile dental caravan proved 'a big draw.'[20] After six months, 'without a real break from soldiering, ... the powers-that-be decided to give us some rest and relaxation in Nicosia, the Island's capital, one company at a time. After the first visit by the Black Watch, the commander of the Royal Military Police declared solemnly that in his entire military career, he had never witnessed so [much] damage inflicted by a single company of soldiers. Well, the Black Watch did have a reputation to maintain.'[21]

When the situation became more peaceful, their lives 'improved'. Beginning their working day in camp at 5 a.m., they finished at lunchtime. 'Leave, too, was granted,' continued Rose. 'The battalion created its own beach where one could stay overnight, get moderately drunk and spend the day swimming and sunbathing. No swimsuits or anything. No women either.' Known as the Beach Camp, it was set up by Captain David Severn: 'each weekend some 200 Officers and men were able to camp in tents by the most beautiful bay and drink to our hearts' content,' related Lieutenant Colin Innes, 'until at 2300 hrs David ordered that a bugle be sounded and everyone had to spend the next five minutes in the sea.' Severn was also responsible for constructing 'an excellent theatre in the hills and we were able to watch Pathé News and some very funny films.'[22] As the last British Army unit to arrive during the Emergency, The Black Watch was chosen as one of three battalions to remain as a permanent garrison, moving in late 1959 to Alexander Barracks, Dhekelia, one of two Sovereign Base areas where Britain retained its authority, the other being Akrotiri. 'Here there were brand new barracks... the troubles were over and it was more or less a return to routine garrison life,' observed Rose. On 25 March 1960 the Battalion, now under the command of Lieutenant Colonel Angus Irwin, provided a Guard of Honour for Earl Mountbatten during his visit as Chief of the Defence

Staff: 'From start to finish it was a success. The harassing period was the preparations for it.'[23] Five months later Cyprus became independent on 16 August 1960. Makarios assumed office as President, The Black Watch again providing a Guard of Honour. Although life continued as before with a combination of training, ceremonial duties and sport, 'the most noticeable impression is one of greatly increased friendliness of the Cypriots'.[24]

1961–62: 'Wind of change'

Leaving Cyprus in December 1961, the 1st Black Watch's return to Britain coincided with a period of social upheaval, the decade memorable as 'the swinging sixties'. As Prime Minister Harold Macmillan had stated in 1960 in reference to the African continent, a 'wind of change' was blowing. With the independence of Britain's former colonies, the requirements of Britain's Armed Forces were diminishing. National Service had been discontinued in 1960, the British Army reverting to a fully professional force, over 300,000 in number, supported by the Territorial Army. By the end of the decade the number of regulars had almost halved, the reduction achieved by the amalgamation or disbandment of regiments and/or battalions.[25] In Black Watch circles the move was resisted. Before handing over as Colonel of the Regiment in March 1960, Major General McMicking had drafted a memorandum which emphasised 'the value of the Regimental System', highlighting how 'the strength of the whole has been based on the individuality of the Regiments contained therein.' Pointing out that the Regimental System was 'the only aspect of the British Army which is universally admired by foreign armies', he continued: 'to jettison it would be a betrayal not only of the past but of our national characteristics, especially in The Highlands.'[26] Nevertheless on 7 February 1961 the Seaforth Highlanders and the Queen's Own Cameron Highlanders were merged to form the Queen's Own Highlanders (Seaforth and Camerons); The Black Watch retained its independence, as did The Gordon Highlanders and The Argyll & Sutherland Highlanders.[27]

Having been briefly stationed at Barton Stacey Camp in Hampshire, where American troops had assembled in June 1944, in April 1962 the Battalion moved to Knook Camp, near Warminster. As the Demonstration Battalion at the School of Infantry 'we were at the behest of the staff of the School of Infantry to show soldiers what new weapons had been produced. That was one of the excitements,' recorded Andy Watson, promoted major in 1961. 'We got the equipment before other soldiers.' 'We were in the public eye and the Jocks lived up to that,' related Private Ronnie Proctor. Training in a newly produced armoured personnel carrier (APC), the prototype Armoured Fighting Vehicle, known as FV432 or the Trojan, the soldiers enjoyed being 'at the biting edge of technology in the British Army'.[28] While one platoon served as the Demonstration Platoon at the Mons Officer Cadet School in Aldershot, another was at Hythe, the Small Arms Wing, and another at Netheravon, which housed the Support Weapons Wing of the School of Infantry. A highlight of the peacetime calendar remained the inter-battalion and inter-regimental sporting competitions. Recollecting his time as Sergeant, Colin Harrison praised his 'very strong platoon' which won 'everything'.[29]

In 1961 the old depot in Queen's Barracks, Perth, was closed as a training depot, the regimental headquarters moving out in 1962. The Black Watch temporarily shared a training depot with the Argyll & Sutherland Highlanders in Stirling Castle before moving to Fort George and then, in 1964, to a new Highland Brigade depot for all four Highland Regiments at Gordon Barracks in Bridge of Don, north of Aberdeen.[30] The Regiment had already found a home in Perth for its archives and artefacts at Balhousie Castle. Formerly owned by the Earls of Kinnoull (the 12th Earl having served in The Black Watch in Egypt in the 1880s), the castle was opened as the regimental headquarters and museum in 1962.

The year was also memorable for being The Queen Mother's Silver Jubilee as Colonel-in-Chief of the Regiment. On 2 September The Black Watch paraded before her in Perth. Also on parade were the 4/5th and 6/7th Territorial Battalions, representatives from the

Affiliated Regiments, the Junior Leaders and Cadets 'and a most impressive turn-out of the members of The Black Watch Association.'[31] Five years later the Territorial Army was reorganised, the 4/5th and the 6/7th becoming part of a new Regiment, the 51st Highland Volunteers, 'so called to keep alive the number made famous by the Highland Division.'[32]

1963: North America, an 'historic tour'

In September 1963 the Pipes and Drums, Military Band and Highland Dancers of The Black Watch again toured North America. Their itinerary took them to fifty-one cities at which they gave sixty-five performances 'seen by countless thousands.'[33] 'In Milwaukee we were furious to find ourselves advertised as the Argyll and Sutherland Highlanders, and soon put that right and in Chicago we played our first stage show, quite unrehearsed, to a capacity crowd.' During the tour the British Ambassador, David Ormsby-Gore, had 'discreetly encouraged' President John F. Kennedy, whose interest in piping related to his Irish ancestry, to invite The Black Watch to perform at the White House. Arriving in Washington on 13 November, 'the President made a very pleasant welcoming speech, outlining the Regiment's previous connections with America in his usual jocular manner, and paying some nice tributes to our traditions.' Invited to sit with the President and the First Lady, Major Mike Wingate-Gray, commanding the detachment, had 'one Kennedy child on one knee and one on the other.' After performing on the White House lawn, refreshments were served. 'There can seldom have been an odder occasion in Regimental annals, 100 soldiers having tea or, in most cases, whiskies and sodas, in the State Dining Room at the White House, entertained by several of the Presidential aides… the President and Mrs Kennedy were kindness itself, behaving in a most free and natural way, with the children running at their feet.' 'I don't know when I have seen The President enjoy himself more,' the First Lady later wrote in thanks.[34] The only moment of tension, recalled Private John Nicoll, was when Wingate-Gray presented the President with a dirk, at which point his security men became 'somewhat perturbed!'[35]

On 22 November, President Kennedy was assassinated in Dallas. Wingate-Gray received an immediate invitation from Jacqueline Kennedy for some pipers to play at his funeral. Pipe Major Anderson and eight pipers flew at once from Knoxville, Tennessee, to Washington. Briefed on the funeral arrangements, Anderson realised that the funeral pace 'was laid down as 100 paces to the minute which accords neither with our funeral march nor with any British marching step'. He therefore spent the night practising 'a selection of four-fours and four-twos to obtain the right speed'. On 25 November as the Black Watch pipers marched forward, President Kennedy's cortège was slowly driven the mile from the White House to the steps of Washington Cathedral. The Regiment's involvement was the only time foreign soldiers had participated in an American state ceremonial occasion. As a result, the end of the tour was, the second-in-command observed, 'more widely publicised and more historic than any of the participants could have dreamt… and one which it would not be presumptuous to say, made the name of the Regiment known to the American man-in-the-street as no other British Army regiment has been known.'[36]

1964–68: 'Endlessly on exercises'

In April 1964 the Battalion moved to Minden on the River Weser, once more forming part of the British Army of the Rhine. 'We were endlessly on exercises,' related Major Adam Gurdon. Exercise Leander in April 1966 was designed to practise water crossings: 'the same sort of idea as using the Buffaloes during the Rhine Crossing in 1945,' as Corporal Proctor commented. Another exercise was Quick Train. 'If you got "Quick Train" over the radio, it meant the Battalion had to appear on the square as soon as possible. Within two hours, we had to collect everybody up and get into our vehicles in full kit,' explained Captain Colin Innes.[37]

Lacking large enough facilities for exercises in West Germany, the

British Army turned to the Libyan desert. 'Apart from Canada, there was nowhere else where we had the ability to conduct exercises over a large area,' explained Major Watson, who recognised the huge task facing the Quartermaster, Major Duff Henderson, when The Black Watch became the first battalion to undertake exercises in Libya in May 1965. Returning the following year in June on Exercise Sea-bird, their exercises had 'added interest': the armoured personnel carrier. 'It was a major effort transporting a battalion's worth of APCs from Minden, down to Marseilles, across the Mediterranean to Malta and on to Tobruk,' continued Watson. 'The idea of transporting so much equipment was that it would be left at El Adem airfield in mothballs for future training.' Bivouacking under the stars and carrying out exercises in the desert the soldiers realised they were operating along tracks once used by the Eighth Army. An unusual distraction was running 'a miniature zoo' whose inmates were tortoises and chameleons. Although 'great value' was gained from the experience, the overthrow of King Idris in a military coup in 1969 put an end to Britain's military presence in Libya.[38]

Almost immediately on returning to Minden, the Battalion was ordered to undertake a six-month unaccompanied tour in Cyprus. After independence in 1960, violence had broken out between the Turkish and Greek Cypriots which President Makarios had been unable to contain. General Grivas' return to take command of the Greek Cypriot National Guard in 1964 had done nothing to allay the Turkish Cypriots' fears that union with Greece remained the ultimate objective. On 15 February 1964 representatives from Britain and Cyprus urged action by the UN Security Council. On 4 March the UN unanimously recommended establishing a United Nations Force In Cyprus (UNFICYP), which became operational on 27 March 1964.[39] Included in the UN force was a platoon from D Company, commanded by Second Lieutenant Paul Sugden, a deployment known as Operation Rocker. On 26 February, the platoon became the first in The Black Watch to wear the UN cap badge 'though certain individuals may have worn it before'. A request to wear the

Red Hackle with the beret was denied, but Major General Michael Carver, Deputy Commander of UN forces, did permit a tartan patch to be worn behind the UN badge.[40]

In October 1966 the whole Battalion deployed, Lieutenant Colonel Earle Nicoll taking command of a detachment at Polymedia camp in Limassol district, while his second-in-command, Major Watson, was appointed district commander, Paphos district. 'In the Paphos district at Ktima, the Turks had been confined into little enclaves at Polis, Paphos itself and Mandria. They lived in tunnels with absolutely no facilities and were being threatened with being pushed almost into the sea,' related Watson, who tried (unsuccessfully) to persuade the Greek Cypriots to let the Turks use a basketball pitch in No Man's Land for recreation.[41]

On 26 January 1967 a group of Turkish Cypriots stopped and searched a bus transporting Greek Cypriots through the town of Kophinou (Kofinou) in the Larnaca district. 'The Greek Cypriot majority in the island was furious and bent on revenge,' related Nicoll. 'The Greek National Guard, commanded in Nicosia by General Grivas, was deployed to Kophinou and the United Nations forces alerted for trouble.' To reinforce the nearby UN police post, which came within the Swedish Army Control Area, two Black Watch platoons based at Limassol were called in. 'The situation was very tense', commented Lieutenant Hamish Gibson, the Battalion's intelligence officer. 'It caught us completely by surprise.'[42] Departing in the middle of the night, in pouring rain, 'by 0600 hrs they were in position blocking any entry into the village. The situation was saved at that time', commented Nicoll, 'but Kophinou remained a potentially dangerous area.' The force was subsequently reinforced by additional Black Watch platoons and by a troop of the 5th Royal Inniskilling Dragoon Guards from their base at Zygi. With the exception of administrative affairs, Force K, as the contingent became known, came under the command of the Swedes.[43]

'This job was no easy task. The Jocks were sort of "pig-in-the-middle": trying to stop the Greek and Turkish Cypriots from fighting one another,' explained Nicoll. 'Day after day in quite bad and cold weather, the Jocks sat out in their sentry posts.' 'It is all very exciting and morale is high. We are determined to keep Peace. Even if we have to fight to do it!' enthused the author of *The Red Hackle*'s General notes. When the Colonel of the Regiment, Brigadier Baker Baker visited Cyprus in early March, affairs in Kophinou 'were humming steadily throughout' making it 'unlikely that a Colonel of the Regiment had ever seen so much of the Battalion in the Field.'[44]

'One other incident blew up in April in our last month in Cyprus,' continued Nicoll. 'This was at Mari… here the Greek Cypriot National Guard had been moving through the village when it was claimed to have been fired on by Turkish Freedom Fighters on the bluff heights around the village. The Turks took a great pounding in this incident and were heavily outnumbered and outgunned.' A UN force was again deployed, with troops from the Kophinou area dispatched to block the roads leading to and from Mari village. 'This time the situation got very nasty and the National Guard fired many rounds of ammunition at the Turks, who for their part offered little resistance. Danish soldiers were called in to reinforce the Black Watch and gradually the Greek National Guard withdrew, leaving the UN forces commanding the situation but once again in a bare hillside observation post in very bad stormy weather.'[45] On 5 May 1967, The Black Watch left Cyprus, Brigadier Mike Harbottle, Commander of UNFICYP, praising the soldiers for their performance. In hindsight, Watson realised their limitations; 'It was very difficult because, as part of the UN force, we were there for peacekeeping. We weren't allowed to take offensive action.'[46]

The situation in Cyprus remained troubled. To bolster Turkish-Cypriot resistance, the Turkish government had begun assisting them by what Watson described as a 'clandestine reinforcement of Turkish soldiers who arrived in Cyprus by sea at night'. In November 1967 the Greek National Guard moved into Kophinou and Ayios Theodorus bringing Greece and Turkey 'to the brink of war'.[47] On 15 July 1974, Makarios was deposed in a military coup, backed by Greece and aided by a faction of EOKA and the Cypriot National Guard. Five days later Turkish forces invaded northern Cyprus. Having initially been deployed across the island, UNFICYP's role became confined to policing a neutral buffer zone indicated by a 'green line' (originally drawn on the map in a green crayon) from Famagusta in the east to Limni in the west.[48] In 1983 the Turkish Republic of Northern Cyprus declared its independence although this was only recognised by Turkey.

Back in Minden, a composite platoon of volunteers, commanded by Second Lieutenant Dick Parata from New Zealand, was detached to reinforce the Argyll & Sutherland Highlanders for its deployment to Aden for an emergency tour from June to November 1967.[49] The Black Watch returned to Scotland in 1968, taking up quarters at Ritchie Camp, Kirknewton. Named after the Regiment's former Colonel, Sir Neil Ritchie, the soldiers were disappointed to find that they were near a small village with only one pub 'in the back of beyond'.[50] In the autumn one company again provided the Royal Guard at Ballater. The rest of the Battalion was busy preparing for the Edinburgh Tattoo, training and fitness exercises, while B Company had a 'stimulating experience' on Exercise Vacuum in Canada, working alongside Canadian and US troops.[51] Christmas 1968 was celebrated with 'the traditional welter of Concerts, Dances and Parties.'[52]

The following year the Battalion, now under the command of Lieutenant Colonel Andy Watson, carried out exercises in jungle warfare in Malaysia. 'Gurkhas played the role of the enemy and the action took place in the challenging environment of the Malayan jungle,' explained Second Lieutenant Hugh Rose, commissioned into the Regiment in 1968 in the footsteps of his father, Lieutenant Colonel David Rose.[53] One minor difficulty was that the maps 'bore no relation to the ground whatsoever' because of all the logging and cultivation which had taken place since they were printed. After four-and-a-half weeks' intensive training, riots in Kuala Lumpur and other parts of Malaysia meant the main Battalion exercise had to be cancelled; instead four separate Company exercises were held in two locations near their camp; 'although shorter and less ambitious' they demonstrated 'how much had been achieved in the previous training period.'[54]

On 1 June 1969 Brigadier Bernard Fergusson became Colonel of the Regiment. 'In all seriousness I am very proud to have done so,' he informed Eric Linklater. 'The succession within my own recollection is Maxwell, Cameron, Wauchope, Wavell, Ritchie, McMicking, Arbuthnott, Baker Baker, and now me. It is no mean line to which to succeed.'[55]

The Black Watch's next posting, in August, was to reinforce the garrison on the Rock of Gibraltar (minus two companies which remained in Scotland and, initially, the Military Band which spent a week in Colombia, South America). For much of the tour, the deputy fortress commander was former Black Watch officer, Brigadier Mike Wingate-Gray. 'The other battalion was the Royal Fusiliers who were at the other end of the Rock at the tip, we were on the airfield in barracks which we shared with the RAF,' related Watson. 'We had to do a lot of guards and parades. The Pipes and Drums were often performing at Government House.'[56]

Since the 4th Black Watch's deployment to Gibraltar during the Second World War, the Crown Colony had been integrated into Britain's administrative system. In 1950 legislative and executive councils were created. In 1964 the Gibraltar Constitution was introduced, followed by the Gibraltar Constitution Order, stipulating that its sovereign status would not be changed without the consent of its 26,000 inhabitants. In response, Spain's military dictator, General Francisco Franco, closed the border and imposed flight path restrictions. 'He also put guided missiles overlooking Gibraltar and Spanish naval vessels kept intruding into Gibraltan waters,' recalled Watson. All necessary items had to come through Tangiers. 'Previously we'd used Spanish labour but now it had to be Moroccan which didn't please the Spanish because they didn't have any work.'[57]

Cut off from mainland Spain, to stave off boredom in the confined space of the Rock, 'adventure training', run by Captain Edward de Broë-Ferguson, was carried out in the Rif mountains, in Morocco. After taking the ferry to Tangiers 'we would travel 150 miles inland by bus,' related Lieutenant Rose. At Tetuan, former capital of Morocco, the platoon would split up into small groups, each taking a different route through the mountains, meeting up again at Tetuan bus station eight days later.[58] Since there was no agreement with the Moroccan government to undertake exercises, they wore civilian clothes 'sometimes looking rather silly in South American sombrero hats pretending we were tourists!' Another activity was mountaineering in the High Atlas mountains to the south, expeditions organised by the padre, Donald Beaton, an experienced climber.[59]

With the frontier officially closed and manned by observation posts (OPs) and detectors, all movement across was forbidden. Even so, Watson was often faced by the problem of men from all three services crossing into Spain 'to have a drink, meet a girl… The Jocks also used to get a boat or swim round to a beach in Spain for a bit of fun.'[60] With the Battalion's commitment to safeguarding the frontier 'paramount', to the soldiers' relief there was no unusual activity on 1 October 1969, the day sanctioned by a United Nations resolution for Gibraltar's return to Spain. 'Despite many well fancied rumours, the day passed extremely quietly except for the many Union flags and red, white and blue bunting that hung from every window and balcony on the Rock.'[61]

By April 1970 the Battalion was back in Britain, returning to Ritchie Camp, Kirknewton after 'a very welcome month's leave'.[62]

As did Drake on Plymouth Hoe,
Watch and wait for Spanish foe,
So does Jock at OP Two,
Standing, watching, wondering who
Would close his frontier gate
To show Gibraltar his love, not hate
For those confined upon the Rock.[63]

20

Emergency Tours in Northern Ireland

Death by 'device, explosive, improvised'
Has no romance, no fairness, no appeal
Only the shredding blast of scarlet murder
Touched off by those who never know or feel
Their victim's terror, see life's light leave his eyes.[1]

The Troubles

For nearly four decades, beginning in the late 1960s, the political life of Britain was overshadowed by Northern Ireland, where tensions had existed throughout the twentieth century. In 1921 the Anglo-Irish Treaty was signed, establishing the Irish Free State in twenty-six southern counties (excluding the six northern counties of Northern Ireland which had opted out under the 1920 Government of Ireland Act).[2] In 1937 the Fianna Fáil political party, founded in 1926 by Republicans who had opposed the Anglo-Irish Treaty, introduced a new constitution which defined the country as consisting of thirty-two counties (theoretically including the six counties of Northern Ireland). It also declared that the name of the state was Éire or Ireland (which, in 1948, became the Republic of Ireland). In response, the following year the British Government passed the Ireland Act, guaranteeing Northern Ireland's status as part of the United Kingdom unless a majority of its inhabitants determined otherwise.

In 1969 growing hostility between Northern Ireland's Roman Catholic minority and its Protestant majority turned violent. A civil rights campaign, organised primarily by members of the Catholic (mainly Nationalist) community and aimed at ending discrimination in local elections, housing and employment, prompted a backlash from Protestant 'Loyalists', leading to widespread sectarian rioting. Members of the Irish Republican Army (IRA), whose historic aim was the reintegration of Northern Ireland into an 'all Ireland' Republic, became increasingly involved in the defence of Nationalist areas as the violence continued. In the opinion of those who supported Northern Ireland's status within the United Kingdom, the IRA's activities were proof of an organised attempt by Republicans to undermine its constitutional position. In late 1969 differences in ideology led to a crisis in the ranks of the IRA, which split into two factions: the 'Official IRA', which was Marxist in nature; and a more militant 'Provisional IRA' (PIRA), which would pursue its aim of establishing a thirty-two-county Irish Republic with a relentless campaign of paramilitary violence.

Opposing the Nationalists politically was the Ulster Unionist Party (UUP), which had governed Northern Ireland since 1921. In addition to ensuring that it remained part of the United Kingdom, the UUP's goal was to reverse the perceived erosion of British culture. In 1971 a more radically pro-Union party, the Democratic Unionist Party (DUP), was co-founded by the evangelical Protestant leader the Reverend Ian Paisley. The DUP had strong links with Protestant churches, especially with Paisley's own Free Presbyterian Church of Ulster. Whereas the Unionists aimed at achieving their aims by political means, the growing body of militant Loyalists were as prepared as the Republicans to take up arms to defend their cause. Countering the Provisional IRA, the most effective Loyalist paramilitary forces were the Ulster Volunteer Force (UVF) formed in the mid 1960s and the Ulster Defence Association (UDA) established in 1971.[3]

The catalyst for the outbreak of violence in 1969 was the pro-Loyalist Apprentice Boys' March in Londonderry, held annually on 12 August to commemorate the city's defence against the Roman Catholic King, James II and his army in 1689.[4] As the triumphant Protestants passed the mainly Catholic Bogside area outside the city walls, fighting began. Recognising that the Royal Ulster Constabulary

(RUC) was unable to control the rioting, which had also broken out in West Belfast, the Prime Minister, the Rt Hon James Chichester-Clark, requested British military assistance. Under the code name Operation Banner, units mainly of the British Army, but including the Royal Navy, Royal Marines and Royal Air Force, all under the direction of Headquarters Northern Ireland, based at Lisburn, were deployed on a rotating basis as roulement battalions on four-to-six-month 'emergency' tours or on longer residential tours.[5]

The deployment of the regular British Army signified a major change for soldiers used to the discipline of operating as a platoon or company. Working in smaller groups not only gave junior NCOs greater responsibility but also required them to take immediate decisions that might have far-reaching consequences. As reported by Tony Geraghty, who covered Northern Ireland for the *Sunday Times*, it 'led to the British Army's adoption of a style of counter-insurgency that ignored the valuable lessons of the successful Malayan campaign, which had stressed the need to win hearts and minds if terrorism was to be beaten by government; it reverted instead to a more primitive security style that alienated the civil population with its collective punishment.'[6] Moreover, the RUC's evidently sympathetic stance towards the Protestant community and the paramilitary Loyalist forces damaged the British Army's non-partisan reputation. The Ulster Defence Regiment (UDR), established in 1970, had similar problems of alleged partisanship since its membership came mainly from the local community and the disbanded Ulster Special Constabulary (B-Specials).[7]

During Operation Banner's thirty-eight-year deployment The Black Watch undertook twelve tours, two in 1970 and two in 1971, as well as in 1974 and 1975, undertaking its first residential tour in 1976. The Battalion returned again in 1982, 1985–86 and 1989–90. Its final two tours were in 1995 and 2005–07.

1970: Belfast, 'shot at in anger'

The purpose of The Black Watch's first emergency tour in 1970 was to protect the Roman Catholic community in Belfast in the event of trouble during the Protestant Orange Parade, held annually on 12 July in celebration of William of Orange's victory at the Battle of the Boyne in 1690. Having just returned from Gibraltar in April, the men were settling back into life at Kirknewton. 'All our equipment, radios, weapons were still on the way', related Lieutenant Colonel Andy Watson, 'when the CGS phoned me up and said "Andy, your battalion has got to go straight away to Belfast".' 'It was the weekend,' related Captain Garry Barnett, 'and so we had to get the Jocks back from the pubs!'[8] 'There was hectic sorting out of kit – and a bit of training,' recorded Second Lieutenant Jeremy Hulme. 'This was still left over from colonial days, where a bit of local rioting was controlled by a bugler, and unfurling a banner in the local language saying "Disperse, or we will shoot your leader". It's hard to imagine our innocence then – no body armour, no rubber bullets.' Travelling by ferry to Belfast, 'we arrived about four in the morning, had an exciting exit from the ferry into the rain-lashed docks, before inevitably getting lost, rescued and directed to the King's Hall', the agricultural exhibition centre where The Black Watch was quartered with the 1st Battalion The Devonshire & Dorset Regiment.[9]

'The Devon and Dorsets had just flown in from Malta and were still in their desert kit with sandy coloured helmets,' related Lieutenant Donald Wilson. 'Two battalions alongside each other in the enormous central arena looked like something out of *Beau Geste*. Rows upon rows of double-tiered beds, all arranged in company and platoon lines, gave an air of ancient martial splendour.' Within two days, the Battalion was dispersed, all but Delta Company moving to a requisitioned school at Dunlambert: 'spacious, modern and well-appointed'.[10] Later, B Company moved to a disused bakery adjoining the Shankill Road, Battalion Headquarters moving to Dunmore Park. D Company was detached to the 1st King's Own Scottish Borderers in the Catholic enclave of the Unity Flats area.

The soldiers' first job was to familiarise themselves with the labyrinth of Belfast's streets, searching for weapons. An early find was a cache in a house in the Falls Road. 'They also turned up a veritable hornet's nest of protest which rapidly got out of hand,' wrote Desmond Hamill in *Pig in the Middle,* a study of the British Army's role in Northern Ireland. 'At first it was a nasty, but fairly straightforward riot and we were not involved,' Captain Lindsay informed his wife, Annie. 'Once that had been dispersed it turned into a rather uglier situation with snipers firing down the streets.'[11] Included in the composite battalion ordered to clear the area were two companies of the Queen's Regiment, one of the King's Own Scottish Borderers and The Black Watch's A Company. 'We drove round to the Falls Road and waited in our trucks,' related Hulme. Since the road had been blocked by an overturned lorry trailer with paving stones stacked up behind, no vehicles could pass by. 'As usual with these things it was a bit chaotic – the other companies were to go in first, each one leapfrogging over the one before, advancing up the road, street by street. We were to be last in. So we sat there in our three tonners for a couple of hours, trying to appear nonchalant, when amid the general noise and confusion, someone noticed a couple of holes appear in the canvas cover… someone said. "I think the b*****s are shooting at us!"' 'There was shooting, people were frightened, smoke grenades were bouncing back on top of us,' related Sergeant Major Hubble. 'It seems extraordinary that the only time I should have been under fire in 10 years service should be in a British city,' commented Lindsay.[12]

'We searched up and down a couple of side streets', continued Hulme, 'but it was hopeless – with those endless little terraced houses and thousands of windows, unless you saw a muzzle flash – there was no chance of seeing anyone. By this time – about 9.30 – it was dark and gloomy – and we were ordered through the barrier, with my platoon leading, but after a hundred yards or so we were told to wait, and so squatted in the doorways, or behind the occasional car, while the odd bullet pinged harmlessly off the tarmac road.' After about an hour, they were ordered forward. When they realised that their route was impeded by a machine-gun firing 'occasional bursts',

Hulme recorded how as platoon commander 'quite democratically' he held a conference to discuss what should be done.

> There were various options – the most obvious being to run across in ones and twos. Then somebody had a brilliant idea (I would like to think it was me, but sadly, I don't think it was), that went something like this: "OK, so this guy's got a machine gun – but unless we're very unlucky, he's not likely to be a professional soldier/machine gunner. So when a novice fires a burst, it's a bit hairy, and they flinch – taking his eye off the ball. If we all get ready, wait 'til he fires a burst, then run like stink, we should be OK". And thus it proved. But in one of those wonderful army moments that people think you must be making up, the Brigadier then arrived and called out "Come back, come back. It's far too dangerous!" So we ran across the street (safely) a second time.[13]

Later that night Hulme's platoon was ordered to attack a building believed to be an IRA headquarters, from where shots had been emanating. Having been issued with CS gas, the soldiers fired some rounds through an open window on the first floor but 'to no avail'. 'So after five minutes or so, with one section, we went storming in, up the stairs straight into the dragon's den – officially known as the Citizens Defence Council (CDC)… we did it all wrong, and were lucky that the opposition were just as green as we were,' disappearing out of the back as the soldiers entered the front. They succeeded, however, in arresting about seventeen men 'mostly harmless, unarmed and very frightened'. They also found 'all kinds of subversive literature, gas masks, wirelesses and ammunition'.[14]

The area was sealed off, and a curfew imposed. A screening operation was then begun, the soldiers spending the next two days 'searching (and finding) weapons, explosives and ammunition – often very cleverly concealed', as Hulme recorded. 'The houses were two up, two down, loo outside the back door – occasionally there would be a pile of used tampons (a very effective hiding place) or an unflushed toilet, with a pistol in a plastic bag hidden "round the bend". Pretty grim stuff – unsurprisingly the Jocks hated it.'[15] 'I cannot describe the squalor these people – or at least most of them, live in,' Captain Lindsay informed his wife. 'Anyway we found quite a number of pistols and fairly went to town on their houses after that – it will be a long time before "Plevna Street" forgets A Company of the Black Watch! In a certain way one felt uncomfortably like the Gestapo – but I had no sympathy for them harbouring gunmen, who had been firing on us.'[16]

'One house was lived in by an elderly widow,' continued Hulme. 'Unlike many others, this house was immaculate, shining clean from top to toe, with photos of her husband (in army uniform) and her wedding on the mantelpiece. Everybody's ideal grandma. And she was terrified. Gunmen had come during the night, and demanded to use her bedroom to shoot from. She pressed tea and cakes on us (very welcome after a long night) and begged us to stay.' Looking back, Hulme admitted that seeing her so afraid was 'deeply shocking. At that moment, I felt her fear and misery justified all that we were trying to do. It was awful leaving her.'[17]

Returning to their quarters in Dunlambert School, 'for most of us it had been a weekend that will long be remembered as the first time we had been shot at in anger'. 'The one good thing about it is that the IRA have received a real shock,' wrote Lindsay. 'They were obviously building up to cause trouble next weekend – and we caught them before they were organised. Almost all the wives and children had been evacuated (or just happened to be away!) whilst some three tiny roomed houses had as many as seventeen young men in them!!'[18]

The imposition of the curfew was widely condemned in the local press. 'A BBC News film crew arrived (after sheltering behind us all night)', recalled Hulme 'and their producer went up and down the street asking for stories of how the residents had had property stolen, been badly treated or abused during the house searches.'[19] While acknowledging the curfew's success in military terms, Hamill described it as 'a disaster, not only alienating a whole community but building up within it an even more active resentment against authority... what the imposition of this "curfew" showed was not only a panic reaction and a paucity of ideas but also that no one had yet grasped a fundamental fact – that an insurgency campaign is a battle for people's minds.' 'It certainly turned the nationalists and Catholic population against the Army,' recorded Lieutenant Donald Wilson. *Sunday Times* journalist Geraghty was in no doubt that the Provisional IRA would be the 'beneficiaries of the British Army's latest fatal mistake in Ireland.'[20] Subsequently the events inspired an Irish folk song, describing The Black Watch, the chorus of which ran:

Strolling down the Falls road with riot guns and gas
Terrorizing women as they're coming out of mass.
A bunch of Scottish traitors we never will forget
Thank god we know the IRA sure aren't beaten yet.[21]

Defending The Black Watch's conduct, the author of the Battalion's notes for *The Red Hackle* wrote: 'there was not one responsible person who had not been extremely impressed by the restraint, sense of compassion and general conduct of the Jocks throughout the operation. Fortunately, because everything had to be so tightly controlled in order to ensure systematic searching we were in a position to know with complete certainty that the accusations were without foundation.' Since the curfew had prevented food and supplies from reaching the inhabitants, 'the Jocks, of their own volition, shared their meals… with many of the families whose needs appeared greatest. So much for the reports of ill treatment and looting that later gained currency among the more incredulous.'[22]

When the Orange Day Parade took place on Monday 13 July (12 July was a Sunday in 1970, and there was no marching) the day passed off 'practically without incident'. The only excitement was when some shots were heard coming from a derelict building. As the soldiers 'surged forward like terriers after a cat', they found 'to their chagrin, that the shots were no more than a motorbike backfiring.'[23] Two days later, the Battalion was ordered home. Donald Wilson's later recollection of The Black Watch's first exposure to 'The Troubles' in Northern Ireland was 'an overriding memory that we didn't have a clue what was going on. The Army first went onto the streets to protect the Catholics, but the briefings we had – such as they were – were very poor and in some cases factually inaccurate. It was a short tour but it revealed how uninformed and ill-prepared we were.' He was also shocked by 'the discrimination against the Roman Catholics'.[24]

1970: Londonderry, being 'rocks'

No sooner was the Battalion back in Kirknewton than it was ordered on another emergency tour to guard against anticipated trouble during the Apprentice Boys' March in Londonderry, the occasion of so much violence the previous August and now known as the Battle of the Bogside. Once again accommodation was rudimentary, the companies dispersed in different locations. In order to 'contain and control' the march, 'rocks' made up of groups of soldiers were positioned along the route so that the thousands of marchers would be forced to keep to the pavements rather than assembling in large and potentially hostile numbers on the road. While B and D Companies formed 'rocks' on the approaches, A Company was on the two-tiered Craigavon bridge across the River Foyle over which the marchers would have to pass. 'All went well as the marchers crossed to the Old City', observed Lieutenant Colonel Watson, and there were only 'a few problems' when they returned to the other side for a rally in St Columb's Park. But 'filled with aggressive enthusiasm' the marchers became more disorderly when they attempted to return to the Old City.[25]

'They poured onto the start of the bridge, yelling obscenities at us, pushing the knife-rests over and threatening to swamp my little command,' related Hulme, whose platoon was positioned on the bridge. 'What the hell was I to do? They would happily tear us limb from limb – yet if we opened fire to defend ourselves, we would kill hundreds – a real massacre. I thought we were all going to die. Then (for us), a small miracle happened.' A battery of Royal Artillery, acting as infantry, fired CS gas grenades over the soldiers' heads into the back of the crowd. 'So as the people pushing from the back retreated, the pressure lifted from those at the front – and we were able to persuade them to disperse. It had been a very nasty moment.'[26] 'We had maintained the law but only just!' concluded Watson. 'So ended the March of the Apprentices. Certainly there had been very little inter-factional incident and the rule of law had been maintained. To this extent the Security Forces had done their job.'[27]

Among those who had been issued with gas masks were the Press. By the end of the day their gas masks had become 'buried somewhere in the back of the car', narrated Simon Winchester of the *Guardian*, while he and his colleagues went out to dinner. On their way back to their hotel, they were stopped at a vehicle checkpoint and the car was searched.

> At first the soldiers found nothing, as they patiently went through the engine, took out the seats, felt under the wings, and tapped the chassis members to test for suspicious hollows. It was obvious that the men, all dour-faced members of The Black Watch… had found nothing all day and were feeling pretty brassed off with their luck. But then, as two of the men combed through the boot, there was a warwhoop of delight… 'And where d'ya get these me laddie?' the Sergeant, a Mr Currie, demanded, holding up two gas masks. 'From the Army,' I said. 'Don't be funny,' he rejoined.[28]

With their gas masks confiscated, the journalists returned to their hotel, only to be telephoned by the adjutant apologising for the confusion and informing him that a further apology would be forthcoming. Soon afterwards 'a nervous looking subaltern' appeared at their hotel with a note of apology signed by Watson 'and a standing offer for dinner in the Mess. That delivered, the gas masks returned… the subaltern slipped out into the night.'[29]

Soon after the Apprentice Boys' March, several rivers burst their banks and the soldiers had to 'bail the locals out of various cold muddy hazards'. 'It was ironic,' observed Lieutenant Wilson, 'one minute you were being stoned, the next thing you are helping them out of their houses. It was the sort of reaction you took for granted.' An unusual hazard was some 'drowned cows [which] lodged under bridges, blew up and exploded, sending us on all sorts of wild-goose chases from reports of IRA bombs going off.'[30] By the end of August The Black Watch was back in Scotland.

A 'landmark' in The Black Watch's history was the grant of the Freedom of the Burgh of Aberfeldy in September, 230 years after the Regiment's first muster in 1740. 'There was a great sense of occasion… those present remarked consistently on the fact that seldom could they remember an occasion when so many Black Watch soldiers, past and present, had met together at one time.' Across the Atlantic, a 'highlight' for the Pipes and Drums was its third tour of North America. Unlike the tours in 1957 and 1963, it was no longer an 'entirely Black Watch show, in fact we only accounted for a third of the overall numbers'. The soldiers also found that resentment against the presence of British troops in Northern Ireland meant that 'the "military" is by no means as popular in America as it was seven years ago,' especially among the Irish-American community. Discussion of American involvement in Vietnam was 'taboo', Lindsay recalled, except in Canada, where a number of draft dodgers had settled.[31]

The year 1970 ended with field firing at Barry Buddon, a battalion exercise 'which included all the four phases of war' and culminated in Exercise Lion Rampant held in the countryside between Aberdeen and Aviemore. 'It did everyone a lot of good to see the whole Battalion out together, functioning as a Battalion would (or might) in war.'[32]

1971: Armagh, keeping the peace

In February 1971 The Black Watch returned to Northern Ireland. Based in the 'more rural setting' of Counties Armagh, Fermanagh and Tyrone, the soldiers were 'engaged in the difficult and exacting task of keeping the peace'. On 6 February the first British soldier had been killed in Belfast, his death coinciding with an upsurge in violence. 'It was the beginning of proper counter-terrorism as opposed to the crisis management we had done in the last two tours,' observed Lieutenant Wilson.[33] The Battalion's duties included patrolling 'a fair slice' of the border and the rural hinterland, setting up road blocks, searching cars, lorries and empty buildings as well as guarding installations. 'It is extraordinary now to think that we used to patrol what later became known as Bandit Country along the border with the South on occasion wearing the kilt with a 9 mm pistol strapped to our belts,' related Lieutenant David Thornycroft, describing how they advertised their platoon symbols by painting them 'on our riot shields so that they could be quickly accessed on call-out'.[34]

'Today we were told to search a series of caves which were marked on the map,' Lieutenant Alistair Irwin, in command of a B Company platoon stationed in Dungannon, informed his fiancé, Nicola. 'We spent a whole morning in fruitless search and abandoned the thing in disgust... We were also supposed to be doing what are called Gosling patrols today. These are roadblocks set up from helicopters and they are quite fun. Having organized the operation at my end I am told that the helicopter had not been ordered. The ground over which we operate is completely boggy at the moment and I can't remember having dry boots for days.'[35]

For the duration of the tour, A Company was detached, coming under the command of the 17/21st Lancers, the resident regiment in Omagh; while Company headquarters and two platoons were in Enniskillen, a third platoon was in Omagh. 'The Jocks went right out into the countryside,' recorded Company Sergeant Major Hubble. 'They had to de-bus, walk along country roads, looking under culverts, every barrel they passed every barn every milk churn that could have been filled with explosives.'[36]

On 10 March 1971 three unarmed off-duty soldiers from the 1st Royal Highland Fusiliers were summarily shot in north Belfast. Their deaths caused a public outcry, with Home Secretary Reginald Maudling declaring that the battle against the terrorists would be fought 'with thc utmost vigour and determination'. 'Wasn't it awful about those three unfortunate RHF Jocks?' exclaimed Irwin. 'It really drags this whole business into a much lower level of downright terrorism. I can't really believe it because it will do the cause of freedom in Ireland absolutely no good at all. I would not be surprised if at last a much tougher line is taken.' That a seventeen year-old was among the dead meant that the minimum age for service in Northern Ireland was raised, as for other operational theatres, to eighteen.[37] In the aftermath the Northern Ireland Prime Minister Chichester-Clark resigned, Brian Faulkner succeeding him on 23 March.

While the Battalion was in Armagh, aware of deteriorating relations between the Catholic and Protestant communities, 'a major effort' was made to promote harmony. Having consulted with the local Education Authority, 'climbing weekends' were organised by The Black Watch's experienced mountaineers, assisted by Padre Donald Beaton, for mixed groups of Protestant and Roman Catholic teenagers in the Mourne mountains. 'Saturday was normally spent climbing the rock faces of Hen Mountain, and learning the basic techniques of mountain rescue. Sunday was usually given over to Map, Compass and First Aid instruction.' The programme was considered a 'huge success', Watson reported, but, under pressure from the IRA, the Catholic children were withdrawn.[38]

'What excitement we had last night!' Irwin was writing in late May. 'Pomeroy [RUC Station] was blown up and this was followed rapidly by a policeman's house going the same way. But both efforts were so remarkably pathetic that only windows were damaged at Pomeroy and only the policeman's garage went up. These are the first explosions since the beginning of April and the interesting thing is that the people responsible for the earlier ones have just been released on bail pending trial so it looks rather as though they are at it again. They ought to be firmly locked away without further ado.' As a result, the soldiers were required to move 'in much larger armed parties behaving in the same sort of warlike fashion that we did when we first arrived.' The new regulations meant that 'individual roamings by platoon commanders have been effectively ruled out!'[39]

A daily danger was monotony 'as the routine of road blocks, guard, ambushes and searches wore on and on.'[40] 'Towards the end of the tour, I could see there might be a problem because nothing had happened and the patrols were going out day in, day out, in all weathers and they were becoming complacent,' related Hubble, whose worst fears were nearly fulfilled in early June. As a landrover was returning from Belleek it 'narrowly-and-miraculously escaped disaster when 15–20 lbs of explosive inside a parked mini-van was detonated when the landrover was only 20 feet away.' Fortunately, the wire was pulled 'too late to cause any casualties, but it gave all the Jocks a big shakeup.'[41]

While the Battalion was in Armagh, the Colonel of the Regiment, Brigadier Bernard Fergusson, made one of his regular visits, during which he heard the story of 'a very English Brigadier' who had encountered some language difficulty. Having asked Private Watt: 'Are you comfy here?' he received the reply: 'No, Sir, I come fae Dundee.' His subsequent narration of the story to the Colonel-in-Chief, the Queen Mother, was a *succès fou*.[42] Another visitor was the Divisional Brigadier, the Battalion's former Commanding Officer Tony Lithgow, who 'toured far and wide throughout the battalion area visiting operations and outposts'. A 'host of very important persons' also visited Northern Ireland in order to see how operations were conducted. For a brief period in June, the Battalion came under the command of 19 Airportable Brigade commanded by Brigadier George Cooper, the Battalion's 'tame Sapper' during the Korean War. By the end of the tour the soldiers had searched 'prodigious numbers of cars, acres of ground and quantities of derelict houses and woods.' 'We found lots of old rifles rusting in attics and in ditches which had been smuggled in in their thousands to arm the Ulster Volunteer Force before the First World War,' observed Wilson. 'If nothing else we've cleaned up the car boots of Ireland and smuggling has taken a downward trend.'[43]

The political situation in Northern Ireland, however, was worsening. On 9 August 1971, Faulkner prevailed upon British Prime Minister Edward Heath to support the reintroduction of internment without trial, which had been used on both sides of the border during earlier troubles in the late 1950s. In Operation Demetrius, over 300 people were arrested. Regarded as a partisan operation since only members of the Provisional or Official IRA were detained, it contributed to the increasing unpopularity of Britain's military presence, not only in Northern Ireland but also among the Irish diaspora worldwide. 'The introduction of internment was one of the greatest errors made by the politicians,' observed Barnett, promoted major in June. 'So many of those arrested were not involved and the result was greater hostility towards the Security Forces in 1971 and thereafter.'[44]

Returning to Kirknewton, the Battalion was now under the command of Lieutenant Colonel Bob Tweedy. In addition to ceremonial duties at Edinburgh, in September a detachment undertook Exercise Eagles Nest, a climbing expedition in the High Atlas mountains in Morocco. Originally planned for the Spring of 1971, it had been postponed first because of the deployment to Armagh and then because of the repercussions from an attempted coup against Morocco's King Hassan II.[45] Other activities included a visit by the Pipes and Drums to Mexico for the country's Independence Day celebrations and the Regimental Highland Games on 25 September, attended by the Queen Mother. In October, having been with the Regiment since 1965, Padre Donald Beaton handed over his 'flock' to Padre Stewart Hynd: 'a worthy successor'.[46] Preparations for The Black Watch's next posting to Hong Kong were interrupted by another emergency tour to Northern Ireland in October 1971.

1971: Belfast, 'a whole new ball game'

'We were operational in East Belfast with prime responsibility for the area known as the Short Strand, a totally Catholic enclave in the midst of the strongly Protestant area south of the River Lagan,' recorded Tweedy. 'We have all moved into an extremely comfortable factory already occupied by some Gunners and some Scots Guards who together run a very strange set up,' commented Irwin, describing B Company's quarters at Carnmoney in north Belfast, also occupied by D Company. 'The whole factory is bristling with defences but women are allowed in at random. The Black Watch is horrified… Our first operation was this morning when we put a block up on a main street out of the city centre. At least Belfast will be fully aware that the Red

Hackle is back in town!' For most of the tour, A Company was in the Short Strand bus depot, where the soldiers were 'a wee bit cramped' in double-decker buses.[47] 'I lived in the booking office with the Colour Sergeant,' related Sergeant Major Hubble.[48]

The increased hostility towards the British Army was palpable: 'When we started patrolling in the Short Strand and Ballymacarrett we were cut dead and it was quite normal to be told to f*** off,' observed Tweedy. 'The Short Strand was a whole new ball game,' related Private David Stacey, who had enlisted in The Black Watch in the footsteps of his father. 'A lot of the boys didn't understand what was going on. As a Catholic, I could see both sides of the Irish question.'[49]

'Generally speaking we go out twice a day into any part of Belfast to show the flag and be on hand if anything should happen. The number of Protestants that have said to us "Thank God The Black Watch has come back" is remarkable,' Irwin was writing on 11 October, indicating that they were looking forward to 'hitting' men of violence whether Republican or Loyalist. 'We have just been told we are being issued with Red Hackles for our steel helmets which is really good news. Now the Irish will always know who their opponents are.'[50]

Mindful of the adverse comments being received by the British Army in Northern Ireland in the press, a regimental broadsheet known as *The Watchkeeper* was issued 'to help dispel all misconceptions concerning our life and work here… the first [platoon] guards the depot and also keeps it clean, the second, on foot and in vehicles, patrols the streets inside our area, while the third just sits and waits – for trouble.' The broadsheet emphasised that the soldiers tried to get to know the people 'in the hope of winning their confidence by so doing. You see if we can succeed in convincing them that we can protect them, then we earn their confidence and support. This in turn makes our job easier and peace more certain.'[51] To boost morale, a nurse in Queen Alexandra's Royal Army Nursing Corps wrote an open letter: 'Dear Soldiers, we realise how fed up you must get sometimes in Northern Ireland and we were wondering if you'd like us to write to you to cheer you up. We want you to know that there are people who care about you out there.'[52]

As the time for The Black Watch's departure approached, Tweedy recollected warning the officers and men that there could be no relaxation of procedure. Sadly, 'right at the very end', Lance Corporal Edwin Charnley, 'an excellent young ex-Junior Leader and outstanding shot', was killed by a sniper from a roof top when running across an open space at the bus depot. When Lance Corporal Robertson, on duty as Regimental Policeman, saw what had happened, he went to help Charnley and was shot through the jaw, but survived.[53] Having immediately searched the block of houses from whence the shots had come, the soldiers found 'that the gunman had chased out the owner, an old lady, and had positioned himself in the skylight using a telescopic sniper rifle,' recalled Captain Colin Harrison, who was present. 'Although he had vanished, two spent empty cases were found.'[54]

By late November, the Battalion was back home. In recognition of those who had served in Northern Ireland for twenty-eight days or more Prime Minister Heath had agreed to the award of a clasp to the General Service Medal 'for specified service in the Province'.[55]

'The Troubles' in Northern Ireland reached a serious low-point on Sunday 30 January 1972 when an anti-internment march in Londonderry was fired upon by the 1st Parachute Regiment; fourteen protesters were killed and seventeen injured, an event remembered as 'Bloody Sunday'. As a result of what was considered (and later acknowledged) to be an unjustifiable act against peaceful protesters, hundreds joined the IRA.[56] On 22 February, in retaliation for Bloody Sunday, the Official IRA initiated a bombing campaign in mainland Britain with a car bomb in Aldershot targeting the 16th Parachute Brigade's headquarters.[57]

The 1st Black Watch did not return to Northern Ireland until 1974, but in July 1972 a platoon under the command of Lieutenant David Thornycroft was posted to Lurgan, County Armagh, to reinforce the under-strength 1st Battalion The Gordon Highlanders. The soldiers had 'all the problems of Belfast in miniature. We have an IRA-harbouring Catholic estate at one end, which we patrol in the certainty of being stoned and the possibility of worse, while at the other we have a militant Protestant area with all the usual paraphernalia of barricades and bonfires. We even have a peace-line between two rival estates, which requires almost constant patrolling.' In July the platoon was withdrawn in order to take part in what was supposed to be 'the highly secret Operation Motorman to take back No Go areas from the IRA', the incentive being the explosion of nineteen bombs in Belfast on 'Bloody Friday' – 21 July – which killed nine people and wounded 130.[58] Undertaken in the early hours of 31 July, British military presence reached its height when 27,000 military personnel were deployed in Belfast, Londonderry and other cities including Lurgan in over 100 locations. Once the operation was over 13 Platoon joined the Battalion which had deployed to Hong Kong in early 1972.

Meanwhile, a different regimental activity was under way. Just as Earl Wavell had requested Bernard Fergusson to write the history of The Black Watch in the Second World War, so Fergusson, as Colonel of the Regiment, had asked Eric Linklater if he would provide the narrative for a 'sumptuous' book, the Regiment's latest official history, *The Black Watch*, which would conclude with the Battalion's service to date in Northern Ireland.[59]

The flags are down today, and quiet
No wild wind whips them proudly to the crack,
But at the half they hang, wet – lifeless;
They mark today no fierce or hot attack.[60]

21

Travelling the Seven Seas

Hong Kong welcomes all who come
In VC10s to seek the sun.[1]

Hong Kong: 'No sinecure'

Following worldwide decolonisation, Hong Kong remained Britain's last imperial outpost. Having become a Crown Colony in 1842 after the First Opium War, in 1860 the colony was extended to include the Kowloon peninsula. In 1898 the British Government signed the Convention for the Extension of Hong Kong Territory with China's Manchu dynasty, leasing Lantau Island and the nearby lands in the north, known as the New Territories, for ninety-nine years.

Unlike previous generations who had travelled to the Far East by sea, in January 1972 The Black Watch went to Hong Kong by air, preceded by twenty-two container loads of regimental and personal baggage sent by sea to accommodate the needs of 700 soldiers and 300 families. Included in the cargo was the Regimental silver and the gong, proudly retained since its appropriation in 1858 during the Indian Mutiny.[2] On arrival, the main body of the Battalion went to Gun Club Hill Barracks in Kowloon on the mainland, while two companies were based at Erskine Camp in the New Territories. Hong Kong's hills and valleys were 'reminiscent of Glencoe, high, steep, rugged and fairly barren. The flat land is either paddy-field or sown with skyscrapers.'[3] According to Private Jim Sandilands, who had been to Hong Kong in the Merchant Navy before enlisting in The Black Watch in 1970, the soldiers had been given a list of all the places they ought not to visit which included the local brothels. 'So this was an open invitation to try the places out!'[4]

As the soldiers soon realised, the posting in Hong Kong would be no 'sinecure'. 'Boredom', the officers and men were warned, 'will not gain a toehold.' 'It was work hard and play hard,' related nineteen-year-old Lieutenant Andrew Ogilvy-Wedderburn. Following a series of incursions from mainland China into the New Territories, units were regularly deployed for guard duty on the Sino-British border and although border duties were not 'constantly gripping', they provided 'an unequalled opportunity to learn some valuable lesson such as observation, reporting, log-writing and sentry duty'. 'We spent a lot of time watching the Chinese who were watching us, but I am not sure what we were going to do if two million Chinese soldiers came across the border!'[5]

Another activity was rounding up 'illegal' immigrants. As Ogilvy-Wedderburn continued:

> There was huge trafficking going on. Our policy was that we did not return them to China. There was an island off Lantau Island, one of the 'freedom' islands which people would try to reach by swimming from mainland China. Early in the morning you would see their heads in the water. We would try and talk the Hong Kong police boat onto the swimmers but we would not pick them up until were in they were in Hong Kong waters. If Chinese gun boats came, they would run them over. There were also shark attacks, and so then the patrol boats would pick up some rather nasty bits and pieces.[6]

The Battalion's main task in Hong Kong was to assist the Royal Hong Kong Police but it was also required to act as the Force Guard, which, in the 'colonial atmosphere' of Hong Kong, meant providing guards for Government House, Flagstaff House and the ammunition depot at Shousan Hill in 'a mixture of ceremonial and tactical' activities.[7]

During the two-year posting, the Governor of Hong Kong was Sir Murray MacLehose, who, under cover of being Vice-Consul in China during the Second World War, had trained Chinese soldiers. Aware of his Scottish background, 'the Jocks nicknamed him "Jock the Sock".'[8] Guard duty at Government House could have its amusing side. 'There was a long curving drive up to the house', related Sandilands, 'and you could hear when a car was coming. So the Guard would be in position presenting arms as the car came round the corner. Some Chinese taxi drivers discovered this and would take tourists up the drive; the Guard would salute and all the tourists would be taking pictures!'[9] Compared with being on tour in the United States or Mexico, life for the Pipes and Drums was 'relatively quiet.' Officers and men also enjoyed a variety of sport, the Battalion becoming 'decimated by sports injuries, grazes, sprained ankles and muscle tears... as many men rise to sport, more fall to bite the dust.' The Climbing Club grew 'from strength to strength.'[10]

On 18 June, 'Black Sunday', two devastating landslides caused by torrential rains at Kwun Tong and Mid-levels buried a number of homes and led to the collapse of a twelve-storey apartment building, resulting in 'a most exhausting week of hopeless digging for an unknown number of Chinese dead.'[11] 'We were digging out the Chinese in mud slides on the Kowloon side which was the shanty side of Hong Kong,' related Captain Hugh Rose, who had taken over as adjutant in April 1972. Sergeant Ronnie Proctor described their efforts as 'quite tragic. We had to dig these poor people out, obviously they couldn't go in with bulldozers; we worked in relays and you began to be infected with the smell of dead bodies. We ended up bringing in the fire brigade and hosing it all down and picking out the bodies.'[12] Reflecting back on dealing with such a 'gruesome' event, Lieutenant Ogilvy-Wedderburn observed:

> You have to remember that 'gallows humour' is what keeps the military together. When something awful happens like that and you are digging up body parts, when you go back to the barracks, you have to laugh. The reason you can get through such terrible

> experiences is because you share such a strong bond. It's something you can't explain to other people but it means you don't crack up on the job. It's only when you go home and there is no one to talk to that you can fall apart and this is of course what people now call 'combat stress'.[13]

Generally their duties were less 'macabre' and included 'the building of bridges to facilitate the morning hike to school of grateful Chinese children', as well as patrolling into 'distant villages which have little contact otherwise with the outside world and its Government'.[14] Exercise Highland Stronghold in the New Territories aimed to teach battle procedure involving 'occupation of a battalion defensive position and ending with a withdrawal operation'. Despite unusually heavy rainfall, the exercise proved 'to be an invaluable shake out for the battalion' before undertaking Brigade exercises, codenamed Celtic Circle. Surveillance of more remote areas in the New Territories was carried out by twelve-man patrols. Travelling by boat, helicopter, land rover and mule, they were accompanied by a policeman, a member of the District Office and, of necessity, two interpreters 'one to interpret from the local tongue to Mandarin Chinese, and the other to interpret from Mandarin to English'.[15]

In the late summer, for the first time in fourteen years, the 'inter-company drill competition' was introduced 'to foster inter-company rivalry still more and also to prepare the Battalion, at company level, for the Parade being held for the Colonel of the Regiment'. The visit of Bernard Fergusson, raised to a life peerage as Baron Ballantrae of Auchairne in the County of Ayrshire and The Bay of Islands in New Zealand, was scheduled for October. The Battalion, Ballantrae later recorded, was 'in tremendous heart, and enjoying a high reputation. Jocks as splendid as ever, and I would guess 90% from the regimental area.' The married families, however, were 'not too happy' having been given quarters in high-rise flats 'with nowhere for the children to play, but almost all… putting the bravest of faces on it, and applying to the situation the most gorgeously undiluted Angus, Fife or Perthshire tongues.'[16]

South Korea: United Nations Honor Guard

During 1972 the Battalion sent three separate contingents to Korea for the United Nations Honor Guard at Yongsan, Seoul. With troops drawn from South Korea, Britain, Thailand and the Philippines as well as a platoon provided by the United States, the Honor Guard's duties involved providing security for the C-in-C of the United Nations Command (UNC), as well as ceremonial guards of honour for visiting dignitaries of the UNC or US Forces in Korea. A third duty was acting as the security guard for the Armistice talks at Panmunjom, held across the Demarcation Line once a month 'on average when both sides can agree on a date'.[17]

The Honor Guard's departure for the first tour coincided with the establishment of diplomatic relations between the United Kingdom and the People's Republic of China on 13 March. This development had angered the Taiwanese whose government 'would not permit the plane carrying the Honor Guard to land for refuelling at Taipei', recalled Proctor, 'so they had to take a circuitous route via the Philippines.' Having arrived as the advance guard, Proctor was one of the first Black Watch soldiers to visit the Demilitarised Zone since the end of the war nineteen years ago. As described in *The Red Hackle*, running 'like an open wound across Korea… here even the most insensitive visitor can feel the tension. In the Guard Posts, OPs and Early Warning System combined, the sentries ceaselessly scan their arcs with their rifles by their hand behind a perimeter fence ringed with claymore mines. Beneath them are the tunnels and bunkers, relics from the days of the war, but all ready for instant occupation, for you cannot tell the Koreans that the war has ended.'[18]

In September, a Black Watch contingent from A Company was again sent to Korea, to be relieved by B Company in November. Taking advantage of the changeover 'a plot was hatched' to enable the five remaining serving Korean War veterans to travel to Korea in the aircraft for a two-day visit in late October, almost coinciding with the twentieth anniversary of the Second Battle for the Hook. Included in the party was the Adjutant, Captain Hugh Rose, whose father, Lieutenant Colonel David Rose, had commanded the Battalion during the war. The timing of the visit was such that there could be no publicity. Not only was a referendum taking place on Korean reunification, but the North Korean Red Cross Mission was in Seoul discussing reuniting families separated during the war. 'We were asked not to go up to the Hook area in case it provoked the North Koreans,' recalled Rose. 'They said they didn't want any old sweats up there who were there during the war,' remarked Sergeant Major Colin Harrison, one of the five war veterans.[19] South Korea was also politically unstable, President Park Chung-hee having declared a state of emergency in 1971, dissolving the national legislature and suspending the constitution.

During their visit the delegation went to the United Nations Cemetery at Pusan. 'We had a service in respect of those who had died during the war and laid a wreath,' recollected Harrison. Their farewell lunch was hosted by the local president of the Korean War Veterans Association, General Kim Kui-Am. Also present was General Park Byung-Kyu, on the staff of the cemetery. As they were leaving, 'with a broad grin and twinkle in his eye' he presented each member of the party with a package which contained ginseng tea renowned for its aphrodisiac qualities![20]

Spread across the hemisphere

Other assignments in 1972 included undertaking a major six-week Company exercise in North Queensland in June, an opportunity given to B Company, commanded by Captain James Arbuthnott. The Regiment's first service in Australia was over 150 years ago when its former 2nd Battalion, the 73rd, was sent to the nascent city of Sydney in 1810, initially under the command of Lieutenant Colonel Lachlan Macquarie, later Governor and renowned as the 'father of Australia'.[21] A contingent had also been present when the colonies of Australia became federated as a Commonwealth in 1901.

During their exercises, the 'enemy', played by members of the 1st Royal Australian Regiment, 'devised excellent contact lanes, ambushes and patrolling… ranging from following blood trails to attacking enemy jungle bases'. A novel experience for the successors of those who had served in Korea was being 'plagued by rats' – Colour Sergeant Scott being confronted by a 'kangaroo' rat, the size of a small terrier. The men also amused themselves by preparing a vocabulary for their Australian counterparts, highlighting the brevity of the Scottish word 'snuff' compared with the English explanation: he is lying on the bar floor because he has had sufficient to drink![22]

In August D Company, under the command of Major David McMicking, undertook Exercise Lacerate in the Jungle Warfare School, (officially called the Malaysian Army Central Training School following the handover to the Malaysian Army). Located in five different places, common to all 'was their distance from Hong Kong (despite the magnificent radio link), their closeness to the equator (which meant much pleasanter weather) and their classification as field conditions.'[23]

The second year of the Battalion's Hong Kong tour began with the departure of A Company, commanded by Major Colin Innes, to New Zealand on Exercise Ladbrooke in late January. 'To send a Company from a Scottish Regiment to New Zealand is to guarantee a fantastic reception for each and every Jock, from the thousands of Scots in the Dominion.'[24] In anticipation of having to entertain their 'military hosts', Innes had collected thirty-six Scottish and Regimental songs, five relating to The Black Watch, in a booklet which he distributed widely during their stay.[25] The object of the exercise was to provide a break 'from the confines of Hong Kong, to carry out limited war training in an unfamiliar environment and to exercise with the New Zealand Army.' Based at Waiouru 'in the heart of the high tussock country in the centre of North Island,' contact was re-established with the New Zealand Scottish, allied to The Black Watch since 1939, the close affiliation highlighted by Lord Ballantrae's visit on 18 February. Having been Governor-General of New Zealand from 1962 to 1967 'he walked into the Sergeants' Mess speaking Maori,' recalled Innes.[26]

A Company's last exercise, Stamina, was a four-day 'orienteering and fitness exercise designed to test the sections on endurance, fitness and day and night navigation'. Leisure time involved 'an incredible assortment of excursions and expeditions that ranged from canoeing down the Waimakariri River, sailing at Lyttleton, sheep dog trialling and touring in the Banks Peninsula, trout fishing, deep sea fishing and plain sight-seeing'.[27] Lance Corporal Henderson and Privates Gear, Lowe and Robertson also had the opportunity to accompany the Army Mountaineering Association on Exercise Snowline in the South Island 'to master snow and ice and climbing techniques, alpine navigation and survival training in the alpine conditions'. Over a five-week period they climbed fifteen peaks as well as climbing or traversing nine major glaciers.[28]

In February 1973 an exchange took place between The Black Watch and the 2nd Battalion the 4th US Marine Regiment based at Camp Hansen, Okinawa, Japan. While twelve members of The Black Watch went to Okinawa, one officer and nine enlisted Marines arrived in Hong Kong for four weeks. 'The "Ladies from Hell" would get their first close working look at the "Devil Dogs" since Korea in 1952,' observed Lieutenant Tim Ireland, US Marines. Among 'training highlights' for those in Okinawa were 'fam-firing' ('familiarisation firing, as opposed to target shooting and classification, weapon-handling with live ammunition) and 'wet-nets' (practice for the Marines' oldest mission, the amphibious assault).[29]

Between March and April, Support Company was in Malaysia, learning, as had their predecessors in D Company the previous year, that 'the jungle is certainly the best place to learn about personal organisation in the field. If you can survive there you can do so anywhere in the Far East.'[30]

From Golden Spur to Winter Gallop

By mid-April the Battalion resumed its full strength in Hong Kong, allowing for a brief period of 'catch up'. The next challenge was Exercise Golden Spur, the Brigade exercise on Lantau Island, west of Hong Kong. This took place in early May at the start of the rainy season, which meant that they had to travel by boat because all the helicopters were grounded. While The Black Watch and the 1st Battalion King's Regiment were 'the good guys,' the Gurkhas were the 'enemy': the 'dreaded Dai Chin a communist infected crew' who were indulging in 'bombings, arms smuggling, murders and other popular terrorist pastimes'. Despite the rain, the exercise 'packed into one week the actions of several months of real Counter Revolutionary Warfare.' One episode, however, was nearly fatal: 'A Sergeant in the mortar platoon was carrying a radio on his back,' recorded Lieutenant Donald Wilson. 'Against regulations he had the long antenna up. When he crossed a road, the antenna touched a power line. There was a huge explosion and he was blown off his feet.' Although the Sergeant survived, his ear drums burst and the soles of his feet had burns. 'But the radio was OK.'[31]

Two more overseas exercises were held: D Company, under Major Giles Le Maitre, undertook a six-week jungle training exercise Tabac in Fiji 'with a very social programme from Friday night to Sunday and back into the jungle on Monday morning', according to Lieutenant David Thornycroft, who had joined the Battalion from Northern Ireland after Operation Motorman.[32] B Company, under Major Ian Ker, went to Brunei, anticipating 'a superb paradise of eternal sunshine, unending sand and palm trees, beautiful girls and beer whenever you wanted it'. To their dismay, because Brunei was a Muslim country 'the girls are untouchable for fear of six months in the local jail and drink in any form is very definitely frowned on.'[33] In their absence, the remainder of the Battalion undertook the various guard duties in Hong Kong which included a summer youth leadership camp for Chinese students.

In August 1973 Lieutenant Colonel Bob Tweedy handed over command to Lieutenant Colonel Thomas McMicking, David's elder brother, both sons of Major General Neil McMicking, Colonel of the Regiment from 1952 to 1960. Among the Battalion's final commitments was Exercise Blue Dragon, a brigade inter-platoon competition involving a 10-mile 'march and shoot'. 'It was up in the New Territories in perfect weather like a good English summer,' related Wilson, who, as the umpire 'was constantly running up and down the hills.' Preparations, meanwhile, were being made for the Hong Kong Military Tattoo as part of the Hong Kong Festival. Due to be held on 25 November 1973, rehearsals began 'with intensity' in October, B Company having been assigned the task of staging the 'modern battle scene,' in which 7 Platoon provided the partisans and enemy, 6 Platoon the helicopter assault force and 5 Platoon the main assault force. Notable for holding the record for being for 'the most rehearsed twelve minute set in history', the performance took place without a hitch.[34]

In mid-January 1974 members of the Battalion were 'squashing' themselves into their riot kit for an internal security exercise, Winter Gallop, in support of the Royal Hong Kong Police. The object was to suppress riots in the Morse Park area of Kowloon, the role of the rioters, known as the Militant Workers Action Group, was again taken by Gurkhas. 'Hotly on the heels', came Cold Comfort, 'billed as positively and irrevocably the final exercise in Hong Kong' and again involving riot procedure, on this occasion against some 'dissident Scots'.[35] Having been informed that The Black Watch's next posting was another Operation Banner tour in Northern Ireland, preparatory training was also undertaken. 'The law had to be understood, shooting had to be modified and improved to a high standard. Reporting drills, arrest procedures, patrolling formations and the equipping of all ranks are only a few of the subjects that had to be covered in this short space of time.'[36]

By March the Battalion was back in Britain, stationed at Roman Camp, Colchester. Before returning to Northern Ireland, intensive training took place in Hythe and Lydd in Kent, where a new unit, the Northern Ireland Training and Advisory Team (NITAT), had been established. 'This is the big difference,' recalled Donald Wilson. 'In the early tours it was *ad hoc*. When we came back in the mid-1970s we went into this systematic training system with intelligence briefings, the history of the conflict, photographs of suspected terrorists and an appreciation of the tactical area.' Urban Close Quarter

Battle (CQB) ranges and the equivalent for rural settings were built. Another range was designed to assist in interpreting the Yellow Card rules of engagement. 'It was all taken very seriously and rightly so, but it was also lots of fun with wonderful resources.'[37]

'The training improved the quality of everything,' observed Major Garry Barnett. 'It focused on likely situations the soldiers might face.' 'An important aspect was riot control,' recorded Lieutenant Roddy Riddell. 'Petrol bombs would be thrown so that you got used to how to react to these different threats. Since the exercise was filmed, you could learn from any mistakes.' 'A special street was set up for live firing,' recollected Private Jim Sandilands. 'Targets would pop up and the soldiers had to decide whether they were locals or IRA.' On at least one occasion Sandilands was informed 'that he had just shot the butcher!'[38]

For these are my mountains
And this is my glen
The brave of my childhood
Will know me again
No land ever claimed me
Though far I did roam
For these are my mountains
And I'm going home.[39]

22
Countering Terror

It had gone from being civil disorder and having to prop up a failing police force to counter-terrorism and a genuine armed insurgency.[1]

The long war

Since The Black Watch's last tour in 1971, Northern Ireland had become explosive, the year 1972 witnessing the worst annual levels of violence.[2] With deadlock existing among the major Northern Irish political parties, on 30 March 1972 Prime Minister Edward Heath reintroduced 'direct rule' from Westminster with the creation of the Northern Ireland Office (NIO) and the dissolution of the Northern Ireland parliament. In May, the Official IRA declared a ceasefire 'except for defensive actions', but the Provisional IRA was transforming itself into a 'lethal' terrorist organisation. Based on a cell structure consisting of groups of four to five men, known as Active Service Units, their attacks (which included the July 1972 'Bloody Friday' attacks leading to Operation Motorman) were fewer but more effective.[3]

In 1973, with the objective of devolving authority back to Northern Ireland and in an attempt at power-sharing, the Northern Ireland Assembly was established. Following elections a Northern Ireland Executive was formed. In May 1974 the pro-Loyalist Ulster Workers' Council staged a general strike which led to the Executive's collapse and the resignation of its Chief Executive, Brian Faulkner. Henceforward military operations were undertaken in 'a local political vacuum which allowed extremism to flourish', commented Donald Wilson. 'It had gone from being civil disorder and having to prop up a failing police force to counter-terrorism and a genuine armed insurgency conducted by the Provisional IRA… Consensual policing was non-existent. All police activities outside secure stations (guarded by Jocks) required close military escorts. The Army, effectively, was the civil power.'[4]

1974: Andersonstown, a political vacuum

In June 1974 The Black Watch was again sent to Northern Ireland. The Battalion travelled from Liverpool to Belfast in RFA *Sir Lancelot* 'an Irish Sea crossing veteran, rumoured to have sailed against the Armada', related Private Sandilands who remembered that the Chinese crew delighted in showing 'blue' movies at the cost of £2. When the soldiers refused to pay, the Chinese taunted them with the certain knowledge that they were all going to be killed in Northern Ireland so 'why not spend the money!'[5]

The picture painted in *The Red Hackle* of the changed environment was grim: 'Vulgar graffiti states everywhere "Go Home You British Pigs", tins, paper and every form of garbage clutter the sidewalks and youths loaf aimlessly.' 'The unreal situation of a normal way of life juxtaposed with violence of startling intensity has persisted and become more strongly entrenched,' observed Lieutenant Irwin. 'There seems to be no solution and no end. If one thought that the Irish could maintain this unreality indefinitely, then we too could expect to be here permanently. It is a far cry from our thoughts of a few years ago.'[6]

Deployed to the Catholic area of Andersonstown, a suburb of West Belfast in the shadow of the Black Mountain, the Battalion was extended across its own 'patch' or Tactical Area Of Responsibility (TAOR): A and B Companies, commanded by Majors Colin Innes and Ian Ker respectively, were both located at Glassmullen Camp with responsibility for Ladybrook, Riverdale, West Andersonstown and Lenadoon; D Company, commanded by Major Garry Barnett, was posted to the southernmost TAOR at Woodburn Police Station covering Twinbrook and the Suffolks where there was 'a Catholic–Protestant interface', resulting in 'many hours' being spent standing at potential flashpoints between the two communities.[7] Support Company, commanded by Major Edward de Broë-Ferguson was at Fort Monagh, with Battalion Headquarters known as 'Tac'. 'Our living conditions are very reasonable,' continued Irwin. 'The Jocks have five-man rooms, each decorated with more bosoms and bare bottoms than the last, all inherited from the Fusiliers and the Devon and Dorsets before them. We have rooms to ourselves, and a very comfortable small mess. Everyone has plenty of hot water all day and night, the cookhouse works overtime to produce really good food, and the chaiwallahs and NAAFI provide other necessary facilities.'[8]

Familiarisation patrols began at once, and the men had 'the nasty feeling of being watched by unseen eyes and rifle sights'. 'What we were trying to do was to look at the daily pattern of life – children going to school, people going to work – and then sense if the pattern had changed and that something was going to happen. For example, there weren't the usual people standing on the streets, or in their doorways chatting,' explained Lieutenant Riddell. 'Our training had taught us to look for windows that were open with a curtain half-drawn across because it meant that a gunman could fire from that window.' But, having arrived in late June 'everybody's windows were open with curtains half-drawn!'[9]

'The patrolling programme at the moment is largely confined to getting to know the area. The four subdivisions of this area have their own distinct characteristics; all of them have slightly illogical road patterns, a situation not helped by the locals, in the Turf [Lodge Housing Estate] particularly, removing the street names, or changing them,' Irwin was recording in his diary. 'The geographical problem apart, personalities have to be memorised.' 'By our presence we were just trying to deter the enemy from taking action,' continued Riddell. From patrolling in 'sections' consisting of ten men, a new system was developed, known as the 'multiple' patrol: 'three patrols of four men each would take irregular routes so that the IRA would feel threatened because they didn't know where a patrol was at a particular moment in time. When the IRA started using command wire IEDs they assigned people called "dickers" to various locations to spot the patrols and report back to their Active Service Units whether it was safe to go ahead with a particular attack. So you were constantly trying to vary routes to avoid setting a pattern and to keep the IRA guessing your whereabouts.'[10]

'A lot of our tactics taught to us by NITAT were to deter the terrorist from launching an attack, by sowing the seed of doubt as to whether he would be able to get away in time,' explained Wilson.[11] 'The hours on duty are long, and as always seems to be the case, rather longer for Jocks than for commanders,' related Irwin. 'Each platoon in the company rotates through a patrol day, a guard day and a standby day. Practically speaking there is no sleep on patrol days, guard days allow a lot of disrupted sleep, while only on standby can we get to bed for a reasonable length of time; and then only if the locals keep quiet and don't make a nuisance of themselves.' In order to 'dominate the ground,' the men did '"lurks and lingers"...instead of moving around we would stay in one place, if for a short period of time, we would "linger", if for a longer period, we would "lurk".'[12] A key objective was preventing terrorists from entering the city by setting up 'an effective and ever changing screen of vehicle check points'.[13]

On 29 June Irwin was describing how Support Company witnessed its first shooting 'albeit one in which [they] were not involved'.

> At quarter to ten in the evening the Mortars were called out from standby to investigate a 'knee-job'. It seemed that a taxi had been driven to the Andersonstown Police Station. Inside was the unfortunate driver, pouring blood from three bullet holes in his legs. Quite naturally, with two knee caps smashed, he was in great pain. The police wanted to find the scene of the crime, and we provided the escort... we followed a trail of blood to a small garage, whose doors were locked. Half inside, half outside, lay an enormous pool

> of fresh blood. But why were the doors locked? Booby trap? After a great deal of ineffective and indecisive to-ing and fro-ing, the police were at last persuaded to look for the owner of the garage, and to all intents and purposes the matter ended there.[14]

Throughout the tour, inhabitants were regularly checked. 'The system, known as "P checking" relies on a collection of cards built up over the last two years listing a large proportion of youths and adults in the area. When a man is asked his name, the Ops Room looks up his card, and the patrol asks a question such as, "Why were you in hospital last month?" If the man is using a false name, he may well not know the rest of his alias's history, a wrong answer results in immediate arrest for screening and possible detention if we are lucky.' As previously, the threat remained high. 'Hand thrown blast/nail bombs were commonplace as were petrol bombs during major disturbances. Stoning was a constant feature of life on the streets,' observed Wilson, who, as the Battalion's adjutant, was not going out on regular patrols but could still 'feel the hostility'.[15]

The Turf Lodge Incident

A direct challenge to authority took place in early July 1974 at Turf Lodge, heartland of the IRA and a depressed housing area where 'a population estimated at 3,000 has been provided with a handful of very second-rate shops, and no form of entertainment whatsoever. There is an outdoor swimming pool in Falls Park but the winter here is long, and the water is always very cold. With nothing to do, the children hang about at all hours, aimless and bitter. This would have been a hard area even without the gunmen. But the "romantic" cause of freedom and Irish patriotism has given the young an interest.'[16]

In what became known as 'the Turf Lodge Incident' during a routine multiple patrol along the top of the flats, Private Duncan observed a man crossing the road with a plastic bag and 'what looked like a Thomson Machine Gun' under his other arm. Having alerted the members of his patrol, Duncan chased the suspicious individual who immediately began to run back from where he had come, with the patrol 'in hot pursuit'. 'As I got to the door,' related de Broë-Ferguson, who was following on behind Private Duncan and another soldier, Private Rennie, 'Duncan was gripping the first chap, while Private Rennie had hold of another man. When [Company] Sergeant Major Adam went into a child's bedroom, he found a machine gun on the balcony of the room. We called the Military Police and it was while we were waiting for them that the crowds built up.' 'Dust bins were clattering, youths were shouting and the atmosphere was in general becoming more hostile.'[17]

To secure the area, the anti-tank platoon was brought forward. Almost immediately the crowd became violent and started throwing bricks, one of which gave Captain Mike Lindsay-Stewart a severe cut on his ear. 'He retired hurt once he had extracted his platoon,' recorded Irwin.

> This was, as it turned out, only the overture to a long night. At about seven o'clock four buses were hijacked from the depot on the Glen Road, and a municipal dust cart was also commandeered. Two of the buses and the dustcart were driven to the Springfield Road/ Monagh Road roundabout and, in the presence of a crowd of 200, were set alight. Over a period of an hour or so half the battalion converged on the scene, positioned for a pincer movement assault on the roundabout... When the moment came, the Mortars led the assault from the South... The next hours saw the Sappers arriving with their heavy machinery to clear the burnt out hulks, and the rest of us hot pursuing into various houses, picking up a number of suspects. We finally pulled out in the pouring rain at midnight, leaving a quiet and subdued Turf behind us.[18]

For an operation involving reinforcements from almost all parts of the Battalion, including the Pipes and Drums, who covered the south of Turf Lodge and escorted prisoners, the results were considered 'pleasing': eighteen men had been arrested, eight of whom were handed over to the police, the rest released.[19] Private Duncan and Colour Sergeant McCutcheon, who, during the second phase of the operation had come under heavy fire as they made their way back into Turf Lodge from the north, were both awarded the newly instituted Queen's Gallantry Medal.[20] 'It was the biggest operation that we ever had in Ireland,' remarked de Broë-Ferguson. Meanwhile, Fort Monagh was being transformed into 'a Black Watch place of residence, as one would expect. Stones painted blue and white, Regimental flag at the gate.'[21]

Constant danger

'Danger here is constant,' Irwin was noting in mid-July, 'not because dangerous things are always happening, but because they might. And the longer nothing happens, the more dangerous the situation becomes. The Jocks relax, concentration is lost and that is the moment our enemy is waiting for.'[22] After the incident at the Turf Lodge, the 'main bulk' of their activities was 'monotonous. Routine has been the major characteristic.' Uneventful days were known as 'periods of SFNI - another of those dreadful jargon terms that have sprung from life in Ireland. It means security forces not involved.' In addition to attacks on the security forces, factional and revenge killings were common. 'Abbreviated individual made his first appearance on our scene, he was the celebrated FNU SNU ANK. Being translated "First name unknown, surname unknown, address not known"!' On this occasion, 'the said gentleman' went to the house of one of his political opponents and shot at him. 'He was taken to hospital, suffering surprisingly only from cuts from flying glass. This was unquestionably attempted murder, carried out by an official against a man who is an ex-internee and a provisional volunteer.'[23]

In an attempt to win over the population and gain information, leaflets – signed by Lieutenant Colonel Thomas McMicking – were distributed:

> I do not believe for one minute that you, the local people, are happy to walk the pavements in your neighbourhood knowing that

> deadly bombs may be concealed under your feet, or to have your families run this terrible risk. Neither do I believe that you wish the terrorists to make use of your cars for their criminal activities. If you have any information which could help us to locate and neutralize a bomb before it explodes, and thereby help us to protect your family, please telephone us on one of the numbers shown overleaf.[24]

As the soldiers realised, the British Army's greatest problem in Northern Ireland was losing people's confidence 'in our ability to protect them. The less the confidence becomes, the greater the support for the various gunmen of the different factions.'[25]

'Listening to patrols returning it is astonishing to hear the flow of intelligence that is gained,' *The Watchkeeper* was recording in August. 'Many of these seemingly trivial observations that might become embarrassing to the reporter are becoming increasingly valuable to the listener.' 'If we could be absolutely certain that plans for terrorism are not being hatched under our noses, there would be cause for relief and relaxation,' continued Irwin. 'As it is, calm can rapidly become storm here, and at this moment the signs point to bad weather ahead. We have been affected by both the Anti-Imperialist Convention and the Sinn Féin Anti-Internment Fortnight. Both have attracted large numbers of press to the area.' 'Propaganda has been the main topic of news,' continued the *Watchkeeper*, attributing 'a smear campaign' against The Black Watch to the presence of so many of the world's press at Turf Lodge. 'The kids of Turf Lodge behaved like angels whilst the press were in their midst, but whenever the chance was given those stones would be flying.'[26]

On 9 August, the anniversary of the introduction of internment, the Observation Post at Glenveagh received 'a bottle and stone attack… accompanied by the martial music of rattling dustbins… the stone throwing and bottling continued for nearly half an hour until every window in the OP had been broken.' Fearing that a petrol bomb would be thrown, there was relief when reinforcements came from the rear, delivering 'a devastating volley [of rubber bullets] at the back of the crowd. The crowd of 150 vanished carrying their injured with them, and again all was peaceful at the OP.'[27]

A week later, on the evening of 13 August, the Battalion HQ at Fort Monagh came under mortar attack. Several officers were watching the news in the mess. 'We were discussing the latest slide in the stock market', related Irwin, 'and I remember hearing two bangs which I assumed to be the corrugated iron fence moving in the wind, as it sometimes does.' Seconds later there was 'a terrific explosion… out we rushed and gradually the facts became established, while a frantic pursuit was organised to attempt, vainly, to snaffle the enemy mortar and its crew.' Only one bomb had exploded, hitting the roof of the school next door. 'Ten minutes earlier it had been full of children, who, on a whim, left the building to play football in the playground. It was a miracle that no children were wounded. The second bomb landed on the roof and failed either to penetrate or to explode… the incident has served in some way to give us some good material for propaganda, and indeed the *Irish News*, usually the most "anti" of the respectable papers published a damning statement on its front page.'[28] On 29 August there was another attack on Fort Monagh, the *Watchkeeper* observing that both attacks had coincided 'with better television shows. On the first occasion that the Fort came under fire, many were enjoying "Dad's Army" and on this occasion most were splitting their sides with "Wish you were here Mum".'[29] During periods of relative calm, the Battalion was inundated with visitors, including MPs on 'familiarisation' visits.[30]

On 16 October internees set fire to the Long Kesh Detention Centre, commonly known as the Maze Prison, on the outskirts of Lisburn, south-west of Belfast. A former RAF base, since the introduction of internment in 1971 it had housed over a thousand paramilitary members from different organisations. The chain of events was begun by an armed robbery at the bookies. On the same day the detention centre was destroyed, and large numbers of warders, soldiers and prisoners injured. When the news broke that evening rioting spread throughout the Province. Buses were burnt and roads blocked. Although the Maze Prison was not within The

Black Watch's TAOR the soldiers were 'at full stretch'.[31]

'The population of Turf Lodge began to get itself going at a quarter to midnight' Irwin related, 'with the women whistling and banging dustbins… Not now content with making a noise, the mob hijacked a car on the top roundabout and set it alight. This seemed to be the signal for the rest of Belfast which spontaneously erupted.' We removed the car in short time by towing it off the scene in a shower of sparks, and that was the end of the night for us. In our innocence, we thought that would be the end of it.' But rioting continued the following day. 'By midday, hijackings and burnings were the order of the day and we were all deployed almost permanently in an effort to calm things down. Bottles and stones filled the air, and mixed with the smell of burning rubber. Eventually we succeeded in arresting a number of hijackers in the act and that particular problem died down.'[32]

While the area remained 'very hostile', there was relative calm until patrols in north Turf reported that more disturbances were being organised. 'The locals had ripped up large quantities of paving stones, and with all sorts of other rubbish had constructed a number of barricades inside the Turf. These, together with the burnt-out hulks, were cleared by the Sappers.' But since their machines could not lift the paving stones 'almost as soon as we had gone the barricades had been rebuilt'. Although no further trouble ensued at the Turf Lodge the Battalion maintained a 24-hour presence. 'The rest of the company area, apart from two isolated and minor barriers elsewhere, remained quiet.'[33]

On 20 October 'about 1,000 men, women and children' started to march in the direction of the Maze. 'It soon became clear that the idea was not to reach Long Kesh but to provoke some sort of trouble either with the Army or with the Protestants. The mob vainly tried to force a way into Orange areas, but were continually outmanoeuvred by platoon or company blocks.' When darkness fell, they dispersed. 'A last minor excitement to the day was added when some clown fired five rounds at the Police Station from the Milltown cemetery. Fire was not returned and the follow up produced nothing.'[34]

After a further week of intense activity, The Black Watch returned to Colchester. Their high spirits were tempered 'by the sobering thought that in eight months we will be back doing the job all over again.'[35] Despite the relative safety of the barracks in mainland Britain, threats against The Black Watch by the Provisional IRA, who accused them of having 'acted like animals' and 'terrorised' the people of Andersonstown, meant precautionary measures had to be taken. 'Strict security has been put into effect to guard against possible attacks,' noted *Daily Telegraph* correspondent James Allan. The bombing of pubs in Guildford and Birmingham in October and December 1974 added to the climate of fear.[36]

On 3 May 1975 the Battalion assembled at Colchester for the presentation of the first new Colours since 1948. Reflecting habitual practice until shortly before the Second World War when the three senior officers of an infantry battalion were mounted during the parade, Lieutenant Colonel McMicking, Major Graham Murray (on attachment from the Queen's Own Highlanders), and the adjutant, Captain Donald Wilson, were on horseback. The rehearsal suffered an 'amusing mishap' when, 'on hearing the Pipes and Drums for the first time, Major Murray's horse took off!' A bitterly cold wind on the day of the presentation, Captain Thornycroft noted, meant that the mounted officers 'struggled hard to prevent their horses from turning their backs on the Queen Mother!'[37]

1975: Andersonstown, a 'meaningless' ceasefire

Following meetings with the Secretary of State for Northern Ireland, Merlyn Rees, a truce was agreed in February 1975 in an attempt to resolve the stalemate of what had become known as 'the long war'. Whereas Rees hoped to integrate the Provisional leadership into peaceful politics, combined with a continuing crackdown on terrorist activity, the Provisional IRA interpreted the ceasefire as a prelude to British military withdrawal.[38] Deployed again to Andersonstown in late June, The Black Watch had the advantage of experience, but there was the danger of 'repetitiveness with its attendant risks of boredom and familiarity. In short, 1 BW knew Andersonstown and Andersonstown knew 1 BW!' recorded Wilson. 'There was a certain amount of overfamiliarity and some complacency.'[39]

As before, the Battalion was dispersed to different locations. Young soldiers deployed for the first time recognised the benefit of improved training. 'The NITAT was fantastic and really tried to cover all eventualities,' observed Private Colin Gray. Emphasising the continuing security threat of exiting and entering a camp, he described the procedure: 'Each four man group of a multiple patrol was called a brick. One of these bricks would burst out; if you were a foot patrol, you just sprinted out into the first available cover –and that first brick would protect the other two coming out. If coming out in a vehicle– you would come out as quickly and as safely as possible. Always while exiting you'd be given cover by men in sangars.'[40]

'I got ambushed on that tour,' recalled Corporal David Stacey.

> We were on the Quick Reaction Force – out on the ground all the time. I had a member of the Women's Royal Army Corps with me that night so we could search females. We were searching on the Falls Road and I got a call from the Ops room that there was a car on fire up at Turf Lodge. We headed up there in two vehicles. Suddenly two gun men opened fire. We immediately debussed (although I must admit, we forgot to take the WRAC with us, so she remained in the vehicle throughout the operation!) As the soldiers approached where the fire was coming from, I gave covering fire. Then an ambulance arrived and took the gunmen away. Either they had suffered real injuries or this was a ruse to enable them to escape.[41]

Inter-sectarian strife had not abated 'with a mixture of selective and indiscriminate executions and attempted murders'. The Battalion also experienced its own 'internal problems' when five NCOs from the same platoon in B Company left the camp early one morning. Having ransacked one of the local clubs they stole 'a vast amount' of alcohol and cigarettes, their actions potentially damaging the

TOP St Andrew's Church, Nairobi, March 1955. The 'biggest' event recorded in the Church diary was the Service of Dedication of a stained glass window presented by the Battalion depicting a Black Watch soldier, flanked by an African with a book in his hand and a white farmer carrying a sheep.

ABOVE The visit of Admiral Lord Mountbatten, Chief of the Defence Staff, to Cyprus, March 1960. 'From start to finish [the visit] was a success. The harassing period was the preparations for it.'

TOP His Majesty King George V reviewing the Royal Guard at Ballater, with the Guard Commander, Major Charles Gilmour, 1935. 'Only a year later I was to slow march behind his coffin with a fine body of NCOs and men at my back,' remarked Lieutenant David Rose.

ABOVE President John F. Kennedy with Major Mike Wingate-Gray, The White House, 13 November 1963. 'I don't know when I have seen The President enjoy himself more,' wrote Jacqueline Kennedy. He was assassinated nine days later.

TOP Her Majesty Queen Elizabeth The Queen Mother's visit to Fort George in celebration of her 60th year as Colonel-in-Chief, 1997.

RIGHT, CENTRE Family day at Glamis Castle, 1998, in the presence of The Queen Mother. 'The entire Black Watch family was present', commented Lieutenant Colonel Roddy Riddell.

RIGHT His Royal Highness Prince Charles, Duke of Rothesay, who described having the 'enormous privilege' of opening the Memorial Gates to his grandmother, The Queen Mother, Balhousie Castle, 2004, with Private S. Rougvie.

Padres hour - Belize style

ABOVE, TOP 1st Black Watch in Werl, BAOR Exercise Liquid Chase, 1983. The soldiers were 'cocooned for much of the time in full chemical protection kit at the hottest time of the year'.

OPPOSITE, TOP Padre's Hour, Belize, 1979, with the Reverend Norman Drummond. 'The moment I had laid out a strip of Black Watch tartan and then the Wooden Celtic Cross, people would begin to gather.'

OPPOSITE, CENTRE Northern Ireland: searching cars. A daily danger was monotony 'as the routine of road blocks, guard, ambushes and searches wore on and on'. w

OPPOSITE, BELOW Northern Ireland: keeping watch. West Belfast was 'home' for Christmas 1982.

ABOVE Berlin: Ruhleben Fighting City, 1987. Exercise Black Highlander was designed 'to lick a Battalion of urban rookies into a veritable FIBUA (Fighting in Built Up Areas) 'A' Team'.

TOP Hong Kong Handover, 1997, Pipe Major Small and Lieutenant Colonel Alasdair Loudon. 'Your smartness, bearing and fortitude in such torrential rain did credit to your regiment, your country and your Sovereign,' observed The Queen Mother.

ABOVE Captain Tim Petransky, 1st Black Watch, Iraq, 2004. 'It was a 360 degree type of war, you were never completely secure because the enemy could pop up anywhere', commented Captain Mark Percy.

TOP *1st Black Watch Operational Orders for Operation Tobruk 2004*, by Edward Cowan, 2005. 'This may be the last attack for the 1st Battalion The Black Watch,' said Lieutenant Colonel James Cowan (in right foreground). 'Let us make sure it goes as well as anything we have done in the past and is one that we can be proud of'.

ABOVE Major Alastair Aitken with the Marsh Arabs, Iraq, 2004. The recruiting process was not straightforward. 'The first offer I had was for the seventy-year-old one-legged brother of the chief!'

ABOVE Last parade in Perth before the Sovereign's and Regimental Colours were laid up at Balhousie Castle, 23 June 2012. The Black Watch was 'turning a page of history', said Her Majesty The Queen.

LEFT Black Watch Corner, Belgium. The statue of a Black Watch Sergeant was unveiled in 2014. 'The Black Watch – a name we know so well,' commented Field Marshal Sir John French in 1914, 'have always played a distinguished part in the battles of our country'.

Regiment's credibility 'as enforcers of the law' as well as jeopardising their own futures.[42]

A day for likely trouble was again the anniversary of the internment law on 9 August. 'Big bonfires which had been built previously were lit on the eve of the 9th, barricades were erected and crowds gathered,' related *The Watchkeeper*. 'Treating it rather like Hogmanay when the law remains at a discreet distance, we reduced patrolling to a minimum and there was no trouble. Several bursts of *feu de joie* were heard which only reinforced the knowledge that guns and gunmen still exist. As the witching hour drew closer small crowds of youths began stoning our posts, banging dustbin lids and blowing whistles. In spite of some alarms and excursions a few small baton charges dispersed the hooligans.' 'But', recorded Irwin, promoted Captain and now second-in-command of A Company, 'as the crowds began to disperse the hooligan element began to roam around looking for trouble. This they created in fine style, producing a fine quality of mob violence which began with stonings, progressed to the hijacking of articulated lorries to create barricades and ended with widespread shooting over the whole of Green Belfast. This died down about midnight. The next day, Sunday, was far worse and ended in full scale gun battles in the Falls, some of which spilled over into our area, with no hits recorded on either side.'[43]

More serious was an incident on 13 September 1975 when Leo Norney, a seventeen-year-old was shot dead 'in disputed circumstances' by Black Watch soldiers on patrol in the Turf Lodge. Although the patrol had come under fire, there was no proof that Norney had fired the shot. Following the inquest into his death, an open verdict was recorded.[44] Subsequently, Lieutenant Colonel McMicking ordered an investigation into the soldiers' general conduct. Although the open verdict on Norney's death was not questioned, the investigation revealed that they had been planting ammunition in cars in Andersonstown. 'It appeared that the junior NCO leading one part of a multiple patrol, Corporal John Ross (Basil) McKay, D Company, who had been convicted of assault during his pre-tour leave, had been anxious to demonstrate that he was an effective soldier,' recorded

Lieutenant Riddell, McKay's platoon commander. 'Having made a legal find of ammunition, instead of handing it in, he and his fellow soldiers planted it in various cars belonging to locals, later being commended by their superiors for their diligence in finding it.'[45]

Following the investigation McKay and four other soldiers were given five-year prison sentences and dismissed from the Army.[46] In hindsight Wilson believed their behaviour was 'an example of a situation where things can go wrong. In conventional operations, soldiers do what they are told, but in counter-insurgency operations, a soldier may be on his own, so he has to be trained to act independently, often making instant decisions under extreme duress. When you instil that type of attitude and approach, you have to accept that on rare occasions the initiatives a soldier takes might lead to him into taking illegal actions.'[47]

During the tour The Black Watch was involved in twenty-three shooting incidents including that of Norney. Although there were only 'about three fully-fledged riots', stoning and bottling was frequent, resulting in twenty-one casualties 'from this form of warfare which was usually, though not always, conducted by children under the age of ten'. Over 165 houses and 37,000 vehicles were searched.[48] At the end of the tour, the officers lunched at 'the often-bombed *Europa Hotel* in Belfast while we waited for our ferry to sail,' related Captain David Thornycroft. Mindful of their activities at the Turf Lodge, they called themselves The Turf Lodge Luncheon Club.[49] By October 1975 the Battalion was back in Colchester.

In early 1976 there was 'some happy sports news', recorded Lieutenant Colonel Duncan Cameron, who had succeeded McMicking as Commanding Officer in November. 'The Battalion football team won through to the final of the United Kingdom section of the Army Football Cup. It was a considerable and very welcome achievement bearing in mind that 135 teams entered the competitions. Furthermore, football is the one sport, apart perhaps from boxing, which really fires the Jocks' enthusiasm.'[50] Having already been informed that The Black Watch would be returning to Northern Ireland as a resident battalion in Ballykinler in 1976, the

Battalion undertook 'rural training' at Stanford in Norfolk, followed by ten days' urban training and range work at Hythe and Lydd in Kent 'during what turned out to be the hottest part of the hottest June on record with the sea tantalizingly close'.[51]

1976–77: Resident in Ballykinler

On 23 January 1976 the IRA truce, initiated in February 1975, was called off. It had already been broken with the retaliatory killing in County Armagh on 5 January of ten Protestants in the 'Kingsmill massacre'. Pending any further attempt to engage with the Republicans, British strategy sought to undermine the IRA's ability to continue its campaign by reorganising the justice system, including 'criminalisation' of those convicted of paramilitary activities. On 1 March Merlyn Rees announced that convicted terrorists would no longer be entitled to Special Category Status and would therefore have to wear prison uniform. This led to the beginning of a five-year 'blanket' protest, starting with eighteen-year-old Kieran Nugent's decision to cover himself with a blanket instead of wearing prison clothes.[52]

In an attempt to 'normalise what was in effect a small-scale war' the British Army had begun changing the way it operated. Following publication of *The Way Forward*, a report produced by the recently established Ministerial Committee on Law and Order, on 23 March Rees announced a policy of 'police primacy'. Known as 'Ulsterisation', henceforward primary responsibility for security was to lie with the RUC, the British Army providing support when necessary. The situation, however, remained volatile and targeted killings continued. On 21 July, only days after The Black Watch's arrival in Northern Ireland, the newly appointed British Ambassador to the Republic of Ireland, Christopher Ewart-Biggs, and his secretary, Judith Clark, were assassinated in a landmine attack on his car in Dublin.[53]

As the residential Battalion in Ballykinler, based in Abercorn Barracks, the soldiers' activities were 'a good deal less hectic than in a roulement battalion', commented Cameron, pointing out that for the first time they could bring their families. 'We worked at a much less high intensity than the emergency tours.' 'One company is mostly tied up with guarding the camp and our immediate security,' he informed the new Colonel of the Regiment, Brigadier Jack Monteith, who had succeeded Lord Ballantrae in May. 'Another company is the Province Reserve and is at two hours notice and has no specific commitments but has already been deployed on several occasions. The other two companies are at respectively 4 and 12 hours notice in their Province Reserve role but have certain other small commitments including responsibility for our own comparatively small and usually quiet rural area in South Down. My plan at the moment is to rotate the company commitments monthly.'[54]

Assistance to the roulement battalions involved 'any number of roles including search duties… prisoner escort tasks, boarding party operations with the Royal Navy, short-term deployments Province-wide, monitoring marches and providing reinforcements for particular operations.' The danger of becoming complacent and therefore 'a soft target in a peaceful part of the Province, had continually to be impressed upon everyone.'[55] The Battalion's 'first excitement' was when Battalion HQ and three companies were sent to the reconstructed and officially renamed Her Majesty's Prison Maze to reinforce the Prison Guard Force 'for an anticipated riot which never took place. However for us it was a useful opportunity to have a critical look at turnout procedures and came at just the right time.' On three occasions the Battalion was deployed to South Armagh on escort duties connected with Operation Tonnage, a major rebuild of the base in Crossmaglen.[56]

In early August the soldiers had to contend again with the annual 'anti-interment' anniversary in Belfast. 'You may have seen some red hackles on the television news,' Cameron was informing Lord Ballantrae prior to a visit of the former Colonel of the Regiment and his wife in September rounding off his '45-year association with the Regiment'. 'Three of the companies were deployed on the streets at one time or another for periods of between a couple of hours to deal with a particular incident and in another case for seven days with its own area of responsibility. All is now quiet again.'[57] Recruitment was a potential problem. 'Ballykinler is not, and never will be, a popular station for single soldiers, albeit it is not so unpopular as to have caused any increase in our wastage rate so far. Indeed the number of soldiers who have purchased their discharge during the first 10 months of this year has been 24 against our annual average of 42 over the last 5 years.'[58]

In late 1976 The Black Watch was again dispersed.

> We have now heard definitely that we will have one company deployed with its own operational area from next week, 28th December. Initially the deployed company will be in East Tyrone with company headquarters and two platoons at Cookstown and one platoon at Pomeroy. From the end of January, the deployed company will move to the south-east of County Armagh and have its headquarters and two platoons at Middletown and one platoon at Keady. The latter deployment, which includes some quite difficult country around Keady as well as a stretch of the border, is likely to remain for the foreseeable future. The deployed company will from the start be commanded by the Armagh regiment who change over every four months.[59]

Among The Black Watch's responsibilities were the activities of the recently established Northern Ireland Patrol Group (NIPG). To improve intelligence gathering, Lieutenant General Sir David Young, Commander Land Forces, HQ Northern Ireland 1975–77, had identified the need 'to have a specialist covert organisation drawn from the best of the Resident Infantry Battalions'. Initially the NIPG had not achieved the necessary successes to engender confidence in its operations. When The Black Watch took over in Ballykinler, a renewed effort was made and Captain Dick Parata was selected as Officer Commanding with a brief 'to make it work'. 'The key to the organisation's success was to produce results,' explained Sergeant Major Mike Smith. 'In many cases it was difficult to see how the information provided would fit into the bigger intelligence picture but it did.'[60] One such operation involved determining which vehicles were making a round trip to and from the Republic of Ireland, potentially bringing weapons into Northern Ireland. 'We set up a series of strategically located Observation Posts on the main road in order to record the number plates going one way in the morning and then in reverse that evening,' recalled Parata. 'After a few days' observation we found only about ten vehicles had done the journey there and back and so it was easy to give those number plates to the police to check the vehicles.'[61]

The importance of the NIPG's work, Parata emphasised in hindsight 'should not be underestimated. On the conclusion of the battalion's tour NIPG became the formally established "Close Observation Platoon" (COP) (meaning that you are an official Army unit and did not have to "beg and steal" as NIPG did).'[62] Cameron also acknowledged the NIPG's contribution, while distancing the Battalion from its operations: since the group was mainly involved in surveillance activity and working with the SAS, 'even the Commanding Officer [was] often in the dark about their whereabouts and activities'.[63]

The year 1977 marked the beginning of a series of attacks on businessmen. IRA snipers also killed three members of the RUC in County Tyrone. In the summer the Battalion was 'fairly fully involved' in counter-insurgency operations during the Ulster Unionist Action Council strike called by Ian Paisley. For its two-week duration, Support Company was based in Newtownards, County Down, 'and did sterling work in an area where regular soldiers are not usually seen. The rest of the Battalion were all involved to some degree but it was a frustrating period for the Jocks particularly, meaning as it did frequent short notice moves, much standing around and no action.'[64]

During available leisure 'keeping sports teams together wasn't easy', related Cameron, himself a keen sportsman. A major success for the Battalion's shooting team was gaining 4th place in the Major Units Championship at Bisley behind three Gurkha battalions. 'You will see that just 2 and a half more points would have given us 2nd place but since no one in the Battalion, even in their wildest dreams, expected the team to be in the top 10, we shouldn't complain,' Cameron informed Brigadier Monteith. 'Credit for the successful results is due almost entirely to Sergeant Major Scott who coached and trained the team as well as performing creditably himself.'[65] Under the tutelage of RSM Fred Beattie the football team had 'another outstanding season, once again reaching the final of the Army Cup, only to be beaten (once again)' by the School of Electrical and Mechanical Engineering.[66]

A major responsibility for the police and the Army was the Queen's security during her first visit to Northern Ireland since 1966 in August 1977 as part of her Silver Jubilee celebrations. A twenty-one-gun salute marked her arrival in Belfast Lough. However, with rioters in Belfast carrying a banner proclaiming 'the Queen of Death' and the Provisional IRA threatening a series of attacks, the Queen did not come ashore. Arriving instead by helicopter, she hosted a Garden Party at Hillsborough Castle, The Black Watch providing an airborne reaction force as well as having responsibility for searching the grounds. 'I like to think we acted professionally all the time,' related Private Colin Gray, 'but with a visit like that you tend to pay even more attention.' Despite the threats, the visit passed off without incident, the Queen emphasising the 'hopeful signs of reconciliation and understanding.'[67]

Towards the end of the tour, The Black Watch was ordered to help in providing fire-fighters during the nationwide firemen's strike, which involved almost 30,000 firemen being called out by the Fire Brigades' Union. In November, the Battalion's second-in-command, Major Ian Ker, moved from Ballykinler to the Northern Ireland Fire Authority Headquarters at Lisburn. Widely deployed across the Province in Operation Bravado over 200 Black Watch soldiers worked alongside fire-fighting crews from the Royal Navy and Royal Air Force in 'green goddess' fire engines.[68]

'You had to ensure that fire hydrants hadn't been booby trapped,' related Lieutenant Riddell, 'that it wasn't what we call a "come on" where you were being sucked into an area to be attacked. So we had to liaise closely with the police as to whether they sensed it was a genuine incident or not.' Fortunately, one hydrant which had been booby-trapped was spotted 'by an alert Jock.' 'We were always concerned about snipers and you felt very vulnerable, standing with your hose to put the fires out,' related Private Gray, stationed at Musgrave Park. 'We had the Gordon Highlanders as our Escort Battalion, when the call came in that there was a fire, the Gordons would go out first to check that it wasn't a set up.' 'In the heart of the Bogside I put out one fire in an empty house; as we were reeling up the hoses, the person next door asked us to feel the walls of his house, claiming they were very hot,' recalled Lieutenant Ogilvy-Wedderburn, who had, in August 1977, succeeded to the baronetcy, aged twenty-five, and was now called 'Sir Sir' by the soldiers. 'We went in and he confessed that there was nothing wrong but he wanted to thank us. He then gave me a bottle of whisky.'[69]

'The last part of the tour has been busy and I think successful,' Lieutenant Colonel Cameron recorded. Although the firemen's strike continued until January 1978, the Battalion was 'conveniently released' from fire-fighting 'in time for Hogmanay'. In addition to praising Major Ian Ker – effectively 'the head Northern Ireland fire officer' – he commended 'the Jocks who, aided by sailors and airmen, fought the fires.'[70] The Black Watch did not return to Northern Ireland for nearly five years but on 19 July 1978 eighteen-year-old Private Mark Carnie, attached to The Queen's Own Highlanders, was killed in a bomb attack in County Tyrone.[71]

Loving a soldier is bitterness and tears,
It's mostly being Young but feeling old,
Reluctantly, painfully, watching him go
Whilst your heart is crying and wanting him so.
You wait for news, no more for a spell
You worry and hope that all is well.[72]

23

Confronting the Cold War

Again we're back in Ireland
For a task which must be done
By all our boys in tartan,
Which of course are next to none.[1]

1978: Training for Out of Area Operations

Back in Britain in early 1978 the Battalion was quartered in Somme Barracks, Catterick, North Yorkshire. To practise conventional tactics 'in different surroundings and climatic conditions' each company was involved in overseas training exercises (OTX).[2]

At the end of May A Company was in Cyprus undertaking Exercise Heron Bill, with platoons based at Dhekelia, Episkopi and in the Troodos Mountains. Although Captain Colin Harrison, who had served in Cyprus in 1958 and 1965, was surprised by 'the vast run-down in the two sovereign bases, and also the deterioration of the buildings, and their surroundings', he was impressed by the newly constructed sea port of Larnaca and the development of luxury hotels. 'It would appear that the Greek Cypriots are going in for the tourist trade in a big way.'[3]

By contrast, D Company was in Scotland on a KAPE (Keeping the Army in the Public Eye) tour. Also present were the Pipes and Drums, which instead of operating independently had been taken under D Company's 'wing'. 'The high point' of the posting took place on 21 June when the old Colours, presented by Earl Wavell at

Duisburg in 1948, were laid up at Balhousie Castle.[4] Exercise Flying Bear took the anti-tank platoon to Berlin in July. In September C Company was in Italy undertaking Exercise Ponte Vecchio near Florence 'to learn something of the ways, customs and methods of operating, at first hand of one of our NATO Allies.' Meanwhile, B Company was providing the Royal Guard at Ballater, Major Stephen Lindsay recording that he had 'a Queen on either arm' for the Grand March at the Ghillies Ball.[5]

Exercise Lead Ball in November took D Company and the recce platoon, commanded by Captain Roddy Riddell, to Guyana for field training at the Takama Battle School. In exchange, members of the Guyana Defence Force went to Catterick. One of the jungle instructors was Private Billy Whytock 'following in the tracks' of his father, Private William Donald Whytock, who had served in what was then British Guiana in the 2nd Black Watch in 1954–56.[6] 'It was a fantastic experience,' observed Corporal Colin Gray, who recorded the prevalence of names 'like Sugar McGregor, McIntosh and Mackenzie' among the Guyanese 'since many of the plantations owners had come from Scotland'.[7] Knowing about Private Robert Howat's extraordinary feat when he swam across the Potaro river in 1955, D Company's Officer Commanding, Major de Broë-Ferguson, and a small party travelled to the Kaieteur Falls to leave a commemorative brass plaque. Also present was Mrs Leila Too Kong, one of the school girls who had helped to rescue Howat, having been 'certain' that he would get washed over the edge.[8]

While in Guyana the officers and men became onlookers to the 'Jonestown massacre', when, on 18 November, 912 people committed suicide by taking poison in a remote part of the jungle. Orchestrated by the founder of the Peoples Temple movement, Jim Jones, it was the single most deadly non-natural disaster in United States' history. 'The Americans were overawed by the number of fatalities and a mortuary unit was flown down from Panama to remove the hundreds of bodies,' observed Riddell.[9] Transported in helicopters to a hanger at Timehri (Cheddi Jagan), the former Atkinson Airfield, 'the smell was indescribable'.[10]

By early December, the Battalion was reunited in Catterick, though A Company's three weeks 'glorious leave' at Christmas was affected by being on call because of a threatened tanker drivers' strike.[11] In preparation for The Black Watch's next tour (to Belize in the New Year) the Battalion went to the Sennybridge Training Area in Wales: normally ideal for practising low-level jungle patrol skills, during the particularly severe weather of early 1979 'there was deep snow,' recorded Company Sergeant Major Ronnie Proctor, who also noted the irony of training for jungle warfare 'in the frozen wilderness of Wales!'[12]

1979: Belize, the smell, the heat, the dust

Under British administration since 1836, Belize was formally declared a British Crown Colony in 1862 as British Honduras. After the Second World War, economic grievances combined with political disaffection resulted in the demand for independence. In 1964 self-government was granted and the country renamed Belize. A dispute between neighbouring Guatemala and Britain concerning sovereignty over Belize led to the deployment of a contingent of approximately 1,500 British troops, divided into two infantry battle groups (North and South) and supported by the RAF, in support of the Belize Defence Force. For the duration of its stay, The Black Watch formed Battle Group North.[13]

'It takes, as in Hong Kong, only a couple of days to get used to the smell, heat and dust,' noted a contributor to the *Bush Telegraph*, 'and in that time the ants and mosquitoes get used to the "new blood" and leave you alone.'[14] While Battalion Headquarters and two companies were deployed at Airport Camp, inland from Belize City, a reinforced company group was posted astride the Western Highway (George Price) near San Ignacio, known as Holdfast Camp, with an outpost at Plassey Camp. 'Our Commanding Officer, Ian Ker, had the right attitude,' related Major Donald Wilson. 'Although it was an operational tour, he treated it as a long period of overseas training.'[15]

A Jungle Warfare School at Guacamallo (Guacamayo) Bridge was set up and administered by Captain Parata with Sergeant Major Al Saunders as chief instructor.[16] An Adventure Training Centre was established on a small island, St George's Cay, commanded by Captain Selby MacDuff-Duncan, whose family had served in the Regiment since the Indian Mutiny.[17] While not wishing to portray their experiences as a 'holiday camp', the officers and men relished the opportunity 'for every type of water sport in addition to the normal facilities one finds in a camp, sailing, swimming, sub-aqua, canoeing, para-ascending, squash, tennis, deep-sea fishing and other assorted sports.' 'It was also very interesting,' observed Captain Andrew Ogilvy-Wedderburn. 'If you were patrolling through the jungle, you would suddenly run into an old Mayan temple or realise you were climbing the steps of an Inca temple.'[18]

Having decided not to bring the Kirk's silver Celtic Cross 'to such humid, operational climes', Lieutenant Colonel Ker had asked the Battalion's Padre, the Reverend Norman Drummond, to commission a local woodcarver 'to carve an exact wooden replica of the Celtic Cross'. Presented to the Kirk at St George's Garrison Church, 'regular Sunday Services were well attended', observed Drummond, highlighting the strong relationship between the Kirk and the Regiment. 'One of the traditions handed-down from Padre to Padre was to go out when the men least expected you, either at dawn or when things were particularly miserable or uncomfortable and, when requested, to conduct an impromptu Service. The moment I had laid out a strip of Black Watch tartan and then the wooden Celtic Cross, people would begin to gather. It was truly remarkable.'[19]

The Battalion's last two months in Belize coincided with the hurricane season. 'Huts were tied down with steel hawsers, torrential rain flooded the Western Highway and contingency plans for moving into Belize City were practised.' In the event only Captain Alastair Watson, with a relief party of signallers, was sent to provide communications and assistance in distributing food to a flooded region of Jamaica where 'walls of water had come down the mountain'.[20] Following the May 1979 General Election which brought a Conservative government under Margaret Thatcher to power, the Armed Forces had been granted a 'timely' pay rise enabling those who wished to enjoy 'the lure of a Caribbean holiday' before going home.[21] The tour was the last time The Black Watch was deployed to Central America, as Belize gained full independence on 21 September 1981.[22]

Back in Catterick in September 1979, the next challenge was preparing to convert to the mechanised infantry role. 'There was an enormous amount of preparatory training and study days in order to learn how mechanised infantry would work and how you cooperate with tanks and the "all arms" battle,' explained Riddell. A rudimentary requirement was for all soldiers to learn to drive.[23]

In late 1979 a specialist team was sent to join the Commonwealth Monitoring Force as part of Operation Agila in Southern Rhodesia (Zimbabwe), becoming part of 'the most convoluted pieces of diplomacy ever undertaken,' according to Brigadier Adam Gurdon, a member of the Monitoring Force.[24] After over a decade of violence against the Rhodesian minority government of Ian Smith, who had made a Unilateral Declaration of Independence (UDI) in 1965, agreement had been reached at Lancaster House in London for a new constitution, paving the way for general elections and independence. In the interim Lord Soames became Rhodesia's Governor. Arriving at Salisbury (Harare) shortly before Christmas 1979, the Commonwealth Monitoring Force spent Christmas under canvas; briefings were held on Boxing Day, 'then the hard work began.'[25] To persuade the guerrilla groups to lay down their weapons a ceasefire had been brokered. Leaving the comfort of the transit camp, 'we all felt slightly apprehensive,' related Lieutenant Ian Thomson, in command of The Black Watch team, one of thirty-nine monitoring groups sent into the African bush. 'Our equipment included two stripped down land rovers with armour plating underneath because of the landmine threat,' related Private Whytock. The Black Watch's job was to persuade the ZANU PF, the Zimbabwe African National Union – Patriotic Front, led by Robert Mugabe 'to come to a rendezvous (RV) point, so that firstly, we could gauge how many there were. Then we wanted to disarm them and take them to our checkpoint in order to give them a safe haven for the duration of the elections. The RV point had an exclusion zone so they could not be targeted by the Rhodesian Security Forces.'[26]

A seven-day assembly phase then began. 'They came across the bush in section formation, heavily armed,' recorded Lieutenant Thomson. 'There were 15 of them, all drunk, but ready enough to accept tea and cigarettes when offered.' When, during their parley, some tea was spilt over a ZANU PF commander, causing him to jump up suddenly, Whytock recalled fearing 'another Rorke's Drift'.[27] But the meeting passed off amicably and the ex-guerrillas departed, promising to return with more of their comrades to surrender their weapons. Once the ceasefire ended, the team moved to the Assembly area with the contingent of ZANU PF who had surrendered their weapons.

Meanwhile Gurdon was in Force HQ assessing the enormity of the task of housing several thousand men. 'The notion that a few tents, blankets and cooking pots would do was rapidly dispelled.' Describing how the 'monitors' had to set up camps from scratch in the bush for anything from 200 to 2,000 he continued: 'this meant proper camps with a full range of camp equipment, stores, cookhouses, latrines etc. Also needed were recreational facilities, radios, newspapers and film shows.' 'We keep separate from the PF, whose camp is 500 metres to our East in low ground,' continued Thomson. 'They hold their own political meetings, early PT runs and mini-cadres during the day. They have their own volleyball courts and football pitches.'[28] Following elections in April 1980, the ZANU PF, supported by the majority Matabele tribe, won 57 out of 100 seats in the newly constituted Parliament. On 18 April Southern Rhodesia officially became independent, adopting its African name, Zimbabwe. Those who served in the Commonwealth Monitoring Force were awarded the Rhodesian Medal and the Zimbabwe Independence Medal.[29]

1980: Werl, West Germany, the pick of the postings

In April 1980 The Black Watch moved to Werl, West Germany, for a five-year tour. Once again part of the British Army of the Rhine

(BAOR), the Regiment now had a place in the 'first eleven', noted David Thornycroft, promoted acting major and Officer Commanding D Company.[30] Since the Battalion's last tour in the late 1960s, West Germany, under the chancellorships of Willy Brandt and Helmut Schmidt and a member of NATO since 1955, had consolidated its position as an ally of Britain and the United States.[31]

Based in Albuhera Barracks, The Black Watch's arrival in West Germany coincided with a new phase of the Cold War. In December 1979, Soviet troops had entered Afghanistan in support of the socio-communist government of President Noor Mohammed Taraki, heightening tensions between the two superpowers. Having warned that the Soviet action was 'the greatest threat to world peace' since the Second World War, US President Jimmy Carter banned the United States' team from participating in the 1980 Moscow Olympics. While the focus of US–USSR rivalry was in Central Asia and potentially the Middle East, vigilance in Europe remained a priority, the British land and air forces still providing a major component of NATO's defensive strategy against a possible incursion from Eastern Europe into West Germany.

'Only 10 per cent of the Battalion was ever allowed to be on leave at one time, even at Christmas,' noted Lieutenant Colonel Garry Barnett who assumed command of the Battalion in October 1980. 'This was standard practice from 1945 until 1989 when the Berlin wall came down.' 'It was all taken desperately seriously,' commented Lieutenant Ronnie Bradford, one of two of Brigadier Bill Bradford's sons commissioned into The Black Watch. 'I can remember going to recce our planned deployment positions for war in civilian clothes with the greatest secrecy.' 'Training to achieve combat effectiveness as part of a combined arms formation in a tri-service battle for a possible war in Europe against the Warsaw Pact was the British Army's Priority 1 role,' observed Major de Broë-Ferguson.[32] To help integrate the officers and men with the local population, experimental language courses were offered, which were 'enjoyed by all students'.[33]

In the twelve-year interval since last serving in a mechanised infantry brigade, the armoured personnel carrier (APC) had evolved.

The soldiers had to spend 'long hours' getting to know 'the front end of an APC from the back end... have we had problems! Name a mechanical ailment – we've had it (in triplicate).' An added drawback to gaining experience driving the APCs was pressure on the defence budget with savings made, among other measures, by restricting the number of miles which could be driven in the APCs 'which meant that the vehicles could seldom leave the tank park.'[34]

NATO's biggest exercise since the Second World War was Crusader 80; held in September 1980, the two-week exercise aimed at testing the military's ability to mobilise and reinforce the BAOR within forty-eight hours. One exercise, Active Edge, required the Battalion, as part of a battlegroup, to mobilise without warning within two hours to concentration areas with vehicles, weapons, ammunition and equipment, invariably when most inconvenient in the middle of the night. 'Deploying a battlegroup was no mean feat', observed de Broë-Ferguson and was only possible 'with copious rehearsals'.[35] During 1981 and 1982 the Battalion continued training activities. In May, while the British public's attention was focused on the South Atlantic where hostilities had broken out between Britain and Argentina over the Falklands Islands, The Black Watch travelled to Canada. For the first time the Battalion had the opportunity to take part in large-scale exercises at the British Army Training Unit Suffield (BATUS), which had replaced Libya as an armoured training facility 'on a vast open prairie on the scale of something like Stirling to Stonehaven with nothing in between,' commented Bradford.[36]

Back in Germany, the routine was interrupted in September by training for another tour in Northern Ireland which began a few days before Christmas, the Regiment's first deployment there in five years. Having gained expertise as a mechanised battalion, the soldiers had to re-train for counter-insurgency. 'Roulement units deployed in Northern Ireland were meant to be drawn from those serving in the United Kingdom,' observed Barnett. 'But not for the first or last time there was overstretch in the British Army and mechanised battalions like 1BW were called upon to put away their armoured vehicles and deploy to the Province.'[37]

1982–83: Belfast, neutralising the enemy

The situation in Northern Ireland remained volatile. Since becoming Prime Minister in 1979 Margaret Thatcher had adopted a hardline approach towards the Republican movement. Not only had her friend and adviser, Shadow Secretary of State for Northern Ireland Airey Neave, been killed by a bomb planted in his car at Westminster in March 1979, but on 27 August 1979 Admiral Earl Mountbatten and members of his family had been assassinated while holidaying in County Sligo. On the same day two bombs were detonated near Warrenpoint on the border with the Republic of Ireland, killing eighteen soldiers and seriously wounding six. But, despite the adverse publicity the attacks created, the Republicans remained defiant, a common refrain being: 'Neave, Mountbatten, eighteen Brits, All the bastards blown to bits.'[38]

In 1981 Bobby Sands, convicted of possessing a revolver from which bullets had been fired at the RUC, began a hunger strike in the Maze Prison demanding the reinstatement of Special Category Status, revoked in 1976 by Merlyn Rees, Secretary of State for Northern Ireland.[39] The issue, which had begun with Nugent's 'blanket' protest, gained worldwide attention, firstly when, in April, Sands was elected a Member of Parliament for Westminster in a by-election and secondly, when, after a sixty-six-day hunger strike, he died, followed by nine other prisoners, also on hunger strike.

The Black Watch's arrival in West Belfast on 21 December 1982 came shortly after another serious attack by the Irish National Liberation Army (INLA) on 6 December, when a bomb exploded in the Droppin Well discotheque in Ballykelly, County Londonderry. Among the dead were eleven British soldiers, mainly from The Cheshire Regiment stationed near by at Shackleton Barracks. The day after The Black Watch's arrival, 'the CO [Lieutenant Colonel Barnett] told me that we were getting a VVIP,' recalled Proctor, now regimental sergeant major. Amid tight security Prime Minister Thatcher, accompanied by her husband and Jim Prior, the Secretary of State for Northern Ireland, arrived in Belfast, going immediately to see the survivors of the Ballykelly bombing in Musgrave Park Hospital.[40]

West Belfast was 'home' for Christmas, with a showing of the film *ET* in the Battalion's HQ at Springfield Road police station among the entertainments. A robbery at a fish-and-chip shop on 27 December had tragic consequences when the nineteen-year-old thief 'was caught red-handed by one of my patrols', related Major Irwin. '[He] refused to stop and pointed what looked like a loaded pistol (it turned out to be a knife) at the corporal who shot him dead… In the end we discovered that he only got £2 from the hold-up and for that he lost his life. What a waste.'[41]

New Year's Day was seen in with the Pipes and Drums playing on the police station's rooftop 'much to the surprise of the local population'. 'Nothing much has happened in Belfast over the last few days,' Lieutenant Rupert Forrest was recording on 2 January. 'Several cassette incendiaries and a culvert bomb containing 550lb were defused. One of my patrols had a brick thrown at it by a yoblet who missed his mark (unusual) and hit an old lady who turned on him and gave him a good hiding, much to the delight of the Jocks.'[42]

Since the Battalion's last tour the accommodation had been fortified, the individual companies again dispersed to different locations at Musgrave Park Hospital Camp, 'The Mill' (North Howard Street Mill) and Macrory Park. The 'most modern' of all the camps was Fort Whiterock, which was protected by sangars and surrounded by corrugated iron overlooking Turf Lodge.[43] A welcome feature was being 'fed 24/7 even if you came back from a patrol at 4 a.m', observed Lance Corporal Brian Baxter, who, as a Catholic, had been apprehensive about his first deployment to Northern Ireland. 'The whole society in the mining community around Fife were in support of the Catholic Irish. My family had their own views against the forces being in Northern Ireland.' 'Very quickly I realised that the hatred was so deep and embedded that it was a real uphill task if we were going to achieve anything at all,' observed Lieutenant Hugo Allen, also undertaking his first operational tour. 'My mother lived on the Isle of Man where there was a strong element who were sympathetic to the Republican cause. Soon after the Battalion arrived, she started getting anonymous telephone calls which scared her, saying "we know your son is in The Black Watch, we are going to get him. We know where he is."'[44]

Lance Corporal Alan McEwen believed, however, that 'only the minority were hostile to the British Army. If the rest of the population was not friendly it was because they were frightened of reprisals.' 'One of the really scary tasks was doing a pub check,' continued Allen, 'when you would take four or five Jocks into a working man's pub or club, and try to identify anyone from the Provisional IRA. There could be up to 100 people.'[45]

Following the introduction of 'coincidental boundaries', the Battalion's TAOR matched that of the RUC's B Division.[46] 'Our aim was to make B Division a place in which the terrorist preferred not to operate, whilst the law-abiding citizen could lead a normal life. While we did not always succeed, every time our adversaries ground their teeth with rage, when there was an act of friendly courtesy between our local population and ourselves, it served our purpose.' 'Victory or success', observed Lieutenant Colonel Barnett, could be measured 'by a neutralised enemy and by days without incidents or better still by many days without incident.'[47]

'There was a change of emphasis from the Army being in the lead,' commented Captain Riddell, who had taken over as adjutant in June 1982. 'Since the police had primacy, we had to seek authority to carry out certain operations. The police now patrolled with us, which they had not previously done on a regular basis and so a close relationship was built up between the RUC, the Command Structure and the soldiers on the ground.' 'The police that I work with are mostly pretty decent and one doesn't feel quite so alone in that respect as we did last time we were here,' observed Irwin on 9 January.[48]

When possible, patrols were carried out wearing the Tam o'Shanter and Red Hackle, and the recently issued Individual Northern Ireland Body Armour (INIBA), reinforced with a Kevlar plate protecting vital chest organs. 'Only when there was a riot situation did we wear helmets,' recalled Proctor.[49] 'While in the past soldiers patrolled without a great deal of significant intelligence and more in a deterrent role, now there was much more emphasis on information gathering and close co-operation with Army Intelligence and the RUC,' noted Barnett. 'We certainly managed to improve hugely the cooperation with other intelligence units,' recalled Bradford, promoted captain and now the Battalion's intelligence officer. 'But although our intelligence was good, it was patchy. There was still plenty going on that we didn't know enough about.'[50]

'The 17th [March] was St Patrick's Day and a public holiday,' remarked Lieutenant Forrest. 'It was no holiday for us.' As two armoured personnel carriers were leaving the base at Macrory Park, a Rocket Propelled Grenade (RPG) 'went straight through and embedded itself above the heads of the occupants in one of the vehicles,' related Proctor. 'Sergeant Johnston, a senior NCO of the Royal Electrical Mechanical Engineers (REME) was badly wounded, the trajectory of the RPG going through his legs.' 'Intelligence units had been tracking this particular weapon. We knew it was ready to be used but we did not know where or when,' continued Bradford, emphasising that those entering and exiting Macrory Park were particularly vulnerable because one of two gates had been out of use for over a week 'and so using only one gate had set a pattern.' 'It was a well planned operation,' commented Forrest. '[With] a quick system for changing cars and hiding the weapons.'[51] Other incidents, 'stolen cars and examples of petty crime aplenty', included the detonation of a remote-controlled bomb in the Falls Road which fatally wounded Corporal G.T. Jeffery, serving with a Devon & Dorsets platoon which had deployed in support of The Black Watch.[52]

On another occasion the Battalion HQ had a timely escape. Before leaving HQ for a weekly briefing, 'we – that is myself, the CO, the 2IC, the adjutant and signals officer – had been standing by a wall in the yard at Springfield Road,' Proctor recalled. 'As we were mounting our vehicles down the Falls Road, we heard a bang, caused by several grenades thrown at the HQ. On our return, I saw that the wall where we had been standing was peppered with shrapnel. If we had still been there when the grenades were thrown, everyone would have been hit, although not me because I am short and the marks were at normal head height directly in line with the others.'[53]

As their experience had demonstrated, a shortcoming of the British Army's equipment remained the vulnerability of the Humber-armoured personnel carrier, known as the PIG. While these could protect against shrapnel, small-arms fire and nail bombs, they were vulnerable to shoulder-launched RPGs. 'These carry a HEAT warhead which explodes into a white hot jet of molten metal able to penetrate even quite thick tank armour,' explained Major Hugh Rose. 'The IRA had learnt that firing an RPG causes a considerable back-blast so it was normal practice for a terrorist to emerge from a house to engage from the pavement.' Having researched reports of previous RPG attacks on vehicles, Rose discovered that there had been none when a sentry was standing up in the vehicle in a position to engage the attacker. 'Our armoured landrovers (PIGLETS) had a hatch in the roof but the PIGS had no such hatch.' A high intensity light beam, known as a fakir torch, which allowed sentries to shine light at likely firing points 'seemed to offer an easy, potential solution to the RPG threat.' Another improvement was fitting a steel protective mesh to deflect or explode the grenade away from the armour. 'A HEAT warhead requires a critical strike angle and 'stand-off' distance to achieve its best effect,' continued Rose. 'The modification request was submitted and a first prototype was delivered for our inspection. The hatch was ideal but the vehicle was entirely encased in heavy-gauge steel netting – the REME workshop price was rumoured to be over £10,000 per vehicle! Comments were submitted and on the last day of our tour an improved prototype was delivered for trial by our successors!'[54]

Easter passed quietly 'with a few fairly small Republican parades and all of us thinking of loved ones in Germany and Scotland'. By the beginning of May 1983, the Battalion was back in Germany. The Provisional IRA, however, was still pursuing its objectives through acts of terrorism. On 12 October 1984 its agents narrowly missed killing the Prime Minister and the British Cabinet when a time bomb was placed in the Grand Hotel, Brighton, during the Conservative Party conference.[55]

1983–85: Farewell to Germany

Back in Werl, among the least appreciated exercises was Liquid Chase designed 'to trial a revolutionary chemical detector known as the Chemical Agent Monitor (CAM) and associated Nuclear Biological and Chemical (NBC) equipment,' recorded Edward de Broë-Ferguson who had succeeded Garry Barnett in command of the Battalion. Lasting three weeks, 'it was the most formative Nuclear Biological and Chemical exercise ever carried out by the BAOR,' observed Captain Riddell. 'It tested an All Arms Battlegroup's ability to operate in full individual protection equipment (IPE).'[56]

Problems immediately surfaced. Fitted out with respirators, 'since everyone was dressed identically with faces covered, you often found you were shouting at the wrong person,' commented Bradford, the Battalion's NBC officer. 'It was so hot that I was pouring sweat out of my rubber boots. A Company was set a particularly testing exercise lasting seventy-two hours which involved digging in, moving and digging in again. When the CO, RSM and others went round to see them after the exercise was declared finished, they found that several were so exhausted that they had collapsed where they stood, their masks still on.' 'For the first time it was acknowledged at the highest level that hard physical work while encased in IPE over a protracted period would degrade individual performance and eventually, through lack of oxygen, cause unconsciousness,' recorded de Broë-Ferguson who was later invited to explain their experiences to a Defence Medical Board in London.[57]

The major Divisional exercise in the autumn of 1983 was Eternal Triangle (which the soldiers were amused to call Infernal Bungle). The Black Watch Battlegroup included two squadrons of tanks of the Royal Scots Dragoon Guards.[58] Soon afterwards a ten-day NATO command-post exercise, Able Archer 83, designed 'to practise Command, Control, and Communications (C3) procedures', simulated conflict escalation. It was so realistic that the Soviet Union readied its nuclear forces, tensions remaining high until the exercise concluded on 11 November.[59] Unaware how strained relations between the two superpowers had become, Battalion activities continued, the annual downhill and crosscountry skiing Exercise Snow Queen taking place in Southern Bavaria. Others undertook a jungle war course in Brunei as well as attachments in New Zealand and Australia. A visit to the 66th Regimento di Fonteria Vattellina in Forli and a return visit by the Italians to Werl resulted in greater understanding 'of each other's world and work.'[60]

Of the various exercises undertaken in 1984, Exercise Base Plate brought The Black Watch 'into the public eye most and for the longest, for better or worse.' This was 'the first ever tactical live-firing exercise designed to put every single mortar platoon in Germany through its paces for four tough days and nights,' recorded Major David Thornycroft, who was responsible for devising the exercise. 'Between them they fired 35,000 rounds in five weeks, during which we were visited by three Generals, nine Brigadiers, COs and staff officers too numerous to mention and the Moderator of the Church of Scotland who memorably arrived by helicopter in his silk stockings, buckle shoes and a tricorne hat.'[61]

The 'culmination and highlight of a busy training year' was a return visit to BATUS in September as part of a Black Watch Battlegroup which included 'squadrons of tanks, artillery, engineers, guided weapons and helicopters and all the supporting arms and services we could expect in war,' continued Thornycroft.[62] One visitor was the Rt Hon John Stanley, MP, Minister of State for the Armed Forces, who had made it known that he wished to be addressed as 'Minister' rather than 'Sir'. 'Out on the prairie he spotted some recce vehicles on the skyline and asked to speak to the crews. Down they came and the Colour Sergeant in charge jumped out of his machine. Remembering imperfectly what he had been told, he gave an immaculate salute and said: "Good morning Padre"'![63]

By the beginning of April 1985 The Black Watch was in Kirknewton, the 'bald statement' that they had been stationed in West Germany for five years concealing 'a multitude of world wide travels' including Northern Ireland. 'Little had changed in thirteen years: Ritchie Camp was still wind swept, sparse and uncomfortable, particularly in cold weather. We had clearly grown soft on the North German plain!'[64] The Battalion's training was now focused on home defence. 'One big shock going back to being dismounted infantry in the UK was having to carry all your kit again,' commented Bradford, who succeeded Roddy Riddell as adjutant in July 1984. 'All we had were the few command and logistic vehicles, whereas in Germany every platoon had armoured fighting vehicles which carried all our personal equipment, ammunition and radios.'[65]

An important event during The Black Watch's absence abroad had been the closure of Dunalistair House which had provided a holiday home for members of the Regiment and their families since 1923. The proceeds of the sale were given to The Black Watch Regimental Association and an endowment was set up to support former members of the Regiment or their dependants.[66] On 17 May for the first time 'the Regiment exercised its right as freemen of Perth since the freedom was accepted by our Colonel-in-Chief Queen Elizabeth the Queen Mother in 1947 and Field Marshal the Earl Wavell on behalf of the Regiment,' observed Lieutenant Colonel de Broë-Ferguson in his address.[67] 'Being busy on Public Duties is, at the moment, a bit of a novelty and cleaning and polishing No. 1 Dress is very much the order of the day,' recorded *The Red Hackle*. 'The Edinburgh Castle esplanade, the Royal Mile and the Forecourt of Holyrood Palace have all echoed to the tramp of Black Watch feet.'[68] On May 8 the Battalion had formed part of a tri-service Guard of Honour at Westminster Abbey commemorating the 40th anniversary of VE Day. 'The presence of the three services was announced on the BBC: "The Royal Navy, the Royal Air Force and The Black Watch" as though we *were* the Army!'[69]

1985–86: Armagh, 'bandit country'

In December 1985 The Black Watch returned to Northern Ireland for another emergency tour, once again leaving their families at home to undertake 'the difficult task of raising children, paying the bills, minding the house and living without "himself"'.[70] Deployed to South Armagh, the Battalion was operating in an area which had gained 'a certain notoriety as the home of some of the world's most skilled terrorists.' 'Multi-tube barrack-buster mortars, radio-controlled bombs and medium machine guns were the mainstays of the terrorist armoury at the time,' observed Lieutenant Colonel Irwin, who had succeeded de Broë-Ferguson in command of the Battalion in September, noting that 'less than a dozen individuals have participated in every tour. About 30% of the Battalion have participated in two or more tours and for the remainder this is their first tour.'[71] Compared with 'the damp streets of Belfast', they now faced 'very damp fields, ditches, rivers and blackthorn hedges.' 'We were patrolling bandit country,' observed Corporal Alan McEwen. 'Do not underestimate the enemy,' one of many Training Directives advised. 'He acts infrequently but when he does it is usually with considerable skill, the result of very careful planning. Our own skills must match and better his. And we must look out for evidence of his planning with the aim of thwarting his actions.'[72]

Since The Black Watch's 1971 deployment in South Armagh, the use of helicopters for 'in and out' movement of troops had developed, the base at Bessbrook Mill becoming the largest heliport in Western Europe. 'We were totally relying on the helicopter to move safely,' related Captain Ronnie Proctor, who, having joined The Black Watch in 1960, had obtained a commission. As Bessbrook's Air Traffic Controller, his 'Radio Appointment Title' was 'Buzzard'. With an average of over 170 helicopter movements in and out of Bessbrook Mill each day, The Black Watch's activities brought back memories of 'the parachute-trained Second Battalion in India in the last war!'[73] Yet even helicopters had their dangers. 'Helicopters are prime targets for terrorists whenever they have to touch down so troops have to learn to board and alight in the minimum time with the chopper still running at full power and the runners barely touching the ground,' noted Maureen Young, the first female reporter to accompany The Black Watch into the 'war zone' of Northern Ireland.[74] Once a patrol had been dropped off at a particular location, the soldiers were self-reliant for three or four days, under orders to sleep in the fields rather than in the barns because the latter could be targeted. 'You could hide in the woods,' observed Corporal Baxter. 'You have got the cover of the ground rather than having thousands of windows looking at you, wondering where a shot is going to come from.' Their main obstacle was the electric fence 'which kept the cattle in but were always at the wrong height!'[75]

'It was a very staunch Republican area; no matter where you were, you had to be vigilant,' related Sergeant Colin Gray, based at 'the Border's worst terror spot' Crossmaglen, abbreviated to XMG.[76] Within the Battalion's TAOR was the often ill-defined border with the Republic of Ireland. 'This border was an inviolable obstacle to British security force movement but was as porous as a colander to the terrorist. From the sanctuary in the south came terrorist weapons, equipment and attacks; into the sanctuary many a terrorist fled after his latest caper,' observed Irwin.[77] To monitor movement across the border various hilltop border observation points had been established, the largest of which was at Slievenaboley, known by the soldiers as Superbowl.

'At the beginning of our tour the IRA launched regular mortar attacks, perhaps one every two nights,' recorded Captain Bradford. 'It was tense every night until you heard that an attack had taken place somewhere else.'[78] Operating covertly was the Close Observation Platoon (COP) which had evolved from the Northern Ireland Patrol Group. 'It was not part of the Battalion order of battle but a Special Branch asset which was chosen from the very best soldiers in the battalion,' explained Captain Hugo Allen, in command of the COP. 'We had a variety of different tasks, such as the covert observation of border crossing points, weapons hides, known terrorist houses. This involved covert infiltration of a particular area.' Answerable to the RUC's Special Branch, the men had undergone 'very specific training', with Northern Ireland Surveillance Systems (NISS) providing 'an Aladdin's cave' of specialist equipment which included microwave cameras and listening devices. 'We were three to five days on the ground, living covertly, eating cold rations.'[79]

Congratulated after the tour by the recently appointed

Commander-in-Chief Land Forces, General Sir John Chapple, for contributing 'significantly to the improved situation in Armagh', the Battalion had experienced some serious incidents and lucky escapes. On 2 January a Lynx helicopter crashed. 'It dropped to the ground from 150 feet and no one was even scratched – shows how strong these machines are. Quite reassuring really,' observed Irwin.[80] On 21 January a patrol, led by Sergeant Pratt, was ambushed by a least five gunmen. 'A short but very fierce battle took place in which the IRA using at least three automatic rifles and two machine guns fired 344 rounds at the patrol.' None of the patrol was hit.[81] Nearly a month later, on 17 February, a home-made landmine, believed to be between 100 and 150 lbs, was detonated remotely just as a patrol, led by Sergeant Kilorn, was crossing a road outside Crossmaglen. Lifted forward by the impact, Private Floan – known henceforward as 'Fast Eddie' – was fortunate in only suffering a broken jaw; pieces of his rifle were found 150 yards away. 'Floan was carried away with the blast,' explained Bradford, describing how the IRA's home-made explosives were more likely to 'shove' objects rather than shatter them. 'Had he been further away he would have been hit by the debris.' Following a similar attack, Private McKelvie was the only soldier to sustain minor injuries, when, like Floan, he was lifted in the air 'some 20 yards', landing on top of his platoon commander, Lieutenant Rikki Dinsmore.[82]

Shortly before the Battalion was due to return home, an attack of a different kind shocked both officers and men. 'Regrettably,' recalled Irwin, 'one of my soldiers, based in Crossmaglen... tried to kill a local resident. It was definite malice aforethought: at night he slipped out of the base with a screwdriver in his hand. He set about a passer-by and stabbed him, allegedly in reprisal for the difficult time his company had had in the area during the previous months. This was one of those rogue soldiers that occasionally came to the surface... luckily for him his victim did not die but he still ended up with a criminal record and I remember having no compunction in discharging him from the Army.'[83]

'The threat remains high until the end,' Forrest was recording on

27 April. 'IEDs and heli-shoots are strong possibilities.' The last incident the Battalion had to deal with was just as it was being relieved. 'Sometime before dawn, with fog obscuring proceedings, a device was placed just 100 feet inside Ulster, under the Dublin–Belfast railway line. The wire by which it was to be detonated was unwound across the Border from where the bomb team waited for the first train to appear from the South. At exactly the right moment the device was detonated, splitting the train in two and wrecking one freight car. The bombers were able to fade safely into the southern countryside, leaving us with quite a good train wreck to sort out.' Given the impact the fatalities could have been more serious.[84] Before departing 'we cleaned the base very thoroughly and handed over with a great sense of joy and also a strange sense of loss… Crossmaglen after all had been our lives and the source of all our toils for over four and half months not including the build-up.'[85]

1986: The Friendly Games

By May 1986 the Battalion was back in Scotland, returning not to Ritchie Camp, which had been closed, but to Redford Barracks on the outskirts of Edinburgh. The main focus was the XIIIth Commonwealth Games held in July–August 1986. 'We provided all the ceremonials for all the venues,' recorded Captain Mike Riddell-Webster.[86] As the adjutant, Captain Alasdair Loudon was responsible for escorting 'athletes, bands and soldiers to Meadowbank Stadium at the right time and in the right order'. Overshadowing events was the threatened boycott in protest at Prime Minister Thatcher's support for maintaining sporting links with apartheid South Africa. 'The 65 countries and 3200 team members gradually reduced to 27 countries with 2120 team members. Yet only two countries formally withdrew, so all our rehearsals had to proceed as if all countries were indeed competing, just in case the nation in question turned up on the day.'[87]

During the rehearsal for the Opening Ceremony the flag party endured 'the huge public embarrassment' of being unable to hoist the Games Flag to the top of the flagpole, since it was faulty. This was rectified on the day, which climaxed with the release of 10,000 balloons and the firing of the gun salute. Reflecting on the two-week games, *The Red Hackle* likened The Black Watch's participation 'to a prize winning rose bush. To the admirer it appears of wondrous form, each bud a perfection. But he will never know the amount of mulching and feeding lavished upon it, nor the frequent waterings it received, the pruning, shaping, hard work and grafting which went into producing the finish[ed] article.'[88] At the Closing Ceremony there was concern that the enthusiastic crowd might mob the Queen, 'and so there were many contingencies relating to how quickly can you form a hollow square to surround the Queen,' related Andrew Ogilvy-Wedderburn, promoted major in 1985.[89]

An unusual activity in August 1986 was providing 'back-up' for Charlie Hankins, who had lost both his legs while serving with the 6th Black Watch in North Africa in 1943. Although equipped with artificial legs, he found that propelling himself around in a Second World War bath chair was 'an occupation suitable for mild recreation'. To raise money for the Royal Star and Garter Home, Richmond, Hankins had undertaken to travel from John O'Groats to Land's End. Known as Exercise Wheel Spin, The Black Watch signal platoon provided support. Having exceeded his target goal of £100,000 by an additional £30,000, a proportion was allocated for an annual award to any Warrant Officer, NCO or soldier who 'by self sacrifice have helped others', 'have saved life or minimized injury', or 'have achieved some unique distinction'. The first recipient of the Charlie Hankins award was Corporal Robertson of the Families Office 'whose labours on behalf of the wives and children of the Battalion have done much to keep the home fires burning brightly.'[90]

Towards the end of 1986 the Battalion entered 'the twilight zone' which often characterised 'the transfer from one station to another'. This included preparing for its next posting in Berlin and, once more, performing the Royal Guard at Ballater with Major Nigel Lithgow in the same role as his father over thirty years previously. The experience was always memorable; Sergeant Colin Gray recorded being 'so lucky' to dance the Dashing White Sergeant with the Queen and the

Queen Mother.[91] The Black Watch was then placed on 'world wide standby' as the 'Spearhead' Battalion which required being ready to move at short notice. With the 'world situation reasonably quiet, the call never came.'[92]

On the streets while on patrols
Do not go through any holes.
Gaps in hedges be aware,
These can give you quite a scare.[93]

24

Closure of Empire

Say 'Farewell to Hong Kong!'[1]

1987–89: West Berlin, 'Tear down this Wall!'

At the end of March 1987 The Black Watch arrived in West Berlin to join the Berlin Infantry Brigade, stationed in Montgomery Barracks, Kladow, on the edge of the city. Since the Battalion's last posting in 1956, the East Germans had divided the city by constructing a wall, reinforcing West Berlin's isolation inside the Soviet bloc. 'Part of the barracks was in East Germany and was unusable. East German watch towers looked directly into the barracks from behind heavily-fortified barbed wire,' observed Lieutenant Colonel Irwin, describing how, on one occasion a soldier from the King's Own Scottish Borderers, who was under arrest in the barracks, tried to abscond. 'But he took the wrong route and was shot at by the East German border guards as he tried to scale the wire.'[2]

In celebration of Berlin's 750th anniversary, the Heads of State of the Allied Powers visited the city, The Black Watch providing the Guard of Honour and gaining the 'sincere gratitude' of the Americans in the US Sector for its 'brilliant performance' during President Reagan's arrival.[3] The President's speech on 12 June in front of the Brandenburg Gate, where the wall divided East and

West Berlin, had greater significance than his listeners realised. Taking as his theme the policy of increased openness introduced by the Soviet Union Communist Party's General Secretary, Mikhail Gorbachev, he made the now famous challenge: 'If you seek peace, if you seek prosperity for the Soviet Union and Eastern Europe, if you seek liberalisation, come here to this gate. Mr Gorbachev, open this gate… tear down this wall!' Lost in the columns of newsprint, onlookers were oblivious that the speech was the prelude to unstoppable change throughout Eastern Europe. 'Of greater impact a year later,' suggested Major Nunneley, was Bruce Springsteen's concert in East Berlin which gave people 'a taste of the freedoms in the West of which they were deprived.'[4]

A traditional ceremonial highpoint was The Queen's Birthday Parade. This was followed by a spectacular parade for The Queen Mother in celebration of her Golden Jubilee as Colonel-in-Chief. Over 400 soldiers were formed into six guards or companies, evoking the original six companies from which the Regiment was formed in 1739. 'We had sized the men by battalion rather than, as normal, by company so that the optical illusion was that all the men in the battalion were the same size!' commented Lieutenant Colonel Irwin.[5] Later thirteen former Commanding Officers of both the 1st and former 2nd Battalions were photographed with The Queen Mother together with Irwin, as Commanding Officer, and the Colonel of the Regiment, Major General Andy Watson.[6] An 'inherited obligation' was running the 'Friendship *Wochenende*', a three-day street festival in Wilmersdorf, attended by approximately 250,000 each year, to explain to young Germans why the British Army's presence remained necessary and to demonstrate that they were in Berlin 'in friendship'.[7] 'We blocked the main roads for Beating the Retreat each night which the Berliners loved,' related the Officer Commanding the Fete, Major Nunneley, who wanted to use the funds raised during the festival to benefit the borough 'but the Burgermeister told us to keep the money. So my vision was to build a garden for the blind at Grunewald, near where prisoners had been loaded in trains to be taken to the extermination camps.' The following year, as a 'singular mark of favour'

The Black Watch received the freedom of Wilmersdorf, the occasion marked by a Freedom Parade.[8]

Regular duties included border patrols and intelligence gathering. 'It was the same deal as before of needing to be prepared against any aggressive action by the Soviets,' observed Captain Mike Riddell-Webster. Exercise Black Highlander at Ruhleben near the Olympic Stadium was designed 'to lick a Battalion of urban rookies into a veritable FIBUA (Fighting in Built Up Areas) "A" Team'. Known as Ruhleben Fighting City, it was believed to be 'one of the finest training facilities in Europe,' where soldiers had to defend an area which combined flat-roofed buildings, cellars and sewage systems, including 'railway embankments, supermarkets, tower blocks of flats, houses, in fact every obstacle that you might find in an urban setting.'[9] Another 'major task', involving most of the Battalion as well as detachments from other units, was planning and conducting the Berlin FIBUA Demonstration for students of the Army and RAF Staff Colleges.[10]

A duty continuing from the Battalion's previous tours in Berlin was the guarding of Prisoner No.7, Rudolph Hess, alone in Spandau since the release of Baldur von Schirach and Albert Speer in 1966. Ever since 1945 the Spandau Guard had been operating under the same standing orders, 'actions on', outlining measures in the event of an attempted escape. These ranged 'from shouting a stern verbal challenge to physical restraint to barking a loud order – "*halt oder ich schieße*" (halt or I will fire),' related Alan McEwen, Sergeant of the Guard during one of the Battalion's tours of duty. Whenever Hess emerged to sit in a glass-fronted portacabin in the prison grounds, which he was permitted to use as a reading room, the soldiers of the Guard had to avert their gaze. Once McEwen found the temptation to observe Hess 'in the flesh' was too strong: what he saw was a 'frail old man walking bent over and very carefully with the aid of two sticks… I could not help uttering under my breath that the "actions on" paragraph in the Guard orders most definitely needed a serious review due to Hess's undoubted inability to walk any faster than a few steps a minute or step from the road to the pavement without the support of a member of the prison staff and that he would most certainly not have been able to scale the 20-ft-high prison wall, topped with broken glass and razor wire.'[11]

On 17 August 1987 Hess was pronounced dead aged ninety-three, having (surprisingly, in the light of McEwen's assessment of his frailty) hanged himself with an extension cord from a window latch in the portacabin. Immediately afterwards, for the first and only time, a platoon of The Black Watch entered the prison, parts of which had been closed off since 1949. 'We visited the condemned cells; saw the guillotine room – the thoughts that this combination conjured up were horrifying.' Lest Spandau become a neo-Nazi shrine, the prison was demolished. With rumours of souvenir hunters offering large sums of money, Hess's personal effects and the portacabin were also destroyed, the bricks buried in an emergency coal pit.[12]

A break from the 'hum-drum routine' of Berlin was provided in late November by a three-week Company, Battalion and Brigade exercise in the hills and forests of the Sauerland. 'We are comfortably installed in a completely empty (of people) but otherwise nearly functional Dracula-style sanatorium amidst tall dark trees,' recorded Irwin. 'It is very weird; a completely abandoned place but with hot running water and central heating!' During the exercise the soldiers 'covered many miles, patrolled, defended, attacked, withdrew, and ambushed.'[13] The Black Watch also had to be prepared for 'Ex Bear Defender – The Berlin Call-out Exercise' which took place four times a year. On two occasions a warning would be given, while on the other two, the exercise would come as a surprise.[14] 'We didn't just play at soldiers,' observed Nunneley. 'We regularly reconnoitered our wartime positions had it come to war with the Russians. There were a number of scenarios, one was closing the corridors to planes, trains and vehicles. This included exercises at Battalion level like Bear Defender but also at Divisional and NATO levels.' As part of a continuing attempt to meet the local population, about 200 unmarried soldiers were invited into German homes for Christmas, several British–German weddings later taking place. The Black Watch also initiated an 'Open Day' in the barracks so local Germans could visit.[15]

Good relations with their allies, the Americans and French, were facilitated by exchanges between garrisons. When, on 8 April 1988, Lieutenant Colonel Irwin handed over command of the Battalion to Donald Wilson, instead of being towed out of the barracks in the customary land rover, his 'chariot' was 'our affiliated French AMX 30 main battle tank', named Buzancy Black Watch in honour of the Regiment's action at Buzancy in 1918.[16] A diversionary event during the summer was being filmed by the BBC for a series on the British Army, 'the Beeb' having decided that The Black Watch 'was worthy of a mention.'[17]

During the posting, the Battalion continued the customary 'flag tour duties', exercising the right of British military access into the Soviet sector of Berlin, the objective being to demonstrate 'to that part of the city, the continued participation of the British in the Quadripartite agreement concerning Berlin'. The Russians had the same rights. 'Every day,' recorded Captain Mike Riddell-Webster, 'someone went to the East, passing through Checkpoint Charlie, as agreed in the original agreements, 'without let or hindrance.' Since they went in uniform, they could not be searched. 'We were also tasked to gather as much low-level intelligence as possible on Soviet military movements. So we spent time in railway sidings as well as counting vehicles and observing number plates,' related Captain Ronnie Bradford.[18] The 'acceptable exchange rate' enabled them to buy china, crystal and carpets 'even Soviet style hats.' 'And Zeiss binoculars,' added Nunneley.[19] Interaction with East German officials also came on the train, which departed daily from West Berlin across East Germany into West Germany, the location of the checkpoint at Helmstedt-Marienborn providing the shortest land route between West Berlin and West Germany. In addition to checking of documents, 'small' presents were exchanged. 'They usually wanted videos of Manchester United,' recorded Captain David Kemmis Betty.[20]

In the spring of 1989 training for another residential tour in Ballykinler began with exercises in Sennelager, the soldiers now equipped with the new SA80, the British Army's new 'Small Arms for the Eighties'.[21]

The Berlin tour concluded with the honour of Trooping the Colour for The Queen's Birthday Parade in June, leading Private Harry Hood to observe how 'fantastic' it was for a seventeen-year-old from Dunfermline to be posted to a major European city.'[22] The Battalion's return to Britain meant that it missed the unexpected outcome of *glasnost*, which led to Germany's reunification and the break-up of the Soviet Union. 'If you had said to me that in a couple of months the [Berlin] wall would come down, I would have asked what you'd been drinking,' observed Captain Riddell-Webster, who felt 'robbed' of the opportunity to witness events first-hand.[23]

1989–91: Ballykinler again

For troops arriving in Northern Ireland in July 1989 and based once again in Abercorn Barracks, the contrast with Berlin was 'startling', but the operational environment 'all too familiar'. Since The Black Watch's last tour, there had been no let up in attacks on the security forces which, in 1988, included the murder of Corporals David Howes and Derek Wood, Royal Signals, caught up in the funeral procession of an IRA member in Belfast in March. On 15 June, the Lisburn 'fun run' bomb killed six soldiers who had just completed a charity marathon.[24] On 20 August a bomb had been placed on a bus in Ballygawley, County Tyrone, bound for Omagh, killing eight soldiers from the Light Infantry and wounding twenty-eight, the single biggest loss of military life since Warrenpoint in 1979.

With a reserve role in 39 Brigade, the soldiers trained for both urban and rural operations. 'You did six weeks down on the border,' commented Major Roddy Riddell, 'then went on leave; a period of pre-deployment training took place over another six-week period. You were then on standby, followed by guards and duties which allowed you to do more training, then you were deployed again.' The targeting of off-duty soldiers resulted in numerous controls and restrictions. 'By this stage', commented Lance Corporal Harry Hood, 'we were wearing helmets and had become anonymous, whereas previously the Battalion wore the Red Hackle.'[25] On 13 December 1989 the continuing threat was again highlighted when the Provisional IRA attacked a permanent vehicle checkpoint manned by the King's Own Scottish Borderers at Derryard, County Fermanagh. Using heavy machine-guns, grenades, rockets and a flamethrower, the attack resulted in a fierce firefight in which two soldiers were killed.

On 29 June, amid tight security, the Queen Mother, shortly to celebrate her 90th birthday, made her only visit to the Battalion in Northern Ireland, which was both 'a tonic and a surprise'.[26] A highlight of the 1990 calendar was celebrating the 250th anniversary of The Black Watch's first muster near Aberfeldy in May 1740, for which a commemorative medal was struck.[27] Having transferred to 3 Brigade in late October the Battalion's role became one of 'roving troubleshooters' operating in the rural and border areas around Newry and Portadown.[28] The move coincided with the aftermath of three proxy bomb attacks on 24 October. Ordered by the Provisional IRA, they were carried out by men coerced into driving vehicles filled with explosives against military targets at Coshquin in the north, Omagh and Cloghoge, south of Newry, when James McAlvoy, allegedly targeted for serving RUC officers at a petrol station, had been forced to drive close to a permanent vehicle checkpoint's accommodation block. Although McAlvoy only suffered a broken leg, Ranger Cyril Smith was killed and thirteen civilians injured. 'The Rangers were on high alert,' recalled Sergeant Baxter, 'and nearly took us out when we arrived.' Among the 'plethora of devices' found in the vicinity was one designed 'to kill as many Jocks as possible in a napalm fire bomb style attack'.[29]

The increased level of violence meant that 'the remaining ten months of the tour were marked by frequent short notice deployments,' noted Lieutenant Colonel Nigel Lithgow, who had replaced Wilson as Commanding Officer in October. 'In one four-month period, I had just four days in camp,' commented Major Bradford. 'I worked in every county in Northern Ireland and was frequently tasked from one operation to the next.' 'We led a schizophrenic life,' observed Captain James Cowan, the Battalion's intelligence officer. 'One day you might be out on patrol in Armagh, the next you might be dancing reels.' 'By the end of the tour, we were knackered,' observed Major Riddell. 'It was a long two years.'[30]

The decision of Iraqi President, Saddam Hussein, to invade Kuwait in August 1990 presaged more conflict in the Middle East. In response the United States launched Operation Desert Shield, involving the build-up of troops in the region for the defence of Saudi Arabia. Among those caught up in events was Black Watch Warrant Officer Jim Paton, a former member of the Northern Ireland Patrol Group, now working as a training adviser in Kuwait. After nearly a month in hiding, Paton and several others were taken prisoner by Iraqi forces and sent to Baghdad. Although women and children were released, the men, among whom were French, German, Japanese and American nationals, were split into groups of four 'and moved out to strategic locations throughout Iraq' as 'human shields'. Realising they were near the Turkish–Syrian border, Paton thought of escaping but, concerned that he might jeopardise the lives of the older civilians, some of whose 'various ailments and complaints' would hinder their escape, he decided 'to continue to get fit and prepare until things got to a stage where we felt threatened'.[31] On 11 December 1990 Paton and his companions were released.

On 17 January a combined UN military force launched Operation Desert Storm to force Saddam Hussein's withdrawal from Kuwait. 'As the Resident Battalion in Northern Ireland,' observed Major Ogilvy-Wedderburn, 'we were releasing equipment to go down to Kuwait.'[32] With the restoration of Kuwait's sovereignty, the Gulf War ended on 28 February 1991. The only Black Watch officer involved in operations was Captain Angus MacDonald, serving on the staff of 1 Armoured Division Rear Headquarters.[33]

Returning from Northern Ireland and posted to Tern Hill, Shropshire in August 1991, the Black Watch's role was 'Military Home Defence'. 'By Christmas all support platoons had been re-formed and trained, an NCOs' cadre had been run and Tern Hill was a truly Black Watch establishment, complete with a 42nd Club,' observed Lithgow. 1992 was a 'full and frantically busy year', the soldiers undertaking a variety of detachments, including duties at the Royal Tournament and Exercise POND JUMP WEST, a six-week training exercise in Alberta, Canada, supported by 'artillery, engineers and aviation assets'.[34]

A newcomer to the Battalion was Rory Stewart, whose father, Brian Stewart, had been serving in the 1st Tyneside Scottish in June 1944. Undertaking a Short Service Limited Commission on his gap year before university, Stewart found his brief service frustrating, instead of the 'heroic life' he had anticipated. He later made his name travelling in the Middle East and Afghanistan before entering politics.[35] By the end of the year, the Battalion was preparing to go to Hong Kong, Lithgow observing that, during their 'somewhat quiet and boring' time in Shropshire, only three soldiers in two separate cases had appeared in local courts 'albeit one was a vicious assault against another Jock' resulting in two privates being imprisoned and dismissed from the Army.[36]

1993–94: Hong Kong, home early

A 'mere handful' of those who had served in Hong Kong twenty years previously remained in the Battalion. Taking up quarters in Stanley Fort in early January 1993 the officers and men were accompanied by 324 families with 382 children, their activities recorded in a new magazine, *The Black Watch (Royal Highland Regiment) Hong Kong Review*. An early news item was Lieutenant Colonel Lithgow's 'unusual exit' in a rickshaw when relinquishing command of the Battalion on 16 April 1993.[37] In retrospect, Lithgow highlighted manpower as a major frustration 'not helped by 12 discharges through DCM [District Court Martial] due to drugs offences... Drugs have now become a much more prevalent problem in the Army; sadly 1 BW is no exception.'[38]

Lithgow's successor was Lieutenant Colonel Sir Andrew Ogilvy-Wedderburn, familiarly known as 'Og-Wed'. He was 'perfect, calm and charming. He just won over Hong Kong,' observed Second Lieutenant Tim Elliott.[39] During the posting, certain activities shelved during the Northern Ireland tour were 'back in vogue', including the Crimean Long Reveille on the 15th of each month, beating the 'Cawnpore' Gong, Pipe and Bugle calls and Regimental sporting fixtures. A highlight of the social calendar was the Dragon Boat Race in June at Stanley Beach, in which the Battalion's teams were appropriately named 'The Royal Highlanders', 'The Forty Twa' and 'The Black Watch Belles'. 'The civilian teams were really competitive as they had practised all year', observed Private John Paul Maestri, 'whereas we were just thrown into boats and told to get on with it!'[40]

One development, a result of the cuts prescribed by *Options for Change 1990,* was the merger of the Regiment's Military Band with the Highland Band. The Pipes and Drums, however, had gone from 'strength to strength', their activities ranging from television (the *Bruce Forsyth Show*) to a Retreat at the British Embassy in Washington, performances at the Royal Albert Hall, the Royal Tournament, the Hong Kong Jockey Club, among others.[41] They also played at the Hong Kong Sevens, the 'premier' tournament of the International Rugby Board Sevens World Series, for which the battalion stewarded, 'making sure people did not run onto the pitch. Once we had a couple of female streakers'.[42]

In addition to ceremonial duties, the Battalion continued operations in the New Territories, including monitoring incidents of smuggling, especially cars and televisions, into mainland China. 'The smugglers would take out the inboard engine of an ocean-going racing boat, leaving sufficient space to fit a Rolls Royce,' related Major Riddell-Webster. 'They would then go hell for leather to China, undertaking "dare and do" stuff like jumping between boats to cut fuel lines.' To counter their activities, the soldiers dug in 'proper Northern Ireland style Observations Posts' overlooking likely loading sites. 'A crane arriving, for example, would be a trigger to the police to intercept the smugglers,' observed Ogilvy-Wedderburn. 'It was quite benign, but basically that form of smuggling was wiped out.'[43]

Competitions to test combat readiness, basic military skills and stamina were held on the 1,912-ft Castle Peak in the New Territories. 'Castle Peak's most demanding phase was the live-firing-platoon attack, which was the first time the platoon had operated together as a conventional Rifle Platoon,' noted Private McGilp.[44] With overseas training exercises in Hawaii, New Zealand and Brunei, the 'Territory', continued Ogilvy-Wedderburn, was 'a great springboard for travel in the Far East. Regrettably many preferred Kirkcaldy to Kota Kinabalu, Perth to Phuket and Tannadice to Thailand. After much haranguing about the benefits of taking leave in the Far East I did receive a post-card from one Jock who wrote "Dear Sir, took your advice, Thailand is Boo (fantastic) yours a very happy Jock".' 'It was an absolutely fantastic post,' observed Private Robert Duncan. 'We were hard worked but we also had the opportunity to travel.'[45]

After less than two years The Black Watch returned home. 'The Hong Kong government was already thinking of the handover in 1997,' explained Riddell-Webster. 'One question which came up in discussion with the British Government was defence expenditure. At which point, the Hong Kong government asked why they were paying seventy per cent of garrison costs to protect them from people they were going to join politically.' Agreement had already been reached about what would be retained. 'Our barracks were going to China. So there was this uncomfortable period when everything started being run down.'[46]

On 13 December 1994, for the last time in The Black Watch's history, a 3rd (Volunteer) Battalion was raised from the 1st Battalion, 51st Highland Volunteers, which, following the cuts recommended by *Options for Change*, had lost two companies. With Headquarters at a new Queen's Barracks in Perth, opened in 1975, the companies were based in Dundee, Forfar and Kirkcaldy. Further mergers were also taking place. After its amalgamation in 1961, The Queen's Own Highlanders merged with The Gordon Highlanders on 17 September 1994, becoming the 1st Battalion The Highlanders (Seaforth, Gordons & Camerons). Despite a continuing requirement for cuts, The Black Watch kept its independent status, its members mindful that, like the Cameronians in 1968, the Regiment could 'fall on its sword', in other words disband rather than be amalgamated.[47]

1995: Belfast, 'pretty much a peace tour'

Having returning briefly to Pirbright, in May 1995 the Battalion began its eleventh tour to Northern Ireland. Since its last posting, the situation had changed dramatically. On 15 December 1993, on behalf of the British and Irish governments, Prime Minister John Major and Taoiseach Albert Reynolds had issued a Joint Declaration on Peace (known as the Downing Street Declaration) stating that 'it is for the people of Ireland alone, by agreement between the two parts respectively, to exercise their right of self-determination on the basis of consent… to bring about a united Ireland, if that is their wish.' For the first time, the British government declared that it had no inherent strategic, political, or economic self-interest in Northern Ireland. The declaration outlined plans for negotiations, in which all parties could participate, including former terrorist organisations which had renounced violence. Although Ian Paisley, leader of the Democratic Unionist Party (DUP), rejected the declaration, others, notably Gerry Adams, President of Sinn Féin since 1983, and James Molyneaux, leader of the Ulster Unionist Party, saw it as the basis for future dialogue.[48]

On 6 April 1994 the Provisional IRA announced a three-day ceasefire followed by the 'cessation of military operations' on 31 August 1994. As a result, the British Army remained virtually confined to barracks. 'No patrols were to be carried out except for administration runs but we were to be ready to revert to patrolling at a moment's notice if the ceasefire broke down,' explained Ogilvy-Wedderburn. 'Headquarters Northern Ireland and 39 Brigade were reluctant to let us out of Belfast to train, so "skillfade" and boredom were potential enemies.' 'It was pretty much what we would call a peace tour,' observed Private Alexander Wilson, undertaking his first tour. 'Gone are the endless frantic days of patrolling, searching and supporting,' observed *The Watchkeeper*. 'They have been replaced by long days of guarding and hurry up and waiting. That said there seems to be enough for everyone to do and frequent forays into the local training areas, hills and playing fields provides a welcome break to urban life.'[49]

'There must have been around 200 soldiers confined to barracks,' observed Captain Tim Elliott, who described Fort Whiterock as like 'living in a shoe box. We were worried we were losing our expertise and were concerned that if we were called out we would just walk into traps because we would not be savvy enough.'[50] In the expectation that the need for an extensive military presence was diminishing, North Howard Street Mill was demolished. A thorough search was made of the building beforehand, but the only item of interest found was a wallet belonging to a Queen's Own Highlander, left behind fifteen years previously.[51]

One controversial incident was the release on licence of Private Lee Clegg, the Parachute Regiment, sentenced to life imprisonment in 1993 for having shot and killed the teenage driver and passenger of a stolen car driven at high speed through a checkpoint. Since the feelings of those opposed to Clegg's release were likely to run high, troops were moved into the nearby RUC stations. As soon as news broke of his release 'West Belfast was sealed by blazing hijacked vehicles'. While the RUC and Sinn Féin argued about whose responsibility it was to move the burning vehicles, the disruption 'angered a large proportion of the population of West Belfast who were beginning to reap the benefits of the ceasefire and this made our job easier… we would get as many cheery waves as we got half bricks thrown at us.'[52] Uneventful as the tour was, during the Battalion's six-month presence there were 80 visits 'of one star and above', including government officials and Prince Charles.[53]

In November 1995 the Battalion returned to Fort George. Among its activities the following year was a six-week exercise, Grand Prix, near Mount Kenya. To meet their water requirements 'each company had a train of camels loaded with cans of water and a camel herder,' recorded the unit press officer, Captain Kemmis Betty. 'It was all very biblical.'[54]

The Black Watch did not return to Northern Ireland for a decade. Although the ceasefire was broken in early 1996 with a bomb attack in London's Docklands followed by a car bomb attack in Enniskillen in July, the shift away from violence continued and in July 1997 the IRA ceasefire was renewed. On 10 April 1998 the Good Friday Agreement was signed in Belfast by the Republic of Ireland and the United Kingdom governments, outlining the constitutional relationship between Northern Ireland and the Republic and the status and system of government between the UK and Northern Ireland. A central component of the talks was the decommissioning of weapons.[55] Although some groups remained active, such as the Real IRA, responsible for the Omagh bomb on 16 August 1998, they were no longer mainstream.[56]

1997: Hong Kong, 'centre stage'

For the last year of Britain's imperial presence in Hong Kong, Lantau Island and the New Territories before the expiry of the ninety-nine-year lease at midnight on 30 June 1997, the Army Board had decided that two British battalions would undertake two successive six-month unaccompanied tours. 'The atmosphere leading up to the handover was amazing,' recalled Lieutenant Colonel Alasdair Loudon, now in command of the Battalion, which arrived in Hong Kong in January. 'We were living in a goldfish bowl. Everyone wanted a story of blood on the streets. But we did the job really well and there were no incidents.' 'It was fantastic to be a part of living history,' commented Second Lieutenant Mark Percy. 'From the British point of view, we were handing over something that had been a huge success.'[57]

'Headquarters was very worried about discipline,' observed Captain Kemmis Betty, 'and so there were fairly dictatorial measures to keep us under control as well as a curfew.' Measures could have been stricter. During a visit by the Commander British Forces, Major General Bryan Dutton, Regimental Sergeant Major Alan McEwen was privy to hearing a suggestion that the Battalion should be 'gated' for the six-month tour. In reply, Loudon had requested that he be allowed 'to gauge the level of ill-discipline and take appropriate action accordingly.' As McEwen observed: 'Gating The Black Watch could have created far more discipline issues than allowing the Jocks to book out, albeit with an imposed curfew. This was without doubt the correct decision. The officers and men of the BW owe Loudon a huge debt of gratitude.'[58]

'We spent six months selling kit. All the kitchens were shut down so we spent our last two or three weeks living on aircraft disposable meals,' recorded Major Riddell-Webster. 'UK PLC had to be clear of Hong Kong at midnight on 30 June so there would be no requirement to go back again.' As part of the drawdown, over a third of the 550-strong Battalion went home, partly so that D Company could prepare itself for the Royal Guard at Ballater. Despite missing the finale to Britain's presence in Hong Kong, Lance Corporal Alexander Wilson had no regrets. 'I was a soldier from a working class background in Fife that danced the slow St Bernard's Waltz with the Queen.'[59]

A daily duty before the handover included raising and lowering the Union Flag at Hong Kong's Cenotaph. On one windy day, a photographer captured Lance Corporal Lee Wotherspoon lowering the flag as a gust of wind raised his kilt to reveal that, as many suspected, Scotsmen wore nothing underneath. The photograph, distributed worldwide, resulted in a number of 'romantic letters' admiring Wotherspoon's 'attributes', the only admonishment apparently being that his 'diced hose tops' were not level! Until the last day of Britain's authority in Hong Kong, The Black Watch kept guard outside the gates of the Headquarters British Forces, mindful that they would be handing over to the Chinese People's Liberation Army, their adversaries in Korea in 1952–53. But 'it was just like a normal guard handover,' recalled Sergeant Gair McCrostie. 'We walked out and they walked in.'[60]

Before the official handover ceremony at midnight on 30 June, Britain's departure was to be marked by a Farewell Parade. In order to choose the participants, McEwen assembled the soldiers. 'He wanted all the Jocks over six feet to take part in the Farewell Parade and all the good-looking ones doing the Handover Ceremony!' related Maestri, now a lance corporal· 'We needed to show the world the best of the best,' explained McEwen, 'lean and mean and good-looking BW soldiers – aesthetically pleasing to the eye.'[61]

The Farewell Parade took place in a stadium erected near the water's edge. Prince Charles represented the Queen, and all 'the great and good' of Hong Kong were present. As The Black Watch prepared to enter the stadium in the footsteps of the Royal Navy, 'all eyes were fixed on the officer at the rear of the Navy and all ears strained for the command that would propel us onto what was quite literally the World Stage. When it came we marched through a gap in the stands and the spotlights suddenly illuminated us… The roar which greeted us was breath-taking and nearly drowned out the massed Bands, but it was also quite the most humbling experience, and probably our only taste of fame.' 'The applause gave us a terrific lift,' related McEwen, describing how, positioned between the Royal Navy and the RAF, The Black Watch was 'centre stage.'[62]

Torrential rain accompanied the proceedings. Having addressed the assembled audience, Prince Charles returned to his seat, reportedly describing his speech as the best he had ever made 'under water'. 'I remember thinking… Christ! My uniform is going to be wrecked,' recalled Drum Major Pat McLinden, 'and I need it for the Edinburgh Tattoo straight away.' After the Union and Hong Kong flags were lowered, Pipe Major Stephen Small played *The Immortal Memory*. The Finale was a performance of the massed bands, pipes and drums, orchestras, choirs and cast of the theme song for the handover, *Rhythm of My Heart*. The ceremony concluded with an exceptional fireworks display as the Guards of Honour marched off to *Auld Lang Syne*. Despite being 'absolutely saturated', Private Duncan recorded the parade as being 'the best' he had ever done.[63] They then went immediately by boat to Kai Tak airport, their progress slowed by large numbers of well-wishers who had come in boats to bid them farewell.[64] Having observed the downpour on the television, the Queen Mother sent her congratulations: 'Your smartness, bearing and fortitude in such torrential rain did credit to your regiment, your country and your Sovereign.'[65]

By the time the handover ceremony at the Convention Centre on the Victoria Harbour riverfront took place, most of the Battalion was airborne. 'Unlike a normal flight, everyone on the plane knew each other,' recalled Riddell-Webster. 'It was like a great cocktail party.' 'A message came over the tannoy,' recorded Kemmis Betty, celebrating his 30th birthday across several time zones: '"Say farewell to Hong Kong!"'[66]

Fort George, a Family day and Fallingbostel

Back at Fort George 'scarcely had the uniforms drenched in that final deluge in Hong Kong had time to dry' before a small party, led by the Colonel of the Regiment, Brigadier Garry Barnett, flew to the United States to dedicate a memorial cairn, made of stones from the homes of many of the clans represented in The Black Watch in 1758, to those who fell at Ticonderoga. Hosted by The Black Watch of Canada, among those present was Second Lieutenant Hugh Campbell, a direct descendant of Major Duncan Campbell of Inverawe, whose premonition that he would be killed at Ticonderoga was recorded in Robert Louis Stevenson's poem. 'The bravery at Ticonderoga,' said Barnett, 'the ability to take casualties not suffered again for over 150 years, until the First World War, owe much to this clan spirit and family loyalty.'[67] In the same year The Queen Mother, aged 97, celebrated her Diamond Jubilee as Colonel-in-Chief of The Black Watch. On 8 September she visited Fort George for the first time, posing, as for her Golden Jubilee, for a photograph with former Commanding Officers.[68]

The following year, on Sunday 20 September, a regimental family day was held at the Queen Mother's childhood home, Glamis Castle, involving soldiers of the 1st and 3rd Battalions The Black Watch as well as cadets and veterans, overseen by Brigadier Barnett and the 1st and 3rd Black Watch's Commanding Officers, Lieutenant Colonels Bradford and Riddell. 'In contrast to Royal visits made wherever the Battalion was based or working, at Glamis the entire Black Watch family was present,' commented Riddell. After a Drumhead service, the Queen Mother visited the tents and stands, a golf buggy, *The Spirit of Angus*, being made available to facilitate her progress. A 'wonderful example of the family atmosphere of the day' was her introduction to WO2 John Wilkinson, who was serving in the 3rd Black Watch, as were his two sons, his grandfather and father having also served in the Regiment. After lunch the Colours of the 1st Black Watch, presented in 1975, were laid up at Glamis Castle; it was the first time in the Queen Mother's long relationship with the Regiment that she had witnessed the ceremony. The 'musical highlight' of the day was a tune composed by Pipe Major Peter Snaddon, 'Salute to our Colonel-in-Chief'.[69]

The 1998 'family day' was the Queen Mother's last engagement with The Black Watch. Having celebrated her 100th birthday in August 2000, Queen Elizabeth the Queen Mother, aged 101, died on 30 March 2002. One of the Royal Company of Archers' vigil teams for her lying in state in Westminster Abbey was provided by serving and retired officers of The Black Watch while Brigadier Barnett was a pall-bearer.[70] In due course Prince Charles, His Royal Highness the Duke of Rothesay (as the heir to the throne is traditionally known in Scotland) was appointed Colonel-in-Chief.[71]

In July 2000 the Battalion moved to Fallingbostel, as part of 7 Armoured Brigade. The first year was spent undergoing extensive training to convert to the role of an armoured infantry battalion equipped mainly with the new 'Warrior' tracked armoured vehicle. 'Germany was a step up professionally, compared to being part of a regional brigade in Fort George which was a bit of a backwater,' observed Captain Angus Philp, who had chosen a commission in The Black Watch because his great-uncle had served in the 2nd Black Watch in Burma during the Second World War. 'It felt as if we were back in the mainstream of the British Army.' 'It was exactly the same feeling of stepping up a gear as we had 20 years previously when we moved from Catterick to Werl,' remarked Lieutenant Colonel Bradford, who handed over command of the Battalion to Riddell-Webster in December 2000.[72]

2001: Kosovo, Supporting Peace

As the 20th century drew to a close, beneath the surface calm unresolved political issues remained. The Gulf War of 1990–91 had left a hostile Saddam Hussein and his ruling Ba'ath Party in control of Iraq. The Middle East remained unsettled. The end of the Soviet Union's hegemony over Eastern Europe had also caused the rise of new nation states convulsed by civil war.

In 1991 the Socialist Federal Republic of Yugoslavia, held together since 1945 under the authoritarian rule of Marshal Tito, fragmented into bloody conflict, with Croatia, Slovenia and Macedonia all declaring their independence, followed by Bosnia and Herzegovina in 1992. This had left a rump state of Yugoslavia composed of Serbia, Montenegro and Kosovo, the latter inhabited by a majority of Albanian-origin Kosovars with a Serb minority. In early 1998 Yugoslav forces had begun fighting rebel Kosovars, grouped together in the Kosovo Liberation Army (KLA). Thousands became homeless. Having failed to reach a diplomatic solution, on the grounds that this was a 'humanitarian war', NATO ordered air strikes to stop the Serbian leadership's increasingly aggressive actions. By the terms of the June 1999 Kumanovo Treaty, Yugoslav forces withdrew from Kosovo and an international peacekeeping force was established, the British contribution named Operation Agricola.[73]

On 14 July 2001 The Black Watch assumed command in Pristina, capital of Kosovo, as part of Operation Agricola VI. Highlighting the 'sheer variety' of the tour, Lieutenant Colonel Riddell-Webster recorded undertaking 'all sorts of operations, urban and rural, static and mobile, from patrols in Pristina to searches in Stmlje. We were privileged to work at all levels alongside people from a vast number of different backgrounds and traditions from the Kosovo civilian language assistants to the sometimes bewildering variety of nations in the UN Police, our comrades in the Multi-National Brigade (Centre) to the tireless volunteers in the international and non-governmental organisations.' 'As a battalion with no corporate Balkans knowledge we had to rely heavily on our Northern Ireland experience and what we could glean from individuals' experiences in Bosnia & Kosovo,' observed Major Rupert Forrest, the Battalion's second-in-command.[74] Describing Kosovo as 'a relatively benign environment,' Captain Mark Percy had 'one of the more interesting jobs' within the Battlegroup area as liaison officer with units of the Kosovo Protection Corps (KPC) based in Pristina. 'It was our first operational tour for the majority of the Battalion and so there was excitement and anticipation, as well as an eagerness to do a good job.'[75]

During the tour the Battalion provided a covert surveillance platoon in support of Brigade HQ. 'It was a bit of a mixture of inherited long-running observation tasks and other new tasks we would plan and run ourselves as Brigade Headquarters received intelligence about particular individuals they were interested in,' related Captain Philp. 'For example, the Serb and Albanian factions within Kosovo or various criminal elements.' 'Tonight our searches of pubs begins,' Major Forrest was recording on 21 August, describing Operation Babylon. 'Many are connected to crime – prostitution & drugs. The heavies are more often than not armed.' 'We were encouraged to go into pubs on patrol and have a pint in order to get information,' recorded Corporal Maestri. 'It was like walking around Perth with your weapon.'[76]

Among other activities was opening the Highland House Orphanage north-east of Pristina, its refurbishment assisted by donations from The Black Watch Wives' Sponsored Walk from London to Fallingbostel. Sadly, an accident during a routine train move of armoured vehicles resulted in the death from severe burns of twenty-four-year-old Private Robert Donkin after he had been struck by overhead power lines.[77] By the time the tour ended on 10 November 2001 and the Battalion returned to Germany, Riddell-Webster believed they were leaving 'at a difficult time' in the closing stages of Kosovo's first genuinely democratic elections. Yet he was confident 'that we left Kosovo in a better state than we found it, and undoubtedly some of this progress is the result of our efforts.'[78]

During The Black Watch's deployment in Kosovo, 'etched in everyone's memories' were the terrorist attacks on 11 September 2001, when hijacked aeroplanes rammed the Twin Towers of the World Trade Center in New York and the Pentagon in Washington, DC, leaving nearly 3,000 dead. In Pristina, the Battalion's first obligation had been to respond to any perceived threat, as well as increasing vigilance around British and American institutions and providing security during 'the many commemorative events that took place.' 'For us little changed but we await the announcement of US intentions with interest,' commented Forrest. 'We didn't really understand the ramifications,' observed Captain Williamson. 'For about 24 hours we put on our helmets and body armour before we realised that what had happened in the United States was nothing to do with Kosovo. In retrospect the biggest thing which happened to us in Kosovo was 9/11.'[79]

But yet the state of things require
These motions of unrest,
And these great spirits of high desire
Seem born to turn them best,
To purge the mischiefs that increase
And all good order mar:
For oft we see a wicked peace
To be well changed for war.[80]

25

Iraq: A Grave and Gathering Danger

There was no issue whether we were going or not going to war.
It was obvious with this huge movement of troops,
we weren't stopping until we got to Iraq.[1]

We were genuinely treated as liberators.[2]

Operation Telic

Following the 9/11 attack by the extremist network Al Qaeda, President George W. Bush had first turned his attention to Afghanistan from where the Saudi dissident Osama bin Laden, leader of Al Qaeda, had been operating. Bush's focus later shifted to confronting the 'grave and gathering danger' presented by Iraq. Included in the conditions for a ceasefire after the 1991 Gulf War, as specified in the UN Security Council's Resolution 687, was the reminder that Iraq had subscribed to the 1989 Declaration of States Parties to the 1925 Geneva Protocol 'establishing the objective of the universal elimination of chemical and biological weapons'.[3] To monitor Iraq's compliance the United Nations Special Commission to Oversee the Destruction of Weapons of Mass Destruction (UNSCOM) was established. On the grounds of non-compliance, in 1998 the United States and Britain launched Operation Desert Fox, a four-day bombing campaign to strike military and security targets which might be used to produce, store, maintain and deliver weapons of mass destruction. The following year United Nations' Security Council Resolution 1284 replaced UNSCOM with the Monitoring,

Verification and Inspections Commission (UNMOVIC), mandated to disarm Iraq of its weapons of mass destruction as well as undertaking a system of monitoring and verification. In February 2001, to protect Allied warplanes operating in the no-fly zones established to protect the Kurdish population in the north and the Marsh Arabs in the south, British and American forces again carried out bombing raids near Baghdad with the objective of disabling Iraq's radar and missile systems.

In support of Bush's 2002 warning at the United Nations, British Prime Minister, Tony Blair, produced a dossier, assessing 'Iraq's Weapons of Mass Destruction'. Known as the 'September Dossier', it indicated that Iraq not only possessed such weapons, but also that Saddam Hussein had reconstituted Iraq's nuclear weapons programme.[4] Following the passage of UN Resolution 1441 on 8 November, stating that Iraq was 'in material breach' of Resolution 687, UN weapons inspectors, led by Swedish diplomat and former head of the International Atomic Energy Authority (IAEA), Dr Hans Blix, travelled to Iraq. On 3 February 2003 the British government produced another dossier, entitled 'Iraq: Its Infrastructure of Concealment, Deception and Intimidation', again affirming that Iraq had not complied with UN Resolution 687.[5]

Reporting to the Security Council on 14 February 2003, Blix detailed how, during an eleven-week period, he had visited over 300 sites and undertaken 400 inspections, all of which were 'performed without notice, and access was almost always provided promptly'. In response to the question: 'How much, if any, is left of Iraq's weapons of mass destruction and related proscribed items and programmes?' he confirmed that 'so far' no weapons had been found, 'only a small number of empty chemical munitions'. He also emphasised that 'many proscribed weapons and items are not accounted for'.[6] Although Blix's findings were inconclusive, the controversial decision had already been taken to invade Iraq. Britain's military contribution was to be codenamed Operation Telic.[7]

'Black Watch Gulf bound'

'The possibility of deployment to Iraq has been on our mental horizons throughout our training in 2002, both in Poland and Canada,' Major Nick Channer, the Battalion's second-in-command, was observing in early 2003, noting that 'resources which might normally have been allocated sparingly have been pushed our way at short notice'. 'We started doing a certain amount of contingency planning before Christmas 2002 looking at gaps in the Battlegroup,' recorded the adjutant, Captain Angus Philp. 'It was obvious with this huge movement of troops, we weren't stopping until we got to Iraq,' noted Captain Jamie Riddell, who was with the Army Training Regiment, Bassingbourn and was 'terrified' of being left behind.[8]

When, on 20 January 2003, the Secretary of State for Defence, Geoff Hoon, announced the deployment of military forces, preparations intensified.[9] 'It was a real war, as opposed to other operations like Kosovo or Northern Ireland,' recorded Philp, who was receiving phone calls 'from guys posted outside the Battalion all desperate to get back'. 'How many people can say "I went to war"?' asked Lance Corporal Jimmy Steele. 'It was the ultimate challenge,' recalled Captain Jules McElhinney. 'Otherwise, it was like training to be a mechanic and never getting to fix a car.'[10]

'We practically doubled in strength,' noted Captain Nick Ord. All soldiers had to be immunised. 'The vehicles had to be cleaned and prepared for special armour to be fitted and painted with desert paint. This sounds an easy task but with limited paint, which is designed to be sprayed onto the vehicles in a heated environment, we found that in the sub-zero temperatures of the garages [in Germany] it was not a simple process, with the paint freezing in the air before it could stick to the surface of the vehicles.' 'We have much to learn about the theatre of operations into which we are to deploy,' continued Channer, describing how Lieutenant Colonel Mike Riddell-Webster was already in Kuwait 'attending a mission rehearsal exercise'.[11]

Part of their training involved becoming familiar with *The Black Watch Battle Group Soldier's Guide to Iraq*, prepared by the intelligence officer, Captain Williamson, which included instructions on desert survival: 'Drink often even if you are not thirsty… Avoid very cold water, it causes cramps… Eat even when not hungry, lack of food is as significant as lack of water.' The booklet also contained a pictorial description of Iraqi military vehicles and army ranks, and Arabic phrases with phonetic pronunciation in Iraqi dialect.[12]

'Black Watch Gulf bound,' announced the *Perthshire Advertiser* on 28 February.[13] 'We flew out of Hanover airport in a passenger aircraft whose markings had been painted over,' continued Riddell. 'Fairly surreal walking off the plane in the dark with lines of other troops doing the same thing,' recorded Lieutenant Will Colquhoun. 'We were moved directly to a holding area in an American camp just on the edge of Kuwait city airport.'[14] Huge tents had been erected to accommodate the gathering contingent. 'We settled into the luxury of a Kuwaiti desert', recalled Corporal Ian Smith, 'where the daily joys of zero visibility, sandstorms and some of the worst sausages ever prepared kept us amused for the weeks leading up to the eventual border crossing date.' 'Managed to beg and borrow some desert combats,' continued Colquhoun. 'We are still due our main issue of desert kit and the rumour is that it will be a while.' 'Waiting in the form-up area, we spent time cleaning our weapons, but if I wasn't doing anything,' recalled Pipe Major Alistair Duthie, 'I'd get out the pipes; it brings out the Caledonian spirit.'[15] An unusual challenge was 'arguing with the wild life', which included rattlesnakes and large black-and-yellow lizards.[16]

The official objective of the mission was 'to disarm Iraq of weapons of mass destruction, to end Saddam Hussein's support for terrorism, and to free the Iraqi people'.[17] Of the invading force, totalling 176,000 troops at its height, the United States contributed the majority. Britain was the only major European country to support the invasion, providing the second largest contingent of over 40,000 troops – involving 'one-third of the British Army'.[18] The Black Watch was one of four battlegroups in 7 Armoured Brigade (the 'Desert Rats' in the Second World War), which was one of three brigades in the 1st UK Armoured Division, under the command of the Major General

Robin Brims. The Black Watch Battlegroup was composed of B and D Companies, and C (Fire Support) Company with two squadrons of armour equipped with the 'Challenger 2' main battle tank – a Squadron from the Royal Scots Dragoon Guards and Egypt Squadron from the 2nd Royal Tank Regiment. There were also units from the Royal Engineers (RE), Royal Electrical and Mechanical Engineers (REME), Royal Army Medical Corps (RAMC), Royal Logistic Corps and Royal Military Police. The Black Watch's A Company was assigned to the Royal Scots Dragoon Guards Battlegroup.[19]

About 70,000 Kurdish irregular troops, whose population had been subjected to genocidal massacre by Saddam Hussein in 1988, supported the operation. Following Turkey's decision to deny passage through its territory, the original plan of assaulting Iraq from the north and south was modified so that entry into Iraq was only through Kuwait. In the line of battle, United States' forces would be the first to cross into the southern province of Basra where the 2nd Black Watch had fought during the 1916 Mesopotamian campaign. Two lines of advance, approximately 60 miles apart, would move in parallel. While the US V Corps secured the Al Rumaylah oilfield near the border, the US 1st Marine Expeditionary Force (MEF) would advance towards Basra. The 1st UK Armoured Division would then carry out a 'relief in place' centred around the town of Az Zubayr. 'Quite a lot of disappointment that we are not to have a very glamorous role,' Riddell-Webster was recording on 1 March.[20]

'Compared with the Americans, I saw what a small part we were and what a small window on the road we would have when the Battlegroup had to move,' recorded Captain Philp, who was responsible for logistics. 'My fear was causing something to go wrong, resulting in a dreadful traffic jam.'[21] With over 100 journalists accompanying British forces, embedded with The Black Watch was Gethin Chamberlain from *The Scotsman* and *The Daily Record* and Ian Bruce from the *Glasgow Herald*. 'They had to strike a balance between reporting objectively and without bias and contributing constructively to the British war effort,' commented Captain Rob Sandford. 'Our embeds candidly admitted that it was hard to rely on the Battle

Group for everything and not to allow that to influence their writing.' 'The BBC television crew arrive tomorrow – and I'm not sure what I am /am not allowed to say to them,' continued Riddell-Webster.[22]

While waiting for orders to move, Captain Williamson had been gathering information. Initially Basra city was not a military objective, the hope being that once the surrounding areas were occupied, fighting (and bloodshed) in the streets could be avoided. Even so, realising the city's importance, Williamson built up a fact sheet and created a map referencing all identifiable strategic locations. 'Someone had talked about cutting the head off Basra, i.e. getting rid of Saddam Hussein, and then making use of what was left,' explained Riddell-Webster. Wondering how to illustrate this concept, Williamson's assistant intelligence officer, Sergeant Major Penman, suggested drawing the city in the shape of a human, known as 'Bertie Basrah'. 'We are to ensure we keep the oxygen and life blood of the city going,' Major David Kemmis Betty, the Battlegroup warfare officer, was writing in his diary on 15 March. 'This is a huge task. We will have to define what is meant by "the head" (all civil & military administration, government infrastructure & organisations linked to the Regime). We must also define what is meant by the Heart & Lungs of the city (the water distribution, food, transport, communications etc.) and ensure we protect it and keep it working.' 'University, Market, Fertile land' constituted one leg, while the other included 'Schools, Industrial Plants, Transport.' Its feet were the civilian population.[23] When eventually Basra became an objective, instead of submitting complicated matrixes, Lieutenant Colonel Riddell-Webster had to hand Bertie Basrah as his 'scheme of manoeuvre and intent'.[24]

The thought of failure did not feature. 'There was no way the Iraqis were going to prevail,' observed Philp who, despite the mission's objective to destroy weapons of mass destruction, did not consider the threat was credible. 'Nobody is fearful,' Lieutenant Colquhoun was recording on 11 March. 'Nobody seems to be thinking that they could be dead within a week. Let's hope nobody is, I am certainly not considering it. Am much more interested in what is going to happen and excited about the unknown and challenge that will confront us.'[25] There were, however, 'a few scares,' recorded Sergeant Robert Duncan. 'We spent quite a bit of time jumping in and out of respirators when warned of Iraqi missile launches', observed Kemmis Betty, 'including a comical "O[rders] Group" held by the CO when we all sat around in respirators discussing battle plans.' 'The first time that "gas gas gas" got shouted (which was the sign to put on our respirators), I was a bit scared,' related Sergeant Shaw, 'but there were lots of false alarms.'[26]

'Cutting off the head'

In the early hours of 20 March 2003 the multi-national offensive began with an air strike on Saddam Hussein's presidential palace in Baghdad, and other key locations. 'We are now at war and I am in a war zone,' Lieutenant Colquhoun was recording. 'Very odd!'[27] Although the initial expectation was that weeks of air strikes would be needed before the ground forces moved, the assault was brought forward, The Black Watch Battlegroup crossing the border in the footsteps of United States' forces on 22 March. 'The night before we deployed, Major Lindsay MacDuff, our company commander, gave us Kipling's poem *If* as part of his orders,' recalled B Company's second-in-command, Captain Riddell. 'There was a heightened sense of edge, we felt it wasn't going to be quite as simple as we had all thought.'[28]

'We had all been waiting for this moment for a long time,' recollected Corporal Robbie Tollan who confessed to having written a 'last' letter to his wife and son, for which 'thankfully' there was no need. 'As we mounted our vehicles in the dark and headed towards the crossing point into Iraq, tensions within our Warrior were high. The silence could be cut with a knife. The only noise was that of the engine, there was no radio net chatter as we were on "radio silence" during the first push into the country.'[29] 'Unlike previous large-scale battles, there was no temporary lull in the firing before a mass of soldiers charged forward,' continued Riddell. 'You could hear the planes overhead but we were so far back in the line of armoured vehicles we could not hear the noise of the guns.' Crossing the frontier in huge lines of armoured vehicles, one of the first things Riddell saw was a sign: 'the 1st Fusiliers welcomes you to Iraq'. 'I remember being slightly irate that they had been allowed to cross first!' 'It was a welcome relief from the monotony of days in the desert responding to rocket attack alarms,' noted Corporal Smith. 'Driving through Iraq, all the local people were keeping out of the way, and there were all these clouds of smoke from burning oil fields, where air strikes had taken place,' recalled Philp. 'As the sun came up, it felt very surreal. As the day went on, we saw a bit more signs of life.' They also started getting 'sporadic contacts with the enemy'.[30]

'The relief in place was something of a rush as there were still quite a few contacts going on in the area,' recorded Riddell-Webster. 'The remainder of the day was spent going around the AO [Area of Operations] and trying to get things sorted out. There was a huge number (8 or 9) of ammunition finds and some were quite large. Not much activity for the rest of the evening.'[31] Badly equipped and demoralised, formal Iraqi resistance, mainly from Saddam Hussein's Ba'ath Party militia, the Fedayeen, had been surprisingly limited. 'We had expected to face an organised military force,' observed Riddell. 'What we were encountering were armed civilians. It was not until later that some of the contacts we had were more coordinated.' 'We found ourselves fighting a different war from what we thought,' recorded Philp. 'All the build-up had been about the Iraqi Army, but once we'd crossed the border, we found these formations did not exist and we ended up fighting irregular troops.'[32] 'You didn't know who was going to be fighting whom,' recalled Williamson. 'If there was a man in uniform with a rifle opposing you, then he was clearly an enemy, but if he had taken his uniform off and was just sitting there with a rifle, that was a different matter.' 'There was a notional front line,' commented Captain Mark Percy, the operations officer. 'It was a 360 degree type of war, you were never completely secure because the enemy could pop up anywhere.'[33]

On 23 March, a task force from D Company, which had been the first Black Watch company 'to cross the line of departure in general war' was called out to 'recover friendly casualties or dead' after two Royal Engineer landrovers had been ambushed in Az Zubayr. 'We got tasked to put in a hasty attack to try and get them back,' related Sergeant Shaw. 'It was just like the film, *Black Hawk Down*, we kept getting shot at from all over the place. It was my first time under fire.' Although they located the landrovers, there was no sign of the occupants. Unable to take further action, the soldiers extracted themselves; the bodies of the Royal Engineers were found a month later in shallow graves.[34]

The following day, C Company's mortar platoon, responding to 'its first Fire Mission in anger since the Korean War', came under RPG attack when two reconnaissance vehicles and a mortar wagon were targeted on the outskirts of Az Zubayr. Lance Corporal Barry Stephen, who had been manning one of the mortars, was hit in the chest. His death was 'something that training cannot prepare any man for,' commented Captain McElhinney, the mortar platoon commander.[35] In a separate incident, back at HQ, Riddell-Webster heard 'a burst of chain gun fire and a scream of pain' when a chain gun mounted on a Warrior returning to base after recovering Stephen's body 'let rip', grievously wounding Colour Sergeant Albert Thomson, Royal Highland Fusiliers. 'By sheer good luck,' recorded Riddell-Webster, 'it happened right next to the RAP [Regimental Aid Post] and so he was kept alive. We then had a drama getting him away, with no helicopters available, but he made it eventually. I went to bed in a pretty grim mood.'[36]

B Company, meanwhile, had been sent to take over 'Bridge 4', one of several bridges across the Shatt al-Basra canal, running almost parallel with the Shatt al-Arab river, Bridges 2 and 3 leading directly into Basra. Their objective was to prevent rebel Iraqis fleeing from Basra city. Although initially quiet, the position on the bridge soon 'hotted up' when about thirty men were seen crossing the wasteland in front of them from the University Complex, the first set of buildings on the way to Basra. 'Then an RPG landed; suddenly we realised that a lot of people were firing at us,' observed Captain Riddell. When they retaliated with their own firepower, the Iraqi rebels withdrew.

Soon afterwards, Riddell was lying on a camp cot beside his vehicle in a nearby warehouse. 'I could hear shrapnel hitting the corrugated iron roof. Then our forward observation officer radioed a message saying that he had seen the enemy "bracket" our position with artillery, and suggesting we get out of there before they hit the position directly.'[37]

Yet not every action ended well. In the early hours of 25 March a 'very serious' Blue on Blue incident occurred when a Challenger tank of the Royal Tank Regiment supporting a B Company platoon mistakenly fired on a tank in the Royal Regiment of Fusiliers Battlegroup, killing Corporal Stephen Allbutt and Trooper David Clarke, both of the Queen's Royal Lancers. 'We were positioned on the road just over Bridge 4,' explained Lieutenant Angus Watson. 'We believed there was a significant amount of hostile artillery in the University Complex in front of us. It had a high wall around it and we'd been told that somewhere in the city a column of tanks was moving towards us. The way it was described to me and where I thought the tank commander was engaging was the corner of this compound and that fitted with our intelligence. The distance was a good few kilometres. It was dark and there was a great deal of smoke from burning oil wells.' Lacking thermal imaging in their Warriors, they were reliant on the tank commander's superior optics to confirm the presence of an Iraqi tank. 'But as it transpired he fired in the opposite direction.'[38]

In hindsight, the operations officer, Captain Mark Percy, believed that the tank commander had become disorientated in the confused situation and fired onto the wrong side of the Shatt al-Arab canal. 'The poor chaps who fired will be devastated,' commented Kemmis Betty, observing that they had been 'under sustained attack for 2 days on the bridge now and were no doubt rather jumpy.'[39]

As British forces tightened their control of the area surrounding Basra, including safeguarding the Az Zubayr petroleum plant, 'known as the "Crown Jewels", due to its importance,' US forces were moving towards Baghdad.[40] In general, the locals' response was friendly 'albeit with some caution,' observed Riddell-Webster. 'Not everyone forthcoming, but most were smiling and willing to talk. Not yet willing to openly express anti-regime feelings until Saddam has gone – they know they are still being watched by those who have remained loyal to the Ba'ath Party.' 'The boys are finding it v. difficult since they are being asked to do a mixture of peace enforcing and war fighting,' Lieutenant Will Colquhoun was telling his fiancé, Francesca. 'Very stressful for them since they are making themselves targets by helping the local population and there is no way of telling who is friend and who is foe. We are beginning to get a feel for it though. It is hard work explaining to them why we can't just flatten Basra and go home!'[41]

Early on the morning of 29 March the Battlegroup's HQ was attacked. 'It was an alarm clock from hell,' recorded Kemmis Betty. 'Woken by the screaming whoosh and intense explosion of mortar & artillery fire right around us. About 10 very accurate shells (possibly air burst). It was rather exciting for a split second or two, then rather terrifying.' 'I was sleeping beside Battlegroup HQ when the first salvo of rockets came in,' recalled Captain Percy. 'I looked over towards Basra city and I could see these streaks coming literally towards us and I realised we had to get under cover. I spent the rest of the night moving the Battlegroup to a safer location. It was just chaos.' Captain Williamson recalled 'a mass scramble for gas masks'. 'A truck nearby was destroyed and 2 chaps hit by shrapnel (looking not too bad). An A Squadron tank had its fuel tank (external) blown off and a number of vehicles had chunks taken out of them. We were *very* lucky,' continued Kemmis Betty. 'We moved to the airfield near B[riga]de HQ.'[42] Following the attack he noted that many of those who normally slept on their vehicles now slept under them. Williamson confessed to noticing the difference between himself and the married men. 'Penman was definitely more scared but that was not because he was less of a man than me but because he was worried about what would happen to his wife and children.'[43]

Meanwhile, regular patrols took place, often during heavy rain, searching for weapons and ammunition. 'At one stage because of delays in re-supply we were limited in the ammunition we had both for mortar barrels and our personal weapons,' commented Captain McElhinney. 'So we would pick up the Iraqi weapons lying about, which we'd use when we needed to fire for effect. This meant we could save the ammunition in our own weapons for proper contacts when we needed greater accuracy'.[44]

On 30 March The Black Watch moved into Az Zubayr. 'We should be able to dominate the place reasonably well,' noted Kemmis Betty, 'but there are a hundred little back streets & if the enemy stick it out they could cause us problems.' Having first patrolled the town in helmet and body armour, on 1 April, accompanied by the press, and conditioned by his experiences in Kosovo, Riddell-Webster decided that 'the feel of the place' meant they could walk about more freely. 'We went in bonnets and without body armour. The reception we received was rapturous.' Photographs of Black Watch soldiers in their Tam o'Shanters with the Red Hackle were broadcast around the world.[45]

On the night of 5 April the advance into Basra city began. On the same day the Colonel-in-Chief, Prince Charles, was writing a personal letter to Riddell-Webster, telling him how much the Battalion was in his thoughts and prayers.[46] 'The Battlegroup had planned a limited raid into central Basra for 6th April, but it became apparent after some initial fierce fighting to gain entry that more could be achieved,' recorded Philp. 'I can remember being in a massive column of armoured vehicles, and then Will Colquhoun got up and played the bagpipes,' related Riddell. 'It was early morning and we were waiting on Bridge 4 going into Basra. Since I'd brought my bagpipes with me I thought it might be the only time I got to play them!' explained Colquhoun. 'Rolling into Al Basrah with the Royal Tank Regiment leading the charge was awe-inspiring,' related Corporal Tollan.[47]

'Basrah population appeared jubilant,' Captain Philp wrote in his diary. 'Lots of waving, smiles and thumbs up. What resistance is left has gone underground largely.' 'What a day!' Riddell-Webster recorded on 6 April. 'It was very hot and the temperatures inside the vehicles were unbelievable. I sweated buckets… the population seem very pleased to see us and there were huge waves and smiles as we arrived. I hope they stay.' 'I remember telling everyone to be careful of an ambush, but as we got closer we realised the people were waving and punching the air, screaming "Welcome to Basrah!"' recorded Kemmis Betty. 'Every place with a Saddam statue is being defaced by the locals.' 'We did not see any fighting, it was just a question of clearing out the odd compound. Thousands of local people were coming out to welcome us,' continued Riddell. 'We were genuinely treated as liberators,' recalled Lance Corporal Ian Smith, 'with the emphasis now changing to the rebuilding of the infrastructure.'[48]

'Finally we have taken Basrah!' Captain Riddell was informing his parents on 6 April. 'I am sitting enjoying the last rays of sunshine inside a military compound having been going since 4 hrs before first light. What was intended as a raid has been transformed by my Commanding Officer into a full-scale seizing of Basrah.'[49] That night, the 'war' was quiet. 'No direct contact, but quite a bit of gunfire about the place,' Kemmis Betty observed on 7 April. 'I think there are scores being settled. Hopefully people taking out the militia & Ba'ath Party men, but it might still be militia taking out those disloyal to the Regime. We patrolled, protecting our backs & projecting ourselves about the area.' An immediate priority was securing the hospitals and vital infrastructure including water pumps, electricity stations, 'some military compounds and a sports complex.'[50] 'We started finding large quantities of weapons and ammunition,' Riddell continued in his letter home. 'We spent the next day just collecting hundreds of RPGs and weapons and lorry loads of ammunition.' 'I went to a compound where a find had been made during the day before and found two full rooms of ammunition and a lorry load that they had been trying to get away,' recorded Riddell-Webster on 7 April.[51]

Amid the jubilation, however, there was a breakdown of law and order including widespread looting. 'Probably some of the people who shot at us were looters trying to get away.' 'We had to guard a hospital because looters were coming in stealing all the medical equipment,' recalled Lieutenant Watson. 'I remember thinking why would you do that to your own people.' At one military hospital

Riddell-Webster found that a doctor, who had tried to prevent the staff from looting, had been killed.[52] As Captain Philp observed,

> The challenge was establishing some kind of law and order without becoming too draconian, which would turn the people against us, making us the enemy. We were supposed to be liberating them and so it was a difficult balancing act. We hadn't been prepared for the scale of looting we ended up having to deal with… People were looting absolutely anything, furniture, stripping taps off sinks, fixtures and fittings – power cables were getting stolen because they were stripping copper wire out of them. They were trying to get a short-term return by selling the copper wire but this created a long-term problem of power shortage.[53]

'Tragically many were electrocuted in the process,' recorded Captain Williamson.[54]

On 9 April American forces entered Baghdad, whereupon Saddam Hussein and his senior leadership disappeared into hiding. Kirkuk was occupied the following day and Tikrit on 15 April. The port of Umm Qasr, where resistance had been unexpectedly strong, had also fallen. With Saddam Hussein's overthrow the 'initial gratitude' of the inhabitants was 'obvious', remarked Corporal Tollan. When Riddell-Webster went for a haircut, the local barber refused to let him to pay. 'He said it was for getting rid of Saddam Hussein.'[55]

From warfighting to peacekeeping

The offensive in Iraq had taken just three weeks. Compared with thousands of Iraqi casualties, Coalition fatalities had been minimal. 'I think we all went back to our Kosovo mentality of peace support operations, trying to do little projects to help the local population,' recalled Lieutenant Angus Watson. 'We spent time guarding hospitals, aiding what was left of the Iraqi police, securing the local markets. One time we got in a wee fire fight,' recalled Sergeant Shaw, 'a laddie who was trying to nick something from a stall was threatening the stall owner with an AK-47 rifle. He'd shot and hurt a small child. When he saw us, he started running off, as we ran round the corner he stopped to try and shoot at us, but two Jocks shot him first.'[56]

With their time divided between patrols, guard duty and rest, greater comfort was achieved by improved quarters, B Company occupying a building which they called Camp Ali Baba 'in honour of the considerably more than 40 thieves around us'. 'The routine is well set,' Captain Riddell wrote home, 'and I have to say the town of Basra is pretty dull most of the week. The inevitable problems have occurred coming from the intensive warfighting phase into a peace-keeping environment where all events are "dull" in comparison. The challenge has and still is to keep the Jocks motivated and sharp in the face of a real threat of the extremist or die-hard trying something.' Returning to Az Zubayr to photograph the various locations where the Battalion had been in action, Kemmis Betty found it hard to believe that the streets, now 'full of happy smiling faces and market activity & kids', had once been empty, the rooftops manned by machine guns.[57]

During the aftermath, 'in jest', Captain Williamson edited a Regimental 'magazine', *Basra 42nd Street*. Using the name 'Bertie', one news item highlighted a new entry into The Black Watch Dictionary: 'A Billy – A common term, used with reference to a soldier who does bugger all except sunbathe. E.g. Question: "Where's Jock?" Answer: "Oh he's on the roof doing a Billy".'[58] Parcels from home were welcome, despite mishaps. 'The avocado you sent exploded like the last one and made everything else in there untouchable!' Riddell informed his parents. 'Unfortunately *The Spectator* was a write-off!' Chocolate club biscuits, he continued, 'don't travel well'.[59]

Still there were occasional scares. 'Saddam's voice was broadcast by Australian Radio saying rise up & start a war against CF [Coalition Forces]!' Kemmis Betty related on 7 May. On another occasion 'over about 5–10 mins the whole city it seemed started to fire weapons in the air. Someone discovered that the TV & Radio had just announced the end of UN sanctions on Iraq. They were celebrating. There must have been many hundreds if not a thousand rifles firing.' As a result, the hospital reported a number of deaths through accidents as well as injuries 'by bullets falling to earth.'[60]

The main concern, however, was the continuing lawlessness. 'People were short of water and they kept tapping into the water supply close to the hospital. We would go and patch it up and the same thing would happen again. There was no police force or army. We did not anticipate what the effect of removing a regime from power would be,' observed Company Sergeant Major Harry Hood. When Kemmis Betty visited the pylon lines in the marshes south of their Area of Operations, he saw a 'truly amazing site… mile after mile of pylons down… Can't they see the damage they are doing to their own future? They have a choice. They can be as rich as Kuwait or Brunei or as poor as Afghanistan.' Having found a letter from an old Security ministry telling all departments 'to loot and sabotage when we arrived, to make our job of reconstruction impossible' he wondered whether the looting was part of an orchestrated plan from the Ba'athists. 'Maybe they are winning!'[61]

By early June the temperature had increased to 'unbelievable levels and the closer we came to coming home the slower the time seemed to pass.'[62] On 11 June The Black Watch began its departure. 'As operations officer,' recalled Captain Percy, 'my aim from the start was to bring everyone home safe. I remember sitting on the plane and thinking thank goodness, with the exception of Barry Stephen, we had brought everyone home alive.'[63] 'Like everything it had its good and bad days but as a soldier's experience I feel fortunate to have been there at such a momentous time for the people of Iraq,' observed Lance Corporal Ian Smith. 'We were still looked on as liberators,' recalled Hood. 'It was still the honeymoon period.'[64]

In retrospect, Mike Williamson, who had been trying to understand the identity of the leaders of the various communities in Basra, admitted: 'We were devoid of policy. There was no plan for reconstruction and re-integration. My particular project was understanding the Ba'ath Party from the bottom up but I had no view on whether or not we should "de-Ba'athify".' Having spent time trying to understand the JAM – the Jaish al-Mahdi (Army of the Mahdi) led by the Shia cleric, Sayyid Muqtada al-Sadr – he believed the warning signs of the growth of the extremist Shia movement and its hardline opposition to the Coalition Forces in southern Iraq were already evident. 'They were establishing themselves as an extreme religious element of the Shias and were already having an amazingly aggressive influence, putting themselves in local positions of power.' 'In terms of a job well done, we were delighted everyone from our platoons got through,' noted Jamie Riddell. 'But the challenge was to deliver – you could see the conditions being set for what later happened. The infrastructure was beginning to fail. You could see that the Iraqis were expecting us to bring development with us. We couldn't meet their dreams.'[65]

Interlude: Fallingbostel

After nearly four months in Iraq, the Battalion returned to Fallingbostel. The period was described by Riddell-Webster as 'a little like the filling in a sandwich' wedged in between Iraq and the Battalion's deployment to the Land Warfare Centre in Warminster scheduled for early 2004.[66] On 18 July 2003 he handed over command of the Battalion to James Cowan, who had been serving as Military Assistant to the Chief of the General Staff, latterly, General Sir Mike Jackson. In Britain detachments took part in several homecoming parades. The town of Aberfeldy came to 'a standstill', the streets lined with people welcoming 'home' their own Regiment. 'Every soldier, to a man, was overwhelmed with the reception he received,' recorded Captain Jules McElhinney.[67]

Reports about insufficient equipment prior to deployment were less welcome. As Cowan explained, the purchase of equipment had been left until the last minute because the government did not want to be seen to be preparing for a war while a debate was continuing at the UN and in Parliament.

> As a result many items of equipment were not available in the right numbers, in the right place, in the right working order at the time they should have been and I think that is widely acknowledged. I

> think there is a clear realisation that if decisions had been taken earlier then the right kit could have been in place, but there is a clear understanding as to why those decisions were not made… the government was walking that political tightrope with the UN Security Council and with its own votes in Parliament, it could not take a decision to commit to war any earlier than it did.[68]

A question mark was also being posed over the future establishment of the British Army. On 11 December 2003 the Secretary of State for Defence, Geoff Hoon, presented a White Paper to Parliament entitled *Delivering Security in a Changing World,* which set out the Government's 'analysis of the future security environment, the implications for defence, and how we intend adapting our planning and force structures to meet the potential threats.' A main objective was reducing the six fighting (armoured and mechanised) brigades by one and creating an all-arms light brigade. As indicated by Jackson, the aim was 'the Defence vision for more deployable, more expeditionary, more capable and better balanced forces'.[69] A key figure in the discussions was Lieutenant General Sir Alistair Irwin, who had succeeded Brigadier Garry Barnett as Colonel of the Regiment in November and, in addition to being Colonel Commandant of the Scottish Division, had been appointed Adjutant-General in January 2003. Having been privy to the discussions regarding the future of the Army, he had been tasked by the Army Board to write a paper setting out the strengths and weaknesses of the regimental system that had evolved since its inception in the reforms undertaken by the Secretary of State for War, Edward Cardwell in the 1870s.[70] At this stage, however, any threat to The Black Watch's future appeared theoretical, prompting Irwin to describe as 'nonsense in the press… so-called plans to disband the Regiment'.[71]

In the New Year the Battalion enjoyed 'a healthy blast of fresh air' taking part in the annual field-firing exercises on the snow-covered Bergen–Hohne ranges, before moving to Warminster in March 2004 as the Demonstration Battalion.[72] Based at Battlesbury Barracks 'we had a phenomenal time pitting one company against another', related Major Tim Elliott. 'We had a free run of Salisbury Plain.'[73] An Overseas Military Assistance Team (OMAT), led by Lieutenant Jono Kelmanson, also went to Kenya for six weeks to train Kenyans for deployment to the Sudan, troubled by genocidal conflict since February 2003.[74] Another task was assembling an infantry training team to assist the Royal Scots Dragoon Guards and the 12th Regiment Royal Artillery before their deployment to Northern Ireland, The Black Watch's counterinsurgency skills in Iraq providing 'a wealth of relevant knowledge and experience.'[75]

Two years after the Queen Mother's death, in commemoration of her long association with the Regiment, on 8 April 2004 Prince Charles opened the Memorial Gates at Balhousie Castle. Speaking of the 'enormous privilege' of opening the gates in memory of his 'darling grandmother', the Prince affirmed his pride in assuming the position of Colonel-in-Chief 'although I am very hesitant to follow in her very beloved footsteps.'[76]

Who would true valour see,
Let him come hither;
Here's one will constant be
Come wind, come weather.[77]

26
Picking Up the Pieces

This may be the last attack for the 1st Battalion The Black Watch.[1]

2004: Return to Iraq

In the wake of the fall of Saddam Hussein's regime, an uneasy peace was prevailing. In early 2004, militias loyal to the Shia religious leader, Sayyid Muqtada al-Sadr, had begun attacking the multinational force, demanding its withdrawal. Simultaneously, Sunni rebels were staging uprisings in Baghdad, Fallujah, Ramadi and Samarra. 'Rumours began to circulate that an armoured infantry battalion would be needed in Iraq,' observed Major Tim Elliott. 'Since we were the Demonstration Battalion we did not think it would be us.'[2] But, although The Black Watch had only recently completed a tour abroad, its operational experience, and the fact that it was one of only ten armoured infantry battalions equipped with Warriors, warranted its return.

On 27 May 2004 The Black Watch was informed that it was to be part of the Multi-National Division (South East) (MND/SE), the British-run division responsible for the southern provinces of Al Basrah, Maysan, Dhi Qar and Al Muthanna. 'The decision to deploy required some rapid planning and training,' noted Lieutenant Colonel James Cowan, a priority being to bring the Battalion up to strength with appropriate supporting tanks and artillery.[3] By mid-July The Black Watch was back in Iraq, stationed at the main British logistics base at Shaibah airfield. 'Very hot out here', Second Lieutenant Nick Colquhoun informed his girlfriend, Rachel, 'air conditioning in the tents (though most isn't working – including ours!!!) showers and such like… good internet facilities and 20 free phone minutes a week.'[4] A Company, which had deployed in advance, was already patrolling the Shatt al-Arab to prevent weapons being smuggled into the Al Faw peninsula.

In Britain, the fate of The Black Watch remained part of the general discussion on the British Army. On 21 July 2004 Geoff Hoon, Secretary of State for Defence, again addressed the House of Commons 'about the need to transform our armed forces to deal with the challenges of the 21st century'. One component was creating a new structure based on 'regiments of two or more battalions, in largely fixed locations'. To achieve the necessary calculated reduction of manpower, four infantry battalions would be cut, one of which would come from the six remaining regiments in Scotland. The infantry arms plot system, whereby the soldiers received 'operational and geographical variety… by moving battalions between locations and roles every few years', was to be phased out. The likely outcome for The Black Watch and the other Scottish regiments was their merger into one or two Super Regiments.[5]

As the news broke, Cowan addressed the Battalion: 'To command the 1st Battalion The Black Watch is the greatest honour of my life and to do so on operations only adds to that sense of pride and responsibility,' he began. 'What I tell you now is perhaps the saddest thing I have had to do, and in some ways I feel the pleasure and pride of command turns to ashes as I do it. What the Secretary of State is announcing is that the Regimental system, as we know and love it, will end and in its place will come a new system of large regiments.' Emphasising that the Battalion had come to Iraq with a specific assignment, he continued: 'But in the morning when the sun rises we must pick up the pieces and continue preparations for operations. In the morning, the day goes on, and we will all still be here. In the morning our struggle begins to make sure the essence of The Black Watch survives.'[6]

Among his listeners was Captain Angus Philp: 'I remember turning around after he had finished the speech and the first person I saw was Captain John Stephenson. Known as 'Peachie' he was a big character and absolutely passionate about The Black Watch. When I saw the look on his face, he was shaking his head in utter disbelief. Everyone felt like that.' 'The immediate assumption was that The Black Watch would form a Regiment with the other Highlanders which looked like it would be a good fit in the circumstances,' related Lieutenant Ben Collis. 'If we went back to being the Royal Highlanders then we would have switched to our historic name. But soon it became clear that wasn't going to happen.'[7] 'After 265 years of loyal service,' Cowan later wrote, 'the impact of this information on a battalion deeply imbued with a sense of its own identity, traditions and ethos cannot be over-stated.'[8]

To compound their dismay, the emergency necessitating the Battalion's presence in Iraq appeared to have receded and the soldiers faced the prospect of a hot summer at Shaibah. To keep them busy, the individual companies moved to separate locations. While A Company remained at Al Faw, supporting the 1st Royal Welch Fusiliers, D went to assist the Danish contingent at Al Qurnah, believed by some to be the location of the Garden of Eden, north-west of Basra.[9] B Company went to Al Amarah, capital of Maysan province, home for centuries of the Marsh Arabs, whose traditional way of life Saddam Hussein had tried to disrupt by draining the marshes.

The relative calm soon ended when, at the beginning of August, fighting broke out in the holy city of Najaf, scene of heavy fighting in 2003. Over the summer, tension had been mounting between supporters of Muqtada al-Sadr's hardline opposition to the secular Coalition-backed interim government of A'yad Allawi and those who accepted the government. Countering al-Sadr in Najaf was a faction led by the Shia cleric, Grand Ayatollah Sistani, absent in Britain for heart treatment.[10] When Prime Minister Allawi closed al-Sadr's newspaper, the latter mobilised his militia, and the situation was aggravated by US operations around Najaf and the Kufa Mosque. From Najaf, fighting spread to Nasiriyah, Basra and Al Amarah. 'While the rebels in Al Amarah had not been very effective in military terms', noted Cowan, 'their principal achievement was to halt most work done to restore the civil infrastructure of Maysan. The electricity supply became less reliable. Deliveries of fresh water became less frequent. Job creation schemes faltered. The result was disaffection in poorer areas and even more young men with nothing to do but listen to the rhetoric of the radicals of the Office of the Martyr [Muqtada al-Sadr's political wing].'[11]

Potential boredom was now replaced by intense activity. D Company's orders to return to Shaibah were postponed in order to help the Danes who had come under fire. 'Half the Company had flown back to Shaibah and the Warriors were already on the trucks so we had to get them off again,' recalled Company Sergeant Major Hood. They soon became part of the action. 'There was a big bang and I was still looking out of the turret,' recorded Lieutenant Alastair Colville, whose Warrior was one of those under RPG attack. 'Stuck my head up again to look for the firing point to have another [RPG] whoosh past my nose. It was my first contact – all over very quickly, much confusion.' On this occasion, the armour plating 'did its job' and the damage to the Warrior was minimal.[12]

An impromptu visit to Shaibah on 9 August by Lieutenant General Irwin to take 'soundings' on the Regiment's future 'was hugely appreciated'. Reflecting on his difficult task, he recalled 'the brief visits in stifling heat to the company locations, the disappointed questions from the men but also their generosity of spirit. There can have been few visits with an unhappier purpose by a Colonel of the Regiment.'[13]

At Al Amarah, B Company was acting in support of the Princess of Wales's Royal Regiment Battlegroup, headquartered south of the city at Camp Abu Naji. On 5 August a patrol led by Second Lieutenant Nick Colquhoun was targeted by over 30 gunmen from the rooftops, signifying the beginning of protracted hostilities. The main location under attack was the headquarters from where civilian aid had been carried out, known as CIMIC (Civil Military Co-operation) House. 'To take the pressure off CIMIC House, the PWRR's 2IC had decided to undertake an operation in the north-west area of Al Amarah with Warriors and tanks to make a show of force and shake them up,' explained Major Tim Elliott, Officer Commanding B Company. 'But they needed to block the insurgents in the south and so a "tethered goat", as the Jocks put it, was deployed in a defensive line to allow them to do their operation. That's where we came in with three Warriors covering each other's positions. We did that for 48 hours non-stop.' During the day the temperature in the turrets 'must have been nearly 50 degrees Centigrade. We were stripped down to just body armour and a T-shirt. It was so hot, we were wrapping sweat rags over our faces.' To quench their thirst, instead of water they drank 'turret tea': 'the water in two-litre bottles was so hot that some of the Jocks vomited drinking it. Then I noticed my signaller, Corporal Duncan, pouring tea and milk sachets into the bottle which tasted much better. So we instructed everyone to do this and the effect was amazing!'[14]

Meanwhile, A Company was in Basra. Having established a base at the Palace, patrols were carried out in the eastern half of the city in support of the 1st Cheshire Regiment and other units. A particular target of the rebel Iraqis was the Old State Building, close to the Office of the Martyr.[15] On 12 August 23-year-old Private Marc Ferns was fatally wounded by an IED while driving a Warrior on patrol in the south of the city, his friends remembering him for 'his sense of humour and kindness.' Sergeant Kevin Stacey was badly injured; Second Lieutenant Chris Baddeley survived unharmed because, at the moment of detonation, his head was down.[16] In the third week of August, D Company replaced A in Basra, the changeover marked by another attack on the Old State Building. 'After a few dull days, we are now in Basrah,' recorded Colville. 'Whole company moved in overnight.' On one occasion, after a Warrior had targeted a sniper on a roof, the house's owner threw a note into the turret, complaining about the damage. 'I don't deserve my house to be shot by yourself 5 holes!! Why it is the only thing I possess along with a car from Saddam's Nation!!!'[17]

Throughout the deployment, the base at Shaibah came under regular rocket attack. Although 'never more than a nuisance', additional security was provided by building walls around each tent. 'A moment of levity' occurred when sudden panic at the sound of explosions and flares was relieved by the realisation that the Iraqis were letting off fireworks to celebrate Iraq's 1–0 football win over Australia in the 2004 Athens Olympic Games. 'So the Iraqis had gone wild,' observed Colville.[18]

On 24 August the Grand Ayatollah Sistani returned from Britain. Setting out a three-point plan to bring peace to Najaf, the terms required the al-Sadr militia to disband, all troops to leave the city and all weapons to be removed. He also called for a 24-hour ceasefire. 'Things have quietened down a lot today as a ceasefire has been called in Najaf, which has had the effect of calming people down a little,' Colquhoun wrote home. 'Long may it last.' Three days later he was noting that the volatile situation meant they carried 'full scales of ammo and weaponry (I sleep at night with amongst other things a couple of grenades under my bed – not good for inducing sleep!)'[19] On 2 September the peace settlement was agreed allowing Coalition Forces freedom of movement in Basra. In return the Office of the Martyr Sadr was permitted to re-enter politics, gaining seats on the Provincial Council.

During the peace negotiations A Company (in reserve since leaving Basra), replaced B in Al Amarah. Since the situation was more stable, A Company's duties were extended to the marshlands on the Iranian border. 'This was one of the most enjoyable periods in a command position,' related Major Alastair Aitken who had taken command of A Company in July. 'We were taking over from another Battalion to interdict the flow of lethal aid coming across the Iraqi border.' Instead of sitting in 'very hot, dusty and rather pointless Observation Posts in the middle of the desert', Aitken decided that 'the better option was to get the Iraqis to do this for us rather than us blustering around in the unknown'. 'We set up a F[orward] O[perating] B[ase] named Camp Ferns in memory of Marc,' recalled Sergeant Alexander Wilson.[20] The recruiting process was, however, not straightforward. 'The first offer I had was for the seventy-year-old one-legged brother of the chief!' continued Aitken. Soon large numbers of Marsh Arabs came forward for training, generally accompanied by the elders and local villagers. 'After a basic training package we presented them all with red hackles and they were now officially "Marsh Scouts". We paid them for each day's work.' Unexpected orders that the Battalion was to be deployed to the American sector meant that care of the Marsh Scouts had to be handed over to another unit. 'I found out later that they had become bored with the project and had abandoned them which was very sad because they had been the most effective and loyal forces I was involved with.'[21]

Since mid-August D Company had been in Basra. After the peace settlement, there was relative calm, which Company Sergeant Major Hood compared to Belfast in 1995 'when you were in lockdown and there was to be no aggressive patrolling'. The lull, however, enabled them to focus on what Cowan referred to as 'the more constructive side of a peace support operation – economic development, civil government and Security Sector Reform.'[22] Meanwhile, B Company was engaged in setting up a leadership course for Iraqi National Guard officers and junior non-commissioned officers. 'Our responsibility was to train some Iraqi National Guard on principles of leadership, map reading, a real mish-mash of bits and pieces, including first aid.' The 250 participants ranged from those ranked as corporal to lieutenant colonel. 'We began with some fundamental ideas for forming teams, how to patrol and gather some evidence so you can hand it over to the police,' recorded Elliott. 'The whole idea was to teach them to lead by example: that the soldiers would not be expected to do anything that the officers would not do.' One challenge was getting up at 'silly o'clock' (because of the heat) to do exercises. 'They had no footwear, only flip-flops, so we got a lorry-load of trainers delivered.' 'I was teaching them about weapons,' recalled Sergeant Duncan, 'some of them wanted to learn and some didn't.' 'It was clear that it could be a high impact task,' related Lieutenant Collis. But the impending move to the American sector meant the course was concluded a week early, the benefits diminishing.[23]

The Super Regiment

In Britain discussions were continuing on the future of the British Army. For those who had served in the Regiment the prospect of merger created an immediate rift between those who accepted the change, albeit with dismay, and those who wanted to fight against the proposals. 'There were an awful lot of meetings and discussions,' related Captain Jamie Riddell, who had returned from Iraq in 2003 and was serving as Lieutenant General Irwin's ADC. 'It was very emotive. Everyone wanted to protect and be seen to protect their battalions. There wasn't the realisation that something was going to have to give.' 'It was a far more revolutionary move than the Childers Reforms in the 1880s,' observed Cowan, who was having to maintain morale and keep the Battalion informed. 'Then it was certain regiments coming together, with one more dominant than the other, in the case of the 42nd which took over the 73rd. What was now proposed was that no regiment would be dominant.'[24]

In the hope of preventing amalgamation, Brigadier Barnett and Major General Watson, both former Colonels of the Regiment, led a campaign to 'Save The Black Watch' which became part of a larger campaign to 'save' all the Scottish Regiments. The strongest weapon in the anti-merger armoury was recruitment. 'Having people coming from the same area means they are far less likely to let down those they are serving alongside because their families all live close together,' noted Barnett.[25] Taking up the cause, on 15 September 2004 Pete Wishart, the Scottish National Party MP for North Tayside, secured time for a 90-minute debate in the House of Commons, which, he said, was part of a campaign to save 'a way of life in our infantry that has served us so well and with such distinction through the centuries'. After he had stated his case, other Members of Parliament representing all the political parties in Scotland voiced their support. Hoon, responding on behalf of the Government, stood firm. 'The world changes and we need to change with it. The programme that I announced in July is about ensuring that our armed forces are prepared to meet the challenges of the 21st century.'[26] As discussions continued, events in Iraq were projecting The Black Watch onto the international stage.

Into 'the Triangle of Death': Operation Bracken

'The US was preparing for its second assault on Fallujah,' explained Lieutenant Colonel Cowan. Codenamed Operation Phantom Fury, the objective was to flush out insurgent Iraqis. But despite considerable 'combat power', there was a gap in the southern cordon around the city, which the Americans wanted to fill with British troops. Prime Minister Blair had therefore agreed that The Black Watch would be deployed, coming under the command of the United States' 24th Marine Expeditionary Unit (MEU). A central part of the agreement was that they would operate under British rules of engagement. When reviewing their assignment, Cowan noted this was the second time that the United States had asked for The Black Watch's support, the first being when President Lyndon Johnson had requested Prime Minister Harold Wilson's help in Vietnam.[27]

'At first we were disappointed, thinking that they could easily have sent the next unit that was coming,' related Sergeant Wilson.[28] Before the deployment, a small group, including Cowan, reconnoitred the area of potential operations, which included responsibility for controlling North Babil (former Babylon) and the routes running south-east out of Fallujah. With limited time and given the dangers of being on the ground, reconnaissance was undertaken by helicopter. 'With only three Warrior companies it was clear that a number of capabilities would be required to convert the Black Watch from a battalion into a Battlegroup,' continued Cowan. Engineers were needed to provide the infrastructure and, given the potentially hostile environment, two extra doctors and Royal Army Medical Corps personnel were attached. 'Numerous other smaller capabilities were added, including logistic troops and a plethora of intelligence personnel.'[29]

On 21 October Geoff Hoon confirmed Britain's participation in the American operation to secure Fallujah. To counter concerns that British troops were being placed under American command, when speaking to the press Cowan stressed that 'the task the Black Watch has been set is an interesting and challenging one and has captured the imagination of my soldiers, who will act as a force for good in a new and different part of this country.' Emphasising their duties were 'well within the experience and abilities of my Battlegroup,' he continued: 'There has been much sensationalist talk about the threat we will face. But frankly, this Regiment beat Napoleon, it beat the Kaiser and it beat Hitler, and for the Jocks of the Black Watch, this is just the latest chapter in our history and another job to be done.'[30]

At home, the press was sanguine: 'British set for Iraqi danger zones,' noted the *Observer*. 'Black Watch prays and prepares for new fight,' Richard Lloyd-Parry wrote in *The Times*. What concerned commentators was that the Battalion was heading into Babil province, known as the Triangle of Death, whose predominantly Sunni population was generally unreceptive to the Coalition Forces and where, in addition to rocket and mortar attacks, improvised explosive devices (IEDs) had been used both to attack and demoralise their opponents.[31] 'For a lot of young soldiers, preparing for an operation like this is the first time in their lives that they face the possibility of dying,' observed the Chaplain, Aled Thomas. 'There are young men making a will for the first time.' 'All the kit is now loaded,' Second Lieutenant Colquhoun wrote home. 'The Warriors prepared and [I am] now sitting in the back of transporters waiting to head north early tomorrow morning.'[32]

Operating under the code name Operation Bracken, on 27 October an advance party, led by Cowan, flew to Baghdad and drove onwards via Kalsu, where the Americans had established the National Liaison Headquarters. The location selected for The Black Watch's headquarters was the site of a former industrial complex, named by the Americans 'Dogwood'. 'There was not a tree for miles around, and certainly not any dogwood,' Cowan noted, believing that the name perhaps originated from the numerous wild dogs in the vicinity. Having selected some ruined buildings in the south-east corner which, in recognition of the Regiment's service in North America, they called Camp Ticonderoga, they settled down to await the

Battlegroup's arrival, armed with their personal weapons for protection. 'It was still very hot and we just slept on the ground,' noted Company Sergeant Major Harry Hood, who had flown up with Cowan. 'It was the calm before the storm. In hindsight the Iraqis must have thought we were crazy for such a small force to be in such a horrible area.'[33]

Meanwhile the main convoy had left Shaibah by road, the 418-mile route passing through several 'high threat zones. The movement plan was complex involving a two-day journey, staying overnight in the US base at Tallil. The convoy was immense and split into nine packets totalling over 300 vehicles (459 including the second convoy).'[34] 'The planning was hugely aided by the Americans,' observed the adjutant, Captain Neil Tomlin. 'All the armoured vehicles were put on what we called "hets" and "lets" – heavy equipment transporters and light equipment transporters. It was something completely out of the capability of the British military at that time.'[35] With the transporters draped in large Union Jack flags to avoid 'friendly fire' from other Coalition Forces, additional protection was provided by American Humvee gun trucks.[36]

Given the media interest in The Black Watch's deployment, journalists were present to report the convoy's departure. Within minutes the news was broadcast worldwide, losing all element of secrecy and potentially enabling the insurgent Iraqis to 'shape the battlefield', noted Lieutenant Collis. But despite the unwanted coverage, the first part of the journey passed without incident. Since they were travelling through airspace controlled by different countries, the aircraft of different nations 'supported us above: British, Dutch and American'. 'For a lot of people it was our first exposure to the Americans,' continued Collis. 'It was exciting to be working with them.'[37]

'We are currently on our move north and are travelling through the desert somewhere just south of Najaf,' Colquhoun was writing on 28 October. He was also reporting the acquisition of some American rations: 'my gunner & driver are fairly resourceful Jocks when left to their own devices. I tend not to ask them where they have been but what I do know is that we now have about 6 slabs of sprite and coke and about 70 days worth of sweeties and choccies stashed in the back of the Warrior.' Other supplies 'foraged' from the Americans, Colville recalled, included 'tinned tuna, Tabasco sauce, tinned tomatoes, Gatorade, the list could go on. So when the vehicle doors opened it was like Christmas!'[38] On 29 October while crossing a bridge in an area interspersed with irrigation ditches, one of the Warriors, driven by twenty-seven-year-old Private Kevin McHale, plunged into the water. Although Private Jonetani Matia Lawaci in the lead vehicle managed to rescue Lieutenant Guy Williams and Privates Ambrose and Wright, by the time he reached McHale, he was dead. Private Allan Stewart, who was in Scotland on leave, realised his good fortune: 'My seat in that Warrior behind the driver was empty. If I'd been in it, I doubt I'd have been able to get out in time.'[39]

Having reached Dogwood, The Black Watch 'wrestled with an area in which no detailed ground reconnaissance had been possible and for which no actionable intelligence existed,' observed Cowan. 'Everything had been looted, the buildings had all been gutted and we took over an old building which had a wall and a roof,' recalled Major Elliott. 'We parked our armoured vehicles around it, dug in defensive positions, put a sandbagged tower up on top to allow us to see a bit of distance and sandbagged all the windows.' 'Dogwood was horrible,' observed Sergeant Maestri. 'It was a completely different environment.'[40] On the basis of experience in Northern Ireland and general instinct, Cowan considered that the soldiers had 'a reasonable understanding of the principles of counterinsurgency' but they had 'few of the capabilities required for implementation'. 'Warriors were very good at taking fire from the sides but poorly prepared from taking a blast from below,' explained Collis.[41]

Among their adversaries was Saddam Hussein's Special Republican Guard as well as Sunni extremists, including Abu Musab al-Zarqawi, responsible for suicide bombings and the execution of hostages. Having joined forces with Al Qaeda, he gained the title 'Emir of Al Qaeda in the country of the Two Rivers'.[42]

While A and D Companies conducted 'familiarisation' patrols, B Company remained in reserve overseeing security around Camp

Dogwood. 'As I write I am sitting in the back of my Warrior enjoying the first few hours of proper rest since we arrived here four days ago (fingers crossed that the quiet will last the few hours!),' Colquhoun was informing his girlfriend. 'Quite a cosy little home really if you forget about the layers of dust, sharp bits of metal to bang your head on and cases of ammo which take up most of the available space!'[43] Meanwhile, a second convoy had left Shaibah. Composed mainly of B Squadron, the 1st Queen's Dragoon Guards and Royal Marines it did not attract the same media interest as the first convoy. Having reached Dogwood in the early hours of 2 November The Black Watch Battlegroup was complete.[44] That the United States' Presidential elections were also taking place did not go unnoticed: '2nd November = US elections,' observed Colquhoun. 'If Bush wins likely to be interpreted as four year extension of US [presence in Iraq].'[45]

Supporting Phantom Fury: The Attack on Fallujah

By 3 November the Battlegroup was at operational capability, signalling the beginning of its thirty-day assignment 'to establish a block to the south of Fallujah to deny the insurgents movement into and out of that city'. While A Company took control of the west bank of the Euphrates (codenamed Angus and Fife), B Squadron of the Queen's Dragoon Guards moved westwards to the desert area (Dundee). B Company remained in reserve. D Company was ordered to establish a forward operating base on the east bank of the Euphrates 'to show that we had a presence and dominate the ground,' observed Company Sergeant Major Hood.[46]

As D Company, commanded by Major Robin Lindsay, headed north, the lead Warrior was badly damaged by a roadside bomb. A second Warrior then slid into a ditch to avoid a rocket attack. Although its damage was limited, under sporadic mortar and RPG attack, it took eight hours to recover the second Warrior. Meanwhile, Lieutenant Colville had gone ahead to secure the entrance to an old industrial power-plant site, which was to be their forward operating base. 'Everywhere there were big holes, thirty metres deep. It was a horrendous foggy night and we felt very vulnerable.'[47] Around 3.30 a.m., the remainder of the Company arrived, slowed down by having to drag the damaged first Warrior.

The next morning Lindsay reviewed his options. The Iraqis arriving to work at the site appeared hostile and he assessed 'that he could not secure the location without denying them access.' He therefore decided to withdraw, the departure delayed because another vehicle had an electrical fire in the turret. Finally setting off 'around 11 am', Colville noted, the plan was to meet up with US troops who would guide them to their forward operating base. Travelling 'at a snail's pace', still towing the damaged Warrior, 14 Platoon, commanded by Lieutenant Alf Ramsay, established a checkpoint in advance of the convoy. Four Warriors were positioned at the crossroads. 'For the next hour', Cowan related, 'all seemed peaceful; cars approached the checkpoint, waited in an orderly queue and were let through once they had been searched.' At 1 p.m. a car driven 'by an unshaven man with pale features, approached the checkpoint at an unremarkable speed. He was seen to smile and then detonated a suicide bomb.' Hood 'didn't hear the blast but just saw a plume of smoke.' As soon as he heard the contact report 'Casualties – Wait Out' he went ahead to the scene of the attack. 'At first I thought the casualties would be civilians but then I saw bodies in desert combats.'[48]

The blast had killed Sergeant Stuart Gray and Privates Scott McArdle and Paul Lowe. 'The scene was devastating,' recorded Colville. 'The interpreter was lying on the ground, obviously missing a leg. There was nothing to be done for him except keep him comfortable until he died.' Eight soldiers were wounded. With mortars also fired at the line of the convoy, the attack, which the insurgents had filmed, had been well-coordinated. 'That incident being put on the internet meant that the distance from the front line to the home front had been obliterated,' related Lieutenant John Bailey, the concern being that the wives of the deceased soldiers would have seen it before being officially notified of their deaths.[49]

While waiting for a helicopter to evacuate the wounded, Privates Currie and McLaughlin, also caught in the blast, administered first aid. 'There was a real mixture of injuries,' continued Colville, who had 'leapfrogged' forward in a Warrior to secure the area beyond where the checkpoint had been attacked. 'It was so horrific I made sure to shut the viewing sight at the back of the Warrior so the Jocks could not look back on it.' Once the wounded were loaded onto the helicopter, Lieutenant Watson and CSM Hood had the distressing task of putting the bodies of their dead comrades into the Warrior. Only on reaching the US forward operating base, could they 'take a deep breath', related Watson. 'We'd had no time to think of the enormity of what had just happened.'[50] 'For a close knit family such as the Black Watch,' Cowan later said, 'their deaths [were] indeed a painful blow. All three of these soldiers were our friends. But as we mourn, so we remember them and give thanks for their contribution to the life of our Regiment. The interpreter had been with the Black Watch since our arrival in Iraq and had become a friend to the soldiers.' His death also meant that the other interpreters left, depriving the Battalion of a vital means of communication. 'In counterinsurgency, being deaf is as bad as being blind.'[51]

'Not a good last couple of days really,' Lieutenant Colquhoun wrote home. 'As I am sure the news has already told you the Battalion has been hit about a wee bit.' Describing how his platoon was 'handling the situation fairly well' he said they were working 'extremely long hours, especially the Warrior crews and in pretty stressful situations, yet there is still a good level of banter. A couple of the younger Jocks are finding things a bit hard – scared really and I can't say I blame them. Have to keep an eye on them.'[52]

On 6 November, with the American attack on Fallujah imminent, the 24th MEU's Commanding Officer, Colonel Ron Johnson, ordered a return east of the Euphrates 'to undertake blocking operations throughout the area in order to disrupt and deter enemy movement through it'. While A Company was told to secure a block across the Euphrates on Saddam Bridge (codenamed Homer from *The Simpsons* television series), B Company, accompanied by the Royal Engineers, was to establish a base in an old ammunition and chemical factory in Al Qaqa, which again, retaining *The Simpsons* theme, was codenamed

Springfield. With the exception of a few men reclaiming scrap metal, the factory was empty 'and resembled Stalingrad. Insurgents had had total control of the area and used it to carry out executions.' The base proved 'highly effective', Cowan reflected, enabling B Company 'to lock down the east side whenever it wished'. A significant asset was the arrival of helicopters from the Army Air Corps and RAF which solved the problem of resupply and 'permitted much greater mobility and responsiveness across the area through the use of dismounted Black Watch and Royal Marine troops as an air reaction force.'[53]

Insurgent attacks, however, continued; a suicide bomb severely injured two corporals, both bomb disposal experts in The Black Watch Battlegroup. When a car failed to stop at the block on Saddam Bridge, Corporal Mitchell, convinced the driver was another suicide bomber, ordered Private Douglas to fire on the vehicle, shooting the driver. 'Everyone was on tenterhooks after what had just happened,' explained Sergeant Shaw.[54] The continuing threat also highlighted 'an essential dilemma', commented Cowan. 'For The Black Watch to search vehicles and to make contact with the local population, soldiers needed to come into close proximity with vehicles and their drivers.' To mitigate their vulnerability to attack, while retaining mobile check points, including Eagle Vehicle Check Points in helicopters, static check points were replaced with roadblocks, forcing vehicles to take another route or to wait until the roadblock was lifted.[55]

On 8 November United States forces initiated Operation Phantom Fury, attacking Fallujah with air strikes and ground forces, while The Black Watch Battlegroup maintained its block to the south. That evening D Company suffered another fatality while out on patrol. 'One Warrior had to go back to refuel', recalled Hood. As it was leaving Dogwood to rejoin the others, it was struck by a roadside bomb, killing the driver, Private Pita Tukutukuwaqa. A Fijian recruit, standing over six-feet tall, 'Big Tukes' was one of a number of Commonwealth soldiers in the British Army. Yet again, the Battalion mourned a fallen comrade, a trained sniper and one of the best rugby players in the Regiment. Two soldiers were injured.[56] 'This incident highlighted the fact that the enemy had a very high sense of awareness and that any sort of pattern would be picked up, particularly as the Warrior track marks left such an obvious signature,' explained Cowan. But avoiding a pattern was 'easier said than done' since the terrain meant that there were few viable routes of entry and exit.[57] B Company, meanwhile, had remained at Al Qaqa. Unable to attack an unseen enemy, tension remained high. 'We've been here 4 days now and everyone is looking a bit tired and weary,' Second Lieutenant Colquhoun wrote again to Rachel. 'Despite the news that is coming through I want to reassure you that I am fine.'[58]

In view of the 'prevailing indirect fire threat', The Black Watch's Remembrance Day service on 11 November was brief.[59] The following day was 'fairly exciting' when a contingent of B Company came across 'an illegal vehicle check point' with ambush positions on either side. 'We were engaged and so had a little fire fight causing the baddies to make their escape in the process leaving behind most of their arsenal,' related Colquhoun. 'A helicopter also tracked one of their escape vehicles resulting in the further capture of two of them along with stuff they had hidden at their house. Quite a good result and good to come face to face with the baddies for a change, far too often we just come across the results of their work.' 'We had begun to identify where the IEDs were,' commented Hood. 'We had tuned in to the environment.' 'We started operating much more on foot,' related Lieutenant Collis. 'Sometimes the IEDs had been hidden, other times not. Given the frequency of attacks, you had to be especially careful when planning patrols to avoid being second-guessed, which was not easy in such a small operating area.'[60]

Living out of their Warriors, 'there were no latrines, just a shovel in the sand', commented Second Lieutenant Will Johnson, who joined D Company in mid-November. Writing letters home 'was a good way of relieving tension. There was not much else to do, apart from cleaning weapons, reading, playing cards or sleeping. We'd also listen to broadcasts of British Forces radio, which relayed messages from home.'[61] Building on previous Regimental lexicons, Company Sergeant Major Penman, the originator of Bertie Basrah, produced a 'Book of Banter', clarifying the Jocks' unique jargon: among varied explanations was the information that 'didnae' meant 'I did', 'speckmental' meant 'someone who is visually impaired', 'schmert': 'not good', 'mong': 'a soldier who can't assimilate information'; 'peepers': 'eyes'; 'chinned': 'tired through lack of sleep'; a 'juice bag' was a 'person who likes drinking a lot' and the inevitable 'widnae' meaning 'I would like to have sexual relations'. 'Fade' meant 'get out of my sight'; skinny': 'obese'; 'straight': 'homosexual'; 'boo': 'fantastic'; 'pucker': 'for real'; and finally 'huvnae': 'I've had sexual relations'![62]

Unlike the searing heat of the summer, nights at Dogwood were cold, and the men slept in a new design of thermal suits. 'I am getting even more skilled at cat napping with my head resting on my sights', Colquhoun informed Rachel: 'quite a knack though you tend to wake up with one or another limb of your body drained of blood'. Five days later Colquhoun was blown to the base of the Warrior's turret, temporarily losing consciousness after a roadside bomb was detonated. His driver, Private Gibson, suffered internal injuries and a shattered pelvis.[63]

In Britain, the Government's proposals to merge the Scottish Regiments had remained headline news; military historian Max Hastings highlighted the irony 'that the Black Watch drove into the Sunni triangle alarmed not by the enemy but by the prospect of amalgamation when they drive out again.'[64] On 17 November Pete Wishart introduced a second debate in the House of Commons, coinciding with the funerals of the three Black Watch soldiers killed at the beginning of the month. 'The thing that Scottish people singularly cannot understand is that, while those regiments and those brave young men are out there doing the Government's bidding in Iraq, the Government plans to stab them in the back by amalgamating the regiments out of existence.' In support, Conservative MP Peter Duncan emphasised that the proposals had 'upset and astounded' people throughout the UK. Speaking on behalf of the government, Adam Ingram, the Minister of State for the Armed Forces, suggested that 'throughout its history, the Army has been subject to change

– sometimes that change has been dramatic'.[65]

'Not to engage in the modernisation of our Armed Forces would weaken our defence at precisely the time it needs to be strong,' affirmed Geoff Hoon, who, on 24 November, had received a delegation led by Brigadier Garry Barnett and Colonel Alex Murdoch. Also present were the Lord Provost of Dundee, the Provosts of Angus, Fife and Perth demonstrating the community's support of the Regiment. Although Hoon listened to their representations, Barnett recalled that 'he did not comment'.[66] The delegation also handed in a petition with over 150,000 signatures to Prime Minister Blair at 10 Downing Street.

Mission accomplished: Operation Tobruk

Having occupied and seized quantities of ammunition as well as detaining a number of Iraqis, the Americans believed that east of the Euphrates could still be an area of resistance, especially the towns in the Triangle of Death in North Babil. Cowan's proposal was for a large-scale cordon-and-search operation in Caraghouli, situated in a bend of the Euphrates, and known to the soldiers as Millionaires' Row because of its large houses and palm groves. Codenamed Tobruk, 'the operation carried some risk. The Battlegroup would need to cross the Euphrates taking its chances with any off-route bombs that might have been pre-positioned. The area would then need to be picketed in order that the assault force could insert and extract unhindered by suicide bombers.'[67]

Realising that the campaign to prevent The Black Watch from being merged had failed, Cowan's order drew the curtain on the Regiment's history. 'This may be the last attack for the 1st Battalion The Black Watch,' he said on 27 November. 'Let us make sure it goes as well as anything we have done in the past and is one that we can be proud of.' 'It was a true Battlegroup operation,' recalled Second Lieutenant Johnson. 'A Company was to be the Assault Company, with B Company undertaking complementary operations on the other side of the river.'[68] D Company's less 'glamorous' role was to secure the routes out of Dogwood and then withdraw until the operation was complete. 'We had loudspeakers attached to one of the Warriors which boomed out pipe music when we arrived on the objective,' related Major Aitken. 'It was quite remarkable to listen to "Highland Laddie" playing while the sun rose behind the river.' As A Company reached its target area, Aitken started a countdown over the Company's radio network. Pausing when he reached 'one' – and taking up Cowan's refrain, he shouted 'Forward the Forty-Twa!', a reminder of Sir Colin Campbell's exhortation as the soldiers moved up the heights of Alma in 1854.[69] 'We had been taught regimental history, and when I heard that it just gave me a real lift,' recalled Sergeant Wilson. 'Black Watch soldiers stormed across the Euphrates river into a suspected insurgent stronghold yesterday, bursting into houses in the middle of the night and arresting scores of males aged 14 and over,' reported *Daily Telegraph* journalist David Harrison. One of the largest offensives since the official end of the war in Iraq in 2003, it was the first large-scale assault by The Black Watch since arriving in Camp Dogwood. The night attack, continued Harrison, 'gave the insurgents little time to organise a fight back: Mission accomplished for Black Watch.'[70]

'Op Tobruk went well in terms of no casualties and we arrested eighty which was narrowed down to twenty-five who are now in the barbed wire chateau behind us,' recorded Lieutenant Colville. Two days later they released sixteen detainees 'of little value. We packed them into the back of three Warriors still cuffed and trundled them across the desert. We did not realise how scared they were... They thought we were going to execute them. Instead we cut the cuffs off and gave them $2 each taxi money to get them home.'[71]

Once the operation was over, plans were begun to extract The Black Watch. 'Various efforts were made to mislead the press by announcing the departure date as 5th December', recalled Cowan, 'while planning proceeded for the 3rd, but this proved superfluous after a D Notice was served preventing all reporting on the subject.' In the early hours of 3 December 2004 the move south began, codenamed Operation

Corunna in memory of Sir John Moore's 1809 retreat during the Peninsular Wars. 'As dawn broke on a cold but crystal clear day, the sight of the entire battle group moving across the desert with sun rising behind it and individual dust clouds from over 100 armoured vehicles and 200 heavy transporters was immensely impressive.' While skeleton crews remained on the Warriors loaded onto the transporters, the majority travelled back to Shaibah by air, Johnson recalled. 'The sense of relief was palpable,' Cowan wrote. 'Operation Bracken was at an end.'[72]

Although the operation to take Fallujah was heavily criticised, especially the number of Iraqi civilian casualties and the American use of cluster bombs and white phosphorous, The Black Watch's thirty-day mission was considered successful. 'We provided an effective block to the south of Fallujah. We interacted well with the local population who had been suspicious of the Coalition up to that point. We also showed that Britain was a good ally.' There had, however, been difficulties. One was the lack of accurate intelligence, prompting the Deputy Coalition Commander, Lieutenant General Kiszely to remark: 'never has a Battlegroup had access to more intelligence assets, but never has a Battlegroup had access to less intelligence.'[73]

The constant threat of attack had also been a strain. During its deployment the Battlegroup experienced 'three suicide bomb attacks, over twenty very large roadside bombs, numerous daily indirect fire attacks, totalling 115 serious incidents'. 'They were all still deeply affected by the trauma of having to pick up the body parts of their friends and store them in the Warrior and then wash it out afterwards,' commented Johnson, referring to the suicide attack in early November.[74] Reflecting on their achievements, Lance Corporal Danny Buist hoped they had made a difference 'for the sake of the guys we lost'. 'I was a different soldier when I came back,' recorded Sergeant Kev Blackley.[75] Major Elliott was disappointed not to be handing the area over to another Battlegroup. 'These people were beginning to confide in us and we had achieved that in a month. I was talking to community leaders and they were talking to me about people they were worried about. Instead we packed everything up and we left. God knows what has happened to these leaders. Their grandfathers had worked with us, the elders wanted to help us. And we just said goodbye, we have done our bit.'[76] British forces remained in Iraq until Operation Telic 13 concluded in April 2009, with some units staying in a training and advisory capacity until May 2011. Subsequently, the emergence of the Islamic State of Iraq and the Levant (ISIL) and the civil war in Syria undermined Western military action, leaving the region in chaos.[77]

In Britain, with the news of the 'Hoon axe' dominating the headlines, grim-faced soldiers marched through Warminster, the pipers playing 'Scotland the Brave', 'Black Bear' and 'Highland Laddie'. Given the continuing publicity about the Scottish Regiments, Lieutenant Colonel Cowan described their experiences as 'surreal'. 'We have never actively sought the limelight, we have had it thrust upon us,' he told journalists. 'We have always thought of ourselves as one of the army's best-kept secrets, and we would now like to return to serving this country for as long as we are allowed in a rather more quiet and anonymous way.'[78]

The Black Watch's deployment was the last time any non-specialist British unit operated outside the Multi-National Division (South East). Recriminations followed: as publicised in the *Daily Telegraph*, a 'Secret UK-Eyes Only' report highlighted the delay between the time The Black Watch was warned of its possible deployment to Dogwood and official confirmation which had 'implications to the Battalion's preparation for a significantly more demanding operational environment… there was insufficient time to assess and then practise appropriate tactics, training and procedures. These had to be developed as the operation progressed.' Once again the limited intelligence was noted.[79]

By December 2004 restructuring the British Army was reaching a critical stage. On 16 December General Jackson wrote a lengthy brief to all Commanding Officers, outlining the Future Army Structure (FAS) and maintaining that creating 'Super' Regiments would prove 'robust for the indefinite future.' Confessing that he had faced some unpleasant comments – 'some addressed to me personally' – Jackson refuted the accusation that he and the Government had destroyed the regimental system. 'What matters is that the regimental system adapts to changing circumstances and operational requirements.' A feature of the new structure, as indicated by Hoon, was ending the infantry 'arms plot' system. Instead of individual regiments rotating their respective roles (armoured, mechanised, light, air assault and public duties) every two to six years, all infantry battalions would be assigned a specific role and location, which would mean families would not be 'uprooted' to go to different postings. Validating the proposal, Jackson maintained that the necessary 'challenge, experience and variety' would be provided 'by individual postings between battalions whilst maintaining continuity of role, increasing the operational availability of battalions and allowing more stability, particularly for families.'[80]

In relation to the Scottish Division, the proposal for a new Royal Regiment of Scotland was formalised: The Royal Scots would be amalgamated with The King's Own Scottish Borderers to become the 1st Battalion, The Royal Highland Fusiliers becoming the 2nd Battalion. As the oldest Highland Regiment, The Black Watch took precedence as the 3rd Battalion, the 4th Battalion being The Highlanders and the 5th The Argyll & Sutherland Highlanders. Two territorial battalions were retained: the 52nd Lowland and the 51st Highland, to be known as the 6th and 7th Battalions The Royal Regiment of Scotland. Unlike other new 'Super' Regiments (for example, the Mercian, merging the Cheshire, the Worcesters & Sherwood Forester and the Staffordshire Regiments where their antecedent names would appear in brackets after the new Regimental name), the regimental names were to be retained in front. 'Unprecedented in format', wrote Jackson. The Executive Committee of the Army Board endorsed the decision taken by the Council of Scottish Colonels for the Battalions to retain their antecedent regimental names 'as the new battalion title foremost, with the new regimental title in brackets'.[81]

Following Jackson's briefing, Lieutenant General Irwin wrote to members of The Black Watch, as well as potential officers and readers of *The Red Hackle,* outlining the new arrangements and highlighting the importance of the retention of The Black Watch's name. Having emphasised that 'there is not a single one of us, serving, retired or related, in the whole regimental family who would have wanted us to face cuts and amalgamations, or would not have wanted to contemplate happily more years of the Regiment as we know it', he stressed the need to move forward 'on the basis that orders have been received and that all serving BW men now have to execute them'. Aware of the personal criticism he had received, he concluded: 'For my part, despite the profound pain of being the Colonel of the Regiment presiding over this change, I intend to do everything that I can to make these new arrangements work for the sake of those who have made Black Watch history in Iraq and who will keep the Black Watch name and Hackle to the fore in the future.'[82]

Don't put away The Black Watch for we will need them by and by
Every man in that old regiment is willing to do or die.[83]

27

Turning a Page of History

O God
Whose strength setteth fast the mountains,
Lord of the hills to whom we lift our eyes:
Grant us grace that we of The Black Watch,
Once chosen to watch the mountains
Of an earthly kingdom,
May stand fast in faith and be strong,
Until we come to the heavenly kingdom of Him
who has bidden us watch and pray,
Thy Son, our Saviour and Lord,
Amen.[1]

Towards merger

Throughout 2005 The Black Watch was reaping the rewards of its service in Iraq. Detachments again took part in a series of homecoming parades in the Regiment's traditional recruiting heartland. 'That was a really powerful time for the Battalion and the communities,' remarked Captain Ben Collis. 'It became very clear how close the connections are with the local towns and the area.' On 7 April a remembrance service was held at St John's Kirk, Perth. Later that day, a monument in the grounds of Balhousie Castle was dedicated to the memory of the six men killed in Iraq in 2003 and 2004. Two days later Pipe Major Scott Taylor was one of three pipers leading the Regiment's Colonel-in-Chief, Prince Charles, and the Duchess of Cornwall away in their car after their wedding reception in Windsor. In a contrasting scenario, on the same day those campaigning to Save The Scottish Regiments marched from Speakers Corner, Hyde Park, to Trafalgar Square. Brigadier Garry Barnett again stressed that 'amalgamation is not a popular move… to be fully up to strength we need to recruit locally and this depends on those links to our local communities.'[2]

Back at the Land Warfare Centre in Warminster 'there was a lot of interest in The Black Watch because we had recently had high intensity battlegroup experience,' continued Collis. But, commented Lieutenant Will Johnson, 'the Jocks would rather have been anywhere else. There were some discipline issues and there weren't many resources in terms of welfare. We had quite a few problems with Jocks going home on leave and not returning. They hadn't really had a chance to get over the Iraq tours. A lot of issues came out from doing those two tours in quick succession.'[3]

Meanwhile the 'old and bold' members of The Black Watch were pledging to fight against amalgamation to the 'bitter end' (defined as the day of formation of the new regiment). Lieutenant Colonel Stephen Lindsay, a descendant of the Regiment's first Colonel, John Lindsay, Earl of Crawford, openly expressed his anger: 'The reality before us is that hundreds of years of sacrifice, courage, honour and tradition are about to be wiped out by pen-pushers and armchair Generals in London.' In contrast, Lieutenant General Irwin, who described the period of discussion as 'profoundly uncomfortable and saddening,' told his listeners at the AGM of the Black Watch Association in April 2005 that 'it was simply inevitable that a process that began in the post-War years would be continued at some time or another to its logical conclusion.' Repeating sentiments expressed in his December 2004 letter, he said that, as Colonel of the Regiment, he 'had no desire whatever to be part of a decision that would see the Regiment's demise'.[4] Fellow former officers, however, remained disappointed at Irwin's involvement as adjutant-general in discussions to end the regimental system. As a serving officer and as Irwin's ADC, Jamie Riddell recognised his dilemma. 'If he had not been on the Army Board we would have lost the regimental names,' he explained. 'For those of us serving, we didn't want The Black Watch to lose its independent status, other regiments felt the same, but unlike those who had retired and were very vocal, we still had a job to do,' remarked Angus Philp. 'The only way we could stay in the Army was to accept the changes – with honour.' For his part, Irwin blamed the government 'bankrolled by the Chancellor, Gordon Brown', who 'persistently declined to fund the Armed Forces to the extent needed to sustain them in the longer term'.[5]

Before the May 2005 General Election, Field Marshal Earl Wavell's grandson, Owen Humphrys, who had retired from The Black Watch as a captain in 1978, organised a 'battle' bus which travelled to Westminster encouraging voters to support those political parties who opposed the merger of the Scottish regiments. Leading the group of veterans was Major Bob Ritchie. In speeches delivered in towns throughout Scotland, he exhorted traditional Labour party supporters, like those in Gordon Brown's constituency of Kirkcaldy and Cowdenbeath, not to vote Labour 'because', reported Magnus Linklater, 'it is a Labour government that has signed the regiment's death warrant'.[6]

After the election, won by Labour with a decreased majority, Barnett wrote to the new Secretary of State for Defence, Dr John Reid, urging him to 'reverse the decision to cut four battalions from the infantry' especially at a time when Britain's military commitments appeared to be increasing. Adam Ingram, Minister of State for the Armed Forces, responded, stating that the government would not be changing its decision 'to move towards larger regiments'.[7] Barnett had also written to General Jackson, questioning his claim that larger regiments would increase recruitment. Jackson responded at length, maintaining that the 'new structure' would be 'better equipped to address the inevitable variations in the regional ability to recruit'. He also explained that once the Executive Committee of the Army Board had decided to stop arms plotting, 'we then had to decide how best to restructure the Infantry to provide our soldiers with the breadth of experience that they previously enjoyed during the arms plot era.' In Jackson's opinion the best way to achieve this was by enabling cross-posting between the battalions of a larger regiment 'recruited from broadly similar areas'.[8]

The 'finale' to the Battalion's posting at Warminster was a Combined

Arms Manoeuvre demonstration on Salisbury Plain at the beginning of October. Preparations were also being made to deploy to Northern Ireland for the first time in a decade. 'There was some disappointment because we hoped that, given our experience in Iraq, we would retain our role as an armoured infantry battalion either in Iraq or in Afghanistan, rather than reverting to a light infantry role in Northern Ireland,' commented Collis.[9] Moving to Palace Barracks outside Belfast in December 2005, The Black Watch's duties included public-order training. Operation Banner was drawing to a close and preparations were being made to reduce troop numbers in accordance with the 1998 Good Friday Agreement.[10]

2006: The Royal Regiment of Scotland

On 28 March 2006 The Black Watch (Royal Highland Regiment) paraded for the last time in front of the Colonel of the Regiment, Lieutenant General Irwin.[11] After a fifteen-minute break the Battalion, still under the command of Lieutenant Colonel Lindsay MacDuff, was then re-formed as The Black Watch, 3rd Battalion The Royal Regiment of Scotland, Irwin now becoming the Battalion's Representative Colonel. The men had been 'wearing our old Tam o'Shanters', recorded Captain Johnson. 'We had our new ones with the cap badge in our pockets which we put on.' Those still upset at the change called the day Black Tuesday. 'The wives had all turned up for the parade in black dresses with black hats and dark glasses. There was a "mourning" party in the evening and the black theme was continued with squid ink pasta and Guinness.'[12] On the same day in Edinburgh, Major General Euan Loudon, Colonel of the Royal Regiment of Scotland, addressed the 'Formation Parade' at Edinburgh Castle. 'On this day we are turning over a new chapter in the story of the Scottish soldier. Today, we are raising a new Regiment… change may be painful but it has come to visit us in our day and generation and it follows on from a remarkable record of service in the antecedent Regiments.'[13]

'We have fought the good fight for what we believed was right for our Regiment and the defence of our country,' Brigadier Barnett said at a service of commemoration at Balhousie Castle attended by veterans, soldiers and politicians from all parties. 'We have now come to the end of an era for The Black Watch, an end to The Black Watch that we have known and loved. None of us would have wished that the decision to amalgamate had been taken but we must recognise that it has and The Black Watch as we have known it is no more.'[14] The Royal Regiment of Scotland was the only 'Super' Regiment, whose battalions were permitted, as promised, to retain their former regimental names and the right to wear their antecedent hackles in combat dress. On ceremonial occasions, however, the new regimental cap badge and Glengarry headdress was to be worn.[15]

'Not everything was ready,' commented Second Lieutenant Andy Colquhoun, the first officer to be commissioned into The Black Watch Battalion. 'There were no Royal Regiment of Scotland buttons, so we were commissioned in our antecedents buttons.'[16] 'We arrived in a new regiment which did not have a new uniform,' commented Second Lieutenant Harry Gladstone, the second officer to be commissioned and grandson of a former Commanding Officer, Brigadier Bill Bradford. 'Yet everybody was very positive,' continued Colquhoun. 'I think they had to be – thinking that there would be more opportunities and more cross postings.' Brigadier Alasdair Loudon was sanguine. 'The gap between reality and emotion was huge. Young commanders will go to whatever battalion they have to.'[17]

As The Black Watch ceased to exist as a regiment, Scottish playwright, Gregory Burke, whose grandfather and two uncles had served in the Regiment, wrote a play, *Black Watch*, for the National Theatre of Scotland. First performed in August 2006, its theme was a soldier's attitude to war and pride in being part of a famous regiment. Critically acclaimed, the actors re-enacted the events leading to the suicide bomb attack in Iraq in November 2004 which killed three Black Watch soldiers. The actor who played the Commanding Officer (Lieutenant Colonel Cowan) in the first performances was Peter Forbes, whose father had served in the Regiment in Korea in the 1950s. For other performances the Commanding Officer's role was played by Johnnie (Jack) Fortune, General Sir Victor Fortune's grandson.[18]

Despite the Battalion's transition from The Black Watch to The Royal Regiment of Scotland, it had remained in Northern Ireland, its duties involving 'a mixture of guarding military sites awaiting "de-construction" (politically correct terminology!)' as well as dismantling the numerous Observation Posts in South Armagh including Crossmaglen.[19] On 16 May Prince Charles, now the Battalion's Royal Colonel and accompanied by the Duchess of Cornwall, visited the Battalion at Palace Barracks 'to see the Battalion in action'.[20] In November, deploying to Iraq for the first time as the Royal Regiment of Scotland, the Battalion's A Company performed the role of an independent company in the Danish Battlegroup at Shaibah. Following its tour, a composite platoon was deployed, The Black Watch Battalion experiencing its first fatalities when Privates Scott 'Casper' Kennedy and Jamie Kerr, both aged twenty, were killed by a roadside bomb south-east of Basra in late June 2007.[21]

On 31 July 2007 Operation Banner was concluded. Fatalities in the British Army, including the Ulster Defence Regiment, totalled 709 out of 3,665 recorded deaths during the period of the Troubles. Recalling nearly four decades of military experience in Northern Ireland, which had 'spawned doctrine, tactics, equipment and knowledge', Lieutenant Colonel MacDuff emphasised the importance of not forgetting 'these hard-learnt lessons' as well as recognising their relevance in other operational theatres.[22] Returning to Fort George, The Black Watch Battalion's main focus in 2008 was completing its conversion to a light infantry battalion, joining 19 Light Brigade in preparation for its first operational tour in Afghanistan.[23]

The Black Watch Battalion (3 Scots): Afghanistan

Following the terrorist attacks in the United States on 11 September 2001 (9/11) and the fall of the Taliban regime in Afghanistan, an International Security Assistance Force (ISAF) had been mandated by the UN to help the new Afghan government maintain security throughout the country. Britain's contribution was codenamed Operation Herrick. In 2003 NATO had taken command of ISAF and its mandate had gradually expanded to include the whole of Afghanistan, with a particular focus on the southern provinces of Kandahar and Helmand where continuing Taliban activity was greatest.[24] In 2007 the Ministry of Defence approved the deployment of a battlegroup to southern Afghanistan as a reserve force. By the time The Black Watch Battalion was deployed as part of Operation Herrick 10 in 2009, the new US President, Barack Obama, had redirected attention towards Afghanistan and away from Iraq. Continuing instability in the region also resulted in the belief that neighbouring Pakistan 'represented an existential threat', widening the conflict to 'the whole of the Pashtun belt'.[25]

'All of you will deploy to Afghanistan [as] part of the same team wearing the badge of the Royal Regiment of Scotland and the Red Hackle of the Black Watch Battalion,' said Lieutenant General Irwin, mindful that the memory of the merger was recent. 'Both symbols are very important. The badge will remind you that the story of your tour will become one of the earliest chapters in the history of the new Regiment. The Red Hackle will remind you of one of the famous and distinguished antecedent regiments, whose ideals, heritage and reputation you are carrying forward into a new era, and from whose example of courage, loyalty and *esprit de corps* you can take inspiration and pride.'[26]

Based in Kandahar and deployed as part of the Aviation Assault Battlegroup, the men were 'operating at a very high tempo', related Captain Collis. 'We were five days in, seven days out. You always had the exhilaration of going somewhere new, partly because of the sheer amount of resources we had at our disposal, most of which came from the Americans.' 'After being up half the night last night I am actually in bed for 10 tonight and am lying listening to the usual cacophony of jets warming up and helicopters taking off,' Captain Nick Colquhoun, the intelligence officer, informed Rachel, now his wife. 'The Battlegroup is back out again tonight on another mission.'[27] 'We were in the thick of everything,' noted Lieutenant Harry Gladstone, describing the contrast between their base in Kandahar 'with Pizza Express' and how 'within forty minutes you could be in the middle of nowhere in a compound with goats'. After reading his grandfather's account of his escape from St Valéry in 1940, Gladstone adopted the system of cryptically indicating his location, prefaced by the same phrase Bill Bradford had used: 'I am not allowed to say where I am.' His mother, Bradford's daughter, 'instantly recognised the ruse!'[28]

Between April and October the Battalion undertook thirteen battlegroup operations and eight company operations 'in areas less frequented by ISAF with the aim of disrupting the insurgents in depth'.[29] Important among them was the British-led air operation, codenamed Panchai Palang, aimed at securing canal and river crossings in order to establish a permanent ISAF presence in Helmand south of Camp Bastion. 'Panchai Palang means Panther's claw,' Gladstone noted in his diary. 'The Panther is the symbol of 19 Brigade showing that this was to be the definitive operation for the brigade over the summer.' 'Our part was to break into Babaji Fasal,' related Colquhoun. 'We planned it from Kandahar, then forward mounted it to Camp Bastion, from where the operation was launched. I did all the intelligence targeting, working out what we were targeting and planning the next area where we were to focus our attention to get a result.'[30] Carried out in three phases and lasting six weeks, at the end of July the operation was declared successful. The Battalion also provided a detachment of fifty soldiers from D Company, commanded by Major Philp, to the 2nd Mercian Battlegroup which was the Operational Mentoring and Liaison Team (OMLT) Battlegroup assisting the Afghan National Army in Helmand. Based at Musa Qaleh, one of six locations in Helmand, their work was 'the unarticulated main effort of the war, in the sense that people had recognised that the key to the long term solution of Afghanistan was making Afghans responsible for their own security.'[31]

In late October The Black Watch Battalion left Afghanistan, its return to Fort George marking the beginning of a six-month 're-set' period. Reflecting on the tour, Private Vincent Byrne emphasised that 'the main thing that keeps you going, and which is seen both in the green zone in Helmand and on the plains in Salisbury, is the camaraderie between the troops that exists even in the toughest of environments.'[32] While in Kandahar, the cousins Rob and Andy Colquhoun had choreographed a new 'Kandahar' Reel. Recalling the 'Reel of the 51st' written in captivity during the Second World War, the Colquhoun cousins wrote their reel in memory of the five Black Watch Battalion soldiers who were killed during operations, Acting Sergeant Sean Binnie, Privates Robert McLaren and Kevin Elliott, Sergeant Gus Millar and Corporal Tam Mason. While the 'hands across' symbolised the blades of helicopters, the steps represented team work. The reel was performed at one-and-half times the normal speed because 'soldiers are constantly asked to give 150%'.[33]

Returning to Afghanistan in October 2011 on Operation Herrick 15, The Black Watch Battalion was deployed as part of a ground-holding battlegroup in Helmand. 'We were transitioning to Afghan supremacy. The Afghan National Army was taking over areas where we were moving out of, so it was hard work in a different way,' explained Captain Harry Hood, who had received his commission in 2008.[34]

On the morning of 11 November, while working with the 1st Princess of Wales's Royal Regiment, a Black Watch patrol was moving through open farmland near the Battlegroup's headquarters at Base Shawqat Nad-e-Ali, as part of a series of operations aimed at disrupting local Taliban activity. When twenty-five-year-old Private Stephen Bainbridge from Kirkcaldy stepped through a doorway, he was 'blown into the air', the sensation of stepping onto an IED 'more like floating. That was until I hit the ground.' Second Lieutenant Robert Weir was hit by debris. 'It seemed to be moving in slow motion. I got launched a few metres and landed on my back.' He then caught sight of Bainbridge, who had one leg missing. 'I saw the other leg was definitely damaged but it was still there at that point. I called for a medic and then started giving my initial first aid'. 'There are words that no soldier ever wants to say', reported journalist Jason Howe, embedded with the patrol group, 'but he [Weir] began to shout into his radio: "Contact IED! One times casualty T1. Wait out!"'[35] 'It happened almost the moment the Remembrance Service started,' recalled Captain Gladstone, who was in the operations room organising the evacuation. 'Outside I could hear the Last Post.' As the service continued there was a recitation of Laurence Binyon's Great War poem 'For the Fallen' and its memorable lines: 'At the going down of the sun and in the morning/ We will remember them.' Realising that Bainbridge was fighting for his life, Gladstone found it 'incredibly moving to draw the parallels between today and yesterday'.[36]

2012: Closing a glorious chapter

In the years following the formation of the Royal Regiment of Scotland, the hope of maintaining the links between the individual battalions and their old recruiting areas was undermined by the imperative to send fully manned battalions on operations overseas. Postings between the battalions for career purposes further loosened local ties. As Gladstone commented: 'In the early days the Battalion had the idea of being Black Watch in camp and 3 Scots outside. But that could never have worked. I think the difficulty was if you remain Black Watch then you exclude everybody who is posted in, so, to make the Battalion a cohesive unit you have to strike a balance between a new Royal Regiment of Scotland identity and a link to the past.'[37] Even so, The Black Watch Battalion, like the other battalions, has managed to retain much of the old ethos symbolised by the Red Hackle and the celebration of Red Hackle Day on 5 January. 'You build your *esprit de corps* by the people you work with,' said Major Neil Tomlin, who commanded a company of The Highlanders Battalion (4 Scots) in Germany between 2009 and 2011. 'You have to be interested in the *esprit de corps* of other battalions to uphold your own.' 'The art of the Commanding Officer is sticking true to the Royal Regiment of Scotland brand but retaining The Black Watch flavour,' observed Major Alastair Colville. 'As the Royal Regiment of Scotland becomes confident in its brand, it will feel less threatened by the brand of its individual battalions.'[38]

After the 2006 amalgamation, the battalions of the Royal Regiment of Scotland retained the Colours of their former Regiments. On 2 July 2011 at Holyrood Park, Edinburgh, The Queen, Colonel-in-Chief of the Royal Regiment of Scotland, presented new Colours to the 1st, 2nd, 3rd, 5th, 6th and 7th Battalions, the first time they had paraded together; only the 4th, in Afghanistan on Operation Herrick 14, was not present. Addressing the officers and other ranks the Queen reminded her listeners that the presentation marked the turning of a page of history in the history of a Regiment. Aware that these were the first Colours bearing the Royal Regiment of Scotland's insignia, she stressed the significance of closing 'one glorious chapter for Scotland's infantry' and the opening of a 'fresh chapter'. 'At the end of the parade,' recalled Brigadier de Broë-Ferguson, in command of the Black Watch Regimental Association on parade, 'all the Associations then marched [their] old Colours past the Queen for the last time'.[39]

The following year, on 23 June, these same Colours were paraded through the streets of Perth. As the pipers played, the soldiers marched, hundreds of Red Hackles moving forward. Young men and women, some of whom had seen active service in Afghanistan and Iraq, middle-aged men who had served in Northern Ireland, old men who had fought in the Second World War, Korea and Kenya, all marched in unison, a few in wheelchairs following on behind. Then came the Colours bearing the name, The Black Watch, held high and gently blowing in the wind. Brigadier Garry Barnett, former Colonel of the Regiment, took the salute.

As those who have served in the Army recognise, the Colours are the Regiment's 'heart and soul'. In days gone by, their purpose was not only ceremonial. During the battle, they served as a rallying point for the men, whose vision was often obscured by smoke and dust. Even when the tradition of carrying the Colours into battle ceased in 1858, they retained their revered status, along with the significance of the Battle Honours inscribed on them. Lacking the space for the 164 Battle Honours granted to The Black Watch, only ten from the First and Second World Wars were emblazoned on the Queen's Colour and only those relating to the battles fought before 1902 on the Regimental Colour, with the addition of *The Hook 1952*,

Korea 1952–53. Al Basrah and *Iraq 2003* were never inscribed.

During its 267-year history The Black Watch fought in nearly every major war in which British troops were involved since its first action at the battle of Fontenoy in 1745, when the opposing French described the soldiers as 'highland furies' rushing upon them 'with more violence than ever did a sea driven by a tempest'.[40] These wars included the French–Indian Wars, the American War of Independence, the Peninsular, Napoleonic and the Crimean Wars as well as actions in India, Egypt and the Sudan. The 2nd Battalion, which became the 73rd Regiment for nearly 100 years, took part in the capture of Seringapatam when Tipu Sultan, the Tiger of Mysore, was killed in 1799. At the beginning of the nineteenth century, it served in Ceylon (Sri Lanka), and in Australia, a place 'so little known', at a time when the journey from Britain by sea took nine months. In 1852, when travelling on board the stricken HMS *Birkenhead*, soldiers of the 73rd were among the first to observe the Birkenhead Drill, a code of conduct which ensured the lives of women and children would be saved first. After fighting in the Second South African War at the turn of the century, The Black Watch saw extensive action in both World Wars and the Korean War, as well as taking part in operations in Palestine, Kenya, Cyprus, Northern Ireland, Kosovo and Iraq.

The destination of the marching soldiers in June 2012, joined by those of the 51st Highland Regiment (now 51st Highland, 7th Battalion The Royal Regiment of Scotland), whose Colours were also being laid up, was a corner of Perth's North Inch where a non-denominational Drumhead service was held near the monument to the 51st Highland Division. As the Queen's and Regimental Colours were handed to the Museum's representatives to be laid up at Balhousie Castle, The Black Watch (Royal Highland Regiment) turned a page of history.

There's a resting-place up yonder
For the feet that march no more;
An' a Billet for the scarlet, an'
The plaids ye proudly wore.
Where the Colours o' the Regiments
Hang in glorious array…
An'Ypres, Mons, an'Alamein are
Topics o' the day.
Where Generals an' Lance Corporals
Can a' let doon their hair:
An' Sergeant-Majors scream the odds,
Intae the empty air!
Where Cameron an' Gordon
Hang their Claymore on the war';
An' yer Silver-Streakin' Seaforths
Greet the Gallant Forty-Twa'.
When golden-mounted pipes, play-in
The famous HLI;
An' the Doric, mixed wi' Gaelic,
Echoes clear across the sky!
Yon' stalwarts o' the Thin Red Line'
The braw lads 'Argyll…
Wi "Swingin' Six", and bonnie dice,
Will aye march-in; fu' style!
Dominion Jocks, an' Exiles a',
Will join wir' gallant band…
An' Transvaal Scots, an' Springboks
March : frae oot Witwatersrand!
They'll sing again the auld, auld sangs,
An' tell o' where they've been…
An' Toast the Lion Rampant, in
The finest Highland Cream![41]

Appendix I: Colonels-in-Chief and Colonels of the Regiment

Colonels-in-Chief

His Majesty King George V, 3 September 1912–20 January 1936
Her Majesty Queen Elizabeth, The Queen Mother, 11 May 1937–30 March 2002
His Royal Highness Prince Charles, Duke of Rothesay, 1 July 2003–28 March 2006

Colonels of the Regiment

John Lindsay, Earl of Crawford, 25 October 1739
Hugh Forbes, Baron Sempill, 14 January 1741
Lord John Murray, 25 April 1745
Sir Hector Munro, KB, 1 June 1787
George Gordon, Marquis of Huntly, GCB, PC, 3 January 1806
John Hope, Earl of Hopetoun, GCB, 29 January 1820
The Rt Hon Sir George Murray, GCB, GCH, 6 September 1823
Sir John Macdonald, GCB, 15 January 1844
Sir James Douglas, GCB, 10 April 1850
George Hay, Marquis of Tweeddale, KT, GCB, 9 March 1862
Sir Duncan Alexander Cameron, GCB, 9 September 1863
Hon Sir Robert Rollo, KCB, 9 June 1888
Sir John Chetham McLeod, KCB, 26 February 1907
Sir John Grenfell Maxwell, GCB, KCMG, CVO, DSO, 11 January 1914
Sir Archibald Rice Cameron, GBE, GCB, CMG, 21 February 1929
Sir Arthur Grenfell Wauchope, GCB, GCMG, CIE, DSO, 28 August 1940
Sir Archibald Percival Wavell, 1st Earl Wavell, PC, GCB, GCSI, GCIE, CMG, MC, 1 March 1946
Sir Neil Methuen Ritchie, GBE, KCB, DSO, MC, 24 May 1950

Neil McMicking, CB, CBE, DSO, MC, 19 June 1952
Robert Keith Arbuthnott, Viscount Arbuthnott, CB, CBE, DSO, MC, 31 March 1960
Henry Conyers Baker Baker, DSO, MBE, 1 June 1964
Sir Bernard Edward Fergusson, Lord Ballantrae, KT, GCMG, GCVO, DSO, OBE, 1 June 1969
John Cassels Monteith, CBE, MC, 6 May 1976
Andrew Linton Watson, CB, 28 September 1981
Garry Charles Barnett, OBE, 28 September 1992
Sir Alistair Stuart Hastings Irwin, KCB, CBE, 28 September 2003

Colonels of the 73rd (former 2nd Battalion)

Sir George Osborn, Bt, 18 April 1786
Sir William Medows, KB, 11 August 1786
Gerard Lake, 1st Viscount Lake, 2 November 1798
George Harris, 1st Lord Harris, GCB, 14 February 1800
Rt Hon Sir Frederick Adam, GCB, GCMG, 22 May 1829
William George Harris, 2nd Lord Harris, CB, KCH, 4 December 1835
Sir Robert Henry Dick, KCB, KCH, 10 June 1845
Sir John Grey, KCB, 3 April 1846
Sir Richard Goddard Hare-Clarges, KCB, 18 May 1849
Robert Barclay Macpherson, CB, KH, 29 July 1852
Chesborough Grant Falconar, KH, 11 February 1857
Sir Michael Creagh, KH, 11 January 1860
Benjamin Orlando Jones, KH, 15 September 1860
Sir Henry Robert Ferguson-Davie, Bt, 17 February 1865

Appendix II: Members of the Regiment Awarded the Victoria Cross (VC)

Indian Mutiny

Lieutenant Francis Edward Farquharson, Lucknow, 9 March 1858
Quartermaster John Simpson, Fort Ruhya, 15 April 1858
Lance Corporal Alexander Thompson, Fort Ruhya, 15 April 1858
Private James Davis, Fort Ruhya, 15 April 1858
Private Edward Spence, Fort Ruhya, 15 April 1858
Colour Sergeant William Gardner, Bareilly, 5 May 1858
Private Walter Cook, Maylah Ghat, 15 January 1859
Private Duncan Millar, Maylah Ghat, 15 January 1859

Ashanti War

Lance Sergeant Samuel McGaw, Amoaful, 31 January 1874

Egyptian Campaign

Private Thomas Edwards, Tamai, 13 March 1884

First World War

Corporal John Ripley, 1st Battalion, Rue du Bois, 9 May 1915
Sergeant David Finlay, 2nd Battalion, Rue du Bois, 9 May 1915
Private Charles Melvin, 2nd Battalion, Istabulat, 21 April 1917
Lieutenant Colonel Lewis Pugh Evans, Commanding Officer, 1st Lincolnshire Regiment, Zonnebeke, 4 October 1917

Korean War

Private William Speakman, attached to King's Own Scottish Borderers, 4 November 1951

Appendix III: Alliances Worldwide

From the beginning of the 20th century The Black Watch (Royal Highland Regiment) developed affiliations with regiments in Australia, Canada, New Zealand and South Africa.[1]

Australia

The 42nd Battalion, The Royal Queensland Regiment, raised as part of the Australian Imperial Force, served on the Western Front from 1916 to 1918. In 1939 the King was 'graciously pleased to approve of the 42nd Battalion (The Capricornia Regiment) Australian Military Forces being allied to The Black Watch (Royal Highland Regiment)'.[2] In 1948 the Battalion was re-formed as part of the re-raised Citizens Military Forces. The 'official' alliance with The Black Watch was lost in the 1960s, Australian Army Regulations demanding 'that such an alliance be on a regimental basis'.[3] Today the battalion's lineage is maintained in the 31st/42nd Royal Queensland Regiment, a light infantry regiment of the Royal Australian Army, based in Queensland.

The New South Wales Scottish Regiment has lineage dating from 1885 when the Sydney Reserve Corps of Scottish Rifles was formed. The 30th Battalion Australian Imperial Force was established in 1915, serving on the Western Front. Having been disbanded in 1919, it was re-raised in 1921. The alliance of the 30th Battalion with The Black Watch is first listed in *The Red Hackle* in 1926, with a New South Wales Branch of The Black Watch Association, 'although not a very strong body', in existence since at least 1921. In 1929, the Honorary Secretary, Mr W. Wilson, who had served with The Black Watch in Egypt and the Sudan in the 1880s, was lamenting that there were 'a good number of Black Watch men out here who should be members that we don't seem to get into touch with owing to the vast size of New South Wales'.[4]

Having been amalgamated with the 51st Battalion as the 30th/51st in the early 1930s, the 30th again became a separate battalion in 1935, adopting the title 'New South Wales Scottish Regiment' with a fund established to raise money 'to help equip the 30th Battalion with The Black Watch dress.'[5]

During the Second World War, after undertaking garrison duties in Australia, the Regiment saw active service in New Guinea in 1944–45. After the war it was disbanded but re-formed again as part of the Citizens Military Force. In 1960 it was absorbed into the Royal New South Wales Regiment following the amalgamation of all the Citizens Military Force infantry battalions in New South Wales.

Canada

The Black Watch (Royal Highland Regiment) of Canada dates from 1812 with the formation of the Highland Rifle Companies. In 1862 the 5th Battalion Volunteer Militia Rifles was formed and in 1884 re-designated the 5th Battalion Royal Scots of Canada. In 1904 it became the 5th Regiment Royal Scots of Canada (Highlanders), signifying the first official 'Highland' designation. The following year it became affiliated with The Black Watch (Royal Highlanders), changing its name in 1906 to the 5th Regiment Royal Highlanders of Canada; the name 'Black Watch' was added the following year. The soldiers, however, had already adopted the custom of wearing a red hackle, permission for which was officially given by Army Order in 1895.

During the First World War three battalions served in the Canadian Expeditionary Force, the 13th, 42nd (Quebec) and the 73rd. The 20th Reserve Battalion was also mobilised. Among those who enlisted was a Danish civil engineer, Private Thomas Dinesen, who was awarded the VC on 12 August 1918 during the Battle of Amiens.[6]

In 1930 the numerical '5th' was dropped, the Regiment's title becoming The Black Watch (Royal Highlanders) of Canada on 1 January 1931. Conforming with the change of title by the parent regiment, in 1935 it became The Black Watch (Royal Highland Regiment) of Canada.[7] The first meeting of the Toronto Black Watch Association was held in 1928. Separate Atlantic and Montreal branches were also established, initially focusing on the needs of veterans.

During the Second World War one company and the mortar detachment of the 1st Battalion suffered heavy losses during the August 1942 raid on Dieppe; in early July 1944 The Black Watch (Royal Highland Regiment) of Canada crossed over to France as part of Operation Overlord, fighting in some thirty operations. After the war it reverted to being a one-battalion militia regiment. On 8 October 1953 the Canadian government announced that the 1st and 2nd Canadian Highland Battalions – formed after the war for service with NATO and in Korea – would become the 1st and 2nd Battalions The Black Watch. The former Montreal Militia Unit became the 3rd Battalion. In July 1970 the 1st and 2nd Battalions were reduced and transferred to the Supplementary Order of Battle, the 3rd Battalion becoming a militia regiment in Canada's Armed Forces.

The affiliation with the parent regiment has lasted for over a century. Both regiments have benefited from having the Queen Mother and, after her death, Prince Charles, as their Colonel-in-Chief. On 23 June 2012 a delegation of The Black Watch (Royal Highland Regiment) of Canada was present when the Colours of The Black Watch (Royal Highland Regiment) were laid up at Balhousie Castle.[8]

The Prince Edward Island Regiment has its origins in the 82nd Abegweit Light Infantry, formed in 1875, two years after Prince Edward Island became a province of Canada. After serving in Halifax, Nova Scotia, during the First World War, the unit was disbanded. Subsequently it was reorganised into the Prince Edward Island Regiment. A further change took place in 1928 when the name 'the Prince Edward Island Highlanders' was adopted. Its affiliation with The Black Watch dates from that time, when the decision was taken 'that the kilt should be worn' since the majority of its members were of Scottish descent. After agreeing that the tartan should be Black Watch 'authority was duly granted'.[9] In 1946 the Regiment was amalgamated with the Prince Edward Island Light Horse, once more becoming the Prince Edward Island Regiment. A further merger with the 28th Light Anti-Aircraft

Regiment took place in 1955. Now a reserve force armoured reconnaissance regiment, based at Charlottetown and Summerside, Prince Edward Island, it has retained the alliance with The Black Watch, 3rd Battalion The Royal Regiment of Scotland; it also maintains an alliance with the 9th/12th Lancers (Prince of Wales's) Regiment.

The Lanark and Renfrew Scottish Regiment originated in 1866 as the Brockville Battalion of Infantry. In 1897 it was re-designated 42nd Lanark and Renfrew Battalion of Infantry. On 15 July 1927 it became the Lanark and Renfrew Scottish Regiment and, on 6 February 1928, the Regiment's alliance with The Black Watch (Royal Highlanders) was approved by the King.[10] Further conversions and re-designations followed. On 10 November 1992 the Regiment was converted to an artillery role and re-named the 1st Air Defence Regiment (Lanark and Renfrew Scottish), based at Pembroke, Ontario. Like The Black Watch, its regimental march is 'Highland Laddie'.

New Zealand

The New Zealand Scottish Regiment has lineage dating from 1863 when a company of Scottish Volunteer Rifles was formed. In early 1939 the New Zealand Government approved the raising of a Scottish regiment which would be allied to The Black Watch (Royal Highland Regiment) 'and wear its tartan'. Companies were formed in Auckland, Wellington, Christchurch and Dunedin, various Scottish societies assisting with raising funds and finding recruits. Although it did not fight in the Second World War as a unit, the New Zealand Scottish was represented by one company of the New Zealand Expeditionary Force, undertaking operations in Greece, Crete, North Africa and Italy. After Japan entered the war a battalion served in New Caledonia, where it remained until disbanded in June 1943, its members being absorbed as reinforcements throughout the Pacific.

After the war the Regiment was re-formed and included in the Order of Battle of the Royal New Zealand Armoured Corps. Known as the 1st Armoured Car Regiment (New Zealand Scottish), in recognition of its relationship with The Black Watch, the Regimental Colours retained the badge of The Black Watch in the right hand corner (in addition to the badge of another affiliated regiment, the Royal Scots Dragoon Guards – formerly the Royal Scots Greys). In the post-war period, the alliance with The Black Watch was strengthened when Bernard Fergusson (later Lord Ballantrae), who had commanded the 1st Battalion The Black Watch (1948–51), served as Governor-General of New Zealand (1962–67); the link was also sustained during his Colonelcy of the Regiment (1969–76). In 1990 the New Zealand Scottish Regiment was disestablished. The Chief of the Defence Force formally disbanded the unit in 2013 and the Colours were laid up in Dunedin on 16 April 2016.[11]

South Africa

The Transvaal Scottish dates back to the formation of the Transvaal Scottish Volunteers in December 1902 as part of the South African Defence Force. One of the founders was John Stewart-Murray, Marquess of Tullibardine, later 8th Duke of Atholl, who had served in South Africa during the Second South African War and helped to raise a regiment of Scottish Horse.[12] Formed from Scottish units who had demobilised and chosen to remain in South Africa, on 11 December 1910 the Transvaal Scottish Volunteers became the Transvaal Scottish. Known formally as the 8th Infantry (Transvaal Scottish) Union of South Africa Active Citizen Force, its alliance with The Black Watch (Royal Highlanders) was approved by the King on 14 July 1927.[13]

Following the outbreak of the Second World War, on 20 May 1940 the 1st Battalion The Transvaal Scottish was mobilised, taking part in the recapture of Ethiopia (Abyssinia) in 1941. The 2nd and 3rd Battalions also served in North Africa. In November 1941 the 1st and 3rd Battalions were part of the Eighth Army, involved in the breakout from Tobruk, 'a historic and moving occasion', signifying the first meeting of the Transvaal Scottish and The Black Watch (Royal Highland Regiment) on the battlefield.[14] United as a single battalion,

The Transvaal Scottish's last operation was at El Alamein in October and November 1942, fighting alongside the 51st Highland Division, with the 1st, 5th and 7th Battalions The Black Watch. The Transvaal Scottish was then ordered back to South Africa; rather than return home a number of officers and men volunteered for service in The Black Watch, fighting in Italy and Greece with the 6th Black Watch.

Southern Rhodesia (Zimbabwe)

There was no affiliated unit in Southern Rhodesia, but in May 1940 a number of men from the colony arrived in Egypt, where two officers and forty-two men joined the 2nd Battalion The Black Watch, fighting in Crete, North Africa and India. On 24 October 1946 a Rhodesian Branch of The Black Watch Association was formed in Bulawayo, with Lieutenant Colonel Gerald Barry as its first President/Chairman. In memory of their service during the war, in 1948 the officers presented a trophy to the 2nd Battalion The Black Watch, to be awarded to the company best at drill. Known as The Rhodesian Platoon Drill Competition Shield, it was first competed for shortly before the 2nd Black Watch left Pakistan in early 1948.[15]

United Kingdom: Royal Navy

Over the years there have been many close but informal links with Royal Navy ships, including an affiliation in 1986 with the nuclear-powered fleet submarine, HMS *Splendid*.[16] There have been two official links. The first was with the guided missile destroyer HMS *Fife*, commissioned in 1966 and later sold to the Chilean Navy. The second link, maintained by The Black Watch, 3rd Battalion The Royal Regiment of Scotland (3 Scots), is with the frigate HMS *Montrose*, commissioned in 1994. Both ships' names are associated with the traditional Black Watch recruiting area in Scotland.

Appendix IV: Military Formations

The principal components of the British Army in the field consist of Army Groups, consisting of two or more armies; armies of one or more corps, each made up of a varying number of divisions, in turn comprising a varying number of Brigades usually of three battalions not necessarily from the same regiment. During the First World War, brigades tended to consist of infantry or cavalry only. By the Second World War, all-arms brigades of armour and infantry were more normal, supported by artillery, engineers and other units.

In 1945 the term 'Battlegroup' came into use, structured around an infantry battalion or armoured regiment headquarters. A battle-group is normally named after its main constituent, e.g. The Black Watch Battlegroup, made up of the 1st Battalion The Black Watch and including squadrons of main battle tanks and supporting arms.

The First World War

Regular Army

1st Battalion on active service in France and Flanders (1914–8), 1 Bde, 1st Div. On 11 Nov 1918 1BW was at Fresnoy-le-Grand, France.

2nd Battalion on active service in France (1914–15), Mesopotamia (1916–17) and Palestine (1918), Bareilly Bde, 7th Meerut Div, Indian Expeditionary Force 'D' (later named 21 Bde, 7th Indian Div). Due to heavy losses, in Feb 1916 amalgamated with the 1st Seaforth Highlanders, becoming the **Highland Battalion**, 19 Bde, returning to 21 Bde when reformed Jul 1916. On 11 Nov 1918 2BW was at Ras el Lados.

3rd (Special Reserve) Battalion based in Nigg, Scotland. Nov 1917 moved to Queenstown, Ireland, and in Mar 1918 to the Curragh. It returned to Britain in Mar 1919.

Territorial Force

1/4th (City of Dundee) Battalion in Feb 1915 joined Bareilly Bde, Meerut Div; due to losses, amalgamated with 2BW (Sep 1915); re-formed Nov 1915 & transferred to 139 Bde, 46th Div, and then 44 Bde, 15th Scottish Div. Jan 1916 transferred to 154 Bde, 51HD, Feb to 118 Bde, 39th Div; 15 Mar 1916 amalgamated with **1/5th** (see below).

1/5th (Angus & Dundee) Battalion, 24 Bde, 8th Scottish Div. In Oct 1915 converted to Pioneer Battalion, 8th Div. Jan 1916 converted back to infantry, joining 154 Bde, 51HD then 118 Bde, 39th Div. 15 Mar 1916 amalgamated with **1/4th**, forming **4/5th Battalion** (see below).

4/5th (Angus & Dundee) Battalion, 118 Bde, 39th Div, serving in France and Flanders (1916–18). May 1918 reduced to company strength, transferring to 46 Bde, then 44 Bde, 15th Scottish Div, absorbing 9BW (see below). On 11 Nov 1918 4/5BW was at Huissignies, south of Ath, Belgium.

1/6th (Perthshire) & **1/7th (Fife) Battalions** in 1915 joined 2 Highland Bde, 1st Highland Territorial Div (which became 153 Bde, 51HD); on active service in France and Flanders (1915–18). On 11 Nov 1918 1/6 & 1/7 BW were at Iwuy, France.

2/4th & **2/5th Battalions** formed in 1914. Oct 1915 joined 191 Bde, 64th (2nd Highland) Div. 2/5 BW absorbed by 2/4BW Nov 1915; 2/4BW disbanded in Dec 1917. Neither 2/4BW nor 2/5BW saw service overseas.

2/6th & **2/7th Battalions** formed in 1914. Oct 1915 joined 192 Bde, 64th (2nd Highland) Div. 2/6BW disbanded Sep 1917; 2/7 BW disbanded in Apr 1918. Neither 2/6BW nor 2/7BW saw service overseas.

3/4th, 3/5th, 3/6th, 3/7th Battalions formed in Mar & Apr 1915. In Apr 1916 all became Reserve Battalions until 1 Sep 1916 when **4th (Reserve) Battalion** Highland Reserve Bde absorbed other units. No third line battalion saw service overseas.

13th (Scottish Horse Yeomanry) Battalion formed in Egypt 1 Oct 1916 from the 1st & 2nd Scottish Horse and details from the 3rd. On active service in Salonika (1916–17) in 81 Bde, 27th Div and France (1918) transferring to 149 Bde, 50th Northumbrian Div. On 11 Nov 1918 it was at Semousies, north of Avesnes.

14th (Fife & Forfar Yeomanry) Battalion formed at Moascar, Egypt, 21 Dec 1916 (officially on 1 Jan 1917). Joined 229 Bde, 74th Yeomanry Div on active service in Palestine (1917) and France (1918). On 11 Nov 1918 14BW was east of Tournai, Belgium.

Kitchener's New Armies (K1, K2, K3, K4)

8th (Service) Battalion formed Aug 1914, 26 Bde, 9th Scottish Div. Served in France and Flanders (1915–18). On 11 Nov 1918 it was at Harlebeke, north of Courtrai.

9th (Service) Battalion formed Sep 1914, 44 Bde, 15th Scottish Div. 1918 transferred to 46 Bde, 15th Scottish Div; reduced to cadre, surplus personnel transferred to **4/5th Battalion** (see above); returned to Britain. Joined 47 Bde, 16th Irish Div, absorbed 15th Battalion (see below), returning to France in Jul 1918 as **2/9th Battalion.** On 11 Nov 1918 it was near Rume, south-west of Tournai.

10th (Service) Battalion formed Sep 1914, 77 Bde, 26th Div. Served in France (Sep–Nov 1915), Salonika (1915–18) & France (1918) attached to 197 Bde, 66th Div; disbanded at Haudricourt on 15 Oct 1918, men joining 1BW, 6BW and 14BW.

11th (Service) Battalion formed Oct 1914, 101 Bde, 34th Div. Apr 1915 it became a second **Reserve Battalion** and Sep 1916 the 38th Training Reserve Bn, 9 Reserve Bde, remaining in Britain for the duration of the war.

Additional battalions

12th (Labour) Battalion formed May 1916; arrived in France Jun. May 1917 became the 5th and 6th Labour Companies of the Labour Corps.

15th Battalion formed 1 Jun 1918; 19 Jun 1918 absorbed in **2/9th Battalion** (see above).

The Second World War

Regular Army

1st Battalion, 12 Infantry Bde, 4th Div, II Corps, deployed to France as part of British Expeditionary Force (BEF) 1939; Mar 1940 exchanged places with 4BW, joining 51HD, II Corps; after the surrender of 51HD at St Valéry-en-Caux Jun 1940, 1BW reformed in Scotland, becoming part of 154 Bde, 51HD (formed from 9th Scottish Div). On operations with Eighth Army, XXX Corps in N. Africa (1942–43), Sicily (1943), and in N.W. Europe (1944–45); briefly under the command of 6 Airborne Div (Jun 1944), before serving as part of 2nd Canadian Corps, First Canadian Army. During the Battle of the Maas (Oct 1944) 51HD formed part of XII Corps, 2nd British Army, returning to XXX Corps Jan 1945.

2nd Battalion, 8th Infantry Div in Palestine and Transjordan 1939-40; joined 23 Bde, HQ, British Troops Egypt; stationed in Aden (Jul); on operations in Somaliland (Aug). 1941, after joining 14 Bde, GHQ, Middle East Force, served in Crete (Creforce) & Syria; later joining 6th Infantry Div (Jul–Oct 1941) & 70th Infantry Div (Oct 1942).

During service in India the Bn also served in 26 Indian Infantry Div & Special Force (the Chindits), serving in Burma Mar–Aug 1944; 1 Nov 1944–31 Aug 1945 part of 14 Airlanding Bde, 44 Indian Airborne Div.

Territorial Army & other Battalions

4th Battalion, 153 Bde, 51HD, II Corps, evacuated from France as part of Ark Force in 154 Bde. From Mar 1941 in Gibraltar as part of 1 Gibraltar Bde, returning to Britain Apr 1943. Dec 1945 to Palestine, then Egypt; disbanded in 1946.

5th Battalion, 27 Bde, 9 Infantry Div, re-designated 153 Bde, 51HD. As part of Eighth Army, XXX Corps, on operations in N. Africa (1942–43), Sicily (1943), N.W. Europe (1944–45). On arrival in Normandy, 5BW was briefly under the command of 8 Canadian Bde then 6th Airborne Div (Jun 1944), before serving as part of 2nd Canadian Corps, First Canadian Army. During the Battle of the Maas (Oct 1944) 51HD formed part of XII Corps, 2nd British Army, returning to XXX Corps in Jan 1945.

6th Battalion, 154 Bde, 51HD. Mar 1940 exchanged places with 1BW, joining 12 Infantry Bde, 4th Div, II Corps; evacuated from Dunkirk (1940); served on operations in N. Africa (1943), Italy (1943–44), Greece (1944–45) where it was disbanded in 1946.

7th Battalion, 28 Bde, 9th Infantry Div, re-designated 154 Bde, 51HD, XXX Corp in the Eighth Army. On operations in N. Africa (1942–43), Sicily (1943), N.W. Europe (1944–45). Briefly came under the command of 6th Airborne Div (Jun 1944), returning to 51HD, serving as part of 2nd Canadian Corps, First Canadian Army. During the Battle of the Maas (Oct 1944) 51HD formed part of XII Corps, 2nd British Army, returning to XXX Corps in Jan 1945.

8th Battalion, formed from 62nd Group of National Defence Companies (Voluntary Military Reserve Force), joining 5 Bde, 47th London Div; 28 Aug 1941 amalgamated with the 9BW (see **8/9th Battalion**).

9th Battalion, formed from 61st Group of National Defence Companies (Voluntary Military Reserve Force); 28 Aug 1941 amalgamated with 8BW.

8/9th Battalion, formed from 8BW and 9BW on 28 Aug 1941 (see above). Jan 1942 was re-designated **30th Battalion,** operating as a mobile counter-attack battalion in Scotland. In Jun 1942 it became the **8th Battalion** (Field Service Formation), units serving in N. Africa (1943) and Italy (1944).

8th Infantry Holding Battalion, formed Dec 1944 to take in medical categories from A1 (fit for general service at home and abroad) to C2 (fit only for home service) of Black Watch officers and men from all theatres where battalions were stationed overseas.

10th Battalion, formed as the 50th Holding Battalion Jun 1940, later becoming the 10th Battalion as part of the Orkney and Shetland Defence Force. 1943 moved to the mainland as 10th Training Battalion.

1st Battalion The Tyneside Scottish, The Black Watch, raised as a duplicate battalion for 9 (Tyneside Scottish) Durham Light Infantry, becoming a territorial battalion of The Black Watch 20 Dec 1939. From Oct 1940–Dec 1941 it served in 70 Bde in Iceland as part of Alabaster Force (renamed Iceland Force). On 18 May 1942 it became part of the 49th West Riding Division, serving with the Division in France Aug–Oct 1944. Disbanded 18 Oct 1944.

For further information: see Select Chronology.

Abbreviations used in the Notes, Select Chronology & Select Bibliography

1BW	1st Battalion The Black Watch
2BW	2nd Battalion The Black Watch, etc.
2IC	Second-in-Command
3 Scots	The Black Watch, 3rd Battalion The Royal Regiment of Scotland
51HD	51st Highland Division
Adjt	Adjutant
Adm	Admiral
AG	Adjutant General
ANA	Afghan National Army
ARIB	Afghanistan Roulement Infantry Battalion
BAOR	British Army of the Rhine
BATUS	British Army Training Unit Suffield
Bde	Brigade
Bde Maj	Brigade Major
BEF	British Expeditionary Force
Bn	Battalion
Brig	Brigadier
BW	Black Watch
BWM	Black Watch Museum
BWRA	Black Watch Regimental Archive
CAC	Churchill Archives Centre
CAM	Chemical Agent Monitor
Capt	Captain
Cdr	Commander
CGS	Chief of the General Staff
C-in-C	Commander-in-Chief
CIGS	Chief of the Imperial General Staff
CO	Commanding Officer
Col	Colonel
col	column
COP	Close Observation Platoon
Coy	Company
Cpl	Corporal
CQMS	Company Quartermaster Sergeant
CSgt	Colour Sergeant
CSM	Company Sergeant Major
Div	Division
FM	Field Marshal
Gen	General
GOC	General Officer Commanding

Govt	Government
HD	Highland Division
HQ	Headquarters
Inf	Infantry
INIBA	Individual Northern Ireland Body Armour
IPE	Individual Protection Equipment
IRA	Irish Republican Army
ISAF	International Security Assistance Force (in Afghanistan)
IWM	Imperial War Museums
LCpl	Lance Corporal
Lt	Lieutenant
Lt Col	Lieutenant Colonel
Lt Gen	Lieutenant General
Maj	Major
Maj Gen	Major General
McMU	McMaster University
MT	Motor Transport
NAAFI	Navy Army and Air Force Institutes
NBC	Nuclear Biological Chemical
NCO	Non-Commissioned Officer
NIPG	Northern Ireland Patrol Group
NISS	Northern Ireland Surveillance Systems
NITAT	Northern Ireland Training and Advisory Teams
NLS	National Library of Scotland
NS	National Service
OC	Officer Commanding
OMLT	Operational Mentoring and Liaison Team
Op	Operation
ORs	Other Ranks, i.e. NCOs and private soldiers
OTC	Officers' Training Corps
PIRA	Provisional Irish Republican Army
PM	Prime Minister
Pte	Private
QM	Quartermaster
QMS	Quartermaster Sergeant
RA	Royal Artillery
RAF	Royal Air Force
RAMC	Royal Army Medical Corps
RE	Royal Engineers
Regt	Regiment
RH	Royal Highlanders
RHR	Royal Highland Regiment
RIR	Royal Irish Rangers/Regiment
RN	Royal Navy

RQMS	Regimental Quartermaster Sergeant
RSM	Regimental Sergeant Major
RUC	Royal Ulster Constabulary
SAS	Special Air Service
Sgt	Sergeant
SM	Sergeant Major
TAOR	Tactical Area Of Responsibility
UDR	Ulster Defence Regiment
UN	United Nations
VE	Victory in Europe
VJ	Victory over Japan
WO	Warrant Officer
WWI	First World War/Great War
WWII	Second World War

Note: Ranks of Officers and Other Ranks (NCOs and private soldiers) appear in the narrative with the rank at the time of the recollection described; the current rank at the time the recollection was written or recorded is listed in the Notes.

Seniority of ranks in the British Army:

Officers
Field Marshal; General; Lieutenant General; Major General;
Brigadier General (abolished 1921); Brigadier; Colonel; Lieutenant Colonel;
Major; Captain; Lieutenant; 2nd Lieutenant; Officer Cadet

Warrant Officers, Non-Commissioned Officers and Private Soldiers
Regimental Sergeant Major, Warrant Officer 1 (WO1);
Company Sergeant Major, Warrant Officer 2 (WO2);
Staff or Colour Sergeant; Sergeant; Corporal; Lance Corporal; Private.

Select Chronology

For a list of abbreviations used in this Chronology, please see *Abbreviations Used in Notes, Select Chronology and Bibliography.*

1899 The South African War. 2BW joins the Highland Bde in S. Africa. *Dec*, Battles of Stormberg, Magersfontein and Colenso, known as Black Week.

1900 Battles of Koedesberg, Paardeberg. Actions at Bavian's Beg, Bloemberg Ridge, Retief's Nek. *Apr*, British forces enter Bloemfontein, capital of Orange Free State & capture Harrismith.

1901 *Jan*, 1BW delegation present at the federation of Australian colonies into the Commonwealth of Australia. Death of Queen Victoria, succeeded by Edward VII. 1BW arrives in South Africa from India.

1902 Arthur Balfour (Con) becomes PM. Treaty of Vereeniging between Britain and South African Boers. 1BW returns to Britain (Edinburgh). 2BW leaves South Africa for India (Ambala). Coronation Durbar in Delhi: Edward VII represented by his younger brother, Arthur, the Duke of Connaught.

1903 Memorial window to the fallen of the South African War unveiled at St Ninian's Cathedral, Perth. Presentation of South African War Medals by Edward VII.

1904 Entente Cordiale (Britain and France). 1BW to Fort George. 2BW moves to Peshawar. Band and pipers of The Black Watch perform at the Toronto Exhibition and at concerts throughout Canada. Russo-Japanese War (until 1905).

1905 Sir Henry Campbell-Bannerman (Lib) becomes PM. The Earl of Minto becomes Viceroy of India. Revolution in Russia.

1906 1BW to Ireland (Curragh, Co. Kildare).

1907 Anglo-Russian Convention. Territorial & Reserve Forces Act. 2BW moves to Sialkot.

1908 H.H. Asquith (Lib) becomes PM. Formation of the Territorial Force.

1909 1BW to Limerick.

1910 Death of Edward VII, succeeded by George V. Lord Hardinge becomes Viceroy of India. Dedication of South African War Memorial, Edinburgh.

1911 Coronation Durbar in Delhi: George V presents new Colours to 2BW. 1BW returns to Edinburgh.

1912 George V becomes Colonel-in-Chief of The Black Watch. Old Colours of 2BW laid up in St Giles Cathedral. 2BW to Calcutta.

1913 1BW leaves Edinburgh for Aldershot.

1914 *Mar,* Curragh Mutiny. *Jun*, assassination of Archduke Ferdinand of Austria. *Aug,* outbreak of war between Central Powers (Austria and Germany) and Triple Entente (France, Russia, Great Britain). H.H. Kitchener becomes Secretary of State for War. Mobilisation of regular and territorial battalions

& raising of Kitchener's New Armies (K1, K2, K3, K4) as well as 2nd and 3rd line battalions (2/4BW, 2/5BW, 2/6BW, 2/7BW and 3/4BW, 3/5BW, 3/6BW, 3/7BW). 1BW embarks for France to join BEF. Allied retreat from Mons. *Sep*, Battles of the Marne and the Aisne. Government of Ireland (Home Rule) Act. *Nov*, First Battle of Ypres. 2BW to Bareilly, leaves India & arrives in France: fights at Givenchy. 5BW arrives in France. *Oct*, Entry of Ottoman Empire into the war on the side of the Central Powers.

1915 *Western Front*: 4BW, 6BW, 7BW, 8BW and 9BW arrive in France. Second Battle of Ypres: Germans use gas for the first time. The 'Shell' Crisis. Battles of Neuve Chapelle, Aubers Ridge, Festubert. Italy declares war on Central Powers. *Sep*, Battle of Loos. Allies use gas for the first time. 'Brodie' steel helmets issued. Britain declares war on Bulgaria. 10BW arrives in France then leaves for Salonika. *Dec*, 2BW embarks for Mesopotamia. FM Sir John French succeeded as C-in-C, BEF by Gen Sir Douglas Haig.

1916 *Mesopotamia:* 2BW engages in attempts to relieve Kut al-Amara at Shaikh Sa'ad, Umm el Hanna and Sannaiyat. Severe losses result in formation of a Highland Battalion with 1st Seaforth. *Apr*, Kut falls to Turkish forces. *Western Front:* 4BW and 5BW amalgamated to form 4/5BW. Death of H.H. Kitchener. *Jul–Nov*, Battle of the Somme; tanks used for the first time. Battle of Ancre Heights (Beaumont Hamel) concludes fighting. Arrival of recently formed 12th (Labour) Battalion (12BW) in France. 1st, 2nd & details of 3rd Scottish Horse formed into 13th (Scottish Yeomanry) Battalion (13BW). *Dec*, David Lloyd George (Lib) becomes PM; Lord Chelmsford Viceroy of India. 3/4BW, 3/5BW, 3/6BW & 3/7BW become reserve battalions; absorbed as 4th Reserve Bn.

1917 *1 Jan*, 14th (Fife and Forfar Yeomanry) Battalion (14BW) formed. Russian Revolution. *Apr*, USA declares war on Central Powers. *Mesopotamia:* 2BW engaged in Battles of Mushaidie and Istabulat. Entry into Baghdad: capture of the 'Baghdad Bell' at Samarra. *Nov*, Balfour declaration supporting creation of a Jewish homeland in Palestine. Fall of Jerusalem. *Western Front: Apr*, Battle of Arras. *Jul–Nov*, Third Battle of Ypres including the 'Battle of Mud', Passchendaele. 12BW becomes part of Labour Corps.

1918 President Woodrow Wilson proclaims 'Fourteen Points' pledging right of self-determination. *Mar*, Treaty of Brest-Litovsk between Russia and Central Powers. *Western Front:* Germans counter-attack in Ops Michael and Georgette known as the 'Kaiserschlacht'. Third Battle of the Somme; 2/9BW, 10BW, 13BW & 14BW arrive in France. Allied counter-attack in Hundred Days Offensive. Over 1 million US troops join Allies. 6BW awarded the Croix de Guerre. *Palestine:* 2BW moves from Mesopotamia to Palestine, fighting at Arsuf and Meggido. *31 Oct*, armistice with Turkey; *11 Nov*, armistice with Germany.

1919 Treaty of Versailles. 1BW to Aldershot, then India (Allahabad). 2BW to Glasgow: reformed incorporating 3rd (Reserve) Battalion. Territorial battalions and New Armies put on peacetime footing/disbanded. Black Watch

Regimental Association establishes 'Red Hackle Day' on 5 Jan.

1920 Dedication of the Tomb of the Unknown Warrior. 2BW to Germany and Upper Silesia.

1921 The Earl of Reading becomes Viceroy of India. *Apr*, first edition of *The Red Hackle* published. Territorial Force renamed Territorial Army.

1922 Andrew Bonar Law (Con) becomes PM. Benito Mussolini becomes PM of Italy. George V makes Solemn Pilgrimage to Belgium and France. 1BW to Quetta, 2BW to Bordon, East Hampshire. Formation of the Union of Soviet Socialist Republics (USSR).

1923 Stanley Baldwin (Con) becomes PM. Opening of Dunalistair House.

1924 Ramsay Macdonald (Lab) becomes PM, replaced by Stanley Baldwin (Con).

1925 Mussolini (Il Duce) sets up dictatorship in Italy. 1BW to Multan; 2BW to Fort George.

1926 General strike in Britain. Lord Irwin becomes Viceroy of India. Memorial at Doiran unveiled.

1928 1BW to Chakrata. Edward, Prince of Wales undertakes Royal tour of India.

1929 Ramsay Macdonald (Lab/Nat Lab) becomes PM. Stock market crash on Wall Street and beginning of the Great Depression.

1930 1BW to Meerut, 2BW to Colchester.

1931 Lord Irwin becomes Viceroy of India. Japanese invasion of Manchuria.

1932 Opening of the Thiepval monument to the 'Missing of the Somme' by Edward, Prince of Wales.

1933 Adolf Hitler becomes Chancellor of Germany; anti-Jewish Nuremberg laws passed. 2BW to Glasgow.

1934 1BW to Barrackpore. *Dec*, the King approves the Regiment's change in title to become The Black Watch (Royal Highland Regiment) effective 1935.

1935 Stanley Baldwin (Con) becomes PM. Mussolini invades Ethiopia.

1936 Death of George V, succeeded by Edward VIII who then abdicates; his brother Albert, ascends the throne as George VI. The Marquess of Linlithgow becomes Viceroy of India. 1BW to Khartoum. Arab revolt in Palestine begins.

1937 Neville Chamberlain (Con) becomes PM. New Colours presented to 2BW by the Regiment's new Colonel-in-Chief, Queen Elizabeth, before departure to Palestine (Jerusalem).

1938 Munich agreement between Britain, Germany, France and Italy permitting Germany's annexation of Sudetenland in Czechoslovakia. 1BW arrives in Dover. 2BW's old Colours laid up at the Scottish National War Memorial.

1939 Black Watch veterans' pilgrimage to WWI battlefields in Belgium and France. *May*, Pact of Friendship and Alliance (Pact of Steel) signed between Germany and Italy. *Sep*, Germany invades Poland; outbreak of war. National Service (Armed Forces) Act passed. 1BW, 4th Div, to France with BEF; takes up position on Maginot line.

1940 4BW & 6BW arrive in France (in 51HD), 6BW transfers to 4th Div & 1BW joins 51HD. *Apr*, German invasion of Denmark & Norway. *May*, battle of France; Winston Churchill (Con) becomes PM in Coalition government.

May–Jun, evacuation of British and French armies from Dunkirk and other ports (including 4BW & 6BW). *Jun*, French armistice with Germany; Vichy government established. Italy enters the war on the side of Germany and invades Egypt from Cyrenaica; *12 Jun*, surrender of 51HD (including 1BW) at St Valéry-en-Caux. *Jul*, 2BW to Aden. *Aug*, fights rearguard action in British Somaliland; returns to Egypt then sent to Crete. *Sep*, Tripartite Pact signed between Germany, Italy & Japan (known as Rome-Berlin-Tokyo Axis) & later joined by Hungary, Romania, Slovakia (& Bulgaria in 1941). *Dec*, British counter offensive, Op Compass, in Western Desert under Wavell's command as C-in-C Middle East.

1941 *Jan*, Allied forces capture Bardia and Tobruk. *Feb*, surrender of Italian Tenth Army at Beda Fomm, fall of Benghazi; German Afrika Korps arrives in Tripoli. *Mar*, 4BW to Gibraltar. *Apr*, fall of Greece to Axis powers; Tobruk under siege. *May*, fall of Crete to German forces: 2BW evacuated. *Jun*, failure of Op Battleaxe to relieve Tobruk. Germany invades USSR. *Jul*, Wavell replaced as C-in-C Middle East by Auchinleck, becomes C-in-C India. *Aug*, 2BW to Syria, armistice between Vichy French and British in Syria. *Sep*, German troops besiege Leningrad (St Petersburg). *Oct*, 2BW to Tobruk; *Nov*, Op Crusader launched to retake Cyrenaica and relieve Tobruk after 241-day siege. *Dec*, Japanese bomb Pearl Harbor, USA enters the war. Sinking of HMS *Prince of Wales* and HMS *Repulse*; fall of Hong Kong to Japanese forces.

1942 *Jan*, 2BW returns to Egypt; Rommel launches new offensive from Mersa el Brega; *Feb*, 2BW travels to India, Singapore falls to Japanese; *Apr*, Benghazi falls to Axis; *Jun*, Tobruk falls to Axis. *Jul*, Allies fall back to El Alamein. *Aug*, Auchinleck replaced as C-in-C by Alexander; Gott (d. in plane crash) then Montgomery put in command of Eighth Army. *Aug*, 51HD (including 1BW, 5BW & 7BW) arrives in Egypt to fight in N. Africa as part of Eighth Army. German troops besiege Stalingrad (Volgograd). German advance halted at Alam el Halfa. *Oct/Nov*, Allied victory at El Alamein; British-American invasion of French N. Africa.

1943 *Jan*, Casablanca Conference. Siege of Stalingrad lifted. 4BW returns from Gibraltar to Britain. *Feb*, Allied capture of Tripoli and advance into Tunisia. *Mar*, fighting at the Mareth Line, Wadi Akarit. 6BW arrives in N. Africa. *May*, Axis surrenders at Tunis, signifying end of war in N. Africa; *Jul*, invasion of Sicily, including 51HD. *Sep*, invasion of Italy: surrenders to Allies; Badoglio Declaration. Mutiny at Salerno. *Oct*, Italy declares war on Germany. *Nov*, 1BW, 5BW & 7BW return to Britain, 6BW to Egypt for training. *India:* Wavell becomes Viceroy of India. First Chindit Expedition behind Japanese lines in Burma.

1944 *Jan*, Siege of Leningrad lifted. *Mar*, 2BW (73 and 42 Cols) takes part in Second Chindit Expedition in Burma. 6BW arrives in Italy, fights at Monte Cassino. *Jun*, Allied entry into Rome. Op Overlord: Allied invasion of Normandy, including 1BW, 5BW, 7BW and 1st Tyneside Scottish, fall of Caen. *Aug*, 2BW to Bangalore. *Dec*, German counter-attack in the Ardennes. 6BW to Greece.

1945 Battle of the Bulge. Battle of the Reichswald. *Mar*, Allied forces (including 1BW, 5BW and 7BW) cross the Rhine. *Apr*, death of US President Franklin D. Roosevelt, succeeded by Harry Truman; Hitler commits suicide in Berlin. *May*, 'Unconditional' surrender of Germany (*8th*, VE Day). *Jul*, Clement Attlee (Lab) becomes PM. *Aug*, atomic bombs dropped on Hiroshima & Nagasaki; Japan surrenders (*15th*, VJ Day); *Sep*, 1BW to Buxtehude. *Oct*, The United Nations established. *Dec*, 4BW to Palestine. Trials of former German leaders at Nuremberg (until 1946).

1946 1BW to Hesedorf, then Duisburg, W. Germany. 2BW to Karachi, W. Pakistan. 4BW moves from Palestine to Egypt where it is disbanded; 6BW disbanded in Greece.

1947 *Mar*, Mountbatten becomes Viceroy of India. *Aug*, independence and partition of India into the Dominions of India and East & West Pakistan. 2BW to Peshawar and Cherat, Malir, W. Pakistan. Reconstruction of Territorial Army leading to formation of 4/5BW, headquartered at Dundee, and 6/7BW, headquartered at Kirkcaldy (serving in amalgamated 51st/52nd Scottish Division). The Black Watch receives the Freedom of Perth.

1948 *Feb*, 2BW leaves W. Pakistan. *Jun*, Mountbatten relinquishes position of Governor-General of India. *13 Jul*, 1BW & 2BW amalgamated at Duisburg. New Colours presented to 1BW by FM Earl Wavell. Beginning of Malayan 'Emergency' (anti-British Liberation War until 1960). Berlin blockade and airlift.

1949 North Atlantic Treaty signed, creating inter-governmental military alliance, North Atlantic Treaty Organisation (NATO). Berlin blockade lifted.

1950 Beginning of the Korean War. *May:* 1BW to Berlin.
51st/52nd Scottish Divisions split into 51st Highland and 52nd Lowland Divisions.

1951 Winston Churchill (Con) becomes PM. 1BW to Buxtehude.

1952 *Feb*, Death of George VI, succeeded by Elizabeth II. 2BW reformed at Colchester, moves to Hubbelrath, W. Germany. 1BW to Korea joining 29 Bde, 1st Commonwealth Div.
Nov, takes part in Second Battle of the Hook. State of emergency declared in Kenya.

1953 *May*, 1BW takes part in Third Battle of the Hook. Ceasefire agreed at Panmunjom signifying end of the Korean War. 1BW deployed to Kenya to counter Mau Mau uprising (1952–60). 2BW to Dortmund.

1954 Formation of The Black Watch Kirk Session in Nairobi. 2BW returns to Britain (Crail), then deployed to British Guiana.

1955 Churchill resigns as PM, replaced by Anthony Eden (Con). 1BW returns to Britain (Crail).

1956 1BW to Berlin. 2BW returns to Britain (Edinburgh) & is disbanded in Perth. 13-day Hungarian revolution.

1957 Eden resigns as PM, replaced by Harold Macmillan (Con). 1BW to Edinburgh. First tour of the Pipes and Drums to North America.

1958 1BW to Cyprus.

1960 National Service ends. Cyprus becomes independent.

1961 1BW to Barton Stacey, Hampshire. Construction of Berlin Wall. Closure of Queen's Barracks as training depot.

1962 HM Queen Elizabeth The Queen Mother's Silver Jubilee as Colonel-in-Chief. 1BW to Warminster as Demonstration Battalion. Closure of Queen's Barracks as Regimental HQ which moved to Balhousie Castle; opening of the Museum.

1963 Macmillan resigns as PM, replaced by Sir Alec Douglas-Home (Con). Independence of Kenya. Second tour of the Pipes and Drums to North America. *Nov*, assassination of President John F. Kennedy: Black Watch pipers play at his funeral.

1964 Harold Wilson (Lab) becomes PM. 1BW to Minden, W. Germany.

1966 1BW to Cyprus as part of UN peacekeeping force. Memorial Garden and Gates opened by Lady Wavell in memory of FM Earl Wavell (d.1950). British Guiana becomes independent
as Guyana.

1967 1BW returns to Minden. Formation of the Territorial and Army Volunteer Reserve: 3rd (Territorial) Battalion raised. 4/5BW and 6/7BW become A Coy and HQ in 51st Highland Volunteers.

1968 1BW to Kirknewton. Soviet invasion of Czechoslovakia.

1969 Beginning of the 'Troubles' in N. Ireland and start of Op Banner. *Aug*, 1BW to Gibraltar. *Dec*, IRA splits (Official and Provisional).

1970 Edward Heath (Con) becomes PM. 1BW returns to Britain (Kirknewton), then deployed to N. Ireland: 1st tour (emergency) in Belfast; 2nd tour (emergency) in Londonderry. 3rd (Territorial) Battalion reduced to cadre.

1971 1BW to N. Ireland: 3rd tour (emergency) in Armagh and 4th tour (emergency) in Belfast. 51st Volunteers split into 2 battalions, BW men forming A and B Coys, 1st Battalion. Secession of East Pakistan which becomes Bangladesh.

1972 *Jan*, 'Bloody Sunday' in N. Ireland; 1BW to Hong Kong.

1974 1BW returns to Britain (Colchester), then deployed to N. Ireland: 5th tour (emergency) in Andersonstown, W. Belfast. Military coup in Cyprus; Turkish invasion in the north. Harold Wilson (Lab) becomes PM.

1975 *May*, Presentation of new Colours in Colchester. 1BW to N. Ireland: 6th tour (emergency) in Andersonstown, W. Belfast. 3rd Battalion, 51st Highland Volunteers formed. Queen's Barracks opened in Dunkeld Rd, Perth.

1976 Harold Wilson resigns, replaced by James Callaghan (Lab). 1BW to N. Ireland: 7th tour (residential) in Ballykinler, Co. Down.

1977 The Queen's Silver Jubilee; she visits N. Ireland for the first time since 1966.

1978 1BW in Catterick. Old Colours laid up at Balhousie Castle.

1979 Margaret Thatcher (Con) becomes PM. 1BW to Belize, then returns to Catterick. Silver Jubilee of the formation of The Black Watch Kirk Session.

1980 1BW to Werl, W. Germany. Southern Rhodesia becomes independent as Zimbabwe.

1982 The Falklands War. 1BW to N. Ireland: 8th tour (emergency) in Belfast.
1983 1BW returns from N. Ireland to Werl.
1985 1BW returns to Britain (Kirknewton) then deployed to N. Ireland: 9th tour (emergency) in South Armagh.
1986 The XIIIth Commonwealth Games. 1BW returns to Britain (Edinburgh).
1987 1BW to Berlin: 750th anniversary celebrations of the city. President Reagan urges Mikhail Gorbachev to 'tear down this wall'. The Queen Mother's Golden Jubilee as Colonel-in-Chief of The Black Watch. Death of Rudolph Hess in Spandau prison.
1989 1BW returns from Berlin, deployed to N. Ireland: 10th tour (residential) in Ballykinler, Co. Down. Berlin Wall is dismantled leading to reunification of East and West Germany.
1990 First Gulf War. Thatcher resigns as PM, replaced by John Major (Con). 250th anniversary of The Black Watch's first muster at Aberfeldy in 1740. The Queen Mother visits 1BW in N. Ireland.
1991 1BW to Tern Hill, Shropshire. Dissolution of the USSR; formation of the Russian Federation.
1993 1BW to Hong Kong.
1994 1BW returns to Britain (Pirbright, Surrey). 1st Battalion 51st Highland Volunteers re-designated 3rd (Volunteer) Battalion. Provisional IRA announces 'cessation of military operations'.
1995 1BW to N. Ireland: 11th tour (emergency) in Belfast. Downing Street Declaration.
1996 1BW to Fort George. Presentation of new Colours to 1BW at Birkhall.
1997 Tony Blair (Lab) becomes PM. 1BW to Hong Kong; takes part in handover ceremony to People's Republic of China.
The Queen Mother's Diamond Jubilee as Colonel-in-Chief of The Black Watch.
1998 *Apr*, Good Friday (Belfast) Agreement signed between UK & Republic of Ireland. *Sep*, Black Watch 'Family day' attended by The Queen Mother; 1BW's old Colours laid up at Glamis Castle.
1999 3rd (Volunteer) Battalion merges with others to form 51st Highland Regiment in British Army's Army Reserve, based at Queen's Barracks, Perth.
2000 1BW to Fallingbostel, Germany: conversion to Armoured Infantry Battalion.
2001 1BW to Kosovo (*Jul–Nov*) Op Agricola VI. *11 Sep* (known as 9/11): attacks on the Twin Towers, New York, and the Pentagon, Washington DC. US/UK launches Op Enduring Freedom against Taliban regime in Afghanistan; UN Security Council establishes ISAF.
2002 Death of HM Queen Elizabeth The Queen Mother.
2003 Second Gulf War. 1BW to Iraq: Op Telic 1. HRH The Prince Charles, Duke of Rothesay, becomes Colonel-in-Chief of The Black Watch. NATO assumes leadership of ISAF in Afghanistan.
2004 Iraq War. 1BW to Warminster as Demonstration Battalion, then Iraq: Ops Bracken, Tobruk, Corunna. Golden Jubilee of the formation of The Black

Watch Kirk Session. *8 Apr*, opening of the Queen Mother's Gates at Balhousie Castle.

2005 1BW deploys to N. Ireland: 12th tour (residential), stationed at Palace Barracks, Belfast. *7 Apr*, dedication of Iraq Memorial, Balhousie Castle.

2006 *28 Mar*, The Black Watch (Royal Highland Regiment) merged to become The Black Watch, 3rd Battalion The Royal Regiment of Scotland (3 Scots). 51st Highland Regiment becomes 7th Battalion The Royal Regiment of Scotland (7 Scots).

2007 Tony Blair resigns as PM, replaced by Gordon Brown (Lab). End of Op Banner in N. Ireland. The Black Watch, 3rd Battalion to Fort George, Inverness; a detachment sent to Iraq.

2009 The Black Watch, 3rd Battalion to Afghanistan: Op Herrick 10.

2010 David Cameron (Con) becomes PM.

2011 The Black Watch, 3rd Battalion to Afghanistan: Op Herrick 15. New Colours presented to The Royal Regiment of Scotland in Edinburgh.

2012 HM The Queen's Golden Jubilee. *23 Jun*, The Colours of The Black Watch (Royal Highland Regiment) are laid up at Balhousie Castle, Perth.

Notes

1. Chasing Back the Boers

1. 'The Black Watch at Magersfontein, 11th December 1899. By a Perthite Who Was There'. There are various claimants to authorship with minor variations in the versions.
2. LCpl James Williams (1877–1961), memoir, p.4, BWRA 0943. Unless indicated otherwise, officers and ORs quoted are in 2BW. The first railway was opened in Natal in 1860 and in the Cape in 1862. A difficulty for the British was that during the war the railways ran through Boer positions presenting problems for transportation. Unnamed officer, Modder River Camp, letter, 18 Dec 1899, BWRA 0800.
3. In atlases Britain and its colonies were traditionally indicated in pink. The casualties at Magersfontein were less than those at Ticonderoga in North America in 1758, which exceeded 600. See Victoria Schofield, *The Highland Furies*, p.67.
4. In Mar 1897 the British Foreign Office had threatened to blockade the German coast if Germany intervened in the Transvaal. In 1905 the RN developed plans for a blockade. Germany passed 5 Naval Laws in 1898, 1900, 1906, 1908 and 1912 committing Germany to build a navy rivalling Britain's.
5. Cecil Rhodes, PC (1853–1902), PM Cape Colony 1890–96. Rt Hon Sir Leander Starr Jameson, KCMG, CB, PC (1853–1917), PM Cape Colony, 1904–08.
6. The First South African War took place between 1880 and 1881. The Second South African War is known as the Boer War or Anglo-Boer War. Alfred Milner, 1st Viscount Milner, KG, GCB, GCMG, PC (1854–1925); Paul Kruger (1825–1904), President of the Transvaal 1883–1900; Martinus Steyn (1857–1916), last President of the Orange Free State (1896–1902).
7. Of the 1,011 officers and men who embarked for South Africa, 581 were serving with 2BW, 430 belonged to the Army Reserve; see A.G. Wauchope, *A Short History of The Black Watch (Royal Highlanders) 1725–1907*, p.151.
8. Gen Sir Redvers Buller, VC, GCB, GCMG (1839–1908); Maj Gen Andrew Wauchope (1846–99).
9. R.H.F. Wallace, 'The Dress of The Black Watch, Part VIII – 1899–Present Day', *Red Hackle*, Oct 1933, pp.5, 6. See also Wauchope, *Short History*, p.153.
10. Wauchope, *Short History*, p.153. Williams, memoir, p.6, BWRA 0943. The Bn had its 'first engagement with the Boers at Arundel', Steve Lunderstedt, 'From Belmont to Bloemfontein', *Diamond Fields Advertiser*, p.37.
11. LCpl Ernest T. Brown, 7 Apr 1900, 'My Experiences in South Africa, 1900,' testimonials, Netley Album (containing brief autograph handwritten accounts of wounds received by British soldiers in the Boer War, 1899–1900), BWRA 0187. FM Paul Methuen, GCB, GCMG, GCVO, DL, 3rd Baron Methuen (1845–1932).
12. '2BW Record of Service 1780–1909', p.175, BWRA 0005. The Highland Bde consisted of approx. 3,500 men. See L. Childs, *Kimberley*, p.75. This was the Battle

of the Modder River on 28 Nov; Methuen had been wounded and had only just resumed command. Gen Piet Cronjé (1836–1911).

13. Williams, memoir, p.7, BWRA 0943.
14. The Guards Bde was under the command of Maj Gen Sir Henry Colvile, KCMG, CB (1852–1907). Capt Charles Edward Stewart, memoir, 13.xii (13 Dec), Wed (1899), p.28, BWRA 0196/1. Later Brig Gen, he compiled his memoir from his diary, BWRA 0197; killed 14 Sep 1916.
15. Wauchope, *Short History*, p.153. Thomas Pakenham, *The Boer War*, p.202.
16. Pte E. Finch, diaries, South Africa 1899–1901, BWRA 0648. Stewart, memoir, Wed 13 Dec (1899), p.28, BWRA 0196/1.
17. Wauchope, *Short History*, p.154.
18. Stewart, memoir, Wed 13 Dec (1899), p.28, BWRA 0196/1. Dykes are stone walls.
19. FM Lord Carver, *The National Army Museum Book of The Boer War*, p.32.
20. Stewart, memoir, Wed 13 Dec (1899), p.29, BWRA 0196/1. The attack was not in fact a direct frontal one, which would have required crossing a 'wide extent of open ground and running the risk of a counter-attack'. See A. Forbes, *The 'Black Watch'*, p.309.
21. Wauchope, *Short History*, pp.83–4, 155. Later Maj Gen Sir Arthur Wauchope, GCB, GCMG, CIE, DSO (1874–1947).
22. Stewart, memoir, Wed 13 Dec (1899), p.29, BWRA 0196/1. Cronjé had initially opposed digging the trenches at the bottom – a tactic also used at Modder River. See G.R. Duxbury, 'Magersfontein', *Battles of the South African War*, p.27; Lunderstedt, 'From Belmont to Bloemfontein', *Diamond Fields Advertiser*, 2000, p.31: 'General de la Rey had learnt two very valuable lessons [from fighting at Graspan and Enslin]. Firstly, that defending kopjes favoured the attackers as the attackers could rest in dead ground at the base before a final assault; and secondly that fire from the crest of the kopjes was not as effective as firing from level ground.' Gen Jacobus Herculaas (Koos) de la Rey (1847–1914), renowned as the 'Lion of the West Transvaal', had been a transport rider at the diamond mines of Kimberley.
23. Brown, 'My Experiences in South Africa, 7 Apr 1900', Netley Album, BWRA 0187; 'Modern commentators dispute the wire', Childs, *Kimberley*, p.83.
24. Pte James McFarlane to Dear Sister, Modder River, Africa, 17 Dec 1899, BWRA 0953.
25. Wauchope, *Short History*, p.84. With the deaths of Wauchope and Coode the chain of command had been broken.
26. Pte James Williamson, 'Testimonials', Netley Album, BWRA 0187.
27. Brown, 'My Experiences in South Africa', 7 Apr 1900, Netley Album, BWRA 0187. The Gordon Highlanders joined the Brigade on 10 Dec 1899. See Lunderstedt, 'From Belmont to Bloemfontein', *Diamond Fields Advertiser* p.37.
28. Capt (later Gen) Archibald Rice Cameron to Dear Father, Wynberg hospital, 17 Dec 1899, letter 9, BWRA 0186. See Duxbury, *Magersfontein*, p.33, for comments about the Gordons.
29. Wauchope, *Short History*, p.85. '2BW Record of Service 1780–1909', p.175, BWRA

0005: 2 leading companies and some mixed details. McFarlane to Dear Sister, Modder River, 17 Dec, and to his father, Modder River, 13 Dec 1899, undated press cutting, BWRA 0953. He died of enteric fever at Bloemfontein on 27 Apr 1900.

30. Stewart, memoir, Wed 13 Dec (1899), pp.31–32, BWRA 0196/1.
31. Brown, 'My Experiences in South Africa', 7 Apr 1900, Netley Album, BWRA 0187. Piper David Welch, testimonials, Netley Album, BWRA 0187. Williams, memoir, pp.8–9, BWRA 0943.
32. Stewart, memoir, Wed 13 Dec (1899), pp.32, 34, BWRA 0196/1. Cameron to Dear Father, Wynberg hospital, 17 Dec 1899, letter 9, BWRA 0186. Col Richard Archibald (Archie) Bulloch, DSO, (1879–1963); see Obit, *Red Hackle*, Jan 1964, p.3. Maj Colin Innes, 'Three Generations', *Red Hackle*, May 2006, p.23.
33. Lt Freddie Tait, quoted in Lunderstedt, 'From Belmont to Bloemfontein', *Diamond Fields Advertiser*, p.42; 'The Black Watch at Magersfontein, 11th December 1899. By a Perthite Who Was There'. See also 'Papers of William Macfarlan (1867–99)', BWRA 0453. From In Memoriam, the *Lorettonian*, Sat 2 Jun 1900: 'When some shouts of "Retire" were raised, he ran up and down his line, calling "Not the 'Black Watch' we don't retire"'. These were his last recorded words. He was wounded in the arm or hand. See also Williams, memoir, p.8, BWRA 0943.
34. Wauchope, *Short History*, p.84; Duxbury, *Magersfontein*, p.32: 'there are few accounts of this battle that agree on the casualties'. Duxbury suggests: Boer forces: 87 killed, 188 wounded; British forces: 69 officers, 879 ORs killed, wounded, missing and taken prisoner (of which 22 officers, 188 ORs killed). From the Highland Brigade: 45 officers and 702 ORs wounded or killed. Cameron to Dear Father, Wynberg hospital, 17 Dec 1899, letter 9, BWRA 0186. 2BW casualties: 7 officers and 86 ORs killed/fatally wounded; 11 officers and 199 ORs wounded, 42 prisoners from a force of 28 officers and 918 ORs who went into action, '2BW Record of Service 1780–1909', p.175, BWRA 0005, & Wauchope, *Short History*, p.158. He states 209 wounded.
35. Tait in Lunderstedt, 'From Belmont to Bloemfontein', *Diamond Fields Advertiser*, p.42. Tait was Amateur Golf Champion 1896 and 1898, and Leading Amateur in Open Golf Championships 1894, 1896 and 1899. His putting cleek was presented to The Black Watch in Jul 1938, 'An Historic Golf Club', *Red Hackle*, Oct 1938, p.11. See Masry MacGregor, *The Moon Behind the Hill*, pp.324, 329. Until the words 'presumed killed' were added to his record, his widow could not receive a pension.
36. William Baird, *General Wauchope*, p.192. *Daily News*, Tues 9 Jan 1900, BWRA 0396/2/Y-Z/3. About a week after the funeral the Hon J.D. Logan obtained permission for Wauchope's body to be exhumed and reburied in the cemetery in Matjiesfontein, over 400 miles south of Magersfontein. See Brig A.S.H. Irwin, letter to the *Red Hackle* Jun 1996, p.8 and Editor's Note.
37. Stewart, memoir, Wed 13 Dec (1899), p.33, BWRA 0196/1. Cameron to Dear Nellie, 2 Jan 1899, letter 11, BWRA 0186.
38. McFarlane to his father, Modder River, 13 Dec 1899, undated press cutting,

BWRA 0953. Brown, 'My Experiences in South Africa', 7 Apr 1900, BWRA 0187.

39. Queen Victoria, quoted in Pte R. Thorburn, 'Message Book', BWRA 0990/1.
40. Capt (later Lt Col) Adrian Grant Duff (1869–1914), 1BW, diary, Sat 16 Dec 1899, BWRA 0705.
41. Wavell, 'A Visit to Magersfontein Battlefield', *Red Hackle*, Jul 1948, p.4, pointed out that Roberts eventually relieved Kimberley by a turning movement which trapped Cronjé's force at Paardeberg; later FM Earl Wavell, GCB, GCSI, CMG, MC, KStJ, PC (1883–1950).
42. E.M. Middleton, poem 'Major General Andrew Wauchope of Niddrie', news cuttings, South African War, II, BWRA 0448.
43. FM Earl Roberts of Kandahar in Afghanistan and of Pretoria in the Transvaal, VC, KG, KP, GCB, OM, GCSI, GCIE, KStJ, PC (1832–1914), as a young man had served as Deputy Asst Quarter Master General to Sir Colin Campbell, C-in-C India, under whom The Black Watch (as the 42nd) had also served. His son was killed at Colenso during 'Black Week'.
44. FM Horatio Herbert Kitchener, KG, KP, GCB, OM, GCSI, GCMG, GCIE, ADC, PC (1850–1916).
45. Maj Gen Sir Hector MacDonald, KCB, DSO (1853–1903). Known as 'Fighting Mac', he had also taken part in the Nile Expedition. Brig Gen Archibald Carthew-Yorstoun, CB (1855–1929).
46. The Volunteer Bns were 1st (City of Dundee) Vol Bn, 2nd (Angus) Vol Bn, 3rd (Dundee Highland) Vol Bn, 4th (Perthshire) Vol Bn, 5th (Perthshire Highland) Vol Bn, 6th (Fifeshire) Vol Bn. See Maj Gen J.M. Grierson, *Records of the Scottish Volunteer Force 1859–1908*, pp.240–57; 'The Black Watch Volunteer Service Companies in the South African War, 1899–1902', J.L.R. Samson, Scrapbook III, pp.253–62, BWRA 0843/12; Wauchope, *Short History*, pp.111–25, 169. Each Vol Coy (which became known as K, L & M Coys respectively) served for a year, the 2nd replacing the 1st in Mar 1901. The end of the war meant the 3rd Vol Coy spent less time on active service.
47. McFarlane, letter, Modder River, 10 Feb 1900, BWRA 0953. Wauchope, *Short History*, p.160, spells it Koedoesberg. In addition to Tait, Capt Cecil Ekyn and 2 men were killed and 7 wounded.
48. FM John French, 1st Earl of Ypres, KP, GCB, OM, GCVO, KCMG, ADC, PC (1852–1925). See G. Cassar, *The Tragedy of Sir John French*, p.49.
49. Wauchope, *Short History*, pp.160 & 85.
50. Stewart, memoir, 20 Feb (1900), p.71, BWRA 0196/1. Wauchope, *Short History*, p.162.
51. Wauchope, *Short History*, p.85: 19 officers and ORs killed; 79 officers and ORs wounded including the CO, Maj Norman Cuthbertson (recovered from being wounded at Magersfontein) taking command. On p.164 Wauchope gives the numbers 18 and 78 respectively.
52. Stewart, memoir, 27 Feb (1900), p.79, BWRA 0196/1.
53. Grant Duff, 1BW, diary, 28 Feb 1900, BWRA 0705. 'Everything comes to those who wait.'

54. Stewart, memoir, 13 Mar (1900), p.87, BWRA 0196/1. 2BW was not involved in the action, '2BW Record of Service 1780–1909', p.176, BWRA 0005.
55. Williams, memoir, p.10, BWRA 0943.
56. Stewart, memoir, 13 Mar (1900), p.88, & 18 Mar, p.89, BWRA 0196/1 (end of Vol.1 of his memoir). Approx. present day values: £4.22 for the tea cake and £38 for the bottle of whisky! (www.measuringworth.com).
57. Pte Francis O'Brien, 1st Vol Coy, diary, Mar 12 (1900), handwritten, p.8, BWRA 0640/2; typescript, p.2, BWRA 0843/02.
58. Pte John McEuan Crearar, 1st Vol Coy, Lecture given at Crieff in 1902, p.4, BWM 2016.95. Anon, *Letters from the Front*, Green Point Common Camp, Cape Town, Mar 1 (1900).
59. Anon, *Letters from the Front*, Naauwpoort Camp, Wed 21 Mar, p.7, and Bloemfontein, Thurs 12 Apr, p.9, BWM.
60. Wauchope, *Short History*, p.86. For further details, see Crearar, 1st Vol Coy, Lecture, Crieff, 1902, pp.13–34, BWM 2016.95.
61. Cpl D. Duff, diary, 1 May, BWRA 0650. He had recently arrived as a volunteer.
62. Pte Charles Rufus Critcher, daily diary, 4 May 1900: handwritten, BWRA 1018/1; typescript, BWRA 1018/3. The last entry is on 15 Sep 1900, BWRA 1018/2. He returned to the UK in Mar 1901.
63. Roberts' daily report in '2BW Record of Service 1780–1909', p.177, BWRA 0005; Wauchope, *Short History*, p.169. Anon, *Letters from the Front*, Winburg, Mon 7 May 1900, p.11, BWM.
64. Wauchope, *Short History*, p.170. These were wide-brimmed hats with a chin strap.'The sun became too hot for felt.' See R.H.F. Wallace, 'The Dress of The Black Watch, Part VIII – 1899–Present Day', *Red Hackle*, Oct 1933, p.5. See also O'Brien, diary, handwritten, 23 May 1900, p.22, BWRA 0640/2.
65. Critcher, diary, 24 May 1900, BWRA 1018/1.
66. O'Brien, diary, 'Twyfontein Ridge', 25/26 May 1900, pp.74–6, BWRA 0640/2. Critcher, diary, 26 May 1900, BWRA 1018/1.
67. O'Brien, diary, 27 May 1900, p.24, & 29 May – reached Heilbron, pp.87–8, BWRA 0640/2.
68. Cameron to Dear Ma, Heilbron, 7 Jun, letter 34, BWRA 0186. See also Cameron, diary, 6 Jun 1900, BWRA 0190; Stewart, memoir, Heilbron, Sun 3 Jun (1900), p.37, BWRA 0196/2.
69. Critcher, diary, 7 & 8 Jun 1900, BWRA 1018/2; Stewart, memoir, Sat 9 Jun (1900), p.40, BWRA 0196/2.
70. Critcher, diary, 24 May 1900, BWRA 1018/1.
71. Gen Louis Botha (1862–1919), later first PM of the Union of South Africa, took over after Kruger crossed into Mozambique.
72. Stewart, memoir, Heilbron, Fri 22 Jun (1900), p.47, BWRA 0196/2.
73. Critcher, diary, 1 Jul 1900, BWRA 1018/2. They reached Bethlehem on 9 Jul. Cameron to Dear Father, Bethlehem, 9 Jul (1900), letter 38, BWRA 0186.
74. Stewart, memoir, Bethlehem, 9 Jul (1900), p.54, BWRA 0196/2.
75. Gen Sir Archibald Hunter, GCV, GCVO, DSO (1856–1936). Gen Marthinus

Prinsloo (1838–1903) had been dismissed by Steyn before Magersfontein because he was considered responsible for their earlier defeats. There was a debate about whether he or General Roux was C-in-C once de Wet escaped; see Pakenham, *Boer War*, p.443.

76. Cameron, diary, Sun 22 & Mon 23 Jul 1900, BWRA 0190.
77. Critcher, diary, 24 Jul 1900, BWRA 1018/2.
78. Pte W. Skidmore, diary, p.41, BWRA 0686. Wauchope, *Short History*, p.86; '2BW Record of Service 1780–1909', p.184, BWRA 0005: 2 officers and 17 ORs killed in BW out of a total of 33 killed and 242 wounded. See also H.W. Kinsey, 'The Brandwater Basin and Golden Gate surrenders, 1900', *Military History Journal*, 11, 3/4, Oct 1999, http://samilitaryhistory.org/vol113hk.html, accessed 20 Jan 2017; Pakenham, *Boer War*, p.444 (information from WO 105/18, TNA).
79. Crearar, 1st Vol Coy, Lecture, Crieff, 1902, p.30, BWM 2016.95. Critcher, diary, 4 Aug 1900, BWRA 1018/2.
80. '2BW Record of Service 1780–1909', p.179, BWRA 0005.
81. Critcher, diary, 14 Aug 1900 and 13 Sept 1900, BWRA 1018/2.
82. Cameron to Dear Mother, Kroonstad, 2 Sep 1900, letter 42, BWRA 0186.
83. Cameron to Dear Mother, Spytfontein, 10 miles S. of Ventersburg, 19 Sep (1900), letter 44, BWRA 0186. This book ends with two more letters, no. 45 dated 22 & 27 Sep.
84. Crearar, 1st Vol Coy, Lecture, Crieff, 1902, p.34, BWM 2016.95.
85. Wauchope, *Short History*, p.174. Crearar, 1st Vol Coy, Lecture, Crieff, 1902, pp.34–5, BWM 2016.95.
86. Roberts, Special Army Order, HQ of the Army, Johannesburg 29 Nov 1900, quoted in Thorburn, Message Book, BWRA 0990/1. On return to Britain he replaced FM 1st Vct Wolseley as C-in-C of the Forces.
87. '2BW Record of Service 1780–1909', p.182, BWRA 0005; Wauchope, *Short History*, pp.176–7. The Regimental Mounted Infantry consisted of 80 men; another detachment was later raised.
88. O'Brien, diary, 11–24 & 25 Dec, pp.58–9, BWRA 0640/2.
89. 'Seasons may roll/ But the true soul/ Burns the same wherever it goes': 'Old Song', at back of Stewart's diary, BWRA 0197; Grant Duff, diary, 23 Jan 1901, BWRA 0705.
90. See Carver, *Boer War*, p.220.
91. '2BW Record of Service 1780–1909', p.180, BWRA 0005.
92. Duff, diary, 1 Oct (1901), BWRA 0650. Stewart, memoir, Bloemfontein, Fri 5 Oct, p.81, BWRA 0196/2. Stewart's diary/memoir concludes here; on 13 Nov 1900 he was appointed Bde Maj.
93. Wauchope, *Short History*, p.182. See also '2BW Record of Service 1780–1909', BWRA 0005.
94. Lt Gen Michael Rimington, KCB, CVO (1858–1928) left the Guides at the beginning of 1901 to take command of the 6th Dragoons.
95. R.J. Collins, *Lord Wavell*, p.45. See Victoria Schofield, *Wavell: Soldier and Statesman*, p.20. He had arrived in South Africa at the end of Oct 1901.

96. '1BW Record of Service 1873–1939', pp.95–95b, BWRA 0080.
97. 2nd Lt James Molesworth Blair, 2BW diary, Wed 25 Dec 1901, p.170, BWRA 0106. He had come to South Africa with the 1st Vol Bn, the Hampshire Rgt, gaining a commission in The Black Watch in Jul 1901.
98. 2nd Lt A.P. Wavell to Nancy, 6 Jan 1902, John Connell fonds, McMU; See Schofield, *Wavell*, p.20.
99. Blair, diary, Tue 14 Jan 1902, at Abrahammoosfontein, p.182, & Wed 12 Feb 1902, Vlakfontein, p.194, BWRA 0106.
100. Maj Hugh Rose of Kilravock, 1BW, handwritten account and drawing. To man the many blockhouses 'all sorts of men were taken, including Bandsmen,' BWRA 0905/1. Acting Sgt David Wood Wilson known as 'Punch' (d.1914 of bronchitis), BWRA 0905/2. LCpl W.G. Scott was killed on 27 Mar 1902. His father was the bandmaster and Capt of the Regimental football team.
101. Limited self-government was granted in 1906 and 1907. In 1910 the Union of South Africa was established. See Carver, *Boer War*, p.250.
102. Lt A.P. Wavell, diary, 1 Jun 1902, quoted in Connell, *Wavell: Scholar and Soldier*, p.42, & Schofield, *Wavell*, p.21. Blair, diary, 1 Jun 1902, p.254, BWRA 0106.
103. Grant Duff, 1BW, diary, 10 Jun 1902, BWRA 0706. Even on official documents 2BW was still referred to as the 73rd (raised in 1786 from the 42nd's 2nd Battalion and merged again in 1881).
104. Ibid, 27 Jun 1902. Schofield, *Wavell*, pp.21–2; Wavell could not raise his left arm straight over his head for the rest of his life as a result of this injury.
105. Grant Duff, 1BW, diary, 20 Sep 1902, BWRA 0706.
106. Lt Col E.G. Grogan, Farewell Order, 5 Aug 1902, '1BW Record of Service 1873–1939', p.96, BWRA 0080.
107. '1BW Record of Service 1873–1939', pp.96b–97, BWRA 0080.
108. 'List of Casualties, South Africa 1899–1902', 'Casualty Roll of The Black Watch (Royal Highlanders) Second Boer War 1899–1902', BWRA 0574/1. Most came from 2BW; see '2BW Record of Service 1780–1909', pp.183–4, BWRA 0005: 11 officers and 114 ORs killed or died of wounds, 54 dying of disease (mainly enteric fever and dysentery), 335 wounded and 2 deserters.
109. See Carver, *Boer War*, p.253. Casualties included men from South Africa, Australia, Canada, New Zealand and Great Britain.
110. The containment of the Boers in 'concentration camps' fuelled a public outcry in Britain. Emily Hobhouse's report on the conditions, presented to the government in Jun 1901, led to an all-female commission, headed by Millicent Fawcett, making a further report confirming Hobhouse's findings, in which the camps in the Orange River Colony and Transvaal were seen as the worst.
111. E.W. McFarland, 'Commemoration of the South Africa War in Scotland, 1900–1910', *Scottish Historical Review*, 89, 2 (228), Oct 2012, p.195. The memorial in South Africa was paid for by contributions to 'Our Heroes Fund'.
112. John 15:13. Address by the Dean of St Andrews, '2BW Record of Service 1780–1909', pp.97–8, BWRA 0005, and 'Order of Service, Dedication of the Memorial, Tue 5 May 1903', BWRA 0452. See *Perthshire Courier*, 5 May 1903. It

was sponsored by the ladies of the Diocese of St Andrews, Dunkeld & Dunblane.

113. '1BW Record of Service 1873–1939', pp.98b–101b, BWRA 0080: 23 officers, 2 WOs (Warrant Officers) and 380 ORs 'were thus honoured'. The 17th Lancers also received medals.

114. *Perthshire Courier*, 18 Aug 1903. The memorial home was closed in 1926, as insufficient funds were available for its upkeep; *Perthshire Advertiser*, 7 Jul 1926.

115. The unveiling was on 25 Feb 1905. 'Chaplain and Parish Minister, Death of Rev James Robertson, DSO, DD', *Perthshire Advertiser*, 20 Nov 1929, p.9. He was Minister of Methven Parish Church, having received the DSO for rescuing an officer under fire at Magersfontein. He also served as a padre during WWI.

116. The Queen Victoria School was supported by former Lord Provost of Edinburgh, Robert Cranston, with money raised from Scottish servicemen and the people. The memorial on the Mound was vandalised when the tips of the soldiers' bayonets were broken off. See *Red Hackle*, Dec 1972. 'It is now maintained by funds voted annually by Parliament as part of the Army Estimates.'

117. Mavor Allan, 'The Charge of the Highland Brigade. Magersfontein – 11th December, 1899', *Celtic Monthly*, Feb 1900, NLS. An earlier verse read: Fell! Fell! And, ah! God! In the foremost, /The Leader they loved more than life:/A sob shook from outpost to outpost, /As Fiercer they flew to the strife,/Black Watch and Infantry, Seaforths, Argyles, /And the Gay Gordons, fill the broken files.

2. Balancing Power

1. Traditional song (as recorded by Thomas B. Smyth, Oct 2014).
2. See David Reynolds, *Summits. Six Meetings That Shaped the World*. Basic Books, 2007, p.23. Mary McGregor's husband, John, had been killed at Magersfontein in 1899 but his body not found. See Masry MacGregor, *The Moon Behind the Hill*, pp.324, 329.
3. Lt Col Hugh Rose to Earl Wavell, 17 Jun 1939, *Red Hackle*, Jul 1948, p.4.
4. The Territorial Force was formally established on 1 Apr 1908, composed of 14 infantry divisions and 14 yeomanry brigades; incorporated into the Territorial Force was the newly formed Officers' Training Corps (OTC), divided into a junior division for public schools and a senior division for universities. See D.C.T(hornycroft), 'Descent of the Volunteer Battalions of The Black Watch', *Red Hackle*, Apr 1993, p.11; 'A History of the 4/5th Bn The Black Watch (TA)', *Red Hackle*, Apr 1967, p.34.
5. George Robert Farrar, Irish Section, 6BW, written in 1961, p.1, BWRA 0999/13. He later received a commission.
6. Alfred Anderson (1896–2005), Obit, Register, *The Times*, 22 Nov 2005. In WWII he served as a Sgt in the Home Guard; John M. Mackenzie, *Alfred Anderson, A Life in Three Centuries*, p.17 (undated) cites Anderson's recollection of briefly being batman to the Hon Fergus Bowes-Lyon, but this is probably his cousin John Bowes-Lyon (who also died in WWI) who was in 5BW, as was Anderson,

while Fergus was in 8BW. See A.G. Wauchope, *History of The Black Watch (Royal Highlanders) in the Great War, 1914–1918*, II, p.40.

7. Bernard Fergusson, *A Short History of the Black Watch*, p.81; D.C.T., 'Descent of the Volunteer Battalions of The Black Watch', *Red Hackle*, Apr 1993, p.11.
8. 'Rifles of the British Army', *Red Hackle*, Jul 1922, p.13. Another model, the SMLE-Mark III, was introduced in 1907.
9. The School of Musketry was set up in 1853; later called the Small Arms School, it was closed in 1968, moving to Warminster, Wiltshire.
10. A.G. Wauchope, *Short History*, p.87.
11. Capt Adrian Grant Duff, diary, Nov 1902, BWRA 0706. See H.N.B. (Blair), 'The Grant Duff Diaries', *Red Hackle*, Apr 1987, pp.8–11, for background on Grant Duff's 'family and characteristics'; 'Lieut.-Colonel Adrian Grant Duff, CB, PSC', *Red Hackle*, Jan 1924, p.5.
12. See Wauchope, *Short History*, p.109. Between 1900 and 1996 The Black Watch performed the Royal Guard at Ballater 13 times.
13. '1BW Record of Service 1873–1939', p.104b, BWRA 0080; Chronology 1729–1905, p.29. Scrapbook relating to tour of Canada by 1BW military band and pipers, 15 Jan 1904–16 Oct 1904, BWRA 0047. The veterans included Ptes William Smeaton, Jock Clarke and Drum Maj Adam Bunch.
14. '1BW Record of Service 1873–1939', p.104b, BWRA 0080: '…by the Officers and Directors of The Canadian Royal Exhibition, Toronto, In commemoration of the visit of the Regimental Band To Canada, 1904', information on wording from Lt J.R. Tait, 10 Jun 2013. Known as the Canada Cup, it is in the Officers' Mess, Fort George. (A second 'Canada Cup' was presented to the Regt in 1950.) Band Master E.J. Murray and the Pipe Maj J. Clark also received presents.
15. Rose to Earl Wavell, 17 Jun 1939, *Red Hackle*, Jul 1948, p.5. The cost was £50. This is a sub-target gun machine for instructing men in marksmanship. 'This remarkable machine makes it possible to engage in effective rifle practice in the armoury, without the expenditure of ammunition.' *Cambridge Chronicle*, 12 Mar 1904, p.13, http://cambridge.dlconsulting.com/cgi-bin/cambridge?a=d&d=Chronicle19040312-01.2.145, accessed 20 Jan 2017.
16. '1BW Record of Service 1873–1939', p.110b, BWRA 0800, & Capt P.P. Hutchison, 'A Brief History of the Canadian Battalions of The Black Watch', *Red Hackle*, Apr 1926, p.16; additional information, Lt Col (retd) Roman Jarymowycz, OMM, CD, PhD (1945–2017), 25 Sep 2016.
17. Pte (later Sgt) William Buchanan (Tug) Wilson, personal diaries, p.13, BWRA 0182/1; Obit, *Red Hackle*, Dec 1966, pp.4–5.
18. Rose to Earl Wavell, 17 Jun 1939, *Red Hackle*, Jul 1948, p.4.
19. Rose to Mrs Marindin, New Barracks, Limerick, 5 Apr 1910, 'Letters 1914–18'. Marindin private papers, 10/B21, Blair Adam House collection.
20. W.B. Wilson, personal diaries, pp.16, 20, BWRA 0182/1. Daniel O'Connell (1775–1847) was a moderate nationalist who had campaigned for the emancipation of Catholics (which became law in 1829) giving them the right to sit in Parliament.
21. The Indian Army was formed in 1895 from the armies of the Presidencies of

Bengal, Bombay and Madras.

22. Details of the C-in-C's Test 4 Jan–17 Feb 1905, '2BW Record of Service 1780–1909', pp.198–9, BWRA 0005.
23. Eric & Andro Linklater, *The Black Watch*, p.135.
24. Col the Hon. C. Malise Hore-Ruthven, CMG, DSO (1880–1969) to Maj Archie John Wavell, John Connell fonds (archives), McMaster University (McMU); Victoria Schofield, *Wavell, Soldier and Statesman*, p.26.
25. '2BW Record of Service 1780–1909', p.199, BWRA 0005.
26. Wauchope, *Short History*, p.88; 'Alas not permanently preserved': in 1980 Lt Gen Sir Alistair Irwin, saw them 'in a state of ruin', additional information, 4 Dec 2014.
27. *Cherat Times and Jalozai Chronicle: A family journal for the million*, 30 May 1907, p.1, produced fortnightly according to 'the pressure of news'. Wavell sent some editions home to his sister. See Schofield, *Wavell*, p.27; 'The Cherat Times: A Link with the Past', *Red Hackle*, Oct 1922, pp.14–15. 'Laudabunt Alii', *Cherat Times*, 30 May 1907, p.5, authorship unknown, although in Wavell's style.
28. GOC the Sialkot Brigade, '2BW Record of Service 1780–1909', pp.210–11, BWRA 0005.
29. Wilson, personal diaries, p.20, BWRA 0182/1.
30. See 'The Colours of The Black Watch,' *Red Hackle*, Oct 1936, p.6.
31. George V, quoted in *The Chronicle of the Royal Highland Regiment, The Black Watch, 1913*, p.98. 'You have since worthily upheld your good name both in Europe and in Africa; and should such a sacrifice as that of 1815 be again required of you, I feel sure that, even though more than half of your numbers should fall in a single action, the remnant will stand firm as they did at Waterloo.' In May 1912 the old Colours were laid up in St Giles Cathedral, Edinburgh.
32. Wilson, personal diaries, p.27, BWRA 0182/1.
33. George V, quoted in *The Chronicle... 1913*, p 99.
34. 'The Black Watch in 1912, 2275 Cpl Frank MacFarlane, MSM, I – A Recruit at the Depot', *Red Hackle*, Apr 1985, p.13, comp. and researched by Diana M. Henderson. MacFarlane (1894–1990) was from Forfar and enlisted in 1912. See Obit, *Red Hackle*, Apr 1990, p.6.
35. *The Chronicle... 1913*, pp.62–3. A caber is a large wooden pole.
36. 'The Black Watch in 1913, 2275 Cpl Frank MacFarlane, MSM, II - Edinburgh and Aldershot', *Red Hackle*, Aug 1985, p.10.
37. Maj Adrian Grant Duff, diary, 31 Mar 1913, p.109, Churchill/AGDF/2/1, CAC. He had spent five years at the War Office, and served as Deputy Assistant Quarter Master General. In 1910 he had been promoted Military Assistant Secretary to the Committee of Imperial Defence (CID).
38. 'MacFarlane, II – Edinburgh and Aldershot', *Red Hackle*, Aug 1985, p.10.
39. *The Chronicle... 1913*, pp.121–2. After George V's death the ornaments were presented by Edward VIII and Queen Mary to The Black Watch Museum.
40. *The Chronicle of the Royal Highland Regiment, The Black Watch 1914*, p.91. This was approved by Army Orders in Jan 1914.
41. 'MacFarlane, II – Edinburgh and Aldershot', *Red Hackle*, Aug 1985, p.11. See also

'Manoeuvres 1913', *The Chronicle... 1914*, p.122.

42. Winston S. Churchill, 'Military Aspects of the Continental Problem', 13 Aug 1911, CAB 38/19/50, TNA, a paper in preparation for one of many meetings of the Cttee of Imperial Defence. See 'Minutes of the 114th Meeting', 23 Aug 1911, CAB 38/19/49, TNA; Churchill, *The World Crisis, 1911–1914*, pp.60–5. Sir Winston S. Churchill, KG, OM, CH, TD, PC, DL, FRS, RA (1874–1965), among other positions held was Home Secretary 1910–11, First Lord of the Admiralty 1911–15, 1939–40, PM 1940–45, 1951–55.
43. See Maj Gen Sir C.E. Callwell, *Field Marshal Sir Henry Wilson, His Life and Diaries*, Cassell, 1927, I, pp.99–100.
44. Grant Duff, diary, 11 Mar 1912, pp.129–31, Churchill/AGDF/2/2, CAC. Credit is sometimes given to Sir Maurice Hankey, who became Secr of the CID in 1912 (having been Naval Asst Secr) and who was responsible for the War Book's application in 1914. But see Hankey to Mrs Grant Duff, 16 Sep 1919: 'I think the best form of words for the record of Adrian's career would be that "he designed and edited the War Book and worked out the detailed coordination of the action to be taken by the various Government Departs on the outbreak of War"', Churchill/AGDF 1/4, CAC. See also Hankey condolence letter to Mrs Grant Duff, 25 Sep1914, Churchill/AGDF/1/3, CAC. The work of Grant Duff and many others 'saved this country from chaos in August 1914,' *Red Hackle*, Jan 1924, p.5.
45. Grant Duff, diary, 5 Aug 1913, Churchill/AGDF/2/2, CAC.
46. See Schofield, *Wavell*, p.38; John Connell fonds, McMU, for correspondence with his father regarding Ireland.
47. 'MacFarlane, II – Edinburgh and Aldershot', *Red Hackle*, Aug 1985, p.11.
48. 'England's Duty', *The Times*, Sat 1 Aug 1914, p.6.
49. Alfred Graf (Count) von Schlieffen (1833–1913), Chief of the Imperial German General Staff 1891–1906. Since Thomas Zuber's 1999 research, some scholars consider that it is inappropriate to talk about Schlieffen's plan as being fully formulated; rather that he was talking about deployment on the understanding adjustments would have to be made depending on circumstances. See Thomas Zuber, 'The Schlieffen Plan Reconsidered', *War History*, 1999.
50. On 2 Aug Germany requested passage through Belgium, on 3 Aug the Belgian Govt refused, 'Five Nations at War', *The Times*, Mon 3 Aug 1914, p.6.
51. Sir Edward Grey, Foreign Secretary, 3 Aug 1914, *Great Britain, Parliamentary Debates, Commons, Fifth Series*, LXV, 1914, cols 1809–34, excerpts at http://wwi.lib.byu.edu/index.php/Sir_Edward_Grey%27s_Speech_Before_Parliament, accessed 20 Jan 2017. See also Grey of Fallodon, *Twenty-Five Years 1892–1916*, II, Hodder & Stoughton, 1925, pp.15–18.
52. H.H. Asquith, 4 Aug 1914, http://hansard.millbanksystems.com/commons/1914/aug/04/violation-of-belgian-neutrality#S5CV0065P0_19140804_HOC_183, accessed 20 Jan 2017. British Summer Time (BST) began in 1916.
53. See Robert Rhodes James (ed.), *Memoirs of a Conservative, J.C.C. Davidson's Memoirs and Papers 1910–1937*, p.20.
54. King George V, diary, 4 Aug 1914, quoted in John Gore, *King George V, A Personal*

Memoir, John Murray, 1949, p.157.

55. 'MacFarlane, II – Edinburgh and Aldershot', *Red Hackle*, Aug 1985, p.11.
56. Pte Joseph Lee, 'Marching', *Ballads of Battle*, v.1, p.86. The two soldiers mentioned are LCpl Linton Andrews and Pte John (Jack) Nicholson. Lee wrote the poem in tribute to Nicholson who was killed in Jul 1915. See Ch.4 for v.2.

3. 1914: The Great War

1. Hilton Webster, 'Bravo, Black Watch' *Montrose Review*, in *Red Hackle*, Oct 1926, p.11. The poem continues: *The Black Watch men were mobilised, all ready for the fight;/And they proudly showed and realised they were sons of Scotland's might.*
2. 'Steady Black Watch', traditional song, in 'The Black Watch in 1913, 2275 Cpl Frank MacFarlane, MSM, II – Edinburgh and Aldershot', *Red Hackle*, Aug 1985, p.10.
3. Rt Hon. H.H. Asquith, Address to Parliament, 6 Aug 1914, www.firstworldwar.com/source/asquithspeechtoparliament.htm, accessed 1 Feb 2017.
4. '1BW War Diary', 7 Aug 1914, BWRA 0237.
5. W.B. (Tug) Wilson, 2BW, personal diaries, p.58, BWRA 0182/1. 2BW had spent most of 1913 in Fort William, Calcutta and a brief stay in Dacca.
6. Capt A.P. Wavell (from the War Office) to his sister, Nancy, 12 Sep 1914, John Connell fonds (archives), McMaster University (McMU), quoted in Victoria Schofield, *Wavell, Soldier and Statesman*, p.49.
7. Lt Gen Sir Horace Smith-Dorrien, GCB, GCMG, DSO, ADC (1858–1930). Grierson died of an aneurism while travelling by train between Rouen and Amiens.
8. Since commanding the Cavalry Division, French had served as Chief of the Imperial General Staff (CIGS) but had resigned over the Curragh mutiny in Mar 1914.
9. Gen Joseph Joffre, GCB, OM (1852–1931).
10. A.G. Wauchope, *The Black Watch in the Great War*, I, p.345. Col R.C. Campbell-Preston (1865–1929).
11. Pte Jim Braid, 1BW, quoted in Derek Young, *Forgotten Scottish Voices*, p.31. He was killed at Loos on 25 Sep 1915.
12. The front-line battalions were known as 1/4th, 1/5th, 1/6th, 1/7th, while the 2nd line – remaining in Britain as training battalions – were known as 2/4th, 2/5th (in 191 Bde), 2/6th and 2/7th (in 192 Bde). See E.A. James, *British Regiments 1914–18*, pp.83–5.
13. The name 'Fighter Writers' remained with them throughout the war. Linton Andrews, *Haunting Years*, p.21; later Sir Linton Andrews, editor of the *Yorkshire Post*, he returned to the UK in early 1918 to sit the exams for a commission.
14. Joseph Gray (1890–1963), 4BW, 'The Fourth Black Watch', *Dundee Advertiser*, Dec 1917. See *Red Hackle*, May 2015, pp.11–12.
15. Kitchener's New Armies were known as the First New Army, Second New Army, etc, numbered: K1, K2, etc. Army Order 382 authorised the raising of 100,000 men for K1, achieved by 24 Aug; orders were then passed for raising K2, K3 and

K4. See W. Reid, *To Arras*, p.102 (for a description of raising 9BW which was not 'properly clad' until 5 months after its formation); Young, *Forgotten Scottish Voices*, p.30.

16. Fraser Brown, 'Black Watch Men from the Argentine', *Red Hackle*, May 2014, p.23: 'The Black Watch had more than its fair share of these… ' Ptes David Lyall and William Adamson had enlisted under age. See also A.L. Holden, *Activities of the British Community in Argentina during the Great War*, 1921. Known as the British Volunteers from Latin America, their status was later recognised with the issue of a gold and blue 'BVLA' patch. The largest contingent (approx. 4,852) came from Argentina.
17. Mark Axe, 'The Oldest Known Veteran of The Black Watch,' *Red Hackle*, Oct 1923. He had enlisted in 1853 and served in the Crimea and India before his discharge in 1864; he died in Aug 1927 aged 92, *Red Hackle*, Oct 1927, p.6.
18. 'MacFarlane, II – Edinburgh and Aldershot', *Red Hackle*, Aug 1985, p.12.
19. Pte John Laing, 1BW, diary, 5 Aug 1914, p.1, BWRA 0768. See '1BW Record of Service 1873–1939', BWRA 0080, p.177 for names of the 27 officers who went to France with the BEF. There were 1,031 ORs.
20. Lt Lloyd Rennie, 1BW, St Nazaire, France, to My Dear Dad, 14 Oct 1914, p.1, Irwin private papers (also in BWM).
21. Lt Victor Fortune, 1BW, postcard franked 20 Aug 1914, Fortune private papers.
22. Lt Lewis Cumming, 1BW, to his parents (undated, probably written on 15 Aug from the rest camp at Harfleur), Irwin private papers. Citation from Macaulay's 'Horatius', *Lays of Ancient Rome*, 1842. See Wauchope, *The Black Watch in the Great War*, I, pp.2–3.
23. Wauchope, *The Black Watch in the Great War*, I, p.3; Laing, diary, Wed 5 Aug 1914, p.1, BWRA 0768. He is writing about subsequent events.
24. Rennie to My Dear Dad, 14 Oct 1914, pp.1–2, Irwin private papers; Wauchope, *The Black Watch in the Great War*, I, p.3. 'We called it "Alle".' 'The Black Watch in 1914, 2275 Cpl Frank MacFarlane, MSM, III – The First Battles, France 1914', *Red Hackle*, Dec 1985, p.10.
25. Capt (later Maj) A.D.C. Krook, 1BW, memoir, p.1, BWRA 0170. He was commissioned into the Regt in 1901.
26. Rennie to My Dear Dad, 14 Oct 1914, p.2, Irwin private papers. Information on movements from 1BW War Diary, p.2, BWRA 0237.
27. Laing, diary, Sun 23 Aug 1914, p.1, BWRA 0768; Krook, memoir, p.2, BWRA 0170.
28. Wauchope, *The Black Watch in the Great War*, I, p.5.
29. Ibid.
30. Krook, memoir, p.2, BWRA 0170; Laing, diary, Mon 24 Aug 1914, p.2. 'On the 28th we marched 31 miles after having only 2 hours sleep the night before,' diary, Sun 30 Aug 1914, p.2, BWRA 0768.
31. Pte A. Mitchell, 1BW, diary and reminiscences, BWRA 0853. He received the DCM for conspicuous gallantry on 22 Oct 1914.
32. Rennie to My Dear Dad, 14 Oct 1914, p.2, Irwin private papers. '1BW War Diary',

27 Aug 1914: 'loss of 7 R & F slightly wounded 3 missing (one probably killed), BWRA 0237. There is no record of their names. See also 'Narratives 1BW', 27 Aug 1914, *Red Hackle*, Oct 1921, p.40.

33. Krook, memoir, p.2, BWRA 0170. Wauchope, *The Black Watch in the Great War*, I, p.5.
34. John Campbell, 'With the B.E.F. in 1914', *Red Hackle*, Aug 1985, pp.12–13.
35. Rennie to My Dear Dad, 14 Oct 1914, p.3, Irwin private papers.
36. Ibid. Wauchope, *The Black Watch in the Great War*, I, p.7, agrees: 'the story was, however, entirely untrue… the only connection between these regiments and The Black Watch is that their patrols passed through the billets of the Battalion during the day.' See also A.A.L.W. (Watson), 'The Charge which never was – St Quentin 1914', *Red Hackle*, Apr 1993, p.10. The 2nd Royal Munsters had not received the messages sent out to the 4 rearguard battalions that it could withdraw.
37. Laing, diary, Sat 29 Aug & Sun 30 Aug 1914, p.2, BWRA 0768.
38. Wauchope, *The Black Watch in the Great War*, I, pp.7, 8.
39. Mitchell, diary and reminiscences, 1 Sep 1914, BWRA 0853.
40. Cumming to his parents, 2 Sep 1914, Irwin private papers.
41. Kaiser Wilhelm, *Weltkrieg II*, p.279, quoted in John Keegan, *First World War*, p.123.
42. '1BW War Diary', 6 Sep1914, BWRA 0237.
43. Mitchell, diary and reminiscences, 6 Sep 1914, p.3, BWRA 0853; Laing, diary, Sun 6 Sep 1914, p.4, BWRA 0768.
44. Rennie to My Dear Dad, 14 Oct 1914, p.4, Irwin private papers. He was in B Coy. On mobilisation in Aug 1914, the reserves of the Prussian Guards were formed into the 1st Guard Reserve Division, which included the Garde-Reserve-Jäger Battalion, Second Army.
45. '1BW War Diary 8 Sep 1914' BWRA 0237. Capt Dalgish and Lt Wilson were killed, Capt Drummond wounded; ORs: 8 killed, 17 wounded. Laing, diary, Battle of the Marne, Between 6th and 10th, p.4, BWRA 0768. They were supported by the 1st Cameron Highlanders (which in early Sep had replaced the 2nd Royal Munster Fusiliers after its heavy losses at Oisy on 27 Aug).
46. Cumming to his parents, 11 Sep 1914, Irwin private papers.
47. See '1BW Record of Service 1873–1939', p.163, BWRA 0080. Moltke quoted in Sewell Tyng, *The Campaign for the Marne*, Oxford, 1935, p.327, & in Keegan, *First World War*, p.133. On 14 Sep, Helmut von Moltke was succeeded by Erich von Falkenhayn (1861–1922), Minister of War. French fatalities of 18,073 included those killed at the Aisne. See I. Sumner, *The First Battle of the Marne*, Osprey, 2010, p.88.
48. Rennie to My Dear Dad, 14 Oct 1914, p.4, Irwin private papers.
49. Pte Harry Ogilvie, 1BW, diary/memoir, 14 Sep 1914, BWM 3504. He joined 1BW after the Marne. Laing, diary, Mon 14 Sep 1914, p.5, BWRA 0768.
50. Pte F.K. Fairweather, 1BW, letter, SS *Carisbrook Castle*, Bay of Biscay, 20 Sep (1914), in 'The Black Watch at the Aisne', newspaper article (undated), Irwin private papers.

51. Ogilvie, diary/memoir, 14 Sep 1914, BWM 3504.
52. Fairweather, letter, 20 Sep (1914), in 'The Black Watch at the Aisne', Irwin private papers.
53. Laing, diary, Mon 14 Sep 1914, p.5, BWRA 0768. Pte J.M. Small, 1BW, 1st Scottish General Hospital, Albyn Place, Aberdeen, to Dear Madame (Mrs Campbell), 28 Sep1914, BWM. See also '1BW Record of Service 1873–1939', p.163, BWRA 0080.
54. Cpl D. Petrie, 1BW, By Dundee to Mr J. Cumming, 3 Mar 1915, Irwin private papers. Lt Kynoch Cumming to My dearest Mater, 6 Oct 1914, Irwin private papers.
55. Guy Rowan-Hamilton to Mrs Adrian (Ursula) Grant Duff, 16 Sep 1914; see Richard Boyle (Adrian Grant Duff's grandson), *Adrian Grant Duff*. Press reports describe Grant Duff carrying the regimental headquarters flag up to the summit and calling out 'Forward 42nd!' *Sunday Post Special*, 18 Jul 1915, Boyle private papers. Rowan-Hamilton's contemporary account does not mention this although Pte Ogilvie describes Grant Duff encouraging the men earlier in the day by shouting: 'Forward the 42nd!'
56. Lord James Thomas Stewart-Murray to Dear Father, 24 Sep 1914. http://www.westernfrontassociation.com/great-war-people/48brothers-arms/300-off-letter-1914.html, accessed 23 Jan 2017. He was in command of A Coy. Wauchope, *The Black Watch in the Great War*, I, p.14.
57. Small to Dear Madame, 28 Sep 1914, BWM. See '1BW Record of Service 1873–1939', p.163, BWRA 0080. Krook, memoir, p.7, BWRA 0170.
58. Laing, diary, Tue 15 Sep 1914, p.5, BWRA 0768.
59. '1BW War Diary', 14 Sep 1914, BWRA 0237. Laing, diary, Tue 15 Sep 1914, p.5, BWRA 0768.
60. Small to Dear Madame, 28 Sep 1914, BWM. See also '1BW Record of Service 1873–1939', p.163, BWRA 0080. Campbell rejoined 1BW and was wounded again at Loos.
61. Rennie to My Dear Dad, 14 Oct 1914, p.4, Irwin private papers. Sgt John Wallace to Mrs Marindin, 'Letters 1914–18', Marindin private papers, Blair Adam. Cpl George Joseph William Snelling's father was a CSM in 10BW.
62. *Sunday Post Special*, 18 Jul 1915, Boyle private papers. Maj J.J.C. Murray, DSO.
63. Laing, diary, Wed 16 Sep 1914, p.6, BWRA 0768.
64. Ogilvie, diary/memoir, 16 & 19 Sep 1914, p.28, BWM 3504.
65. '1BW Record of Service 1873–1939', p.163, BWRA 0080; Krook, memoir, p.7, BWRA 0170.
66. Scout Joe Cassells's account describing members of The Black Watch (including himself) helping to dig the bodies out as related in Cassells, *With The Black Watch: The story of the Marne*, Andrew Melrose (1918), p.110, is not corroborated by either 1st Camerons, 'War Diary', 25 Sep 1914, App 2, nor 'Records of the Cameron Highlanders, 1914', pp.59–60 (courtesy The Highlanders Museum). Other aspects of his account are also uncorroborated, correspondence with Lt Gen Sir Alistair Irwin/Alistair Hogg/David Miers, Nov–Dec 2014; Neil McMicking, 8 May 1957: 'I have read this book. It is inaccurate in almost all details & the writer would appear to have little knowledge of the 42nd in France in 1914. Most atrocities,

possibly all in this book, attributed to the Germans are false.' In 1915 Cassells had received a medical discharge, emigrating to the US in 1916.

67. The maximum extent of the line held by the British was 123 miles (out of 466 miles). But the terrain presented challenges not shared by the French. Only at Arras did the British hold the high ground. See Linklater, *The Black Watch*, p.140.
68. Fortune, postcard, 30 Sep1914, Fortune private papers.
69. Laing, diary, Sun 4 Oct & Fri 16 Oct 1914, pp.10, 13, BWRA 0768.
70. Wauchope, *The Black Watch in the Great War*, I, p.347.
71. Wilson, 2BW, personal diaries, pp.58, 59, BWRA 0182/1. Also in the Division were the 1st Seaforth Highlanders (Dehra Dun Brigade) and the 2nd Leicestershires (Garhwal Brigade). Divided into the Indian Cavalry Corps and the Indian Corps, the Indian Expeditionary Force (IEF) 'A' was composed mainly of Indian soldiers. According to Wilson, the Seaforths refused to wear the Broderick caps, the soldiers marching through the streets of Marseilles 'glengarrys on and pipes playing an inspiring Gaelic air… Eventually the battalion got rid of the Broderick caps and instead folded up the Balaclava helmet issued in India in such a way as to resemble a Glengarry. This became popular until we had issues of Balmoral bonnets.'
72. Wauchope, *The Black Watch in the Great War*, I, p.165.
73. Wilson, personal diaries, p.61, BWRA 0182/1. Pte James McGregor Marshall, 2BW, reminiscences (written in Australia, 1937), p.2, BWRA 0793.
74. 'The Black Watch in 1914, 2275 Cpl Frank MacFarlane, MSM, MM, IV – The Winter of 1914', *Red Hackle*, Apr 1986, p.11.
75. Wauchope, *The Black Watch in the Great War*, I, p.16.
76. '1BW Record of Service 1873–1939', p.164, BWRA 0080.
77. Lt C.L.C. Bowes-Lyon (1885–1914) was a first cousin of Elizabeth Bowes-Lyon, (later Queen Elizabeth). Wauchope, *The Black Watch in the Great War*, I, p.17.
78. Wauchope, *The Black Watch in the Great War*, I, pp.18, 19. More than three-quarters of the Coy became casualties, 1BW casualties on 29 Oct: 5 officers and 250 ORs. On 7 Nov 1914 the London Scottish joined 1 Guards Bde.
79. Krook, memoir, p.12, BWRA 0170. He was taken prisoner on 29 Oct 1914.
80. '1BW Record of Service 1873–1939', p.164, BWRA 0080.
81. Wauchope, *The Black Watch in the Great War*, I, pp.19–20; '1BW Record of Service 1873–1939', p.164, BWRA 0080. A total of 5 ORs were killed, 21 missing and 34 wounded. Lt R.P.D. Nolan was also killed. Harold Amery was an interpreter in Arabic, German and Persian, who had served in the Sudan in the 1890s. He died a year later. His brother was Rt Hon Leopold Amery (1873–1955) politician and journalist.
82. Alfred Anderson, Obit. Register, *The Times*, 22 Nov 2005. 2nd Lt Hugh Scott Quekett, 5BW, 'Jottings of an Ordinary Man, from childhood to the end of the Great War 1914–1918', p.12, BWRA 0992. Quekett had served as a private with the London Scottish Volunteers and was commissioned into The Black Watch on the outbreak of war. 5BW formed part of 24 Bde, 8th Div (which included 1st Worcesters, 2nd Northamptonshires, 2nd East Lancashires, 1st Sherwood Foresters).

83. '1BW Record of Service 1873–1939', p.164, BWRA 0080. Mitchell, diary and reminiscences, 8 Nov 1914, BWRA 0853. Brig Gen Charles FitzClarence, VC (1865–1914).
84. '1BW War Diary', 5,6,7,8,9,10 Nov 1914, BWRA 0237. Pte Andrew Somers Mackie, 1BW, 'Notes from a Prisoner of War Camp 1914', p.1, BWRA 0756. See also '1BW War Diary', 11 Nov 1914, BWRA 0237.
85. 'MacFarlane, IV – The Winter of 1914', *Red Hackle*, Apr 1986, p.11. *Die Wacht am Rhine* (The Watch/Guard on the Rhine) was a popular German song, rooted in Franco-German enmity.
86. Mackie, 'Notes from a Prisoner of War Camp', p.2, BWRA 0756. Capt C.E. Stewart, in '1BW War Diary', App B, 11 Nov 1914, BWRA 0237. The 1st Camerons and 1st Scots Guards also suffered from the German onslaught. Wauchope, *The Black Watch in the Great War*, I, p.22, gives McNeill the initial 'M' but it should be 'N' – Neil.
87. See *Black Watch Corner, Flanders*, memorial brochure 3 May 2014, p.11; 4 other 'strong points' had been established: '1BW War Diary', 11 Nov 1914, BWRA 0237.
88. Stewart, in '1BW War Diary', App B, 11 Nov 1914, BWRA 0237. See illustration in *London Illustrated News* and commentary, in *Black Watch Corner, Flanders*, p.12. Cpl Robert Redpath was killed in 1917.
89. Wauchope, *The Black Watch in the Great War*, I, pp.22–23.
90. 'MacFarlane, IV – The Winter of 1914', *Red Hackle*, Apr 1986, p.11.
91. Capt Fortune to Dear Mrs Lawson, 13 Nov 1914, newspaper cutting, Fortune private papers. 18 ORs were killed; 2 officers, Sprot, McNeill and 49 ORs missing, presumed dead or taken prisoner; 4 officers and 52 ORs wounded.
92. '1BW War Diary', 12 Nov 1914, BWRA 0237.
93. Lt Col Hugh Rose, HQ 3rd Army Corps, BEF, to Mrs Marindin, 20 Nov 1914, 'Letters 1914–18', Marindin private papers, Blair Adam.
94. Moltke to Kaiser Wilhelm in David Bilton, *The Germans in Flanders, 1914*, Pen & Sword, 2012, p.81. Minor attacks were mounted over the next few days. In the official German history the 1st Battle of Ypres ended on 30 Nov 1914.
95. Lyn MacDonald, *1914: The Days of Hope*, p.412; *1914*, p.421.
96. Keegan, *First World War*, p.143. German casualties during Oct and Nov were assessed at 50,000 cf. 24,000 British.
97. Extracts from speech by FM Sir John French, 'In the Field', 26 Nov 1914, 'taken down from memory immediately after the parade', C.E. Stewart, '1BW War Diary', App C, BWRA 0237; '1BW Record of Service 1873–1939', p.165, BWRA 0080.
98. Designed by Edinburgh sculptor, Alan Herriot. Engraved on the plinth are the words: 'Near this spot in November 1914 the 1st Battalion The Black Watch (Royal Highlanders) as part of 1st (Guards) Brigade halted the Prussian Guard – First Battle of Ypres'.
99. Wauchope, *The Black Watch in the Great War*, I, pp.165, 166. Wilson, personal diaries, p.64, BWRA 0182/1. The gun mentioned by Wilson could have been the very heavy howitzer, developed by the armaments manufacturing firm Krupp and known as the 'Big Bertha' (possibly after Krupp's owner, Bertha).

100. Wauchope, *The Black Watch in the Great War*, I, pp.166, 168–9. Capt R.E. Forrester, Ptes Venters, Boyd, McIntosh and Stewart received the DCM for their part in the counterattack.
101. Wauchope, *The Black Watch in the Great War*, I, pp.170–1. Strachan (also spelt Strahan)'s death given as Oct in Samson (ed.), *Officers of The Black Watch*, p.94. Wauchope recorded a corporal receiving 'thirty-two separate wounds from one German grenade'.
102. Marquis de Ruvigny's 'Roll of Honour 1914–18', II, p.218; Wauchope, *The Black Watch in the Great War*, I, p.172.
103. '1BW War Diary', 21 Dec 1914, BWRA 0237.
104. Wauchope, *The Black Watch in the Great War*, I, p.28.
105. Sgt John Wallace, Officers' Mess Sgt, 1BW, 'In the Field', 26.12.14 (26 Dec 1914), to Mrs Marindin, 'Letters 1914–18', Marindin private papers, Blair Adam. Wallace was promoted 2nd Lt in Mar 1915; killed in action, Aubers Ridge, 9 May 1915. Evie Marindin's husband Maj (later Maj Gen) Arthur Marindin CB, DSO (1868–1947) was appointed GSO2 Scottish Coast Defence in 1914, GSO1 in 1915.
106. 'MacFarlane, IV – The Winter of 1914', *Red Hackle*, Apr 1986, p.12. Aged 90, he still had the cigarettes which he said had her initial 'M' on them.
107. Wilson, personal diaries, pp.73–4, BWRA 0182/1. 2BW was in billets at Amettes, near Lillers.
108. Wallace, In the Field, 26.12.14, to Mrs Marindin, 'Letters 1914–18', Marindin private papers, Blair Adam.
109. Quekett, 'Jottings of an Ordinary Man', p.14, BWRA 0992.
110. 'Narratives 1BW', *Red Hackle*, Oct 1921, p.53. 1BW casualties: 22 officers killed, 29 wounded and 1 missing. ORs: 255 killed, 457 wounded and 148 missing; 2 BW: 2 officers killed, 7 wounded; ORs: 56 killed, 122 wounded and 1 missing; Wauchope, *The Black Watch in the Great War*, I, pp.130, 322; II, p.56. Pte George Reid, 1BW; his younger brother William was in 5BW and Stewart in 2BW.
111. '1BW Record of Service 1873–1939', p.165, BWRA 0080. Later Pipe Maj (Acting Sgt) Dugald McLeod was killed at Albert in 1916. See Wauchope, *The Black Watch in the Great War*, I, p.28. He is not to be confused with Pipe Maj Daniel McLeod, 4/5BW.
112. Hilton Webster, 'Bravo, Black Watch', *Montrose Review*, in *Red Hackle*, Oct 1926, p.11.

4. 1915: Trench Warfare – Hell on Earth

1. Lance Corporal Linton Andrews, 4BW, *Haunting Years*, p.40.
2. Adam Macgregor Wilson, 8BW, diary, 17 May 1915, BWRA 0889. He had served as a Sgt in 1BW in 1914.
3. Pte John Laing, 1BW, diary, 1 Jan 1915, p.24, BWRA 0768. Pte James McGregor Marshall, 2BW, reminiscences, p.3, BWRA 0793.
4. 2nd Lt Hugh Scott Quekett, 5BW, 'Jottings of an Ordinary Man, from Childhood to the End of the Great War 1914–1918', p.14, BWRA 0992.

5. F.'Taff/Jock' Dawkins, 'Correspondence, First World War', *Red Hackle*, Apr 1979, p.6. He was on active service at Passchendaele and Ypres: 'all trench warfare and a few times over the top'. After contracting frozen toes, he was sent home. In 1918 he returned to Nivelles for demobilisation work.
6. Pte Jim Braid, 1BW, & 2nd Lt Lionel Sotheby, Argyll & Sutherland Highlanders, attached to 1BW, quoted in Young, *Forgotten Scottish Voices*, pp.97–8. On 3 Dec 1914 Gen Rawlinson had requested a special unit to assist with mining duties. In early 1915 eight tunnelling Coys were formed. By mid-1916 there were about 25,000 trained tunnellers, those recruited preferably with mining experience; see also Robert K. Johns, *Battle Beneath the Trenches: The Cornish Miners of 251 Tunnelling Company*, Pen & Sword, 2015.
7. 13 Platoon Comd, D Coy, 1BW (unsigned), In the Field, 26 Jan 2015, to Mrs Marindin, 'Letters 1914–18', Marindin private papers, 10/B21, Blair Adam House collection. This is possibly 2nd Lt R. Mackenzie who joined D Coy on 15 Jan 1915 (died of wounds on 11 Apr 1915). See '1BW War Diary', 4 Jan & 11 Apr 1915, App 2, BWRA 0237.
8. 13 Platoon Comd, D Coy, 1BW (unsigned), In the Field, 26 Jan 1915, to Mrs Marindin, 'Letters 1914–18', Marindin private papers, 10/B21, Blair Adam. Statistics from A.G. Wauchope, *History of The Black Watch in the Great War*, I, p.32 (13 Platoon Comd says 8). One of the officers was 2nd Lt C.W. Murray-Menzies, who had only arrived in France on 3 Jan 1915. His body was not found until 10 Feb.
9. LCpl John Morrison's body was only identified 100 years later and buried with full military honours on 27 Jul 2016. See '100-year-old service spoon find that led to soldier's burial', *Daily Telegraph*, 28 Jul 2016; Capt N.J.T. Coles, 'The Interment of Lance Corporal John Morrison,' *Red Hackle*, Nov 2016, pp.28–9.
10. '1BW War Diary', 16 Feb 1915, BWRA 0237.
11. LCpl A.B. Thomson, 4BW, diary (handwritten in two books and incomplete type-script), 27 Feb 1915, p.21, BWRA 0712/1. Joseph Gray, 'The Fourth Black Watch', *Dundee Advertiser*, 6 Dec 1917, p.6.
12. Andrews, *Haunting Years*, p.40.
13. Thomson, diary, 10 Mar 1915, p.49, BWRA 0712/1. Gray, 'The Fourth Black Watch', *Dundee Advertiser*, 14 Dec 1917, p.8.
14. Andrews, *Haunting Years*, p.57. Gray, 'The Fourth Black Watch', *Dundee Advertiser*, 15 Dec 1917, p.6. See also Wauchope, *The Black Watch in the Great War*, II, pp.7, 9.
15. Wauchope, *The Black Watch in the Great War*, I, pp.176, 179. In II, pp.9–10, Wauchope describes the German prisoners as deliberately firing their rifles. 'Needless to say, this treachery was at once summarily avenged.' Among the wounded during the battle was Lt Neil McMicking.
16. Quekett, 'Jottings of an Ordinary Man', p.16, BWRA 0992.
17. Wauchope, *The Black Watch in the Great War*, II, p.44. Although not involved in the initial assault 5BW's casualties numbered over 80, including 14 fatalities. No details for 4BW.

18. Gray, 'The Fourth Black Watch', *Dundee Advertiser,* 18 Dec 1917, p.7.
19. Wauchope, *The Black Watch in the Great War,* II, p.10.
20. Gray, 'The Fourth Black Watch', *Dundee Advertiser,* 19 Dec 1917, p.7.
21. Wauchope, *The Black Watch in the Great War,* I, pp.179–80.
22. Sir John French, addressing 4BW, quoted in Wauchope, *The Black Watch in the Great War,* II, p.11; see also p.45, & Gray, 'The Fourth Black Watch', *Dundee Advertiser,* 24 Dec 1917, p.6. Pte William Cuthill, 4BW, to his parents, undated, quoted in Young, *Forgotten Scottish Voices*, pp.237–8. He was killed at Loos on 25 Sep 1915.
23. Wauchope, *The Black Watch in the Great War*, I, p.33. Lt John Burdon Sanderson Haldane (1892–1964), a child prodigy, could read by the age of 3. Later acclaimed as a 'polymath' for his study of physiology, genetics and evolutionary biology.
24. Pte John Laing, 1BW, diary, 9 & 11 Apr 1915, p.33, BWRA 0768.
25. Lt Col Hugh Rose to Mrs Marindin, 26 Apr 1915, 'Letters 1914–18', Marindin papers, 10/B21, Blair Adam.
26. 6BW & 7BW were in Gordon Bde with the 5th and 7th Gordon Highlanders. On 11 May the 1st Highland Territorial Div was renamed 51st Highland Div. In Mar 1915 the 3/4th and 3/5th Black Watch were established at Dundee and Forfar, in Apr the 3/6th and 3/7th in Perth and St Andrews. After the summer at the Bridge of Earn, they moved to Ripon in Yorkshire. See Wauchope, *The Black Watch in the Great War,* II, p.345.
27. Sir Robert Moncrieffe of Moncrieffe, CB, CMG (1856–1931) had been in command of the 4th Volunteer Bn 1893–1911. Farrar, 'Notes on Irish Section, 6BW', pp.33, 42–3, BWRA 0999/13.
28. CSgt Alexander (Alick) C. Guthrie, B Coy, 6BW, envelope dated 9 May 1915, BWRA 0926.
29. Quekett, 'Jottings of an Ordinary Man', p.16, BWRA 0992. Chocolate Menier Corner was so-called because of an advertisement nailed on the wall of a house; see Wauchope, *The Black Watch in the Great War*, I. p.33.
30. Thomson, diary, 8 May 1915, pp.96–8, BWRA 0712/1.
31. Gray, 'The Fourth Black Watch', *Dundee Advertiser,* 28 Dec 1917, p.6. Thomson, 4BW, diary, 8 May 1915, pp.98–100, BWRA 0712/1.
32. Piper Daniel McLeod, 4BW, diary, 1 & 9 May 1915, BWRA 0981.There are 6 diaries (23 Feb 1915–4 Jan 1919); he left the Regt on 19 Jan 1919. Andrews, *Haunting Years,* pp.122–3.
33. Gray, 'The Fourth Black Watch', *Dundee Advertiser,* 31 Dec 1917, p.6.
34. Quekett, 'Jottings of an Ordinary Man', p.16, BWRA 0992. Sgt Joseph Webster received the DCM. Wauchope, *The Black Watch in the Great War,* II, p.60, incorrectly lists him as killed on 11 Nov 1914.
35. 'Narratives 2BW', 9 May 1915, *Red Hackle,* Jan 1922, p.38. Approx. 430 went 'over the top', of which 7 officers and 262 ORs were casualties (almost all due to rifle or machine-gun fire).
36. Thomson, diary, 9 May 1915, pp.101–2, 104–6, BWRA 0712/1. The other Scottish Regts involved were the 1st and 4th Seaforth Highlanders and 4th Cameron Highlanders.

37. McLeod, diary, 1 & 9 May 1915, BWRA 0981.
38. '5BW War Diary', 9/10 May 1915, App 2–3: 8 officers wounded, 22 ORs killed and 108 wounded, 8 reported missing, 2 later reappearing, BWRA 0241. See also stats from Wauchope, *The Black Watch in the Great War,* II, p.47: 8 officers wounded, 31 ORs killed and 106 wounded.
39. 'Narratives 1BW', 9 May 1915, *Red Hackle,* Oct 1921, p.44. 14 officers (including 'bombing' officer, Lt Haldane who was wounded), and 461 ORs were casualties, see Wauchope, *The Black Watch in the Great War*, I. p.39.
40. Brigade Staff Officer, quoted in Eric and Andro Linklater, *The Black Watch,* pp.141–2. An officer, 1st Scots Guards, quoted in Young, *Forgotten Scottish Voices,* p.121. Pte J. Braid, 1BW, quoted in ibid, p.122.
41. Correspondent, *Frankfurter Zeitung*, quoted in Young, *Forgotten Scottish Voices,* pp.121–2.
42. Gray, 'The Fourth Black Watch', *Dundee Advertiser,* 31 Dec 1917.
43. 2nd Lt Lionel Sotheby, attached to 1BW, letter, 11 May 1915, quoted in Young, *Forgotten Scottish Voices,* pp.120–1.
44. See Wauchope, *The Black Watch in the Great War,* II, p. 250; '1BW Record of Service 1873–1939', p.172, BWRA 0800; citation, *London Gazette*, 29 Jun 1915, Supplement. Cpl John Ripley, VC (1867–1933) had served in 7BW in which his son was still serving.
45. *London Gazette*, 29 Jun 1915. LCpl (later Sgt) David Finlay, VC (1893–1916) was killed in action in Mesopotamia on 21 Jan 1916. See Wauchope, *The Black Watch in the Great War,* I, pp.180–2. Of the 450 men engaged in 2BW, 270 (i.e. 60 per cent) were killed, wounded or missing.
46. Andrews, *Haunting Years,* p.131. See Gray, 'The Fourth Black Watch', *Dundee Advertiser,* 1 Jan 1918. The fatalities were Pte Donald Pyott, son of Sgt Maj Pyott, and Sgt Archie Troup, father of Pte John Troup.
47. Military Correspondent (Lt Col Charles à Court Repington), Northern France, 12 May, 'Need for Shells – British Attacks Checked – Limited Supply the Cause', *The Times,* 14 May 1915, p.8; 'Shells and the Great Battle', *The Times,* 14 May 1915, p.9.
48. *Perthshire Advertiser*, 15 May 1915, quoted in *Scotland and the Great War,* ed. C.M.M. Macdonald & E.W. McFarland, pp.164–5.
49. The Bdes were numbered 152, 153, 154; 6BW and 7BW were in 153 Bde. The 7th Div is not to be confused with the 7th Meerut Div combining various units from the British Empire.
50. LCpl David Simpson, 2BW, diary, 17 May 1915 (Apr–Sep), BWRA 0998. Wauchope, *The Black Watch in the Great War,* I, gives no details of 2BW fighting at Festubert. There is also very little on 4BW in vol. II. 'Narratives 2BW', *Red Hackle*, Jan 1922, p.39, also gives no details.
51. Farrar, 'Notes on Irish Section, 6BW', p.46, BWRA 0999/13.
52. Ibid, pp.44–7.
53. Wauchope, *The Black Watch in the Great War,* II, p.251. Guthrie, 6BW, to Crissie, 23 May 1915, BWRA 0926.

54. The 7th Meerut Div suffered 2,521 casualties, of which 102 were officers.
55. Gray, 'The Fourth Black Watch', *Dundee Advertiser,* 1 Jan 1918, p.6.
56. Lt Jack Mackintosh (1888–1915), 8BW, to Mother Darling, Apr 1915, Noble private papers. His nephew, Nigel Noble was commissioned into The Black Watch in 1939, commanding 1BW 1961–4.
57. Wilson, 8BW, diary (written in pencil), 9 May 1915, p.1, 12 May 1915, p.4, 13 May 1915, pp.7–8 (no pagination after p.11, 15 May), BWRA 0889.
58. '8BW War Diary', 1/2 May 1918, In the Field, BWRA 0248. See Wauchope, *The Black Watch in the Great War*, III, p.6. Wilson, diary, 19, 25 May 1915, BWRA 0889.
59. Mackintosh to Dearest Mary, 25 May 1915, Noble private papers.
60. Ibid. Gen Sir Neil Ritchie, 1BW, 'Recollections', p.13, BWRA 1025/83. He described BW casualties at Aubers Ridge 'as the heaviest experienced by The Black Watch in a single engagement since the debacle of Ticonderoga in 1758'.
61. Wilson, diary, 25 May 1915, BWRA 0889. See also Wauchope, *The Black Watch in the Great War*, III, p.6. 2nd Lt Lionel Sotheby, attached to 1BW, quoted in Young, *Forgotten Scottish Voices*, p.88. Forrester had been severely wounded with 2BW, Nov 1914.
62. Guthrie, Trenches in Flanders, to Crissie, 13 Jun 1915, BWRA 0926.
63. Farrar, 'Notes on Irish Section, 6BW', p.49, BWRA 0999/13.
64. Guthrie, Somewhere in France, to Crissie, 1 Jul 1915, BWRA 0926. There were five soldiers named Ferguson in 6BW who were killed during WW1 (3 on the same day: 13 Nov 1916) so it is probable that this Piper Ferguson was one of them.
65. Farrar, 'Notes on Irish Section, 6BW', pp.50–3, BWRA 0999/13.
66. Ibid. 2nd Lt George Mitchell was killed on 22 Jul 1915. His boxing opponent was Georges Carpentier (1894–1975). Mitchell's sister Elsie was the mother of Isabel Sanders who married Black Watch officer Neville Blair.
67. Wauchope, *The Black Watch in the Great War,* I, pp.42, 184.
68. Gray, 'The Fourth Black Watch', *Dundee Advertiser*, 2 Jan 1918; on 1 Jun Gray was sent to Bde HQ to do sketches. Thomson, diary, 8 Jun 1915 (2nd book), pp.33–4, BWRA 0712/2. Capt Patrick Duncan, 4BW, to Bob, 1 Aug 1915, quoted in Young, *Forgotten Scottish Voices,* p.235. Duncan was wounded at Loos on 25 Sep 1915.
69. Wilson, diary, 1 Jul, 6 Jul (re Festubert), 7 Aug (re cemetery), & 14 Aug (re Hell…) 1915, BWRA 0889.
70. Sgt Joseph Miller Barber, 9BW, to Dear Dick, 7 Jul 1915, BWRA 0963. Major John (Jack) Stewart, 9BW, A certain place, France, to Dearest One, 9 Jul 1915, BWM 2014.2A, transcr. Margaret Bowman, 2015. He had retired from the Regular Army in 1906.
71. [The kilt] 'is good for making love, but not for fighting a war'! Farrar, 'Notes on Irish Section, 6BW', pp.54–8, BWRA 0999/13. 51HD was now part of X Corps, Third Army. The CO of the French Tenth Army was Gen Victor d'Urbal (1858–1943); see Wauchope, *The Black Watch in the Great War,* II, p.254.
72. Guthrie, Somewhere in France, to Crissie, 9 Sep.1915, BWRA 0926. Farrar, 'Notes on Irish Section, 6BW', pp.54–8, BWRA 0999/13. On returning from leave, Farrar fell ill with rheumatic fever, missing the battle of Loos.

73. See Wauchope, *The Black Watch in the Great War*, II, pp.132–3. Maj William Alexander was awarded the DSO for his 'able handling of a dangerous situation'.
74. H.J. Humphrys, CBE, DSO, MC, a member of 139th Tunnelling Coy; information from his great-nephew, Charles Kenyon. Pte McHowe was rescued at the same time. Sgt Paterson had attempted the rescue operation but was overcome by gas and had to come out; Capt Peter Alabaster to his wife, 1 Sep 1915, Kenyon private papers. See Wauchope, *The Black Watch in the Great War*, II, p.255, for details of tunnellers, who included 2nd Lt John Galt Rowan.
75. Wauchope, *The Black Watch in the Great War*, I, p.185. Obviously named by the Germans after the Royal House of Hohenzollern.
76. Wauchope, *The Black Watch in the Great War*, II, p.48. Having 'expended all of its bombs' it rejoined 5BW and was reassigned as a 'pioneer' battalion. Its duties included counteracting the increasing mining activities of the Germans, 'having been selected for this duty on account of the large number of skilled tradesmen in its ranks'.
77. Capt J.S.S. Mowbray, 8BW, to Capt E.M. Murray, 5 Sep 1915. Murray had been wounded on 27 Jul 1915. He corresponded regularly with officers and ORs, sending them food parcels. Pte J.A. Ireland, 8BW, to Capt Murray, 9 Sep 1915, Clark family private papers.
78. Wilson, diary, 15 Sep 1915, BWRA 0889. Lt Sidney Steven, 4BW, Pont du Hem, 22 Sep 1915, quoted in 'The Battle of Loos', *Courier & Advertiser*, 100 Year Souvenir Supplement, 2015, p.13; see docs 5525, IWM. Gray, 'The Fourth Black Watch', *Dundee Advertiser*, 4 Jan 1918, p.6. Barber, 9BW, to Dear Father and Mother, 24 Sep 1915, BWRA 0963.
79. For statistics of rounds fired compared with Neuve Chapelle, see WO 158/259, TNA; approx 500 guns took part in the opening barrage at Loos. Pte J.A. Ireland, 8BW, to Capt E.M. Murray, 23 Sep 1915, Clark family private papers. Wauchope, *The Black Watch in the Great War*, III, p.122.
80. Mowbray to Murray, 5 Sep 1915, Clark family private papers. Sgt Charles Forman, 8BW, 'My Life', handwritten memoir, BWRA 0804, p.3. Born in 1890, he was the 9th of a family of 13. Signed by Colin Forman, dated 1965, who it seems is writing his father's memoirs in the first person. Forman was batman to Capt D'Alteyrac Steward, OC C Coy. See Wauchope, *The Black Watch in the Great War*, I, p.186, & Niall Cherry, *Most Unfavourable Ground*, Heilon & Co., 2005. Chlorine was a serious irritant to lungs and mucous membranes. Prolonged exposure was fatal.
81. Lt Col Harry Walker, Operation Order No.5, 24 Aug 1915, in front of notebook, BWRA 0296. McLeod, diary 2, 25 Sep 1915, BWRA 0981. See also '4BW War History', 25 Sep 1915, App, p.7, BWRA 0241.
82. Forman, 'My Life', p.4, BWRA 0804. He observed that the Germans' gas masks were 'the same type our civilians had in the 2nd World War 25 years after.' See Wauchope, *The Black Watch in the Great War*, III, pp.9–10.
83. LCpl McGee to Mrs Charles Broad (Mary Mackintosh), 3 Dec 1915, Noble private papers. Forman, 'My Life', pp.4–5, BWRA 0804. Hamilton died on 27 Sep 1915.

84. Forman, 'My Life', pp.4–5, BWRA 0804. John Forbes-Sempill was the 18th Lord Sempill (1863–1934). The 12th Lord Sempill had commanded the 42nd, 1741–5. Wauchope, *The Black Watch in the Great War,* II, p.12.
85. Piper Alexander MacDonald, quoted in Thomas McCluskey, 'The Other Pipers of Loos', *Red Hackle*, May 2009, p.26.
86. Wauchope, *The Black Watch in the Great War*, I, pp.186, 193–4. 'Narratives 2BW', *Red Hackle*, Jan 1922, pp.39–40. 2BW: out of 21 officers and 796 ORs, 4 officers and 38 ORs were killed, 10 officers and 261 ORs wounded and 49 missing. Among the wounded was Maj Charles Gordon, 2IC, whose father, Col William Gordon, was a former CO, 1BW. He was killed in action in Jul 1917.
87. MacDonald, in McCluskey, 'The Other Pipers of Loos', p.26. A week later MacDonald was badly wounded, requiring amputation of his leg. He died of tuberculosis in Apr 1917.
88. 'Narratives 2BW', *Red Hackle*, Jan 1922, p.40. 2nd Lt M.M. Thorburn, MC, 2BW, quoted in Young, *Forgotten Scottish Voices*, p.103.
89. '4BW War Diary', 25 Sep 1915, App, pp.8–9, BWRA 0241. 'Narratives 4BW', *Red Hackle,* Oct 1923, p.41. Gray, 'The Fourth Black Watch', *Dundee Advertiser*, 5 Jan 1918, p.6.
90. McLeod, diary 2, 25 Sep 1915, BWRA 0981. Gray, 'The Fourth Black Watch', *Dundee Advertiser*, 5 & 7 Jan 1918, pp.6, 8.
91. McLeod, diary 2, 25 Sep 1915, BWRA 0981. Thomson, 26 Sep 1915, 2, p.92, BWRA 0712/2. The 2IC Maj Elmslie Tosh had also been wounded on 9 May 1915. Out of 20 officers and 420 ORs who had taken part in the attack, 19 officers and 230 ORs were killed or wounded. 'Narratives 4BW', *Red Hackle,* Oct 1923, p.41, says 20 officers and 300 ORs killed, wounded, missing. Among the wounded was Maj Francis Rowland Tarleton. See '4BW War Diary', 25 Sep 1915, App, p.7, BWRA 0241.
92. Lt Harvey Steven, 4BW, Merville, 26 & 28 Sep 1915, quoted in 'The Battle of Loos', *Courier & Advertiser*, 100 Year Souvenir Supplement, p.13. Harvey Steven was killed on 7 Oct. '4BW War Diary', 25 Sep 1915, App, p.10, BWRA 0241. Wauchope, *The Black Watch in the Great War*, II, p.20.
93. 2nd Lt George Young, 1BW, diary 6, 25 & 26 Sep 1915, BWRA 0958. 1BW casualties: 4 officers, 60 ORs killed; 6 officers, 151 ORs wounded, 61 missing; 'Narratives 1BW', *Red Hackle*, Oct 1921, p.45. See also Wauchope, *The Black Watch in the Great War,* I, p.46 for stats. 1BW was withdrawn on 27 Sep to brigade reserve in the old front line, returning to the front on 5 Oct.
94. Gen Sir Neil Ritchie, 'Recollections', p.14, BWRA 1025/83. After recovering he went to 3BW, Nigg; he was reprimanded by the War Office for being 'too young' to go to the front 'this of course after I had already been there and had been wounded. Anyhow, within a month, I was sent to the Mesopotamian front,' p.14.
95. Wauchope, *The Black Watch in the Great War,* III, pp.124, 127. Maj M.W. Henderson had retired from the Territorial Force as Lt Col but rejoined as a Maj. 9BW total casualties: 10 officers, 360 ORs killed or missing; 11 officers, 320 ORs wounded out of 940 who went into action on 25 Sep.

96. Wauchope, *The Black Watch in the Great War*, III, pp.124, 126–7, 128, 131. Brig Gen Henry Thuillier was Director of Gas Services, RE, part of the 'special companies' formed to develop chlorine gas in response to German use of gas in Apr 1915.
97. Stewart, Same place that we were before, to My darling, 27 Sep 1915, BWM 1024. A. Wauchope, *The Black Watch in the Great War,* III, p.126. The machine-guns were brought near the front line on motorcycles.
98. Wauchope, *The Black Watch in the Great War,* III, p.128.
99. See Barber to Dear Dick, 7 Jul 1915, BWRA 0963, & W. Reid, *To Arras, 1917*, p.110.
100. Stewart, Same place that we were before, to My darling, 27 Sep 1915; Back somewhere else, to My very own darling, 28 Sep 1915, and Somewhere, to Dearest of Women, 1 Oct 1915, BWM 1024.2A. This is Lt A. Sharpe. Stewart said: 'The B.W. took very few prisoners.'
101. Pte Jock Young, 'Jock's Story', pp.1–9, BWRA 1002, written in the 3rd person. He had to have his hand amputated, and 'hung between life and death for several days,' p.17. The official name for the Regiment was The Black Watch (Royal Highlanders), hence the 'RH' on the shoulder straps.
102. Stewart, Somewhere back, to My dear old Boy (his son), 29 Sep 1915, BWM 1024.2A. Emilienne Moreau-Evrard (1898–1971) was awarded the Croix de Guerre 1914–1918, the MM, the Royal Red Cross (first class) and the Venerable Order of St John. She joined the French Resistance during WWII. Capt F.A. Bearn, DSO, MC, Royal Army Medical Corps.
103. Wilson, diary, 26 Sep 1915, BWRA 0889. His last diary entry was on 16 Oct. He was later commissioned and seconded to 15th Royal Scots. He died on service in Baghdad 10 Aug 1920.
104. Forman, 'My Life', p.6, BWRA 0804; see Wauchope, *The Black Watch in the Great War,* III, p.14. Lt G.B. Gilroy to Lady Strathmore, 27 Sep 1915, original in Glamis Castle, photocopy, BWRA 0985. Bowes-Lyon, after retiring from the Army in early 1914, had rejoined on the outbreak of war. Gilroy wrote to Lady Strathmore, Capt Bowes-Lyon's mother, rather than to his wife, Lady Christina, because his mother was noted as next of kin. Gilroy added: 'I am sorry to say that we could not bury his body as we were ordered to attack again that day & never came back to that part of the line. He was actually killed in a trench running from the Hohenzollern redoubt to the main German line.' His sister, Lady Elizabeth, hand-copied the letter reporting her brother's death; now framed as an exhibit in BWM. Capt Gilroy died of wounds on 15 Jul 1916.
105. Wauchope, *The Black Watch in the Great War,* III, pp.14–15. During 3 days' fighting, 8BW lost 19 officers and 492 ORs.
106. Forman, 'My Life', p.7, BWRA 0804.
107. Reid, *To Arras 1917*, p.111. 2nd Lt George Young, 1BW, 30 Sep 1915, diary, book 6, BWRA 0958. Three divisional commanders were killed including Maj Gen George Thesiger, commanding the 9th Scottish Div.
108. Wauchope, *The Black Watch in the Great War,* I, p.269. See also '2BW War Diary', App 2, 11 Nov 1915, and list of recipients, App 5, BWRA 0238.

109. Stewart, Somewhere, to Dearest and Best of Girls, 29 Sep 1915, BWM 1024.2A. Among those he commended for performing 'splendidly' was 9BW's medical officer, Capt F.A. Bearn, and the stretcher-bearers.
110. Gen Rawlinson to Lord Stamfordham, quoted in Fergus O'Connell, *Candlelight*, p.117. The end of the Battle of Loos is recorded as 15 or 19 Oct 1915.
111. Wauchope, *The Black Watch in the Great War,* III, pp.208, 272. For a further breakdown of statistics see ibid, I, pp.130, 322; II, pp.111, 216, 324; III, pp.84, 186, 261, 281, 290, 306.
112. Young, diary, book 7, (13) Oct 1915, BWRA 0958.
113. Ibid. 'Narratives 1BW', *Red Hackle*, Oct 1921, p.45. Of the 14 officers and 536 ORs in 1BW who went into action, 6 officers were killed and 4 wounded; 33 ORs were killed, 163 wounded, and 33 missing. Wauchope, *The Black Watch in the Great War,* I, pp.47–8.
114. Gray, 'The Fourth Black Watch', *Dundee Advertiser,* 7 Jan 1918, p.8. This ends Joseph Gray's account: 'Some time must yet elapse before details of the glorious work of the reconstituted Fourth after Loos may be revealed.'
115. Wauchope, *The Black Watch in the Great War,* I, p.196.
116. LCpl Dan McLeod, 4BW, diary, 2 & 8 Oct 1915, BWRA 0981. McLeod was promoted LCpl on 7 Oct. Wauchope, *The Black Watch in the Great War,* I, pp.197–8.
117. 2nd Lt Charles Vernon Somers Cocks, 2BW, diary, 31 Oct–5 Nov 1915, p.4, BWRA 0555; born in 1895 he served in 2BW 29 Sep 1915–19 Apr 1916. Lt A.B. Cumming, 2BW, The Trenches, Tues 12.15 p.m. (Nov 1915), 'Letters Home', p.7, BWRA 0924.
118. Miller, 4BW, 'Fifty Years After', memoir, *Red Hackle*, Nov 2015, p.18. 'Although, from the text, it was apparent the writer was named Miller, no other clues as to his identity were available. Then in 1992 a militaria dealer had on his listing a similar photocopy of the typescript which was entitled, by Miller, "Fifty Years After".' Thomas Moles, Introduction, to Miller, 'Fifty Years After', *Red Hackle*, Nov 2015, p.17. His rank is unclear but since he had just enlisted it is assumed he began as a Pte, later promoted Sgt.
119. '4BW War Diary', 15, 16, 17 Dec 1915, BWRA 0241.
120. Forman, 'My Life', p.8, BWRA 0804.
121. Wauchope, *The Black Watch in the Great War,* III, pp.214–15: Since no mail had arrived, and consequently no packages, their Christmas dinners consisted of 'what was known as "Balkan Stew"'.
122. Guthrie, 6BW, 9 Oct 1915; Somewhere in France, 23 Oct 1915, BWRA 0926.
123. George V's visit was cut short when he was thrown from his horse, resulting in his evacuation home on a stretcher.
124. Wauchope, *The Black Watch in the Great War,* II, pp.133, 256–7, 135.
125. See *Douglas Haig, War Diaries and Letters 1914–1918,* ed. Gary Sheffield & John Bourne, Weidenfeld & Nicolson, 2005, p.172; Gerard de Groot, *Douglas Haig, 1861–1928*, p.216; J.P. Harris, *Douglas Haig and The First World War,* p.546. FM Sir William (Wully) Robertson, GCB, GCMG, GCVO, DSO (1860–1933) had acted as C-in-C of the BEF in Sep when French fell ill and might have been a

better choice 'despite his lack of command experience'. Instead he became Chief of the Imperial General Staff (CIGS). French became C-in-C Home Forces.

126. Wauchope, *The Black Watch in the Great War,* I, p.198. Reid, *To Arras*, p.118. In 1915 John Leopold Brodie took out a patent on a steel helmet, modelled on medieval kettle hats.
127. Cpl Ian Maclaren, 6BW, quoted in Young, *Forgotten Scottish Voices,* p.41.
128. Donald's late father never returned to Scotland. 'Dundee Romance', *Dundee Advertiser,* 8 Oct 1915; Alexander McKay, 'Together Again', *Japan Society Journal*, 134 (Winter 1999), pp.51–8; James Rougvie, *Scotsman,* 11 Aug 1999; McMicking (ed.), *Officers of The Black Watch*, II.
129. Pte James McGregor Marshall, 2BW, 'Reminiscences', p.3, BWRA 0793. Cumming, 2BW, Billets, to my Dearest All (undated, 1915), 'Letters Home', p.13, BWRA 0924. Wauchope, *The Black Watch in the Great War,* I, p.199 n1.
130. Cumming, At sea, to my Dearest All, 15 Dec 1915, 'Letters Home', p.19, BWRA 0924. No. 2 Coy sailed in advance with the Seaforth Highlanders. 2nd Lt Robert Stevenson Morrison, diary, 25 Dec 1915, p.5, BWRA 0769.
131. Wauchope, *The Black Watch in the Great War*, I, p.199. In contemporary usage: al-Basrah or Basrah.
132. Joseph Lee (1876–1949), 'Marching', *Ballads of Battle*, v.2, p.86. See Ch.2 for v.1 and details about the poem.

5. 1916: Attrition

1. Sgt (later Capt) R. Wood, MC, DCM, MM, 7BW. After 4 months in the Labyrinth, 51HD had come out for a rest, marching about 20 miles to Franqueville, a remote location, i.e. Blanqueville. *Red Hackle,* Jul 1921, p.3.
2. Gen Sir John Nixon, GCMG, KCB (1857–1921). Maj Gen Charles Townshend (1861–1924) had fought with Kitchener at Omdurman. Baron Wilhelm Leopold Colmar von der Goltz (1843-1916), known as Goltz Pasha, was a respected military historian. He spent the 1880s and 1890s modernising the Ottoman Army; see J. Keegan, *The First World War*, p.323.
3. A.G. Wauchope, *The Black Watch in the Great War,* I, p.207. Lt Gen Sir Fenton Aymler, VC, KCB (1862–1935).
4. Maj Gen Sir George Younghusband, KCMG, KCIE, CB (1859–1944) was the elder brother of the better-known Lt Col Francis Younghusband.
5. Pte John Haig, 2BW, 'With the Highland Brigade in Mesopotamia', *The War Illustrated,* 5 Aug 1916, 'Press Cutting Album 1916–1919', p.5, BWRA 0116. Pte J.M. Marshall, 'France to Mesopotamia', II, reminiscences, p.4, BWRA 0793. Unless stated otherwise all officers and ORs mentioned in the Mesopotamia sections are 2BW.
6. Haig, 'With the Highland Brigade in Mesopotamia', BWRA 0116.
7. 'Narratives 2BW', *Red Hackle,* Jan 1922, p.41. Lt Charles Vernon Somers Cocks, 2BW, diary, 6 Jan 1916, p.5, BWRA 0555; also in Samson Scrapbook III, p.311, BWRA 0843/12.

8. Wauchope, *The Black Watch in the Great War*, I, p.209. Haig, 'With the Highland Brigade in Mesopotamia', BWRA 0116. .
9. Wauchope, *The Black Watch in the Great War*, I, pp.211, 212. Lt R.H. Dundas, 2BW, diary (typescript), Sat 8 Jan 1916, BWRA 0640/3.
10. 'Narratives 2BW', *Red Hackle*, Jan 1922, p.41. Wauchope had a fractured shoulder and spine injury, Samson Scrapbook III, BWRA 0843/12.
11. Lt A.B. Cumming, 2BW, to My Dearest All, 25 Jan 1916, 'Letters Home', p.27; diary, 7 Jan 1916, p.32, BWRA 0924. Morrison died on 8 Jan 1916. The last entry in his diary was 5 Jan: 'very hot sun indeed', BWM 2014.357. 2nd Lt Henry Bowie, diary, 7 Jan 1916, BWRA 0960/1.
12. Haig, 'With the Highland Brigade in Mesopotamia', BWRA 0116. Somers Cocks, diary, 7 Jan 1916, p.6, BWRA 0555.
13. Dundas, diary, Sat 8 Jan 1916, BWRA 0640/3. Somers Cocks, diary, 7 & 8 Jan 1916, p.7, BWRA 0555; evacuated to Bombay, having contracted dysentery Somers Cocks' health did not improve and he returned home in Mar 1916, his attachment to 2BW ending on 19 Apr 1916. Bowie, diary, 8 & 9 Jan 1916, BWRA 0960/1.
14. Dundas, diary, Sat 8 Jan 1916, BWRA 0640/3.
15. Wauchope, *The Black Watch in the Great War*, I, p.214.
16. Cumming, diary, 7 Jan 1916, 'Letters Home', p.32, BWRA 0924. Due to his groin injury he was evacuated to Bombay to convalesce. He returned to Basra on 6 Apr 1916. Recorded figures were 58 killed, 301 wounded and 19 missing. 'Narratives 2BW', *Red Hackle*, Jan 1922, p.42.
17. Bowie, diary, 12 Jan 1916, BWRA 0960/1.
18. Wauchope, *The Black Watch in the Great War*, I, p.216: one officer died of his wounds, 5 ORs were killed, 1 missing. Lt Gen Sir Percy Lake, KCB, KCMG (1855–1940). In 1917 an official enquiry blamed Nixon for failing to provide adequate medical facilities. He died in 'eclipse' in 1921, Jan Morris, *Farewell the Trumpets*, Faber & Faber, 1978, pp.170, 172n1.
19. Wauchope, *The Black Watch in the Great War*, I, p.216.
20. Dundas, diary, Fri 21 Jan 1916, BWRA 0640/3. Sections in round brackets were added by Dundas later. Sections in square brackets are the author's.
21. Wauchope, *The Black Watch in the Great War*, I, p.220.
22. Dundas, diary, Fri 21 Jan 1916, Sun 23 Jan 1916, & Tues 25 Jan 1916, BWRA 0640/3.
23. Wauchope, *The Black Watch in the Great War*, I, pp.220–1. Another fatality was 2BW's former CO in 1914–15, Brig Gen St John Harvey: 'a soldier of commanding personality and the broadest outlook' he was killed while commanding the Dehra Dun Bde on 1 Feb.
24. Gen Sir Neil Ritchie, 2BW, 'Recollections', pp.14–16, BWRA 1025/83.
25. Wauchope, *The Black Watch in the Great War*, I, p.224.
26. Cumming, to My Dearest All, 6 Apr 1916, 'Letters Home', p.43, BWRA 0924.
27. Wauchope, *The Black Watch in the Great War*, I, p.226. The Highland Bn lost 11 officers and 187 ORs.

28. Cumming to My Dearest All: The 1st Line, 12 & 14 Apr 1916; & The Trenches, 21 Apr 1916, 'Letters Home', pp.44–5, 48, BWRA 0924.
29. Wauchope, *The Black Watch in the Great War*, I, p.229.
30. Wauchope, *The Black Watch in the Great War*, I, p.230. Lt Col W.M. Thomson to Mrs Carver, 26 Apr 1916, 'Letters Home', p.51, BWRA 0924. 2BW casualties were: 10 officers and 321 ORs; Seaforth: 9 officers and 233 ORs.
31. Chaplain Andrew Macfarlane to Mrs Carver, 26 Apr 1916, 'Letters Home', p.51, BWRA 0924. Ritchie, 'Recollections 1916–45', p.16, BWRA 1025/83.
32. Capt T.E. Lawrence CB, DSO (1888–1935) and Capt Aubrey Herbert, MP (1880–1923) were sent as negotiators; see Dr Norman F. Dixon, *On the Psychology of Military Incompetence*, Pimlico, 1994, pp.95–109. Townshend died in partial disgrace in 1924 after reports surfaced about how badly his troops had suffered in captivity while he had lived in relative comfort.
33. The capitulation was eclipsed by the surrender of Singapore to Japanese forces in 1942. See David Fromkin, *A Peace to End All Peace*, p.203, and *Statistics of the Military Effort of the British Empire, 1914–1920*, HMSO, 1922. Lt Gen Sir Frederick Stanley Maude, KCB, CMG, DSO (1864–1917).
34. Ritchie, 'Recollections', p.18, BWRA 1025/83. He was appointed adjt of the Highland Bn late Jun 1916.
35. By May married men were no longer exempt. In 1918 a 3rd Act was passed increasing the age to 51. The Derby Scheme, introduced in 1915 by the Director of General Recruiting, Edward Stanley, 17th Earl of Derby, KG, GCB, GCVO, TD, KStJ, PC, JP (1865–1948), which required each eligible man to make a public declaration that he would enlist, gained insufficient recruits.
36. Wauchope, *The Black Watch in the Great War*, I, pp.53–4.
37. 4/5BW was in 118 Bde which included the 6th Cheshires, 1st Hertfordshire, 1st Cambridgeshire. The other bdes in the 39th Div were 116 and 117. Sceales remained as CO. Before amalgamation the 4th and 5th briefly joined 51HD. '4BW War Diary', 16 Feb 1916, & '5BW War Diary', 15 Mar 1916, BWRA 0241. See also Wauchope, *The Black Watch in the Great War*, II, pp.67–8.
38. He later published 4BW's war history in the *Dundee Advertiser*.
39. Miller, 4/5BW, 'Fifty Years After', *Red Hackle*, Nov 2015, p.18.
40. CSgt Alick Guthrie, 6BW, letter, 14 Mar 1916, France, BWRA 0926. Wauchope, *The Black Watch in the Great War*, II, p.259.
41. 2nd Lt Hubert Arnold Clement, 8BW, memoir (written before May 1917) unpaginated, BWRA 0894 (BWM 2014.110.1). See also letters to his sister, Gertrude Herzfeld, and others, BWM 2014.110.3. Also in the 9th Scottish Div, Jan–May 1916, the CO of 6 Royal Scots Fusiliers was former Home Secretary and First Lord of the Admiralty, Winston Churchill, who had resigned from the government after the disasters of the Gallipoli campaign.
42. J. Putkowski & J. Sykes, *Shot at Dawn*, p.63; see '9BW War Diary', App, Feb 1916, p.5, BWRA 0249. Docherty was buried in a civilian cemetery at Mazingarbe. He was suffering from neurasthenia (a mechanical weakness of the nerves) but the doctors had been unable to confirm shell-shock, which would have entitled

Docherty to be classified as 'wounded'.

43. Maj John (Jack) Stewart, 9BW, to Dearest and Best Beloved! Somewhere, 20 Apr 1916, BWM 1024.2A.
44. Clement to Dear W & D, 7 Jun 1916, BWRA 0894.
45. Sir Philip Gibbs (1877–1962), quoted in Reid, *To Arras*, p.127: one of only five official British reporters during WWI for the *Daily Telegraph* and the *Daily Sketch*. He reluctantly submitted his articles to censorship in order to be given permission to go to the front. He was knighted in 1920.
46. Clement to Dear Gertrude, 30 Jun 1916, BWRA 0894. Fought in three phases, and consisting of 13 major actions, the 1st phase lasted throughout Jul, the 2nd Jul–Sep, and the 3rd mid-Sep–mid-Nov.
47. Reid, *To Arras*, p.126. Keegan, *First World War*, p.317, says out of 100,000 men, '20,000 had not returned; another 40,000... were wounded... a fifth of the attacking force was dead, and some battalions... had ceased to exist.' German records also reveal that the offensive was compromised by German intelligence sources. See Peter Barton, 'The Somme 1916 – From both sides of the wire', BBC 2, 18 & 25 Jul 2016.
48. Lt Col Charles William Edward Gordon, 5 Jul (recd 11th), 'Letters' (transcribed), p.81, BWRA 0236. He took command of 8BW on 9 Apr, having come from the 8th Gordon Highlanders; he relinquished command on 22 Sep 1916.
49. Wauchope, *The Black Watch in the Great War*, I, pp.56–7.
50. Clement, from hospital, Manchester, to dear Walter & Dolly... best love to you all from Uncle Hubert, 25 Jul 1916, BWRA 0894. He was wounded in the neck, later returning to 8BW.
51. Gordon, 20 Jul (recd 25th), 'Letters', p.88, BWRA 0236.
52. Brevet Maj John Ewing, MC & bar., *History of the 9th Scottish Division*, pp.126–35. The assaulting forces included the 1st South African Inf and the 11th Royal Scots. Ewing served with the 6th King's Own Scottish Borderers, which joined the Div in 1916. See also Wauchope, *The Black Watch in the Great War*, III, p.24; 8BW's strength was reduced to 6 officers and 165 ORs. Gordon, 20 Jul (recd 25th), 'Letters', p.89, BWRA 0236.
53. Wauchope, *The Black Watch in the Great War*, III, p.26. Lt Col Stewart had been evacuated due to illness. His successor, Lt Col Sydney Armitage Innes, DSO and bar (d.1960), began a family tradition: his son and grandson both served in The Black Watch, Wauchope, *The Black Watch in the Great War*, III, p.136.
54. Farrar, 'Notes on Irish Section, 6BW', p.73, BWRA 0999/13. He had rejoined the Bn at Vimy Ridge. He joined 4/5BW in Jan 1918 as a 2nd Lt, promoted Lt in Sep 1918.
55. Wauchope, *The Black Watch in the Great War*, II, pp.140, 266; 9 officers and 31 ORs were killed, 98 wounded, with 14 missing.
56. Maj (later Brig) Frederick William Bewsher, CBE, DSO, MC (1886–1950), *History of the 51st Highland Division*, pp.84–5. Bewsher served as GSO2, 51HD.
57. Cpl Ian Maclaren, 6BW, to his mother, 11 Aug 1916, quoted in Young, *Forgotten Scottish Voices*, p.172.

58. See 'Narratives 6BW' & 'Narratives 7 BW', Aug–Sep 1916, *Red Hackle*, Jul 1921, pp.38–9, 45.
59. Wauchope, *The Black Watch in the Great War*, III, p.140. Casualties numbered 9 officers and 240 ORs. Having received the MC at Loos, Capt F.A. Bearn was awarded the DSO after the Somme.
60. Pte H.L. Junks, 3/4BW, 'The Diary of a Soldier in the Great War', 11 Sep 1916, BWRA 0949. On 1 Sep the 3rd line bns 3/5, 3/6 and 3/7 BW, were amalgamated with 3/4BW to form the 4th Reserve Battalion The Black Watch, under the command of Col Sir Robert Moncrieffe, Wauchope, *The Black Watch in the Great War*, II, p.345. The Palladium Picture House in Ripon was opened in Mar 1916.
61. Capt R.E. Badenoch, MC (a former member of the Highland Cyclist Battalion), 7BW, 'My Recollections of the First World War', pp.7–8, BWRA 0771. Pte Black was shot at 5.47 a.m. & was buried in the cemetery near Bailleul. See '7BW War Diary', BWRA 0244. Writing in later life, Badenoch added: 'Today the most premeditated cold blooded murder can be perpetrated in the knowledge that there is no death sentence for the murderer and yet in 1916 some poor soldier who possibly lost his nerve for a short time and ran the wrong way could be shot for desertion.' In 2006 the Armed Forces Act was passed allowing the soldiers to be pardoned posthumously, but Section 359(4) states that the pardon does not affect any conviction or sentence. See Putkowski & Sykes, *Shot at Dawn*, p.114.
62. Miller, 'Fifty Years After', *Red Hackle,* Nov 2015, p.18.
63. '4/5BW War Diary', 2 Sep 1916, App, BWRA 0240.
64. Pipe Maj Daniel McLeod, 4/5BW, diary 3, 3 Sep 1916, BWRA 0981. Promoted Cpl on 7 Jan, Pipe Cpl 8 Jan, Acting Pipe Maj 9 Jan, Lance Sgt 12 Jan, & Bn Sgt Piper 20 Jan (Pipe Maj), he turned 25 on 31 May 1916.
65. Wauchope, *The Black Watch in the Great War*, II, p.72. See also Lt Col G.McL. Sceales, Account of the Battle, '4/5BW War Diary', 3 Sep 1916, App, pp.12–18, BWRA 0240.
66. Miller, 'Fifty Years After', *Red Hackle,* Nov 2015, p.18.
67. Wauchope, *The Black Watch in the Great War*, I, p.59: 37 ORs were killed, 123 wounded, 36 missing.
68. Bewsher, *History of the 51st Highland Division*, p.88. Newspaper report dated Sep 1916; Fortune did not officially assume the rank of Lt Col until 10 Jan 1927, when he took command of the Seaforth Highlanders, Fortune private papers. See Ch.1 for Capt C.E. Stewart's memoir of South Africa.
69. See Reid, *To Arras*, p.131. Wauchope, *The Black Watch in the Great War,* III, pp.140–1. Statistics from 'Narratives 9BW', *Red Hackle,* Apr. 1921, p.35. The 15th Scottish Division was relieved on 19 Sep 1916.
70. Initially there were 50 tanks but 14 broke down due to the difficult terrain. The tank's importance was recognised by Maj Gen Sir Ernest Swinton, KBE, CB, DSO (1868–1951), RE; see John Keegan, *First World War,* p.320. Tanks were assigned to the Heavy Branch of the Machine Gun Corps. Actions were fought at Flers and Courcelette until 22 Sep, Morval 25–28 Sep, Thiepval 26–28 Sep, the Transloy Ridges 1 Oct–11 Nov; Ancre Heights 1–11 Nov; the last battle

known as the Battle of Ancre 13–18 Nov.

71. 'Narratives 1BW', *Red Hackle*, Oct 1921, p.47. 2nd Lt L.J. Sarjeant, 'War Diary', 26 Sep 1916, BWRA 0862/1&2 (BWM A63380). He had fought at Aubers Ridge and Loos. At the end of 1916 he was appointed adjt & QM 1st Divisional School. His diary was written daily, with indelible pencil on small sheets of paper, later transcribed by his daughter Ailie Harrison and Elizabeth Miller.
72. Wauchope, *The Black Watch in the Great War*, I, p.61; Sgt W.B. Wilson, Obit., *Red Hackle,* Dec 1966, p.4. Wilson had transferred to 1 BW. Capt McLaren Stewart's mud-spattered kilt is in BWM.
73. 2nd Lt Robert Keith Arbuthnott, diary, 29 Sep 1916, Arbuthnott private papers. Wauchope, *The Black Watch in the Great War*, I, p.62. Sarjeant, 'War Diary', BWRA 0862/1&2. Sarjeant remained with 1BW until Nov 1917 and was then was sent with XIV Corps to Italy.
74. Wauchope, *The Black Watch in the Great War*, II, pp.73, 76: 4 officers and 27 ORs were killed, 220 wounded and 30 missing.
75. Miller, 'Fifty Years After', *Red Hackle,* Nov 2015, p.19.
76. Wauchope, *The Black Watch in the Great War*, III, pp.28–9. The CO of 8BW was now Lt Col Sir George Abercromby. The Butte was taken by the 2nd Australian Div in Feb 1917, retaken by the Germans in Mar 1918, retaken by the 21st Div in Aug 1918.
77. Ewing, *History of the 9th Division*, App IV, p.409: 'Approximate' numbers: 118 officers, 3,137 ORs; Wauchope, *The Black Watch in the Great War,* III, p.31.
78. Wauchope, *The Black Watch in the Great War*, III, p.142. Lt Ernest Reid, 9BW, to his brother Ronald, 28 Oct 1916, quoted in Reid, *To Arras*, p.133.
79. Wauchope, *The Black Watch in the Great War*, II, p.143. Bewsher, *History of 51st Highland Division*, p.99.
80. Wauchope, *The Black Watch in the Great War*, II, p.270. The Reserve Army (previously Reserve Corps) was under the command of Lt Gen Hubert Gough, GCB, GCMG, KCVO (1870–1963).
81. Pte William Couston, 7BW to My Dearest Mum, France, 13 Oct 1916, BWRA 0806.
82. Wauchope, *The Black Watch in the Great War*, II, p.272. Those attacking were 152 and 153 Bdes – 154 was in reserve, Bewsher, *History of the 51st Highland Division*, p.103. Maj Gen G.M. Harper, KCB, DSO (1865–1922): his name was used in the nickname assigned to the 51HD when it was considered to have under-performed –'Harper's Duds'. See Colin Campbell, *Engine of Destruction, The 51st Highland Division in the Great War* for his assessment that the Germans feared the Division more than any other British or Empire Division in the war.
83. Badenoch, 'My Recollections', p.9, BWRA 0771.
84. Sgt W. Mitchell, quoted in Wauchope, *The Black Watch in the Great War*, II, pp.151–2.
85. Wauchope, *The Black Watch in the Great War*, II, p.150: 12 officers and 214 ORs were killed, wounded or missing. Lt Col John Wylie to Mrs Maclaren, 17 Nov 1916, quoted in Young, *Forgotten Scottish Voices*, p.174. Wylie was CO of 6BW

1–30 Oct, replaced by Lt Col Booth, Gordon Highlanders. He took command again on 3 Dec 1916.

86. *Perthshire Constitutional and Journal*, 25 Dec 1916.
87. Baron Hubert de Reuter (1878–1916) succeeded to the Barony in Apr 1915, when his father, the 2nd Baron, committed suicide following the sudden death of Hubert's mother. He resigned his commission in the Essex Regt, preferring to serve as a private. Lt Col G.R.H. Cheape, 1st Dragoon Guards, had succeeded Allen in command of 7BW after Allen was wounded at High Wood. Allen resumed command in Feb 1917.
88. Badenoch, 'My Recollections', pp.9–10, BWRA 0771.
89. Bewsher, *History of the 51st Highland Division*, pp.120, 123.
90. Casualties are contested; see Keegan, *The First World War,* p.321: 'The Germans may have lost over 600,000 killed and wounded… the Allies had certainly lost over 600,000.' See also Farrar-Hockley, *The Somme,* pp.210–12. The duration of the battle of the Somme is generally set at 141 days excluding the bombardment. Peter Barton suggests that fighting did not conclude until the spring of 1917. See 'The Somme 1916 – From Both Sides of the Wire', BBC 2, 18 & 25 Jul 2016.
91. Wauchope, *The Black Watch in the Great War,* I, pp.232–3, 234–5, 243. Maude reorganised the forces in I and II Corps: 2BW remained in I Corps.
92. Lt Alexander Neville Blair, 2BW, to his son, 18 Nov 1916. Envelope addressed to Master Neville Blair. 'To be opened and read to him after my death: I should also like it kept for him to read from time to time as he grows up.' Cheetham/Metcalfe private papers. His forebear, Maj James Blair, served in The Black Watch in the 1790s.
93. Lloyd George's successor as Secretary of State for War was Edward Stanley, Earl of Derby. Kitchener died en route to Russia when the ship was torpedoed. See e.g. Farrar-Hockley, *The Somme,* p.209 for details on the crisis which brought about Asquith's downfall.
94. Couston, to My Dearest Mum, 13 Dec 1916, BWRA 0806. Badenoch, 'My Recollections', p.10, BWRA 0771.
95. Wauchope, *The Black Watch in the Great War*, II, p.77; III, pp.31–3. On 23 Nov the 9th Scottish Div was transferred from the Fourth to the Third Army, commanded by Gen Sir Edmund Allenby. On 28 Dec a German gas attack lasting three hours resulted in the death of 2 sergeants from gas poisoning with 65 soldiers hospitalised.
96. Lt Archibald Don to Prof T. McKenny Hughes, 10 Feb 1916, quoted in *Archibald Don, A Memoir*, ed. Charles Sayle, p.136; Wauchope, *The Black Watch in the Great War*, III, p.216. The mammoth tusk, probably dating from the Pleistocene geological epoch, was found near Aivatli and specimens of it are among the Sedgwick Museum of Earth Science's exhibits. His brother Lt R.M. Don, also in 10BW, was killed in May 1917. Additional information, Matt Riley, Sedgwick Museum, Dec 2015.
97. '13 BW (Scottish Horse) War Diary', WO 95/4892, TNA. Pte Sandy R. Stratton, 13BW, 'Letters Home from the Front', 3 Nov 1916, BWRA 1004. Title given on 15

Oct, official confirmation 22 Dec 1916; conforming with other bns, its companies became known as A, B, C and D instead of 1, 2, 3 and 4, Wauchope, *The Black Watch in the Great War*, III, pp.293–4. No BW battalions fought at Gallipoli but some officers were attached to other units. Capt William Thomas Kedie, 2BW, was killed in action at Gallipoli on 20 Aug 1915. Capt Guy Rowan-Hamilton and his batman, Pte Harry Ogilvie, were also at Gallipoli. Capt George Ogilvie, correspondence, 8 Mar 2016.

98. Maj D. Douglas Ogilvie, *Fife & Forfar Yeomanry*, p.41. Maj Ogilvie joined 14BW in Jan 1918. He used the War Diaries and Lt Col Younger's diary for his account. 'Narratives 14BW', *Red Hackle*, Jan 1922, p.51. The official date for its formation is 1 Jan 1917. See '14BW War Diary', 17, 1–31 Jan 1917, WO 95/4677, TNA. Also BWRA 0251, Jan 1917, App 1; Wauchope, *The Black Watch in the Great War*, III, p.317. The Fife & Forfar Yeomanry was in 229 Bde, 74th Div; Members of the Lanarkshire & Ayrshire Yeomanry were also posted to the Bn.
99. See Wauchope, *The Black Watch in the Great War*, I, pp.130, 322; II, pp.111, 216, 324; III, pp.84, 186, 261, 281, 290, 306 for a further breakdown.
100. Clement, memoir, BWRA 0894.
101. Neil Munro (1863–1930), 'To Exiles'. Munro was a Scottish journalist and newspaper editor. See http://www.scottishpoetrylibrary.org.uk/poetry/poems/exiles, accessed 24 Feb 2017.

6. 1917: Blown to Pieces

1. Cpl Albert A. Hay, 1BW, formerly 2/2nd Scottish Horse, 'Soldiering', memoir, 1917–21, 'There runs a road in Flanders', v.3, BWRA 0073.
2. Pte William Cameron, Scottish Horse, 7BW, 'Army Life and Trials, Reminiscences', (written 22 Feb 1918), p.5, BWRA 0805. Lt R.K. Arbuthnott, 1BW, diary, 28 Jan 1917, Arbuthnott private papers. Promoted Lt on 5 Jan 1917. Rev Coll Macdonald, 8BW, to Dear Mary, 4 Jan 1917, BWM 2014.689. Macdonald left to join the Royal Scots Fusiliers in Britain, returning to 8BW in May 1917.
3. Pte Sandy Stratton, 13BW, to Mother, 7 Jan 1917, 'Letters Home from the Front', BWRA 1004.
4. By 21 Feb 1917, 1,362 ORs had been sent abroad, Wauchope, *The Black Watch in the Great War*, III, p.276. By Nov 1918 the Labour Corps formed nearly 10% of the British Army Establishment.
5. Paul von Hindenburg (1847–1934) was President of Germany 1925–34. He had replaced Gen von Falkenhayn as CGS in Aug 1916. The United States Army 'ranked in size –107,641 men – 17th in the world. It had no experience of large-scale operations since the armistice at Appomattox 51 years earlier,' John Keegan, *The First World War*, p.401.
6. A.G. Wauchope, *The Black Watch in the Great War*, I, p.245. General Maude, quoted in ibid, p.244.
7. Also in 7th Indian Division were 19 and 28 Bdes. The 'Punjabis' were the 20th Duke of Cambridge's Own Infantry (Brownlow's Punjabis). It was Col J. Alban

Wilson, 1/8th Gurkhas, who had given 2BW the diary of Capt McGregor, 73rd Regiment, found in a Hindu temple at Manipur in 1891. See Schofield, *The Highland Furies*, p.635n72; Wauchope, *The Black Watch in the Great War*, I, p.243n1.

8. Gen Sir Archibald Murray, GCB, GCMG, CVO, DSO (1860–1945) took command of the EEF in Jan 1916. On 26 Feb 1917 the Anglo-French Conference reversed the War Cabinet's decision of 11 Jan 1917 to reduce operations in Palestine. The EEF was now ordered to capture Gaza as a prelude to taking Jerusalem. These shifting objectives illustrated the divergent views of 'westerners' (Haig and Robertson) who favoured concentrating efforts in the west and 'easterners' (Lloyd George) who favoured operations in the east.
9. T.E. Lawrence, was known as Lawrence of Arabia; his first desert raid was on 3 Jan 1917.
10. Wauchope, *The Black Watch in the Great War,* I, pp.246–8. Among those commended for doing 'fine work' were the stretcher bearers, including Cpl Hutchison who received the DCM for bringing in a wounded Punjabi.
11. Wauchope, *The Black Watch in the Great War,* I, p.249.
12. Gen Sir Neil Ritchie, 2BW, 'Recollections', pp.18–19, BWRA 1025/83. The 'golden domes' he saw were domes of the Holy Shrine of the Imam Musa el-Kazmin.
13. Ritchie, 'Recollections', pp.18–19.
14. Wauchope, *The Black Watch in the Great War,* I, pp.251–2. The Baghdad railway (also known as the Berlin-Baghdad railway) ran from Hamburg (via Berlin, Dresden, Prague, Vienna, Budapest, Belgrade to Basra. In the Ottoman Empire the main towns it passed through from Basra were Baghdad, Samarra, Mosul, Aleppo, and Constantinople).
15. Wauchope, *The Black Watch in the Great War,* I, pp.255–6, 257. Lt Gen A.S. Cobbe, I Corps Cdr. Casualties were 5 officers, 36 ORs killed, 5 officers, 184 ORs wounded out of 525; 27 medallions were presented in Jan and 20 in Mar 1918. See '2BW War Diary', Jan 1918, App , & Mar 1918, App 6 , BWRA 0238.
16. The Median Wall formed the outline of the defences of the Kingdom of Babylon under Nebuchadnezzar II in the seventh century BC. Wauchope, 'The Battle That Won Samarrah', *Blackwood's Magazine*, Apr 1918, pp.427, 429, and *The Black Watch in the Great War*, I. p.261.
17. Artillery officer quoted in ibid, p.264. Lt Col John (Jack) Stewart, 2BW, to Dearest and Best, 4 May 1918, BWM 1024.2A. He was disappointed that when he read Wauchope's article, 'The Battle That Won Samarrah', '[He] hardly gave the Regt sufficient credit for their marvellous advance over an absolutely flat plain in the face of our "somewhat" heavy fire.'
18. Pte Charles Melvin, VC, *London Gazette* (Supplement) No. 30400, pp.12330-1, 26 Nov 1917. His VC is in The Black Watch Museum.
19. Wauchope, 'The Battle That Won Samarrah', *Blackwood's Magazine*, Apr 1918, p.431, and *The Black Watch in the Great War*, I. p.266: 4 officers and 41 ORs killed, 6 officers and 132 ORs wounded. On Palmer, see Wauchope, *The Black Watch in the Great War*, I, p.267n1.

20. 2BW, General, *Red Hackle*, Jul 1955, p.15; Ritchie, 'Recollections', p.19, BWRA 1025/83. 2BW, 21 Bde was the first to enter Samarrah (Samarra). The 'Baghdad Bell' is in BWM.
21. Stewart, Samarrah, to Dearest and Best, 3 May 1917, BWM 1024.2A.
22. Stewart, Samarrah, to My Sweetheart, Friday 27 Jul 1917, BWM 1024.2A. Pte George Cutmore was tried 2 Jul, executed 25 Jul 1917, Obit., *Red Hackle*, Apr 1931, pp.7–8, and Putkowski & Sykes, *Shot at Dawn*, p.227. He was the last soldier to be shot for desertion in Mesopotamia during the war.
23. Ogilvie, *Fife & Forfar Yeomanry*, p.44.
24. '13BW War Diary', 11 Apr, WO 95/4892, TNA. He was assisted by Ptes Wrench and McNiven.
25. See '10BW War Diary', 8/9 May 1917, App.10, BWRA 0250, 'Narratives 10BW', *Red Hackle*, Apr 1921, p.42, and Wauchope, *The Black Watch in the Great War*, III, p.238: 5 officers (including Lt R. M. Don whose brother, also 10BW, had died of malaria in Sep 1916) and 63 ORs were killed; 6 officers and 309 ORs were wounded; an estimated 12,000 Allied forces were killed, wounded or missing.
26. '10BW War Diary', 1 Jun 1917, BWRA 0250, and Putkowski & Sykes, *Shot at Dawn*, p.228. Pte Brown was already serving a suspended sentence of a year's hard labour for striking a superior officer.
27. Stratton to Jean 18 May 1917, 'Letters Home', BWRA 1004. Lt Col G. Railston, Precautions Against Malaria, '13BW War Diary', 6 Jul 1917, App 1, p.9, BWRA 0251. See also Linklater, *The Black Watch*, p.167.
28. Arbuthnott, diary, 18 Mar 1917, Arbuthnott private papers.
29. Robert Georges Nivelle (1856–1924); FM 1st Viscount Edmund Allenby, GCB, GCMG, CVO (1861-1936). Haig, created FM on 1 Jan 1917, remained in supreme command of the BEF.
30. Maj Gen Douglas Wimberley, CB, DSO, MC (1896–1983), 'Alamein, the story of the 51st Highland Division in North Africa', 23 Oct 1942, Samson Scrapbook III, p.330, BWRA 0843/12. He commanded 51HD in WWII. See also Maj F.W. Bewsher, *History of the 51st Highland Division*, p.205.
31. General Erich Ludendorff, Deputy and Quartermaster General (*Erster Generalquartiermeister)* (1865–1937); General Alexander von Falkenhausen (1878–1966).
32. Capt R.E. Badenoch, MC, 7BW, 'My Recollections of the First World War', pp.10–11, BWRA 0771. On 31 Mar he was hit in the shoulder about 5 miles behind the line. Describing his wound as the 'cushiest wound imaginable', after recovering he went to the 4th Reserve Bn at Ripon. He returned to France in Oct 1917 and was posted to 4/5BW.
33. Bewsher, *History of the 51st Highland Division,* pp.151, 158. Pte W. Cameron, Scottish Horse, 7BW, 'Army Life and Trials', p.6, BWRA 0805. Suffering from trench foot he was sent to hospital at the end of Apr, returning at the end of May.
34. Pte Alexander Black, 8BW, quoted in Reid, *To Arras, 1917*, p.157.
35. Wauchope, *The Black Watch in the Great War*, III, p.40. He suggests (p.152) that the casualties were less than at Loos in 1915 because the Division was no longer

being asked to 'push on to the full extent of its power'; instead the individual battalions were set specific tasks, after which it was expected other battalions would pass through; '9BW War Diary' stats for Apr: 28 officers, 472 ORs killed, wounded or missing, 30 Apr 1917, App 6, recorded by Lt Col S.A Innes, BWRA 0249.

36. Reid, *To Arras,* p.175. Ernest was Walter Reid's uncle; his father, Ronald, 'never truly got over' his older brother's death , p.13. Wauchope, *The Black Watch in the Great War*, III, pp.147–8, II, p.283. Capt E.J. Blair died on 11 Apr 1917.
37. Wauchope, *The Black Watch in the Great War*, II, pp.284–5. See also '8BW War Diary', 15/16 Apr 1917, BWRA 0248.
38. Pte William Couston, 7BW, to My Dearest Mum, 24 Apr, and to Dearest Mum, 29 Apr 1917, BWRA 0806. Losses for 6BW: 5 officers, 25 ORs killed, 4 officers, 123 ORs wounded and 48 missing; 7BW: 7 officers, 64 ORs killed, 5 officers 194 ORs wounded and 65 missing, Wauchope, *The Black Watch in the Great War*, II, pp.160, 285.
39. '9BW War Diary', 23 Apr 1917, BWRA 0249.
40. Lt Hubert Arnold Clement, 8BW, to dear G[ertrude], Sat evening 28 Apr 1917, BWRA 0894. '8BW War Diary', App A, Operations from Apr 27–May 10, The Attack, p.4, BWRA 0248; see also Wauchope, *The Black Watch in the Great War*, III, pp.40–1.
41. Lt Col G. Abercromby, CO 8BW, to Miss Herzfeld, 16 May 1917, BWRA 0894.
42. Macdonald to Angus, 26 May & to My Dear Mary, 28 May 1917, BWM 2014.689.
43. See Keegan, *The First World War*, pp.355–7. 'The objects of the mutinies had been achieved. The French army did not attack anywhere on the Western Front, of which it held two-thirds, between June 1917 and July 1918.' It was also described as a military strike. Gen (later Marshal) Henri Philippe Pétain (1856–1951).
44. Lt José Penney, 7BW, *Diary of a Black Watch Subaltern*, 20 May 1917, pp.26–7.
45. Information from Salmond's 2nd cousin, Patrick Anderson 28 Jul 2012 and 11 Aug 2014. Salmond edited *The Hydra*, while Wilfred Owen (killed on 4 Nov 1918) was sub-editor. Salmond later wrote the history of 51HD. Lt Siegfried Sassoon, Artists' Rifles, also spent time at Craiglockhart. Patrick Anderson's uncle and namesake, Lt Patrick Anderson, served with 10BW, dying in 1921 of wounds sustained in 1918. Anderson ensured that his name appeared on the Roll of Honour, Scottish National War Memorial. See *Red Hackle,* Nov 2012, pp.4–5.
46. 2nd Lt George Young, 1BW, diary 8, 3 & 7 Jun 1917, BWRA 0958; he had just returned to 1BW after being wounded at the Somme. Arbuthnott, diary, 20, 24 Jun 1917, Arbuthnott private papers.
47. Miller, 'Fifty Years After', *Red Hackle*, Nov 2015, p.19.
48. Penney, *Diary of a Black Watch Subaltern*, 22–24 Jul & 30 Jul 1917, pp.74, 84–6, BWM.
49. Ibid, 31 Jul, 3.50 a.m., p.87.
50. '9BW War Diary', 31 Jul 1917, App 3–4, BWRA 0249. By the end of the day, 9BW mustered 'only 7 officers & 137 O.R. but there were many stragglers to come in, who had got mixed up with other battns. Estimated casualties to rank & file killed 30. – wounded 150. Strength going into action 18 officers & 520 O.R.' Pipe Maj

Daniel McLeod, 4/5BW, diary 4, 31 Jul 1917, BWRA 0981. Miller, 'Fifty Years After', *Red Hackle,* Nov 2015, pp.19-20. Wauchope, *The Black Watch in the Great War,* II, p.87: 4/5BW's casualties: 8 officers and 228 ORs.

51. Pte W. Cameron, Scottish Horse, 7BW, 'Army Life and Trials', pp.11–12, BWRA 0805. Penney, *Diary of a Black Watch Subaltern,* 31 Jul 1917, pp.88–90.
52. 'A man of D Coy', quoted in Wauchope, *The Black Watch in the Great War*, II, pp.166–7.
53. Penney, 7BW, *Diary of a Black Watch Subaltern*, 31 Jul, 9 p.m. & 1 Aug, 1917, pp.93–4. His diary ends on 26/27 Aug. He was evacuated to England because of his wounded leg. His younger brother, Colin, also in The Black Watch, lost an eye & two toes from trench foot.
54. Lt Col McL Sceales, '4/5BW War Diary', Operations 31 Jul–6 Aug, 1917, App 13–14, BWRA 0240. McLeod, diary 4, 31 Aug 1917, BWRA 081.
55. The Tank Corps was formed on 27 Jul 1917. Lt Edward M. Wolf to Mrs Murray-Menzies, 19 Sep 1917, BWM 2010.21.56. He was with Murray-Menzies. Pte James Wallace to Dear Madam, 29 Aug 1917, BWM 2010.21.34. See also letter dated 2 Sep 1917, BWM 2010.21.36. Menzies (killed on 22 Aug 1917) was descended from Capt Archibald Menzies, who served in the 42nd in the early 19th cent. Lt Col Victor Fortune to Mrs Murray-Menzies, 1 Sep 1917, BWM 2010.21.51. His body was eventually recovered and buried and a cross erected where he fell in Oct, Sidney Charrington to Mrs Murray-Menzies, 4 Sep & 28 Oct 1917, BWM 2010.21.61 & 64, BWM 2010.21.64. His brother was 2nd Lt Clive William Murray-Menzies, 1BW, killed on 25 Jan 1915. See 'Regimental Museum', *Red Hackle,* May 2009, p.10. The two brothers' portraits are in BWM.
56. Lt Gen Ivor Maxse, Commanding XVIII Corps, '8BW War Diary', Sep 1917, App 12–13, BWRA 0248. See Bewsher, *51st Highland Division,* pp.216–17, Wauchope, *The Black Watch in the Great War,* II, p.168 & p.270. The attack opposite Poelcapelle was mainly carried out by 154 Bde and the 9th Royal Scots.
57. Wauchope, *The Black Watch in the Great War,* III, p.166. See Putkowski & Sykes, *Shot at Dawn,* p.205; http://www.telegraph.co.uk/news/1526443/The-306-executed-men.html, accessed 18 Feb 2017.
58. '8BW War Diary', 28 & 29–31 Jul 1917, App 2, BWRA 0248. McLeod, diary, 5 & 9 Oct 1917, BWRA 0891.
59. Maj John Ewing, *History of the 9th Scottish Division,* pp.239–240.
60. Maj W. French (for Lt Col), Narrative of Operations 10–14 Oct 1917, '8BW War Diary', App 8, BWRA 0248. Casualties were 7 officers and 294 ORs (3 officers and 40 ORs killed, 4 officers and 166 ORs wounded, 1 officer dying of his wounds, 82 ORs missing.) Ewing, *History of the 9th Scottish Division,* pp.243–4.
61. Macdonald to My Dear Mary, 4 Nov 1917, BWM 2014.689. Ossian was the narrator in the epic poems of James Macpherson (1736–96).
62. Badenoch, 4/5BW (from 7BW), 'My Recollections', p.13, BWRA 0771. See '4/5BW War Diary', 8–14 & 19 Oct, 1 & 8 Nov 1917, BWRA 0240.
63. Lt P. King, 2/5th East Lancashire Regiment, quoted in Lyn Macdonald, *They Called it Passchendaele,* p.218.

64. Macdonald to My Dear Mary, 4 Nov 1917, BWM 2014.689. Maj W. French for Lt Col, '8BW War Diary', Nov 1917, App, BWRA 0248.
65. Lt Col V.M. Fortune, quoted in Topp, *The 42nd, C.E.F. Royal Highlanders of Canada in the Great War*, p.172. Wauchope, *The Black Watch in the Great War*, I, p.70 says that the Canadians helped to guide 1BW to their positions (in recognition of which they were granted the right to wear the Red Hackle. This is not mentioned in Topp nor in '1BW War Diary', Nov 1918, App, II, 2, BWRA 0237).
66. See Lyn Macdonald, *They Called it Passchendaele*, p.241. She says a quarter of a million were killed wounded or missing 'in the last three months alone'. German casualties were comparable. Wauchope, *The Black Watch in the Great War*, I, p.71 records 1BW casualties: 4 officers, 86 ORs.
67. *Lokal-Anzeiger*, 18 Mar 1917, quoted in Bewsher, *History of the 51st Highland Division*, p.233.
68. '6BW War Diary', 13 Nov 1917, BWRA 0243.
69. Haig, quoted in Bewsher, *History of the 51st Highland Division*, p.235.
70. Bewsher, *History of the 51st Highland Division*, p.238. Cameron, 7BW, 'Army Life and Trials', pp. 14–15, BWRA 0805.
71. '6BW War Diary', Narrative of Events during the Battle, 20 Nov 1917, App F, p.12, BWRA 0243. Cameron, 'Army Life and Trials', p.15, BWRA 0805.
72. '7BW War Diary', 20–21 Nov 1917, App 3, BWRA 0246.
73. '6BW War Diary', Narrative of Events during the Battle, 20 Nov 1917, App F, pp.14–15, BWRA 0243; Cameron, 'Army Life and Trials', pp.15–16, BWRA 0805.
74. '6BW War Diary', Narrative of Events during the Battle, 20 Nov 1917, App F, p.15, BWRA 0243. '7BW War Diary', 22–23 Nov 1917, App 4, BWRA 0246.
75. Cameron, 'Army Life and Trials', p.16, BWRA 0805, talking specifically about the Scots Guards which relieved 7BW. He developed an abscess on his shoulder requiring an operation and was sent home to convalesce.
76. See Liddell-Hart, *A History of the First World War*, pp.443–8 & Bryn Hammond, *Cambrai: The Myth of the First Great Tank Battle*, pp.83–6, 431. Lt Col N.D. Campbell states 6BW casualties: 1 officer & 8 ORs killed; 2 officers and 34 ORs wounded, '1/6BW War Diary', 28 Nov 1917, App 6, BWRA 0243.' Maj Hugh Mackintosh states 7BW casualties: 1 officer & 8 ORs killed; 1 officer & 94 ORs wounded, 1 missing, '1/7BW War Diary', Dec 1917, App, 3.
77. The Battle of Caporetto (24 Oct–19 Nov 1917) led to the collapse of the Italian Second Army. After Caporetto the Italians were reinforced by 6 French and 5 British Inf Divs. A year later Italy defeated Austria-Hungary at Vittorio Veneto, concluding the war on the Italian front.
78. Wavell, *Allenby*, p.168. Wavell's service in the trenches in 1914–15 had resulted in the loss of his left eye. Brevet i.e. promotion to a higher rank but without the corresponding pay. He had been promoted major in May 1916.
79. Cpl David Livingstone, 14BW, 'On Active Service and Otherwise, some notes and recollections from a Wanderer's Diary', pp.19–21, BWRA 0892.
80. Wavell, *The Palestine Campaigns*, p.117. Livingstone, 'On Active Service', pp.21, 22, BWRA 0892.

81. Livingstone, 'On Active Service', p.23, BWRA 0892. Livingstone had dislocated his ankle and was 'hors de combat for good in this affair'.
82. Ogilvie, *Fife and Forfar Yeomanry*, p.68. See also Wauchope, *The Black Watch in the Great War*, III, pp.318–19: 3 officers and 47 ORs were killed, 5 officers and 182 ORs wounded, of whom 13 later died. When Lt Col Gilmour was wounded Maj J. Younger assumed command. Lt John Donaldson Kinniburgh died on 6 Nov 1917 aged 23.
83. Livingstone, 'On Active Service', pp.26–7, BWRA 0892.
84. '14BW War Diary', App.2, 12-23 Dec, 1917 & 8 Dec 1917, BWRA 0251. See Ogilvie, *Fife & Forfar Yeomanry*, p.87 & p.104, repeated in Wauchope, *The Black Watch in the Great War*, III, p.321. The guard was made up of 1 officer and 50 ORs.
85. Ogilvie, *Fife & Forfar Yeomanry*, pp.99–100; '14BW War Diary', App 4, 28 Dec 1917, BWRA 0251. Wauchope, *The Black Watch in the Great War*, III, p.321: 3 officers, 11 ORs killed, 3 officers, 38 ORs wounded. Figures in '14BW War Diary' differ: see 27 & 28 Dec 1917 App 3–4, BWRA 0251.
86. Wauchope, *The Black Watch in the Great War*, I, p.268. Maude died on 18 Nov 1917.
87. Stewart to Sweetheart from Somewhere, Sat 15 Dec, & to his wife from Basra, 25 Dec 1917. The 'sudden' orders were received at 8 a.m. on 7 Dec 1917.
88. Eric Linklater (1899–1974), 4/5BW, *The Man on my Back*, 1941, pp.34–6; see also *Fanfare for a Tin Hat*, 1970 and *Private Angelo*, 1946 (fiction).
89. Macdonald to My Dear Mary, 8 & 7 Dec 1917, BWM 2014.689.
90. The 11 were 1st, 2nd, 4/5th, 6th, 7th, 8th, 9th, 10th, 12th, 13th, 14th. See Wauchope, *The Black Watch in the Great War*, I, pp.130, 322, II, pp.111, 216, 324, III, pp.84, 186, 261, 290, 306, 335 for a further breakdown.
91. Stratton to Jean, 24 Dec 1917, 'Letters Home', BWRA 1004.
92. Tom E. Kempshall, FSA Scot. The poem (dated Feb 1979) is dedicated to those of the 42nd and 13th Royal Highlanders of Canada who fought at Passchendaele. Sgt Kempshall, who served in both 1BW and 2BW, was known as a horticulturist, botanist, ornithologist, numismatist, cartophilist, antiquarian, Scottish historian, author, lecturer and ex-schoolmaster! Samson Scrapbook III, pp.315–16, BWRA 0843/12.

7. 1918: Weary of War

1. Charles Chaloner Lindsey, C.F., May 1918, 'The Old "Jocks" (A Medley)', *Red Hackle*, Jul 1923, p.32. He became temporary Chaplain to the Forces, 12 Mar 1917, Supplement to the *London Gazette*, 28 Mar 1917, p.3071.
2. Rev Coll Macdonald, 8BW, to Dear Mary, 8 Jan 1918, BWM 2014.689.
3. Capt R.E. Badenoch, MC, 4/5BW, 'My Recollections of the First World War', pp.13–14, BWRA 0771.
4. Lt Col Evans had won the VC at Zonnebeke, Oct 1917, as CO, 1st Lincolnshire Regt, 21st Div.

5. 2nd Lt R.K. Arbuthnott, 1BW, diary, 8 Jan 1918, Arbuthnott private papers. Cpl Albert Hay, 1BW, 'Soldiering', memoir, 1917–21, handwritten in 1935, p.64, BWRA 0073; A.G. Wauchope, *The Black Watch in the Great War*, I, pp.75–6. Pte Eric Linklater, 4/5BW, quoted in Eric & Andro Linklater, *The Black Watch*, p.169.
6. Linklater, *The Black Watch*, pp.169–70. Miller, 4/5BW, 'Fifty Years After', *Red Hackle*, Nov 2015, p.20.
7. Pte William Couston, 7BW, to My Dearest Mum, 8 Mar 1918, BWRA 0806. 51HD was now commanded by Maj Gen Carter Campbell; Harper was commanding IV Corps, Third Army to which 51HD belonged. Macdonald to Dear Mary, 16 Jan 1918, BWM 2014.689.
8. Wauchope, *The Black Watch in the Great War*, III, p.167. The number of battalions in a division had been reduced from 13 to 10, involving some reorganisation: 9BW moved from 44 Bde to 46 Bde.
9. Maj John Ewing, *History of the 9th Scottish Division*, p.260.
10. Wauchope, *The Black Watch in the Great War*, II, p.93.
11. Miller, 4/5BW, 'Fifty Years After', *Red Hackle*, Nov 2015, p.20.
12. Ibid. See also Wauchope, *The Black Watch in the Great War* II, p.96, & '4/5BW War Diary', 23 Mar 1918, App 3, BWRA 0240. Lt Col Neill Campbell had sprained his ankle.
13. Badenoch, 'My Recollections', p.14, BWRA 0771. Wauchope, *The Black Watch in the Great War* II, p.94, says only about 150 men remained out of the 600 who had gone into action on the 21st. Between 21 and 31 Mar 1918, 27 officers were killed, wounded, missing, or sick, '4/5BW War Diary', App 9, BWRA 0240.
14. Eric Linklater, *The Man on my Back*, p.38.
15. Maj W.D. Campbell, Report on Fighting 21–26 Mar 1918, '6BW War Diary', App A, p.3, BWRA 0243; also in Wauchope, *The Black Watch in the Great War*, II, pp.186. During 5 days' fighting 6BW's casualties were 20 officers and 620 ORs.
16. Pte Josiah Ashworth, 7BW, 'A POW's Tale', p.7, BWM. Wauchope, *The Black Watch in the Great War*, II, pp.299–300, 301. By the afternoon of 22 Mar, only 2 officers (Lt Col McClintock and the Adjt Capt Reid) remained fit, out of 19 who had gone into action; 23 officers and 627 ORs were recorded as killed, wounded or missing from the 39 officers and 941 ORs who went into battle.
17. Maj Keir was wounded on 14 Apr, command passing to Lt Col Millar, 'Narratives 7BW', *Red Hackle*, Jul 1921, p.49.
18. Couston, to My Dearest Mum, 28 Mar 1918, BWRA 0806.
19. Ewing, *History of the 9th Scottish Division*, pp.261, 293–4. Wauchope, *The Black Watch in the Great War*, III, pp.52, 55–6: 12 officers and 437 ORs killed, wounded or missing (many of the latter found later as POWs).
20. XVII Corps CO, later Gen Sir Charles Fergusson, GCB, GCMG, DSO, MVO (1865–1951), quoted in Wauchope, *The Black Watch in the Great War*, III, p.171.
21. Linklater, *The Man on My Back*, p.42.
22. Wauchope, *The Black Watch in the Great War*, II, p.95. Badenoch, 'My Recollections', p.14, BWRA 0771.

23. Linklater, *The Man on My Back*, p.44. The Special Order of the Day was issued on 11 Apr 1918. Linklater was wounded soon afterwards concluding his 'little while of active service', p.46. His tin hat is in the possession of his son, Magnus.
24. Arbuthnott, diary, 3 Apr 1918, Arbuthnott private papers. Hay, 'Soldiering', 12 Apr 1918, p.64 & p.70, BWRA 0073.
25. F.W. Bewsher, *History of the 51st Highland Division*, p.296.
26. Bewsher, *History of the 51st Highland Division*, p.319, describes congestion but does not mention reports that the 51st, in poor visibility, mistakenly fired on Portuguese troops. Nor does Churchill, *The World Crisis, 1916–1918*, p.430.
27. Maj W.P. Campbell, '6BW War Diary', 11 Apr 1918, Movements 9–15 Apr 1918, App B, p.10, BWRA 0243. Wauchope, *The Black Watch in the Great War*, II, pp.303, 187.
28. Campbell, '6BW War Diary', 12 Apr 1918, p.10, BWRA 0243.
29. Bewsher, *History of the 51st Highland Division*, p.318. It was also known as the Battle of the River Lawe.
30. Lt Col Rowland Tarleton had been wounded at Loos serving with 1BW. Wauchope, *The Black Watch in the Great War*, II, pp.186–8. See also '6BW War Diary', Movements 9–15 Apr 1918, App B, p.9, BWRA 0243. Between 9 and 13 Apr, 7BW losses recorded as 1 officer and 7 ORs killed, 5 officers and 660 ORs wounded, with 2 officers and 162 ORs missing; among the wounded was Maj Keir.
31. Rev Coll Macdonald, 8BW, letter, 14 Apr 1918, BWM 2014.689.
32. Hay, 'Soldiering', memoir, pp.72–4, 76–80, BWRA 0073.
33. Ibid, p.84. 'Narratives 1BW', 18 Apr 1918, *Red Hackle*, Oct 1921, p.49.
34. Hay, 1BW, 'Soldiering', 18 Apr 1918, pp.84–8, 90, BWRA 0073. Two soldiers, Ptes Bernard Carson and Robert Sime, were killed; whereas Carson was an old soldier, Sime, aged 19, had been in France for only 2 weeks.
35. Since Albert Hay wrote his memoir in 1935 he must have been aware of the novel by Erich Remarque (1898–1970), *All Quiet on the Western Front*, published in English in 1929.
36. Hay, 'Soldiering', pp.92–100, BWRA 0073. Wauchope, *The Black Watch in the Great War*, I, p.89: 15 officers and 366 ORs were casualties.
37. Hay, 'Soldiering', pp.104–6, BWRA 0073. Statistics from 'Narratives 1BW', *Red Hackle*, Oct 1921, p. 50. Lt Arbuthnott was kept as a POW in Mainz.
38. See W.S. Churchill, *The World Crisis 1916–1918*, p.446. Churchill was now Minister of Munitions.
39. 'Reduced to cadre': reduced in strength to a basic core.
40. Badenoch, 'My Recollections', p.15, BWRA 0771. Lt Col Richard Archibald (Archie) Bulloch took command on 17 May, the amalgamation officially recorded as taking place on 9 Jun 1918, Wauchope, *The Black Watch in the Great War*, II, p.97.
41. Miller, 'Fifty Years After', *Red Hackle*, Nov 2015, p.21. He was now a Lewis gun Sgt. The 70th Inf Div was the first US Div to arrive; the 30th Inf Div was one of two US Divs (the other being the 27th) to break through the Hindenburg Line in the Battle of St Quentin Canal.

42. Wauchope, *The Black Watch in the Great War*, III, pp.174–5. There is no information on 15BW other than that it was formed on 1 Jun in Deal, Kent; see E.A. James, *British Regiments*, p.85.
43. Lt Col Jack Stewart, 2BW, EEF, to Dearest One, 1 Feb 1918, BWM 1024.2A. Ritchie, 'Recollections', p.22, BWRA 1025/83.
44. Stewart, EEF, to Dearest One, 20 Mar 1918, & Somewhere, to Dearest One, 29 Mar 1918, BWM 1024.2A. Cpl David Livingstone, 14BW, 4 Mar 1918, 'On Active Service and Otherwise: some notes and recollections from a Wanderer's Diary', p.27, BWRA 0892.
45. '2BW War Diary', 31 Mar 1918, WO 95/4713; Wauchope, *The Black Watch in the Great War*, I, p.273, 274n1, 279. On 5 Jun a General Routine Order was received prohibiting the wearing of the Red Hackle in the khaki helmet; see '2BW War Diary', 5 Jun 1918, & App 15, 15 Jun 1918, requesting sanction. The order was reversed by 'verbal telephone message from 7th Divisional HQ… to the effect that permission is about to be granted for the wearing of the Red Hackle in the Khaki helmet', WO 95/4713.
46. Wauchope, *The Black Watch in the Great War*, I, p.274; '2BW War Diary', 19 Apr 1918, WO 95/4713; Ritchie, 'Recollections', p.23, BWRA 1025/83.
47. Stewart, Somewhere, to Dearest One, 11 & 15 Apr 1918, BWM 1024.2A.
48. Livingstone, 1 May 1918, 'On Active Service', p.28, BWRA 0892.
49. Quoted by Wavell, in A.P. Wavell, *Allenby*, p.215.
50. Wauchope, *The Black Watch in the Great War*, I, p.275. Stewart, 2BW, to Dearest One, Tues 23 Jul 1917, BWM 1024.2A. Ritchie, 'Recollections, p.23, BWRA 1025/83.
51. John Keegan, *The First World War*, p.401.
52. Livingstone, 14BW, 'On Active Service', pp.30–1, BWRA 0892.
53. 10BW was in 197 Bde, 66th Div, Wauchope, *The Black Watch in the Great War*, III, p.251. Disbanded at Haudricourt in Oct 1918, its members joined 1BW, 6BW and 14BW.
54. Pte Sandy Stratton, 13BW, to Jean, 26 Jun 1918, 'Letters Home from the Front', BWRA 1004.
55. Wauchope, *The Black Watch in the Great War*, III, pp.174–5. It was in 47 Bde, 16th Div.
56. Hay, 'Soldiering', p.130, BWRA 0073.
57. Wauchope, *The Black Watch in the Great War*, I, pp.90–1.
58. Badenoch, 'My Recollections', p.15, BWRA 0771.
59. Ibid, p.16. B Coy was attached to 8th Seaforth Highlanders. Lt McGregor was 'a Canadian'.
60. Ibid, p.17. Badenoch was awarded the MC: 'I may say quite undeservedly but I was glad to say that Sgt Dickson got the DCM and the French decoration *Médale Militaire* which is only given to Generals and ORs and carries with it the Croix de Guerre.'
61. Pipe Maj Daniel McLeod, 4/5BW, diary 5, 1 Aug 1918, BWRA 0981.
62. GOC 17th French Div to GOC 15th Scottish Div, 27 Aug 1918, quoted in

Wauchope, *The Black Watch in the Great War,* II, pp.100, 101 & photograph. Built 'with the material at hand' by Lt René Puaux, the monument is believed to be the only one erected by the French Army 'on any battlefield in memory of a British formation.' Badenoch, 'My Recollections', p.18, BWRA 0771: 'Lt Stewart reached the furthest point.' Badenoch returned to Buzancy 'in the early '30s'.

63. '6BW War Diary', 27 Jul, App F (Tarleton), 'Operations 19–31 Jul 1918', pp.16–22, BWRA 0243; see also Wauchope, *The Black Watch in the Great War,* II, pp.193–6 (& pp.307–9 for details on 7BW). 6BW casualties in Champagne were 5 officers and 45 ORs killed, 20 officers and 350 ORs wounded, 1 officer, 33 ORs missing.
64. Macdonald to My Dear Mary, 30 May 1918, BWM 2014.689.
65. '8BW War Diary', App A, 'Narrative of Operations on 19 Jul 1918', p.3, BWRA 0248.
66. 'Narratives 8BW', 19 & 21 Jul 1918, *Red Hackle,* Apr 1921, p.31; Wauchope, *The Black Watch in the Great War,* III, p.61: a total of 226 killed, wounded or missing.
67. '2BW War Diary', 'Strictly Secret' instructions, (Sd) N.M. Ritchie, Capt & Adjt, 19 Sep 1918 (4), WO 95/4713, TNA. See Wauchope, *The Black Watch in the Great War,* I, p.281.
68. Wavell, *Allenby,* p.225.
69. Lt Col J. Stewart, 'British attack on the Tabsor system of enemy trenches, 19 Sep 1918', pp.1–3; see also Stewart, 'Account of the movements of the 2nd Battalion The Black Watch, 18 Sep–20 Oct', p.2, BWRA 0172. He dated this account 1917 but the events he describes are in 1918.
70. Ritchie, 'Recollections', pp.23–5, BWRA 1025/83.
71. Wauchope, *The Black Watch in the Great War,* I, pp.289–90. Ritchie, 'Recollections', p.25, BWRA 1025/83, & Stewart, 'Account of the movements… 18 Sep–30 Oct', p.1, BWRA 0172. A brigade of Australian Light Horse passed through Damascus on 1 Oct 1918. See Stewart's description of 'mopping up' actions, 'British attack on the Tabsor system of enemy trenches', p.5, BWRA 0172.
72. Wavell, *Allenby,* p.245. See Schofield, *Wavell,* pp.78–9.
73. The Battle of Amiens, also known as the Battle of Picardie. Black Watch battalions active: 1BW, 4/5BW, 6BW, 7BW, 8BW, 2/9BW (which had arrived in late July, 1/9BW having been absorbed by 4/5BW), 10BW, 13BW and 14BW. 2BW was in Palestine.
74. Hay, 'Soldiering', pp.154–8, BWRA 0073.
75. Ibid. 1BW also fought at Épehy (with 14BW) and at St Quentin Canal.
76. Wauchope, *The Black Watch in the Great War,* II, p.103. 4/5BW was now in the 15th Scottish Division.
77. Pte James Jack, diary, Sat 1 Sep 1918, BWRA 0970. Livingstone, 14BW, p.36, 'On Active Service', pp.34–6, BWRA 089; he was wounded on 22 Sep 1918.
78. See Wauchope, *The Black Watch in the Great War,* III, pp.64–9; casualties amounted to 178 all ranks.
79. Hay, 'Soldiering', pp.208–10, BWRA 0073.
80. Gen Guillaumat, quoted in *The Scotsman,* 8 Feb 1919, 'Press Cutting Album 1916–1919', p.201, BWRA 0116. The Croix de Guerre, represented by a bronze

cross patée with two crossed swords and a green-and-red ribbon band, continued to be worn by members of 6BW and its successor battalion, 3BW. The Croix de Guerre was pinned on the Regimental Colour on 12 Jul 1919, Wauchope, *The Black Watch in the Great War*, II, pp.196–7, 202. 'Public Notice, French Honour', *Perthshire Constitutional*, 20 May 1919.

81. Stratton to Father, 9 Oct 1918, 'Letters Home from the Front', BWRA 1004. 'Narratives 13BW', 17 Oct 1918, *Red Hackle*, Oct 1921, p.54.
82. Hay, 'Soldiering', pp.216–18, BWRA 0073.
83. Jack, diary, 22 Oct 1918, BWRA 0970. Lt Col J. Mackenzie, 14BW, The Field, to Mrs Carver, 27 Oct 1918, 'Letters Home', p.55, BWRA 0924. Cumming had joined 14BW from 3BW on 11 Sep 1918. Of the 32 casualties, Cumming was the only officer, Ogilvie, *Fife & Forfar Yeomanry*, p.138.
84. Hay, 'Soldiering', pp.228–30, BWRA 0073.
85. Stratton to Lill, 12 Nov 1918, 'Letters Home from the Front', BWRA 1004. See 'Narratives 13BW', *Red Hackle*, Oct 1921, p.55.
86. Badenoch, 'My Recollections', p.20, BWRA 0771. Austria agreed peace terms on 3 Nov.
87. Hay, 'Soldiering', p.234, BWRA 0073.
88. PM Lloyd George, 5th Lord Mayor's Banquet, Guildhall, quoted in *The Times*, 11 Nov 1918. Jack, diary, Sat 9 Nov 1918, BWRA 0970. Livingstone, 14BW, 'On Active Service', pp.37–8, BWRA 0892.
89. Jack, diary, Mon 11 Nov 1918, BWRA 0970.
90. Livingstone, 'On Active Service', pp.38-9, BWRA 0892. See also Ogilvie, *Fife & Forfar Yeomanry*, p.139.
91. Hay, 'Soldiering', p.234, BWRA 0073. Stratton to Lill, 12 Nov 1918, 'Letters Home from the Front', BWRA 1004.
92. Badenoch, 'My Recollections', pp.20–1, BWRA 0771. Miller, 'Fifty Years After', *Red Hackle*, Nov 2015, p.21.
93. Ritchie, 'Recollections', p.25, BWRA 1025/83, & Wauchope, *The Black Watch in the Great War*, I, p.290. It is believed the 'Spanish influenza' was brought in by US troops. Ashworth, 7BW, 'A POW's Tale', 21 Mar–20 Dec 1918, BWM. Wauchope, *The Black Watch in the Great War*, III, p.69. See also '13BW War Diary', 11 Nov 1918, App 4, BWRA 0251, & '14BW War Diary', 11 Nov 1918, App 2, BWRA 0251 for their movements.
94. FM Sir Douglas Haig, 'Special Order of the Day, General HQ 13 Nov 1918', Misc. Files, Marindin private papers, Blair Adam.
95. See Wauchope, *The Black Watch in the Great War*, I, pp.130, 322; II, pp.111, 216, 324; III, pp.84, 186, 261, 290, 306, 335 for a further breakdown of casualties. Hay, 'Soldiering', p.4, BWRA 0073.
96. Lindsey, C.F., May 1918, 'The Old "Jocks" (A Medley)', *Red Hackle*, Jul 1923, p.32.

8. Their Name Liveth For Evermore

1. Anon. *Red Hackle,* Jan 1922, p.27. Ecclesiasticus 44:14 was used by Rudyard Kipling when serving on the Imperial War Graves Commission (now Commonwealth War Graves Commission) and on the Stones of Remembrance in all but the smallest of the cemeteries. Also inscribed on the monument in the gardens of Balhousie Castle, Perth.
2. A.P. Wavell, *Other Men's Flowers,* p.372.
3. Arthur Mee, *Enchanted Land, King's England,* Hodder & Stoughton, 1936, identified 32 'Thankful Villages' in England and Wales, which had not lost a member of the community.
4. *Statistics of the Military Effort of the British Empire, 1914–1920*, p.739, gives the figure of 1,048,053 killed, missing or taken prisoner, 2,035,965 wounded in all theatres to 11 Nov 1918; Bernard Fergusson, *Short History*, p.99; A.G. Wauchope, *History of The Black Watch,* I, p.vii, says 'some thirty thousand' & 8,000 killed. See Trevor Royle, *Flowers of the Forest*, p.284, who says 10,000, emphasising that 'it is impossible to get absolute agreement on the exact number of Scottish casualties'. Statistics for The Black Watch on the Scottish Memorial: 566 officers and 9,459 ORs.
5. 'The Black Watch in 1914, 2275 Cpl Frank MacFarlane, MSM, III – The First Battles, France 1914', *Red Hackle,* Dec 1985, p.10. See 'Narratives 1BW', *Red Hackle,* Oct 1921, p.52, & 'Narratives 2BW', *Red Hackle,* Jan 1922, p.50, for list of officers & ORs who served continuously. *North-China Daily News,* 24 Mar 1937 states that Capt Richard Wood joined 2BW in 1914 serving 'for the full duration of hostilities,' but he is not in BW records.
6. Gen Sir Neil Ritchie, 'Recollections', p.25 & p.9, BWRA 1025/83.
7. Their eldest son and heir, Patrick, Lord Glamis, 5BW, had returned home in 1915 having been accidentally wounded cleaning his pistol. See *The Dundee Advertiser,* 9 Feb 1915, *The Scotsman,* 15 May 1915, *Daily Telegraph,* 12 Oct 1915, Press Cutting Album BWRA 0500 & 0114.
8. Ritchie, 'Recollections', p.25, BWRA 1025/83.
9. Reduced to cadre i.e. reduced in strength to a basic core. 'Narratives 8BW, 9BW, 10BW', *Red Hackle,* Apr 1921, pp.27–44. There were further cuts in army wages in 1925 and 1931. See John Muir, CO 4th/5th to Maj A.C.C. Brodie, 14 Apr 1952, BWRA 0844/085. Miller, 'Fifty Years After', memoir, *Red Hackle,* Nov 2015, p.21.
10. Eric & Andro Linklater, *The Black Watch,* p.174. See also 'The Strength of a Regiment', p.1, Acc 101588/58, NLS.
11. 'Service Chart 1914–18', Fortune private papers. Having briefly commanded 46 Bde, 15th Scottish Div, before its disbandment, Lt Col Fortune took command of 8BW in Apr 1919. Maj Colin Innes, 'Three Generations', *Red Hackle,* May 2006, p.23. On his death, Lt Col Sydney Innes requested all his diaries to be destroyed.
12. Andrews, *Haunting Years,* pp.5–7. Joseph Gray's history of 'The 4th Black Watch in the Great War' was published in the *Dundee Advertiser*, 3 Dec 1917–7 Jan 1918. He acknowledged the assistance of 'many of my comrades' especially Sgt John

Bowman, RQMS Dryden, CQMS Beedie and Sgt Maj John Milne for assistance in writing about 'incidents in which I did not myself take part'. His paintings included: *The 4th Black Watch Bivouac on the Night of the Battle of Neuve Chapelle*, *A Ration Party of the 4th Black Watch at the Battle of Neuve Chapelle 1915* and *The 4th Battalion The Black Watch in the Attack, 1915*.

13. The BW Association had its origins in the Old Comrades Association. See H.McL. Clark, 'A Brief History of the Black Watch Association', *Red Hackle*, Dec 1998, p.17–18. He says attempts to found the Association were made in 1874 but the date normally given is 1873, since the BW Association was in its '46th year' in 1919.
14. Minute book, General Committee & Annual General Meetings, 27/9/1919–28/4/1934, BWRA 0880/1. It is generally agreed that the wearing of the Red Hackle evolved as a means of identification until the right was exclusively granted to the Regiment in 1822. See Victoria Schofield, *The Highland Furies*, pp.186–8; Jack Fortune, research on Geldermalsen, Fortune private papers; 'How the Red Hackle was Won,' *Red Hackle*, Apr 1921, p.11, which, in contemporary thinking, highlights the significance of 5 Jan.
15. Vol. 1, No.1, issued in 1921. No. 162 was issued in Nov 2016. An earlier magazine was published as a 'regimental paper' during 1BW's postings in Subathu and Sitapur, India, in Sep, Oct & Nov 1897, and Jan, Feb, May & Sep 1898. Capt Sammy Watson, MC, worked to ensure *The Red Hackle* recommenced publication after a break during WWII. He also took a great interest in Dunalistair House; see 'Biographical notes' (undated) prepared by his son, late Maj Peter Watson, MC, who served in 7BW in WWII. A feature of the contributions in *The Red Hackle* was for both regular and territorial bns to give a digest of their news, listed as 1st Battalion, 2nd Battalion Notes (1BW, 2BW) etc., with subsections from the various Coys. This practice continues to the present day. Unless on a specialised subject, no authorship is generally given.
16. 'The Black Watch Memorial Home', *Red Hackle*, Apr 1921, p.7. 'Mrs Ethel Shepherd, R.R.C.', *Red Hackle*, Jan 1951, p.4. For her services during the war Mrs Shepherd (d. 1950) was awarded the Royal Red Cross (Second Class), *Dundee Advertiser*, Fri 3 Jan 1919, p.7. The wording on the memorial crest commemorates 'the undying memory of the 8000 officers, non-commissioned officers and men of the Regiment who gave their lives for King and Country in the Great War 1914–1918'. When the memorial home was closed in the 1980s, the crest was sited in the gardens at Balhousie until refurbishment in 2013 when it was placed in the Museum.
17. Museum Notes, *Red Hackle*, Dec 1973, p.4. Now a considerable collection, it is housed in The Black Watch Museum, Balhousie Castle, Perth. Queen's Barracks had become the depot in 1881, with postings there in 1830, 1852 and 1873.
18. Cpl Albert A. Hay, 'Soldiering', memoir, 1917–21, pp.268–70, pp.284, 302, BWRA 0073. After completing 4 years' service he was discharged from the Army in Mar 1921.
19. 'Visit of HRH The Prince of Wales to Allahabad', *Red Hackle*, Apr 1922, p.16.

'Corporals' Mess Notes – 1st Bn', *Red Hackle,* Apr 1922, p.17.

20. 'Refusal to Embark at Dover', reprinted in the *Dundee Advertiser,* 13 Jun 1919, p.2; 'Black Watch Trouble Smoothed Over', *Dundee Advertiser,* 16 Jun 1919, p.2.
21. 'With the Families in Cologne', *Red Hackle,* Apr 1922, p.21.
22. Ritchie, 'Recollections', p.30, BWRA 1025/83.
23. Sgt J. Erskine, 'The Second Battalion in Silesia', *Red Hackle,* Jul 1921, pp.6–7. Wauchope became Col Commandant, 18 Inf Bde, Londonderry. See 'Colonel-Commandant A.G. Wauchope, CMG, CIE, DSO', *Red Hackle,* Oct 1922, p.39. 'The passing of a Commanding Officer is not an uncommon occurrence, coming as it does every four years, but, when the Commanding Officer possesses the soldierly qualities and the personality of Arthur Wauchope, the loss is far more felt.'
24. Erskine, 'The Second Battalion in Silesia,' *Red Hackle,* Jul 1921, p.7. See also Lt Col R. Steward, '2BW, Account of Operations in Silesia', p.3, BWRA 0841/1.
25. Also in 1 Silesian Bde was the 1st Durham Light Infantry, 2nd Prince of Wales's Leinster Regt; 2 Silesian Bde included 1st Royal Irish Regt, 2nd Connaught Rangers and 3rd Middlesex Regt sent from England. 'Narratives 2BW', *Red Hackle,* Jan 1922, p.17, & Apr 1922, pp.18–19.
26. 'The Handing over of Tarnowitz to Poland, 25th June 1922', *Red Hackle,* Oct 1922, p.8.
27. T.E. Kempshall, FSA Scot, written at Coventry in Apr 1979. 'The story is fact – the writer was at the time a Sgt in the 73rd, i.e. 2BW (1922)', Samson Scrapbook III, p.314, BWRA 0843/12.
28. '1BW, Miscellaneous', *Red Hackle,* Apr 1923, p.16 & Jul 1923, p.15. '1BW Notes, Multan', *Red Hackle,* Apr 1926, p.21.
29. Kempshall, 'British Baluchistan 1923', re-constructed from memory at Coventry 1983, from verses written in 1923, Samson Scrapbook III, p.328, BWRA 0843/12. The Afridis inhabit the Tirah around the Khyber Pass.
30. '1BW Notes', Multan, *Red Hackle,* Apr 1926, p.21. Col R.A. Bulloch, Obit. by W.R.N.C., *Red Hackle,* Jan 1964, p.3. He succeeded Lt Col the Hon. Malise Hore-Ruthven.
31. '1BW Record of Service 1873–1939', p.191, BWRA 0080; see pp.192–4 for additional information on 1BW's activities. *India With Pen and Sword: Selected Journalism of F.G. Woolnough,* ed. Keith Woolnough, pp.85–121, privately published 2005. 'The Unseen Messenger' was published in the *Civil and Military Gazette.*
32. '2BW Notes', *Red Hackle,* Oct 1922, pp.17–18.
33. Rt Hon Sir Eric Campbell-Geddes, PC, GCB, GBE, KCB (1875–1937) had been First Lord of the Admiralty (1917–18) before taking up a new office as Minister of Transport (1919–21). '2BW Notes', *Red Hackle,* Oct 1922, p.19.
34. '2BW Notes', *Red Hackle,* Apr 1923, p.18. '4th/5th and 6th/7th Black Watch,' *Red Hackle,* Oct 1922, pp.23, 24. '2BW Notes', *Red Hackle,* Jul 1923, p.18.
35. '2BW Notes', *Red Hackle,* Jan 1924, p.17.
36. '2BW Notes', *Red Hackle,* Jan 1926, p.29, & Apr 1926, p.36.
37. '2BW Notes', *Red Hackle,* Jan 1927, p.31. Bernard Fergusson, *The Watery Maze,*

The Story of Combined Operations, Collins, 1961, p.36, describes combined operations in the 1920s and 30s: 'Occasionally, also, by local enterprise, some *ad hoc* manoeuvre was arranged.' These exercises were the forerunners of amphibious landings so necessary during WWII.

38. Lt Col Guy Rowan-Hamilton was CO 1930–33; his two sons Lt Col Denys Rowan-Hamilton and Maj Angus Rowan-Hamilton both received commissions in 1939. Lt Col Harold Neville Blair (1910–89) was commissioned 31 Jan 1930. His brother James served with 4BW during WWII. His uncle (on his mother's side) was 2nd Lt George Mitchell, killed in 1915 (see Ch.4). Bernard Fergusson was later Brig Baron Ballantrae, KT, GCMG, GCVO, DSO, OBE (1911–80). George Patrick Campbell-Preston, later Lt Col Campbell-Preston, MBE (1911–60) was the son of Col R.C. Campbell-Preston (1865–1929). When David Rose, later Lt Col Rose, DSO, (1912–2010), was 'warned' to join 1BW in Meerut in India, he didn't 'much want to go', having recently lost his father, and so upon payment ('probably for the price of a polo pony'), Campbell-Preston went in his place. See *Off the Record,* p.9, & Lt Col David Rose, DSO, Obit, Rose private papers. His elder brother, Rhoddy, joined the Highland Light Infantry, the second brother Angus, the Argyll & Sutherland Highlanders, while his younger brother Neil served in the French Foreign Legion. See also 'Recruiting Notes', *Red Hackle,* Apr 1925, p.28.
39. David Walker, MBE (1911–92), *Lean, Wind, Lean,* p.35. Lt Neill Grant Duff from Meanee Barracks to Shiela Grant Duff, 13 Oct & 27 Jul 1931, Sokolov Grant Collection, Bodleian Library, Oxford. Another officer commissioned in 1930 was 2nd Lt Charles Neil Molesworth Blair (no relation of 2nd Lt Alexander Neville Blair and his son Col Harold Neville Blair); he chose The Black Watch in succession to his father, Capt James Blair, who fought in South Africa with 2BW. See Ch.1.
40. Rose, *Off the Record,* p.9. Fergusson, *Trumpet in the Hall,* p.18; Gen Sir Arthur Wauchope was his mother's cousin, p.31. Dave Hutton, interview, 'This Happens in War', 4 Nov 2008, BWM. He enlisted in the Army in 1934 aged 17 (having tried to join aged 16 but was turned away!) and celebrated his 100th birthday on 9 Apr 2017.
41. Rose, *Off the Record,* p.12. Earlier tours were in 1775, 1790, 1816–17, 1837–38, 1893–94, *Red Hackle,* Apr 1933, p.3. Hutton, interview, 'This Happens in War', 4 Nov 2008, BWM.
42. 'Pageant, 1934, Olympia – Edinburgh', *Red Hackle,* Jul 1934, pp.40–1. Rose, *Off the Record,* p.13. See the novel by Alexander McArthur & H. Kingsley-Long, *No Mean City,* Neville Spearman, 1956 (first published 1935).
43. Ritchie, 'Recollections', pp.33–4, 37, BWRA 1025/83. Walker, *Lean, Wind, Lean,* p.48.
44. Comments by Maj Alexander C.C. Brodie, DSO, OBE, MC, commissioned in 1932. Col Sir Alan Gomme-Duncan, MC, Obit., *Red Hackle,* Jan 1964, pp.3–4.
45. Walker, *Lean, Wind, Lean,* p.62.
46. Ibid, pp.66–7, 71–2. Walker played golf with the CO, Lt Col Vesey Holt; see p.66 for his description of this 'remarkable man'.

47. '1BW Record of Service 1873–1939', p.201, BWRA 0080. The Maidan was the Brigade Parade Ground. Ritchie, 'Recollections', p.38, BWRA 1025/83.
48. 'Regimental Notes & News', *Red Hackle,* Jan 1935, pp.13–14. Letter from the War Office signed A.L. Widdows, 10 Dec 1934.
49. Rose, *Off the Record,* p.15. Lt Neville Blair, diary, 21 Jan 1936, Cheetham/Metcalfe private papers. '1BW, Khartoum', *Red Hackle,* Apr 1938. See also *Red Hackle*, Oct 1935, pp.41–7. In Dec 1937, a diamond brooch in the shape of the Regimental insignia was presented to Queen Elizabeth, with a Black Watch tartan scarf and a miniature shoulder brooch. See *Red Hackle,* Jan 1938 (between pp.22 & 23).
50. Details of movements from Samson, ed., *Officers of The Black Watch, 1725 to 1986*, p.106, and '1BW Record of Service 1873–1939', pp.201–5, BWRA 0080; Maj Richard Wallace Fleming, memoirs, p.14, BWRA 0974. The other three subalterns were: 'Charles Burrell a very good polo player, young Archie Wavell of whom I was most fond and Jack Monteith.'
51. '1BW, Khartoum', *Red Hackle,* Oct 1937, p.24, & Apr 1938, p.21.
52. Balfour declaration, 17 Nov 1917. http://www.history.com/this-day-in-history/the-balfour-declaration, accessed 18 Feb 2017. See Lt Col A.P.L. Halford-MacLeod, '2nd Battalion The Black Watch in Palestine 1937–1938', *Red Hackle*, Nov 2013, pp.22–4.
53. 'Queen Elizabeth & Lt Col Alexander McLeod', *Red Hackle,* Oct 1937, p.33. The old Colours were handed over at a ceremony at the Scottish National War Memorial on 16 Jul 1938, *Red Hackle,* Oct 1938; Rose scrapbook, private papers. See also 'The Retirement of Lieut.-Colonel A.K. McLeod', *Red Hackle,* Oct 1938, p.11. His father was John Chetham McLeod, Col of the Regiment 1908–14; he had fought in the Indian Mutiny and commanded 1BW 1868–77. See photograph in *Red Hackle,* Dec 1996, p.1.
54. Wauchope had previously served in Berlin as chief of the British Section, Military Allied Commission of Control, Commander of the Home Counties Division and GOC Northern Ireland District. Wavell took command of 6 Infantry Bde on Salisbury Plain and then the 2nd Div at Aldershot.
55. The 'milk and honey advertisement' began: 'To Let.- Maryhill Barracks. Commodious residence in N.W. Glasgow. Owners going abroad. Suitable conversion into flats. Water, h.c. and rain. Usual offices, and some very unusual ones. Apply Messrs Watt & Steward, Jerusalem. Telegraphic address – Milk and Honey, Palestine', *Red Hackle,* Oct 1937, p.33; Palestine Supplement, *Red Hackle,* Oct 1937–38.
56. Maj Harold McLoy (Nobby) Clark, MBE, audio interview, undated (probably 1980s), BWM. He was promoted Sgt Maj in Palestine, & commissioned in 1947. '2BW Notes, Officers' Mess', *Red Hackle,* Jan 1938, p.33. The barracks were later named Allenby Barracks. In the British Mandate period 1920–48 a large military base ('the Aldershot of Palestine') was established at Sarafand.
57. Clark, interview, BWM. Linklater, *The Black Watch,* p.175. See Sgt Maj James Findlay, MBE, MSM, Obit, *Red Hackle,* Aug 1976, p.9. 'It does not mention the near mutiny, but I remember hearing the story from the late Harry Wharton, who

was there,' Thomas B. Smyth to the author, May 2013. See '2BW, Historical Record, Bn Digest Nov 1937', 5 Nov 1937, BWRA 0069. See also Fergusson, *Trumpet in the Hall*, pp.42–4; the fathers of the murdered privates had both served in the Regiment. Cpl Dave Hutton, interview, 12 Mar 2010, Perth.

58. Wavell, quoted in John Connell, *Wavell, Scholar and Soldier,* p.194. Fergusson, *The Trumpet in the Hall,* p.44. Clark, interview, BWM; Linklater, *The Black Watch,* p.175.
59. Matthew Hughes, 'A Very British Affair? British Armed Forces and the Repression of the Arab Revolt in Palestine, 1936–39', *Journal of the Society of Army Historical Research*, 87 (2009), p.357.
60. Maj Richard Fleming, memoirs, BWRA 0974, pp.15, 18. The other officers were 2nd Lt Charles Burrell, 2nd Lt John Monteith, and Lt Robert George 'Wuz' Pollock-McCall.
61. '1BW Notes and News, Details – Dover Castle', *Red Hackle,* Jan 1938, p.23. NB 'details' arrived first, hence the earlier date.
62. '2BW Notes', *Red Hackle,* Apr 1938, p.36.
63. Fleming, memoirs, BWRA 0974, pp.18–19.
64. Clark, interview, BWM. Hutton, interview, Perth, 12 Mar 2010.
65. '2BW Notes, Officers' Mess', & 'Petra' by G.W.M, *Red Hackle,* Jul 1938, pp.32 & 7.
66. '2BW Notes, The departure of HE the High Commissioner', *Red Hackle,* Apr 1938, p.36. Wauchope's successor was Sir Harold MacMichael GCMG, DSO (1882–1969), formerly Governor of Tanganyika (Tanzania) (1934–38). '2BW Notes, Officers' Mess', *Red Hackle,* Jul 1938, p.32. Wavell's official history, *The Palestine Campaigns,* was published in 1929. While in Palestine Wavell was writing a biography of Allenby.
67. Victoria Schofield, *Wavell: Soldier and Statesman,* p.122. This was in Jul 1938. The armoured car had been christened 'Araminta', after Sir Harold MacMichael's daughter, a friend of the Wavell family. Fleming, memoirs, p.18, BWRA 0974.
68. Fleming, memoirs, p.16, BWRA 0974. According to McMicking's son, David, (who heard the story from Fleming) his father was concerned the officers were 'partying too well' and was dressed as a taxi driver. 'As he dropped them off he raised his cap and said "Gentlemen it is not every night that your Commanding Officer gets you back safely".' Maj David McMicking to Lt Gen Sir Alistair Irwin, 26 May 2015. History does not relate whether Fleming was one of the 'inebriated young officers'!
69. Rev David Railton, MC to Herbert Ryle, Dean of Westminster, Aug 1920, quoted in David Crane, *Empires of the Dead,* p.248; see pp.249–53 for the sequence of events leading to the dedication. CSM McRobbie, 'The Funeral of the Unknown Warrior', *Red Hackle*, Apr 1921, p.9; 'How They Chose the Unknown Warrior', *Red Hackle,* Dec 1969, p.5.
70. 'Graves of our dead – The King's Message to the Bereaved', by Harold Child, Boulogne, 13 May, *The Times,* 15 May 1922, pp.10, 18. The speech was written by Rudyard Kipling and delivered at Terlinchtun Cemetery, Boulogne, *The Cambridge Edition of the Poems of Rudyard Kipling*, ed. Thomas Pinney,

Cambridge University Press, 2013. The Tyne Cot Information Centre attributes the quotation to the King's visit to Tyne Cot on 11 May.

71. The Last Post Association, Ypres, www.lastpost.be, accessed 2 Feb 2017. The figure 54,896 is given on the Menin Gate which was completed in 1927. Names are removed as remains are found and identified. Capt the Hon Fergus Bowes-Lyon's name was among those on the Loos Memorial. In 2015 it was confirmed that he was buried in a quarry near Loos and he now has his own headstone in the nearby Quarry Cemetery. See Tom Morgan, 'Queen's search for uncle lost on First World War battlefield', *Daily Telegraph,* 6 Nov 2015.
72. '42nd and 79th High Wood Memorial', *Red Hackle*, Apr 1923, p.4. The location was where the 42nd right joined the 79th left in the Worcester Trench. 'Unveiling and Dedication of High Wood Memorial', 13 Jul 1924, *Red Hackle,* Oct 1924, p.6.
73. The memorial at Dorian was unveiled on 25 Sep 1926 'in glorious memory of 418 officers and 10,282 other ranks' as well as commemorating 1,979 of all ranks who have 'no known grave'; Fraser Brown, 'Black Watch Men from the Argentine', *Red Hackle,* May 2014, pp.23–4.
74. 'Black Watch Memorial at the Royal Military College', *Red Hackle,* Jan 1922, p.10. The dedication is: 'to the memory of the Officers of the Regiment' who were cadets, including 'all other Officers, Warrant Officers, NCOs and Men of the Black Watch who gave their lives in The Great War, 1914–1919'.
75. Inscription, the Black Watch Bay, Edinburgh Castle. The Regimental records state the number of Black Watch dead as 8,960. The three surviving VC holders were present at the dedication ceremony, the 4th recipient, Sgt David Finlay, had been killed in Mesopotamia in 1916.
76. Edward, Prince of Wales, quoted in Gavin Stamp, *The Memorial to the Missing of the Somme,* Profile Books, 2007, pp.148–9.
77. Rudyard Kipling, 'The King's Pilgrimage', 15 May 1922, commemorating George V's visit to the War Cemeteries in France, May 1922, *The Cambridge Edition of the Poems of Rudyard Kipling*, ed. Thomas Pinney, 2013, II, ll.17–18, 50–54, pp. 1399–1401.

9. 1939: Marching Off to War

1. PM Neville Chamberlain, broadcast 3 Sep 1939, http://www.bbc.co.uk/archive/ww2outbreak/7957.shtml?page=txt, accessed 10 Jan 2017.
2. RQMS Ed Meekison, 5BW, 'The Story of a Quartie's War whilst Serving with the 5th Black Watch (RHR)', p.2, BWRA 0878/2.
3. Bernard Fergusson, *The Black Watch and the King's Enemies*, p.17. See Victoria Schofield, *The Highland Furies*, p.7.
4. '1BW Notes, Current Events', *Red Hackle,* Jul 1938, p.23. The bren gun was introduced in 1938, replacing the Lewis gun.
5. '1BW Record of Service 1873–1939', 15 Sep, 24 Sep, 7 Oct 1938, BWRA 0080; '1BW Notes, Current Events', *Red Hackle,* Oct 1938, p.19.
6. Lt Col C.G. (Steve) Stephen, 'History of The Black Watch 1939–41, 1BW', p.1,

BWRA 0902/6. See also Fergusson, *King's Enemies,* pp.17–18.

7. 'Reunion at Battlefield of Waterloo', *The Times,* 25 Aug 1939. See also *Red Hackle,* Apr 1939, pp.46–7, & Jul 1939, p.48. (There were no more issues of *The Red Hackle* until 1946.) They arrived at Zeebrugge on 20 Aug and were to spend 3 nights in Arras, 1 in Brussels and 1 in Ypres. See also *Perthshire Advertiser,* 23 Aug 1939, p.8, col. 5. Stephen, 'History of The Black Watch', p.2, BWRA 0902/6.
8. PM Neville Chamberlain, 3 Sep 1939, http://www.bbc.co.uk/archive/ww2outbreak/7957.shtml?page=txt, accessed 10 Jan 2017. Stephen, 'History of The Black Watch', p.2, BWRA 0902/6.
9. The Hon Mrs Grant Duff to My darling Neill, Tue 5 Sep 1939, Ormond private papers. He was in the Supplementary Reserve.
10. André Maginot (1877–1932) was Min of War 1922–1924, 1929–1930, 1931–1932. At the outbreak of war France had 20 regular divisions and 74 reserve. Lt Col P. Campbell-Preston, 'Saar Spring 1940' (written after the war), transcribed by Andrew Bradford, Feb 2006, BWRA 0902/2.
11. Stephen, 'History of The Black Watch', p.3, BWRA 0902/6.
12. Lt Noel Jardine Paterson, personal diary, quoted in Andrew Bradford, *Escape from St Valéry-en-Caux,* p.17. He had been commissioned into the Regt in 1936, serving with 2BW in Palestine and transferred to 1BW. Stephen, 'History of The Black Watch', p.4, BWRA 0902/6. Once the parade was over the instruments had to be taken to France because the train for Scotland had already left.
13. CSM MacGregor, quoted in Fergusson, *King's Enemies,* p.18–19, and in Trevor Royle, *A Time of Tyrants*, p 52. But see Saul David, *Churchill's Sacrifice*, p.10, who says few men 'were sad to see the back of the kilt.' Stephen, 'History of The Black Watch', p.5, BWRA 0902/6. By minimising the visible differences between units, it was believed that they were contributing to the intelligence vacuum in which they hoped the Germans were operating. The privilege of wearing metal badges was withdrawn 1 Jan 1941.
14. 'French positions improved,' From our own correspondent, Paris, 13 Sep, *The Times,* 14 Sep 1939, p.8.
15. Stephen, 'History of The Black Watch', p.6, BWRA 0902/6.
16. Bradford, *Escape from St Valéry-en-Caux,* pp.18–19. Stephen, 'History of The Black Watch', p.6, BWRA 0902/6.
17. Stephen, 'History of The Black Watch', p.7, BWRA 0902/6. 1BW was in 12 Bde, 4th Div, II Corps. Lt Bill Bradford, 16 Oct 1939 and Jardine Paterson, both quoted in Bradford, *Escape from St Valéry-en-Caux,* p.20.
18. Stephen, 'History of The Black Watch', p.8, BWRA 0902/6.
19. Lt Neill Grant Duff to Mr Perkins, 3/11/39, Ormond private papers. Jardine Paterson quoted in Bradford, *Escape from St Valéry-en-Caux,* p.21.
20. Bradford, 6 & 10 Nov 1939, quoted in Bradford, *Escape from St Valéry-en-Caux,* pp.21, 22. Johann Georg Elser (1903–45) held Hitler responsible for creating misery for the poor by instigating a war. Bad weather meant that Hitler had shortened his speech and left the hall earlier than expected, his early departure saving his life. Elser was held without trial for five years and executed on 9 Apr

1945 in Dachau concentration camp.

21. Stephen, 'History of The Black Watch', p.11, BWRA 0902/6. Bradford, 30 Nov 1939, quoted in Bradford, *Escape from St Valéry-en-Caux*, p.22.
22. Stephen, 'History of The Black Watch', pp.11–12, BWRA 0902/6. After the fall of France in 1940, Emilienne Moreau-Evrard (1898/9–1971) worked for the French Resistance, one of only 6 women to receive the *Ordre de la Libération*. See Bradford, *Escape from St Valéry-en-Caux*, p.22. The visit to Black Watch Farm was on 3 Dec and it is likely the two visits were made on the same day. The 'history' was undoubtedly A.G. Wauchope's *History of The Black Watch*.
23. Stephen, 'History of The Black Watch', p.12, BWRA 0902/6. In mid-Sep, French forces had attacked the German Siegfried line near Saarbrucken, which after WWI had come under French control but, following a plebiscite in 1935, had reverted to Germany. Although a breach was made, the Germans counter-attacked pushing the French back to behind the Maginot Line where their position stabilised.
24. Campbell-Preston, 'Saar Spring 1940', BWRA 0902/2. Bradford, 18 Dec 1939, quoted in Bradford, *Escape from St Valéry-en-Caux*, p.22. Stephen, 'History of The Black Watch', pp.13, 15, BWRA 0902/6.
25. Chamberlain, quoted in Robert C. Self, *Neville Chamberlain: A Biography*, Ashgate, 2006.
26. Bradford, quoted in Bradford, *Escape from St Valéry-en-Caux*, pp.23, 25. He could not write to his family to tell them what they were doing until after 1BW was withdrawn.
27. Stephen, 'History of The Black Watch', p.13, BWRA 0902/6. Bradford, letter home, Hogmanay 1939, quoted in Bradford, *Escape from St Valéry-en-Caux*, p.24.
28. Winston Churchill gave this name to Book II, Vol. I, of his *The Second World War*, describing the period 3 Sep 1939–10 May 1940.
29. David Rose, *Off the Record*, p.22. Maj Lindsay-Orrock-Graham-Scott was known as KB for short.
30. Rose, *Off the Record*, pp.22–3.
31. Col Neville Blair to Rose, 29 Apr 1962, Rose private papers. Blair's position was difficult because 'for security reasons' Tidbury had not given written orders and initially disclaimed responsibility. There is no record of what Tidbury or McMicking said or thought about the incident.
32. Gen Sir Richard O'Connor, KT, GCB, GBE, DSO, MC (1889–1981), Cdr of the 7th (later 6th) Division 1938, Cdr of the Western Desert Force 1940, was taken prisoner 1941. Blair to Rose, 29 Apr 1962, Rose private papers.
33. Rose, *Off the Record,*, p.23. They left 'with clapping and handshaking and mended feelings'.
34. Matthew Hughes, 'A Very British Affair? British Armed Forces and the Repression of the Arab Revolt in Palestine, 1936–39,' *Journal of the Society of Army Historical Research*, 87 (2009), p.358. The other episode took place at Al Bassa in September 1938; see 'Palestine: The First Intifada', BBC *Timewatch*, 27 Mar 1991. Juliet Cheetham to the author, 6 Jan 2015.
35. '2BW, Regimental Milestones', 25 Sep 1939, BWM. Maj Richard Wallace Fleming,

memoirs, p.19, BWRA 0974. Fleming does not comment about Halhul or Muckmas (he was in command of the signals pl).

36. Walker, *Lean, Wind, Lean*, p.132.
37. RSM Docherty who was 'a little old for the post', 5BW War History (draft, sheet 1 of Ch.2), BWRA 0844/082. 5BW was commanded by Lt Col William Cox, a veteran of WWI, having served in 4BW and 4/5BW. He relinquished command on 21 Jul 1940.
38. RQMS Ed Meekison, 'Quartie's War', pp.1–2, BWRA 0878/2. In fact they were only going as far as Dundee – 'quite a few of the lads were back in town the same night.' He went to the Recce Corps until disbanded in 1943, returning to 5BW.
39. '5BW War History' (draft, sheet 1 of Ch.2), BWRA 0844/082. The 9th Div was a second line Territorial division.
40. B.J.G. Madden, DSO, *History of the 6th Battalion The Black Watch*, p.1. He had been commissioned into the Regt in 1929, and served as adjt, 2BW, 1934–37. 6BW was commanded by Lt Col R.H. Hamilton Smith.
41. Henry McKenzie Johnston, interview, London, 22 Sep 2014. He had served in the Young Soldiers Home Defence Bn before joining 6BW. The Croix de Guerre was awarded after the action at Bois de Corton in 1918 (see Ch.7).
42. D.F.O. Russell, *War History of the 7th Bn The Black Watch (R.H.R.)*, pp.1–3. The abbreviation VP might also stand for Vital Points. 7BW was commanded by Lt Col R.H. Robertson.
43. See Maj Gen Sir Victor Fortune, Obit, *Red Hackle*, Apr 1949, p.12. In the interwar years he had commanded the 52nd Lowland Div (also referred to as 52nd Div and Lowland Area, while 51HD was called the 51st Div and Highland Area). Fortune to GOC-in-C Scotland, 'Training of Division (Highland), Dec 1939, Fortune private papers. Fortune, 'Order of the Day, HQ Perth, 15 Sep 1939', quoted in Ernest Reoch, *The St Valéry Story*, p.10.
44. Lt Col Purvis Russell Montgomery, 'Notes on the War Service of 9BW, 1939–44', BWRA 0162/1.
45. Lt Col N. Baxter, 'Notes on 8BW', pp.1–5, BWRA 0157. W.W. Mustard was promoted RQMS and Lt in 1940.
46. Montgomery, 'Notes on the War Service of 9BW', BWRA 0162/1.
47. J.L.R. Samson, *Geordie and Jock*, p.11. Army Order 260/2939. It had been raised in May as a duplicate battalion to the 9th Durham Light Infantry.
48. Walker, *Lean, Wind, Lean*, p.304.

10. 1940: A Colossal Military Disaster

1. Lt Col Frederick (Freddy) Burnaby-Atkins to Andrew Bradford, 2007, quoted in Andrew Bradford, *Escape from St Valéry-en-Caux*, p.55.
2. Lt Col C.G. Stephen, 'History of The Black Watch 1939–41, 1BW', p.17, BWRA 0902/6; Lt Noel Jardine-Paterson, quoted in Bradford, *Escape from St Valéry-en-Caux*, pp.25, 26.
3. Stephen, 'History of The Black Watch', p.18, BWRA 0902/6.

4. Additional elements included the RA, RE, the Royal Corps of Signals, RAMC and the Royal Army Service Corps. A number of attached troops included machine-gunners from the 1st Princess Louise's Kensington Regt and the 7th Royal Northumberland Fusiliers. When 1BW replaced 6BW, the 2nd Seaforth replaced the 6th Seaforth, 152 Bde, and the 1st Gordons, the 6th Gordons, 153 Bde.
5. B.J.G. Madden, *History of the 6th Battalion, The Black Watch*, p.2. Pte George Morrison Daily, 6BW, 'A Soldier's Tale', BWRA 0961; his memoir was written aged 81; he died aged 84. Capt Bill Bradford, letter home, 9 Mar 1940, quoted in Bradford, *Escape from St Valéry en-Caux*, p.27. He was not promoted until Sep 1940 but was given the brevet rank of captain.
6. Capt Neill Grant Duff to Darling Shiela, 3 May 1940, Sokolov Grant papers, Bodleian Library, Oxford.
7. Lt Col P. Campbell-Preston, 'Saar Spring 1940', BWRA 0902/2.
8. Pte Alan Brierley, A Coy, 1BW, quoted in Saul David, *Churchill's Sacrifice*, p.14.
9. Daily, 'A Soldier's Tale', BWRA 0961. Pte Jamie Garvie, 6BW, diary (handwritten), 2 May & 20 Apr 1940, BW 2010.116.1 The diary is incomplete; the last entry for 1941 is 10/7: 'nothing much to relate. Lovely weather'. He then starts again on 14 May 1943: 'resolved to start diary after looking through it'. But there are only a few entries in May and then 4 for Jan 1944.
10. Gen Franz Halder (1884–1972), Hitler's chief of the *Oberkommando des Heeres* (Supreme High Command) (1938–42).
11. Gen Gamelin, 'Special Order of the Day', in '1BW War Diary', WO 167/710, Sep 1939–Jun 1940, TNA. See Richard Doherty, *None Bolder*, p.18; David, *Churchill's Sacrifice*, p.23.
12. Madden, *History of the 6th Battalion*, p.3.
13. W.S. Churchill, *Never Give In!*, p.206. Lord Halifax, former Viceroy of India, remained as Sec of State for Foreign Affairs while Anthony Eden became Sec of State for War. Clement Attlee, 1st Earl Attlee, KG, OM, CH, PC, FRS (1883–1967) was later PM.
14. Madden, *History of the 6th Battalion*, p.3. Garvie, diary, 11 & 13 May 1940, BW 2010.116.1. Daily, 'A Soldier's Tale', BWRA 0961.
15. Capt Ian Macrae, 'War Diary B Coy, 6 BW', p.1, BWRA 0975. Garvie, diary, 14 & 17 May 1940, BW 2010.116.1.
16. Madden, *History of the 6th Battalion*, pp.4, 5.
17. J.L.R. Samson, *Geordie and Jock*, p.11. 1st Tyneside Scottish was in 70 Bde, 23rd Div. See Kevin Baverstock, *Breaking the Panzers*, p.5; A.P. Whitehead, *Harder Than Hammers*, Hunter's of Perth, 1947, p.7. Only about 140 survivors returned to England. In Oct 1940 The Tyneside Scottish joined Alabaster Force, renamed Iceland Force in Iceland, where it remained until Dec 1941.
18. Madden, *History of the 6th Battalion*, p.5. Garvie, diary, 22 & 24 May, BWM 2010.116.1. Daily, 'A Soldier's Tale', BWRA 0961. Daily must be referring to Pte Edward Murphy, killed travelling from Bergwijk/Caster/Smeir on 22 May 1940. He calls him the first casualty, but perhaps he was the first in Daily's platoon.
19. Madden, *History of the 6th Battalion*, p.6. He thought some hot soup given at

Coutrai acted as a soporific!

20. RQMS Ed Meekison, 5BW, 'The Story of a Quartie's War whilst Serving with the 5th Black Watch (RHR)', p.4, BWRA 0878/2; the account starts when he was a Company Clerk but he was quickly promoted CQMS. Lt Col N. Baxter, '8BW Notes', p.6, BWRA 0157.
21. Pte Andrew Meldrum, 'Memoirs of a Conscript', pp.2–3, BWRA 0873.
22. Madden, *History of the 6th Battalion*, p.6. Garvie, diary, Tues/Fri, BWM 2010.116.1.
23. Madden, *History of the 6th Battalion*, p.6; Macrae, 'War Diary B Coy, 6BW', BWRA 0975.
24. Madden, *History of the 6th Battalion*, pp.7–9. He says that the next Christmas, a card was received from Gen Franklin, Cdr, 5th Div, 'thanking the Battalion for their fine counter-attack'.
25. Madden, *History of the 6th Battalion*, p.9: 5 units – 'ourselves, Royal Fusiliers of our Brigade and the Grenadier Guards, Oxfords and Bucks and Gordons – had troops in the area.' Garvie, diary, Mon 27 May 1940, BWM 2010.116.1.
26. Madden, *History of the 6th Battalion*, pp.9, 13.
27. Macrae, 'War Diary B Coy, 6 BW', p.4, BWRA 0975. Madden, *History of the 6th Battalion*, p.14. Lt Col Archibald Morden Carthew had dropped his double-barrelled name (Carthew-Yorstoun), under which his father had commanded 1BW during the Boer War.
28. Garvie, diary, BWM 2010.116.1; the dates of his diary at this stage are unclear.
29. Madden, *History of the 6th Battalion*, pp.14–15. Garvie, diary, 31 May 1940, BWM 2010.116.1.
30. Madden, *History of the 6th Battalion*, p.15. He says the 'blood-stained beaches' was 'largely a journalistic phantasy'. Information on singing 'The Gallant Forty-Twa' from Fergusson, *King's Enemies*, p.31.
31. Daily, 'A Soldier's Tale', BWRA 0961. Maj George Grant, 6BW, interview, Perth, 17 Oct 2013.
32. Daily, 'A Soldier's Tale', BWRA 0961.
33. Ibid. Grant, interview, 17 Oct 2013. Madden, *History of the 6th Battalion*, pp.16 & 9n*.
34. Daily, 'A Soldier's Tale', BWRA 0961. Between 20 May and 3 Jun, there were 66 fatalities in 6BW, many on the beaches of Dunkirk.
35. Richard Holmes, *Oxford Companion to Military History*, p.267: 338,000 in total; Max Hastings, *All Hell Let Loose*, p.66. Churchill, *Never Give In!*, pp.216, 218.
36. Capt Neill Grant Duff to Dear Mum, 23 May 1940, handwritten in pencil, Ormond private papers. Unless otherwise stated all officers and ORs cited in notes 36–76 are in 1BW.
37. Lt Col Honeyman, 'Notes on Operations in France 24 May–12 Jun 1940', p.1, BWRA 0902/4, also BWRA 0141 (Stephen was no longer with 1BW. When he wrote his 'History' he included Honeyman's account verbatim). He says they boarded the train on 24/25 May but this appears to be incorrect.
38. Bradford, quoted in Bradford, *Escape from St Valéry*, p.42. Honeyman, 'Notes

on Operations in France', p.1, BWRA 0902/4, also BWRA 0141. See also T.W. Garside, 'Withdrawal from the Somme, France 1940', BWM.

39. Burnaby-Atkins to Lt Gen Sir Alistair Irwin, 23 Sep 2004, File d/ag.006/4 correspondence, Irwin private papers; Burnaby-Atkins, 'One Short Day in May', *Red Hackle*, May 2005, p.20. See also Bradford, *Escape from St Valéry*, p.44: the attack took place 'on French orders without consultation with Divisional HQ. This was in direct contravention of the agreement between the French and British.'

40. Later Gen Charles de Gaulle (1890–1970), leader of the Free French, founder of the French 5th Republic, President 1959–69. See Linklater, *Highland Division*, frontispiece; Lt Col Swinburn, quoted in Ernest Reoch, *The St Valéry Story*, p.81. While in captivity Swinburn wrote the Divisional Diary. Reoch, Royal Army Service Corps, was a former journalist for the *Evening News*, Perth. He remained a POW throughout the war, *Evening News,* 28 Mar 1945, Fortune private papers.

41. Bradford, *Escape from St Valéry*, p.45.

42. Maj Gen Victor Fortune, 5/6 Jun – Midnight 1940, to Dear General (via Liaison Officer, Capt G. Koch de Gooreynd), communicated to Lt Gen James Marshall-Cornwall, HQ French Tenth Army, in Norman Force, & Marshall-Cornwall to Fortune, 6 & 7 Jun 1940, both in WO 167/1405, TNA.

43. Honeyman, 'Notes on Operations in France', p.2, BWRA 0902/4. Walker, *Lean, Wind, Lean,* pp.134–5.

44. Honeyman, 'Notes on Operations in France', p.2, BWRA 0902/4. Pte James Clarke, 1BW, memoir, p.2, BWRA 0915. Burnaby-Atkins to Bradford, 2007, quoted in Bradford, *Escape from St Valéry*, p.55.

45. An evacuation from Dieppe was not considered. See David, *Churchill's Sacrifice*, p.166: 'Perhaps the greatest tragedy of this campaign was that General Fortune chose the port of Le Havre and not Dieppe as his point of embarkation… at least part of the explanation is that General Fortune had been led to believe that Dieppe harbour was unsuitable for embarkation.'

46. After 1BW was put in 153 Bde, 4BW had gone into Divisional Reserve 'and then took our place in 154 Bde, which explains why ourselves and 1 Gordons (two Regular Bns) were captured with 153 Bgd at St Valéry', says Honeyman, 'Notes on Operations in France', p.2, BWRA 0902/4. See H. Sebag-Montefiore, *Dunkirk*, p.459, for information about the stand made by the 4th Border Regiment, at Incheville on the river Bresle.

47. Fortune, quoted in Reoch, *The St Valéry Story*, p.192.

48. Gen Erwin Rommel (1891–1944) was known as the Desert Fox. The 7th Panzer Div was nicknamed the Ghost Division for the speed with which it advanced.

49. Bradford, quoted in *Escape from St Valéry*, p.56. Pte J. McCready, writing to Maj J.A. Hopwood to whom he had been batman, quoted in Linklater, *The Highland Division*, p.84.

50. Clarke, 1BW, memoir, p.2, BWRA 0915. See Linklater, *The Highland Division*, p.82: 'Fog had come down, delaying the return of the ships and obscuring from view all the coast.' Lt R.U.E.A. Sandford, memoir, BWRA 0902/5. He was one of 1,350 British and 930 French soldiers who were evacuated. Statistics from

Linklater, *The Highland Division*, p.89. See also his letter to Bradford, 26 Oct 1941 quoted in Bradford, *Escape from St Valéry*, pp.55–8.

51. McCready, quoted in Linklater, *The Highland Division*, p.90. See Roderick Grant, *The 51st Highland Division at War*, p.16; Hugh Sebag-Montefiore, *Dunkirk*, p.478. David, *Churchill's Sacrifice*, p.217, gives statistics of 1,300 British and 900 French. See Pte Victor Mons Osborne, 1BW, 'Flight to Safety', BWM. Under orders to blow up bridges, he was detached from the Div and escaped to Le Havre.
52. Account of Pte Robert Mitchelson, 1BW, POW, 'A Wartime Log for British Prisoners', gift from the War Prisoner Aid of the YMCA, 37 Quai Wilson, Geneva, BWRA 0719. See 'Fallingbostel 1944/45', *Red Hackle*, Nov 2000, pp.18–19.
53. Honeyman, 'Notes on Operations in France', p.1, BWRA 0902/4: 'About 1200 the Chasseurs Alpins forestalled the C.O. by deciding to capitulate' but he has already said that he received orders to capitulate 'about 09.30'; see also Fergusson, 'The Black Watch and the King's Enemies', *Red Hackle*, Apr 1951, p.20. Irwin, later Brig A.D.H. Irwin CBE, DSO, MC, JP (1917–1997), to David, quoted in *Churchill's Sacrifice*, p.323; *Herald Scotland*, 23 Dec 1997.
54. Bradford, quoted in Bradford, *Escape from St Valéry*, pp.56–7. Honeyman, 'Notes on Operations in France', p.1, BWRA 0902/4, says that it was not until those Companies which had been fighting separately joined the rest of the Division about 3 pm that they heard of the general capitulation.
55. Reoch, *The St Valéry Story*, p.214.
56. Bradford, quoted in *Escape from St Valéry*, p.59. Clarke, 1BW, memoir, p.3, BWRA 0915.
57. Maj Gen Victor Fortune to Hon Mrs Adrian Grant Duff, 7 Nov 1940, written with 'special permission of the German authorities', Oflag VIIC/H, Ormond private papers. Official confirmation of Grant Duff's death was not given until Dec 1940. See also: A.V. Holt to Mrs Grant Duff, 4 Nov 1940, Ormond private papers; 'Letters from a Prisoner of War', *Red Hackle*, Apr 1970, pp.8–9.
58. 2nd Lt David Campbell to Barbara (Mrs Neill) Grant Duff, 16 Dec 1940, Oflag VII C/H, Ormond private papers. He received an MC for his command of a fighting patrol. See Doherty, *None Bolder*, p.25; War Diary, WO 167/455, 1BW, 1940, TNA.
59. Churchill, *The Second World War*, II, p.134. See David, *Churchill's Sacrifice*, p.238 for a detailed account. On 12 Jun 2010, Veterans of 51HD attended a commemorative ceremony for the 70th Anniversary of the surrender.
60. Hastings, *All Hell Let Loose*, p.72. Statistics quoted in David, *Churchill's Sacrifice*, p.242. Another prisoner was Andrew Ross, correspondence from his nephew Jack Ross, letter 27 Jun 2012.
61. Walker, *Lean, Wind, Lean*, p.139. He had taken command of A Coy after Capt Nigel Noble was evacuated on 7 Jun due to illness. Bradford, quoted in Bradford, *Escape from St Valéry*, p.59.
62. Clarke, 1BW, memoir, p.3, BWRA 0915. Bradford, quoted in *Escape from St Valéry*, pp.61, 64, 65.
63. Bradford, quoted in *Escape from St Valéry*, p.65. Maj John Mackintosh-Walker,

Seaforth Highlanders, in command of 4th Camerons.

64. Maj Mackintosh-Walker, 'The Diary of an Escape from Germans, 21st June 1940 to 4th August 1940', *Red Hackle*, Jan 1946, p.21; Apr 1946, pp.25–6; Jul 1946, pp.25–7. Over 4,000 Allied service personnel escaped or evaded capture during WWII. Archives available in TNA.
65. See Bradford, Leguevin, Hte Garonne to My Darling Mummie, 8 Oct 1940, quoted in Bradford, *Escape from St Valéry*, p.139. Clarke, 1BW, memoir, pp.13–14, BWRA 0915; Obit, *Red Hackle*, Apr 1990, p.6. Donald Caskie, *The Tartan Pimpernel*, foreword by Mike Hughes, p.viii.
66. Sgt David Philp (c.1920–90), undated letter c.1947, individual accounts of POWs, BWRA 0151. He rejoined 1BW. See his account *Un Ecossais dans le Maquis*, pp.53–4 for Davie Wilson's recapture and death (English version, *Maggy Savoye presente… David Philp, A Scot in the French Resistance: A fantastic adventure throughout occupied France*, p.53). See 'Saint Valéry 1940', *Red Hackle*, May 2000, pp.15–18.
67. 2nd Lt John Moon, 'A Pair of Boots', memoir, BWRA 0714. Depending on where captured, they marched for 14 days covering 220 miles, then travelled in boats, barges & steamers 130 miles taking over 2 days to Wesel on the Rhine and then by train. Information from Donald McLean, 1992, 'POWs, individual accounts, WWII', BWM.
68. Walker, *Lean, Wind, Lean*, p.139–40; 2nd Lt Leslie Hunt, East Surrey Regt, *The Prisoners' Progress: An Illustrated Diary of the Last of the British Army in France – June 1940*, Hutchinson & Co., 1941, gives a pictorial account of the journey which would have been similar to the 51st Highland Div. Stalags were mainly for NCOs and privates but not exclusively. Many in The Black Watch went to Stalag XXB in Marienburg, near Danzig.
69. CSgt D. McKenzie, 'Life as a POW in Germany', individual accounts of POWs, BWRA 0151. Another inmate of Stalag XXA was William Rumgay who managed to escape and join the Polish resistance; he died in 2015 aged 94.
70. LCpl John Grieve, enlisted 1932 with 2BW posted to 1BW 1939, 'Oral History 1999', Thomas B. Smyth research material. McKenzie, 'Life as a POW in Germany', BWRA 0151.
71. Lt Frederick Burnaby-Atkins to Darling Dumps [his mother], 30 Sep 1941, in 'Escape from Prisoner of War Camp Oflag VB', compiled by his nephew, Hugh Burnaby-Atkins, BWM 2012.371. There is an interesting description of constructing the tunnel. Known as 'the Great Escape of Biberach (Oflag VB)' it was made on the night of 13/14 Sep 1941. See 'Message to all families and friends of the 26 escaped British officers', Rowan-Hamilton private papers. During their captivity David Walker and Patrick Campbell-Preston also tried to escape.
72. Col David Thornycroft, '*Nigel and Corona*', Book Reviews, *Red Hackle*, Nov 2011, p.17. First published as *Fowler's Moon*, republished by Nigel Thornycroft's nephew David in 2001.
73. Moon, 'A Pair of Boots', BWRA 0714. 'John was always cheerful in the Bag', J.R.P. Moon, OBE, Obit by EFDC, *Red Hackle*, Apr 1979, p.11. Pte Cameron Walker,

4BW, was repatriated home in 1945, but died soon afterwards from illness. In July 2004 the Hubert family visited Cameron Walker's home village of Dunning. See 'Gratitude to a French Family', *Red Hackle,* Nov 2004, p.5; also Lorne Wallace, 'Private Cameron Walker's Story', *Red Hackle,* Nov 2003, p.5.

74. Lt K.H Sutherland, 'Oral History 1999', Thomas B. Smyth research material. See Major K.H. Sutherland, Obit. by FJB-A., *Red Hackle,* Dec 1968, pp.7–8. His health remained impaired after the war and he retired from the Army in 1955, dying in 1968 aged 46. Walker, *Lean, Wind, Lean*, pp.118, 144; see also pp.107–17 for account of one attempted escape.
75. J.R.L.S(amson), 'But Two Got Home Later', *Red Hackle,* Dec 1987, pp.18–19. Gare died on 29 May 1959, Sgt D. Reid, 1BW, *London Gazette*, 12 Feb 1942, p.705. Reid was also helped by the Tartan Pimpernel, Rev Caskie. Both were later awarded the MM.
76. See Walker, *Lean, Wind, Lean*, p.139. Hon Terrance Prittie, 'At a POW Camp', *Cricketer*, 1944, Fortune private papers. See 'Letters from a Prisoner of War', *Red Hackle*, Apr 1970, pp.8–9 for a number of letters from POW camp. Fortune spent over two years in Schloss Spangenberg, moving to Hadamar and then Limberg hospital when he had a stroke in 1944. The reel was written by Lt Jimmy Atkinson, 7th Argyll & Sutherland Highlanders.
77. Capt (later Lt Col) Gerald Barry, 'War Diaries 1', 1 May 1940, p.8, BWRA 0067. Already in his 40s, he had transferred from the Coldstream Guards and was posted to D Coy. Unless otherwise stated all officers and ORs cited in notes 77-98 are in 2BW.
78. David Rose, *Off the Record,*, p.25; he was 2IC, A Coy. Dave Hutton, 2BW, interview, 'This Happens in War', 4 Nov 2008, BWM.
79. Barry, 'War Diaries 1', 12 Jun 1940, p.13, BWRA 0067.
80. Maj Richard Wallace Fleming, memoir, pp.15, 21, BWRA 0974. In addition to Fleming, three officers transferred back from the 1BW to 2BW: Charles Burrall, Archie John Wavell and Jack Monteith.
81. '2BW Regimental Milestones 1939–1945', BWM. Hutton, interview, 4 Nov 2008, 'This Happens in War', BWM.
82. Fleming, memoir, pp.21-2, BWRA 0974. Barry, 'War Diaries 1' , 8,9,10,11 Aug 1940, p.21, BWRA 0067. Later Maj Gen Arthur Reginald Chater, CB, CVO, DSO, OBE (1896–1979). He had commanded the Somaliland Camel Corps 1927–30 & 1937–40; when he was put in command of the whole force he requested promotion to brigadier. See Andrew Stewart, *The First Victory,* p.72.
83. 'Black Watch Operation Orders. Secret. 16 Aug 1940', Lt Col David Rose scrapbook, Rose private papers. Later Gen Reade Godwin-Austen, KCSI, CB, OBE, MC (1889–1963).
84. Rose, *Off the Record*, p.27.
85. Hutton, interview, 4 Nov 2008, 'This Happens in War', BWM.
86. Fleming, memoir, p.22, BWRA 0974.
87. Rose, *Off the Record*, p.28. He was evacuated to India. Fleming, memoir, p.22, BWRA 0974. Cdr Maurice Vernon, RN, 'Evacuation of Somalia', transcript of

tape (undated), enclosed with letter from Edward Lee, dated 25 Nov 1987, p.19, BWRA 0514. He believed that Gen Wavell intended to evacuate Berbera since it had no value as a port whereas Aden did. 'This information we kept very secret because it wasn't to be generally known – we didn't want the Itis to know that we were evacuating from Berbera.' BWRA 0514. See Stewart, *The First Victory*, pp.71–94, for detailed analysis of the evacuation.

88. 'An epic of Somalia', from Our Correspondent, Durban, 3 Oct 1946, David Rose scrapbook, Rose private papers. Recollection of Sgt Kavanagh, Somaliland Camel Corps, who was repeating 'our General's comments after the attack'.
89. 'How Somaliland was evacuated,' Arthur Merton, *Natal Mercury*, Special Correspondent at Aden (undated), David Rose scrapbook, Rose private papers. Vernon, 'Evacuation of Somalia', transcript, pp.20–1, BWRA 0514.
90. Vernon, 'The Evacuation of British Somaliland', *Red Hackle*, Apr 1988, p.7. David Mountbatten, OBE, DSC (1919–70) had become 3rd Marquis of Milhaven in 1938.
91. Piper MacDonald is commemorated on the Hargeisa memorial. Stats from '2BW Regimental Milestones 1939–45', BWM. Less than 20 from 2BW were wounded.
92. Gen Sir A.P. Wavell to Churchill, telegram, Aug 1940; Dill quoted in Lewin, *The Chief*, p.25, Schofield, *Wavell*, p.153.
93. Barry, 'War Diaries 1', 15 Aug 1940, p.26, BWRA 0067. Fleming, memoir, pp.22–3, BWRA 0974: 'I was made an honorary member of The Black Watch for life.'
94. Fleming, memoir, pp.22–3, BWRA 0974. Barry, 'War Diaries 1', 4–11 Sep 1940, pp.33–4, BWRA 0067; Hutton, interview, 4 Nov 2008, 'This Happens in War', BWM. A popular film was *Three Smart Girls* with Deanna Durbin (Hutton remembered her as Shirley Temple).
95. Meldrum, 'Memoirs of a Conscript', p.4, BWRA 0873. After failing to reach 51HD before the fall of France he joined 2BW in Oct 1940.
96. John McVay to David Rose, 15 Aug 1996. Response to *Off the Record*, Rose private papers. Hutton, additional information, 13 Jan 2016.
97. Fleming, memoir, p.24, BWRA 0974. Fergusson, *King's Enemies*, p.71. Hamish Stewart-Peter, 'Service in the Middle East', p.4, BWRA 0717.
98. Meldrum, 'Memoirs of a Conscript', p.5, BWRA 0873.
99. Douglas Hugen Tobler, 1BW, 'A Brigade Intelligence Officer's Recollection of Manoeuvres', pp.5–6, BWRA 0509. See also D.H. Tobler, *Intelligence in the Desert*, Morriss Printing, 1978, p.16.
100. John McGregor, *Spirit of Angus*, pp.7–9.
101. Adrian Searle, *Isle of Wight at War*, p.93.
102. Baxter, '8BW Notes', pp.6–7, BWRA 0157.
103. Lt Col Purvis Russell Montgomery, 'Notes on the War Service of 9BW 1939–44', BWRA 0162/1.
104. See '10BW Notes', *Red Hackle*, Oct 1946, p.21; Montgomery 'Notes on 10BW', BWRA 0162/2.
105. Stephen, 'History of The Black Watch', BWRA 0902/6. Also included were those who had escaped from France.
106. McGregor, '5BW War History' (draft, sheet 1 of Ch.2), BWRA 0844/082. A new

arrival in The Black Watch was the renowned travel writer, Eric Newby, CBE, MC (1919–2006), who gained a commission as a 2nd Lt in Oct 1940. He later transferred to the Special Boat Section and was captured during an operation off Sicily in Aug 1942, spending the rest of the war as a POW.

107. Churchill, quoted in Hastings Lionel Ismay, *The Memoirs of Lord Ismay*, Heinemann, 1960, p.195. Wavell to Dill, 17 Dec 1940, WO 106/5127, TNA. See Schofield, *Wavell*, pp.157, 158–64.
108. Alfred Tennyson, 'Ulysses', *Idylls of the King and a Selection of Poems*, 1842.

11. 1941: All Hell Broke Loose

1. Pastor Bill Lark, poem, c.1996, in response to *Off the Record*, Rose private papers.
2. Lt Col C.G. Stephen, 'History of The Black Watch 1939–41, 1BW', p.21, BWRA 0902/6.
3. John McGregor, *Spirit of Angus*, p.11.
4. D.F.O. Russell, *War History of the 7th Bn The Black Watch (R.H.R.)*, p.6.
5. See *Red Hackle*, Jul 1946 for more details on 6BW 1940–43. Gibraltar garrison also included battalions from the Somerset Light Infantry, the Devonshire Regiment & the King's Regiment. See Adrian Searle, *Isle of Wight at War.*
6. Lt Col N. Baxter, '8BW Notes', p.7, BWRA 0157.
7. Until his death Wavell maintained that assisting Greece was the correct decision. See A.P. Wavell, 'The British Expedition to Greece', *Army Quarterly*, LIX (Jan 1950), & Victoria Schofield, *Wavell, Soldier and Statesman,* pp.190–3. See also Robin Higham, 'Duty, Honor and Grand Strategy: Churchill, Wavell and Greece, 1941', *Balkan Studies,* 46, pp.180–2.
8. Capt the Hon H.N. Dalrymple, '63 Years on – Some Random Recollections', *Red Hackle,* May 2010, p.22. Unless otherwise stated, all officers and ORs quoted in this chapter are in 2BW.
9. Maj Richard Fleming, memoirs, p.25, BWRA 0974. Maj Hamish Stewart-Peter, 'Service in the Middle East', p.6, BWRA 0717 (he wrote these memoirs in his 80th year, see p.18). Pte Andrew Meldrum, 'Memoirs of a Conscript, Nov 1939–Sep 1945', p.5, BWRA 0873.
10. John McVay to Lt Col David Rose, 15 Aug 1996, in response to *Off the Record*, Rose private papers. 2BW had travelled to Crete on board HMS *York*.
11. Fleming, memoirs, pp.25–6, BWRA 0974. Fleming commended Leigh Fermor's bravery in 'returning to Crete after the evacuation and carrying out a most arduous and again hare-brained operation of capturing and kidnapping a German general.'
12. Fleming, memoirs, p.26, BWRA 0974. Later the 2nd Leicesters and the 1st Argyll & Sutherland Highlanders joined the Brigade. Capt (later Lt Col) Gerald Barry, 'War Diaries, 1', 10 May 1941, p.98, BWRA 0067.
13. 'Most Secret Appreciation – German plan for attack on Crete', prepared by BGS Keith Stewart, quoted in Freyberg, *Bernard Freyberg VC*, p.283. See pp.284–9 for an explanation regarding the use of Ultra intelligence. According to Freyberg,

Wavell wrote in a letter (subsequently destroyed) that 'the authorities in England would prefer to lose Crete rather than risk jeopardizing ULTRA,' Ibid, p.286.

14. J.C. Donaldson, 'Crete – 1941', Correspondence, *Red Hackle,* Dec 1987, p.5. Meldrum, 'Memoirs of a Conscript', p.5, BWRA 0873. Dave Hutton, 2BW, interview, 4 Nov 2008, 'This Happens in War', BWM. McVay to Rose, 15 Aug 1996, in response to *Off the Record*, Rose private papers.
15. Barry, 'War Diaries 1', 20–24 May 1941, p.106, BWRA 0067.
16. Fleming, memoirs, p.26–7, BWRA 0974. Hutton, interview, 4 Nov 2008, 'This Happens in War', BWM. Barry, 'War Diaries 1', 20–24 May 1941, p.107, BWRA 0067. On 20 May 2BW lost 14 men, among them 2nd Lt George 'Snowy' Snowden 'as he tried to bring his carrier into action'; see Fergusson, *King's Enemies*, p.80. He gives the initials T.M. for Snowden, who is listed as George on the Roll of Honour.
17. Capt George Ogilvie to Maj Ronnie Proctor, 18 May 2015, Proctor private papers.
18. Freyberg to Wavell, 20 May 1941, quoted in Churchill, *Second World War*, III, p.254.
19. Barry, 'War Diaries 1', 20–24 May 1941, p.107, BWRA 0067.
20. Hutton, interview, 4 Nov 2008, 'This Happens in War', BWM. Donaldson, 'Letters, Crete 1941', *Red Hackle,* Dec 1987, p.5.
21. Barry, 'War Diaries 1', 20–24 May 1941, p.108, BWRA 0067. Barry, 'Parachutes over Crete', *Blackwood's Magazine*, Feb 1944, pp.81–94, reproduces many of Barry's diary entries; see esp. p.87.
22. Wolfgang Henner, Leberecht Wilhelm and Hans-Joachim Gebhard von Blücher, aged respectively 24, 19 and 17. A 4th brother, Adolf Graf, serving in the German Navy, was relieved of his duties. He died from a gunshot wound while stalking deer in 1944.
23. Dalrymple, '63 Years on – Some Random Recollections', *Red Hackle,* May 2010, p.23.
24. Barry, 'War Diaries 1', 20–24 May 1941, 27 & 28 May 1941, pp.107, 108, 109, BWRA 0067.
25. Fergusson, *King's Enemies*, pp.84, 85. Maj Sir Keith (Colin) Dick-Cunyngham died on 31 Oct from injuries sustained at Tobruk while supervising his Coy's ration truck which hit a minefield.
26. Fleming, memoirs, p.28, BWRA 0974. He does not remember much else until preparing for the evacuation.
27. Wavell to Churchill, 27 May 1941, CHAR 20/39/33, CAC. See also Schofield, *Wavell*, pp.201–2. Fleming, memoirs, p.29, BWRA 0974.
28. Barry, 'War Diaries 1', 29 May 1941, pp.110–11, BWRA 0067. Fergusson, *King's Enemies*, pp.87–8. Stewart-Peter, 'Service in the Middle East', p.20.
29. Freyberg to Wavell, quoted in Freyberg, *Bernard Freyberg VC*, pp.311–12, & Schofield, *Wavell*, p.202.
30. Fleming, memoirs, p.30, BWRA 0974. 'As this entailed delaying the force to a reduced speed of 15 knots for our now overloaded *Hotspur* to catch up, a very brave decision for Admiral Rawlings to have taken.'
31. Meldrum, 'Memoirs of a Conscript', pp.5–6, BWRA 0873.

32. Stewart-Peter, 'Service in the Middle East', pp.21–2, BWRA 0717.
33. Donaldson, 'Letters, Crete 1941', *Red Hackle*, Dec 1987, p.5. HMS *Orion* was Rear Admiral Rawling's flagship. During the crossing, at least 100 had been killed and 200 wounded, including the Captain (fatally).
34. See Fergusson, *King's Enemies*, pp.90–1. Capt George Ogilvie, 1st Royal Highlanders of Canada, Germany, 24 Nov 1960, Graphics Box HMS Dido File, BWM. The painting, *HMS Dido* by Noel Syers (1916–2007), is in the BWM. Capt George Ogilvie, telephone interview, 4 Aug 2015; letter to Maj Ronnie Proctor, 18 May 2015, Proctor private papers. Col Neville Blair, 'Piper George Ogilvie', Correspondence, *Red Hackle*, Apr 1979, p.7, mistakenly states that Ogilvie was evacuated on board HMS *Dido*. See also Blair, 'The Battle of Crete', *Red Hackle*, Aug 1981, p.12, in which he endorsed the evacuation since 'the scant resources then available to the Middle East Headquarters would have made it impossible to continue to supply us from Egypt'.
35. Wavell to Commanders of Formations which served in Crete, and Officers Commanding Units which Served in Crete, GHQ, quoted in A.P. Wavell, *Speaking Generally*, p.24. See Schofield, *Wavell*, p.202.
36. Churchill, *Second World War*, III, p.268. McVay to Rose 15 Aug 1996, in response to *Off the Record*, Rose private papers. During May, 66 officers and men from 2BW were killed, more than a third during the evacuation at sea.
37. Hutton, interview, 4 Nov 2008, 'This Happens in War', BWM. Pipe Maj Roy to Papi, from Middle East Force (undated but probably 19 Sep 1941), 'from your old friend Bobbie'. 'Correspondence, Photographs & Press Cuttings', BWRA 0906, & typewritten memoir of escape, 'Waifs & Strays', BWM. (In the memoir he says he escaped on 21 Jul but in letter to Papi he says 19 Jul.) He left his bagpipes with a Greek family. See Fergusson, *King's Enemies*, pp.85, 95, 328, and Obit, *Red Hackle*, Oct 1960, pp.7–8.
38. Hutton, interview, 4 Nov 2008, 'This Happens in War', BWM.
39. Meldrum, 'Memoirs of a Conscript', p.7, BWRA 0873. FM Henry Maitland Wilson, 1st Baron Wilson, GCB, GBE, DSO (1881–1964).
40. Fleming, memoir, p.32, BWRA 0974. Meldrum, 'Memoirs of a Conscript', pp.7–8. Allied casualties during the 5-week campaign numbered over 3,000, but only 3 of the BW are buried in Damascus.
41. Fleming, memoir, p.32, BWRA 0974.
42. Barry, 'War Diaries 2', 15 & 17 Aug 1941, pp.19–20, BWRA 0067; Fergusson, *King's Enemies*, p.94.
43. Fergusson, *King's Enemies*, p.95. Roy, 'Waifs & Strays', BWM. Lt Col Rusk took command on 19 Aug 1941. While in Somalia he had been seconded to command a Bn of the King's Own African Rifles. Pitcairn who had been commanding the Bn became 2IC.
44. Barry, 'War Diaries 2', 18 Sep & 22 Oct 1941, pp.30 & 40, BWRA 0067.
45. The Afrika Korps was formed 11 Jan 1941, and was officially subordinate to the Italian chain of command in Africa. In mid-1941 an enlarged command structure involved the creation of a German–Italian force, Panzer Group Afrika. On 30 Jan

1942 it was renamed Panzer Army Afrika. In Oct 1942 it became the German-Italian Panzer Army until Feb 1943, and finally Army Group Afrika until May 1943.

46. Op Brevity's objective was the same but Rommel counter-attacked, retaking the pass.
47. 14 Bde was under Brig Chappel's command, with the 1st Bedfordshire & Hertfordshire and the 2nd Yorkshire & Lancashire. Also in the Div were 16 and 23 Bdes, supported by the Polish Carpathian Bde and Czechoslovak 11th Infantry Bn (East) and supporting units. Maj (later Lt) Gen Sir Ronald Scobie, KBE, CB, MC (1893–1969). See Maj J.E. Benson, '2 Black Watch – Tobruk, etc', memoir (written 50 years later), Cheetham/Metcalfe private papers (reprinted as 'Tobruk, Nov 1941', *Red Hackle,* Apr 1992, pp.8–12).
48. Barry, 'War Diaries 2', 23 Oct 1941, p.42, BWRA 0067. Meldrum, 'Memoirs of a Conscript', pp.6–7, BWRA 0873.
49. Benson, '2 Black Watch – Tobruk', p.3, Cheetham/Metcalfe private papers. Barry, 2 Nov 1941, 'War Diaries 2', p.47, BWRA 0067. Capt Dick-Cunyngham's uncle had commanded 10BW during WWI.
50. Fergusson, *King's Enemies,* pp.100–1.
51. '2BW, War Diaries', Tobruk, dated 11 Nov 1941, BWRA 0346. Fergusson, *King's Enemies,* p.101; he was currently serving as Wavell's private secretary in India.
52. Later Gen Sir Alan Cunningham, GCMG, KCB, DSO, MC (1887–1983). See Fergusson, *King's Enemies,* pp.102, 105; '2BW, War Diaries', Tobruk, BWRA 0346.
53. Meldrum, 'Memoirs of a Conscript', p.7, BWRA 0873.
54. '2BW, War Diaries', Tobruk, BWRA 0346. Meldrum, 'Memoirs of a Conscript', p.7, BWRA 0873.
55. Benson, '2 Black Watch – Tobruk', p.4, Cheetham/Metcalfe private papers. '2BW, War Diaries', Tobruk, BWRA 0346. Other strongpoints were East Butch, East Tugun, Jack, Lion and Wolf.
56. Capt Gerald Barry, OC HQ Coy, 'Account of the Battle for Tiger on Nov 21st, 1941', BWRA 0346. Benson, '2 Black Watch – Tobruk', pp.5–6, Cheetham/Metcalfe private papers. Barry, 'War Diaries 2', 22 Nov 1941, p.56, BWRA 0067.
57. G.A. Rusk, 'Tobruk Breakout', notes written 30 Aug 1971, BWRA 0346. Reprinted as 'Tobruk, November 1941', *Red Hackle,* Apr 1992, pp.8–12. Anon, quoted in Fergusson, *Black Watch,* p.108. See Obit., 'RSM Robert Roy, MBE, DCM', *Red Hackle,* Oct 1960, p.7.
58. Barry, 'War Diaries 2', 22 Nov 1941, p.56, BWRA 0067. See also Blair, 'Tobruk, Nov–Dec 1941';'Descriptive account of Tobruk, 18 Oct–31 Dec 1941', BWRA 0138, & Barry, OC HQ Coy 'Account of the Battle for Tiger on Nov 21st, 1941', BWRA 0346. Benson, '2 Black Watch – Tobruk', p.6, Cheetham/Metcalfe private papers.
59. Meldrum, 'Memoirs of a Conscript', p.7, BWRA 0873.
60. Rusk, 'Tobruk Breakout', BWRA 0346. Maj P.R. Birkin was 107th South Notts Hussars, Royal Horse Artillery. The problem of the missing tanks arose at the start line. 'Whoever laid the tapes apparently ignored the fact that units in depth required several hundred yards behind the actual line. Hence, in the dark, there

was confusion and C Squadron 4 RTR must have got involved with Squadron 7 RTR instead of covering my left forward Company to Jill.' See also Fergusson, *King's Enemies*, p.107: the tanks were four (Benson says 20) minutes late and they crossed the wrong bridge across the anti-tank ditch, getting muddled up with the King's Own on another objective, Butch. Realising their mistake, they changed direction, but were followed by some of the King's Own, 'who thought that these particular tanks were those which had been allotted to them: seeing them moving off to Jill, this party of King's Own began to think that Jill must be Butch.'

61. Rusk, 'Tobruk Breakout', BWRA 0346. J.L.R. Samson, *Concise Account*, p.30, says 25 officers and over 300 ORs were killed or wounded 'in taking all its objectives'. In 1991, marking the 50-year anniversary, 'a retired officer' stated: 'of the 32 officers and 600 men who crossed the start line, 6 and 160 took Tiger', 'The Breakout from Tobruk', *Red Hackle*, Dec 1991, p. 11.
62. Barry, 'War Diaries 2', 22 Nov 1941, p.55, BWRA 0067.
63. Blair, 'Tobruk, Nov–Dec 1941', BWRA 0138. Capt George (Mungo) Stirling died of his wounds on 14 Dec; a memorial window was dedicated to him and LCpl Alistair Hamilton in St Andrew's Memorial Church, Jerusalem. See 'Two Worlds in Turmoil', *Red Hackle*, Dec 1987, p.13. Rusk was awarded the DSO and 9 other decorations were given.
64. Blair, 'Tobruk, Nov–Dec 1941', BWRA 0138. LCpl James McGraw, recollection to Alice Soper, 'The Piper of Tobruk', unpublished typescript. Fergusson, *King's Enemies*, p.110.
65. 'Descriptive account of Tobruk', BWRA 0138; Barry, 'War Diaries 2', 24 Nov 1941, p.61, BWRA 0067.
66. Gen Sir Neil Ritchie, GBE, KCB, DSO, MC, Obit., *Red Hackle*, Apr 1984, pp.6–10; Ritchie, 'Recollections', p.42, BWRA 1025/83. Having been Brig Gen Staff to Alan Brooke, he commanded the 2nd Army Corps in the BEF; in Oct 1940 he took command of 51HD. It is beyond the scope of this narrative to go into detail over Auchinleck's decision but it is important to note Ritchie's belief that he was not experienced enough to have been given the command.
67. Barry, 'War Diaries 2', 26 & 27 Nov 1941, pp.62, 63, BWRA 0067.
68. Benson, '2 Black Watch – Tobruk', p.10, Cheetham/Metcalfe private papers. Among the German POWs was Gen von Ravenstein, formerly in command of 21st Panzer Div. HMS *Chakdina*'s sister ship, HMS *Chakala*, had brought 2BW from Aden to Berbera in 1940.
69. Capt Neville Blair, 'Notes on *Chakdina* Sinking' and 'Report on the sinking of HMS *Chakdina* on 5 Dec. 1941', BWRA 0138.
70. Benson, '2 Black Watch – Tobruk', p.10, Cheetham/Metcalfe private papers. Blair, 'Notes on *Chakdina* Sinking', BWRA 0138. Of the 5 wounded BW officers, the only one who did not survive was 2nd Lt Harvey.
71. Blair, 'Notes on *Chakdina* Sinking', BWRA 0138.
72. Lt Col G.A. Rusk to 2nd Battalion The Black Watch, 11 Dec 1941 (via Capt David Rose), BWRA 0346. 'Eighty of our comrades have left us for good and 183 are seriously wounded.' A memorial service for those who fell at Tobruk was held 11

Jan 1942 in Egypt, Cheetham/Metcalfe private papers.

73. 'Descriptive account of Tobruk', BWRA 0138. Less D Coy, 2BW left on 31 Dec, arriving 3 Jan 1942. Fergusson, *King's Enemies*, p.115; *Trumpet in the Hall*, pp.126–7. See Benson, '2 Black Watch – Tobruk', p.8, Cheetham/Metcalfe private papers, for information on Fergusson's work bringing 2BW up to strength. Mrs J. Nisbet to Capt Blair, 31 Jan 1942, Cheetham/Metcalfe private papers.
74. Barry, 'War Diaries 2', 31 Dec 1941, p.88, BWRA 0067.
75. Fergusson, 'Towards the East', v.1, *King's Enemies*, p.116.

12. 1942: The Desert Was Their Battlefield

1. Anon. poem by two 'English' Jocks about Alamein, written in pencil on a scrap of paper later found after they were both killed 19 Mar 1943 at the Mareth Line, 'Fifth Black Watch War History: The Gay and Gallant Black Watch, the Battle of Alamein', *Red Hackle*, Apr 1986, p.10.
2. Sgt Robert Penman, 7BW, 'One Man's War, reminiscences of WW2', p.20, BWRA 0928. He enlisted on 15 Dec 1939 and was in the mortar pl 1940–44. The manuscript was written without his family's knowledge and only found following his death in 1998.
3. Maj Douglas Hugen Tobler, 1BW, 'A Brigade Intelligence Officer's Recollection of Manoeuvres and Other Odds and Ends', 1975, p.12, BWRA 0509.He was promoted temporary captain in Mar 1942.
4. Maj Graham A. Pilcher (1916-2009), 4BW, interview, 11 Nov 2008, 'This Happens in War', BWM. He had been wounded on 8 Jun 1940 at Bresle during the retreat to St Valéry and had rejoined his former Bn as signals officer.
5. H.B. McKenzie Johnston, 6BW, 'Recollections of Service', p.6, BWRA 1023. For a fuller account of 6BW movements, see *Red Hackle*, Jul 1946, & B.J.G. Madden, *History of the 6th Battalion*, p.16.
6. Lt Col Purvis Russell Montgomery, 'Notes on War Service of 9BW, 1939–45', pp.5–6, BWRA 0162/1. Detachments were at Crail and Milnathort aerodromes as well as at Lunan Bay, Montrose aerodrome and Brechin.
7. J.L.R. Samson, *Geordie and Jock*, p.11. 1st Tyneside Scottish had been deployed to Iceland with 70 Bde Oct 1940–Dec 1941. It joined the 49th West Riding Division on 18 May 1942 whose two bdes 146 and 147 had also been in Iceland.
8. P.J.W. (Watson), MC, 7BW, 'The Gallant Forty Twa, Oct 9th, Kirkcaldy', *Red Hackle*, Apr 1983, p.7. He continued: 'A Cameron he might be, but a fearsome inspiration to us all!'
9. Pte David Chalmers, 'Six Years of My Life', memoir, 2 Apr 1940–6 Jul 1946, BWM 2014.530. He joined 5BW in Apr 1940.
10. Brig J.A. Hopwood, '1BW History' (draft), N. Africa, Ch.1, p.1, BWRA 0727. He was serving (2IC) in 7BW, becoming CO of 1BW in 1943.
11. Alexander was later FM 1st Earl Alexander of Tunis, KG, GCB, OM GCMG, CSI, DSO, MC, CD, PC (1891–1969). Lt Gen William (Strafer) Gott, CB, CBE, DSO & Bar, MC (1897–1942) was a former commander of the 7th Armoured

Division and of XIII Corps. Montgomery became FM 1st Viscount Montgomery of Alamein, KC, GCB, DSO, PC (1887–1976).

12. See A.P.Wavell, 'Ballade of the Second Front', 16 Aug 1942, quoted in FM Lord Alanbrooke, *War Diaries,* ed. Alex Danchev & Daniel Toldman, 16 Aug 1942, p.307: 'Prince of the Kremlin/ Here's a fond farewell/ I've had to deal with many worse than you;/ You took it though you hated it like hell/ NO SECOND FRONT in 1942'.
13. Tobler, 'A Brigade Intelligence Officer's Recollection', pp.14–15, BWRA 0509. Hopwood, '1BW History' (draft), N. Africa, p.1, BWRA 0727.
14. Tom Renouf, *Black Watch,* p.59. Renouf was not in North Africa but gained his information from others who served there.
15. Lt George Morrison, 7BW, to his mother, 29 Aug 1942, IWM, quoted in Alistair Borthwick, *Battalion*, Baton Wicks, 1994, p.17; Richard Doherty, *None Bolder*, pp.63–4.
16. Hopwood, '1BW History' (draft), N. Africa, Ch.1, p.1, BWRA 0727. Tobler, 'A Brigade Intelligence Officer's Recollection', p.16, BWRA 0509. Pte William Fisher, 7BW, to My Dear Wife, 28 Aug 1942. (While retaining original text, I have corrected Fisher's spelling for greater fluency of reading). His wife gave birth to a son while he was away. 'I bet he a Wee Smsher', undated letter Oct 1942, Victor Herd (Fisher's son-in-law) private papers.
17. Tobler, 'A Brigade Intelligence Officer's Recollection', p.27, BWRA 0509. Hopwood, '1BW History' (draft), N. Africa, Ch.1, pp.2 & 1, BWRA 0727. Churchill wanted Montgomery to attack at full moon in Sep, but Montgomery insisted on waiting until Oct, by which time he guaranteed success. Doherty, *None Bolder*, p.68.
18. Tobler, 'A Brigade Intelligence Officer's Recollection', p.34, BWRA 0509. Brig Ralph Bagnold, FRS, OBE (1896–1990).
19. Linklater, 'El Alamein', I, p.5, Acc. 5665, Box 11/5, NLS.
20. Lt Col W.N. Roper-Caldbeck, 1BW, to Gen Sir Arthur Wauchope, 11 Nov 1942, BWRA 0799/1. See also Roper-Caldbeck, quoted in Bernard Fergusson, *King's Enemies,* p.125. Capt (temp. Maj) Sir Arthur Wilmot, Bt, (1909–42) was killed on 3 Oct.
21. Hopwood, '1BW History' (draft), N. Africa, Ch.1, p.3, BWRA 0727.
22. Fergusson, *King's Enemies,* p.126. Main formations of the Eighth Army were XXX, XIII and X Corps. 51HD was in XXX Corps together with the 9th Australian, 2nd New Zealand, 1st South African, 4th Indian Divs. XIII Corps included the 44th and 50th Infantry Divs and the 7th Armoured Div (known as the Desert Rats).
23. D.F.O. Russell, *War History of the 7th Bn The Black Watch (R.H.R.),* pp.15, 17. He had been appointed temporary captain in Apr. See Fergusson, *King's Enemies,* p.127; the Commanders of the two flanking platoons were both killed. See also Linklater, 'El Alamein' II, p.4, Acc. 5665, Box 11/5, NLS.
24. Lt George Morrison to his mother, 16 Oct 1942, IWM, quoted in Doherty, *None Bolder*, p.70. Chalmers, 'Six Years of My Life', memoir, BWM 2014.530.
25. 'Eighth Army, Personal Message from the Army Cdr (To be read out to all Troops)', 23 Oct 1942, quoted in Russell, *War History of the 7th Bn*, p.16.

26. Maj Peter Watson, 'My helmet flew six feet in the air', *Daily Telegraph*, 24 Oct 1992. His father was Capt Sammy Watson who had fought in WWI and was Secretary of The Black Watch Association from 1919–46. Tobler, 'A Brigade Intelligence Officer's Recollection', p.19, BWRA 0509.
27. Pte (later LCpl) Henry Scivity Barker (1919–1996), 1BW, 'Memoirs 1939–46', p.16, BWRA 0966/1, compiled while undergoing treatment for cancer. Another typescript (BWRA 0966/2) has different pagination. Hopwood, '1BW History' (draft), N. Africa, Ch.1, p.4, BWRA 0727. The idea of the crosses was to show the artillery observation officers where they were. That it was a St Andrew's Cross, 'potent symbol of Scottish national pride', was 'most likely' Wimberley's idea, John Bierman & Colin Smith, *Alamein*, p.271.
28. Letter from Libya, 12 Dec 1942 (unsigned), in Linklater papers, Acc.10328/14, NLS. The author of the letter had just rejoined his battalion after being in hospital. Watson, 'My helmet flew six feet in the air', *Daily Telegraph*, 24 Oct 1992.
29. Bierman & Smith, *Alamein*, pp.275, 278. See Fergusson, *King's Enemies*, p.129. Linklater, 'El Alamein' II, p.1, Acc. 5665, Box 11/5, NLS.
30. Hopwood, '1BW History' (draft), N. Africa, Ch.1, p.4, BWRA 0727. Pte Sid Lunn, quoted in Bierman & Smith, *Alamein*, p.278. Barker, 'Memoirs 1939–46', p.16, BWRA 0966/1. The authors interviewed Lunn in Oct 1999.
31. Chalmers, 'Six Years of My Life', BWM 2014.530.
32. Fergusson, *King's Enemies*, p.128.
33. John McGregor, *Spirit of Angus*, p.39.
34. Chalmers, 'Six Years of My Life', BWM 2014.530.
35. Roper-Caldbeck to Wauchope, 11 Nov 1942, BWRA 0799/1. This was Capt David Johnstone.
36. J.B. Salmond, *51st Highland Division*, p.42. Fergusson, *King's Enemies*, p.129. Penman, 'One Man's War', pp.22–3, BWRA 0928. Lt George Morrison, quoted in Doherty, *None Bolder*, p.70.
37. Watson, 'My helmet flew six feet in the air', *Daily Telegraph*, 24 Oct 1992. Watson felt 'quite ashamed' to have to retire because of loss of blood. He lived to his 90s, dying in 2015. See Maj J.P. Watson, MC, Obit by R.M. Riddell, *Red Hackle*, May 2015, pp.22–3.
38. Linklater, 'El Alamein', II, p.4, Acc. 5665, Box 11/5, NLS.
39. Brig Howard Kippenberger, *Infantry Brigadier*, OUP, 1949, p.234. Hopwood, '1BW History' (draft), N. Africa, Ch.1, p.5, BWRA 0727. In recognition of his 'outstanding example' in the attack on Miteriya Ridge, Lt Col Oliver, 7BW, was awarded the DSO.
40. The conduct of the campaign led to a heated argument between Montgomery and X Corps's Commander, Maj Gen Herbert Lumsden, CB, DSO and Bar, MC (1897–1945) following which he was replaced by Maj Gen (later Lt Gen Sir) Brian Horrocks, KCB, KBE, DSO, MC (1895–1985), formerly in command of XIII Corps. Lumsden died in a kamikaze attack in the Pacific in Jan 1945.
41. Hopwood, '1BW History' (draft), N. Africa, Ch.1, p.5, BWRA 0727.
42. Fergusson, *King's Enemies*, p.134. See Doherty, *None Bolder*, p.84.

43. Wimberley, 'Scottish Soldier', II, pp.43–4, docs 430, IWM. He originally thought it was a mortar bomb.
44. B.H. Liddell-Hart, ed., *The Rommel Papers*, pp.304–6.
45. Doherty, *None Bolder*, pp.82, 87. Penman, 'One Man's War', p.27, BWRA 0928.
46. Doherty, *None Bolder*, pp.88–9, gives a very concise account of events.
47. McGregor, *Spirit of Angus*, pp.41–2, 44.
48. Hopwood, '1BW History' (draft), N. Africa, Ch.1, p.5, BWRA 0727.
49. Russell, *War History of the 7th Bn*, p.21; Roper-Caldbeck to Wauchope, 11 Nov 1942, p.4, BWRA 0799/1.
50. Wimberley, 'Scottish Soldier', II, docs 430, IWM, p.51. Wimberley sent this message as a 'postscript' to the congratulatory message received by 51HD from Lt Gen Sir Oliver Leese, XXX Corps Commander. Penman, 'One Man's War', p.69, BWRA 0948.
51. 2nd Lt Hugh Rose of Kilravock, 1BW; *Roses of Kilravock Society*, 10th ed., privately published, 2008, p.21. Roper-Caldbeck to Wauchope, 11 Nov 1942, BWRA 0799/1. Fergusson, *King's Enemies*, p.130. See BWRA 0905/1. McGregor, *Spirit of Angus*, p.44.
52. Roper-Caldbeck to Wauchope, 11 Nov 1942, p.4, BWRA 0799/1. Russell, *7th Black Watch War History*, p.21. Capt Gerald Osborne's son, Bruce, was later commissioned into The Black Watch.
53. Pte J.J. Cosgrove & Pte Charles Reid, 'MM of The Black Watch, WW2', Thomas B. Smyth research material.
54. Fergusson, *King's Enemies*, pp.128–9. See also Doherty, *None Bolder*, p.74. McIntyre (born 15 Jan 1914) was 28. The song was written by an unknown soldier in 5BW. See 'El Alamein, A Soldier's Tale', notes written by R. Simpson, ex-Drummer, 1/4/5BW. McIntyre's sister unsuccessfully petitioned for her brother to get the VC. See also Bierman & Smith, *Alamein*, p.278.
55. Maj Hew Blair Imrie, 5BW, to his wife from hospital, 31 Oct–2 Nov 1942, pp.13–14 (of 17), BWRA 0801. Wounded in the right hand, he adapted to writing with his left. After recovering he became 2IC, 5BW. He was killed in action while CO of 5th/7th Gordons on 18 Aug 1944. In 1986 his widow loaned the letters to McGregor for his official history of 5BW. See excerpts, *Spirit of Angus*, pp.45–6.
56. Roper-Caldbeck to Wauchope, 11 Nov 1942, p.8, BWRA 0799/1.
57. Winston Churchill, Lord Mayor's Luncheon, Mansion House, 10 Nov 1942, quoted in *Never Give In!, The Best of Winston Churchill's Speeches*, p.342.
58. Roper-Caldbeck to Wauchope, 11 Nov 1942, p.9, BWRA 0799/1. Lt Gen Sir Oliver Leese, KBE, CBE, DSO (1894–1978). McGregor, *Spirit of Angus*, p.50; Fergusson, *King's Enemies*, p.136.
59. Hopwood, '1BW History' (draft), N. Africa, Ch.1, p.6, BWRA 0727.
60. Fisher to My Darling Wife, 10 Nov & 15 Nov 1942, Herd private papers. An example of Fisher's poor spelling is as follows: 'our Bige gunes ar kiping gerey bisey we ar up all night and slepe all day But it is getting very cold out hear.' He realised his ignorance and said he wanted his children better educated: 'I don't wont them to be a dope like thar dad for I wish I cood right and spel to right a Big

litter to you but it cant be help... pless right soon,' Letter 16 Jun 1942. He was in 'dock' for 2 months with a burnt arm and so appears to have missed El Alamein.

61. Roper-Caldbeck to Wauchope, 11 Nov 1942, p.10, BWRA 0799/1. The 42nd was the old name for the Regiment, but it was commonly used to refer to the 1BW while the 73rd was used in reference to 2BW.
62. Fergusson, *King's Enemies*, pp.136–8. Wimberley, 'Scottish Soldier', II, docs 430, IWM, quoted in Doherty, *None Bolder*, p.93.
63. Fergusson, *King's Enemies*, p.140.
64. Barker, 'Memoirs 1939–46', p.20, BWRA 0966/1. S-mine in German meaning 'Schrapnellmine, Springmine or Splittermine.' Also known as the Bouncing Betty because it bounded in the air.
65. Fergusson, *King's Enemies*, p.140. Russell, *War History of the 7th Bn,* CO's account, p.24. Barker, 'Memoirs 1939–46', p.20, BWRA 0966/1.
66. Russell, *War History of the 7th Bn,* CO's account, p.25. Hopwood, '1BW History' (draft), N. Africa, Ch.2, p.2, BWRA 0727.
67. Hopwood, '1BW History' (draft), N. Africa, Ch.2, p.2, BWRA 0727. Rennie took over from Brig Harry Houldsworth who returned to the UK as Commandant of the recently established School of Infantry, Barnard Castle, Co. Durham.
68. General Dwight Eisenhower, (1890–1969) became 34th President of the United States. John Laffin, *Scotland the Brave,* p.126. Laffin does not provide a source for this story but it sounds credible! The First Army eventually consisted of British V and IX Corps, the United States' II Corps and the French XIX Corps.
69. Brig Keith Arbuthnott took command of 11 Bde, 78th Division in Sep 1943; he became acting GOC 78th Division in Jul 1944, formally taking over the position in Nov 1944.
70. Admiral François Darlan (1881–1942) was France's 81st PM (as Vice-President of the Council). Although his assassin confessed to having been himself opposed to Darlan's pro-German stance, he was encouraged to carry out the assassination by men believing the only solution to France's problems was a restoration of the monarchy; see http://realite-histoire.over-blog.com/article-24209065.html, accessed 6 Feb 2017. Given Darlan's collaboration with Hitler, the Free French and de Gaulle were also angered by the Allied deal. General Henri Giraud (1879–1949).
71. 'Christmas with the Eighth Army', unsigned, 23 Dec 1943 (1942), Linklater papers, Acc 10328/15, NLS. Although the letter is dated 1943 the Eighth Army was not in North Africa and so this is an error.
72. McGregor, *Spirit of Angus,* pp.56, 60. Russell, *War History of the 7th Bn*, p.26. Fisher to My Darling Wife, 31 Dec 1942, Herd private papers.
73. Capt (later Lt Col) Gerald Barry, 2BW, 'War Diaries 3', 22 Feb & 24 Feb 1942, p.13, BWRA 0067. Fergusson, *King's Enemies,* pp.223–4.
74. See William Slim, *Defeat into Victory*, p.116. The Burma Corps (formed in Mar 1942, disbanded in May) was under the command of Acting Lt Gen Slim (1891–1970). Later FM Viscount William Slim, KG, GCB, GCMG, GCVO, GBE, DSO, MC, KStJ.

75. Barry, 'War Diaries 3', 19 May & 21 Jun 1942, pp.40, 48; 'War Diaries 4', 1 Aug 1942, p.14, BWRA 0067.
76. Barry, 'War Diaries 4', 25 Aug 1942, p.28, BWRA 0067. Fergusson, *King's Enemies,* p.225.
77. The National Government existed from 17 Dec 1942 to 8 Aug 1944.
78. '2 BW, Regimental Milestones, 1939–45', 16 Oct 1942, BWM; see also account in '2BW War Diary, India, Jun 1941–May 1944', BWRA 0066. C Coy Diary, quoted in Fergusson, *King's Enemies,* p.226; see Capt the Hon H.N. Dalrymple, '63 Years on – Some Random Recollections', *Red Hackle,* Nov 2010, p.28. Pte Andrew Meldrum, 2BW, 'Memoirs of a Conscript', p.8, BWRA 0873.
79. Barry, 'War Diaries 4', 18 Oct 1942, p.50, BWRA 0067. Citation, signed Lt Col (Rusk) Commanding 2nd Bn, 30 Nov 1942, 'Cyclone Contai District Pichaboni River, 2BW, 17 Oct 1942, India', BWRA 0343. Donaldson was 18 Pl, D Coy. See also '2BW War Diary', Oct 1942, pp.55–67, BWRA 0066. Capt Paul LeButt, previously Mentioned in Despatches for his actions in Crete, was also awarded the MBE.
80. Citation, signed Lt Col (Rusk) Commanding 2nd Bn, 30 Nov 1942, BWRA 0343. See Fergusson, *King's Enemies,* p.231.
81. '2BW, Regimental Milestones', 16 Oct 1942, BWM. Meldrum, 'Memoirs of a Conscript', p.8, BWRA 0873.
82. Fergusson, *King's Enemies,* p.230; Barry, 'War Diaries 4', 19 Oct 1942, p.50, BWRA 0067.
83. Barry, 'War Diaries 4', 25 Oct & 5 Nov 1942, pp.52, 58, BWRA 0067. His diary concludes on 10 Jan 1943. Note: Archie John Wavell joined 2BW in Nov 1942. See Barry, 'War Diaries 4', 2 Nov 1942, p.56.
84. Churchill, *The Second World War,* Vol. IV, p.541.
85. Sung by The Agheila Angels, 24 Dec 1942, quoted in McGregor, *Spirit of Angus*, p.56. The Ladies from Hell was a nickname given to all kilted troops by the Germans in WWI.

13. 1943: Fighting in the Front Line

1. LCpl Charlie Hankins, 6BW, *A Part of My Life in a Family at War*, p.120.
2. Maj Robert (Bobby) Hutchison, 7BW (1914–1943), 'Letter Home', 4 Jul 1943, *Red Hackle*, Dec 1993, p.12.
3. B.B. Schofield, 'Glad Waters', unpublished memoir, p.163. Churchill, accompanied by Lord Moran, addressed this remark to my father, Capt (later VAdm) B.B. Schofield, Director of Trade Division at the Admiralty, as they met walking in the gardens of the Anfa Hotel where the Conference was taking place.
4. 'Milestones 1937–1945', https://history.state.gov/milestones/1937-1945/casablanca, accessed 7 Feb 2017. The meeting took place between 14 & 24 Jan 1943.
5. The 4th Div was in V Corps, which also included the 1st & 78th British Infantry Divs, as well as the 25th Tank Regt. Also in 12 Bde, known as the Royal Bde, were the 2nd Royal Fusiliers and the 1st Royal West Kent Regiment; Maj George Grant, interview, 17 Oct 2013, Perth.

6. Pte William Fisher, 7BW, to My Darling Wife, 4 Jan 1943, Victor Herd private papers. He is probably referring to those lost in the Mersa Brega minefields.
7. Brig J.A. Hopwood, '1BW History' (draft), N. Africa, Ch.2, pp.3–4, BWRA 0727. D.F.O. Russell, *War History of the 7th Bn The Black Watch (R.H.R.)*, p.28. Lt Col Roper-Caldbeck, 1BW, 'Notes on the Advance of the 42nd Royal Highlanders from Buerat to Tripoli (253 miles)', included in a letter to Gen Sir Arthur Wauchope, 12 Jan 1943, signed on behalf of the CO by the Adjt, Nigel Noble, BWRA 0799/2. Brig James Stirling, DSO, TD (1898–1968), Seaforth Highlanders, then assumed command of 154 Bde until Rennie's return.
8. 'Eighth Army, Personal Message from the Army Commander', signed B.L. Montgomery, 12 Jan 1943, quoted in Russell, *War History of the 7th Bn*, p.29.
9. J. B. Salmond, *51st Highland Division*, p.62. He gives date of 14 Jan for start of the attack.
10. Roper-Caldbeck, 'Notes on the Advance of the 42nd', 15 & 16 Jan 1943, BWRA 0799/2.
11. Russell, *War History of the 7th Bn*, p.39. A heavy gale on 17 Jan 1943 had destroyed much of the restoration work on Benghazi harbour. Brig J.A. Hopwood, '1BW History' (draft), N. Africa, Ch.2, p.4, BWRA 0727.
12. Russell, *War History of the 7th Bn*, p.32.
13. Ibid. Hopwood, '1BW History' (draft), N. Africa, Ch.2, p.5, BWRA 0727.
14. Roper-Caldbeck, 'Notes on the Advance of the 42nd', 20 Jan 1943, BWRA 0799/2, See also Bernard Fergusson, *King's Enemies*, p.147. Bruce Fortune was the son of Maj Gen Sir Victor Fortune.
15. Russell, *War History of the 7th Bn* (CO's Account), pp.34–5. Fergusson, *King's Enemies*, p.148. Salmond, *51st Highland Division*, p.66. They were supported by the 2nd Seaforth attacking a feature known as El Nab as well as the 5th Seaforth and Hammerforce which included tanks and artillery.
16. Russell, *War History of the 7th Bn* (CO's Account), p.36. Hopwood, '1BW History' (draft), N. Africa, Ch.2, p.4, BWRA 0727; see also Roper-Caldbeck, 'Notes on the Advance of the 42nd', BWRA 0799/2. John McGregor, *Spirit of Angus*, p.62.
17. 'Eighth Army, Personal Message from the Army Cdr', 23 Jan 1943, quoted in Russell, *War History of the 7th Bn*, p.38.
18. B.L. Montgomery, *Memoirs*, p.154. 'A note in my diary dated the 20th January reads as follows: "Sent for the GOC 51st (Highland) Division…"; but see Wimberley, 'Scottish Soldier', II, p.72n31, docs 430, IWM: he says that he did not see Montgomery but received a 'sharp message' in the form of a personal letter. 'He probably tried to get hold of me on the 20th, and having failed, wrote me this note I have referred to.'
19. Hopwood, '1BW History' (draft), N. Africa, Ch.2, p.6, BWRA 0727.
20. Fergusson, *King's Enemies*, p.154; Russell, *War History of the 7th Bn*, pp.39–40. See also Hopwood '1BW History' (draft), N. Africa, Chs 2 & 3, BWRA 0727. Created in 1921, the NAAFI (Navy, Army, and Air Force Institutes) provided recreational facilities and sold goods to servicemen and their families.
21. Churchill, *History of the Second World War*, IV, p.646; see also Fergusson, *King's*

Enemies, p.154. Russell, *War History of the 7th Bn*, p.40. Churchill visited Turkey to persuade the Turks to join the war; which they did on 23 Feb 1945 allegedly to qualify for membership of the UN. See John Bierman & Colin Smith, *Alamein*, p.361n*.

22. Wimberley, 'Scottish Soldier', II, p.86, docs 430, IWM.
23. Churchill, *History of the Second World War*, IV, p.646.
24. Alexander was also Deputy C-in-C.
25. In Feb Rommel had defeated US forces at the Kasserine Pass. The 'Army Group Afrika' was composed of the 1st Italian Army commanded by General Giovanni Messe and the 5th Panzer Army under the command of General Hans-Jürgen von Arnim. Although its official titles changed, to the Allies it was familiarly known as the Afrika Corps; see Liddell-Hart, ed., *The Rommel Papers*, p.390. Hopwood, '1BW History' (draft), N. Africa, Ch.3, p.3, BWRA 0727. See also Richard Doherty, *None Bolder*, p.107; Russell, *War History of the 7th Bn*, p.43.
26. Russell, *War History of the 7th Bn*, p.45.
27. See John McGregor, *Spirit of Angus*, p.67.
28. Pte (later LCpl) Henry Scivity Barker, 1BW, 'Memoirs 1939–46', p.24, BWRA 0966/1. Hopwood, '1BW History' (draft), N. Africa, Ch.3, pp.4–5, BWRA 0727. See Fergusson, *King's Enemies*, p.157. The infantry battalions in 131 Bde were the 5th, 6th and 7th Queen's Royal Regiment – and so it was called the Queen's Bde.
29. Russell, *War History of the 7th Bn*, pp.49–50.
30. Liddell Hart, ed., *The Rommel Papers*, pp.418–19.
31. 'Eighth Army, Personal Message from the Army Commander (To be read out to all Troops)', 19 Mar 1943, quoted in Russell, *War History of the 7th Bn*, p.51; also in Salmond, *51st Highland Division*, p.80. 7BW was put under the command of 23 Armoured Bde, and with supporting artillery was known as the Mace Force.
32. Fisher to My Dear Wife, 22 Mar, & to my Darling Wife, 23 Feb 1943, Herd private papers.
33. Russell, *War History of the 7th Bn*, p.53.
34. See Wimberley, quoted in McGregor, *Spirit of Angus*, p.71; Salmond, *51st Highland Division*, p.83.
35. Russell, *War History of the 7th Bn*, p.53.
36. Russell, *War History of the 7th Bn*, p.54. Fisher, 7BW, to My Dearling [sic] Wife, 31 Mar 1943, Herd private papers. This was Fisher's last surviving letter.
37. Russell, *War History of the 7th Bn* (CO's Account), p.55.
38. Sgt Robert Penman, 7BW, 'One Man's War, reminiscences of WW2', p.40, BWRA 0928. Russell, *War History of the 7th Bn* (CO's Account), p.57.
39. Penman, 'One Man's War', p.41, BWRA 0928. Hopwood, '1 BW History (draft)', N. Africa, Ch.4, p.4, BWRA 0727. Brig J.A. Hopwood, Obit by A.O.L.L (Tony Lithgow), *Red Hackle*, Dec 1987, p.7.
40. McGregor, *Spirit of Angus*, p.73. Russell, *War History of the 7th Bn*, p.58.
41. 'Eighth Army, Personal Message from the Army Commander (To be read out to all Troops)', 8 Apr 1943, quoted in Russell, *War History of the 7th Bn*, p.59. Wimberley, 'To all Ranks of the 51st Highland Division', 10 Apr 1943, In the

Field, 5BW War History (draft prepared by Brodie) BWRA 0844/084. Wimberley, 'Scottish Soldier', II, p.113, docs, 430, IWM.

42. Russell, *War History of the 7th Bn* (CO's Account), p.58. See also Salmond, *51st Highland Division*, pp.91–4.
43. Russell, *War History of the 7th Bn* (CO's Account), p.60. Maj J.P. Watson, MC, Obit by R.M. Riddell, *Red Hackle*, May 2015, p.23. Watson had been wounded at El Alamein. Pte G. Clark, *London Gazette*, 27 Jul 1943, 'MM Notes WW2,' Thomas B. Smyth research material.
44. Reid was kept in a POW hospital before being transferred to a POW camp outside Modena. After the Italian surrender, the camp was taken over by the Germans and he escaped. See Howard Reid, *Dad's War*, Bantam Press, 2003, his account of his own journey of discovery regarding his father's capture and escape; also Ian Reid, *Prisoner at Large*, Futura, 1976; Fergusson, *King's Enemies*, p.333.
45. Moreland (Bill) Johns (1913–2005); having trained with 10BW he had been sent to North Africa to join 51HD, fighting at Alamein and Wadi Akarit, Biographical information, BWM.
46. 4th Bn Memorial in Gibraltar. *Red Hackle*, Oct 1955, p.9. He was the son of Col Sydney Innes.
47. J.L.R. Samson, *Geordie and Jock*, p.11. Brian Stewart, *Scrapbook of a Roving Highlander*, p.35; letter to George, 12 May 1943, p.49.
48. H.B. McKenzie Johnston, 6BW, 'Recollections of Service', p.7, BWRA 1023. Charlie Framp, *Crimson Skies*, 6BW, p.49. He said the Scots regiments were 'that bit more glamorous than their English counterparts', p.43. Born in 1922, he published his memoir in 1988.
49. W.B. Wilson, MM, Obit (by J.A. MacL Stewart), *Red Hackle*, Dec 1966, p.4.
50. McKenzie Johnston, 'Recollections of Service', p.8, BWRA 1023.
51. Framp, *Crimson Skies*, pp.51, 55–6.
52. McKenzie Johnston, 'Recollections of Service', p.8, BWRA 1023. Framp, *Crimson Skies*, p.57.
53. LCpl Charlie Hankins (1920–2004), *A Part of My Life in a Family at War*, p.22. Evacuated to Britain, he became 'fully mobile' with tin legs (p.31).
54. B.J.G. Madden, *History of the 6th Battalion*, pp.19–21. McKenzie Johnston, 'Recollections of Service', p.9, BWRA 1023. Barclay died on 21 May 1943. His son was also serving in 6BW. 'I was with him when they told him his father had been killed,' Maj George Grant, interview, 17 Oct 2013, Perth. There were 22 6BW fatalities at Djebel Rmel.
55. Peter's Corner was named after the CO of the Derbyshire Yeomanry who had undertaken numerous patrols of the area. Framp, *Crimson Skies*, p.74.
56. McKenzie Johnston, 'Recollections of Service', p.10, BWRA 1023. Pte George Morrison Daily, 6BW, 'A Soldier's Tale', BWRA 0961.
57. Framp, *Crimson Skies*, pp.75, 77–8. He relates an amusing episode of encountering a German while sheltering in a trench. See Madden, *History of the 6th Battalion*, p.23ff. & 'Sidi Medienne 1943 and 1988', *Red Hackle*, Aug 1988, pp.9–10 (article written following a visit to the battlefield 45 years later).

58. Daily, 'A Soldier's Tale', BWRA 0961.
59. Madden, *History of the 6th Battalion*, pp.27–8. Fatalities in 6BW numbered over 50.
60. McKenzie Johnston, 'Recollections of Service', p.11, BWRA 1023. Montgomery had exhorted all troops to 'Drive the Enemy into the Sea!' 'Eighth Army, Personal Message from the Army Commander (to be read out to all Troops)', 8 Apr 1943, quoted in Russell, *War History of the 7th Bn*, p.59.
61. Madden, *History of the 6th Battalion*, pp.31–2, 34.
62. McKenzie Johnston, 'Recollections of Service', p.12, BWRA 1023. After 2 months in N. Africa, 6BW had suffered 95 fatalities.
63. Russell, *War History of the 7th Bn*, pp.62–3; see '153 Bde War Diary, Jan–May 1943', WO 169/8959, TNA. Barker, 'Memoirs 1939–46', p.25, BWRA 0966/1. See also McGregor, *Spirit of Angus*, p.79. Pte G. Marchant, 20 May 1943, 'Extracts from Letters', 51HD, p.47, BWM.
64. 'Eighth Army, Personal Message from the Army Commander (to be read out to all Troops)', Tunisia, 14 May 1943, quoted in Russell, *War History of the 7th Bn*, p.63. The 18th Army Group was then disbanded. Between Oct 1942 & May 1943, 1BW, 5BW and 7BW casualties amounted to 1,453 men killed, wounded or missing (16 Officers & 275 ORs killed); see Salmond, *51st Highland Division*, p.99.
65. McKenzie Johnston, 'Recollections of Service', pp.12–13, BWRA 1023. Madden, *6th Battalion History*, p.35*.
66. 'Eighth Army, Personal Message from the Army Commander (to be read out to all Troops)', Tunisia, 14 May 1943, in Russell, *War History of the 7th Bn*, p.63; see John Follain, *Mussolini's Island*, p.310. The German Divisions were commanded by Maj Gen Fridolin von Senger und Etterlin and the Italians by Generale d'Armata Alfredo Guzzoni.
67. Maj Gen Wimberley, quoted in Salmond, *51st Highland Division*, p.104. 51HD was again part of XXX Corps, under Leese's command. RQMS Meekison, 5BW, 'Quartie's War', memoir of service in 5BW, p.7, BWRA 0878/2. LCpl Ernest Lewis, 1BW, was recorded as dying from seasickness; see Fergusson, *King's Enemies*, p.173; '1BW War Diary', WO 169/10178, TNA: 'Sea became very rough and all ranks suffered accordingly,' 9 Jul 1943. 'One man died of sea sickness during voyage,' 10 Jul 1943; Hopwood, '1BW History' (draft), Sicily, Ch.1, p.1, BWRA 0727. See also Maj Archie Murray to Dear General (Wauchope), 30 Jul 1943, Sicilian campaign report, BWRA 0799/3.
68. Maj Robert Hutchison, 7BW, 'Letter Home', 4 Jul 1943, *Red Hackle*, Dec 1993, p.12. He had been wounded at Alamein.
69. Meekison, 'Quartie's War', p.7, BWRA 0878/2. Barker, 'Memoirs 1939–46', p.27, BWRA 0966/1.
70. Russell, *War History of the 7th Bn*, pp.67, 68. Some explanation for the lack of opposition was Operation Mincemeat, a deceptive strategy indicating that the invasion would be elsewhere, which resulted in the strengthening of Axis defences on Sardinia, Corsica and Greece at the expense of those on Sicily. Hopwood, '1BW History' (draft), Sicily, Ch.1, p.1, BWRA 0727.

71. Russell, *War History of the 7th Bn,* p.69; Hopwood, '1BW History' (draft), Sicily, Ch.1, p.1, BWRA 0727, who says 8 ORs killed, 27 wounded. See '153 Brigade War Diary', WO169/8959, TNA; also Doherty, *None Bolder,* p.130.
72. McGregor, *Spirit of Angus,* p.91.
73. Meekison, 'Quartie's War', pp.6–8, BWRA 0878/2. He was in B Echelon with the stores. The Reconnaissance Regt was staffed from the various regiments of the HD. Meekison was posted to A Coy, under John McGregor's command. '(Better known as Honest John) [he] was an enthusiastic Deck Tennis convert and soon had me as keen on this strenuous but healthy game, as himself. It was good fun and kept us fit too. We became very good friends.'
74. Barker, 'Memoirs 1939–46', p.27, BWRA 0966/1. Russell, *War History of the 7th Bn,* pp.69, 70. Hopwood, '1BW History' (draft), Sicily, Ch.1, p.1, BWRA 0727.
75. Maj Gen Rennie, 'The Battle of Gerbini. Secret'. Z/544/G. 14 Aug 1943, http://51hd.co.uk/accounts/gerbini_combs, accessed 7 Feb 2017.
76. Russell, *War History of the 7th Bn,* pp.70–1. Barker, 'Memoirs 1939–46', pp.27–8, BWRA 0966/1.
77. Hopwood, '1BW History' (draft), Sicily, Ch.1, p.4, BWRA 0727; '1BW War Diary', 19 Jul 1943, WO169/10178, TNA. Rennie, 'The Battle of Gerbini', 14 Aug 1943; '1BW War Diary', 28 & 29 Jul 1943, WO 169/10178, TNA. Baker Baker became 2IC in place of Maj A.J. Murray who had assumed temporary command when Neil Blair was injured (this is Charles Neil Molesworth Blair, not to be confused with Neville Blair).
78. McGregor, *Spirit of Angus,* p.97. Meekison, 'Quartie's War', p.9, BWRA 0776.
79. Hopwood, '1BW History' (draft), Sicily, Ch.2, p.1, BWRA 0727. Maj Archie Murray to Dear General (Wauchope), 30 Jul 1943, Sicilian campaign report, BWRA 0799/3. Hopwood was absent 5–16 Jul because of a leg injury. Russell, *War History of the 7th Bn*, pp.72–6. 'Throughout the whole battle, very heavy concentrations of fire were put down by our artillery.'
80. John McLaren, telephone interview, 27 Sep 2016, describing the recollections of his father, Capt Stewart McLaren (1919–2006).
81. Lt J.R.B. Murray, 1BW, diary, 15 Aug 1943, 'Notebook 7', p.20, BWRA 0823. 'Eighth Army, Personal Message from the Army Cdr (to be read out to all Troops)', Sicily, 17 Aug 1943, quoted in Russell, *War History of the 7th Bn*, p.75.
82. See Carlo D'Este's *Bitter Victory: The Battle for Sicily 1943*; Steven J. Zaloga, *Sicily 1943, The debut of Allied joint operations*, Osprey, 2013, for discussion of Montgomery and Patton's 'race' to Messina.
83. The armistice is known as the Badoglio Declaration. Italy declared war on Germany on 13 Oct.
84. Statistics from Salmond, *51st Highland Division*, pp.133–4: 124 officers and 1,312 ORs killed, wounded, missing in 51HD which had suffered 'some 7,000 casualties within a year'.
85. Barker, 'Memoirs 1939–46', p.28, BWRA 0966/1. LCpl Francis Barrett, 5BW, 'MM Notes WW2', Thomas B. Smyth research material. Salmond, *51st Highland Division,* p.117; see also the story of Pte John Travena's bravery, pp.116–17.

Statistics from 'The Gerbini Battle', unsigned, BWRA 0799/3.

86. Maj Gen Douglas Wimberley, 'Order of the Day/Farewell Message', 19 Aug 1943, '1BW War Diary', App O, WO 169/10178, TNA; Wimberley, 'Scottish Soldier', II, pp.200–1, docs 430, IWM.
87. Pte Alec McMichael, 5BW, quoted in Saul David, *Mutiny at Salerno*, p.43. See also Wimberley, 'Scottish Soldier', II, pp.209–10, docs 430, IWM. The 192 men (the largest number to be charged at any one time in British military history) who refused to join the new units were taken to Algiers and found guilty of mutiny: 3 sergeants were sentenced to death, commuted to forced labour.
88. '1BW War Diary', 28 Oct 1943, WO 169/10178, TNA. See Doherty, *None Bolder*, p.140.
89. Murray, diary, 4 Nov 1943, 'Notebook 8', p.3, BWRA 0823. He was liaison officer, 154 Bde.
90. Hopwood, '1BW History' (draft), Sicily, Ch.2, p.10, BWRA 0727. 1BW arrived home on 1 Dec 1943.
91. Russell, *War History of the 7th Bn*, p.83. McGregor, *Spirit of Angus*, p.108.
92. McKenzie Johnston, 'Recollections of Service', pp.13–14, BWRA 1023.
93. Pte Andrew Meldrum, 2BW, 'Memoirs of a Conscript', p.11, BWRA 0873, & '2BW War Diary, India, Jun 1941–May 1944', 19 Feb 1943, p.109, BWRA 0066. Unless otherwise stated all BW sources in this section are in 2BW. 'Maj Boyle MC and Lt J.C. Reid and other spectators immediately dived in to assist these men.' LCpls Saunders and Nobby Clark from Rhodesia both drowned.
94. Bernard Fergusson, *Beyond the Chindwin*, pp.16–17, 35. Included in the force was the 13th King's (Liverpool) Regiment, Burma Rifles, Hong Kong Volunteers, Gurkhas, & West African troops.
95. What became known as the First Arakan Campaign began in Dec 1942 but when the Japanese counter-attacked in Mar 1943, the troops were forced to withdraw.
96. See Christopher H. Sykes, *Orde Wingate*, Collins, 1959, p.385; also John Connell, *Supreme Commander*, p.257.
97. Fergusson, *Beyond the Chindwin*, p.50.
98. See Philip D. Chinnery, *March or Die*, p.73. Fergusson, *Beyond the Chindwin*, pp.176, 187,nL, 248–9, 250; he says over 65% got out safely, where Gordon Thorburn, *Jocks in the Jungle*, p.45, says 2,182 out of 3,000 (73%). 'Most of the 818 missing were missed for ever. Of the men who returned, only 600 recovered sufficiently from their ordeals to fight again in that war.' Fergusson, BBC Home Service, quoted in Thorburn, *Jocks in the Jungle*, p.46.
99. Fergusson, *Beyond the Chindwin*, p.241.
100. 'Commando in the Jungle – Raids into Burma, from our Special Correspondent, GHQ, India, 20 May', *The Times*, 21 May 1943, p.4. Operation Chastise took place on 16–17 May 1943. Slim, *Defeat into Victory*, p.164.
101. Meldrum, 'Memoirs of a Conscript', pp.8–9, BWRA 0873. See '2BW, Regimental Milestones, 1939–45'. Cox's Bazaar was named after the 18th cent. East India Company officer, Captain Hiram Cox.
102. First Quebec Conference (codenamed Quadrant), 17–24 Aug 1943, attended by

Roosevelt, Churchill, & combined chiefs of staff. Wingate was also present. (A second conference codenamed Octagon was held in Quebec in 1944.) See '2BW War Diary', 8 Sep 1943, p.200, BWRA 0066.

103. Fergusson, *King's Enemies*, p.232. Gen Joseph Stilwell (1883–1946) had an acerbic temperament which meant he acquired the names 'Vinegar' or 'Dextrose' Joe. The Chinese force had retreated from Burma under his command into India in 1943. He had served as military attaché at the US Legation in Beijing 1935–9 and spoke Mandarin fluently.
104. Frederick C. Patterson, *From Rattray & Beyond*, pp.43–4. Patterson joined The Black Watch but was sent with a draft to the 1st Cameronians. He wrote his memoirs in his 80s having ended the war as a mortar platoon sgt.
105. Cpl Jim McNeilly, quoted in Thorburn, *Jocks in the Jungle*, pp.31–2. In addition to documentary material, his book is based on interviews c. 2006 with Lt Col David Rose, Cpl Jim McNeilly and Piper William (Bill) Lark. His father, LCpl Andrew Douglas Thorburn, 2BW, 'was there but never said a thing about it', p.x.
106. The conference at Cairo (codenamed Sextant) was held between 22 & 26 Nov 1943, that at Teheran (codenamed Eureka) between 28 Nov & 1 Dec 1943. The Soviet–Japanese Neutrality Act 1941 precluded Stalin attending a meeting at which Chiang Kai-Shek was present.
107. Michael Drayton (1563–1631), 'Agincourt', v.1, quoted in Salmond, *51st Highland Division*, p.135.

14. 1944: Only Numbers Can Annihilate

1. Frederick C. Patterson, *From Rattray & Beyond*, p.57.
2. Charlie Framp, *Crimson Skies*, p.131.
3. Cpl Andrew Dow, 'Memoirs, France, Holland, Belgium, Germany 1944–45', typescript, p.4, BWRA 0604/4; see also 'Material assembled for *The Spirit of Angus*', BWRA 0844. Dow was previously a private in 7BW but transferred to 5BW because of its losses and was promoted LCpl on arrival in Normandy, p.3.
4. See William Slim, *Defeat into Victory*, pp.216–17 for an account of the changing nature of the long-range penetration force. The bdes and commanders were: 16 British, Brig Bernard Fergusson; 77 Indian, Brig Mike Calvert, DSO; 111 Indian, Brig (later Lt Gen) Joe Lentaigne, CB, CBE, DSO (1899–1955); 14 British, Brig Thomas Brodie; 3 West African, Brig Gillmore; 23 British under Brig Perowne was diverted to Assam. Various landing strips in forest clearings were established, codenamed Broadway, Chowringhee and Piccadilly (which proved unusable), see Philip D. Chinnery, *March or Die*, pp.110, 113.
5. Pte Andrew Meldrum, 2BW, 'Memoirs of a Conscript', Ch.12, p.12, BWRA 0873. (His chapters and pagination are not consistent.) Roosevelt had been distressed to know that there had been no way of evacuating the wounded on the first expedition. The aircraft was the WACO (originally Weaver Aircraft Company of Ohio) CG-4A, just under 50 ft long, with a wingspan of over 80 ft, which the British called the Hadrian. 2BW in fact flew in in Dakotas 'our first time ever

on a powered plane'; Meldrum, 'Memoirs of a Conscript', Action, p.1. He was in 42 Col under Rose 'the Daddy of the Battalion', aged 32 on 23 Mar! See Gordon Thorburn, *Jocks in the Jungle*, p.73. Unless otherwise stated, all BW sources in this section are from 2BW.

6. Bernard Fergusson, *King's Enemies*, p.233. A column comprised 4 platoons, a support group, a demolition group and a recce platoon, including Burmese hill tribesmen who also acted as interpreters. Also in 14 Bde were bns of the Bedfordshire and Hertfordshire, the Royal Leicestershire and the Yorkshire and Lancashire Regts.
7. Patterson, *From Rattray and Beyond*, p.57. Meldrum, 'Memoirs of a Conscript', Ch.12, p.12, BWRA 0873.
8. David Rose, *Off the Record*, pp.40, 42.
9. Pte William (Cocky) Cochrane, 2BW, 'Over the Hills', memoir, BWRA 0947; written in the third person, it was told c. late-1990s to his son, Stewart, who published it as *Chindit Special Force, Burma 1944*, p.27. Characters in Cochrane's section were given pseudonyms.
10. Rose, *Off the Record*, p.42. Stewart Cochrane, *Chindit Special Force*, p.49.
11. Patterson, *From Rattray and Beyond*, pp.49–50; see Fergusson, *King's Enemies*, p.243.
12. Cochrane, *Chindit Special Force*, p.33.
13. Piper Bill Lark, quoted in Thorburn, *Jocks in the Jungle*, pp.76 & 66. See Chinnery, *March or Die*, p.231; Pipe Cpl William Henry Lark, Obit, *Red Hackle*, Nov 2012, pp.18–19. At Tobruk Lark had been told to pick up a rifle rather than play the bagpipes (which he had wanted to do). He later became a pastor.
14. Cochrane, *Chindit Special Force*, p.37. Meldrum, 'Memoirs of a Conscript', Action, p.1, BWRA 0873.
15. Nine were killed, including Wingate's ADC. Fergusson, *King's Enemies*, pp.237 & 235; *Trumpet in the Hall*, p.191. See '2BW War Diary' (17 Jun 1942–31 May 1944), pp.263–4, BWRA 0066, & Chinnery, *March or Die*, p.161, for explanations of his death including the possibility that the pilot received an electrical shock from an aerial left trailing in flight. In *Defeat into Victory*, Slim says 'three different officers each informed me that Wingate had told him he was to be his successor should one be required', p.265, Calvert being one of the most likely. See also Chinnery, *March or Die*, pp.161–2.
16. '2BW War Diary: India, Jun 1942–May 1944', 28 Mar 1944, pp.264–5, BWRA 0066: 'killing two and wounding two'.
17. '2BW War Diary', 29 Mar 1944, p.266, BWRA 0066; Fergusson, *King's Enemies*, pp.238–9. Capt the Hon H.N. Dalrymple, '63 Years on – Some Random Recollections', *Red Hackle*, Nov 2010, p.28.
18. Meldrum, 'Memoirs of a Conscript', Ch.12, p.12, BWRA 0873. See '2BW War Diary', 1 May 1944, p.296, BWRA 0066.
19. Cpl Jim McNeilly, quoted in Thorburn, *Jocks in the Jungle*, p.102. The Black Watch had two fatalities but the supply drop was not interrupted: '2BW War Diary', 5 Apr 1944, p.275, BWRA 0066.

20. See Fergusson, *King's Enemies*, p.240. 'Some of the old buffers at GHQ were not convinced, believing that aircrew could not be accurate enough to avoid hitting their own men,' Thorburn, *Jocks in the Jungle*, p.106.
21. Rose, *Off the Record*, p.45. His 'recuperation' meant riding a horse; once he felt better he walked with the men. Prickly heat infected the wound which caused 'severe blood poisoning' and he was evacuated on 24 May. His successor was Maj Michael Condon, 2nd Burma Rifles. Fergusson, *King's Enemies*, p.252, says this was 'the only occasion in the war when a unit of the Regiment was commanded by an officer from outside it. See Lt Col David Rose, DSO, Obit, Rose private papers.
22. Lark, quoted in Thorburn, *Jocks in the Jungle*, p.113. Lt Col Green, quoted in Fergusson, *King's Enemies*, p.241.
23. Cochrane, *Chindit Special Force*, p.42.
24. McNeilly, quoted in Thorburn, *Jocks in the Jungle*, p.102.
25. Cochrane, *Chindit Special Force*, p.43.
26. Lark, quoted in Thorburn, *Jocks in the Jungle*, pp.111, 114, 118.
27. Meldrum, 'Memoirs of a Conscript', Action, p.2, BWRA 0873. Cochrane, *Chindit Special Force*, p.33. Lark, quoted in Thorburn, *Jocks in the Jungle*, p.152.
28. '2BW War Diary', 2 May 1944, p.296, BWRA 0066.
29. '2BW War Diary', 5 May 1944, p.299, BWRA 0066. See Fergusson, *King's Enemies*, pp.244–5. Rose repeated Fergusson's account in full in *Off the Record*, pp.45–51. Since Rose was present and Fergusson wasn't, it is possible that Rose wrote it; see *Red Hackle*, Apr 1951, p.21, in which Fergusson acknowledges Rose as one of the 'principal written authorities' of 2BW's history.
30. Cochrane, *Chindit Special Force*, p.78. McNeilly, quoted in Thorburn, *Jocks in the Jungle*, pp.129–30. See also 2BW War Diary, 6 May 1944, p.300, BWRA 0066.
31. McNeilly, quoted in Thorburn, *Jocks in the Jungle*, pp.129–30; see '2BW War Diary', 6 May 1944, p.300, & App C No.5, referring to events 6 May 1944, pp.304–5, BWRA 0066. Cochrane, *Chindit Special Force*, pp.79–80, 85, 87. Cochrane and Lark say Pte McLuskie fired the shot which killed the rider of the white horse but Pte W. McGreary claims to have done so; see *Sunday Mail*, 10 Sep 1944. McNeilly says that he thought Geordie Ballantyne fired the shot!
32. Cochrane, *Chindit Special Force*, pp.93–6. McNeilly, quoted in Thorburn, *Jocks in the Jungle*, p.135; '2BW War Diary', 9 May, p.307, BWRA 0066. Fergusson, *King's Enemies*, p.249. Losses were 26 killed, 35 wounded and 'a few missing'.
33. Fergusson, *King's Enemies*, pp.249–50.
34. McNeilly, quoted in Thorburn, *Jocks in the Jungle*, p.139. Cochrane, *Chindit Special Force*, pp.124, 127. Fergusson, *King's Enemies*, p.251.
35. Lark, quoted in Thorburn, *Jocks in the Jungle*, pp.140–1.
36. '2BW War Diary', 26 May 1944, p.315, BWRA 0066; '2BW, Regimental Milestones, 1939–45', 27 May 1944, p.10, BWM; Patterson, *From Rattray and Beyond*, p.64.
37. John Masters, *The Road Past Mandalay*, p.259; Lt Col John Masters, DSO (1914–83), 4th Prince of Wales's Own Gurkha Rifles. It is not known if any belonged to The Black Watch contingent with the Cameronians. See Patterson, *From Rattray and Beyond*, p.64: 'I ran into Jack Masters… I asked if I could take any wounded

with me. He said "No, they are being looked after. You look after yourself and keep going."' Chinnery, *March or Die*, p.199, says 49 men were shot.

38. McNeilly, quoted in Thorburn, *Jocks in the Jungle*, p.155.
39. Fergusson, *King's Enemies*, pp.254–5. Over 1,000 sick and wounded were evacuated in the flying boats. Gertie and Doris were the stage names of two comedians, Elsie and Doris Waters, the sisters of Horace John Waters (alias Jack Warner), who played Dixon of Dock Green. One of those evacuated was Capt Dalrymple, wounded in the wrist. Fergusson, *King's Enemies* (p.253) incorrectly stated that Dalrymple lost two fingers. See *Red Hackle*, Apr 1951, p.20; Capt the Hon H.N. Dalrymple, '63 Years on…', *Red Hackle*, Nov 2010, p.29. He lived to 102!
40. FM Lord Wavell became Viceroy of India in Oct 1943, see A.P. Wavell, *Viceroy's Journal*, ed. Penderel Moon, 8 May & 13 Jun (1944), pp.71, 74. Capt A.J. Wavell had fallen ill with typhus during training and missed leaving with 2BW, but joined 77 Bde, attached to the 1st South Staffordshire Regiment. Regarding himself less seriously injured than others he refused to be evacuated. Chinnery, *March or Die*, p.213: 'A light plane kept coming back to fetch Archie, but he was adamant and nearly sixty men had been evacuated before Calvert arrived to force him on the plane.'
41. '2BW War Diary', 26 Jun & 30 Jun 1944, pp.71, 72, BWRA 0345. Graham Bishop, Intelligence Officer, 42 Col, to Rose, 29 Aug 1944, in Rose, *Off the Record*, p.53.
42. Cochrane, *Chindit Special Force*, pp.130, 133–4. The account differs slightly from his original memoir, 'Over the Hills'. '2BW War Diary', 13 Jul 1944, p.78, BWRA 0345. Bowie was pl cdr, Sec 1, A Coy, 73 Col. His pseudonym in Cochrane's account is Muir.
43. Quoted in Thorburn, *Jocks in the Jungle*, pp.169, 175.
44. '2BW War Diary', 31 Jul 1944, p.81, BWRA 0345. Another medical report revealed that from 73 and 42 Cols, only 2 officers and 48 ORs were considered fit to carry on fighting, Fergusson, *King's Enemies*, p.258. Mountbatten, later Admiral of the Fleet 1st Earl Mountbatten of Burma, KG, GCB, OM, GCIE, GCVO, DSO, PC, FRS (1900–1979), was given the rank of acting Adm in Aug 1943, VAdm in 1949 and full Adm in 1953.
45. Scottish *Sunday Mail*, quoted in Thorburn, *Jocks in the Jungle*, p.181.
46. Pte W.S. Anderson to Rose, 31 Aug 1944, quoted in Rose, *Off the Record*, p.54; Anderson was Rose's batman. Graham Bishop to Rose, 29 Aug 1944, quoted in ibid, p.53. Anon., Yorks & Lancs, quoted in Thorburn, *Jocks in the Jungle*, pp.185–6. McNeilly, quoted in ibid, p.184. McNeilly had his leg re-set in India. Cochrane, *Chindit Special Force*, p.150.
47. Meldrum, 'Memoirs of a Conscript', Action, p.4, BWRA 0873: 'Unfortunately, I didn't write all the words.' See *Songs and Ballads of Dundee*, ed. Nigel Gatherer, John Donald Publishers, Edinburgh, 1986, p.143.
48. Cochrane, *Chindit Special Force*, pp.153–4, 159. Fergusson, *King's Enemies*, p.261.
49. Psychiatric Report on 14 Inf Bde, pp.287–8, quoted in *Crisis Fleeting*, comp. & ed. by James H. Stone, Book Four: Maj Gen W.J. Officer, *With Wingate's Chindits, A Record of Heedless Valour*, Historical Unit, US Army Medical Dept, 1969.

http://history.amedd.army.mil/booksdocs/wwii/crisisfleeting/bookfour.htm, accessed 15 Feb 2017.

50. Lark, quoted in Thorburn, *Jocks in the Jungle*, p.189.
51. '2BW War Diary', 31 Jul 1944, p.104, BWRA 0345. Of the 944 killed, 452 missing and 2,434 wounded during the Second Chindit Expedition, 59 men in 2BW had died between May and Sep 1944, excluding fatalities from illness; 70 died from typhus during Jul and Aug, 'Roll of Honour and Medical History of the Second World War: Army Medical Services, Campaigns, Vol.4', HMSO, quoted in http://www.chindits.info/Thursday/FinalBattles.htm, accessed 18 Jan 2017. In 14 Bde total casualties were 354 killed, wounded, missing. Fatalities were proportionately less than for the First Chindit Expedition.
52. Lentaigne, in Cochrane, *Chindit Special Force*, pp.170–2. In 2016 a memorial was dedicated at Henu, site of the 'White City' stronghold in Myanmar; see Jeremy Archer, 'Dedication of the Chindits Memorial White City, Mawlu by 77th Brigade', 17 Mar 2016, *Red Hackle*, Nov 2016, p.31.
53. 'Whoever had that mountain was the master!', Kurt Langeluddecke, German artillery observation officer, stationed in the monastery after its destruction, quoted in Matthew Parker, *Monte Cassino*, p.209. Pte George Morrison Daily, 'A Soldier's Tale', BWRA 0961. Unless otherwise stated, all quotations in notes 53–88 are from BW officers and ORs in 6BW. H.B. McKenzie Johnston, 'Recollections of Service', p.15, BWRA 1023; see also his account: 'Monte Cassino – the Final Battle – May 1944', *Red Hackle*, May 2009, pp.23–4.
54. Eighth Army included: XIII British Corps (4th Div: 10 Bde, 12 Bde – incl 6BW, 2nd Royal Fusiliers & 1st Royal West Kents – 28 Bde, 6th Armoured Div, 8th Indian Div), I Canadian Corps, II Polish Corps. See Parker, *Monte Cassino*, pp.436–7; B.J.G. Madden, *History of the 6th Battalion*, p.37. In Jul 1944 Brig (later Maj Gen Viscount) Keith Arbuthnott took command of 78th Div (having commanded 11 Bde). Gen Clark later gave him a carbine rifle now in BWM.
55. Fergusson, *King's Enemies*, p.200. The German fortifications across Italy were collectively called the Winter Line, while the primary fortifications were along the Gustav Line; others were established along the Volturno Line and the Barbara Lines to the south, and the Caesar C and Rome Switch Lines in the north. Subsidiary lines north and south of the Gustav Line were called the Bernhardt and Adolf Hitler Lines.
56. It was later found that the Germans had agreed not to occupy the monastery; an estimated 230 Italian civilians who had taken refuge were killed during intensive bombing which also killed German and Allied troops in the surrounding region. See Hapgood & Richardson, *Monte Cassino: The Story of the Most Controversial Battle of World War II*, Da Capo (reprint ed.), 2002.
57. Framp, *Crimson Skies*, p.86. See also Eric Linklater, *The Campaign in Italy*, HMSO 1951. H.B. McKenzie Johnston, 'Recollections of Service', p.15, BWRA 1023. Daily, 'A Soldier's Tale', BWRA 0961.
58. Framp, *Crimson Skies*, p.87. McKenzie Johnston, 'Recollections of Service', p.16, BWRA 1023. Madden, *History of the 6th Battalion*, p.39. Maj George Grant,

interview, 17 Oct 2013, Perth.

59. McKenzie Johnston, 'Recollections of Service', p.16, BWRA 1023. Since AD 79 when Pompeii was destroyed, Vesuvius has erupted 30 times, but at the time of writing the last eruption was 1944.
60. McKenzie Johnston, 'Recollections of Service', p.17, BWRA 1023.
61. Geordie Cox, 'Monte Cassino – the Final Battle – May 1944', *Red Hackle*, May 2009, p.22; the painting is in BWM. Framp, *Crimson Skies*, p.103.
62. W.B. Wilson, MM Obit (by J.A. MacL Stewart), *Red Hackle*, Dec 1966, p.4. Stewart's brother, Deb, killed at the Somme in 1916, had served with Wilson in WWI. As he was carried off on a stretcher, Wilson was heard to say: 'Jist as weel ah've already had a long married life'. See Fergusson, *King's Enemies*, p.207.
63. Madden, *History of the 6th Battalion*, p.54; Fergusson, *King's Enemies*, pp.206, 207.
64. McKenzie Johnston, 'Recollections of Service', p.18, BWRA 1023.
65. Gen Alexander, in Parker, *Monte Cassino*, p.288. Nelson's actual quote is 'Numbers can only annihilate,' Nelson to Rt Hon George Rose, 6 Oct 1805 on board HMS *Victory*, 'Letters and Dispatches of Horatio Nelson', *War Times Journal*, http://www.wtj.com/archives/nelson/1805_10b.htm, accessed 15 Feb 2017.
66. Madden, *History of the 6th Battalion*, p.62, says zero hour was 11.45 pm. Vietinghoff, Cdr Tenth Army to Kesselring, in John Ellis, *Cassino: The Hollow Victory*, p.277.
67. Framp, *Crimson Skies*, p.127.
68. Maj F.G. Sutton, memoir written in 1949, p.36, docs 6018, IWM.
69. Framp, *Crimson Skies*, p.131.
70. McKenzie Johnston, 'Recollections of Service', pp.18–19, BWRA 1023. 'Now began four months away from the war.' He returned to 6BW in Sep 1944. Sgt R. Bonella, St Andrew's Day programme, BBC, in 'MM Notes WW2', Thomas B. Smyth research material. Bonella was awarded the MM for his actions at Monte Savino on 5 Jul 1944.
71. Daily, 'A Soldier's Tale', BWRA 0961.
72. Madden, *History of the 6th Battalion*, p.70; Fergusson, *King's Enemies*, p.211. After the collapse of Tunis, no more South African units fought in Europe but individuals were permitted to do so. Fergusson, *King's Enemies*, p.210, mistakenly wrote that RSM Dyce was among the fatalities, see *Red Hackle*, Apr 1951, p.20.
73. Sgt J.D. Lewis, account of service in 8BW, 7 May 1998, p.4, BWM. He says 8BW landed with 2 Sherwood Foresters 'on 22-1-44, broke out on 25-5-44' (22 Jan & 25 May 1944); the original 8BW had been merged with 9BW in Aug 1941; in Sep 1942, 30BW became 8BW. The Adolf Hitler Line was renamed the Senger Line (after Gen Fridolin von Senger und Etterlin) since Hitler did not want to give the Allies a propaganda advantage if the 'Adolf Hitler Line' was broken.
74. The sub-title of John Ellis' book *Cassino, The Hollow Victory: The Battle for Rome Jan–Jun 1944*; see pp.469–70.
75. Daily, 'A Soldier's Tale', BWRA 0961.
76. Madden, *History of the 6th Battalion*, p.79. Framp, *Crimson Skies*, p.153.
77. The poem has been described as by 'Various, 1944-5', Ellis, *Cassino*, p.468. It has

also been attributed to LSgt Harry Pynn but see Timothy Neat, *Hamish Henderson*, I, p.152 who gives authorship to Hamish Scott Henderson (1919–2002), who was serving in the Intelligence Corps, and later commanded some partisans.

78. Madden, quoted in Col Vesey Holt, 'Occasional Letter No.1', *Red Hackle,* Aug 1980, p.25. Once Overlord began Wauchope asked Holt, CO of the Regimental Depot, to write 'occasional letters' informing him of any 'regimental gossip'. Madden wrote to Holt who transmitted the news to Wauchope. Framp, *Crimson Skies,* p.148.
79. Madden, *History of the 6th Battalion*, pp.85–6. Gian Caspare Napolitano, *To War with The Black Watch,* tr. Ian Campbell Ross, Birlinn, 2007.
80. Madden, *History of the 6th Battalion,* pp.91, 96. Madden's wound required evacuation and he did not return to 6BW in Italy.
81. Henry McKenzie Johnston, interview, 19 Sep 2014. Madden, *History of the 6th Battalion*, p.87.
82. Framp, *Crimson Skies,* pp.152-3.
83. Pte G.A. Wombwell, diary, 1 Sep 1944, BWRA 0986.
84. Framp, *Crimson Skies,* p.156.
85. Wombwell, diary, 15 Sep 1944, BWRA 0986. Framp, *Crimson Skies*, pp.163–5; he was evacuated, arriving home shortly before Christmas 1944 (having also been wounded at Monte Cassino); Madden, *History of the 6th Battalion*, p.99. The requirements of the campaign in Normandy meant that no more reinforcements were being sent to Italy and D Coy was disbanded.
86. Madden, *History of the 6th Battalion*, p.102. Casualties were 'about 70'.
87. McKenzie Johnston, 'Recollections of Service', p.21, BWRA 1023. Lt Col Graham Macpherson-Smith was suffering 'extreme fatigue', and as 'the only other officer with him at Bn HQ', McKenzie Johnston briefly took command. See Madden, *History of the 6th Battalion*, pp.103, 106.
88. McKenzie Johnston, 'Recollections of Service', p.21, BWRA 1023. Maj Archie Callander died of wounds on 21 Oct 1944, Madden, *History of the 6th Battalion*, p.101.
89. Statistics for 11 May–5 Jun 1944 from Ellis, *Cassino,* p. 469. Allied casualties for the whole Cassino/Rome campaign of 105,000 casualties for the Allied armies and *at least* 80,000 Germans, p. 469n*.
90. Pte Graham Shand, 5BW, diary, 6 Jun 1944, BWRA 0844/20; he had transferred to 5BW from 4BW in Apr. Diaries were forbidden but he wrote on scraps of paper, later transcribing his daily activities into a diary.
91. RQMS Edward Meekison, 'The Story of a Quartie's War whilst Serving with the 5th Black Watch (RHR), p.12, BWRA 0878/2.
92. John McGregor, *Spirit of Angus*, p.114; he was in command of A Coy, 5BW.
93. Meekison, 'Quartie's War', p.13, BWRA 0878/2. McGregor, *Spirit of Angus*, p.115. Since 153 Bde had been in the rear during operations in Sicily, it had been chosen to be in the advance here, becoming 51HD's only unit to land on D-Day. As a 'follow up' formation it was to be deployed 'piecemeal'; see J.B. Salmond, *51st Highland Division*, p.139n1.

94. McGregor, *Spirit of Angus*, p.117: 4 ORs were killed, 3 wounded; Canadian casualties were comparable.
95. Brig J.A. Hopwood, '1BW History' (draft), N.W. Europe, Ch.1, p.7, BWRA 0727. Part of the account was compiled by John Benson, 2IC Aug 1944–Jan 45, Hopwood to Capt. J. McIntyre, undated letter.
96. LCpl Henry Scivity Barker, 1BW, 'Memoirs 1939–46', p.34, BWRA 0966/1. The 1st Tyneside Scottish was under the command of Lt Col R.W.M. De Winton; Hopwood, '1BW History' (draft), NW Europe, Ch.1, pp.7–8, BWRA 0727.
97. See J.L.R. Samson, *Geordie and Jock*, pp.11–12; Tom Renouf, *Black Watch*, p.96; Brian Stewart, *Scrapbook of a Roving Highlander*, p.53. Capt Donald Mirrielees (1915–44) to My dearest family, 14 Jun 1944, Rose Laycock private papers. Capt (later Maj) Mirrielees (1915–44) served with 2BW in Palestine 1937–38, and with 1BW and 4BW before being attached to 1st Tyneside Scottish in Nov 1943.
98. Stewart, *Scrapbook of a Roving Highlander*, p.54.
99. McGregor, *Spirit of Angus*, pp.119–20. 153 Bde was under the command of 3 Para Bde (composed of the 1st Canadian and the 8th and 9th Parachute Bns); 5BW's casualty list was 19 officers and 285 ORs, '153 Bde War Diary', Jun 1944, WO 171/678, TNA. Meekison, 'Quartie's War', p.15, BWRA 0878/2.
100. McGregor, *Spirit of Angus*, pp.121–2, 123; 30 officers and men were killed on 12 Jun.
101. Ibid, pp.123–4. McGregor compared these figures with 529 casualties in the whole North African campaign and 111 in the Sicilian campaign. There is no corroboration for the claim made by Lt Col Terence Otway, CO, 9th Parachute Bn, when aged 86 in 2000, that he had to take a battalion of the Black Watch, i.e. 5BW, under his command because 'the CO broke down'. Otway, recollections, SWWEC; Anthony Beevor, *D-Day*, p.187.
102. Shand, diary, 12 Jun 1944, BWRA 0844/20; Meekison, 'Quartie's War', pp.15, 19, BWRA 0878/2. The survivor was disbelieved at first 'but months later there came confirmation that his story was true. They had been shot in the back as they stood,' Fergusson, *King's Enemies*, p.267; also Salmond, *51st Highland Division*, p.142, & Richard Doherty, *None Bolder*, p.153. See also Neil Barber, *The Day the Devils Dropped in, the 9th Parachute Battalion in Normandy – D-day to D+6, The Merville Battery to the Château St Côme*, Leo Cooper, 2004, p.222n1, which cites a recollection from Padre Tom Nicol & correspondence with Thomas B. Smyth, Jun–Jul 2010, re- Pte Arthur Fisher, killed at Château St Côme, and his son Michael's anxiety to find out more about his father's fate. See also 153 Bde HQ War Diary, WO171/678, TNA.
103. Barker, 'Memoirs 1939–46', p.35, BWRA 0966/1. See Salmond, *51st Highland Division*, p.144. Dow, 'Memoirs', p.3, BWRA 0640/4.
104. John McLaren, telephone interview, 27 Sep 2016, recollections of his father, Stewart McLaren, wounded on 26 Jun 1944. Penicillin had only come into relatively widespread use to treat infection in 1942. McLaren spent the rest of the war helping to train soldiers, many of whom he taught to read; he recovered sufficiently to play cricket for Scotland 1947–9.

105. See Shand, diary, 24 Jun 1944, BWRA 0844/20; McGregor, *Spirit of Angus*, p.126. Renouf, *Black Watch,* p.104. The Germans also brought up reinforcements, including the 12th SS-Panzer Division, known as *Hitlerjugend*, under the command of Kurt Meyer.
106. Pte P. Lawton, 18 Pl, D Coy, quoted in Kevin Baverstock, *Breaking the Panzers*, 26 Jun 1944, p.33.
107. See Baverstock, *Breaking the Panzers*, 1 Jul 1944, pp.63ff; '1st Tyneside Scottish War Diary', BWRA 0907/13 & 0907/14, App B: 'In personnel we lost two officers killed, five wounded and two missing. Thirty-one ORs were killed, seventy-nine wounded and thirteen are missing.' OC A Coy, Maj W.L. McGregor, was badly wounded by a mortar bomb.
108. Renouf, *Black Watch*, pp.99–100.
109. Stewart to Mother, 1 Jul 1944 (evening), *Scrapbook of a Roving Highlander*, pp.55–6, 60.
110. 'Bn ceases to administer itself and now exists in name only,' '1st Tyneside Scottish War Diary', 9 Sep 1944, BWRA 0907/14 (also WO/171/1382, TNA). The Bn was briefly employed in the Tilly-sur-Seulles and Caen sectors. On 18 Oct 1944, The Tyneside Scottish went into 'suspended animation', becoming 670 Light-Anti Aircraft Regiment RA (TA) on 1 Jan 1947, Samson, *Geordie and Jock*, p.12.
111. Renouf, *Black Watch*, p.132. See Maj J.L.R. Samson (1926–88), Obit by G.C. & by H.B.B., *Red Hackle*, Aug 1988, p.8. He was commissioned on 31 May 1946; see *Officers of The Black Watch 1725–1986.*
112. Operation Epsom, also known as the First Battle of the Odon, was carried out by VIII Corps, under the command of Lt Gen Sir Richard O'Connor who had been a veteran of Wavell's 1940 Western Desert campaign. In support of Epsom, 51HD had carried out a preliminary attack from east of the Orne. Caen was finally taken in Operation Charnwood, 8–9 Jul 1944.
113. Capt A.C.C. Brodie to Dear family, 2 Jul 1944, BWRA 0844/10. Reinforcements were by drafts from Midland Regiments: 'Quite a nice lot and fairly intelligent', Brodie said of his subalterns. See also Col A.C.C. Brodie, 'My time with the 51st (Highland) Division', p.7, BWRA 0844/09; Roderick Grant, *51st Highland Division,* p.111.
114. Shand, diary, 10 Jul 1944, BWRA 0844/20.
115. Roland Dane, 7BW, interview, 20 May 2015, Banbury. Shand, diary, 11 Jul 1944, p.6, BWRA 0844/20. Douglas Sinclair Roger, 5BW, interview, 7 Jul 2009, Perth. Roger was a Coy Clerk and so 'not very far forward in engagements… I think you worked on the principle if your name was on it, you would get it'.
116. McGregor, *Spirit of Angus*, pp.129, 131. Brodie returned to 5BW after convalescing in Inverness. He contradicted Fergusson's claim, in *King's Enemies*, p.301, that he was abandoned by stretcher-bearers. See *Red Hackle,* Apr 1951, p.20. In the action, from 5BW 5 officers and 66 ORs were killed or missing, 3 officers and 54 ORs were wounded; *7th Black Watch History*, p.95, gives 2 killed and 13 wounded from 7BW.
117. Report by Lt Col C.N. Thomson, DSO, 23 Jul 1944, quoted in McGregor, *Spirit of*

Angus, pp.127, 129. Brig (later Gen Sir) Horatius (Nap) Murray, GCB, KBE, DSO (1903–89) to Lt Col Thomson, 16 Jul 1944, quoted in ibid, p.130. Dane, interview, 20 May 2015.

118. McGregor, *Spirit of Angus*, pp.131–2.
119. Shand, diary, 18 Jul 1944, BWRA 0844/20.
120. Rommel never returned to the battlefront: accused of being complicit in the 20 Jul 1944 plot, rather than face a People's Court, which would have consigned his family to a concentration camp, he agreed to take cyanide; his death on 14 Oct 1944 was announced as a result of injuries sustained on 17 Jul.
121. See Salmond, *51st Highland Division*, pp.150–2 for appreciation of Rennie. The change of command was on 26 Jul. Montgomery had become dissatisfied with 51HD's performance, writing to Brooke on 15 Jul: '51st [Highland] Division is at present not – NOT – battleworthy. It does not fight with determination and has failed in every operation it has been given to do.' Quoted in Beevor, *D-Day*, p.279.
122. Lt Gen Guy Simonds, CC, CB, CBE, DSO, CD (1903–1974) had fought in N. Africa and Sicily. At Dieppe over half the force of over 6,000 men were killed, wounded or captured, including nearly all of the 325 men in The Black Watch (Royal Highland Regiment) of Canada.
123. Maj Gen Thomas Rennie, 'Special Order of the Day, 7 Aug 1944', quoted in Salmond, *51st Highland Division*, p.155; McGregor, *Spirit of Angus*, p.133; Doherty, *None Bolder*, p.170.
124. Referred to as Totalisator in '153 Bde HQ War Diary', WO171/678 quoted in Doherty, *None Bolder*, p.168.
125. Dow, 'Memoirs', p.4, BWRA 0640/4.
126. Sgt Robert Penman, 'One Man's War, reminiscences of WW2', p.69.
127. Capt Donald Mirrielees to Darling Netia, 10 Aug 1944. He was OC B Coy, 5BW, having transferred from the 1st Tyneside Scottish. He was killed by 'a direct hit' on the chest, H.B. Boyne to Mrs Mirrielees, 8 Sep 1944, Laycock private papers. A monument to those killed at Mauny was erected in 2013; see Dr Tom Renouf, MM, 'The Mauny Pilgrimage – 1st June 2013', *Red Hackle*, Nov 2013, pp.24–5.
128. Gen Montgomery, 'Personal Message', 11 Aug 1944, quoted in Salmond, *51st Highland Division*, p.156, & McGregor, *Spirit of Angus*, p.134. 'Piobaireachd', 12 Aug 1944, WW2 Box N, BWM; the newsletter was first published on 14 Jun 1944.
129. Maj Gen Rennie, message to the Division, quoted in McGregor, *Spirit of Angus*, p.141–2, & Salmond, *51st Highland Division*, pp.170–1.
130. Barker, 'Memoirs, 1939–46', p.37, BWRA 0966/1. Dow, 'Memoirs', p.9, BWRA 6404/4. See Hopwood, '1BW History' (draft), NW Europe, Ch.3, p.32, BWRA 0727.
131. McGregor, *Spirit of Angus*, p.142. The force involved mainly Canadians, with some British and Americans, including The Royal Highland Regiment (The Black Watch) of Canada.
132. Shand, diary, 2 & 3 Sep1944, BWRA 0844/20. McGregor, *Spirit of Angus*, p.142. Lt Col Bill Bradford, Maj Graham Pilcher and Pte Graham Shand had all served in the original 51st Highland Division.
133. See Salmond, *51st Highland Division*, p.173. The Derbyshire Yeomanry were the

first troops of the Division to enter, with claims that Capt Dawson, 5th Seaforth, 152 Brigade, was the first infantryman from a Regiment with a prior connection. Dow, 'Memoirs', p.9, BWRA 0640/4.

134. Maj Gen Thomas Rennie, message to the Division, typescript, Ormond private papers. See also Ernest Reoch, *The St Valéry Story*, p.225; Saul David, *Churchill's Sacrifice*, p.249.
135. Dow, 'Memoirs', p.9, BWRA 0640/4.
136. Ibid.
137. Lt Col Bill Bradford, 'Diary of 5BW movements', 5–9 and 10 Sep 1944, p.7, BWRA 0844/12.
138. Dow, 'Memoirs', p.10, BWRA 0640/4. See Salmond, *51st Highland Division,* p.176; Fergusson, *King's Enemies*, p.279. Col Eberhard Wildermuth (1890–1952) was not a general although Dow refers to him as such. The refusal to permit the evacuation of civilians during the bombardment became controversial when Lt (acting Capt) William Douglas-Home, 141st Regiment Royal Armoured Corps, refused to follow orders; his letter of protest published in the *Maidenhead Advertiser* prompted his temporary arrest.
139. Barker, 'Memoirs 1939–46', p.37, BWRA 0966/1. Dow, 'Memoirs', p.10, BWRA 0640/4.
140. Salmond, *51st Highland Division,* p.183. Dow, 'Memoirs', p.11, BWRA 0640/4. Maj Gen Rennie, message to all troops in 51HD, 13 Sep 1944, quoted in McGregor, *Spirit of Angus*, p.144. The port had been so badly destroyed during the attack that it was not usable until a month later.
141. Montgomery, Personal Message, 17 Sep 1944, quoted in Salmond, *51st Highland Division*, pp.179–180. Max Hastings, *All Hell Let Loose,* p.581.
142. Roland Dane, 7BW, 'Memoir 2014', p.1, Dane private papers; D.F.O. Russell, *War History of the 7th Bn The Black Watch (R.H.R.),* p.105; Salmond, *51st Highland Division*, pp.180–1. Later Brig Walter Michael Wingate-Gray, OBE, MC and bar (1921–95).
143. Barker, 'Memoirs 1939–46', pp.38–9, BWRA 0966/1; Dow, 'Memoirs', p.11, BWRA 6404/4.
144. Salmond, *51st Highland Division*, pp.184–5. XII Corps included the 51st Highland Div with its affiliated 33rd Armoured Div as well as the 7th Armoured, 15th Scottish and 53rd Welsh Divs.
145. Shand, diary, 23 Oct 1944, p.11, BWRA 0844/20.
146. Bradford to Gen Sir Arthur Wauchope, 8 Nov 1944, p.10, BWRA 0844/12. Capt James Borthwick, 'Belgium and Holland', *With the Scottish Troops in Europe,* p.22. Borthwick had enlisted in The Black Watch in 1940 and was an original member of the reconstituted Highland Division. He served in Egypt and before Alamein was seconded to Public Relations as officer-observer, 51st HD, writing 400 stories. As a civilian he was a well-known journalist for the *Southern Reporter*. See 'Capt James Borthwick, Officer-Observer', *51st Highland Division in North Africa and Sicily,* p.43.
147. Maj Gen Rennie, message to the Division, 8 Nov 1944, in Salmond, *51st Highland*

Division, p.192. Rennie noted casualties: 44 officers and 630 ORs, of whom 7 officers and 115 ORs were killed. 2,408 Germans were taken prisoner 'and enemy casualties must have been heavy'. Dane, interview, 20 May 2015. The Sgt could have been Sgt Anthony Foy, the only one listed on the Roll of Honour as killed on 30 Oct 1944.

148. See Salmond, *51st Highland Division,* pp.194–5; Bradford to Wauchope, 3 Dec 1944, BWRA 0844/12. Fergusson, *King's Enemies,* p.289.
149. Meekison, 'Quartie's War', p.28, BWRA 0878/2. Russell, *War History of the 7th Bn,* p.117. Dow, 'Memoirs', p.16, BWRA 6404/4.
150. Hopwood, '1BW History' (draft), NW Europe, Ch.5, p.59, BWRA 0727. See Pieter Stolte, *The 51st Highland Division in the Ardennes.* Meekison, 'Quartie's War', p.28, BWRA 0878/2.
151. See Samson, *Concise Account of the Black Watch and its Movements,* p.29; Bradford, 'Occasional Letter No.1', 21 Jul 1944, BWRA 0844/12. In Jul 1944 4BW moved to 165 Infantry Bde, after 8 months in 5 London Infantry Bde. In Dec 1944, an 8th Infantry Holding Bn was formed from the 8th Infantry Training Centre, Perth, growing 'rather like a mushroom'. See *Red Hackle,* Jan 1946, p.15.
152. McKenzie Johnston, 'Recollections of Service', p.22, BWRA 1023. The Communist Party was the Kommounistikó Kómma Elládas (KKE). ELAS = *Ellinikós Laïkós Apeleftherotikós Stratós,* i.e. The Greek People's Liberation Army. Daily, 'A Soldier's Tale', BWRA 0961; Madden, *History of 6th Battalion,* p.108. See Fergusson, *King's Enemies,* pp.218–22.
153. McKenzie Johnston, 'Recollections of Service', p.23, BWRA 1023; Capt R.M. Honey, 'Episodes in Greece', typescript, McKenzie Johnston private papers.
154. Daily, 'A Soldier's Tale', BWRA 0961. Pte Edward Hawthorne was killed on 26 Dec during an attack on a platoon. McCartney's death is recorded as occurring on 1 Jan 1945.
155. 'Piobaireachd', 31 Dec 1944, WW2 Box N, BWM. Shand, diary, 31 Dec 1944, p.12, BWRA 0844/20.
156. William Shakespeare, *Richard III,* Act 1, Sc.1.

15. 1945: Unconditional Surrender

1. Derek Howard-Smith, telephone interview, 12 Jun 2015. He was a private in 7BW.
2. RQMS Edward Meekison, 'The Story of a Quartie's War whilst Serving with the 5th Black Watch (RHR)', p.37, BWRA 0878/2.
3. Winston S. Churchill, House of Commons, 18 Jan 1945, in *Never Give In!,* p.371.
4. Pte George Morrison Daily, 6BW, 'A Soldier's Tale', BWRA 0961; H.B. McKenzie Johnston, 6BW, 'Recollections of Service', p.23, BWRA 1023.
5. Capt James Borthwick, 'The Ardennes', *With the Scottish Troops in Europe,* p.73. McGregor, *Spirit of Angus,* p.163. Pte John Mitchell, 5BW, quoted in Stolte, *51st Highland Division,* p.12.
6. Pte Alexander Barr, Carrier Pl, 7BW, quoted in Stolte, *51st Highland Division in the Ardennes,* p.17, an account which includes many interviews from research

carried out in 1997. Lt Col Bill Bradford to Gen Sir Arthur Wauchope, 'Operations 1–23 Jan 1945', p.12, BWRA 0844/12. Roland Dane, 7BW, interview, 20 May 2015, Banbury. Borthwick, 'The Ardennes', *With the Scottish Troops in Europe*, p.73; a nicky-tam was a pair of straps or pieces of string tied around the leg below the knee to raise trousers above the level of farmyard dirt.

7. Pte Stanley Whitehouse, 1BW, quoted in Stolte, *51st Highland Division*, p.18. Pte Percy Lawton, 5BW, quoted in ibid, p.61.
8. Lt William M. Chisholm, 5BW, quoted in Stolte, *51st Highland Division*, p.23. The PIAT bomb first introduced in Sicily in 1943 was the Projector Infantry Anti-Tank weapon, capable of launching a small (2.5lb) bomb.
9. Tom Renouf, *Black Watch*, pp.202–3.
10. D.F.O. Russell, *War History of the 7th Bn The Black Watch (R.H.R.)*, p.119.
11. LSgt J. Rowe, 1BW, quoted in Stolte, *51st Highland Division*, pp.34–5. This could have been Lt James McKillop, buried in Geel War Cemetery.
12. Sgt Jim Burrow, 1BW, quoted in Stolte, *51st Highland Division*, p.36. Maj Ambrose Walton, quoted in Stolte, *51st Highland Division*, p.37.
13. J.B. Salmond, *51st Highland Division*, p.209.
14. Pte Charles Gate, 7BW, quoted in Stolte, *51st Highland Division*, pp.38–9. 'Monty's moonlight' was artificial moonlight created by reflecting light onto the clouds, used during previous campaigns since the Normandy invasion.
15. 'Piobaireachd', 12 Jan 1945, WW2 Box N, BWM. Pte Graham Shand, 5BW, diary, 13 Jan 1945, BWRA 0844/20. Pte Tom Renouf, 5BW, quoted in Stolte, *51st Highland Division*, p.58. See also McGregor, *Spirit of Angus*, pp.163–4.
16. Renouf, quoted in Stolte, *51st Highland Division*, p.57. John McGregor, *Spirit of Angus*, pp.165–6.
17. Salmond, *51st Highland Division*, p.212; Stolte, *51st Highland Division*, p.76. XXX Corps had 325 fatalities, 969 wounded and 114 missing.
18. Stalin was unwilling to allow France to occupy a zone, unless this came from the zones occupied by the US and UK. Yalta was the second of three wartime conferences attended by the Big Three represented by Churchill (UK), Roosevelt (USA) and Stalin (USSR), preceded by the Teheran Conference (1943). The third was at Potsdam in Jul 1945 attended by the newly elected British PM Clement Attlee, Stalin and Roosevelt's successor, Harry S. Truman (1884–1972), 33rd US President. On 9 Aug 1945 Soviet forces attacked Manchukuo.
19. Cpl Andrew Dow, 5BW, 'Memoirs, France, Holland, Belgium, Germany, 1944–45', p.18, BWRA 6404/4.
20. Russell, *War History of the 7th Bn*, pp.122-3. (Russell was no longer present, after being seriously wounded at Le Havre in Sep 1944.) The 3rd Canadian Div was on the left flank, 51HD on the right, with the 2nd Canadian, 15th Scottish and 53rd Welsh in between.
21. Shand, diary, 7 & 8 Feb 1945, BWRA 0844/20. Salmond, *51st Highland Division*, p.215. It was one of the heaviest artillery bombardments of the war, using 5.5 inch guns. See Kevin Baverstock, 'Clearing a Path to the Rhine – February 1945', *Red Hackle*, May 2005, p.23.

22. Russell, *War History of the 7th Bn*, p.123. Roland Dane, interview, 20 May 2015. LCpl Henry Scivity Barker, 1BW, 'Memoirs 1939–46', p.42, BWRA 0966/1.
23. Salmond, *51st Highland Division*, p.215. Lt Col Hopwood was on leave. Horrocks had resumed command of XXX Corps, having been absent during the Battle of the Bulge.
24. Dow, 'Memoirs', p.18, BWRA 6404/4.
25. Ibid.
26. Salmond, *51st Highland Division*, pp.218–19, 221. Maj Donald Ian Molteno was the first cousin of Maj Donald Mirrielees MC, killed at Mauny in Aug 1944, whose family lived at Garth House, once the home of the Regiment's early historian, David Stewart of Garth. His nephew is Lt Col R.M. Riddell.
27. Graham Pilcher, interview, 11 Nov 2008, 'This Happens in War', BWM. Shand, diary, 11 Feb 1944, p.14, BWRA 0844/20.
28. See Dennis Hall, '7th Battalion – Black Watch – 60 Years on!', *Red Hackle*, Nov 2005, p.20. Capt Brodie, 5BW, letter to his family, 25 Feb 1945, General Hospital, B.L.A.; & 28 Feb 1945, QE Hospital Birmingham, BWRA 0844/10.
29. Brodie, ibid. The second letter repeats the information in his more detailed letter dated 25 Feb 1945. For his 'courageous and heroic leadership, his dauntless determination and devotion to duty', Brodie was later awarded the DSO. Citation, Maj A.C.C. Brodie. Also wounded was D Coy's runner, Pte Malcolm McInnes.
30. Gen Harry Crerar, CH, CB, DSO, KStJ, CD, PC (1888–1965).
31. Dow, 'Memoirs', pp.21–2, BWRA 6404/4. The Buffaloes were one of 'Hobart's Funnies', amphibious vehicles and tanks, whose development had been overseen by Maj Gen Sir Percy Hobart, KBE, CB, DSO, MC (1885–1957), British 79th Armoured Div.
32. Col Ian Critchley, 7BW, interview, 21 Nov 2012, Crieff. Although commissioned into the Regt in Nov 1944, Critchley was not permitted to serve abroad until after his 19th birthday on 7 Feb 1945. Prof Karl Joseph Leyser (1920–92) was a German Jew, evacuated to Britain in the 1930s by his parents (who remained in hiding in Holland). He was released from internment by enlisting in the Pioneer Corps (reportedly the only British unit in which 'enemy aliens' could serve) and commissioned into The Black Watch in 1944. He was later the Chichele Professor of Medieval History and a Fellow of All Soul's Oxford.
33. FM Montgomery, quoted in Salmond, *51st Highland Division*, pp.229–30.
34. See Brig J.A. Hopwood, '1BW History' (draft), NW Europe, Ch.1, pp.78–9, BWRA 0727: 154 Bde on the left, 153 Bde on the right, with 152 Bde behind 153 Bde and 9 Canadian Bde on the left flank; Salmond, *51st Highland Division*, p.231. Part of Hopwood's account was compiled by John Benson, 2IC from Aug 1944–Jan 45 since Hopwood had been injured.
35. Critchley, interview, 21 Nov 2012, Crieff. Barker, 'Memoirs 1939–46', pp.43–4, BWRA 0966/1.
36. Hall, '7th Battalion – Black Watch – 60 Years On!', *Red Hackle*, Nov 2005, p.20. Critchley, interview, 21 Nov 2012 & 18 Apr 2015, Crieff; interview, 4 Nov 2008, 'This Happens in War', BWM. See Russell, *War History of the 7th Bn*, p.130;

Salmond, *51st Highland Division*, p.233. The Schu-mine 42 was a German anti-personnel blast landmine, consisting of a wooden box with hinged lid containing a block of TNT. It was cheap to produce and the wooden box made detection more difficult. Rollo's contingent had been hit by Spandau fire resulting in two fatalities, while Rollo was wounded and shell-shocked.

37. Dow, 'Memoirs', pp.22–3, BWRA 6404/4.
38. Lt Col Bill Bradford, 'Operations War Diary 5BW', 24 Mar 1945, p.19, BWRA 0844/12. Shand, diary, 24 Mar 1945, p.16, BWRA 0844/20.
39. Critchley, interview, 21 Nov 2012, Crieff; & 4 Nov 2008 'This Happens in War', BWM. Buried in the village of Appeldorn alongside four soldiers, Rennie was re-interred in the Reichswald Forest War Cemetery. His former batman, LCpl Davy Chalmers, visited his grave 'three or four times', 'Six Years of My Life', p.9, BWM 2014.530. Richard Boyle was Bernard Fergusson's cousin. Before returning to the Regiment in time to take part in the Reichswald offensive he had been on the staff of IV Corps. Hopwood, '1BW History' (draft), NW Europe, Ch.1, pp.86–7 & 'The Final Advance and German Capitulation, 8 Apr–4 May, Op. Eclipse', p.1, BWRA 0727.
40. Gen Gordon MacMillan, KCB, KCVO, CBE, DSO, MC & two bars (1897–1986) was wounded in Aug 1944, but returned to France in Nov 1944 to take command of the 49th West Riding Div.
41. Hall, '7th Battalion – Black Watch – 60 Years On!', *Red Hackle*, Nov 2005, p.21. Hopwood, '1BW History' (draft), 'The Final Advance and German Capitulation, pp.1–2, BWRA 0727. Derek Howard-Smith, telephone interview, 12 Jun 2015.
42. Lt Col Bill Bradford to Gen Sir Arthur Wauchope, 27 Apr 1945, BWRA 0844/12. By 27 Apr 51HD was at Westertimke. Maj Graham Pilcher, OC C Coy, was seriously wounded, when a fragment of shell went through his neck and came out of his stomach; he spent three months in hospital, but then lived until the age of 92!
43. Pte Robert Mitchelson, POW, extract from 'A Wartime Log for British Prisoners', 12 Apr 1945, p.3, BWRA 0719. In Aug 1944 he was moved from Stalag 357 to Fallingbostel (Stalag IXB).
44. LCpl John Grieve, 1BW, 'Oral History 1999', Thomas B. Smyth research material. Dave Hutton, interview, 4 Nov 2008, 'This Happens in War', BWM. In 2003 he went to Prague and contacted the son of one of the Czechs who had helped him in 1945.
45. Mitchelson, extract from 'A Wartime Log for British Prisoners', 16 Apr 1945, p.3, BWRA 0719.
46. Bombardier E.E. Rafferty, RA, written statement. He was a POW in Stalag XXB, Marienburg, (Malbrok), East Prussia, POWs 1945, Thomas B. Smyth research material. The distance from Marienburg to Putlitz was approx 525 km. Since Jul 1944 a series of forced marches (known mainly as The March but also called the Long March) had been undertaken when the Germans decided to evacuate prisoners from the camps in territory soon to be occupied by the Soviet Union. Weather conditions were extreme and hundreds died. One of the small Union Jacks made is on exhibition in the BWM.
47. Meekison, 'Quartie's War', p.37, BWRA 0878/2. Others were not so lucky: Sgt

Peter Prentice was killed on 4 May and Pte Harry Kirk on 6 May at Hipstedt. 7BW's last recorded fatality during WWII was Pte William Ness on 7 May. 1BW had no fatalities in May.

48. 'Piobaireachd', 5 May 1945, WW2 Box N, BWM. Meekison, 'Quartie's War', p.37, BWRA 0878/2. Renouf, *Black Watch*, p.287; he was awarded the MM for his actions crossing the Rhine, 'LCpl Tom Renouf', 'MM Notes WW2', *London Gazette,* 7 Jun 1945, Thomas B. Smyth research material.
49. Meekison, 'Quartie's War', p.37, BWRA 0878/2. Dow, 'Memoirs', p.29, BWRA 6404/4.
50. Barker, 'Memoirs 1939–46,' pp.46, 47–8, BWRA 0966/1.
51. Critchley, interview, 18 Apr 2015.
52. Renouf, *Black Watch*, pp.288–89.
53. Ibid, p.290. He wrongly says the river was the Weser.
54. Ibid, pp.291–4 (NB misprint on p.291 states Mar instead of May). The official version is that Himmler killed himself intentionally; other accounts suggest he accidentally bit on the cyanide pill during a scuffle or that he was killed by British Intelligence to prevent him revealing details of secret peace negotiations. He was buried anonymously on Lüneburg Heath. The file on Himmler's death cannot be opened until 2045.
55. Meekison, 'Quartie's War', p.39, BWRA 0878/2. Renouf, *Black Watch,* p.295.
56. Meekison, 'Quartie's War', p.41, BWRA 0878/2. He ended his service in 1945, arriving home on 6 Dec 'more than six long years since I marched out of Arbroath a raw Private of C Company, 5th Bn, The Black Watch (RHR)', p.42. He visited Belsen with Eddie Macmillan and Frankie Stuart, the MT Stores Specialist Sgt.
57. Adm Lord Mountbatten to Brig Mike Calvert (undated), quoted in Chinnery, *March or Die,* pp.236–7. Reunions of the 44/2 Indian Airborne Div were held regularly.
58. Bernard Fergusson, *Trumpet in the Hall,* p.196. Also in 14 Bde were the 4th/6th Rajputana Rifles and 6th/16th Punjab Regt. Two other Bdes – the Indian 50th and 77th Parachute – made up the Div.
59. Cochrane, *Chindit Special Force*, p.201.
60. Pte Edward Graves, 2BW, 'My First Year Abroad', pp.52–5, BWRA 0914.
61. '2BW War Diary', Sep 1944–Dec 1946 (handwritten), 9 May 1945, p.83, BW 2433/3.
62. Graves, 'My First Year Abroad', pp.57–61, BWRA 0914.
63. '2BW War Diary', Sep 1944–Dec 1946 (handwritten), 15 Aug 1945, p.122, BW 2433/3.
64. Graves, 'My First Year Abroad', pp.62–3, BWRA 0914. Col Ian Critchley, 'Last Days in India', *Red Hackle,* May 2008, p.18.
65. See account by John Benson, 'The 2nd Battalion becomes a Parachute Battalion, 1945', reprinted from *Red Hackle*, in 'Newsletter, The Black Watch (RHR), 44/2 Indian Airborne Division, Apr 1993', BWM. Additional information, Col Ian Critchley, 4 Feb 2016.
66. Max Hastings, *All Hell Let Loose,* p.xv. Statistics also given as between 50 and 70

million, at least 2.5% of the population in 1939.

67. Roll of Honour, Scottish National War Memorial, BWRA 0260 gives statistics of 142 officers, 1,237 ORs. See Salmond, *51st Highland Division*, p.273, '51st Highland Division – Battle Casualties, N.W. Europe from D-Day, 6 Jun 1944–5 May 1945' (5th Camerons lost almost as many as 5BW).
68. C.K. Bate and M.G. Smith, *For Bravery in the Field*, p.261.
69. Lt Col Peter Taylor, DSO, MC, TD. See J.B. Salmond, *51st Highland Division*, p.215, & Fergusson, 'The Black Watch and the King's Enemies', *Red Hackle*, Apr 1951, p.20. Others who rose from the ranks were Edward (Eddie) Robertson, who had enlisted in 1911, rising to the rank of acting Lt Col in 1942; see Maj Edward Robertson, MBE, MC, Obit by Bernard Fergusson, *Red Hackle*, Apr 1959, p.5; James (Tam) Irons, RSM 2BW in 1939, became Col Commanding the Training Depot in Cyprus; see Col J. Irons, OBE, Obit by J.McK., *Red Hackle*, Aug 1981, p.10. In WWI, Lt Col James Kennedy, DSO & bar, MC, DCM, rose from the ranks.
70. Eleanor Fortune to Hon Mrs Adrian (Ursula) Grant Duff, 4 Jan 1944, Ormond private papers. See Gen Sir Victor Fortune, Obit by N. McMicking, *Red Hackle*, Apr 1949, pp.11–12. Slightly paralysed by a stroke in 1944, he died on 2 Jan 1949 aged 65. Susan Fortune, interview with G. & M. Makins, 15 Feb 2001, http://www.auchencairn.org.uk/index.php?option=com_content&task=view&id=208&Itemid=102, accessed 19 Jan 2017. 2nd Lt David Campbell was one of those repatriated in Oct 1943, having feigned deafness; to Flavia Ormond, 1959. Information from Flavia Ormond, 5 Dec 2014, London.
71. Grieve, 'Oral History 1999', Thomas B. Smyth research material. Grieve later became batman to Bernard Fergusson, and played the bagpipes with Rab Roy for Eisenhower. Among others Pat Campbell-Preston rejoined the Regiment as did Freddy Burnaby-Atkins, briefly serving as ADC to the Viceroy, Lord Wavell, while David Walker became his Household Comptroller.
72. Russell, *War History of the 7th Bn*, p.138. The motto was originally that of the Royal Stuart dynasty, which became a Scottish national motto and was adopted by The Black Watch and other regiments.
73. McKenzie Johnston, 'Recollections of Service', pp.24–5, BWRA 1023.
74. '2BW War Diary', 31 Dec 1945 & 1 Jan 1946, p.154, BWRA 0345.
75. Mrs J.G. Moir, 'The Black Watch (RHR)', 1944, inspired by R.L. Stevenson, *Memoirs and Portraits* (who said that after years abroad, returning soldiers kissed the earth at Port Patrick). Her husband was in the jute business in Calcutta during WWII and often entertained Black Watch officers on leave. Mrs Moir wrote numerous poems which were dropped, wrapped up in comforts, for the troops in Burma, 'Museum Notes', *Red Hackle*, Apr 1963, p.6.

16. The Illusion of Peace

1. Joshua 9:23.
2. George Morrison Daily, 'A Soldier's Tale', memoir, BWRA 0961.
3. H.B. McKenzie Johnston, 'Recollections of Service', p.28, BWRA 1023.

4. Tom Renouf, *Black Watch*, pp.295–6.
5. '4th Battalion', *The Red Hackle*, Jul 1946, p.13. 'Service of Thanksgiving & Remembrance on the Disbandment of the 6th Bn The Black Watch (R.H.R.), Kifissia – Greece, 26th May 1946', BWRA 0986. Henry McKenzie Johnston, interview, 19 Sep 2014. See also '6th Battalion', *Red Hackle*, Jul 1946, pp.16–17.
6. 'Re-organisation of the TA', *Red Hackle*, Apr 1967, p.9, & 'A History of the 4/5th Battalion', *Red Hackle*, Apr 1967, pp.34–41. When the 6/7BW Drill Hall in Crieff was sold to Dodds the Builders in the 1980s (belonging to the family of Lt Col Peter Taylor,) the Coat of Arms was removed to be preserved in another building in Crieff where it can be seen to this day; see Lt Col R.M. Riddell, 'Arms and the Man', *Red Hackle*, Nov 2010, p.46. The training battalions were also disbanded. See Lt Col Purvis Russell Montgomery, 'Additional Note', undated, BWRA 0162/2.
7. Wavell, 31 Dec 1947, *Viceroy's Journal*, ed. Penderel Moon, p.439. See Obit, 'The Late General Sir Arthur Wauchope', by FM Earl Wavell, *Red Hackle*, Jan 1948, pp.4–5, where it is stated that Wauchope 'financed, edited and partly wrote' *A History of The Black Watch (Royal Highlanders) in the Great War, 1914–1918*.
8. For information on the negotiations leading to independence and Wavell's role in particular, see Victoria Schofield, *Wavell, Soldier and Statesman*, pp.348–69.
9. '2BW War Diary (Jun 44–Dec 46)', 19 Jan 1946, p.157, & 16, 18, 23 Apr 1946, p.176, BWRA 0345; '2BW, General Activities', *Red Hackle*, Jul 1946, p.7.
10. '2BW, Four Walls and a Roof', *Red Hackle*, Oct 1946, p.12; Col Ian Critchley, 'Last Days in India', *Red Hackle*, May 2008, p.18. '2BW War Diary', 31 Dec 1944, p.239, BWRA 0345.
11. Critchley, 'Last Days in India', *Red Hackle*, May 2008, p.18. See also 2BW, 'General', *Red Hackle*, Jul 1947, p.14.
12. D.H.W(alker), 'The Presentation of the Freedom of the City of Perth to The Black Watch on 19th July, 1947', *Red Hackle*, Oct 1947, pp.19–21. City of Perth and Royal Burgh, 'To the Colonel, Officers and Other Ranks of The Black Watch (Royal Highland Regiment)', 13 Jul 1947, Freedom scroll in BWM.
13. Critchley, 'Last Days in India', *Red Hackle*, May 2008, p.20. Ghulam Nabi Hussain Bux were the Black Watch's contractors for 40 years.
14. Ibid. Col Neville Blair, 'Partition and the North-West Frontier', *Red Hackle*, Apr 1988, p.10. Geoffrey Cowper-Coles, interview, 21 Oct 2015, London.
15. Blair, 'Partition and the North-West Frontier', *Red Hackle*, Apr 1988, p.10.
16. Critchley, 'Last Days in India', *Red Hackle*, May 2008, p.19.
17. '2BW, General', *Red Hackle*, Oct 1947, p.15. Blair, 'Partition and the North-West Frontier', *Red Hackle*, Apr 1988, p.10.
18. Ibid, pp.10–11.
19. Ibid, p.11.
20. Ibid, pp.11, 29.
21. Critchley, 'Last Days in India', *Red Hackle*, May 2008, p.20. Elizabeth Irwin to Dearest Mummy and Daddy, 18 Sep 1947, Irwin private papers; she had already been evacuated from Peshawar to Karachi by plane.
22. E. Irwin to Dearest Mummy and Daddy, 18 Sep 1947, Irwin private papers.

23. Blair, 'Recollections of the Second Battalion and the Final Days of the Indian Idyll', typescript, p.1, BWRA 0842; Elizabeth Irwin to her parents, 24 Sep 1947, Irwin private papers. Information to Elizabeth Irwin from Lt Alec Carver, rear-guard party.
24. Blair, 'Recollections… Indian Idyll', p.2, BWRA 0842. Louis Manson, interview, 17 Jul 2015, London.
25. Blair, 'Recollections… Indian Idyll', p.6, BWRA 0842.
26. Ibid, p.7.
27. Juliet Cheetham, correspondence, 5 Jan 2015. Critchley, 'Last Days in India', *Red Hackle*, May 2008, p.19.
28. Cpl F. Norfolk, Ex D Coy, Correspondence, 2BW, 1947/48, *Red Hackle,* Aug 1988, p.5; See Maj A.C.C. Brodie, DSO, MC, 'Royal Highlanders in Jerusalem', *Red Hackle,* Jul 1948, p.5.
29. Blair, 'Recollections… Indian Idyll', pp.10–11, BWRA 0842.
30. Ibid.
31. Ibid.
32. Ibid. The war became 'official' in May 1948 when members of the Pakistan Army crossed the international frontier.
33. Bernard Fergusson, *King's Enemies,* p.374; Critchley, 'Last Days in India', *Red Hackle*, May 2008, p.21.The Baghdad Bell is in BWM; the gong at Fort George, Inverness. See 'The amalgamation of the 1st and 2nd Battalions of The Black Watch (RHR)', *Red Hackle,* Oct 1948, pp.10–11. It was the first time since 1881 that the Regiment had only one regular bn. It still had two territorial bns.
34. Poem dated Duisburg, Amalgamation Day, 1948. Material relating to FM Wavell, Col of the Regiment, BWRA 0988/8.
35. Col Ian Critchley, interview, Crieff, 21 Nov 2012. See Bernard Fergusson, *Portrait of a Soldier,* p.84.
36. Maj K.L. Prendergast (1910–54), Obit, *The Times,* 4 Jun 1954, p.8. Having studied geology, Maj Prendergast gained a PhD in palaeontology before studying medicine. Information courtesy Sandra Freshney, archivist, Sedgwick Museum of Earth Sciences, 18 Dec 2015.
37. Maj Gen Andrew Watson, interview, 7 Dec 2012, London.
38. Brig O.R. Tweedy, interview, 19 Oct 2013, Perth.
39. Fergusson, *King's Enemies,* pp.374–5. In *Red Hackle*, Apr 1951, p.21, he thanked over 50 sources and corrected a number of errors. Fergusson to Linklater, from 1st Bn. The Black Watch (RHR.) BAOR, 26 Mar 1949, Acc 10282, No. 12/1, NLS.
40. FM Earl Wavell, Col of the Regt, Foreword, in Fergusson, *King's Enemies,* p.13.
41. He was suffering from primary carcinoma of the hepatic duct. Wavell, 'Recollections', in John Connell, *Wavell: Scholar and Soldier,* p.149, & Schofield, *Wavell*, p.88.
42. Bernard Fergusson, *Trumpet in the Hall,* p.251. He had had a mild heart attack; he handed over temporarily and then officially in Feb 1951.
43. WO2 Joe Hubble, interview, 17 Sep 2013, London. He joined the motor transport platoon as a driver. His elder and younger brothers also served in The Black Watch because their father, serving in the Royal West Kent Regiment during WWI, had

seen Black Watch soldiers coming out of their trenches and going over the top. 'He decided that if he survived and had sons they would go into The Black Watch because it was the best disciplined Regiment.'

44. 'Visit of The Black Watch (RHR) of Canada, 3–5 Oct 1950', *Red Hackle,* Jan 1951, p.4. The inscription reads: 'Instructions to Past Present and Future Officers The Black Watch (Royal Highland Regiment) of Canada. The undersigned [i.e. the Regimental Commandant, The Black Watch (RHR) of Canada] has today committed you upon entering this mess for the first time in any calendar year to charge this trophy with whiskey and invite all present to toast with you The Black Watch (Royal Highland Regiment).' The cup, known as the Montreal Trophy, was one of the earliest won by the Canadian Regiment, originally presented in 1863 in a rifle match. Like the Toronto Cup, it is in the Officers' Mess, The Black Watch, 3rd Battalion RRS (3 Scots). Information from Lt J.R. Tait, 10 Jun 2013.
45. Adam Gurdon, 'Berlin 1950', *Red Hackle,* Apr 1988, pp.8–9. The episode happened in Sep 1950. In a letter to *The Red Hackle,* R. MacDougall maintained that the Russians first blocked the road. He did not remember the white line being painted. Editor's Note suggested that he was describing the beginning of the incident whereas Gurdon's account described the sequel. 'Correspondence', 'Berlin 1950', *Red Hackle,* Aug 1988, p.4. The painting of the white line confirmed by Brig O.R. Tweedy, interview, 19 Oct 2013, Perth.
46. In Mar 1947, US policy had been formalised in the Truman Doctrine, indicating American willingness to become involved in disputes beyond its frontiers in an attempt to contain Soviet expansion. This entailed building up a network of alliances with friendly states which the United States would aid militarily.
47. 'The Moon Behind the Hill', ll.1–8, quoted in Mary MacGregor, *The Moon Behind the Hill,* p.8 (found in John McGregor's songbook after he was killed at Magersfontein 1899).

17. Korea: The Forgotten War

1. Anon, poem written by a Prisoner of War, Camp 3, North Korea, 1952, in *Poems of the Korean War,* compiled by D.W. Hall, 1952, Korea/Kenya box, BWM.
2. Harold Davis, *Tougher than Bullets,* p.34.
3. Kim Il Sung (1912–1994) had fought in a Korean unit with the Soviet Army during the war. Dr Syngman Rhee (1875–1965) changed his name from Yi Sung-man while living in the USA.
4. Linklater, *Our Men in Korea,* p.7. 'The problem of the Republic of Korea', UN General Assembly Resolution 195, 3rd session. A.J. Barker, *Fortune Favours the Brave,* p.xiv.
5. The resolution was passed on 7 Jul 1950. Communist China was not recognised as a permanent member of the UN Security Council until 1971.
6. The 16 members of the UN who supplied troops were: Australia, Belgium, Canada, Colombia, Ethiopia, France, Greece, Luxembourg, Netherlands, New Zealand, Philippines, South Africa, Thailand, Turkey, UK and USA, which

supplied the largest contingent. Humanitarian aid came from Denmark, India, Italy (which joined the UN in Dec 1955), Norway and Sweden. In Jul 1951 the Commonwealth Bdes were united as 1st Commonwealth Div: 25 Canadian Inf Bde, 28 Commonwealth Inf Bde (made up mostly of Australian as well as UK and New Zealand units) and 29 Independent Inf Bde, which the 1st Battalion The Black Watch joined in 1952.

7. Gen of the Army Douglas MacArthur (1880–1964) was replaced by Lt Gen Matthew Ridgway (1895–1993) in Apr 1951.
8. On 6 Dec 1950 top US generals including MacArthur considered atomic strikes but the idea was rejected by the Pentagon and State Dept in case the war escalated. The option was reconsidered (but rejected) in 1953 when Eisenhower succeeded Truman as US President.
9. See Jung Chang & Jon Halliday, *Mao: The Unknown Story*, who claim that, by withholding agreement over the return of the prisoners-of-war, Mao 'milked the Korean War' for his personal benefit.
10. William Speakman-Pitt (b.1927), *London Gazette*, 25 Dec 1951, http://www.gazettes-online.co.uk/issues/39418/supplements/6731, accessed 13 Feb 2017. See *Red Hackle*, Jan 1952, frontispiece.
11. Peter Stormonth Darling, *Forgotten War*, pp.2, 4. LCpl Jim Laird, quoted in Royle, *The Best Years of their Lives*, p.239. Davis, *Tougher Than Bullets*, p.24. 'Selective National Service' was not popular since many men felt they were being picked 'in place of their less dispensable contemporaries'; 80% of the British troops in Korea were National Servicemen, Barker, *Fortune Favours the Brave*, p.7. National Service ended in 1945 for women in 1960 for men.
12. WO2 Joe Hubble, interview, 17 Sep 2013, London. Laird, quoted in Royle, *The Best Years of their Lives*, p.223.
13. Stormonth Darling, *Forgotten War*, p.41.
14. Lt Col David Rose, *Off the Record*, p.64. Lt Col Campbell-Preston had suffered a 'serious' heart attack, hence relinquishing command.
15. Col Ian Critchley, additional information, 26 Apr 2013. He was MT officer in charge of all vehicles within 1BW and appointed 2IC, B Coy before the Battle of the Hook in Nov 1952. He left Korea in Dec 1952.
16. Stormonth Darling, *Forgotten War*, p.43. Eric Linklater, *Our Men in Korea*, prepared for the Admiralty, War Office, and Air Ministry by the Central Office of Information. His account stops in mid-1951 after the battle of the Imjin and the battle of the Kapyong river, fought by Australians and Canadians.
17. Maj Gen Andrew Watson, interview, 7 Dec 2012, London. See also 2BW, *Red Hackle*, Jul 1952, p.18.
18. '1BW, Officers' Mess', *Red Hackle*, Jul 1952, p.9; '2BW, General', *Red Hackle*, Oct 1952, p.19. The name 'Old Mangalores' was given in India during the Mysore Wars.
19. '2BW, General', *Red Hackle*, Jan 1953, p.18. In Jul 1953 2BW moved to Minden Barracks, Dortmund, under the command of Lt Col Bill Bradford, who took over from Lt Col Neville Blair on 23 Apr 1953.

20. '1BW, General', *Red Hackle*, Apr 1952, pp.6–7; '1BW, Officers' Mess', *Red Hackle*, Jul 1952, p.11.
21. Brig Adam Gurdon, interview, 27 Nov 2012, London. 'There was one instance in my platoon, and that's how I dealt with it.'
22. Maj Angus Irwin to Elizabeth, 22 Jun1952. See '1BW, Sergeants' Mess', *Red Hackle*, Oct 1952, p.12.
23. Stormonth Darling, *Forgotten War*, pp.55–6.
24. '1BW, Intelligence Section', *Red Hackle*, Oct 1952, p.18. Lt John Moncrieff was intelligence officer. See also '2nd Hook Reports', BWRA 0148/BWM 2012.274.
25. Lt Col Hon David Arbuthnott, (younger son of Viscount Arbuthnott), 'The Black Watch in Korea 1952–53' (undated), BWM. The advance party's journey lasted 25 May–9 Jun, stopping at Tripoli, El Adem (to avoid Egypt due to political difficulties over Suez), Habbaniya in Iraq, Mauripur in Pakistan, Negombo in Sri Lanka, Singapore, Manila and Kure in Japan! As MT officer, Critchley was with the advance party. In Singapore, he visited the grave of his 'best man', Capt Rowland Tarleton, who had been killed on 12 Apr 1952 while serving with the 5th Malay Regt (the third BW officer to die in Malaya); his father had commanded 6BW in 1918. Critchley, additional information, 26 Apr 2013. See Barker, *Fortune Favours the Brave*, App A, p.151.
26. Gurdon, interview, 27 Nov 2012; he was a pl cdr, D Coy. In addition to A, B, C (mortar) and the 'golden' Don, D Coy, Support Coy included mortar and machine-gun platoons. HQ Coy (comprising signals and administrative platoons) remained at Bn HQ.
27. Hubble, interview, 17 Sep 2013.
28. Lt Col Hon David Arbuthnott, 'The First Battalion in Korea', *Red Hackle*, May 2002, pp.20–1. LCpl Robert McKee, Pte John Nicoll and Pte Neil McDougall had died in 1951 while attached to 1KOSB. See www.theblackwatch.co.uk/regimental-association/roll-of-honour; accessed 16 Feb 2017.
29. Gurdon, interview, 27 Nov 2012. The QM was Capt H.McL (Nobby) Clark, who received his commission in 1947.
30. Sgt Brian Gait, 'All the Redcaps were Valiant', memoir, p.19, Gait private papers.
31. Arbuthnott, 'The Black Watch in Korea 1952–53', BWM.
32. George Jackson, 'Working Holiday - All Expenses by H.M. Government', memoir, 13 Nov 1987, Korea/Kenya Box, BWM. He undertook his National Service 1947–49. Posted to the Hara Mura Battle Training School in Japan, he reached Korea in Jun 1952. He was wounded by a mortar shell on 18 Apr 1953 and did not fight at the Third Battle for the Hook. He left the Regt on 29 Oct 1954 after serving in Kenya.
33. 2nd Lt Brian Mann, 'Korea 1952–53', memoirs, Korea/Kenya box, BWM.
34. '1BW, General', *Red Hackle*, Oct 1952, pp.9–10. Gait, 'All the Redcaps were Valiant', p.24, Gait private papers.
35. Critchley, additional information, 26 Apr 2013.
36. Rose to his wife, 26 Jul 1952, quoted in *Off the Record*, pp.75–6. See Obit, *Red Hackle*, Oct 1952, p.3. 'The code-word for calling up defensive fire was "Christie."'

When Renny-Tailyour used it, he did not think it would come so quickly,' Lt Col Hon David Arbuthnott to the author, 2013.

37. Stormonth Darling, *Forgotten War*, p.76. See Obit, *Red Hackle*, Oct 1952, p.3. Nicoll was also a National Serviceman. See George Cooper, *Fight, Dig and Live*, p.128: 'Accidents in our own minefields continued all the year round. As most of the fields had been laid by sappers we felt a responsibility for preventing casualties to our own side… There were 350 minefields within the divisional area, many of them marked insufficiently or even not at all.'
38. Pte Jack Erskine, interview, 18 Nov 2008, 'This Happens in War', BWM. Irwin to his son Alistair, 3 Aug 1952, Irwin private papers.
39. Arbuthnott, 'The First Battalion in Korea', *Red Hackle*, May 2002, p.20, 'Points 210, 159, and 355, Yong Dong and of course the Hook and Point 121.' During the period in reserve one company was stationed under the command of the Royal Fusiliers at Yong Dong 'considered to be the cushy billet as the enemy were a long way away'.
40. '1BW', *Red Hackle*, Oct 1952, p.10. '1BW, General', *Red Hackle*, Jan 1953, p.8.
41. Lt Col David Rose to Gen Neil, 19 Aug 1952, quoted in *Off the Record*, p.80. 'A load of amateurs who could play anything.' Brig Adam Gurdon, interview, 15 Jan 2013, London.
42. '1BW, General', *Red Hackle*, Jan 1953, p.8.
43. Elizabeth Irwin, interview, 17 Nov 2012, Comrie. Maj Angus Irwin who had auburn hair was known as 'Red' Angus to distinguish him from the dark-haired 'Black' Angus Rowan-Hamilton, OC B Coy. See Maj Angus Rowan-Hamilton, Obit, *Red Hackle*, by Maj Alistair Irwin, Aug 1978, p.9.
44. Irwin to Elizabeth Irwin, 28 Aug 1952, Irwin private papers. Mann, 'Korea 1952–53', Korea/Kenya box, BWM. Rose said the sweaters were not necessary since they had 'quite a lot of stock' from their predecessors', Rose to Gen Neil, 19 Aug 1952, quoted in *Off the Record*, p.80.
45. '1BW, Officers' Mess', *Red Hackle*, Oct 1952, p.10. Critchley, interview, 21 Nov 2012; additional information, 26 Apr 2013: he also spent time taking photographs for the regimental archives and for use by instructors, i.e. at University OTCs, RMA Sandhurst or Eaton Hall, or the Junior Leaders Bn. 'Notably, *The Times* published my photograph of Angus Irwin for his obituary.'
46. Hubble, interview, 17 Sep 2013. He was protected by his 'top gun', Pte Jim Bowers and delivered mail as well as dispatches which could not be transmitted.
47. Stormonth Darling to his father, 16 Oct 1952, quoted in *Forgotten War*, pp.103–4.
48. Derek Halley, *Iron Claw*, p.68. Stormonth Darling, *Forgotten War*, p.105.
49. Maj Allan C. Bevilaqua, USMC (Ret), 'The Hook, Korea 1952,' *Leatherneck*, Nov 2002, p.19, Korea/Kenya box, BWM. Salient features were Point 121, Sausage and Point 146.
50. Rose to his wife, 4 Nov 1952, *Off the Record*, p.95; see also *Red Hackle*, Jan 1953, p.7. Critchley, additional information, 26 Apr 2013; he continued: 'David Arbuthnott reported that the same situation existed at command post level in that the line to Brigade was a mass of cables as thick as a tree trunk. His platoon soon

sorted out the situation for us on the Hook.'

51. Lt Col David Rose to Gen Neil, 15 Nov 1952, quoted in *Off the Record*, p.97; additional information from David Rose notes, Rose private papers. The Chinese used the same tactic. Cooper, *Fight, Dig and Live*, p.87.
52. L.S. Wood, 'National Service 1951-53', memoir, Korea/Kenya box, BWM. He initially found wearing the tam o'shanter and the red hackle 'strange after the beret and badge'.
53. 2nd Lt Sandy Younger, 'Account of Ronson Patrol as told by 2 Lt Younger of A Coy App A to 1BW/Int/1', dated 17 Jan 53, Gait private papers. Stormonth Darling, *Forgotten War*, p.108.
54. Statistics from *Red Hackle*, Jan 1953, p.7. Kerry was on standing patrol, Doig on reconnaissance patrol. 'The Military Medal', citation 28 Nov 1952, *London Gazette*, 9 Jan 1953, in *Red Hackle*, Jan 1953, p.5. Gurdon, interview, 27 Nov 2012.
55. 1BW, A Coy, *Red Hackle*, Jan 1953, p.11. John Ridley, *Daily Telegraph* and *Scotsman* correspondent, 'How Black Watch won Battle of the Hook' (undated but probably Nov 1952). George Jackson, 'Working Holiday', memoir, Korea/Kenya Box, BWM. He was promoted Sgt on 25 Oct 1952.
56. Lt Col Hon David Arbuthnott, interview, 18 Nov 2008, 'This Happens in War', BWM.
57. Douglas Fairey, Weekend True Life Drama… 'shovels will do', 1–7 May 1963; also Gurdon, interview, 11 Dec 2012. See John Ridley, *Daily Telegraph* and *Scotsman* correspondent, 'How Black Watch won Battle of the Hook' and '2nd Battle of the Hook, Outline of Events', BWRA 0178.
58. Arbuthnott, 'The Black Watch in Korea 1952–53', BWM.
59. Critchley, interview, 21 Nov 2012; additional information, 26 Apr 2013. He continued: 'Most of our fire positions in the trenches had "shelves" cut in the mud walls upon which fully primed British "Mills 36 Grenades" were kept for easy access and use.' It was one of these grenades that a Chinese threw at Rowan-Hamilton and his batman. See also Critchley, interview, 4 Nov 2008, 'This Happens in War', BWM. Rowan-Hamilton's death aged 58 in 1978 was as a result of blood poisoning from a transfusion received because of his injuries, so technically his death was caused by his Korean war wound, Guy Rowan-Hamilton, additional information, 18 Sep 2016.
60. Rose, *Off the Record*, p.98.
61. Pte Robert Clark, quoted in Douglas Fairey, Weekend True Life Drama… 'shovels will do', *Weekend* (*Daily Mail*), 1–7 May 1963.
62. 'Perth soldier killed, another wounded,' *Perthshire Advertiser*, 22 Nov 1952, BWM. Gait, 'All the Redcoats were Valiant', p.76, Gait private papers. Since 23 Oct, 35 men had died and 15 were recorded as missing in action or taken prisoner, mostly from A and B Coys; 69 had been wounded, Pipe Maj Dick Erickson losing his left leg. See Obit by Lt Col Hon David Arbuthnott, *Red Hackle*, May 2003, p.13. Roll of Honour, *Red Hackle*, Jan 1953, p.7. Royle, *The Best Years of their Lives*, p.235, says 12 men killed, 67 wounded and 20 missing. The 'first' Battle took place in Mar 1952. See also *Perthshire Advertiser*, 26 Nov 1952, p.7 & '1BW, Sergeants'

Mess', *Red Hackle*, Jan 1953, p.9. Pte G. Coley was attached to 1BW from the Royal Leicestershire Regt.

63. J.G. Moncrieff, intelligence officer, 'Second Battle of the Hook', 26 Nov 1952, Rose private papers. See also 'Intelligence report' and 'Second battle of the Hook, Reports, Medical', p.2 BWRA 0148. Initially there were insufficient stretchers but the shortage was 'rectified rapidly'.
64. Rose to My dear Rhoddy, 23 Nov 1952, quoted in *Off the Record*, p.101. Lt Col Rhoddy Rose was CO, the Highland Light Infantry in Malta.
65. Cooper, *Fight, Dig and Live*, p.90. Maj Gen A.H.G. Ricketts, CBE, DSO (1905–93), was a veteran of the 1944 Second Chindit Expedition. Maj Gen Sir Douglas Anthony Kendrew, KCMG, CB, CBE, DSO (1910–1989), later Governor of Western Australia, was 'Joe' Kendrew, a rugby union player for England.
66. 'Preliminary Report on Action in area A Coy 1 BW Night 18/19 Nov 52'. Details of the escape of 26 Nov 1952 from Pte Stanley of A Coy, App F, Gait private papers. Derek Hall, 'Poems of the Korean War 1952', Korea/Kenya box, BWM.
67. Gait, 'All the Redcoats were Valiant', p.85, Gait private papers. They had been training at the Divisional Battle School at Hara Mura in Japan. Jack Erskine (b. 1931), interview, 18 Nov 2008, 'This Happens in War', BWM; Pte Derek Halley (1933–2013).
68. Rose to the Chairman of the Comforts Fund, 'Korean Comforts Fund', *Red Hackle*, Jan 1953, p.3.
69. The Queen Mother from Buckingham Palace to Gen McMicking, 26 Nov 1952, quoted in Rose, *Off the Record*, p.109. She continued: 'I feel so deeply for those who have lost relatives in this unending & unsatisfactory war – it makes sorrow doubly hard to bear.' A photocopy of the letter is in Rose's file of letters received in response to *Off the Record*, Rose private papers. Permission to publish '*in toto*' was given by the Queen Mother, Dame Frances Campbell-Preston, Lady-in-Waiting, to Lt Col David Rose, 31 Jan 1997.
70. Maj Angus Digby Hastings Irwin, MC, Citation 29 Nov 1952; *London Gazette*, 9 Jan 1953; *Red Hackle*, Jan 1953, p.3; Irwin to Elizabeth, 22 Nov 1952, Irwin private papers. See also 'Second Battle of the Hook, Reports', BWRA 0148.
71. Lt Richard John Haw, 2nd Lt Michael Donald Gordon Black, Citations 27 Nov 1952, *London Gazette*, 9 Jan 1953; *Red Hackle*, Jan 1953, p.4. Col Michael Anstice, MC, OBE (1929–2011) was a troop leader, B Squadron; Obit, *The Scotsman*, 25 Jul 2011.
72. See Citations 28 Nov 1952; *London Gazette*, 9 Jan 1953; *Red Hackle*, Jan 1953, pp.4–5. Sgt (Acting) A.B. Hutchison, Sgt (Acting) W.F. Kerry, LCpl (Acting) R.A. Manning were awarded the MM. See also 'Preliminary Report on Action in area A Coy 1 BW Night 18/19 Nov 52', Gait private papers; Royle, *The Best Years of their Lives*, p.235. Several others were Mentioned in Despatches, including late Pte Coley.
73. Derek Halley, interview, 18 Nov 2008, 'This Happens in War', BWM. Stormonth Darling, *Forgotten War*, p.82.
74. Halley, *Iron Claw*, p.67: 'the company urinals [were] nothing more than artillery

ammunition tubes sticking out of the ground or sandbags'.

75. Davis, *Tougher than Bullets*, pp.70–2.
76. Irwin to Elizabeth, 4 Dec 1952, Irwin private papers. 1BW, *Red Hackle*, Apr 1953, p.8.
77. Cooper, *Fight, Dig and Live*, p.91; LCpl Derek Hurst, memoir, Korea/Kenya box, BWM.
78. Rose, 8 Dec 1952, quoted in *Off the Record*, p.106; Irwin to Elizabeth, 9 Feb & 10 Mar 1953, Irwin private papers. Irwin writes frequently about playing bridge. 1BW, *Red Hackle*, Apr 1953, p.8.
79. Gait, 'All the Redcoats were Valiant', p.107, Gait private papers.
80. Mann, 'Korea 1952–3', Korea/Kenya box, BWM. Some of the fighter ground attack was carried out by the South African Air Force, Brig Adam Gurdon, interview, 11 Dec 2012, London.
81. Gurdon, interview, 27 Nov 2012. Halley, *Iron Claw*, p.69.
82. Hurst, memoir, Korea/Kenya box, BWM; another National Serviceman, he had requested to join The Black Watch because his uncle had served in the Regt in WWII. Wood, 'National Service 1951–53', Korea/Kenya box, BWM. Halley, *Iron Claw*, pp.69–70. Gurdon, interview, 27 Nov 2012.
83. Ian E. (Danny) Kaye, formerly Argyll & Sutherland Highlanders, 'I Have!', quoted in Cooper, *Fight, Dig and Live*, pp.141–2. See Obit, *Red Hackle*, Aug 1993, p.7 & Dec 1993, p.8; *Poetry of the Korean War*, ed. Reuben Holroyd, British Korean Veterans Association, 2003, p.30. Also Ian E. Kaye, 'They only fade away', *Pick & Shovel Poems*, Arthur H. Stockwell Ltd, 1960.
84. Mann, 'Korea 1952–53', Korea/Kenya box, BWM; see also Stormonth Darling, *Forgotten War*, p.130. Arbuthnott, 'The First Battalion in Korea', *Red Hackle*, May 2002, p.20.
85. Irwin to Elizabeth, 18 Feb 1953, Irwin private papers. This seems to have been a rare occurrence.
86. Mann, 'Korea 1952–53', Korea/Kenya box, BWM.
87. Hugh S.W. Blakeney, 'National Service', memoir, pp.18–19, Blakeney private papers.
88. Capt A.O.L. Lithgow had been serving as Brigade Maj, 153 Brigade.
89. Halley, interview, 18 Nov 2008, 'This Happens in War', BWM. Anthony Laycock, 'The Hook Again, 1953', *Red Hackle*, May 2003, p.20. 'It was rather strange for the Chinese had a kind of unwritten agreement whereby if we didn't drop phos on them they would not drop it on us,' Halley, *Iron Claw*, p.103.
90. Capt Colin Harrison, telephone interview, 23 Nov 2012.
91. Gen Sir George Cooper to Lt Col David Rose, 14 Nov 1996, in response to *Off the Record*, Rose private papers. Lt David Haugh belonged to the Seaforth Highlanders.
92. Halley, *Iron Claw*, p.104.
93. Rose to Mrs Iris Blakeney, 11 May 1953, Blakeney private papers.
94. Davis, *Tougher Than Bullets*, p.17. He was able to play football for Rangers 1956–64. Royle, *The Best Years of their Lives*, p.236.

95. Gurdon, interview, 11 Dec 2012. He was now in command of the mortar platoon.
96. Rose to his wife, 8 May 1953, quoted in *Off the Record*, p.121. Publication of Rattray's MC for the Nov 1952 battle had been made 2 weeks previously; Lt Alec Rattray, Citation 27 Nov 1952, *London Gazette,* 24 Apr 1953; *Red Hackle,* Jul 1953, p.4, & see also pp.8–10. In 2010 Rattray's family was awarded the Elizabeth II medal. His brother Alistair Rattray attended the 60th Reunion in Perth, Scotland, organised by The Black Watch Regimental Association, 16/17 Nov 2012. He presented the Regimental Association with a print of the painting by Terence Cuneo CVO, OBE, RGI (1907–96) showing Cooper and Alec Rattray discussing building defensive tunnels.
97. Hubble, interview, 17 Sep 2013.
98. Rose to Dearest Mother, 11 May 1953, quoted in *Off the Record*, p.122. The rain delayed the relief for 24 hours. One company temporarily remained in the line.
99. Rose, 'Telling the Story', a general letter to be circulated to other battalions quoted in *Off the Record*, pp.123–5. See also Lt Col Rose, 'Third Battle of the Hook, Reports', BWRA 0149. He wrote the letter to be circulated to other battalions.
100. 'Regimental News', *Red Hackle,* Jan 1954, p.3. 'Honours and Awards', *Red Hackle,* Jan 1954, pp.3–4.
101. Hurst, memoir, Korea/Kenya box, BWM.
102. Rose to his wife, 25 May 1953, quoted in *Off the Record*, p.126.
103. Gurdon, interview, 27 Nov 2012.
104. Arbuthnott, 'The First Battalion in Korea', *Red Hackle,* May 2002, p.20. '1BW, General', *Red Hackle,* Jul 1953, p.10. Irwin was among the party who returned home for the coronation, Irwin to Elizabeth, 23 & 28 Jan 1953, Irwin private papers.
105. Gurdon, interview, 11 Dec 2012. See also Adam Gurdon, 'The Coronation in Korea,' Letter to the Editor, *Red Hackle,* Nov 2003, p.11. 'Not a shot was fired by the Chinese all day – It shows that there is still some chivalry,' Gen Sir George Cooper, interview, 17 Jun 2013, Harlow.
106. Brig Kendrew quoted in '1BW, General', *Red Hackle,* Oct 1953, p.5.
107. Arbuthnott, interview, 18 Nov 2008, 'This Happens in War', BWM. See The Rev T.J.T. Nicol, LVO, MBE, MC, DD, Obit, by W.D. Arbuthnott, *Red Hackle*, Dec 1998, pp.11–12.
108. Hubble, interview, 17 Sep 2013.
109. Wood, 'National Service 1951–3', Korea/Kenya box, BWM. Gurdon, interview, 15 Jan 2013.
110. Rose, *Off the Record*, p.130. Arbuthnott, 'The First Battalion in Korea', *Red Hackle,* May 2002, pp.20–1.
111. Over 1,000 British soldiers died and a comparable number were missing or prisoners-of-war. Among those of The Black Watch in Camp 3 were D. Dow, Derek Hall, J. Lafferty, T. Swan, J. Macpherson, Korea/Kenya box, BWM. Statistics 'Roll of Honour', *Red Hackle,* Jul 1953, p.8.
112. Halley, interview, 18 Nov 2008, 'This Happens in War', BWM; additional information to the author, 21 Nov 2012, & *Iron Claw*, p.159. Dewar was 1BW's last fatality

in Korea. Halley was annoyed at the demands for compensation by regular soldiers who claimed to have been traumatised by 'ten days of fighting' during the 1982 Falklands War and decided to write his own memoir of Korea; see also *Perthshire Advertiser,* 8 Jul 1953. Statistics from 'The Black Watch in Korea', address by Revd Alex R. Forsyth, Service of Commemoration, Parish Church of St John the Baptist, Perth, 19 Nov 2002, Korea/Kenya box, BWM.

113. Pres Kim Dae-Jung, 'Letter of Appreciation, 25 Jun 2000', Rose private papers. A gold 'Ambassador for Peace' medal with a certificate of thanks from the Korean War Veterans Association is still presented. Initially they were only given to those who revisited South Korea; this was extended to all veterans who might have liked to visit but were unable to do so. Hubble, interview, 17 Sep 2013. Peter Stormonth Darling received his on 8 Oct 2015!
114. There are 110 Korean pine trees (one for every ten Britons who died in the war) and 1,090 birch trees (one for each fatality). A 'United Nations Avenue' is lined by 21 trees, representing the 21 nations involved. Opened on 27 Jun 2013, it is maintained by the Korean War Memorial Trust. See *Red Hackle,* May 2002, p.11, & R.C.B. Ritchie, Letter to the Editor, *Red Hackle,* May 2005, p.11.
115. See T. Hubble, 'Memorial to a Forgotten War', Letter to the Editor, *Red Hackle,* May 2015, p.15. A memorial was dedicated in St Paul's Cathedral in Mar 1987, *Red Hackle,* Sep 1987, p.50.
116. Cpl Raymond Carriage, 1BW, sent to Lt Col David Rose, 20 Nov 1997, in response to *Off the Record,* Rose private papers. The poem has several verses with, as Carriage admitted, some artistic licence!

18. Small Wars: Kenya and British Guiana

1. 'To 39 Bde, With apologies to the sender of your priority unclas. Sig. 113/3/AQ of 30 Oct 53', v.1, *Red Hackle,* Jan 1954, p.8. The poem was written for the Limuru Hunt Ball held in Limuru, north-west of Nairobi, Kenya, on the east of the Great Rift Valley, on 31 Oct 1953. Vs 2 & 3 are given at the end of the chapter.
2. Mau Mau Uprising, also known as a revolt, rebellion or the Kenya Emergency. There are about 40–70 tribes in Kenya, the Kikuyu comprising about one-fifth of the population. No 1BW War Diary exists, & the accounts of individual Companies are lost, so this chapter is dependent on *The Red Hackle* and individual accounts and recollections. Subsequently a number of Mau Mau wrote their memoirs but most history is from European sources. For an indigenous perspective see Jim Bailey, *Kenya: The National Epic,* ed. Carole Cooper, Kenway Publications, 1993.
3. Sir Evelyn Baring, later 1st Baron Howick of Glendale, KG, GCMG, KCVO (1903–73) was Governor of Kenya 1952–59. The Emergency was declared to quell protests against the arrest of Jomo Kenyatta (1891–1978), President of the banned Kenya African Union. The Mau Mau was proscribed as a terrorist movement until 2003. Figures of those taking part in the Lari massacre are disputed; 24 Kikuyu were sentenced to death. The military presence was increased in line with the

Appreciation of the Situation by Maj Gen W.R.N. Hinde at Nairobi, 5 Mar 1953 in 'Ops against Mau Mau Policy Directives', WO 276/411 or 410, TNA. This figure included African regular soldiers. See Karari Njama, *Mau Mau from Within*, who describes guerrilla fighters dressed in ordinary clothes aged between 25 and 30, armed either with European or homemade guns, swords and machetes (pangas). In time they became more organised but disagreements between leaders were frequent. Marshall S. Clough, *Mau Mau Memoirs*, p.134.

4. '1BW, General', *Red Hackle*, Oct 1953, p.5; 'The 1st Battalion in Kenya', *Red Hackle*, Dec 1993, p.12, both written by David Rose.
5. Gen Erskine, quoted in 'The 1st Battalion in Kenya', *Red Hackle*, Dec 1993, p.12. See *Red Hackle*, Jul 1954, p.12, for map listing main areas of deployment; also '1BW, General', *Red Hackle*, Jan 1955, p.8.
6. Harry Ellis, interview, 2 Dec 2008, 'This Happens in War', BWM. HQ Coy and A Coy, under the command of Angus Irwin, were at Nakuru; B Coy under Tony Lithgow at Gilgil, south-east of Nakuru; C and D Coys under Keith Dennison and Claud Moir respectively at Ol Joro Orok, a few miles from Thomson's Falls.
7. Lt Col David Rose, 'The 1st Battalion in Kenya', 2 & 5 Aug 1953, *Off the Record*, p.133.
8. Pte Alexander Farmer, 'Mau Mau Rifles', *Red Hackle*, May 2011, p.21.
9. D. Rose, 'Life with The Black Watch in Kenya', *Courier and Advertiser*, 31 Dec 1953. See also '1BW, General', *Red Hackle*, Oct 1953, pp.5–7; '1BW, General', *Red Hackle*, Jan 1954, p.6.
10. Bob Mitchell, interview, 2 Dec 2008, 'This Happens in War', BWM; he was a National Serviceman in the mortar platoon. WO2 Joe Hubble, recollection, 13 Jan 2003, BWRA. A knobkerrie was an African club, also written *knobkierie*. Both are now in the BWM. It is not clear when this incident happened.
11. D. Rose, 'Life with The Black Watch in Kenya', *Courier and Advertiser*, 31 Dec 1953; repeated in '1BW, General', *Red Hackle*, Jan 1954, p.6.
12. A.G. Somerhaugh, Deputy Public Prosecutor to Asst Dir of Army Legal Services, 1 Mar 1954. He repeated much of the information given by the Commissioner of Police, Chas. King, to the Attorney General in his letter dated 20 Feb 1954, 'Emergency, Unrest, Discipline of Security Forces, Allegations of Brutality/Complaints against Security Forces', FCO 141/5692. This file is one of the 'migrated archives' currently held in TNA. Those in relation to Kenya run to nearly 2,000 files, FCO 141/5595–FCO 141/7224. Somerhaugh was writing to the Army Legal Services to see if Lindsay could be made available to conclude the enquiry.
13. Chas. King, Commissioner of Police to Attorney General, Nairobi, 20 Feb 1954; the compensation given to the respective families of the deceased was according to 'full Kikuyu rates': for a man: 110 goats and 9 fat sheep, valued at £132.10 and for a woman: 60 goats and 6 fat sheep with a value of £75, Provincial Commissioner, Central Province to Hon Chief Secretary, 23 Dec 1953, 'Allegations of Brutality/Complaints against Security Forces', FCO 141/5692, TNA.
14. E.D. Bevan Lt Col GSO I to Deputy Director of Operations to Hon Chief Secretary, 28 Jan 1954. 'Allegations of Brutality/Complaints against Security Forces', FCO

141/5692. D Coy's notes for *The Red Hackle* do not mention this episode. Date for Lindsay's departure is given as 30 Nov when he is 'towed from the Camp in a Land Rover… to the strains of the pipes', '1BW, D Coy', *Red Hackle,* Jan 1954, p.15. He transferred to 2BW in command of A Coy, retiring from the Army in 1958.

15. 'Lord Wavell killed – long battle with terrorist gang', From our correspondent, Nairobi, *The Times,* 27 Dec 1953, p.6; one private soldier and Assistant Inspector Pratt were wounded. Statement of Mr Colin MacDonald, Kenyan Police Reserve Officer of Section 12, Klambu District concerning the incident on the night of 24/25 Dec 1953 near Thika. Transcript of document contained in 'Log Book D Coy', Korea/Kenya; '1BW, The Black Watch, 1952–4', BWRA 0178. Harry Ellis, interview, 2 Dec 2008, 'This Happens in War', BWM. The pipes and drums were at Thika at the time.
16. D. Rose to My Dear General Neil, 30 Dec 1953, *Off the Record*, p.136; Due to the loss of his arm in Burma, Wavell had not served in Korea; as an unmarried man, he had volunteered to rejoin 1BW in Kenya so that a married officer of equivalent rank could return to the UK to be with his family for Christmas. In his spare time, he had been compiling material for his father's biography. 'The file was with me when he was killed. The War Office wired for its recovery and return immediately by 'safe hand,' '1BW', *Red Hackle*, Apr 1954, p.6; see Major the Earl Wavell, MC, Obit by Bernard Fergusson, *Red Hackle,* Jan 1954, p.2. He was buried in the City Park Cemetery, Nairobi, the epitaph on his grave: 'He found the poetry of Man's endeavor'.
17. '1BW, Sergeants' Mess', *Red Hackle,* Apr 1954, p.8.
18. D. Rose, 'The Wives', *Off the Record*, p.138; 2nd Lt John Rankin, 'Subaltern's Diary', p.13, Rose private papers. Illness was another hazard for families: in 1954 there was an outbreak of polio.
19. Rev Norman Drummond, 'The Kirk Session of 1st Battalion, The Black Watch, Royal Highland Regiment, The first twenty-five years 1954–79', p.11, BWM. See 'The Kirk of The Black Watch', *Red Hackle,* Apr 1987, pp.33–5; '50th Anniversary of the Kirk Session', *Red Hackle*, May 2005, pp.5–6. A Battalion Kirk was established at Gilgil supported by Rev. W.G.A. Wright, Tom Nicol's successor as Padre. Additional information, Rev Norman Drummond, telephone interview, 4 Feb 2016.
20. 'Hitlerism in Kenya, Allegations by dismissed Army Officer', *New Milton Advertiser & Lymington Times*, Sat 5 Dec 1953; 'Allegations of Brutality/Complaints against Security Forces,' FCO 141/5692, TNA.
21. 'New Assessment in Kenya,' From Our Correspondent, Nairobi, *The Times,* 26 Jan 1954, p.8. The delegation included Walter Elliott representing the govt and opposition politician, Arthur Bottomley. 'Police reforms urged', From Our Special Correspondent, *The Times,* 24 Feb 1954, p.8.
22. Rankin, 'Subaltern's Diary', p.2, Rose private papers. '1BW, General', *Red Hackle,* Jan 1954, p.6. This is probably Lt Col Rose writing but authorship is not given.
23. (D. Rose), '1BW, General', *Red Hackle*, Apr 1954, p.6. Gen Kago wa Mboto (c.1920–54), see Anthony Lavers, *The Life and Death of 'General' Kago Mboto*,

Press Office, Dept of Information, 1954 and Gucu Gikoyo, *We Fought for Freedom*, 1979, cited in Marshall S. Clough, *Mau Mau Memoirs*.

24. Peter Grant, *Letters from the Forest*, p.43. His great-great uncle was Ensign William Grant (1810–36) who served in the 42nd in Gibraltar and Malta. See Part Four, 'Letters Home,' *Letters from the Forest*, pp.229–320.
25. D. Rose, 'White Highlands', *Off the Record*, p.136.
26. Rankin, 'Subaltern's Diary', pp.4, 8, Rose private papers.
27. Pte Alexander Farmer, 'Mau Mau Rifles', *Red Hackle*, May 2011, p.21. Two rifles were retrieved, now in the BWM.
28. Grant, *Letters from the Forest*, pp.41, 83.
29. Rankin, 'Subaltern's Diary', p.9, Rose private papers.
30. Peter Grant, 'Rhino Patrol', Correspondence, *Red Hackle*, Nov 2011, p.15.
31. Rankin, 'Subaltern's Diary', pp.14–15, Rose private papers. See Grant, *Letters from the Forest*, cover for illustration of how a 'terrorist' should surrender.
32. In addition to the use of airpower for reconnaissance, Lincoln (not Lancaster) bombers made a number of missions between Jul 1953 and Nov 1955. See Grant, *Letters from the Forest*, pp.208-10, on the cost of bombing the forests which he said did most damage to the wildlife. Rankin, 'Subaltern's Diary', p.15. See also '1BW, C Coy', *Red Hackle*, Jul 1954, p.16.
33. Ibid, p.17.
34. Rankin, 'Subaltern's Diary', p.16, Rose private papers.
35. '1BW, Officers' Mess', *Red Hackle*, Jul 1954, p.13; Rankin, 'Subaltern's Diary', p.17; '1BW, B Coy', *Red Hackle*, Jul 1954, p.16–17. Harry Ellis, interview, 2 Dec 2008, 'This Happens in War', BWM. The transcript reads 'Floors' Hotel but this must be a mistake for Torr's Hotel. See '1BW, Pipes and Drums', *Red Hackle*, Jul 1954, p.20.
36. Rankin, 'Subaltern's Diary', p.16. Also present were the 1st Buffs, Kenya Regiment, 1st Royal Inniskillings, 6th KAR, 1st RNF, 'Operation Anvil,' FCO 141/6573.
37. Draft for Press handout explaining reason for sweep, from The Secretariat, Nairobi, 22 Apr 1954, p.2, 'Operation Anvil,' FCO 141/6573. Grant, *Letters from the Forest*, p.63–4.
38. Rankin, 'Subaltern's Diary', pp.17–18. Grant, telephone interview, 13 Aug 2015.
39. Peter Grant to Dear Pop, 6 May 1954, *Letters from the Forest*, pp.71, 75.
40. See Draft to Secretary of State for the Colonies by Acting Governor, Sir Frederick Crawford, KCMG, OBE, 10 May 1954, 'Operation Anvil,' FCO 141/6573: the total number picked up for investigation was c.30,000, of which approx c.19,000 were held for screening. Over 2,000 women and 4,000 dependent children were repatriated to the Central Province; an additional 1,050 women and 2,000 were repatriated by their own request. See Arthur Young, Police Commissioner, to Governor Evelyn Baring, 22 Nov 1954, quoted in *The Times*, 11 Apr 2011, describing the horrors of some of the 'so-called screenings camps'.
41. With HQ and B Coys at Gilgil, the others were dispersed, A and D Coys going on operations to North Kinankop, one of the settled farming areas at an altitude of 10,000 feet bordering the Aberdares, near Pencil Slats: 'I understood that graphite for pencils had been mined in the past near the location', wrote Grant, *Letters*

from the Forest, p.82. He worked as a signaller at Fort Jericho and Fort Jerusalem, A Coy.

42. Grant, telephone interview, 7 Jan 2013; & letter to Dear Pop, 1 Jul 1954, *Letters from the Forest*, p.97.
43. Rankin,' Subaltern's Diary', p.24 & pp.41–2, Rose private papers. See '1st Battalion The Black Watch (Royal Highland Regiment) Historical Record: Jul 1953–Apr 1955', WO 305/230.
44. '1BW, C Coy', *Red Hackle*, Oct 1954, p.11. 'Kerito Ole Kesio [also written Kiseu] and Mundet Ole Ngapian' Two Typical Mau-Mau Leaders, *Red Hackle*, Apr 1955, p.3. Rankin, 'Subaltern's Diary', p.39, Rose private papers. Ngapian was hanged in Jan 1955.
45. Rankin, 'Subaltern's Diary', p.39.
46. Ibid, p.46.
47. Rankin, 'Subaltern's Diary', p.51, Rose private papers. See Bob Mitchell, interview, 2 Dec 2008, 'This Happens in War', BWM. Pte Graham was the last BW fatality on operations until Northern Ireland in 1971.
48. Rankin, 'Subaltern's Diary', pp.52 & 44, Rose private papers.
49. '1BW, B Coy', *Red Hackle*, Apr 1955, p.15. Grant, *Letters from the Forest*, p.135.
50. '1BW, D Coy', *Red Hackle*, Apr 1955, p.16.
51. '1BW, A Coy', *Red Hackle*, Apr 1955, p.14. Brig Adam Gurdon, interview, 15 Jan 2013, London. Grant, *Letters from the Forest*, p.129. Rankin, 'Subaltern's Diary', p.53, Rose private papers.
52. '1BW, C Coy', *Red Hackle*, Apr 1955, pp.15–16. Rankin, 'Subaltern's Diary', p.53, Rose private papers.
53. '1BW, D Coy', *Red Hackle*, Jul 1955, p.14. Rankin, 'Subaltern's Diary', p.59, Rose private papers.
54. Rev. R.G.M. Calderwood, sermon preached at the Black Watch Parade Service, 13 Mar 1955; see '1BW, Padre's Notes', *Red Hackle*, Apr 1955, pp.12,14. The window was crafted by Douglas Hamilton of Glasgow. St Andrew's was the Church of Scotland in Nairobi. In 2005 John Rankin found that the window had been removed and stored within the building, *Red Hackle*, May 2005, p.6. In 2003 the congregation had voted to remove all items relating to the Church's colonial past, which including all stained-glass windows, plaques, & archives; information from the caretaker to Lt Gen Sir Alistair Irwin; additional information Angus Macdonald, 8 Mar 2016. See photograph in Grant, *Letters from the Forest*, p.H.
55. Rankin, 'Subaltern's Diary', pp.62–3, Rose private papers. D. Rose, 'Farewell to Kenya', *Off the Record*, p.140. 1BW had lost 3 ORs and 1 officer.
56. FM Dedan Kimathi (1920/3–57) was a former teacher and clerk, 'Notes on 10 Prominent Mau Mau leaders, signed for Asst Commissioner of Police, I/C Special branch Hqrs Nairobi' 31 Dec 1955', in 'General Headquarters Nairobi, Mau Mau Organisation & Strengths', WO 276/426, TNA.
57. Dominic Casciani, 'British Mau Mau abuse papers revealed', BBC News, 12 Apr 2011, http://www.bbc.co.uk/news/uk-13044974, accessed 30 Jan 2017.
58. Grant, telephone interview, 7 Jan 2013; see also his comments in *Letters from the*

Forest, pp.148–58. See 'Mau Mau Uprising: Bloody History of Kenya Conflict', http://www.bbc.co.uk/news/uk-12997138, accessed 14 Feb 2017.

59. Ian Cobain, Richard Norton-Taylor, 'Mau Mau Massacre Cover-Up Detailed in Newly-Opened Secret Files', http://www.guardian.co.uk/world/2012/nov/30/maumau-massacre-secret-files, accessed 30 Jan 2017. See Anthony Cary's report, 'The Migrated Archives: what went wrong and what lessons should we draw?' 24 Feb 2011, https://www.gov.uk/government/publications/cary-report-on-release-of-the-colonial-administration-files, accessed 30 Jan 2017. See Editorial, *The Guardian,* 11 Apr 2011, & Editorial, *The Times,* 13 Apr 2011: 'Taking on the Boss: the quiet whistleblowers on events in Kenya deserve praise'.
60. Ian Cobain, 'Mau Mau Torture Case: Kenyans win ruling against UK', http://www.guardian.co.uk/world/2012/oct/05/mau-mau-veterans-win-torture-case, accessed 30 Jan 2017. In 2013 the British government paid out compensation of £19.9m to 5,228 Kenyans who suffered torture. A second claim was made in May 2014 by 41,005 Kenyans for a range of alleged offences, including false imprisonment, forced labour and an interference with their right to education. See Katie Englehart, '40,000 Kenyans Accuse UK of Abuse in Second Mau Mau Case', *Guardian,* 29 Oct 2014, http://www.theguardian.com/world/2014/oct/29/kenya-mau-mau-abuse-case, accessed 30 Jan 2017.
61. Rankin, 'Subaltern's Diary', p.65, Rose private papers. A 'sad postscript' was that the officer responsible for throwing the grenade committed suicide soon afterwards 'though for reasons unconnected with the incident.' See also '1BW, Officers' Mess', *Red Hackle*, Jul 1955, p.11, which describes it as tear gas.
62. Rankin, 'Subaltern's Diary', p.67, Rose private papers. Grant, excerpt from his diary, Apr 1955, quoted in *Letters from the Forest*, p.144.
63. '1BW, A Coy', *Red Hackle*, Jul 1955, p.13.
64. '1BW, D Coy', *Red Hackle,* Jul 1955, p.14. Bob Mitchell, interview, 2 Dec 2008, 'This Happens in War', BWM.
65. Maj Gen Neil McMicking, quoted in '1BW, General', *Red Hackle,* Jul 1955, p.11. D. Rose, 'Farewell to Kenya', *Off the Record*, p.140. Rankin, 'Subaltern's Diary', p.51.
66. Grant, *Letters from the Forest*, p.206. Lt Col Henry Conyers (Mick) Baker Baker had been commanding the Regimental Depot.
67. '1BW, General', *Red Hackle*, Oct 1955, p.12. 2BW had provided the Royal Guard in 1926, 1935 & 1952. The previous time 1BW did so was in 1912. It undertook the Royal Guard again in 1958, 1968, 1978, 1981, 1986, 1996.
68. Capt Colin Harrison, telephone interview, 26 Nov 2012. Harrison's recollection relates to when 1BW provided the Royal Guard in 1958. See also '1BW, General', Jan 1959, p.17; & 'Her Majesty's Guard', *Red Hackle*, Jan 1959. Gurdon, interview, 15 Jan 2013. He took pride in initiating the 'bread and butter' letter of thanks addressed to the Queen's Equerry. 'Those letters made the Royal Family's day!' The Queen continues to inspect the Guard at Ballater even though the station no longer exists.
69. Cheddi Jagan (1918–97) and his wife Janet (1920–2009) became the 4th and 6th Presidents respectively.

70. '2BW, General', *Red Hackle*, Jul 1954, p.22; additional information, Maj Gen Andrew Watson, interview, 7 Dec 2012, London. French Guiana was a prison for hardened French criminals, as recorded in Henri Carrière's *Papillon*! Dutch Guiana (Suriname) was in fact British Guiana's direct neighbour, then French Guiana.
71. Lt Col Ian Blacker Leslie, Obit by O.R. Tweedy, *Red Hackle*, May 2007, p.11. David Steavenson, interview, 7 Jan 2014, London. Lord Wilson of Tillyorn, KT, GCMG, FRSE, telephone interview & correspondence, Jul 2015.
72. Watson, interview, 7 Dec 2012. Maj R.C.B. Ritchie, interview, 2 Dec 2008, 'This Happens in War', BWM. David Steavenson, interview, 7 Jan 2014, London.
73. '2BW, Pipes and Drums', *Red Hackle*, Jan 1955, p.25. '2BW, C Coy', *Red Hackle*, Jan 1955, p.22.
74. 2nd Lt the Hon Malcolm (now Viscount) Davidson to Darling Granny, 9 Dec 1954, Davidson private papers.
75. '2BW, General', *Red Hackle*, Apr 1955, p.20. 2nd Lt the Hon Malcolm Davidson to his parents, 27 Dec 1954, Davidson private papers.
76. See map in *Red Hackle*, Apr 1955, p.20. See also '1BW, Kaieteur revisited', *Red Hackle*, Apr 1979, p.31; & Ch.19 in this volume.
77. 2nd Lt David Wilson, 'The Lost World', *Red Hackle*, Jan 1956, p.8. Conan Doyle's *Lost World* (1912) concerned an expedition up the Amazon Basin in Brazil, to a secret location where prehistoric animals were to be found. See Lt Col Ian Blacker Leslie, Obit by O.R. Tweedy, *Red Hackle*, May 2007, p.11, for an account of Leslie's journey with Lt Eddie Orr-Ewing: they returned 'absolutely black with sun burn, covered in horrid sores and having lost an enormous amount of weight; something that Ian [Leslie] fortunately could well afford.'
78. '2BW, General', *Red Hackle*, Apr 1955, p.20. '73rd Reunion', *Red Hackle*, Apr 1956; '2BW, General', *Red Hackle*, Oct 1956, p.15.
79. 'To 39 Bde, … Sig. 113/3/AQ of 30 Oct 53', vs 2 & 3, *Red Hackle*, Jan 1954, p.8.

19. What The Black Watch Does is News

1. Maj Gen Douglas Wimberley, CB, DSO, MC, paper, 1962, cited by Brig the Hon H.B.H.E. Monro CBE (Col, The Highlanders) to Lt Gen Sir Alistair Irwin, 17 Nov 2004, Irwin private papers. Monro said he was struck by the quotation in the context of the discussion about regimental names.
2. Ian Tarnish, 'Missing Glory,' *Evening Telegraph*, 11 Nov 1968, republished in *Red Hackle*, Dec 1968, p.4.
3. R. MacDougall, Letters, *Red Hackle*, Apr 1988, p.5. Jim Anderson, interview, 2 Dec 2008, 'This Happens in War', BWM.
4. Philip Howard, 'When I guarded Hess', *The Times*, reprinted in *Red Hackle*, Dec 1987, p.17.
5. Brig Duncan Cameron, interview, 19 Sep 2012, Perth. See Victoria Schofield, *The Highland Furies*, pp.434–55 for details of Gen Sir Duncan Cameron's service. All four occupying armies had the right to cross into the others' respective sectors.

6. '2BW', *Red Hackle*, Apr 1957, p.28.
7. Cameron, interview, 19 Sep 2012. See '1BW, General', *Red Hackle*, Oct 1958, pp.19, 28.
8. '1BW, A Coy', *Red Hackle*, Apr 1959, p.20. B Coy was on detachment at Tobruk protecting King Idris until the end of Jan 1959, when it joined 1BW in Cyprus.
9. For details of the poem and incident, see Schofield, *The Highland Furies*, pp.500, 502–3; 'Sergeant Samuel McGaw VC', *Red Hackle*, Nov 2015, p.23.
10. Ethniki Organosis Kyprion Agoniston (EOKA) translates as National Organisation of Cypriot Fighters. Georgios Grivas (1898–1974) used Digenis as his *nom de guerre*.
11. Born Michail Christodolou Mouskos (1913–1977), he became Makarios III, Archbishop and primate of the autocephalous Cypriot Orthodox Church in 1950, then first President of the Republic of Cyprus from 1959, over three consecutive terms (to 1977), interrupted by the 1974 coup. He survived 3 assassination attempts and died of a heart attack.
12. Cameron, interview, 19 Sep 2012. Maj Gen Andrew Watson, interview, 7 Dec 2012, London.
13. Christopher Rose, 'The Black Watch (RHR) in Cyprus', memoir, originally published in 2008 on www.britains-smallwars.com, ed. David Carter (accessed 2013, currently off-line); he served as a volunteer private soldier from 1957–60; correspondence with Christopher Rose, 29 Jan 2017.
14. '1BW, D Coy', *Red Hackle*, Apr 1959, p.22.
15. '1BW, QM's Dept', *Red Hackle*, Apr 1959, p.28.
16. '1BW, A Coy', *Red Hackle*, Apr 1959, pp.20, 22. B Coy was on its way back from Tobruk, C Coy was sent on detachment from Polis to Nicosia guarding Greek Cypriots detained under the emergency regulations. C. Rose, 'The Black Watch (RHR) in Cyprus'.
17. Ibid.'1BW, A Coy', *Red Hackle*, Apr 1959, p.20.
18. Ibid, pp.20, 23.
19. C. Rose, 'The Black Watch (RHR) in Cyprus'.
20. Ibid. '1BW, M.I. Room', *Red Hackle*, Apr 1959, p.28.
21. C. Rose, 'The Black Watch (RHR) in Cyprus'.
22. Ibid. Maj David Severn, Obit by Maj Colin Innes, *Red Hackle*, Nov 2011, p.20. He was the son of Lt Col B.A. Innes and grandson of Col Sydney Innes.
23. C. Rose, 'The Black Watch (RHR) in Cyprus'.'1BW, A Coy', *Red Hackle*, Jul 1960, p.27; Lt Col Angus Irwin took over from Monteith on 27 Jul 1959. He commanded the Regimental Depot 1955–57 and had been acting as British Infantry Liaison Officer to the School of Infantry, Fort Benning.
24. '1BW, General' *Red Hackle*, Oct 1960, p.13.
25. See White Paper, The Infantry Re-Organisation of 1957; also http://hansard.millbanksystems.com/lords/1957/jul/31/army-estimates-and-reorganisation-1, accessed 30 Jan 2017. One proposal was for the Highland Regiments to be formed into a Brigade Regiment, which would mean a loss of name and tartan.
26. Maj Gen Neil McMicking, memorandum (undated), Watson private papers; &

memorandum, 24 Nov 1958, Cheetham/Metcalfe private papers. McMicking's successor as Colonel was Maj Gen Viscount Arbuthnott, who, like McMicking, had served in both World Wars as well as being Hon Col of the 6/7th Black Watch. Both had sons in the Regiment.

27. Following the *Options for Change Defence Review* in 1994, the Queen's Own Highlanders was again amalgamated with the Gordon Highlanders to form The Highlanders. In 2006 all remaining Highland and Lowland Regiments were merged to form the Royal Regiment of Scotland, see Ch.27.
28. Watson, interview, 7 Dec 2012. Maj Ronnie Proctor, interview, 16 Oct 2013. 'The Trojan was on display and used from time to time on demonstrations at Warminster 1962–64.' Production of the FV432 started in 1962 and ended in 1971. Proctor had enlisted in the Army in May 1960 as an infantry junior leader aged 15, later completing the Highland Brigade Junior NCOs course.
29. Shortly before National Service was abolished in 1960 the Mons Officer Cadet Training Unit and the Eaton Hall Training Unit were amalgamated to form the Officer Cadet School. Capt Colin Harrison, telephone interview, 26 Nov 2012.
30. See 'The Highland Brigade Depot', *Red Hackle,* Apr 1964, p.4; also Apr 1962, p.6. It had formerly been the depot for the Gordon Highlanders.
31. 'Regimental Headquarters', *Red Hackle,* Apr 1962, p.6, & Oct 1962, p.2. See also T.J.M., 'Marching through Perth – 17 May 1985', *Red Hackle,* Aug 1985, p.21.
32. D.C.T(hornycroft), 'Descent of the Volunteer Battalions of The Black Watch', *Red Hackle,* Apr 1993, p.11. The 4/5th and 6/7th were disbanded on 1 April 1967. The 6/7th became HQ Coy and still claimed 'the privilege of wearing the Croix de Guerre lanyard'. See also 'Re-organisation of the TA', *Red Hackle,* Apr 1967, p.9.
33. '1BW', *Red Hackle,* Jan 1964, p.11.
34. 'The Black Watch, Royal Highland Regiment Wed. Nov 13, 1963, South Lawn of the White House', *Red Hackle,* Supplement, Jan 1964. Programme, 'The Black Watch, Royal Highland Regiment, Wed, Nov 13, 1963'. 'Tour of the United States and Canada by the Pipes and Drums, Military Band, Highland Dancers from Sep to Dec 1963', *Red Hackle,* Jan 1964, Supplement. Mrs Jacqueline Kennedy to Maj Wingate-Gray, 14 Nov 1963.
35. Pte (later) CSgt John Nicoll, interview, 19 Oct 2015, London.
36. 'The Black Watch, Royal Highland Regiment, Wed. Nov 13, 1963, South Lawn of the White House', *Red Hackle,* Jan 1964, Supplement; footage of The Black Watch Pipers playing is still part of the exhibition in the Sixth Floor Museum, Dallas, Texas. 'Tour of the United States and Canada by the Pipes and Drums, Military Band, Highland Dancers from Sep to Dec 1963', *Red Hackle,* Supplement, Jan 1964. Cameron, interview, 19 Sep 2012, Perth. He was 2IC of the detachment.
37. Gurdon, interview, 15 Jan 2013, London. He had been promoted captain in 1958 and major in 1965. Proctor, interview, 16 Oct 2013, Perth. Maj Colin Innes, interview, 17 Oct 2013, Perth.
38. Watson, interview, 7 Dec 2012; see '1BW, General', *Red Hackle,* Aug 1966, p.10 & '1BW, Sergeants' Mess, B & D Coys', *Red Hackle,* Aug 1966, pp.12, 17, 19. 1BW carried out exercises with B Squadron, The Royal Scots Greys. The military coup

was led by Muammar Qaddafi (Gaddafi), who was overthrown and killed in 2011. At least two RAF bases also had to be abandoned.

39. '1BW, A (Grenadier) Coy', *Red Hackle*, Dec 1966, p.18. UNFICYP mandate, see http://www.un.org/en/peacekeeping/missions/unficyp/mandate.shtml, accessed 30 Jan 2017.
40. The platoon was acting in support of the 3rd Division (Strategic Reserve); see 'Rocker Platoon Notes', *Red Hackle*, Jul 1964, p.19.
41. 'Officers' Mess', *Red Hackle*, Aug 1966, p.27. Lt Col Earle Nicoll, the first Roman Catholic commanding officer, replaced Tony Lithgow in Aug 1966. Watson, interview, 7 Dec 2012.
42. Lt Col E.W. Nicoll, 'Six months in Cyprus with the United Nations Forces', *Red Hackle*, Aug 1967, p.11. Hamish Gibson, telephone interview, 21 Aug 2015. On a visit to Ayios Theodorus, Gibson met Col Mehmet, Turkish Army, who made it clear that Turkey already had an invasion plan, indicating the relevant drop zones. 'I wrote a confidential report for Colonel Nicoll and when, five years later, Turkish troops did invade, Col Mehmet's predictions were entirely accurate.'
43. Nicoll, 'Six months in Cyprus with the United Nations Forces', *Red Hackle*, Aug 1967, p.11. '1BW, General, Kophinou', *Red Hackle*, Apr 1967, p.15.
44. Nicoll, 'Six months in Cyprus with the United Nations Forces', *Red Hackle*, Aug 1967, p.11.
45. Ibid.
46. Watson, interview, 7 Dec 2012. The Black Watch did not return to Cyprus until 2015 when it was deployed as The Black Watch, 3rd Bn The Royal Regiment of Scotland (3 Scots).
47. Watson, interview, 7 Dec 2012. Brig Francis Henn, *A Business of Some Heat, The United Nations Force in Cyprus before & During the 1974 Turkish Invasion*, p.24.
48. Henn, *A Business of Some Heat, The United Nations Force in Cyprus before & During the 1974 Turkish Invasion*, pp.497–8. Maj Gen P.G.F. Young, in charge of British troops, which had first deployed from the sovereign bases in 1963, had used a green pencil which explains the name.
49. Maj Dick Parata, telephone interview, 29 Jul 2014; additional information 17 Sep 2016. He had met Bernard Fergusson serving as Governor-General of New Zealand 1962–67. On 30 Nov 1967 British forces withdrew from Aden and the independent People's Republic of South Yemen was proclaimed.
50. Maj R. Ritchie, 'Ritchie Camp, Kirknewton', Correspondence, *Red Hackle*, Nov 2011. During WWII the camp served as a POW camp and a US Air Force communications base.
51. '1BW, General', *Red Hackle*, Dec 1968, p.11. '1BW, B Coy and Exercise Vacuum', *Red Hackle*, Dec 1968, p.19.
52. '1BW, General', *Red Hackle*, Apr 1969, p.11.
53. Maj Hugh Rose, interview, 18 Nov 2012, Comrie.
54. 'Behind the Bamboo Curtain with the First Battalion, Exercise Preparation', *Red Hackle*, Aug 1969, pp.17, 22.

55. Brig Bernard Fergusson to Eric Linklater, from Ayrshire, 3 Jun 1969, Acc 10282, No.12/5, NLS. Fergusson was the 22nd Colonel of the Regiment since the Regiment's formation in 1739.
56. See 'Rock Island Lines, The First Battalion in Gibraltar', *Red Hackle,* Dec 1969, pp.11–14. Watson, interview, 7 Dec 2012. The Black Watch was posted to Gibraltar in 1795, 1800, 1805, 1825, 1827 (73rd Regt), 1878, 1889, & 1940.
57. Watson, interview, 7 Dec 2012. The economic blockade lasted until 1985.
58. 'Rock Island Lines', *Red Hackle,* Dec 1969, p.14. H. Rose, interview, 18 Nov 2012.
59. Brig Edward de Broë-Ferguson, interview, 7 Mar 2013, London. There is no mention of Beaton's expeditions in *The Red Hackle.*
60. Watson, interview, 7 Dec 2012.
61. 'Rock Island Lines', *Red Hackle,* Dec 1969, pp.20 & 11.
62. '1BW, General', *Red Hackle,* Aug 1970, p.9.
63. Anon, 'Stag' ll.1–7, quoted in 'Rock Island Lines,' *Red Hackle,* Dec 1969, p.14.

20. Emergency Tours in Northern Ireland

1. K.R.C(raig), 1BW, 'Remembrance', ll.9–13, *Red Hackle*, Aug 1983, p.18. It was written when the flags were at half-mast for the funeral of Cpl Gerald Jeffery, 1st Devon & Dorsets, who died of wounds received from a booby-trap bomb in Apr 1983. See McKittrick et al., *Lost Lives,* p.941.
2. The six counties were Antrim, Armagh, Down, Fermanagh, Londonderry, Tyrone. Three further counties of the original province of Ulster – Donegal, Cavan and Monaghan – remained part of the Republic of Ireland (Éire).
3. See Alvin Jackson, *Ireland 1798–1998*, for background information. Smaller violent non-legal groups included the Red Hand Commandos (1972) and the Ulster Freedom Fighters (1973). In 1974 a delegation from the UDA visited Libya 'intent on sounding out the Gaddafi regime about possible aid in the event of independence.' Ian Paisley, Baron Bannside, PC (1926–2014) became a Protestant Evangelical minister in 1946.
4. The Marching Season, when Protestants in towns throughout Northern Ireland held marches or parades, lasted from Apr to Aug. There had already been Protestant attacks on civil rights demonstrations in Aug & Oct 1968.
5. See Operation Banner Restricted Army Code 71842, 'An Analysis of Military Operations in Northern Ireland & Special Order of the Day, The End of Operation Banner' from Gen Sir Richard Dannatt, KCB, CBE, MC, Chief of the General Staff, 25 Jul 2007, BWM. (Earlier version has the Foreword by Gen Sir Mike Jackson GCB, CBE, DSO, ADC Gen, Jul 2006.) Residential units served in permanent barracks accompanied by their families.
6. Brig Garry Barnett, correspondence, 22 Oct 2015. Tony Geraghty, *The Irish War*, p.29.
7. In deciding to deploy the British Army, the British Govt had been alarmed by newsreel footage of RUC and 'B-Specials' laying into Nationalists, which caused international outrage. The Ulster Special Constabulary (B-Specials) was

disbanded in May 1970 in an attempt to attract more Catholic recruits into the police. It had been accused of carrying out revenge killings against the Catholic community in the 1920s. In 1992 the UDR was amalgamated with the Royal Irish Rangers to form the Royal Irish Regiment. It was the only unit of the British Army in Northern Ireland to serve continuously 1970–92.

8. Maj Gen Andrew Watson, interview, 7 Dec 2012, London. Brig Garry Barnett, interview, 19 Oct 2013, Perth. See also selected interviews, 'This Happens in War', Northern Ireland, BWM.
9. Jeremy Hulme, '1BW's first visit to Northern Ireland', Hulme private papers. He received his commission in 1968.
10. Brig Donald Wilson, interview, 9 Jul 2013, London. See also '1BW Notes, A Coy, Part 1 – Belfast: Eye-witness Account', *Red Hackle,* Dec 1970, p.17. '1BW, Belfast', *Red Hackle,* Dec 1970, p.11.
11. Desmond Hamill, *Pig in the Middle,* p.37. Capt Stephen Lindsay to his wife, Annie, 1970, Lindsay private papers.
12. Hulme, '1BW's first visit', Hulme private papers. WO2 Joe Hubble, interview, 17 Sep 2013, London. He believes he fired the first shot by 1BW. Lindsay to Annie, 1970, Lindsay private papers.
13. Hulme, '1BW's first visit', Hulme private papers.
14. Ibid. Lindsay to Annie, 1970, Lindsay private papers.
15. '1BW, Bravo Bravo Bravo', *Red Hackle,* Dec 1970, p.19; Hulme, '1BW's first visit', Hulme private papers. The 'curfew' was in fact 'a movement restriction on the civilian population of that area for the sake of their own safety and the safety of the soldiers.' Permission for a curfew would have taken 'too long', Hamill, *Pig in the Middle*, p.37.
16. Lindsay to Annie, 1970, Lindsay private papers. The action took place on the crossroads between Plevna Street and Varna Street.
17. Hulme, '1BW's first visit', Hulme private papers.
18. '1BW Notes, A Coy, Part 1 – Belfast: Eye-witness Account', *Red Hackle,* Dec 1970, p.18. Lindsay to Annie, 1970, Lindsay private papers.
19. Hulme, '1BW's first visit', Hulme private papers. The aftermath of the Falls Curfew deepened the divide between the Official and Provisional IRA (which had split in 1969) when the Officials blamed the Provisional IRA for starting the fight and then leaving them on their own, resulting in the loss of many weapons. In 1972 the Official IRA had declared a ceasefire, reserving the right of self-defence.
20. Hamill, *Pig in the Middle,* p.39. Wilson, interview, 9 Jul 2013, London. Tony Geraghty, *The Irish War*, p.34.
21. Writer unknown, recorded by Athenry and Shebeen; guitar music by Marc Fahrbach: http://www.irish-folk-songs.com/the-black-watch-lyrics-and-chords1.html, accessed 15 Feb 2017. There are different versions to this song; one line goes: 'Thank god we know the IRA will shoot the bastards dead.'
22. '1BW, Belfast', & '1BW, Bravo Bravo Bravo', *Red Hackle,* Dec 1970, pp.12, 19.
23. Ibid, pp.12, 20.
24. Wilson, interview, 9 Jul 2013.

25. Maj Gen Andrew Watson, 'The Battalion's Tours in Northern Ireland, Jul 1970–Jun 1971, Londonderry, Operation Banner Aug 1969–Jul 2007, Northern Ireland: An overview', *Red Hackle*, May 2007, p.18.
26. Hulme, '1BW's first visit', Hulme private papers. Since the bridge was two-tiered, soldiers on the lower tier also got gassed. Brig Garry Barnett, interview, 19 Oct 2013, Perth.
27. Watson, 'Londonderry', *Red Hackle*, May 2007, p.18. '1BW, Londonderry', *Red Hackle*, Dec 1970, p.14. See also 'A Coy, Part 2 – Londonderry: Eye-witness Account', *Red Hackle*, Dec 1970, p.18.
28. Simon Winchester, 'Holy Terror', *Red Hackle*, Dec 1996, p.16.
29. Ibid. The adjt was P.G. Forster.
30. '1BW, Slow Down, I Want to Get Off', *Red Hackle*, Dec 1970, p.22. Wilson, interview, 9 Jul 2013. Hulme, '1BW's first visit', Hulme private papers.
31. '1BW, Aberfeldy', *Red Hackle*, Dec 1970, p.14. '1BW, Pipes and Drums Tour of North America', *Red Hackle*, Apr 1971, p.23. Lt Col Stephen Lindsay, interview, 27 Feb 2014, Crieff.
32. '1BW, A Coy, Part 3 – Other Events: Eye-witness Account', & '1BW, Slow Down, I Want to Get Off', *Red Hackle*, Dec 1970, pp.19, 22. Another exercise was Highland Fury; see *Red Hackle*, Aug 1970, p.14.
33. '1BW, The Black Watch and Ireland', *Red Hackle*, Apr 1971, p.13, also Watson, interview, 7 Dec 2012; Watson, 'Armagh', *Red Hackle*, May 2007, p.18. Wilson, interview, 9 Jul 2013.
34. '1BW, General', *Red Hackle*, Apr 1971, p.12. Col David Thornycroft, 'Ypres 2014', memoir, Thornycroft private papers.
35. Lt Alistair Irwin to Nicola, 17 Feb 1971, Irwin private papers; the son of Brig Angus Irwin, CBE, DSO, who commanded 1BW 1959–61, Alistair Irwin (b.1948) was commissioned in 1969. Later Lt Gen Sir Alistair Irwin KCB, CBE, Col Commandant of the Scottish Division (1999–2005), Chairman of the Council of Scottish Colonels, Adjutant-General (2003–05), Col of The Black Watch (2003–06), Representative Colonel of The Black Watch, 3rd Battalion, The Royal Regiment of Scotland (3 Scots) until 2009. He commanded 1BW 1985–88. His diaries and letters are the most comprehensive primary source material available.
36. Hubble, interview, 17 Sep 2013, London.
37. Rt Hon. Reginald Maudling, Hansard, 11 Mar 1971, see http://hansard.millbanksystems.com/commons/1971/mar/11/british-soldiers–northern-ireland-murder#S5CV0813P0_19710311_HOC_300, accessed 15 Feb 2017. Irwin to Nicola, 11 Mar 1971, Irwin private papers. A memorial has been dedicated to the three soldiers at Ballysillan, who were lured from a city centre bar by some Republican women. Fusiliers John & Joseph McCaig were brothers, aged 17 and 18 respectively: the third soldier was Fusilier Dougald McCaughey, aged 23.
38. '1BW, Climbing Club', *Red Hackle*, Aug 1971, p.23. Watson, 'Armagh', *Red Hackle*, May 2007, p.18.
39. Irwin to Nicola, 23 May 1971, Irwin private papers.
40. '1BW, General', *Red Hackle*, Aug 1971, p.10.

41. Hubble, interview, 17 Sep 2013. '1BW, A (Grenadier) Coy', *Red Hackle,* Aug 1971, p.14.
42. Brig Bernard Fergusson to Eric Linklater, from Ayrshire, 15 Apr 1971, Acc 10282,12/8, NLS. The story has been told on a number of occasions. Pte Watt was at Pomeroy RUC station, Co. Tyrone.
43. '1BW, General', *Red Hackle,* Aug 1971, p.10. Wilson, interview, 9 Jul 2013. '1BW, D Coy', *Red Hackle,* Aug 1971, p.18.
44. Brig Garry Barnett, correspondence, 22 Oct 2015.
45. '1BW, Exercise Eagles Nest', *Red Hackle,* Apr 1972, p.26. (NB the date given on p.24 should be 1971 not 1972.) See 'The Kirk Session of the 1st Battalion The Black Watch 1954–79'.
46. '1BW, At Home, Sat. 25 Sep. 1971', *Red Hackle,* Aug 1971, p.2. '1BW, General', *Red Hackle,* Dec 1971, p.13.
47. Brig O.R. Tweedy, 'East Belfast Oct–Dec 1971, Op Banner Aug 1969–Jul 2007, Northern Ireland – an overview', *Red Hackle,* May 2007, p.19. Irwin to Nicola, 8 Oct 1971, Irwin private papers. '1BW, The Black Watch in Belfast', *Red Hackle,* Dec 1971, p.21. B Coy later moved to a hangar at Sydenham airfield by the docks and then to Ballymacarrett; C Coy and HQ were at the Royal Naval Air yard/Sydenham.
48. Hubble, interview, 17 Sep 2013. He wanted to put the current hostility in a historical context by recognising the contribution of the 36th Ulster Division, 32,186 of whom were killed, wounded or missing during WWI.
49. Tweedy, 'East Belfast Oct–Dec 1971', *Red Hackle,* May 2007, p.19. WO1 David Stacey, interview, 28 Feb 2014, Perth; he served in the Regt for 38 years.
50. Irwin to Nicola, 11 Oct 1971, Irwin private papers.
51. *The Watchkeeper – Belfast '71,* pp.4–5. '... and also the gloom which inevitably arose as a result of this further period of separation. It was also a tribute and a gesture of thanks to our wives for the tremendous way they have endured, a fact too often forgotten in the excitement of the Irish situation.' '1BW, General', *Red Hackle,* Dec 1971, p.13.
52. '1BW, Dear Soldiers', *Red Hackle,* Dec 1971, p.25.
53. Brig O.R. Tweedy, interview, 19 Oct 2013, Perth, & 'East Belfast Oct–Dec 1971', *Red Hackle,* May 2007, p.19. Charnley died on 18 Nov 1971. Obit, *Red Hackle,* Dec 1971, p.9, gives the date of evening 19 Nov 1971. See McKittrick et al., *Lost Lives,* p.118.
54. Capt Colin Harrison, telephone interview, 26 Nov 2012; he was at the bus depot when the attack happened.
55. See Geraghty, *Irish War,* p.42. The General Service Medal, combining previous General Service Medals, was introduced in 1962; a total of 13 clasps were awarded.
56. The Widgery Tribunal, which investigated the actions of the security forces, whitewashed events; it was not until 15 Jun 2010 that the Saville Inquiry (instigated in 1998) conceded that the paratroopers had fired the first shot, had fired on fleeing unarmed civilians, and had shot and killed one man who was already wounded. Following the report's publication, PM David Cameron said he was 'deeply sorry' and described the actions on Bloody Sunday as 'unjustified and

unjustifiable', in the House of Commons. http://www.bbc.co.uk/news/10320609, accessed 25 Feb 2017.

57. The Parachute Regt was stationed abroad at the time, but 7 civilian staff were killed and 19 wounded.
58. Thornycroft, 'Ypres 2014', memoir, Thornycroft private papers. This was 13 Platoon, D Coy. Operation Motorman was the largest operation mounted by the British Army since Suez in 1956.
59. Fergusson to Linklater, from Ayrshire, 12 Nov 1971, Acc 10282, No.12/10 NLS; Linklater was restricted to writing 80,000 words by the publisher, Barrie & Jenkins. See also correspondence Acc 10155/3, NLS. Eric Linklater died on 7 Nov 1974; his son, Andro Linklater (died 3 Nov 2013), completed the book.
60. K.R.C(raig), 'Remembrance', ll.1–4, *Red Hackle*, Aug 1983, p.18.

21. Travelling the Seven Seas

1. '1BW, Thirsty Work', *Red Hackle,* Apr 1972, p.24. I have no diaries or letters for this chapter and so am dependent on interviews and *The Red Hackle.*
2. 'Largest single container cargo for Hong Kong', *Red Hackle,* Apr 1972, p.2. The only broken items on arrival were four soup plates, ibid, p.12.
3. '1BW, General', *Red Hackle,* Apr 1972, p.12.
4. Pte Jim Sandilands, interview, 9 Dec 2008, 'This Happens in War', BWM.
5. '1BW, General', *Red Hackle,* Aug 1972, pp.12, 28. Lt Col Sir Andrew Ogilvy-Wedderburn, Bt, interview, 17 Oct 2013, Perth; born in 1952, he was commissioned in 1971.
6. Ogilvy-Wedderburn, interview, 17 Oct 2013. The island is not to be confused with Tung Ping Chau (or vice versa), another island of the same name also off the coast of Hong Kong.
7. '1BW, D Coy Force Guard', *Red Hackle,* Apr 1972, p.18.
8. Lt Gen Sir Alistair Irwin, interview, 19 Feb 2014, London.
9. Sandilands, interview, 9 Dec 2008, 'This Happens in War', BWM.
10. '1BW, Pipes and Drums', *Red Hackle,* Apr 1972, p.16. '1BW, Medical Memorandum by the RMO', *Red Hackle,* Apr 1972, p.16. '1BW, Exercise Eagles Nest', *Red Hackle,* Apr 1972, p.26.
11. '1BW, General', *Red Hackle*, Aug 1972, p.9.
12. Maj Hugh Rose, interview, 18 Nov 2012, Comrie. Maj Ronnie Proctor, interview, 16 Oct 2013, Perth.
13. Ogilvy-Wedderburn, interview, 17 Oct 2013.
14. '1BW, General & Community Relations', *Red Hackle*, Aug 1972, pp.9, 21. 1BW's first 'community relations' task was constructing a 50 ft bridge at Man Wo.
15. '1BW, Training & Remote Patrol Areas', *Red Hackle*, Aug 1972, pp.18, 22. The interpreters were Chinese soldiers in the British Army.
16. '1BW, The Inter-Drill Competition', *Red Hackle*, Dec 1972, p.30. Brig Bernard Fergusson to Eric Linklater, from Ayrshire, 4 Jan 1973, Acc 10282, No.12/15, NLS.
17. '1BW, Korea, The Honor Guard', *Red Hackle,* Aug 1972, pp.12, 13.

18. Ibid, p.14. Proctor, interview, 16 Oct 2013.
19. (Hugh Rose), '1BW, Korea, The Pilgrimage', *Red Hackle,* Apr 1973, p.23. See also '1BW, Korea Honor Guard', *Red Hackle,* Apr 1973, p.22. Harrison, interview, 26 Nov 2012. The other veterans were WO2 Pedro Hird, CSgt Dave Anderson, Cpl William Thomson and Nobby Clark. Ed. Note, *Watchkeeper,* Hong Kong, 1973.
20. Harrison, interview, 26 Nov 2012. Rose, interview, 18 Nov 2012; see also '1BW, Korea, The Pilgrimage', *Red Hackle,* Apr 1973, p.24. Park Byung-Kyu told them he was not in fact a General but a Colonel but his friends all said that he looked like a General!
21. See '1BW, In Hong Kong', *Red Hackle,* Aug 1972 p.9; also Victoria Schofield, *The Highland Furies,* pp.254–70.
22. '1BW, Australian Adventure', *Red Hackle,* Dec 1972, p.18. '1BW, Strines Learn Scottish', *Red Hackle,* Dec 1972, p.21.
23. '1BW, Malaysia, Exercise Lacerate', *Red Hackle,* Dec 1972, p.22.
24. '1BW, New Zealand', *Red Hackle,* April 1973, p.18.
25. Innes was assisted by the CSM, CSgt and one Cpl., 'Foreword and Acknowledgements', *Songs of the Regiment, The Black Watch (Royal Highland Regiment),* Jan 1973. Maj Colin Innes, interview, 18 Oct 2013, Perth.
26. '1BW, New Zealand', *Red Hackle,* Apr 1973, p.18, & '1BW, The Black Watch and the New Zealand Scottish Regiment', *Red Hackle,* Aug 1973, p.13. Innes, interview, 20 Oct 2013. The New Zealand Scottish Regiment was disestablished in 1990 and disbanded in 2013; the Colours were laid up on 16 Apr 2016; see *Red Hackle,* Nov 2016.
27. '1BW, The Black Watch and the New Zealand Scottish Regiment', *Red Hackle*, Aug 1973, p.14.
28. '1BW, Black Watch in All Black Country, Exercise Snowline', *Red Hackle,* Aug 1973, p.16.
29. 'The Okinawa Platoon', & Lt Tim Ireland, USMC, 'Letter from America', *Red Hackle,* Aug 1972, pp.15, 16.
30. '1BW, Exercise Lamar Kite', *Red Hackle,* Aug 1973, pp.18–19.
31. Brig Donald Wilson, interview, 9 Jul 2013, London. '1BW, Exercise Golden Spur', *Red Hackle,* Aug 1973, pp.17–18.
32. Col David Thornycroft, interview, 20 Jul 2014, London.
33. '1BW, B Coy', *Red Hackle,* Dec 1973, p.14.
34. '1BW, A–D Coys' *Red Hackle*, Apr 1974, pp.15–18; Wilson, interview, 9 Jul 2013. 'Hong Kong Tattoo', *Red Hackle,* Apr 1974, p.18.
35. '1BW, B Coy, 7 Platoon', *Red Hackle*, Apr 1974, pp.16–17.
36. '1BW, General', *Red Hackle*, Aug 1974, p.12.
37. Wilson, interview, 9 Jul 2013.
38. Brig Garry Barnett, interview, 20 Oct 2013, Perth. Lt Col R.M. (Roddy) Riddell (b.1953), interview, 19 Jun 2013, London; he was commissioned in 1973 and was the nephew of Major Donald Molteno, killed in action in 1945. Sandilands, interview, 9 Dec 2008, 'This Happens in War', BWM.
39. 'For These Are My Mountains', Songs of the Regiment, no.14, p.8.

22. Countering Terror

1. Brig D.R. (Donald) Wilson, interview, 9 Jul 2013, London.
2. See David McKittrick et al., *Lost Lives*, p.1473, Table 1; also Tony Geraghty, *Irish War*, p.41; 496 people were recorded as having been killed in 1972: over half (259) were civilians, 151 British security forces (108 Army), the remainder from the Republican and Loyalist paramilitary organisations (RUC/RUCR 17, UDR 26, Republican and Loyalist paramilitaries 85, other 9).
3. 'Special Order of the Day, The End of Operation Banner from Gen Sir Richard Dannatt, KCB, CBE, MC, Chief of the General Staff', 25 Jul 2007, pp.2–12, BWM.
4. Wilson, interview, 9 Jul 2013; Wilson for CO the late Brig T. N. McMicking, 'Andersonstown Jun–Oct 1974, Operation Banner Aug 1969–Jul 2007, Northern Ireland: An overview', *Red Hackle*, May 2007, pp.19–20. He also stated that in addition to fuelling terrorist activity in Northern Ireland, the IRA was sustaining a number of similar movements in Spain (ETA), Germany (the Baader Meinhof) and Italy (the Red Brigade).
5. '1BW, 7 Pl, B Coy', *Red Hackle*, Dec 1974, p.17. Three brothers from Kirkcaldy were serving: Jimmy, Alex and Tommy Kinnaird, while a fourth brother, Andrew, later enlisted, *Red Hackle*, Aug 1974, p.1. This was not as unusual as it might seem: the brothers Jim, David and John Atkinson also served in the Regiment. Pte Jim Sandilands, interview, 9 Dec 2008, 'This Happens in War', BWM.
6. '1BW, General', *Red Hackle*, Aug 1974, p.16. Lt Alistair Irwin, 'N. Ireland Diary, Jun–Oct 1974', p.3, Irwin private papers.
7. Lt Col R.M. (Roddy) Riddell, interview, 19 Jun 2013, London.
8. Irwin, 'N. Ireland diary Jun–Oct 1974', Sun 23 & Wed 26 Jun, pp.7, 11, Irwin private papers. The chaiwallahs were from the same family Ghulam Nabi as those in Cyprus and in India/Pakistan 1947/8.
9. Ibid, Wed 26 Jun 1974, p.11. Riddell, interview, 19 Jun 2013.
10. Irwin, 'N. Ireland diary', Thurs 27 Jun 1974, p.13, Irwin private papers. Riddell, interview, 19 Jun 2013. IED = Improvised Explosive Device.
11. Wilson, interview, 9 Jul 2013. He went on to say that in the current state of warfare, terrorists are no longer concerned about saving their own lives.
12. Irwin, 'N. Ireland diary', Fri 28 Jun 1974, p.15, Irwin private papers; & interview, 20 Feb 2014.
13. '1BW, General', *Red Hackle*, Dec 1974, p.10.
14. Irwin, 'N. Ireland diary', Sat 29 Jun 1974, p.17, Irwin private papers.
15. Ibid, Mon 1 Jul 1974, p.21. Wilson for McMicking, 'Andersonstown, Jun–Oct 1974', *Red Hackle*, May 2007, p.20.
16. Irwin, 'N. Ireland diary', Fri 5 Jul–Sat 6 Jul 1974, pp.28–30, Irwin private papers.
17. '1BW, General', *Red Hackle*, Aug 1974, pp.21–2. Brig Edward de Broë-Ferguson, interview, 3 Feb 2014, London.
18. Irwin, 'N. Ireland diary', Tues 2 Jul–Thurs 4 Jul 1974, pp.25–7, Irwin private papers.
19. M.L.M. (probably Michael Landale Melville), '1BW, The Turf Lodge Incident', *Red Hackle*, Aug 1974, p.23.

20. Wilson for McMicking, 'Andersonstown, Jun–Oct 1974', *Red Hackle*, May 2007, p.20. The Queen's Gallantry Medal was introduced in Jun 1974 to replace the OBE for Gallantry, the British Empire Medal for Gallantry and the Colonial Police Medal for Gallantry. Duncan and McCutcheon were among its first recipients.
21. Broë-Ferguson, interview, 3 Feb 2014. Irwin, 'N. Ireland diary', Fri 5 Jul–Sat 6 Jul 1974, p.30, Irwin private papers.
22. Irwin, 'N. Ireland diary', Fri. 7 Jul–Sat. 13 Jul 1974, p.34, Irwin private papers.
23. '1BW, General', *Red Hackle*, Dec 1974, p.10. Irwin, 'N. Ireland diary', Sun 21 Jul–Sat 27 Jul 1974, p.46, Irwin private papers.
24. 'Leaflet to Residents of Andersonstown, Riverdale, Ladybrook, Suffolk, Lenadoon, Turf Lodge and Twinbrook', kept in ibid, p.31, Irwin private papers.
25. Irwin, 'N. Ireland diary', Sun 21 Jul–Sat 27 Jul 1974, p.48, Irwin private papers.
26. 'Continue to Dominate', *Watchkeeper*, Aug 1974, pp.1, 8. Irwin, 'N. Ireland diary', Sun 28 Jul–Sat 3 Aug 1974, p.54, Irwin private papers.
27. '1BW B Coy 5 Platoon', *Red Hackle*, Dec 1974, p.15.
28. Irwin, 'N. Ireland diary', Sun 11 Aug–Sat 17 Aug 1974, pp.66–8, Irwin private papers.
29. 'A Final Fling', *Watchkeeper*, Sep 1974, p.1, Irwin private papers.
30. '1BW General', *Red Hackle*, Dec 1974, p.10.
31. Wilson for McMicking, 'Andersonstown Jun–Oct 1974', *Red Hackle*, May 2007, p.20. The Maze Prison formally became known as HM Prison Maze with the end of internment in Dec 1975 and the ending of Special Category status in 1976. It was closed in 2000 and demolition began in 2006.
32. Irwin, 'N. Ireland diary', Sun 13 Oct–Sat 19 Oct 1974, pp.142–44, Irwin private papers.
33. Ibid, pp.146–50.
34. Ibid, Sun 20 Oct–Thurs 24 Oct 1974, p.154. See also '1BW Support Coy', *Red Hackle*, Dec 1974, p.18.
35. Irwin, 'N. Ireland diary', Conclusions, p.168, & Anatomy of a Tour, Irwin private papers, p.159: statistics of having completed 858 headchecks, 240 house searches, 278 arrests, 90 arrests handed over to RMP/RUC, 8 bomb hoaxes, 9 armed robberies, 5 riots, 15 hostile shootings, 6 internal shootings, 5 bombings, 9 marches/military funerals, 1 major attack, 12 hijacks, 8,714 car searches.
36. James Allan in Belfast, 'Black Watch threatened by Provos,' *Daily Telegraph*, undated newspaper cutting. Two pubs in Guildford were bombed on 5 Oct 1974, killing 5 and wounding 65; two pubs in Birmingham were bombed on 21 Nov killing 21 and wounding 182.
37. Lt Gen Sir Alistair Irwin, interview, 19 Feb 2014, London. Col David Thornycroft, interview, 20 Jul 2014, London. See '1BW, The Colours Parade', *Red Hackle*, Aug 1975, p.7. The old Colours were laid up at Balhousie on 21 Jun 1978, see *Red Hackle*, Apr 1978, pp.2 & 11, Aug 1978, p.9.
38. 'Special Order of the Day, The End of Operation Banner from Gen Sir Richard Dannatt, KCB, CBE, MC, Chief of the General Staff', 25 Jul 2007, pp.2–12, BWM. Critics of the ceasefire, notably Gerry Adams and Martin McGuinness believed the ceasefire was disastrous for the IRA leading to a feud with the Official IRA.

The truce broke down in Jan 1976.

39. Wilson for McMicking, 'Andersonstown Jun–Oct 1975', *Red Hackle*, May 2007, p.20, & additional information, 9 Jul 2013, London.
40. Maj Colin Gray, interview, 27 Feb 2014, Perth. D Coy and Bn HQ were in Fort Monagh, A and B Coys at Glassmullen Camp, with an Observation Post in the Lenadoon. Support Coy was in Woodburn Police Station. Echelon, with the medical officer and supplies, was at Musgrave Park.
41. WO1 David Stacey, interview, 28 Feb 2014, Perth.
42. Irwin, 'N. Ireland diary', Fri 20 Jun–Fri 4 Jul 1975, p.3, & Sat 5 Jul–Thu 17 Jul, p.5, Irwin private papers. See also 'Special Order of the Day, The End of Operation Banner from Gen Sir Richard Dannatt, KCB, CBE, MC, Chief of the General Staff', 25 Jul 2007, pp.2–12, BWM.
43. 'Judging the Pace', *Watchkeeper*, Sep 1975, p.1, Irwin private papers. Irwin, 'N. Ireland diary', Fri 25 Jul–Sun 10 Aug 1975, p.9, Irwin private papers. This was Irwin's last entry. Promoted captain on 25 Jul, he took up a posting as an instructor at the School of Infantry at Warminster.
44. See '1BW, Operations in Belfast, Shootings', *Red Hackle*, Dec 1975, p.11. McKittrick et al., *Lost Lives*, p.577.
45. Riddell, interview, 19 Jun 2013; Tony Geraghty, *Irish War*, p.137; see *Red Hackle*, Dec 1975, p.11.
46. Although McKay and his patrol were charged for illegally planting ammunition, no soldier was charged in connection with the Norney killing. See McKittrick et al., *Lost Lives*, p.1472; Brian J. Brady, Denis Faul & Raymond Murray, *A British Army Murder*, & Ciara Quinn, 'Family appeals for information over the 1975 murder of Turf Lodge teen,' *Andersonstown News*, 20 Jul 2011. In Apr 1977 the Norney family were awarded 'a small amount of compensation' for their son's killing & in Feb 2014 the N. Ireland Attorney General, John Larkin, directed that an inquest be held into Norney's killing. After some delay, the inquest was scheduled for November 2021. John Ross McKay died in Sep 2015.
47. Wilson, interview, 9 Jul 2013.
48. '1BW, Operations in Belfast, Riots', *Red Hackle,* Dec 1975, p.11.
49. Col David Thornycroft, 'Ypres 2014', memoir, & interview, 20 Jul 2014, London. The menu consisted of prawn cocktail, roast rib of beef and chocolate profiteroles! Thornycroft private papers.
50. Lt Col E.D. Cameron to Brig the Lord Ballantrae, 5 Mar 1976, Cameron private papers.
51. '1BW, The Cadet Leadership Course', *Red Hackle,* Aug 1976, p.11. There was a record heat-wave in 1976 lasting Jun–Aug.
52. Kieran Nugent (1958–2000) was imprisoned in Sep 1976 for hijacking a vehicle. He said the prison authorities would have to 'nail' the prison uniform to his back. He died of a heart attack aged 42.
53. See Aogán Mulcahy, *Policing Northern Ireland: Conflict, Legitimacy and Reform,* Willan Publishing, 2006, pp.108–27. Christopher Ewart-Biggs, CMG, OBE (1921–76).

54. Brig Duncan Cameron, interview, 19 Sep 2012, Perth, & Brig E.D. Cameron, 'Ballykinler 1976–78, Operation Banner Aug 1969–Jul 2007 Northern Ireland: An overview', *Red Hackle*, May 2007, p.22. Cameron (as Lt Col) to Brig J.C. Monteith, 6 Aug 1976, Cameron private papers.
55. Cameron, 'Ballykinler 1976–78', *Red Hackle*, May 2007, p.22.
56. Cameron to Monteith, 6 Aug 1976, Cameron private papers. Cameron, 'Ballykinler 1976–78', *Red Hackle*, May 2007, p.22.
57. Cameron to Ballantrae, 20 Aug 1976, & Ballantrae to Cameron, 17 Sep 1976, Cameron private papers.
58. Cameron to Monteith, 2 Nov 1976, Cameron private papers.
59. Ibid, 22 Dec 1976.
60. Lt Gen Sir David Young, KBE, CB, DSC, (1926–2000). (Lt Col Mike Smith), 'The Northern Ireland Patrol Group (NIPG) The Black Watch Ballykinler 1976–1978', Parata private papers. The NIPG was distinct from the 14 Intelligence (the Dets) who wore civilian clothes, whereas the NIPG were in uniform; later the COP formed the basis for the Special Reconnaissance Regiment.
61. Maj Dick Parata, telephone interview, 30 Jun 2014. He added: 'With today's technology, the numbers would have been photographed and put into a computer!'
62. Parata, correspondence, 23 Mar 2015. He continued: 'Although the COP finished with the end of the hostilities, the legacy of NIPG/COP skills has been adopted in future Army planning albeit with much more sophisticated equipment and support. Specialist reconnaissance regiments are now an important part of the Army structure.' For his services, Parata received the MBE.
63. Cameron, 'Ballykinler 1976–78', *Red Hackle*, May 2007, p.22.
64. Cameron to Monteith, 24 May 1977, Cameron private papers.
65. Cameron, 'Ballykinler 1976–78', *Red Hackle*, May 2007, p.22. Cameron to Monteith, 15 Jul 1977, Cameron private papers.
66. Cameron, 'Ballykinler 1976–78', *Red Hackle*, May 2007, p.22.
67. See http://www.bbc.co.uk/history/topics/queen_elizabeth_ii_northern_ireland, accessed 16 Feb 2017. WO1 Colin Gray, interview, 28 Feb 2014, Perth.
68. Maj Colin Innes, 'Black Watch – Fire Watch', *Red Hackle*, Dec 1977, p.34. Innes, serving as GS02, 51 Highland Bde, was on a visit.
69. Riddell, interview, 19 Jun 2013. Innes, 'Black Watch – Fire Watch', *Red Hackle*, Dec 1977, p.34. Gray, interview, 28 Feb 2014. Lt Col Sir Andrew Ogilvy-Wedderburn, Bt, interview, 17 Oct 2013, Perth.
70. Cameron to Monteith, 24 Jan 1978, Cameron private papers.
71. Pte Mark Donald Carnie, Obit, *Red Hackle*, Dec 1978, p.9.
72. Anon, 'The Love of a Soldier', ll.13–18, *Red Hackle*, Apr 1978, p.20.

23. Confronting the Cold War

1. Anon, 'Just a Rhyme', v.1, quoted in 'Red Hackles in West Belfast Once Again!' *Watchkeeper*, p.4, West Belfast, Dec 1982–May 1983, Irwin private papers.
2. 'Heron Bill', *Red Hackle*, Aug 1978, p.19. Additional information, Lt Col R.M.

(Roddy) Riddell, 6 Oct 2015.

3. Capt Colin Harrison, 'A Look at Cyprus today', *Red Hackle*, Aug 1978, p.21.
4. 'D Coy Notes', *Red Hackle*, Aug 1978, p.24. 'Laying up the Old Colours', *Red Hackle*, Aug 1978, p.25. '1BW, D Coy', *Red Hackle*, Aug 1978, p.24.
5. See 'Visit to Berlin, Jul 1978', *Red Hackle*, Dec 1978, p.30. 'Exercise Ponte Vecchio', *Red Hackle*, Dec 1978, p.28. '1BW, General', *Red Hackle*, Aug 1978, p.14; Lt Col Stephen Lindsay, interview, 27 Feb 2014, Crieff. It was the first time in 10 years they had provided the Royal Guard; the Regiment's 10th time since 1900.
6. WO1 Billy Whytock, interview, 17 Oct 2013, Perth. He had joined the Regiment in Colchester in 1975 and was also a member of the Northern Ireland Patrol Group. He was among a group of NCOs sent on a Jungle Instructors' Course in Brunei before deploying to Guyana.
7. Maj Colin Gray, interview, 27 Feb 2014, Perth.
8. 'Kaieteur Revisited', *Red Hackle*, Apr 1979, pp.30–2. The event was reported in the *Guyana Chronicle*, 4 Nov 1978. See *Red Hackle*, Dec 1978, p.3. Brig Edward de Broë-Ferguson, correspondence, 11 Apr 2013 & 26 Oct 2015. See also Ch.16.
9. Lt Col R.M. Riddell, interview, 19 Jun 2013, London. Congressman Leo Ryan, who had come to Guyana to investigate conditions in Jonestown, and five others were shot, bringing the total number of deaths to 918 (of which 276 were children).
10. Brig de Broë-Ferguson, interview, 3 Feb 2014, London; correspondence 26 Oct 2015. See *Guyana Chronicle*, 21, 22, 23 Nov 1978; *Citizen*, 29 Nov 1978; de Broë-Ferguson private papers.
11. '1BW, A Coy', *Red Hackle*, Apr 1979, p.26. On 15 Dec Pte Christopher Munro died of cancer aged 17½. As a member of D Coy, he had recently taken part in jungle training in Guyana and 'at no time did he complain that he could not carry his full battle load of equipment'. *Red Hackle*, Apr 1979, p.11.
12. Maj Ronnie Proctor, interview, 16 Oct 2013, Perth.
13. See P.A.B. Thomson, *Belize: A Concise History*, pp.165–78 on the dispute with Guatemala.
14. 'First impressions of Belize', *Bush Telegraph*, 1979, Belize, p.1, BWM.
15. Brig Edward de Broë-Ferguson, correspondence, 26 Oct 2015; additional information, Riddell, 27 Sep 2105. '1BW', *Red Hackle*, Aug 1979, p.25. Brig Donald Wilson, interview, 9 Jul 2013, London; he was OC B Coy.
16. '1BW, Jungle Warfare Course – How to Survive', *Red Hackle*, Aug 1979, p.33.
17. See 'Adventure Training Team', *Red Hackle*, Apr 1979, p.26.
18. 'First impressions of Belize', *Bush Telegraph* 1979, Belize, p.1, BWM. Lt Col Sir Andrew Ogilvy-Wedderburn, Bt, interview, 17 Oct 2013, Perth.
19. Rev Norman Drummond, 'The Kirk Session of 1st Battalion, The Black Watch, Royal Highland Regiment, The first twenty-five years 1954–79', p.11, BWM, pp.24–5. On Sun 9 Sep 1979 a lectern with the Regimental Badge was presented to the Church. The woodcarver was Frank Lisame of the Belize National Craft Centre. Rev Norman Drummond, telephone interview, 4 Feb 2016.
20. Broë-Ferguson, correspondence, 26 Oct 2015; '1BW, General', *Red Hackle*, Aug 1979, p.19. Watson is the son of Maj Gen Andrew Watson.

21. Following Margaret Thatcher's assumption of office, the Armed Forces received a 35% pay rise (promised by Labour but instituted under the Conservatives), followed by a 15% pay rise in 1980–1.
22. A detachment served in Belize in Aug 1987 with the 1st Queen's Own Highlanders. See 'Back to Belize', *Red Hackle,* Dec 1987, pp.11–12.
23. Riddell, interview, 19 Jun 2013; '1BW, General', *Red Hackle,* Dec 1979, p.19.
24. A.B.D.G(urdon), 'The View from the Top, The Black Watch in Rhodesia 1979–80', *Red Hackle,* Apr 1980, pp.8–9.
25. Whytock, interview, 17 Oct 2013.
26. I.R.T(homson), 'Worm's Eye View, The Black Watch in Rhodesia 1979–80', *Red Hackle,* Apr 1980, p.9. Whytock, interview, 17 Oct 2013.
27. Whytock described 'over 250 coming in in arrowhead formation', Whytock, interview, 17 Oct 2013.
28. (Gurdon), 'The Black Watch in Rhodesia 1979–80', *Red Hackle,* Apr 1980, p.8. He was awarded the CBE for his work in Rhodesia, *Red Hackle,* Aug 1980, p.2. (Thomson), 'Worm's Eye View, The Black Watch in Rhodesia 1979–80', *Red Hackle,* Apr 1980, p.9.
29. (Gurdon),'The Black Watch in Rhodesia 1979–80', *Red Hackle,* Apr 1980, pp.8–9. Robert Mugabe (b.1924) has been President of Zimbabwe since 1980.
30. Col David Thornycroft, interview, 21 Jul 2014, London.
31. Willy Brandt (1913–1992), Chancellor, Federal Republic of Germany 1969–74, resigned when a close associate was found to be an agent of Stasi, the East German secret service. He was succeeded by his Minister of Finance, Helmut Schmidt (1918–2015).
32. Brig Garry Barnett, interview, 19 Oct 2013, Perth. Col Ronald (Ronnie) Bradford, skype interview, 11 Jan 2016. Capt Robert (Bertie) Bradford (1952–2009) received a Short Service Commission in 1975, and left the Army in 1981. See Capt Robert Bradford, Obit by R.J.K. Bradford, *Red Hackle,* May 2010, pp.11–12. Broë-Ferguson, correspondence, 29 Oct 2013.
33. 'German Speaking Classes', *Red Hackle,* Aug 1979, p.44. '1BW, A Coy, Sprechen sie Deutsch?', *Red Hackle,* Aug 1980, p.17.
34. '1BW, B Coy', *Red Hackle,* Aug 1980, p.18. Riddell, interview, 19 Jun 2013. Additional information, Lt Gen Sir Alistair Irwin, 28 Dec 2015.
35. Bradford, skype interview, 11 Jan 2016. Crusader 80 included Exercises Spearpoint, Jog Trot and Reforger. Involving forces from the UK, USA, Belgium, Holland and Germany, exercises on this scale were carried out every 4 years. Broë-Ferguson, correspondence, 29 Oct 2013; Barnett, interview, 20 Oct 2013. In Minden, Active Edge was called Quick Train.
36. Bradford, skype interview, 11 Jan 2016. BATUS was established in 1972 with the grant of a 10-year lease between the British and Canadian govts; the lease has now been extended indefinitely. The Falklands War lasted 2 Apr–14 Jun 1982.
37. Brig G.C. Barnett, '1 BW in Belfast 21 Dec 1982–3 May 1983, Operation Banner Aug 1969–Jul 2007, Northern Ireland: An overview', *Red Hackle,* May 2007, p.23; Barnett, additional information, 15 Dec 2015. This was the first unaccompanied

tour since 1BW deployed to Cyprus as part of UNFICYP in 1965–66. Most of the wives with children at school stayed in Werl.

38. Lt Rupert Forrest, diary, 1982–83, Forrest private papers. The bomb which killed Neave had been planted by the Irish National Liberation Army (INLA), formed in 1974 from disaffected members of the Official IRA who opposed the ceasefire.
39. Special Category Status had been granted by Willie Whitelaw, Secretary of State for Northern Ireland, in Jul 1972 as part of a negotiated settlement with the Provisional IRA.
40. The attack in Droppin Well Inn was the worst since Warrenpoint in 1979. Proctor, interview, 26 Feb 2014. PM Thatcher had not visited N. Ireland since 1981 at the height of the hunger strikes. See photograph, '1BW', *Red Hackle*, Apr 1983, p.23; http://www.nytimes.com/1982/12/23/world/around-the-world-mrs-thatcher-visits-ulster-blast-survivors.html, accessed 16 Feb 2017. Barnett, interview, 18 Oct 2013.
41. Maj Alistair Irwin to Nicola, 29 Dec 1982, 'Letters, West Belfast 1982–3', Irwin private papers. According to Forrest, diary, 28 Dec 1982: '[Patrick] Elliott was on bail and was wanted for attempted murder of an RUC constable. He had 30 other offences on record. The Yellow Card (Rules governing the use of weapons NI) were applied and no further comeback is expected.' Another man was wounded but despite a night-long search he was never found, Forrest private papers.
42. Barnett, '1 BW in Belfast, 21 Dec 1982–3 May 1983', *Red Hackle*, May 2007, p.23. Forrest, diary, 2 Jan 1983, Forrest private papers. He was 16 Pl Cdr, D Coy, moving to 4Pl, A Coy.
43. '1BW, General', *Red Hackle,* Apr 1983, p.23.
44. Sgt (later Capt) Brian (Spatts) Baxter, interview, 26 Feb 2014, Perth. Capt Hugo Allen, interview, 20 Jun 2016, London. As part of the British Army's PR activities, Allen's achievements as a ski champion were publicised, revealing both his hometown and a photograph!
45. Capt Alan McEwen, interview, 17 Oct 2013, Perth. Allen, interview, 20 Jun 2016.
46. Barnett, interview, Oct 2013. The idea behind the introduction of 'coincidental boundaries' was to avoid one police superintendent having to deal with different battalions in different TAORs.
47. '1BW The Black Watch, 21 Dec 1982–3 May 1983', memento booklet, Irwin private papers. Barnett, '1 BW in Belfast 21 Dec 1982–3 May 1983', *Red Hackle*, May 2007, p.22.
48. Riddell, interview, 19 Jun 2013. Maj Alistair Irwin to Nicola, 9 Jan 1983, 'Letters, West Belfast 1982–3'. See also 'Red Hackles in West Belfast Again!', *Watchkeeper*, West Belfast, Dec 1982–May 1983, p.1, Irwin private papers.
49. Proctor, interview, 26 Feb 2014.
50. Barnett, '1 BW in Belfast 21 Dec 1982–3 May 1983', *Red Hackle*, May 2007, p.23; additional information, Brig Garry Barnett, interview, 19 Oct 2013. Bradford, skype interview, 11 Jan 2016; Bradford's assistant, WO2 Kenny Glasgow, was Mentioned in Despatches for his work.
51. Forrest, diary, 20 Mar 1983, Forrest private papers. Proctor, interview, 26 Feb

2014. See 'Echoes of Belfast: RPG Attack', *Red Hackle*, Aug 1983, p.18. Bradford, skype interview, 11 Jan 2016. The main gate had fallen off its hinges due to high winds, so the vehicle was using the back gate, which meant going round a blind corner making it more vulnerable to attack.

52. '1BW, A Coy', *Red Hackle*, Apr 1983, p.27. 'Marching on to May', *Watchkeeper*, West Belfast, Dec 1982–May 1983, p.1. Jeffery died on 7 Apr 1983, Irwin private papers. The Devon & Dorsets was the Resident Battalion in Ballykinler.
53. Proctor, interview, 26 Feb 2014.
54. Maj Hugh Rose, interview, 18 Nov 2012, Comrie, & correspondence, 1 Aug 2014; Rose was OC B Coy. Information also from Riddell, interview, 19 Jun 2013. The acronym HEAT (High Explosive Anti Tank) has sometimes made people think the missiles rely on heat to be effective; in fact high-velocity pressure enables the warhead to penetrate through armour.
55. 'Marching on to May', *Watchkeeper*, West Belfast, Dec 1982–May 1983, p.1, Irwin private papers. In the Brighton bombing, 5 people were killed and 31 injured.
56. Broë-Ferguson, correspondence, 26 Oct 2015. 'Exercise Liquid Chase', *Red Hackle*, Dec 1983, pp.15–18; '1BW', *Red Hackle*, Apr 1984, p.32. Riddell, interview, 25 Feb 2014, Crieff.
57. Bradford, skype interview, 11 Jan 2016. Broë-Ferguson, correspondence, 26 Oct 2015: 'Following a visit to the Battalion from the Deputy Assistant to the US Secretary of Defence for Chemical Matters he told the Commander 1st British Corps that he planned to incorporate the lessons of the exercise into US programmes.'
58. '1BW, Our Winter's Tale', *Red Hackle*, Apr 1984, p.36. The Black Watch Battlegroup was in 33 Armoured Bde.
59. 'Able Archer simulated the use of tactical nuclear weapons by NATO after a Warsaw Pact chemical attack. The timing of the chemical trial Liquid Chase carried out by the Black Watch Battlegroup in the summer was coincidental', additional information, Brig Edward de Broë-Ferguson, 23 Feb 2016.
60. See 'Skiing Exercise Snow Queen, Nordic Ski Team', *Red Hackle*, Apr 1984, pp.22–3, 24. 'Italian Exchange', *Red Hackle*, Apr 1984, p.17.
61. 'Exercise Base Plate One: Five weeks in a concentration camp', *Red Hackle*, Aug 1984, p.18. Col David Thornycroft, 'Ypres 2014', memoir, Thornycroft private papers; he was OC C Coy.
62. '1BW, Training in Canada', *Red Hackle*, Dec 1984, pp.28–30. Thornycroft, 'Ypres 2014', memoir, Thornycroft private papers. He had taken command of A Coy. A contingent also went to Nordegg in the Canadian Rockies, see pp.31–3.
63. Lt Col Alistair Irwin to Nicola, fn to N. Ireland, 7 Jan 1986, 'Letters, N. Ireland, 1985–6', Irwin private papers. The Rt Hon Sir John Stanley (b.1942), was Min of State for the Armed Forces 1983–87, Northern Ireland Office 1987–88.
64. 'Association News', *Red Hackle*, Apr 1984, p.55.
65. Bradford, skype interview, 11 Jan 2016.
66. 'Association News', *Red Hackle*, Apr 1984, p.55.
67. T.J.M., 'Marching through Perth – 17 May, 1985', *Red Hackle*, Aug 1985, p.21.

Broë-Ferguson, correspondence, 26 Oct 2015; he made the comment to the Provost of Perth Mr Mathieson and council.

68. '1BW, General', *Red Hackle,* Aug 1985, p.26.
69. Bradford, skype interview, 11 Jan 2016. See also 'Commemoration of VE-Day 8 May, 1985', *Red Hackle*, Aug 1985, p.17.
70. '1BW, Families Office', *Red Hackle,* Apr 1986, p.47.
71. '1BW, General', *Red Hackle*, Apr 1986, p.24. 1BW was the Armagh Roulement Battalion (ARB). 'A.S.H. Irwin, Lt Col, 1st Bn The Black Watch (Royal Highland Regiment) Armagh Roulement Battalion, Handover Brief Feb 1986', Irwin private papers. 1BW took over from 3rd Royal Regiment of Fusiliers on 17 Dec 1985. Lt Gen Sir Alistair Irwin, 'South Armagh Dec 1985–May 1986, Operation Banner Aug 1969–Jul 2007, Northern Ireland: An overview', *Red Hackle*, May 2007, p.23. For details of Operation Bewilder, a spoof to confuse and embarrass new subalterns regarding the identity of the senior officers, see '1BW Notes, Officers' Mess', *Red Hackle,* Sep 1986, p.21.
72. '1 BW South Armagh, Jan 1986', commemorative booklet. McEwen, interview, 17 Oct 2013. BW Training Directive 2/85 (NI), Restricted, Irwin private papers.
73. Proctor, interview, 25 Feb 2014; others were Baseball (Air traffic controller), Brimstone (Padre), Mushroom (Watchkeeper), Snapper (Guard Dog), Ground Hog (Tracker Dog), etc., 'Radio Appointment Titles', Forrest private papers. '1BW, General', *Red Hackle,* Apr 1986, p.24.
74. Maureen Young, 'X.M.G. – stands for terror!', *Perthshire Advertiser*, 22 Apr 1986, Irwin private papers.
75. Baxter, interview, 26 Feb 2014.
76. Gray, interview, 26 Feb 2014. He was platoon sgt, B Coy. Young, 'X.M.G. – stands for terror!', *Perthshire Advertiser,* 22 Apr 1986, p.8, Irwin private papers.
77. Irwin, 'South Armagh Dec 1985–May 1986', *Red Hackle*, May 2007, p.24.
78. Bradford, skype interview, 11 Jan 2016.
79. Allen, interview, 20 Jun 2016.
80. Gen Sir John Chapple to Lt Col Alistair Irwin, 8 Jun 1987, Irwin private papers. '1BW, General', *Red Hackle,* Apr 1986, p.24. Lt Col Alistair Irwin to Nicola, 2 Jan 1986, 'Letters, N. Ireland, 1985–6', Irwin private papers. See also Forrest, diary, Forrest private papers. The official report was that there had been a severe down draught. Among the passengers was Maj Michael Lindsay-Stewart.
81. '1 BW South Armagh', Feb 1986. The patrol was from B Coy.
82. '1BW, General,' *Red Hackle,* Apr 1986, p.24. '1 BW South Armagh', Mar 1986, p.1. The patrol was from D Coy. Sgt Kilorn was known as Jubilee Jim, by virtue of being awarded the Queen's Silver Jubilee medal. Bradford, skype interview, 11 Jan 2016.
83. Lt Gen Sir Alistair Irwin, interview, 16 Feb 2009, quoted in Andrew Sanders & Ian S. Wood, *Times of Troubles*, p.157. In the same incident three other BW men appeared in court, stating that they had been under the influence of alcohol (Sanders and Wood incorrectly state that this was a different incident). Additional information, Lt Gen Sir Alistair Irwin, 24 Sep 2016.

84. Forrest, diary, 27 Apr 1986, Forrest private papers; he was 2IC B Coy, Maj Nigel Lithgow was OC. '1BW, General', *Red Hackle,* Sep 1986, pp.18, 31, & Sgt Gair McCrostie, telephone interview, 14 Aug 2013.
85. Forrest, diary, 27 Apr 1986, Forrest private papers. '1BW, Officers' Mess', *Red Hackle,* Sep 1986, p.21. Bradford, skype interview, 11 Jan 2016: 'The tour was notable as the first time Lieutenant Colonel Irwin instructed me to obtain the Battalion's computers', the preferred make being Amstrads 'because they came with a printer.'
86. Maj Gen M.L.(Mike) Riddell-Webster, interview, 13 Dec 2012, Cupar. He was commissioned into the Regt in 1979. His uncle and grandfather had both been in command of the Cameronians which had been disbanded in 1968, so his father suggested he join The Black Watch.
87. 'The Friendly Games', *Red Hackle,* Dec 1986, p.16.
88. Ibid, p.17.
89. Ibid, p.18. Ogilvy-Wedderburn, interview, 17 Oct 2013.
90. 'Exercise Wheel Spin', *Red Hackle*, Dec 1986, p.14. Riddell-Webster, interview, 13 Dec 2012. See Charlie Hankins, BEM, *A Part of my Life in a Family at War.* 'The Black Watch was his life,' observed Riddell Webster, who, as Regimental signals officer, planned Hankins' six-week trip and accompanied him to the border. 'The Charlie Hankins Award', *Red Hackle,* Apr 1988, p.16. The Charlie Hankins Trophy continues to be awarded annually.
91. Gray, interview, 28 Feb 2014.
92. '1BW, General', *Red Hackle*, Apr 1987, p.20. The Spearhead Battalion is a component of the British Army which has to be in readiness for non-combatant operations, for example disaster relief.
93. 'A Soldier's Ode', v.1, 'Red Hackles in West Belfast Again', p.9, *Watchkeeper*, West Belfast, Dec 1982–May 1983, Irwin private papers.

24. Closure of Empire

1. Message over tannoy recorded by Maj David Kemmis Betty, interview, 13 Jun 2013, London.
2. Additional information, Lt Gen Sir Alistair Irwin, 3 Jan 2016. The King's Own Scottish Borderers (KOSB) and the Gloucester Regt were also in Berlin Bde. In addition to the anti-tank platoon's deployment in 1978, 1BW had served in Berlin twice before, in 1950 & 1956. Statistics of those who died attempting to cross from East to West are contested, ranging from 98 to 200, with the figure of 136 generally accepted.
3. 'Ceremonial Parades: Queen's Birthday Parade', *Red Hackle,* Sep 1987, p.19. Maj Gen John Mitchell, US Army to Maj Gen Patrick Brooking, GOC Berlin, 23 Jun 1987, Irwin private papers.
4. President Reagan's remarks on East–West relations at the Brandenburg Gate in West Berlin; http://www.historyplace.com/speeches/reagan-tear-down.htm, accessed 17 Feb 2017. Lt Col Richard Nunneley, interview, 18 Mar 2014, London.

The Springsteen concert was in Jul 1988.

5. Additional information, Maj Rupert Forrest, 18 Aug 2016; Lt Gen Sir Alistair Irwin, 14 Sep 2016.
6. 'HM Queen Elizabeth the Queen Mother's visit to the 1st Bn The Black Watch: Wed 8 Jul 1987', *Red Hackle,* Sep 1987, p.29. In order of seniority of service those present were: J.E. Benson, H.N. Blair, B.C. Bradford, DSO, MBE, MC, J.C. Monteith, MC, A.D.H. Irwin, DSO, MC, N.G.A. Noble, MC, A.O.L. Lithgow, MC, E.W. Nicoll, CBE, LVO, A.L. Watson, CB, O.R. Tweedy, T.N. McMicking, E.D. Cameron, OBE, R.I.L. Ker, G.C. Barnett, OBE, E.N. de Broë-Ferguson, MBE. David Rose, DSO, was unable to come.
7. 'Aspects of Berlin', *Red Hackle,* Sep 1987, p.22. The majority of Berliners were under 25 and exempt from military service. They did not understand why British military presence remained necessary.
8. Nunneley, interview, 18 Mar 2014. 'A Just So Story, Wilmersdorf Freedom Parade', *Red Hackle*, Aug 1988, p.22.
9. Maj Gen M.L. (Mike) Riddell-Webster, interview, 13 Dec 2012, Cupar. 'Exercise Black Highlander', *Red Hackle,* Sep 1987, p.32. Nunneley, interview, 18 Mar 2014.
10. '1988 Berlin Brigade Army Staff Course FIBUA demonstration', *Red Hackle*, Aug 1988, p.21. Held at Ruhleben village on the site of a former WWI internment camp for British civilians, the demonstration was done by 1BW in 1987 and 1988. Nunneley, interview, 18 Mar 2014.
11. 'Aspects of Berlin: the Spandau Guard', *Red Hackle*, Sep 1987, p.22. Additional information, Capt Alan McEwen, 11 Feb 2014.
12. There were claims that Hess had been killed by the British Secret Service, his son stating that his father was too old and frail to have hanged himself. He had attempted suicide in 1977 and been under 24-hour surveillance but this was discontinued as an invasion of privacy and impracticable, Wulf Schwarzwaller, *Rudolf Hess: The Deputy*, Quartet Books, 1988, p.2. See 'The End of Spandau', & '1BW, Introduction', *Red Hackle,* Dec 1987, pp.18, 21. Additional information, Riddell-Webster, interview, 13 Dec 2012; Kemmis Betty, interview, 13 Jun 2013, London. In Jul 2011 Hess's remains were exhumed, cremated and scattered at sea; the plaque marking his grave was destroyed. Information regarding the bricks from Nunneley, interview, 18 Mar 2014; he says they were 'uniquely marked' which gave them a market value of DM200 each.
13. Lt Col Alistair Irwin, 'Letters, West Germany, Nov 1987', Irwin private papers. '1BW, A (Grenadier) Coy', *Red Hackle,* Apr 1988, p.19.
14. 'Ex Bear Defender', *Red Hackle,* Aug 1989, p.17.
15. Nunneley, interview, 18 Mar 2014.
16. '1BW, Introduction', *Red Hackle,* Aug 1988, p.28.
17. 'In the Highest Tradition – BBC Visit', *Red Hackle,* Aug 1988, p.23. The programme was screened in 1989.
18. 'Flag Tours in East Berlin', *Red Hackle*, Dec 1987, p.16. Riddell-Webster, interview, 13 Dec 2012. Col R.J.K. Bradford, skype interview, 11 Jan 2016.
19. 'Flag Tours in East Berlin', *Red Hackle*, Dec 1987, p.16. Nunneley, interview,

18 Mar 2014.

20. Kemmis Betty, interview, 13 Jun 2013. See http://www.baor-locations.org/BMT.aspx.html, accessed 16 Feb 2017; they were originally established to maintain a link between the British zone of Germany and the British sector of Berlin.
21. See *Red Hackle*, Aug 1988, p.10. Lt Col R.M. (Roddy) Riddell, interview, 25 Feb 2014, Perth: 'With an optical sight it was a great improvement over the Self Loading Rifle (SLR) and led to enhanced shooting standards.'
22. Capt Harry Hood, interview, 6 Dec 2013, Harrogate. See also '1BW, Introduction', *Red Hackle*, Sep 1987, p.29; '1BW, Nightlife in Berlin', *Red Hackle*, Aug 1988, p.30.
23. Riddell-Webster, interview, 13 Dec 2012.
24. Brig D.R. Wilson and Col N.C.D. Lithgow, 'Ballykinler Jul 1989–Aug 1991, Operation Banner Aug 1969–Jul 2007, Northern Ireland: An overview', *Red Hackle*, May 2007, p.24. In the Lisburn attack, 4 soldiers were from the Royal Signal Corps, 1 from the Green Howards, 1 from the Royal Army Ordnance Corps; see McKittrick et al., *Lost Lives*, pp.1130–1.
25. Riddell, interviews, 25 Feb 2014 & 23 Nov 2015, Perth. Hood, interview, 6 Dec 2013.
26. '1BW, Alarms, Excursions and a Surprise', *Red Hackle*, Aug 1990, p.18.
27. See '1BW, 250th Anniversary', *Red Hackle*, Aug 1990, p.23.
28. Wilson & Lithgow, 'Ballykinler July 1989–Aug 1991', *Red Hackle*, May 2007, p.25. 39 Bdc was commanded by Brig Mike Jackson, and had its headquarters in Lisburn.
29. See 'Ranger Cyril J Smith QCM – 2nd Bn Royal Irish Rangers', Regimental Roll of Honour, http://royalirishrangers.co.uk/role.html, accessed 16 Feb 2017: 'Cyril died a hero instead of running to safety he tried to save his colleagues by running to warn them. He was awarded The Queen's Gallantry Medal Posthumously.' He was the first regular Royal Irish Ranger soldier to be killed. See McKittrick et al., *Lost Lives*, p.1216. Sgt Brian Baxter, interview, 26 Feb 2014, Perth. Wilson & Lithgow, 'Ballykinler Jul 1989–Aug 1991', *Red Hackle*, May 2007, p.26.
30. (Nigel Lithgow), '1 BW Oct 1990–Apr 1993, A Review, Staff in Confidence', The Regiment, part 1, p.1, Cowan private papers. Bradford, skype interview, 11 Jan 2016. Maj Gen James Cowan, interview, 11 Sep 2012, London. Riddell, interview, 23 Nov 2015.
31. WO1 J. Paton, 'Saddam Hussein's Guest', *Red Hackle*, Apr 1991, pp.10–1.
32. Lt Col Sir Andrew Ogilvy-Wedderburn, Bt, interview, 17 Oct 2013, Perth.
33. Information from Capt Angus MacDonald, 15 Mar 2016, who was promoted in the field and awarded the MBE for his part in developing logistic support for an armoured division conducting offensive operations. 34 nations joined the UN military force.
34. (Lithgow), '1 BW Oct 1990–Apr 1993, A Review, pp.2, 9, Cowan private papers.
35. Rory Stewart, *The London Gazette*, 52792, 13 Jan 1992, Supplement, p.493. Roderick James Nugent (Rory) Stewart, OBE, FRSL, MP (b. 1973), interview with Rachel Savage, *Cherwell*, 8 Aug 2013, http://www.cherwell.org/comment/interviews/2013/08/08/interview-rory-stewart, accessed 16 Feb 2017. He became

Member of Parliament for Penrith and The Border in Cumbria in 2010.

36. (Lithgow), '1 BW Oct 1990–Apr 1993, A Review', pp.2, 9, Cowan private papers.
37. *The Black Watch (Royal Highland Regiment) Hong Kong Review*, Sep 1993, p.13. There were editions in Sep & Dec 1993, and Jul 1994.
38. (Lithgow), '1 BW Oct 1990–Apr 1993, A Review', p.9, Cowan private papers. 1BW had its first major investigation for drugs in N. Ireland.
39. Maj Tim Elliott, interview, 3 Sep 2013, London.
40. (Lithgow), '1 BW Oct 1990–Apr 1993, A Review', p.11, Cowan private papers. *The Black Watch... Hong Kong Review*, Sep 1993, p.13. Sgt Maj J.P. Maestri, interview, 17 Oct 2013, Perth.
41. (Lithgow), '1 BW Oct 1990–Apr 1993, A Review', pp.9–10, Cowan private papers. The Military Band was merged in early 1994.
42. Riddell-Webster, interview, 13 Dec 2012. The band also played in Jakarta for the Java St Andrew's Society's 25th anniversary, with contingents performing in Moscow, Beijing, South Korea and the Philippines (with the Royal Navy).
43. Ogilvy-Wedderburn, interview, 17 Oct 2013. Capt Rikki Dinsmore was police liaison officer.
44. Pte McGilp, recce platoon, 'A Jock's view of the platoon competition', *The Black Watch... Hong Kong Review*, Jul 1994.
45. Ogilvy-Wedderburn, quoted in *The Junk*, Jun 1994, p.2. Sgt Robert Duncan, interview, 26 Feb 2014, Perth.
46. Riddell-Webster, interview, 13 Dec 2012.
47. Following 3BW's conversion into a Fire Support Bn on 1 Apr 1995, B Coy was reduced under A Coy, its machine-gun and mortar platoons based in Dundee with an anti-tank platoon in Forfar; K Coy's mortar and machine-gun platoons were based in Kirkcaldy with an anti-tank platoon in Perth; see D.C.T. (David Thornycroft), 'Descent of the Volunteer Battalions of The Black Watch', *Red Hackle*, Apr 1993, p.11. The suggestion that the Coys would be numbered 4, 5, 6 & 7 'to make clear their descent' from the original Territorial Bns did not materialise. The 1994 amalgamation left 6 regular Scottish Regiments, Brig Edward de Broë-Ferguson, interview 3 Feb 2014, London.
48. Downing Street Declaration, http://www.oxfordreference.com/view/10.1093/acref/9780199295678.001.0001/acref-9780199295678-e-682, accessed 16 Feb 2017. Gerry Adams (b.1948) had been joint Vice President of Sinn Féin since 1978. James Molyneaux, Baron Molyneaux of Killead, KBE, PC (1920–2015), leader of the UUP 1975–95, opposed the Good Friday Agreement but had been succeeded as leader of the UUP by David Trimble, Lord Trimble, PC (b.1944).
49. Lt Col Sir Andrew Ogilvy-Wedderburn, 'Belfast May–Nov 1995, Operation Banner Aug 1969–Jul 2007, Northern Ireland: An overview', *Red Hackle*, May 2007, p.26. Sgt Maj Alexander Wilson, interview, 26 Feb 2014, Perth. '1 BW Belfast,' *Watchkeeper*, 1 Jul 1995.
50. Elliott, interview, 3 Sep 2013. He was a platoon commander in B Coy.
51. Ogilvy-Wedderburn, 'Belfast May–Nov 1995', *Red Hackle*, May 2007, p.26.
52. For the story behind the removal of the hijacked vehicles see Ogilvy-Wedderburn,

'Belfast May–Nov 1995', *Red Hackle*, May 2007, p.27. The conviction for murder was quashed in 1998 and a re-trial ordered, in which Clegg was convicted for 'attempting to wound' the driver. In 2000, on appeal that conviction was also overturned.

53. Ogilvy-Wedderburn, 'Belfast May–Nov 1995', *Red Hackle*, May 2007, p.26. 'One star' refers to ranks of Brigadier and above.
54. Kemmis Betty, interview, 13 Jun 2013; Capt Harry Hood, interview, 6 Dec 2013.
55. Space does not permit narrating the negotiations leading to the Good Friday Agreement. A referendum was held in Northern Ireland and the Republic of Ireland in May 1998; the Agreement came into force in Dec.
56. The Omagh bomb killed 29 civilians, 15 of whom were 21 and under, in the largest civilian loss of life during the Troubles. On 1 Mar 2016, the case against Seamus Daly, held responsible for the Omagh bombing, collapsed due to lack of evidence.
57. Brig Alasdair Loudon, interview, 22 Aug 2008, Islamabad. Maj Mark Percy, interview, 2 Aug 2013, London.
58. Kemmis Betty, interview, 13 Jun 2013, London. Additional information, Capt Alan McEwen, Feb 2014.
59. Riddell-Webster, interview, 13 Dec 2012. Alexander Wilson, interview, 26 Feb 2014.
60. See 'Canadian Bagpipes Links – What is worn under the kilt?' 24 Apr 1997, http://canadianbagpipelinks.info/under_the_kilt.html, accessed 1 Mar 2017. Sgt Gair McCrostie, telephone interview, 14 Aug 2013. See Neil & Jo Craig, *Black Watch, Red Dawn*, pp.1 & xiv. Neil Craig spent his National Service in the 1BW.
61. Maestri, interview, 17 Oct 2013. Additional information, Capt Alan McEwen, Feb 2014. See also 'Withdrawal from Hong Kong, B Coy', *Red Hackle*, Dec 1997, p.26.
62. Ibid, p.27.
63. RSM Alan McEwen, quoted in Craig & Craig, *Black Watch, Red Dawn*, pp.224–5. Capt Alan McEwen, interview, 17 Oct 2013, Perth. Drum Maj Pat McLinden, quoted in Craig & Craig, *Black Watch, Red Dawn*, pp.211, 226. Sgt Duncan, interview, 26 Feb 2014.
64. McEwen, interview, 17 Oct 2013.
65. Queen Mother quoted in Craig & Craig, *Black Watch, Red Dawn*, p.xv.
66. Riddell-Webster, interview, 13 Dec 2012. Kemmis Betty, interview, 13 Jun 2013.
67. Editorial, p.3; 'Black Watch Visit to Ticonderoga', *Red Hackle*, Dec 1987, p.30. See Victoria Schofield, *The Highland Furies*, pp.57–66, for an account of the Battle of Ticonderoga. Brig Garry Barnett, speech, Ticonderoga, 5 Jul 1997, Barnett private papers.
68. 'Visit to Fort George', *Red Hackle*, Dec 1997. To mark the occasion, the artist Anna Redwood did a number of sketches and oil paintings.
69. Elliott, interview, 3 Sep 2013. See '1BW, A Coy', & '3BW, The Visit of HM Queen Elizabeth the Queen Mother', *Red Hackle*, Dec 1998, pp.26, 41–4. Additional information, Lt Col R.M. Riddell, 3 Nov 2015; '3BW, The Visit of HM Queen Elizabeth the Queen Mother', *Red Hackle*, Dec 1998, p.44. A painting of the occasion was commissioned and completed by artist Anna Redwood and which now

hangs in the Officers' Mess, Fort George. Following the Strategic Defence Review three Territorial Bns (3rd Black Watch, 7th/8th Argyll & Sutherland Highlanders, Highlanders) were amalgamated in 1999 to form the 51st Highland Regiment (51 HD) with its HQ at Queen's Barracks.

70. See *Red Hackle*, May 2002, pp.3, 10–11. The Royal Company of Archers is the Sovereign's Bodyguard in Scotland, performing ceremonial functions at her request. The Black Watch vigil team included Lt Gen A.S.H. Irwin, Brig E.D. Cameron, Maj D.J. McMicking, Maj J. Duncan Millar, Maj J.M.K. Erskine.
71. In 1469 an Act of the Scottish Parliament confirmed that the heir apparent would hold the Dukedom of Rothesay (created in 1398).
72. Lt Col Angus Philp, skype interview, 17 Jan 2013; his great-uncle was Lt Stanley MacKintosh, MC. Bradford, skype interview, 11 Jan 2016.
73. The Kosovo Liberation Army (KLA) was formed in 1991 and began attacking government installations in the mid-1990s. It was disbanded soon after the Kumanovo Treaty in 1999. NATO's aerial bombardments were controversial partly because they were not sanctioned by the UN Security Council. Op Agricola lasted Jun–Aug 1999. The Brigade consisted of 1 Challenger II Regt (Royal Scots Dragoon Guards), in a dismounted role less 1 Squadron and their recce cars. 1BW was part of UK Battlegroup 1 (UK BG1) which included other multi-national units.
74. Lt Col M.L. Riddell-Webster, Introduction, '1st Battalion The Black Watch (Royal Highland Regiment) Operation Agricola VI, 14 Jul–Nov 2001', Riddell-Webster private papers. Maj Rupert Forrest, diary, 'Kosovo 2001', Forrest private papers.
75. Percy, interview, 2 Aug 2013. The Kosovo Protection Corps was active 1999–2009 as a civilian emergency service, undertaking humanitarian assistance as well as search and rescue operations; many of its members had belonged to the now disbanded Kosovo Liberation Army, which was replaced by the Kosovo Security Force.
76. Philp, interview, 17 Jan 2013. Forrest, diary, 'Kosovo 2001', 21 Aug 2001, Forrest private papers. Maestri, interview, 17 Oct 2013.
77. See Capt A.H. Ferguson, 'Operation Agricola VI Jul–Nov 2001 – The End of the Kosovo Tour', *Red Hackle*, May 2002, p.23. Pte Robert Donkin died on 14 Nov 2001; LCpl Hamilton lost his leg trying to save him, *Red Hackle*, May 2002, p.14.
78. Riddell-Webster, Introduction, 'Operation Agricola VI, 14 Jul – Nov 2001', Riddell-Webster private papers.
79. '1BW, B Coy', *Red Hackle*, May 2002, p.27. Forrest, diary, 'Kosovo 2001', 13 Sep 2001, Forrest private papers. Maj Mike Williamson, interview, 30 Aug 2013, London. He was 2IC, A Coy.
80. Samuel Daniel (1562–1619), 'Ulysses and the Siren', ll.57–64, in *The Complete Works in Verse and Prose of Samuel Daniel*, ed. Alexander B. Grosart, privately published, London, 1885–96 (ll.13-16 were quoted in Bernard Fergusson, *Beyond the Chindwin*, p.17).

25. Iraq: A Grave and Gathering Danger

1. Capt Jamie Riddell, interview, 10 Dec 2012, London. He is the nephew of Lt Col R.M. Riddell.
2. WO2 Ian Smith, 'Op Telic 1 Recollections', 15 Mar 2013, recorded for the Regimental Archive.
3. President Bush made his comments about the 'grave and gathering danger' at the UN General Assembly on 12 Sep 2002. Resolution 687 (1991) adopted by the Security Council, 3 Apr 1991; http://www.un.org/Depts/unmovic/documents/687.pdf, accessed 20 Feb 2017.
4. 'Raid shows Bush–Blair bond on Iraq,' http://www.guardian.co.uk/world/2001/feb/19/usa.iraq2, accessed 20 Feb 2017. Iraq's Weapons of Mass Destruction: The Assessment of the British Government, 24 Sep 2004, http://news.bbc.co.uk/nol/shared/spl/hi/middle_east/02/uk_dossier_on_iraq/pdf/iraqdossier.pdf, accessed 20 Feb 2017. There were no citations, supposedly to protect the sources and the information has subsequently been proved to be false.
5. Known as the 'Dodgy' Dossier, it was released by Blair's Director of Communications and Strategy, Alastair Campbell.
6. Dr Hans Blix briefing to the Security Council. http://www.guardian.co.uk/world/2003/feb/14/iraq.unitednations1, accessed 20 Feb 2017. Additional information, St Antony's College, Oxford, 26 Nov 2004. In 2005 the CIA released its final report stating that no weapons of mass destruction had been found in Iraq. http://www.nbcnews.com/id/7634313/ns/world_news-mideast_n_africa/t/cias-final-report-no-wmd-found-iraq/#.UfWYLVO9xrg, accessed 20 Feb 2017.
7. 'Telic' means a purposeful or defined action; since much planning took place over Christmas 2002, it was jokingly referred to as Tell Everyone Leave Is Cancelled. Telic 1 constituted the invasion, followed by 12 roulements known as Telic 2–13 (II–XIII), the last of which took place from Dec 2008 to Apr 2009. As a battalion The Black Watch was involved in Telic 1 and Telic 4; elements of the battalion took part in other roulements.
8. Maj N.H. de R. Channer, RHF, 2IC, 'The Build up to Operation Telic', *Red Hackle*, May 2003, pp.45–6. Lt Col Angus Philp, skype interview, 17 Jan 2013. Riddell, interview, 10 Dec 2012. The ATR, Bassingbourn, was closed in 2012.
9. Channer, 'The Build Up to Operation Telic,' *Red Hackle*, May 2003, p.45. Statements regarding the deployment of the RN were made on 7 Jan 2003 and regarding the RAF on 6 Feb 2003.
10. Philp, skype interview, 17 Jan 2013. LCpl (later Cpl) Jimmy Steele, interview, 20 Jan 2015, Fort George. Lt Col Jules McElhinney, telephone interview, 26 Aug 2016.
11. Capt N.E. Ord, Brigade liaison officer for operations and the media, 'Operation Telic – A Battle Group Overview,' *Red Hackle*, Nov 2003, p.21. Channer, 'The Build up to Operation Telic', *Red Hackle*, May 2003, p.46. There were other deficiencies in terms of equipment, especially replacement of 'snatch' landrovers which offered inadequate protection. See Sir John Chilcot, *Report of the Iraq Inquiry*.

http://www.iraqinquiry.org.uk/the-report/, accessed 21 Feb 2017.

12. Maj Mike Williamson, interview, 30 Aug 2013, London. 'The Black Watch Battlegroup Soldier's Guide to Iraq', scrapbook, Riddell-Webster private papers. Williamson's task was simplified because the Royal Scots Dragoon Guards were in the same camp in Fallingbostel and had been deployed during the 1991 Gulf War.
13. Paul Reoch, 'Black Watch Gulf bound,' *Perthshire Advertiser*, 28 Feb 2002, scrapbook, Riddell-Webster private papers.
14. Riddell, interview, 10 Dec 2012. There had been an exercise in Kuwait in Jan. Lt Will Colquhoun, war diary, 27 Feb 2003, Colquhoun private papers. See also '1BW, 5 Platoon – 'For'ard the Forty Twa (Deployment and Build up to War)', *Red Hackle*, Nov 2003, p.25.
15. Smith, 'Op Telic 1 Recollections', 15 Mar 2013. Colquhoun, war diary, 27 Feb 2003, Colquhoun private papers. Pipe Maj Alistair Duthie, interview, 25 Feb 2014, Perth.
16. RSM Scott Shaw, interview, 22 May 2014, Bassingbourn.
17. See Ben Connable, 'Blog', 'The Deeply Mixed Results of the Iraq War', 21 Mar 2013, http://www.rand.org/blog/2013/03/the-deeply-mixed-results-of-the-iraq-war.html, accessed 20 Feb 2017.
18. Colquhoun, 20 Jan 2002, war diary, Colquhoun private papers. The operation was comparable to Operation Granby (Gulf War 1991) and Operation Musketeer (Suez Crisis 1956). It was larger than Operation Corporate (Falklands War). But see Chilcot, *Report of the Iraq Inquiry*, emphasising that such a large British contingent was unnecessary. http://www.iraqinquiry.org.uk/the-report/, accessed 21 Feb 2017.
19. C (Fire Support) Coy, consisting of reconnaissance, anti tank and mortar platoons. Also in 7 Armoured Bde (commanded by Brig Graham Binns): 3rd Regt Royal Horse Artillery & 1st Irish Guards. The other 2 bdes in the UK 1st Armoured Div were: 3 Commando Bde (Brig Jim Dutton) & 16 Air Assault Bde (Brig 'Jacko' Page). The three other battlegroups were: The Royal Scots Dragoon Guards, 2nd Royal Tank Regt & 1st Royal Regiment of Fusiliers (with elements of the Queen's Royal Lancers). The medical section doubled the size of medical support available.
20. 'Plans had to be radically changed because of the Turks', Maj David Kemmis Betty, interview, 13 Jun 2013, London. See Maj Angus Beaton, ed., *The Fight for Iraq*, p.31; Lt Col (later Maj Gen) M.L. Riddell-Webster, diary, 1 Mar 2003, scrapbook, Riddell-Webster private papers.
21. Philp, skype interview, 17 Jan 2013.
22. Capt Rob Sandford, 'Working with the Media on Op Telic', *Red Hackle*, Nov 2003, pp.35–6. Riddell-Webster, diary, 3 Mar 2003, scrapbook, Riddell-Webster private papers.
23. Maj Gen M.L. Riddell-Webster, interview, 15 Dec 2012, Cupar, & correspondence, 9 May 2014. Williamson, interview, 30 Aug 2013. The project was called 'Reviving Al Basrah'. Maj David Kemmis Betty, diary, 15 Mar 2013, Kemmis Betty private papers.

24. Riddell-Webster, correspondence, May 2014. 'I thought it high risk (from a career point of view!), but when Maj Gen Brims saw it he liked it because it let him know that the Battalion had received and understood his intent.'
25. Philp, skype interview, 17 Jan 2013. Colquhoun, war diary, 11 Mar 2003, Colquhoun private papers.
26. Sgt Robert Duncan, interview, 26 Feb 2014, Perth. Kemmis Betty, correspondence, 13 May 2014. Shaw, interview, 22 May 2014; he was a platoon Sgt, D Coy, commanded by Maj Dougie Hay.
27. Colquhoun, war diary, 20 Mar 2003, Colquhoun private papers.
28. Riddell, interview, 10 Dec 2012. Times were given in 'Zulu' (Z) time i.e. GMT.
29. WO2 Robbie Tollan, 'Op Telic 1 Recollections', 15 Mar 2013, recorded for the Regimental Archive.
30. Riddell, interview, 10 Dec 2012. Smith, 'Op Telic 1 Recollections', 15 Mar 2013. Philp, skype interview, 17 Jan 2013.
31. Riddell-Webster, diary, Sat 22 Mar 2003, scrapbook, Riddell-Webster private papers. The US Marines moved on to Baghdad.
32. Riddell, interview, 10 Dec 2012. Philp, skype interview, 17 Jan 2013.
33. Williamson, interview, 30 Aug 2013. Maj Mark Percy, interview, 1 Aug 2013, London.
34. 'D Coy', *Red Hackle,* Nov 2003, p.30. Shaw, 'Op Telic 1 Recollections', 15 Mar 2013, & interview, 22 May 2014; he was Mentioned in Despatches for this action. The Engineers, Sapper Luke Allsopp and Staff Sgt Simon Cullingworth, were from a specialist bomb disposal unit of the RE.
35. 'Mortar Platoon', *Red Hackle,* Nov 2003, p.27; McElhinney, telephone interview, 26 Aug 2016. These were 81mm mortars mounted in armoured vehicles. They had a range of several thousand metres and could fire HE, smoke and illuminating rounds.
36. Riddell-Webster, diary, Mon 24 Mar 2003, scrapbook, Riddell-Webster private papers. The shortage of helicopters to take Thomson to a field hospital was suggested as the reason why his leg could not be saved. See Capt Hugo Guthrie, RAMC, quoted in Gethin Chamberlain, *The Scotsman,* 21 Jan 2004, 'Medic: Why Scots sergeant lost his leg'. NB Lt Col Cowan to Lt Gen Irwin, 20 Jan 2004: 'Our RMO (who stabilized him and thereby saved his life) is clear that at the point of leaving the RAP he was lucky to be alive. If a helicopter could have got him to a Field Hospital, then there was a very faint hope the leg could have been saved, but he thinks this unlikely, as it remained attached only very loosely to the torso.' Charged with firing the chain gun negligently, Sgt Tam Henderson was fined two weeks' pay and posted out. On appeal, he argued that the gun was faulty and his sentence was quashed. See 'WO2 Henderson – Summary Appeal, Judgment, 23 Jun, 2004', ColComdt/06/2, Irwin private papers. See also Capt Tam Henderson QM & John Hunt, *Warrior: A True Story of Bravery and Betrayal in the Iraq War*, Mainstream Publishing ebooks, 2008.
37. Riddell, interview, 10 Dec 2012. For his prompt action withdrawing the troops under fire and the engagement on the first night, Riddell was given a Joint

Commander's Commendation.

38. Kemmis Betty, diary, 25 Mar 2003, Kemmis Betty private papers. Maj Angus Watson, interview, 26 Feb 2014, Perth. At the Coroner's inquest in Britain, MacDuff, OC B Coy, was held responsible for failing to tell Watson about an alteration to the no-fire zone in the area where they were situated, 'Iraq Widow Condemns Officer's Promotion, *Telegraph*, 3 Jul 2007, http://www.telegraph.co.uk/news/uknews/1556309/Iraq-widow-condemns-officers-promotion.html, accessed 20 Feb 2017, & 'Officer Blamed for Army Deaths,' http://news.bbc.co.uk/1/hi/england/staffordshire/6266072.stm, accessed 20 Feb 2017.
39. Percy, interview, 2 Aug 2013; he added: 'I don't believe if Lindsay had briefed on the supposed change to the inter-unit boundary this would have prevented the accident.' Kemmis Betty, diary, 25 Mar 2003, Kemmis Betty private papers.
40. 'D Coy', *Red Hackle*, Nov 2003, p.30.
41. Riddell-Webster, diary, Wed 26 Mar, & Cdr's Diary, 31 Mar 2003, scrapbook, Riddell-Webster private papers. Lt Will Colquhoun to Francesca, 28 Mar 2003, Colquhoun private papers.
42. Kemmis Betty, diary, 29 Mar 2003, Kemmis Betty private papers; interview, 13 Jun 2013; on 30 Mar 2003, he wrote: 'the thought is that the previous night we were hit by multi-barrel rocket launchers not mortars.' Percy, interview, 2 Aug 2013. Williamson, interview, 30 Aug 2013, London.
43. Kemmis Betty, diary, 29 Mar 2003, Kemmis Betty private papers; interview, 13 June 2013. Williamson, interview, 30 Aug 2014.
44. McElhinney, telephone interview, 23 Aug 2016.
45. Kemmis Betty, diary, 30 Mar 2003, Kemmis Betty private papers. Riddell-Webster, Cdr's Diary, Tues 1 Apr 2003, scrapbook, Riddell-Webster private papers. Gethin Chamberlain, *Scotsman/ Daily Telegraph,* 2 Apr 2003. Riddell-Webster, interview, 13 Dec 2012: he said he had been 'pretty knackered' patrolling in full combat gear.
46. HRH The Prince of Wales to Lt Col M.L. Riddell-Webster, from Birkhall, 5 Apr 2003, scrapbook, Riddell-Webster private papers.
47. Capt A.M. Philp, adjt, 'The Black Watch Battlegroup in Iraq 2003,' enclosed with letter dated 24 Jul 2003 to Lt Cdr Alastair Graham RN, Equerry to HRH The Prince of Wales, 24 Jul 2003, Irwin private papers, BW Association, D/AGG/006/1. Capt Jamie Riddell to his parents, 6 Apr 2003, J. Riddell private papers, & interview, 10 Dec 2012. Lt Will Colquhoun was B Coy intelligence officer. Tollan, 'Operation Telic 1 Recollections', 15 Mar 2013.
48. Philp, diary, & skype interview, 17 Jan 2013. Riddell-Webster, diary, 6 Apr 2003, scrapbook, Riddell-Webster private papers. Kemmis Betty, diary, 6 Apr 2003, Kemmis Betty private papers & interview, 13 Jun 2013. Riddell to his parents, 6 Apr 2003, J. Riddell private papers, & interview, 10 Dec 2012. Smith, 'Op Telic 1 Recollections', 15 Mar 2013.
49. Riddell to his parents, 6 Apr 2003, J. Riddell private papers.
50. Kemmis Betty, diary, Mon 7 Apr 2003, Kemmis Betty private papers.
51. Riddell, interview, 10 Dec 2012, & letter to his parents, 6 Apr 2003, J. Riddell private papers. Riddell-Webster, diary, Mon 7 Apr 2003, scrapbook, Riddell-Webster

private papers.

52. Riddell, interview, 10 Dec 2012. Watson, interview, 26 Feb 2014. Riddell-Webster, diary, Mon 7 Apr 2003, scrapbook, Riddell-Webster private papers.
53. Philp, skype interview, 17 Jan 2013.
54. Williamson, interview, 30 Aug 2013.
55. In Dec 2003 Saddam Hussein was found hiding near Tikrit. He was executed for war crimes on 30 Dec 2006. Tollan, 'Operation Telic 1 Recollections', 15 Mar 2013. Riddell-Webster, diary, Mon 28 Apr 2003, scrapbook, Riddell-Webster private papers.
56. Watson, interview, 26 Feb 2014; he left mid-May to go on a platoon cdr's course; see also '1BW, 6 Platoon - Peace Support Operations in Basrah', *Red Hackle*, Nov 2003, p.26. Shaw, interview, 22 May 2014.
57. '1BW, 6 Platoon - Peace Support Operations in Basrah', *Red Hackle*, Nov 2003, p.26. Riddell to his parents, Camp Ali Baba, 28 Apr 2003, J. Riddell private papers. Kemmis Betty, diary, Mon 2 May 2003, Kemmis Betty private papers.
58. *Basra 42nd St*, 15 May 2003. There were two more editions: 22 May 2003 and undated.
59. Riddell to his parents, Camp Ali Baba, 28 & 24 Apr 2003, J. Riddell private papers.
60. Kemmis Betty, diary, Wed 7 May & Thu 22 May 2003, Kemmis Betty private papers.
61. Capt Harry Hood, interview, 6 Dec 2013, Harrogate; he was CSM for D Coy. Kemmis Betty, diary, Tue 27 May 2003, Kemmis Betty private papers.
62. '1BW, 6 Platoon – Peace Support Operations in Basrah', *Red Hackle*, Nov 2003, p.26.
63. Percy, interview, 2 Aug 2013; 21 Mar–22 Apr 2003 there were 16 British fatalities; thousands of Iraqis were killed. See Beaton, *The Fight for Iraq*, p.149.
64. Smith, 'Op Telic 1 Recollections', 15 Mar 2013. Hood, interview, 6 Dec 2013.
65. Williamson, interview, 30 Aug 2013. Riddell, interview, 10 Dec 2012. Brig Graham Binns later stated to Jane Corbin that the UK had 'over-promised and under-delivered', BBC Panorama, 29 Jun 2016. See also Ben Farmer, *Telegraph,* 29 Jun 2016: http://www.telegraph.co.uk/news/2016/06/29/britain-over-promised-and-under-delivered-in-iraq-general-admits/, accessed 20 Feb 2017.
66. '1BW, CO's Foreword', *Red Hackle,* May 2004, p.17.
67. Capt J. McElhinney, 'Homecoming Parades,' *Red Hackle,* Nov 2003, p.42.
68. RQMS and Lt Col James Cowan, quoted in Gethin Chamberlain, 'Black Watch Commander: how the MOD let us down in Iraq,' *Scotsman,* 22 Jan 2004, ColComdt /06/2, Irwin private papers,. The main complaint was that 1BW deployed 'without enough [NBC] protection suits to go round, without equipment to decontaminate vehicles after an attack and with unusable detection equipment intended to provide early warning of an attack.'
69. Rt Hon Geoff Hoon, MP, Foreword, Defence White Paper, *Delivering Security in a Changing World,* http://webarchive.nationalarchives.gov.uk/20121026065214/www.mod.uk/NR/rdonlyres/051AF365-0A97-4550-99C0-4D87D7C95DED/0/cm6041I_whitepaper2003.pdf, accessed 20 Feb 2017. Gen Sir Mike Jackson,

Defence White Paper, *Implications for the Army*, D/CGS/50/01, 11 Dec 2003. The cuts were a continuation of *Options for Change* 1990.

70. Lt Gen Sir Alistair Irwin, 'What is Best about the Regimental System?' *RUSI Journal*, 149, 5, 2004, pp.32–6. The Scottish Division was formed on 1 Jul 1968 to replace the Highland and Lowland Bdes. An earlier paper, 'Thinking the Unthinkable', had prompted Barnett to ask Riddell-Webster 'without causing any alarm to sound out the battalion on what they would see as the best way forward were there to be cuts of say one or two battalions in the Scottish Infantry,' Brig G. Barnett to Lt Col Riddell-Webster, 10 Sep 2001. On 28 Mar 2002, Riddell-Webster responded saying that because of the increasing frequency of battalion transfers, 'a large regiment would therefore present them with no fears. There was also an almost unanimous opinion that there should be no move for an amalgamation… and that people would prefer to see a complete end to the current system and a large regiment.' In 1962 Maj Gen Douglas Wimberley had proposed a Highland Brigade Regt to face up to the likely 'reforms'.
71. Lt Gen Sir Alistair Irwin to Lt Cdr A. Graham RN, Equerry to HRH The Prince of Wales, 25 Nov 2003, Irwin private papers. See also Philip Howard, 'Tradition Will Watch Over The Black Watch', *The Times,* 28 Nov 2003.
72. '1BW, CO's Foreword', *Red Hackle,* May 2004, p.17.
73. Maj Tim Elliott, interview, 3 Sep 2013, London. '1BW, A Coy', *Red Hackle,* May 2004, p.21.
74. '1BW, CO's Foreword', *Red Hackle,* May 2004, p.17. On 9 Jan 2005, the Nairobi Comprehensive Peace Agreement was signed, leading to the 2011 referendum which resulted in South Sudan's secession.
75. '1BW, Infantry Training Team', *Red Hackle,* May 2004, p.27.
76. HRH The Prince of Wales, quoted in 'Regimental News,' *Red Hackle,* May 2004, p.4. He added: 'She used to tell me about the Regiment when I was very small so I have grown up with it second-hand.'
77. John Bunyan, 'To Be a Pilgrim', v.1.

26. Picking Up the Pieces

1. Lt Col (later Maj Gen) James Cowan, quoted in *Daily Telegraph,* Nov 2004. He gave the Regiment its full title – Royal Highland Regiment, the 42nd Foot, Capt Will Johnson, interview, 18 Jul 2013, London.
2. Maj Tim Elliott, interview, 3 Sep 2013, London.
3. Lt Col James Cowan, 'The Black Watch in Iraq 2004', *Red Hackle,* Nov 2004, p.21, & 'The Black Watch in Iraq 2004', Cowan private papers. The only significant town was the fishing port of Umm Qasr. The strategic significance of Al Faw was that it gave access to the Shatt al-Arab waterway and the port of Basra.
4. 2nd Lt Nick Colquhoun to Rachel, 15 Jul 2004, Colquhoun private papers.
5. Geoffrey Hoon, Westminster Hall, Hansard, http://www.publications.parliament.uk/pa/cm200304/cmhansrd/vo040721/debtext/40721-08.htm, accessed 26 Feb 2017.

6. Cowan, Statement given at Shaibah airfield, 21 Jul 2004, Cowan private papers. He continued: 'while it is right and proper that we have a moment to mourn what is past, it is also right to celebrate what is ahead.'
7. Lt Col Angus Philp, skype interview, 17 Jan 2013. Capt B.R. (Ben) Collis, interview, 2 Jul 2003, London; commissioned into the Regt in 2003, he had had a 'taster' of operations in Oct 2003 as part of a small range team running 20 Armoured Bde's acclimatisation training package; see Lt B.R. Collis, 'Op Telic 3 – Iraq Four Months On', *Red Hackle*, May 2004, p.24.
8. Cowan, 'The Black Watch in Iraq 2004', *Red Hackle*, Nov 2004, p.22.
9. Ibid, pp.22, 38.
10. A'yad Allawi (b.1944) was in office as interim PM 1 Jun 2004–3 May 2005, having been President of the Governing Council of Iraq 1–31 Oct 2003 (later Vice President of Iraq 2014–15). Ali al-Hussayni al-Sistani (b.1930) became Grand Ayatollah in 1992 and is regarded as the spiritual leader of Iraqi Shias.
11. Cowan, 'The Black Watch in Iraq 2004', *Red Hackle*, Nov 2004, p.22.
12. Capt Harry Hood, interview, 6 Dec 2013, Harrogate. Maj Alastair Colville, interview, 13 Aug 2013, Shrivenham, & diary, 9 Aug 2004, Colville private papers.
13. Cowan to Lt Gen Sir Alistair Irwin, from Shaibah Airfield, 10 Aug 2004, ColComdt/06/2, Irwin private papers; see also Cowan, 'The Black Watch in Iraq 2004, D Coy at Al Qurnah, Nov 2004', *Red Hackle*, p.22. Irwin, interview, 21 Jan 2015, Craigellachie.
14. Elliott, interview, 3 Sep 2013.
15. See Cowan, 'The Black Watch in Iraq 2004, A Coy in Basrah', *Red Hackle*, Nov 2004, p.25.
16. Marc Ferns, Obit, *Red Hackle*, p.14. Cowan, 'The Black Watch in Iraq 2004, A Coy in Basrah' , *Red Hackle*, Nov 2004, p.25. Sgt Kevin Stacey was the 3rd generation of his family to serve in The Black Watch.
17. Colville, diary, 20 Aug 2013, & quotation from note which he had kept in his diary, Colville private papers.
18. Cowan, 'The Black Watch in Iraq 2004, D Coy in Basrah', *Red Hackle*, Nov 2004, p.25. Colville, interview, 13 Aug 2013. Iraq came 4th in the men's football.
19. Cowan, 'The Black Watch in Iraq 2004, Return of the Grand Ayatollah', *Red Hackle*, Nov 2004, p.25. Colquhoun to Rachel, 27 & 30 Aug 2004, Colquhoun private papers.
20. Brig Alastair Aitken, correspondence, 23 Dec 2015. Sgt Maj Alexander (Sandy) Wilson, interview, Feb 2014, Perth; he had replaced Stacey as platoon Sgt.
21. Aitken, correspondence, 23 Dec 2015.
22. Hood, interview, 6 Dec 2013. Cowan, 'The Black Watch in Iraq 2004', *Red Hackle*, Nov 2004, p.34.
23. Elliott, interview, 3 Sep 2013. Sgt Robert Duncan, interview, 26 Feb 2014, Perth. Collis, interview, 2 Jul 2013.
24. Capt Jamie Riddell, interview, 10 Dec 2012 London. Maj Gen James Cowan, interview, 10 Sep 2012, London.
25. Brig Garry Barnett, interview, 20 Oct 2013, Campsie.

26. Peter Wishart (b.1962), MP for Tayside North 2001–05, Perth and N. Perthshire 2005–present day. Westminster Hall, http:// https://www.publications.parliament.uk/pa/cm200304/cmhansrd/vo040915/halltext/40915h01.htm#40915h01_spnew29, accessed 21 Feb 2017. Wishart was supported by a number of MPs including Rachel Squire, Labour, Dunfermline West, John Thurso, Conservative, Caithness, Sutherland & Easter Ross, Annabelle Ewing, SNP, Perth.
27. Cowan, 'The Black Watch in Iraq 2004', *Red Hackle*, May 2005, pp.28, 56. The US's first attempt to take Fallujah in the autumn of 2003 had received 'a bloody rebuff', p.28. See p.56 for explanation of why the US required British troops. 'As the Shi'a uprising subsided and the Sunni insurgency gathered momentum, senior British officers in Baghdad recognised that the British reputation for flexibility was at jeopardy unless the United Kingdom was prepared to assist her principal ally.' 24th MEU was commanded by Col Ron Johnson. Cowan, 'Counterinsurgency in Iraq and Afghanistan', Cowan private papers. See also Philip Ziegler, *Wilson: The Authorised Life of Lord Wilson of Rievaulx*, Weidenfeld & Nicolson, 1993, p.222.
28. Sgt Maj Alexander Wilson, interview, 26 Feb 2014, Perth.
29. See Cowan, 'The Black Watch in Iraq 2004', *Red Hackle*, May 2005, p.32 & 'Op Bracken – CO's Personal Perspective', Cowan private papers.
30. Cowan, statement to the press, Oct 2004, Cowan private papers.
31. Peter Beaumont and Martin Bright, 'British set for Iraqi danger zones', *Observer*, 17 Oct 2004; Richard Lloyd-Parry, Shaibah logistic base, 'Black Watch prays and prepares for new fight,' *The Times*, 25 Oct 2004. Between 28 Aug and 27 Sep, in three incidents, 22 US and 7 Spanish soldiers, and a number of civilians, had been killed in bomb attacks.
32. Chaplain Aled Thomas (who had replaced Duncan Macpherson), quoted in Richard Lloyd-Parry, 'Black Watch prays and prepares for new fight,' *The Times*, 25 Oct 2004. Colquhoun to Rachel, 26 Oct 2004, Colquhoun private papers.
33. See Cowan, 'The Black Watch in Iraq 2004', *Red Hackle* , May 2005, p.30. Hood, interview, 6 Dec 2013.
34. Cowan, 'The Black Watch in Iraq 2004', *Red Hackle*, May 2005, p.32.
35. Maj Neil Tomlin, interview, 13 Aug 2013.
36. Cowan, 'The Black Watch in Iraq 2004', *Red Hackle*, May 2005, p.32.
37. Collis, interview, 2 Jul 2013. Tomlin, interview, 13 Aug 2013.
38. Colquhoun to Rachel, 28 Oct 2004, Colquhoun private papers. Colville, interview, 13 Aug 2013.
39. Pte Allan Stewart, interview, 28 Feb 2014, Perth.
40. Cowan, 'The Black Watch in Iraq 2004', *Red Hackle*, May 2005, p.33. Elliott, interview, 3 Sep 2013. Sgt Maj J.P. Maestri, interview, 17 Oct 2013, Perth.
41. Cowan, 'Counterinsurgency in Iraq and Afghanistan,' Cowan private papers. Collis, interview, 2 Jul 2013. Additional information Cowan, interview, 10 Sep 2012. The Battlegroup did not have integral Joint Fires capability, i.e. the coordination of two or more forces of fire support, for example artillery and helicopters. (They initially lacked helicopters.)
42. Cowan, 'The Black Watch in Iraq 2004', *Red Hackle*, May 2005, p.33. Abu Musab

al-Zarqawi (1966–2006), a Palestinian-Jordanian, was killed by a US air strike.

43. Colquhoun to Rachel, 1 Nov 2004, Colquhoun private papers.
44. Cowan, 'The Black Watch in Iraq 2004', *Red Hackle,* May 2005, p.34.
45. Colquhoun, notebook, Colquhoun private papers. George W. Bush did win a 2nd presidential term.
46. 'Op Bracken – CO's Personal Perspective', Cowan private papers. Hood, interview, 6 Dec 2013.
47. Hood, interview, 6 Dec 2013. Colville, diary, & interview, 13 Aug 2013. Lindsay had judged the ground around Al Qaqa as too 'complex' for a base, so chose the industrial power-plant site to the north. The deployment across the Euphrates caused protests of 'mission creep'. The MOD rejected the allegation and said it was 'mission essential'. See John Parker, *Black Watch,* p.343.
48. Colville, diary, & interview, 13 Aug 2013. Cowan, 'The Black Watch in Iraq 2004', *Red Hackle,* May 2005, p.35. Hood, interview, 6 Dec 2013.
49. Colville, diary, & interview, 13 Aug 2013. Maj John Bailey, interview, 22 Jan 2015, Fort George. He had been in the lead Warrior struck by a roadside bomb the previous day. See Nicholas Rufford and Abul Taher, 'London Muslim puts Black Watch deaths on internet', *Sunday Times,* 14 Nov 2004.
50. Colville, interview, 13 Aug 2013. Watson, interview, 26 Feb 2014.
51. Cowan, 'The Black Watch in Iraq 2004', *Red Hackle*, May 2005, p.36; 'Counterinsurgency in Iraq and Afghanistan,' Cowan private papers. The casualties and fatalities were from 14 Pl, 'which had served together for many years as the Pipes and Drums'.
52. Colquhoun to Rachel, 5 Nov 2004, Colquhoun private papers.
53. Cowan, 'The Black Watch in Iraq 2004', *Red Hackle,* May 2005, pp.36–7. 'Op Bracken – CO's Personal Perspective', Cowan private papers.
54. The Cpls were Michael Brennan, Royal Signals, and Neil Heritage, Royal Logistics Corps; see Richard Lloyd-Parry, Camp Dogwood, 'Two Gravely Hurt as Black Watch Hit by New Suicide Attack,' *The Times,* 8 Nov 2004, & Cowan, 'The Black Watch in Iraq 2004', *Red Hackle*, May 2005, pp.36–7. RSM Scott Shaw, interview, 22 May 2014, Bassingbourn.
55. Cowan, 'The Black Watch in Iraq 2004', *Red Hackle,* May 2005, p.37. See also Parker, *Black Watch*, pp.346–51, for diary of events 6 Nov–5 Dec 2004.
56. Hood, interview, 6 Dec 2013. Tom Newton Dun, 'The Black Watch mourns the loss of its quiet Fijian', *The Times*, 10 Nov 2004.
57. Cowan, 'The Black Watch in Iraq 2004', *Red Hackle,* May 2005, p.38.
58. Colquhoun to Rachel, 10 Nov 2004, Colquhoun private papers.
59. Cowan, 'The Black Watch in Iraq 2004', *Red Hackle*, May 2005, p.38.
60. Colquhoun to Rachel, 13 Nov 2004, Colquhoun private papers. Hood, interview, 6 Dec 2013. Collis, interview, 2 Jul 2013. 1BW had been reinforced by a 'close observation' platoon of the 1st Welsh Guards.
61. Johnson, interview, 18 Jul 2013. He replaced Lt John Bailey who returned to the UK.
62. C.S.M. Penman, 'Book of Banter', known as the 'Bantasorous', Cowan private papers.
63. Colquhoun to Rachel, 13 Nov 2004, Colquhoun private papers. Capt Nick

Colquhoun, interview, 30 Jul 2013, Gloucester. He made no mention of the incident in his letters home lest he worry his family.

64. Max Hastings, 'We are in this together: if America fails, we fail,' *Sunday Telegraph*, 7 Nov 2004, Irwin private papers, BW/006/3.
65. Peter Wishart, Peter Duncan & Adam Ingram, Westminster Hall, Wednesday 17 Nov 2004, https://www.publications.parliament.uk/pa/cm200304/cmhansrd/vo041117/halltext/41117h01.htm, accessed 21 Feb 2017. Wishart was again supported by several Scottish MPs, including Iain Luke (Lab), Russell Brown (Lab), Michael Moore (LibDem), Annabelle Ewing (SNP), Mohammad Sarwar (Lab), Peter Duncan (Con). Pte Lowe's funeral was on 17 Nov, Pte McArdle's on 16 Nov, with Sergeant Gray's funeral still to take place. Ingram emphasised that the SNP's support of Scottish independence included the proposal to withdraw from NATO and downgrade the Scottish regiments 'to occasional peacekeeping missions… so, I question the motives of the SNP on the issue.'
66. Geoffrey Hoon, quoted in George Jones and Neil Tweedie, 'Hoon still backs cuts in face of protests from serving soldiers', *Daily Telegraph*, Nov 2004. Members of the London Black Watch Association were also present. He made this statement on the second day of the Queen's Speech debate. Brig Garry Barnett, 24 Nov 2004, Barnett private papers; additional information, 15 Dec 2015.
67. Col Ron Johnson had proposed Operation Plymouth Rock (originally called Op Thanksgiving Day Massacre, but this was considered too provocative; as was Op Turkey Shoot). Cowan, 'The Black Watch in Iraq 2004', *Red Hackle*, May 2005, p.42. This was the culmination of ten Battlegroup operations 'based partly on informed speculation and partly on a developing intelligence picture'; 'Op Bracken – CO's Personal Perspective', Cowan private papers. It revived an earlier proposal, Op Hood.
68. Cowan, quoted in David Harrison, with The Black Watch on the Eastern Euphrates, 'Scores Arrested in Rebel Stronghold as British Troops Storm "Millionaires' Row"', *Daily Telegraph*, Nov 2004. Johnson, interview, 19 Jul 2013.
69. Aitken, correspondence, 23 Dec 2015.
70. Wilson, interview, 26 Feb 2014. David Harrison, with The Black Watch on the Eastern Euphrates, 'Mission Accomplished for Black Watch,' *Telegraph*, Nov 2004.
71. Colville, diary, 25 & 27 Nov 2004, Colville private papers.
72. Cowan, 'The Black Watch in Iraq 2004', *Red Hackle*, May 2005, p.45. Johnson, interview, 19 Jul 2013. The D notice was the first since the Falklands War.
73. Cowan, 'Counterinsurgency in Iraq and Afghanistan', & 'Op Bracken – CO's Personal Perspective, Accomplishments', Cowan private papers. Cowan, 'The Black Watch in Iraq 2004', *Red Hackle*, May 2005, p.45. Comment by Lt Gen Sir John Kiszley, KCB, MC.
74. 'Op Bracken – CO's Personal Perspective', Cowan private papers. Johnson, interview, 19 Jul 2013.
75. LCpl Danny Buist, quoted in Ian Dow, 'We'll never forget the heroes who won't come back home,' *Daily Record*, 6 Dec 2004. Sgt Maj Kev Blackley, interview, 22 Jan 2015, Fort George.

76. Elliott, interview, 3 Sep 2013.
77. In Jun 2014 a group referring to itself as the Islamic State (*ad-Dawlah al-Islāmiyah*) and also known as Daesh (an acronym for its name in Arabic), proclaimed a worldwide caliphate, extending its authority to large areas of Iraq and Syria. The group originated in 1999 pledging allegiance to Al Qaeda. The Chilcot Report, released in Jul 2016, concluded that the invasion of Iraq was based on 'flawed intelligence and assessments'. The UK went to war before 'peaceful options' for disarmament were exhausted', not as 'a last resort' and there was 'no imminent threat' from Saddam Hussein. See http://www.iraqinquiry.org.uk/the-report/ accessed 21 Feb 2017.
78. The Pipes were invited by Warminster's Mayor Martin Baker, 'Black Watch Wins Hearts and Minds,' *Warminster Journal*, 17 Dec 2004. Lt Col Cowan, statement to press, Warminster, quoted in Kenny Farquharson, 'Black Watch Return to Uncertain Future,' *Scotland on Sunday*, Dec 2004. As of Jul 2007 there were over 500 Coalition operations undertaken in Iraq.
79. Report prepared by a team of officers from the Army's Land Warfare Centre at the behest of the Chief of Joint Operations at the Permanent Joint Headquarters in Northwood, quoted in Sean Rayment, 'Army Report Says Government Delay Put The Black Watch at Risk in Iraq/ Black Watch Sent In "at bomber's mercy"', *Sunday Telegraph*, 19 Dec 2004.
80. Gen Sir Mike Jackson to The Army Chain of Command, All Commanding Officers, 16 Dec 2004, DGS/11/4/7 (CGS), BWM, Irwin private papers. On 8 Oct 2004, 'by a large majority decision', the Council of Scottish Colonels had agreed to the creation of The Royal Regiment of Scotland. Mike Jackson, *Soldier*, p.351.
81. Jackson to The Army Chain of Command, 16 Dec 2004, DGS/11/4/7 (CGS), BWM, Irwin private papers. The amalgamation of The Royal Scots with the King's Own Scottish Borderers took place on 1 Aug 2006. Irwin was succeeded as Col Commandant by Maj Gen W.E.B. Loudon, Col of the Royal Highland Fusiliers on 5 Jan 2005.
82. Irwin, 'The Future of the Regiment', Dec 2004, BWM. In his letter to potential officers Irwin outlined the better career opportunities. He also wrote to Association Branch chairmen, local MPs, MSPs and the Lord Provosts. To obtain the views of past and present members of the Regiment, he had circulated a questionnaire to determine whether, if retaining separate regiments were not possible, they would prefer the three Highland and three Lowland Regiments to become one regiment or two (Lowland and Highland). The majority appeared to prefer retaining the distinction of a Highland and Lowland Regiment. See questionnaires in 'Future of the Regiment', BWM. When the issue of having 'two small/large regiments as opposed to one large/large regiment' was voted on by the Council of Scottish Colonels, Irwin was outvoted five to one.
83. Miss A.B. Millar, 'Don't put away The Black Watch', Correspondence, *Red Hackle*, Nov 2004, p.10. Her grandfather and his two sons had served in The Black Watch. The words of the song had been taught to her by her mother 'over 50 years ago'. In the same issue, 92-year-old James A. Sinclair published his poem: 'Save the

Watch': 'The name O'The Watch/Is known the World ower/But we canna stop the madness/for Scotland disnae hae the power', ll.1–4.

27. Turning a Page of History

1. Anon, The Black Watch Collect. On 4 Mar 1964 at the Kirk Session in the vestry of the Kirk, Knook Camp, Warminster, the Regimental Collect was discussed to see if any changes should be made in the wording. It was unanimously agreed that the words should remain unaltered, signed by Roy Dear, Session Clerk and Rev B.J.L. Hay, Moderator, Kirk Session Minute Book, 1961–78, BWRA 0576: 'O God whose strength setteth fast the mountains. Give thy grace we pray Thee to The Black Watch, Once chosen to Guard the mountains for our King, That we may stand fast in the faith and be strong, As we watch for the coming of Him, Who has bidden us watch and pray, Our Saviour Jesus Christ. Amen.' See Duncan Bengough, correspondence, *Red Hackle,* Nov 2007, p.11, & David Arbuthnott, *Red Hackle,* May 2008, p.11: 'By 1981, in Norman Drummond's time as Chaplain', however, the amended version was being used.
2. See *Red Hackle,* May 2005, p.4 for list of recipients of awards. Capt B.R. (Ben) Collis, interview, 2 Jul 2013, London. Towns were: Cupar, Methil and Leven, Cowdenbeath, Dunfermline, Kirkcaldy, St Andrews, Blairgowrie, Aberfeldy, Crieff, Arbroath, Montrose, Forfar, Ballingry, Kelty, Dundee, Perth – the parades lasted from 28 Feb to 5 Mar. Brig Garry Barnett, speech at the March in London, 9 Apr 2005.
3. Collis, interview, 2 Jul 2013. Capt Will Johnson, interview, 18 Jul 2013, London.
4. See BW Campaign Cttee Meeting 27 Jul 2005, Report to Regimental Council. Arthur MacMillan, 'Veteran takes aim at "armchair generals"', *Scotland on Sunday*, 6 Mar 2005. Lt Gen Sir Alistair Irwin, President's address, BW Association AGM, Apr 2005, pp.2–3, Irwin private papers.
5. Capt Jamie Riddell, interview, 10 Dec 2012, London; 'I also think General Alistair, by being on the Army Board, ensured the Scottish Division did not have a second battalion cut at this time – it was obviously bad enough losing one battalion in Scotland but two would have made it much harder,' additional information, 27 Apr 2014. Lt Col Angus Philp, skype interview, 17 Jan 2013. Irwin, 'Reflections on the Scottish Military Experience,' *A Military History of Scotland,* ed. Spiers et al., p.805. Irwin retired as AG in Apr 2005.
6. Magnus Linklater, see *Scotsman* at http://www.scotsman.com/lifestyle/linklater-s-scotland-1-1389809, accessed 21 Feb 2017. Humphrys also entered a TV interview with Gordon Brown, behind whom he held up a banner saying 'Save our Regiments, Don't Vote Labour!' before being removed! Gordon Brown replaced Tony Blair as PM in 2007.
7. Brig Garry Barnett to Rt Hon Dr John Reid, MP, 6 May 2005; Rt Hon Adam Ingram, MP, to Brig Garry Barnett, 31 May 2005, Irwin private papers.
8. Brig Garry Barnett to Gen Sir Mike Jackson, 3 Apr 2005; Gen Sir Mike Jackson to Brig Garry Barnett, 8 Jun 2005, Irwin private papers. Another exchange of letters

on 18 Jun/ 8 Jul 2005 had a similar outcome, i.e. both retained their respective positions.

9. Collis, interview, 2 Jul 2013.
10. Included in the terms of the agreement was a commitment by the British govt to reduce its armed forces in Northern Ireland 'to levels compatible with a normal peaceful society'.
11. The parade was primarily D Coy, the other Coys being deployed in South Armagh, Collis, interview, 2 Jul 2013; Lt Gen Sir Alistair Irwin, interview, 9 Apr 2014, Craigellachie.
12. Johnson, interview, 18 Jul 2013. 75 Officers were still serving: see 'Location of Serving Officers', *Red Hackle*, Nov 2007, p.7. By 1 Sep 2012 the list of former Black Watch officers was reduced to 35.
13. Col Commandant's address to the Formation Parade of the Royal Regiment of Scotland, Edinburgh Castle, 28 Mar 2006.
14. Brig Garry Barnett, speech, 28 Mar 2006, Barnett private papers. See also 'Emotional Farewell to the Black Watch', *Evening Telegraph*, 28 Mar 2006.
15. The Glengarry was a traditional Scottish cap made of thick cloth, distinct from the Tam O'Shanter (named after the hero in Robert Burns' poem) worn by The Black Watch. The Pipes and Drums of each Battalion could still wear the ceremonial uniforms and tartans of their antecedent regiments, only the buttons and cap badges changed, additional information, Alistair Duthie, 8 Jul 2016.
16. Capt Andy Colquhoun, skype interview, 12 Dec 2012. He was a cousin of the three Colquhoun brothers, Will, Nick and Rob, and another cousin, Alastair Colville, all serving in 1BW; their extended family's service in The Black Watch dates back to 1725.
17. Capt Harry Gladstone, interview, 30 Jul 2013, Gloucester. A. Colquhoun, skype interview, 12 Dec 2012. Brig Alasdair Loudon, interview, 28 Aug 2008, Islamabad.
18. He was 2nd Lt A.K. Forbes; see photograph in *Red Hackle,* Jul 1952, p.8. In addition to being an actor, Jack Fortune is an authority on Red Hackle Day and Geldermalsen in 1795.
19. 'B Coy', *Red Hackle,* May 2007, p.37.
20. 'Battalion Events', *Red Hackle,* Nov 2006, p.35. Prince Charles also made a 'much appreciated' visit on 4 Jun 2009 to the families during The Black Watch Battalion's first tour to Afghanistan. On 20 Jan 2010 he presented medals at Fort George. Also in 2010 he visited 11 Light Bde, commanded by Brig James Cowan, in Afghanistan. See 'A Royal visit to Afghanistan', *Red Hackle,* May 2010, p.21.
21. This was Op Telic 9. The platoon's role was as dismounts – i.e. they were the soldiers on the ground out of armoured vehicles. See Obit, *Red Hackle,* Nov 2007, p.15. A third fatality was not from The Black Watch.
22. Lt Col L.R. MacDuff, 'Palace Barracks, Belfast, Dec 2005–Dec 2007, The End of Op Banner, Aug 1969–Jul 2007', *Red Hackle*, May 2007, p.28. Statistics from McKittrick et al., *Lost Lives*, pp.1494–5: British Army, 503; UDR/RIR, 206. Op Banner was replaced by Op Helvetic, providing specialised assistance in ordnance disposal.

23. After 1945, 19 Infantry Bde was part of 3rd Armoured Div; disbanded after the end of the Cold War, it became 3rd UK Div. In 2003 19 Bde became a 'Light' formation, designated 19 Light Bde on 1 Jan 2005. Also in 2007 B Coy, under the command of Andrew Tait, one of the first Coy Cdrs to be posted in, undertook a 3-month tour of The Falklands. Another exercise, codenamed Grand Prix, was held in Kenya.
24. Op Herrick began in 2002 when Britain handed over command of ISAF to Turkey. In 2003 the deployment in Kabul was expanded to the size of a Bn together with a Rapid Reaction Force, known as the Afghanistan Roulement Infantry Bn (ARIB). Op Herrick 17 concluded in Apr 2013. Individual officers also served in Afghanistan; see Col R.J.K. Bradford, 'Afghanistan, HQ ARRC'; WO2 C. (Chipper) Davidson, 'Op Herrick 4 – Operational Mentoring and Liaison Team (OMLT)'; Capt B.R. Collis, 'Mogging with the Marines', *Red Hackle,* May 2007, pp.29–33. In 2008 Brig James Cowan was responsible for reforming 11 Light Bde which served in Afghanistan in 2009–10 during Op Herrick 11.
25. Brig J.M. Cowan, 'Counterinsurgency in Iraq and Afghanistan: Background to Herrick 11', Cowan private papers. In addition to The Black Watch Battalion, under the command of Lt Col Stephen Cartwright (the first CO from outside the 'Regimental family'), 19 Bde included The Light Dragoons, 1st Squadron, 2nd Royal Tank Regiment, 1st Welsh Guards, 2nd Mercian Regiment (Worcester & Foresters) and the 2nd Rifles, as well as supporting units from the Royal Artillery and Royal Engineers.
26. Lt Gen Sir Alistair Irwin to officers of The Black Watch Battalion, quoted in *A Military History of Scotland*, ed. Spiers, p.812. He saw them off from Fort George at 4 a.m. on 3 Apr: 'my last duty as the Representative Colonel'.
27. Collis, interview, 2 Jul 2013; he was adjt and alternating with Capt Alastair Colville as Battle Capt at their base in Kandahar. Capt Nick Colquhoun to Rachel, 9 Jun 2009, Colquhoun private papers. See *Aviation Assault Battle Group, The 2009 Afghanistan tour of The Black Watch 3rd Battalion The Royal Regiment of Scotland,* 2011, for a full account.
28. Gladstone, interview, 30 Jul 2013. See Andrew Bradford, *Escape from Saint Valéry-en-Caux,* pp.19, 137.
29. Lt Col Stephen Cartwright, 'Introduction', *Aviation Assault Battle Group,* p.13.
30. Lt Harry Gladstone, Op Panchai Palang – 19 Jun–9 Jul diary/scrapbook, Gladstone private papers; Gladstone thought that 'too much pressure' had been placed on the operation by Obama's announcement of a 'big push in Afghanistan' and the suggestion by the ISAF Commander in Kabul that US foreign policy would be 'won or lost in Helmand this summer'. N. Colquhoun, interview, 30 Jul 2013.
31. Philp, skype interview, 28 Aug 2013; in Jul 2009, Philp handed over to Maj Nigel Jordan-Barber. See Maj Nigel Jordan-Barber, 'Part 3- D (Light) Coy, OMLT', *Aviation Assault Battle Group,* pp.168–73.
32. Pte Vincent Byrne, 'A Coy, Living in the Field in Afghanistan', *Aviation Assault Battle Group,* p.253.
33. See http://www.scottish-country-dancing-dictionary.com/dance-crib/kandahar-

reel.html, accessed 13 Feb 2017, & *A Collection of Pipe Music of The Black Watch*, pp.321–2. Cpl Tam Mason died on 25 Oct of wounds sustained on 15 Sep.

34. Capt Harry Hood, interview, 6 Dec 2013, Harrogate.
35. 2nd Lt Robert Weir, quoted in Jason P. Howe, 26 Mar 2012, http://www.telegraph.co.uk/news/worldnews/asia/afghanistan/9165695/Afghanistan-moment-Private-Stephen-Bainbridge-stepped-on-an-IED.html, accessed 26 Feb 2017, & *Red Hackle*, May 2012, p.27. Howe was embedded with the Princess of Wales's Royal Regt in Afghanistan. Bainbridge was in hospital 36 mins after the explosion. He was present when the Battalion paraded through Inverness, 3 Apr 2012. T1 requires an urgent response based on the Triage process of determining the priority of wounded men's treatment.
36. Gladstone, interview, 30 Jul 2013; Laurence Binyon (1868–1943), 'For the Fallen', *The Times*, 21 Sep 1914. Lt Col Ed Fenton received the DSO; his actions in Nad-e Ali were credited with advancing the transition of responsibility to Afghan forces by six months. Sgt Daniel Buist and Col Sgt Ian Smith were Mentioned in Despatches. Bainbridge recuperated at Headley Court Military Hospital, Surrey, where the doctors were 'much impressed' by his determination to walk with prosthetic limbs. On 31 Dec 2014 the British Government concluded withdrawal of its military presence as part of a planned hand-over by the US-led Coalition to the Afghan National Army (ANA).
37. Gladstone, interview, 30 Jul 2013.
38. Maj Neil Tomlin, interview, 13 Aug 2013, Shrivenham. Maj Alastair Colville, interview, 13 Aug 2013, Shrivenham.
39. https://stv.tv/news/east-central/260961-queen-to-present-regiment-with-colours/, accessed 13 Feb 2017. Brig Edward de Broë-Ferguson, interview, 3 Feb 2014, London.
40. Victoria Schofield, *The Highland Furies*, p.33.
41. The monument to 51HD was dedicated in 1995, commemorating 50 years since the end of WW2. Ian E. Kaye, 'They only fade away', *Pick & Shovel Poems*, Arthur H. Stockwell, 1960, p.46. The Colours were carried by Lts Christopher McRobbie and Christopher Voce-Russell and were handed over to former Regimental Sgt Majors, Lt Colonel Fred Beattie and Maj Bob Ritchie (1936–2014).

Appendix III Alliances Worldwide

1. See Bernard Fergusson, 'The Allied Regiments', *King's Enemies*, pp.342–72.
2. By Army Order No. 43/39 (Mar 1939), *Red Hackle*, Jul 1939, p.10.
3. Capt B.W. Palmer, '42nd Battalion The Royal Queensland Regiment, Australian Military Forces', *Red Hackle*, Apr 1969, p.31.
4. 'Allied Battalion of Australian Infantry', *Red Hackle*, Apr 1926, p.4; 'Sydney Branch Notes', *Red Hackle*, Jan 1929, p.41. See Editorial, *Red Hackle*, Jul 1921, p.2, & Oct 1921, p.32.
5. 'New South Wales', *Red Hackle*, Apr 1935, p.50, & 'The 30th Bn. The Australian Military Forces', *Red Hackle*, Oct 1935, pp.54–5.

6. Thomas Dinesen, VC (1892–1979) later received a commission. After the war he lived in East Africa, helping his sister, the writer Karen Blixen, manage her farm. He was one of 6 VC winners in The Black Watch of Canada. See http://www.blackwatchcanada.com/en/heritage-and-history/a-brief-history, accessed 22 Feb 2017.
7. '1BW Record of Service 1873–1939', p.110b, BWRA 0800; Capt P.P. Hutchison, 'A Brief History of the Canadian Battalions of The Black Watch', *Red Hackle*, Apr 1926, p.16. Additional information Roman Jarymowycz, 25 Sep 2016.
8. See Roman Jarymowycz, *The History of The Black Watch (Royal Highland Regiment) of Canada,* 2 vols, Black Watch of Canada Foundation, forthcoming.
9. *Abegweit* means 'resting on the wave', in reference to its geographical location. Mention of the affiliation first appears in *The Red Hackle,* Jul 1931, p.7, & 'A Brief Sketch of the Prince Edward Island Highlanders', p.19.
10. See 'History of The Lanark and Renfrew Scottish Regiment', BWRA 0142; *Red Hackle,* Apr 1928, p.6.
11. See Editorial, *Red Hackle,* Apr 1939, p.3; 'The Black Watch and the New Zealand Scottish Regiment', *Red Hackle,* Aug 1973, p.13; *A History of the Second Battalion, New Zealand Scottish* compiled by The Ex-Members Association, 1981, for history of 2nd Battalion. Additional information from Brett Pierce, 4 Sep 2013, Oct 2016; & Lt Col K.L. Forrest, 'Reply to the Toast', 16 Mar 1991. 'End of an Era – The Laying up of the New Zealand Scottish Regiment Colours', *Red Hackle,* Nov 2016, p.30.
12. John Stewart-Murray, 8th Duke of Atholl, KT, GCVO, CB, DSO, PC, ADC (1871–1942), Marquess of Tullibardine until the death of his father the 7th Duke in 1917.
13. '1BW Notes & News', *Red Hackle*, Oct 1927, p.15.
14. Fergusson, *King's Enemies*, p.357.
15. See 'Rhodesian Branch', *Red Hackle,* Apr 1947, p.27; 'Rhodesians' gift to the Regiment', *Red Hackle,* Apr 1948, p.26; & '2BW Farewell Notes', *Red Hackle,* Jul 1948, p.18. It was won by 4 Pl, B Coy. The Rhodesian Shield is with 3 Scots, Fort George. It was last competed for in 1994. Information from RSM Kevin Stacey, 27 Oct 2016.
16. 'Under the Ocean Wave', *Red Hackle,* Dec 1986, p.21. It was initially affiliated to B Coy but then subsumed by the Battalion. There appears also to have been a brief affiliation with HMS *Onslaught*. See 'Visit to HMS Onslaught', *Red Hackle*, Dec 1987, p.29.

Select Bibliography

Unpublished sources

Interviews with Black Watch officers & other ranks

Brig Alastair Aitken, OBE; Capt Hugo Allen; Col the Hon David Arbuthnott, MBE

Maj John Bailey; Brigadier Garry Barnett, OBE; Capt Brian Baxter; Sgt Major Kevin Blackley; Col Ronald Bradford; Brig Edward de Broë-Ferguson, MBE; Dr Fraser Brown; Lt Col Freddy Burnaby-Atkins*

Brig Duncan Cameron, OBE; Capt Ben Collis; Capt Andrew Colquhoun; Maj Nicholas Colquhoun; Maj William Colquhoun; Maj Alastair Colville; Maj Gen James Cowan, CBE, DSO; Geoffrey Cowper-Coles*; Keith Craig; Col Ian Critchley, OBE*

Roland Dane*; The Viscount Davidson*; Rev Norman Drummond; Sgt Robert Duncan; Pipe Maj Alistair Duthie

Maj Tim Elliott; Maj Rupert Forrest, MBE

Hamish Gibson; Capt Harry Gladstone; Maj George Grant, MBE, MM*; Peter Grant; Maj Colin Gray; Brig Adam Gurdon, CBE*

Derek Halley*; Capt Colin Harrison*; Capt Harry Hood; Derek Howard-Smith*; WO2 Joe Hubble*; Jeremy Hulme; Cpl Dave Hutton*

Maj Colin Innes; Lt Gen Sir Alistair Irwin, KCB, CBE; Capt William Johnson; Maj David Kemmis Betty, MBE

Lt Col Stephen Lindsay; Brig Alasdair Loudon, OBE*

Sgt Maj John Paul Maestri; Louis Manson*; Sgt Gair McCrostie; Lt Col Jules McElhinney; Capt Alan McEwen; Henry B. McKenzie Johnston, CB*

John Nicol; Lt Col Richard Nunneley, MBE; Capt George Ogilvie, CD*; Lt Col Sir Andrew Ogilvy-Wedderburn, Bt

Maj Richard Parata, MBE; Maj Mark Percy; Lt Col Angus Philp; Maj Ronnie Proctor, MBE

Dr Tom Renouf, MBE, MM*; Capt Jamie Riddell; Lt Col Roderick Riddell; Maj Gen Michael Riddell-Webster, CBE, DSO

Douglas Sinclair Roger*; Christopher Rose; Maj Hugh Rose

Capt Scott Shaw; Sgt Maj Ian Smith; WO1 David Stacey; David Steavenson*; Jimmy Steele; Allan Stewart; Peter Stormonth Darling*

Sgt Maj Dave Taylor; Col David Thornycroft, OBE; Lt Col Neil Tomlin; Brig O.R. Tweedy*

Maj Gen Andrew Watson, CB; Maj Angus Watson; Maj Peter Watson, MC*; Sgt Ronald White; WO1 William Whytock; Lt Col Mike Williamson, MBE; Sgt Maj Alexander Wilson, Brig Donald Wilson, CBE; Lord Wilson of Tillyorn, KT, GCMG, FRSE.

(*since deceased)

The Black Watch Museum (BWM)
(incorporating the Black Watch Regimental Archive (BWRA))

Correspondence, diaries and memoirs
Anderson, LCpl W.M.D., 'Captivity', memoir, 1918
Ashworth, Pte Josiah, 'A POW's Tale, 21 Mar–20 Dec 1918'
Badenoch, Capt R.E., 'My Recollections of the First World War', memoir (1978)
Barber, Sgt Joseph Miller, letters home, 1915
Barker, LCpl Henry Scivity, memoirs 1939–46 (1990s)
Barry, Maj (later Lt Col) Gerald, 'War Diaries', 1 & 2, 3 & 4; 'Account of the Battle for Tiger on 21st Nov 1941'
Blair, Col Harold Neville, 'Tobruk, Nov–Dec 1941'; 'Notes on *Chakdina* Sinking'; 'Recollections of the Second Battalion and The Final Days of the Indian Idyll'
Blair, Col James Molesworth, diary, South Africa, 1901
Blair Imrie, Maj H.A.C., DSO, MC, letters to his wife in 1942
Bowie, 2nd Lt (later Lt) Henry, diary, Mesopotamia, 1916
Bradford, Brig Bill, DSO & Bar, MBE, MC, 'One Day in the Saar 1940'; 'Occasional letters' to Gen Sir Arthur Wauchope, GCB, GCMG, CIE, DSO; 'Activities between Jun 1944 and May 1945'; 'Operations 1–23 Jan. 1945'
Brodie, Lt Col Alec, DSO, OBE, MC, letters to his family, 29 Jun 1944–28 Feb 1945
Brown, LCpl Ernest, 'My Experiences in South Africa', in 'Testimonials', 1899, Netley Album
Burnaby-Atkins, Lt Col Freddy, letter to his mother describing his escape, 1941
Cameron, Capt Archibald Rice, letter book and diary, South Africa, 1899–1901
Cameron, Pte William, 'Army Life and Trials', 1917
Campbell-Preston, Lt Col Patrick, MBE, 'Saar Spring 1940', memoir
Chalmers, Pte David, 'Six Years of My Life, 2 Apr 1940–6 Jul 1946', memoir
Clark, Maj H. McL, oral memoir (recorded 1980s)
Clarke, Pte James, 'POW escapee 1940', memoir
Clement, Lt Hubert A., correspondence and diary, 1916–17
Cochrane, Pte William, 'Over the Hills and Far Away, 1944', memoir as told to his son
Cocks, Lt Charles Vernon Somers, diary, 1915–16
Couston, Pte William, letters to his mother, 1916–18
Crearar, Pte John McEuan, lecture 1902, Second South African War
Critcher, Pte Charles Rufus, diary, Second South African War
Cumming, Lt Alexander Bryant, letters home, 1915–16
Daily, Pte George Morrison, 'A Soldier's Tale', memoirs (c.2000)
Dow, Cpl Andrew, memoirs, France, Holland, Belgium, German, 1944–45 (1980)
Duff, Cpl D., diary, Second South African War
Duke, Maj A.W., papers and correspondence
Dundas, Capt R.H., diary, Mesopotamia, 1915–16
Farrar, George Robert, memoir of the Irish Section, 6BW, 1915–16
Finch, Pte E. diaries, South Africa 1899–1901
Fleming, Maj Richard Wallace, memoirs, 1936–41

Forman, Sgt Charles, 'My Life, 1914–18', memoir (1965)
Garside, T.W., 'Withdrawal from the Somme', France, 1940
Garvie, Pte Jamie, diary, 1940–41
Gilroy, Lt G.B., letter to Lady Strathmore, 27 Sep 1915
Gordon, Lt Col (later Brig Gen) C.W.E., letters, 1916
Grant Duff, Capt (later Lt Col) Adrian, diaries, 1899–1902
Graves, Pte Edward, 'My First Year Abroad', memoir, 1944–45
Grieve, Cpl A., pocket diary, 1945
Gunter, J.E., 'Experiences of Draft 2 Jul 1941–30 Aug 1941'
Guthrie, Colour Sgt Alexander Cameron, 'Letters from the Front', 1914–16
Hall, D.W., 'Poems of the Korean War', 1952
Harrison, LCpl David, 'Six Years in The Black Watch', 1940–46
Hay, Cpl Albert A., MM, 'Soldiering', memoir, 1917–21 (1935)
Honeyman, Lt Col G.E.B., DSO, 'Operations in France 24 May–12 Jun 1940' (Oct 1946)
Hopwood, Brig J.A., 'History of the 1st Battalion in the Second World War' (draft)
Hubble, WO2 Joe, recollection of Kenya (13 Jan 2003)
Hurst, Cpl Derek, memoir (Korea)
Kempshall, Tom, poems relating to service in The Black Watch, 1920s (1979) in J.L.R. Samson, Scrapbook III
Krook, Maj A.D. Campbell, memoir, 1914
Jack, Pte James, war diary, 1917–19
Jackson, George, 'Working Holiday – All Expenses by H.M. Government', memoir (13 Nov 1987)
Jackson, Gen Sir Mike, GCB, CBE, DSO, DL, letter to Army Chain of Command, All Commanding Officers, 16 Dec 2004
Johns, William (Bill), biographical information
Junks, Cpl Herbert L, 'Diary of a Soldier', 1916–19
Laing, Pte John, diary, 1914–15
Lewis, Pte J.D., account of service in 8BW in 1944 (7 May 1998)
Livingstone, Cpl David, 'On Active Service and Otherwise: Some notes and recollections from a Wanderer's Diary', 1917–18
Macdonald, Rev Coll, letters home (typescript and handwritten), 1917–18
Macfarlane, Pte James, letters, Second South African War
Mackie, Pte Andrew Somers, notebook, 1914–15
Macrae, Capt Ian, 'War Diary', WWII
Mann, Brian, 'Korea 1952–53', memoirs
Marchant, Pte G., 'Extracts from Letters', 51st Highland Division, 1943
Marshall, Pte James McGregor, reminiscences, (1937)
McAskill, Malcolm, memoirs, 1939–45
McKenzie, Colour Sgt D., 'Life as a POW in Germany'
McKenzie Johnston, Henry B., CB, 'Recollections of Service in 6BW', 1939–45
McLeod, Pipe Maj Daniel, diary 1915–19
Meekison, RQMS Ed, 'The Story of a Quartie's War', memoir of service in 5BW, WWII

Meldrum, Pte Andrew, 'Memoirs of a Conscript', Nov 1939–Sep 1945
Mitchell, Pte A., diary and reminiscences, 1914
Mitchelson, Pte Robert, 'A Wartime Log for British prisoners', memoir
Moon, 2nd Lt John, 'A Pair of Boots', memoir, 1940
Morrison, Lt Robert Stevenson, diary, 1915–16
Muir, Cpl J.R., diary, 1915–16
Murray, Lt J.R.B., diaries (1–9), 15 Jan 1940–22 Aug 1944
Murray-Menzies, Mr & Mrs, correspondence enquiring into death of their son, Duncan, including with Lt Edward M. Wolf, Pte James Wallace & Sidney Charrington, 1917
O'Brien, Pte Francis, diary, Second South African War 1900–02
Ogilvie, Capt George, memoir, 1941
Ogilvie, Pte Henry, diary/memoir, 1914
Osborne, Pte Victor Mons, 'Flight to Safety', memoir, 1940
Penman, Sgt Robert, 'One Man's War, reminiscences of WW2'
Philp, Sgt David, letter describing his escape as a POW, 1940
Quekett, Lt H.S., 'Jottings of an Ordinary Man, from Childhood to the End of the Great War, 1914-1918'
Rafferty, Bombardier E.E., RA, written statement, 1945
Ritchie, Gen Sir Neil, GBE, KCB, DSO, MC, KStJ, 'Recollections'
Robertson, Colour Sgt, 'Life as a POW in Germany', 1BW, in 'Waifs & Strays'
Roper-Caldbeck, Lt Col A.R., letters to Gen Sir Arthur Wauchope, including notes on the advance from Buerat to Tripoli, 1942–43
Roy, Pipe Maj Robert (Rab), letters home, 1941
Rose, Lt Col David, DSO and bar, 'Third Battle of the Hook', reports
Rose, Capt Hugh of Kilravock, letters and sketches, Second South African War
Rusk, Lt Col George, DSO, MC, Tobruk 'Break out' notes, written 1971; Cyclone Contai District Pichaboni River, 2BW citation, 30 Nov 1942
Samson, J.L.R., Scrapbook III
Sandford, Lt R.U.E.A., memoir, 1940
Sarjeant, L.G., 'War diary', WWI
Shand, Pte Graham, diary, WWII
Simpson, LCpl David, 'Diary of My Doings', 1915
Skidmore, Pte W., 'Second South African War diary'
Small, Pte J.M., letter from hospital to Dear Madame (Mrs Campbell), 28 Sep 1914
Stephen, Lt Col C.G., 'History of The Black Watch 1939–41'
Steward, Lt Col R., diary, Nov 1940–41; 'An Account of Operations in Silesia'
Stewart, Capt (later Brig Gen) Charles Edward, diaries and memoir, South Africa, 2 vols: I, 22 Oct 1899–18 Mar 1900; II, 18 Mar–5 Oct 1900
Stewart, Lt Col John, diary, letters, 1915–16 France, 1917–18 Mesopotamia; 'British attack on the Tabsor system of enemy trenches, 19 Sep 1918'; 'Account of the movements of the 2nd Battalion The Black Watch, 18 Sep–20 Oct'
Stewart-Peter, Hamish, 'Service in the Middle East', memoir, 1940–42
Stratton, Pte Sandy, 'Letters Home from the Front During the Great War'

Sutherland, Lt Kenneth Henry, POW, statement of experiences under the Gestapo 24 Sep 1942–11 Dec 1942, extracted from Padre Platt's diary, 12 Jan 1943
Thomson, Capt Alex, diary/memoir, 1914–18
Thorburn, Pte R., message book, 1899–1900
Tobler, Maj Douglas Hugen, 'A Brigade Intelligence Officer's Recollection of Manoeuvres and Other Odds and Ends' (1975)
Vernon, Cdr Maurice, RN, 'Evacuation of Somalia', transcript of tape (undated), enclosed with letter from Edward Lee, dated 25 Nov 1987
Walker, Lt Col Harry, miscellaneous papers, 1914
Welch, Piper David, 'Testimonials', 1899, Netley Album
Williams, Lance Cpl James, memoir, Boer War, 1899
Williamson, Pte James, 'Testimonials', 1899, Netley Album
Wilson, Adam Macgregor, 'On Active Service', diary, 1915
Wilson, Pte (later Sgt) W.B., Memoirs (personal diaries), 1891–1965
Wimberley, Maj Gen Douglas, 'Alamein, the story of the 51st Highland Division in North Africa', 23 Oct 1942, in J.L.R. Samson, Scrapbook III
Wombwell, G.A., diary, Italy 1944
Wood, L.S., 'National Service 1951–53', memoir (11 Jan 2001)
Young, 2nd Lt George R., diaries, 1915–17
Young, Pte Jock, 'Jock's Story', memoir, 1915

Battalion and Brigade war diaries & histories
First World War:
War Diaries (also available in TNA): 1BW 1914–18; 2BW 1914–19; 4BW 1915–16; 5BW 1914–16, 4/5BW 1916–19; 6BW 1917–19; 7BW 1915–16, 1917–19; 8BW 1915–19; 9BW 1915–18; 10BW 1915–18; 13BW 1916–19; 14BW 1917–19

Second World War:
1BW: Brigs J.A. Hopwood & W.N. Roper-Caldbeck; Cols C.G. Stephen, B.C. Bradford and G.P. Campbell-Preston, Maj J.N. Davies-Colley; Capts A.O.L. Lithgow, W.M. Wingate-Gray and V.M. Fortune (used by Bernard Fergusson in *The Black Watch and the King's Enemies*); Normandy Bridgehead 1944
2BW: History of operations provided by Brig A. Gilroy; Cols G.G. Green, H.N. Blair, G. Barry and C.V. Watson-Gandy; Majs D.McN.C. Rose, J. Ewan, D. Ross; Capts E. Lee and I. Scott-Hyde; RSM J. Walker (used by Bernard Fergusson in *The Black Watch and the King's Enemies*); 'Regimental Milestones, 1939–45' (by Donald Maclean, 1948); 'War Diaries', Tobruk, Nov 1941; 'War Diary, India', 17 Jun 1942–31 May 1944; 1 Jun 1944–31 Dec 1946 (typescript); 1 Sep 1944–31 Dec 1946 (handwritten) ; 'War History 1939–45' (by Douglas Ross)
4BW: History of operations by Brig R.C. Macpherson, Majs Douglas Murray and R.St G.R. Maxwell (used by Bernard Fergusson in *The Black Watch and the King's Enemies*)
5BW: History of operations provided by Maj Gen H. Murray, Lt Col Chick

Thompson and Maj Aldo Campbell (used by Bernard Fergusson in *The Black Watch and the King's Enemies*); 'War History and Reminiscences' prepared by A.C.C. Brodie (used by Roderick Grant in *The 51st Highland Division at War*); John McGregor, *The Spirit of Angus*

6BW: 'War Diary (B Company), May 1940 – Belgium and France' (by Capt Ian Macrae); 'War Diary (D Company) 12–30 May 1940' (by 2nd Lt Ben S. Leslie); Col B.J.G. Madden, *History of the 6th Battalion*; 'Notes on Greece 1944'

7BW: Maj D.F.O. Russell, *War History of the 7th Bn The Black Watch* (R.H.R.) (*Fife Territorial Battalion*)

8BW: Notes by Lt Col N.E. Baxter

9BW: Notes by G.F. Underwood & Lt Col Purvis Russell Montgomery; 'Notes on the War Service of 9BW, 1939–44'

10BW: Notes by Lt Col Purvis Russell Montgomery;

1st Battalion The Tyneside Scottish, The Black Watch: 'War Diary', I, Jan–Jun 1944; II, Jul–Sep 1944

Additional sources

Campaigns, operations and battles:

Korea: '2nd Battle of the Hook, Outline of Events & Reports'; Second/Third Battle of the Hook, reports

North Africa: 'Extracts from Letters', 51st Highland Division; 'Start Line, El Alamein, 23 Oct 1942'; Tobruk Break out', 2nd Battalion, 1941; 'Report on the sinking of HMS *Chakdina* on 5 Dec. 1941'; translations from Italian & German diaries of the North African Campaign

Northern Ireland: 'Operation Banner: An Analysis of Military Operations in Northern Ireland'; 'Special Order of the Day, The End of Operation Banner from Gen Sir Richard Dannatt, KCB, CBE, MC, Chief of the General Staff', 25 Jul 2007

North-West Europe 1944: 'Piobaireachd', daily bulletins of the Highland Division, 14 Jun 1944–8 May 1945

'Op Telic 1 Recollections' (recorded for the Regimental Archive, Mar 2013)

Second South African War: 'Casualty Roll of The Black Watch (Royal Highlanders) Second Boer War 1899–1902'; 'Highland Heroes of Magersfontein', scrapbook; 'List of Casualties, South Africa 1899–1902'; 'News Cuttings, South African War', vols I, II, III; Order of service, Dedication of the [South African] Memorial, Tues 5 May 1903; 'Testimonials' of wounded soldiers in 1899, Netley Album

Sicily 1943: Sicilian campaign report 1943, including account of The Gerbini Battle; 'Statistics from the Gerbini Battle', unsigned

Miscellaneous:

Minute Books: General Committee & Annual General Meetings, 27 Sep 1919–28 Apr 1934, The Black Watch Association; Aberdeen & District Branch of The Black Watch Association Press Cutting Album

Newsletters: The Black Watch (Royal Highland Regiment), 44/2 Indian Airborne Division

Prisoners-of-War: individual accounts, WWII; 'Wartime Log for British Prisoners: Issued by the War Prisoners' Aid of the YMCA', Switzerland, including notes and drawings by Pte R. Mitchelson, POW, Germany, 1940–45

Regimental records: '1st Battalion The Black Watch 1910–39, Historical Record';'1st Battalion The Black Watch Record of Service 1873–1939'; '2nd Battalion The Black Watch, 1909–39, Historical Record'; '2nd Battalion The Black Watch Record of Service 1780–1909'; 2nd Battalion scrapbooks; Regimental and General Order Books

Scrapbook relating to tour of Canada by 1st Battalion Military Band and Pipers, 1904

'This Happens in War': video interviews/transcripts with officers and ORs recorded in 2008

'Waifs and Strays', miscellaneous drafts for Bernard Fergusson, *The Black Watch & The King's Enemies*

Bodleian Library, Oxford

Shiela Sokolov Grant papers: Capt Neill Grant Duff correspondence

Churchill Archives Cambridge (CAC)

Amery, Rt Hon Leopold, CH, papers relating to his brother, Maj Harold Amery (1877–1915);

Churchill, Winston S., KG, OM, CH, RD, PC, DL, FRS, RA, correspondence

Grant Duff, Lt Col Adrian, diary & miscellaneous papers including correspondence after his death with Sir Maurice Hankey 1912–30

The Imperial War Museum (IWM)

Sutton, Maj F.G., 'Pioneer Platoon and War Crimes and Interrogations, 1943–1945', memoir (1949)

Wimberley, Maj Gen D.N., CB, DSO, MC, 'Scottish Soldier, II, An Autobiography' (1958–60)

McMaster University (McMU)

John Connell William Ready Division of Archives & Research collection: Col the Hon. C. Malise Hore-Ruthven, CMG, DSO, recollections; Wavell, FM the Earl, GCB, GCSI, CMG, MC, KStJ, PC, diary, 1902, & letters to his sister, 1902, 1914

The National Archives (TNA)

1BW 'Historical Record', Jul 1953–Apr 1955; 1 Apr 1955–1 Apr 1956

1BW 'War Diary', Jan–Dec 1943

Churchill, Winston S., 'Military Aspects of the Continental Problem', 13 Aug 1911

4th Division, 'War Diary', 1944

51HD, 153 Infantry Brigade, 'War Diary', 1943, 1944

Kenya/ Mau Mau insurgency: 'Emergency, Unrest, Discipline of Security Forces, Allegations of Brutality/Complaints against Security Forces' (migrated archive); 'Mau Mau Organisation & Strengths'; 'Operation Anvil, Kenya' (migrated archive);

'Operations against Mau Mau/ Policy Directives'; 'Organisation of Mau Mau'
Norman Force, Jun 1940 (documents from Lt Gen James Marshall-Cornwall)

The National Library of Scotland (NLS)
Linklater, Eric, CBE, TD, 'El Alamein I & II'; correspondence with Bernard Fergusson (Lord Ballantrae) GCMG, GCVO, DSO, OBE

Second World War Experience Archive (SWWEA)
Otway, Lt Col Terence, DSO, recollections

Private collections
Anderson, Patrick, correspondence relating to his uncle, Lt Patrick Wright Anderson, & his cousin, J.B. Salmond
Arbuthnott, Col the Hon David, MBE, diaries 1916–19 of his father Maj Gen Viscount Robert Keith Arbuthnott, CB, CBE, DSO, MC, DL
Blair Adam Muniments, letters to Evie Marindin from officers and ORs, 1914–15
Blakeney, Hugh S.W., 'National Service', memoir (2014)
Boyle, Richard, correspondence relating to his grandfather, Lt Col Adrian Grant Duff; letter from Capt Guy Rowan-Hamilton to Mrs Adrian Grant Duff
Cameron, Brig Duncan, OBE, correspondence with Brig J.C. Monteith, CBE, MC, as Lt Col Cameron commanding 1st Battalion The Black Watch
Cheetham, Juliet (née Blair) & Tina Metcalfe (née Blair), letter from their grandfather, 2nd Lt Alexander Blair, to his son, Neville, 1916; Col Neville Blair, correspondence and diaries; J.E. Benson, '2 Black Watch -Tobruk, etc', memoir (c.1991); Maj Gen Neil McMicking, memorandum (c.1960)
Clark, John, correspondence of his great-grandfather, Capt Edward M.Murray, with serving officers and other ranks, 1915
Cochrane, Stewart, correspondence relating to his father, Pte William Cochrane
Colquhoun, Maj Nicholas, letters to Rachel & notebook, Iraq 2004
Colquhoun, Maj William, war diary, Iraq 2003
Cooper, Gen Sir George, GCB, MC, DL, correspondence relating to service in Korea
Cowan, Maj Gen James, CBE, DSO, documents and scrapbook, Iraq 2004
Dane, Roland, 'Company Carrier Driver', memoir (2014)
Davidson, Viscount, journal & letters home, British Guiana, 1954
Gait, Lt Col Brian, DSO, DCM, RMP, 'All the Redcoats were Valiant', memoir (courtesy his son-in-law, Lt Col Mike Bullen); 2nd Lt Sandy Younger, 'Account of Ronson Patrol, 17 Jan 1953'
Gladstone, Capt Harry, diary and scrapbook, Afghanistan 2009, 2011–12
Forrest, Maj Rupert, MBE, diaries, N.Ireland 1982–83, 1985–86, Kosovo 2001
Fortune, Jack, research material relating to Geldermalsen and the Red Hackle; correspondence relating to his grandfather, Maj Gen Sir Victor Fortune, KBE, CB, DSO
Herd, Victor, letters home from N. Africa from his late father-in-law, Pte William Fisher, 1942–43

Hulme, Jeremy, '1st Battalion The Black Watch's first visit to Northern Ireland 1970', memoir

Jarymowycz, Roman, correspondence relating to The Royal Highland Regiment (Black Watch) of Canada, 2016

Kemmis Betty, Maj David, MBE, diaries, Iraq 2003

Kenyon, Charles, correspondence relating to his great-uncle, H.J. Humphrys, CBE, DSO, MC

Kiszely, Lt Gen Sir John, Senior British Military Representative, Iraq & Deputy Coalition Cdr 2004, extracts from reports of the SBMR/CoalitionCom Reports to the Chief of Defence Staff

Irwin, Lt General Sir Alistair, letters home, 1914, from his great-uncle, Lt Lewis Cumming; letter from Lt Kynock Cumming, 1914; letter from Cpl D. Petrie to Mr J. Cumming, 1914; letter from Lt Lloyd Rennie to his father, 1914; Elizabeth Irwin, letters to her parents from India 1947; letters of Brig Angus Irwin, CBE, DSO, MC, to Elizabeth Irwin 1952–53; diaries and letters of Lt Gen Sir Alistair Irwin relating to service in 1BW 1969–1989; correspondence with Lt Col Freddy Burnaby-Atkins, 2004

Laycock, Rose, letters home from her uncle, Captain Donald Mirrielees, 1944

Lindsay, Lt Col Stephen, letters to Annie, N. Ireland 1970

McLaren, John, oral recollections of his father, Robert Stewart McLaren, WWII

McKenzie Johnston, Henry B., CB, 'Recollections of Service in 6BW', 1939–45; memoir by Capt R.M. Honey, 'Episodes in Greece'

Noble, James, letters home from his great-uncle, Lt Jack Mackintosh, 1915

Ormond, Flavia (née Grant Duff), correspondence relating to her father, Capt Neill Grant Duff and grandfather, Lt Col Adrian Grant Duff; correspondence from Maj Gen Sir Victor Fortune, KBE, CB, DSO and from his wife, Eleanor; letter to her mother, Barbara, from Lt David Campbell

Parata, Maj Richard, MBE, 'The Northern Ireland Patrol Group', Smith by Lt Col Mike Smith

Riddell, Capt Jamie, letters to his parents, Iraq 2003

Riddell-Webster, Maj Gen M.L., CBE, DSO, diary, Commander's diary, scrapbook, Iraq 2003

Rose, Christopher, 'The Black Watch (RHR) in Cyprus', memoir, 1958–59

Rose, Major Hugh, miscellaneous correspondence in 1996 relating to his father Lt Col David Rose, DSO and bar, in response to *Off the Record*, including letters from Col Neville Blair, John McVay, Pastor Bill Lark, Gen Sir George Cooper, GCB, MC, DL

Rowan-Hamilton, Guy, correspondence relating to his father, Maj Angus Rowan-Hamilton

Smyth, Thomas B., research material: 'Casualty Roll of The Black Watch (Royal Highlanders), Second Boer War 1899–1902'; 'Croix de Guerre 6th Battalion The Black Watch'; 'Prisoners of War, 1945'; 'Formations of Battalions of The Black Watch, WW2'; 'Military Medallists of The Black Watch WW2', 'Oral History 1999'; 'The Black Watch and the Victoria Cross'

Soper, Alice, 'The Piper of Tobruk', memoir of her father, Pipe Major 'Rab' Roy, MBE, DCM

Thorburn, Gordon, correspondence relating to his father

Thornycroft, Col David, OBE, 'Memoir –Ypres 2014'

Watson, Maj J.P., MC, biographical notes on his father, Capt Sammy Watson

Wylie, Alasdair, diaries, notes and scrapbook of Lt Col John Wylie, 6BW, 1915–16

Published sources

Books and articles

Army List of Serving Regular, Militia or Territorial British Army Officers

Alanbrooke, FM Lord, *War Diaries*, ed. Alex Danchev & Daniel Todman, University of California Press, 2001

Allan, Mavor, 'The Charge of the Highland Brigade. Magersfontein – 11th December, 1899', *Celtic Monthly*, Feb 1900

Allan, Stuart, & David Forsyth, *Common Cause, Commonwealth Scots and the Great War*, National Museums of Scotland, 2014

Andrews, W. Linton, *Haunting Years*, Hutchinson & Co., 1930

Anon, *Letters from the Front, by a Black Watch Volunteer on Active Service in South Africa, 1900–1901*, reprinted from the *Evening Telegraph*, John Leng & Co., Dundee, 1901

Arbuthnott, David, 'The First Battalion in Korea', *The Red Hackle*, May 2002

Baird, William, *General Wauchope*, Oliphant Anderson & Ferrier/T. & A. Constable, 1901

Barber, Neil, *The Day the Devils Dropped in: The 9th Parachute Battalion in Normandy – D-day to D+6, The Merville Battery to the Château St Côme*, Leo Cooper, 2004

Barclay, C.N., *The History of the Cameronians (Scottish Rifles)*, III, 1933–1946, Praed, 1949

Barker, A.J., *Fortune Favours the Brave: Battle of the Hook, Korea, 1953*, Leo Cooper, 1974

Bate, C.K. & M.G. Smith, *For Bravery in the Field*, Bayonet, 1991

'The Battles for Monte Cassino 12 Jan–5 Jun 1944', *The Second World War 60th Anniversary Series*, Ministry of Defence and New Opportunities, UK, 2004

'The Battle of Loos', *Courier & Advertiser*, 100 Year Souvenir Supplement, 2015

Baverstock, Kevin, *Breaking the Panzers*, Sutton, 2002

Baynes, John (with John Laffin), *Soldiers of Scotland*, Brasseys, 1988

Beaton, Angus, ed. *The Fight for Iraq*, Army Benevolent Fund, 2004

Beaumont, Peter, & Martin Bright, 'British set for Iraqi danger zones', *Observer*, 17 Oct 2004

Beevor, Antony, *Ardennes 1944: Hitler's Last Gamble*, Viking, 2015

Beevor, Antony, *D-Day*, Viking, 2009

Benson, John, 'Tobruk Breakout', *The Red Hackle*, Apr 1992

Bewsher, F.W., *History of the Fifty-First (Highland) Division 1914–18*, Naval & Military Press, 2001 (first pub. Blackwood, 1921)
Bierman, John, & Colin Smith, *Alamein, War without Hate*, Viking, 2002
Blair, Neville, 'Partition and the North-West Frontier', *The Red Hackle*, Apr 1988
Borthwick, James, *51st Highland Division in North Africa and Sicily*, selected articles, Tripoli, Jan 1943
Borthwick, James, *With the Scottish Troops in Europe*, selected articles, R.G. Lawrie Ltd, Glasgow, undated
Boyle, Richard, *Adrian Grant Duff*, Real Press, 2014
Bradford, Andrew, *Escape from Saint Valéry-en-Caux: The Adventures of Captain B.C. Bradford*, History Press, 2009
Brady, Fr. Brian J., Fr. Denis Faul & Fr. Raymond Murray, *A British Army Murder*, Abbey Printers, 1975
Brown, Fraser, 'Black Watch Men from the Argentine', *The Red Hackle*, May 2014
Burnaby-Atkins, F.J. 'One Short Day in May', *The Red Hackle*, May 2005
Burrows, Bob, *Fighter Writer: The Eventful Life of Sergeant Joe Lee, Scotland's Forgotten War Poet*, Breedon Books, 2004
Campbell, Colin, *Engine of Destruction: The 51st Highland Division in the Great War*, Argyll Publishing, 2013
Carver, FM Lord, *The National Army Museum Book of The Boer War*, Pan Books, 2000
Caskie, Donald, *The Tartan Pimpernel*, Birlinn, 1999
Cassar, George S., *The Tragedy of Sir John French*, Associated University Presses, 1985
Chamberlain, Gethin, 'Black Watch Commander: How the MOD let us down in Iraq,' *Scotsman*, 22 Jan 2004
Chamberlain, Gethin, 'Medic: Why Scots sergeant lost his leg', *Scotsman*, 21 Jan 2004
Chang, Jung, & Jon Halliday, *Mao: The Unknown Story*, Vintage, 2007
Childs, Lewis, *Kimberley: Battleground South Africa*, Leo Cooper, 2001
Chinnery, Philip D., *March or Die*, Airlife, 1997
Chronicle of the Royal Highland Regiment, The Black Watch, T. & A. Constable, 1913/14
Chronology of the 42nd Royal Highlanders, The Black Watch from 1729 to 1905, 4th ed., printed for the Regiment, Berwick-on-Tweed, 1906
Churchill, Winston S., *Never Give In!, The Best of Winston Churchill's Speeches*, selected & edited by his grandson Winston S. Churchill, Pimlico, 2003
Churchill, Winston S., *The Second World War*, I–VI, Cassell & Co, 1951–54
Churchill, Winston S., *The World Crisis, 1911–1914, 1915* & *1916–1918*, II, Thornton Butterworth Ltd, 1923 & 1927
Cochrane, Stewart, *Chindit Special Force, Burma 1944*, XLibris, 2000
Collins, R.J., *Lord Wavell, 1883–1941*, Hodder & Stoughton, 1948
Connell, John, *Wavell, Scholar and Soldier: To June 1941*, Collins, 1964
Connell, John, *Wavell: Supreme Commander*, Collins, 1967
Cooper, George, *Fight, Dig and Live: The Story of the Royal Engineers in the Korean War*, Pen & Sword, 2011

Cornford, Leslie Cope, & Frank William Walker, *The Story of the Regiments: The Great Deeds of The Black Watch*, J.M. Dent & Sons, 1915
Cowan, James, 'The Black Watch in Iraq 2004', *The Red Hackle*, Nov 2004
Cox, Geordie, 'Monte Cassino – the Final Battle – May 1944,' *The Red Hackle*, May 2009
Craig, Neil, & Jo Craig, *Black Watch, Red Dawn: The Hong Kong Handover to China*, Brassey's, 1998
Cram, Sandy, Alistair Duthie, Alistair Irwin, & Scott Taylor, *A Collection of Pipe Music of The Black Watch*, Balhousie Publications, 2012
Crane, David, *Empires of the Dead*, Collins, 2013
Creswicke, Louis, *South Africa and the Transvaal War*, I–VI, T.C. & E.C. Jack, Edinburgh, 1900/01, VII, Caxton Publishing (undated)
Critchley, Ian, 'Last Days in India', *The Red Hackle*, May 2008
Dalrymple, H.N., '63 Years on – Some Random Recollections', *The Red Hackle*, May 2010
Danskin, Julie S., *A City at War: The 4th Black Watch Dundee's Own*, Abertay Historical Society, 2013
David, Saul, *Churchill's Sacrifice of the Highland Division, France 1940*, Brasseys, 1994
David, Saul, *Mutiny at Salerno: An Injustice Exposed*, Brassey's, 1995
Davis, Harold (with Paul Smith), *Tougher Than Bullets*, Mainstream Publishing, 2012
De Groot, Gerald, *Douglas Haig, 1861–1928*, Unwin Hyman, 1988
Delaforce, Patrick, *Monty's Highlanders: 51st Highland Division in the Second World War*, Pen & Sword, 2007
D'Este, Carlo, *Bitter Victory: The Battle for Sicily 1943*, Collins, 1988
Devine, T.M., *To the Ends of the Earth: Scotland's Global Diaspora*, Allen Lane, 2011
Doherty, Richard, *None Bolder: The History of the 51st Highland Division in the Second World War*, Spellmount, 2006
Don, Archibald, *A Memoir*, ed. Charles Sayle, John Murray, 1918
Douglas, George, *The Life of Major-General Wauchope*, Hodder & Stoughton, 1904
Drummond, Norman, *The Kirk Session of the 1st Battalion The Black Watch 1954–79*, The Black Watch Regiment, 1979
Duxbury, Col George R., 'The Battle of Magersfontein, 11th December, 1899', *Battles of the South African War, 1899–1902*, 9, S.A. National Museum of Military History, Johannesburg, Feb 1974
Ellis, John, *Cassino: The Hollow Victory*, Andrew Deutsch, 1984
Ewing, John, *History of the 9th (Scottish) Division*, John Murray, 1921
Farrar-Hockley, A.H., *The Somme*, Batsford, 1964
Fergusson, Bernard, *Beyond the Chindwin*, Collins, 1945
Fergusson, Bernard, *The Black Watch and the King's Enemies*, Collins, 1950
Fergusson, Bernard, 'The Black Watch and the King's Enemies', *The Red Hackle*, Apr 1951
Fergusson, Bernard, *The Black Watch: A Short History*, Woods of Perth (Printers), revised ed. 2002 (first published 1955, revised eds 1968, 1985, 1996)
Fergusson, Bernard, *The Trumpet in the Hall*, Collins, 1970

Fergusson, Bernard, *The Wild Green Earth*, Collins, 1946
Follain, John, *Mussolini's Island*, Hodder & Stoughton, 2005
Forbes, Archibald, *The "Black Watch": The Record of an Historic Regiment*, Cassell & Co, 2nd ed. 1910 (first published 1896)
Framp, Charlie, *Crimson Skies*, Richard Kay, 1988
Fraser, George MacDonald, *Quartered Safe Out Here*, HarperCollins, 1995
Freyberg, Paul, *Bernard Freyberg VC, Soldier of Two Nations*, Hodder & Stoughton, 1991
Fromkin, David, *A Peace to End All Peace: Creating the Modern Middle East*, Andre Deutsch, 1989
Geraghty, Tony, *The Irish War: The Military History of a Domestic Conflict*, HarperCollins, 2000
Grant, Peter, *Letters from the Forest*, Peter Grant, 2016
Grant, Roderick, *The 51st Highland Division at War*, Ian Allan, 1977
Gray, Joseph, 'The Fourth Black Watch', *Dundee Advertiser*, Dec 1917–Jan 1918
Grierson, J.M., *Records of the Scottish Volunteer Force 1859–1908*, Blackwood & Sons, 1909
Gurdon, Adam, 'Berlin 1950', *The Red Hackle*, Apr 1988
Haig, Douglas, *War Diaries and Letters 1914–1918*, ed. Gary Sheffield & John Bourne, Weidenfeld & Nicolson, 2005
Halley, Derek, *The Iron Claw: A Conscript's Tale*, Finavon Print, 2009
Hamill, Desmond, *Pig in the Middle: The Army in Northern Ireland 1969–1984*, Methuen, 1985
Hammond, Bryn, *Cambrai: The Myth of the First Great Tank Battle*, Weidenfeld & Nicholson, London, 2008
Hankins, Charlie, *A Part of My Life in a Family at War: The Charlie Hankins Story*, privately published (undated)
Harris, Douglas, *Haig and The First World War*, Cambridge University Press, 2008
Harrison, Colin, 'A Look at Cyprus today,' *The Red Hackle*, Aug 1978
Hastings, Max, *All Hell Let Lose: The World at War 1939–1945*, HarperPress, 2012
Hastings, Max, *Catastrophe: Europe Goes to War 1914*, HarperPress, 2013
Henderson, Tam, & John Hunt, *Warrior: A True Story of Bravery and Betrayal in the Iraq War*, Mainstream Publishing, 2008
Henderson, Hamish, *Elegies for the Dead in Cyrenaica*, Polygon, 1948
Henn, Francis, *A Business of Some Heat: The United Nations Force in Cyprus before and during the 1974 Turkish Invasion*, Pen & Sword, 2004
Holmes, Richard, ed., *The Oxford Companion to Military History*, Oxford University Press, 2001
Holt, Ivo Vesey, 'Occasional Letters', *The Red Hackle*, Aug 1980
Hughes, Matthew, 'A Very British Affair? British Armed Forces and the repression of the Arab Revolt in Palestine, 1936–39,' *Journal of the Society for Army Historical Research*, 87, 2009
Innes, Colin, 'Three Generations', *The Red Hackle*, May 2006
Innes, Colin, ed., *Songs of the Regiment: The Black Watch (Royal Highland Regiment)*,

privately published, 1973

Irwin, Alistair, 'Operation Banner Aug 1969–Jul 2007, Northern Ireland: An overview', including contributions from A.L. Watson, O.R. Tweedy, D.R. Wilson, E.D. Cameron, G.C. Barnett, *The Red Hackle*, May 2007

Jackson, Alvin, *Ireland 1798–1998, Politics and War*, Wiley-Blackwell, 2010

Jackson, Mike, *Soldier: The Autobiography*, Bantam Press, 2007

James, E.A., *British Regiments 1914–1918*, Naval & Military Press, 5th ed., 1998

Keegan, John, *The First World War*, Hutchinson, 1998

Laffin, John, *Scotland the Brave: The Story of the Scottish Soldier*, Cassell, 1963

Lee, Joseph, *Ballads of Battle*, John Murray, 1916

Liddell-Hart, B.H., *A History of the World War 1914–1918*, Faber & Faber, 1934 (first published as *The Real War*, 1930)

Liddell-Hart, B.H., ed., *The Rommel Papers*, tr. Paul Findlay, Collins, 1953

Lindsay, Stephen, ed., *The Black Watch Photographic Archive*, Tempus Publishing, 2000

Linklater, Eric, *The Highland Division*, *The Army at War*, HMSO, 1942

Linklater, Eric, *The Man on my Back*, Macmillan, 1941

Linklater, Eric, *Our Men in Korea*, HMSO, 1952

Linklater, Eric, & Andro Linklater, *The Black Watch*, Barrie & Jenkins, 1977

Lloyd-Parry, Richard, 'Black Watch prays and prepares for new fight,' *The Times*, 25 Oct 2004

Lloyd-Parry, Richard, 'Two Gravely Hurt as Black Watch Hit by New Suicide Attack,' *The Times*, 8 Nov 2004

Lunderstedt, Steve, 'From Belmont to Bloemfontein', *Diamond Fields Advertiser*, 2000

MacDonald, Callum, *Britain and the Korean War*, Basil Blackwell, 1990.

Macdonald, Catriona M.M., & E.W McFarland, eds, *Scotland and the Great War*, Tuckwell Press, 1999

Macdonald, Lyn, *1914*, Michael Joseph, 1987

Macdonald, Lyn, *1914: The Days of Hope*, Penguin, 1989

Macdonald, Lyn, *Somme*, Penguin, 1983

Macdonald, Lyn, *They Called it Passchendaele*, Penguin 1978

MacFarlane, 2275 Cpl Frank, compiled and researched by Diana M. Henderson: 'The Black Watch in 1912, I – A Recruit at the Depot and stationed in Edinburgh', *The Red Hackle*, Apr 1985; 'The Black Watch in 1913, II – Edinburgh and Aldershot', *The Red Hackle*, Aug 1985; 'The Black Watch in 1914, III – The First Battles, France 1914', *The Red Hackle*, Dec 1985; 'IV – The Winter of 1914', *The Red Hackle*, Apr 1986

MacGregor, Masry, *The Moon Behind the Hill*, Holman's Press, 1997

Mack, David, & Gillian Shaw, eds, *Aviation Assault Battlegroup: The 2009 Afghanistan Tour of The Black Watch, 3rd Battalion The Royal Regiment of Scotland*, Pen & Sword, 2011

McCluskey, Thomas, 'The Other Pipers of Loos', *The Red Hackle*, May 2009

McFarland, E.W., 'Commemoration of the South African War in Scotland, 1900–1910', *Scottish Historical Review*, Oct 2012

McGregor, John, *The Spirit of Angus: The War History of the County's Battalion of The Black Watch*, Phillimore, 1988

McKenzie Johnston, Henry, 'Monte Cassino – the Final Battle – May 1944', *The Red Hackle, May 2009*

McKittrick, David, Seamus Kelters, Brian Feeney, & Chris Thornton, *Lost Lives: The Stories of the Men, Women and Children Who Died Through the Northern Ireland Troubles*, Mainstream Publishing, 1999

McMicking, Neil, ed., *Officers of The Black Watch 1725 to 1986*, 2nd revised ed. by J.L.R. Samson, Samson Books, 1989 (first pub. 1937)

McMicking, Neil, *Officers of The Black Watch*, II, Thomas Hunter & Sons (undated, post-1952)

Madden, B.J.G., *A History of the 6th Battalion, 1939–1945*, Leslie, 1948

Madden, B.J.G., 'Sidi Medienne 1943 and 1988', *The Red Hackle*, Aug 1988

Mallinson, Allan, *Fight the Good Fight: Britain, the Army and the Coming of the First World* War, Bantam Press, 2013

Martin, H.G., *History of the 15th Scottish Division 1939–1945*, Blackwood & Sons, 1948

Masters, John, *The Road Past Mandalay*, Michael Joseph, 1961

Montgomery, Bernard, *The Memoirs of Field Marshal Montgomery*, Collins, 1958

Moon, Penderel, ed., *Wavell, The Viceroy's Journal*, Oxford University Press, 1973

Napolitano, Gian Gaspare, *To War With the Black Watch*, tr. Ian Campbell Ross, Birlinn, 2007

Neat, Timothy, *Hamish Henderson*, Polygon, 2007

Nicoll, E.W., 'Six months in Cyprus with the United Nations Forces', *The Red Hackle*, Aug 1967

Ogilvie, D.D., *The Fife and Forfar Yeomanry*, 1914–1919, John Murray, 1921

Pakenham, Thomas, *The Boer War*, Abacus, 2004

Parker, John, *Black Watch: The Inside Story of the Oldest Highland Regiment in the British Army*, Headline, 2005

Parker, Matthew, *Monte Cassino*, Headline, 2003

Patterson, Frederick C., *From Rattray & Beyond*, Wm Culross & Son, 2010

Penney, José, *Diary of a Black Watch Subaltern*, privately published (undated)

Philp, David, Maggy Savoye, *Un Ecossais dans le Maquis: Une épopée fantastique à travers la France occupée*, Bertout, 1994

Putkowski, Julian, & Julian Sykes, *Shot at Dawn*, Leo Cooper, 1992

Reid, Walter, *To Arras 1917: A Volunteer's Odyssey*, Tuckwell Press, 2003

Renouf, Tom, *Black Watch, Liberating Europe and Catching Himmler – My Extraordinary WW2 with the Highland Division*, Little, Brown, 2011

Reoch, Ernest, *The St Valery Story*, Highland Printers, 1965

Reoch, Paul, 'Black Watch Gulf bound,' *Perthshire Advertiser*, 28 Feb 2002

Riddell, Lt Col R.M., 'Lean, Wind, Lean', *The Red Hackle*, May 2012

Rose, David, *Off the Record: The Life and Letters of a Black Watch Officer*, revised ed., privately published, 1998

Royle, Trevor, *The Best Years of their Lives: The National Service Experience 1945–63*,

Coronet Books/Hodder & Stoughton, 1986
Royle, Trevor, *The Black Watch*, Mainstream Publishing, 2006
Royle, Trevor, *The Flowers of the Forest: Scotland and the First World War*, Birlinn, 2006
Royle, Trevor, *A Time of Tyrants*, Birlinn, 2011
Royle, Trevor, *War Report*, Grafton Books, 1987
Rufford, Nicholas, & Abul Taher, 'London Muslim puts Black Watch deaths on internet', *Sunday Times*, 14 Nov 2004
Russell, D.F.O., *War History of the 7th Bn The Black Watch (R.H.R.) (Fife Territorial Battalion)*, Markinch Printing, 1948
Salmond, J.B., *The History of the 51st Highland Division 1939–1945*, Blackwood, 1953, repr. Pentland Press, 1994
Samson, J.L.R., *A Concise Account of the Black Watch and Its Movements*, Samson Books, 2nd ed., 2001
Samson, J.L.R., *Geordie and Jock*, Samson Books, 1978
Samson, J.L.R., *Officers of The Black Watch 1725 to 1986*, 2nd revised ed., Samson Books, 1989 (1st & 2nd eds 1937/1953, compiled & revised by Neil McMicking)
Sanders, Andrew, & Ian S. Wood, *Times of Troubles: Britain's War in Northern Ireland*, Edinburgh University Press, 2012
Schofield, Victoria, *The Highland Furies: The Black Watch, 1739–1899*, Quercus, 2012
Schofield, Victoria, *Wavell: Soldier and Statesman*, Pen & Sword, 2010
Searle, Adrian, *Isle of Wight at War 1939–1945*, Dovecote Press, 1990
Sebag-Montefiore, Hugh, *Dunkirk: Fight to the Last Man*, Viking, 2006
Slim, William, *Defeat into Victory*, Reprint Society/Cassell, 1957
Spiers, Edward M., Jeremy A. Crang, & Matthew J. Strickland, eds, *A Military History of Scotland*, Manchester University Press, 2015
Stamp, Gavin, *The Memorial to the Missing of the Somme*, Profile Books, 2007
Statistics of the Military Effort of the British Empire during the Great War, 1914–1920, HMSO, 1922
Stewart, Andrew, *The First Victory: The Second World War and the East African Campaign*, Yale University Press, 2016
Stewart, Brian, *Scrapbook of a Roving Highlander: 80 Years Round Asia and Back*, Acorn, 2002
Stiles, Richard G.M.L., *'Mayhem in the Med': A Chronicle of the Cyprus Emergency 1955–1960*, Savannah, 2009
Stolte, Pieter, *The 51st Highland Division in the Ardennes, Dec 1944–Jan 1945*, Arnhem, 1999
Stormonth Darling, Peter, *Forgotten War: Remembering Korea 1951–1953*, privately published, 2007
Thomson, P.A.B., *Belize: A Concise History*, Macmillan Caribbean, 2004
Thorburn, Gordon, *Jocks in the Jungle: Black Watch and Cameronians as Chindits*, Pen & Sword, 2012
Thornycroft, D.C., 'Descent of the Volunteer Battalions of The Black Watch', *The Red Hackle*, Apr 1993

Topp, C. Beresford, *The 42nd, C.E.F. Royal Highlanders of Canada in the Great War*, Gazette Printing (Montreal), 1931

Walker, David, *Lean, Wind, Lean*, Collins, 1985

Wauchope, A.G., 'The Battle That Won Samarrah', *Blackwood's Magazine*, Apr 1918

Wauchope, A.G., *A History of The Black Watch (Royal Highlanders) in the Great War, 1914–1918*, I–III: Medici Society, 1926

Wauchope, A.G., *A Short History of The Black Watch (Royal Highlanders) 1725–1907*, Blackwood & Sons, 1908

Wavell, A.P., *Allenby: Soldier and Statesman*, George G. Harrap & Co, 1946

Wavell, A.P., *Other Men's Flowers*, Jonathan Cape, 1948

Wavell, A.P., *The Palestine Campaigns*, Constable & Co, 1929

Wavell, A.P., *Speaking Generally*, Macmillan, 1946

Wavell, A.P., 'A Visit to Magersfontein Battlefield', *The Red Hackle*, Jul 1948

White, Peter, *With the Jocks: A Soldier's Struggle for Europe 1944–45*, Sutton, 2006

Young, Derek, *Forgotten Scottish Voices from the Great War*, Tempus, 2005

Young, Derek, *Scottish Voices from the Second World War*, Tempus, 2006

Additional journals & magazines

1st Battalion The Black Watch (Royal Highland Regiment), 21 Dec 1982–3 May 1983*

The Black Watch Battlegroup Photographs, Second Gulf War, Iraq 2003*

Black Watch Corner, Flanders, Memorial Brochure, 3 May 2014*

Black Watch (Royal Highland Regiment), Hong Kong Review, Sep 1993, Jul 1994*

Bush Telegraph, 1979*

Cherat Times & Jalozai Chronicle, A Family Journal for the Million, collected ed., Commercial Press, 1907

The Daily Telegraph

The Junk (for the British Forces in Hong Kong), Jun 1994

Peoples' Journal, including *The Dinna Forget Book of the 4th, 6th and 7th Black Watch*

Perthshire Advertiser

Perthshire Constitutional and Journal

Perthshire Courier

*The Red Hackle, 1921–2016**, selected articles

The Scotsman

The Times

*The Watchkeeper**

*available in BWM

Online sources

51st Highland Division Online Museum, a general historical digest relating to the 51HD, at www.51hd.co.uk

The Gazette, Official Public Record, www.thegazette.co.uk

Report of the Iraq Inquiry by Sir John Chilcot, *www.iraqinquiry.org.uk/the-report*

List of Illustrations

Unless otherwise stated all illustrations are from the collection of The Black Watch Museum at Balhousie Castle.

27. Northern Ireland: keeping watch, Belfast 1982–83.
28. 1st Black Watch in Werl, BAOR Exercise Liquid Chase, 1983.
29. Berlin: Ruhleben Fighting City, 1987.
30. Hong Kong Handover, 1997, Pipe Major Small & Lieutenant Colonel Alasdair Loudon.
31. The Black Watch in Iraq, 2003/04.
32. *1st Black Watch Operational Orders for Operation Tobruk 2004* by Edward Cowan, 2005.
33. Major Alastair Aitken with the Marsh Arabs, Iraq 2004. (Aitken collection)
34. Last parade in Perth before the Sovereign's and Regimental Colours are laid up at Balhousie Castle, 23 June 2012. (Schofield collection)
35. Statue of a Black Watch Sergeant unveiled in May 2014, Black Watch Corner. (Schofield collection)

End papers: Detail from Panel 37, The Menin Gate, photographed by Erwin Ureel.

Index

NB Battalions, divisions and military ranks are listed according to the list of Abbreviations on pp. 615–17. Where identifiable, the ranks cited are the most senior at retirement/to date, including some temporary/acting appointments.